Taken at the Flood

Taken at the Flood

Robert E. Lee and Confederate Strategy in the Maryland Campaign of 1862

Joseph L. Harsh

THE KENT STATE UNIVERSITY PRESS
Kent, Ohio

Library of Congress Catalog Card Number 98-41614
ISBN 978-0-87338-631-9 (cloth)
ISBN 978-1-60635-188-8 (paper)

Manufactured in the United States of America

Library of Congress Cataloging-in-Publication Data
Harsh, Joseph L.
Taken at the flood : Robert E. Lee and Confederate strategy in the Maryland campaign of 1862 / Joseph L. Harsh.
p. cm.
Includes bibliographical references and index.
ISBN 0-87338-631-0 (alk. paper) ∞
1. Maryland Campaign, 1862. 2. Lee, Robert E. (Robert Edward), 1807-1870—Military leadership. 3. Strategy—History—19th century. 4. Confederate States of America—Military policy. I. Title.
E474.61.H37 1999
973.7'33—dc21 98-41614
CIP

British Library Cataloging-in-Publication data are available.

17 16 15 14 13 7 6 5 4 3

For

Trudy, Laura, Drew, and Greg

with love

Brutus: Well, to our Work alive. What do you think
Of marching to Philippi presently?
Cassius: I do not think it good.
Brutus: Your reason?
Cassius: This it is:
'Tis better that the enemy seek us:
So shall he waste his means, his soldiers,
Doing himself offense; whilst we, lying still,
Are full of rest, defence, and nimbleness.
Brutus: Good reasons must, of force, give place to better.
The people twixt Philippi and this ground
Do stand but in forc'd affection;
For they have grudged us contribution:
The enemy, marching along by them,
By them shall make a fuller number up,
Come on refresh'd, new-aided, and encourag'd;
From which advantage shall we cut him off
If at Philippi we do face him there,
These people at our back.
Cassius: Hear me, good brother.
Brutus: Under your pardon. —You must note beside,
That we have tried the utmost of our friends,
Our legions are brimful, our cause is ripe:
The enemy increaseth every day;
We, at the height, are ready to decline.
There is a tide in the affairs of men
Which, taken at the flood, leads on to fortune;
Omitted, all the voyage of their life
Is bound in shallows and in miseries.
On such a full sea are we now afloat;
And we must take the current when it serves,
Or lose our ventures.

William Shakespeare, *Julius Caesar*, IV.3

Indeed, wherever we turn, and in whatever aspect we look at the contest which engages our hearts and hands, we find multiplied reasons for hope and encouragement. Our cause is on the advance—our star in the ascendant. The tide is swelling in our favor: shall we take it at its flood? Shall we push on the path which Fortune and the God of Battles kindly beckons us? or shall we rest upon our arms, boast of the wonderful things we have accomplished, and supinely wait for the enemy to recover from our terrible blows? What says the government? What says the President? The army and the people say, advance—seize the golden opportunity—repeat the blows—and never stop until we have wrung from the foe an acknowledgment of our birthright to be free.

Fortune favors only the brave. She spurns the timid, the doubting and the boastful. An opportunity lost, seldom ever returns. The tide, if not taken at the flood, sweeps past us forever.

Richmond Whig, August 7, 1862

Contents

List of Maps xii
Preface xiii

Introduction. "On such a full sea . . ." 1

Antietam Creek and the Stream of History 1
Historical Sights: Fore, Hind, Over, and In 6

Reprise. "From the interior to the frontier": Lee Reaches the Potomac, September 1, 1862 11

1. *"We cannot afford to be idle": Lee's Strategic Dilemma, September 2–3, 1862* 16

Pope Escapes, September 2 16
Dilemma of a New Campaign 19
Confederate Tide at Flood 25
The Strength of Lee's Army 33
The Mettle of Lee's Army 39
The Maryland Option: A New Turning Movement 46
The Open-Ended Decision 50
The Dranesville Dispatch, September 3 54

2. *"More fully persuaded": Lee Crosses the Potomac, September 4–6, 1862* 66

The March to Leesburg, September 4 66
Clearing the Decks 70
Leesburg War Council 80
Jackson's Crossing, September 5 85
Frederick Occupied, September 6 99

3. *"In this I was disappointed": Lee Revises His Strategy, September 7–9, 1862* 110

Restful Sabbath, September 7 111
Lee Dabbles in Politics, September 8 120
The Intrusion of Jeff. Davis, September 9 127
The Walker Interview 133
Frederick Council of War 145
The Writing of Special Orders, No. 191 152

4. *"Intercept such as may attempt escape": Lee's Best-Laid Plans, September 10–12, 1862* 168

The First Day of the Valley Expedition, September 10 168
The Second Day of the Valley Expedition, September 11 182
Lee at Hagerstown, September 12 190
The Watershed of the Maryland Campaign 198

5. *"More rapidly than convenient": Lee's Plans Unravel, September 13, 1862* 212

Some Concern in the Morning 213
The Pendulum Swings Back 223
The Lost Orders Found 237
The Crisis by Eventide 242

6. *"The day has gone against us": Lee Stands at the Mountain Gaps, September 14, 1862* 253

Lee to the Rescue 254
The Battle of Boonsboro 256
Jackson Tightens the Noose 267
The Battle of Crampton's Gap 275
Evening: The First Retreat 284

7. *"We will make our stand on these hills": Lee's Hope Renewed, September 15, 1862* 298

Lee Stands at Sharpsburg 299
The Pursuit Ends 308
The Surrender of Harpers Ferry 315
Lee's Resolve Strengthened 322

8. *"All will be right": Lee's Last Chance for Maneuver, September 16, 1862* 330

Lee Sees a Window 330
Lee and the Whims of War 334

McClellan Shuts the Window 344
Lee Accepts Battle at Sharpsburg 354

9. *"A hard day's work before us": Lee's Bloodiest Day, September 17, 1862* 368

The Opening Attack by Hooker, 5:15 to 9:00 A.M. 370
Lee and the Morning Crises on the Left, 5:30 to 9:30 A.M. 377
McLaws and Walker Restore the Confederate Left, 9:00 A.M. to 1:00 P.M. 385
Federal Success on Four Fronts, 9:30 A.M. to 1:30 P.M. 395
Lee and the Midday Crisis, 9:30 A.M. to 2:00 P.M. 401
Burnside's Attack and Lee's Final Crisis, 2:00 to 5:00 P.M. 413
Night of Reckoning 424

10. *"Until none but heroes are left": Antietam Endgame, September 18–21, 1862, and After* 430

Lee Defies Fate, September 18 430
Williamsport, the Last Gambit, September 18–19 444
Checkmate at Shepherdstown, September 19–21 452
Echoes of Maryland 471

Finale. "We have tried the utmost": Lee's Ventures Risked and Lost 480

Verdicts of History 481
Lee's Overland Campaign of 1862—A Shore Too Far 490

Notes 497
Bibliography 591
Index 613

List of Maps

Lee's strategic dilemma, September 2 17
Confederate march, September 3 56
Confederate march, September 4 68
Confederate march, September 5 87
Confederate march, September 6 101
The line of the Monocacy, September 7–9 151
The first day of the Valley expedition, September 10 172
The second day of the Valley expedition, September 11 184
The third day of the Valley expedition, September 12 191
The fourth day of the Valley expedition, September 13 243
The fifth day of the Valley expedition, September 14 255
Battle of South Mountain, September 14, noon 277
Battle of South Mountain, September 14, evening 286
Concentration at Sharpsburg, September 15 323
Pre-Antietam maneuvering, September 16 355
Battle of Sharpsburg, September 17, first phase 371
Battle of Sharpsburg, September 17, second phase 379
Battle of Sharpsburg, September 17, third phase 386
Battle of Sharpsburg, September 17, fourth phase 394
Battle of Sharpsburg, September 17, fifth phase 398
Battle of Sharpsburg, September 17, sixth phase 416
Sharpsburg, the morning after, September 18 432
Retreat from Sharpsburg, September 18–20 449
Echoes of Maryland 473

Preface

THIS IS A BOOK I probably could not escape writing. Born in Hagerstown, Maryland, and graduated from North Hagerstown High School, I grew up thirteen miles from Antietam battlefield. From an early age the Civil War mesmerized me, and at least from the second grade on I frequently roamed the rolling fields around Sharpsburg listening for echoes of the great event that had once made the ground tremble there. I remember that my eighth-grade math teacher, Elmer Poffenberger, a direct descendent of Joseph Poffenberger and heir to the farm behind the North Woods, took me into the barn where Fighting Joe Hooker had slept on the night before the First Corps launched the sunrise attack that opened the battle. I also recall that I went with John Eavey, my high school friend and biology lab partner, to visit his grandparents in Sharpsburg at their prewar ancestral home. We drank from a spring in the backyard that had quenched the thirst of Confederate soldiers.

One winter I spent every Sunday afternoon copying down onto index cards the information from the cast iron plaques that line Antietam's avenues. My Uncle Bunt Long accompanied me on most of these trips, and behind Bloody Lane, near the spot where the marker said that Gen. George B. Anderson had been mortally wounded, he found a blunted and brown-stained bullet, which he was sure was the one that had "done in" the general.

As a high school junior, I volunteered (with others) to put together an hour-long lesson on the Maryland campaign that was telecast to all of the eleventh-grade U.S. history classes in Washington County. Mercifully, little is remembered of the finished product, except that we kept a running count of the stupid mistakes committed by George McClellan, and in so doing quite filled a large poster. The summer before going off to college, I frequently went to Sharpsburg with my friend Jim Murfin, who was then at work on the manuscript that in time became *Gleam of Bayonets*, the first full-length study devoted solely to the Maryland campaign. In a kind paragraph in his preface, Jim predicted I would be a candidate "for future Antietam honors."

At Gettysburg College, as a history major and in the shadow of the bigger battle that most historians proclaim the turning point of the war, I retained my fascination with Antietam. When the time came to choose a topic for my bachelor's thesis, I decided to undertake a study of the attack and repulse of Sedgwick's division in the West Woods.

In 1963, perhaps still under the spell of the charismatic professor I had recently heard speak during the Antietam centennial, I quickly chose to accept the fellowship offered by Rice University and with it the opportunity to study under Frank E. Vandiver. After several false starts on other Civil War topics, I turned to the Maryland campaign as the subject of my master's thesis. Under the title "Taken at the Flood," the thesis examined the campaign from the opening to the finding of the "lost orders." Looking at both sides, it pursued such subjects as Lee's reasons for entering Maryland and dividing his army at Frederick and McClellan's reorganization of a field army and his response to the invasion of the North.

It was during work on the thesis that two new interests began to pull me in a different direction. First, the bigger picture of the war for the North became increasingly attractive. The presence of green regiments in the Army of the Potomac, the issuance of the Preliminary Emancipation Proclamation immediately after the battle, the timing of McClellan's removal from command only after the fall elections had passed, and like subjects led me to the question of the cross-pollination of politics and the military in the conduct of the war. Second, about halfway into the thesis I concluded that the information which kept turning up simply did not support the stereotypical interpretation of George B. McClellan inherited from other historians. Hence, the subject of my research for the next nearly thirty years would become the Federal side of the Civil War, with a particular focus on McClellan.

In 1973, upon joining the history department of George Mason University in Fairfax, Virginia, I returned physically to the Eastern theater. Since then, in a variety of ways, connections with Antietam have been renewed. Not a year has passed without my taking at least one class on a battlefield tour. I reactivated my membership in the Hagerstown Civil War Round Table, developed a cordial and now long-standing relationship with the National Park Service staff that preserves and interprets the battle site, and have twice been honored by being asked to deliver lectures in the James Murfin Memorial Lecture Series.

Still, although it has been in the back of my mind, I never quite got around to writing a book on Antietam.

It was my good friend Ted Alexander, National Park Service historian at Antietam, who finally prodded me into action. At the close of one hot summer's day, after we had jointly guided a group of Smithsonian Associates around the battlefield, Ted asked—in language more colorful than here reported: "Joe, when the heck are you going to write a book about Antietam." He went on to proclaim that it would be a "shame" if all of my years of work and my "many peculiar notions" (I call them insights) never found print.

So, in January of 1991 the long-delayed task was undertaken. In the beginning I doubted that a full-scale narrative could be justified. Stephen Sears's *Landscape Turned Red* was less than a decade old, and, although in disagreement with many of its conclusions, I did not believe that a complete retelling of the Maryland campaign, including all of its many familiar anecdotes, was needed. Instead, I decided to write a series of essays, each around a single theme, which would permit me to focus directly on the traditional views that were to be challenged. The original plan called for one volume to include studies of Confederate strategy, Federal strategy, the Lost Orders, the strengths of each army, and the tactics at the Battle of Antietam.

I soon discovered (and probably should have recognized all along) that strategy is not a theme which can be studied in a vacuum. In particular, an understanding of Lee's decision to enter Maryland—because it was much more than a sudden impulse—required an analysis of Confederate war aims, policy, and strategy prior to September 2, 1862. Also, an assessment of Lee's strategy during the campaign demanded more attention to the condition of the Army of Northern Virginia and its command structure, to logistics, to intelligence gathering, and to a host of other details than I had originally intended. It was necessary to identify and analyze all of the small strategic decisions that Lee made before his grand strategy became clear; and it was equally necessary to evaluate the many factors that impacted on Lee's decisions before it was fair to judge them.

Hence, the project that was supposed to take several months stretched into five years, and the work that was intended as two or three chapters in a single volume became an eleven-hundred-page typescript that has yielded two books. The first six chapters covering the origins of the Maryland campaign were published last year as *Confederate Tide Rising;* the remaining two-thirds, comprising the campaign itself, is here presented as *Taken at the Flood.*

In closing, it is proper to explain several features of the work that follows. First, much of the research spade-work for a companion study of the Northern side of the Maryland campaign has already been carried out, and this has allowed me to include in the present work capsule summaries of Federal operations on a day-to-day basis. Although this will inevitably lead to some duplication, the redundancy in this instance is unavoidable. There is no way to fully appraise Lee's strategy without at the same time comparing the Confederate commander's understanding of the enemy's position with the actual Federal situation.

I should also reemphasize that—in spite of its increase in size—this is not a full narrative of the Maryland campaign. It focuses on Robert E. Lee's strategy and the context necessary to understand his strategy. In other words, no anecdote—no matter how famous or droll—is included that does not contribute to the topic under study. For example, the story of Stonewall Jackson falling asleep in church at Frederick will not be found (unless it seems possible that Confederate boredom impelled Lee to move against Harpers Ferry as an entertaining diversion!). On the other hand, I have taken particular pains to establish, where possible, precise locations and routes, times, weather conditions, and other such factors that impact on deciding and executing strategy.

Similarly, everything extant that Lee wrote or said about the Maryland campaign, during it or afterward, has been included and subjected to close textual scrutiny. In this regard, I should explain both my usage and my citation of the three postwar occasions on which Lee commented about the campaign. Fortunately for students, William Allan and Edward C. Gordon made memoranda of these conversations. Allan's original notes are at Washington and Lee University, but a copy made by an Allan family member is in the William Allan Books at the University of North Carolina, Chapel Hill. Gordon's memorandum, along with a cover letter, is in the Allan Books at North Carolina. My research is based on the Chapel Hill collection, but for the ready reference of readers I originally cited printed versions of the memoranda in volume 2 of Douglas Southall Freeman's *Lee's Lieutenants* and Charles Marshall's *An Aide-de-camp of Lee.* Subsequently, however, Gary Gallagher has reprinted all three in *Lee the Soldier.* Believing the latter to be the most convenient, all citations herein have been changed to this latest work.

Finally, I must confess how much pleasure I derived from the method I employed. In attempting to see the campaign through Lee's eyes, I came to feel—almost—that I was a member of his staff. I would rise each morning and set out to follow in his footsteps. Throughout the day I would ask: What is he doing now? Why is he doing it? To the best of my recollection, I never found myself actually talking to him. And, aware of the pitfall of identifying too closely with one's subject, I frequently reminded myself that had I lived in the 1860s I would likely have been a small farmer of German descent residing in western Maryland; and, like my ancestor, Benjamin Franklin Kreps, I too would have fought to save the Union.

A detailed acknowledgment of the debts I owe to others has been made in the preface of *Confederate Tide Rising*, but I would be remiss if I did not again call attention to those whose special contributions made this present book possible: Frank Vandiver, Richard Sommers, Thomas Clemens, John Divine, John Hennessy, Mike Miller, Bill Miller, Jim Murfin, Will Greene, Dennis Frye, Ted Alexander, Paul Chiles, David Nathanson, Harry Butowsky, Mike Musick, Dawn Sobol, Lynda Crist, Mary Dix, Mike Pinkston, John Hubbell, Julia Morton, Joanna Hildebrand Craig, Diana Dickson, Will Underwood, Nancy Fuchs, Michael Snyder, Will Johnson, Lois Brock, Cora Jacobson, Sherree Derocher, Leon Tenney, John Allen, John Scully, Ethan Rafuse, Betty Lockhart, Charlene Calder, Ann McCauley, Jane Constantine, Betsy Rowe, Joe Hudson, and Dick Lemmon.

To this list I would like to add the names of Vince Armstrong, for his many stimulating conversations and for the discovery of important documents relating to Edwin Sumner and the Second Corps; and Erina Moriarity, former student and latest addition to George Mason's history department secretarial staff.

To my wife, Trudy, and our three children, Laura, Drew, and Greg, I dedicate this work of love.

Taken at the Flood

INTRODUCTION

"On such a full sea . . ."

Antietam Creek and the Stream of History

FOR ONE BRIEF, coruscating moment Antietam stood as the undisputed turning point of the Civil War. The battle carried the war into wholly new dimensions. The man-made cyclone that engulfed the hills around Sharpsburg on September 17, 1862, scaled a fury previously unknown in the Civil War. It was as though the two days of Shiloh or the Seven Days around Richmond had been collapsed into a single bloody dawn to dusk. For the Union, Antietam ended a summer of stinging defeats, blunted the threat to Washington, and turned back the Confederate invasion of the North.

Beyond the course of military events, the Maryland campaign also influenced Northern politics and society. Five days after the battle, President Abraham Lincoln announced his intention to issue in one hundred days a proclamation that freed the slaves in regions still in insurrection against the United States government. And in October Mathew Brady exhibited in his gallery in New York City a collection of photographs taken of the battlefield covered with freshly dug graves and grotesque, bloated corpses. These pictures brought home to the public the horrors of battle with an immediacy never before known. Wrote a *New York Times* reviewer, the photographer has "brought bodies and laid them in our door-yards."[1]

Confederates did not—indeed at the time they could not—view Sharpsburg (as they called it) as the turning point in the war. Unable or unwilling to envision their own eventual defeat, they would not acknowledge that their failed campaign represented the best chance they would ever have to achieve independence. Still, many, at least in Robert E. Lee's Army of Northern Virginia, glimpsed that their cause had been dealt a severe setback in Maryland. In recrossing the Potomac, they had sprung the coil of pressure it had taken a summer of hard-fought victories to tighten. Back in Virginia, it would be necessary to start over from the beginning.

Antietam's shining moment lasted less than a year. More battles were fought, and both sides came to recognize that the war would stretch on many more months. In the North, George B. McClellan, the commander of the Army of the Potomac at Antietam, was put on the shelf in Trenton, and it became politically unfeasible to accept an achievement by him as the most important event of the war. For the South, there was another advance beyond the frontier, one that carried the Army of Northern Virginia much deeper into enemy territory. Thus, although no other battle of the war ever exceeded the single-day losses at Sharpsburg, Antietam yielded preeminence to Gettysburg.

For the next nine decades Antietam languished in the long, obscuring shadow cast by Gettysburg. There were, of course, compelling reasons. Gettysburg was bigger. It lasted three times longer and witnessed twice as many casualties. It was also the only significant fighting to occur on the free soil of the Union. But, perhaps most of all, Northerners in looking back perceived Gettysburg as marking the end of the string of early Confederate victories in the East and the beginning of the path to Appomattox. Naturally, they proclaimed Gettysburg to be the turning point of the Civil War. Southerners, in rare accord, came to agree that their own best chance to win independence ebbed on the hills around the small Pennsylvania town and that their Cause had washed to its high tide on the gentle slopes of Cemetery Ridge.

Perceptions born during the war persisted. Gettysburg became the apotheosis of the war for the reunited states. Its fields hosted the encampments of the aging veterans who had fought there, and its meadows witnessed old men shaking hands over the stone wall where Pickett's charge had crested. In the last decade of the nineteenth century, the War Department included both Gettysburg and Antietam among the first five battlefields developed as historical memorials.[2] Gettysburg was designated a "military park" and launched lavishly with $250,000 and nearly four thousand acres. Antietam began as a "battlefield site" with a meager $60,000 and twenty-two acres.[3] Antietam never caught up either in largess or in fame.

Over the years, thousands of veterans and millions of their descendants flocked to the Round Tops, the Bloody Angle, and the cemetery where Lincoln delivered his Address. During the same time, but one-fourth that number trudged through the West Woods, down the Bloody Lane, and across the Burnside Bridge at Sharpsburg.[4] From the founding, hundreds of cannon have guarded the military avenues at Gettysburg, while for nearly a century only two lonely and widely separated four-gun batteries stood sentinel on Antietam's hallowed ground.[5] At its nadir, Antietam even lost its autonomous identity. For two decades it existed as a branch under the authority of the superintendent at Gettysburg.[6]

Scholarship trailed where popular attention led. A long shelf grew heavy with volumes on Gettysburg, while for over a hundred years not a single serious historical study appeared that was devoted entirely to the Maryland campaign.[7] In the famous Scribner's *Campaigns of the Civil War* series of the 1880s it comprised but half of Francis Palfrey's volume on *The Antietam and Fredericksburg*. Although Palfrey was a veteran of the battle, he wrote before the operational reports had been published, and the study he produced was shallow and frequently confused. Isaac Heysinger's *Antietam and the Maryland and Virginia Campaigns of 1862*, while devoting most of its attention to September 1862, also covered the Peninsula and Second Manassas campaigns and was, in any case, more of a polemical defense of George McClellan than a study of any of the campaigns. As late as 1959, Edward J. Stackpole (retired military officer and publishing house founder), in his series of books on the Eastern theater, combined the Second Manassas and Maryland campaigns in his *From Cedar Mountain to Antietam*.[8]

Ironically, there was an exclusive study of the Maryland campaign written, but it was never published. Ezra Carman, a veteran of the battle and member of the Antietam Battlefield Board, spent most of the 1890s composing "The Maryland Campaign of 1862." This huge work—1,800 manuscript pages—is in several respects amateurish. Carman lacked objectivity; he was weak when treating disputes and controversies; and his plodding prose is frequently convoluted and not always clear. Nonetheless, his history is perhaps the best study produced by any participant of the war. Based on hundreds of letters and maps sent to him by veterans upon his request for information, an unknowable number of hours of oral interviews, and years of his own study of the field, his work is an invaluable source of anecdotes and insights that historians have barely begun to utilize. Why Carman never published his manuscript—whether he never finished it to his satisfaction or, more simply, never found a publisher—is not known.[9]

Not until the mid–twentieth century did interest revive in Antietam. Historian Bruce Catton drew Antietam back into the historical spotlight. In 1957, with interest in the Civil War swelling in anticipation of the centennial, Catton's widely read account of the Union side of the Civil War, *This Hallowed Ground*, proclaimed Antietam, not Gettysburg, as the turning point of the war. Not only did the Federal victory stop Lee's invasion of the North, Catton argued, but it also provided Abraham Lincoln with the impetus to issue the Preliminary Emancipation Proclamation; and the combination of Lee's failure and the promise of the death of slavery combined to end any hope of foreign recognition of the Confederacy. Catton reasoned that since the South could not win without support from Britain or France, the Confederate high tide had crested and begun to recede along the banks of Antietam Creek and not the following year with Pickett's charge against Cemetery Ridge.[10]

Although subsequent historians have hardly stampeded to acclaim Antietam the watershed of the war, Catton's spotlight attracted considerable attention to the Maryland campaign. The ensuing generation witnessed a comparative flood of books devoted to the campaign and its climactic battle. The Maryland campaign finally received its due as the sole subject of a monograph with the appearance of James V. Murfin's *Gleam of Bayonets* in 1965, only to be followed in less than two decades by another, Stephen W. Sears's *Landscape Turned Red* (1983). Both are full-scale narratives of the campaign from Lee's crossing of the Potomac to his retreat, based on research in a wide variety of sources, and full of colorful stories and dramatic quotations from participants. Subsequently, there has been a third monograph, Perry Jamieson's *Death in September* (1995), a more condensed telling of the story.[11]

Works of narrower focus have also appeared: a series of local historical works; a study of the photographs of the battle; the published papers of a seminar held on Antietam; a collection of original articles; a difficult-to-categorize melange of eyewitness accounts; two guide books; a study of the artillery; even monographs on parts of the campaign, one on South Mountain and two on Harpers Ferry. And all have been crowned with the unfailing proof of academic worthiness, a bibliography devoted exclusively to the Maryland campaign.[12]

It is true that interest in Antietam still falls considerably short of the popular and scholarly fascination with Gettysburg. Scott Hartwig's bibliography lists only 688 items on the Maryland campaign, even though he includes manuscript collections and general reference works, in addition to memoirs and studies that deal only in small part with Antietam. Richard Sauers, using largely the same criteria, has listed four times as many items (2,757) for the Pennsylvania campaign.[13] Moreover, Gettysburg's front-rank status was probably clinched for all time with the appearance of Michael Shaara's Pulitzer Prize–winning novel *Killer Angels* in 1974 and the epic motion picture based on it in 1993.

Still, Antietam is arguably the next most studied Civil War battle after Gettysburg. Merely being second is scarcely sufficient justification for additional investigation. It would not be unreasonable to assume that 688 books and articles might provide adequate coverage for a twenty-day campaign and a one-day battle. Anyone who picks up the present work and reads its title could legitimately ask, "Why should more trees be sacrificed for yet another look at the Maryland campaign?"

And it is probably true that a new full-scale narrative of the Maryland campaign is not now needed. Another recounting of the twenty-day story from Lee's crossing the Potomac at White's Ford to his recrossing at Shepherdstown, replete with anecdotes and descriptive prose, would serve little purpose. Most of the best tales are well known and oft told. Additional quotes—no matter how scintillating—from heretofore unknown diaries and letters, attesting to the pain and suffering of the soldiers, would not deepen comprehension of the campaign. Indeed, it is possible the very wealth of human-interest stories surrounding Antietam have blurred focus on the larger questions of the campaign and helped to make it difficult for writers to see beyond the individual trees of the North, West, and East Woods.

What is needed is a rethinking of the Maryland campaign. Certain sweeping assumptions have controlled accounts of Antietam almost from the first telling. It has been assumed that Robert E. Lee, who was bold and daring by nature, risked destruction of his army by invading the North to court foreign intervention, to influence the coming fall elections, and to liberate Maryland from the heel of the despot's boot. It is said that George B. McClellan, also acting true to his character, responded slowly, timidly, and ineffectively to the invasion. And it is held that only "fate" spoiled Lee's plans, when the orders detailing the wide separation of his army accidentally fell into the hands of the enemy. Yet, even with this stroke of luck, described as more revealing than the "most spectacular code-breaking accomplishments of World War II," McClellan frittered away his golden opportunity to crush Lee and end the war.[14] Although the Federals outnumbered the Confederates better than two to one, the best McClellan could do at Sharpsburg was to fight to an inconclusive draw. Finally, it is averred that Lee dominated McClellan by reading his mind, "almost as if Lee was pulling the strings of a Federal puppet."[15]

This traditional interpretation ought to be challenged for three reasons. First, it is simply unhealthy for historical assumptions to go untested for 130 years, especially when these particular assumptions, which originated with the participants themselves, are unlikely to be either as objective or as perspicacious as they might be. Second, the meaning and lessons of the Maryland campaign have been consistently reduced to the level of the personal peculiarities of its chief antagonists: Robert the Bold versus George the Timid. Such a personality-centered and atomistic view is not only a highly oversimplified understanding of life but an equally oversimplified explanation of life in the past, and it forms a barrier to full enlightenment of the rich complexities of a major historical event.

Finally, Antietam studies, along with much other Civil War literature, have suffered by being viewed through faulty historical "sights." Authors have unhesitatingly employed hindsight to condemn historical figures for not exercising foresight or in some cases, it would seem, for not possessing second sight. A basic premise of the following study, indeed a major reason for its undertaking, is that before even the limited lessons possible from history can be validated, events must be studied as they unfold and in the light of what is known at the time. Before historians reach judgment, they ought to render justice.

Historical Sights: Fore, Hind, Over, and In

The primary job of the historian is to understand the past and to explain it to the present. To carry out this responsibility the historian cannot avoid using some form of hindsight. He cannot study historical events while they are still happening. Even in the unusual case where he is a participant in the event, he can do no more than create one individual's record of observations and reflections. He cannot operate as a historian until enough time has passed to collect and study other firsthand accounts. He is stuck with hindsight.

And hindsight is a tricky business. It means by definition the historian always knows more than the men and women he is studying. In the first place, he knows more about the world surrounding them, what others are saying and doing and planning, than any participant could possibly know. Also, the historian knows the participants' future; for to the historian that future is simply the less-distant past. Thus a historian will know the results of an action even as he studies its unfolding and the consequences of a decision even as he analyzes how it was made.

It is such godlike knowledge that makes hindsight a tricky business. It is tempting to take the next step and to render godlike judgments on persons and events in history that are both unfair to them and unrealistic in light of what was likely or even possible given all of the constraints of a particular situation. It is certainly unrealistic to expect that anyone in the past be clairvoyant. At most, it is possible to suggest that certain persons, given their knowledge, experience, and intelligence, might have had insights or perceptions which they did not. But even here the historian needs to tread with considerable caution. As Lee once remarked to one of his generals, "after it is all over, as stupid a fellow as I am can see the mistakes that were made."[16]

Historians too frequently forget that even though they know some things participants in historical events could not have known, those who come later can never achieve omniscience. On another occasion Lee wryly observed that the South might lose the war because of a mistake it had made at the outset. "In the beginning," he explained, "we appointed all our worst generals to command the armies, and all our best generals to edit the newspapers."[17] When historians pretend to the status of "know-it-all," they are heirs to the armchair generalship of the editors Lee lampooned. Historical participants knew many things that can never be learned after the fact. Students of history must constantly remind themselves that many documents have disappeared and that much information was never documented in the first place.

It would be unreasonable to assume that among this vast body of lost knowledge there were not pieces of evidence which if known would radically alter our view of persons and events. While historical study must proceed in spite of missing information—if there is to be any historical study at all—it behooves historians to be humble where they must be tentative. There is a long-standing admonition to writers that too many "ifs," "perhapses," and "maybes" will soon weary readers. Nonetheless, certainty where not justified is nothing less than distortion. Most bold and unqualified assertions warp understanding of the past.

Hindsight is tricky for still another reason. In the natural desire to understand the reasons for success and failure, one is easily trapped in a framework that focuses exclusively on the final results. Thus, virtually everything preceding success is seen as right and good, and everything coming before failure is viewed as wrong and bad. According to Machiavelli, if a commander wins the battle, "it cancels all other errors and miscarriages."[18] Civil War history provides an amplitude of examples of this distortion by hindsight. Because Ulysses Grant and Abraham

Lincoln (and to a lesser extent William Sherman, Philip Sheridan, and Henry Halleck) won the war, their mistakes are passed over as "learning" along the way to victory. George McClellan, on the other hand, proves the reverse is true. He did not win the war, and virtually every significant decision of his military career has been subjected to adverse criticism. Hindsight can obscure a truth that is rediscoverable every day in life: decisions can be made that are right in terms of everything knowable when they are made but that lead to bad results.

Explanations imprisoned within the success/failure framework sometimes take curious shape. For example, Robert E. Lee, in spite of not winning the war, is adjudged an overall success because he accomplished so much with so little. Hence, although Lee failed in the Maryland campaign, his failure has been largely excused as the result of unkind fate. George B. McClellan, however, whose overall career is considered a failure, succeeded in the Maryland campaign but is blamed for not accomplishing more.

Unfair and unrealistic judgments make good propaganda but bad history. Historical interpretations need to be as objective as possible and need to be based on a realistic assessment of potentialities and limitations in particular and discrete situations. Otherwise they fail to answer the two most primitive reasons for studying history. At the most basic level, the study of history is meant to satisfy human curiosity: What happened? And why did it happen? While complete objectivity may be unobtainable, if objectivity is not the overriding goal in historical research and explanation, then the resulting study will inevitably yield gross distortions and false answers to the "whys." The second most basic reason for turning to history is to learn as much as possible from the past to help in our understanding of the present and to cast some light, no matter how dim, upon the future. In this instance also, the history turned to must be fair and realistic, or it will be of no help in understanding the present or enlightening the future. At worst, it will lead to misapprehending the present and obscuring what is yet to come.

The Maryland campaign of 1862 is one of the most interesting, critical, dramatic, and potentially enlightening episodes in all of United States history. It is a neatly defined canvas on which to study leaders compelled to make decisions of momentous consequence while stumbling forward with confused and conflicting information and while under the press of time and rapidly changing conditions. With the fate of their governments teetering on swaying scales, two men bore the responsibility for comprehending their situations and responding quickly and correctly. For a moment in history, Lee and McClellan became the focus of their nations' destinies. There is much to be learned from their predicaments and their solutions, if understanding is the goal.

It would be frivolous, even counterproductive, to reduce such a richly instructive story to a Grimm's fairy tale replete with fair heroes and foul villains. It is not necessary to oversimplify history to make it entertaining. The historian needs to admit frankly that no event, or any of its parts, can ever be known with certainty and then invite the reader to join the quest for the most probable answers. That the answers when found will never reach the finality found in Hansel and Gretel will be unsatisfying only to those who seek escape rather than understanding. The ambiguity in history is the residue of the ambiguity that existed when the past was the present. Ambiguity is long, and life is short.

In focusing on the two commanders in the Maryland campaign, there is also the temptation of yielding to the more subtle distortion of attributing to each general more control over events than either possessed. Both the railroad and the telegraph had been in use for several decades, but their potential for military application was just being explored. Lee and McClellan understood that troops and supplies on the one hand, and information on the other, could now travel much faster than ever before. They used the modern inventions when opportunity permitted; but armies on the march were seldom able to obtain full advantage of these technological advances.

Neither the rail nor the wire played a significant role in the Maryland campaign. While the telegraph was used (at least in part) to maintain contact with Richmond and Washington, it was not available for coordinating the units of the army. The commanders perforce relied upon the mounted courier and the signal flag for sending orders and receiving information. Such primitive communications did not permit tight control or provide accurate, timely intelligence. It must be remembered that the famous "fog of war" of Karl von Clausewitz also interposed (albeit less densely) between a commander's eyes and his own army.

The fog became much denser, and at times impenetrable, when it came to knowledge of the enemy. During the Maryland campaign Lee and McClellan seldom knew much that was useful about the location, strength, or organization of the opposing army. Usually, what they thought they knew was highly distorted, and sometimes it was flatly false. Spies were conspicuous only by their absence in the Maryland campaign, and the commanders knew only what they were told by excited civilians and cavalry scouts. When it is recalled that the troopers on both sides were recent volunteers and had received virtually no training in gathering intelligence, it is not surprising that the information they provided was not substantially better than that of their civilian counterparts.

A fair appraisal of Lee and McClellan requires a full exploration of the circumstances under which each labored. It is necessary to attempt to discover what they believed their responsibilities to be and what they tried to accomplish; to evaluate the human and logistical resources at their disposal, both in quantity and quality; and to determine what they knew and when they learned it. Only after understanding their intentions, resources, and knowledge is it possible to grade their performance. Only after recognizing their limitations and ignorance is it fair to judge their achievements.

REPRISE

"From the interior to the frontier"

Lee Reaches the Potomac, September 1, 1862

MONDAY, SEPTEMBER 1, dawned clear and warm. The first morning of a new and momentous month in Confederate history promised to be a typical summer's day and offered no premonition of the savage thunderstorm already building behind the Blue Ridge Mountains. In northern Virginia, on the border between Loudoun and Fairfax Counties, one-half of Robert E. Lee's army was on the march to interpose itself between the retreating Federal army of John Pope and the forts of Washington, D.C. Lee was determined to inflict maximum damage upon Pope and to reap the greatest results from the victory at Second Manassas. Unable to attack the Federals at Centreville, where Pope had sought refuge in the entrenchments the Confederates had built the previous year, Lee had the day before sent Stonewall Jackson on a turning movement to reach the enemy's rear.

At an early hour on the 1st, Jackson resumed his march eastward down the Little River Turnpike with his divisions in reverse order from the preceding day. Jackson's division (under Starke) led the way, followed by Ewell (under Lawton), and last came A. P. Hill. Stonewall had heard nothing from the cavalry about what lay ahead, and necessarily the column moved slowly and cautiously. By late morning he had covered a scant four miles to Chantilly plantation, where he was joined by Jeb Stuart, who had just returned from a ride to Frying Pan.[1]

Stuart could tell Jackson that nothing but Pope's wagontrain and its guards lay ahead, but the information was old and apparently did not satisfy Stonewall, who wisely directed the cavalry to undertake a fresh scout of the ground up to Fairfax Court House. While sending Fitz Lee's brigade directly east to Ox Hill, Stuart accompanied Robertson's brigade in a sweep south of the Little River Turnpike. Although most of Pope's army was now strung out along the Warrenton Turnpike—which because of its acute angle brought the enemy within two miles of

Ox Hill—Stuart reported he found "no force but a small one of cavalry was to be found nearer than Centreville."[2]

The sun had long since been cast over with clouds by the time the cavalry chief joined Robertson's brigade at Ox Hill. Here he waited until Jackson covered the two miles from Chantilly and arrived with the van of the infantry at about four o'clock. As towering thunderheads topped the horizon, Stonewall ordered Stuart to push skirmishers ahead to Fairfax Court House. When the Confederate horsemen had advanced about two miles and reached the headwaters of Difficult Run, just west of Jermantown and a mile short of Fairfax Court House, they encountered "wooded ridges . . . firmly held by infantry and artillery," which "plainly indicated" the enemy intended to "make a stand." Jackson deployed the four brigades of the Stonewall division under William Starke, and then he decided—or at least so was Stuart's understanding—that he would wait for the arrival of Longstreet's men before pushing forward. In the meantime, Stuart set out for Flint Hill with Fitz Lee's brigade to uncover and, if possible, turn the Federal flank to the north.[3]

John Pope, forewarned by the capture of his cavalry patrols and the shelling of his trains on the previous day, acted in a timely fashion to counter the threat to his rear and right flank. He ordered Joseph Hooker with elements of McDowell's and Franklin's corps into line at Jermantown to cover the retreat to Fairfax Court House. At two o'clock Pope had also ordered Reno's corps to move northward from the Warrenton Turnpike to take an advanced position at Ox Hill.

Shortly after Jackson's arrival at Ox Hill at four o'clock, Confederate scouts reported an enemy force (Reno) was approaching on the Confederate right flank from the south.[4] Thus, Stonewall was forced to shift his attention from Hooker in his front to the new threat on his right side, and Lee's offensive to turn Pope's position became a defensive battle to protect the exposed flank of the attacking column.

Jackson drew two brigades from his rear division under A. P. Hill and threw them into the thick woods south of the Little River Turnpike. Before they had advanced more than several hundred yards, skirmishers from the brigades of Branch and Field (Brockenbrough) encountered the advancing skirmishers of Isaac Stevens's small division of Reno's corps near the Reid farmhouse. It was a classic meeting engagement in which the two sides discovered each other by running into one another. The battle that ensued was confused and desperate. Eventually all twelve regiments of Reno's small command became engaged, and Jackson committed brigade after brigade of his own until nearly all of his three divisions formed an arc south of the turnpike.

At five o'clock the skies finally gave way and torrents of water drenched the armies. Violent winds drove the rain into the soldiers' faces, while lightning rent the gloomy woods and thunder louder than the artillery shook the trees.[5] At the start of the battle, Jackson outnumbered his foe nearly ten to one; yet due to fatigue and the storm, it was nearly six o'clock before his men began to press Reno from the field. Philip Kearny's division of the Third Corps arrived in time to stabilize the Federal line, and when darkness came early to the stormy field both sides were back approximately to where they had begun. The Union lost both of its major generals, Stevens and Kearny, killed in the vicious little fight. The Confederates suffered approximately 700 casualties out of 15,000 on the field, while the Federals lost 500 out of 6,000.[6]

In the last half-hour of twilight, the head of Longstreet's column approached Ox Hill on the Little River Turnpike, and Old Peter offered his lead brigades to join the fray. He also had the gall to comment to Jackson, "General, your men don't appear to work well today." Considering the extra share of work Jackson's men had shouldered since August 25, Stonewall might have been forgiven a sharp reply. Instead, he said simply, "No, but I hope it will prove a victory in the morning" and declined to commit any further forces to the waning battle.[7] Although Longstreet's barb was ungenerous, it struck close to the truth. As Dorsey Pender, brigade commander in A. P. Hill's division, would confess in a letter to his wife the next day, "None of us seemed anxious for the fight or did ourselves much credit."[8]

Lee's movements on September 1 are not well chronicled. Likely he was in great pain from the accident of the previous day, when he had fallen and sprained both hands and broken bones in his right one. He may have spent the forenoon confined to his tent. Nonetheless, around midday he set out before Longstreet and arrived by ambulance sometime before the battle to establish headquarters in a small farmhouse along the Little River Turnpike between Chantilly and Ox Hill. Here he first discovered the extent to which his injured hands restricted his capacity to command. On foot he was unable to find a vantage from which he could see much or get a feel for the tactical situation.[9] After the fighting started he made no apparent attempt to influence the action. Indeed, untypically, he allowed his mind to drift to other matters.

Around five o'clock, Lee summoned Col. Thomas Munford of the 2d Virginia Cavalry to headquarters for a special assignment. The Confederate commander showed Munford a letter that had just arrived from an old friend in Leesburg. John Janney, who as president of the Virginia Secession Convention had conferred on Lee the command of the Virginia state forces the previous spring, had written asking for protection. The Loudoun Rangers, a company of Union loyalists under Capt. Sam Means, were in the town threatening to arrest and carry away prominent Confederates on the next day. "We must crush out those people," Lee told Munford, ordering him to leave behind his wagons so he might travel quickly. "I shall expect to have a good report from you tomorrow." As an afterthought revealing his concern over his dwindling food supply, Lee added that upon returning Munford should help the commissary department "to collect beef cattle for this army."[10]

About 6:30, as an early darkness descended on the water-logged field, the rain settled into steady drizzle, the temperature began to drop, and the fighting gradually ceased. Both sides broke off the contest and withdrew a short distance to reform. Jackson returned Starke's division to the Little River Turnpike to face east, while the divisions of Ewell and A. P. Hill lay on their arms in the soggy woods south of the road in anticipation of renewing the struggle on the morrow.[11] Stuart in the meantime had ridden north with Fitz Lee's brigade in search of the Federal right flank only to find it firmly anchored at Flint Hill two miles away. When word of these developments reached army headquarters, the commanding general had to acknowledge that his turning movement had failed. Pope had found time to form a strong defensive line that stretched in a four-mile arc across the front of Fairfax Court House from the Warrenton Turnpike to Flint Hill.

The battle at Ox Hill—named Chantilly by the North—proved the fighting capacity of the Federal army was at least equal to that of the bone-tired Confederates. It also suggested that a frontal assault the following day would be bloody and perhaps useless. Wisdom—as well as Lee's long-standing strategic policy—dictated the Confederates should probe the Federal flank at Flint Hill in the morning. Yet, Lee was rapidly running out of room for another turning movement, for seven miles behind Flint Hill lay Fort Buffalo and the perimeter of the forts that encircled Washington. On the cold, wet, dreary night of September 1, Lee might have begun to sense the strategic dilemma into which the very magnitude of his successes had carried him. It should not have come as a total surprise, since it was the logical outcome of a victory gained at Manassas.

Lee was now within twenty miles of Washington. He was as near to the Northern capital as McClellan at Harrison's Landing had been to Richmond. "The war was thus transferred," he would later observe in his report, "from the interior to the frontier."[12]

Masked behind the staid prose lay miles of dusty roads, many moments of high anxiety, and excruciatingly large casualties that had in the end yielded final triumph from innumerable uncertainties. Lee must have sensed the even greater opportunity that was unfolding as the summer lengthened. Through chance, risk, and much bloodshed, he and the Army of Northern Virginia were cobbling together the series of rapid victories that might lead to Northern demoralization and Confederate independence.

Yet Lee must also have known he was not going to get much closer to Washington. Even if the morrow should bring the opportunity to deal Pope's army a final blow, what could be accomplished on the day after next? Was he not fast approaching on the Potomac the stalemate he had faced on the James? Were his very victories to render him impotent again? On the other hand, was not the plain lesson of Chantilly that his tired army needed rest?

Heavy decisions lay on the horizon for September 2.

CHAPTER ONE

"*We cannot afford to be idle*"

Lee's Strategic Dilemma, September 2–3, 1862

WITH A BRIGHT sun rising in a cloudless sky, a sodden dawn broke glistening over the spongy meadows and dripping forests of Fairfax. Weary, hungry soldiers of the Army of Northern Virginia awoke expecting another fight. It would have been the fifth day out of the last six spent in battle—a record to match the week of incessant struggle along the banks of the Chickahominy. But Tuesday, September 2, was not to be a day of combat. There would be rest for all save the cavalry, and there would be food for the fortunate. Still, "idle" would ill-depict one of the most momentous days in Confederate history. By noon Lee would end his fortnight's campaign against John Pope. But ere the sun had set, he would start another. And it would be the most ambitious of his career thus far.[1]

Pope Escapes, September 2

There can be no doubt that Robert E. Lee awoke on the morning of the 2d determined to strike Pope a blow that would wring even greater advantage from the Confederate victory. At an early hour the Army of Northern Virginia stood under arms in column of march ready for pursuit.[2] Concurring misfortunes had stymied Lee's first attempt to expand success. Jeb Stuart's casual disclosure of Confederate whereabouts, when combined with the battle fatigue of Stonewall Jackson's troops and the surprising resilience of the enemy, had foiled the fourth turning movement of the summer. Still, the Confederate commander was not ready to admit the campaign was over. He might yet be able to deliver a coup de grace to the fleeing Federal regiments. It was a question of time and maneuvering space.

Stuart put his troopers in the saddle at daybreak to probe the enemy position. Unfortunately, Jeb had only Fitz Lee's brigade at hand for the

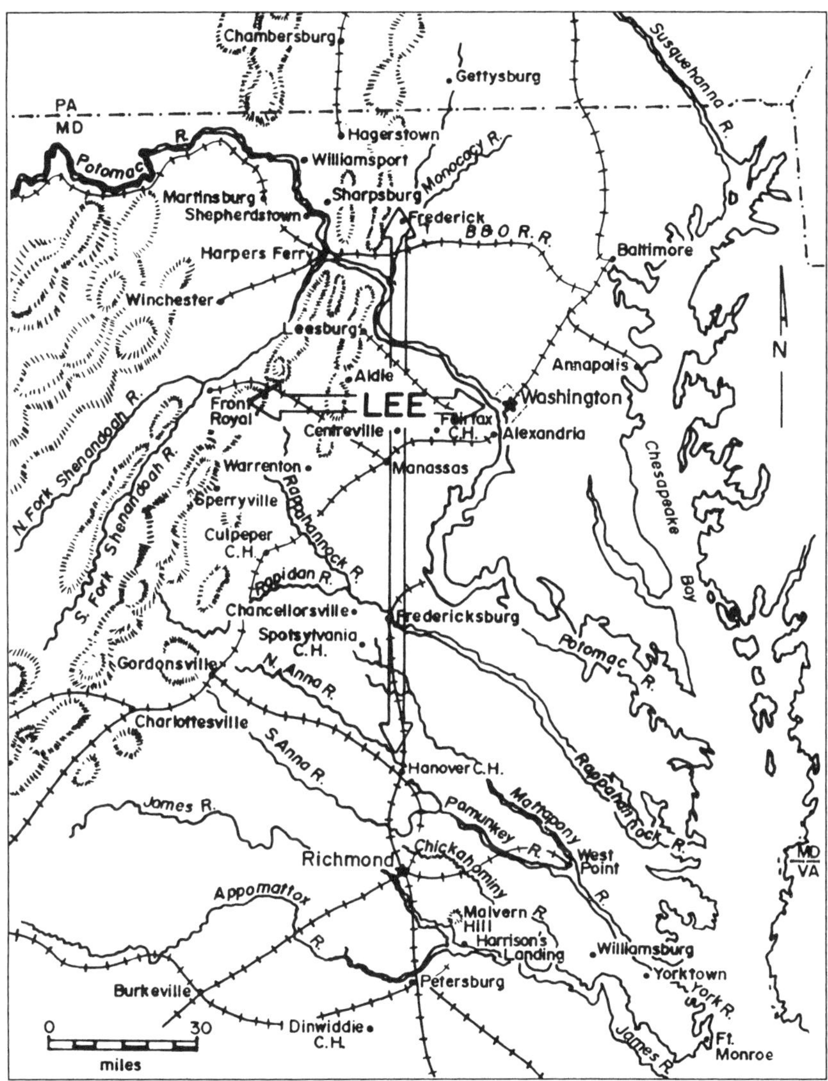

Lee's strategic dilemma, September 2

work, since Robertson's brigade (by a "misapprehension" of orders) had returned to the vicinity of Chantilly in the rear of the Confederate army. Scouts soon reported the Federals had withdrawn from the Ox Hill battlefield and from Centreville, but the enemy remained in a strong defensive line behind Difficult Creek, which ran south from Flint Hill to the Little River Turnpike. Pope's compact front covering the western face of Fairfax Court House did not invite assault. At this timely juncture,

Wade Hampton's brigade of cavalry arrived on the field after its long journey from Richmond and reported to the cavalry chief. Stuart immediately took the fresh regiments of horse along with two pieces of Pelham's flying artillery to try to turn the Federal flank at Flint Hill. But, as had been true the previous evening, Stuart could find no soft spot in the enemy's position. And by midmorning the two sides fell into desultory skirmishing.[3]

To Lee, who spent the morning near Ox Hill conferring with Longstreet and Jackson and receiving frequent reports from the cavalry, it may have seemed for a brief moment as if the frustrating stalemate on the Rappahannock was to reemerge in northern Virginia.[4] But the precedent was to be the Rapidan and not the Rappahannock, for once again John Pope had lost the will to defend a strong position. In spite of the presence of five fresh divisions in Sumner's Second and Franklin's Sixth Corps, Pope decided early in the morning he must abandon the field and retire to Washington.[5] Lee's continued aggressiveness had shaken him, and, lacking faith in many of his subordinates—especially those from McClellan's Army of the Potomac—the Federal commander decided he could only pull his shattered army together within the capital's defenses.

At 7:30 in the morning, Pope wired Halleck that his men had gotten "an intense idea among them that they must get behind the intrenchments." He characterized the enemy as "in very heavy force," and he urged Halleck to ride to the front to see the situation for himself. He correctly divined that the Confederates would again try to turn his right flank; and then he ended darkly, "You had best look out well for your communications. The enemy from the beginning has been throwing his rear toward the north, and every movement shows that he means to make trouble in Maryland." Pope poked all of the right sensitive spots to panic Halleck, and in midmorning the new Federal general-in-chief took upon his own shoulders the onus of ordering a retreat. "You will bring your forces as best you can," he telegraphed in reply, "within or near the line of fortification. . . . Do not let the enemy get between you and the works."[6]

So anxious was Pope to get away that he drew up and issued orders within the hour, and the retreat was underway before noon. The Federal army fled for safety by three routes. Sigel's corps led the western column, taking the Chain Bridge Road from Flint Hill through Vienna to Upton's Hill, followed by Porter, with Sumner in the rear covered by

Buford's cavalry brigade. To the east, Heintzelman led on the Braddock Road, with Banks covering the rear. And in the center, Reno's battered corps set out immediately on the Little River Turnpike for Annandale, to be followed by McDowell's corps and eventually Franklin's. Hooker's mixed temporary command, composed of elements of McDowell, Franklin, and Couch, would hold the line at Difficult Creek until four o'clock and then retreat through Fairfax Court House with Bayard's cavalry covering its rear.[7]

On this occasion, Jeb Stuart justified his reputation for alert reconnaissance. Almost instantaneously he perceived and reported to Lee the enemy's rapid withdrawal.[8] He also ordered Hampton to pursue and harass the Federal column retiring from Flint Hill toward the Chain Bridge. Into the hours of darkness, Hampton closely pressed the Federal tail under Sedgwick, lobbing shells into the panicky main body until the heavy casualties suffered by the 1st North Carolina Cavalry in an "ambuscade" laid by the 71st Pennsylvania Infantry bought breathing space for the retreating Federals.[9] Meanwhile, in the center of the line, where Stuart had only Fitz Lee's tired troopers, the Confederate horsemen pressed more gently and permitted Hooker to withdraw through the county seat virtually unscathed. Heros von Borcke, Stuart's Prussian chief of staff, planted the Confederate colors on the courthouse green, while deliriously happy Southern sympathizers mobbed the troopers, and damsels showered Stuart with kisses. Jeb even found time to visit his friend and "spy" Antonia Ford.[10]

Dilemma of a New Campaign

News of the Federal escape reached army headquarters shortly after noon and presented Lee with a strategic dilemma as perplexing as any he had yet confronted. To be sure, it was an embarrassment from successes he faced and was far preferable to being nailed to the doorstep of his capital or spread-eagled by a triple pincer. Still, to know he must exploit his costly victories while the opportunity lasted, but not to see any attractive avenues for action, was no less frustrating. His achievements in three months far exceeded anything he could have realistically expected when he took command on June 1. In eastern Virginia, he had pushed the battlefront "from the interior to the frontier" and thus cleared rich and productive regions of Federal troops, confining the foe to toeholds in the vicinity of Fort Monroe and Alexandria and a few garrisons in the lower Shenandoah Valley. He had caused the enemy to weaken drastically their armies along the south Atlantic coast and in the Kanawha Valley of western Virginia. Thus, he had restored to Confederate control areas essential to carrying on a protracted war. At the same time, he had harassed, baffled, and embarrassed—indeed he had destroyed—the Federal grand offensive that McClellan had so painstakingly constructed and that had seemed so close to success.[11]

Lee had accomplished all of this by concentrating Confederate forces, seizing the initiative, and pursuing the offensive. He had relied upon infantry, cavalry, and maneuver in the open field, especially the turning movement, to overslough the enemy's superiority in numbers, engineering, artillery, and naval forces. True, he had made some mistakes, and he had benefited from both the greater mistakes made by his enemy and from good fortune. There had been attacks that should not have been made, subordinates whose faulty judgment had subverted his plans, and losses larger than he could afford. But the balance sheet was overwhelmingly favorable, and the desperate risks he had taken—had been compelled to take—had been justified by the results.

Yet, all that had been gained was still at hazard. The enemy had hoisted no white flags. Every sign indicated that Federal leaders were calling upon Northerners to recommit and regroup—as they had after First Bull Run—and that they would soon return to invade the Confederacy once again. Lee had been pursuing a variation on the strategy of exhaustion, but he was not foolish enough to believe he could exhaust the vast physical resources of the North. What Lee sought to destroy was the Northern will to put forward large numbers of men and vast amounts of money. His observation that the North thought it needed a speedy war—a concern he believed Lincoln frequently exhibited—had led Lee to conclude the South might win if he could deny the enemy the possibility of easy success.

There could be no better chance to test the soundness of this strategy than the opening days of September 1862. A full year's Federal effort in the East lay in ruins. Virtually, the Northern people were being called upon to start over again. Might not one more crushing blow at this time—especially if delivered in a sensitive location—dispel all hope of a speedy victory? And, conversely, if Northerners got out of this crisis without further injury, would not their hopes, and with them the war, drag on for at least another season? Fortune might give the Confederates another chance. Yet, with the amount of resources they had already depleted, what was the likelihood that they could arrange through genius and fortuitous happenstance a further series of victories that would bring them to another moment so critical for achieving independence?[12] The tide must be taken at the flood and pressed on to victory.

The decision to strike came easily to Lee. Where to deliver the blow was not so readily apparent. His initial assessment indicated there were strong reasons for not moving in any of the four points of the compass. And that was his strategic dilemma.

Lee at once dismissed the idea of marching east against Washington. He ordered his infantry, who had been waiting in column for pursuit, to stack arms and go into camp for a much needed rest.[13] His aim all along had been to "intercept" the enemy before they reached their fortifications. He wasted no time considering an attack on these forts with their 643 large-caliber cannon and seventy-five mortars permanently emplaced.[14] He knew that his summer's successes had caused the enemy to pull troops from its scattered armies throughout the East—just as he intended should happen in order to free Confederate resources—but now most of these forces were concentrated around Washington. Likely more than double his own number of infantry manned the fortifications, along with more than three hundred pieces of field artillery. Lee bluntly described a direct assault on these frowning works as "injudicious," "useless," and "folly."[15]

The Confederates had neither the forces nor the guns and equipment needed to besiege the thirty-seven miles of fortifications that completely encircled the city and were bisected by the Potomac River, navigable by the largest class of naval vessels. And a partial investment would have been worse than useless, since it would have recommitted Southerners to the very mode of warfare at which the North excelled. It would have returned them to McClellan's "battle of posts" that Lee had fought so hard to escape. On top of which, to mount an assault or to lay a siege he must necessarily have operated out of war-ravaged Fairfax. Eight years later, while visiting Alexandria, Lee would point at Fort Ward and confess, "I could not tell my men to take that fort when they had had nothing to eat for three days."[16]

Indeed, it is not likely Lee would have ordered his men to attack the forts even if they had been well fed. Nonetheless, his postwar comment underscored the second easy decision he reached. He could not long remain in Fairfax County. The region had been picked clean of food and forage by the continuous fifteen months of occupation by the armies of both sides. Even wood for fires had all but disappeared, except in the westernmost part of the county around Chantilly. Thousands of acres of timber had been felled to construct the Federal fortifications around Washington and the Confederate defenses around Centreville and to build shelters and fuel the fires of the troops during the long winter of 1861–62.

Nor could Lee hope to freight in enough supplies either quickly or efficiently for his large body of soldiers, many of whom had gone two or three days without food except for what they had gleaned from the countryside. Although the Orange and Alexandria and the Virginia Central provided a continuous rail link between Fairfax Station and Richmond, the railroad bridges over the Rapidan, the Rappahannock, and the Bull Run had been destroyed. In addition, in its first long, overland campaign the Army of Northern Virginia suffered from a severe shortage of wagons. After the war, Lee would write, "I could not have maintained the army in Fairfax, so barren was it of subsistence and so devoid were we of transportation."[17]

Even if the Confederates could have solved their supply problem, it would have been unsound strategy for them to remain in Fairfax. An army based in northern Virginia was vulnerable to being turned on either flank. Lee would have had neither the navy to control the river on his east nor the additional forces to secure the Shenandoah Valley to the west. The first year of the war had been an extended lesson in military geography of the strategic weakness of the ground immediately in front of Washington. George McClellan provided the first demonstration when he bypassed Johnston's army at Manassas and carried the Army of the Potomac to the Peninsula. McClellan gave the second when he arranged for the safety of Washington in his absence by posting his main defensive force at Winchester, where it would be on the flank of an enemy advancing directly on the Northern capital. Lincoln and Stanton had not understood the military geography, and they believed they were making Washington more secure when they dismantled McClellan's arrangement and shifted the bulk of the Federal troops back to Manassas and Fredericksburg. They had, of course, simply opened the way for Jackson's turning movement down the Valley, which threatened Washington from the upper Potomac and threw the Northern administration into such a tizzy that significant reenforcements were withheld from McClellan's offensive against Richmond. Lee, who certainly understood the military geography of his theater as well as McClellan, could scarcely have failed to draw the conclusion that it would be foolish to position himself directly in front of Washington.[18]

Sound strategy dictated that Lee could not remain in Fairfax many days, but it was the scarcity of food which compelled him to move immediately. Within hours of learning from Stuart of Pope's escape to the forts, Lee reached two decisions: he could not attack Washington and he could not stay in his present position. Other answers would have to be found and found quickly, so Lee likely spent the afternoon consulting with his chief lieutenants.[19]

One option Lee may not have even discussed—since he does not mention it in any of his writings—was to retire south to a defensive position behind the Rappahannock, either at Fredericksburg or to the west near Culpeper. While the move would assure him the leisure to rest, refit, and reorganize his army, it would give the same respite to the enemy, who needed it much more desperately. It would abandon the agricultural and manpower resources of northern Virginia so recently liberated. It would also surrender the initiative to the Federals and reduce Lee to reacting to any new offensive launched at the time and place of the enemy's choosing. Finally, it might be interpreted by Northerners as demonstrating Lee was too weak to pursue even a smashing victory and thus encourage in them the belief that they could win the war in spite of their current low fortunes. All of this ran so completely contrary to everything Lee had been trying to accomplish that it is likely he never considered retreating or making any move that might be seen as a retreat.[20]

It is also unlikely that on the afternoon of September 2, the Confederate commander gave more than passing thought to an invasion of the North. To Lee "invasion" meant more than a mere incursion across the border. In his mind it was a "very decided offensive movement" and involved deep penetration and occupation of the free states themselves.[21] Looking backward in February of 1864, Lee would declare bluntly, "We are not in a condition, and never have been, in my opinion, to invade the enemy's country with a prospect of permanent benefit."[22] An invasion of conquest would clearly exceed Confederate war aims, and such a drastic departure from policy ought not be undertaken without approval from Richmond. More to the point was the obvious question of what Lee would do with either land or cities he might capture. He dare not spread his forces too thin and become bogged down in a military occupation.

It is true there had been loose talk from time to time of "carrying the war into Africa." Conceivably, Lee might have felt justified in invading the North in the more limited sense of a raid to avenge injuries to the South and to make Northerners comprehend the horrors of war. It is also possible—although no direct evidence exists on the point—that he perceived any attempt to visit devastation on Northerners would more likely increase their hostility, deepen their determination to prosecute the war, and thus undermine his own grand strategy for victory.[23] Clearly, what Lee did believe was that his army was neither large enough nor sufficiently well equipped in ordnance and munitions to launch an offensive deep into enemy country for whatever purpose.[24]

West was the only point of the compass that offered several attractive possibilities, albeit it possessed serious drawbacks as well. If Lee marched west as far as the Shenandoah Valley, he could clear out the Federal garrisons at Winchester and Martinsburg, open a safe line of communications to Richmond through Charlottesville or Lynchburg, and threaten Harpers Ferry and the upper Potomac. This move possessed three inherent weaknesses. First, operations based from Winchester might not sufficiently threaten the Federals to cause them to abandon a period of rest and refitting. Second, it might give the enemy sufficient room to mount a flank movement against Richmond, especially one by water down the Chesapeake. And third, even if the Federals did respond to the menace from the upper Potomac, they might move against it from south of the river, thus reoccupying recently freed northern Virginia and at the same time effectively securing Washington from danger.

There was a variation on this move that made more sense. If Lee marched only so far west as Loudoun County, he could take advantage of a region lightly touched by the war and one rich in food and forage while simultaneously securing the flank of Fairfax and Manassas.[25] The prospects for this more modest westward movement were tempered by the fact that it seemed to offer no long-range prospects. The first few days of a Confederate encampment at Leesburg might cause the enemy to fear a movement against its western flank. But as Lee's stay lengthened, it would become obvious to the Federals that they could continue their reorganization and plan for their next offensive at their own pace. He could not, in other words, be certain of maintaining the initiative from Loudoun County.[26]

What, then, was Lee to do? It seemed as if any action he might take—including making no move at all—would diminish the hard-won momentum gained by his summer's successes. Perhaps at no time in his career did Lee face the need to decide on a strategy so quickly and with such inadequate and contradictory information.

Confederate Tide at Flood

Ironically, three tangents did exist to help Lee escape going around the four points of the compass in strategic circles, but it is doubtful that his limited knowledge allowed him to perceive more than one of them. Viewed from afar, a heavy mist of ripeness hovers over the opening days of September 1862. Forces were at work carrying Confederate military fortunes toward their flood. To the extent Lee understood the broader context surrounding the decision he had to make, he would have also known there were powerful swells pulling him northward to Maryland. There were two concurrent chains of events developing, even as Lee sat in perplexity at Ox Hill, that would have weighed heavily in his thinking—if he had known about them. Across the Atlantic, British sympathies toward the South were rapidly approaching their apogee amid talk of foreign mediation in the war and recognition of the Confederacy. Simultaneously, six Confederate armies beyond the Eastern theater were either already on the march, or were preparing to advance northward.

The seductive possibility exists that British and French recognition of the Confederacy—and with it the further possibility (although scarcely certainty) of foreign intervention—depended on one more major victory by Lee in the late summer or autumn of 1862. At the outbreak of hostilities, many foreign observers assumed that the sprawling South was too large for the North to subdue. Throughout the war, however, European attention focused heavily on the Eastern theater. Hence, upon reading reports of McClellan's seemingly inexorable advance upon Richmond in the spring of 1862, many Europeans changed their minds and concluded that the Confederacy was on the verge of defeat. News of Lee's victories in the Seven Days battles sparked anew the belief that the task of conquering the South was too big for the North.

The French emperor Napoleon III, addicted to all manner of foreign adventures, from time to time seemed inclined to aid the Confederacy. The American Civil War was not one of the emperor's priorities, however, and it soon became apparent, in spite of the suffering of the French textile industry from the cotton drought, that he would not act unilaterally.[27] The question of whether or not there would be any form of foreign intervention came to hinge upon the decision of the British government.

On July 18 the British House of Commons debated mediation, and, although the question was temporarily remanded to the cabinet, the degree of sympathy revealed during the debate encouraged leaders of the governing Liberal party to believe the time was near when parliament might support some level of action. News of Lee's further victory at Second Manassas brought speculation that Washington and Baltimore were in danger. In mid-September, a cabinet meeting was scheduled for late October to discuss what measures ought to be taken. With the great Liberal triumvirate—Prime Minister Viscount Palmerston, Chancellor of the Exchequer William Gladstone, and Foreign Minister Lord John Russell—all showing varying degrees of sympathy, it is impossible to dismiss entirely the notion that Great Britain might have acted in some manner that would have benefited the Confederacy. Nevertheless, the postponement of the discussion for six weeks indicated that the leaders remained unconvinced and needed further proof of the viability of the Confederacy. Idleness by Lee might not have weakened the Southern cause abroad, but neither would such inactivity have strengthened it. Even more, a Confederate success in Maryland might have provided the push to recognition.[28]

Such questions must be forever moot, since Lee would neither stay idle nor be able furnish the timely, additional victory. The moment, and with it the possibility of foreign intervention, would pass unfulfilled into history.

One pertinent question does remain. What bearing, if any, did foreign affairs have on Lee's determination of strategy in September 1862? The answer—based on the lack of any connecting evidence—is little, if any at all. The British decision to hold a cabinet meeting on the American question was made two weeks after Lee determined to cross the Potomac, and thus there cannot have been a causal relation. The most that might be said is reports of the debate in Commons could have reached Lee by September 2; and such news could conceivably have then induced Lee to believe Confederate military success might favorably influence the actions of foreign governments toward the Confederacy. Such speculation, doubly hypothetical, must be balanced against Lee's professed belief that no foreign nation would significantly contribute to Confederate independence, as well as against the absence of evidence that the general gave any weight to foreign considerations while deciding the strategy he would pursue.[29]

There was another series of events—more immediate and more strategically relevant—that had indeed already been set in motion by September 2. The long-delayed Confederate offensive push of the third phase of the war was at last under way. Six Confederate columns on a front stretching from western Virginia to northern Mississippi were set to embark on a drive to the Ohio River, and a seventh under Kirby Smith had already entered eastern Kentucky. From August through October 1862 the Confederacy mounted its greatest effort to expel the invaders from its borders and to claim the provinces irredenta. Kirby Smith would be joined in Kentucky by the bulk of the Army of Mississippi under Braxton Bragg and a smaller force from southwestern Virginia under Humphrey Marshall. Armies in northern Mississippi under Sterling Price and Earl Van Dorn were to advance northward through western Tennessee to join the gathering host in Kentucky. In the meantime, William W. Loring launched his own army and a separate cavalry column under Albert Jenkins to clear the mountainous counties of western Virginia.[30]

All of these movements at their origin were encouraged by Davis and Lee. All grew from the Confederate recommitment in the third phase to mobilize, concentrate, and return to the offensive; and all may have been invigorated by the success of Lee's campaigns in June and August in clearing eastern Virginia. Most importantly, all were approved by Richmond.

On the other hand, none was controlled or even coordinated in any meaningful way from the Confederate capital. Following his customary policy, Jefferson Davis established the grand strategic framework, but he did not attempt to dictate the details of timing and geography of the campaigns. It could not have been otherwise. Mid–nineteenth century communications and transportation could not operate in time over the distances involved to provide efficient coordination.[31] As Davis wrote to Bragg on September 4, "You have the field before you and I rely on your judgment."[32] In consequence, the grand Confederate offensive was a web of nearly random design held together by the most diaphanous threads.

There can be little doubt that knowledge of a massive Confederate advance in the West would have nudged Lee toward mounting a northward offensive of his own. There is considerable doubt, however, about how much the Confederate commander knew of what was happening in the mountains and beyond. Although Lee was never officially relieved of his duties as general-in-chief, the burdens of commanding the Army of Northern Virginia and the continuing crisis in the Eastern theater prevented him from paying much attention to Confederate affairs elsewhere. So long as he remained in the Richmond area and in close touch with Davis and the War Department, some news from other fronts filtered through to him, and occasionally his advice was still sought.

At the time he moved to field command, Lee knew generally that other Confederate commanders had stalled, and no one anywhere was making forward progress. In mid-June, upon hearing that Halleck had dispersed the large Federal army at Corinth, Lee urged that Bragg, who had just succeeded Beauregard, seize the opportunity to go on the offensive.[33] For over a month nothing had come of the suggestion. As late as the middle of July, the great Confederate attempt of the spring to reverse the tide of the war appeared to be exhausted without much to show for the effort. To balance the serious defeats at Shiloh and Seven Pines, the maximum push of the third phase had yielded only Jackson's success in the Shenandoah, Lee's tactical victory on the Chickahominy, and the modest cavalry raids of John Hunt Morgan in Kentucky and Nathan Bedford Forrest in Tennessee.

The Confederate offensive-defensive was not dead, however, but merely dormant. It took Bragg five weeks to acclimate to his new command and to decide on the best response to the Federal dispersal of force. He finally focused on the Federal column under Don Carlos Buell, which had set out from Corinth in June and was working its way eastward slowly across northern Alabama, building and repairing railroads as it aimed toward Chattanooga. By July 23 Bragg had decided to split his own army to prevent Buell from occupying east Tennessee. Bragg would move with the bulk of his force (some 35,000) by rail from Tupelo via Mobile to Chattanooga, where he would join with Kirby Smith's 20,000 men based at Knoxville. Initially the plan called for Bragg and Smith to maneuver against Buell in middle Tennessee, while Earl Van Dorn and Sterling Price (each with about 16,000 men) held the line of the Mississippi River and the position at Tupelo respectively.[34]

Lee, who was still in the Richmond vicinity, must have been privy to Bragg's plans as communicated to the War Department. When he also learned of Morgan's raid into Kentucky in mid-July and heard the reports that Kentuckians were ready by the thousands to flock to the Confederate banner, Lee put the strands of information together on July 26 to devise a comprehensive strategy for the West. He suggested that Bragg and Smith advance into Kentucky and be supported on their right flank by the forces of Humphrey Marshall and William Loring from western Virginia.[35] On August 5, Jefferson Davis presented a considerably watered-down version of the plan to Bragg. The president hinted that after Buell had been "crushed" in middle Tennessee—but only after—the way "may" be open for the liberation of Kentucky. He made no mention of possible cooperation from Marshall and Loring.[36]

It was at this point that affairs in the West started to take on a life of their own and, simultaneously, that Lee began to lose touch with happenings outside of the Eastern theater. On August 9 Kirby Smith took the initiative to propose a drastic change in the plan he had agreed upon with Bragg. Impressed with Morgan's reports of the ripeness of Kentucky, Smith told Bragg that time should not be wasted in reducing the Federal force at Cumberland Gap preparatory to a pincer movement against Buell. Instead, if the enemy at the Gap were found to be well entrenched, Smith would bypass them and head directly for Lexington, Kentucky. Next, Smith violated the chain of command by arranging for Humphrey Marshall (from Loring's department) to come to Knoxville for an interview, at which time the two generals decided that Marshall with 3,000 men would cross over the mountains to join Smith's expedition.[37]

Bragg's reply of the following day virtually adopted Smith's plan. While it is true that Bragg merely affirmed his "inclination" to move on Lexington with his own army as well, and also confessed that he could not make any move for a week or so, until his artillery, cavalry, and wagons had arrived from their overland march from Tupelo, nonetheless, his enthusiasm for a direct advance into Kentucky was evident. He even expanded the offensive plans by adding that he would instruct Van Dorn and Price to strike for west Tennessee in Buell's rear. Referring to the five cooperating Confederate columns, Bragg concluded, "I trust we may all unite in Ohio."[38]

It is clear that by August 14 the Confederate War Department had become generally aware of the "extensive plan of operations" evolved by Bragg, Smith, and Marshall.[39] How much Lee knew about the proposed offensive is not at all clear, however. The 14th was his last hectic day in Richmond before leaving for Gordonsville, the day he had not even been able to find time to stop at home and say goodbye to his wife. It is reasonable to assume that some word reached him of an undertaking of such magnitude. Still, since no one had yet taken a step toward Kentucky, the most he could have learned at this early date was that plans were being laid.

From mid-August onward, Lee became so involved with Pope and so isolated in the field that he apparently lost track of affairs in the West. Moreover, Lee seems to have been equally ignorant of affairs in the mountain theater between East and West. Although he several times suggested to the War Department that William Loring clear the Federals from the Kanawha and then march east to the Shenandoah Valley, the Confederate commander seems to have had little idea of what was happening in western Virginia. Apparently he did not know that Loring would in fact try to carry out the nearly impossible mission and had even added his own touch by planning a cavalry raid across the Ohio River.

From the documents that have survived there is no indication that either Davis or the War Department forwarded information to Lee about Confederate armies elsewhere. Even Northern newspapers, usually a favorite source of intelligence, apparently were either scarce or unavailable in central Virginia. The drumbeat of parallel happenings rolled with such rapidity in East and West that Lee moved for a time in a shadow of ignorance. On August 16, as Lee laid plans to flank Pope on the Rapidan, Kirby Smith's vanguard crossed the Kentucky border. On August 22, as Lee danced with Pope on the Rappahannock, Loring dispatched Albert Jenkins on a cavalry raid to the Ohio River. On August 25, as Jackson set out for Thoroughfare Gap, Bragg ordered Van Dorn and Price to start their advance on western Tennessee. On the 28th, as Jackson launched his attack against King's division on the Brawner farm, Bragg's Army of Mississippi left Chattanooga for Kentucky. Finally, on the 30th, as Longstreet smashed Porter's flank on the plains of Manassas, Kirby Smith won an equally brilliant tactical victory on a smaller scale at Richmond, Kentucky.

Thus, three days later, as Lee sat at Ox Hill on September 2 contemplating his own strategic dilemma, the greatest Confederate offensive of the war was beginning to unfold. Kirby Smith had just entered Lexington, and the armies of Bragg and Marshall were on the march toward Kentucky. Van Dorn and Price had not yet moved but were under orders to do so. Jenkins was within two days of the Ohio River, and Loring was but four days from launching his advance northwest through the Kanawha Valley. Had Lee known of this rising Confederate tide, the knowledge would surely have been a powerful inducement to throw the Army of Northern Virginia into the balance to create a maximum effort and bring the war to a successful closure. Apparently, he did not know.[40] Indeed, so ignorant was Lee of what was happening elsewhere, he would, on the following day (September 3), suggest to Jefferson Davis that—if Bragg was not being usefully employed—a few troops be left in garrison and the remainder of the Army of Mississippi be transferred to Virginia.[41]

On the basis of this statement, it does not seem likely Lee was aware of his opportunity to become part of a multiprong offensive during the time he had to decide upon his new course of operations. In fact, the opposite may have been true. If he suspected that other Confederate armies were not being effectively employed elsewhere, he may have felt the increased need to press his own advantage to the fullest. In the days that followed, Lee would learn more of what was happening in the West. The belated revelation that he was coincidentally part of a joint offensive would stiffen his resolve to push his campaign to victory. No doubt it would also be one of the influences driving him to scramble for alternatives long after most commanders would have abandoned the campaign.

There was a third tangent that might have helped Lee escape from going around in strategic circles, and about it he knew something more than the other two. Indeed, he could not have failed to grasp that events were at work which portended the opening of a new phase of the war—one in which the odds would be weighted even more heavily against the Confederacy than they were on September 2. Unavoidably, the disparity in strength between the South and the North had dominated his thinking throughout the summer of 1862. It had been the hard truth that focused his strategy on wearing down the enemy while husbanding his own resources, which reminded him the war's clock was running against the Confederacy and compelled him to take normally unacceptable risks. Now it seemed, in spite of his successes, the gap between the size of the forces in the field was going to increase.

Of course, Lee could not have known with any degree of precision the odds he faced at any given moment. The inefficient record keeping of his own government could only provide him with gross estimates of the numbers raised by Southern mobilization, and the enemy's figures were necessarily a greater mystery to him. He could not have known with exactness that the 477,000 men the South had in the field in July and August represented 76 percent of the 624,000 of the North, giving it a disparity of slightly better than 3 to 4.[42] But he must have realized the Confederacy currently enjoyed the best odds it could hope to obtain after the brief opening months of the war. The South had nearly reached the peak number of men it could put into the field at any one time, while the North had just begun to tap its potential.

It is certain Lee knew that Lincoln on July 1 had called upon the loyal states for an additional 300,000 three-year volunteers to push the war "to a speedy and satisfactory conclusion."[43] Once mustered, this force would raise the Federal total to 924,000 and tip the scales against the Confederacy at odds of worse than 2 to 1. Even with the new volunteers, the North would still have mobilized scarcely 20 percent of its potential military manpower. The South, on the other hand, had already put into the field almost twice that proportion (39.8 percent) from its pool of white males aged eighteen to forty-five.[44]

It is not certain whether or not Lee knew the Federal War Department on August 4 drafted an additional 300,000 men from the state militias for nine-months' service. If he had learned of it, the knowledge could only have heightened his sense of desperation. This second call would increase the total of Northern soldiers to 1,224,000 and raise the odds against the South to 2.6 to 1. Even then, the North would have summoned only 27.5 percent of its manpower resources.[45]

Lee was not prescient. He could not foretell how far the North would go to compel the South to remain in the Union. He could not know that the Lincoln government was fast approaching the decision to enlist blacks as soldiers. But he could not fail to grasp the desperate plight of the Confederacy. He knew the Federals were not yet employing compulsory service, while the Confederates had already resorted to conscription and were beginning to scrape the bottom of the manpower barrel. He also knew he had all but stripped the south Atlantic states three months earlier and that new regiments raised from the Conscription Act had slowed to a trickle.

And, he knew the moment was ripe for action. Although the Federals had concentrated nearly 110,000 veterans in the environs of Washington, these old soldiers were the demoralized and dispirited fragments of five different armies.[46] He believed they were unlikely to give a good account of themselves if called into a campaign immediately.[47] Nearly 20,000 of the new troops had already reached Washington; but they had been organized into entirely separate regiments, and their greenness rendered them almost useless for the time being.[48] The Army of Northern Virginia, on the other hand, was flushed with victory and confident in itself and its leaders. It was also now stronger by half than it had been at Manassas, for on this pivotal September 2 the van of the long-awaited third wing arrived from Richmond.

The Strength of Lee's Army

The size of the Army of Northern Virginia on the eve of the Maryland campaign has been somewhat understated in the past. Most of the diminution has derived from a failure to appreciate the strength of the reenforcements that reached Lee at Ox Hill. In fact, not much attention has been paid to the history of the column from Richmond. It is usually supposed these troops had been freed from the defense of the capital by McClellan's withdrawal, did little more than make good Confederate losses from Manassas, and exerted negligible influence on Lee's considerations of strategy. Their full story is markedly different and is worth tracing from its origin.

The massive Confederate army that Davis and Lee had pried loose from localities across the South and collected at Richmond in June was intended to thwart the dire threat posed by McClellan on the Chickahominy. It is not clear whether either leader initially envisioned that the emergency force would—after the immediate crisis had passed—evolve into a field army to serve at a distance from the capital. From the start, however, Lee did consider all of these troops to be part of his Army of Northern Virginia. As the strategic situation in Virginia developed during the summer (with the appearance of Pope on the Rapidan and the withdrawal of McClellan from the James), the Confederate commander moved to transfer his army and the scene of fighting to central Virginia. Ironically, he encountered the same sort of political friction that had hobbled McClellan when the Federal general removed the Army of the Potomac from the immediate vicinity of Washington. Fortunately for Lee, Jefferson Davis would rise to the occasion. After some hesitation, the president would fully commit the Confederate resources at hand.

By late July, Lee had concentrated one-third of the Army of Northern Virginia (three infantry divisions and one cavalry brigade) under Jackson at Gordonsville to confront Pope's threat along the Rapidan River. Starting on August 9, Lee dispatched another third under Longstreet (three infantry divisions and a cavalry brigade) to force the issue in the north and then quickly return to Richmond. By the time Lee himself left for Gordonsville six days later, he guessed that McClellan was withdrawing from the Peninsula, and he took with him an additional division of infantry.[49] He left behind on the James fully one-third of his army in three infantry divisions, one cavalry brigade, and four battalions of the artillery reserve.

Lee viewed the forces left at Richmond as the third wing of his Army of Northern Virginia. Clearly, he anticipated they would soon join him in the field, and he issued orders to facilitate their departure. Perhaps for that reason he seems not to have paid too close attention to which units he took into the field and which remained. Still, it is interesting that he sent both purely Virginia cavalry brigades north and retained the mixed brigade under Hampton at Richmond. Of the infantry he left behind, the divisions under D. H. Hill and LaFayette McLaws were fine, battle-tested units from the Seven Days campaign, while the one under Walker was composed of lightly seasoned regiments from the district of North Carolina.[50]

August 17 started the chain of events that unrolled to form the story of the reenforcing column. At the time, Lee sat near Gordonsville with Jackson and Longstreet, attempting to overslough inertia and launch his turning movement against Pope across the Rapidan. While the Confederate field army was weak in both men and provisions, the three brigades of R. H. Anderson's division competed for space with supplies on the woefully inadequate facilities of the Virginia Central Railroad. On the same day, Lee ordered D. H. Hill's division to move forward to Gordonsville.[51] Coincidentally, reports coming into the War Department confirmed McClellan's withdrawal from Harrison's Landing, and the administration approved the release of the additional division.[52]

The intent was to ship Hill's five brigades by rail, but the effort was clearly beyond the capacity of the overburdened Virginia Central. Adj. Gen. Samuel Cooper suggested to Lee that the troops be sent by three different railroads on a circuitous route via Lynchburg to arrive in Gordonsville from the west. Lee sensibly pointed out that this would interfere with the shipping of needed supplies from the Valley, and he urged that the men simply be marched northward instead.[53] In the end, the division waited for the traffic to clear, and, finally, on the 19th space was found on the cars for the nine regiments of Roswell Ripley and Alfred Colquitt. The two brigades reached Gordonsville by midnight, detrained, and marched eight miles farther north to bivouac at Orange Court House.[54]

The delay proved fatal for the rapid reenforcement of Lee. In the three intervening days, rumors grew of phantom Federal threats against Richmond, and a nervous administration reversed its decision. On the

19th, even as the first troops embarked, Secretary of War Randolph telegraphed Lee that three enemy brigades were advancing on Richmond from Fredericksburg, while McClellan's army was reported to be sailing up the York to the White House. In consequence, the divisions of Hill and McLaws would be retained at the capital. Randolph had the grace to add, "What do you think of it?"[55]

By this point, Lee believed he would be attacking Pope so soon that no reenforcements could reach him in time to be of help. Moreover, he also had heard that an enemy force was moving south from Fredericksburg. Hence, he made the best of the changed situation. He urged all available troops at Richmond be assembled on the line of the North Anna River. It was a creative compromise.[56] A force on the North Anna would be directly between Fredericksburg and Hanover Junction and on the left flank of an enemy advancing up the York and Pamunkey Rivers. At the same time they would have taken an important first step in joining him in the field. They could "then be moved," as he put it, "according to circumstances."

Lee's plan appealed to Davis, and the president acted immediately to put it into effect. On the 19th, he ordered not only the three remaining brigades of Hill's division, but also the four battalions of the Artillery Reserve under William Nelson Pendleton to Hanover Junction. With a forced march the troops arrived the following day.[57] During the next several days, McLaws's division and Hampton's cavalry brigade were added to the swelling numbers, and D. H. Hill arrived to take command of the entire wing.[58] It was a formidable force on the North Anna. Only the three brigades from the District of North Carolina stationed in the vicinity of Petersburg and a hodgepodge of miscellaneous troops remained solely committed to the defense of the capital.

Unfortunately for Lee, it became difficult for the administration to take the second step, and the plan froze halfway to completion. The ghost of McClellan on the York evaporated, and the threat from Fredericksburg dissipated. At the same time, events to the north rushed toward a climax. Lee chased Pope from the Rapidan and sparred with the Federals along the Rappahannock, all the while asking what had become of his third wing. Yet, for seven days from their first arrival, the reenforcements idled behind the North Anna.

On August 25—the same day Lee held a war council at Jeffersonton and ordered Jackson on the sweep through Thoroughfare Gap—Harvey Hill, depicted as "crazy to get to the front," could brook the delay no longer.[59] Hill "begged" William Pendleton, who had been a West Point classmate of Davis, to visit Richmond and persuade the authorities to release the stalled column. Pendleton mounted a passing train, and, upon his arrival in the capital that evening, he went directly to see the president. He discovered that Lee's letter of the 24th, in which the general had forced the issue by ordering the reenforcements forward subject only to a positive veto, was already on Davis's desk. Pendleton sat in on two long meetings—one that evening and one the following morning—in which Davis, Secretary Randolph, and Gen. G. W. Smith discussed the ramifications of the situation.

Regrettably, the details of those conversations have been lost. Who, if anyone, protested against stripping the capital of its defenders, and who argued that the momentum Lee was building must be sustained, cannot now be known. Only the results are certain. In the end, the president decided—"whatever risks might ensue"—he would not only release the North Anna column but augment it with two of the three brigades at Petersburg.[60] Orders were issued at once, and Davis sent his extraordinary dispatch to Lee in which he declared, "Confidence in you overcomes the view which would otherwise be taken of the exposed condition of Richmond."[61]

Once released, the reenforcing wing moved forward in three columns. Ripley and Colquitt, who had reached Orange before stopping, comprised the vanguard. These two brigades made reasonably good time. Setting out on the 27th, they waded the Rapidan and Rappahannock and reached Manassas Junction by the afternoon of the 30th in time to hear the raging battle but too late to participate in the climactic attack against Porter's corps.[62]

Contrary to normal practice, the main column (Hill's remaining three brigades, McLaws's four, the Artillery Reserve, and Hampton's cavalry) actually started a day earlier than the vanguard. Immediately upon the conclusion of the presidential meeting on the morning of the 26th, the War Department telegraphed orders to Hanover Junction. When Pendleton returned to his camp later in the day, he found his command already on the road.[63] In spite of the early start and regardless of Harvey Hill's determination, the main body of the reenforcements would not reach Lee until September 2. For reasons that are not clear but undoubtedly had to do with heavy traffic and Hill's impatience, none of this column used the railroad for even part of the way.[64] The whole column marched the entire distance to Leesburg. According to the reckoning Sgt. Mike Hubbert kept in his diary, the 13th Mississippi (Barksdale's brigade of McLaws) covered 145 miles in nine days, an average of sixteen miles per day.[65]

The tail of the reenforcing wing was comprised of the two brigades (Walker and Ransom) under John G. Walker on loan from the District of North Carolina and stationed on the south side of the James. Although they had the farthest to travel, their journey was the easiest. The men began boarding trains at Richmond on the 26th, and by the evening of the following day they had concentrated at Rapidan Station, thus leapfrogging the van and the main body. Here Walker waited four days for his wagons to catch up and did not commence his march until September 1. By the 2d, Lee knew only that Walker was on the way, but not where he was or when he would arrive.[66]

Lee no doubt should have had all of these reenforcements earlier in his campaign, and it is interesting to speculate what more he might have accomplished with a greatly augmented army against Pope. Still, the most remarkable part of the story was not the hesitation and delay—which, considering what was at stake and the primitive rail facilities, were minimal—but the president's willingness to strip so completely the Confederate capital of its defenders to support an offensive on the frontier. Such fulsome support bespoke not only Jefferson Davis's confidence in Robert E. Lee, but also his sense that the moment for decision was at hand and his determination to provide all possible resources to press the momentum on to final victory. At this critical juncture, Davis rose to the challenge of history and his office and proved himself—at least on this occasion—a great wartime president.

After August 26, the total forces available for the defense of Richmond, stretched from the Rappahannock to Petersburg, numbered 17,000. Of these, 11,000 were in green regiments just mustered into service, and the remainder were a miscellany of heavy artillery units, local militia, convalescents, sailors without ships, and recently paroled prisoners of war.[67] Into Lee's army on the distant Potomac, Davis entrusted one-third of all the regiments in the entire Confederacy.

Even before the arrival of the reenforcements, Lee already possessed a sizable number of regiments in his field army. Jackson's command contained 67.5 infantry regiments, Longstreet's 55.6, and the reserve division of R. H. Anderson 13.5. Combined with Stuart's 9.8 cavalry regiments and the equivalent of 4.4 artillery regiments, Lee had available a total of 150.8 regiments for the Battles of Second Manassas and Chantilly. D. H. Hill, McLaws, and Walker brought him another 47.7 infantry regiments; Hampton added 4.1 cavalry regiments; and the new divisional and Reserve Artillery contributed the equivalent of 3.2 regiments for a total of 55 regiments in the reenforcing column. Thus, by September 2, the Army of Northern Virginia comprised a grand total of 205.8 regiments of all arms. On that date the Confederacy had 621.5 regiments mustered and in the field, and Lee had 33.11 percent of them.[68]

Strictly in terms of numbers of regiments, this army certainly was one of the largest, and may indeed have been the largest field army ever commanded by Lee.[69] If, on September 2, all of Lee's regiments had been at the full 750-man strength of new units after their initial shakedown, his army would have numbered 154,000. If the regiments had averaged even 500, as they had when he took over three months earlier, he would have had 103,000 men.

It is possible that the impression of strength created by such a large number of units exerted a subtle influence on both Lee and his opponents. The organizational structure, hierarchy, and staff functionaries; the number of battleflags; and even the intervals in the columns on the march were the same as they would have been for a much larger army. This may explain in part the inflated estimates that would flow without contradiction into Federal headquarters on the size of the Confederate army.[70] And, in spite of his knowing full well most of his regiments were below optimum strength, it may have influenced Lee. Because he had not yet inculcated conscientious record keeping habits among his officers, the Confederate commander did not know on September 2—and would not know throughout the campaign ahead—the precise number of men in his army. Still, if nothing else, even a foggy perception of the prodigious percentage of the power of the Confederacy placed in his hands must have increased his determination to pursue his advantage of the moment.

Moreover, although Lee's regiments were indeed worn down from fighting and marching, they were not so anemic as claimed by the Confederates writing after the war. They ranged in size from the 85 officers and men present for duty in the 8th Georgia in D. R. Jones's division to the 983 in the conscript-swollen 3d North Carolina in D. H. Hill's division.[71] Jackson's regiments were appreciably the smallest, averaging 285; while Longstreet's averaged 364 and R. H. Anderson's 377. Understandably, the forces just arrived from Richmond were the largest, averaging 454. The average for the combined forces was 360.[72]

The army commanded by Lee as he sat at Ox Hill and contemplated his next move was not as large as it might have been. The continuing and complicated problem of "estrays" reduced the figure from the 90 to 100,000 men he should have had after deducting the losses from Second Manassas. Yet, it was larger by 50 percent than the Confederates looking back through the mists of the Lost Cause would have their posterity believe. According to the partial figures of the trimonthly muster for September 1, supplemented by estimates based on earlier returns, Jackson's infantry and artillery totaled 20,600 officers and men present for duty; R. H. Anderson's 5,700; Longstreet's 19,600; and Stuart's cavalry and artillery 5,600. The reenforcements, which it has been said only made good the 9,000 losses of Second Manassas, actually counted 23,900 officers and men present for duty in infantry and artillery. Thus, Lee had a combined force of about 75,500.[73]

One of the ironic side affects of the determined postwar effort by Confederates to deflate Lee's numbers has been to raise doubts about the soundness of his judgment in undertaking the Maryland campaign. Yet, his army was now significantly larger than the one with which he had defeated what he believed to be the combined armies of Pope and McClellan four days earlier. There was no reason for Lee to be unduly worried, therefore, that numbers alone would prevent him from undertaking any new campaign that strategy and his sense of urgency dictated.[74]

The Mettle of Lee's Army

The size of an army is but part measure of its strength, of course. Just as important is its ability to fight. Rosters kill not a single enemy, and numbers alone do not gain victories. The fighting capability of an army derives from an imprecise mixture of its combat experience and training, its physical condition, its morale and confidence in itself and its leaders, and the quality of its officer corps. From the perspective of his army's battle effectiveness, Lee could find more reasons to be optimistic than otherwise.

On September 2, 1862, there was no army of either North or South to match the battle experience of the Army of Northern Virginia: 61 percent of Lee's infantry regiments had fought in three or more major battles, and 81 percent had fought in two or more. And all 184 infantry regiments were veterans of at least one major battle. Even the handful of regiments mustered within the last two months had already received their fiery initiation at Second Manassas.[75] It is true, there were about

2,200 conscripts and recruits from North Carolina too recently arrived to have been properly drilled, but these had been distributed throughout the old Tar Heel regiments. Thus, the new men would likely give much better account of themselves than the green Yankee troops now coming into the field who were being formed into wholly new regiments.[76]

Not only could Lee rely on an army of veteran regiments, but at the next highest level he could also count on considerable experience and continuity. The effectiveness of a regiment in line of battle depended in part on its good relations with neighboring units, and in the Civil War the esprit of brigades was second only to the camaraderie of the regiment. Confederate brigades had started to solidify early in the war, and Lee had three which dated to First Bull Run and had engaged in five major battles. Another three brigades had gone through four battles with their organization essentially intact, and an additional nine had experienced three battles together. In all, twenty-seven (or 67.5 percent) of Lee's forty brigades were veterans of two or more major battles. All of the remaining thirteen brigades had fought in either the Seven Days or Second Manassas campaigns in essentially, if not exactly, their current formation.[77]

The division was the largest combat unit recognized by Confederate law. Neither Lee nor his predecessor, Johnston, believed the cohesiveness of the division quite so important as that of the brigade. Lee in particular recognized the heavy responsibility of the divisional commander made it more important for the unit to be competently led than that its organization remain unchanged.[78] Nevertheless, all eleven of the divisions with the army as it bivouacked near Chantilly had fought at least one battle as a unit, and seven of them had engaged in three or more battles with essentially the same organizations.[79]

It was at the very tip of the military hierarchy where Lee remained most fluid in his structure. When he inherited the Army of Northern Virginia, it had been on the verge of solidifying into two corps. Joseph Johnston had collected his divisions into a right wing under Longstreet and a left wing under G. W. Smith for the Battle of Seven Pines. Lee abandoned this organization by returning Longstreet to divisional command and not replacing Smith, who had taken a leave of absence. At the opening of the Seven Days campaign, only Jackson commanded more than one division. And Stonewall brought with him to Richmond the two divisions he already commanded in the Valley District. At the outset, Jackson had been given another division (Whiting), and before the week was over he was assigned a fourth (D. H. Hill). Longstreet was also given temporary command of an additional division (A. P. Hill).

Immediately after Malvern Hill, however, Lee reverted to his simpler structure by divisions. It is not unlikely that his displeasure with the awkward and sometimes incompetent working of the army caused him to hesitate in creating larger units. It is also true that three of his most senior generals (Magruder, Huger, and Holmes, who had commanded independent departments and were in line for higher commands) had proven the least reliable in battle. After the three had disappeared for other assignments, Lee gradually began to experiment with combining divisions again. Still, Jackson's command did not increase beyond his own two divisions until after A. P. Hill was sent to him at Gordonsville in late July. And Longstreet did not return to de facto corps level until August 9, when he was dispatched to the Rapidan and Hood was ordered to report to him.[80]

During the Second Manassas campaign, it was not so much that Lee operated with two corps as that he recognized the need for a unit larger than the division to undertake detached operations. The rest of the army remained under Lee's immediate direction; and when R. H. Anderson arrived on the Rapidan, he was not added to Longstreet's responsibilities but kept as a general reserve and reported directly to Lee. It is nonetheless true; Lee began to use Jackson and Longstreet as corps commanders from the start of the campaign against Pope. It is not at all clear, however, whether this meant he had already decided to organize his army in two halves or was considering the formation of a third corps from the reenforcements.

The arrival of the three new divisions from Richmond provided a perfect opportunity for Lee to demonstrate whether he intended to enlarge the commands of Jackson and Longstreet or to create a new corps. That he did neither is the surest sign that he had not yet made up his mind. D. H. Hill was the next senior major general, and Lee's indecision may have reflected his continuing doubts about Hill since the fiasco at Coggins Point had failed to dislodge McClellan from Harrison's Landing. Whatever the case, before September 2 was over, Lee would make it clear he did not intend to take further steps toward solidifying the army into corps. For the present, four divisions—McLaws, Walker, D. H. Hill, and R. H. Anderson—would continue to operate independently.[81]

If lingering doubts over personnel made Lee hesitate before formalizing organization at the highest level in his army, there is no indication he experienced concern over its leadership at the lower grades. Yet, he perhaps ought to have, because the cost of obtaining a battle-tested army in so short a period was an inevitably high attrition in officers. In slightly less than four months, parts of Lee's army had engaged in six major battles and had lost through casualties or transferral seven division and twenty-six brigade commanders. The loss of regimental colonels was equally high. As a consequence, on September 2, less than half of the Army of Northern Virginia's regiments, brigades, and divisions were under officers appropriate in rank to their level of command.

Casualties had taken their heaviest toll in Jackson's corps, and especially in the division he formerly commanded himself. To be properly officered the Stonewall division should have had one major general, four brigadier generals, and a colonel for each of its eighteen regiments. Instead, it could now count for duty one brigadier and nine colonels, four of whom were temporarily removed from their regiments to head their brigades. This extraordinary depletion was mitigated by the fact that the units themselves were so reduced as to not require a full complement of field officers. It also helped that the four colonels commanding brigades—Alexander Grigsby, Bradley Johnson, Edward Warren, and Leroy Stafford—were solid and reliable officers, and William E. Starke, who led the division, was adequate for the role.

Ewell's division was in the next worse shape. With the severe wounding of its able leader, Richard S. Ewell, at the Brawner farm on August 28, senior brigadier Alexander Lawton had taken over command. The only other general present was Jubal Early, so three of the four brigades were led by colonels. In fact, Trimble's brigade was in the sorriest state of any in the army. It had not an officer present above the rank of captain, requiring that Col. James A. Walker of the 13th Virginia be transferred from a neighboring brigade to take temporary command. Even counting those heading brigades, there were only seven colonels in Ewell's entire division.

The remainder of the army was much better served. In A.P. Hill's division four of the six brigades were commanded by generals. Of Longstreet's four divisions and Anderson's reserve division, only one was headed by a major general (D. R. Jones), but two (Kemper and Wilcox) were somewhat informal arrangements and were under the brigadiers who had commanded them from their formation.[82] In the three divisions just arrived from Richmond, there were two major generals and ten generals for eleven brigades. In sum, four of Lee's eleven divisions were commanded by major generals, twenty-one of his forty brigades by brigadier generals, and sixty-eight of his 179 full-sized infantry regiments by colonels.[83]

Nonetheless, rank appropriate to the level of command is at best an imprecise measure of quality. When promotion is slow to keep up with fast-paced campaigning, it is not even an accurate gauge of experience. John Bell Hood, arguably the best division commander in the army, had his promotion to major general blocked simply because William H. C. Whiting, titular head of the division, was on a prolonged leave of absence. It is just as true that a number of Lee's commanders, even though they held appropriate rank, were unequal to their responsibilities. All in all, however, Lee had every reason to believe his officer corps was adequate. It was the core of his optimistic, best-case approach to conducting war that he did not measure himself or his army against an abstract standard of perfection but against what he had to accomplish and the foe he had to defeat. After the Seven Days and Second Manassas he could conclude that his army and his officers were superior to the Federal forces he would be facing in a new campaign.[84]

The physical condition of the Army of Northern Virginia was clearly another matter, and inescapably a cause for serious concern. Battle fatigue had hobbled Jackson's assault at Ox Hill the day before and thwarted the attempt to outflank Pope before the Federals could reach the safety of Washington's forts. The men in Jackson's three divisions had reached and passed the point of exhaustion. Since setting out on the march for Thoroughfare Gap on August 25, they had spent an entire week marching and fighting and had gone to sleep every night under the tension of contact with the enemy and imminent prospect of battle the next morning. Years later, gunner Edward Moore of the Rockbridge Artillery recalled riding a caisson on the night of September 1 so weary he could not keep his eyes open for more than five seconds at a stretch in spite of the danger of being crushed beneath the wheels if he fell.[85]

Fortunately, only Jackson's command was in such dire condition. Longstreet's and R. H. Anderson's men had marched as far but not so hard, and they had fought less. The reenforcements from Richmond had not seen combat in two months and were certainly fresh in that regard. Still, the forced march of both the vanguard (Ripley and Colquitt) and the main body under D. H. Hill that covered more than a hundred miles in seven days in the brutal heat of August had blistered feet and strewn stragglers in its wake. It was literally a killing pace, and it left soldiers dead from heat stroke along the side of the road. Most of those who broke down were able to rest and then struggle onward to rejoin their regiments several days later.[86] Lee's army would be stronger by thousands if he waited for these men to arrive. It would be weaker by thousands if he did not rest the men already with him.

The scarcity of food presented an even graver problem, since its impact was felt everywhere. The fighting capability exhibited by Lee's army in its first field campaign had far exceeded the capacity of its commissary, quartermaster, and ordnance departments to match its wants. Lee faced the compounded problems of too few vehicles and the inability of the supply trains to keep up with the rapid movements and uncertain destinations of his evolving strategy. Sensibly, he left behind at Orange Court House the wagons carrying baggage and camp equipage, but even the wagons carrying food and ammunition had soon fallen behind. For days at a time the troops had been forced to scavenge the meager pickings from the fields and orchards of a ravaged land and to profit from the occasional generosity of sympathetic civilians. Some of the regiments had not been issued rations for three days, and few of the wagons with food were up on the morning of the 2d. There was, of course, a direct correlation between food scarcity and many of the temporarily absent soldiers. As LaFayette McLaws observed shortly after joining Lee, "our men do not grumble. They only straggle."[87]

The nature of the food substituted for the missing army rations also contributed to the attrition from the ranks. A common refrain in Confederate memories of the late summer of 1862 was the prevalence of a green diet. In Civil War parlance "green" frequently meant fresh as opposed to dried, salted, or pickled. While fresh beef and fresh corn were treats when properly cooked and preserved, the ardors of campaigning too often led to undercooking, and fresh provisions did not keep well in the haversacks during hot August days. Half-spoiled beef and pork and a surfeit of roasted ears of corn and raw apples prevented starvation, but in many cases such a menu produced a severe and debilitating dysentery, which could not be cured without prolonged rest and a more balanced diet. Already some of Lee's best soldiers were dropping from the ranks because they were too weak to keep up with their comrades. Whatever the Confederate commander might decide to undertake in grand strategy, he had no choice but to do something about the food supply for his army.[88]

In addition—as if all of this were not enough—Lee had marched many of his troops out of their uniforms. The wagons carrying extra clothes had been left far behind and would not be seen again for weeks. Grimy trousers and jackets were reduced to shreds. Yet, tattered clothing was not critical during summer months to an army that never aspired to a spit-and-polish appearance. It mattered considerably, however, that thousands in the army had become shoeless, and bare heels and soles had not had time to toughen as would happen later in the war. Many who straggled simply could not keep up with their units on blistered, bleeding feet.[89]

As a final concern, Lee knew his ordnance supplies were running low. Some infantry units had exhausted their ammunition during the fight at Ox Hill. But the greatest shortage was with the artillery, and orders had been issued to "economize" what was on hand, "as it cannot be replaced immediately." Lee realized that a large ammunition train was on its way from Richmond under Ordnance Chief Porter Alexander, but on the 2d its whereabouts was unknown.[90]

Nothing could ameliorate the lack of ammunition except acquiring bullets, shot, and shell. But, ironically, the other deficiencies worked in a beneficent way to strengthen the army. The hunger, the exhaustion, and the privations purged the Army of Northern Virginia of its weaker soldiers. Bradley Johnson would later assert, "The troops who were left after these campaigns were as hard and tough as troops ever have been, for the process of elimination had dropped out all of the inferior materials."[91] And this is one Rebel boast that is not far off the mark. The rigorous marching and fighting of the summer of 1862 were a crucible in which the impurities of physical softness and faint hearts burned off to leave an army of superlative fighting mettle. Not all who fell by the side of the way were weak, for even good fighters succumbed to dysentery and bleeding feet. But all who remained had to be strong.

As might be expected after a season of impressive victories, the morale of those who survived to answer morning muster stood extremely high. Men were not only cheering the appearances of Robert E. Lee and Stonewall Jackson, but they were writing home comparing their campaigns to those of Napoleon, the pinnacle of military genius to the nineteenth-century imagination.[92] Within the week a Union doctor experienced in dealing with the military would have the chance to observe the Army of Northern Virginia and talk with its soldiers, and he would record in his diary, "They all believe in *themselves* as well as their generals, and are terribly in earnest. They assert that they have never been whipped, but have driven the Yankees before them whenever they could find them."[93] A general could achieve as much with men such as these as he could from a much larger number from which the dross had not been leached.

The weaknesses in food, munitions, and fatigue Lee could not ignore but must take steps to rectify, whatever strategic option he chose to pursue. Still, in themselves the deficiencies were not persuasive arguments against immediately undertaking a new campaign. Certainly, none of the problems were so overwhelming as to prevent the Confederate commander from seizing upon the brightest prospects that might ever come the way of his desperate cause. Clearly, the ideal movement for Lee now to make would be one that kept the initiative in his hands—but that allowed time for rest and refitting and opened new resources for supply. By the late afternoon of September 2, just such a plan had begun to take shape in his mind.

The Maryland Option: A New Turning Movement

In his brief career as a field commander, Lee had thus far relied exclusively on the turning movement to achieve his twin objectives of hurting the enemy at the same time as husbanding his own resources. Four times in three months—indeed, in every major strategy he launched—he laid plans to bypass strong positions and move instead against sensitive points that would compel the enemy to abandon chosen ground and come out into the open to be destroyed. Although the vagaries of war had prevented any of the four from being executed exactly as planned, nonetheless, the turning movement had brought such success to Confederate arms as to reverse the tide of the war in the Eastern theater. And it was to the turning movement that Lee understandably resorted to exploit the advantages of his successes and to minimize the weaknesses of his present condition.

It is doubtful Lee gave any serious thought to turning Washington in the classic sense of breaking the city's supply lines. He could not get at the rail link which ran through Baltimore to the north without abandoning his own communications. And, even if besieged on all sides, the Northern capital could be supplied by water from its vast fleet of transports on the Potomac. In theory, however, a turning movement did not need to aim at severing enemy communications. It might intend only to threaten supply lines, or it might target some altogether different enemy weak point—just as long as the enemy viewed that point as so vital that there was no choice but to defend it immediately. The plan emerging in Lee's mind on the afternoon of September 2 envisioned a combination of both of these variations.[94]

At Ox Hill Lee had run out of room for offensive maneuvering in Virginia. Any new turning movement would require crossing the Potomac and entering Maryland. Lee's new plan assumed that this simple move might be enough. Maryland itself might be such a sore point that the sudden appearance of Confederates on its soil would cause the enemy to react precipitously. In the Confederate view, the Lincoln administration had already exhibited such anxiety over the capital being surrounded by a slave state that it had suspended the writ of habeas corpus, arrested nine members of the state legislature, and committed other outrages with a heavy-handed occupation by Federal troops. Would not the mere presence of a Rebel army in the midst of these disaffected people strike terror into the heart of the Union government?[95]

In addition, Northerners must necessarily assume the move was an invasion and would imagine Lee as a threat to Harrisburg, Philadelphia, and Baltimore, as well as to Washington. The political and psychological peril could work as effectively as the physical interruption of supplies to force the foe to leave his fortifications while still groggy from defeat. Moreover, by presenting a multiple threat, Lee would compel the Federals to divide their large army to provide for several contingencies. The Confederate commander could then maneuver to engage a fraction of their forces in the open field. Finally, although he could not entirely cut off supplies to Washington, he could drastically curtail them by destroying sections of the Chesapeake and Ohio (C&O) Canal and the Baltimore and Ohio (B&O) Railroad, both of which ran parallel to the Potomac.[96]

With a turning movement into Maryland Lee would retain his hold on the initiative. He would create the opportunity to inflict another and even more shattering blow to the armies of Pope and McClellan. And there can be no doubt Lee would intend battle—engaged at the time and place of his choosing—to be the endgame of his maneuver.[97] It always was. He might also expect that a victory gained on soil, viewed by the enemy as home ground, would be especially damaging to their morale. Then, Northerners in increasing numbers might ask why prolong a year-and-a-half effort costing thousands of lives and millions of dollars only to be farther from success than when it had all started. It was raising this question in enough Northern minds that would lead to Confederate independence. Lee must have sensed—might have palpably felt—that fortune had brought the well-nigh impossible of three months ago within the reach of a courageous grasp.

A multitude of other advantages to be gained in entering Maryland came readily to mind once the possibilities were canvassed. It was the single move most likely to lift the spirits of the army even higher and to make the men forget their weariness, hunger, and privations. Lee's hard-used soldiers would be given the chance to reap the rewards their fortitude had earned. Better still, the army would probably not encounter any opposition at the outset, and, if the marches were set in easy stages, there would be time for rest, even days of leisure, while waiting for the Federals to react. And, best of all, the move promised to ameliorate the Confederate supply problem.

Operating out of western Maryland, Lee could run a lengthy but workable and secure line of communications through Winchester and up the Shenandoah Valley to Staunton where the Virginia Central Railroad connected with Richmond. Moreover that line would bear a lighter burden, because he could tap into the resources of a region as lush as any in Virginia and as yet unravaged by the scourge of marching armies. The Maryland counties of Frederick and Washington compared favorably with Augusta, Rockingham, Fauquier, and Loudoun, the best Virginia had to offer. Farmers around Hagerstown and Frederick City owned tens of thousands of horses, "milch cows," beef cattle, and swine, and annually harvested millions of bushels of wheat and Indian corn from their fields and fruit from their orchards.[98] Food and forage would be plentiful.

And every pound of Maryland provender consumed would be one less drained from the dwindling reserves of the Old Dominion. Indeed, the longer Lee could keep the seat of war north of the Potomac, the longer central and northern Virginia would have to recuperate from the Federal occupation and regain their productive capacity for supporting the war effort. This consideration alone—if Lee's own words during and after the war are to be believed—weighed heavily with the Confederate commander. To "relieve" Virginia was not simply the romantic notion of a devoted native son, it was a condition necessary to enable the Confederacy to carry on the war long enough to win it.[99]

Lee knew full well that his government recognized the Potomac as its national boundary. Unlike Kentucky and Missouri, Maryland had no star on the Confederate flag, nor did any Marylanders sit in the Congress at Richmond. Yet, Maryland was a sister slave state, and its citizens had shed the blood of Massachusetts soldiers on the streets of Baltimore on April 19, 1861, to protest Lincoln's call for troops to suppress the rebellion. Thousands of Maryland's sons now served in the Confederate army, and hundreds more, including a recent governor, lived as expatriates behind Southern lines.[100] So confident was the Confederate Congress that Maryland belonged in the new nation and was held in the Union only by Federal bayonets that it had proclaimed the liberation of the state to be a war aim.

The joint resolution passed on December 21 authorized the use of "appropriate measures to facilitate the accession of Maryland, with the free consent of her people, to the Confederate States." Furthermore, the resolution declared no peace treaty would be acceptable that did not mandate a "fair" plebiscite for the citizens of the state to decide their future in the absence of troops from either side. Nor was the resolution mere paper bravura. In February, Jefferson Davis instructed Confederate envoys to inform the governments of France and Great Britain that Maryland's free election must be a condition for peace and a necessary aim for any alliance formed to intervene in the war on the Confederacy's behalf. In consequence, Lee might well assume his entering Maryland would be politically acceptable to the Confederate government.[101]

He also knew the possibility of crossing the Potomac had been raised previously in Confederate strategy debates, and it had been discussed entirely in terms of military feasibility without regard to political appropriateness. Lee had been absent in western Virginia during the fall of 1861, when Davis traveled to Fairfax Court House to consult with Generals Johnston, Beauregard, and Smith on the advisability of launching an offensive into Maryland. No evidence survives to testify what, if anything, Lee knew about that meeting. Yet, it is likely in his subsequent role as general-in-chief with his almost daily strategy talks with Davis he learned something of its details. It is even more likely he discerned the permissive attitude of the president, who was so excited by the possibility that he brought charts of the Potomac fords with him to the meeting in Fairfax.

In any case, Lee had participated in the series of meetings of the past April in which Johnston and Smith had proposed a joint offensive of the Eastern and Western armies to cross the Potomac and Ohio Rivers to negate the threats of McClellan at Yorktown and Halleck at Corinth. And he had himself—only days after assuming command of the Army of Northern Virginia—forwarded with his approval Jackson's plan to enter Maryland as a means to break the enemy's tightening grip on Richmond. At no point had the idea of setting foot on Maryland's soil been ruled beyond the pale of consideration. Each plan had fallen through because the commanding general could not be given the requisite force he demanded. On September 2, the Confederacy now had a general who was willing to undertake the move with the troops at hand. Could not that general assume his action would be approved?

As Lee pondered his options on this late summer's afternoon in his camp near Ox Hill, it must have seemed clear that the most logical and desirable course open to him was to cross the Potomac and turn Washington's fortifications. And yet, just as clearly, the move was fraught with policy ramifications and strategic and logistical vagaries. Even with an expectation of Davis's likely concurrence, should he undertake such a momentous action without his government's specific authority? Would Marylanders warmly welcome the Confederates and willingly share the riches of their fields and workshops? How might he obtain ammunition and other strictly military supplies that could not be expected from even the most sympathetic civilians? Where would be the best place to cross the Potomac to exert pressure on Washington? And what of the Federal garrisons in the Shenandoah at Winchester and Harpers Ferry? Would they not block his communications and threaten his flank and rear?

It must have also occurred to Lee that this move would hazard all of the hard-earned capital he had accumulated with his summer of success? A defeat suffered on enemy soil would shatter his army's aura of invincibility, reveal to all the world its limitations, and immeasurably encourage the North to struggle on to the end. And what if his army were not merely defeated but destroyed? There would be no force left capable of protecting Richmond or Virginia. After the war, William Allan heard Lee say, "in referring to criticisms that had been made on the great risks he had taken . . . that such criticisms were obvious, but that the disparity of forces between the contending armies rendered the risks unavoidable."[102] It is likely that such was Lee's thinking on September 2. Still, it was imperative to take only the right risks.

The Open-Ended Decision

It is not surprising Lee felt compelled to gather more information or reflect further before committing to such a momentous course. Yet, so convinced was he of the ripeness of the moment, he refused to procrastinate. By some point on the afternoon of the 2d, he decided on a compromise plan that permitted him to get the army under way but kept open his best option. He determined to march to Leesburg and avail himself of the supplies of Loudoun County. His presence there would threaten both Maryland and the Union garrisons in the Shenandoah, and he would be in position to cross the Potomac, if it still seemed like a good idea after further consideration.[103] He may even have hoped this modest move would in itself draw the bulk of the Federal forces north of the river. In any case, he believed this preliminary step exposed his army to little risk.[104]

It is highly likely that Lee reached his halfway answer to the strategy quandary after discussing the ponderables of a new campaign with Jackson and Longstreet and seeking their advice on entering Maryland. Both were camped conveniently at hand, and it had become Lee's habit to consult with his chief subordinates while thinking through knotty questions of strategy. Certainly, sometime before reaching Leesburg, he did talk with them about Maryland, and it makes sense to believe he did so before taking the preliminary steps to open the campaign.[105] Lee's interest in crossing the Potomac was no doubt strengthened by learning that both officers—even the often defensively minded Longstreet—warmly supported the idea. After the war, Longstreet would even claim to have helped convince Lee, who "hesitated a little" in deciding.[106] And Jackson, when asked, may have argued for the even bolder course of "carrying the war into Africa" by invading Pennsylvania "to cripple the enemy's industry and transportation."[107]

How much Lee benefited from the advice of his subordinates is unknown, but it is clear that he opened the chapter on his next campaign less than six hours after closing the old one on Second Manassas. In the waning hours of the afternoon of the 2d, he issued verbal orders setting in motion the new venture. Jackson and Longstreet were instructed to take separate country roads that ran north from the Little River Turnpike and led to the Ox Road; they were then to follow this road past Frying Pan Church; cross the Alexandria, Loudoun and Hampshire Railroad at Herndon Station; and finally strike the Leesburg Pike near Dranesville, where they were to make camp. They were to set an easy pace and were not to cover more than ten miles on the first day.[108] Interestingly, the Washington Artillery of Louisiana received orders to cook three days rations in preparation for the march. It is doubtful the order was repeated widely throughout the army, since so many of the veterans later claimed there was no food on hand.[109]

For the commanders at a distance from headquarters, Lee had to resort to written communications, and, because of his bandaged hands, these necessarily were composed and sent out over the signature of his adjutant, Robert H. Chilton. D. H. Hill and McLaws, with Hill in the lead, had reached the Little River Turnpike at a point near Pleasant Valley. They were ordered to travel parallel roads northward to the Leesburg Pike and to camp at or near Leesburg. Anticipating a stay of several days at Leesburg and hoping to re-victual from the bounties of Loudoun, Lee ordered both division commanders to unload their subsistence train as quickly as possible and turn them over to the army's commissary chief to take on new provisions. Hill had taken charge of McLaws in the march from Richmond, but the orders ignored the arrangement and treated each as an independent commander. At this time Lee apparently had no intention of creating a third corps or of assigning the newly arrived units to either Jackson or Longstreet. The Reserve Artillery, the ordnance train, and Walker's division—all reported at or nearing Manassas—were instructed not to follow the army to Fairfax but to proceed directly to Leesburg.[110]

Lee's plans for the employment of his cavalry were thorough, although somewhat curiously directed considering the aim of his strategy. Whether he crossed the Potomac or remained south of the river at Leesburg, his main object now was to threaten Washington from the west and induce the Federals to draw their troops out of Virginia. Yet, Lee did not send Stuart to lead the van of the army to clear the way or to scout the fords or even to mount a preliminary raid into Maryland to exert pressure as soon as possible on John Pope and the dispirited Federal armies. Instead, Lee's orders for the cavalry for the 3d were to feint against Washington from the south and east and to cover the front and rear of the Confederate infantry columns on the march. Fitzhugh Lee's brigade was to ride twelve miles east to demonstrate against Alexandria and threaten the Federal left flank. In the meantime, Hampton was to strike the Leesburg Pike at Hunter's Mill and lead the army to Dranesville, while Robertson was merely to follow the rear of the column.[111]

Lee's cavalry dispositions make most sense if it is assumed that he believed it was necessary to have several uninterrupted days at Leesburg for rest, refitting, and thinking through his plans but that he was not entirely certain the enemy was in such bad shape as to give him the opportunity. In addition, he could be relatively confident he would not encounter any resistance in the march to Leesburg. Happily, he had dispatched Thomas Munford and the 2d Virginia Cavalry just the day before to secure the town. At noon on September 2, Munford swept through Leesburg, surprising and routing the Loudoun Rangers and part of Cole's Battalion of Maryland Cavalry.[112] It is doubtful that news of this small victory could have traveled the twenty-some miles to reach Lee before he issued his orders, but he likely was counting on Munford for warning of any serious opposition from the west. Finally, it is also true that Fitz Lee's diversionary skirmishing at Alexandria was planned to last only one day, and thus it would not divert the enemy's attention in the wrong direction for too long.

Whatever the explanation, it should not be assumed that Lee undervalued the role to be played by the cavalry in the campaign he was considering. He would need an effective screen to shield the condition and exact location of his army and to keep the enemy ignorant of the true object of his strategy. Equally, his success would depend on receiving accurate and timely information of the Federals' response to the Confederate threat. Hence, to ensure that his horsemen would be equal to any service they might be called upon to perform, Lee issued special orders to weed out the troopers with unfit mounts. He sent them back to the "late battle-fields" to shoe and rest their horses.[113]

He chose the site for recuperation specifically so that the men freed from combat duty could collect the abandoned arms and equipment scattered across the fields of Manassas. Far too precious to be squandered, the war matériel was to be stacked along the Warrenton Turnpike. Such wagons as could be spared were sent back under Capt. William Allan to ferry the arms to empty railroad cars returning to Richmond, where they could be inspected and repaired.[114] In the same vein—and as further reflection of Lee's concern "to relieve the heavy stress upon the commissary department"—he had Chilton write to Secretary of War Randolph urging the "rapid completion" of the reconstruction of the railroad bridge across the Rapidan River. Apparently, Lee had received reports that the civilians were not "working with the energy required by the occasion."[115] The route from the Rapidan via Warrenton to Manassas would probably not be a safe line, if he carried the army into western Maryland. But not having as yet fully decided, he wanted to keep open all of his options.

All in all, September 2 had been a vexing day for Robert E. Lee. Embarrassingly, as the Confederate tide approached its flood, his heavily bandaged hands could not grasp the reins of his horse; nor could they button his blouse or trousers or hold a pen to write the fateful dispatch to Jefferson Davis that had already begun to take shape in his mind. At least he could tell himself he had not allowed his physical crippling to interfere with the attempt to reap fullest advantage from the discomfiture of the enemy. The search for a new tangent to escape the concentric circles of a complicated strategic situation and the worn condition of his army had stopped him short of a vigorous and instantaneous start to a new campaign. Still, he could retire for the night satisfied that a beginning had been made. History might fairly judge that few commanding generals would have done so much under the circumstances.

The Dranesville Dispatch, September 3

The night was clear but unseasonably cold, with temperatures dropping into the high forties, and the army woke to a bright sun and a light frost.[116] Whether or not the verbal orders had specified an early march, most of the columns got off to a sluggish start.[117] Even Lee set an unhurried pace. Before striking his tent, he dictated two dispatches, both of which this time he sent over his own name.[118] He addressed the secretary of war in the briefer of the two and revealed his continuing search for ways to wring full advantage from repossession of northern Virginia. He did not want to miss this chance to fill the depleted ranks of his Virginia regiments. He reminded Randolph that the Conscription Act had never been enforced in the counties occupied by the Federals, and he also mentioned the estrays who had drifted from their commands and returned to their homes. Lee may have believed that as many as 4,000 to 5,000 men could be collected by state officers and sent to Richmond for distribution throughout his army.[119]

In his second and longer dispatch, Lee reopened communication with Jefferson Davis after a four-day lapse. Now that the Second Manassas campaign had concluded, he felt it appropriate to submit a preliminary report to the president. The document is interesting in that it reveals Lee's comprehension of his situation at this critical time, as well as for the several topics he does not mention. He estimates the enemy casualties to be at least 15,000, but, except for naming killed and wounded generals and colonels, he makes no reference to his own losses. He pays tribute to the indomitable "gallantry and endurance" of his soldiers, "who have cheerfully borne every danger and hardship, both on the battlefield and march," but he makes no mention whatsoever of the problem of straggling. In fact, the only problem to which he alludes is the "progress and protection of our trains," which he says have "caused the greatest difficulties."

The most conspicuous omission, however, is Lee's failure to refer to his future operations. He brings the report down to the time of his writing by mentioning the arrival of the divisions of McLaws and D. H. Hill and his belief that the ordnance train is not far behind. He also summarizes the "great advantage" of his success as being "the withdrawal of the enemy from our territory." But he includes not a word about the impending march to Leesburg or the possibility of crossing the Potomac. It is conceivable Lee was still so uncertain of the larger move that he was uncomfortable in even mentioning it to Davis. At the very least, he recognized it was not a notion to be introduced casually and was probably already planning a special dispatch devoted exclusively to the subject.[120]

The 3d turned out to be a rare day in the annals of the Army of Northern Virginia. The sky remained cloudless and the temperature became comfortably warm, gradually reaching the high sixties. On the western flank, LaFayette McLaws displayed the most enterprise in the army. He formed his division at sunrise and marched north on the Gum Spring Road. Turning left on the Leesburg-Alexandria Turnpike, he reached Leesburg by five o'clock and marched through the town to encamp at Big Spring farm two miles beyond on the road to the Potomac. D. H. Hill set out later in the day and followed the route taken by McLaws.

Under a bright half-moon, the two divisions passed through Leesburg until well after midnight. The lateness of the hour meant nothing to the deliriously happy citizens, as they brought forward food and shouted words of encouragement. In appreciation, each regiment sent up "deafening yells" as it filed by. When the crowds thronging the sidewalks recognized the Mississippians of William Barksdale's brigade who had been their protectors the previous fall at Ball's Bluff, they surged forward and completely disrupted the marching formation to mingle with officers and men.[121]

Farther to the east, the columns of Jackson and Longstreet swung along at a more leisurely pace on parallel country lanes through a beautiful countryside and a sympathetic populace. Some regiments had still not seen their subsistence wagons and were reduced to dusting the crumbs from their haversacks. But there were orchards and friendly farms to blunt the hunger of many, and there were subjects of conversation to divert the attention of all. Knowing how close they were to the Potomac, their march north for most of the day must have sparked

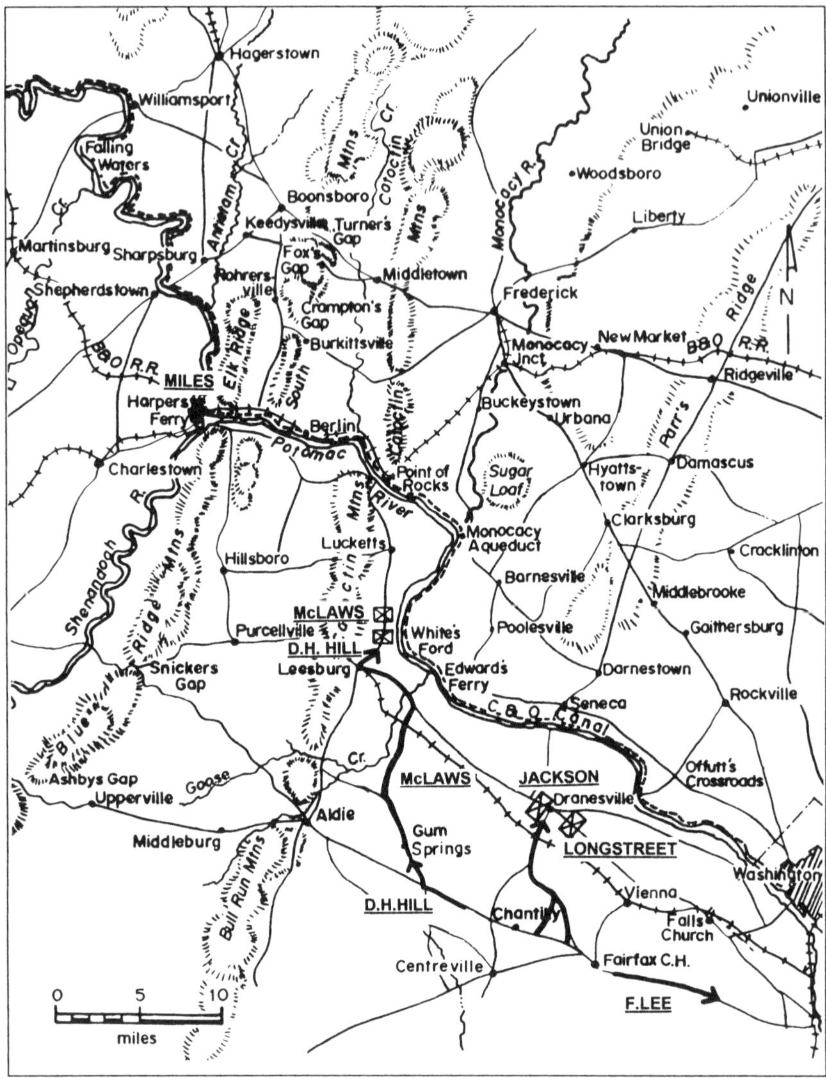

Confederate march, September 3

considerable speculation in the ranks. Then, when they turned away from the river in midafternoon and headed west on the Leesburg Turnpike, the noncommissioned strategists were given a deeper puzzle to solve.[122]

Stuart in particular seems to have had a good time. At the head of Hampton's brigade he rode in the very van of the main body; and as he cantered down the Leesburg Turnpike, he described to his staff the battle he had fought near Dranesville the previous December. He seemingly gave no thought to the demonstration Fitzhugh Lee had been ordered to carry out against Alexandria, although perhaps he ought to have. Whatever Fitz did by way of feinting made no apparent impression on the Federals, but, fortunately for his uncle who commanded the army, the enemy was in no shape to press the flank or rear of the marching columns.[123]

By late afternoon the main body of the army reached Dranesville and went into camp for the night. Stuart appropriated the Drovers' Inn for his headquarters. Longstreet stopped short of the village, while Jackson marched through to bivouac on the banks of Sugar Land Run. Thus, by the close of the day, the Army of Northern Virginia stretched over sixty miles of the region for which it was named. While the van was beyond Leesburg and the main body at Dranesville, the Artillery Reserve had only reached Gainesville, and Walker's division had just passed through Warrenton.[124]

After making camp, Lee took another step toward making his decision. Still not prepared to roll the dice, he was now ready to shake them. He called Armistead L. Long, his military secretary, into his tent to take down the dictation of his second letter of the day to Jefferson Davis.[125] "Mr. President," Lee began, "the present seems the most propitious time since the commencement of the war to enter Maryland." Thus, at the outset did he establish an aggressive tone. He framed his dispatch as an argument to be expounded and not as a request seeking approval. And he started with the unstated premise that crossing the Potomac was a long-standing Confederate goal awaiting only its proper season. The question to be examined was one of timing and not of propriety. He took for granted Davis's agreement in principle.

"The two grand armies of the United States that have been operating in Virginia," he commenced his argument, "though now united, are much weakened and demoralized." It is revealing that Lee's first consideration should be the condition of his opponents, and even more revealing that he was willing to act upon his perception of their weakness. It was another indication of his best-case or optimistic approach to the conduct of war. It was easy to see an opponent's strengths, but Lee took a step beyond and tried to comprehend his problems and limitations as well.

There is also in this sentence a glimpse of a state of mind that would remain with Lee throughout the campaign ahead and help to shape several major decisions that are otherwise difficult to understand. He believed his own soldiers—at least for the time being—marched better and fought better than the Federals, and he would be willing to rely on this Confederate superiority in tight spots when time and numbers seemed to be against him.[126] At the outset this belief convinced him the Federals in their present condition would be unable to react quickly enough to oppose the potentially risky operation of crossing a major river.

In the same vein, he went on to point out, it was necessary to deny the North the interval to profit from Lincoln's recent call for more volunteers. "Their new levies, of which I understand 60,000 men have already been posted in Washington, are not yet organized, and will take some time to prepare for the field." It would be interesting to know if Lee got this information from newspapers (and if so, of what date) or from Southern spies. In either case, this inflated figure no doubt caused him considerable alarm. The statement also confirms his awareness that the unfavorable odds he faced were about to worsen.[127]

Then, as he was to do a number of times in this dispatch, Lee proceeded with a non sequitur. Perhaps because he was accustomed to thinking out his communications while writing them down in his own hand; and perhaps because his mind was so full of revolving pros and cons, he found it difficult to organize his topics with his usual precision.

"If ever it is desired to give material aid to Maryland," he went on somewhat randomly, "and afford her an opportunity of throwing off the oppression to which she is now subject, this would seem the most favorable." The point of view is still that of seizing the moment, but this time Lee applied it to a political consideration. It may be that at this early stage in his thinking, he did somewhat naively believe Marylanders would rise up in large numbers to cast off the "despot's heel." The attempt would certainly be in line with the stated congressional aim of not ending the war without giving Maryland the opportunity to join the Confederacy. Yet, it may be doubted that such a political aim would have held much weight with Lee had it not coincided with his assessment of both military objectives and realities.

Once again, he then shifted topics randomly.

"After the enemy had disappeared from the vicinity of Fairfax Court-House, and taken the road to Alexandria and Washington, I did not think it would be advantageous to follow him farther." Implicit is Lee's resignation that he could not get at Pope before the Federals reached the

Washington fortifications. Even if there had been maneuvering room for a turning movement to interpose between Pope and the forts—and there probably was not—the fatigued condition of the Army of Northern Virginia as revealed at Chantilly would have prevented him from taking advantage of it.

"I had no intention of attacking him in his fortifications, and am not prepared to invest them." Here Lee merely states the obvious. No rational commander would have contemplated attacking an enemy twice his size ensconced in strong fortifications. But, beyond the obvious, Lee would not have returned voluntarily to a "battle of posts"—as he had referred to McClellan's approach to Richmond—a mode of warfare he had admitted the Confederates could never win, because it put a premium on engineering and artillery. Lee must stick with open field fighting, where surprise maneuvers and the elan of Confederate infantry and cavalry might prevail.

"If I possessed the necessary munitions, I should be unable to supply provisions for the troops." It is not certain why Lee felt it necessary to belabor the foolhardiness of attacking Washington, except that it introduced his second greatest concern—after deciding his next strategic move—was his weakness in supplying his army. Had he based his operations in burned-out Fairfax County he would have put the entire burden of provisioning his troops on the inadequate commissary department. He believed he must avoid this by drawing a substantial proportion of his food and forage from a local region.

He then informed Davis of the preliminary decision he had reached the previous afternoon.

"I therefore determined, while threatening the approaches to Washington, to draw the troops into Loudoun, where forage and some provisions can be obtained, menace their possession of the Shenandoah Valley, and, if found practicable, to cross into Maryland." With this move he had thus addressed his two major concerns. He had found a way to continue exerting pressure on the defeated enemy while moving toward subsistence for his men. His occupation of Leesburg would not only cause alarm in Washington, it would also threaten to isolate the garrisons at Winchester and Harpers Ferry.

"The purpose, if discovered, will have the effect of carrying the enemy north of the Potomac, and, if prevented, will not result in much evil." Here, of course, Lee is referring simply to the move into Loudoun and not to crossing the Potomac. Since it is not likely he believed the

Federals would so easily abandon their fortifications in Alexandria and Arlington, he presumably anticipated their withdrawal from the Shenandoah Valley. It was also a move that, in fact, did not carry with it much risk.

Lee then reverted to the proposition with which he had opened the dispatch and which was his primary reason for writing.

"The army is not properly equipped for an invasion of an enemy's territory. It lacks much of the material of war, is feeble in transportation, the animals being much reduced, and the men are poorly provided with clothes, and in thousands of instances are destitute of shoes." This time when he considers the option of advancing north, he confesses it does not make sense if undertaken as a full-scale invasion. His failure to consider subsistence as a problem probably reflects his belief that sufficient food would be obtainable from Marylanders. He mentions only military equipment, clothing, and his transportation system—in other words, the sort of supplies he could not count on acquiring from the countryside.

Nevertheless, even though a full-scale invasion might be out of the question, he was on the verge of deciding to undertake a modified version of one. The reason he gave cut to the heart of the grand strategy he believed the Confederacy must pursue to win the war. "Still, we cannot afford to be idle," he dictated to Long, "and though weaker than our opponents in men and military equipments, must endeavor to harass if we cannot destroy them." This is the key sentence in the dispatch and a succinct statement of the principle behind all of Lee's operations in the summer of 1862.[128] He recognizes that Confederate victory must necessarily result from the frustration rather than the destruction of the enemy. He acknowledges that the clock is running against the South and that he has a limited time within which he can achieve victory before his own resources are exhausted. He must, therefore, seize every opportunity coming his way and press it to its fullest advantage. For the first and only time in the dispatch, Lee mentions the disparity in numbers; but he does it in such a general way as to seem to be referring to the odds in the war, rather than his particular situation on September 3.

"I am aware that the movement is attended with much risk, yet I do not consider success impossible, and shall endeavor to guard it from loss." Unlike the march into Loudoun, Lee admitted that crossing the Potomac raised many potential hazards. He may have recognized that he would endanger not only his army but also the momentum he had built at such high cost. But he could not seize the moment without the risk of losing the momentum. It is interesting that Lee understates his chances of success as not "impossible," and it is unclear what he believed he could do to minimize his risks. Curiously, if read standing alone, this sentence implies Lee had made up his mind by the evening of the 3d. Perhaps "if I undertake it" is an unstated clause.

After raising the issue of the risks involved in crossing the Potomac, Lee's thinking naturally turned to the one danger that would likely be of greatest concern to Davis—the exposure of the Confederate capital. "As long as the army of the enemy are employed on this frontier I have no fears for the safety of Richmond," he dictated to allay the president's possible fear. The statement was a strikingly familiar variation on what Charles Marshall would recall as his chief's favorite saying: "Richmond was never so safe as when her defenders were absent." Indeed, Lee not only believed Richmond could be defended at a distance, but that it must be in order to avoid coming under siege. Still, although he believed the Lincoln administration would be too preoccupied by its "inordinate fear" for its own capital to mount a serious offensive against Richmond, he could not guarantee against a raid by the enemy army or navy.[129]

So he went on prudently, ". . . yet I earnestly recommend that advantage be taken of this period of relative safety to place its defense, both by land and water, in the most perfect condition. A respectable force can be collected to defend its approaches by land, and the steamer Richmond, I hope, is now ready to clear the river of hostile vessels." Here is just a glimpse of Lee's hope that he would be able to prolong his stay on the Potomac—either above or below—for a period of some duration.[130] Clearly, he still worried about the threat to Richmond from the James, which he felt necessary to mention only as "the river." It is not at all clear, however, how he thought a "respectable force" could be collected. He knew that virtually no troops remained in North Carolina or Florida. He also knew it would be difficult and time consuming to pry loose additional regiments from the diminished forces in Georgia and South Carolina. Indeed, awareness of his overoptimism in this respect may have led Lee to cast farther afield in his thinking for a source for reenforcements.

"Should General Bragg find it impracticable to operate to advantage on his present frontier, his army, after leaving sufficient garrisons, could be advantageously employed in opposing the overwhelming numbers which it seems to be the intention of the enemy now to concentrate in Virginia." Lee's desperation in seeking to provide forces for Davis at Richmond, as well as reenforcements for his own army to reap full advantage from his victories, led him to suggest reducing the Confederate Western army to garrisons so that troops might be shifted east. He surely knew that time would be required to reorganize the Western forces and transfer part of them to Virginia, and this reconfirms his intention to extend his stay on or beyond the frontier for as long as possible.

It also confirms that as of September 3, Lee was unaware that Bragg had launched his own campaign northward from Chattanooga on August 28 to reclaim Kentucky. Otherwise, the notion of Bragg not being able to operate "to advantage on his present frontier" is nonsense. Apparently the Confederate government had not yet notified Lee of the parallel moves in the West, nor had he learned of them from the newspapers. Hence, at least during the critical period during which he decided whether or not to cross the Potomac, Lee assumed his move would be solitary and not in concert with a major offensive advance into Kentucky.[131]

"I have already been told by prisoners that some of Buell's cavalry have been joined to General Pope's army, and have reason to believe that the whole of McClellan's, the larger portion of Burnside's and Cox's, and a portion of Hunter's, are united to it." Lee here simply reiterates information already passed on to Davis about McClellan's army from the Peninsula, Burnside's corps from North Carolina, and Cox's division from western Virginia. The presence in Washington of part of Hunter's troops from South Carolina was new, however, and may have been acquired from prisoners taken at the Battle of Chantilly, where a major portion of the fighting was borne by Isaac Stevens's division. Lee also takes the opportunity to slip in the information—actually a false rumor—that the Federals had shipped some of Buell's forces from the West to meet the crisis, hoping possibly to buttress the argument to bring some of Bragg's men east.[132]

Lee's main point, no doubt, was to underline the desperateness of his situation, but he may also have meant to emphasize the degree to which his success had opened new opportunities which might now be exploited. After the war, Charles Marshall would maintain that one of Lee's major strategic aims from the start of his command was to pose such a threat to Federals in Virginia that they would reduce their forces elsewhere and thus relieve other parts of the country. In three months he had achieved exactly this to such an extent that the Federals posed virtually no threat anywhere east of the Appalachian Mountains.[133] Was he now suggesting this principle be carried to its logical conclusion and that the entire burden of the war be put on the shoulders of the Army of Northern Virginia? Was he suggesting that the Western armies be shifted to the East, because the West would never be so safe as when its defenders were absent?

Finally, it is significant that at this critical juncture in his thinking about crossing the Potomac, Lee believed the combined enemy armies belonged to John Pope and he assumed Pope would be the Federal commander faced in a campaign in Maryland.[134]

For one final time, Lee abruptly shifted topics and returned to expand on the supply weaknesses of his army. "What occasions me most concern is the fear of getting out of ammunition. I beg you will instruct the Ordnance Department to spare no pains in manufacturing a sufficient amount of the best kind, and to be particular, in preparing that for the artillery, to provide three times as much of the long-range ammunition as that for smooth-bore or short-range guns." These are two moderately ambiguous sentences. It is not clear whether Lee is worried about running out of ammunition only in the case of entering Maryland, where he certainly cannot count on acquiring it from citizens as he might with subsistence, or whether his concern is regardless of what strategy he pursues. It is also unclear whether Lee is equally concerned over all types of ammunition—including that for small arms—or just that for long-range artillery.

The most reasonable reading is that Lee probably was worried whether or not he crossed the Potomac, and his concern was primarily, although not exclusively, for artillery ammunition. Not only did the Confederates have the opportunity to replenish small arm munitions from captured and dead Federals, but orders had already been issued for rationing that for the artillery. Nevertheless, it is curious that Lee should display such acute worry over ordnance in the afternoon after announcing in his morning letter to Davis the approach of Porter Alexander's large ordnance train from Richmond.

"The points to which I desire the ammunition to be forwarded will be made known to the department in time." Lee must have realized that his requisition could not be filled and shipped overnight, and this statement again confirms Lee's anticipation that his campaign on the frontier could be prolonged at least for a matter of weeks and that he is planning in long-range terms. Implicit also is Lee's uncertainty at the time of dictating this dispatch over what strategy he would pursue and precisely where events would carry him during the campaign.

Then Lee brought the dispatch to a close somewhat anticlimactically: "If the quartermaster's Department can furnish any shoes, it would be the greatest relief. We have entered upon September," he concluded, "and the nights are becoming cooler." His second mention of the deficiency in shoes indicates his awareness of the extent of the problem, and the unseasonable frost of the previous night had underscored the urgency in finding a solution. Still, it was a curiously low-key note on which to end one of the great strategy documents of the war.[135]

Almost as interesting as the subjects covered by Lee in the wide-ranging dispatch are the points omitted. First, he does not specifically ask for Davis's approval; nor does he indicate that he intends to ask or even to wait long enough for a reaction from the president to arrive. Considering the great pains Lee had taken and would thereafter take to consult Davis on matters small and large and to keep smooth relations with the president, this omission must mean either that Lee was confident in advance of Davis's approbation or that he considered the opportunity so great and the time so short he was willing to risk acting contrary to Davis's wishes in order to pursue a strategy he believed might end the war victoriously for the South. Had Lee dispatched a trusted staff officer on a fast mount—he probably would not have entrusted such a sensitive communication to the telegraph even at Rapidan Station—he might have received a reply in three days. But it might have been the wrong answer. And that may have been one risk he was not willing to take. Instead, he would draw on the capital he had been building for months in Davis's trust.

Secondly, Lee made no request for reenforcements except for the improbable mention of Bragg. This may have been no more than a simple realization there were none to be had. Moreover, without knowing the exact figure was one-third, Lee should have had a reasonably accurate appreciation—from his months as general-in-chief—that the arrival of the column from Richmond gave his Army of Northern Virginia a large percentage of all of the regiments the Confederacy had in the field. He may also have guessed that any new troops scraped together in the East in the foreseeable future would be retained by Davis at Richmond.

In fact, it is interesting in regard to strength that except for his general reference to the Confederacy being outnumbered in the war, Lee does not reflect special concern over the size of his army while considering the decision to enter Maryland. His later comments would emphasize that at this time he seemed to worry more about food and ammunition than he did the strength of his army. He seemed satisfied that the

Army of Northern Virginia had proven itself superior to its enemy and would be equal to the demands he would make of it.

And, finally, he does not mention the problem of straggling, which later would become such a constant theme in his communications. Either he had not yet perceived it to be a pressing problem, or more likely he wished—consciously or unconsciously—to avoid mentioning a serious negative consideration against the idea of crossing into Maryland.

Lee retired for the night to his tent near Dranesville under a half-moon and a high black sky salted with shimmering stars. Someone must have pulled off his boots and helped him undress. Someone likely covered him with a blanket, for the evening was already turning cool. Whether the pain in his hands allowed him a peaceful rest is not known. Whether the grave ponderings of the last two days troubled his mind, there is no record. Of the dreams which visited his sleep, history cannot say.

CHAPTER TWO

"More fully persuaded"
Lee Crosses the Potomac, September 4–6, 1862

WITH THE PASSING of twelve hours, Robert E. Lee would fully determine "to make the movement" into Maryland. Deciding to start "at once," he immediately ordered a Confederate division to ford the Potomac. The first Southern regiments in Maryland were not so much the vanguard of the army, however, as they were a raid to explore possibilities and obstacles. Lee needed a little more time to decide where the main body would cross. He would take even more time to think through the other details of his plan and to prepare his army for the fateful and delicate operations beyond the Confederate frontier. Yet, in the end, the turning movement was conceived, organized, and launched in a remarkably brief three days. Whatever faults Lee might possess as a military chief, procrastination was not among them.

The March to Leesburg, September 4

The weather of Thursday, September 4, rivaled that of the 3d. Under cloudless heavens, a cool morning turned into a pleasantly warm afternoon. The Army of Northern Virginia stepped out with more purpose and greater alacrity than it had the day before. Still, there were signs that rest had not completely banished the fatigue from battle.

Stonewall Jackson—his thoughts already on Maryland and fretting over yesterday's sloppy marching—ordered his division commanders to set out at exactly four o'clock in the morning. His determination was thwarted by the laxity of subordinates and the high waters of Goose Creek, which forced the column to detour to find a crossing. It was sunset before his command completed the twelve miles to Leesburg, passed through the town, continued several miles beyond on the road taken by D. H. Hill, and went into camp at George Washington Ball's farm at Big Spring. Nonetheless, night found Jackson's much-used men sinking down to rest in a grassy meadow as welcome as a "downy couch" only one mile from Conrad's Ferry on the Potomac. Longstreet's four small divisions brought up the rear and stopped for the evening two miles short of Leesburg at Newton Hall.[1]

Once again Lee gave somewhat strange employment to his horsemen. Jeb Stuart, along with Hampton's fresh brigade, spent the day in "blessed, uninterrupted quietude" at Dranesville. According to Heros von Borcke, "We rested at headquarters—the officers, the soldiers, the negroes, the horses, the mules, all wrapped in the *dolce far niente* which marked the termination of our eventful summer campaign in Virginia." Stuart did find time to forward recommendations for promotion directly to the War Department, and he sent money to his wife, writing that he would be in Maryland before she received it. In the meanwhile, Fitzhugh Lee and his brigade returned without incident from the feint against Alexandria and joined Stuart in the sweetness of doing nothing at Dranesville.[2]

The serious cavalry action of the day was assigned to Beverly Robertson, who was ordered to demonstrate against the western end of the Federal forts covering Chain Bridge. Taking with him the 7th and 12th Virginia Cavalry, his only regiments present, along with three guns from Chew's Horse Artillery, Robertson rode east on the Lees-burg Pike until he encountered the enemy cavalry at Pimmitt Run near Lewinsville. Deploying his troopers as skirmishers, he sparred with the Federals from 1:30 that afternoon until dark, when he perceived the enemy were being reenforced with infantry. Satisfied he had "fully accomplished" his assignment, Robertson withdrew to Dranesville.[3]

One incident of the day's march soon became part of the folklore of the army and an often-cited example of the defect in Jackson's character that made him a stickler for details and an overly stern taskmaster to his subordinates. Having taken special pains to ensure an early start, he was upset to discover that his lead division under A.P. Hill was not under way a half-hour after the appointed time. Stonewall publicly rebuked Hill and thereafter kept a close eye on the progress of the division. It soon became apparent that Hill next went to the opposite extreme by setting a pace that was too fast for his men and by ignoring the appropriate rest breaks. Jackson intervened to order Gregg's brigade to halt for its midday meal. When Hill discovered that Jackson had meddled in the internal operation of his division, he angrily proffered his sword in resignation. Jackson refused the sword but arrested Hill. For ten days thereafter, the irate Hill would march on foot at the rear of his men, and

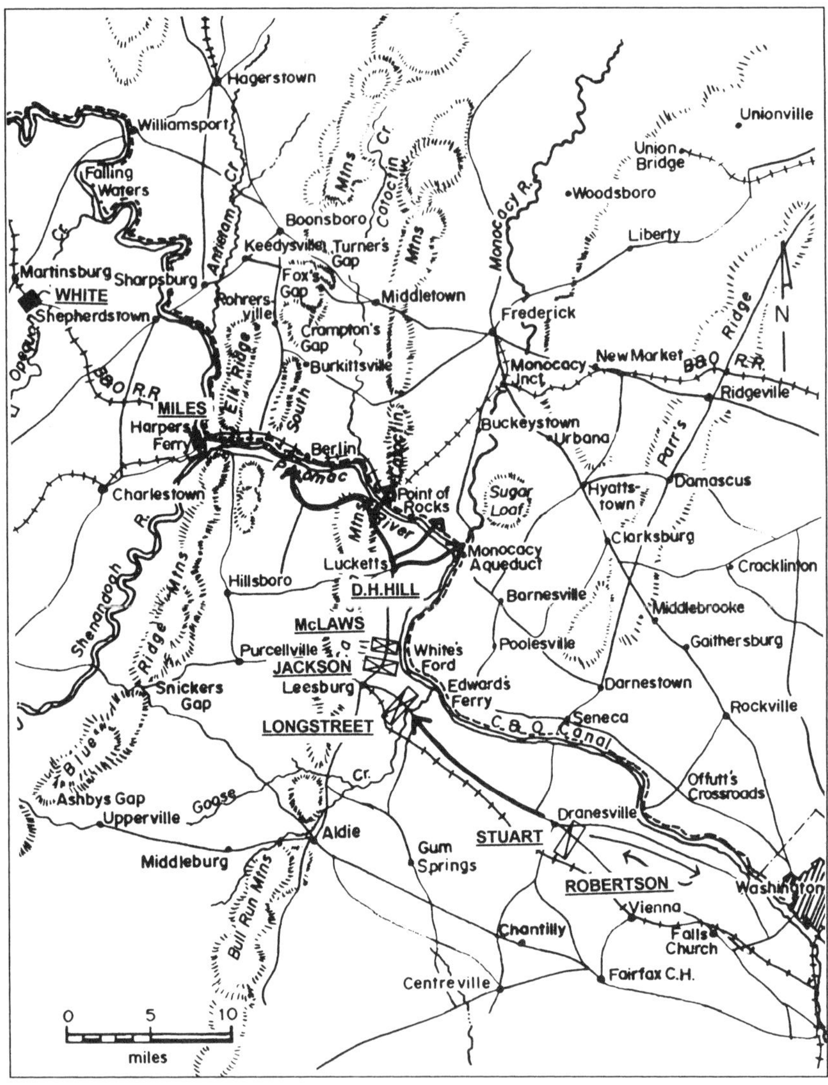

Confederate march, September 4

his division would be led by its senior brigadier, Lawrence Branch, until the eve of the surrender of Harpers Ferry.[4]

Curiously, John Hood—the only rival to Powell Hill as a division commander left in the thin officer corps—also marched to Leesburg behind his men and under arrest. During the latter stages of the Second Manassas campaign, Longstreet had placed Nathan Evans's unattached brigade with Hood's small division of two brigades. While the consolidation gave Longstreet a neatly symmetrical command structure of four divisions of three brigades each, Evans's earlier commission date made him commander of the newly formed division. Hood had continued to operate independently during the battle due to separation of the units on the field, a factor that no doubt contributed to Confederate success.

After the three brigades came together on August 31, Evans chose to exert his authority in a way Hood found unacceptable. Scouts from the Texas brigade turned in a number of captured Federal ambulances. Evans demanded the vehicles be given to him, but Hood refused. Ironically, the Texas scouts had appropriated the wagons from Stuart's troopers, who were returning them along with prisoners from the pursuit of Pope to Centreville. Whether or not Hood knew the ambulances were not "fresh captures" is uncertain, but that fact may have been the basis of the dispute with Evans. In any case, Hood was placed under arrest for disobedience of orders. Longstreet approved and ordered Hood to Culpeper to await a court-martial. Lee intervened to keep Hood with the army, although he did not restore him to command.[5]

Both arrests became minor grist for the rumor mills in the ranks, but neither was sufficiently interesting to divert attention for long from the major topic of September 4. Before the day was over, it was clear to nearly all that the army was bound for Maryland. Not only did the direction of march seem aimed at the fords of the Potomac, but by evening General Orders were read which mentioned portentously that the "most important operations" were pending and word spread that D. H. Hill's regiments had already crossed the river.[6]

It was inevitable that the movement would appear in the simplified view of the private soldier to be an invasion. And, when considered as such, a minority judged it to be a bad idea. Some thought it unwise to take the risk, while others believed it morally wrong to leave their own country. Necessarily, the dissidents failed to understand what Lee aimed to achieve and what desperate circumstances compelled him to attempt the move. In any case, the doubters were few and their impact negligible, although it is possible that a small number became conscientious stragglers when the time came to cross the Potomac.[7]

The overwhelming majority of the soldiers of the Army of Northern Virginia celebrated the notion of entering Maryland, even if they could not appreciate the subtleties of Lee's strategy. Many assumed Pennsylvania must be the ultimate goal, and they looked forward to the chance to visit revenge upon the Yankees who had ravaged Southern homes and fields. Others believed Maryland would welcome the opportunity to "burst the tyrant's chains" and join the Southern Confederacy. But nearly all aspired to ride the victorious tide to its high-water mark and "hailed with joy the advance to the Potomac."[8]

Soaring Confederate spirits rose even higher in response to the jubilant and generous reception by the loyal natives of lower Loudoun County. Showers of food, gifts, and blessings rejuvenated the weary soldiers as they passed through Leesburg. And such was the day's run of good fortune that even the army's long errant subsistence wagons magically appeared by evening.

To the Confederate veterans looking back over the years, a golden mist enshrouded these cloudless days of early September 1862, when all things were still possible and fate had not yet decreed their cause lost. After the passing of thirty years, Lt. Robert Healy could conjure an image from the memory of that day that tied together the diverse threads of his emotions. Swinging through the streets of Leesburg, the 55th Virginia beheld "an old woman with upraised hands and tears in her eyes," shouting as they passed, "The Lord bless your dirty ragged souls!"[9] Such moments made much suffering bearable.

Clearing the Decks

Although it cannot be fixed to the moment when Robert E. Lee made up his mind to enter Maryland, it is apparent he decided during the morning of the 4th. Either before he broke camp at Dranesville or while on the march to Leesburg, he cast the die. Then, eager to capitalize on the paralysis of the Federal armies—and perhaps anxious to commit before gainsaid by word from Richmond—the Confederate commander acted instantly to implement his decision. During the morning, he issued two verbal orders that revealed he had determined the main question, even if numerous important details remained to be settled.

Although he was yet uncertain where he wanted the main body to cross, Lee decided he would immediately establish a foothold in Maryland with a raid across the Potomac. He would interrupt Federal communications west of Washington, gain more precise information about the fords in the area, and learn what enemy forces were in place to dispute his passage. He must have recognized that he would at the same time send an early alert to the enemy of his intentions, and it may have been his purpose to do so. The quicker the Lincoln administration panicked the better. The sooner the Federal army left the Washington forts the weaker and less prepared it would be.

For the preliminary raid into Maryland, Lee chose a convenient force at hand, the division under D. H. Hill, which had already passed beyond Leesburg on the road to Point of Rocks. He instructed Hill to cross the Potomac at several different fords, disrupt the B&O Railroad and the C&O Canal, and destroy the aqueduct carrying the canal over the Monocacy River. Seemingly, Lee was unwilling to rely entirely on the demoralization of the enemy to guarantee the security of the raiding parties. He instructed Stuart to exert pressure on Washington's fortifications long enough to distract and confuse the Federals, while Hill was in the act of crossing. Thus, the purpose of Robertson's demonstration at Pimmitt Run was to cover Hill's raid.[10]

Daniel Harvey Hill, who may not have seen Lee since arriving from Richmond, had no idea the mission was part of any larger scheme. And Hill may have wondered why he was given no cavalry support. Still, with commendable energy he split his division of five brigades into four columns and launched his strike against Federal communications beyond the Confederate frontier. He sent G. B. Anderson's brigade northwest along the Virginia shore to a point opposite Berlin, where the B&O approached the river close enough to come under artillery fire. By three o'clock Ripley was crossing the Potomac at Point of Rocks, Garland was splashing across at Noland's Ferry, and Colquitt and Rodes were brushing away a small Federal force at Cheek's Ford near the mouth of the Monocacy. Once on the Maryland side, the four brigades spent the night and the next morning destroying the locks and cutting the banks of the canal, although "for want of powder and tools" they were unable to destroy the aqueduct. Hill was not too busy to avail himself of Maryland's bounties, however, and he purchased a large field of corn for his men. Diplomatically, he paid for it in Federal currency.[11]

About noon, the ambulance carrying Lee entered Leesburg on East Market Street, turned right at the courthouse onto King Street, and stopped two blocks north at Harrison Hall, the home of distant kinsman Henry T. Harrison. After being helped from the wagon, the injured general walked up the boxwood-bordered path to the brick mansion, where he received a warm welcome and the house was put at his disposal. In his enfeebled condition and with much work to do, Lee forsook his customary tent on this occasion and accepted the proffered hospitality. A guard was posted at the door, and his headquarters flag planted at the gate. But, before Lee could get down to work, he submitted to the concern of his host, who summoned physician Samuel K. Jackson from the house next door. Dr. Jackson's diagnosis confirmed "serious ligamentous strain" in both hands and a "fracture in one." He rebandaged the hands and made the General "as comfortable as possible."[12]

When politeness would permit, Lee broke away from the social calls which threatened to engulf him for hours and plunged into the details of preparing for his campaign in Maryland. Leaving to one side the question of where the army would cross until he had collected more information, he set to work stripping the army "of all incumbrances" and raising it to the highest possible level of efficiency. Plainly, Lee understood the importance of doing all that he could in advance to assure his army would be able to move swiftly and strike forcefully. He also recognized that operating in Maryland demanded a higher degree of discipline than the army had so far exhibited. As his first step, he issued General Orders, No. 102, which were circulated at once to be read at the head of the assembled troops at the first convenient moment.[13]

Lee not only ordered but also "earnestly enjoined" all commanders "to reduce their transportation to a mere sufficiency" for "cooking utensils and the absolute necessaries of a regiment." All horses and mules "not actually employed for artillery, cavalry, or draught purposes" were to be turned over to the chief quartermaster. Lee wanted both to shorten the trains and also to lessen the forage consumed. Although it is not entirely clear, he presumably considered the wagons carrying food to be among the "absolute necessaries." To the extent possible, he would want to reduce his dependence on the generosity of Marylanders for acquiring subsistence.

Next, having addressed the weaknesses in the cavalry two days earlier, Lee now turned to the artillery. On paper this arm appeared impressively strong. The forty-three batteries available for Second Manassas had been augmented by twelve with D. H. Hill, McLaws, Walker, and Hampton and another nineteen in the Artillery Reserve. The total of seventy-four batteries averaged slightly over four guns each and gave Lee in excess of three hundred cannon, or almost four guns for each one thousand infantrymen. In reality, however, the artillery was Lee's weakest arm.

In fielding a military force from scratch, the Confederacy had been compelled to acquire its cannon where it could, and its collection included relics of ancient wars, moldy pieces long stored in arsenals, some guns captured from the enemy, and some purchased abroad, as well as the few now being produced in their own foundries. The hodgepodge of types and calibers made training difficult and supply of ammunition in battle a nightmare. Proportionately, too few of the guns were either rifled or of heavy caliber—about one-quarter of the guns were the light 6-pounders—and too many of the officers and men were indifferent or incompetent artillerists. In addition to these problems common to all Confederate artillery early in the war, many of Lee's best batteries had suffered severely during the summer's campaigns. Their horses and equipment had worn down, and their ranks had been reduced below the minimum necessary for efficient operation.[14]

Lee could not solve all of these problems, and he had time only to ameliorate a few of them through consolidation. He ordered all batteries adjudged below standard to be left behind and their men and best guns and horses to be temporarily distributed among the other organizations. As a means of sparing the horses, he ordered that cannoneers be prohibited from riding on the guns or caissons. He assigned Gen. William Pendleton, chief of the Reserve Artillery, to supervise the refitting. But, a variety of causes would thwart Lee's intentions in the matter. Partly because Pendleton at his best was somewhat below his responsibility and was currently ill, partly because Confederate law prohibited mixing men from different states in the same unit, and partly because of the fierce resistance from the units themselves, only six batteries were broken up even on a temporary basis. Hence, Lee's artillery would not be as prepared for the great undertaking as it ought to have been.[15]

Then, tucked away in the middle of the Orders, came confirmation of the widespread rumors about Maryland. Although the wording was ambiguous, the meaning was clear. "This army is about to engage in most important operations," they announced, "where any excesses committed will exasperate the people, lead to disastrous results, and enlist the populace on the side of the Federal forces in hostility to our own." Where it was going, the army would avail itself of food and forage but only by purchase and only through the authorized agencies of the quartermasters and commissaries. It is likely D. H. Hill was operating under these orders, or similarly worded instructions, when he purchased the field of corn for his men later in the day.

Lee recognized, of course, that depredations and pillage were least likely to come from the good soldier plodding obediently along in the ranks, and most likely to be the work of the detritus flowing in the army's wake. Half of the orders were devoted to straggling, the bane for which Lee had found no antidote thus far. In his most stringent measures yet, Lee charged brigade commanders to create provost guards who were to be held to a "strict accountability" to prevent the men "from leaving the ranks, right, left, front or rear." Since similar measures had proven inadequate in the past, this time Lee created a special provost guard for the entire army, to be commanded by Lewis Armistead and to follow in the rear of the main body. Armistead was given the power to "punish summarily all depredators," a vague and ominous phrase—and perhaps Lee intended it to be so—which meant he could mete out unnamed punishments on the spot without the formality of a trial.

Finally, using uncommonly harsh words and making no allowances for physical disabilities, Lee branded stragglers as cowards and appealed to the pride of his soldiers to aid their officers in "checking the desire for straggling among their comrades." In plain language, he asserted, "stragglers are usually those who desert their comrades in peril" and are "unworthy members of an army which has immortalized itself" in its recent campaigns. Jackson in his confrontation with A. P. Hill earlier in the day had simply anticipated his chief's stern policy on straggling. Those in the army at the time, as well as subsequent commentators, who marked the incident down to the quirkiness of Stonewall the martinet, have missed the point. If veteran and well-liked leaders such as A. P. Hill would not exhibit discipline themselves and demand it of their subordinates, there was little hope the straggling problem could be solved or the army be put in the best possible shape to exploit "such momentous occasions" now in the offing.

In fact, Lee's stirring words did spur conscientious officers at various levels in a new effort to control the fractious soldiers of the citizen-army. That very night, when Company A of the 19th Virginia, Pickett's brigade in Kemper's division, ended its march and went into camp in the "pitch dark," its acting commander 3d Lt. William Wood found himself summoned to the head of the regiment. "Lieutenant," demanded Col. John B. Strange, "did you not hear the orders about straggling?" "I did, Sir," replied Wood. "One of the men under your command has just been discovered ahead of his company," Strange continued, "Consider yourself under arrest."[16] Such an extreme rendering of Lee's orders seemed unfair to Wood, and perhaps it was. In light of the severity of the problem, however, it was also necessary. It is likely that the straggling which continued to plague the army in Maryland would have been even worse without Lee's orders and the efforts of subordinates such as Jackson and Strange.

Sometime during the afternoon or early evening, Lee also dictated to Jefferson Davis his second dispatch within twenty-four hours.[17] He began by acknowledging receipt of a letter from the president which had taken an unwonted six days to reach army headquarters. "I am extremely indebted to Your Excellency for your letter of the 30th ultimo, and the letter from Washington which you enclosed to me." Davis had forwarded a letter from a Southern sympathizer, whom he described as of "high intelligence and good opportunity to be well informed," warning the Confederates that a substantial portion of McClellan's Army of the Potomac had reached Washington.[18] "You will already have learned all that I have ascertained subsequently of the movements of McClellan's army," Lee proceeded diplomatically to inform his chief that he possessed more accurate information on the enemy; "a large part, if not the whole of which participated in the battle of Saturday last, as I have good reason to believe."

It is not surprising that Lee made no further reference to the content of Davis's dispatch, since events had rendered obsolete most of what the president had written. When Davis had penned his lines, he had available only Lee's telegram of August 29 and knew only that Pope's assaults had been repulsed on two successive days. He was unaware of the crushing victory of the 30th and the rout and demoralization of the Federal armies. Understandably sensitive to his capital's vulnerability, Davis reminded Lee that releasing the last reenforcements had "uncovered Richmond to such an extent as to make its safety depend upon the ignorance and want of enterprise of the enemy." No doubt, Lee's perception of Davis's own ignorance of subsequent events and the several intervening dispatches, which discussed the safety of Richmond, led the general to pass over the president's pointed remark.

In fact, after a brief allusion to the president's letter, Lee quickly turned to the subject currently occupying his full attention. "Since my last communication to you with reference to the movements I propose to make with this army, I am more fully persuaded of the benefits which will result from an expedition into Maryland, and I shall proceed to make the movement at once, unless you should signify your disapprobation." Lee's phrase "more fully persuaded" is curious because it suggests a remaining tentativeness. Nevertheless, when taken in conjunction with his announcement that he is going to act "at once," it is implicit he has fully decided. The qualification concerning Davis's "disapprobation" is somewhat disingenuous. Considering that Lee had already ordered D. H. Hill to enter Maryland—indeed, depending upon the hour of this dispatch Hill may have already crossed the Potomac—and that Davis's last letter took six days to reach him, it would seem there was no way the president could have disapproved in time. It is barely possible that this sentence reflects Lee's view that Hill's movement stood as an independent raid, which did not necessarily commit him to entering Maryland with the entire army. In light of his other preparations, however, it is more likely that Lee—to use A. L. Long's explanation—acted "in anticipation of the president's concurrence."[19] At the same time, he apparently engaged in verbal camouflage to give the impression he was truly consulting Davis.

Revealing also is that Lee does not characterize his move as an invasion, or in any terms overly grand, but simply as an "expedition." And, consistent with his thinking to this point, he refers only to operations in Maryland, when describing his overall plan of campaign.

"The only two subjects that give me any uneasiness," he continued, "are my supplies of ammunition and subsistence." The significance of this sentence is not just that Lee confesses concern about ammunition and subsistence, but that he claims they are the "only" subjects that give him "any uneasiness." By implication, he is not uneasy about operating in Maryland, about being heavily outnumbered, about straggling from his ranks, or about any countermoves the enemy might take.

"Of the former, I have enough for present use, and must await results before deciding to what point I will have additional supplies forwarded." This reflects the knowledge Lee gained on the 3d of the arrival of Porter Alexander with the reserve ordnance train. It also reveals that Lee had not fully determined whether he would base his operations in Maryland east or west of the Blue Ridge Mountains, and hence he could not yet designate his best line for supplies or his depots. The fact that one hundred wagons of munitions were only "enough for present use," and that he anticipated the necessity of "additional" ordnance supplies in the near future, indicates Lee was planning a campaign of some duration in which he believed there would be hard fighting. This is consistent, first, with his statement in his report of his aim "to detain the enemy upon the northern frontier until the approach of winter." And, second, it conforms to Lee's use of the turning movement to create favorable conditions under which to deliver battle.[20]

"Of subsistence, I am taking measures to obtain all that this region will afford, but to be able to collect supplies to advantage in Maryland, I think it important to have the services of some one known to the people and acquainted with the resources of the country." The measures Lee took to collect supplies in Loudoun County are not known, nor the success they met. Presumably, his commissaries purchased such food as was available, so the trains could be as full as possible when crossing the Potomac.[21] Apparently, also, Lee was experiencing some doubts about the largesse of western Maryland—or the generosity of her people—and as yet had found no one in the army sufficiently familiar with the region to answer his questions.

"I wish therefore that if ex-Governor Lowe can make it convenient, he would come to me at once, as I have already requested by telegram. As I contemplate entering a part of the State with which Governor Lowe is well acquainted, I think he could be of much service to me in many ways." The telegram referred to has not been found and was presumably sent on the 4th from Leesburg.[22] Lee's use of "contemplate" probably does not mean that any real doubt remained in his mind about "entering" Maryland. Instead, it more likely reflects his indecision about "the part of the state." Or, it may be an unconscious attempt to disguise further the fact that he has already made up his mind.

Enoch Louis Lowe (1820–1892) was born at the Hermitage, a thousand-acre estate on the Monocacy three miles from Frederick. He was a Democrat, the thirty-second governor of Maryland (1850–53), and a Breckinridge elector in 1860. In 1861 he cast his lot with the Confederacy and exiled himself to Richmond, although after the war he would practice law in Brooklyn. In addition to using Lowe as an adviser, it is likely Lee hoped to employ him as a figurehead and rallying point for Southern sympathizers in the state. Lee later made clear he planned to have Lowe issue a proclamation to Marylanders.[23]

Having broached the issue of political sensitivity, Lee then proceeded to make an offhand statement that would whet the expectations of Jefferson Davis when he read it and would also lead later commentators to conclude that the general planned from the beginning a full-scale invasion of the North. "Should the results of the expedition justify it," Lee wrote, "I propose to enter Pennsylvania, unless you should deem it unadvisable upon political or other grounds."

In spite of its somewhat casual tone, this is clearly a critical sentence in understanding Lee's strategy, and it has sometimes been used to prove that Lee intended from the start a penetration deep into the

Northern territory. Such is not the most likely interpretation, however. Everything else written by Lee up to this point indicates that he did not believe he had the men or materiél to undertake an "invasion." He was already greatly concerned about establishing his communications for future supplies and in this state of mind must have doubted his ability to maintain the attenuated line that would be required to threaten Philadelphia or even Harrisburg. Equally, the entire thrust of Lee's thinking, as reflected in his writing to Davis, indicates he expected to spend an extended period—perhaps months—in Maryland.

One reasonable reading of this sentence would be that in writing "should the results of the expedition justify it," Lee meant "should the course of the campaign require it." The Confederate commander knew enough about the geography of western Maryland—or he could glean it from a simple glance at the map—to realize how narrow its neck becomes in the vicinity of Hagerstown. In a campaign of maneuver, he might be tempted to cross the Mason-Dixon line to gain advantage over his opponent. In a subsequent letter to Davis, written as the army was about to leave Frederick, Lee would indicate he was moving as "originally intended" in the direction of Hagerstown or Chambersburg to open communications through the Shenandoah Valley. Chambersburg is a scant fifteen miles inside Pennsylvania and located in the interconnected Cumberland, Hagerstown, and Shenandoah Valley system. It was here that Lee intended to operate for as long as conditions would permit, in order to allow Virginia a season to recover.

Another reasonable reading of this sentence would emphasize the conditions Lee set for entering Pennsylvania. He proposed to do so only if the "results" in Maryland justified it. In other words, the move was not the aim of his campaign but a contingency. In contemplating his present turning movement, Lee may have allowed his anticipations to soar far in advance. He may have speculated that—after he had delivered a crushing defeat to a Federal army in western Maryland—it might be difficult to induce the enemy to come out from the safety of Washington's forts a second time. Then, it might be necessary to undertake a new turning movement—one that presented a more immediate threat to Harrisburg, or Philadelphia, or even New York—in order to compel the Federals to expose their demoralized forces soon after a third Manassas.

One thing which is clear is that Lee understood the difference between crossing into Maryland and entering Pennsylvania. Although the dotted line on the map that separated Hagerstown from Chambersburg may have had no meaning in military topography, Lee clearly recognized its political significance. While he might anticipate the president's concurrence in entering Maryland, with good reason he might hesitate to set foot on the soil of a free state. There might be something of the charade in his appearing to consult about crossing the Potomac at nearly the same time his troops were splashing into the river, but his request for approval to enter Pennsylvania was likely genuine. Moreover, there would be ample time for guidance from Davis to arrive from Richmond on this question. It might also be noted, when Lee did reach Hagerstown, he would be careful to advance his pickets to, but not beyond, Middleburg on the state boundary.[24]

Whatever Lee intended, he must have believed his meaning unambiguous, for he quickly passed on to the topic of information about the Federals. "As to the movements of the enemy," he continued, "my latest intelligence shows that the army of Pope is concentrating around Washington and Alexandria in their fortifications." This indicates Lee had no serious worries about offensive movements by the Federals, or concern that they would be able to oppose his crossing the river. It also shows Lee still believed his opponent to be John Pope.

Lee closed his dispatch with a piece of news of great importance to his future plans. "Citizens of this county report that Winchester has been evacuated, which is confirmed by the *Baltimore Sun* of this morning, containing extracts from the *Washington Star* of yesterday." This gives an interesting glimpse into Lee's intelligence gathering operations. He derived this information not from Stuart but from local residents and from Northern newspapers—in this case one from the current day. It also strongly argues that Lee composed this letter in the afternoon—perhaps even late afternoon or early evening—as some time must be allowed for the Baltimore paper to reach his camp. Brig. Gen. Julius White had indeed evacuated his force of three thousand men from Winchester on the night of September 2 and taken refuge with the garrison at Harpers Ferry.

"This will further relieve our country, and I think leaves the Valley entirely free. They will probably concentrate behind the Potomac."

On one level, Lee is pointing to the evacuation of Winchester as another fruit of his offensive strategy in clearing a region of Virginia from occupation and making its citizens and resources once again available to sustain the Confederate war effort.[25] But, on another level, he sees the Federal retreat as clearing the Valley as a safe line for his communications with Richmond. His failure to mention the Federal garrison at Harpers Ferry is curious, since he must have known of its existence. He may have assumed it would also fall back in order to avoid being cut off, but his reference to concentrating "behind" the Potomac is even more puzzling. It seems to mean he initially believed the Federal troops from the Shenandoah Valley would fall back only a short distance and regroup behind the river. This should have caused him some concern, since these enemy forces would then be in his rear or on his flank after he himself had crossed. Either this had not yet occurred to him, or he was already anticipating that his crossing the Potomac would further isolate the Valley forces and compel them to retire farther northward.

In any case, Lee's closing sentences to Davis emphasized the uncertainties which remained in his mind. True, he had decided to enter Maryland, and D. H. Hill was already on the way to test the waters of the Potomac and destroy Federal communications west of Washington. But, he had not yet determined where he would run his supply line, where he would base his operations in Maryland, or where he would cross the river with the main body. All three decisions were so interdependent that they must be resolved together. Lee may have naturally inclined toward establishing a base west of the Blue Ridge, but he also felt the need to operate initially east of the mountains in order to exert maximum pressure on Pope to come after the Confederates before the Federal army had much time to recover. Lee needed to talk with someone intimately familiar with western Maryland. During the evening, Stonewall Jackson brought him that someone in the person of Bradley Johnson.

Leesburg War Council

Riding at the head of the Stonewall division's second brigade as it left camp along Sugar Land Run on the morning of the 4th, Bradley Tyler Johnson was a man without a home in more ways than one. He had abandoned his native state in the spring of 1861 and joined with fellow exiles in Richmond to form the 1st Maryland Infantry, the regiment that became the bulwark of the Maryland Line in the Confederate army. Promoted from major to colonel, Johnson led the regiment with distinction through the Valley campaign and the Seven Days. When the depleted unit was unable to recruit its strength with men from its own state—as required by Confederate law—it was disbanded at Gordonsville on August 11, and in exile Johnson found himself doubly orphaned and without a home in the army. Jackson held too high an opinion of Johnson's abilities to see them wasted, however, and appointed him to the temporary command of the second brigade in the absence of John R. Jones. Johnson had performed so "ably" in defense of the railroad cut at Second Manassas that Jackson would take time on his busy September 4 to recommend with "pleasure" his promotion to brigadier general.[26]

Jackson had Johnson on his mind for another reason this day, and he sought out the company of the Marylander on the march to Leesburg. Stonewall had known for some time—probably since a conference with Lee on the 2d—that the army might enter Maryland. He had argued with his chief that the army should first move to the west and clear the Federals from the Shenandoah Valley and then cross the upper Potomac at or above Harpers Ferry.[27] As they rode west on the Leesburg Turnpike, Jackson asked Johnson for a "detailed description of the country in Maryland on the other side of the Potomac," including the "topography, resources and political condition." Johnson, born and reared in Frederick, was especially well qualified to supply the wanted information. Although without military training, he was well educated, having graduated from Princeton and attended Harvard Law School, and after election as state district attorney he had risen to the leadership of the Maryland Democratic party. In 1859 he became chairman of the state central committee; in 1860 he attended the Democratic conventions in Charleston and Baltimore, and in the fall he served as a Breckinridge elector.

Unaware he was intruding in an ongoing debate, Johnson no doubt boasted of the agricultural richness of his native countryside, but it is certain he also emphasized that the reaction of its citizens was likely to be cool. Jackson may have believed the information buttressed his own arguments for not operating in Frederick County; he may, as well, have intended to exert a subtle influence on Lee in favor of an invasion of Pennsylvania; or, he may have simply felt it his duty to pass on important intelligence to his commander. That night after making camp, Stonewall took Johnson into Leesburg to visit Lee at the Harrison house. He requested the Marylander to "repeat our conversation of the day," and Johnson "did so at length" in a meeting that lasted several hours.[28]

Although Johnson's brief memoir of the meeting gives few details of what he said, it is likely he pointed out the facts of the state's culture and economy that made it improbable there would be a popular uprising in response to the presence of the Confederate army. Maryland's slaveholders—and therefore its most ardent Southern sympathizers—were heavily concentrated in the counties of the eastern and western shores of the Chesapeake Bay. The Federal armies occupying Washington and Baltimore would stand between these supporters and a Confederate force in western Maryland. The counties now open to Lee were peopled largely by German Americans, who worked small farms, owned few slaves, and were predominantly Unionist in sentiment.[29]

Johnson's narrowly partisan views may have prevented him from giving Lee a realistic assessment of the political climate in the state. It may have seemed to Southerners that Maryland was being held against its will in the Union, and in the volatile days of April 1861—in the absence of hard evidence either way—it cannot be stated with finality that the possibility of secession was not real. By the fall of the same year, the predominantly loyal sentiment of the state asserted itself, however. In the September elections, Unionist Augustus Bradford out-polled states' rights candidate Benjamin Howard two to one, and safe majorities in both houses of the new state legislature were firmly opposed to secession.[30]

Johnson may have been blinded by his passion, or he may simply have been out of touch with developments in his state, because he told Lee that sentiments in Maryland were about evenly divided. Nonetheless, the expatriate plainly predicted the Confederates would receive little "material aid" in the beginning. He argued that Marylanders could not be expected to hazard life and fortune in an uprising unless the occupation offered promise of "at least some permanence."[31] It is doubtful Lee was much dismayed by what he heard, since his primary reason for entering the state had always been military and not political, but he may have been disappointed. After hearing the pessimistic views of one of its most ardent secessionists, it is even less likely he placed much reliance on substantial support from the state.

In fact, Johnson's memoir gives the impression that Lee displayed considerably more interest in the geography of Maryland than in its politics. As late as the night of the 4th, the Confederate commander was still debating with himself where the main army should cross the Potomac. If Jackson believed that Johnson's information would show Lee the futility of basing operations in Frederick County and thus dissuade him from crossing east of the Blue Ridge, he missed the point of his chief's dilemma. Lee was balancing, on the one hand, the desire to cause enough fear among the Federals for their capital to induce them to abandon northern Virginia and come after him in their demoralized condition against, on the other hand, his concern for a safe line of communications with Richmond. He questioned Johnson closely about the banks of the Potomac and the fords in Loudoun County, as compared with those farther up the river around Harpers Ferry and Williamsport.

At the end of the long conversation, Jackson "sat bolt upright asleep." And Lee, staring into the distance as if speaking to himself, mused, "When I left Richmond, I told the President that I would, if possible, relieve Virginia of the pressure of these two armies." Neither president nor general could have then foreseen such success as would lead to the quandary over the fords of the Potomac.[32] According to Johnson, Lee then continued his soliloquy, "If I cross here, I may do so at the cost of men, but with the saving of time. If I cross at Williamsport, I can do so with saving of men, but at cost of time."

The passing of the years must have garbled Lee's words in Johnson's memory, because as stated they make no sense. The Confederate commander's reference to cost in men could only mean he expected the Federals to dispute his crossing east of the mountains, but he could avoid casualties by crossing farther west. Yet, by this time, Lee must have been certain he could cross the river from Loudoun without opposition. Not only had he written Davis earlier in the day that his intelligence showed the Federals were cowering in the Washington forts, but D. H. Hill had by now demonstrated that only token forces guarded the fords. Indeed, it is possible Lee might have said almost the reverse. He may have remarked that moving against the Federal forces in the Valley risked needless losses, since they would surely retire of their own volition.

In spite of this inconsistency, Johnson's observations on Lee's intentions in the Maryland campaign are worth weight. After the war he wrote, "It seems beyond dispute that the first Maryland campaign was undertaken by General Lee solely and entirely as part of his defensive operation for the protection of Virginia." Johnson concluded, "It was an offensive-defensive operation, having as its objective neither the invasion of Pennsylvania nor the redemption of Maryland, but only the relief of the Confederacy, as far as the means at his command would permit."

The meeting finally broke up, and Jackson and Johnson rode back through the cool September night to their bivouac at Big Spring, ignorant of Lee's decision. But Lee was very close to deciding, and either that same night or early the next morning, he determined he would cross the Potomac east of the mountains. In fact, he would cross even nearer to Washington than had D.H. Hill. Common sense—and the example of the Winchester garrison—argued that the problem of the Federal forces in the Shenandoah would solve itself. Once the Confederates entered

Maryland, the enemy at Harpers Ferry would have to fall back to avoid isolation and the risk of capture.[33]

This decision completed Lee's strategy in its original form. He would cross the lower Potomac and threaten Washington and Baltimore to draw Pope's army north of the river. After the demoralized Federals had started to respond, he would move into western Maryland and threaten Pennsylvania. With Confederate communications running securely through the Shenandoah Valley, Lee would cause the enemy supply line to lengthen until it was vulnerable to a campaign of maneuver. Confident of the ability of his own army, he would depend on the enemy in two respects. First, he needed the Federals to abandon the Shenandoah Valley in a timely manner. Second, he needed an opposing commander who would cooperate—not necessarily a timid opponent, but one who would give him openings for maneuver.

Unknown to Lee, John Pope had already been stripped of army command. The very panic that Lee had worked so hard to create had impelled Lincoln—over the angry protests of his cabinet—to restore George McClellan to a measure of authority. Since the morning of the 2d, McClellan had been in charge of the defenses of Washington and all of the troops therein. With his customary energy he was working to disentangle the mixed commands and restore order to the disorganized ranks. His presence alone virtually banished the demoralization.

By the morning of the 4th, McClellan had the small but reliable force of cavalry which had arrived from the Peninsula operating in Lee's rear, and he had established a string of signal stations along the Potomac as far west as Maryland Heights at Harpers Ferry. He knew of the arrival of the first Confederates in Leesburg on the night of the 3d, and his cavalry chief, Alfred Pleasonton, correctly interpreted Beverly Robertson's feint near Falls Church as a cover for crossing the Potomac—an interpretation that McClellan immediately accepted. By noon he had the corps of Sumner, Banks, and Burnside north of the Potomac and Couch's division following close behind. By dusk he had relinquished the northern Virginia front to the fatigued troopers of Pope's army and ordered his dependable cavalry under Pleasonton across the river to push reconnaissance to the northwest. Thus, McClellan anticipated the reports that came in during the night from the signal station on Sugar Loaf Mountain via the telegraph at Poolesville and from Point of Rocks via Harpers Ferry of D. H. Hill's fording the Potomac.[34]

On one level, the return of an old opposing chess mate—if indeed McClellan were to be given command of the Federal force taking the field—would be good news for Lee. It would be comforting to confront a professional who knew the science of war and whose actions would therefore be calculable if not predictable. At the same time, however, it would mean the Confederates would be facing the Federal general whose innate deliberateness would make him difficult to catch off guard for a third Manassas-like victory. Would Lee have still undertaken his "expedition into Maryland" had he known his opponent was to be McClellan and not Pope? Undoubtedly, he would have. What better choice of action did he have? Besides, although he already knew of McClellan's deliberate nature, he had yet to learn of McClellan's power to reinvigorate the dispirited Union armies.

Jackson's Crossing, September 5

On Friday, September 5, a brilliant and cloudless dawn spread slowly up the Potomac River Valley, ushering in the fourth consecutive day of beautiful late-summer weather for the recuperating Army of Northern Virginia. This day would be different, however, for even as a pleasant coolness lingered in the long shadows of the morning, the temperatures began to climb. This was the first in a stretch of hot, dry days during which the sun boiled away the last moisture from the Chantilly thunderstorm and baked the earth into a hard crust that crumbled under hooves and boots into choking clouds of dust. The 5th was also the day weariness evaporated from the army. The rattling drums and shrilling bugles that echoed for miles across the rolling Loudoun countryside summoned the Army of Northern Virginia to a new campaign and the promise of establishing independence for the South.

Lee arose early for his busy day. Dr. Samuel Jackson, the Harrison's neighbor, returned to put splints on both his hands and support his arms with slings. The Confederate commander was then called to a breakfast table groaning with delicacies, where a lady of the house cut his food and fed him.[35] At some point in the morning—probably immediately after breakfast—Lee went into council with his senior lieutenants, Stonewall Jackson and James Longstreet. He must have then told them of his decision to enter Maryland opposite Leesburg and ordered Jackson to proceed at once to cross the river at White's Ford. Stonewall was to take temporary charge of D. H. Hill's division and move northwest toward

Frederick. Longstreet was to move forward to occupy the camp vacated by Jackson and cross at the same ford the following day. Lee himself intended to remain in Leesburg another day and supervise the details of preparation.

In the course of the meeting, Stuart arrived from Dranesville, having halted his cavalry a mile outside of Leesburg, because the streets were blocked with wagons and troops. On this occasion, Lee demonstrated his growing appreciation of concentrating the cavalry to screen the movements of the infantry. He ordered Stuart to interpose the horsemen between Jackson and Washington. But, once again, Lee either underestimated the coordination that would be required, or he relied too heavily on the discretion of his subordinates. Whatever verbal orders the Confederate commander gave did not leave Stuart feeling under any obligation to expedite the cavalry crossing by using a different ford or to provide reconnaissance north and west in the direction of Frederick or to open communication with Jackson once both were in Maryland.

After attending a brief prayer meeting with Lee in the parlor of the Harrison home, Jackson rode rapidly back to Big Spring and ordered his command into column for the march. With Jackson himself and the Stonewall division in the van, the striking arm of the Army of Northern Virginia proceeded a mile down a farm lane and by midmorning reached the banks of the Potomac.[36]

The 10th Virginia of Taliaferro's brigade was the first to enter the water. Preceded by a band and waving the dark-blue colors of the Old Dominion, the regiment set the bow-shaped route the army would follow. Instead of wading directly across the half-mile breadth of the river, the column inclined to the right to break its passage on a sandy strip eroded from the tip of Mason's Island and then veered left again to return to the lower banks of the ford on the other shore. When the musicians reached dry land, they struck up "Maryland! My Maryland!" to the cheers of the soldiers. The scene repeated throughout the day, as succeeding bands took up the Maryland air amid shouts of enthusiasm.[37]

The exuberant passage of the river occurred without serious incident and under the eyes of a mere handful of Yankees who immediately "scampered away" to safety. But it consumed more time than Jackson had anticipated. Lee had chosen an "obscure" ford and its little-used precipitous banks had to be "dug down" on the Virginia side to provide a gentler grade for the wagons and artillery. The river still flowed moderately fresh from the storms earlier in the week, and at places the water

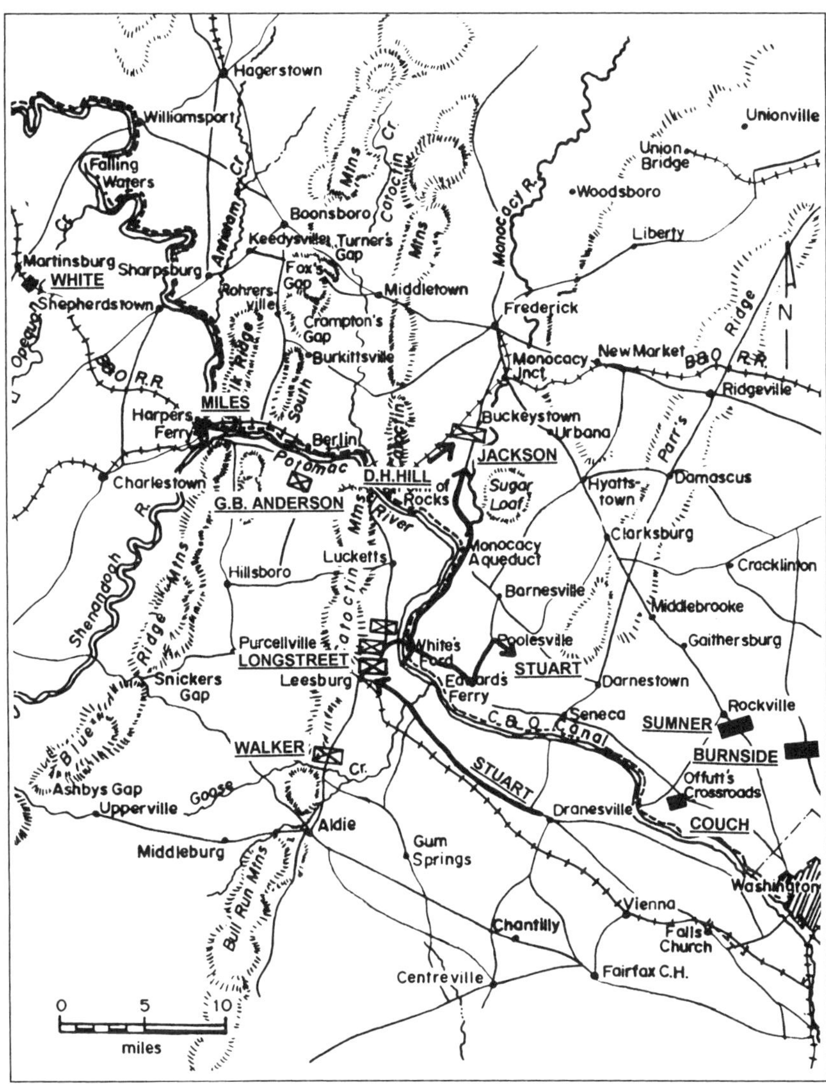

Confederate march, September 5

reached the upper chests of both horses and men. Most not only removed their shoes but also took off their trousers and drawers, leading a member of the 49th Georgia to confide to his diary, "Never did I behold so many naked legs in my life." An occasional wagon sank into a mud hole, and some of the mules decided they preferred the cool water to the hot sun and had to be "cussed" into Maryland by Maj. John A. Harmon, Jackson's quartermaster. At least one battery commander ignored the recent general order and allowed his cannoneers to ride across on their caissons and limbers. Ironically, it was the Rockbridge Artillery, which included Lee's youngest son, Rob, that reached Maryland dryshod. Its commander, Capt. William Poague, soon found himself under arrest, because the breach in discipline was observed by Jackson's adjutant.[38]

Stonewall intended to reach the B&O Railroad bridge over the Monocacy River—a march of about fifteen miles—by nightfall. On gaining the Maryland shore, Jackson turned his column to the left and headed west several miles on the tow path of the C&O Canal until it reached the locks just below the mouth of the Monocacy. A rough bridge was quickly laid down at the locks, and the army then marched northward on the Furnace Road and forded the Monocacy. Finally, after midnight had been reached and passed, the vanguard bivouacked at Three Springs near Buckeystown, near the railroad but about six miles shy of the B&O bridge and nine miles from Frederick.[39]

Once in Maryland, Jackson's progress may have been hampered by his lack of cavalry. He had with him only the Black Horse troop of the 4th Virginia under Capt. Robert Randolph, and a company of scouts under Capt. Lige White. Stuart did not start crossing the Potomac until midafternoon, and in the meanwhile Jackson had to make do with a handful of horsemen to feel his way forward in an unfamiliar country and to protect the vulnerable right flank of his marching column against enemy attack from Washington. Surviving scraps of evidence plainly indicate Jackson worried about marching almost blindly into territory he considered unfriendly. At three o'clock he sent orders to Lawrence Branch, who commanded while A. P. Hill was under arrest, to keep sharp watch for the enemy and be prepared to throw his division into line of battle a mile east of the road "to prevent the enemy's artillery from annoying our trains."[40]

Jackson also moved immediately to open communications with D. H. Hill, who had been engaged since the previous afternoon with four brigades west of the Monocacy destroying sections of the canal. Lee had charged Jackson with temporary command of all of the Confederate forces north of the Potomac, and Stonewall justifiably felt the safety of the column outweighed the importance of cutting canal banks.[41] At two o'clock, he sent a politely worded dispatch—that was more request than order—informing Hill of the mission to destroy the railroad bridge over the Monocacy. He asked Hill to suspend his work and move forward to join him "during the evening or night at furthest." He carefully noted

Lee had "authorized" the move and added it was important to "effect the junction, as we may meet with opposition before we can destroy the bridge."

The two generals had married sisters, and as a friendly gesture Hill rode across country to report in person to his brother-in-law. He found Stonewall studying a map held by Lige White, and, as Hill would later recall it, Jackson told him, "You have been placed under my orders. I wish your division to join me, to-night, near Frederick." The conversation could not have taken place before three o'clock, and by the time Hill gathered his four scattered brigades and reached the Frederick road night had fallen. He fell in at the rear of Jackson's last division (Lawton) and followed on to the vicinity of Buckeystown.[42]

For Stonewall Jackson the day had been a strange blend of promise, worry, and frustration. He would keep his topographical engineer, Jed. Hotchkiss, awake most of the night drawing a map of the vicinity of Frederick, because he still "expected opposition in going there."[43] And he closed the day with a curious incident that has never been explained. After midnight when the troops were in camp, he summoned his scout, Lige White, and asked to be conducted back over the route of march. Through the darkness the two men rode in silence almost to the Potomac before turning around and returning to Three Springs. Had Jackson dropped a glove? Was he afraid some regiments had been left by the wayside? Was he so concerned over the vulnerability of his position that he felt the need to familiarize himself with every detail of his potential escape route? These and a dozen other possibilities seem unlikely in pitch blackness. Did his horse need exercise? Was he himself too excited to welcome the embrace of Morpheus just yet? The uncommunicative Stonewall did not open his mouth during the entire trip.[44]

In the meanwhile, Jeb Stuart discovered the tribulations of traveling in the wake of a large army. Returning at about two o'clock from the early morning conference with Lee—either the Confederate chief had found much more to discuss with Stuart than his other lieutenants or Stuart had found other business in Leesburg—Jeb observed the streets were jammed with troops, artillery, and wagons, and he decided to bypass the town. He detached Robertson's undersized brigade to remain as rear guard, sent orders to Hampton to follow when possible, and set out on an easterly detour with Fitzhugh Lee's brigade. But Stuart's determination to cross the river at White's Ford—whether by his own choice or Lee's orders—forced him eventually to join the same road already clogged by Jackson's creeping column. "After a dusty and very much impeded march of two hours, winding through infantry columns, and compelled frequently to halt," the horsemen—who probably were not singing "Jine the Cavalry" by this time—reached the Potomac. Fording took another two hours.[45]

Thus, it must have been about six o'clock before Stuart was in place to carry out his mission to screen Jackson's entrance into Maryland. Turning to the right and away from the infantry, he traveled south a short distance on the River Road and then took the road that ran almost due east to Poolesville. The cavalrymen covered the six miles to the village in good time, and the van of Fitz Lee's brigade reached the outskirts at dusk. Here, in Friday's falling shadows, the Confederate expedition encountered its first serious opposition.

A squadron of about one hundred troopers of the 1st Massachusetts Cavalry had deployed as skirmishers, unaware they confronted fifteen times their number in gray horsemen. The Federal squadron had arrived with its regiment just two days before by ship at Alexandria from service along the coast of South Carolina. Alfred Pleasonton in his search to patch together a force to scout the prowling Confederate army rushed the unit to the Maryland front and scattered its companies widely. The Massachusetts troopers and their commander, Capt. Samuel Chamberlain, were totally ignorant of their surroundings, apprehensive from the rumors of a massive Confederate invasion, and nervous because of the evident Southern sympathies of the residents of Poolesville. Consequently, their resistance was brief, and they quickly broke to the rear, intending to ride through the town to safety. Instead, they found the village street a jumble of rocks, furniture, and other obstacles the citizens had strewn about to block their escape. Chamberlain and thirty of his troopers were captured in the melee.[46]

Poolesville was located in Montgomery County, the most westerly bastion of slavery and Southern sympathy in Maryland, and excitement reached a fever heat as the small town greeted its liberators. Young boys eager to join the cavalry rode up on their farm horses, and two merchants declaring their intention to enlist liquidated their stock of goods "upon the spot for Confederate money." More than an an hour was spent in revelry and stuffing pockets and saddlebags with oddments soon to be discarded. Finally, the brigades of Lee and Hampton—the latter having arrived after the skirmish—moved two miles east of the village in the direction of Darnestown and went into camp. There is no evidence Stuart communicated with Jackson after his crossing or during the night.[47]

The Confederate reception in Poolesville was not typical of the reaction by Marylanders upon finding the Army of Northern Virginia suddenly in their midst. A march of five miles carried Jackson's men from a friendly Montgomery County, where slaves comprised nearly one-third of the population, to the less hospitable clime of Frederick County, where only 7 percent were in bondage.[48] In general, the first day established a pattern of relations between the uninvited visitors and their hesitant hosts that held true for the entire campaign. On their part, the soldiers exhibited a discipline and self-restraint that reflected their understanding of the gravity of the occasion. Lee's words and Jackson's example did sink in. In a scene that may have been repeated elsewhere, William Dorsey Pender called together all of the officers of his brigade of A. P. Hill's division before the march had started that morning. He lectured them on their duties as "officers and gentlemen," telling them to keep "a firm hand on the men of their commands" and warning them "he would hold them strictly responsible for their conduct."[49]

Still, among the multitude of veterans' memoirs that bear witness—with variation in detail—to "thousands of troops pass[ing] the very orchards, whose red and golden burdens overhung the road, without touching a fruit"; there are an amazing number of gleeful stories—again with differing details—of ferocious pigs that had to be killed in self-defense. It is safe to say the army's diet did not suffer decline in Maryland, and many of the soldiers ate quite well. While D. H. Hill and Jackson purchased fields of corn for their men, the men themselves bought apple butter and other delicacies and gladly accepted gifts when offered. The overriding impression, however, is that the Confederates behaved quite well for a Civil War army, a comparison made plainer to the residents by the conduct of the Federals who passed through the same area within a week.

For their part, Marylanders displayed a full range of emotions in response to the Confederate presence. A sympathetic minority welcomed the Southerners. Jackson received a "noble" melon and a big gray mare, and he and his staff were "cordially invited to many houses" and "handsomely entertained" at their encampment near Three Springs. One host boasted he fed over 600 soldiers. As word spread of the Confederate presence, admirers traveled from as far as Baltimore to catch a glimpse of their heroes. Still, curiosity and civility predominated among the majority. Wonderment was to be expected in rural nineteenth-century communities that would gossip for months when a passing circus broke its dull routine. And politeness no doubt seemed appropriate in the face of a mighty army fresh from the fields of its latest victory. One farmer captured the spirit of resignation when told that his fence rails must be consumed to cook the soldiers' rations. "Burn away," he said, "that's what rails are for when there's no other wood around."[50]

Friday, September 5, passed a bit more quietly for the Confederates who remained south of the Potomac. William Pendleton struggled to implement Lee's orders to bring efficiency to the artillery of the army. He named Maj. Charles Richardson to take charge of the fatigued horses and deficient equipment and open a refitting depot at Winchester, and he set nine o'clock the next morning as the hour for the Reserve Artillery to join the march for the Potomac. Suffering from a "crisis of diarrhea of some two weeks duration," Pendleton had submitted to a blistering of his right side and understandably took to his saddle as little as possible. His physical disability combined with the reluctance—in some cases near mutiny—of commanders to see their batteries even temporarily disbanded retarded his progress.[51]

During the day, Longstreet's command and R. H. Anderson's division marched through Leesburg and occupied the camp at Big Spring vacated by Jackson. There they joined the four brigades of LaFayette McLaws, who had arrived two nights before. This brought to seventy-seven the infantry regiments crowded around the generous watering hole on the farm of George W. Ball. Twenty-five feet in diameter, the limestone spring would earn the unique distinction of providing drinks of cold, pure water to all of the foot soldiers of Lee's army, as they bivouacked on four successive nights.

Citizens from the neighborhood visited the grand encampment, bringing food and inviting soldiers to their homes. Officers inspected transportation and other accouterments in preparation for the expedition that was now common knowledge in the ranks. As darkness fell and hundreds of campfires dotted the rolling countryside, excitement and anticipation banished tiredness. A gunner from Chew's battery of Robertson's cavalry brigade, which was also camped nearby, wrote in his diary of the "joyous gayety" surrounding him. "As I am writing,"

George Neese noted, "I hear soldiers shouting, huzzahing all around us." Then a brass band struck up "to swell the cheer of the merry throng." It would seem that the Army of Northern Virginia was prepared to meet its fate.[52]

After his busy morning, Lee spent a relatively quiet day, one which in part assumed the nature of a family reunion. He received visits from his nephew, Fitzhugh Lee, who commanded a brigade under Stuart; his second son, Rooney, colonel of the 9th Virginia Cavalry in the same brigade; and his youngest son, Rob, a private in the Rockbridge Artillery. He also walked several blocks to Cornwall Street to pay a courtesy call on John Janney, who, as president of the Virginia secession convention, had made an eloquent speech tendering the command of the state forces to Lee in April 1861, and whose threatened harassment had caused Lee to send Munford to Leesburg four days earlier. On the way, a soldier, who may not have recognized the Confederate commander, asked the distance to White's Ford. Lee replied, "It makes no difference to you, my man. Keep up with your regiment."[53]

The Confederate commander also devoted his attention to minor details of the preparation, which he published in Special Orders, No. 188. He released Brig. Gen. Richard B. Garnett from arrest and ordered him to report to Longstreet for duty. Garnett had been charged by Jackson with dereliction of duty in the battle of Kernstown in March and was traveling with the army, because the court-martial hearing his case had been interrupted by the Second Manassas campaign. Lee may or may not have viewed the accusations to be substantial, but in any case he believed the army needed all of its experienced generals. Longstreet recognized the interim nature of the assignment and gave Garnett the brigade of Virginians left temporarily without an officer of appropriate rank by the wounding of George Pickett at Gaines' Mill.[54]

Lee also adopted several reforms in the cavalry that had undoubtedly been urged by Stuart during the morning meeting. He relieved Beverly Robertson, who was unpopular with both Stuart and Jackson, from command of a cavalry brigade and ordered him to report to North Carolina to train new regiments of horse. This vacancy elevated the capable Col. Thomas Munford of the 2d Virginia to command of the brigade that had belonged to Turner Ashby in Jackson's Valley campaign. In addition, in a move to unify the cavalry for its operations in Maryland, Lee ordered companies that had been detached to serve with infantry commands to report to Stuart for service with their regiments. Experience in the war was demonstrating that, while artillery served more efficiently when disbursed to divisions, cavalry required centralization to be effective.[55]

Special Orders were usually employed to direct individual or small groups of persons or units and were circulated in separate parts on a need-to-know basis, whereas General Orders were promulgated when the subject matter applied to the whole or large segments of the army and usually appeared in complete form. Embodied in the middle of Special Orders, No. 188, of September 5 was an article that seemed more appropriate to general orders. It showed Lee's continuing desire to perfect his policy concerning straggling and was probably meant for every command in the army. Apparently, a question had arisen over the authority of the guards established at the rear of each brigade to deal with strays from other commands. Lee felt it necessary to make clear that all stragglers were to be arrested, and they were to be carried along until the end of the day's march and then returned to their respective units.

Finally, at some point during the day or early evening, Lee composed and dictated another dispatch to Jefferson Davis, his fourth in three days. He thus established the new practice of maintaining unusually close contact with the president, which he would continue for the duration of the Maryland campaign.[56] "As I have already had the honor to inform you, this army is about entering Maryland," Lee began, seeming to belie the apparent tentativeness of his letter of yesterday, "with a view of affording the people of that State an opportunity of liberating themselves," implying the possibility of an uprising was his main reason for the movement. Immediately, however, he set the record straight.

"Whatever success may attend that effort, I hope at any rate to annoy and harass the enemy." In this candid sentence Lee revealed his true aims for the campaign. Having spoken at length with Bradley Johnson, he no longer harbored—if indeed he ever had—serious expectations of an insurrection in Maryland. In his report submitted almost a year later, Lee would confess he expected "more assistance" from the "fears of the Washington Government than from any active demonstration" by Marylanders.[57] It is all the more persuasive that he wrote much the same thing even before he set foot on Maryland soil. It is also revealing that Lee employed his favorite terms, "annoy and harass"—his code words for an offensive to thwart the enemy and push him closer to abandoning the war against the South—to describe what he hoped to gain from the campaign.

Lee then turned rather abruptly to the details of logistics. "The army being transferred to this section, the road to Richmond through Warrenton, has been abandoned as far back as Culpeper Court House and all trains are directed to proceed by way of Luray & Front Royal from Culpeper Court House to Winchester. I desire that everything coming from Richmond may take that route, or any nearer one turning off before reaching Culpeper Court House." There are three interesting conclusions to be derived from Lee's statement. First, he believed that a line of communications running east to Manassas and then south to Warrenton and Culpeper was too exposed even from his position at Leesburg. Undoubtedly he was correct, since at its best the line ran at a right angle to his front and at its worst bowed out toward the enemy. Second, he was willing to act on newspaper reports that Winchester had been abandoned by the Federals. And, third, this confirms he had ordered his supply line to be shifted to the Shenandoah Valley before he left Virginia.

"Notwithstanding the abandonment of the line above mentioned," Lee continued, "I deem it important that as soon as the bridge over the Rapidan shall be completed, that over the Rappahannock should be constructed as soon as possible, and I have requested the president of the road to have timber prepared for that purpose." Apparently, he feared that Richmond would route his supplies through Lynchburg or Charlottesville and fail to complete the repairs to the bridges over the Rapidan and the Rappahannock.

"My reason for desiring that this bridge shall be repaired is, that in the event of falling back, it is my intention to take a position about Warrenton, where should the enemy attempt an advance on Richmond, I should be on his flank, or, should he attack me, I should have a favorable country to operate in, and the bridges being repaired, should be in full communication with Richmond." This is a curious and interesting revelation. It proves Lee had thought through his plans to the extent of deciding what he would do if repulsed from Maryland. It also reconfirms that Lee understood the best position from which to defend Richmond against a potential overland attack was not on a direct line south (which would have placed him at Fredericksburg) but from a point farther west, which would put him on the flank of a column advancing from Washington. Lee is here concurring in a military truth that was axiomatic with McClellan but seemed unimaginable to Northern politicians. It is no small irony that Lee's forethought about lines of retreat might have called down upon his head the wrath of the Joint Committee on the Conduct of the War had he worn blue.

"I have had all the arms taken in the late battles collected as far as possible, and am informed that about ten thousand are now at Gainesville. All empty trains returning to Rapidan are ordered to take in arms at Gainesville to transport to Rapidan. They should be sent at once to Richmond to be put in order, as arms may be needed in Maryland." Lee not only reflects his concern that much needed ordnance not be lost to the Confederacy, he also again implies his expectation of remaining in Maryland for a period of some duration—at least long enough for muskets to be sorted out, repaired, and shipped back to him. He may have foreseen their use in arming Maryland recruits. In referring to "trains" here, Lee means wagons.

"I desire that Col Gorgas will send some one to take charge of these arms at once, as the cavalry regiment now on duty in the vicinity of Gainesville will have to be withdrawn. We shall supply ourselves with provisions and forage in the country in which we operate, but ammunition must be sent from Richmond. I hope that the Secretary of War will see that the Ordnance Department provides ample supplies of all kinds. In forwarding the ammunition it can be sent in the way above described for the other trains, or it can be sent to Staunton, and thence by the Valley road to Winchester, which will be my depot." Once again Lee states his confidence in obtaining food and forage in Maryland, but he repeats his recurring fear of running out of ammunition. This latter also emphasizes his intention of fighting in Maryland.

"It is not yet certain that the enemy have evacuated the Valley, but there are reports to that effect, and I have no doubt that they will leave that section as soon as they learn of the movement across the Potomac. Any officer however proceeding towards Winchester with a train will of course not move without first ascertaining that the way is clear." It is interesting that Lee was certain enough the Federals in the Valley would scamper to safety to base his own moves upon it, but he hedged his bets when it came to the movements of others. He may have believed that, if he were wrong, he could correct his error by driving the enemy away, but he did not want to take the chance of losing precious ordnance supplies.

In closing, Lee reverted to a proposal he had urged almost two weeks earlier. "I am now more desirous that my suggestion as to General Loring's movements shall be carried into effect as soon as possible so that with the least delay he move to the lower end of the valley about Martinsburg, and guard the approach in that direction." On August 25, after launching Jackson's column toward Thoroughfare Gap, Lee had proposed to Secretary Randolph that Loring be ordered to clear the Kanawha Valley and then march to the Shenandoah to join with the Army of Northern Virginia. In the interim, events had pulled Lee eastward to Manassas and were currently propelling him north across the Potomac. But he had not forgotten Loring, and he now wished to incorporate the five thousand men from the Department of Southwestern Virginia into his Maryland strategy. Presumably, a Confederate force at Martinsburg would guard against interference from the Federal forces which Lee anticipated would concentrate at Cumberland after fleeing from Winchester and Harpers Ferry.

"He should drive the enemy from the Kanawha Valley, if he can, and afterwards, or if he finds he cannot accomplish that result, I wish him to move by way of Romney towards Martinsburg and take position in that vicinity." Here Lee simply restates—albeit in very confusing syntax—his proposal for Loring. Lee's idea had never been a practical one, a fact instantly grasped by Loring. In spite of his own experiences in western Virginia less than a year earlier, Lee expected Loring to travel two hundred miles northwest to Charleston and then to march an even greater distance northeast to Martinsburg—and nearly every step of the route was either up or down rugged mountainous terrain. Even if Loring had been ordered to proceed directly from his base at the Narrows west of Blacksburg northeastward to Martinsburg, and even if a perfectly straight road had been available, he would have faced a journey of 225 miles. Either Lee quixotically ignored the itinerary of his proposal or projected his own stay in Maryland would last until mid-October or beyond.

In any case, Loring was well along in maturing his own, more modest plans to recapture the Kanawha Valley. On August 22, he had launched his cavalry under Albert Jenkins on a raid to the northwest to clear the way. Traveling fast and bypassing Charleston, Jenkins had covered three hundred miles in two weeks. And on September 4—just twenty-four hours before Lee wrote this dispatch and at about the time D. H. Hill crossed the Potomac—Jenkins crossed the Ohio River near Ravenswood. On September 6—less than twenty-four hours later—Loring would set out himself to undertake the capture of Charleston. If the small army in western Virginia would not play the role assigned them by Lee, it would at least contribute to the atmosphere of confusion and panic that gripped the North in September of 1862.[58]

As Lee retired for the night on September 5, he could be well satisfied. About 40 percent of the Army of Northern Virginia was in Maryland.

Another 50 percent was poised and ready within a mile of the Potomac, and even John Walker's division had arrived within seven miles of Leesburg during the evening.[59] Thus, the remainder of the army was in hand and could cross in short order. The Confederate commander believed the problem of his line of communications had been solved. And, he must have been especially pleased to discover the enemy had proven powerless to interfere with the beginning of his turning movement—just as he had anticipated.

What Lee did not know, of course, was precisely what the Federals were doing in response to his movements. Had he known he would have been for the most part pleased. Pleasonton spent his first full day on the Maryland front attempting to gain information on the Confederate crossing. Operating in country largely unknown to himself and his subordinates and with only about a thousand horsemen, the Federal cavalry chief pushed forward too cautiously to gain any useful information. The disappearance of the squadron from the 1st Massachusetts at Poolesville late in the day made him even more careful. News coming in from elsewhere was confusing and contradictory. The Confederates were either advancing on Frederick, or they remained near the river destroying the canal and the aqueduct. They either numbered up to 40,000 men of all arms, or they were a small force composed only of cavalry.

Amidst the swirl of conflicting reports, the Federal high command drifted haphazardly as the crisis deepened. Halleck perceived the danger to Harpers Ferry, but his first response was to pass on the responsibility of whether its garrison should be withdrawn to John Wool, commanding the Middle Department and headquartered in Baltimore. One level of confusion was removed when John Pope was relieved of command of the defunct Army of Virginia and ordered to report to the secretary of war. But, even at the moment of the gravest military danger yet faced by the Union, politics threatened to emasculate the leadership of the army. President Abraham Lincoln directed that Fitz John Porter, William Franklin, and Charles Griffin—the first two commanding corps, and all three veteran and capable officers—be relieved to face charges stemming from Pope's preliminary report on Second Manassas. At the same time, no one would take the responsibility for naming a commander to lead a field army against the Confederates, although Halleck seemed to hint that Edwin Sumner might be Lee's opponent.

There were, nonetheless, developments on the Federal side which ought to have given Lee concern had he known about them. Even now, two separate strands were being woven that would eventually intertwine to catch the Confederates in a strategic web. Contrary to common sense, elements were at work determining that the garrisons in the Shenandoah Valley would not be withdrawn to safety. When Julius White evacuated Winchester, he had not fallen back north of the Potomac but only twenty-five miles to Harpers Ferry. More ominously, John Wool, given the responsibility, decided he did not want a cowardly retreat attributable to him. He ordered Dixon Miles to hold Harpers Ferry to the last extremity and to shoot dissenters. Hence, it began to look as if Lee would have to deal with an enemy blockage of his intended supply line.

At the same time, solid progress was underway to reorganize the Army of the Potomac. George McClellan assumed he had whatever authority he required and set about the task for which he was well suited. Although his command was strictly limited to the defenses of Washington, he was preparing a force to take the field. With the Ninth Corps (Burnside) on the Seventh Street Road to the north; the Second (Sumner) and Twelfth (Banks) in the center at Rockville; and Couch's division (Fourth Corps) on the left at Offutt's Crossroads, he too had about 40 percent of his army north the Potomac. Of course, the mere fact the Federals were preparing pursuit would not have dismayed Lee. It was exactly what he wanted, and the sooner the better. The disquieting news for Lee—had it been available—was the rapidly reviving morale in the Federal ranks.[60]

Frederick Occupied, September 6

On Saturday, September 6, Confederate reveille rent the silence of the vermilion dawn as it broke across the Monocacy River valley. One week ago, Jackson's old division had defended the railroad cut against the furious assaults of Porter's corps on the third and decisive day of Second Manassas. Now—seven days later and seventy zigzagging miles northward—Stonewall's division fell into column to lead the army forward to the occupation of Frederick, the second largest city in Maryland. In the van was the second brigade led by Bradley Johnson, the Frederick native, and stretching behind were the veterans of Ewell under Lawton and A. P. Hill under Branch, while D. H. Hill brought up the rear with his four brigades recently arrived from Richmond. The morning augured another clear but hot and dusty day, and indeed, the temperature would reach eighty degrees by the afternoon.[61]

Mishap marred the march before it started. When Jackson was ready to mount, he called for the big gray mare an admiring Marylander had given him the previous day. Unused to Stonewall's way—at least his way with the spur—the "strong-sinewed, powerful" horse reared on her hind legs and fell over backward. Jackson lay on the ground "stunned and severely bruised" for over thirty minutes before his staff felt it safe to carry him to an ambulance. D. H. Hill, the only other major general north of the river, was summoned from the rear of the column to take temporary command. Jackson traveled by wagon during the day's short march, but he kept control through his staff to make certain his plans were carried out, and by evening he was not only able to resume command but mount a horse.[62]

With little, if any, delay caused by the change in commanders, the column quickly covered the four miles from Buckeystown to Monocacy Junction, where the Frederick spur line joined the main B&O line just west of the river. Here, Jackson's division turned left onto the Frederick-Urbana road and proceeded toward Frederick. The next two divisions filed to the right to cover the Junction and the railroad bridge, Lawton taking position to the north to guard the approaches from Baltimore and Branch to the south to protect those from Washington. Jackson himself remained for some time near the Junction, supervising details of defense to ensure against surprise from any Federal force from the east.[63]

Frederick awaited its conquerors with dread and trepidation. The 14th New Jersey Infantry, not two weeks in the service but the only sizable force in the area, had retreated from Monocacy Junction toward Baltimore the day before. The town's small garrison, a company of the Maryland Potomac Home Brigade under the aptly named Capt. William Faithful, had labored most of the night to fill railroad cars and wagons with stores, records, and movable convalescents from the hospital and ship them safely to Baltimore or Gettysburg. Before dawn the infantry departed for Harpers Ferry, leaving only a handful of cavalry in the western outskirts to report the advance of the enemy. Defenseless and vulnerable, the predominantly Unionist citizenry anticipated its sons would be impressed into the Confederate army, its old men sent to Southern prisons, and its wealth pillaged in retribution by a vengeful foe. Some fled, while many hid their valuables, shuttered their windows, and bolted their doors, but a surprising number milled about the streets with irrepressible curiosity and passed along the latest rumors of the Confederate approach.[64]

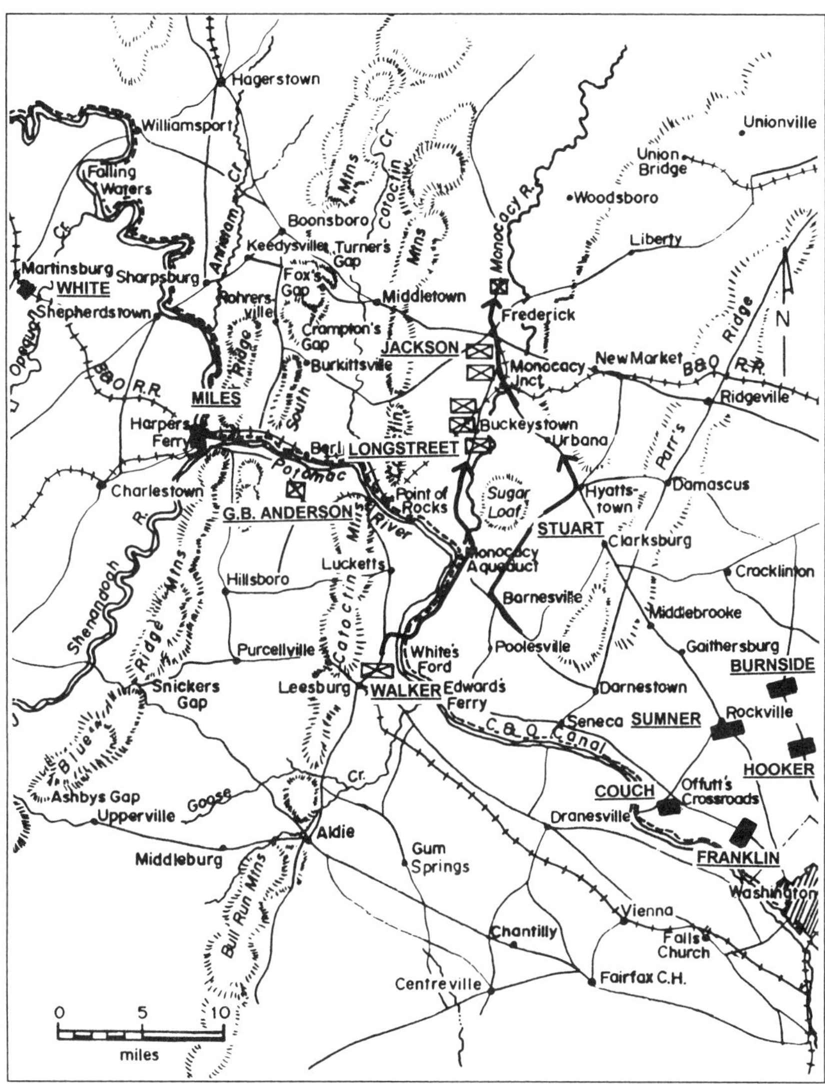

Confederate march, September 6

The suspense was mercifully brief. At nine o'clock two "seedy-looking" horsemen dressed in "dirty, faded gray" galloped up Market Street from the direction of Urbana, pausing at the intersections to huzzah for Jeff. Davis. Greeted with indifference, the two retraced their route at a trot. They were soon followed by a cavalcade of fifty or so that included Bradley Johnson, D.H. Hill, and the scouts of Lige White. Johnson harangued the crowd that "the time of your deliverance has come" and met with scattered cheers from the boldest of the Southern sympathizers. The cavalry cantered on to seize the military hospital set up on the fairgrounds that still held seven hundred patients who had been too critically ill to remove. Hill rode over to the telegraph office and cut the wires, a needless precaution since the retreating Federals had taken the instruments with them.[65]

An hour later, the 21st, 42d, and 48th Virginia and the 1st Virginia Battalion, the brigade temporarily commanded by Johnson, came swinging through the town. To all but the staunchest pro-Confederate citizens, the soldiers appeared the motliest group ever assembled. Their "multiforms" were filthy; their faces "had not been acquainted with water for weeks"; and their hair was "shaggy and unkempt." Adding to the bizarre scene, many of the men carried under their arms watermelons they had just appropriated from the depot of the B&O Railroad. Even their bands, playing "Maryland" and "Dixie" in "execrable style," failed to impress favorably. The Virginians "strolled" through the town—"marching it could not be called without doing violence to the word"—and went into camp on the fairgrounds in the northern suburbs.[66]

Johnson's men had been designated provost guard and were the only troops officially authorized to remain in Frederick. The other three brigades of Jackson's division passed through the town and bivouacked two miles north on the Emmittsburg Road. Later in the day, D. H. Hill's four brigades stopped short of Frederick and set up camp two miles south on the Best farm. Thus, all of the town's key points were covered, except for its western approaches. Jackson was determined to prevent pillaging and other incidents that might sour relations with Marylanders. Guards were established around all of the camps, including Johnson's at the fairgrounds, to prevent the men from visiting the town, and officers conscientiously attempted to enforce the ban. The request of a lieutenant in Pender's brigade to find some milk for one of his ill soldiers was turned down with the note: "Let the sick man eat a little beef." On the following day, Stonewall would even write a pass for himself and his staff before attending church services.[67]

Still, if the veterans who wrote memoirs represent a fair sampling, a large number of officers and soldiers evaded the security net with or without passes to forage in the town and the surrounding countryside. The precautions perhaps worked best to convey the need for exemplary behavior, and, although the businesses of the town of eight thousand soon were crowded, the unpleasant incidents were remarkably few in number. There was some drunkenness, an occasional impolite repartee, a few articles disappeared unpaid for, and late in the day an attempt was made to destroy the local Unionist newspaper, which was quickly protected by the provost guard. The seven hundred Federal patients were promptly paroled, and the hospital and its supplies otherwise unmolested. The civility of the occupying force was returned in kind by the residents. Many merchants accepted Confederate scrip, although none were coerced, and a large number of Unionist families—without changing their political views one whit—responded in human and religious terms to the need for food and clothing.[68]

While the vanguard of the Army of Northern Virginia established its hold on central Maryland, the main body moved to close the gap by following the route taken by Jackson the previous day. Longstreet's wing, now organized into three divisions, crossed at White's Ford early in the morning. His command had been slightly rearranged by the consolidation of the three brigades of D. R. Jones with the three of Kemper into a single division under Jones. The merger ran contrary to Longstreet's preference for divisions composed of three brigades, but it probably resulted from the worn condition of the regiments and the desire to keep divisions to the same approximate fighting size. At this time, Longstreet's command also incorporated the divisions of Cadmus Wilcox and Nathan Evans, the latter general still in charge of his own and Hood's two brigades.[69]

The second day of the crossing was no less merry than the first had been. With flags waving and bands blaring the Maryland anthem, the soldiers shouted and joked in their excitement.[70] Once again many stripped off their pants and drawers and assaulted the Old Line State in "nature's uniforms."[71] Ignorant that they were in Maryland as soon as setting foot in the Potomac, some who had potables celebrated upon reaching the far shore with a "big drink."[72]

Fording later in the day, and in uncertain order, were the divisions of R. H. Anderson and LaFayette McLaws, neither of which had yet been included into the wing structure of the army. Thus, nineteen brigades of infantry with their attendant batteries of artillery, along with the ordnance and subsistence trains of the army, comprised the massive marching column of the 6th.[73] Hooves and wheels and boots further pulverized the dirt roads leading to the campground at Three Springs near Buckeystown that Jackson had vacated in the morning. At places the dust was so thick it obscured a man at fifty feet. Following along behind the army, a staff officer found a soldier who had crawled into a fence corner, unable to speak and barely breathing, his mouth and nose clogged with dust.[74]

Lee himself set out from Leesburg in his ambulance early in the morning, anticipating that his entire army would cross into Maryland by nightfall. Although he apparently would not learn of it until later in the day, the inertial drag of a large army still imperfectly organized prevented some units from meeting the expectations of his fast-paced strategy. Pendleton had not been able to complete the refitting of the Artillery Reserve in time, and he would not cross until the following day. John Walker, who had just reached the vicinity the previous evening, would believe his division too fatigued for an extended march. He would pass through Leesburg and occupy the vacated camps at Big Spring.[75]

Along with Pendleton and Walker, the cavalry brigade that Thomas Munford had just taken over from Beverly Robertson remained south of the Potomac, under orders to act as rear guard. By sunset, Munford decided he was intended to guard the rear of the main body and attempted to cross the river, but the ford was so choked with trains and artillery that he did not get his own wagons and guns over until after midnight.[76] Still in Virginia was the "lost" brigade under George B. Anderson that D. H. Hill had sent up the Potomac to fire on B&O trains at Berlin and seems to have forgotten.[77]

Curiously, no eyewitness accounts testify to Lee's crossing of the Potomac. Considering the excellent time he would make and that he would likely want to avoid the suffocating dust of the army in motion, his ambulance must have forded the river early in the morning.[78] Shortly after entering Maryland and probably just before passing the Monocacy several miles west of Barnesville, Lee dictated a dispatch to be sent by telegraph to Jefferson Davis: "TWO DIVISIONS OF THE ARMY HAVE CROSSED THE POTOMAC. I HOPE ALL WILL CROSS TO DAY. NAVIGATION OF THE CANAL HAS BEEN INTERRUPTED AND EFFORTS WILL BE MADE TO BREAK UP THE USE OF THE BALTIMORE AND OHIO RAILROAD." The brief message served to notify Davis that the expedition was well under way, and it was the only communication Lee would send to Richmond during his busy day. His reference to "two divisions" must have meant either that two of Longstreet's divisions had crossed that morning; or else, using division loosely to denote command, he meant that Jackson and Longstreet were across and several independent commands remained.[79]

Lee was correct in claiming interruption of C&O traffic. Along a twenty-five-mile distance, the embankment had been cut to let in the waters of the Potomac. Floodgates had been destroyed and huge boulders rolled into the canal. Only the aqueduct over the Monocacy had proven impervious to Confederate tools. Still, it would probably have been frustrating for the Confederates to know that in less than two months and at a cost of only $50,000 (in repairs and lost business) the waterway would be back approximately to normal.[80]

At some point after the passage of the Potomac, Longstreet fell in beside Lee's wagon, and the two struck up conversation. While talking, they detected the sound of artillery fire from the direction of Harpers Ferry some fifteen miles to the west. The enemy had obviously not yet scurried from the Shenandoah Valley, and the news concerned Lee. He speculated that the Federals might not pursue the wise course of fleeing to safety upon hearing the Confederates had cut them off from Washington. They might instead concentrate their scattered garrisons for the defense of Harpers Ferry. He proposed that Longstreet lead an expedition to clear the Valley and perhaps capture the foolhardy foe. Longstreet opposed the movement on the grounds that the Confederate army should not be divided while on enemy soil. He argued that the Federals would soon learn of the expedition and move against the fragmented army before the expedition could succeed. He concluded it was "a venture not worth the game."[81]

Apparently, not even with the hindsight available in writing his memoirs, did Longstreet grasp the importance of the Shenandoah Valley in Lee's strategy. The Confederate commander had already cut loose from his communications through Warrenton and named Winchester as his depot. With a large Federal force remaining at Harpers Ferry, the Army of Northern Virginia would have no reliable supply line while operating in a territory where the acquisition of supplies was at best uncertain and, in the case of munitions, improbable. Lee did not press the point with Longstreet, and the latter assumed it was because his arguments had won over his chief. Instead, Lee was willing to give the Federals more time to react to threat of the Confederates crossing the Potomac. He would not waiver, however, in his conviction that both his ability to stay in Maryland for an extended season and to wage battle while there would depend upon safe communications through the Valley.

Lee and Longstreet did not halt with the troops at Three Springs but continued on by way of Monocacy Junction to Best's Grove about two miles from Frederick, where Jackson and D. H. Hill had already established their headquarters. It became a rare occasion when, later in the afternoon, Jeb Stuart arrived, and the five leading generals of the Army of Northern Virginia pitched their tents in the same woods. Word soon spread, and the curious flocked to see the famous men. Lee kept mostly to his tent and continued to work.[82]

He issued General Orders to the army on two subjects that seemed unrelated but which together addressed the discipline and morale of the troops. Two days earlier he had appointed Brig. Gen. Lewis Armistead to command a provost guard to follow after the army and arrest stragglers. Now that Lee expected the army to remain stationary for some days, he changed the nature of Armistead's responsibility by naming him provost marshal and assigning him the task of maintaining "good order and military discipline" in the camps and preventing "depredations upon the community" of Frederick. Armistead occupied the provost marshal headquarters previously used by the Federals in the town and entered on his duties at once.[83]

Lee used the second and larger article of the General Orders to announce to the army the "signal success" of Kirby Smith at the battle of Richmond, Kentucky, on August 30, in "capturing General Nelson and his staff, 3,000 prisoners, and all his artillery, small-arms, wagons, &c." The news of victory—seldom heard from the West—was especially cheering, but word of this victory on the soil of Kentucky was electrifying. The rank and file now became aware that a parallel offensive was underway by another Confederate army. And Lee tried to make the most of the stirring moment. "Let the armies of the East and the West vie with one another in discipline, bravery, and activity," he urged, and independence will soon "be established on a sure and abiding basis."

It does not seem likely Lee yet knew that Kirby Smith was but one of five columns intending the northward offensive and aiming to unite on the Ohio River. Braxton Bragg had not left Chattanooga with the Army of Mississippi until August 28, and he would not cross into Kentucky until September 10. Humphrey Marshall was setting out from Abingdon in southwestern Virginia on this very day, September 6. Earl Van Dorn and Sterling Price were still in Mississippi and not near a departure for west Tennessee. Hence, Lee could not have read of any of their missions in Northern newspapers.

It is reasonable to assume Lee first learned of Kirby Smith's Kentucky victory from a brief report that appeared in the *Baltimore Sun* of September 4, a paper he mentioned having read in his dispatch to Davis of the same date. Since that article gave no figure for Federal losses and clearly stated that Gen. William Nelson, although wounded, escaped, it is evident, however, Lee must have also had additional news of the battle. Once in Frederick he may have had access to other Northern newspapers, or he may have received official word from Richmond among the recaptured documents presented to him by Stuart that afternoon. The latter is perhaps more likely, since Northern newspapers ought not to have included the erroneous information on Nelson's capture.[84]

In any case, by September 6 (if not slightly before), Lee became generally aware that his advance into Maryland coincided with a similar—although possibly more modest—northward thrust in the West. Apparently, the Eastern and Western offensives were coincidental and not coordinated. Clearly Lee decided to enter Maryland based on the circumstances of his own situation and not as part of concerted, large-scale plan. Still, once aware that a bigger game was under way, he likely came to attach even more importance to his own campaign. He was no longer acting alone. Now the Federals were being frustrated and embarrassed in the West as well. The chances for winning the war in the autumn of 1862 must have suddenly seemed even brighter.

Lee also held two conferences during the afternoon of the 6th. He called Jackson to his tent and presumably requested a report on the occupation of Frederick and the state of affairs in Maryland. It is interesting to speculate that Lee may have raised the issue of Harpers Ferry with Stonewall, whom he knew would be a more receptive audience than Longstreet had been. If the security of communications through the Shenandoah Valley were discussed, however, the decision to act was postponed.[85] Lee held a separate meeting with Stuart to discuss matters of more pressing immediacy.

Stuart had departed Poolesville early that morning with the brigades of Hampton and Fitz Lee and quickly covered the twelve miles to Urbana. During the ride, Jeb noticed a Federal signal station on Sugar Loaf Mountain busily sending messages in the direction of Washington. He sent a detachment to capture the wigwaggers and end their spying on Confederate movements. The expedition yielded unexpectedly valuable results. Aware of their danger, the Federals had closed the station and hurried down the mountain. At its foot, they captured a courier from Richmond bearing dispatches from Jefferson Davis to Lee. While in the act of searching the messenger, the signalmen were in turn taken prisoner by the Confederate cavalry. Stuart established bivouac for his horsemen at Urbana and then set out with the rescued dispatches to find Jackson's headquarters. Five miles down the road at Best's Grove he discovered that Lee had arrived from Leesburg.[86]

When Stuart reported to his commander's tent, he learned that Lee had a carefully thought-out program of operations for the cavalry for the second phase of the campaign. Stuart was to divide his brigades and threaten both Baltimore and Washington, "giving out on each flank that he (Lee) was behind with his whole force." Lee clearly intended to confuse the enemy by making him think the Confederates were at two places simultaneously. Yet, just as certainly, his purpose was not to buy time with this plan. On the contrary, he was putting pressure on the Federals to leave their fortifications and come out to fight before they had fully recovered from Second Manassas. Had Lee simply wanted to rest at Frederick for awhile, he would not have poked the enemy in the ribs with a sharp stick.

For the second part of his assignment, Stuart was to keep careful watch for a Federal movement from Washington and to report the slightest sign of an advance. It was probably also in this meeting that Lee told Stuart of a secret service fund of several hundred dollars in greenbacks that he could draw upon through Col. Porter Alexander. The money would be useful to buy news about the Federals and to sell false information about the Confederates. After receiving his orders, Stuart decided not to pitch his tent permanently at Best's Grove but rode back to Urbana to establish his headquarters nearer his troopers. Apparently, he postponed setting about his new task until the morrow.[87]

Thus, as night fell on September 6, Lee had virtually completed the first phase of his turning movement. He had passed the Potomac without opposition, and 90 percent of his army now rested in the vicinity of Frederick. The response by Marylanders had been near to what Bradley Johnson had predicted, but food and forage had so far been adequate. Except for the small cloud on the horizon at Harpers Ferry, Lee could be well pleased as he retired for the night.

What Lee did not know was that the Federals were already being deluged with contradictory reports and wild rumors even before his planned deception went into effect. Telegrams were coming in from all directions, and Lee was observed to be marching on Harpers Ferry, Frederick, and Baltimore all at once. The only reasonable note in the day's news were the numbers that were being reported as between 30,000 and 60,000. The Federal cavalry was in contact with the enemy along Seneca Creek, and their chief discounted the rumors about Baltimore. Alfred Pleasonton believed Lee was moving on Washington and the Confederate attack would center on Rockville.

McClellan acted upon the best information available to him. He held both the Second (Sumner) and Twelfth (Banks) Corps at Rockville to anchor the center of his line. He pushed the Ninth (Burnside) Corps forward to Leesborough to cover his right flank from the north, while Couch's division (Fourth Corps) maintained its position at Offutt's Crossroads to cover the left flank near the Potomac. He ordered two additional corps to cross the river. The First Corps (McDowell) was on the march to join Burnside, and the Sixth (Franklin) was moving to Tennallytown to act as general reserve. By nightfall he had 60 percent of his army stretched in an arc ten miles, on average, north and west of Washington. No one had yet been designated to command a Federal army beyond the defenses of Washington.[88]

In the military chess game under way, Lee was at least two full moves ahead of his opponents.

CHAPTER THREE

"In this I was disappointed"

Lee Revises His Strategy, September 7–9, 1862

IRONICALLY, BEING two moves ahead was not an advantage in Lee's present strategy. It would have been otherwise had he intended to capture Baltimore or to seize any specific geographic target. In that case, he would have wanted to move as quickly as possible to preempt Federal countermeasures. Likewise, if it had been his plan to penetrate deeply into Pennsylvania, he would have wanted to cover as much ground as possible, as quickly as possible, before meeting opposition. Lee intended neither, however. He wanted simply to compel the Federal army to leave its strong position while still groggy from defeat and fight him on ground of his choosing in western Maryland. Hence, Lee's own strategy forced the Confederates into a period of waiting. He must now bide his time until the enemy came out to find him.

Idleness in an army carries with it inherent risk. In waiting, Lee took the chance of losing the initiative through mishap, inadvertence, or an unforeseen move by the foe. Still, this was inaction to a purpose, and not the corrosive inertia he had warned against in his dispatch to Davis only four days earlier. Lee believed he would remain master of the situation so long as he continued to exert pressure on Washington. The Federals would be limited in the movements they could make while their capital was in check—just as he had been on June 1 with the Army of the Potomac poised on the Chickahominy. He had been compelled to remove the direct threat to Richmond before he could consider any other move, and the enemy was now likewise constrained.

On the other hand, might not the enemy do to him what he had done to them under similar circumstances? Might not the Federals attempt to break his long supply line? Lee's specific answer to this important question of strategy is unknown. But, enough is known about his thinking to suggest he assumed there were two major differences between his position on September 7 and McClellan's on June 26. First, Lee was not nearly so vulnerable. While resting at Frederick, the Confederates were able to draw provisions from the country around them and needed to worry only about wagoning munitions from a distance. Also, a supply line established through the Shenandoah Valley would run to the southwest and obliquely away from Washington. To get at Confederate communications, a Federal column would be separated from the army covering the capital by a minimum of fifty miles and by the Potomac River. Second, Lee probably did not think the enemy would undertake an elaborate or complicated response. With a demoralized and disorganized army—and a panicky government to boot—the Federal commander was likely to make a straightforward attempt to drive the Confederates from Maryland.

So, Lee settled down to wait. Events of the next three days would disappoint him. To his dismay, he would discover it was possible to be right in all of his major assumptions about the Federal army around Washington, and yet have his campaign threatened from a different direction. Inexplicably, the garrisons at Martinsburg and Harpers Ferry would not flee to safety but remained in place squarely athwart his line to Winchester and the Valley. Lee made the mistake of supposing his foe knew the rules of warfare and would obey them. Considering Henry Halleck had written a book on those rules, it was not an unreasonable assumption to make.

Restful Sabbath, September 7

Sunday, September 7, would be another clear, dry day, the warmest of the campaign, with the temperature climbing to the low eighties. Longstreet's command and the divisions of Anderson and McLaws quickly covered the four miles from Buckeystown and went into permanent camp at Monocacy Junction.[1] Fortunately, since no other marching was required of the main body, the heavy clouds of dust slowly drifted back to earth to reveal the beauty of the lush countryside. A few of Jackson's men labored to tear up the tracks of the B&O, while the engineers puzzled over the best method to destroy the iron railroad bridge over the Monocacy.[2] Most of the soldiers of the Army of Northern Virginia, however, spent the day resting in the shade, swimming and washing clothes in the muddy waters of the river, and cadging passes or evading the camp guard to visit Frederick.[3] There was also much speculation as to whether the army was bound for Baltimore, Washington, or Pennsylvania, and a rumor circulated that there was fighting in the streets of Baltimore in anticipation of its liberation by the Confederates.[4]

Lee himself passed a restful sabbath in his camp among a "beautiful grove of oaks" on the Best farm, two miles southeast of Frederick. He took the opportunity to dictate four letters to Richmond on a wide variety of subjects.[5] In the first of two dispatches to Davis, he continued his practice of making almost daily reports to the president on the progress of the campaign, even when there was little news to recount. Perhaps instinctively, he was trying to allay the understandable anxiety Davis could be expected to feel with the army at a great distance from the capital.

"I have the honor to inform you that all the divisions of the army have crossed the Potomac," he announced, "unless it may be Genl Walker's from whom I have had no report since his arrival at Leesburg on the evening of the 5th instant. They occupy the line of the Monocacy."[6] It is interesting to note Lee's description of his position on the 7th. He does not see himself as occupying Frederick, but, in terms more reflective of active military operations, he depicts his army as holding the "line of the Monocacy."

There also seems to be a mild rebuke of John Walker for not maintaining communications with general headquarters. Actually, on the previous day Walker had advanced his division of two large brigades to the camp at Big Spring. On the morning of the 7th, he marched six miles up the Potomac to avoid the congestion at White's Ford, and by midmorning he started to cross at Cheek's Ford at the mouth of the Monocacy. Here Walker discovered George B. Anderson's errant brigade of D. H. Hill's division just returning from its mission to fire on B&O trains. The three brigades marched only six miles into Maryland and bivouacked short of Buckeystown.[7] Although Lee does not mention it, a substantial portion of the army's artillery also forded the Potomac on the 7th. Having at last completed his assigned reorganization, William Pendleton crossed at White's Ford with the Reserve Artillery. He was apparently joined by the battalions of J. B. Walton and S. D. Lee attached to Longstreet's command. Pendleton did not break his march at Buckeystown but proceeded on to the vicinity of Frederick, although he too did not report until the next morning.[8]

Lee then turned to the subject that would occupy most of his dispatch to Davis, the relations between his army and Marylanders. He started with the good news. "I find there is plenty of provisions and forage in this country, and the community have received us with kindness." Lee accurately reflected the situation as it existed during the first several days of the army's encampment. In spite of the good discipline that undeniably prevailed, most of the Confederate soldiers fared very well during their stay in the Frederick area. While not all were able to drink champagne as were members of the Washington Louisiana Artillery, there was cider for the rest, as well as eggs, chickens, and butter.[9] A surprising number also found a way to get into town to purchase articles of clothing, shoes, books, and sundry other items. Some even bought ladies' apparel and shoes to send home to families and sweethearts. Because there was no such thing as a rate of exchange between currencies, the soldiers found themselves in the prosperous position to spend inflated Confederate dollars for goods at prices they had not seen since the war started.[10]

Unfortunately for Lee, the army did not carry with it much money in the form of gold or Federal greenbacks, and he anticipated Marylanders might make a distinction between accepting Confederate scrip from soldiers for their private needs, as opposed to selling large quantities of supplies to an agency of the Southern government. "There may be some embarrassment in paying for necessaries for the army, as it is probable that many individuals will hesitate to receive Confederate currency. I shall in all cases endeavor to purchase what is wanted, and if unable to pay upon the spot, will give certificates of indebtedness of the Confederate States, for future adjustment." This was Lee's way of avoiding the confiscation of supplies, a practice that would have surely alienated Marylanders and further weakened the Southern cause in the state.

"It is very desirable that the Chief Quartermaster and Commissary should be provided with funds," he went on, presumably meaning greenbacks, "and that some general arrangement should be made for liquidating the debts that be incurred to the satisfaction of the people of Maryland, in order that they may willingly furnish us with what is wanted. I shall endeavor to purchase horses, clothing, shoes, and medical stores for our present use, and you will see the facility that would arise from being provided with the means of paying for them." Clearly, once again, Lee was thinking in terms of his stay in Maryland stretching into weeks, and he underscored the point when he continued, "I hope it may be convenient for ex-Governor Lowe or some prominent citizen of Maryland to join me, with a view of expediting these and other arrangements necessary to the success of our army in this state."

Still, in order that the president not be led into false hopes, Lee repeated the lowered expectations for Maryland's response, which he had held at least since his conference with Bradley Johnson. "Notwithstanding individual expressions of kindness that have been given, and the general sympathy in the success of the Confederate States, situated as Maryland is, I do not anticipate any general rising of the people in our behalf. Some additions to our ranks will no doubt be received, and I hope to procure subsistence for our troops." It would be interesting to know whether Lee had already determined to issue a proclamation to the citizens of the state when he dictated these lines. It would not seem likely he expected rhetoric alone would impel Marylanders to revolt.

In closing his dispatch, Lee passed on to Davis his knowledge of what the Federal army was doing in response to his expedition. "As yet we have had no encounter with the enemy on this side of the river, except a detachment of cavalry at Poolesville, which resulted in slight loss on both sides, thirty-one of the enemy being captured." This was two-day-old news, although Lee maybe did not learn of the skirmish until the previous afternoon's meeting with Stuart. While Lee might have wanted to commit much to paper—the fate of the recent Richmond dispatches certainly emphasized the vagaries of his long-range communication—still, his description of the enemy's movements seemed not only brief, but his perception to be both superficial and flawed.[11] "As far as I can learn, the enemy are in their entrenchments around Washington. General Banks with his division, has advanced to Darnestown."

There are a number of confusions and contradictions in Lee's summary of the activities of the enemy. In the first place, he conveys the chief impression that the Federals are awaiting an attack within their fortifications. Yet, his observation that a division has advanced to Darnestown—which was twelve miles beyond the line of forts—seems to controvert the fact. Possibly, Lee may have viewed the move as nothing more than a reconnaissance in force. Second, whatever the explanation, the information was wrong, since it placed Federal infantry almost twice as far from the forts as they had actually advanced. Third, Lee's assignment of a division to Nathaniel Banks, who commanded the Second Corps in Pope's army, reveals an imperfect understanding of the organization of the Union forces. And, finally, Lee fails to mention that Federal cavalry reoccupied Poolesville during the afternoon.[12]

All of which suggests that Stuart's performance in the Maryland campaign has perhaps been somewhat overrated. It was his first and most important responsibility to provide Lee with accurate and timely information on the movements of the enemy—a task that depended solely on Stuart's own diligence and persistence. The operations of the 7th were the first indication that Lee might not get the quality of information he would need to make his turning movement successful. Stuart's second major responsibility was to screen the Confederate army and its intentions from the eyes of the enemy. This role he seems to have executed with greater success, although that success may have resulted nearly as much from the inadequate numbers and cautious scouting by the opposing cavalry as from the activities of the Confederates.

As reflected in the reports and memoirs of the Southern cavalry, September 7 is depicted as a relatively quiet day—which may have been part of the problem. Heros von Borcke, Stuart's chief of staff, appears to have been largely occupied with the planning of a dance for the following evening. And, while the headquarters horses "stood saddled day and night" as witness to "constant vigilance," there is less evidence as to how much they were ridden. As one staff member recalled, "There was nothing to do but await the advance" of the enemy, and "General Stuart like a good soldier knew how to improve the passing hour in the enjoyment of the charming society the country round afforded."[13]

Following the instructions he had received from Lee the previous day, Stuart did extend his cavalry line on the 7th. He retained Hampton at Urbana and Hyattstown to anchor the center and cover the approaches from Washington. And he sent most of Fitzhugh Lee's brigade north to New Market on the National Pike, which connected Frederick with Baltimore. Since no Federal advance was expected from that direction, Lee's role presumably was to convey the impression of a Confederate threat to Baltimore.

Stuart must have been less concerned with his right flank, which stretched south to the Potomac. He entrusted its safety to a single regiment, the 5th Virginia of Fitz Lee's brigade, which had probably been left behind the day before when the main column moved on to Urbana. It was this weak spot that the Federals found, when the 8th Illinois Cavalry captured Poolesville during the afternoon. There is no indication this threat from the south caused Stuart any particular worry. At sunset, Thomas Munford arrived at Urbana with his brigade, having traveled first to Frederick after crossing the Potomac. Stuart assumed this additional force would allow him to retake Poolesville on the following day.[14]

The dispatch to Davis revealed that Lee was operating under another false impression about the enemy. "The Shenandoah Valley has been evacuated," he told the president, "and their stores at Winchester, &c., are stated to have been destroyed." This is a curiously ambiguous sentence. Lee mentions specifically only Winchester and covers Martinsburg and Harpers Ferry, if at all, with his sweeping "and so forth." Yet, he must have believed the Federals had left or were leaving the other two towns—which are certainly in the Shenandoah Valley—or he could not have declared the Valley "evacuated." Some light is shed on Lee's thinking on this point in two additional letters he dictated on the 7th.

He sent a dispatch to the secretary of war devoted entirely to the subject of opening his line of communications through the Valley.[15] He told Randolph he had already designated Winchester as the new depot for the army, requested repair shops be opened there, and suggested that the convalescent Edward Johnson be named to command the post. Lee also summarized a report he had received from Col. John Funk, 5th Virginia Infantry, of the occupation of Winchester on the morning of September 3; and he enclosed a captured report from Federal general Julius White, who had commanded the garrison that fled the town.[16] Lee thus demonstrated he now had positive confirmation of the story he had first read in the *Baltimore Sun* of the 4th that the Federals had abandoned Winchester. More importantly, Lee went on to tell Randolph that White's troops had "retired in the direction of Harpers Ferry and Martinsburg, and, as I learn from rumor, have retreated to Pennsylvania." Lee must have assumed that White's not stopping to join the other garrisons proved the Federals did not intend to make a stand in the Valley. Unfortunately, the Confederate commander was in error. White had halted at Harpers Ferry and then returned to Martinsburg. He was still very much a threat to Lee's proposed new communications.

It is possible Lee's mistaken assumption about the Valley merely reflected his largely optimistic frame of mind on this September sabbath. The grand strategy he had implemented to give the desperate South a chance to win the war seemed to be working. He had stripped the Atlantic states of their defenders to concentrate Confederate forces and launch an unrelenting offensive. He believed the Federals would be compelled to abandon their widely scattered campaigns—which were gradually eating away the frontiers of the Confederacy—and be forced to concentrate their own columns in response to his initiatives. And now, everywhere, this seemed to be coming to pass. In another letter dictated on the 7th, Lee wrote to Gustavus Smith that he had seen official accounts of the complete evacuation of Fredericksburg."[17] And, then, elaborating on his comment to Randolph, he told Smith, General White, commanding at [Winchester], is stated to have retired into Pennsylvania. I think the enemy will concentrate about Washington."

Another indication of the generally optimistic outlook of the Confederate commander on the 7th was the apparent non sequitur with which he closed his dispatch to Davis. "By the enclosed unfinished note from an officer of the Federal Army, dated at Poolesville, you will perceive that the enemy are withdrawing troops from Hilton Head." Although the note has not been preserved, it was likely from a member of the 1st Massachusetts Cavalry—a regiment directly off the ship from South Carolina—and had been captured by Stuart in the skirmish on the 5th. Still, this was week-old news. Lee had known since fighting Stevens's division at Chantilly on the 1st (and had reported to Davis on the 3d) of the arrival in the Washington area of forces from David Hunter's Department of the South. Lee's mentioning the fact simply underscored his prevailing optimism.

One thing did concern Lee greatly as he rested with his army behind the Monocacy on the 7th, and he wrote a second letter to Davis devoted to it exclusively. The old problem of estrays continued unabated. Lee made it clear he was not referring to deserters, for ample authority existed to deal with those who left the ranks permanently; nor, to the "sick and feeble" who dropped from the ranks "from necessity." Stragglers were soldiers officially counted as present for duty, but who came and went from their units as they saw fit, without regard to orders or the movements and needs of the army. Lee was so vexed that he suggested stragglers be dropped from the rolls "if they cannot be improved by correction." He confessed that he believed he and his "higher officers" had "done all in their power to stop it." Out of frustration, he asked the president to change the laws if necessary to allow the appointment of a commission of high-level officers and inspectors general to travel with the army and "see to the execution of orders." In unusually strong language, Lee called stragglers the "cowards of the army," and told the president, "I assure you some remedy is necessary."[18]

Undoubtedly, Lee was at least partially correct in his assessment. In spite of the understandable reluctance of veterans to write much about such a sensitive topic, it is clear there were a relatively large number of men—even in the fabled Army of Northern Virginia—who fit the contemporary definition of coward. Swept off their feet by the enthusiasm of the moment to enlist with their neighbors, some soldiers discovered in their first battle they lacked the temperament to play a military version of Russian roulette. Others found they could not always be as brave as they sometimes could. Whenever the prospect of fighting became imminent, some men found a way—legitimate or otherwise—to be absent from the firing line. During the Maryland campaign, William Dorsey Pender, commanding a brigade in A. P. Hill's division, discovered he could not bring anything like his effective strength into battle. "Men find it safer," he wrote his wife, "to get behind [the] lines than to fight. We will have to shoot them before it stops." On one occasion, when a threatened battle did not develop, he lamented that over half of his brigade, including six out of ten officers in one regiment, "skulked out and did not come up until they thought all danger over."[19]

Still, it is not clear that most cases of straggling aptly fit even the broader definition of cowardice accepted in the nineteenth century. By modern standards Civil War armies failed to achieve an efficient level of discipline. Confederate armies were the worst, and the Army of Northern Virginia was no exception. The diaries and memoirs of Lee's veterans attest to the fact that a large number of men who considered themselves good soldiers—and whom historians have also considered good soldiers—frequently meandered from camp or the march to seek food or other necessities or simply break the boredom of routine. To cite but one example, on the morning of September 17, while awaiting the Federal attack on the Lower Bridge at Sharpsburg, four men from the 17th Virginia left the regiment for the rear in search of food. They did not return until four o'clock, after Burnside had carried the bridge and their regiment was in retreat. A veteran would later relate the incident solely because of the amusing vicissitudes undergone by the men in baking their biscuits, and not because anyone thought them stragglers, let alone cowards.[20]

In addition, even Lee recognized that extenuating circumstances existed in the late summer of 1862 that worsened the degree of straggling. He admitted that defective organization, the rushing of improperly trained units into the field, and his recent "forced marches and hard service" had contributed to the evil. It is not clear, however, that he fully appreciated the degree to which his policy of continually pressing forward to seize opportunities, while outstripping his supply branches, may have been the primary culprit. Since August 25, he had been willing to leave his wagons behind in a cloud of dust, as he pushed his army on to one victory after another. He had forced his men to live off the land, and in many cases to straggle for food or face starvation. Now, he had knowingly undertaken a campaign in which he intended to feed off the countryside; and, when commissaries were slow to purchase provisions, or bought substandard fare, such as fields of green corn, the soldiers knew how to rectify the oversight. Certainly, Lee was not wrong to try to wring the most from his successes, but he was wrong in thinking he could escape paying the overhead costs of his strategy.

As Robert E. Lee went to sleep for the second night under the northerly skies of western Maryland, there was much that he did not know about the enemy and some that he thought he knew—such as the assumed flight of Julius White to Pennsylvania—was not so. Still, most of the information that lay beyond his ken would not have troubled him greatly had it been available to him. He would have been delighted to learn that Federal intelligence was becoming even more spooked by Confederate ghost movements. Pleasonton no longer believed Washington the primary target. The Federal cavalry chief now reported Lee was aiming for Baltimore, a conclusion that perhaps reflected the appearance of Fitz Lee on the National Pike. But Pleasonton also passed on a rumor that a column of 35,000 Confederates lay at Barnesville near the Potomac.

Henry Halleck saw this dispatch and worried that the whole enemy dash into Maryland was a feint intended to lull the Federals into exposing Washington from the south, a fear that would remain with him for the next week. The elderly John Wool, who was becoming increasingly excited in his post at Baltimore, chimed in with a tale that Braxton Bragg was advancing down the Shenandoah Valley with 40,000 troops. Wool's telegram came under Lincoln's eye, and the president peppered his Western commanders for assurances that Bragg remained across the mountains.[21] Neither would it have bothered Lee that no Federal infantry had yet reached Darnestown but still lay seven miles southeast at Rockville.

On the other hand, some developments on the 7th might have caused Lee to pause had he been aware of them. Not only were the Federals not huddling behind their fortifications, but, with the advance of Franklin's Sixth Corps from Tennallytown to Offutt's Crossroads, McClellan had created a strong left wing to connect with his center and right and complete a curved battleline ten miles beyond the forts. More portentously, the Federals were not digging in for defense, because this battlefront was not intended to be stationary. It would be moved forward, mile by mile, with its communications covered, until the Confederates were brought to bay.

This was the day also on which McClellan decided the field army could no longer be without a commander. Late in the afternoon—and without written orders—he put Nathaniel Banks in charge of Washington's defenses and moved his own headquarters to Rockville in the middle of the battleline.[22]

Lee Dabbles in Politics, September 8

To the idling soldiers in the ranks of the Army of Northern Virginia there was nothing in particular about Monday, September 8, to set it apart in recollections of their stay on the Monocacy. It was another fair, warm, languorous day they passed in loafing, swimming, mending clothes, and finding clever ways to escape camp and avail themselves of the bounties of the Frederick area. Even Robert E. Lee opened his daily report to Davis by confessing there was little news to relate about the army. "Since my letter to you of the 7th instant nothing of interest in a military point of view has transpired."[23] And it was almost literally true. Only Walker's brigades were on the move, and they made but small progress, marching the short distance to Buckeystown and stopping a mile beyond on the road to Frederick. Still—although there is no certain evidence—it is likely Lee learned of the near arrival of the lost division.[24] Hence, when Pendleton reported in person during the morning with the Reserve Artillery, the last of the scattered units were finally at hand and the army united for such work as its commander might direct.

Shortly after his arrival, Pendleton precipitated an incident, trivial in itself but one that provided a rare glimpse into the obscure matter of the measures taken by Lee to defend his position on the line of the Monocacy. The five batteries under Lt. Col. Allen Cutts, nominally one of the battalions in the reserve artillery, had been detached to serve with D. H. Hill's division on its early crossing of the Potomac on the 4th. When Pendleton tried to reassert control over Cutts, he was informed by Lee's headquarters that Hill had posted Cutts's guns "to command the Washington road," and they should not be moved.[25] Why Lee took this precaution—and presumably there were similar defensive steps for which evidence no longer exists—is not clear. It is unlikely he expected to wait behind the Monocacy for a Federal assault. He had come to Maryland to maneuver, and he intended to draw the enemy beyond the mountains before offering battle. His present location resembled the position he had abandoned at Ox Hill, because it was too near both the Potomac and the Washington forts to leave sufficient room for operations against the enemy's communications. On the other hand, with Stuart's cavalry screen in place, Lee should not have been seriously concerned about a surprise attack from the direction of Washington. Yet, it is only this latter explanation that makes any sense.

Another event of the 8th underscored the distinction Lee made in the protection of private property. While doing all in his power to shield the personal possessions of Marylanders from plunder, he continued to destroy even privately owned facilities that constituted a military resource for the enemy. Engineering officers of Jackson's staff ignited kegs of black powder to blow up the B&O's bridge across the Monocacy. A soldier of Kemper's brigade became one of the earliest casualties of the campaign when killed by a flying fragment of iron while bathing in the river. The incident also illustrated the futility of trying to nullify Yankee ingenuity. After the Confederates had left the area, railroad crews would have the span repaired within five days and at a cost of less than four thousand dollars, making it questionable that the bridge's destruction was worth the loss of even a single life.[26]

From the single sentence Lee devoted to news about the enemy in his dispatch of the day to Davis, it would seem he believed the Federals to be as indolent as the Confederates. "As far as I can learn the enemy are not moving in this direction," he wrote, "but continue to concentrate about Washington." Apparently, Stuart had not pierced the screen of blue horsemen to discover that much of the Federal army was on the move on the 8th. The entire right wing of the Army of the Potomac, the First and Ninth Corps under Burnside, advanced from Leesborough ten miles north to Brookeville. In thus straightening his front, which had bent eastward to protect Washington from the north, McClellan extended coverage to Baltimore. The Federal commander also shifted Sykes's division of regulars from south of the river to Rockville. At the close of his first full day away from Washington, McClellan had some 66,000 men in a sixteen-mile-wide battleline, which was on average twelve miles beyond the forts. He determined from improved intelligence reporting that the Confederates had not advanced in force to Parr's Ridge but were in line behind the Monocacy. He was prepared to move his own army forward as an interlocking front to engage the enemy, while covering both the capital and Baltimore and protecting its own communications.[27]

Also surprising is that Stuart either did not discern, or detected but failed to alert Lee of, the considerable increase in the activity of the Federal cavalry on the 8th. Pleasonton now had 2,000 troopers, and—although still outnumbered two to one—he had established a cavalry line from Poolesville in the south through Clarksburg and Damascus to Unity in the north. His reports allowed McClellan to determine that the Confederates were not currently marching eastward against Washington or Baltimore, and the enemy apparently had only cavalry east of the Monocacy River. The spirited skirmishing that began on the 8th and extended along the entire front between the two armies should have alerted the Confederates that the anticipated Federal advance was under way.[28]

One of these Federal attacks came around midnight and fell on Hampton's pickets at Hyattstown, the heart of Stuart's line. It has received an unusual amount of historical attention, because it contributed to one of the most romantic scenes of the war. Heros von Borcke's grand ball was in full swing at the Female Academy in Urbana. Stuart and his staff, attired in their best uniforms, swirled blushing maidens in white gowns to the music of a band borrowed from the 18th Mississippi while the candlelight flickered on the battle flags draping the walls. Suddenly, a grim-faced courier arrived, and the warriors rode off into the night. After repelling the assault, the cavaliers returned to the dance. At the time, the affair was dismissed as a nuisance, but it was eagerly seized upon by the troopers to appear even more gallant in the eyes of their female companions.[29]

Earlier in the day, however, occurred a serious encounter that ought to have alarmed the Confederates. That morning Munford set out from Urbana with the 7th and 12th Virginia Cavalry regiments and two guns of Chew's Horse Artillery to reclaim Poolesville and anchor the Confederate line on the Potomac. A mile from the town he ran into Col. John Farnsworth with the 3d Indiana and 8th Illinois and a section of Battery M of the 2d U.S. Artillery. After several hours of charge and countercharge, Munford abandoned his mission and gave the enemy the victory in the first major engagement of the campaign. The Federals fought so well that one of Chew's gunners complained "the confounded Yankees can shoot better in the United States than they can when they come to Dixieland." Munford first fell back to Barnesville, but later he retired to Comus at the foot of Sugar Loaf Mountain to establish the right flank of the Confederate cavalry. By nightfall there was a four-mile-wide gap in Stuart's line at the mouth of the Monocacy.[30]

In continuing his letter to Davis, Lee made only a casual reference to the question of his supply line. "I am endeavoring to break up the line of communication as far back as Culpeper Court House and turn everything into the Valley of Virginia, in accordance with the plan which I have heretofore made known to you." It is interesting that as late as the 8th, Lee reflects no particular concern over the presence of the Federal garrisons at Martinsburg and Harpers Ferry. He would make it even clearer, in a dispatch he sent to Adjt. Gen. Samuel Cooper on this same date, that his attention focused on the line he was abandoning rather than the one he was establishing.[31] Apparently, there was a stream of convalescents and recruits trailing behind the army like the tail on a comet. Traveling alone or in small groups without officers, this human detritus not only preyed on the countryside but were vulnerable to capture, as there were no longer any Confederate forces in the area to protect them. Lee recommended such men be held and employed in Richmond until they could be sent forward in large detachments with officers.

Lee also hinted to Davis—but made plain to Cooper—that he still intended his new communications to run from Rapidan Station north to Culpeper, and thence westward to Luray before turning north again to Front Royal and Winchester. This is an important point for two reasons. First, it indicates Lee was confident the bridge over the Rapidan either had been repaired or soon would be. Second, that Lee remained satisfied with this line, which ran fifty miles farther north and hence that much closer to Washington, rather than a more secure route from the Rapidan to Charlottesville, is additional circumstantial evidence that he intended to remain in western Maryland for some time. Had he been thinking of a deep penetration into Pennsylvania it is doubtful he would have wanted his line to extend as far to the northeast and as near to Washington as Culpeper.

In his dispatch to the president, Lee did not mention the problem of convalescents, but he dwelt at length on another difficulty arising from the abandonment of the old line. "I fear that the arms captured on the plains of Manassas, of which some ten or twelve thousand were collected at Gainesville, will all be lost for want of transportation to remove them. I made the best arrangements in my power, being compelled to move the army away, and the wagons ordered to go by Gainesville to take arms back were taken to transport sick and wounded to Warrenton. I can get no satisfactory account of these arms. The last I heard of them they were still at Gainesville." In spite of the admitted importance of these weapons to the Confederacy, it is a bit puzzling Lee would devote fully half of his letter to the subject.

By way of contrast, Lee covered the vitally important topic of obtaining current supplies in a single closing sentence. "So far we have had no difficulty in procuring provisions in the country," he concluded, "though we have not relied exclusively upon them for our subsistence." Apparently, this was one more area critical to the success of his plan, which as late as the 8th, gave him no cause for particular concern. Unless Lee dissembled in the letter, and there is no imaginable reason he should have, he projected the impression of a commander who was content with the progress of his campaign in all of its major phases—and one who had the time to spend worrying about minor annoyances.[32]

It is interesting that Lee ended the dispatch to Davis without mentioning the Proclamation to Marylanders, which he must have already issued or was even then having printed for distribution. In fact, Lee seemingly attached so little importance to the public pronouncement that he did not mention it to Davis until four days later, and even then he did not seek approval of the text until the following day, after he had received a proposed proclamation from Davis himself. It is likely whatever hopes Lee may have originally entertained for a revolt in Maryland had evaporated by the 8th, and he viewed his Proclamation as an effort to calm the public, rather than excite it.

As the Confederate visit at Frederick stretched into the third day of what augured to be an indefinite stay, understandably the "citizens were embarrassed as to the intentions of the army." Ex-governor Enoch Lowe had not appeared, nor had any other prominent Marylander stepped forward to speak for the Confederates and address the political questions raised by their presence.[33] It is also possible Lee was responding to a rumor circulating in the army that fighting had broken out in the streets of Baltimore. It would be regrettable if misapprehension of his intentions led to the useless shedding of the blood of pro-Southern civilians.

Lee, in consequence, found it necessary to wade into the turbid pool of politics himself to put the proper public face on his sudden appearance north of the Potomac. By happy coincidence, the staff officer whose eloquent pen was called upon to draft important papers, Charles Marshall—although a native Virginian—had resided in Baltimore at the outbreak of the war and could be counted on to appreciate the nuances required in the document. And, in spite of several dramatic references to the "outrages" the North had "inflicted" on the state with arbitrary arrests and the suppression of free speech, the Proclamation clearly aimed to reassure Marylanders that the Confederates would not be a new despot's heel on their shore. "We know no enemies among you," wrote Marshall for Lee, "and will protect all of every opinion. It is for you to decide your destiny freely and without constraint. This army will respect your choice, whatever it may be." And, he concluded, "the Southern people . . . will only welcome you when you come of your own free will." It is entirely possible the major benefit Lee hoped to gain from the Proclamation was an increase in the supplies available for purchase from a reassured public.[34]

It fell to Bradley Johnson, the Frederick native and only prominent Marylander at hand, to use empurpled prose to induce his fellow citizens to join the ranks of the Confederate army. The impassioned proclamation he issued on the 8th—peppered with exclamation points—exhorted the free staters to overthrow "sixteen months of oppression more galling than the Austrian tyranny" and to "strike for liberty and right." Avengers were invited to step forward at the recruiting offices in the town to be armed and mustered in at once. And then—in an inspired attempt to turn an undeniable negative into a propaganda plus—he told the volunteers to bring with them only "a stout pair of shoes, a good blanket and a tin cup," as "Jackson's men have no baggage." Recruits were even offered a choice of units, for in addition to Johnson, Lige White announced the formation of a cavalry regiment, and the former editor of the *Frederick Herald*, John Heard, published a card calling for volunteers for a company of his own.[35]

All of the efforts yielded few results. The local press estimated that perhaps up to 130 men from Frederick and another forty from Middletown were swept up in the enthusiasm. Johnson would always believe his failure stemmed from the absence of an existing Maryland regiment to serve as a rallying point. The 1st Maryland Infantry (C.S.A.) had served with distinction through Jackson's Valley campaign and the Seven Days battles, but it had been disbanded on August 11 because of a dispute over the length of its term of service. Still, there is no reason to believe its presence would have significantly increased the interest in joining the Southern army in pro-Union western Maryland. It is possible that a prolonged stay by the Confederates would have allowed men from Baltimore and the eastern counties to reach the recruiting offices, but it is equally possible that most of the pro-Southern young men who possessed the zeal to fight had already left the state and were scattered in the units of other states throughout the Confederacy.[36]

Lee's final communication of the 8th may have been the most extraordinary letter he sent during the entire war. For the second day in a row, he dictated an additional dispatch to Jefferson Davis to treat at length a subject he felt too delicate to include in his daily report. This time, instead of a military matter such as straggling, Lee addressed a question that lay at the outer boundaries—and perhaps beyond—of a soldier's realm of responsibility. He opined that the time was ripe for a bid to end the war. "The present posture of affairs, in my opinion, places it in the power of the Government of the Confederate States to propose with propriety to that of the United States the recognition of our independence."[37] Once again, it was his strong belief in carpe diem, plucking the moment, that led him into crossing the limits, just as it had five days earlier induced him to seize "the most propitious time" to ford the Potomac.

"For more than a year," he continued, "both sections of the country have been devastated by hostilities which have brought sorrow and suffering upon thousands of homes, without advancing the objects which our enemies proposed to themselves in beginning the contest." Might not the frustration of Northerners, he asked by inference, have finally reached the point where they would be willing to consider permitting the South to leave the Union?

Nor, could the move be interpreted as a sign of weakness on the part of the Confederacy. "Such a proposition coming from us at this time, could in no way be regarded as suing for peace, but being made when it is in our power to inflict injury upon our adversary, would show conclusively to the world that our sole object is the establishment of our independence, and the attainment of an honorable peace."

It is noteworthy that Lee's sweeping reference to world opinion—indirect as it may be—is the sole allusion in any form to foreign affairs by him, or any one in a position to know his thinking, during the entire Maryland campaign. In it Lee gives no hint he is aware of events across the Atlantic, nor does he give the impression he would base his military operations on foreign considerations. He merely avers that he does not believe a peace proposal at this time would appear as a weakness in the eyes of other nations.[38]

It was not until the penultimate sentence of the second dispatch that Lee revealed the sophisticated thinking that lay behind his suggestion. He assumed the Lincoln administration would reject the proposal, and in fact it was this negative response he counted upon to help the Confederate cause. "The rejection of this offer would prove to the country that the responsibility of the continuance of the war does not rest upon us, but that the party in power in the United States elect to prosecute it for purposes of their own."

All along Lee believed the surest, if not the only, path to Confederate success lay in demoralizing Northerners and weakening their will to continue the war. And it was precisely this end he sought to further. "The proposal of peace would enable the people of the United States to determine at their coming elections whether they will support those who favor a prolongation of the war, or those who wish to bring it to a termination, which can but be productive of good to both parties without affecting the honor of either."

There is no clearer indication than this letter of the enormous stakes Lee believed were riding on the results of his campaign in Maryland. Only his appreciation of the high tide his military fortunes had reached, combined with his understanding of the desperateness of the Confederate cause, could have induced him to make this extraordinary suggestion to the president. There is no evidence and therefore no way of knowing whether Lee may have had this proposal in the back of his mind since September 2. He may have, or he may only have conceived it after reaching Frederick.

Ironically, even as he dictated the dispatch, forces beyond Lee's reach were already causing his tide to ebb. He was on the eve—apparently without knowing it—of the last day in the campaign in which he would exercise absolute control over strategy.

The Intrusion of Jeff. Davis, September 9

From its sullen gray dawn, Tuesday, September 9, portended change. For the first time since the Confederates crossed the Potomac, the sun did not shine on their expedition. Although the heat continued unabated, clouds overcast the skies of western Maryland. Yet, to the soldiers in the ranks nearly the whole day passed without a hint that the idle phase of the campaign was coming to a close. Not until a late hour would the familiar orders that always presaged imminent action filter down through the command hierarchy. The men were to cook three days rations and be ready to march at daybreak.[39]

Even the army's commander started his day without a sense of pressing urgency. Lee opened his daily report to the president—which circumstantial evidence suggests he composed early in the morning—by blandly asserting, "Nothing of interest in a military point of view has transpired since my last communication."[40] Curiously, the body of Lee's dispatch did not bear out its vacuous beginning. He went on to discuss three developments of seemingly serious import. Certainly, when viewed together with the benefit of hindsight, the news Lee possessed can be seen to mark clearly the start of the third and decisive phase of the strategy of the expedition. Just as certainly, from the tone of his dispatch, Lee underestimated the significance of the developments. Without his realizing it, the initiative was beginning to slip from his grasp.

In the first place, something had happened since the day before—when Lee had reported "no difficulty in procuring provisions"—to change his mind about the availability of food in the Frederick area. "We are able to obtain forage for our animals, and some provisions, but there is more difficulty about the latter. Many of the farmers have not yet gotten out their wheat, and there is a reluctance on the part of the millers and others to commit themselves in our favor." And not only bread, but also meat, the second basic staple for the army, was in short supply. "Some cattle, but not in any great numbers, are obtained in this country, the inhabitants are said to have driven many off to Pennsylvania."[41]

It is unclear whether prior to the 9th Lee had been unaware of the extent of the problems encountered by his commissary officers in purchasing supplies, or whether these problems had worsened significantly as the Confederate stay lengthened. The latter is perhaps more likely, since the army must have exhausted within a few days the supplies available from Southern sympathizers and the nonpartisans willing to accept Confederate money. Also, there is evidence Frederick merchants had begun to raise their prices, demand U.S. currency, and hoard such stock as remained from their dwindling stores.[42] Farmers and millers, when given the choice, were probably even less inclined to risk a year's income, when the request came from official agents of a government they viewed as the enemy. And this led to the second development that had occurred since Lee's last letter to Davis.

Seventy thousand men consume an enormous amount of food daily.[43] Because the army had brought scant provisions with it, the moment Lee realized local supplies were failing, he could not long delay taking corrective action. He must either confiscate from unwilling citizens, or resort to wagoning food from Virginia. Because he would not do the former—indeed could not in his anomalous position as protector of the rights of Marylanders—he was compelled to undertake the latter. He wrote to Davis, "I shall now open our communications with the Valley, so that we can obtain more supplies."

Lee's ambiguous statement offers little insight into either what he knew, or what actions he intended to take at the writing of this dispatch on early Tuesday morning. He makes no reference to the Federal garrisons at Martinsburg and Harpers Ferry; nor is there any indication that he believes opening communications with the Valley will require military action. In fact, it is uncertain whether he had yet determined if it would even be necessary for the army to leave its line on the Monocacy. It is clear only that he had decided he could no longer neglect his communications, as he had been doing for nearly a week.

The third piece of news Lee passed on to Davis—after declaring that "nothing of interest" had occurred—demonstrated positively he now knew the Federals had put a force into the field and were advancing toward his position. "From reports that have reached me, I believe that the enemy are pushing a strong column up the River (Potomac) by Rockville and Darnestown, and by Poolesville towards Seneca Mills. I hear that the commands of Sumner, Sigel, Burnside and Hooker are advancing in the direction above mentioned."

The clear impression of this statement, especially when taken in the context of the entire dispatch, is that Lee saw nothing alarming in the fact that the Federals had advanced a "strong" force—comprised of at least four corps—and had reached Poolesville, the nearest of the three towns mentioned, within fifteen miles of his own position. Apparently, Lee was judging Federal progress in terms of the total distance covered since the 4th and assumed the small number of miles averaged over that longer period would continue to mark their progress in the future. He missed the fact that the Federals had spent several days in organization and refitting and were only now starting in earnest the attempt to bring the Confederates to bay. In other words, he either failed to grasp, or else Stuart failed to provide him with the information that would allow him to grasp, the fact that the Federal advance had become serious within the last two days.

These two sentences constitute the only direct, contemporaneous evidence on the extent and quality of information Lee possessed about his enemy on this critical 9th of September, but they contain inaccuracies that help to explain why he underestimated the Federal threat. First, he may have been the victim of faulty maps. He noted the Federals were advancing on Seneca Mills by way of Poolesville, and yet Poolesville is almost ten miles beyond Seneca Mills to the west. Thus, it is possible Lee did not realize the enemy were within fifteen miles of his position. Second, he depicts the Federal column as hugging the Potomac River, since all of the places he mentions are within five miles of the river. Yet, by the 9th McClellan's right flank extended fifteen miles to the northwest at Middlebrook and Brookeville, and the Federal cavalry extended to Damascus, which is even closer to the National Pike that runs from Baltimore to Frederick.

It is not surprising Lee would have worried most about a river column, as such may have portended an attempt to turn his own right flank and cut his communications with Virginia. Still, the Confederate commander's report to Davis suggests a faulty perception of the lengthy enemy battlefront that was advancing toward him. Third, Lee also conveys a confused picture of the Federal units arrayed against him. Sigel's Eleventh Corps was still south of the Potomac guarding Arlington and Alexandria, while Stuart had not yet reported that Franklin (Sixth Corps), Banks (Twelfth Corps) and the divisions of Couch (Fourth Corps) and Sykes (Fifth Corps) had joined McClellan's field army.

Finally, although not an inaccuracy, there is also Lee's curious depiction of the enemy force. He habitually referred to the opposing army as the enemy, as the Federals, or by the name of its commander, but in this letter he mentions only the names of subordinate officers and gives no indication he knows who is in overall command of the Federal column. And under the circumstances it would be reasonable if he had not yet learned. Such confusion and hesitation dominated the highest levels of the Federal military hierarchy that no order was ever published—indeed none was ever written—assigning a commander to the Army of the Potomac once it moved beyond the Washington fortifications.

It was common knowledge and hence available to Lee through Northern newspapers that Pope had been relieved and that McClellan had been appointed to a strictly limited assignment for the defenses of the capital. Not until late on the 7th, however, had McClellan transferred his headquarters to Rockville and acted on his own authority to fill the vacuum. News that McClellan had left the city for Rockville appeared in Washington newspapers on the afternoon of the 8th as a simple announcement and without comment on the ramifications of the move in regard to field command. Even so, there is no evidence Lee had such timely access to Washington newspapers during this period, and the Baltimore papers he did sometimes read would not carry the report until the 9th.[44]

It seems likely, therefore, that Lee's description of the Federal column reflected his current uncertainty over the identity of the Federal commander he would eventually face in western Maryland. While there can be no doubt Lee judged the Federal advance from Washington to be slow and cautious, he probably based that conclusion on his erroneous analysis of the enemy's rate of march, his perception of the demoralized condition of the Federal army, and his understanding of the Lincoln administration's anxiety for the safety of the Northern capital. It is much less likely at this point in the campaign Lee would have evaluated enemy movements—let alone decided to undertake critical operations—based upon his insights into the character traits of George McClellan or of any other potential opponent. Simply put, there was too much doubt about whom that opponent would be.

After closing his report to Davis, Lee probably had no intention of writing the president again on the 9th. Sometime during the morning, however, he received a letter from Davis that seemed to demand an immediate reply. The president was on his way to visit the army. "I have just received your letter of the 7th instant from Rapidan," Lee dictated, "informing me of your intention to come on to Leesburg."[45] Apparently, Lee had not misjudged his man, except perhaps to underestimate his enthusiasm for the expedition across the Potomac. The dispatch Lee sent from Dranesville late on September 3 proposing the movement could not have been received by Davis earlier than the 5th, and the 6th was more likely in view of the customary delivery time for nontelegraphic messages. Yet, by the 7th, Davis had traveled ninety miles by rail to Rapidan Station and was on his way to visit the Army of Northern Virginia. He brought with him former Maryland governor Enoch Lowe.[46]

The news from Lee must have fanned a fiery excitement already smoldering in the breast of the president of the Confederacy. He alone was in a position to appreciate fully the grand offensive unfolding across half the continent. From northern Mississippi to the Kanawha, eight Confederate columns were either on the march or were preparing to advance to liberate Kentucky and western Virginia and to carry the war into enemy territory. While Loring's vanguard under Jenkins had already crossed the Ohio, Kirby Smith and Humphrey Marshall were on Kentucky soil and Braxton Bragg was within one day of the state's border. Not only were Sterling Price and Earl Van Dorn under instructions to join the offensive, but John Breckinridge's small army had been ordered from Port Hudson to reenforce Bragg. The word from Lee meant a ninth arrow was to be launched against the body of the enemy and this one aimed at his heart. This must have been good news indeed to the man who had gathered maps of the Potomac fords the year before—

and who had written to a friend just six weeks earlier that he would, "if I could to-night issue orders to an army adequate to the work of invasion."[47]

Unfortunately, Davis's letter of the 7th has not been found and is known only as it is reflected in Lee's reply on the 9th. Apparently, the president assumed Lee would spend a longer period in preparation for the crossing and by leaving at once he would have time to reach the army while it was still in Virginia. Whether Davis knew when he wrote from Rapidan that Lee had already reached Frederick is unclear, but Lee's reference to the president's intention of coming to Leesburg suggests he was ignorant of the army's progress. Hence, there is no evidence Davis ever contemplated leaving the boundaries of the Confederacy, although Lee apparently feared the president might do just that, when he discovered the changed circumstances.

"While I should feel the greatest satisfaction in having an interview with you and consulting on all subjects of interest," Lee assured Davis, "I cannot but feel great uneasiness for your safety should you undertake to reach me." It would be most interesting to know how specific Davis had been in his letter of the 7th in regard to the subjects he wished to discuss with Lee. It is possible he had been as vague as was Lee in his reply, and it is probable that he did not specifically mention a proclamation at this time.[48]

The heading of Lee's letter, "Headquarters, Near Fredericktown," and his phrase "to reach me" implicitly told Davis that the Confederate commander could not return to Leesburg for a conference. For a meeting to take place, the president would have to come to the army. It is possible that in spite of his good relations with Davis, Lee preferred not to be fettered by the presence of his superior. Since leaving Richmond, Lee had been free to plan and execute his operations without a supervisor looking over his shoulder. The results had more than justified the freedom; and it would have been an instinctive human reaction on his part to try to avoid returning to a restrictive relationship no matter how affable, especially in the midst of a critical and delicate campaign.

However understandable such a reaction might have been on Lee's part, it can only be inferred from his excessive solicitude for Davis's comfort and safety. "You will not only encounter the hardships and fatigue of a very disagreeable journey, but also run the risk of capture by the enemy." And, apparently to make certain the president did not continue his journey, Lee sent back a staff officer to intercept him. "I send my aide-de-camp, Maj. Taylor back to explain to you the difficulties and dangers of the journey, which I cannot recommend you to undertake."

In his effort to discourage Davis from attempting to visit the army, Lee elaborated on the movement he was currently pondering but had barely mentioned in his first dispatch. "I am endeavoring to break up the line through Leesburg, which is no longer safe, and turn everything off from Culpeper Court House towards Winchester. I shall move in the direction I originally intended, towards Hagerstown and Chambersburg, for the purpose of opening our line of communication through the Valley, in order to procure sufficient supplies of flour. I shall not move until tomorrow, or perhaps next day, but when I do move, the line of communication in this direction will be entirely broken up. I must therefore advise that you do not make an attempt that I cannot but regard as hazardous."

It cannot be known whether Lee was merely providing additional details to his simple statement in the earlier letter that he would "now open our communications with the Valley" or whether his plans had further developed as the day progressed. In either case, it is clear he now intended to move with the entire army from Frederick. It would not seem that he had yet determined to send an expedition against Harpers Ferry. Indeed, the most plausible reading of his statement is that he intended to open communications through the Valley simply by moving toward Hagerstown. He must have believed at this point that increasing the pressure on the Federal garrisons by threatening to isolate them from the north would be enough to make them abandon their positions. His uncertainty as to whether he would move "tomorrow, or perhaps the next day," proves this dispatch was written before the details of his move had been fixed. And it is reasonable to assume that it was also written prior to Lee's receiving the information that would make it necessary to send a force against Harpers Ferry, and before the discussions that led to the issuing of Special Orders, No. 191.

The Walker Interview

At some point during the afternoon of the 9th, Lee decided he could not rely on the Federal garrisons in the lower Shenandoah Valley to withdraw on their own accord, even if he put additional pressure on them by marching to Hagerstown. He concluded it would be necessary to move directly against the Federals to make certain they would not remain to block the new Confederate line of communications. Later in the afternoon, he would hammer out the details of the expedition to the Valley in a meeting with Jackson and Longstreet. Before the war council, however, the commander of the last division of the Army of Northern Virginia to reach Frederick reported to army headquarters. What—if anything—can be learned from this meeting between Lee and Walker, is open to serious question.

Twenty-four years after the event, Brig. Gen. John George Walker would claim that when he reported in person to Lee, the Confederate commander divulged to him in minute detail not only his current thinking but also the entire strategy of the Maryland campaign. Walker would demonstrate an uncanny memory in recalling gestures and facial expressions and reciting long speeches by Lee in quotation marks to indicate the Confederate commander's exact words had been captured. Unfortunately, Walker's account is marred by inaccuracies, inconsistencies, and implausibilities and contradicts other statements that Lee made either at the time or afterward about the campaign; and it is at variance, as well, with the official report that Walker himself submitted a little less than a month after the event.[49]

Virtually every secondary study of the campaign has accepted Walker's memoir, however, and many have relied heavily upon it for insight into Lee's thinking and intentions. Walker's account has been so widely accepted and his claims so finely interwoven into the traditional understanding of Lee's strategy in the Maryland campaign that a detailed analysis is required to justify and explain the rejection of many of its assertions.

Significantly, the confusion starts with the date on which the meeting occurred. According to Walker, "on the night of the 6th of September my division reached the vicinity of Leesburg, and the next morning crossed the Potomac at Cheek's Ford. . . . The next day we reached the neighborhood of Frederick. I went at once to General Lee, who was alone." Walker thus asserts he reached Leesburg on the 6th, crossed the Potomac on the 7th, and met with Lee on the 8th. In Walker's account, his division covered the distance from the Potomac to Frederick in a single day's march.

According to the unpublished diary of a soldier of the 30th Virginia, however, the command barely passed Buckeystown, seven miles from Frederick, by the evening of the 8th and did not reach the vicinity of

Frederick until the 9th. Pvt. Isaac Hirsch's diary entry for September 9th records that the division reached Frederick and rested there three hours before returning to Buckeystown. Then, at five o'clock in the evening, they set out on a mission to destroy the C&O aqueduct. Of course, it is possible Walker left his division at Buckeystown on the 8th and rode ahead alone to report to Lee. Nonetheless, it would have been bizarre, to say the least, if Walker had learned of his special mission on the 8th and then marched his division seven miles in the wrong direction on the following day—only to rest three hours and then retrace his steps. It makes sense to believe that Walker did not report on the 8th, but that he set out on the 9th with his division unaware of any new assignment. He met with Lee during the late morning, received instructions about the aqueduct, returned to his men idling in the Frederick suburbs, and countermarched them to Buckeystown. Finally, in his official report, Walker flatly states that he received instructions from Lee on the 9th.[50]

Telescoping a two-day march into one and misdating an event by twenty-four hours is not a capital memory offense. It is merely a single, small piece of evidence that Walker's recollection of the interview was not as sharp as his postwar account implies. Ironically, if Walker had reported to Lee on the 8th, there would be even more reason to doubt Lee made the remarks alleged to him.

In Walker's memoir of the substance of the meeting, Lee at once plunged into a full explanation of Confederate strategy for the campaign. "After listening to my report, he said that as I had a division which would often, perhaps, be ordered on detached service, an intelligent performance of my duty might require a knowledge of the ulterior purposes and objects of the campaign." It stretches credulity to believe the usually secretive Lee—who did not discuss grand strategy beyond the small circle of Davis, Longstreet, and Jackson—would have promptly unburdened himself to a nonintimate acquaintance such as Walker. On the basis of the reasoning assigned by Walker, Lee should have been equally forthcoming to both LaFayette McLaws and D. H. Hill, who would also be ordered on detached service and as major generals were a full grade senior to Walker. The Confederate commander did no such thing. He would later in the day give verbal instructions to McLaws but only on the specifics of the Harpers Ferry expedition. There would be no mention of grand strategy. And he would speak not at all to D. H. Hill. In fact, Lee had sent Hill as vanguard of the army splashing across the Potomac with no knowledge of the larger purposes of the mission.[51]

Walker continued: "'Here,' said he, tracing with his finger on a large map, 'is the line of our communications, from Rapidan Station to Manassas, thence to Frederick. It is too near the Potomac, and is liable to be cut any day by the enemy's cavalry. I have therefore given orders to move the line back into the Valley of Virginia, by way of Staunton, Harrisonburg, and Winchester, entering Maryland at Shepherdstown.'" In the first place, with both hands in splints and bandages and at least one arm in a sling, it is certain Lee did no tracing with his finger. And, it is surprising that with Walker's claimed recall of details, he would not have remembered the general's injured hands. Second, even with an elbow, Lee would not have pointed to the line through Manassas and called it "our communications," nor would he have depicted his new line as running through Staunton and Harrisonburg. Lee had been trying to break up traffic on the Manassas line since the 5th and had, in effect, been operating without communications since that time. Even more to the point, his new line was not to enter the Valley at Staunton but at Luray, over fifty miles to the north. If Lee spoke to Walker at all about the army's communications, Walker either did not understand what he heard at the time, or he freely embellished a frail memory and guessed the wrong details.

Then, according to Walker, Lee assigned him a special mission. "I wish you to return to the mouth of the Monocacy and effectually destroy the aqueduct of the Chesapeake and Ohio canal." This part of the memoir is undoubtedly true. Lee did order Walker on an expedition—independent of the move against Harpers Ferry—to destroy the aqueduct; and, since no written orders have been found, it is reasonable to assume he issued verbal instructions at the time Walker reported. Walker's language in his report, "I was instructed by General Lee," also suggests verbal orders.[52]

Lee did not stop with assigning this mission, however; he went on to reveal his future plans. "By the time that is accomplished you will receive orders to cooperate in the capture of Harper's Ferry, and you will not return here, but, after the capture of Harper's Ferry, will rejoin us at Hagerstown, where the army will be concentrated." Walker's assertion here is not entirely beyond possibility. By the time he met with Lee, which was probably late in the morning or early afternoon, the Confederate commander may have begun to think about moving against Harpers Ferry. Certainly, Lee had already written to Davis that he intended to "open" communications with the Valley, and the fact that he had implied he would effect this by moving to Hagerstown did not exclude the possibility he was also considering an expedition against the Federal garrisons. Furthermore, it would have been reasonable for Lee to alert Walker in advance of orders he might receive while at a distance from the army.

However plausible, it did not happen that way. The events of the next twelve hours as described in Walker's official report contradict his postwar claim that he had any foreknowledge of an expedition against Harpers Ferry, let alone knew of his own participation in one. When Walker reached the aqueduct at about eleven o'clock that night, he set his engineers to work drilling holes for placing the gunpowder to blow up the arches. They discovered the "solidity and massiveness of the masonry," combined with dull augers, made the work before them "one of days instead of hours." Walker decided he could not risk remaining that long at the mouth of the Monocacy, because Lee had told him the "main army" was going to march "from Frederick toward Hagerstown" on the 10th. Believing his small division would be too much exposed to the enemy, he "determined to rejoin General Lee by way of Jefferson and Middletown, as previously instructed by him."

Thus, it would appear—according to Walker's memory twenty-eight days after the event—that Lee had said much the same thing to him in the late morning or early afternoon that Lee had written to Davis earlier in the day. If the Confederate commander said anything at all to Walker about Harpers Ferry, it may have been that the move toward Hagerstown was intended to open communications with the Valley. Such a remark might account for the later confusion and telescoping in Walker's memory. In any case, several hours after midnight a courier delivered Special Orders, No. 191, which instructed Walker to proceed to Loudoun Heights, and the general canceled his plans to return to the main army by way of Middletown.[53]

From this point on in the interview, as Walker would have it in 1886, Lee became unusually garrulous. "My information is that there are between 10,000 and 12,000 men at Harper's Ferry, and 3,000 at Martinsburg. The latter may escape toward Cumberland, but I think the chances are that they will take refuge at Harper's Ferry and be captured. Besides the men and material of war which we shall capture at Harper's Ferry, the position is necessary to us, not to garrison and hold, but because in the hands of the enemy, it would be a break in our new line of communications with Richmond."

Beginning with these statements, the Lee portrayed by Walker is not only suspiciously chatty, but he is credited with intelligence details and gifted with a foresight into the future that are also suspect. In regard to Harpers Ferry, for example, later on the 9th, Lee would tell LaFayette McLaws that the garrison "was not more than, perhaps, 3000 or 4000."[54] Nor is there reason to believe that Lee expected the Federal garrisons at either Martinsburg or Harpers Ferry would remain stationary to be captured in place. On the contrary, for nearly a week he had been anticipating their flight to avoid capture, and the orders he would draft later on the 9th would clearly imply he continued to believe the enemy would attempt to escape. Finally, based on the experience of the recent evacuation of Winchester—in which Lee reported to Davis the enemy's "stores, &c. . . . are stated to have been destroyed"—he had no basis for confidence in the capture of a large amount of supplies.[55]

According to Walker, Lee then expounded on the additional benefits he expected to gain by taking time out from his campaign to capture Harpers Ferry. "A few days rest at Hagerstown will be of great service to our men. Hundreds of them are barefooted, and nearly all of them are ragged. I hope to get shoes and clothing for the most needy." Even this statement is also at variance in subtle ways with Lee's known thinking. In the first place, in both letters to Davis on the 9th, Lee emphasized the food he hoped to obtain in Hagerstown and made no mention of clothing. Second, on the 12th Lee would estimate the shoeless problem of the army to run into the thousands. And, third, when it is remembered that the move was in conjunction with the Harpers Ferry expedition, it is obvious that less than half of the army would be resting at Hagerstown, while the remainder would become considerably more fatigued by tramping around western Maryland.[56]

"But the best of it," Lee allegedly continued, "will be that the short delay will enable us to get up our stragglers—not stragglers from a shirking disposition, but simply from inability to keep up with their commands. I believe there are not less than from eight to ten thousand of them between here and Rapidan Station." Again, Walker's version belies contemporary evidence. First, on September 7, Lee's dispatch to Davis had used a far different tone in describing stragglers—worse than shirkers, they were cowards, according to Lee—and asked for authority to employ stern measures. Secondly, after four days of rest at Frederick, it is hard to imagine what Lee would have had in mind in thinking that a few more days at Hagerstown—farther from the Potomac and more difficult to reach—would accomplish.[57]

"'Besides these we shall be able to get a large number of recruits who have been accumulating at Richmond for some weeks. I have now requested that they be sent forward to join us. They ought to reach us at Hagerstown. We shall then have a very good army, and,' he smilingly added, 'one that I think will be able to give a good account of itself.'" This flatly contradicts the dispatch Lee had sent to the adjutant general the day before that requested recruits and convalescents be detained in Richmond until they could be sent forward in an organized body at some unspecified future date.[58]

Walker then came to the crux of the conversation in which Lee supposedly revealed the heart of his reason for entering Maryland. "'In ten days from now,' he continued, 'if the military situation is then what I confidently expect it to be after the capture of Harper's Ferry, I shall concentrate the army at Hagerstown, effectually destroy the Baltimore and Ohio Road, . . .'"

From the start of the soliloquy, the words Walker puts in Lee's mouth are suspect. By the terms of the Special Orders Lee would draft later in the day, the columns operating against Harpers Ferry would be given three days (i.e., the 10th through the 12th) to carry out their missions. And, in several postwar remarks Lee would reiterate his expectation that the army would only be divided three or four days.[59] Yet, in this conversation the Confederate commander estimates his concentration will require an additional six days. Also, Lee would have been spouting nonsense to say that after reaching Hagerstown he will destroy the B&O. With every step toward Hagerstown the Confederates would be moving away from that railroad, which ran south from Frederick to Harpers Ferry, where it crossed into Virginia before heading west. Whatever Lee hoped to accomplish against the B&O would need to be "effectually" carried out while at Frederick or as part of the operations against Harpers Ferry and not after he had moved northward.

But, there is more, as Lee supposedly went on, "'. . . and march to this point,' placing his finger at Harrisburg, Pennsylvania. 'This is the object point of the campaign. You remember, no doubt, the long bridge of the Pennsylvania railroad over the Susquehanna, a few miles west of Harrisburg. Well, I wish effectually to destroy that bridge, which will disable the Pennsylvania railroad for a long time. With the Baltimore and Ohio in our possession, and the Pennsylvania railroad broken up, there will remain to the enemy but one route of communication with the west, and that very circuitous, by way of the Lakes.'"

Nothing else Lee said or wrote before, during, or after the campaign indicated he contemplated a deep penetration into Pennsylvania, let alone that a railroad bridge was the "object point" of his entire expedition.

The fact that he once mentioned to Davis the possibility of entering Pennsylvania, and that on the morning of the 9th, named Chambersburg in addition to Hagerstown as his intended direction, must be taken in the context of his clearly and consistently stated aim to draw the Federal army beyond the mountains into western Maryland, where he hoped to inflict upon it another defeat of the magnitude of Second Manassas. It is also revealing that no other contemporary who was in a position to know something of Lee's thinking and later wrote about the campaign—not James Longstreet or D. H. Hill or Bradley Johnson or Charles Marshall or Walter Taylor or Armistead Long—ascribes this or a remotely similar objective to Lee in crossing the Potomac. Significantly, William Allan, who undertook careful research in producing his *Army of Northern Virginia in 1862* in the early 1890s and who had the opportunity to speak to Lee several times after the war on this topic, ignored the Walker memoir.[60]

Lee then proceeded, according to Walker, to top off his strategy with a sweeping flourish. "After that I can turn my attention to Philadelphia, Baltimore, or Washington, as may seem best for our interests."

Coming from a commander who had realistically described his army as "not properly equipped for an invasion" and who had been continually worried about replenishing his ordnance supplies, this is simply not credible. While Lee might have talked about threatening to cut off Baltimore and Washington—indeed he was doing just that from Frederick—it is absurd from the viewpoint of strategy and military reality that he would have even mentioned Philadelphia. Moreover, nowhere is there any reference to his primary objective, which was to bring the enemy army to battle in a situation favorable to the Confederates. Ten months later, in his official report Lee declared that his object after leaving Frederick was to "establish our communications with Richmond through the Valley of the Shenandoah, and, by threatening Pennsylvania, induce the enemy to follow, and thus draw him from his base of supplies." After the war, Lee would declare flatly "I did not propose to invade the North, as I did not believe that the Army of Northern Virginia was strong enough for the purpose," and there is no evidence except Walker's assertion to contravene his plain statements.[61]

Walker must have realized the objectives he ascribed to Lee would appear extreme, and he had Lee himself provide the explanation. "I was very much astonished at this announcement, and I suppose he observed it, for he turned to me and said: 'You doubtless regard it hazardous to leave McClellan practically on my line of communications, and to march into the heart of the enemy's country?' I admitted that such a thought had occurred to me."

Leaving aside for the moment the question of Lee's information about McClellan being in command of the Federal field army, it will be noted that Lee admits his movement on Harrisburg will virtually abandon his communications to the enemy. Why would a commander who on the very same day decides to undertake a troublesome expedition to establish his communications, promptly turn around and abandon them? If he would not care about his communications in a week, why care so keenly about them on September 9?

Lee then allegedly described the role he assigned to McClellan in Confederate strategy. "'Are you acquainted with General McClellan?' he inquired. I replied that we had served together in the Mexican war, under General Scott, but that I had seen but little of him since that time." This in itself is a curious exchange, as it seems to inform Lee, who had been a member of Scott's staff, of something he should already have known.

"He is an able general but a very cautious one. His enemies among his own people think him too much so. His army is in a very demoralized and chaotic condition, and will not be prepared—or he will not think it so—for three or four weeks. Before that time I hope to be on the Susquehanna."

This statement also is replete with implausibilities. In the first place, there is no contemporaneous evidence that Lee knew as early as the 9th it would be McClellan he would face as the enemy commander. Although he several times refers to the arrival of "McClellan's army" in Washington, not once in his dispatches from the 3d onward does Lee mention McClellan himself. As previously noted, it is possible—but unproven—that he might have read Northern newspapers of the 8th which stated that McClellan had left Washington for Rockville. Lee might have interpreted this to mean McClellan would command the Federal field army. It is also possible that information garnered by Stuart from civilians or enemy prisoners suggested that McClellan had taken the field. What is reasonably certain, however, is that even if by midday of the 9th Lee did surmise he would be contending against McClellan, his assumption was based on inconclusive information he had received within the last twenty-four hours. In spite of this, Walker would have Lee hazard his expedition—not to mention his army—on the Confederate commander's analysis of McClellan's character. Moreover, the clear implication is that Lee had planned his campaign from the start on the presumption that he could count on McClellan's foibles. On the contrary, however, from September 2 to 4, it was John Pope whom Lee referred to as the Federal commander.

Second, although the portrait of McClellan as able but cautious would probably match Lee's evaluation, it also reflects the widespread and common Confederate view of the Federal commander, and the reference to his enemies in the North sounds suspiciously like hindsight gained after the war. Moreover, the thrust of Lee's comments elsewhere is that he counted on the demoralization and disorganization of the Federal army without reference to its commander.[62] Walker's version of Lee's strategy is clearly inconsistent in this respect. If Lee assumed McClellan would not move until he thought his army prepared, then, obviously, when the Federal army moved it would in fact be recovered. And this was exactly what Lee did not want. Lee's whole reason for crossing east of the mountains, for remaining in the Frederick area, and for putting out rumors of impending attacks on Baltimore and Washington was to force the Federal army into the field before it had time to recover from Second Manassas. Yet, according to Walker, Lee now blithely announced his confidence that he would be given three or four weeks to destroy a railroad bridge deep in the interior of Pennsylvania.

Third, although the chronology ascribed by Walker to Lee is somewhat ambiguous, it is far-fetched in all of its several possible readings. It is not clear whether Walker's Lee is counting his three or four weeks from the crossing of the Potomac on September 4 or from the interview on September 9. If the former, the end of the grace period he expected would be from September 25 to October 2; if the latter, which is the likely reading, it would be from September 30 to October 7. In either case, Lee was projecting an extraordinarily long time that he would be allowed to roam about unmolested in enemy territory, especially in light of his known belief in the panicky nature of the Lincoln government.

Fourth, the arithmetic of the chronology is also curious. If Lee concentrated at Hagerstown by the 19th and rested there until the 21st, he was estimating it would require eight days to reach the Susquehanna, some eighty miles away. As a rate of march, ten miles a day would be considerably below the standard Lee usually set for his army. And all of this leisure, it will be remembered, was taken for granted by Lee on the day after the enemy cavalry had seized Poolesville, a town within fifteen miles of the position the Confederates occupied before even setting out for Harpers Ferry.

Walker concluded his story by introducing a third witness to the interview, but a witness who also would be dead by the time the memoir appeared in print. "Our conversation was interrupted at this point by the arrival of Stonewall Jackson, and after a few minutes Lee and Jackson turned to the subject of the capture of Harper's Ferry. I remember Jackson seemed in high spirits, and even indulged in a little mild pleasantry about his long neglect of his friends in 'the Valley,' General Lee replying that Jackson had 'some friends' in that region who would not, he feared, be delighted to see him. The arrival of a party of ladies from Frederick and vicinity, to pay their respects to Lee and Jackson, put an end to the conversation, and soon after I took my departure."

Walker's memoir first appeared as an article in *Century Magazine* in 1886 and was reprinted the following year in that magazine's popular anthology, *Battles and Leaders of the Civil War*. After its publication, no ex-Confederate writer subsequently adopted Walker's views on Lee's grandiose plans to penetrate deeply into Pennsylvania during September of 1862. At least four authors who were in a position to know something of Lee's thinking—James Longstreet, Walter Taylor, William Allan, and Porter Alexander—covered the Maryland campaign in books that appeared in the 1890s or later but ignored the Walker account. These later writers had available Volume 19 of the *Official Records*, which appeared in 1887 and included Lee's report and his dispatches to Jefferson Davis, and they chose to follow the explanation provided directly by Lee and to avoid the torturous path required to reconcile the discrepancies between it and the Walker claims. They were, perhaps, reluctant to challenge the veracity of a former comrade on the contents of a conversation of which he was the only survivor and which, in any case, involved mostly hypothetical events that had never had the chance to occur.[63]

Bradley Johnson and Henry Kyd Douglas did directly challenge a later segment of the article, however, in which Walker claimed that he had saved Lee's army by precipitating the surrender of Harpers Ferry. Johnson and Douglas not only demonstrated Walker's faulty memory, but they also implied he was awarding himself credit he did not deserve.[64]

Subsequent authors have been less discriminating. Indeed, it was the usually meticulous Douglas Southall Freeman, who in 1934 elevated Walker's account to the status of a major source for understanding Lee's intentions in crossing the Potomac. Without questioning why, Freeman even noted in passing, "It is curious that this plan, which was plainly set forth in Lee's conversation with General J. G. Walker, should have been overlooked in published accounts of General Lee's reasons for dividing his army."[65] Since that time, historians have accepted the Walker account without hesitation; and they have buttressed its authority by reference to Lee's September 5 request for permission from Davis to enter Pennsylvania and his September 9 mention of Chambersburg.

Although historians should be slow to reject a firsthand account without direct contradictory evidence, the cumulative weight of the inconsistencies and implausibilities of Walker's narrative of his conversation with Lee justify rejection. Whether he did so consciously or not, it seems likely that Walker expanded upon his brief sojourn with the Army of Northern Virginia and inflated his relatively minor role in the Maryland campaign into a major speaking part. Within two months of the army's return to Virginia, Walker would be ordered to the Trans-Mississippi Department, the Siberia of the Confederacy. Although he served with considerable distinction in the southwest for the remainder of the war, he returned to settle in Winchester, Virginia. He may have found comparatively little interest among his neighbors in the heart of Lee country in his achievements west of the Mississippi, and he was never able to publish a book-length study that he wrote of the war in the far West.[66]

Because of its pervasive flaws, it is difficult to conclude which parts of the Walker account may have provided the foundation for the elaboration and can therefore be credited as having occurred. Nevertheless, there are four points that may be accepted with varying degrees of assurance. First, Walker almost certainly did report in person and meet privately with Lee on the late morning or early afternoon of the 9th. Second, Lee probably did inform Walker of the special mission to destroy the C&O aqueduct over the Monocacy River. Third, Lee may have told Walker in very general terms of the problem arising from the Federal garrisons in the Valley and that he intended to move the army toward Hagerstown on the following day to increase the pressure on them to withdraw. And, fourth, since other evidence suggests that Lee and Jackson met on the 9th to plan the movement, Jackson may have come to Lee's tent toward the end of the interview and joined in the discussion on Harpers Ferry, although it seems unlikely in view of Walker's official report that anything definite was said about an expedition against the garrison.

Beyond these four points, Walker's account of the interview with Lee is not reliable. Unless additional, confirming evidence is found, it cannot be used to understand Lee's strategy in the Maryland campaign.

Frederick Council of War

During the afternoon of September 9, Lee decided the Federal garrisons at Martinsburg and Harpers Ferry were not responding to the threat of being cut off, as common sense dictated, and a Confederate march to Hagerstown probably would not be enough to make them withdraw. He met with Jackson, and the two generals evolved a plan to eliminate this threat to the new line of communications through the Shenandoah Valley. Longstreet joined the war council near its close and offered several modifications to the proposed operations. That evening the instructions were embodied in Special Orders, No. 191, and issued to the commanders who were to play an independent role in the expedition. Four days later a copy of this document fell into the hands of the Federals, and—ever after known as the "lost orders"—they became the most famous orders of the Civil War. Historical fascination has centered on the mysteries surrounding their loss, their discovery, and the inability of George McClellan to capitalize on the incredible opportunity fate provided him. What has been obscured in the controversy is the equally significant story of the writing of Special Orders, No. 191.

Prior to the 9th, Lee had not viewed the Federal garrisons as posing a serious problem. Of course, he realized that enemy troops could not be allowed to sit squarely on his proposed supply line, and he had worried briefly on his ride to Frederick on the 6th about the sound of artillery fire from the direction of Harpers Ferry. He had put the matter out of mind, however, confidently assuming "that as soon as it was known that the army had reached Fredericktown, the enemy's forces in the Valley of Virginia . . . would retreat altogether from the State." He had logically expected the garrisons to withdraw as soon as they perceived the danger of being isolated, because he saw nothing that the Federals stood to gain by sacrificing these troops. "In this I was disappointed," he would write to Davis in hindsight from Hagerstown three days later.[67] He had failed to account for the confusion and cross-purposes among the Federal high command that would defy logic and order the garrisons to hold out to the last man with no larger gain in view than avoiding the appearance of cowardice.

So confident had Lee been that he may also have been somewhat careless. There is no firm evidence that he monitored the situation in the lower Shenandoah as closely as he should have. It would have been reasonable to leave a cavalry force south of the river to scout toward Harpers Ferry and vicinity, but, if Lee did so, he left only a very small force and did not receive timely intelligence from it.[68] It was not until after he reached Frederick—and then almost by accident—that Lee is known to have taken concrete action to gather information about the Valley by sending Lige White and his company of scouts to the area.

On the 6th or 7th, after the task of guiding Jackson's column into Maryland had been completed, White and his previously autonomous command were ordered to report to Jeb Stuart. Both cavalry leaders possessed towering egos, and on this occasion they clashed spontaneously. Stuart saw no immediate use for a band of irregulars of doubtful discipline, and he ordered White to return to Leesburg and remain in Virginia to watch for Federal movements from the direction of Dranesville and Fairfax. As a Marylander, White was outraged at being ordered away from the campaign to liberate his native state. The two carried their argument to Lee's tent, where the Confederate commander rendered a decision that pleased both men. Lee ordered White "to scout towards Harpers Ferry" and report back directly to him.[69]

Quite possibly, therefore, it was a report sent back by White that Lee received on the afternoon of the 9th that convinced him the Federal garrisons were not going to withdraw of their own volition. Whatever the impetus, Lee apparently concluded he ought to reconsider his plan for a simple movement of the army in the direction of Hagerstown. His experiences in Frederick suggested that such provisions as he might acquire in Hagerstown would be insufficient to feed his army; and, "in order to remain for any time" in western Maryland, he would have "to haul from the Valley of Virginia" food and clothing, as well as ordnance supplies.[70] This he could not do so long as the enemy continued to block communications with the depot he had established at Winchester. He might be able to accomplish several objectives at once, however, if he sent part of his army against the Federal garrisons, while moving with the remainder to Hagerstown. He assumed the enemy—no matter how foolish until now—would not stand in the face of a direct movement against them. The operation could be completed in a matter of days, and the army reunited in ample time to maneuver against the slowly advancing column from Washington. Naturally, as soon as he contemplated an independent mission, he turned to Stonewall Jackson.

Whether Lee called Jackson to headquarters, or simply took advantage of a coincidental visit, is not known.[71] In either case, Lee's proposal may have taken Jackson by surprise. The fact that Jed. Hotchkiss, Jackson's topographer, spent the 9th making a map of Hagerstown's Washington County suggests that Stonewall was not thinking about recrossing the Potomac, when he visited Lee's tent during the afternoon. If so, Jackson had his own surprise for Lee, for, in the beginning, Stonewall advised against sending an expedition to clear the Valley. After the battle of Fredericksburg in December, Jackson told his brother-in-law, D. H. Hill, in confidence, "At the council held in Frederick, I opposed the separation of our forces in order to capture Harper's Ferry. I urged that we should all be kept together." As Jackson understood the situation outlined by Lee, there were three options. First, the army could move toward Hagerstown and ignore the Federal garrisons. Jackson agreed this would be unwise. Second, the army could divide and simultaneously move on Hagerstown and eliminate the Federal garrisons. Jackson thought this would be too complicated and too risky. Third, the army could remain united east of the mountains and await the advance of the Federals from Washington. This course Jackson suggested as best.[72]

From this point in the meeting until Longstreet's arrival near its close, the only direct evidence on what occurred is a brief remark made by Lee after the war. Indirect evidence comes from the inferences that can be drawn from the orders issued as a result of the council.

Lee may have explained that Jackson's preferred course was out of the question. The Confederates could not remain east of the mountains, due to the growing difficulty in finding supplies in the Frederick area and because the line through Leesburg and Warrenton had to be abandoned as unsafe. Additionally, it was necessary to draw the Federals as far from Washington as possible before engaging them, as the opportunity for maneuver would increase in proportion to the length of their supply line and their distance from their base. It was not a question of whether to move westward, but of what to do about the Federal garrisons in the Valley. Presumably, when the problem was put in this light, Jackson dropped his objections and joined with some enthusiasm in planning the details of the operation.[73]

The original plan for the reduction of the Federal garrisons has been obscured both by the modifications made to it even before Special Orders, No. 191, was issued as well as the changes adopted afterward. By concentrating on the wording of the orders as issued and by removing the suggestions made by Longstreet, it is possible to see the operations as first envisioned by Lee and Jackson. It is also possible to discern the two suppositions on which the plan was originally based, and why at least Lee believed the expedition would succeed.

The first and most obvious assumption underlying the plan was that, as Lee put it in his report, "The advance of the Federal army was so slow at the time we left Fredericktown as to justify the belief that the reduction of Harper's Ferry would be accomplished and our troops concentrated before they would be called upon to meet them." After the war, Lee would make it clear that he had relied on the reports from Stuart, whose "cavalry was close up to the enemy," that the Federal army "was moving only a few miles every day, feeling its way with great caution." In fact, he would remember being told that the "uneasy and uncertain" enemy had only reached Rockville.[74] If Lee projected that same rate of advance into the future, he could have concluded the Federals would not even reach Frederick by the time the expedition had finished.

The second assumption underlying the plan was Lee's belief that the expedition would be carried out quickly and easily. This assumption is equally plain, but it has been obscured because subsequent events proved it entirely wrong. Initially, Lee allocated a relatively small force for the expedition, and he allotted only three days for its completion from start to finish. He did not foresee a siege as necessary, because the garrisons—which he believed to be weak[75]—would attempt to escape as soon as they perceived a force moving directly against them. In his report and in two postwar letters Lee used "dislodge" to describe what he expected the expedition to do to the Federal garrisons.[76] This does not mean he aimed merely to chase the enemy from the Valley, although he probably would have settled for that result. He hoped to move so rapidly that the Federals would be caught in flight, or, as he explained in an 1868 conversation, he wanted "to overwhelm . . . and if possible catch them."[77]

The specific objective of the mission, therefore, would be to move as rapidly as possible to block the Federals' routes of escape. Both garrisons would probably attempt to retreat northward, and a force moving on Martinsburg by way of Sharpsburg would be likeliest to intercept them. This would be the most important Confederate column, and it would need be the largest and best led. This would be Jackson's assignment, and he could take with him as much of his command as he believed would be required.

If any of the Federals should be caught in Harpers Ferry itself, Confederate possession of the towering Maryland Heights across the Potomac would quickly compel their flight or surrender. Both Jackson and Lee understood thoroughly the topography of Harpers Ferry, and both believed the capture of Maryland Heights was tantamount to the capture of the town. Stonewall had demonstrated this belief as early as May 1861.[78] The secondary column sent to occupy the heights could be composed of one of the newly arrived and unattached divisions, such as McLaws's.

Finally, Federal flight either south or east was not likely. Nonetheless, Walker's small division, already on its way to the mouth of the Monocacy, could be utilized to block that route as well. If Walker could move quickly enough, he could recross the Potomac and advance on Loudoun Heights in time to ensnare any enemy fleeing from that direction.

In the meanwhile, Lee with the main body, consisting of Longstreet's three divisions (D. R. Jones, Evans, and Wilcox), R. H. Anderson's division, and the Reserve Artillery, would march on to Hagerstown to secure provisions rumored to be in that region and threaten Pennsylvania. Stuart and the cavalry would remain east of the mountains to observe and retard the movements of the Federals from Washington. And, as the last element of the plan, D. H. Hill would take position at Boonsboro at the western foot of South Mountain "to intercept fugitives from Harpers Ferry and support the cavalry, if needed."[79]

It was after these essential points had been established that Lee heard Longstreet's distinctive voice beyond the tent fly and immediately invited him to join the conference.[80] Whether Lee had intentionally excluded his senior subordinate from the planning of the expedition, perhaps because of Longstreet's earlier opposition to any movement against Harpers Ferry, or the exclusion was accidental, the result was the same. Longstreet found himself confronting a fait accompli. With Jackson apparently "heartily approving" the plan, Longstreet did not attempt to oppose the movement. He did try to reform it considerably, however.

First, he argued that the entire Army of Northern Virginia ought to be used to move against the garrisons. Lee rejected this suggestion, probably because he was confident so large a force would not be required, and because he may have feared the flour and beef in Hagerstown might be sent out of his reach in the meantime. More fundamentally, however, Lee may have wished to avoid giving even the appearance that his crossing the Potomac was a mere raid to isolate Harpers Ferry—a rumor already afloat in Northern newspapers. If he were going to set the stage for inflicting so crushing a blow on the enemy that it might tilt the scales of the war, then he needed the Federals to take his campaign with such grave earnestness that they would hazard their demoralized army to thwart him.

Thus far, it seemed Lee had been almost too successful in threatening Washington and Baltimore. Stuart's reports suggested that one reason the enemy advanced so slowly was that they had formed an "extended front" to protect both cities from attack. This was the reason the Confederates must shift the threat to Pennsylvania and try to induce the enemy to move away from his capital. To move the entire army toward Harpers Ferry would give the wrong impression and might encourage the Federals to focus their attention south of the Potomac.[81]

Undaunted, Longstreet next urged that the Confederate army should not be so badly fractured and that the main body should remain at Boonsboro with D.H. Hill. To this Lee acquiesced, although the final rendering in Special Orders, No. 191, would read ambiguously that the army was to reunite at either Boonsboro or Hagerstown. Apparently, Lee was willing to consider foregoing both the provisions at Hagerstown and the immediate threat to Pennsylvania, so long as the central column maintained pressure on Maryland and Washington and avoided the appearance of a retreat to Virginia. Finally, Longstreet successfully persuaded Lee to augment the force to be sent directly against Harpers Ferry from Maryland Heights. He suggested the three brigades of R.H. Anderson's division be added to McLaws. Again, Lee agreed—at least to the extent that he would offer part of Anderson to McLaws.[82]

Although Longstreet's modifications only slightly affected the strategy of Lee's plan, they substantially altered the strength of the columns. Lee originally intended to send Jackson with 20,000 men and twenty-one batteries to Martinsburg, McLaws with 7,000 men and five batteries to Maryland Heights, and Walker with 5,000 men and two batteries to Loudoun Heights. Thus, the expedition would have totaled 32,000 men with twenty-eight batteries and have comprised 48 percent of the army's infantry. Longstreet and the Reserve Artillery with 26,000 men and thirty-seven batteries (39 percent) would have gone on to Hagerstown, while D. H. Hill with 8,000 men and nine batteries would have remained at Boonsboro.

According to the revised plan which transferred Anderson to McLaws and retained Longstreet and the Artillery Reserve at Boonsboro, the army would be divided into four columns instead of five. The expeditionary force would now total 38,000 men with thirty-two batteries, or more than half (58 percent) of the army. The central column, or main

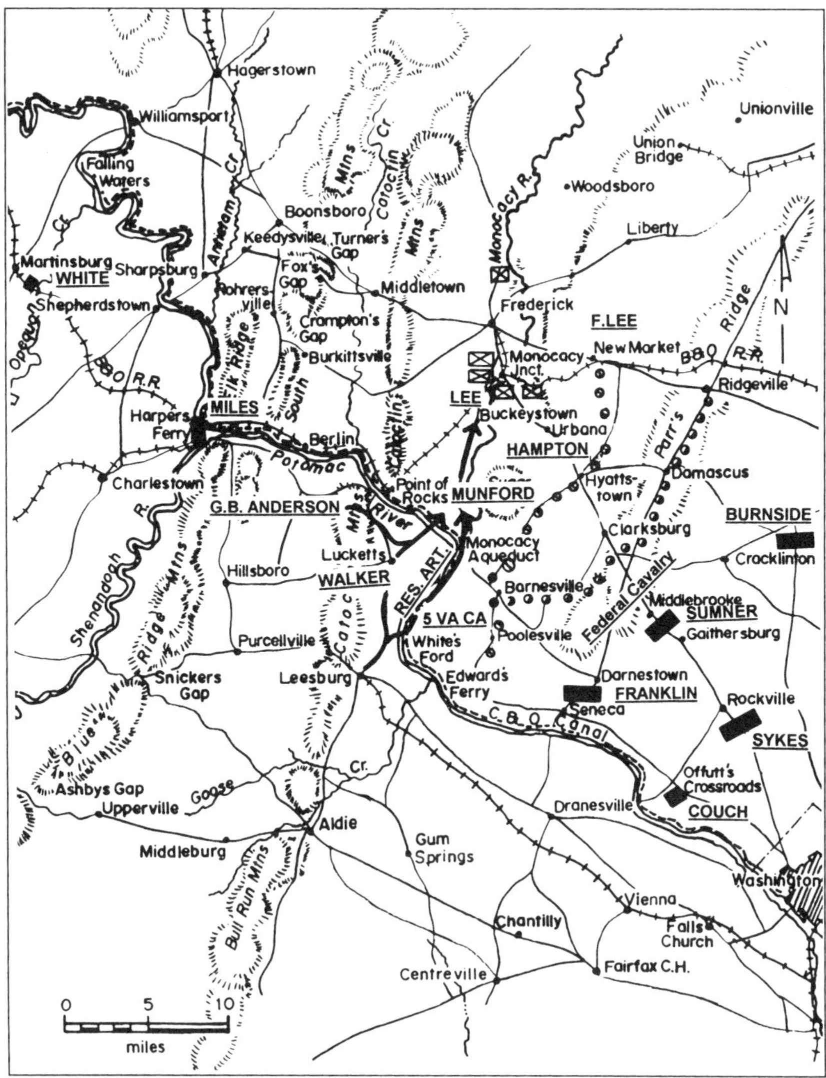

The line of the Monocacy, September 7–9

body, would combine Longstreet and D. H. Hill and comprise 28,000 men and forty-two batteries, or 42 percent of the army.[83]

At some point during the meeting—whether before or after Longstreet joined is unclear—it was decided that the movement ought to be launched with some haste. Lee and Jackson undoubtedly wanted to increase the chance of capturing the garrisons before they escaped to safety. On the other hand, Longstreet—and perhaps Jackson agreed on this point as well—wished to shorten the time the army would be divided. Even though the conference broke up in the late afternoon or early evening, it was determined that the orders would be issued immediately and the march set to start at dawn the following morning. Hence, seven sets of the famous S.O. 191 were hastily copied on the night of the 9th and delivered to Jackson, Longstreet, McLaws, Walker, Stuart, Pendleton, and D. H. Hill. To five of these commanders the orders must have come as quite a surprise.[84]

The Writing of Special Orders, No. 191

As finally issued, the format and language of this controversial document would not be the least of the ambiguities and mysteries surrounding it. Three extant copies have been located. The first is the copy sent to Richmond and entered into the permanent files of the Confederate adjutant and inspector general. Presumably, it is the copy Lee included in his dispatch to Davis on September 12 from Hagerstown. It was this version that was published by the editors of the *Official Records.* Today it is in the National Archives and is referred to below as the Lee-DNA copy.[85]

Ironically, both the second and third copies were addressed to D. H. Hill. The one sent from Lee's headquarters—which after the war Hill and his adjutant would swear was never delivered to Hill's headquarters—is the copy the Federals found on September 13 on the ground in Frederick wrapped around three cigars. Today it is in the McClellan Papers at the Library of Congress and is referred to below as the McClellan-DLC copy.[86]

The other is a copy sent by Jackson in his own hand to D. H. Hill. Stonewall assumed that military protocol demanded he notify Hill, since the latter had been assigned to him at the time of the crossing and had not subsequently been officially detached. Hill would go to great lengths after the war to demonstrate that this was the only copy he received and the only one he should have received. He had Joseph G. Morrison, Jackson's brother-in-law and aide, certify the authenticity of the handwriting, although this was hardly necessary since Hill was also Jackson's brother-in-law. He acquired an affidavit from his adjutant, J. W. Ratchford, swearing that only one copy of the order arrived at headquarters; and he secured a statement from his quartermaster, John D. Rogers, attesting that all orders regarding wagontrains and supplies had been issued through Jackson. Today this version of the orders is in the D. H. Hill Papers in the North Carolina State Archives and below is referred to as the Hill-Nc-Ar copy.[87]

Hill was unquestionably correct in his explanation of the reason Jackson sent him a copy of Special Orders, No. 191. Lee's staff and Lee himself came to the same conclusion after the war.[88] Yet, at the time, Lee had not intended Jackson's control over Hill to extend beyond September 5 and part of September 6, the period when Jackson commanded everything north of the Potomac. Once Lee reached Frederick the special arrangement ended, and Hill was again considered unattached. For that reason Lee's staff prepared a copy of S.O. 191 to send to Hill directly. Apparently, Lee was careless in not making it clear to either Jackson or D. H. Hill that the command arrangement was temporary.

How the copy from Lee to Hill was lost is one of the great mysteries of the war. The sensitive nature of the information in Special Orders, No. 191, should have been obvious to all who were aware of its contents. Longstreet memorized the details and then chewed up the orders; Walker pinned his inside his coat; and Jackson did not trust the copying to a staff member. It is true that—except for the one masticated by Longstreet—the ultimate fate of the copies to McLaws, Stuart, Pendleton (if indeed he received one), and even those of Walker and Jackson, are unknown.[89] But, their fate is irrelevant to the story of the lost orders, since none would have had D. H. Hill's name on it, as did the copy that ended up in McClellan's hands.

It would seem that the errant orders were lost at Hill's headquarters, or Lee's, or somewhere in between. The likelihood of their loss in transmission, or the presence of a traitor among the couriers, has been discounted, because orderlies were required to obtain signed receipts to verify safe delivery of documents.[90] The favored theory among historians has been that two copies did reach Hill; and, once one was perceived as a duplicate, it was treated carelessly. There is absolutely no proof, however, that the copy ever left Lee's headquarters, or that it was not returned as a duplicate. Moreover, at least up until the present, the fact that Hill and Lee were camped "within sight of each other" in Best's Grove, while the orders, as best as can be determined, were found two miles away on the Myers farm, had merely deepened the mystery.[91] The newly discovered fact that clogged roads prevented Hill's division from marching through Frederick on the 10th and that he spent the night near the Myers farm would seem to bear out the conclusion that the orders were lost from his headquarters.

Although of consuming interest to many, the manner in which the orders were lost—at least in light of the few details of that story as are now known—is not of great importance to an understanding of Lee and his strategy in the campaign. What is crucial to such an understanding is what the orders did and did not say.

The text explicated below is the version most widely accepted as the "real" S.O. 191. It is the Lee-DNA copy as printed in the *Official Records* and consists of ten articles.[92]

> Special Orders, No. 191
>
> Hdqrs. Army of Northern Virginia
>
> September 9, 1862
>
> I. The citizens of Fredericktown being unwilling, while overrun by members of this army, to open their stores, in order to give them confidence, and to secure to officers and men purchasing supplies for benefit of this command, all officers and men of this army are strictly prohibited from visiting Fredericktown except on business, in which case they will bear evidence of this in writing from division commanders. The provost-marshal in Fredericktown will see that his guard rigidly enforces this order.

While of little direct significance to the strategy of the campaign, the mysteries of this first article are among the most intriguing of the entire order.

(1) What is it even doing here? Special orders were supposed to instruct an individual or a small group and were intended for restricted circulation. These instructions regarding passes applied to everyone in the army, and they should have been issued in general orders to be read at the head of each regiment.

(2) Although they have not been found in written form, orders requiring passes to visit Frederick were already in effect. This is demonstrated in the well known anecdote of Jackson writing himself a pass to attend church on the night of the 7th.[93] Were new orders required because the old ones had proven ineffective? Were the old ones merely verbal? Had they been issued from only Jackson's headquarters? Had they permitted commanders at lower levels—say, brigade or regiment—to issue passes?

(3) The first sentence, which may have been hastily transcribed, is a poorly constructed and monstrous run-on that appears to be missing a

word or phrase. It is not clear what is to be secured to "officers and men purchasing supplies for the benefit of this command"? The most likely intent of the order is to clear the city of soldiers transacting private business to make it easier for officials of the commissary and quartermaster corps to acquire supplies for the entire army. Perhaps a word such as "advantage" or "benefit" should have been inserted after "secure." If this reading is correct, it would confirm the impression that the citizens of Frederick had responded humanely to the needs of individual soldiers, but most did not wish to conduct business with agents of the rebel government.[94]

(4) Why would this article have been issued in any manner or form late on the 9th of September? Why issue orders governing visits to Frederick, when the army would be leaving the area in less than twelve hours?

(5) Was this paragraph drafted either on the 8th, or very early on the 9th, and awaiting additional articles before being issued? In other words, was it written before Lee decided to leave the area? Were the Harpers Ferry instructions appended casually, almost inadvertently to an "in-preparation" general order?

(6) In fact, this first article may never have been issued. It is omitted in both the McClellan-DLC and Hill-Nc-Ar copies. Or, perhaps, it may have been issued standing alone earlier than the 9th and entered incorrectly in the headquarters order book. Maj. Walter Taylor, who usually "supervised the promulgation" of orders, left for Leesburg before S.O. 191 was issued, and whoever filled his function may have been careless or unfamiliar with the routine.[95]

> II. Major Taylor will proceed to Leesburg, Va., and arrange for transportation of the sick and those unable to walk to Winchester, securing the transportation of the country for this purpose. The route between this and Culpeper Court-House east of the mountains will no longer be traveled. Those on the way to this army already across the river will move up promptly; all others will proceed to Winchester collectively and under command of officers, at which point, being the general depot of this army, its movements will be known and instructions given by the commanding officer regulating further movements.

(1) There is no mention of Taylor's mission to Jefferson Davis. Was this assignment already determined and this paragraph already drafted,

when Lee received Davis's letter? Did he then decide to use Taylor to stop the president in addition to the other tasks? On the other hand, it is possible Lee got the idea of sending Taylor back after receiving Davis's letter and decided his aide could also be effective in directing traffic into the Valley. For security reasons, he may have intentionally avoided mentioning the fact that the president of the Confederacy was traveling near the country's frontier.

(2) As it is written, this article is not necessarily connected with the Harpers Ferry expedition. For nearly a week, Lee had been trying to break up the route through Manassas and Leesburg as unsafe, and he could well have decided to send back a staff officer to force traffic into the Valley even before he had determined to move from Frederick. Indeed, the permission granted to those on their way to continue reads as if Lee did not expect to be leaving within twelve or so hours. Moreover, since Taylor left Frederick at noon, this article was almost certainly drafted before the conference with Jackson and Longstreet.[96]

(3) This article was clearly meant to be special instructions for Taylor, as well as his authority for ordering higher ranking officers to cooperate with his mission. It was omitted from the McClellan-DLC and Hill Nc-Ar copies, and likely it was not included in any of the copies sent to commanders of the Harpers Ferry expedition. Taylor, on the other hand, would have received only this second paragraph, if indeed it was ready by the time he departed.[97]

(4) In regard to the responsibilities assigned to Taylor, it is not easy to see how one man traveling alone could be expected to impound sufficient transportation and collect the widely scattered sick and wounded soldiers. The orders seem to imply Taylor was to travel as far as Culpeper. After learning Davis had returned to Richmond, however, Taylor would go no farther than Warrenton before heading west to Winchester. In fact, the major spent no longer than a night in Leesburg. He seems to have paid relatively little attention to his task of shifting communications and within four days was hurrying back to join the army at Hagerstown. It raises the possibility that Lee invented a cover story for Taylor's true mission, which was to divert Davis. This suspicion is strengthened by a letter Taylor wrote to his sister from Winchester on the 12th. In it he implies the only reason he went to Winchester was because the route back through Leesburg was no longer safe: "I was sent from Frederick City Maryland to meet his Ex. the President & Ex Govr Lowe. Failing to meet them at Leesburg, I proceeded to Winchester [Warrenton] & there learned that his Ex had returned to Richmond &

the Govr had left for this place—so I was compelled to trudge along this way, since I could not return by the old route the army having moved & that being considered unsafe."[98]

> III. The Army will resume its march to-morrow, taking the Hagerstown road. General Jackson's command will form the advance, and, after passing Middletown, with such portions as he may select, take the route toward Sharpsburg, cross the Potomac at the most convenient point, and by Friday morning take possession of the Baltimore and Ohio Railroad, capture such of them as may be at Martinsburg, and intercept such as may attempt to escape from Harper's Ferry.

(1) This is the first article of Special Orders, No. 191, to deal with the expedition against the Federal garrisons in the Shenandoah Valley. It is also the first to appear in the McClellan-DLC and Hill-Nc-Ar copies, although it is headed III in both.

(2) Curiously, no time is set for the start of the march even though the vanguard would set the pace for the entire column. This may mean that a specific time was not determined until after the orders were issued. Or, it may be an example of the discretion that Lee frequently—and sometimes injuriously—extended to his subordinates. In any case, Jackson issued his own orders late on the 9th, setting dawn (which would have been around 5:45) as the starting time, and Longstreet put out a circular naming five o'clock for his command to be ready.[99]

(3) Apparently, Lee and Jackson had not determined in conversation how many of his three divisions Stonewall should take with him on the expedition. Possibly the two had mildly disagreed on the point. In any case, Lee must not have believed the mission absolutely required all of Jackson's men, or he would not have given his subordinate this discretion. There is no evidence, however, that Jackson ever considered taking less than his whole command.

(4) Jackson is specifically ordered toward Sharpsburg, but he is given the freedom to select where he will ford the Potomac. He may have been allowed this additional discretion either to take advantage of local information about the fords, or to be able to respond to any countermoves the enemy might have made. The route through Sharpsburg would have brought Jackson directly against Martinsburg from the east, and it was not well suited to block an alert enemy trying to escape northward.

(5) This article reads as if it were not contemplated that Jackson would have to go to Harpers Ferry. He was to operate against the B&O and Martinsburg and "intercept" any enemy trying to escape from Harpers Ferry. Stonewall was to do this by "Friday morning," the same time given in Article V for McLaws to capture Maryland Heights and the enemy at Harpers Ferry. Lee clearly gives the impression that he expected the enemy to flee to avoid capture and that a siege would not be necessary.

(6) In his official report, Lee stated Jackson's mission differently: "General Jackson was directed to proceed with his command to Martinsburg, and, after driving the enemy from that place, to move down the south side of the Potomac upon Harper's Ferry."[100] Plainly, these were not the directions embodied in Special Orders, No. 191. Did Lee conveniently modify history to reflect the way events turned out? Or, were there verbal instructions to Jackson in addition to S.O. 191?

(7) A controversy that developed after the war sheds some light on the discrepancy. In February 1868, D. H. Hill published an article in defense of his role in regard to S.O. 191. Not only did he maintain he was not responsible for losing the orders, but he went on to argue that the orders confused McClellan and their loss was actually a boon to the Confederates. Hill contended that S.O. 191 implied Jackson was to return directly to Boonsboro from Martinsburg and this implication misled the Federals into believing a considerable body of Confederates opposed them at South Mountain.[101] After reading Hill's article, Lee reacted angrily to the suggestion that Jackson had violated orders and commented that Hill was: "mistaken in regard to Genl. Jackson's move to Harper's Ferry being contrary to or without orders. That even if he did not receive written orders to that effect, he remembers distinctly that in a private conversation with Genl. Jackson, the movements were agreed upon."[102] In another conversation on the same day, Lee said: "but this had all been fully explained to Jackson verbally, and no one could imagine that the order did not contemplate just what Jackson did."[103]

Lee's postwar remarks should be taken to mean that in the council of war the two discussed the possibility the enemy might not flee from Harpers Ferry, and Jackson had been given the authority to follow through on the mission to its completion, whatever that might require. Lee's comments do not contradict the clear implication of S.O. 191, however, that at the time he did not anticipate such a course would be necessary. And, finally, this is confirmed by a statement Lee would make in a letter to Jefferson Davis on the 12th from Hagerstown, while awaiting the results of the expedition. After telling the president that the Federals had not withdrawn from Martinsburg and Harpers Ferry as earlier expected, he would write: "Generals Jackson and McLaws have been detached with a view of capturing their forces at each place should they not have retired."[104]

(8) The assignment of Jackson with permission to take his entire command—a force of 20,000 infantry and artillery present for duty, including twenty-one batteries—confirmed that Lee believed this column was the most critical part of the expedition.

(9) Finally, there is another indication of carelessness or haste in the preparation or transcription of Special Orders, No. 191. In the phrase "capture such of them" that appears near the end of the second sentence, the pronoun has no antecedent. In the McClellan-DLC and Hill-Nc-Ar copies "them" is replaced by "the enemy."

> IV. General Longstreet's command will pursue the main road as far as Boonsborough, where it will halt, with reserve, supply and baggage trains of the army.

(1) Thus, according to orders as published, Longstreet was to halt at Boonsboro. This indicates that at least temporarily Lee had accepted Longstreet's suggestion and suspended his plans to proceed on to Hagerstown during the Harpers Ferry expedition.

(2) This main body, after the transfer of Anderson to McLaws, would total 15,000 infantry and artillery, with thirty-three batteries.

(3) As is made clear in the next article, Longstreet was to be second in the column of march. Thus, somewhat curiously, the organization of S.O. 191 is patterned after the sequence of the column. If Lee had viewed the expedition as a tightly knit force under Jackson, it would have made sense to treat it as such in the orders. Instead, each unit is simply split off from the line and sent on what appears to be an independent mission.

> V. General McLaws, with his own division and that of R. H. Anderson, will follow General Longstreet. On reaching Middletown will take the route to Harper's Ferry, and by Friday morning possess himself of the Maryland Heights and endeavor to capture the enemy at Harper's Ferry and vicinity.

(1) Notice that the assignment of this column was to capture the Federal force and not the town. There may be no mention of blocking an

escape route, because it was not expected the enemy would flee to the northeast, as that would have been toward Frederick and the known direction of the Confederate army.

(2) The assumption underlying McLaws's mission was that possession of Maryland Heights would be enough to assure the enemy would vacate Harpers Ferry or surrender. And, according to McLaws's report, he did indeed act on the belief that "if we gained possession of the heights, the town was no longer tenable to them."[105]

(3) Lee must not have viewed the task of this column as particularly difficult or critical, or he would not have assigned it to the recently arrived and relatively untested McLaws. If he believed this to be the key role in the expedition, he ought to have given it to Jackson and sent someone else to Martinsburg. Or, he could have assigned the occupation of Maryland Heights to Longstreet, or even to D. H. Hill, who had led the army in the crossing of the Potomac. Was Lee testing his new people? Would he have done so, if he believed the fate of the expedition was at stake?

(4) Lee originally intended this mission to be entrusted solely to McLaws with his division of 7,000 infantry and artillery present for duty, including five batteries. This is another indication the Confederate commander viewed the Maryland Heights column to be of secondary importance to Jackson's. After Longstreet convinced Lee to add R. H. Anderson's division—and the following day talked Lee into adding Wilcox's three brigades to Anderson—McLaws would take with him nearly 18,000 infantry and artillery present for duty, with nine batteries. Hence, as finally constituted, McLaws's column would approximate Jackson's in men. It is curious, however, considering the nature of McLaws's assignment, that he would be much inferior to Jackson in cannon, and that no high-ranking artillerist would be sent along to supervise the firing from the Heights.

(5) McLaws was also assigned the deadline of Friday morning, September 12. In his case, however, the deadline was for both possession of Maryland Heights and the capture of the enemy in the area. Once again the two are viewed as virtually synonymous.

(6) Finally, as another indication of the carelessness or haste surrounding S.O. 191, it should be noted that the first clause of the second sentence of this article is missing a subject. The McClellan-DLC copy is exactly the same, while the Hill-Nc-Ar copy—which Jackson copied from his own copy—inserts an ampersand to create a run-on sentence, indicating Stonewall perceived the grammatical flaw and corrected it.

> VI. General Walker, with his division, after accomplishing the object in which he is now engaged, will cross the Potomac at Cheek's Ford, ascend its right bank to Lovettsville, take possession of Loudoun Heights, if practicable by Friday morning, Key's Ford on his left, and the road between the end of the mountain and the Potomac on his right. He will, as far as practicable, co-operate with Generals McLaws and Jackson, and intercept the enemy.

(1) This indicates Lee had not only previously given Walker the assignment to destroy the aqueduct but that he knew the general had already departed. Since Walker's division left Frederick at five o'clock, this suggests S.O. 191 must have been written after that time.[106]

(2) Walker is given more precise directions than any other commander. Why? His task was not more difficult. Does it suggest Lee had not talked in detail with him about the Harpers Ferry expedition in the interview earlier in the day?

(3) Walker's division totaled 5,000 infantry and artillery (two batteries) present for duty, and was significantly the weakest of the columns.

(4) With "practicable" twice repeated in this article, it would seem Lee did not place great reliance on Walker being able to accomplish his mission in the time allotted. Clearly Walker's role was considered to be the minor one in the expedition. Apparently, his main job was to prevent enemy escape by Key's Ford on the Shenandoah River and by the road next to the Potomac. Of course, unless Walker had been able to occupy Loudoun Heights and vicinity, there could have been no true siege.

(5) In this article is the only mention of cooperation during the expedition—and it is specifically "to intercept retreat of the enemy." Again, it seems Lee anticipated he would catch the enemy in flight, and it would not be necessary to undertake a siege.

> VII. General D. H. Hill's division will form the rear guard of the army, pursuing the road taken by the main body. The reserve artillery, ordinance, and supply trains, &c., will precede General Hill.

(1) With this last bit of information, the sequence of the column of march for the 10th was set as follows: Jackson, Longstreet, McLaws, the trains, and D. H. Hill.

(2) Hill had 8,000 infantry and artillery (nine batteries) present for duty, including Cutts's battalion of the Artillery Reserve, which was still attached to his command.

(3) Curiously, no destination is named for Hill. The implication is that he is now part of the "main body" and would proceed all the way to Boonsboro. Longstreet's recollection that Hill was to support the cavalry is not specifically reflected in Special Orders, 191. This responsibility may not have been added until after the decision to split the central column on the 10th.

> VIII. General Stuart will detach a squadron of cavalry to accompany the commands of Generals Longstreet, Jackson and McLaws, and with the main body of the cavalry, will cover the route of the army, bringing up all stragglers that may have been left behind.

(1) According to the trimonthly estimate of September 1, Stuart then had available 5,664 cavalry and artillery present for duty with three batteries. His strength was probably about 4,500 on the 10th, allowing for detachments and the losses due to the series of skirmishes that had taken place daily.[107]

(2) Lee's distribution of this sizable cavalry force is curious in several respects. The phrase "will cover the route of the army" would seem to imply Stuart was to accompany and protect the entire column on the march. If Lee believed, as he probably did, that the only danger to the army came from the Federal force advancing from Washington, it is possible to stretch this phrase to mean Stuart's main force would remain east of the mountains and thus protect the distant rear of the Confederate army. Still, from that position he would not be able to bring up the stragglers left behind in the march. While it is entirely possible that Lee explained the role of the cavalry to Stuart in person, it is unlikely the cavalry chief received much useful information from S.O. 191.

(3) As reflected in S.O. 191, Lee once again—as in the case of the march through Thoroughfare Gap and the crossing of the Potomac—seems to have placed relatively small value on the use of cavalry to lead and protect columns marching into unknown situations. The orders assign a squadron (two companies) each to Jackson and McLaws. Approximately one hundred troopers would perhaps be enough to scout in advance and prevent running into a trap, but they would be scarcely sufficient to protect the flanks and rear or to engage an enemy cavalry force of any size. Lee must have had no clue that the enemy had 1,300 horsemen at Martinsburg and Harpers Ferry.

(4) Even granting Lee such ignorance, however, a squadron each seems a woefully inadequate force for Jackson and McLaws to accomplish their mission to capture an enemy expected to flee. Not only were there myriad possible escape routes to be covered, but, once the direction of the enemy was discovered, cavalry would be needed to harass and slow his progress until the infantry arrived. Also, inexplicably, no cavalry whatsoever was assigned to Walker.

(5) Furthermore, if Lee did intend from the start for the bulk of the cavalry to remain east of the mountains to confront the Federals advancing from Washington—in spite of the contrary wording of S.O. 191—then he had assigned only a single squadron of cavalry to cover the entire main body of the army, including Longstreet, the trains, and D. H. Hill. Whether this central column remained at Boonsboro or went on to Hagerstown, it would be seriously deficient in cavalry protection. Accustomed to operating in his home territory, where sympathetic citizens could be relied upon to provide intelligence, Lee apparently saw no reason to adjust his thinking north of the Potomac.

(6) As originally written, the cavalry provisions of S.O. 191 may have reflected both the haste in which the orders were issued and Lee's optimism in the speed and ease with which the various missions could be concluded. Lee modified these instructions almost at once, probably as early as the 10th. The 7th Virginia Cavalry (of Munford) would accompany Jackson's column; and the 1st Virginia Cavalry (of Fitz Lee) would be assigned to Longstreet. There is no evidence, however, that any cavalry operated with McLaws, Walker, or D. H. Hill.

> IX. The commands of Generals Jackson, McLaws, and Walker, after accomplishing the objects for which they have been detached, will join the main body of the army at Boonsborough or Hagerstown.

(1) There is no indication these columns were to join each other at any point, or to come under Jackson's command. Each commander was separately responsible for returning to the main body after the completion of his mission.

(2) At this point, before later modifications, the main body is presumably meant to include Longstreet, D. H. Hill, the trains, and Lee.

(3) The final three words of this article indicate Longstreet had not entirely won his point with Lee. Although article 4 specified that

Longstreet was to halt at Boonsboro, Lee here reserved his option to move on to Hagerstown during the several days required for the Valley expedition.

> X. Each regiment on the march will habitually carry its axes in the regimental wagons, for use of the men at their encampments, to procure wood, &c.

(1) This is a curious anticlimax to an important order. It was included in both the McClellan-DLC and Hill-Nc-Ar copies and must be considered as an integral part of S.O. 191. Apparently, some special problem had developed in regard to axes not being conveniently at hand, which required emphasis be given to this standard procedure.

> By command of General R. E. Lee:
>
> R. H. Chilton
> Assistant Adjutant-General

(1) This is the normal closure, and Chilton was the officer who more often than not who signed general and special orders in Lee's name.

(2) Nevertheless, Walter Taylor makes a special point in his memoirs that he had left for Leesburg and was not present to "supervise the promulgation" of S.O. 191.[108] This suggests it was normally Taylor's responsibility to make the copies, see to their delivery, verify receipt, transcribe the headquarters copy, and in general supervise the clerical aspects of issuing orders. If this were the case, and someone less familiar with the procedures acted in his stead, some of the inconsistencies and seeming carelessness surrounding Special Orders, No. 191, become more understandable.

After the war council with Jackson and Longstreet had ended, and while the Special Orders were being drawn up and issued, Lee called two division commanders to his tent. In two separate meetings, Lee orally explained part of the details of the Valley expedition. His words give further insight into how the Confederate commander originally conceived the problem of the Federal garrisons and how he intended to solve it.

Maj. Gen. LaFayette McLaws, who was encamped on the left bank of the Monocacy, later recalled that evening had fallen when an orderly summoned him to army headquarters.[109] With little in the way of preliminaries, Lee told McLaws: "the whole army would move the next morning (Wednesday), taking the Hagerstown road, and that Gen. R.H.

Anderson of South Carolina would be directed to report to me, and that I would follow with Anderson's and my own division in the rear of the army, until, reaching Middletown, I would take the route to Harpers Ferry, and by Friday morning, the 12th, possess myself of Maryland Heights, and endeavor to capture the enemy at Harpers Ferry and vicinity."[110] The startled McLaws at once confessed that he "had never been to Harpers Ferry," nor even "in the vicinity." Lee replied "intimating that it did not matter."

The Confederate commander went on to observe that reports placed seven or eight thousand men in the garrison, but he "inclined to think the number was exaggerated." He believed there was not more than three or four thousand at Harpers Ferry.[111] On that basis, he asked McLaws if the mission might not be carried out with his own division alone, or at most the addition of a brigade or two from Anderson.

In response, and thinking quickly no doubt, McLaws assembled every argument he could conceive to bolster his odds for success in the independent operation suddenly thrust upon him. He noted that the strength of the enemy garrison was unknown. If in fact the highest report were accurate, his lone division would be outnumbered. McLaws's "preference would be to have the whole of Anderson's division." He added that Richard Anderson "was a classmate and friend, and I would like to have him with me particularly." Lee probably sensed at this point that the argument was lost. According to McLaws, "but little more passed between us, and I returned to my headquarters." Later in the evening he received a copy of Special Orders 191.

Then, for reasons that are not clear, Lee sent for Maj. Gen. Richard Heron Anderson, whose tent was nearby.[112] Once again, the Confederate commander launched into an explanation of the expedition against Maryland Heights and Harpers Ferry, giving in detail "his objects—his expectations and his opinions as to the best steps to be taken, &c." According to Anderson, Lee repeatedly said, "Harpers Ferry must be taken against Thursday evening." Whether Anderson misremembered, or Lee advanced the schedule for the mission is not known.

The conference so puzzled Anderson, who was to be second in command to McLaws, that he wondered if Lee was mistaken as to who was the superior officer.[113] When reporting to McLaws on the following morning, Anderson was careful to repeat all the commanding general had said to him. Anderson did not receive a copy of S.O. 191.

The meetings with McLaws and Anderson underscore two assumptions implicit in the orders. Lee expected the expedition against the

Federal garrisons would meet with little resistance and would be rapidly concluded. His remarks to McLaws suggest that one reason for his confidence was his underestimation of the strength of the enemy. He also did not anticipate that Julius White at Martinsburg would fall back on Harpers Ferry and thus increase the total Union force to nearly 12,000.

Written in haste and hurriedly delivered, S.O. 191 must have caused a sudden tremor to ripple through the camps of the Army of Northern Virginia after three days of quiet rest. Myriad orders need have flown to prepare the army to march at dawn.[114] Amidst the bustle, only a handful knew the purpose of the abrupt departure from Frederick, and the rest were left to wonder if Lee had decided to move against Washington, Baltimore, or Pennsylvania. Results would indeed justify the anticipation of great events, although the shape of the outcome would defy speculation. The movement would yield a treasure of wagons, medical supplies, ordnance, munitions, and the largest capture of United States troops in the war. But, it would also lead to the unraveling of Lee's strategy.

Lee made a critical mistake in issuing S.O. 191 and dividing his army to undertake an expedition against Harpers Ferry on September 10. He was wrong in believing the enemy garrisons would flee to safety and wrong in assuming the movement could be completed in three days. More importantly, he misjudged the Federal advance from Washington. Either Lee misinterpreted the information he was receiving from his cavalry chief, or Stuart was supplying faulty intelligence.

The scant evidence available suggests the latter to be the case. Nothing indicates Stuart on the 9th perceived the Army of the Potomac to be pressing in a menacing way. He and his staff awoke late after the revelries of the previous night and spent the day enjoying the amenities of the Cockey family in Urbana. The report of a "brisk skirmish" at Barnesville, according to von Borcke, "did not prevent" the cavalry staff "from spending the evening with our fair friends at Mr. C's, nor from paying them the compliment of a serenade."[115] Likely the news passed on from such an indolent headquarters would lead Lee to believe the Confederates could spare three days to secure their communications through the Valley.

Yet, the perception that the Federals had only reached Rockville, one-third of the thirty-five miles from Washington's fortifications to Frederick, was a dangerous underestimation of the enemy advance. By the 9th, McClellan's left under Franklin had reached Darnestown, the center under Sumner reached Middlebrook, and the right under

Burnside reached Cracklinton, so that the Federal battlefront averaged seventeen miles from the forts, or almost exactly halfway to Frederick. Moreover, with the capture of Barnesville on the left and Ridgeville on the National Pike on the right, McClellan's leading elements were only ten miles from the Confederate encampment on the Monocacy.[116] The decision Lee made on the 9th put at risk his campaign in Maryland and possibly even the safety of his army. It did so at the time he wrote Special Orders, No. 191, and long before events prevented these orders from a timely execution—or before they fell into the hands of his enemies.

CHAPTER FOUR

"Intercept such as may attempt escape"

Lee's Best-Laid Plans, September 10–12, 1862

LEE LAUNCHED the third phase of his campaign in Maryland with high expectations. So far as he knew, he was still master of the situation. For the moment, his army was rested, reasonably well fed, and supremely confident of its prowess. He held the initiative in the chess game of strategy firmly in his own hands—or so he believed—and he would be able to determine both the time and the place he would inflict the next crushing blow on the Federal army in the Eastern theater. Further, he expected at the end of the third phase to be in an even stronger position, because with a secure supply line he would have access to munitions and be less dependent upon the whims of unsympathetic Marylanders for provisions.

In three short days, Lee's expectations would come crashing down around his ears. His plan for the new phase—as modified in S.O. 191 and further amended in execution—failed to provide either for the true rate of the enemy's advance from Washington or for even minimal resistance by the Federal garrisons in the Valley. As a consequence, by September 12, when the expeditionary forces had fallen considerably behind their schedules and the vanguard of the Army of the Potomac entered Frederick, Lee lost control of the campaign. The afternoon of the 12th was the watershed of the campaign. Thereafter, the initiative flowed from the Federal side of the divide.

The First Day of the Valley Expedition, September 10

Three hours before dawn, under the pallid light of a waning three-quarter moon, crashing drums and crowing bugles summoned Jackson's groggy foot cavalry to fall into the column of march. By four o'clock the van of the Stonewall division stepped out to the willing if discordant notes of its regimental bands, shattering the silence of the darkened streets of Frederick and alerting the town's citizens to the welcome news that their uninvited guests were at last departing.

All day long, under a bright and cloudless sky, the Army of Northern Virginia swept westward with the sun toward the mountain wall on the horizon. The broad turnpike allowed a compact formation of "three close parallel columns, artillery and trains in the center, and infantry on each side."[1] And for two hours past sunset the procession of wagons, guns, men, horses and mules pounded the baked road into choking clouds of dust. After Jackson's three divisions came Longstreet's three; then McLaws's command newly increased with Anderson's division; and finally the Reserve Artillery and the ordnance, commissary, and quartermaster trains.

For the first time in the war, nearly all of Lee's army passed in review before the eyes of a northern audience. Among the observers was one who came near to being an official spy. Lewis H. Steiner, a son of Frederick and a volunteer inspector for the U.S. Sanitary Commission, was visiting Washington, when he heard the Confederates had crossed the Potomac. Dr. Steiner claimed it was "anxiety as to the fate of my friends, as well as to the general fate my native place would receive at rebel hands" that impelled him to catch the last B&O train that made it across the Monocacy to the small Maryland town on September 5. A large dose of curiosity no doubt augmented his anxiety, for the doctor proceeded to keep a copious diary of the Confederate occupation of Frederick. As a physician and chemistry professor, Steiner was a trained observer; and his employment for the past year in visiting the camps and hospitals of the Army of the Potomac gave him practiced judgment in dealing both with the size and the quality of the enemy army.[2]

Having watched for four days the dribs and drabs of the various commands who evaded the provost marshal's net to visit the town, Steiner then had the opportunity to witness the bulk of the Army of Northern Virginia parade before him on the 10th. First, he was startled to discover the presence of "over 3,000 negroes" who "were manifestly an integral portion of the Southern Confederacy Army." The blacks were "clad in all kinds of uniforms" that were "not shabbier than those worn by white men in the rebel ranks." Most were armed in some fashion, including "rifles, muskets, sabres, bowie-knives, dirks" or the like, and many were supplied with knapsacks, haversacks, and canteens. "They were seen riding on horses and mules, driving wagons, riding on caissons, in ambulances, with the staff of Generals, and promiscuously mixed up with all the rebel horde."

Steiner could not refrain from noting the irony—if not hypocrisy—of Southern condemnation of Northern talk of enlisting blacks as soldiers, while at the same time employing them in such obviously military capacities in the Confederate army. From the Southern point of view, the blacks traveling with the army were servants not soldiers, and they were not included in military formations, deployed for fighting, or ever counted in the strength of the army. Yet, in their roles as teamsters, cooks, foragers, nurses, and the like, they freed an equal number of whites from these extra-duty jobs to shoot on the firing line. Scattered references in diaries, letters, and memoirs indicate that privates were as likely to have brought their servants to war as generals. It is interesting that there was apparently no hesitation in carrying slaves within a stone's throw of the dreaded Mason-Dixon line, which separated Maryland from the free state of Pennsylvania. There is no evidence to reveal how many servants took advantage of the Maryland campaign to escape from bondage. It may be speculated that the blacks who were carried along with the army represented the elite of the enslaved class and included those who had formed special relations with their masters based on privilege and trust.[3]

Steiner subjected the marching Confederates to a close scrutiny, and he found them wanting in many respects when compared to their Federal counterparts. Each regiment had but one or two wagons, and the soldiers carried but few knapsacks or blankets, although he was professionally gratified to see an occasional toothbrush "pendant from the button-hole." He was unpleasantly surprised to discover that Lee's army appeared "to have been largely supplied with transportation by some United States Quartermaster," as "Uncle Sam's initials were on many of its wagons, ambulances, and horses." He also estimated that "about 150" of their cannon were stamped with the letters "U. S." In spite of their raggedness, loose marching, and "vile" regimental bands, he was impressed with their physical fitness and high morale.[4]

Preconditioned by Northern newspapers to believe Lee's host totaled more than 100,000, Steiner was also surprised to discover a substantially smaller number march through the streets of Frederick. Apparently, he took some pains to estimate accurately the size of the Confederate army. "Some of the rebel regiments have been reduced to 150," he noted, and "none number over 500." After watching the sixteen-hour parade, he came to the conclusion that "the most liberal calculations could not give them over 64,000 men," and he included in this total the

3,000 blacks serving in extra-duty roles. Although Steiner's reaction was surprise at the smallness of the Confederate army, his reckoning supports the belief that Lee's force was not so weak at this stage of the campaign as has sometimes been suggested.

In fact, Steiner's estimate parallels the figures from the reconstructed trimonthly report for September 1 and suggests that any straggling since that date may have been more than made good by returning soldiers and the arrival of conscripts during four days of rest on the Monocacy. With the entire army on the march, the columns passing through Frederick would have included the extra-duty men and nearly reflected its complete present for duty strength. His "most liberal calculation" of 61,000 (excluding blacks) was 6,000 greater than the 55,000 present for duty credited by the estimate for the commands of Jackson, Longstreet, McLaws (including Anderson), and the Reserve Artillery for September 1. Moreover, considering that on the 10th Steiner would not have seen the divisions of Walker, D. H. Hill, and Stuart, his calculations support the conclusion that in midcampaign Lee commanded a force of between 70,000 and 75,000 present for duty.[5]

Confederates during and after the war, including Lee himself, claimed an effective fighting strength of 40,000 for the Army of Northern Virginia at the Battle of Sharpsburg, and there are good grounds for accepting this figure, or one only slightly larger. That strength should not, however, be read backwards to earlier dates in the campaign. The larger figure makes more reasonable not only Lee's decision to cross the Potomac, but also his willingness on September 9 to divide his army and undertake the expedition against Harpers Ferry.

When not counting Rebels and their guns, Steiner watched the reactions of the citizens of Frederick as the Confederates took their departure. The doctor believed the Southern soldiers had long overstayed their modest welcome. Not only were Unionist sympathizers happy to see them go, but even "their friends were anxious to get rid of them and of the penetrating ammoniacal smell they brought with them." By and large the crowds watched silently, and among the few flags to be seen along the route several bore the stars-and-stripes. While Barbara Frietchie's banner may not have been among them, one incident touched with pathos did occur. A one-legged civilian, who had been traveling on horseback with the army—perhaps a zealous early war casualty—became incensed at two small girls waving candy store Union flags. He was threatening to snatch away the flags, when Jubal Early

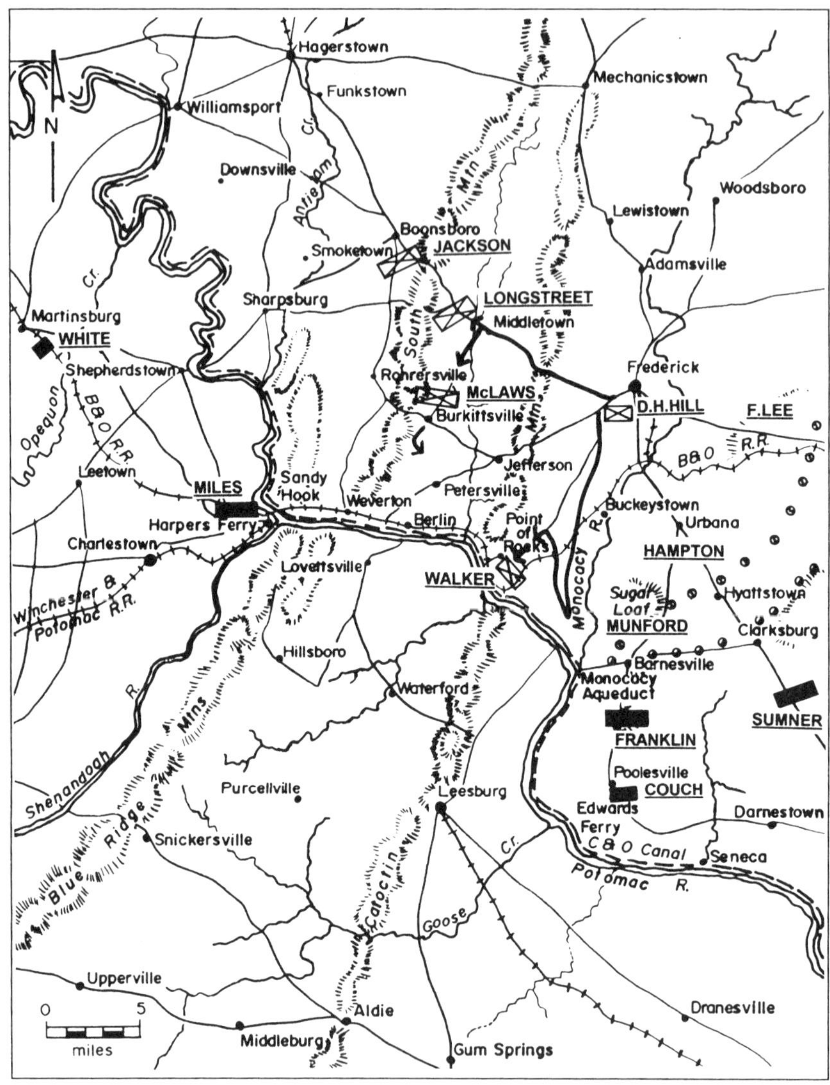

The first day of the Valley expedition, September 10

intervened. Detecting the aroma of alcohol, Early told the man he was a fool and sent him on his way.[6]

Following reveille at three o'clock, Jackson's old division reunited on the march. Three Brigades came south on the Emmitsburg Road to join with the Stonewall brigade at the fairgrounds and enter Frederick on Market Street. Lee's most battle-scarred division, now commanded by Brig. Gen. John R. Jones, then headed west on Patrick Street, the route of the old National Turnpike through the town.[7] From their bivouac at Monocacy Junction, Jackson's other divisions came onto Market Street from the opposite end of town. During the night Jackson had rearranged the order of march and Ewell's division under Alexander Lawton came second, with A. P. Hill's division still under Lawrence Branch bringing up the rear.[8] Powell Hill, chafing at continuing under arrest, followed along behind in an ambulance in a temper so vile that on one occasion he jumped from his seat to thwack an insolent teamster with the flat of his sword. Finally overcoming his pride, Hill sent a humbly worded request to Jackson to be allowed to lead his division into battle. In the anticipation that action would soon be upon them, Stonewall acquiesced, although the formal order was not issued until the following day.[9] Seemingly in a forgiving mood, before the day was over Jackson also restored to command the artillery captains who had been suspended for allowing their men to ride on the caissons across the Potomac.[10]

Jackson himself entered the town near the head of the column, but he soon pulled off to the side with his staff and commenced to make an uncharacteristically loud and ostentatious scene. He demanded from his engineer James Boswell a map of Chambersburg and vicinity, and then he made inquiries of the citizens standing about regarding the various roads leading to Pennsylvania. No doubt Stonewall intended to plant misleading information that would find its way to Federal headquarters and direct attention away from the expedition to the lower Valley. When he pulled the ruse he must have believed—as outlined in Special Orders, No. 191—that the remainder of the Confederate army would be waiting at Boonsboro. Had he known that Lee would revise the plans later in the day and march a part of his force in the direction of Chambersburg, it is possible Jackson would have tried a different deception.

After the public display, Jackson called to his side Henry Kyd Douglas, his young aide-de-camp whose family lived at Ferry Hill on the Maryland side of the Potomac just opposite Shepherdstown. According to Douglas's memory twenty-four years later, Jackson then told him of the mission to "capture Harpers Ferry." Stonewall explained he would recross the Potomac at Shepherdstown or Williamsport, or somewhere in between, "depending upon the movements of the enemy at Martinsburg." He asked Douglas about the different fords available.[11]

In several respects, Douglas's memory is at variance with the actual words of S.O. 191. In the first place, it seems unlikely that on the morning of the 10th, Jackson was focusing on the "capture" of Harpers Ferry, when the instructions written less than twelve hours before directed him to capture the enemy at Martinsburg and "intercept such as may attempt to escape from Harpers Ferry." It is possible Douglas superimposed knowledge of later developments on the conversation in this regard. More to the point, S.O. 191 directed Jackson "after passing Middletown" to "take the route toward Sharpsburg" and "cross the Potomac at the most convenient point." This implies that Jackson was to follow the Old Sharpsburg Road, which branched off the National Turnpike two miles west of Middletown, crossed South Mountain at Fox's Gap, and proceeded in a meandering fashion to Sharpsburg. After reaching that town, he had the discretion to select the "most convenient" ford for crossing the Potomac. It seems unreasonable that Lee intended that discretion to extend to Williamsport eleven miles upriver and not connected to Sharpsburg by a direct route.

In this case, however, Douglas's testimony must be taken seriously, because Jackson would indeed decide to extend his march and cross the Potomac at Williamsport. What is questionable is whether Jackson debated the choice between Sharpsburg and Williamsport as early as four A.M. on the 10th as he set out from Frederick. If so, either the wording of S.O. 191 must have very poorly reflected the understanding reached between Lee and Jackson the previous day, or the two must have met subsequently to the war council and verbally revised the plan. It is certainly possible that in a wide-ranging discussion of the best way to capture the garrison at Martinsburg, the two generals covered the contingencies that the Federals might flee to the northwest toward Cumberland, or northward on the Valley Pike to Williamsport and Chambersburg to escape the Confederates approaching directly from the east from Shepherdstown by way of Sharpsburg. Should such a course by the enemy appear likely, it would make sense for Jackson to continue on to Williamsport before crossing the Potomac, so that he could advance on Martinsburg from the west.

Nevertheless, among all of these ambiguities and uncertainties, what seems most likely is that Jackson set out on the 10th intending to remain flexible until he had gathered sufficient information to select the best route for his mission; and at this early hour his focus was on Martinsburg. It was no doubt for this very reason Jackson rode ahead of his troops the entire day. After a detour to visit a Presbyterian clergyman whose household had not yet awakened, Stonewall and his staff rode rapidly through Frederick's back streets and gained the head of the column on the outskirts of town. Jackson continued about a half-mile in advance of his infantry for the remainder of the day. He was preceded only by his personal escort, the Black Horse Troop, whose commander had orders to let no civilians pass to the front to spread word of their approach.[12] Curiously, Jackson deployed the 7th Virginia Cavalry of Munford's brigade—which Stuart had assigned to him in excess of the requirements of S.O. 191—at the rear of his command.[13] It may be surmised that Stonewall intended to net any strays who left the ranks.

If so, Jackson was probably responding to Lee's concern that the heat and dust would cause considerable straggling and that those who left the ranks would be in danger of capture, as they passed through increasingly unfriendly territory. The Confederate commander had ordered that the rate of march should be limited to three miles per hour and that ten minutes of rest should be included in each hour. Lee specified that those who could not keep up should be carried in the ambulances and wagons, contravening Jackson's usual practice of leaving stragglers by the wayside.[14]

In spite of the restrictions on his wonted celerity, Jackson made good time, passing through the gentle Catoctin mountain range at Hagan's Gap and reaching Middletown around eight o'clock. The snug village, situated in the center of the Valley bearing its name, appeared deserted by its mostly Unionist citizens. The exception was two young girls who waved small U.S. flags at Stonewall. Commenting, "We evidently have no friends in this town," he continued west without pausing toward the more rugged South Mountain.[15]

Apparently, Jackson had already decided not to take the Old Sharpsburg Road two miles beyond Middletown—at least not immediately—for by nine o'clock he had passed beyond the turnoff and continued westward through Turner's Gap in South Mountain. Then, strangely, he stopped within a mile of Boonsboro and set up camp. He was no more than fourteen miles from Frederick, and it could not have been later than ten in the morning. It is possible that initially Jackson intended the bivouac to be temporary, while he gathered information that would allow him to decide in which direction to proceed. The impression is strengthened by the fact that the divisions of Lawton and Branch were stopped short of South Mountain near the junction with the Old Sharpsburg Road. If this was the case, the information must have been hard to come by, as the bivouacs became permanent for the night.[16]

Thus, Jackson's progress on the first day of the expedition becomes something of a puzzle. Obviously determined to get off to a fast start, he had aroused his men in the middle of the night, marched them as hard as Lee's orders would allow until midmorning, and then did not stir them for the remainder of the day. The most likely explanation would be that sometime during the march he learned—perhaps from Douglas—that the route to Sharpsburg via the road just beyond Middletown would carry him over a rough and meandering road. Alternatively, he could proceed on the National Turnpike to Boonsboro, where a decent road would carry him to Sharpsburg and the distance covered would only be two miles greater. From Boonsboro, he could also march farther west and take a macadamized road to Williamsport, if that option should seem more desirable. Unable to decide between the three routes, he paused with one division at Boonsboro and two at the turnoff to the Old Sharpsburg Road. For whatever reasons, he was unable to make up his mind before the day was far advanced, and his resting point became his camp for the night.[17]

After Jackson ordered his headquarters tents to be pitched in a meadow a mile east of Boonsboro, he sent a squad of the Black Horse Troop ahead on the National Turnpike to reconnoiter in the direction of Hagerstown. Since Jackson had no intention of going to Hagerstown, the scout may have been caused by a rumor that a Federal force was advancing from that direction. Shortly after the Confederate horsemen had passed through Boonsboro, Henry Kyd Douglas rode into the village with an aide to visit friends and collect information on the fords across the Potomac. Douglas had just reached the center of town, where the Sharpsburg Road joined the National Turnpike, when he heard the "clatter of unseen cavalry" approaching from his left.[18]

The Confederates almost paid dearly for taking lax precautions while advancing through enemy territory. Lt. Col. Stephen W. Downey, commander of the Federal outpost at Kearneysville midway between Martinsburg and Harpers Ferry, had led a patrol of the 1st Maryland Cavalry across the Potomac at Shepherdstown and was now approaching Boonsboro on the Sharpsburg Road. Seeing the two lone Confederates, Downey and his twenty troopers charged. As Douglas and his companion dashed back toward their camp, they saw Stonewall Jackson walking down the hill just outside the town, leading his horse and alone. Jackson quickly understood the signals of alarm, "mounted and galloped to the rear." To make certain his chief had time to escape, Douglas pretended to be directing unseen support from the other side of the hill and charged the enemy. At the same time, the Black Horse Troop, returning at the sound of gunfire, appeared from the north end of town. The Federals fled toward Sharpsburg after suffering several casualties, including Colonel Downey. This well-known incident, famous for the near capture of Stonewall, may have convinced Jackson not to take the route to Martinsburg by way of Sharpsburg and Shepherdstown. After the skirmish, he may have concluded that the enemy garrison would be unlikely to attempt flight in this direction; and in order to surprise and capture them, it would be necessary to take the longer route to Williamsport.[19]

The unsatisfactory progress of the Army of Northern Virginia on September 10 is a cautionary reminder of the military truism that large armies seldom move rapidly even under the best of conditions. With a predawn start in fine weather on a good road, the head of Lee's column covered but thirteen miles, and the tail did not budge an inch. As is usually the case, the best of conditions fall short of perfection, and unforeseen complications thwart expectations. Since Jackson had the greatest distance to cover, it made sense to put his command in the van of an army traveling on a single road. And, had Stonewall taken the Old Sharpsburg Road two miles beyond Middletown, it is likely the entire army would have covered considerably more ground. But because of the discretion Lee gave Jackson to react to terrain and the movements of the enemy; and because of Jackson's inability to obtain timely information, the lead divisions of the column became a bottleneck blocking the flow of the march.

Longstreet's reduced command, now consisting of about 14,000 men in nine brigades under D. R. Jones and Nathan Evans and two artillery battalions, were ready to march almost an hour before dawn. By the time Jackson's men had cleared the way, the sun was well above the horizon. As Longstreet entered Frederick, the audience had grown larger and filled the sidewalks, porches, and balconies, but the reception remained "decidedly cool." The watching crowds displayed "positively no enthusiasm, no cheers, no waving handkerchiefs and flags—instead a death-like silence" surrounded the marching troops. Kemper's brigade responded by bursting into "The Girl I Left Behind Me," but many of the Confederate officers declared their pleasure at departing such "a damned Union hole." To their regret, the soldiers would only find the "Union sentiment stronger as we go northwest."[20] By late afternoon, the head of Longstreet's column came upon the rear of A. P. Hill's division halted for the night two miles beyond Middletown. Thus, Longstreet would make camp only ten miles out from Frederick on the 10th.[21]

The doings of Robert E. Lee on September 10 have been lost to history. It is not known at what hour he struck his headquarters tent, which part of the army he accompanied, when he passed through Frederick, how far he traveled, or where he stopped for the night. For the first time in a week he did not write to Jefferson Davis, and he issued no general or special orders, or circulars, nor send any correspondence that has survived. No doubt his continued travel by ambulance explains the lack of reported sightings by soldiers or civilians, while his four full days of rest at Frederick had allowed him to catch up with all of his important paperwork. He probably rode with Longstreet's command, as was his wont, and encamped just beyond Middletown with the bulk of the army.[22] Late in the day he may have received word of a rumor—although it is just as likely he did not hear of it until the following morning—that a Federal force was approaching Hagerstown from the direction of Chambersburg.

Lee's only known action on the 10th was his consent to another modification in Special Orders, No. 191, at the request of Longstreet. Apparently a growing concern over the size and possible resistance of the garrison at Harpers Ferry prompted Longstreet to offer the three brigades of Cadmus Wilcox to accompany McLaws. Lee accepted and Wilcox was merged into R. H. Anderson's division.[23] With this addition of five thousand men, McLaws's column totaled nearly eighteen thousand and approximated the size of Jackson's command. The shift also meant that two-thirds of the army was now engaged in the expedition, while the remaining one-third comprised the so-called "main body."

Thus, it came to pass that about noon Maj. Gen. LaFayette McLaws, who had never directed more than four brigades, nor had been in independent command, rode through Frederick at the head of eleven brigades—in effect a wing of the Army of Northern Virginia—entrusted with the mission of removing the enemy nuisance at Harpers Ferry. He must certainly have felt the sudden increase in responsibility, and he may have wondered if he were being groomed, or at least tested for promotion.

McLaws had broken camp on the Monocacy at daybreak, only to spend the morning waiting for the streets of Frederick to clear of the commands of Jackson and Longstreet.[24] His column did not reach Middletown until late afternoon, but happily he did not need to worry about the pileup of regiments just west of the village. His route branched off from the center of town and headed southwest to the Potomac. Five miles brought McLaws to Burkittsville and the need to decide where he would cross South Mountain. Due west lay Crampton's Gap, but only a little over a mile farther south was the Brownsville Pass. Neither mountain crossing was served by good roads, and apparently McLaws decidedly simply on the basis of which would bring him closer to his goal. The head of his column, Kershaw's brigade, marched a mile beyond Burkittsville and went into camp for the night at the foot of the mountain near the Brownsville Pass.[25]

Had McLaws known the details, he could have been modestly proud, because his men's fourteen-mile march was slightly the longest by any of Lee's troops on the first day of the expedition. He was, moreover, only seven miles on a straight line from Harpers Ferry. Unfortunately, two mountain ranges also lay between him and the enemy, and the key strategic point he must possess was the peak of one of the mountains. There is evidence McLaws did have at least the handful of cavalry which S.O. 191 assigned to him.[26] There is no indication, however, that he was lucky enough to have along a staff officer familiar with the area, as Jackson had in Douglas. In truth, McLaws was troop rich and information poor, and his troubles had only just begun.

Although each division, brigade, and regiment possessed its own supply wagons for its immediate use, there were also reserve trains for the entire army. While the Confederates carried less impedimenta with them than the Federals, their reserve trains were still immense, and included three battalions of artillery, a hundred ordnance wagons; and a vast number of vehicles for the commissary and quartermaster departments. The reserve trains were ready in early morning, but they were not able to take up their place in the column after McLaws until midafternoon, and it is doubtful their tail cleared Frederick until early evening. Whether or not all of the wagons were able close up on the main body beyond Middletown by nightfall is unknown.[27]

As a result of the snags and delays, the day was too far advanced for the rear guard to make more than a feeble start. Along with the rest of the army, D. H. Hill's five brigades had been roused from sleep at daylight. They "soon found," in the words of a member of the 4th North Carolina, "everybody and thing had been ordered to march at the same time." Viewed from the ranks, it appeared the "confusion" was the result of poor planning. By noon the division had barely covered three miles to reach the outskirts of Frederick. There it became obvious that further progress was unlikely, and Hill went into camp for the night near the Myer Farm.[28]

At about the same hour (3:00 A.M.) that Jackson's men were rubbing the sleep from their eyes, John Walker—twelve miles to south—was concluding Lee had given him an impossible assignment. Walker had arrived at the C&O aqueduct at the mouth of the Monocacy River at eleven o'clock on the night of the 9th. After chasing away a small Federal cavalry force, Walker spent several hours futilely searching for a way to destroy the bridge that carried the canal over the river. Knowing the army was leaving Frederick for Hagerstown that morning, he feared he would be isolated in the face of the enemy, and he decided to rejoin Lee by way of Jefferson and Middletown. He had withdrawn from the aqueduct, and at least a part of his division had marched several miles northward, when a courier delivered S.O. 191 with his new assignment.[29]

Walker's hasty retreat now presented him with a problem. His new instructions called for him to recross the Potomac at Cheek's Ford, which lay just a mile below the aqueduct, but after his withdrawal the enemy had returned in what he believed to be—albeit mistakenly—large force. For the greater part of the daylight hours of the 10th, he pondered his dilemma and allowed his weary troops to rest and cook rations. At two o'clock he retraced his steps toward Buckeystown until he reached the road to Point of Rocks. By this circuitous ten-mile route, he reached Point of Rocks about midnight. Long after the rest of the army to the north had bedded down, Walker's tired and befuddled soldiers were bridging the canal with railroad sills; and, then stripping to cross the Potomac at an unfriendly, boulder-strewn ford, where the water was shoulder high on the shorter men. After daylight he went into camp a mile south of the river. In spite of the cross-purposes and countermarching, Walker was on course to complete his mission in the allotted time.[30]

On this day critical to the success of Lee's campaign in Maryland, there is no indication that Stuart undertook any special measures to gain information or to increase security as the army headed westward. The 10th was "one day more of rest at headquarters" for the cavalry chief, and the only incident worth noting was a "sharp but unimportant skirmish" on Munford's front near Sugar Loaf Mountain.[31] Also, Stuart detached the 7th Virginia Cavalry (of Munford) to accompany Jackson;

the 1st Virginia Cavalry (of Fitz Lee) to report to Longstreet; and an unknown force to join McLaws, to fulfill the revised requirements of S.O. 191.

Still, apparently Stuart's troopers were doing a reasonably effective job in screening the whereabouts of the Confederate army. Nothing in any of Alfred Pleasonton's reports suggests Federal scouts discovered Lee was marching west from Frederick. Indeed, on the basis of the presumed inactivity of the Confederates, McClellan concluded his enemy did not intend to move on either Washington or Baltimore, and the Federal commander inclined to rule out a move to the northeast toward York or Gettysburg as well. By elimination, he believed Lee either planned to move northwest toward Chambersburg or to stand and fight on the line of the Monocacy.

Ironically, Stuart's complaisance on the 10th indicates that he was as ignorant of McClellan's movements behind the screen of opposing cavalry, as was Pleasonton of Lee's. Stuart missed a significant advance by the left and center of the Federal battlefront. On the left, Franklin (Sixth Corps) marched ten miles to occupy Barnesville, which lay only twelve miles southeast of Frederick; and, in the center, Sumner (Second Corps) moved forward five miles to Damascus, fourteen miles from Frederick and only five miles from Stuart's headquarters at Urbana. Indeed, McClellan's intelligence on this one day was a bit better than his foes, for by ten that night his pickets at the mouth of the Monocacy reported the advance of a Confederate force on the aqueduct.

In truth, McClellan's information ought to have been much better, however. Henry Halleck received reports from Hagerstown by way of Pennsylvania's governor Curtin in Harrisburg and from Martinsburg by way of Dixon Miles in Harpers Ferry of the Confederate advance westward from Frederick. There is no evidence Halleck passed these reports on to the man who most needed to know of them—the commander of the Army of the Potomac.[32]

By the close of September 10, Lee still possessed the initiative, but his margin for error had narrowed appreciably. At this time, it was the success of his gamble in crossing the Potomac that was at stake, however, and not the fate of his army. With a third of his force in the vicinity of South Mountain to slow the advance of the enemy and the remainder on the move toward the Potomac, Lee was—to say the least—in a good defensive posture. It is a reasonably safe bet, nevertheless, the Confederate commander spent little time thinking of defensive combinations this night.

The Second Day of the Valley Expedition, September 11

Once again reveille sounded through Jackson's camps in the blackness before there was any hint of dawn. Sometime during the night Stonewall learned that the Federal garrison had not yet fled from Martinsburg, and there was still a chance to catch the enemy in flight. He decided not to take the direct approach through Sharpsburg and Shepherdstown, therefore, but to swing in a wide western loop and try to gain control of the most likely escape path before the Federals had passed out of reach. The detour added eleven miles to the distance as prescribed in Special Orders, No. 191, and it meant that he would have to make double progress of the previous day, if the deadline of noon on the 12th were to be achieved. Jackson rode at the head of the Stonewall division as it marched through Boonsboro at about four o'clock. A mile west of town, the column abandoned the National Turnpike and turned left onto the macadam road that led to Williamsport. Sunrise came without the sun, and the overcast sky and heavy air promised rain. An uneventful march of twelve miles brought Jackson to Williamsport.[33]

During a halt for rest at the small river town, Stonewall's practiced scavengers slipped from the ranks to fill their stomachs and haversacks.[34] In the afternoon, as a misting rain descended on the Potomac valley, Jackson marched his command to Light's Ford, directly across from Williamsport. The men approved the crossing point. The river was knee-deep, with a gentle current, a "smooth, gravelly bottom," and water clear enough to avoid sharp rocks and sudden holes. With the bands playing "Carry Me Back to Old Virginia," and many in the ranks believing the experiment in Maryland concluded, they broke into song as they returned to the Old Dominion.[35]

Operating on the assumption the enemy would still attempt to escape, Jackson immediately spread a net to intercept any Federals moving westward. Stonewall himself, with the divisions of Lawton and J. R. Jones, marched nine miles to the south toward North Mountain Depot, a station on the B&O Railroad seven miles west of Martinsburg. He stopped a mile and a half short at Hammond's Mill and made camp. But, he sent a small force, including a gun from the Rockbridge artillery, to seize the depot, while his men engaged in the sport of heating rails and twisting them around trees. A. P. Hill's division, with its impetuous commander released from arrest, moved eight miles directly down the road from Williamsport toward Martinsburg. Jackson sent the 7th Virginia Cavalry fifteen miles south to cover the Berkeley and Hampshire Turnpike.[36]

Hence, as darkness fell and the rain increased, Stonewall had covered on average twenty-three miles. His exhausted men dropped to the ground, and some who had fallen by the way did not come up during the night.[37] The boom of a solitary cannon, assumed to be the enemy's "evening gun," signaled that the Federals had not departed from Martinsburg.[38] Still, Jackson was within an easy two-hour march of the town; he had destroyed another section of the B&O Railroad, and he had his troops positioned to meet the enemy. He was back on schedule and prepared to carry out his role in the expedition on time, even if it seemed increasingly doubtful the garrison intended to flee.

Jackson's early start cleared the National Turnpike for Longstreet's two divisions to start their march by five o'clock.[39] Four miles carried the six brigades under D. R. Jones and three under Evans over South Mountain at Turner's Pass and into Boonsboro. Thus, by seven or eight o'clock in the morning Longstreet had completed the easy role assigned to him in S.O. 191, and he had only to wait for the other columns to carry out their task and return to join him. Such was not to be, however.

For the second day in a row, Lee's activities are obscured by a lack of evidence. Again, he issued no written orders and neither wrote nor received any correspondence, at least none that has survived. On the 11th he did reach an important decision, however, and made one final deviation in his plan as outlined in S.O. 191. Sometime during the morning, he put together various reports he had received about Federal activities to the northwest and concluded he ought not to remain idle at Boonsboro.[40] He learned that an ample supply of flour existed at Hagerstown, but Union sympathizers were hurrying it off to safety in Pennsylvania. He also heard stories about a nebulous enemy force supposed to be at Chambersburg. It is likely he was more enticed by the former than he was worried by the latter. It is true that if the Federals occupied Hagerstown, they might seize the Williamsport Road and threaten Jackson's rear; but Chambersburg was over twenty miles north of Hagerstown, and it was unlikely that an enemy there would have time to interfere with Jackson's mission.

In truth, it is probable Longstreet had never fully sold Lee on the idea of retaining the entire main body at Boonsboro, and, given the

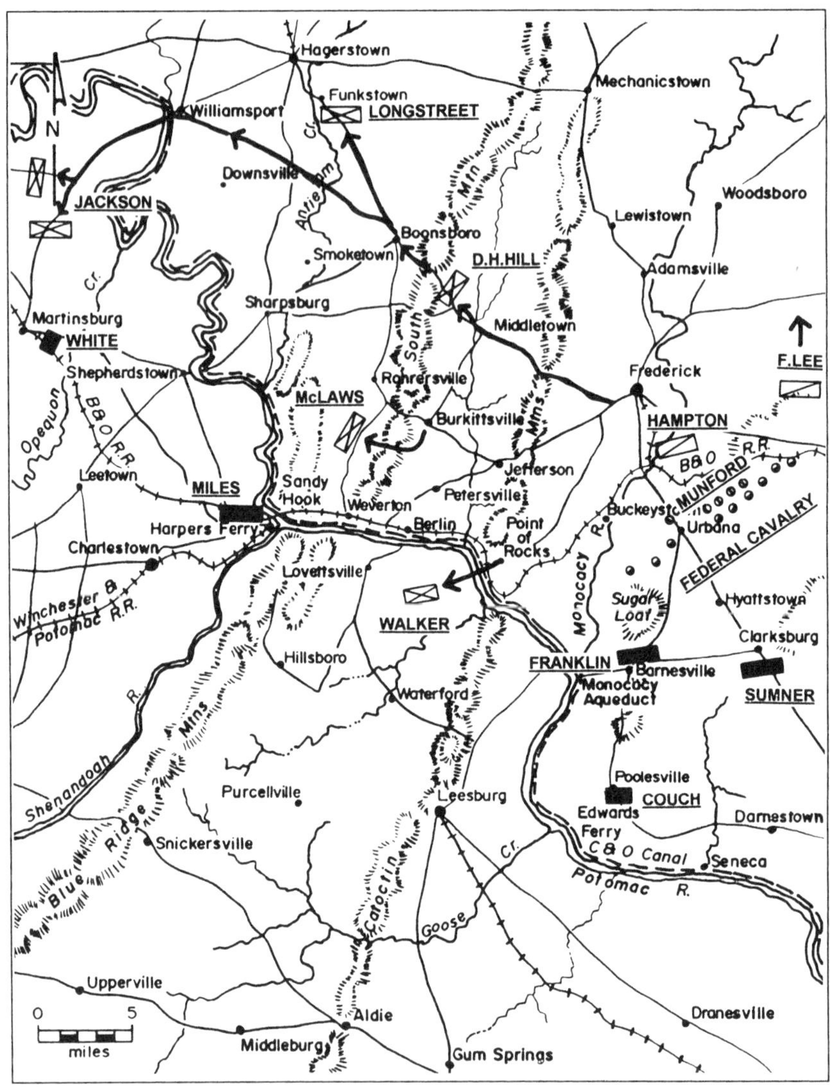

The second day of the Valley expedition, September 11

slightest excuse, the Confederate commander reverted to his original plan. When Longstreet heard that he was to march on to Hagerstown and only D. H. Hill was to remain at Boonsboro near South Mountain, he lodged one more protest. As Lee recalled after the war, his senior subordinate huffed, "General, I wish we could stand still and let the damned Yankees come to us!"[41]

Longstreet's crusty complaint reflected a misperception of Confederate strategy in the Maryland campaign. Lee had no intention of preventing the enemy from passing through the South Mountain range. The Confederate commander wanted the Federals to extend their communications and make themselves vulnerable to maneuver.[42] As Lee saw it, the only use for a force at Boonsboro was to guard escape routes from Harpers Ferry, and for that purpose D. H. Hill's division was sufficient. In consequence, the decision stood. Preceded by the 1st Virginia Cavalry, Longstreet's column resumed its march northward on the National Turnpike in the late morning or early afternoon. Toombs's brigade entered Hagerstown and seized the terminus of the Cumberland Valley Railroad, while the remaining brigades bivouacked several miles to the southeast in the vicinity of Funkstown.[43]

It is clear, moreover, Lee was not merely mounting a raid to seize flour and chase away an annoying enemy force. Not only did he personally accompany Longstreet, but also he took with him three of the five battalions of the Reserve Artillery, the reserve ordnance trains, and the bulk of the commissary and quartermaster wagons.[44] As late as midday on the 11th, the Confederate commander was sufficiently satisfied with the progress being made to carry out the plan in S.O. 191 that he went ahead with the next step in his strategy. He moved his "main body" to Hagerstown to secure both the base from which he intended to operate and the northern end of his proposed line of communications.

At the same time, nothing he was hearing from Stuart about the Federals' advance from Washington caused him to hesitate about further dividing the Army of Northern Virginia. Now there would be five rather than four independent columns operating at a distance from each other. The gravest risk involved in Lee's decision, however, was one he did not perceive. Although Lee did not wish to prevent the Federals from passing South Mountain, neither could he permit them to cross while the Confederate army was still scattered widely over western Maryland. Originally, one-third of his army had been assigned to Boonsboro and could have disputed the enemy passage of South Mountain. Now Lee's rear guard was reduced to a single division of less than 8,000 men present for duty.

That responsibility fell to the five brigades of D. H. Hill, which broke their overnight camp in the suburbs and marched through Frederick during the morning. According to the observant critic, Lewis Steiner, Hill's division seemed to be composed of superior materials. Not only were the men better dressed and equipped—which may have resulted merely from their missing the arduous Second Manassas campaign—but they also "marched in better order, had better music," and generally exhibited "more of military discipline" than their predecessors. The fact they moved noticeably "more rapidly" through town was taken by the citizens as a hopeful sign of "the approach of the National army."[45] It is likely, however, that their apparent speed resulted from nothing more than a clear road being before them for the first time.

Indeed, there is no reason to believe Harvey Hill was any more concerned about the Federals advancing from Washington than was Lee. The hour at which he passed through Frederick is not known, nor is the time he halted for the night. The thirteen miles he covered, however, while a respectable distance, was far off the torrid pace he set when marching from Richmond to join the army. It is possible that Lee's delay at Boonsboro may have caused Hill to encounter the rear of the trains and impeded his progress. Whatever the reason, Hill did not cross South Mountain on the 11th but went into bivouac two miles east of Turner's Gap.[46]

Lee's confidence in the unfolding events was not well placed. Only Jackson made the kind of progress on the 11th to justify the belief that the Valley expedition would be carried out on time. The inaccurate assessment of the Federal advance from Washington was merely the first fundamental flaw of S.O. 191. The plan's additional defects became clear on the 11th.

Lee had assumed the enemy garrisons would elect to flee to safety as soon as they perceived the Confederates advancing directly upon them. He had not foreseen the necessity for complicated and time-consuming operations, nor had he envisioned the need for extensive coordination between the three independent forces. Based on this mistaken assumption, the Confederate commander had, in the first place, allowed insufficient time for the completion of the expedition; and second, he had selected recently arrived and inexperienced commanders to lead two of the three columns; and third, he had failed to provide the neophytes with either adequate information or the means for obtaining it efficiently.

As a result, when the enemy refused to cooperate and did not immediately flee, it became necessary to plan offensive operations against a strong force in a defensive posture. Confronted by this unexpected and unwelcome development, both John Walker and LaFayette McLaws all but stalled on the second day of the expedition. A last-minute escape attempt by the enemy was certainly still possible and had to be taken into account, but interception would now require a more intimate knowledge of the road network in the immediate vicinity of Harpers Ferry. Moreover, the possibility of a siege loomed increasingly large. Neither Walker nor McLaws knew the regions about them; nor did they have guides or adequate cavalry to obtain quickly the information they needed. Consequently, both spent the 11th trying to find out where they should go next.

McLaws, at least, knew something more of the complications he faced. He knew Federal scouts had been spotted and the enemy was now aware of his presence. More ominously, he learned from a sympathetic farmer that the garrison at Harpers Ferry numbered at least 10,000, a figure three times larger than Lee had predicted.[47] The simple had become seriously complex. Except for attempting to gain more information, McLaws seems to have done little on the 11th. He advanced a mile or so through the Brownsville Gap to the edge of Pleasant Valley and concentrated his forces.[48]

On the other hand, John Walker suffered from nearly total ignorance. There is no reason to believe he knew anything of the strength, disposition, or intentions of the enemy garrisons. What he did know was that his men had missed the days of rest at Frederick and were worn down from the nearly continuous marching that had started at Rapidan Station two weeks earlier. He had not completed crossing the Potomac until after dawn, and he spent the entire day in bivouac a mile beyond Point of Rocks.[49]

The activities of the Confederate cavalry on September 11 make perfect sense, if considered within the context of Special Orders, No. 191. The last Confederate infantry and artillery had departed Frederick, and the independent columns would complete their missions by noon of the next day. Lee himself was in the act of transferring his base to Hagerstown. The time had also come to shift the cavalry front that ran from Sugar Loaf in the south through Hyattstown to New Market in the north. According to Stuart, he had already held that line "longer than was contemplated by the instructions" in the special orders.[50] The cavalry commander never stated exactly where he intended to establish his new front, and, since events prevented it ever being formed, its location can only be surmised. It would appear, however, that he expected to construct a curved line stretching from Frederick to the Pennsylvania border and facing southeast. Such a posture would have protected Lee's army while operating from either Hagerstown or Chambersburg. And, on the 11th Stuart did pull his horsemen back an average of eight miles and in a northwesterly direction.

Outside of the illusory world created by S.O. 191, and in light of the real situation that existed, Stuart moved too early and his execution was too casual. On this day critical to discovering the movements and intentions of the Federals, Stuart collapsed his twelve-mile front and lost contact with both wings of the enemy army. He united two of his brigades on the Washington Road that ran from Frederick through Urbana, and he sent the third due northward and away of the scene of active operations. Thus, his operations not only exposed the rears of Walker and McLaws to the south, but they also left uncovered in the center the National Turnpike, one of the two avenues along which the vanguard of the Federal infantry was now advancing.

Fitzhugh Lee could have fallen back directly from New Market on the National Road to the Monocacy and protected the center. Instead, in the steady rain that had already started falling east of the mountains, he led his brigade seven miles north to Liberty and then continued six miles west to cross the Monocacy.[51] Alternatively, Wade Hampton could have moved a short distance north and replaced Lee on the turnpike. Instead, during the late morning, Hampton retreated from Hyattstown through Urbana, crossed the Monocacy, and bivouacked at Frederick, throwing out pickets on the roads leading into town.[52]

The only attempt to keep the enemy at bay on the 11th fell to the depleted and overused brigade of Thomas Munford. After holding Sugar Loaf Mountain against repeated assaults by the Federal horse, Munford, who had only two regiments remaining after detachments, rode north to become the rear guard of the army. By two o'clock, he was holding the outskirts of Urbana with the 2d and 12th Virginia and being pushed steadily backward by enemy skirmishers. In the meanwhile, Stuart and his staff "lingered in the verandah with the ladies" of the pro-Southern Cockey family. Finally, when shells began to explode around the porch, the cavaliers galloped out of town, and within ten minutes Urbana fell to the Federals. Munford formed in line behind the Monocacy, three miles away, with Chew's Horse Artillery in the center at the bridge.[53]

Stuart rode ahead and established new headquarters at a farmhouse near Frederick. Shortly before nine o'clock, he wrote a report to Lee. In the dispatch (which has not been found and must be reconstructed from Lee's reply of the following day) Stuart apparently advised his chief that the old line had been abandoned and that Frederick would probably fall to the Federal cavalry in several days.[54] He seems also to have noted that a large number of stragglers remained behind and would be captured if some action were not taken. There is no indication he sounded an alarm over any danger developing in the rear. That night Stuart and his staff had a "lively little dance" with the "spirited Irish girls" of the farm household.[55]

September 11 was a good day for George McClellan and the Army of the Potomac. The best news—that Lee had further divided Confederate forces even while the expedition to clear the Valley was falling behind schedule—McClellan did not know. Yet, there was solid progress and cause for cautious optimism. At the start of the day, the Federal commander believed Lee occupied Frederick with a force of more than 100,000 and intended either to fight a major battle in the vicinity or to invade Pennsylvania. To counter Lee, McClellan still had approximately 60,000 men, and he continued to move with deliberation.

By nightfall the situation had brightened considerably. Federal cavalry, still outnumbered by their Confederate counterparts, pressed forward along the entire front. On the left flank, Pleasonton captured Sugar Loaf, which, once the weather cleared, would give the Federals an unparalleled view of Confederate activities around Frederick and all the way to the Catoctin Mountains. In the center, the Union horsemen occupied Urbana, six miles from Frederick, and to the north they entered New Market on the National Road, seven miles from Frederick. Reports accumulated during the day that Lee had marched west in the direction of Hagerstown, and McClellan ordered the right wing under Burnside to press forward the following day to occupy Frederick. In addition, McClellan pried loose reenforcements from Washington. Fitz John Porter would soon be on the way with another 12,000 men to bring the contending armies closer to equality.

One other development favorable to the Federal strategic situation was unknown to both McClellan and Lee, and it represented one final, ironic twist to the convoluted story of Harpers Ferry. Up to this stage in the campaign, the decision to hold the Valley garrisons in place had been wrong from both the Federal and Confederate point of view. Now, however, a stubborn defense by the garrisons would imperil Lee's army and provide McClellan with the opportunity to catch his foe badly divided. Until the 11th, neither Dixon Miles at Harpers Ferry nor Julius White at Martinsburg believed they were in any danger. But, during the day, just as Miles found his "eastern front" was threatened from Pleasant

Valley, White discovered he was about to be surrounded by Jackson from the west. True to their orders, neither commander considered leaving the Valley. White abandoned Martinsburg during the night, but he retreated east to Harpers Ferry. And Miles, preparing to defend his post to the last, wired "Good bye" to Halleck in Washington.[56]

Lee at Hagerstown, September 12

Friday, September 12, was a pleasantly warm day, with the temperature reaching the high seventies. The rain had stopped during the night, and conditions for marching were the best during the campaign. While an overcast sky shielded the sun, the showers had been sufficient to lay the dust without turning the roads into quagmires. This came as welcome news, for most of Lee's army still was on the move to meet the midday deadline imposed by S.O. 191. The 12th was a day critical to the success of Lee's campaign in Maryland. It would not be a lucky day for the Confederates.

The least significant role on this fateful Friday fell to James Longstreet and the diminished column that did not deserve to be called the main body of the Army of Northern Virginia. Although the road was clear before them, Longstreet's two infantry divisions did not form ranks on the National Turnpike until seven o'clock, and it was nine before the cavalry vanguard had covered the five miles through Funkstown to Hagerstown. Longstreet distributed his troops in an arc to cover the roads leading into the town. James Kemper took the three brigades he had formerly commanded as a separate division through the town and a mile north on the road leading to Chambersburg. His pickets were pushed forward toward the Pennsylvania line four miles beyond. David R. Jones with the remaining two brigades of the division proceeded through the town, turned left, and went into camp a mile west on the road to Williamsport. Nathan Evans passed Funkstown but stopped two miles short of Hagerstown to cover the National Road from the east. Toombs's brigade continued to occupy the town itself. Sometime before noon, Lee and Longstreet established their headquarters just beyond Funkstown, where they were joined by the Reserve Artillery and the army's trains not left behind at Boonsboro.[57]

When Lee pitched his tent on the 12th, he settled in for a stay of several days. He may not yet have decided whether he would base the next stage of his campaign from Hagerstown or Chambersburg, and he still

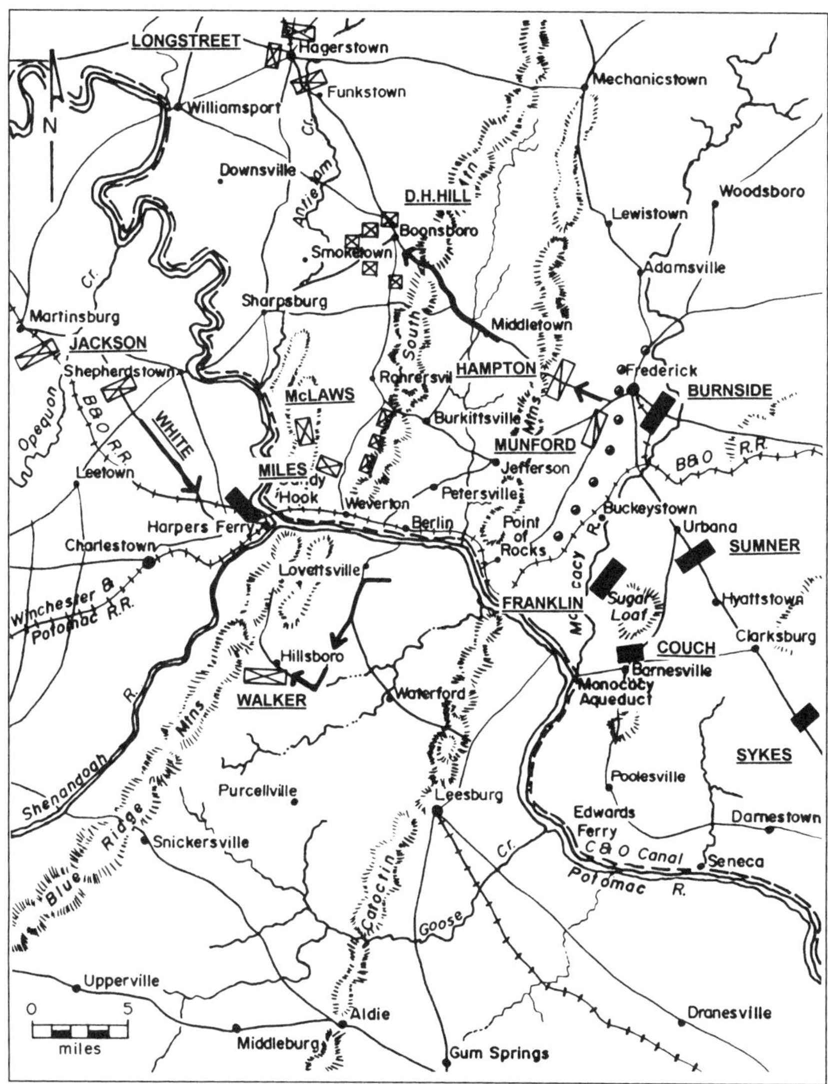

The third day of the Valley expedition, September 12

did not suspect that the Valley expedition was running behind schedule. Nevertheless, even if the detached columns completed their tasks on time, he must have anticipated it would be the 14th before his army would be reunited and he could move on to the next phase. It may be that Lee's false sense of security derived from more than a flawed perception—whether Lee's or Stuart's—of McClellan's advance from Washington. He may also have been the victim of lopsided intelligence from the expedition itself. Jackson, who had made good progress on the 11th, kept in communication with his commander through a "constant line of couriers." From McLaws and Walker, however, who were falling seriously behind, he had heard nothing at all. Lee may have interpreted the good news from Jackson as an indication Confederate operations were developing on time.[58]

It was with an optimistic frame of mind, therefore, that Lee settled into his new camp and turned to correct the unusual two-day lapse in his correspondence with Jefferson Davis. He began with a rare contemporary glimpse into the thinking behind his strategy. "Before crossing the Potomac," he wrote, "I considered the advantages of entering Maryland east or west of the Blue Ridge. In either case it was my intention to march upon this town."[59] This is the sole indication that Hagerstown was from the start the focus of Lee's campaign in western Maryland.

"By crossing east of the Blue Ridge," he explained, "both Washington and Baltimore would be threatened, which I believed would insure the withdrawal of the enemy's troops north of the Potomac. I think this has been accomplished." Here, Lee means not only that he wished to free northern Virginia of Federal troops, but also that he realized an enemy force south of the river would have seriously threatened his attenuated communications with Richmond.

The Confederate commander then confessed another assumption that had governed his actions until September 9. "I had also supposed that as soon as it was known that the army had reached Fredericktown, the enemy's forces in the Valley of Virginia, which had retired to Harper's Ferry and Martinsburg, would retreat altogether from the State." Lee had been mistaken, however, and he went on to describe his countermove in most revealing language. "In this I was disappointed, and you will perceive from the accompanying order of the 9th instant that Genls Jackson and McLaws have been detached with a view of capturing their forces at each place, should they not have retired."

With the exception of Special Orders, No. 191, themselves, this statement by Lee is the most revealing evidence in existence on his thinking behind the Valley expedition. Written before he knew of the developments that knocked his plan askew—indeed, even before he knew White had fled from Martinsburg to Harpers Ferry—Lee's words confirm several simple conclusions that would be obvious in the orders, if they had not been obscured by subsequent changes caused by unforeseen events. First, Jackson and McLaws are depicted as operating separately against the enemy "at each place." Second, even at this late date, Lee seems to believe it a fifty-fifty proposition whether the enemy could be captured, or would flee to safety. And, third, he makes no mention of Walker, underscoring the impression that he was not certain Walker's assignment, in the language of S.O. 191, was "practicable" and that he did not view Walker's contribution as absolutely necessary to the success of the expedition.[60]

Lee then shifted from the past to the present. "The army has been received in this region with sympathy and kindness," he told the president, putting a decidedly diplomatic face on the humane but cool reception by the residents of Hagerstown. Washington County had been settled by German Lutherans and Baptists. Their small but prosperous farms had all but choked out slavery, and their descendants remained overwhelmingly loyal to the Union.[61] To the aristocratic eye of the Reverend William Nelson, the people were "cousins-german to Pennsylvania Yankees" who lived in an bland "state of society where all is one dead level."[62] Still, the civilians treated the Confederates who slipped from camp to forage with "polite attention" and, in some cases, with surprising generosity.[63]

"We have found in this city about fifteen hundred barrels of flour," he went on, "and I am led to hope that a supply can be gathered from the mills in the country." This is a considerable amount of flour, and its acquisition must have pleased Lee greatly. The fact that he could report obtaining it so soon after reaching Hagerstown indicates his agents must have set to work immediately. Also, if he had not brought a substantial portion of the commissary trains with him, he must have ordered them up from Boonsboro at once.

There were disappointments, however. "The supply of beef has been very small, and we have been able to procure no bacon." Although Lee does not so state, the scarcity of beef may have derived from the residents driving their herds to safety, or hiding them from the Confederates.[64] According to the 1860 census it did not result from the poverty of the area. Washington County ranked first in Maryland in beef cattle and was second only to Frederick County in swine; and it compared favorably in both categories with the richest counties in Virginia.[65] Also, as in Frederick, Lee may have suffered from residents declining to become official purveyors to an enemy government. Individual soldiers fared well in finding butter, honey, bacon and "excellent lager beer," and even the critical Pendleton admitted he and his staff had no trouble finding "some place where we get wholesome food."[66]

Turning to the other great need of the army, Lee could only report mixed results. "A thousand pairs of shoes and some clothing were obtained in Fredericktown, two hundred & fifty in Williamsport, and about four hundred pairs in this city." This indicates Lee had heard from Jackson within the last twenty-four hours. He admitted, "They will not be sufficient to cover the bare feet of the army."

Lee then returned to his strategic situation. "Our advance pickets are at Middleburg on the Pennsylvania line. I await here the result of the movements upon Harper's Ferry and Martinsburg." These two sentences are sometimes seen as evidence that Lee intended to invade Pennsylvania. In absolute terms they prove no such thing. "Advance" may mean no more than "farthest," and "await" does not necessarily denote any further movement, and certainly not a northward movement after the army had reunited. Still, admittedly, the implication here is strong that Lee does not intend simply to remain at Hagerstown and allow the enemy to come to him. And it may be that Lee had already begun to favor Chambersburg as his next base in order to draw McClellan even farther from Washington and to allow even greater room for Confederate maneuver.[67] He may also have had in mind a fresh source for food and shoes. Additionally, this sentence also indicates Lee had not yet heard of the enemy flight from Martinsburg.

That Lee had either decided by the 12th, or was near to deciding on his next move after the army had reunited, is hinted in another action he took sometime during the day. He issued a circular to all division commanders requiring that they forward "at once" a field return of their strength to his headquarters.[68] The circular may have been nothing more than another round in Lee's continuing attempt to establish regular reporting habits in an army that resisted bureaucratic details. Nevertheless, the admonition that these returns were "indispensably necessary for the information of the commanding general and to govern him in his movements" suggests he had an ulterior motive for counting his troops at this particular time. What that motive was is open to contradictory conclusions. On the one hand, his concern over the impact of straggling may have grown to such an extent he was concerned about his ability to carry through with the objects of his campaign. On the other, flushed by his success thus far, he may have been assessing his strength to determine if he might undertake even more than he had originally intended.[69]

There is another, simpler explanation that accounts for both the sense that Lee was preparing for his next move and his audit of strength, and it is supported by Lee's own recollection of what he intended to do. Three years after the war, in two different conversations that occurred on the same morning, when he reminisced about the Maryland campaign, Lee stated unequivocally he had decided to move against the enemy. First, he told Edward Gordon he "proposed as soon as possible after the reduction of Harpers Ferry to collect his troops and deliver battle."[70] Then, within an hour or so, he explained to William Allan that if the Federals had continued their cautious advance "for two or three days longer, I would have had all my troops reconcentrated on Md. side, stragglers up, men rested, and *intended then to attack McClellan.*"[71]

If, in fact, Lee correctly remembered his state of mind at Hagerstown—and there is no good reason to doubt his memory—he must necessarily have somewhat modified his view of the rate of progress of McClellan from Washington. While he was clearly still not worried about being caught with his forces divided, he must have judged the enemy would be west of the Blue Ridge sooner than originally anticipated. Otherwise, he could not have planned to attack McClellan. It is inconceivable Lee would have contemplated recrossing east of the mountains himself to deliver battle, and, indeed, in his report, he admitted he had not even intended to oppose the Federal army's "passage through South Mountain, as it was desired to engage it as far as possible from its base."[72]

It is also interesting to note that Lee's decision to move forward his timetable was seemingly at odds with his earlier desire to prolong the campaign beyond the Potomac and provide a season of relief for Virginia. Perhaps, his concern over supplies caused him to become impatient. Or, perhaps, he assumed that another victory that drove the routed Federals into Washington's forts would allow him to stay beyond the Confederate borders for an even longer period—if it did not bring a suit for peace.

In closing Lee reverted to the topic of relations with Marylanders and finally got around—four days after the fact—to apprising Davis that he had dabbled in politics. "I have the honor to enclose to you a copy of the proclamation which I issued to the people of Maryland," he wrote. Apparently feeling the need for justification, he added, "I waited on entering the State for the arrival of ex-Governor Lowe, but finding that he did not come up, and that the citizens were embarrassed as to the intentions of our army, I determined to delay no longer in making known our purpose." Although it was a clever propaganda concept to use a well-known native as a political figurehead, slow communications and difficult travel conditions rendered it impractical. Lowe did respond to Lee's call. The ex-governor left Richmond with Jefferson Davis on the morning of September 7, but he would not reach Winchester until the 13th.[73] Moreover, there is no reason to believe that Lowe's presence with the army would have significantly changed the views of Unionist western Maryland.

After completing the dispatch to Davis, Lee received two important communications from subordinates that would alter his perception of unfolding events. The first was from Jackson and announced that the enemy had evacuated Martinsburg and retreated to Harpers Ferry. The second came from Stuart and advised that the Confederate cavalry would abandon Frederick in several days. Taken together the news might have alerted Lee that considerable danger loomed on the horizon. Neither dispatch has been found, and both are known only from the reply Lee sent to Stuart.[74]

At two-thirty in the afternoon, Lee dictated a response to Stuart, which opened: "Your note of 8.40 P.M., Sept 11th, has just been received." It is interesting that it took Stuart's dispatch eighteen hours to travel less than thirty miles from Frederick to Hagerstown. At under a mile and half per hour, it was not delivered in hot haste. Lee's reference to "note" suggests a brief communication, rather than a detailed report.

Lee turned first to a point apparently raised by Stuart. "Positive orders were given that all the sick of the command should accompany it," he stated with some asperity; and, "those only who would be injured by the journey to be left behind, of whom Dr. Guild was under the impression that there were about forty, and had made an arrangement with Dr. Woolten of Frederick for their attendance."

Stuart's dispatch must have called Lee's attention to a relatively large number of sick (or those who claimed to be sick) who remained in Frederick and vicinity. It is revealing to discover that Lee had taken such pains to ensure that few prisoners would be captured by the enemy. This is in line with similar actions taken by the Confederate commander, such as having the cavalry travel at the rear of the columns and allowing exhausted soldiers to ride in wagons rather than be left by the wayside. And, it is additional evidence that Lee issued instructions supplemental to S.O. 191 to govern the departure from Frederick.[75]

"Dr. Wingfield has been sent back to see what can be done," Lee continued, "but I fear the enemy will be in Frederick before he can get there, as I presume they will follow in your footsteps." There is much of interest in this statement. Perhaps the least important observation is that Lee ordered back a physician and not a provost guard. This suggests Stuart must have referred largely, if not exclusively, to sick soldiers and not laggards.

More importantly, Lee's comment indicates the main purpose of Stuart's note must have been to alert the Confederate commander that the cavalry were on the verge of abandoning Frederick. This does not mean Stuart anticipated leaving Frederick on the 12th, however. If that had been the case, at midafternoon on the 12th, Lee would have known it was too late to effect any further removal of the sick. On the contrary, it makes sense to assume Stuart had announced the last of his command would leave the town on the 13th, and Lee believed there was still a narrow window of opportunity to remove additional sick. Lee's reference to the enemy following in Stuart's "footsteps" is ambiguous, but, as the subsequent sentences suggest, likely referred to Federal cavalry and not the main body of the Army of the Potomac.

"I do not wish you to retire too fast before the enemy," Lee continued, "or to distribute your cavalry wide apart." This is the first indication that a small concern was growing in the Confederate commander's mind. The instructions were so vague, however, as to have offered little guidance to Stuart. Still, there is the definite implication that Stuart was not only to observe but also retard the advance of the enemy. Lee could not have expected this, unless he—and Stuart—believed that only Federal cavalry was pressing the Confederate rear.

Lee went on, "Gen. D. H. Hill's division is posted at Boonsboro; while Gen. Longstreet's is at this place." This information was probably included to alert Stuart that the army was even more fractured than had been called for in Special Orders, No. 191. It suggests that Lee had not previously informed Stuart of the modifications in the orders, and that the cavalry commander had operated under the mistaken impression that a much larger Confederate force was at Boonsboro.

Then, Lee added significant news. "I have just heard from Genl Jackson at Martinsburg that the enemy retired from that city last night to Harper's Ferry." Thus, it must have been shortly past noon on the 12th—the deadline named in S.O. 191 for the completion of the various missions—when Lee discovered that the Valley expedition was not proceeding as planned. The obstinate enemy refused to cooperate by fleeing from the Valley. Now, there was no doubt that the operation would take longer than anticipated. This was the likely reason Lee did not wish Stuart "to retire too fast."

"He will move down against them," Lee explained, "and I wish you to guard the road leading from that point through Maryland, and notify Gen McLaws who is on the north side of the Potomac, of any movements affecting him." Jackson—in the dispatch not found—must have informed Lee that it was necessary to go beyond the instructions in S.O. 191. Stonewall would move against the combined enemy forces at Harpers Ferry. There is as yet no hint that siege operations were contemplated, and both Lee and Jackson may have still contemplated last-moment flight by the enemy. Hence, Stuart is instructed "to guard" the roads leading east from Harpers Ferry. The phrase is not entirely clear, however, and may have been Lee's first recognition of the vulnerability of the rear of McLaws's column at Maryland Heights.

Lee concluded, "Keep me advised of the movements of the enemy, and do not let him discover, if possible, our movements." Lee's final sentence may suggest that Stuart had not communicated frequently enough to suit his chief. It certainly indicates Lee did not want the enemy to learn of the wide separation of the columns of the Confederate army.

Taken as a whole, the dispatch does not reveal the mind of a commander who is greatly concerned over the news that Frederick will soon be abandoned, or that the Valley expedition will take longer than planned. Lee recognized that modifications were necessary, but the revisions he made at this point were minimal. Nothing suggests he glimpsed the approach of disaster.

The Watershed of the Maryland Campaign

"By Friday morning," the phrase thrice repeated in S.O. 191, established the deadlines for completion of the Valley expedition. It was the time by which Jackson was to have captured the enemy at Martinsburg and intercepted "such as may attempt to escape from Harpers Ferry." By the same date, McLaws was to be in possession of Maryland Heights and endeavoring to capture "the enemy at Harper's Ferry and vicinity." And, meanwhile, Walker was to have taken Key's Ford on the Shenandoah River and the road between Loudoun Heights and the Potomac to "intercept retreat of the enemy."

Noon of the 12th came and went, and with it Friday morning passed. Lee did soon learn from Jackson that not all went well with the plan according to S.O. 191. But, not until another twenty-four hours had elapsed would the Confederate commander realize how baldly fortune had turned against him this Friday. This was the day the initiative in the campaign passed from Lee's hands. Hereafter, he would not act but react.

Although the usual sources do not record the hour that Jackson marched on the 12th, it may be assumed he got off to his customary predawn start. If so, Stonewall's progress was unwontedly slow. Either he was unaware Julius White had evacuated Martinsburg during the night, or he refused to rely on such rumors as he had heard. "Moving cautiously," he waited for his cavalry to confirm the town was abandoned, and it was midmorning before A. P. Hill's division covered the five miles from its bivouac and entered Martinsburg. The divisions of Lawton and J. R. Jones, having swung slightly to the west to Hedgesville to intercept any enemy in flight, covered nine miles and arrived soon thereafter.[76]

Such had been White's haste to avoid the tightening noose, there had not been time to save all of the military stores. Although the Confederates entered on streets strewn with salt, they found no fires such as had destroyed several blocks of Winchester, nor storehouses that had been stripped of bounty; and they captured rations of bacon and bread, as well as quartermaster and ordnance supplies.[77] Official plunder was the least of the memories Jackson's men carried with them from Martinsburg, however. For the first time in many days, they entered a Confederate town; and they came as conquering heroes. The residents showered the soldiers with adulation and food. "I saw a ton of bread devoured that day," recalled a South Carolinian of Gregg's brigade. The appearance of Stonewall "excited a perfect furor." They begged for buttons, clamored for locks of hair—from either the general or his horse—and "almost suffocated him with crowding around him."[78] In spite of the distractions, Jackson closeted himself in a room at the local hotel long enough to write a report to Lee on his progress.[79]

This would be the communication from Jackson that Lee wrote to Stuart, who had arrived in Hagerstown shortly before 2:30 in the afternoon.[80] Unfortunately, this report is among the many lost dispatches of the Civil War, but it may be assumed with some confidence that Jackson announced to Lee that he had—with God's blessing, of course—accomplished his task as set out in S.O. 191 and in the time allotted. He would not be returning to rejoin the army at Hagerstown immediately, however, for complications had arisen. Jackson must have learned as soon as he entered the town that White had not fled for safety from the Valley, but instead the 3,000 Federals had retreated to the southeast to join Dixon Miles at Harpers Ferry. Hence, although Jackson had literally carried out his assignment, the object of the expedition remained unfulfilled.

It would have been unreasonable, under the circumstances, for Jackson to have decided otherwise than to advance on Harpers Ferry, and it is not unlikely that he and Lee had discussed this contingency on the 9th while plotting S.O. 191. It had now become a real possibility that the reenforced garrison at Harpers Ferry would not attempt escape and that a siege operation would be necessary. Such a job would not only be too big for McLaws and Walker by themselves, but it would require Jackson's experience and rank to coordinate the operations successfully. On the other hand, even if the enemy still attempted last-minute flight, Jackson would need to be in place nearer to the town to block escape from the west.

There is nothing to suggest that Jackson asked Lee's permission, or waited for approval to move on Harpers Ferry. On the other hand, perhaps from the need to mull over the complications of the new situation, Stonewall made only moderate progress during the remainder of the day. While the divisions of Lawton and A. P. Hill advanced three miles eastward and bivouacked on the banks of Opequon Creek, J. R. Jones went into camp on the outskirts of Martinsburg.[81] In terms of distance traveled, September 12 was not one of Jackson's better days, as he covered only a total of eleven (Jones), ten (Lawton), and eight (Hill) miles.

There might be reasonable explanations, but the results were the same. The deadline had come and passed, and Jackson was now fifteen miles from his new objective and moving into an operation that was likely to be complicated and time consuming. He would have to coordinate three columns separated by two rivers and three mountains. And, he had no word—either direct or roundabout—of Walker and McLaws. Unless the enemy untowardly cooperated, the expedition was bound to fall seriously behind the timetable of Lee's expectations.

Out of touch with the rest of the Confederate army and isolated in a mountain-walled world of his own, LaFayette McLaws had no notion of the changes then occurring that were inflating his role from secondary to primary importance. The entire Valley expedition had rapidly narrowed to focus on a single object—the capture of Harpers Ferry. Since the key to Harpers Ferry was Maryland Heights, and since the taking of Maryland Heights was McLaws's responsibility, his task had perforce become the crucial element in the success of Special Orders, No. 191.

Simultaneously, that task had become considerably more difficult. With the addition of Julius White's men from Martinsburg, the Harpers Ferry garrison now totaled 13,000. For those who could read them, the signs increasingly suggested that the Federals intended to stand and defend their last foothold in the Valley.

Of all this, the commander from Georgia knew naught. After spending the 11th attempting to gather information, McLaws formulated a plan aimed not only at seizing Maryland Heights but also at closing to the enemy any possible escape routes. While the fifth article of S.O. 191, addressed specifically to him, had not mentioned intercepting the flight of the enemy, he was certainly well within the spirit of the overall instructions to worry about catching the Federals in precipitate retreat.

McLaws's tactical situation was complicated by a quirk of nature that placed before him overlapping and nonconnecting mountain chains. At Burkittsville, he confronted the same South Mountain the main army had crossed eight miles to the north to reach Boonsboro. It ran six miles to the south to Weverton Cliffs on the Potomac and extended into Virginia as the gradually declining Short Hills until it finally disappeared. But he also faced a parallel chain farther to the west, which came out of Virginia as the Blue Ridge (including Loudoun Heights) and ran about eight miles into Maryland as Elk Ridge before also disappearing. Maryland Heights was located on Elk Ridge, where it abutted the Potomac. At a width of two to three miles, Pleasant Valley separated South Mountain and Elk Ridge.

Anxious to perform well in his first independent command, McLaws had devised a complicated tactical plan in response to the tortuous topography. He intended to form his ten brigades in a wide net to prevent the enemy from slipping by him unnoticed, while at the same time he moved to possess Maryland Heights. He planned to put a force on the crest of each mountain to advance simultaneously toward the Potomac with a line stretched across the valley floor. Unaware the enemy had no intention of fleeing, McLaws proceeded to carry out this plan on the 12th; and thus he consumed both time and effort better spent in concentrating on Maryland Heights. In fairness to the general—had the Federal garrison not been nailed in its coffin by orders from Washington—McLaws's plan could have worked; and it could have been completed no more than a half-day late of his deadline.

At six o'clock on the morning of the 12th, McLaws set his brigades in motion. He sent the troops he considered most reliable, the brigades of Kershaw and Barksdale, directly across Pleasant Valley to ascend Elk

Ridge at Solomon's Gap. This pass was little more than a slight indentation and was five miles on the crest line of the mountain away from Maryland Heights. He ordered Cobb's brigade to march along the foot of Elk Ridge keeping pace with the troops on the summit. At the same time, Wright's brigade climbed South Mountain and advanced south toward Weverton Cliffs, while Pryor's brigade marched below them with orders to capture Weverton, the small hamlet on the Potomac. McLaws formed a line with three brigades (Armistead, Wilcox, and Featherston) across the valley floor to connect Cobb and Pryor and to complete the complex web. His provisions to protect his rear indicate he was not at this point particularly worried about an enemy threat from behind. McLaws charged his two remaining brigades (Semmes and Mahone) not only to guard both passes through South Mountain at Crampton's and Brownsville, but also to occupy Solomon's Gap in Elk Ridge after it had been secured by Kershaw.[82]

There was one gaping hole in the net spread by McLaws. The River Road that connected Weverton with Sandy Hook continued westward at the base of Maryland Heights and then turned due north to Antietam Furnace and Sharpsburg. The Federals in Harpers Ferry had access to the road by a railroad and a pontoon bridge. It is virtually impossible McLaws did not know of this unstoppered escape route. Not only had he taken pains to glean information from the residents of Pleasant Valley, but he had also by this time gained a local guide in the person of a young son of Confederate congressman Alexander Boteler of Shepherdstown. More likely, McLaws believed that blocking this road was beyond his resources. He probably decided he could not penetrate between Harpers Ferry and Maryland Heights, while both were in enemy hands; and he could not extend his net west of Elk Ridge, because he lacked sufficient manpower. It is true that instead of assigning two brigades to the crest of Elk Ridge, he might have ordered one to continue through Solomon's Gap and advance along the western foot of the mountain. That he did not do so probably resulted from the impression McLaws gained from local inhabitants that Maryland Heights was held in such strength by the Federals as to require both brigades to carry it.[83]

The Confederate left flank made good progress on the 12th. Ambrose Wright pulled two mountain howitzers with him along the ridge of South Mountain and took Weverton Cliffs without opposition. By sunset Roger Pryor held Weverton and the road at the base of the mountain. Under the supervision of Richard Anderson, second in command of the column, the brigades of Lewis Armistead and Howell Cobb moved forward to the River Road that connected Weverton with Sandy Hook but stopped well short of the base of Maryland Heights.

On the right it would be otherwise, however, for Joseph Kershaw encountered obstacles from both the enemy and nature. Federal pickets opened on him at his approach to Solomon's Gap, confirming his suspicion that he would have to overcome desperate defenders on Elk Ridge itself. Although Kershaw judged it impractical to dismount artillery and haul it with him, as soon as he reached the top he attempted to form a battleline. Throwing out eight companies as skirmishers and keeping the 2d South Carolina in reserve, Kershaw advanced the 3d, 7th, and 8th South Carolina with regimental front. His line extended well down either side of the ridge, and as it advanced it quickly lost cohesion.

At some places no more than fifty feet wide, the crest table was strewn with rocks, cleft with crevices, and occasionally blocked by large boulders. There was a road, but it was little more than a logging trail and frequently disappeared down one side or the other. Following Kershaw's South Carolina brigade came William Barksdale's Mississippi brigade, and neither were from states that gave their soldiers much practice with rugged terrain. At times the troops had "to pull themselves up precipitous inclines by the twigs and undergrowth" and "hold themselves in position by the trees in front."[84] All the while, enemy skirmishers peppered them with an annoying fire which ricocheted off stone to make a single bullet count as two or three.[85]

Kershaw passed one lightly held defensive work about a mile from Solomon's Gap and beat off a small cavalry force on his right flank. Then, at about six o'clock and within a mile of the ridge crown at Maryland Heights, he encountered an abatis "extending across the mountain" and "flanked on either side by a ledge of precipitous rocks." By this time, the Confederates had also come under artillery fire from Federal cannon on the western slope of the heights. A sharp skirmish convinced Kershaw that the enemy "occupied the position in force," and he pulled back slightly to rearrange his line and prepare for battle. As the shadows lengthened, he made the sensible decision to postpone an attack until the morning. His men would spend an uncomfortable night on the mountain, however, with almost no water and nothing to eat but corn and apples from their haversacks.[86]

Thus, by the close of the day, McLaws had not only failed to accomplish his mission, but he could not have known how much longer it would take him to capture Maryland Heights. He had kept in touch with Kershaw by signal flags, and he must have learned that his goal was blocked by a sizable force of the enemy holding a strong defensive position, which could not be flanked in its immediate vicinity. There is no indication McLaws considered trying to turn the position by advancing on the road that ran along the Potomac at the base of Elk Ridge and thus threatening to separate the Federals on Maryland Heights from the garrison at Harpers Ferry. His men in Pleasant Valley had already come under fire from the artillery in battery on the mountain, and he decided Kershaw would have to carry the position with a frontal assault.

Alone and with but a handful of cavalry, having heard not a word from the remainder of the army, and guided by the skimpiest instructions, by the fall of night on the 12th, LaFayette McLaws may have begun to question the desirability of independent command.[87]

With the consolidation of the garrisons at Harpers Ferry and the decreased likelihood the Federals intended to attempt escape, John Walker's mission was also promoted in importance. Whereas Lee originally had been uncertain whether Walker could even arrive in time to contribute to catching the enemy in flight, now Walker would have to occupy the third side of a siege triangle. Equally important, his possession of Loudoun Heights would turn out to be critical for the success of the siege. High enough for artillery placed there to devastate Harpers Ferry's defenses, but more easily accessible than Maryland Heights, Loudoun would prove the key position in forcing the Federal surrender.

Walker knew nothing of this on the 12th, and his actions during the day did not auger well for the eventual success of the overall expedition. In spite of having rested his troops on the 11th, he got off to a relatively late start, his rear guard not leaving the camp opposite Point of Rocks until eight o'clock. During the morning his column marched "very slow and rested often" in covering the seven miles of winding road to Lovettsville. Here, Walker faced a decision. He could continue westward another six miles on a similarly bad road and reach one of his destinations, the northern foot of Loudoun Heights at the Potomac. He decided instead to turn left and take the Berlin Turnpike south, so as to swing in a loop and approach the mountain from the opposite direction.[88]

In itself, it was not a bad decision, as it promised a better chance to block the escape routes from Harpers Ferry, which is what his instructions were all about; and it moved him in the direction of Key's Ford on the Shenandoah River, an objective mentioned in S.O. 191. Still, with the slow pace he set for himself, and the increased distance he now had to travel, Walker determined he would fall farther behind schedule. He marched only six more miles before bivouacking on the outskirts of Hillsboro for the night. Although he covered thirteen miles on the 12th, a greater distance than achieved by any other part of Lee's army, Walker was still six miles from Key's Ford, eight miles from Loudoun Heights, and ten miles from the escape route by the road along the Potomac. Realistically, he would need another full day to occupy his assigned positions. If the enemy resisted, then that time might be extended indefinitely.

Even as unforeseen forces worked to lengthen the time it would take to complete the Valley expedition, the unexpected quickening of the Federal advance from Washington shortened the number of hours available to Lee. By the morning of the 12th, Stuart had awakened to the suspicion that something was happening he did not fully understand. He was unable to pierce the Federal cavalry screen to discover if he was dealing only with a vigorous reconnaissance, or if the main body of the enemy were close behind. To obtain information about McClellan's intentions, he ordered Fitz Lee, who had crossed the Monocacy west of Liberty, to retrace his steps eastward and probe around the northern flank of the Federals. Stuart would gain little from this move which deprived him of over one-third of his available force.

Fitz Lee promptly rode so far to the north as to remove his brigade from the campaign for two days. At 7:30 that evening his troopers charged through the streets of Westminster, a town twenty-five miles northeast of Frederick, firing their pistols, capturing the local provost marshal, burning the conscription enrollment books, and damaging a small bridge of the B&O. His subsequent doings are obscure until he appeared at Boonsboro late on the 14th, but there is no evidence he discovered anything useful, or that his movement did more than add another small mystery for the Federals to solve.[89]

Although Stuart had become puzzled by the 12th, apparently, he was not unduly concerned by the increased Federal pressure he felt. He knew this was "the day on which, by the calculation of the commanding general, Harpers Ferry would fall." Aware that "the garrison was not believed to be very strong," and having heard nothing of the delays the expedition was encountering, he assumed the operation was proceeding on schedule.[90] The eyes and ears of the Confederate army, while neither blind nor deaf, saw and heard very little on September 12.

Hence, largely in ignorance, Stuart proceeded to take the second step to reform his line to guard the rear of an army based in Hagerstown. This time he factored in—as he had advised Lee the evening before—the loss of Frederick in a day or so. He withdrew Munford's small brigade from Monocacy Junction and sent it seven miles southwest to Jefferson, a village just beyond the Catoctins. This move belatedly provided protection for McLaws's rear, since Jefferson was but four miles from Burkittsville. There is no evidence that this was Stuart's purpose, however, since he believed the Harpers Ferry operations were winding down. Instead, he intended to establish the southern anchor for a line that would run north to Frederick (or Middletown after Frederick was lost), and eventually end at whatever point Fitz Lee returned to after his raid, perhaps Catoctin Furnace. Moving at a leisurely pace, Munford did not reach Jefferson until "a little before night."[91]

These dispositions gave Stuart only Hampton's brigade to hold Frederick and the rear of the center of Lee's divided army. Hampton's men were broken into squadrons and dispersed to picket the roads leading into the town. After the morning passed quietly, at about noon scouts reported the Federals advancing in "heavy force" on the National Turnpike. Unaccountably, Hampton was unprepared for a battle, and he rushed a squadron of the 2d South Carolina Cavalry and a rifled gun to strengthen the two guns already on the pike to buy time to collect his scattered troopers. As soon as he could, Hampton fell back through Frederick to post his men and guns farther to the west. The only force remaining in the town was a provost guard of twenty-four sabers selected from each regiment in the brigade. All morning the small body of troopers had been shepherding stragglers westward to safety. Now they were ordered to retard the progress of the enemy.

The Federal column approaching Frederick was nothing less than the vanguard of Burnside's Ninth Corps, the Kanawha Division under Brig. Gen. Jacob Cox, composed of six regiments of infantry and two batteries of artillery. The 6th New York Cavalry, which had been the eyes of the right wing, had been sent off earlier in the day to counter the move of Fitz Lee's brigade to the north, and Cox found himself leading with his infantry. After crossing the Monocacy, he had formed Moor's brigade in advance—stretching on both sides of the National road—supported by Scammon's brigade. In the very front was Col. Augustus Moor, accompanied by a single cannon and a personal escort, a troop of Chicago Dragoons. In a moment of excess ardor, Moor dashed ahead of his infantry supports and entered the town.

Seeing an opportunity too good to resist, Hampton's rear guard charged down the street in a furious attack that even the jaundiced Dr. Steiner admitted was "in grand style." The Federals, having just rounded a sharp bend, were taken completely by surprise. In a swirl of dust, horses thudded into one another, saddles were emptied, and the cannon discharged accidentally as it overturned. The Confederates captured ten prisoners, including Colonel Moor, but they could not bring off the gun as five of its horses were dead in their traces. At the sound of the commotion, Cox rushed forward at the double-quick with the 11th Ohio, only to find Hampton's men escaping through the western end of the town. By 4:30 Frederick was in the hands of the Federals. A half-hour later, Pleasonton's cavalry arrived on the road from Urbana. The citizens threw open their windows, unfurled their flags, and tossed flowers at their deliverers.[92]

Thus, for the second day in a row Stuart had been forced to move his headquarters under enemy fire. He still did not seem unduly concerned. Leaving the Jeff. Davis Legion and two guns at Hagan's Gap in the Catoctins, he traveled on with the remainder of Hampton's brigade and settled for the night in a farmhouse near Middletown. Here he and his staff enjoyed a plum cake that had been foist on his adjutant, as they galloped out of Frederick. He found time to compose a chatty letter to his wife, in which he made casual mention of Hampton's escape from Frederick. He also sent word to Lee through D. H. Hill of the loss of Frederick and included the observation that Catoctin Gap would be a "very strong position for infantry and artillery."

It is also clear, however, that Stuart assumed that the various columns in the Valley expedition had completed their missions during the day. It was no longer important to delay the enemy but only to skirmish with him "in order to develop his force." The enemy's intentions and strength continued to be a mystery to Jeb, however, as he knew only that a portion of Burnside's command occupied Frederick. The Federals refused to cooperate, as they lighted no campfires that night that might have been counted from the mountains.[93]

The command most immediately affected by the fall of Frederick was the division of D. H. Hill, which had started the day only thirteen miles west of the town. Hill's five brigades resumed their march at an early hour, passing through patches of fog, and toiled two miles up the eastern slope of South Mountain at Turner's Gap. The day soon turned warm, and the men in the ranks "suffered for water very much." The column did not stop at Boonsboro but continued northward on the National Pike, causing the men to speculate that the destination was Hagerstown, where Longstreet had already encamped.[94]

Once across the mountain, however, Hill focused on the "two objects" he understood to constitute his assignment: guarding such trains as remained at Boonsboro and watching "all the roads leading from Harper's Ferry, in order to intercept the Federal forces that might make their escape." The original positions established by Hill are not known, although he later recalled that there was a "considerable separation" of his brigades; and that his headquarters four miles west of town on the National Turnpike was in the center of his division. It is likely that his line faced south and west and covered the roads to Pleasant Valley, Sharpsburg, and Williamsport. It is certain he did not initially post any infantry in his rear to guard Turner's Gap, nor did he cover the approaches to Boonsboro from the east.[95]

What should have been a shock tremor—the news that Frederick had fallen prematurely—seems to have caused barely a ripple on its first stop, as it passed along the Confederate communications network. D. H. Hill's response certainly was minimal, when word reached him after dark. He sent the brigade of Alfred Colquitt, the only force he had not committed to watching the roads from Harpers Ferry, back from the divisional camp four miles west of Boonsboro, "to occupy the commanding points" around the town itself. He sent no force to the pass in the Catoctins commended by Stuart, nor did he even move to defend the vastly more important Turner's Gap in South Mountain, which was immediately in his own rear.[96] As was the case with Stuart, Hill may believed that the missions assigned in Special Orders, No. 191, had now been completed.

Robert E. Lee knew better, of course. Since the arrival in the early afternoon of Jackson's dispatch from Martinsburg, he had known the Valley expedition would miss its deadlines. The Confederate commander would not learn in a timely fashion, however, of the capture of Frederick by Federal infantry. Jeb Stuart would later recall that he "conveyed" the information "through General D. H. Hill."[97] This may mean the cavalry courier had orders to go no farther than Boonsboro, and it then became Hill's task to forward the word to Hagerstown. Whatever the case, Lee would not learn of this important development until about noon of the following day, twenty-four hours after the fact.

• • •

Once McClellan reached Frederick, the simple arithmetic of geography put him closer to either wing of Lee's army than they were to each other. Neither arithmetic nor geography could help the Federal commander, however, until his intelligence provided him with accurate information about the enemy's location. The reports coming into headquarters on the 12th yielded tantalizing glimpses into Confederate movements, but taken together they provided a confusing picture of Confederate intentions. At dawn, Burnside reported that the Confederates had left Frederick taking the roads to Hagerstown, Gettysburg, and Harpers Ferry, but he admitted the information did not make sense. "If they are going into Pennsylvania," he wired McClellan, "they would hardly be moving on the Harper's Ferry road, and if they are going to recross [the Potomac], how could they be moving upon Gettysburg?" By ten in the morning, however, McClellan felt "perfectly confident" Lee had left the town "moving in two directions," using both the Hagerstown and Harpers Ferry roads.[98]

During the course of the day, McClellan began to suspect that a part of Lee's army had been detached to capture Harpers Ferry. Receiving word from Washington that the garrison was now under his command, he issued orders to press reconnaissance in the direction of Harpers Ferry to discover if it were under direct attack. By evening the picture that had started to come into focus lost its resolution. Nothing had been heard from Dixon Miles, nor was there any sound of firing from Harpers Ferry; in addition, there were new reports that Jackson had recrossed the Potomac as far away as Williamsport. The latter news made it appear the enemy might be merely retreating into Virginia, rather than moving on Harpers Ferry. Indeed, when Lincoln saw a telegram from Curtin to that effect, he wired McClellan begging, "Please do not let him get off without being hurt."[99]

The uncertainty that had settled on McClellan's mind by the end of the day was reflected in his instructions to the vanguard under Burnside for the pursuit on the 13th. After carrying the Catoctins and approaching Middletown, if Burnside could determine the main body of the enemy had taken the National Turnpike toward Hagerstown, he was to pursue. But, if intelligence, including merely the sound of cannon fire, indicated Harpers Ferry was under attack, Burnside was to move to the relief of the garrison.[100] It is not surprising that McClellan did not immediately decide to employ his left wing under Franklin to relieve Harpers Ferry. In focusing on Frederick for the past several days, the

Federal right had not only advanced quicker and farther, but the left had angled northward toward Frederick. In consequence Burnside was now considerably nearer Harpers Ferry than Franklin. Moreover, McClellan needed to refuse his left flank along the Potomac until he learned the meaning of the rumor that Jackson had recrossed the river at Williamsport. Lincoln may have jumped to the conclusion that the Confederates were retreating, but the possibility of a turning movement could not be dismissed lightly.

All in all, the Army of the Potomac made solid progress on the 12th. With the vanguard of the Ninth Corps in Frederick and the remainder nearby, the First Corps, the other component of the right wing, advanced ten miles from Poplar Springs to New Market. In the center, Sumner's Second Corps marched seven miles from Clarksburg to Urbana, and Williams's Twelfth Corps moved six miles from Damascus to Ijamsville Crossroads. On the left, Franklin's Sixth Corps advanced five miles from Barnesville to Licksville Crossroads, and Couch's division of the Fourth Corps marched six miles from Poolesville to Barnesville. It was on this day that Washington finally released the Fifth Corps from the defenses of the capital, and McClellan ordered Sykes's division of regulars eleven miles forward from Middlebrook to Urbana. Morell's division of the Fifth crossed the river from Arlington and advanced twenty miles to Brookeville. A third division had been created from new regiments and assigned to the Fifth Corps, but it would not likely be able to take the field for some days yet.

As McClellan retired for the night at his headquarters at Urbana, he could be pleased with the day's developments on several levels. His army occupied the line of the Monocacy and stood a day's march from the mountains. With the addition of Porter's Fifth Corps, that army now totaled about 95,000 officers and men present for duty, a figure that approached his estimate of the size of the enemy. And, finally, although several key questions remained unanswered, he had a better understanding of his foe's movements than at any time in the campaign. Washington and Baltimore were now safe. Lee had but three broad options: the Confederate commander could head north in an invasion of Pennsylvania, but this would be an unwise move with the Federals now so close on his communications; he could stand and fight in western Maryland; or he could launch a turning movement against the Army of the Potomac. This latter option was not only the best move the enemy could make, it was also the most characteristic of the strategy

Lee had pursued since he took command. The reports that Lee had already divided his army suggested the turning movement may have already commenced.

McClellan knew that the momentum in the campaign was shifting toward the Federals. What he did not know was that the initiative had already slipped from Lee's grasp. It would not come unbidden into his own hands, however. It would not be his until he seized it.

CHAPTER FIVE

"More rapidly than convenient"

Lee's Plans Unravel, September 13, 1862

From its dawning warm and sunny, Saturday, September 13, promised to be a typical day in the Maryland campaign. It was the tenth day of the Confederate sojourn north of the Potomac and the fourth day of the expedition to clear the Federal forces from the Valley of Virginia. But, it was also the day on which Lee learned that the Federals were advancing against his rear "more rapidly than was convenient." Before another sun could clear the horizon, the Confederate commander would be scrambling frantically to reunite his army and salvage his campaign. The 13th was a day of discovery and awakening. Lee would not employ the phrase "more rapidly than convenient" until three days later in a dispatch to Jefferson Davis.[1] The context of that letter makes it clear that Lee was referring to the vigorous Federal advance from Frederick to South Mountain on the 13th, which Lee assumed was entirely due to his plans falling into McClellan's hands. Indeed, after the war, the Confederate commander asserted his belief that until the Federals found a copy of Special Orders, No. 191, McClellan had been in "complete ignorance of the whereabouts and intentions of the Southern army." Furthermore, as Lee remembered it, "McClellan's army, widely extended, with its left on the Potomac, was moving only a few miles every day, feeling its way with great caution."[2]

Lee's testimony confirms—albeit in the manner of rationalization—that he did not become greatly alarmed until the evening of the 13th. With but a single exception, his words and actions during the day largely bear this out. At the time Lee did not perceive—and after the war he would not admit—that his army was in considerable danger before the orders were found. It is now clear, however, that Lee's lack of alarm, at least on September 13, was ignorance due to faulty intelligence.

Some Concern in the Morning

On the morning of the 13th, Lee knew that Stuart planned to evacuate Frederick during the day, and he was also aware that complications had arisen in clearing the Valley of Virginia of Federals. This combination of information was sufficient to cause him concern in one respect. Clearly, it was past time to find out what was happening with the column designated to operate directly against Maryland Heights and Harpers Ferry. At an early hour, Lee dictated to his military secretary, Armistead Long, the essence of a message to be dispatched to LaFayette McLaws.[3]

"General Lee desires me to say," Colonel Long began with a reprimand, "that he has not heard from you since you left the main body of the army. He hopes that you have been able to reach your destined position." Since there is no indication Lee had issued instructions about reporting or provided McLaws with special couriers or opened communication from the other end to pass on important news affecting McLaws (such as the move to Hagerstown or the evacuation of Martinsburg), the rebuke seems unmerited. Likely, Lee's initial belief that the expedition would be doing little more than chasing away a nuisance had forestalled elaborate precautions for coordination and communication. The reference to "destined position" meant Maryland Heights.

"He is anxious that the object of your expedition be speedily accomplished," Long wrote. And then he explained, "The enemy have doubtless occupied Frederick since our troops abandoned it, and are following our rear." These two sentences are the most revealing evidence of Lee's state of mind during the morning of the 13th. Before the enemy had advanced to the foot of South Mountain, before he was even certain of the Federal occupation of Frederick, Lee was "anxious." He perceived that McClellan was "following our rear" closely enough to pose a threat to McLaws, unless the operations against Harpers Ferry were "speedily" concluded. These sentences suggest that with more timely information Lee might have perceived the strategic momentum in the campaign had shifted to the enemy. Undoubtedly, he would have been even more anxious, if he had known that, as he dictated this dispatch, Federal infantry and artillery were swarming through the streets of Frederick, and Federal cavalry had entered the Middletown valley and was probing toward Crampton's and Turner's Gaps.

Long then went on to report developments in the Valley expedition as known to Lee. "The enemy have abandoned Martinsburg and retreated to Harper's Ferry, about 2,500 or 3,000 strong. General Jackson will be at Harper's Ferry by noon today to cooperate with you." This strongly suggests that Lee dictated the dispatch early in the morning, and he expected it to reach McLaws before midday. It is impossible to tell, however, whether the information about the strength of the Martinsburg garrison and the estimated arrival of Jackson had been embodied in Jackson's report of the previous noon or came from a subsequent dispatch.

By announcing Jackson's arrival "to cooperate," Lee confirmed that S.O. 191 had not specifically called for Stonewall to march to Harpers Ferry. It is interesting that Lee did not tell McLaws that Jackson would take charge of the operations. Certainly, it is possible that Lee felt no need to state the obvious fact that Jackson's senior rank would give him command. Nonetheless, the use of "cooperate"—and the failure to mention John Walker's column—suggests something more. It is reasonable to infer that Lee still did not foresee the necessity of a siege. The strength of the Martinsburg garrison may have confirmed his belief that the force at Harpers Ferry was of approximately the same size. Whether Lee thought the combined garrison to be half their actual numbers, or whether he thought the Federals would still attempt flight—or both—he continued to believe the problem could be "speedily" solved.

In providing additional information, Long revealed the extent of Lee's knowledge about the positions of the remainder of the Confederate army. "General Stuart, with his cavalry, occupies the Middletown Valley," he wrote. Hence, even while Lee only guessed that the Federals were in Frederick, he assumed that Stuart had evacuated the town. This implies Lee had not heard from the cavalry commander since the dispatch of the 11th two nights before, in which Stuart declared his intention of abandoning Frederick, probably on the 13th.

"General D. H. Hill is a mile or two west of Boonsboro at the junction of the Sharpsburg and Hagerstown roads, and General Longstreet is at Hagerstown." This acknowledges that Lee knew Hill was observing the escape routes from Harpers Ferry but not guarding the South Mountain passes. There is no indication at this point that the Confederate commander was displeased by Hill's dispositions. It is worth noting that there still is no mention whatsoever of John Walker's division.

Long then went on to warn McLaws to guard his own rear: "You are particularly desired to watch well the main road from Frederick to Harper's Ferry, so as to prevent the enemy from turning your position." Lee was likely referring to the road that ran southwest from Frederick through Jefferson to Knoxville, where it connected with the River Road that led to Weverton and Harpers Ferry.

When taken in conjunction with the previous sentence, this indicates that Lee believed it more likely McClellan would move south from Frederick to the relief of Harpers Ferry, than that the Federals would march northwest against Turner's Gap and Boonsboro. It also suggests that Lee was either unaware, or at least unconcerned, about Franklin's left wing, which had been advancing along the Potomac River. This would certainly help to explain why the Confederate commander was anxious but not greatly alarmed on the morning of the 13th. He perceived some danger to McLaws and the success of the Valley expedition—but none as yet to his army or to the overall campaign.

In closing, Long reiterated and thus emphasized, "The commanding general hopes that the enemy about Harper's Ferry will be speedily disposed of, and the various detachments returned to the main body of the army." Lee's anxiety was apparently sufficient that he approved the use of "speedily" twice in the dispatch. He also implied in employing "dispose of" that he would accept a resolution of the problem posed by the Federal garrison that fell short of their capture.

Finally, in case the opening of the letter had been too subtle, Long admonished McLaws, "You are also desired to communicate as frequently as you can with headquarters."

Just as Lee began to grow "anxious" over the pace of the Valley expedition, a distraction arose to divert his attention. When last heard from, Jefferson Davis had reached Rapidan Station on his way to visit the Army of Northern Virginia. On the 9th, Lee not only wrote to discourage the president from traveling farther, he had also dispatched Maj. Walter Taylor to dissuade Davis from continuing the journey. Now, after four days without further word, Lee received a lengthy letter from the Confederate president. Unfortunately, the dispatch has been lost. Its location and date of composition are unknown, and its contents must be surmised from Lee's reply.

Davis had reached Warrenton before abandoning his trip on his own accord, probably after learning the army had already crossed the Potomac. He returned to Richmond on either the 8th or 9th, as Taylor would hear on the 10th at Warrenton that the president had already departed.[4] Frustrated in his attempt to consult on the broad policy implications of the movement into Maryland, Davis had committed his thoughts to paper and sent them to Lee. It is likely, he also took this opportunity to send along the draft of a proclamation for Lee to issue. If he sent the dispatch before leaving Warrenton, it had taken an unusually long time to reach the army. More likely, Davis wrote after he returned to Richmond, and, with a hard-riding courier, his dateline may have been as late as the 11th.

Presumably, Davis's letter reflected the high expectations which abounded in Richmond in response to Lee's move and which the president's attempt to join the army suggested he fully shared. The Confederate Congress had defeated a motion to send peace commissioners to Washington only on the grounds that previous overtures had been rejected discourteously and that any new move must be initiated by the Federals. A House resolution under debate, as Davis wrote, declared:

> Congress has heard, with profound satisfaction, of the triumphant crossing of the Potomac by our victorious army, and, assured of the wisdom of that military movement, could repose with entire confidence on the distinguished skill of the commanding general and the valor of his troops, under favor of the great ruler of nations, to achieve new triumphs, to relieve oppressed Maryland, and to advance our standards into the territory of the enemy.

Although there was near unanimity in approving the entry into Maryland, a significant minority was trying to strike the final phrase with its implied authorization of an invasion of Pennsylvania.[5] Doubtless, Davis realized that both the high hopes of the majority and also the reservations of the minority imbued Lee's actions with political delicacy and increased the importance of providing the military commander with political guidance.

In the reply Lee dictated to Davis on the morning or afternoon of the 13th (no time is given or implied), the Confederate commander revealed that in several ways he appreciated the delicate nature of the exchange. He began, perhaps somewhat ingenuously, by lamenting their inability to meet. "I regret," he assured Davis, "that you should have exposed yourself while indisposed, to the fatigue of travel, though I should have been highly gratified at an opportunity of conferring with you on many points."[6] This is the only indication Davis had undertaken the journey even though ill, and it suggests one reason he may not have persevered beyond Warrenton. At the same time, it also underscores the enthusiasm the president felt over Lee's expedition. Lee's reference to "many points" suggests Davis either raised many issues in his letter or at least alluded to the fact there was much he had wished to talk about in their meeting.

"You will perceive," Lee went on, "by the printed address to the people of Maryland which has been sent to you, that I have not gone contrary to the views expressed by you on the subject." Minimally, this must mean Davis told Lee to issue a proclamation to Marylanders and provided some instructions about its contents. It more likely means that Davis sent a draft proclamation, and it was probably the one printed in the *Official Records* and dated "September 7[?]" by the editors.[7] If the first possibility be true, Davis may have simply instructed Lee to remind Marylanders that the Confederacy was committed to ensuring them a free voice in their own destiny. In this case, Lee's confidence that he had anticipated Davis's wishes is understandable. If Davis did send the version of the draft proclamation as printed, however, a number of curiosities arise.

In the first place, the manner in which the draft found its way into the *Official Records* is unusual. No copy was a found among the records of the Army of Northern Virginia or in any collection of Lee papers. In 1882, upon request of the War Department, Davis furnished copies of seven letters he had written to Lee during the war, including the draft proclamation. As copied in Davis's "Letter Book," the draft is in the form of an undated letter with three blanks in place of the name of a specific state and its citizens, and includes a note that originals were sent to Generals Lee, Bragg, and Kirby Smith. Davis filled in the first blank with "Maryland" and assigned the date of the 7th with a question mark when he forwarded a copy to Washington. This indicates Davis believed he had sent the draft to Lee, but the date probably indicates either the time of composition or the trip to Rapidan, and not the day the letter was sent. It is not positive proof, of course, that Lee ever received the draft.[8]

The second curiosity about the draft proclamation derives from its contents. Of the eight articles that comprise the draft none is aimed at the people of a border state such as Maryland, or at a state claimed to be already in the Confederacy such as Kentucky. In fact, the last three articles specifically address those who were waging war against the Confederacy. It would seem as though this proclamation were intended for Pennsylvania and Ohio. Considering the political unanimity on entering Maryland and Kentucky but the debate over the propriety of crossing the Mason-Dixon Line and the Ohio River, it is reasonable to assume Davis directed his attention to the subject of occupying avowedly enemy territory.

The president may also have been motivated by knowledge of debate on another resolution then before the Confederate Congress that would be passed on September 12. It called upon him to instruct commanders "as soon as they approach or enter the territory of the United States bordering on the Mississippi River," or its tributaries, to issue a proclamation assuring all concerned that the Confederacy stood for the free navigation of the Mississippi.[9] Although this issue would seem to have been of little interest to Marylanders, it formed the subject of article three of Davis's draft proclamation.

Possibly, Lee's comment that his own proclamation had "not gone contrary to the views" of the president was the general's contorted way of acknowledging that the Davis draft had not exactly suited his purposes. It may also explain Lee's next sentence: "Should there be anything in it to correct, please let me know." He may have felt a bit uncomfortable about the dissimilarities between his own and the president's suggested proclamation.[10]

It is interesting that, as late as the writing of this letter, Lee would think there was time for him to hear from Davis and still issue a revised statement to the people of Maryland. This suggests Lee believed he would be in the area at least another week, and it places the dispatch to Davis earlier, rather than later on the 13th.

In his fourth sentence, and without beginning a new paragraph, Lee seemed to shift topics drastically.[11] "I have received as yet no official list," he wrote, "of the casualties in the late battles, and from the number of absentees from the army, and the vice of straggling, a correct list cannot now be obtained." In fact, however, Lee introduced a discussion of the condition of his army in order to put into perspective his response to Davis's high expectations for its achievements. "The army has been so constantly in motion, its attention has been so unremittingly devoted to what was necessary, that little opportunity has been afforded for attention to this subject." Lee felt it necessary to remind the president that the fast-paced Confederate victories of the summer had been purchased through hard service and considerable expense in wear on the Army of Northern Virginia.

Lee's point was to dampen Davis's enthusiasm. "I wish your views of its operations could be realized," he cautioned, "but so much depends upon circumstances beyond its control, and the aid we may receive, that it is difficult for me to conjecture the result." The only firm conclusion to be drawn from Lee's remark is that Davis must have expressed ambitious hopes for the campaign. The reference to dependence on aid received suggests at least one of those hopes involved adding Maryland's star to the Southern cross.

Lee's next comment hints that Davis did not confine his expectations to Maryland. "To look to the safety of our own frontier," he observed, "and to operate untrammeled in an enemy's territory, you need not be told, is very difficult." It is highly likely that the reference to "enemy's territory"—which in Confederate eyes Maryland was not—meant that Davis had approved Lee entering Pennsylvania. This interpretation is rendered all the more reasonable when it is recalled that on the 4th Lee had specifically asked Davis to let him know if setting foot in Pennsylvania must be ruled out for political reasons. Lee's cautionary response on the 13th suggests Davis not only approved but had conjured grander visions of invasion than Lee had intended to imply. The Confederate commander was reminding the president that the farther his army marched north, the more difficult it would be to guard his communications, or to prevent the Federals from mounting a counterstroke against Richmond.

No doubt, the difficulties Lee was experiencing in opening a safe line of supply, combined with his rising concern over the pace of the expeditionary forces, contributed to his cautious response to Davis's expectations. Still, no one better appreciated the ripeness of the moment than did Lee, and no one could have been more determined to harvest its fruit. "Every effort however will be made," he assured the president, "to acquire every advantage which our position and means may warrant."

Lee could not leave the subject without returning to what he perceived to be the single greatest obstacle to his achieving full success. "One great embarrassment," he lamented "is the reduction of our ranks by straggling, which it seems impossible to prevent with our present regimental officers." Unless he sacrificed accuracy to brevity, Lee's remark indicates a shift in opinion. In his letter of the 7th devoted exclusively to straggling, he had blamed the system at different levels, including the lack of patriotism of many of the soldiers.

Lee then proceeded to make the only contemporary estimate of the size of his army. "Our ranks are very much diminished," he told Davis, "I fear from a third to a half of the original numbers, though I have reason to hope that our casualties in battle will not exceed five thousand men."

The fact that Lee had to guess at the approximate size of his army, and even more that his guesses ranged tens of thousands apart, reveals the extent of his ignorance. It also explains his call for divisional returns on the previous day.

Unfortunately, it is impossible to know what Lee meant by "original numbers." In theory, he may have meant the total initially mustered into the regiments, a figure represented by the "present and absent" category on returns. In one respect, this would have been a reasonable figure for him to use as a benchmark, as it would show the greatest diminution and emphasize his point. Yet this is unlikely, because two-thirds or one-half of 180,000 would mean Lee believed he had an army of 90,000 to 120,000 on September 13.

It is equally unlikely that he was referring to the 75,000 present for duty total of the trimonthly estimate for September 1, as the context makes clear his "original" indicates a period earlier than Second Manassas. It would also mean Lee estimated his army to be no more than 37,000 to 50,000 men. While this would harmonize with his statement of "less than 40,000" men in his official report, that later estimate referred to the day of the Battle of Sharpsburg, which occurred after the losses at South Mountain and Harpers Ferry and did not include the significant straggling yet to occur.[12]

It is most likely Lee referred to the present for duty totals of the army he inherited in June. In this case, one-half to two-thirds of 112,000 would mean Lee estimated he had 56,000 to 75,000 at the time he wrote to Davis.[13] This figure would accord with the report by Dr. Steiner of the number of troops he saw marching through Frederick three days earlier. In any event, Lee's estimate may have been so ill informed as to be meaningless. After all, his projection of Confederate losses at Manassas and Chantilly were wrong by nearly half.[14]

Lee then turned to less pressing matters, and, in fact, proceeded to ramble a bit among scattered topics. "I am glad to hear," he declared, "that the railroad bridge over the Rapidan is in a fair way to completion." Apparently the span had not been completed by the 9th, when Davis had left for Richmond. And then, because Manassas was much on his mind, Lee ruminated, "I fear all the locomotives and cars captured at Bristoe & Manassas have been destroyed either by the enemy or ourselves." Carrying forward with his thought, the Confederate commander continued, "As I before stated, having only Jackson's & Longstreet's corps in the battle of Manassas, I was unable to spare men to save property, though I knew and felt its value." This is an interesting glimpse into Lee's current thinking about organization. Not only does he employ "corps" instead of command or wing, but he implies he may still be thinking in terms of more than two.

Lee then returned for a third time to the topic of the casualties of Manassas. "I fear there was much suffering among the wounded," he lamented, "but it was impossible to prevent it. Dr. Guild, the Medical Director, with detachments from each brigade, was left upon the field, and all the wounded committed to their care." This is the only known mention that brigade detachments were left behind on the battlefield; and there is no way of knowing how large they were or how long they stayed. He then added an explanation with somewhat confusing syntax: "All the means of transportation at our command were given to him, including the wagons, with directions that they must receive the first attention and be sent to Warrenton. They were ordered to be forwarded thence to Gordonsville, as fast as possible, and as they were able to bear the transportation." Not only are the pronouns carelessly employed, but the phrase "including the wagons" makes no sense, as there was no other means of conveyance. Nevertheless, however many vehicles were detached for this purpose increased the strain on the army's inadequate transportation system and impacted on Lee's ability to haul victuals to his hungry men.

Finally, Lee closed by tying his diverse strands of thought together. "Only one regiment of cavalry is in front of Warrenton," he wrote, referring to the 6th Virginia of Munford's brigade, "and that I fear my necessities will oblige me to withdraw." Alluding directly only to Warrenton, he warned, "Unless Genl Smith can organize a force and advance it, it will be liable to raids from Washington and Alexandria by the enemy's cavalry." Lee must have realized—and he must known Davis would instantly grasp—that what was true of Warrenton, was just as true of all of northern and central Virginia.

It was, therefore, a comment not merely on the tactical vulnerability of the wounded, but an incisive observation on the strategic gamble taken by Lee, when he carried nearly all of Richmond's defenders across the Potomac. If Lee had started to feel the weight of his gamble by the morning of the 13th, he did not so say to Davis. Instead, steeling himself to any sentiment over danger, either to his wounded men or to the capital, he stated philosophically, "It is a risk we must necessarily run to use the troops elsewhere."[15] Such steel, forged from an awareness of the moment to be seized and the resources already sacrificed to create it, would harden Lee's determination to persevere with his campaign in Maryland beyond when most generals would have lost heart—and, perhaps, beyond logic.

It is impossible to predict whether Lee would have been amused or embarrassed to learn that someone else in the Army of Northern Virginia was writing a letter to Jefferson Davis on September 13, a letter that was in effect a clandestine report on him and the campaign. Artillery chief William Nelson Pendleton, who at West Point had been one year behind Lee and two behind Davis, had been commissioned by the president to submit "occasional confidential memoranda of the positions, doings, &c of the army."[16] It is highly unlikely that either hostility or lack of confidence in Lee motivated the president's furtive assignment. On the other hand, the incident does reveal the lengths to which Davis would go to acquire information and divergent views.

Lee certainly need not have worried that his old friend would undercut his authority. According to Pendleton, Lee was "bold, prompt, energetic, sagacious." The army was in high morale, and the food was ample. If anything, Pendleton's report was overly optimistic. His one small concern was that rumor had the army staying in Hagerstown for ten days, when he believed that celerity was necessary for "great results at this juncture." What results he expected, Pendleton did not divulge.

The forenoon concluded for Lee with the arrival of a message from Jeb Stuart. This is yet another unfound dispatch known only from the response to it. Apparently, it is the one dashed off by the cavalry commander early in the morning, while awaiting the attack of the enemy at Hagan's Gap in the Catoctins.[17] It had taken about five hours to travel seventeen miles, pass through D.H. Hill's hands, and reach Lee in Funkstown. From it Lee learned that Federal infantry had occupied Frederick on the previous day. As is evident from Lee's answer, however, Stuart must not have depicted the developing situation as desperate.

At 12:45, Lee replied over his own signature, "Your note of this date has been received."[18] Responding to the news that a mixed force of the enemy was pressing entrance into the Middletown valley, he advised Stuart, "If you find that the enemy intends more than a reconnaissance, and is too strong for your cavalry, Gen. Hill can reinforce you with a brigade of infantry, and some artillery." Lee's calm counsel indicates he did not perceive a crisis to exist. Indeed, his casual suggestion that Hill's single infantry brigade might return east of South Mountain demonstrated his belief that Stuart contended with a minimal Federal force. At the same time, since Lee never intended to stop the enemy from crossing South Mountain, his willingness to send infantry back to the Catoctins also showed his growing concern to buy time for the flagging Valley expedition to complete its mission.

That this was in fact on Lee's mind was revealed in his next sentence. "I have as yet heard nothing from Harper's Ferry of the troops in that region." This meant not only that Lee had not heard at all from McLaws, but also that he had not heard recently from Jackson.

Then Lee made a truly startling proposal. "If there is a prospect of drawing the force you mention under Reno, within reach of Hill, so that he can strike at them with his whole force, do so. Keep Hill advised of any movements affecting him." It may be that Lee was victim of an obsolete picture of the organization of Federal forces and that he believed Reno commanded the mere handful of regiments he had led on the Rappahannock, at Second Manassas, and at Chantilly. Even so, the idea that Hill's entire division should retrace its steps and undertake an offensive is puzzling. It cannot be fully explained by either an underestimation of Federal strength, or a mild concern for the vulnerability of McLaws's rear, although both no doubt made the thought seem feasible. The notion must have derived from Lee's determination to seize every opportunity—and to create one where none existed—to baffle and harass the enemy.

It is also a clear indication that at midday on the 13th Lee did not recognize he had lost the initiative. He was attempting to employ something he no longer possessed.

The Pendulum Swings Back

By first light of the 13th, LaFayette McLaws, the object of Lee's concern, was himself growing anxious about his situation, and there were ample reasons. His troops would today consume the last of the four days of rations they had carried with them from Frederick. In Pleasant Valley his commissary found only twenty barrels of flour and "a few head of cattle," while the wheat acquired could not be ground by the mills on the C&O Canal, because the banks had been cut to let out the water.[19] Moreover, he had heard nothing from Lee, Walker, or Jackson. The dispatch written by Long for Lee must cover twenty-five to thirty miles, depending upon the route taken by the courier, and it would not arrive until late that night.[20] Hence, McLaws knew nothing of the consolidation of the Federal garrisons at Harpers Ferry or of the diminution of the Confederate force at Boonsboro or of the inconveniently rapid advance of McClellan's army.

In his envelope of ignorance, McLaws stolidly plodded forward to fulfill and exceed the letter of his instructions. At daybreak his line stretched from Weverton Cliffs at the tip of South Mountain and ran diagonally northeastward across the floor of Pleasant Valley to a point on Elk Ridge, a mile short of Maryland Heights. Only on Elk Ridge, where Kershaw's brigade, supported by Barksdale's, had come upon strong fortifications, were the Confederates confronted by the enemy. The remainder of McLaws's eight brigades were watching escape routes from Harpers Ferry. While watching, they were also cowering from the occasional shells lobbed at them from Maryland Heights; and it was the fear of this fire that had prevented McLaws from advancing farther west on the River Road to turn the enemy position.[21]

Skirmishing commenced on Elk Ridge at daylight. Kershaw formed his own brigade into two lines, with the 7th and 8th Carolina in front and the 2d and 3d in the rear; and he ordered Barksdale to extend the first line to the left down the eastern slope of the mountain. At 6:30, without waiting for Barksdale to get into position, the first two South Carolina regiments advanced. It took them fifty minutes to cross the boulder-strewn, crevice-cleft terrain and reach an enemy line behind an abatis. Here the 8th South Carolina encountered a deep precipice across their front and had to turn right and struggle down the western slope of the mountain to get around it. The soldiers of the 7th, now all alone on the crest, drove the enemy from the tangled, sharpened branches and through three hundred yards of "open growth of hickory and chesnut" trees. Their reward was a second abatis, this time supported in the rear by extensive log breastworks, and a galling fire from a clearly superior number of the enemy.[22]

The 7th could make no further progress, and its colonel, David Aiken, was compelled to call for help. Kershaw ordered forward the 3d South Carolina. Because of the lack of space and the broken ground, the 3d had to pass through the 7th and form for attack while under fire. Fortunately for the Confederates, their parallel movements converged at about the same moment. Around 10:30, Barksdale gained a position on the left and rear, and the 8th South Carolina reappeared up the mountain on the right. The Federals were subjected to a brisk three-way cross fire. It was equally good luck for the Confederates that the log breastworks were held by the 126th New York Infantry, a green regiment that had been mustered in at Geneva only three weeks before. The raw recruits broke in panic at the thought of being surrounded and started a stampede of the defenders down the backside of the mountain.[23]

Victory must have caused nearly as much confusion in the ranks of the Confederates, as it took them six hours to advance the final mile and secure the remainder of Maryland Heights by 4:30 in the afternoon.[24] Shortly past noon McLaws felt sufficiently confident to send the following announcement to Lee: "Have carried the enemy entrenchments on the Maryland Heights with considerable loss in the S.C. Brig. The enemy still occupy the height next to the river on this side and are shelling from Bolivar Heights. Am occupying the R. R. and Turnpike in force."[25]

At about the same time, McLaws pushed forward his line in the valley; he sent Cobb's brigade to occupy the village of Sandy Hook at the base of the mountain and to close the road from Harpers Ferry, at least its eastern end.[26] For reasons never explained, McLaws sent no force forward the additional two miles to cover the railroad and pontoon bridges across the Potomac to Harpers Ferry. Hence, contrary to all of the injunctions in Special Orders 191, and in spite of all the precautions McLaws himself had taken, an escape route was left open for Federal flight.

By nightfall McLaws had achieved only one of his goals. Although he possessed the key to Harpers Ferry, he had not yet accomplished his mission. The enemy garrison remained at Harpers Ferry and seemed inclined to stay there. Apparently, it would be necessary to attack them in place. While this prospect promised enormous profit in captured men and supplies, it could have posed a perplexing problem for McLaws. All alone, how was he to dispose of an enemy force he believed to be about equal in size to his own?

Fortunately, McLaws never had to ask himself this question. In the best news of the day, he had earlier learned that help was on the way. A courier arrived from Jackson announcing that Stonewall would be continuing on from Martinsburg and expected his leading division would be approaching Harpers Ferry by two in the afternoon. The sound of firing from the direction of the head of the peninsula between the Shenandoah and Potomac Rivers suggested that Stonewall had arrived.[27] Surprisingly, just before sunset the signal party on Maryland Heights established contact with Walker—at first he was mistaken for A. P. Hill—on Loudoun Heights across the Potomac.[28]

Even with the welcome help of Jackson and Walker, much remained to be done, and tomorrow would be a busy day for McLaws. Infantry on Maryland Heights would not subdue the enemy. Since the Federals had managed to save part of their artillery and had spiked the cannon they could not carry off, he must find a way to get his own guns to the top of the two-thousand-foot mountain. There were also the sounds of cannon fire to the northeast and annoying reports from scouts that Federals were approaching in the rear "from various directions." Still, McLaws seemed not to worry unduly about the enemy from behind, as the "lookouts from the mountains saw nothing to confirm" the rumors.[29]

South of the Potomac, John Walker, who was just as isolated from the rest of the army as McLaws, broke camp at about 6:30. His two brigades marched south through Hillsboro and then turned right, heading west on the road from Leesburg. Having no notion of the situation he might encounter, Walker decided to mask his approach from the enemy in Harpers Ferry. He stopped short of Vestal Gap in the Blue Ridge and proceeded north on the road that ran between the Blue Ridge (Elk Ridge in Maryland) and the Short Hills (South Mountain in Maryland). Known locally as "between the Hills," this dale was a continuation of Pleasant Valley across the Potomac.

Passing through Neersville, Walker reached the eastern foot of Loudoun Heights, the crown of the Blue Ridge on the Potomac, by ten o'clock. Here he was greeted by the ominous sound of a cannonade in the water gap beyond the mountain. The mysterious firing was soon explained, as up rode a party of engineers and signal officers sent by Jackson to guide the placement of artillery and open communications between the columns. Walker thus learned that the nature of his mission had changed. He had now become one element in a complicated siege operation.

While putting six of his regiments into camp, Walker sent the 48th North Carolina to hold the road between the mountain and the river. He also ordered Col. John Rogers Cooke with two regiments to occupy Loudoun Heights. Setting out at about noon with the 27th North Carolina and 30th Virginia, and accompanied by Jackson's officers, Cooke followed a torturous, snaking route up the steep slope. Under instructions to avoid being seen, the troops frequently left the road to hack through the underbrush with hatchets and knives and did not reach the crest until five o'clock.[30]

From the summit, the Confederates enjoyed a spectacular view. They saw activity on Maryland Heights and soon learned through signal flags that McLaws was in possession of the neighboring peak. They saw Jackson's camps near Halltown, although they were unable to establish communication with Stonewall. They also saw the Federal camps spread out on the peninsula in such detail that even an ignorant private could accurately guess the enemy force numbered about ten thousand. And they in turn were seen, as Federal batteries lobbed several shells over their heads. Secrecy scarcely mattered any longer. Indeed, the sooner the Federals realized their plight, the sooner they might contemplate surrender.

As night fell, Walker's situation was strikingly similar to McLaws. He too had carried out the specific instructions of S.O. 191. Yet he, too, had not achieved his mission. He held Loudoun Heights and had blocked the escape routes. The enemy remained at Harpers Ferry, however, and showed signs of fight. Walker too would have to drag artillery up his mountain and play his role in pounding the Federals into submission. The outcome seemed inevitable, but the time it would require could not be foretold.

Stonewall Jackson awoke on the 13th knowing that the expedition to clear the lower Valley of Federals had fallen short of the swift, clean strike he and Lee had originally planned. He was already a day behind schedule; and the enemy, instead of scampering to safety, had consolidated into a considerable force of 13,500, which would now have to be subdued by assault. Fortunately, the Federal commander, Dixon Miles, had chosen to make his stand at the bottom of a topographical bowl. Just as happily, no general of the Confederacy was better suited to conduct operations against Harpers Ferry than Jackson. The post had been his first command in the spring of 1861, and he had spent several months thinking about its defense. A year later, the success of his famed Valley campaign had carried his offense to the outskirts of the town, and he had the chance to view the tactical situation from the reverse.

Jackson knew that S.O. 191 contained all of the elements necessary to construct a siege of Harpers Ferry. With McLaws assigned to capture Maryland Heights and Walker to approach Loudoun Heights, once Stonewall's three divisions moved from the west to block the neck of the peninsula, the Federal garrison would be surrounded. On the morning of the 13th, however, he did not know if McLaws and Walker were in place, nor could he foresee the degree of resistance the enemy would mount. He seemed to grasp at once that it was his responsibility as senior commander to coordinate the siege and—in addition—to make certain the operation did not drag on interminably. As his first step, he sent couriers to find the commanders of the other two columns to apprise them of the changed situation. He also told them he expected his own lead division to approach Harpers Ferry by two o'clock that afternoon.[31]

Jackson's command had been in motion at daylight, as was its custom. A. P. Hill and Lawton left their bivouac on the Opequon and traveled by a series of roads directly southeast toward Harpers Ferry thirteen miles distant. J. R. Jones's division passed through Martinsburg—dropping off the 2d Virginia (Stonewall brigade) and 10th Virginia (Taliaferro's brigade) as provost guard—and brought up the rear. Although the infantry and artillery traveled in a single column, Jackson spread his cavalry in a wide net to ensure against any attempt by the Federals to make a belated escape. Throughout the morning small groups of prisoners were brought in, nearly all of whom were shoeless. In response to the jeers of the infantry, the horsemen swore the enemy had been captured in their stocking feet. Making better time than expected, A. P. Hill's van reached the turnpike from Charlestown, turned north, and stopped just short of Halltown at eleven o'clock. Jackson could now see the enemy's defenses on Bolivar Heights two miles to the front, but he decided not to develop his line until he had scouted the position and established contact with McLaws and Walker. Jones and Lawton were halted in the rear of Hill.[32]

Assuming that Walker and McLaws had met their deadlines the previous day, Jackson posted flagmen to open communication with Loudoun and Maryland Heights. Simultaneously, he sent a party of engineers and signalmen to cross the Shenandoah at Key's Ford, apparently believing Walker might be deficient in both. By late in the afternoon, visible activity indicated a Confederate presence on the two mountains, but direct communications could not be established with either.[33]

In the end, as the Confederates attempted to change plans in mid-operation, the 13th slipped by in half measures. No artillery yet frowned from either Maryland or Loudoun Heights. Jackson's men were not in position across the mouth of the peninsula, nor was their commander yet in control of the cooperating columns. Stonewall may have hoped it possible to force the issue on the morrow, but it was not a reasonable expectation. At this point, however, he had no reason to believe a few more days added to the expedition would be of consequence.

• • •

At nine o'clock in the morning, when George McClellan rode into town, Frederick erupted with expressions of "deep-seated feelings of gratitude" seldom seen in a "matter-of-fact age." Politics cast no shadow on the "whole-souled reception" by the effervescent citizens. "Old and young shouted with joy," observed Dr. Steiner. "Matrons held their babes towards him as their deliverer from the rule of a foreign army, and fair young ladies rushed to meet him on the streets, some even throwing their arms around his horse's neck." The good doctor, who was not without sympathy for the abused general and his army, mused that "years of obloquy and reproach might have been considered compensated for by such a reception."[34]

More important than the ephemeral acclaim and even the fleeting vindication, when McClellan rode down Frederick's streets, he was nearer to either Lee or Jackson than they were to one another.[35] Although the Federal commander did not know the exact details of the strategic situation—and could not have known it from the information available to him—he understood the strategic relationships had changed for the better. Indeed, from the night of September 12, McClellan acted as if he realized the momentum of the campaign had shifted in his favor and the initiative, while not yet in his hands, was within his grasp. Once the Federals held Frederick, he knew Lee could no longer move on either Washington or Baltimore without first defeating the Army of the Potomac in the field. He knew also he was close enough to Lee's rear to make the enemy pay a heavy price for their boldness, if they headed north into Pennsylvania. Finally, he had convincing reports that Lee had fragmented the Confederate army and had sent part on roads heading north and part marching south.

Of course, McClellan needed to find out the meaning of the enemy machinations. Did the rumors of the Confederates taking the Harpers Ferry road indicate a move to capture Miles and his garrison? Did the reports of Jackson crossing the Potomac much higher upriver at Williamsport portend a turning movement from the south against the Federals' left flank? Or, although it seemed less likely, did the news of Lee in Hagerstown and Rebel cavalry in Westminster mean the enemy would try to turn their right flank? If McClellan could learn something concrete on the whereabouts of the divided enemy forces, he would have an opportunity to take advantage of their vulnerability.

Under orders that had been issued the night before, the Army of the Potomac moved forward at daylight on the 13th to locate the enemy and pierce Lee's intentions. On the far left, near the Potomac,

Charles Whiting's brigade of the 5th and 6th U.S. Cavalry rode forward from both Point of Rocks and from Buckeystown toward Jefferson to discover if the Confederates had moved on Harpers Ferry. Meanwhile, the bulk of the left wing, Franklin's Sixth Corps, marched to Buckeystown to be ready either to move to the relief of Dixon Miles, or to join the rest of the army at Frederick. Couch's division advanced from Barnesville to Licksville to protect the rear and flank from the south.

On the other flank, McClellan spared one cavalry brigade, the 1st New York and 12th Pennsylvania under Andrew McReynolds, to find out if the reports of the enemy in Westminster posed a threat from the north. At the same time, he consolidated his center and right wing into a compact front by bringing the First, Second, and Twelfth Corps—and even the division of regulars under Sykes that had been acting as his general reserve—into Frederick to join the Ninth Corps.

At an hour early enough to be worthy of Stonewall Jackson, Pleasonton pushed westward from Frederick, followed by the vanguard of the Ninth Corps. His was the responsibility to discover whether McClellan should head toward Hagerstown or Harpers Ferry. The Federal cavalry chief sent Richard Rush's brigade (4th and 6th Pennsylvania) down the road to Jefferson, supported by Harrison Fairchild's infantry (9th, 89th, and 103rd New York.) He thrust straight ahead on the National Turnpike with John Farnsworth's cavalry brigade (8th Illinois, 3d Indiana, 1st Massachusetts, and 8th Pennsylvania), followed by Edward Harland's infantry (8th and 11th Connecticut and 4th Rhode Island).

These operations—well under way before noon—brought the Federals by evening to the foot of South Mountain at both Turner's and Crampton's Gaps. These were the movements that would panic Lee when he learned of them later that night. And they were conceived before and pursued independently of the Federal discovery of a copy of S.O. 191 left behind in Frederick.[36]

Jeb Stuart did not at first recognize the threat imminent in the advance of the Army of the Potomac. Laboring under the mistaken notion that the expedition to the Valley had completed its mission and that the fragments of Lee's army were already reuniting, he did not grasp that time was running against the Confederates. Equally pernicious, he failed to perceive that in close order behind the enemy cavalry screen marched the long, snaking columns of infantry and artillery of the main body of the Federal army. In looking back a year and a half later, Stuart would protest that the "enemy had studiously avoided displaying any force" and had lighted no campfires during the night to help him count their numbers.[37] In spite of knowing from captured prisoners that infantry from the Ninth Corps had chased his rear guard from Frederick on the previous day, Jeb persisted in believing he faced a reconnaissance in force.

Still, he had doubtless now received Lee's admonition not "to retire too fast"; and, determined to retard the progress of the reconnaissance, he established a new defensive line along the Catoctin Range five miles west of Frederick. On the right, he sent Munford's brigade south to Jefferson, immediately behind the mountains; in the center he held Hampton at Hagan's Gap on the National Pike. There could be no Confederate left wing, since Fitz Lee's brigade had been sent far to the northeast to raid Westminster and threaten the Federal flank. Stuart almost paid dearly for this futile mission, because McReynolds's Federal troopers forced Lee to beat a hasty retreat and nearly captured Maj. John Pelham and the Horse Artillery.[38] The rest of Stuart's line would not fare much better on the 13th.

Thomas Munford faced a truly formidable task. Only two regiments, the 2d and 12th Virginia, remained in his brigade, and they had, in turn, been reduced by detachments to about three hundred troopers and the three guns of Chew's battery. With this inadequate force he was expected to anchor the right flank and protect McLaws's rear. Skirmishing began on Munford's front at daylight, and he soon found himself being pressed from three directions. While Whiting's regulars probed his defenses from Point of Rocks to the south and Buckeystown to the east, Rush's two regiments of Pennsylvania horsemen, supported by an infantry brigade, advanced on him from the Frederick road to the northeast.

By noon the inevitable could be held at bay no longer, and Munford began to fall back slowly on Burkittsville. He sent his trains in advance and covered his rear with sharpshooters from the 2d Virginia. Chew's battery retired toward Middletown, but, finding the enemy too far advanced on the National Road, the gunners were forced to cut across country on farm lanes to rejoin their command. Late in the afternoon, Munford abandoned Burkittsville and posted his guns and thin line of troopers in Crampton's Gap in South Mountain. Curiously, there is no indication Munford communicated with McLaws, although he was now virtually within shouting distance of Semmes's brigade at Brownsville.[39]

It is likely this was the firing McLaws heard during the day but dismissed, because spotters on the mountain saw nothing to worry about.

As McClellan had intended, however, Alfred Pleasonton directed the main Federal effort against Stuart's center, where the Jeff. Davis Legion held the National Road at Hagan's Gap. It is possible the vigor of the probe surprised the Confederate cavalry commander. When heavy skirmishing and artillery fire erupted at daybreak, Stuart rushed the rest of Hampton's brigade back from Middletown to defend the pass. The contending cavalry forces were about equal in size, but the Federals had three batteries to the Confederates' one, and from their view on the mountain the Southerners saw what appeared to be two blue infantry brigades winding westward from Frederick.[40]

Stuart had no prospect for reenforcements, and he knew he must eventually yield the pass. He may even have begun to sense that events were veering from his control. If he did not yet view the situation as critical to the survival of the Confederate army, still, he recognized that time had to be bought for D. H. Hill to prepare at Turner's Gap; and there was no better defensive position before South Mountain than the one Hampton held. Although the Catoctins were not a high range, the pass at Hagan's was a relatively sharp declivity and offered no opportunities for the enemy to turn either flank. Hence, Stuart sent two dispatches—one apprising Lee of the Federal advance and the other advising Hill to send an infantry brigade to Turner's Gap—and then he prepared to hold on as long as he could.[41] With their better view of the field, Stuart and Hampton were able to parry every Federal thrust until heavy lines of infantry punched through the center at two o'clock.

The Confederate horse withdrew in good order to Middletown, three miles farther west. Here Stuart decided to make a second stand to delay the enemy. He posted the 1st North Carolina Cavalry in front of the town and formed the remainder of Hampton's brigade behind Catoctin Creek west of the village. The troopers dragged combustibles onto the covered bridge (known locally as Koogle's) to prepare it for instant destruction. Suddenly, the Federals—who had advanced with an alacrity surprising to the Confederates—were upon them. This time the terrain did not favor Stuart. The enemy infantry deployed and extended beyond both his flanks. The 1st North Carolina broke in panic and fled through the town, where citizens shot at them from windows. They reached the creek only to find the bridge had been prematurely fired. While some troopers braved the smoke and flames, others dashed through the small stream to safety. Stuart got off several volleys from his main body before deciding he had "held the enemy in check sufficiently long" to give D. H. Hill "ample time" to man Turner's Gap. He withdrew at once from his second defensive position of the day and fell back slowly along the National Turnpike.[42]

By five o'clock, as Stuart approached the crossroads called Bolivar, about a mile east of Turner's Gap, information had accumulated that changed drastically his perception of the Confederate situation. He learned from Munford that the two small cavalry regiments at Crampton's Gap were in danger of being overrun, and he must have also heard at the same time that Harpers Ferry had not yet surrendered. This immediately focused Stuart's attention on the peril at the pass six miles to the south, which he now viewed as the "weakest point of the line."

Of vastly greater importance, at this point a breathless local resident dashed into the Confederate lines on a heavily lathered horse from a twelve-mile ride from Frederick. The Southern sympathizer had been outside McClellan's tent when the Federal commander had received a document so revealing that McClellan had thrown his hands in the air and exclaimed, "Now I know what to do!"[43] Whether or not Stuart deduced the document was a copy of S.O. 191 cannot be known for certain, but he did conclude that McClellan now knew Lee had divided the Confederate army for the purpose of eliminating the garrisons in the lower Valley.

Also, although no one, including Stuart himself, ever commented on the fact, he could not have heard the story of the civilian without grasping the implication that both McClellan and the main body of the Federal army was already in Frederick. While there is no reason to believe Jeb underestimated the value of this news, from it and all else he had recently learned, he drew the wrong conclusion. He assumed that McClellan would move at once to relieve Harpers Ferry.[44]

On this basis, and in spite of the heavy pressure the Federals had been exerting from Frederick all day against the National Road, Stuart decided to send nearly all of Hampton's brigade to reenforce Munford. Keeping only the Jeff. Davis Legion and Hart's battery, Stuart dispatched Hampton with the remainder of the brigade on the road from Bolivar to Burkittsville. As Hampton traveled south along the base of the mountain, his scouts discovered they were being paralleled on a road to their left by enemy cavalry. It turned out to be no more than a detachment of Farnsworth's brigade, which Pleasonton had sent out from Middletown, and Cobb's Legion rode across country and quickly dispersed the small

Federal force. In the meanwhile, Munford, who had heard from his own scouts of the enemy's approach, was waiting at Crampton's Gap with shotted guns and taut lanyards when Hampton's van cantered up the road. Someone in the advancing column grasped the situation just in time to wave a white flag and avert disaster. The combined cavalry force spent the night together at Crampton's Gap.[45]

After dispatching Hampton, Stuart fell back with the Jeff. Davis Legion and Hart's guns on the National Turnpike and reached Turner's Gap in South Mountain at about six o'clock. As he surmounted the crest of the pass, he encountered Col. Alfred Colquitt, who, with four Georgia and one Alabama regiments and Lane's North Carolina battery, was just arriving from Boonsboro. D. H. Hill had sent back Colquitt's brigade in response to Stuart's request—as Hill understood it—for infantry support for the cavalry to hold the pass.[46] Much to the surprise of Colquitt, Stuart ordered the foot soldiers to the side of the road, so that his troopers could continue on down the mountain. The cavalry chief conferred briefly with Colquitt near the old stagecoach inn, known as the Mountain House, and rejected the colonel's suggestion that the cavalry be employed to guard the flanks of the infantry. As Colquitt recalled the conversation after the war, Stuart conveyed no sense of urgency or alarm. "He informed me that he could not remain—that he should move with his cavalry towards Harper's Ferry—that I would have no difficulty in holding my position—that the enemy's forces he thought consisted of cavalry and one or two brigades of infantry."[47]

Colquitt, who had no cavalry whatsoever of his own, then requested Stuart detach two companies to serve as pickets and to scout the approach of the enemy. This Jeb also declined and continued on down the mountain to Boonsboro, leaving behind the impression of indifference to the fate of Turner's Gap.[48] In fairness to Stuart, he had but one regiment (actually a battalion) left with him after sending Hampton south to Burkittsville. At Boonsboro, when he discovered one regiment of Fitz Lee's brigade had returned from its futile mission to Westminster, he sent Thomas Rosser's 5th Virginia to occupy Fox's Gap located a mile south of Turner's. Rosser was given but vague instructions, however, and he was not ordered to report to Colquitt. All in all, the judgment rendered by Rosser after the war seems inescapable: "Stuart did not expect the enemy would advance on Boonsboro, and was careless in guarding the roads leading that way."[49]

From Boonsboro Stuart sent another series of dispatches to Lee and to D. H. Hill. That he did not attempt to find Hill and report in person is additional indication he did not perceive an emergency existed at Turner's Gap. Neither did he alert Hill that the enemy now possessed special knowledge of the vulnerability of the Confederate army. That information was sent to Lee, but apparently only camouflaged within the interpretation that the Federals were moving energetically to relieve Harpers Ferry and without mentioning that a lost document had been found.[50] Finally, weary after fourteen hours of hard riding and skirmishing, Stuart then settled in for the night, intending to ride with his staff to join Munford and Hampton at Crampton's Gap in the morning.

Since leading the Confederates across the Potomac and unsuspectingly launching the great adventure in Maryland, D. H. Hill and his division had melded quietly into the Army of Northern Virginia. In fact, since September 10 he and his men had performed the lightest duties of any of Lee's troops. After the short march from Frederick, Hill's five brigades had been closely watching empty roads from Harpers Ferry and waiting for fugitives that never materialized.[51] On the 13th, however, events pushed Harvey Hill to the center of the stage and toward a spotlight of scrutiny that would follow him for the remainder of his life. For more than twenty-four hours the fate of the Army of Northern Virginia—and therefore in part the destiny of the Confederacy—rested on his shoulders. Ironically, although he performed well under the circumstances, he would never entirely escape the suspicion that in one way (or another) he lost the Maryland campaign for Lee.[52]

The news of Frederick's fall on the 12th had perturbed Hill no more than it had Stuart or Lee. Hill's solitary response had been to pull Colquitt's brigade from its road watching and send it along with Lane's battery to occupy a prominence on the eastern outskirts of Boonsboro. Late on the morning of the 13th, while reconnoitering the position with Colquitt, Hill received the word from Stuart at the Catoctins that a modest enemy force—cavalry and one or two infantry brigades—would probably reach the foot of South Mountain by evening. Obviously, Stuart's message, which has not been found, must have been ambiguous. Jeb believed that he was alerting Hill to prepare to defend Turner's Gap. As Hill understood it, the defense of the Confederate rear was Stuart's responsibility, and the dispatch merely requested support.[53]

It was in this spirit that Hill ordered back Colquitt with the battery to Turner's Gap, but Hill did not ride to the pass himself, nor did he disarrange his other brigades. Stuart upon his arrival at Boonsboro apparently felt that neither protocol nor the tactical situation obliged him to report to a senior officer and the man he believed responsible for the defense of Turner's Gap. The first premonition of pending disaster came to Harvey Hill from a courier sent by Colquitt after darkness had fallen.[54]

Once Stuart had abandoned the mountain, Col. Alfred Colquitt watched with growing alarm in the gathering twilight as great plumes of dust ascended from the floor of the Middletown Valley. It occurred to the colonel that the cavalry chief's notion of the size of the enemy force might have been understated, and he immediately scrambled to find the best defensive posture for his fifteen hundred men and four guns. Turner's Gap itself was a strong position, but it was flanked both right and left by passes scarcely more than a mile away. Passable roads led from the National Turnpike to Fox's Gap to the south and Frosttown Gap to the north, and both auxiliary passes were joined by mountaintop roads to Colquitt's position at Turner's. In other words, Colquitt was vulnerable to being turned on either flank.

Initially, it seemed as if the enemy intended to ascend the mountain in the failing light, and Colquitt hurried his brigade halfway down the eastern slope and deployed on either side of the National road. At darkness the enemy withdrew from contact, and the colonel had time to reconsider his position. He retreated back up the mountain and formed line just behind the road cutting across the crest. He stretched his numbers thinly along the ridge and posted strong pickets at the gaps on either side. Then, he watched as Federal campfires began to twinkle in the valley below. The pinpoints of light multiplied by the hundreds until they stretched for miles to the horizon and soon were "far in excess" of the number required by two brigades. Indeed, although unknown to Colquitt, all four divisions of Burnside's Ninth Corps, along with two cavalry brigades, lay spread before him. Colquitt did know for certain he was in trouble, however, and he dispatched a message to Hill declaring "Genl Stuart must have been mistaken as to the strength of the enemy." He requested immediate reenforcement.[55]

Colquitt's message must not have conveyed a strong sense of emergency, as it did not cause his commander to concentrate the division or to ride the three miles back to the gap. Hill did order Samuel Garland's North Carolina brigade and Bondurant's Alabama battery to march at once to the mountain, and he ordered the remaining three brigades (Ripley, Rodes, and G. B. Anderson) to cook rations and be prepared to march in the morning. He also sent a dispatch to Hagerstown advising Lee of the increased threat. Hill then retired for what he thought would be the night.[56]

Garland's five North Carolina regiments marched through the moonshine back to the mountain and bivouacked halfway up the western slope. Their young brigadier, Samuel Garland, rode to the crest of the pass and conferred with Colquitt. The two officers insightfully guessed the greatest vulnerability lay with the more accessible Fox's Gap to the south, and Garland agreed he would extend the line in that direction at first light. Thereupon, the Confederates, most of whom were without blankets, settled down in the chilly mountain air to try to sleep for the few hours remaining before dawn.[57]

D. H. Hill was not as prepared for the morrow as his critical situation demanded, but—although he did not know it—neither was he as prepared as he was going to be. Robert E. Lee would see to that before the night was over.

The Lost Orders Found

All of the events of September 13, as thus far described—with the single exception of Stuart's mistaken assumption that McClellan would focus on the relief of Harpers Ferry—occurred independently of one of the most famous incidents of the entire Civil War.

After McClellan's arrival in Frederick about nine o'clock, he had established his headquarters in a field on the family farm of Dr. Lewis Steiner west of town.[58] Here he began to assess the information coming in from Pleasonton and Burnside to determine whether he should push toward Harpers Ferry or Hagerstown. Shortly before twelve a messenger arrived from Alpheus Williams, acting commander of the Twelfth Corps, with a copy of Lee's S.O. 191 that had been found on the ground by several soldiers of company F of the 27th Indiana Infantry. At noon an elated McClellan telegraphed to Abraham Lincoln, "I have all the plans of the rebels. . . . My respects to Mrs. Lincoln. . . . Will send you trophies."[59]

The Federal commander's ebullience is understandable. With his heart still pounding from his triumphant entry into Frederick, he saw spread before his eyes a document marked "Confidential" and addressed to Maj. Gen. D. H. Hill that detailed the marching orders for the Army of Northern Virginia. It answered in an instant several of the most puzzling questions confounding him. It not only confirmed the fragmentation of the enemy army, it also explained Lee's separation of his forces. Apparently, the Confederates had paused in their invasion of Pennsylvania to scoop up the Federal garrisons in the Valley. It also relieved McClellan's fears that Jackson was engaged in a turning movement from south of the Potomac, as Stonewall had crossed higher up the river to capture Martinsburg and block escape routes to the west. Finally, it indicated that only two divisions were operating in Pleasant Valley against Maryland Heights and Harpers Ferry from the north.

That McClellan did not immediately strike his tent and charge hell-bent westward to smite his hamstrung foe is also explained by S.O. 191—both in what it erroneously implied and what it did not reveal at all. First, it contained no information whatsoever about the strength of the Confederate army or any of its units. In this respect, McClellan's find was much less helpful than had been Lee's capture of Pope's dispatch of August 20, which had conveyed numbers for the Federal units. Second, it provided an ambiguous picture of the structure of the Confederate army. McLaws, Anderson, Walker, and D. H. Hill were said to lead divisions, but there was no way of telling what constituted the "commands" of Jackson and Longstreet. Ironically, even if Federal intelligence had been sufficiently sophisticated to piece together a chart of the Confederate army it had confronted at Second Manassas, its information would have been hopelessly skewed by the multiple changes effected by Lee since then.

Third, there was the possibility that the details in S.O. 191 were not accurate. McClellan did not doubt the authenticity of the document. Although Col. Samuel Pittman, Twelfth Corps adjutant, validated Chilton's signature, it might have been a clever enemy ruse. McClellan correctly put more weight on the fact that the orders seemed to corroborate the reports he had been receiving from Pleasonton, Curtin, and others. Still, the orders were four days old, and significant changes could have occurred.

Fourth, even if accurate and unchanged, there were ambiguities of wording that critically impaired an outsider's ability to exploit the opportunity. How much of his "command" had Jackson taken to Martinsburg? And, conversely, how much had remained with the main body? Most importantly, had the main body itself remained at Boonsboro just behind South Mountain, or had it marched on to Hagerstown?

Quite properly McClellan determined to answer as many as possible of these questions before directing his army forward. Nor, did he take an inordinate amount of time to pursue them. At three o'clock, he sent a copy of S.O. 191 to Pleasonton with instructions "to ascertain whether this order of march has thus far been followed by the enemy." Then, in a phrase that well reflected the ambiguity of his information, he warned Pleasonton to approach Turner's Gap with caution as it "may be disputed by two columns."[60] Presumably, he meant Longstreet and D.H. Hill.

From the moment McClellan first read S.O. 191, he believed Lee had "made a gross mistake" and could be "severely punished for it." He perceived the Confederates had exposed themselves in laying a snare for Harpers Ferry, and he might "catch them in their own trap."[61] If, however, while waiting for Pleasonton's report he studied a map of the terrain and reviewed all of the information available to him, his euphoria must have begun to thin. Knowledge of the enemy's divided forces was in itself of limited usefulness.

First, there was also the matter of the enemy's strength as compared to his own. Everything McClellan had heard to date suggested Lee had at least 100,000 men in Maryland, and some of the reports gave the Confederates half again as many. What Lee referred to as the "main body" likely contained 50,000 to 60,000 soldiers, therefore, and could scarcely be regarded as a insignificant force. McClellan himself had but 65,000 in the Frederick area in the First, Second, Ninth, and Twelfth Corps, Sykes's division of regulars and Pleasonton's cavalry.[62] The absence of 40,000 to 50,000 Confederates on the Harpers Ferry expedition evened the odds, but it did not make Lee a walkover.

Second, there was the matter of geography. If Lee's main body was at Boonsboro, just fifteen miles away behind South Mountain, McClellan's strategic flexibility was limited. If the Federals attempted to move to the relief of Harpers Ferry, Lee would be immediately on their flank or rear. Even if the Confederate main body had marched on to Hagerstown, it would be only thirteen miles farther distant. On the other hand, there would be objections to bringing Franklin's left wing of 19,000 men to Frederick to give McClellan a significant advantage over the enemy main body. Not only would the move cost a day's delay, but any Federal force punching through Turner's Gap would then have Jackson and McLaws on its flank or rear. The unhappy prospect McClellan believed he confronted was that a large army divided could easily become a vise. While there is no evidence to suggest McClellan suspected Lee intentionally created a pincer movement, the Federal commander's actions indicate he recognized the potential for one existed.

By six o'clock—just three hours later—McClellan had gathered such information as he could expect to acquire in a timely fashion, and the general, correctly known for his cautious temperament, had decided on an untypically bold[63] plan to maximize his opportunities under the conditions known to him.[64] Officers of the signal corps had spotted McLaws's column in Pleasant Valley, and heavy firing from the direction of Harpers Ferry indicated Miles had not surrendered. McClellan had also concluded, presumably on the basis of reports from Pleasonton, that a strong Confederate force held Turner's Gap. Unfortunately, he could have no way of knowing if this meant Lee's main body had remained at Boonsboro, or if only D. H. Hill's "corps" defended the pass.[65] He was compelled to render his plan with this important piece of information lacking.

McClellan decided he would avoid falling prey to pincers by attacking in two columns and pressing forward at both Turner's and Crampton's Gaps. He would hazard less than decisive odds against the Confederates due west at Boonsboro in order to attempt to relieve Harpers Ferry and, perhaps more importantly, to guard his left flank by putting pressure on McLaws. If all went well on the morrow, Burnside and Hooker would carry Turner's Gap and break through to the Hagerstown Valley. Simultaneously, Franklin would carry the pass at Crampton's and either defeat McLaws or chase him away. Miles could then cross the Potomac with his 13,000 men to safety. Franklin with his augmented column must then turn to help against the enemy main body. If Burnside had not successfully carried Turner's Gap, Franklin was to move north along Pleasant Valley on the Confederate flank at Boonsboro. If the Federals had already carried Boonsboro, however, Franklin was to march west toward Sharpsburg and Williamsport to cut off enemy escape and prevent Jackson recrossing the Potomac. Sumner, Williams, and Sykes would be in close support of Burnside, but a portion could be diverted to Franklin if necessary.

Considered within the context of the information as known to McClellan, his plan was probably overly ambitious. It was not certain Couch's division could come up in time to participate with the two divisions of Franklin's Sixth Corps. Nor did McClellan account for the presence of Walker's division, which at Loudoun Heights would be on Franklin's flank. He was also relying on Jackson, a commander known for his speedy responses, to remain idle at Martinsburg for an improbably long time. Finally, McClellan seems not to have considered that Lee's known propensity for moving by his left flank might induce the Confederate commander to cross South Mountain farther north—say at Hamburg Pass—and threaten the long and unprotected Federal columns on the National Road. In this latter case, McClellan might have been justified in assuming the already fragmented Confederates would lack the strength to attempt such a move.

Considered beyond the facts as McClellan knew them and in the context of the situation as it actually existed, McClellan's plan was a good one. It offered the chance to inflict severe punishment on McLaws and D. H. Hill, to raise the siege of Harpers Ferry and rescue the garrison and supplies there, to harry Lee back across the Potomac and bring to an inglorious conclusion the Confederate adventure in Maryland. It did not give promise for the destruction of Lee's army, but then no plan McClellan had the ability to execute could have looked for that result. Jackson and Walker were already south of the Potomac, and the Federals could not have prevented Longstreet from recrossing unhampered at Williamsport, only six miles from Hagerstown. Nor, should D. H. Hill have much difficulty in getting away, as it was only twelve miles from Boonsboro to the Potomac through Sharpsburg, and he would have had Stuart's cavalry to cover his retreat. Under severe duress even McLaws might escape on the road from Sandy Hook through Antietam Furnace to Boteler's Ford below Shepherdstown. No matter who commanded it, the Army of the Potomac did not have the discipline, the officers, or the legs to outrun the Army of Northern Virginia.

On the other hand, returning to reality as it appeared to the participants on September 13, McClellan had no reason to believe Lee would cut and run. The Federal commander would need to have known that his foe totaled only 70,000 or so men, and that only 8,000 troops guarded Turner's Gap, to have worried the Confederates might scamper out of harm's way and spoil his opportunity to punish them. Ironically, if McClellan had known the size of the Confederate army, and if he had planned his strategy on the assumption Lee would flee for Virginia, he would have been mistaken, and perhaps dangerously so. In order to succeed, what McClellan needed to know in addition to the strength of the Confederates—and no document could have been found to tell him this—was the iron determination Lee possessed to prevent the Maryland campaign from failing. The finding of Special Orders, No. 191, did not give McClellan a realistic opportunity to destroy Lee, but Lee himself was about to provide that chance.

The Crisis by Eventide

Although there is no evidence that Robert E. Lee left the confines of his camp on the outskirts of Hagerstown, Saturday, September 13, was a long, wearisome day for the Confederate commander. As the hours dragged on, reports accumulated at headquarters which revealed that his campaign in Maryland was unraveling at an ever increasing rate. He had been mildly concerned to learn the previous day that Stuart was evacuating Frederick. That news had caused him to send a sharp note to McLaws to "speedily" dispose of the Federals around Harpers Ferry. Then, this noon came the dispatch from Stuart indicating the Federals were already pressing forward from Frederick in such force that the Confederate cavalry could not hold the pass at the Catoctins and would be obliged to retire to South Mountain. Despite the fact that this meant the Confederate rear would collapse thirteen miles in one day; and that the enemy would be within five miles of intersecting a straight line drawn between Hagerstown and Maryland Heights, there is no known evidence of any action taken by Lee during the afternoon in response. At this point, he apparently trusted to Stuart, supported by D. H. Hill, to hold Turner's Gap for several days longer.[66]

Moreover, Stuart must have expressed his news in such a way as to depict the Federal force—although too large for the Confederate cavalry to resist—as not representing an overwhelming threat to D. H. Hill. In his conversation with Colquitt, his note to Hill, and his later official report, Stuart referred to Federal cavalry supported by a brigade or two of infantry, and he must have used similar language to Lee. Through early afternoon, in fact, Stuart's assessment was essentially correct; he was being pursued by Farnsworth's cavalry and Harland's infantry brigade. What Stuart did not perceive was that Burnside's entire Ninth Corps was moving west from Frederick in support of the pursuit. Stuart implies in his report that he sent another message to Lee, when Middletown was abandoned about two o'clock. This report would have reached Lee around four, but it is not likely it did more than confirm Stuart's earlier prediction.[67]

Then occurred the one piece of good luck to befall the Confederates on September 13. About five o'clock, the pro-Southern civilian found Stuart at the eastern foot of South Mountain and reported witnessing McClellan receive a document so important that the Federal general had thrown his hands in the air and exclaimed, "Now I know what to do!" The civilian did not pretend to know what the paper was, may not even

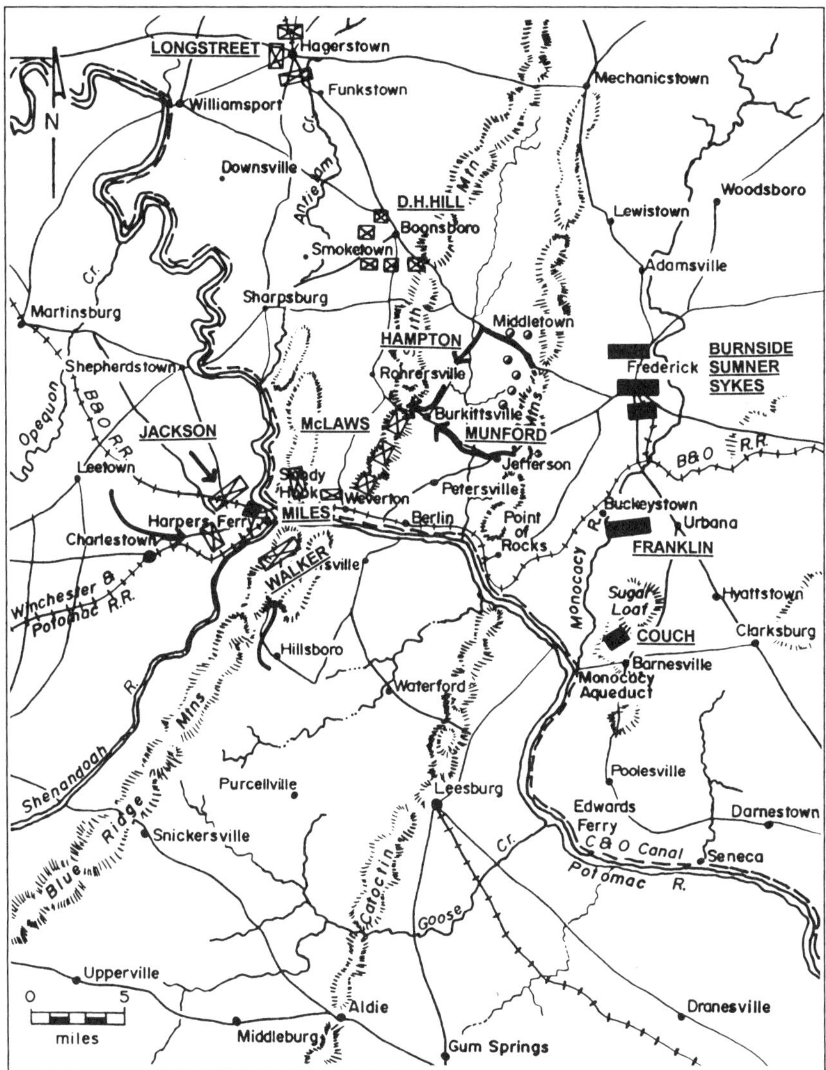

The fourth day of the Valley expedition, September 13

have known it was Confederate, but he grasped its great importance from the way orders flew in every direction and that the Federal army intended to move forward rapidly because of it.[68]

Whether or not Stuart correctly guessed from what he heard that a copy of Special Orders 191 had fallen into McClellan's hands is unclear, but the cavalry chief did conclude that the Federals knew Lee's army had divided to capture Harpers Ferry. When Jeb combined the citizen's report with the intelligence that Harpers Ferry had not yet surrendered and that Munford had been forced back to Crampton's Gap, he concluded that McClellan was moving to the relief of the beleaguered garrison and McLaws was in imminent danger. On this basis, Stuart ordered all but one of Hampton's units south to reenforce Munford, and thereafter he became somewhat careless about the defense of Turner's Gap. He may have waited for an hour or so, until after he had established his headquarters for the night near Boonsboro, before communicating with Lee.[69]

Stuart's dispatch probably reached Lee at Hagerstown shortly after dark, at about eight o'clock, and it is likely the one Lee would later refer to as the "note" from Captain Blackford. It did not mention either the story of the pro-Southern civilian or the possibility that the enemy possessed S.O. 191.[70] Nonetheless, it must have contained the disturbing news that McClellan was aware of the division of the Confederate army and was advancing with quickened stride to the relief of Harpers Ferry. This was bad news indeed, and it increased the fear Lee already felt for McLaws.

Lee scarcely had time to digest this disturbing development, before a message arrived from D. H. Hill with equally disconcerting news. Based on Colquitt's alarming view of the enemy campfires blanketing Middletown Valley, Hill asserted McClellan was approaching Turner's Gap with the main Federal force. Thus, Lee received almost simultaneously apparently contradictory reports regarding two threats to his army.[71]

By nine o'clock, Lee's tent was aglow with candlelight, as the Confederate commander bent over his map of western Maryland. With no means to resolve the conflicting statements, Lee assumed that, taken together, they indicated McClellan was pressing both passes for the purpose of relieving Harpers Ferry. Still, he must have quickly grasped that his army was not in mortal danger. Jackson and Walker were certainly safe south of the Potomac in Virginia, and both Longstreet and D. H. Hill could likely recross the river before McClellan could intercept them. Only McLaws's position was precarious. With the Army of the Potomac within three miles of his rear and with Miles's garrison in his front, McLaws might be crushed between the two; and neither Jackson nor Walker would be in position to prevent it from their positions across the river. Yet, even McLaws was not trapped. He could march northward up Pleasant Valley to Rohrersville, where he could then either continue on to Boonsboro, or head west to Sharpsburg. Both of the latter towns were only fourteen miles distant by this route.

The question was not, therefore, one of saving the Confederate army but one of protecting the Harpers Ferry expedition and salvaging the Maryland campaign. If Lee ordered a precipitate retreat, whether all the way back into Virginia or to a point just short of the Potomac—say, Sharpsburg—where he could reunite his columns, he would forfeit the capture of a sizable garrison and a vast store of much needed supplies. Of even greater importance in Lee's mind must have been the realization that retreat would be the admission of strategic defeat. If he allowed himself to be maneuvered out of Maryland, he would appear fallible and his army weak. The chain of Federal defeats would be snapped, and the North be given the hope to revitalize its morale and the time to reorganize its resources. This sort of setback would strengthen the Union's resolve to prosecute the war—the only chink Lee perceived in his enemy's armor—and thus immeasurably, perhaps irretrievably, diminish the Confederacy's chances to win independence.

The risks Lee had already taken—first in crossing the Potomac, and second in dividing his army—were small compared to the one he now determined to hazard. Although he now knew that he had lost the strategic initiative and that he had no choice but to react defensively, he would not abandon his campaign. Rather, he would assume the most aggressive possible defense. It is probable, although far from certain, that Lee had heard from Jackson late in the day that the Confederates had gained possession of Loudoun and Maryland Heights. It is also possible, although even less certain, that Stonewall had conveyed the impression Harpers Ferry would capitulate on the 14th.[72] Finally, at this point, Lee knew only that McClellan had learned a Confederate force had been detached to capture Harpers Ferry; he did not yet know that the Federals possessed a copy of S.O. 191 and the details of the splintering of the Army of Northern Virginia.

Whatever the source of his optimism, Lee decided to act on two shaky guesses. First, he assumed that Harpers Ferry would surrender relatively soon; second, he calculated that he could hold McClellan at the South Mountain passes until the surrender occurred. He would rely on the cavalry, presumably with some help from McLaws, to hold Crampton's Gap, and Stuart and D. H. Hill to do the same at Turner's, until he could determine which pass was more seriously threatened. In the meantime he would post Longstreet in a position from which he could move to the support of either.[73]

After Lee had thought through his problems and drawn his solutions, he called Longstreet to his tent. He was still bent over the map in study, when his senior subordinate arrived. Lee outlined for Longstreet the information from Stuart and D. H. Hill. Then, he explained that he had decided to leave the trains and one brigade in Hagerstown, while sending Longstreet with D. R. Jones and Evans to take up position on Beaver Creek, three miles northwest of Boonsboro on the National Road. The position chosen, five miles behind Turner's Gap and fourteen miles north of Crampton's, along with his decision not to split Longstreet's force between the two passes, indicates that Lee anticipated the greater danger would come at Turner's. His leaving the Reserve Artillery and trains behind at Hagerstown reflected his determination to return to his original plan to give battle in the Hagerstown-Chambersburg area after he had fought off the Federal threat. It was a strategy aimed to regain the initiative.

As Longstreet remembered it long after the war, he objected to Lee's tactics, arguing his troops would be too exhausted from their march to render effective support. He suggested instead that his divisions and Hill's be withdrawn and united for a stand at Sharpsburg. Behind the Antietam, the Confederates would be fresh and in position to "strike the flank or rear of any force that might be sent to the relief of Harpers Ferry." According to Longstreet, "Lee listened patiently enough, but did not change his plans." Indeed, if Longstreet correctly recalled his own objections, it is not surprising Lee dismissed them. In the first place, the position on Beaver Creek was only seven miles distant, and Longstreet's concern about exhaustion must have seemed like overprotection of his troops. Secondly, it might not be possible to protect McLaws from Sharpsburg due to the intervening and massive Elk Ridge. Finally, at Sharpsburg the only likely options open to Lee would be to stand and fight a defensive battle or to retire into Virginia. And Lee was not yet ready to admit he had lost his chance to strike a blow that might affect the outcome of the war.

Unable to sway Lee, Longstreet returned to his own tent and tried to go to sleep. His "mind was so disturbed," however, as the imagined "perils seemed to grow," that he arose, lighted a candle, and wrote a note to his commander. Again, he urged Lee to concentrate immediately at Sharpsburg. Although he received no reply, he would claim his sense of duty had been satisfied, and he was thereafter able to rest.[74]

• • •

Lee, however, was far from through for the night. Issuing the orders to Longstreet was but the first step to put his plans into action. He also attempted to communicate with his far-flung detachments. Around ten o'clock he sent three dispatches to try to arrange affairs for the 14th. One was a message to Jackson, explaining "the necessity for bringing to a prompt conclusion the operations at Harper's Ferry."[75] The second—and the only one known to have survived—he dictated to Maj. Thomas Talcott, his aide-de-camp, for LaFayette McLaws, and it is timed at ten o'clock.[76] This document is the only contemporary evidence of Lee's state of mind on the night of the 13th.

"General Lee directs me to say," wrote Talcott, "that, from reports reaching him, he believes the enemy is moving toward Harper's Ferry to relieve the force they have there." This indicates Lee had accepted Stuart's interpretation that McClellan was moving to the relief of the garrison, but it is ambiguous as to whether the main Federal thrust was to be made at Crampton's or Turner's Gap.

"You will see, therefore, the necessity," the dispatch continued, "of expediting your operations as much as possible." This seemingly obvious statement is critical. It announced that Lee intended the expedition to continue to a successful conclusion. "As soon as they are completed, he desires you, unless you receive orders from General Jackson, to move your force as rapidly as possible to Sharpsburg." After the fall of Harpers Ferry, McLaws would have three routes open to him for a march to Sharpsburg. He could move north through Pleasant Valley to Boonsboro; take the road at the foot of Maryland Heights that passed through Sandy Hook and Antietam Furnace; or recross the Potomac into Harpers Ferry and pass up the Virginia side to Shepherdstown. Lee's only guidance in this dispatch is that McLaws should take the quickest route. Finally, this sentence suggests that Lee recognized Jackson's seniority at Harpers Ferry but did not yet understand Stonewall to be in complete control of the siege.

Talcott then apprised McLaws that "General Longstreet will move down tomorrow and take position on Beaver Creek, this side of Boonsboro." This is firm evidence Lee did not originally intend for Longstreet to march directly to Turner's Gap. In conclusion, the dispatch promised, "General Stuart has been requested to keep you informed of the movements of the enemy." In this respect, it is curious that Lee made no mention of the presence of Munford and Hampton at Crampton's Gap, nor did he even hint that McLaws ought to position infantry at the pass.

Lee's third dispatch, addressed to D. H. Hill, must also have been written around ten o'clock, since Hill remembers receiving it about midnight. As Hill would recall over twenty years later, the essence of Lee's message was that the commanding general "was not satisfied with the condition of things on the turnpike or National road" and "suggested" he "go in person to Turner's Gap the next morning and assist Stuart in its defense."[77] Even though Hill had heretofore believed the pass to be primarily the concern of Stuart and the cavalry, after receipt of this dispatch he was clearly given joint responsibility; and, as senior officer on the field, he would in fact be in command. In consequence, Hill took one final step on the night of the 13th. He pulled four more regiments, Roswell Ripley's mixed brigade of Georgians and North Carolinians, from watching the roads from Harpers Ferry.

After occupying the ridge east of Boonsboro previously held by Colquitt, Ripley was to report to Stuart for information about the roads and gaps in the area and to be prepared to march to the mountain in the morning. Apparently Stuart was none too happy at being roused from sleep to supply information about a "locality where General Hill had been lying for two days with his command." Although Jeb claimed he "cheerfully" provided full information, somehow Ripley got the false impression of a threat at Hamburg Pass, three miles to the north, where the old Frederick stagecoach road crossed the mountain. This mistake would effectively take one of Ripley's regiments (the 4th Georgia) out of the fighting on the next day.[78]

After sending off his flurry of dispatches, Lee may have thought his long day had ended. It had not. Sometime later, probably several hours after midnight, another message arrived from Stuart. It may be speculated that after Ripley had roused the cavalry chief from sleep—perhaps disclosing the new orders for Hill that reflected Lee's increased alarm for Turner's Gap—Jeb had decided to send fuller particulars to Lee about the source and scope of the intelligence on Federal movements. Unfortunately, Stuart's message has been lost, and exactly what he wrote is unknown. According to Lee's postwar testimony, however, the dispatch revealed Stuart "had learned from a citizen of Maryland" that McClellan "was in possession of the order directing the movement of our troops."[79]

Since the sympathetic Marylander had not known the contents of the document, Stuart must have guessed that it was a copy of S.O. 191. It was a relatively easy conjecture, because no other paper would likely have excited the reaction by McClellan and his staff. That Stuart did identify the document—either hypothetically or positively—is demonstrated not only by Lee's recollection but also by Stuart's assumption from the late afternoon forward that McLaws at Maryland Heights was in grave danger. It was Lee who recalled that part of the story was McClellan's exuberant response in throwing up his hands and exclaiming, "Now I know what to do."

Even if couched only in terms of strong possibility, the news that McClellan possessed a copy of S.O. 191 was stunning. That it meant there had been either treachery or extreme carelessness Lee must have grasped at once, but that could be dealt with later.[80] It is hard to imagine that he did not immediately ask himself what his opponent could learn from the order. It is possible he even reread it carefully and tried to view it through McClellan's eyes. It is not beyond reason that he took some comfort in knowing that no strengths were divulged.

Almost certainly, Lee must have reviewed his plan for the morrow and the assumptions on which it was based. Could he still count on holding the enemy at South Mountain until the columns at Harpers Ferry rejoined him? Yet what were his options? If he fell back to Sharpsburg, as Longstreet had suggested, he ran the serious risk of sacrificing the divisions of McLaws and R. H. Anderson. If he retreated to Virginia, he not only sacrificed the divisions, but he also terminated the campaign. If he retreated, could the Confederacy ever again create such favorable circumstances for winning the war? Not only were his opponents in the East battered and demoralized, but, as Lee now knew, in the West, Confederate armies were sweeping through Kentucky toward the Ohio River. His nation's fortunes were at floodtide. Could he and his army be the ones to reverse the tide? For three months they had outmarched and outfought the enemy. Could they not do it one more time? Did he have any choice but to try?

There is no way of knowing whether these or different thoughts ran through Lee's mind in the early hours of what had now become September 14. But his conclusion is known. He would stand by his plan.

Although he must have been exhausted from his nearly interminable day, Lee dictated two more dispatches before returning to his cot to attempt sleep. First, he responded to Stuart. "I have received your note & also Capt Blackford's," began his short letter.[81] Lee likely referred to the dispatch he had received at about eight o'clock, which must have been sent over the name of Stuart's engineer, William Blackford. Lee's language suggests he had not replied to the earlier message, and the designation "note" suggests both were brief.

"The gap must be held at all hazards," he continued, "until the operations at Harper's Ferry are finished." In this sentence Lee confirmed his intent to hold to the plan he had devised some six hours earlier. No doubt, Lee intended this statement to be an unequivocal order, but it was seriously weakened by the failure to mention a specific gap. Perhaps, in his weariness, Lee chose this unhappy way to refer to South Mountain and all of its gaps. Or, more likely, he assumed Stuart would understand Turner's was meant, since the cavalry chief had written from Boonsboro. In either case, it is scarcely credible Lee intended to write anything that would deflect Stuart from his responsibility to defend the pass where the National Turnpike crossed the mountain. Unlike Stuart, Lee believed the greatest threat lay at Turner's. Nevertheless, since reading this letter would not change Stuart's mind to ride to Munford's aid in the morning, it is possible Jeb believed Lee was referring to Crampton's Gap.

"You must keep me informed," Lee went on, "of the strength of the enemy's forces moving up by either route." This sentence revealed that Lee was concerned about both gaps, but it did nothing to resolve the ambiguity of the previous sentence. If anything, it may have compounded the confusion by implying Stuart's responsibility for both passes. Of course, Lee probably had in mind that all intelligence, including that from Munford and Hampton, would naturally be channeled through Stuart. Lee's desire to learn the size of the different enemy columns no doubt derived from his anxiety to know which gap represented the more pressing danger.

"Gen Longstreet is moving down this morning," Lee concluded, "to occupy the valley about Boonsboro." This sentence, along with Lee's postwar statement that he received Stuart's dispatch "early on the morning of the 14th," places the exchange between midnight and dawn.[82] It is also the second indication that Lee originally intended Longstreet to occupy a reserve position and not march directly to South Mountain. Since this time he does not specify Beaver Creek north of Boonsboro, however, it may mean he has slightly modified his thinking and plans to post Longstreet nearer the gap.

Finally, for the third time within twenty-four hours, Lee sent a dispatch to LaFayette McLaws. Because of the distance, the darkness, and the uncertainty as to McLaws's exact location, the Confederate commander may have feared his ten o'clock message had not gotten through. But, he also wrote because he had changed his mind on several important points. This time Lee spoke in the first person and affixed his own signature, and, for the first time, he sounded a single note approaching panic.

Lee opened the dispatch with a concise reiteration of the situation and his plans: "General Longstreet moves down this morning to occupy the Boonsborough Valley, so as to protect your flank from attack from forces coming from Frederick, until the operations at Harper's Ferry are finished."[83] It reconfirms Lee's intended use of Longstreet and adds nothing to what he had previously written McLaws, except, as in the case of the message to Stuart, it is more ambiguous about Longstreet's destination.

But, then, Lee revealed that Stuart's latest news had finally shaken his confidence in the ultimate success of the plans outlined in S.O. 191. "I desire your operations there to be pushed on as rapidly as possible, and, if the point is not ultimately taken, so arrange it that your forces may be brought up the Boonsborough Valley." This is the only known indication that Lee admitted to himself the possibility the expedition might fail of its goal and Harpers Ferry not be captured. It also reveals he believed McLaws could not safely take the road through Sandy Hook at the foot of Maryland Heights as long as the Federals occupied Harpers Ferry. Lee was mistaken in this assumption. The road was practicable, even at night, as the escape of the Federal cavalry from Harpers Ferry would prove in less than twenty-four hours. During daylight, McLaws might have endured a gauntlet of fire for several miles, but aggressive cover from Walker and Jackson would probably have gotten him through with relatively small loss. It is important that Lee believed McLaws to be blocked in this direction, however, and helps to explain the Confederate commander's increased concern. Lee probably believed the route up Pleasant Valley through Rohrersville to Boonsboro to be second best and only to be taken if Harpers Ferry did not fall, because it exposed McLaws's flank to any Federal force penetrating a gap in South Mountain.

Lee then provided McLaws with his only unequivocal explanation of his view of the arrangements to defend South Mountain: "General Stuart, with a portion of General D.H. Hill's forces, holds the gap between Boonsborough and Middletown, and Hampton's and Munford's brigades of cavalry occupy Burkittsville and the pass through the mountains there." This confirms that Lee did understand Stuart as holding the primary responsibility at Turner's Gap. It also proves that in his last dispatch to Stuart the unspecified gap was indeed Turner's.

In closing, Lee reverted to the more optimistic view that the expedition would be successful: "If Harper's Ferry should be taken, the road will be open to you to Sharpsburg. Around the mountains from Sharpsburg the road communicates with Boonsborough and Hagerstown." Significantly, Lee does not mention Virginia or recrossing the Potomac. If McLaws is able to march to Sharpsburg, it is to be preparatory to rejoining the main body at Boonsboro or Hagerstown. Clearly, and notwithstanding all of the bad news, if he possibly could, Lee still intended to reconstruct his campaign and recapture the initiative.

Within the space of one day the fortunes of the Maryland campaign had turned half-circle, and the bottom was now on top. Because the finding of S.O. 191, one of the most dramatic episodes and spinable yarns of the war, coincided with the reversal, the discovery has been accorded disproportionate importance. The watershed of the campaign occurred on the evening of September 12 and the morning of the 13th, when the Federals entered Frederick, and McClellan set in motion the pursuit to the foot of South Mountain. The information in the lost orders did not materially affect the movements of the Federal army on the 13th, except to cause Pleasonton and Burnside to approach Turner's Gap with greater caution. Nor, did Lee's discovery of their loss change the plans he had already laid for the 14th. D. H. Hill's postwar rationalization that the discovery of the orders may have saved Lee's army exaggerates a minute possibility.[84] The finding of Special Orders, No. 191, may, however, have spared McLaws much discomfort and doomed Harpers Ferry by directing McClellan's attention toward the Confederate "main body" at Boonsboro.

Lee's fortunes in the Maryland campaign did not turn because the enemy found his orders. Lee lost the initiative, first, because he underestimated the rate and character of the advance of the Federal army, and, second, because he attempted to accomplish too much with the limited resources available to him. It did not augur well for his regaining control of the campaign that his plans for the coming day exhibited the same two weaknesses.

CHAPTER SIX

"The day has gone against us"

Lee Stands at the Mountain Gaps, September 14, 1862

So opened the fourth and final phase of the Maryland operations. Only six days of life remained to the turning movement that Lee intended to last long enough to keep his enemy north of the Potomac until winter closed active operations for the season. Worse yet, Lee had lost the initiative in his ambitious offensive launched to swell to flood tide his summer's victories and grasp a long-shot chance for the Confederacy to win the war. In spite of his best efforts, he could not regain control. During the entire week the Confederates remained nailed to the defensive and, at times, came perilously close to destruction. Many then and since have concluded that the Confederate commander should not have prolonged the campaign for six more days; he should have retired at once to Virginia to avoid outrageous risks. His decision to remain north of the Potomac after his plans had gone awry has been dubbed his greatest blunder.

But Robert E. Lee would not go gently into defeat. Four times he would reject the notion of retreat and stand to offer battle in the teeth of overwhelming odds. Once he stood to gain time for his scattered army to reunite, but thrice he stood to keep from being pushed from Maryland. In the struggle to keep his campaign alive, Lee would carry his army—and perhaps the country dependent upon it—to the brink of catastrophe. In the blood lust of competition, did the general allow ambition or frustration or personal pique or some other murky mental miasma to becloud his perception of reality and to blunt his sense of duty to his men and his nation? There is a simpler, nobler explanation that fits the facts as known. Lee doubted fate would ever again arrange conditions so favorably for achieving Confederate independence, and he was determined to try his tide to its utmost.

Lee to the Rescue

No restful Sabbath would this Sunday be. In the chilly predawn of September 14, under an eastern sky ribboned with orange-pink clouds, the dwarf that was by default the main body of the Army of Northern Virginia fell into column to march to the rescue of its imperiled limbs. Although filled with misgivings, Longstreet had issued the late-night orders to prepare his command for an unusually early start.[1] By five o'clock the division of David R. Jones was assembling on the National Turnpike, which led to the mountain where the sun had not yet risen.[2] Nonetheless, the haste of the sudden decision would tell in its sloppy execution. Inadvertently, the 11th Georgia Infantry was not relieved from its all-night guard duty, and Robert Toombs, whose brigade had been designated to remain in Hagerstown to guard the trains, was left to guess his mission from the failure to receive marching orders.[3] In spite of the early reveille, Jones's lead brigades (Drayton and G. T. Anderson) did not set out for Boonsboro until eight o'clock; and it was one o'clock before the rear of Evans's division departed Hagerstown.[4] Only then could the Reserve Artillery and the ordnance train follow. Lee had decided at the last moment that both must be on hand for the major battle in the offing.[5]

Driven by anxiety, Lee traveled in his ambulance near the head of the column in the company of his ordnance chief, Porter Alexander.[6] Although the sun wholly disappeared during the morning, to the Confederate commander's consternation it soon became apparent that the weather was not ideally suited for the rapid movement of an army. The 14th was the first of a run of five days that veterans would remember as "very warm," and the moisture from Friday's rain had long since evaporated.[7] Once again thousands of feet and hooves pounded the dirt roads into a blanket of grit that stung the eyes and choked the breath. Although Longstreet called his march "forced" in his official report, he would later amend his description to confess, "We marched as hurriedly as we could over a hot and dusty road."[8]

Even with frequent stops for rest, which reduced the rate of progress to about two and a half miles an hour, the column dwindled as exhausted men dropped from the ranks.[9] It was nearly noon before the vanguard covered the ten miles from Hagerstown and began to approach Boonsboro. Here Lee quickly forgot his idea of forming Longstreet's command on the heights along Beaver Creek east of the town. As South Mountain loomed larger and larger, the sounds of serious battle rever-

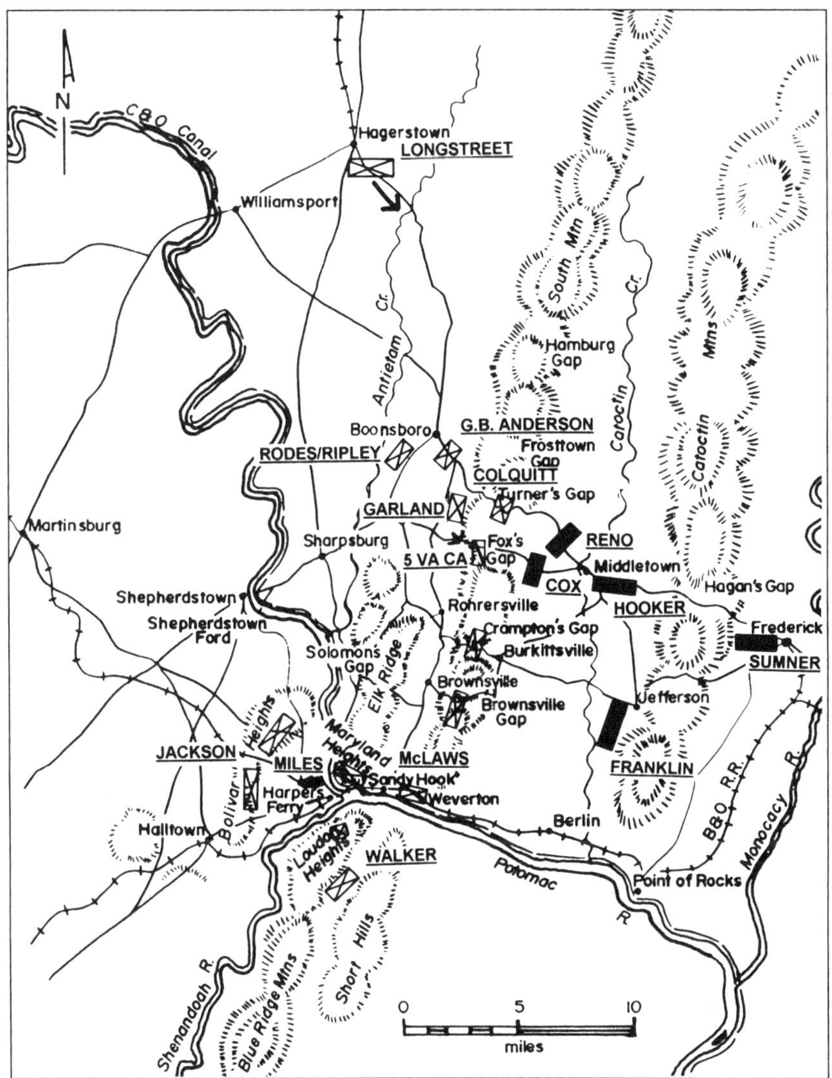

The fifth day of the Valley expedition, September 14

berated among its spurs and ridges. The boom of artillery and the rattle of musketry echoed through the valleys, while balloons of smoke rose from the slopes and filled the sky above. It was manifest that Harvey Hill was heavily engaged even before his messenger arrived to tell Lee that the Confederates were being overwhelmed and were in imminent danger of losing the pass.[10]

There would be no time for rest. Longstreet's weary men must be thrown into the gap at once. On through Boonsboro Jones's division tramped, while Longstreet ascended the mountain to consult with Hill. Unhappily for Lee, there was no question of traveling to the battlefront in his ambulance. The old engineer—who always felt the need to see the ground through his own eyes—sent off his entire staff, except for Adj. R. H. Chilton, to gather information that would be at best secondhand.[11] At about three o'clock Lee dismounted from his vehicle at the base of the gap and stood by a fence near the National Road to encourage his troops as they marched to a field he would never see. No Civil War commander could ever exert efficient control over a large battle, but never would Lee be so helpless as he was this afternoon at South Mountain. He would have no feel whatsoever for the dispositions of Hill or the enemy, and he would exert absolutely no influence over the placement of the reenforcements. He was denied not only the use of his hands but also of his eyes and ears.

One small contribution only was his to make. As the Texas brigade filed past Lee—and it became clear to the men they were about to enter battle without their trusted commander—the cry arose, "Give us Hood!" Lee shouted back, "You shall have him, gentlemen," and he dispatched Chilton to fetch the general from the rear of the column. Although Hood refused to make even the mildest apology for the affray over the captured wagons, Lee was in no mood for punctilio and suspended the arrest.[12]

Perforce, Lee thereafter watched from afar and waited.

The Battle of Boonsboro

At four o'clock in the morning, while the rest of the scattered Confederate army slumbered through its final hour of sleep, Maj. Gen. Daniel Harvey Hill arose at Boonsboro and breakfasted on a cup of coffee. By 5:30, with a still-invisible sun illumining a partly cloudy sky, Hill rode up to the Mountain House near the crest of Turner's Gap.[13] At what hour he would have traveled the two and a half miles from Boonsboro without prodding will never be known. He had returned because of Lee's urgent midnight directive that he personally supervise the defense of the pass. Even on the spot, Hill could not have grasped at once the full extent of the danger facing him. In the dawn's feeble twilight, neither the constellation of campfires that had frightened Colquitt the night before nor the endless writhing columns of blue that would later take shape disturbed the tranquil Middletown Valley. Hearing from Colquitt that the enemy had retired from the foot of the mountain and knowing that Longstreet was returning to Beaver Creek, Hill failed to perceive the urgency of the crisis.[14]

Still, Hill at once appreciated the difficulty of his position. Without being relieved of the responsibility to watch the roads from Harpers Ferry, he had been assigned the additional task of blocking the enemy's passage through South Mountain in his rear. His division of five brigades totaled something between seven and eight thousand men present for duty.[15] Had there been but one pass to defend, Hill's job might have been manageable, but there were four gaps (Hamburg, Frosttown, Turner's, and Fox's) within a five-mile front. To complicate matters, Hill received a message from Stuart that the cavalry chief had departed for Crampton's Gap with Hampton's brigade. Unaware of the arrival of Fitz Lee's brigade at Boonsboro, Hill assumed there was no cavalry available to reconnoiter and discover where the Federals intended to attack. Under the circumstances, Hill was slow to commit his forces. He held Colquitt's brigade in line at the top of Turner's Gap, with Garland in reserve, while he sent the 4th Georgia of Ripley's brigade to the north to man Hamburg Pass on the far left. He ordered George B. Anderson's brigade to march to the mountain, while Rodes and Ripley remained to watch the Harpers Ferry routes.[16]

Sometime after six, Hill set out with his adjutant along the mountain-crest road to examine Fox's Gap, one mile to the south. About three-quarters of the way to his destination, the sounds of shouted commands and rumbling wheels convinced Hill that the Federals had already secured a foothold in the gap. As he hurried back to his command post on the National Turnpike, he was puzzled to hear firing break out in his rear, as he was unaware of any Confederate troops on the right flank. Unbeknownst to Hill, Stuart, before leaving to help McLaws, had posted Thomas Rosser's 5th Virginia Cavalry to watch Fox's Gap. Rosser had reported the advance of a heavy enemy column to Stuart as the cavalry chief passed east of the mountain, but Stuart had sent neither instructions to Rosser nor warning to Hill.[17]

Yet, the mere presence of the 5th Virginia Cavalry may have saved Confederate fortunes at South Mountain. While Rosser could not hope to stop the enemy, he not only slowed their progress by causing them to deploy battlelines in tangled woods and rocky terrain, but he also unknowingly changed their direction. Had the Federals continued only a half-mile farther west—as they would have in the time it took Hill to bring troops from the center—they would have passed through the mountain, turned Hill's line, and made the Confederate position at Boonsboro untenable. Instead, Rosser's fire on their right flank turned the Federals off the Sharpsburg Road and against the crestline road that carried them deeper into the mountain. In effect, the turning movement became a flank attack over terrain that minimized the superiority of Federal strength.[18]

When Hill regained the National Turnpike near the Mountain House, he found Samuel Garland's brigade under arms and ready to march. As best he could, Hill explained the situation to Garland, but the instructions reveal that Hill misunderstood the geography of the position he defended. He did not direct Garland to prevent the enemy's passage through Fox's Gap; rather, he simply emphasized the necessity of holding the road that ran along the mountain top. Seldom has a general gone into battle in more profound ignorance than did Garland. To the sound of unexplained firing, the thirty-one-year-old graduate of the Virginia Military Institute rode onto rugged and unscouted ground to confront an enemy not yet seen.

Happily, before he met any Federals, Garland encountered Tom Rosser. The cavalry colonel explained that the 5th Virginia had deployed as skirmishers and were holding a large force of the enemy at bay. Rosser also supplied information on the lay of the ground and helped form the infantry line. The Federals had consumed so much time in preparing their attack, they had made virtually no progress; and Garland was able to post his five North Carolina regiments almost at the junction of the Old Sharpsburg and crestline roads. The nature of the ground, however, prevented him from forming a connected line. The Confederates were already in position, and Garland and Rosser were seated under a chestnut tree in conversation, when the assault opened.[19]

When battle was joined with Scammon's brigade of the Kanawha division (Ninth Corps) at about nine o'clock, it was from the start a disjointed fight between isolated regiments. Not well understood by the participants while engaged, the confused fighting cannot be completely unraveled by historians. Garland's death early in the battle ended any Confederate coordination. His successor, Col. Duncan McRae of the 5th North Carolina, had neither staff nor horse to exert control over the brigade. With each regiment acting on its own, the right flank soon gave way, opening a gaping hole in the Confederate line.[20]

The enemy had no notion of the Confederate plight. The new Federal commander on the ground, Jacob Cox, understood that it was his task to pursue the mountaintop road, rather than to force passage of Fox's Gap. This notion ensured that his men would remain tangled in the rugged terrain. Cox also concluded the trees, ravines, and boulders concealed a considerable Confederate force. Hence, the Federals sat down to await reenforcements.

In the meanwhile, as the crash of musketry and artillery signaled a furious fight at Fox's Gap, D. H. Hill climbed the lookout station at Turner's Gap for a better view in the center. He saw before him a chilling spectacle of Federal might. "The marching columns extended back as far as eye could see in the distance," he later recalled. He had never before and would never after see "so tremendous an army" visible at one time. Curiously, Hill took satisfaction in this indication that McClellan was mounting his main attack against Boonsboro rather than against McLaws at Harpers Ferry, as Stuart had anticipated. This can only be explained by Hill's assumption that the sacrifice of his own division would buy ample time for the escape of both McLaws and Longstreet.[21]

When the routed portion of Garland's brigade came streaming along the crest of the mountain, Hill at last knew the full extent of his own crisis. Anderson's troops had not yet arrived, and there was no infantry at hand other than Colquitt. Hill advanced two cannon to the right and a "line of dismounted staff officers, couriers, teamsters and cooks . . . to give the appearance of battery supports." It was of this moment that Hill later recalled, "I do not remember ever to have experienced a feeling of greater loneliness."[22] He finally forgot the Harpers Ferry escape routes and ordered up his remaining brigades, Rodes and Ripley. He also sent an urgent request to Lee for support, or, as Hill put it in a postwar letter to Longstreet, "It was then I called so loudly for your help."[23]

Hill did not know that a portion of Garland's brigade remained in line, or that the Federals had decided to await reenforcements. After a half-hour's suspense, George B. Anderson's brigade arrived at around 10:30, and Hill rushed the four North Carolina regiments south to restore a right flank that had already stabilized thanks to the enemy. Anderson divided his command and extended the remnant of Garland's line on both flanks, but by then the battle at Fox's Gap had settled down into light skirmishing.[24] When the brigades of Ripley and Rodes reported at the Mountain House at eleven, or shortly thereafter, Hill remained sufficiently concerned about the threat to his right flank that he ordered Ripley's one Georgia and two North Carolina regiments to reenforce

Anderson. Hill also ordered Roswell Ripley, who as senior brigadier had commanded the division for two months during Hill's absence in North Carolina, to take command at Fox's Gap.[25]

Finally satisfied he had done all he could for his right, Harvey Hill turned his attention to his other flank. About a mile north was the Frosttown Gap, which was also approached by a feeder road that branched from the National Turnpike at Bolivar in the valley and was also connected to Turner's Gap by a crestline road. Between these two gaps there was a high knoll that commanded both. Having no artillery to spare, Hill had been forced to rely on badly aimed artillery fire from Cutts's battalion to secure the promontory. Now he ordered Rodes's six Alabama regiments forward to plug this hole.

Thus matters stood at noon. Hill had committed his entire division and had not a man in reserve.

On the morning of the 14th, George McClellan had no reason to expect that he could take Lee by surprise at Turner's Gap. It is true—assuming the details of S.O. 191 remained accurate—a third to a half of the Confederate army was absent on independent missions. Still, according to all reports, the enemy in the Boonsboro-Hagerstown area numbered 60,000 or more and approximated the size of the four corps McClellan had at hand near Frederick. Moreover, it was certain Confederate cavalry had reported the approach of the Federals to the foot of South Mountain the day before. It had to be assumed that, once alerted, Lee had moved in force to man the strong defensive barrier nature had placed at his disposal. Any attempt to punch through the center at Turner's Gap would likely entail heavy casualties and, even if successful, might so shatter the fragile, convalescing Army of the Potomac as to render it unable to follow up its success. McClellan's surprise for Lee was that he intended to punch through Crampton's Gap, while holding the Confederate main body at Boonsboro. The enemy position at Turner's Gap must be approached forcefully but prudently, and if possible be carried by a turning movement.

Alfred Pleasonton, whose cavalry led the advance on the 14th, may have consulted personally with McClellan. At the very least, he instinctively understood his chief's thinking. At an early hour his troopers scouted both Confederate flanks, and he learned of the roads to the north and south that led to the passes that circumvented Turner's Gap. He also made the correct strategic choice in deciding to move against Fox's

Gap to the south, as success there would drive a wedge between Lee and McLaws at Crampton's Gap, while pushing through Frosttown to the north might have driven Lee back on McLaws.

If Pleasonton could have grasped that he faced only Rosser's regiment at Fox's Gap, there would not have been a battle at South Mountain. Had Pleasonton gained the rear of the mountain before nine o'clock, Hill must have retired from Turner's Gap with Garland and Colquitt and formed a defensive line somewhere north or west of Boonsboro. Lee would then have been hard pressed not to abandon his Maryland campaign and retire with Longstreet and Hill to Virginia. The Confederate commander might also have felt he had to order McLaws to escape by way of Shepherdstown and thus have raised the siege of Harpers Ferry.

Perceptions, not realities, rule history, and the pursuit of possibilities depends upon the information available as well as on the assessment of that information. In this case, the far-ranging possibilities were stillborn. Pleasonton not unreasonably—in light of the situation as he understood it—decided not to risk the needless sacrifice of his command once he discovered the Confederate presence in the pass. He immediately sent back to the Ninth Corps for the infantry support that had been promised the night before. As prearranged, Eliakim Scammon's brigade of the Kanawha division set out from its camp west of Middletown to reenforce the cavalry.

Jacob Cox, the division commander, rode along as a spectator out of curiosity. Unlike Pleasonton and McClellan, Cox was ignorant of the general strategic situation and had no idea of what lay ahead. After crossing Catoctin Creek near the burned Koogle's bridge, Cox was surprised to see the 28th Ohio's Col. August Moor, who had been captured in the streets of Frederick on the evening of the 12th by Hampton's cavalry. Moor had spent the 13th behind Confederate lines—he had probably been carried all the way back to Boonsboro by Stuart before being paroled—and he knew something of the enemy's strength. In passing through Turner's Gap he had certainly seen Colquitt's line, and he may have seen Garland's brigade as well.

"Where are you going?" Moor asked. Cox replied that Scammon was advancing to support a reconnaissance into Turner's Gap. "My God!" Moor exclaimed without thinking, "Be Careful!" Then, remembering that he was under parole and honorbound not to divulge information, Moor abruptly turned and walked away. Not unlike the discovery of S.O. 191, the ambiguous intelligence from this brief exchange probably harmed the Federal cause as much as it helped. It convinced Cox that heavy Confederate forces lay ahead and left to his imagination their number. He immediately rode down the length of his column to alert each regimental commander of the imminent danger, and then he hurried back to his camp to order out his other brigade under George Crook. He also sent a warning message to Jesse Reno, who commanded the Ninth Corps while Burnside directed the right wing. Not waiting for Crook, Cox hastened back to the front, where he found Pleasonton conferring with Scammon.

Cox discovered that Pleasonton did not intend to attack Turner's Gap but instead had requested the infantry to force Fox's Gap to the south. In his alarmed state of mind, Cox quickly agreed to the indirect approach, but he informed Pleasonton that once Crook's brigade arrived, he would assert his own seniority and take command of the field. At this point, it is not clear whether Pleasonton remained on the National Turnpike or whether he traveled with Cox on the Old Sharpsburg Road. In either case, by nine o'clock Scammon's brigade was approaching Fox's Gap after a march with frequent halts, Crook's brigade was in near support, and Cox had become the general in charge of operations.

From first to last, there is no indication that Cox ever thought in terms of a turning movement or that he intended to punch west through the pass and gain the rear of the mountain. From the moment his skirmishers opened battle with Garland's North Carolinians, Cox was drawn to the right (north) into a direct assault on the Confederate flank, and thereafter he fought to gain possession of the road that traveled the crest of the ridge. Instead of passing through the mountain, Cox pushed deeper into it. After that his movements through the tangled terrain were as confused and sporadic as those of his enemy. By midday the Kanawha division was exhausted, and its attack had run out of steam. Cox sat down to await the arrival of the remainder of the Ninth Corps.[26]

Burnside arrived in the vicinity of Middletown about noon. He discovered Orlando Willcox's division forming battlelines north of the National Pike. At the suggestion of Pleasonton, Willcox was preparing to assault the Frosttown Gap. Burnside decided the first order of business must be the support of Cox at Fox's Gap, however, and he ordered Willcox to reform column and march south on the Old Sharpsburg Road. Indeed, so intently was Burnside's focus riveted on Fox's Gap that he sent orders to Jesse Reno to bring up the remaining two divisions of the Ninth Corps and to take personal command of the attack at the pass. The result of Burnside's decisions was that the lull in the fighting was considerably lengthened, as Reno would not have all of his forces aligned and ready to attack until nearly five o'clock.

Still, based on the information available to him, Burnside apparently did not feel confident that even an attack by the entire Ninth Corps on the Confederate right flank would be sufficient to sweep the enemy from the mountain. Not understanding that it was possible to advance through Fox's Gap and bypass the Confederate flank—and since Cox did not realize this, there is no reason to expect Burnside would have—Burnside looked elsewhere for a way to dislodge the enemy. Probably on the basis of information supplied by Pleasonton, he forbore to attack the center at Turner's Gap which could be assumed to be strongly defended. He decided instead "to turn the enemy's left and get in his rear." As the units of Joseph Hooker's First Corps arrived west of Middletown, they were sent to the north to force passage through the Frosttown Gap. Burnside reserved Gibbon's brigade from Hatch's division to press against the center, while sending word to Reno to prepare to attack upon receiving word that Hooker was well advanced.[27]

Shortly thereafter, McClellan arrived at Burnside's headquarters to learn that he had been committed to one of the most difficult tactical maneuvers in warfare, the double envelopment, which in this case was rendered all the more difficult because it was to be executed in a mountain range. Hearing Burnside's explanations, McClellan approved the tactical plan, and there is no indication that he was then, or ever after, unhappy with the arrangements.

From the vantage of hindsight that allows a view of the strengths and positions of both armies, Federal operations on the 14th appear overly cautious and misdirected. To the Federal generals west of Middletown, who could see the looming mountains ahead but not into or beyond them, and who believed they faced an army about equal to their own, the division of force to attack simultaneously two gaps almost two miles apart must have seemed fraught with risk.

From the viewpoint of Harvey Hill, who knew what was on the mountain and could see something of what was in front of it, the situation by three o'clock seemed more desperate than ever. On his right, he held a position near Fox's Gap with Garland, G. B. Anderson, and Ripley (or so he thought); in the center at Turner's Gap, Colquitt's brigade remained as yet unbloodied; and on the left, Rodes had been shifted to the ridge north of the Frosttown Gap, leaving the knoll between Rodes and Colquitt undefended. All afternoon, line after line of blue was seen marching south from the National Road in the direction of Fox's Gap, and now at least two divisions were forming battlelines in front of Frosttown Gap to the north.

At this most opportune moment a note reached Hill that Longstreet had arrived at Boonsboro. In reply, Hill not only urged Longstreet "to hurry forward troops," but he also specifically requested help in preventing the enemy from pushing through the mountain at Fox's Gap. When the message was passed on to general headquarters, Lee ordered Longstreet to divide the division of David R. Jones to comply with both of Hill's needs. Lee sent the brigades of Drayton and George T. Anderson directly up the mountain on the National Turnpike to report to Hill. At the same time, he instructed Jones with the brigades of Kemper, Garnett, and Jenkins (Walker) to advance south along the western base of the mountain toward Fox's Gap.[28]

This latter move might have yielded brilliant tactical results had Jones continued far enough to strike the Old Sharpsburg Road. He could have then proceeded east into the gap and struck the flank of the Ninth Corps. Whether his two thousand men could have broken Reno's ten thousand will never be known, however, since Jones never made contact with the enemy. Why Jones did not go far enough—if he followed the wrong road, or if he was deceived by the lull in the battle and the thick woods—is not clear, but it is certain he came to the wrong conclusion. In about an hour he reported back that he had reached the pass and found the rumor the enemy was "flanking our army" to be "incorrect." He was thereupon ordered to retrace his steps, and it was nearly dark before he brought his now thoroughly exhausted troops back to a useful position at Turner's Gap.[29]

In the meantime, Drayton and George T. Anderson reported to Hill at the Mountain House. It is revealing that—in spite of repeated requests from Rodes for support and the existence of a half-mile hole on the left-center toward which the enemy could already be seen advancing—Hill sent the first reenforcements to reach him off to the right to support Ripley at Fox's Gap. Hill would later explain that he wanted to defeat the enemy on his southern flank before the major assault commenced from the north. Hill's decision, although bold, was not unreasonable. Rather than continue to spread his forces in a thin defense, he would concentrate and attack. Along with the remnants of Garland's brigade, he was amassing four brigades of some four thousand men (G. B. Anderson and Ripley from his own division, and Drayton and G.T. Anderson from

Longstreet) that as yet had seen little or no fighting—although the recent arrivals could scarcely be called fresh.

Hill conferred with Ripley, who was commanding on the right, and with Drayton and Anderson to outline a plan of attack. It is possible that at the time there was a vague understanding among the four—subsequently forgotten in the chaotic events that followed and never reported—that Ripley was to push his line down the mountain to connect with the force under D. R. Jones that Lee had sent along the western base of the mountain. This would explain the disaster that ensued. In any case, whether from good intentions or ignorance, when Ripley formed his line, he extended his right so far down the western slope that his own and a portion of G. T. Anderson's brigade became separated, left the scene of fighting altogether, and, as he later put it, "didn't pull a trigger." In consequence, it was a diminished and uncoordinated Confederate attack that swept through the woods and broke weakly on the Ninth Corps, which had just completed its own preparations. Reno's men counterattacked—with Reno himself falling mortally wounded—and began to chase the Confederates along the crest of the mountain. Only the arrival of Hood's two brigades prevented the Federals from reaching Turner's Gap from the south before darkness finally fell.[30]

Meanwhile, Rodes and the 1,200 muskets in his six Alabama regiments dangled isolated and exposed in front of the 9,000 men in Hooker's First Corps.[31] Rodes's position was made doubly excruciating; first, from his mountain vantage he could see the enemy masses forming to attack him; and, second, he was aware that a half-mile opening existed between his right and the left of Colquitt's brigade at Turner's Gap. The hole in the Confederate line had resulted from the nature of the terrain and the paucity of defenders. As Rodes had discovered after taking up position on the left of Colquitt, the Frosttown Gap was actually dual clefts in South Mountain about a half-mile apart. Both gorges were steep and rocky and far inferior to the passage at Turner's, but both had roads that infantry, and even artillery, could traverse to gain the Confederate rear.

Initially, Rodes occupied the first ridge north of Turner's Gap, but, when it was discovered both roads from Frosttown flanked his position to the left and the ridge to his left dominated his position, he was ordered to hopscotch to the second ridge. This meant he now held the highest ground in the immediate area, but he had a passable road on either flank and a half-mile opening on his left. What Rodes saw before him was the unfolding of the entire First Corps from its column of march. The thirteen regiments of the Pennsylvania Reserve Corps, comprising the three brigades of Meade's division, formed in his immediate front, and they were supported by another twelve regiments in the three brigades of Ricketts's division. On his right, the thirteen regiments in the three brigades of Hatch's division were moving in the direction of the undefended ridge. Hatch's fourth brigade was held in reserve near the National Turnpike. In response, Rodes stretched his line as thin as he dared, and he sent repeated and urgent requests to Hill for additional troops.

Shortly after three o'clock, and not long after Hill had sent the first of Longstreet's arrivals (Drayton and G. T. Anderson) in the other direction to support the attack at Fox's Gap, the Federal skirmishers reached Rodes's position and the lines of blue began to lap around both of his flanks. Rodes and his regimental commanders—many of whom fought independently in detached engagements—waged a brilliant delaying action. Yet, inexorably he was borne back, even as he contested every foot of ground lost. The steep incline slowed the Federals, and the wooded and undulating terrain hid from them the weakness of the Confederates.[32]

At this critical juncture, Longstreet arrived at Hill's headquarters near the Mountain House. He would later claim he grasped the hopelessness of the situation "at first sight," and his first order of business was to dispatch a note to Lee that it would be necessary to retreat during the night. His second action was to assert his seniority over Hill and take command of the field to see if he could stave off disaster until darkness would cover a withdrawal.[33] Longstreet then sent Evans's brigade of South Carolinians—just up from Boonsboro—forward to occupy the undefended ridge between Rodes and Colquitt. Evans arrived too late to beat the Federals to the ridge, however, and he had too few men to retake it. His men were tired and his ranks thinned by the exhausting march, and he was able to do little but slow Hatch's rate of advance.[34]

It was now after five o'clock, and the roar from the south, accompanied by a stream of fugitives, revealed that the Ninth Corps had broken the Confederate line at Fox's Gap. Thus, when Hood arrived with his two brigades—the last troops available so far as Longstreet knew at the time—they were rushed down the mountaintop road to the right to stem the rout. Charging with fixed bayonets, Hood was able to stabilize the flank just short of Turner's Gap.[35]

One crisis had been solved at the expense of the other, however, for on the left Meade and Hatch continued to push back the brigades of Rodes and Evans, while John Gibbon's black-hatted brigade of westerners moved forward against Colquitt in the center. Only the stubborn stand on the National Pike by Colquitt and the support of Evans and Rodes by the last-minute arrival of D. R. Jones and his three brigades (from their ill-fated detour west of the mountain) allowed the Confederate defense to stretch and hold until the sun set.[36]

By the close of the day, both Confederate flanks had been smashed back upon the center, and Fox's Gap was now open for the passage of Federal troops to intervene between Lee and McLaws. As Longstreet and Hill rode through the darkness down the mountain to report to Lee, both knew they had to urge retreat. The choice was obvious for the subordinates who needed to concentrate only on the problems immediately at hand. Lee, the chief who must make the decision, would have to consider a broader canvas, however, including the well-being of the entire army, the fate of the Maryland campaign, and even the ramifications on Confederate chances to win the war. And, if that were not enough, he would also have to take into account several other critical developments that had occurred on September 14 beyond the field of Boonsboro. Some of the news was good. Most of it was bad.

Jackson Tightens the Noose

Jedediah Hotchkiss, Stonewall Jackson's mapmaking engineer, noted in his diary that he spent a "cold night on the Mt." He was referring to the night of the 13th and the mountain was Loudoun Heights. Hotchkiss was a member of the party of engineers, signal men, and artillerists Jackson had sent to supply the deficiencies of John Walker's small divisional staff, as Walker took his position in the encirclement of Harpers Ferry. Hotchkiss recalled that it had been understood at Stonewall's headquarters that "Gen. Jackson intended to advance and storm the place today," and the engineer noted in puzzlement, "but he did not advance; why I know not."[37]

The simple answer to Hotchkiss's question was that Jackson needed time to adjust to a set of new, although not entirely unforeseen, circumstances. Even though it is likely Lee and Jackson had discussed the possibility that one or both of the Federal garrisons might resist, the underlying assumption of Special Orders 191 had been that the Federals would to attempt escape from superior numbers. After it became certain on the

13th that Dixon Miles did not intend to abandon Harpers Ferry, Jackson's initial impulse "to storm the place" had yielded to complications and reflection. The interdiction of rivers and mountains meant that Stonewall could bring the infantry of only his own three divisions to assault an enemy force the size of a small corps d'armée. Although it is unclear how accurately he understood the odds to be 15,000 Confederate to 13,000 Federals, he did understand it would be foolish to mount a straight-on foot assault on Miles's strong defensive position on Bolivar Heights.[38]

The great vulnerability of Harpers Ferry was that it sat in a bowl dominated by Loudoun and Maryland Heights. It made plainest sense to use the plunging fire of Confederate artillery from those mountains to reduce enemy resistance. In fact, Jackson's second thought seemed to be that it might be possible to force the surrender without resort to infantry assault. Unfortunately, Jackson had not been able to open signal communication with either Walker or McLaws during the afternoon of the 13th. When he did hear from Walker by messenger after dark, Jackson learned that Loudoun Heights had just been occupied and no artillery was yet in place; and he also soon learned the same situation held true for McLaws and Maryland Heights.[39] Inevitably, this meant delay in opening the attack.

When Jackson arose on the morning of the 14th and laid his plans for the day, he did not think a modest delay would be a problem. Shortly after seven, he sent a dispatch to McLaws that detailed the tactics to be followed by the three cooperating columns.[40] Batteries were to be established on Maryland and Loudoun Heights to sweep the enemy camps and, in particular, to take in reverse the Federals' fortified line atop Bolivar Heights facing Jackson. When all of the batteries were in position, including Jackson's own, Stonewall intended to demand the surrender of the garrison. Should Colonel Miles refuse, a truce would be offered for the removal of "non-combatants." After that, Jackson wrote, "let the work be done thoroughly. . . . Demolish the place." It is clear from the letter, Jackson intended to take the operations by stages in order to minimize Confederate losses. First, there was always the chance that Miles would see the hopelessness of his plight and accede to the surrender demand. Second, there was an even better chance that a severe artillery bombardment would secure the same results. Finally, if an infantry assault became necessary, Jackson wanted McLaws and Walker to "draw attention from Furnace Hill," an earlier name for Bolivar Heights, so that he might "have the opportunity of getting possession of the hill without much loss." This last sounds very much as if Jackson from the outset—even before he knew how he would accomplish it—planned to turn the flank of the enemy line.

There is strong presumptive evidence that Jackson sent an appropriately modified version of this dispatch to Walker.[41] Indeed, to launch his plan he would have had to send similar instructions with explanations to the commander of the forces on Loudoun Heights. It would be most interesting to know something of the schedule Jackson had in mind when he framed his plan early in the morning. Even if he underestimated the time it would take McLaws and Walker to get artillery up their respective mountains, and even if he expected their guns to be ready at an unreasonably early hour, he had built in other steps bound to protract operations considerably. The process of sending out a flag of truce with a demand for surrender and waiting for a reply must consume several hours, the time to negotiate for the evacuation of noncombatants several more hours, and the removal of the civilians a half-day at least—and all of this before the bombardment that would determine whether or not an assault would take place. Even if this plan were put into effect early on the 14th, Jackson could not have expected to take Harpers Ferry before midday on the 15th, assuming Miles determined to hold out.

John Walker, in the same postwar article that described his strategy tête-á-tête with Lee, asserted that he received a message from Jackson by signal flags that instructed him to hold fire until after a twenty-four-hour truce had been offered for the removal of citizens. Since all of the messages signaled from Jackson's headquarters have apparently survived and none such is among them, Walker likely mistakenly remembered the written dispatch he received similar to the one sent to McLaws. It is even possible, since the document has not survived, that Walker's version did specify a time duration for the truce. Defenders of Jackson, Henry Kyd Douglas and Bradley T. Johnson, wrote strong letters denying Jackson ever intended a full day's delay. In this particular instance, although yet another example of Walker's confused recollections, the general is more nearly correct than his critics, who fail to grasp the sizable delay implicit in Jackson's dispatch to McLaws.[42]

Walker is wrong, however, in his immodest claim of saving the Confederate army from destruction. In his article, he argued that because he understood better than Jackson the danger from McClellan's advance, he provoked the garrison's guns into opening fire and thus circumvented a truce and precipitated the surrender. Had operations dragged on according to plan, Walker asserted, Jackson could not have reached

Sharpsburg in time "and General Lee would undoubtedly have been driven into the Potomac." All of this is wrong for several reasons. First, Walker assumes without basis that Lee would have stood at Sharpsburg without assurances of the fall of Harpers Ferry. Second, he is ignorant of—or at least he ignores—the revisions Jackson made in the plan during the course of the day, including the abandonment of a demand for a surrender or a truce. And, last, Walker did not even open fire without Jackson's approval.

For one of the few instances of the war, the complete messages sent and received by a Confederate signal station have survived. Capt. Joseph Bartlett, who was the only signal officer remaining at Jackson's headquarters and who wrote his report on the evening of the 14th, included the text of all messages sent and received at his station.[43] They provide a firm basis for the conclusion that Jackson changed his early morning plan as the day progressed.

The first significant signal Bartlett received came at ten o'clock from Loudoun Heights: "Walker has six rifle pieces in position. Shall he wait for McLaws?" Starting at first light, Walker had managed to get the long-range guns from the batteries of French and Branch onto Loudoun Heights in a timely fashion.[44] It is impossible to tell from the ambiguous language of the message if Walker asked permission to fire because he had received written orders similar to those Jackson had sent to McLaws or because he had not yet received them. Whatever the case, Jackson replied curtly, "Wait."

Shortly thereafter Jackson personally visited the signal station to dictate a lengthy message to both Walker and McLaws. The signal from Walker may have caused Stonewall to doubt that his early-morning orders had yet reached their destinations, but equally important he had changed his mind in the interval. The message Jackson sent around 10:30 differed in several important respects from the written instructions he issued some three hours before. He began by repeating his desire that batteries be posted to fire on the enemy's camps and particularly the line on Camp Hill—which indicates he was not positive his early morning orders had yet arrived—but he went beyond to ask for "any suggestions by which you can operate against the enemy." Then Jackson dictated two revealing sentences. "Cut the telegraph line down the Potomac if it is not already done. Keep a lookout against a Federal advance from below." Thus, by midmorning, Jackson not only alerted McLaws and Walker to watch out for their rears, but he also wanted to make certain that word of approaching relief did not reach Colonel Miles to stiffen his determination to hold out.

Jackson then went on to reiterate, "I do not desire any of the batteries to open until all are ready on both sides of the river." But this time he made no mention of any sort of delay, and added, "except you should find it necessary, of which you must judge yourself." It is reasonable to assume that had Jackson still intended to send a white flag for either surrender or truce, he would have restated his purpose in this message; and he certainly would not have granted his subordinates discretionary authority to open fire.

In a concluding postscript, Jackson urged both generals "to take steps at once" to supply themselves with rations. This alert sounded very much as if Jackson believed all of them would soon—for whatever reason—be on the march.

The most plausible explanation for the changed attitude Jackson manifests in this signal would be the arrival during the morning of an alarming dispatch from the commanding general in Hagerstown. Likely Lee had written to Stonewall shortly before midnight—around the same time as the dispatches to McLaws and D. H. Hill—to warn him of the inconveniently rapid advance of McClellan to South Mountain.[45] The courier must have traveled through the darkness hours a circuitous twenty miles by way of Shepherdstown and located Jackson sometime after 7:30. Assuming Lee used language in this lost dispatch similar to that in the ten o'clock letter to McLaws, he not only urged a speedy conclusion to the Harpers Ferry operations, but he may have also implied the necessity of abandoning the expedition, if it could not be terminated quickly enough. Thereupon, Jackson would have alerted McLaws and Walker to watch their rears and have given up any thought of a truce.

Jackson and his entire staff then rode away from the signal station to inspect the left of the line. Soon thereafter, Bartlett received the following message from Walker: "General McLaws informs me that the enemy are in his rear, and that he can do but little more than he has done. I am now ready to open." Apparently, McLaws could not for some reason communicate directly with Jackson—Bartlett recorded no messages all day long from Maryland Heights—but had to relay his signals through Walker. It would now have been near noon, and McLaws had indeed begun to worry at least mildly about the Federal advance toward Crampton's Gap. It is curious that McLaws did not specifically mention what "he has done." In fact, he had been able to bring only four guns up the rugged slope, and they were not yet in place.

All alone at the signal station, Bartlett himself had to carry the message to Jackson, whom he found reconnoitering Bolivar Heights on the left. To the double-layered message, Stonewall dictated a reply each for Loudoun and Maryland Heights, and he sent Henry Kyd Douglas back with Bartlett to act as courier. In the message to Walker, and the first part of the one to McLaws,[46] Jackson asked the two generals to predict what their artillery could "probably effect" against Harpers Ferry. It is reasonable to assume that Jackson was continuing to evaluate his options in light of the increasing pressure for a speedy finish to the job at hand. In questioning the potential effectiveness of the artillery, while examining the enemy lines on Bolivar Heights, he must have been considering the desirability, perhaps even necessity of forcing the issue to a quick conclusion with an infantry assault.

The second part of the message addressed to McLaws affords a revealing glimpse into Jackson's information at the time: "Notify General D. H. Hill, at Middleburg, of the enemy's position, and request him to protect your rear. Send the same message to General Lee, near Hagerstown." This proves, first, that at noon Jackson had no idea of the battle that had been raging at Turner's and Fox's Gaps for the past three hours and was fully engaging D. H. Hill's attention. Second, it shows that Jackson carried with him—he was at the front and away from headquarters papers—a fuzzy mental picture of S.O. 191. He should have known that Hill was located at Boonsboro, not Middletown. (The misidentification as Middleburg is of no consequence.) It is not likely, however, that Jackson thought Hill was east of the mountains. He probably simply transposed the two towns in his mind's map. Third, he assumed that Lee and army headquarters were still located at Hagerstown.

The only information Jackson received in answer to his queries about the potential effectiveness of a cannonade from the mountains was Walker's message that he could not bring his guns to bear on an island in the Shenandoah where an enemy battery was believed to be located. Stonewall did receive, however, the additional alarming signal from Walker that "the enemy are advancing on Purcellville, and have possession of the passes from the valley." Whether Walker actually believed the Federals held the Catoctins in Virginia in his own rear, or whether he was relaying a message from McLaws and meant to specify Burkittsville, Jackson would have known that Purcellville was six miles west of Leesburg and thirteen miles south of Harpers Ferry. Even had Stonewall had the insight to translate the information from Walker's to McLaws's rear, he must have been startled to learn the Federals possessed the passes. Clearly, delay was no longer possible. Jackson signaled to both Walker and McLaws: "Fire at such positions of the enemy as will be most effective."

Nevertheless, at about one o'clock Walker did apparently open fire of his own volition in response to Federal batteries that were raking his position. Whether he provoked the fire by parading his infantry in clearings on the mountain, and whether he never received Jackson's order, are facts for which the only evidence is Walker's word in his flawed recollections.[47] Whatever the case, he did not force Jackson's hand, nor did he go contrary to Jackson's wishes at the time. Shortly after one, Jackson's own guns opened fire, and by two o'clock McLaws's battery had joined in from Maryland Heights.[48]

Although all of the reports would boast of brilliant results for the Confederate fire from Loudoun and Maryland Heights, it soon became apparent to Jackson that, due to the "distance and range of their guns, not much could be expected from their artillery" against the Federal line on Bolivar Heights.[49] Hence, shortly before three o'clock, he proceeded to set in motion a plan he had been evolving in the meanwhile. He ordered A. P. Hill's division to move to the right and attempt to turn the enemy's flank on the Shenandoah River. Lawton was to support the move by advancing down the Charlestown Turnpike and threatening the center; and one brigade from Jones's division was to make a demonstration against the left near the Potomac. The remainder of Jones was to be held in reserve.[50]

The tactical logic of Jackson's plan argued that the moves be made simultaneously, so that Lawton and Jones could divert enemy attention while Hill probed the flank. For some reason, however, the divisions advanced piecemeal, with considerable gaps of time between their moves. Lawton did not take up position on School House Hill, straddling the Charlestown Pike and in front of the main Federal line on Bolivar Heights, until so late in the day that his last units filed into place after dark.[51] And Winder's and Starke's brigades of Jones's division did not set out for the left flank on the Potomac until night had fallen.[52] Fortunately for Jackson's plan, A. P. Hill, who set out at about three o'clock, encountered no opposition in his approach to the Shenandoah. Even more fortunately, Hill discovered that the enemy left flank was weakly defended, was not supported by artillery, and did not reach all the way to the Shenandoah. During the night, Hill worked two of his brigades through the ravines along the riverbank and gained the rear of the Federal position.[53] Even later, Jackson put the finishing touch on his preparations by sending his artillery chief, Stapleton Crutchfield, with a ten-gun battery across the Shenandoah to occupy a foothill of Loudoun Heights, which gave a raking fire along Bolivar Heights.[54]

Such progress had been made by eight o'clock that Jackson felt confident of Confederate success on the following day. Thus, he was not unduly alarmed, when a dispatch arrived from Lee announcing that McClellan had all but forced passage through Turner's Gap.[55] To have covered the twenty-one miles and reached Jackson by eight, Lee's courier must have left Boonsboro before six and thus before Lee had finally concluded the position at South Mountain must be entirely abandoned.[56] It is not likely, therefore, that Lee was nearly so pessimistic when he dictated this message, as he would later become, after learning McLaws had lost Crampton's Gap. Indeed, Lee's language must have been sufficiently mild as to give Jackson no cause to think of abandoning operations on the verge of victory. In his response addressed to Lee's adjutant, R. H. Chilton, Jackson acknowledged the dispatch "respecting the movements of the enemy and the importance of concentration," but he adopted a wholly optimistic attitude.[57] Giving no hint that he was considering leaving his work unfinished, he stated flatly he expected "complete success tomorrow."

Boldness—like bliss—sometimes stems from ignorance. It may be questioned whether Jackson would have replied in quite the same vein had he understood the full depth of the crisis facing the Army of Northern Virginia. Not only was he likely misled by Lee's understatement of the situation at Turner's Gap, but it seems Jackson also did not fully appreciate the disaster that had befallen in McLaws's rear. Although the firing at Crampton's Gap had been audible to Jackson's men opposite Bolivar Heights, it may have been interpreted as part of D. H. Hill's battle to the north, or it may have been assumed McLaws had successfully blocked the Federal advance.[58] In any case, lacking direct signal communication with McLaws, Jackson seems to have been unaware at this point that the Federal Sixth Corps had captured Crampton's Gap, which lay but three miles in McLaws's rear.[59] Apparently, Lee in his message complained of not hearing from McLaws, because Jackson suggested, "Can you not connect the headquarters of the army, by signal, with General McLaws." Had Jackson himself possessed information about McLaws and Crampton's Gap he surely would have passed it along to Lee.

Thus, when Jackson wrote his optimistic reply to Lee at 8:15 on the evening of September 14, he may have inadvertently painted an overly rosy prospect for his chief. Undoubtedly he was correct in believing—to use the words of A. P. Hill's report—"the fate of Harper's Ferry was sealed." Still, the ultimate outcome of his operations had become secondary to the amount of time they would consume. The clock now measuring the success of the Maryland campaign—and possibly the survival of McLaws's command—was no longer calibrated in days but in hours.[60]

The Battle of Crampton's Gap

September 14 was not one of Jeb Stuart's best days as cavalry chief of the Army of Northern Virginia. Early in the morning he rode away from Turner's Gap, when Colquitt and D. H. Hill—and even Lee, ten miles away in Hagerstown—had begun to realize how critical holding the pass would become during the day. Stuart continued to believe McClellan would focus on Crampton's Gap and the rear of McLaws's command as the best way for the Federals to exploit their newly gained knowledge of the separation of the Confederate army. Jeb took with him the Jeff. Davis Legion, which Hampton had left behind the previous evening, and set out along the western base of South Mountain for Pleasant Valley. He did order Col. Thomas Rosser with the 5th Virginia—the only unit of Fitz Lee's brigade that had returned from the abortive Westminster raid—to guard Fox's Gap. Yet, he did not give Rosser instructions or alert D. H. Hill to Rosser's presence; and, when Rosser sent a message to Stuart warning of the Ninth Corps's advance on Fox's Gap, Stuart continued riding southward without reply.[61]

By midmorning, Jeb had covered ten miles and proceeded directly to Crampton's Gap.[62] Here he found Hampton's brigade (1,200 men); Munford's brigade (about 400 men in the two regiments that had not been detached); two small infantry regiments of Mahone's brigade (300 men); and three batteries (the horse artillery of Chew and Hart and Grimes's Portsmouth Artillery of Anderson's division).[63] Although lopsided in horse soldiers, in an emergency it was a force that could have harassed and slowed a much larger force attempting to penetrate the mountain pass. Once again, however, Confederate cavalry intelligence failed at a critical moment. Either Munford and Hampton had not scouted eastward from Burkittsville that morning, or Stuart misinterpreted what was reported to him. Because there was no active Federal pressure immediately in front of Crampton's Gap, Stuart decided he had misjudged McClellan's intentions. He seems not have considered that the Federal attack was still in the stage of development nor to have reconsidered that the main Federal thrust might be aimed at Turner's Gap. Instead, he decided the enemy must be moving directly along the Potomac River to the relief of Harpers Ferry.

On the basis of this speculation—for which there could have been no hard evidence—Stuart withdrew Hampton and sent his brigade and Hart's battery to occupy the River Road and scout toward Knoxville, the small river village that was the terminus of the road from Frederick by way of Jefferson and Petersville. Here Hampton would remain until the morning of the 16th, and for two days his brigade would be essentially useless to the Confederate army.[64] Leaving Munford with two small cavalry regiments, two even smaller infantry regiments, and two batteries to guard Crampton's Gap, Stuart for the second time that morning rode away from a position that would within hours become the scene of a battle crucial to the safety of Lee's army. Pursuing his notion that McClellan intended to relieve Harpers Ferry through the water gaps, Stuart with his staff proceeded to Weverton at the foot of South Mountain. He spent the rest of the morning and the early afternoon visiting the headquarters of Roger Pryor, whose brigade was stationed at Weverton.[65]

Somewhat belatedly, Stuart rode several miles northwest to McLaws's headquarters at the foot of Maryland Heights.[66] It was approaching two o'clock, and he found McLaws was about to ascend the mountain to supervise the opening of his battery. It had taken since dawn to clear a rough road and drag by hand four cannon to the crest. Across the river, Walker and Jackson had already opened fire, and McLaws was anxious to contribute to the reduction of Harpers Ferry. Stuart decided to ride along, and as the two generals picked their way up the steep, rocky slope they exchanged information. Jeb reminisced about his service at Harpers Ferry during the John Brown raid in 1859. This reminded him, he later reported, to warn McLaws specifically to guard the road that ran from the base of Maryland Heights westward (passing near the farm Brown had rented) and eventually reached Sharpsburg.

McLaws had a more pressing concern he wanted to talk about. He told Stuart that about noon he had received a report the enemy was advancing on the passes into Pleasant Valley in his rear. In response, McLaws had ordered Semmes, who held Brownsville Gap, to withdraw

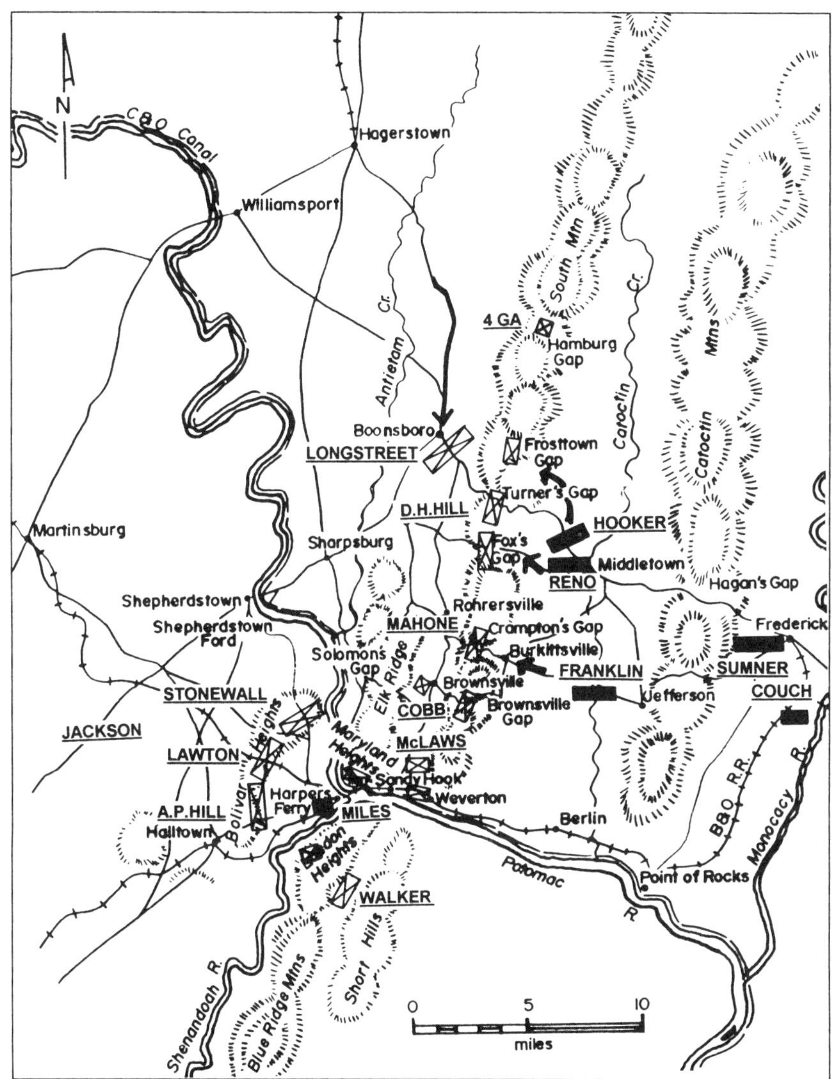

Battle of South Mountain, September 14, noon

the force holding Solomon Gap in Elk Ridge and return it to Crampton's. Unsure if the enemy were threatening the pass at Brownsville or Burkittsville (Crampton's) or both, McLaws had also ordered Howell Cobb to return to Brownsville, where his brigade would be in position to reenforce either gap. Ironically, Cobb had been posted at Sandy Hook and would have been the only force available to close the road Stuart had just called to McLaws's attention.[67]

Why McLaws chose Cobb's brigade is a mystery. Even if he did not know that he thereby opened an escape route, it is hard to fathom why he selected the unit that had the farthest distance to travel and—except for Kershaw and Barksdale on Maryland Heights—would take the longest time to reach Brownsville. It is also unclear why McLaws indiscriminately mingled the brigades from his own division and that of Richard H. Anderson and why he did not use Anderson, a major general and West Point class mate, as a second in command with responsibility for protecting the rear of the column. Surface appearances suggest McLaws either did not trust Anderson and Anderson's men or was strongly biased toward his own division. McLaws chose his own brigades for all of the assignments he believed most important: he assigned Kershaw and Barksdale to carry Maryland Heights, Semmes to remain as rear guard at Brownsville, and Cobb to return as reenforcement when the threat was reported. It may be that with independent command and major responsibilities thrust suddenly upon him, McLaws could not delegate authority and trusted only the subordinates he knew best.

In any case, McLaws was able to report to Stuart that he had three infantry brigades in the vicinity of the Brownsville and Burkittsville passes (Semmes, Mahone, and Cobb) and another two at the Weverton water gap (Wright and Pryor). Stuart was able to add that Munford's cavalry brigade was at Crampton's Gap and Hampton was now in front of Weverton. Equally important, Stuart, who, in McLaws's words, "had just come in from above," said "he did not believe there was more than a brigade of the enemy" pressing against the rear. Either Stuart was the victim of highly erroneous scouting reports—and there is no indication he was receiving any reports—or else he irresponsibly reassured McLaws on the basis of stale, early-morning intelligence that had been hastily and inaccurately drawn in the first place.

In consequence, McLaws would claim he "felt no particular concern" when the roar of artillery burst forth from the direction of Brownsville around three o'clock. Although the noise of the battle in the rear coincided almost precisely with the opening of his guns on Maryland Heights, the distracted McLaws took time to send his adjutant, Maj. James Goggin, with orders to Cobb that the mountain passes must be held, even "if he lost his last man in doing it." Concern must have continued to play in the back of McLaws's mind, because around five o'clock he and Stuart rode down the mountain and toward Brownsville. On the way, they met an excited Major Goggin, who announced that the Confederates at Crampton's Gap had been routed. The Federals had already debouched into Pleasant Valley. McLaws immediately ordered Wilcox's brigade to Brownsville, and then he and Stuart rode on to Crampton's Gap to assess the damage.[68]

Maj. Gen. William B. Franklin, commanding the left wing of the Army of the Potomac, started on the 14th as early as any of his opponents. He was encamped with the two divisions of his Sixth Corps three miles east of Jefferson on the road from Urbana. Six miles behind at Licksville was Darius Couch's division of the Fourth Corps, which thus far in the campaign had acted as reserve to guard against an enemy crossing of the lower Potomac. The previous evening, McClellan had ordered Franklin to force passage into Pleasant Valley and "cut off the retreat of or destroy Mclaws' command." The Federal chief had begged of his subordinate, "at this important moment, all your intellect and the utmost activity that a general can exercise."[69] Duly impressed, Franklin set Henry Slocum's division in motion before daylight around five o'clock.

After advancing the three miles to Jefferson, however, Franklin halted. In spite of McClellan's specific instructions not to wait for Couch's division to come up, Franklin did just that. Not until noon did he decide he would be compelled to move against McLaws with the 12,000 men at hand in the divisions of Slocum and William Smith and not wait for the lagging 6,000 of Couch. (It was as well he did not wait, as Couch would not reach Jefferson until eight o'clock that night.) It took Franklin an additional three hours to cover the four miles to Burkittsville and prepare his men for an assault. The Sixth Corps commander is justly open to criticism for taking ten hours to advance eight miles. Still, it ought to be remembered, he operated under the same conditions of heat and dust as Longstreet, who took the same time to cover ten miles and arrived at Boonsboro with depleted and exhausted ranks. While the Sixth Corps reports do not mention adverse marching conditions, neither do they indicate straggling that significantly weakened their force.[70]

From the start Franklin focused on Crampton's Gap, rather than Brownsville Gap a mile to the south, and he seems never to have considered advancing on the Weverton water gap, as anticipated by Stuart. By three o'clock, Slocum's division of three brigades had formed on the right of the road leading from Burkittsville to Crampton's Gap. Smith's division took position to the south, sending William Brooks's brigade along the left of the road to Crampton's Gap and Winfield Hancock to demonstrate against Brownsville Gap and holding William Irwin in reserve. It was a sensible plan, and according to the Confederates viewing the movement from the mountain crest, it was carried out with impressive precision.[71] Countless armchair generals in subsequent years have marveled that Franklin did not sweep unhesitatingly up the mountain and punch through the lightly defended pass. "Fortune favors the bold" is often the battle cry once victory is assured. After a foolish assault has failed, however, the appropriate axiom is "Look before you leap." True wisdom lies in knowing know ahead of time which aphorism to apply. Except for the late start, the importance of which must not be underestimated, Franklin performed better than his Confederate counterparts.

No sooner had Hampton's brigade departed and Stuart galloped away from Crampton's Gap to other imagined dangers—indeed, it must have been frustratingly soon thereafter—than Thomas Munford and his small band of defenders caught their first glimpse of the "Yankee host" unfolding in the valley before them.[72] By noon Federal skirmishers had reached Burkittsville, a mile from the mountain, and long lines of blue could be seen stretching from Jefferson three miles farther east. "As they drew nearer," observed a Confederate gunner standing by his piece, "the whole country seemed to be full of bluecoats. They were so numerous that it looked as if they were creeping up out of the ground."[73]

"Hold the gap at all hazards," Stuart had ordered, but he had left Munford with only the 16th and 41st Virginia Infantry, reduced to about three hundred men; Munford's own cavalry brigade, which had only two hundred men apiece left in the 2d and 12th Virginia Cavalry because of detachments; the four guns of Chew's Horse Artillery; and the two boat howitzers of Grimes's Portsmouth Artillery. Munford placed the infantry behind a stone wall at the base of the eastern slope of the mountain; he dismounted his cavalry and divided it on either flank and posted his cannon halfway up the gap. He also sent back to McLaws an urgent call for help. It was no doubt this plea that caused McLaws to send Cobb back to Brownsville.[74]

Col. Edgar Montague, with the 32d Virginia of Semmes's brigade, held the Brownsville Gap a mile to the south. As Franklin's Sixth Corps approached from the southeast on the Jefferson road, it was impossible to tell which pass the Federals would attack, or if they would attack both simultaneously. Montague sent back to his brigade commander, Paul Semmes, for support, and he was soon joined by the 15th Virginia, the 53d Georgia, and four guns from a mixed battery. This uncertainty over Federal intentions prevented a sizable reenforcement from being sent to Munford's support. Although Semmes's artillery was able to harass

Franklin's flank with an annoying fire from the Brownsville Gap, three of the four regiments of his brigade were wasted there for the remainder of the day and contributed nothing to the battle.[75]

Fortunately for Munford, other support—albeit meager—did reach him in time. Marching under the orders McLaws had issued at noon, Col. William Parham (commanding Mahone's brigade in the absence of Mahone, who had been wounded at Second Manassas) arrived with the 6th and 12th Virginia from Solomon's Gap. Munford would recall these two "very small regiments" numbered "scarcely 300 men." Help also came from the 10th Georgia Infantry, which Semmes had left to guard the road from Rohrersville to Boonsboro. Although conflicting orders caused Maj. Willis Holt to send two companies back into Pleasant Valley, he added 173 officers and men to the Confederate defense. With about 800 infantry protected by stone walls to hold the center, 200 dismounted cavalry on each flank, three rifled guns at the crest of Crampton's Gap, and a battery enfilading from Brownsville Gap, Munford held the cautiously advancing Federals at bay for over two hours.

Caution is not the sole explanation, however, for the Federal delay in carrying Crampton's Gap. Munford held a naturally strong defensive position, he posted his forces wisely, and his men fought extremely well. Munford reported that "the firing was as heavy as I ever heard," and the Sixth Corps suffered 538 casualties. Whether or not Franklin should have pressed harder, he can be excused in believing for several hours that he faced a well-defended mountain pass.[76]

It was four o'clock before Howell Cobb reached Brownsville with the 1,300 men in the four regiments of his brigade. He had covered the six miles from Sandy Hook in three hours, which was not a bad marching record for the norm established by both sides on September 14. Inexplicably, the politician-turned-soldier then put his men into camp, even though the sound of battle from Crampton's Gap two miles away must have been crashing about his ears. Even if the firing from Brownsville Gap made Cobb uncertain which mountain pass most required assistance, the question remains why he made no attempt to find out.[77]

An hour passed before a courier from Munford (who had no way of knowing Cobb was at Brownsville) showed up to beg immediate help for Crampton's Gap. Cobb sounded the assembly for the 15th North Carolina and the 16th Georgia, intending to leave the 24th Georgia and the Cobb Legion behind in camp as reserve.[78] Before the first two regiments had "filed into the road," however, an alarming message arrived from

Parham indicating that overwhelming enemy numbers were about to force the pass. Cobb thereupon called out his remaining two regiments and set out with them for Crampton's Gap. On the way, he was overtaken by a member of McLaws's staff with the message that Cobb "must hold the gap if it cost the life of every man" in his command. Finally impressed with the seriousness of his mission, Cobb galloped to the head of his column.

Through seniority, field command at the gap passed to Cobb upon his arrival at about 5:30, but he quite correctly requested that Munford post the brigade as it arrived. By this point in the battle, the Sixth Corps having made little headway against the center, Franklin had extended his lines on both flanks. Munford feared envelopment and rushed Cobb's first two regiments to the left. Just as he was attempting to place the last two regiments on the right, that flank was turned by Brooks's Vermont brigade of Smith's division advancing from the south. The 24th Georgia and the Cobb Legion panicked and fled down the mountain. The panic spread from right to left, and Munford's entire line dissolved.

As darkness fell, Stuart and McLaws approached the foot of the mountain to discover soldiers streaming down the western slope in one of the worst routs suffered by the Army of Northern Virginia during the entire war. In about thirty minutes the Confederates had lost half of their men in killed, wounded, and captured.[79] "Dismount, Gentlemen!" the distraught Cobb cried out to them, "if your lives are dear to you! The enemy is within fifty yards of us." Stuart volunteered Heros von Borcke to scout how near disaster loomed, and the less-than-enthusiastic Prussian advanced cautiously through the gloom to discover the enemy had stopped at the gap and were not within a mile of the Confederates. After learning there was no immediate threat, McLaws and Stuart and their staffs, along with Paul Semmes, who had ridden over from Brownsville Gap, were able to form a thin defensive line from the fugitives of Cobb and Mahone.[80]

As blackness closed in across Pleasant Valley and hundreds of enemy campfires flared up on the near horizon, LaFayette McLaws may have been led again to wonder what charms men saw in independent command. In his view he was boxed into a most desperate situation. He believed he was caught between a force about equal to his own at Harpers Ferry and one much larger ("25,000 and upward") in his rear. Even if he wanted to cut and run, he quickly learned it was not possible. He sent a staff officer and a guide with a courier down the Boonsboro road bearing a message to Lee with news of his plight. The party soon ran into enemy pickets who chased them back, killing the courier. Thereafter, McLaws assumed he was cut off from Lee and the main body of the army. He took some small comfort in knowing Stuart sent messages that apparently did get through.

In McLaws's eyes his command was virtually trapped. In his report, he recalled his strategic analysis: [81]

> I could not retire under the bluffs along the river, with the enemy pressing my rear and the forces at Harper's Ferry operating in conjunction, unless under a combination of circumstances I could not rely on to happen at the exact time needed; could not pass over the mountain except in a scattered and disorganized condition, nor could have gone through the Weverton Pass into the open country beyond to cross a doubtful ford when the enemy was in force on the other side of the Blue Ridge and coming down in my rear. There was no outlet in any direction for anything but the troops, and that very doubtful. In no contingency could I have saved the trains and artillery.

McLaws's assessment was comprehensive if not entirely accurate. He was undoubtedly correct in assuming that escape by way of the barely perceptible notch in Elk Ridge called Solomon's Gap was impractical. He probably overestimated the risk, however, of withdrawing on the road through Sandy Hook at the base of Maryland Heights. If McLaws had moved in conjunction with a demonstration by Walker and Jackson, the garrison at Harpers Ferry could have spared little attention to his column passing along the river. Finally, he was completely mistaken in the belief he could not march east through the Weverton water gap and recross the lower Potomac. Ironically, the one contribution that Hampton's misplaced brigade operating toward Knoxville could have made was to assure McLaws that this route was open.

Still, as is always the case, it is what is known and believed that is important. Moreover, believing he was virtually trapped helped McLaws decide to hold to his mission. He concluded, "I had nothing to do but defend my position. . . . I therefore determined to defend myself in the valley, holding the two heights and the two lower passes in order to force a direct advance down the valley, to prevent co-operation from Harper's Ferry, and at the same time to carry out my orders in relation to the capture of that place."

In other words, since he could not be sure of escape without great loss, he might as well go down with colors flying. Two factors made this decision especially agonizing. First, he apparently had no notion whatsoever how long it might take for Harpers Ferry to surrender. Second, having seen during the afternoon that his guns on Maryland Heights had limited ability to influence the reduction of the garrison, his must be the merely passive role of blocking escape routes. It appeared he would have little control over his own destiny.

Having cast his die, McLaws took the steps necessary to defend himself. He ordered up the brigade of Wilcox to strengthen the line at Brownsville, and he instructed the brigades of Kershaw and Barksdale to descend Maryland Heights as additional support. Only the 13th Mississippi and two guns were to remain behind on the mountain, a tacit confession that the fire from Maryland Heights had not been judged effective. By early morning, the only units absent from the Brownsville line would be the brigades of Wright and Pryor, watching the Weverton water gap, and those of Armistead and Featherston guarding the road below Maryland Heights from the eastern end.[82] The latter were posted so far east, however, that McLaws inadvertently kept open an escape route for the enemy. During the night, 1,300 Federal cavalry under Col. Grimes Davis rode across the bridges from Harpers Ferry and took the open road through Sharpsburg to safety in Pennsylvania.[83]

To add to McLaws's misery, before dawn he received three dispatches from Lee—including the one to Munford that the cavalry leader forwarded from Rohrersville—all calling upon him to abandon his position immediately. With much misgiving he decided to disobey the peremptory instructions from his army commander. He sent several messages to Lee, but none got through. Then, he waited, as he would write after the war, to "see what fortune would bring me on the morrow."[84]

McLaws was right, of course. He properly exercised the discretion—which any commander of a detached force must hold—to depart from orders due to circumstances unknown to a superior. McLaws's perception of his situation was far from perfect, but his decision to disobey Lee and hold his position was correct.

Evening: The First Retreat

It was nearly four o'clock when Lee stood by the turnpike fence and watched Hood's division disappear down the National Road in a swirl of dust. After the rear guard of Longstreet's column had passed out of sight and started to climb the mountain, the Confederate commander had not a single regiment left at his disposal. It was an anxious moment for Lee, and could his bandaged hands have bridled Traveller, he might well have tried in person to lead the Texans into battle, as he would twenty months later on another grim day for Confederate fortunes. Here and now he could only agonize in ignorance, two miles in the rear of the fighting.

Lee's wait was ruthfully short, although he might have traded the first news that reached him for a return to uncertainty. Longstreet—whose heart was not in the stand at the mountain—had ridden at once to the top of the gap to take command. His first glimpse of the "disjointed condition" of the Confederate position convinced him the situation was hopeless. In one sweeping glance, he decided Hill had wrongly posted the troops, the enemy were too great in numbers, and the Confederate reenforcements too few and too late. Clearly, Longstreet correctly assessed the odds, even if he were predisposed to withdraw. He immediately dispatched a note to Lee "to prepare his mind for disappointment, and give time for arrangements for retreat."[85]

Lee may have clutched at the optimistic note in Longstreet's report that suggested the gap could be held until nightfall. He may also have reflected that situations often appear worse than they turn out to be. Still, he could not ignore the dire warning. When William Pendleton arrived around four-thirty and reported with three battalions of the Artillery Reserve, over sixty guns in fourteen batteries, Lee took the first step in his retreat. Since the guns would be awkward to employ in the rugged terrain in any case, he used Pendleton to prepare a position for falling back. Lee ordered Pendleton to form a superbattery on the heights crowning Beaver Creek three miles west of Boonsboro. This early decision reveals that Lee did not at first intend to fall back very far. A defensive line behind Beaver Creek would forfeit his most convenient escape route to Virginia, the road from Boonsboro to Sharpburg and Shepherdstown; also, it would even uncover the most direct road to Williamsport. There were other, if more circuitous, routes to Williamsport, however, and Lee must have intended to stand as near to South Mountain as possible in order to threaten the flank of the Federals should they attempt to turn south against McLaws after emerging from Turner's Gap.[86]

In planning for McLaws's safety, Lee's thinking naturally turned to the Harpers Ferry expedition. It was now two full days behind the original schedule, and he had no clear idea of when the two-thirds of his army

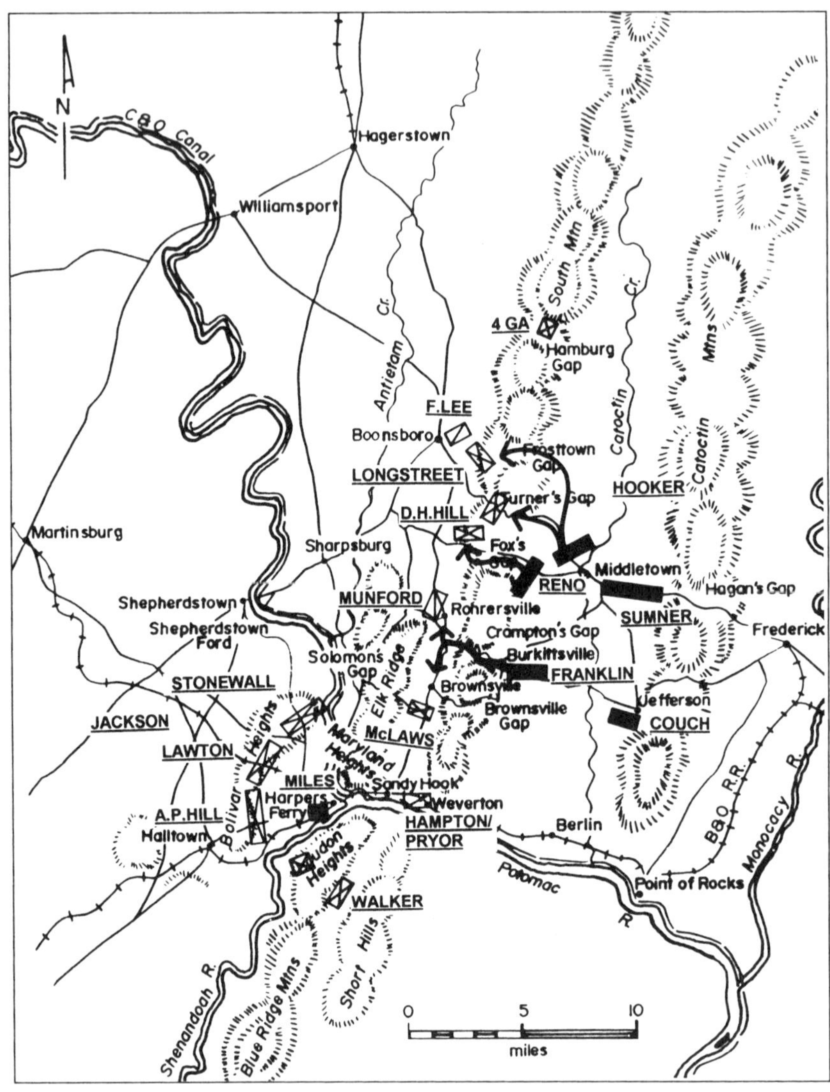

Battle of South Mountain, September 14, evening

operating there would be free to rejoin him. Shortly thereafter (it must have been by five o'clock if not before) Lee dispatched a hard-riding courier to Jackson with a message drafted by Chilton. It is possible to tell from Jackson's reply that Lee discussed McClellan's movements, and he may have specifically mentioned that Turner's Gap would be abandoned that night and a new line formed behind Boonsboro. The Confederate commander emphasized the need for the rapid reuniting of the army, and he may have directly asked Jackson to estimate the time needed to finish at Harpers Ferry.[87] Curiously, there is no evidence Lee tried to communicate with either McLaws or Walker at this time.

Nor is there any indication that he had heard from McLaws or Stuart or Munford during the day. It is likely, therefore, Lee was unaware a battle had been raging simultaneously at Crampton's Gap. The mountain-shaking roar from Turner's would certainly have precluded hearing a fight six miles away, and Lee may have been misled—as D. H. Hill had been—into believing the heavy Federal assault in his immediate front meant Stuart had been wrong about the threat at Burkittsville. Of course, even had Lee been aware of a battle at Crampton's Gap, he could not yet have known of the disastrous defeat that was just then occurring there. His ignorance helps to explain why his first planned retreat was such a modest one.

By sunset, at 6:15, the artillery fire gradually diminished around Turner's Gap until finally it ceased, while the crack of musketry grew sporadic but continued on into the night. The exhausted soldiers collapsed where the fighting ended, and the opposing lines snaked erratically through the mountain woods and ravines. In truth, darkness saved the Confederates. On the left, Meade had cleared the Frosttown Gap and held the road that ran to the rear. In the center, Hatch's flank was within 1,500 feet of Turner's Gap. On the right, thanks to Hood's last-minute countercharge, the Confederates held the mountain almost a mile along the crest, but Fox's Gap was now open to the enemy.

After struggling to straighten the alignment of his division in the failed light, John Hood rode down the road along the crest to the Mountain House. He found D. H. Hill and other officers huddled on the gallery, and when he asked, as he dismounted, about affairs on the left, he was greeted with, "Pshe—Pshe," and a whispered, "The enemy is just there in the cornfield; he has forced us back." Quite reasonably, Hood suggested, presumably in a whisper as well, that they "repair without delay to General Lee's headquarters, and report the situation."[88] Down the mountain came Hood and Hill and found Lee at the Widow Herr's house in the eastern outskirts of Boonsboro. The Confederate commander was already in consultation with Longstreet.

Apparently, Lee said little in the war council that ensued, except to inquire about the "prospects for continuing the fight." Longstreet, who was already on record in favor of withdrawal, simply deferred to Hill, as the officer best acquainted with the ground. Hill declared that both flanks had been turned, and the toehold the Confederates retained was subject to a murderous cross fire from enemy batteries already in place. He saw no alternative to retreat. When Longstreet and Hood concurred, Lee found himself facing the unanimous advice of three generals fresh from a field he had never seen. He had no choice but to acquiesce.[89]

Indeed, what Lee heard had shaken him badly. The generals—at least Hill and Longstreet—must have so emphasized the exhaustion and disorganization of their commands as to cause Lee to decide it would be unwise to attempt the stand at Beaver Creek. Although he probably did not mention it to his subordinates, he determined to abort his campaign in Maryland and withdraw to Virginia.[90] He would take the shortest, quickest route and follow the road from Boonsboro to Sharpsburg and recross the Potomac at Shepherdstown. McLaws—there was no help for it—would have to abandon Maryland Heights and find his own way to safety. Jackson must break off operations against Harpers Ferry and march up the river to cover the crossing at Shepherdstown.

Lee must have been aware that he was forfeiting every advantage he had hoped to gain from his movement into Maryland. By returning to Virginia now, he would have nothing to show for the great risk he had taken except a handful of recruits whose numbers were so few as to mock Confederate pretensions to Maryland. More importantly, by being chased ingloriously across the Potomac, he would destroy the aura of invincibility from his string of summer's victories and thereby unwittingly feed the starving morale of the enemy. How bitter must have been the knowledge that he and his army would be the first to turn back from the grand continental offensive. He might even be retreating from the best chance the Confederacy would ever have to win the war. It was likely the hardest, most distasteful decision Lee had yet rendered in his career.

He may even have purposefully hidden the final destination from his subordinates at Boonsboro. The complicated withdrawal from the mountain would necessarily consume time, and perhaps Lee hoped something would turn up to divert fate. Still, he could not delay alerting McLaws, who must be given the longest possible time to plan his own escape; nor could he postpone telling Jackson. Hence, at eight o'clock Lee dictated to Chilton two painful dispatches. The one to Jackson, ordering Stonewall to leave Harpers Ferry and march to Shepherdstown to cover the crossing of the main body, has been lost,[91] but its tone was no doubt reflected in the message addressed to McLaws at Weverton, which has survived.[92]

"The day has gone against us," he opened bluntly to McLaws, "and this army will go by Sharpsburg and cross the river." There is no way to read this sentence except to mean that at the time he spoke it, Lee fully intended to quit. In consequence, he instructed McLaws, "It is necessary for you to abandon your position tonight."

Lee then went on to lecture McLaws on the steps he should take in a didactic, repetitive, and somewhat rambling manner that reflected the strain under which the Confederate commander labored:

> Send your trains not required on the road to cross the river. Your troops you must have well in hand to unite with this command, which will retire by Sharpsburg. Send forward officers to explore the way, ascertain the best crossing of the Potomac, and if you can find any between you and Shepherdstown leave Shepherdstown ford for this command. Send an officer to report to me on the Sharpsburg road, where you are and what crossing you will take. You will of course bring Anderson's division with you.

It is noteworthy that in this dispatch there is no indication that Lee yet knew of the battle of Crampton's Gap. He seems to have assumed that McLaws was free of any close pressure from the enemy and certainly seems unaware that McLaws would have to disengage from the Federals in order to retreat.

In preparing for the return to Virginia, Lee promptly set about following part of the advice he had given McLaws. Shortly after eight, he remembered to call in the forces he had left behind in Hagerstown. He ordered Toombs's brigade to take up position at Sharpsburg, three miles southwest of Keedysville on the Boonsboro Pike and nearer the river, where the four Georgia regiments would provide the only fresh troops available to cover the crossing from the north bank. Lee had also to provide for the considerable trains at Hagerstown. Not only had some fifty of Longstreet's reserve ordnance and supply wagons been left behind in the hurried departure of the morning, but there were another fifty or so at Funkstown, including those carrying the provisions collected in Maryland. There were also the trains of D. H. Hill, which had been sent northward during the day for safety. Lee ordered that all of these wagons recross the river at Williamsport. To escort them he designated the 11th Georgia Infantry, which George T. Anderson had forgotten to call in from guard duty, and the 1st Virginia Cavalry, which was still picketing the Pennsylvania line. For reasons that are not clear, Lee delayed taking any action on the trains at Boonsboro, including the Artillery Reserve.[93]

Meanwhile, the withdrawal from Turner's Gap had started slowly and in considerable confusion. It seems to have been Lee's intention to pull Hill's division—weary from a full day's fight—from the line first, to be followed in turn by Longstreet's command.[94] It is difficult to tell from the existing records, whether Lee's desire was carried out in the timing or sequence the units withdrew from the mountain. It is doubtful many officers struck a light to check their watches, and the reports they wrote afterward are ambiguous and contradictory. Col. Montgomery Corse of the 17th Virginia reported receiving orders to retire "shortly" after 7:30. If true, this means that Corse's regiment—part of Kemper's brigade and one of the last of Longstreet's units to arrive—was not only one of the first to leave but received its instructions virtually at the same time as the war council.[95] Similarly, Hood, whose postwar memoirs claimed the council met after ten, reported two weeks after the fact that his division had been ordered to withdraw "soon after night."[96] Considering all the evidence, however, the actual withdrawal seems to have started around ten o'clock, and movements prior to that time must have been merely realignments.[97]

Once started, the generals and their staffs faced a daunting task in extracting exhausted troops from the broken terrain in darkness. "We had a bad night on the mountain," recalled Longstreet's adjutant, Moxley Sorrel, and "had to make sharp play with the flats of our swords on the backs of these fellows." Likely, the officers—many of whom were so near the enemy they had to crawl forward on hands and knees—simply took the regiments as they could find them. Many of the soundly sleeping soldiers were unknowingly left behind, while others groggily wandered off in the wrong direction.[98] Several of many incidents illustrate the chaos of that night. Two units were overlooked in the muddle. Roswell Ripley forgot that he had sent George Doles's 4th Georgia to guard the Hamburg Pass, three miles to the north at the start of the fight. If one of Doles's fellow colonels, William DeRosset of the 3d North Carolina, had not missed his presence and dispatched a courier, the regiment would have been captured. The next morning Doles passed through Boonsboro ten minutes ahead of the Federals.[99]

More extraordinarily, Allen Cutts and his artillery battalion were ordered off the mountain and back to their old camp a half-mile from Boonsboro. There Cutts sat with his twenty-eight guns, caissons, and wagons without further instructions until he finally decided on his own to hurry after the army to Sharpsburg.[100] Lastly, and most curiously, Roswell Ripley reported that while still on the mountain he received orders from Longstreet "to renew the attack as early as practicable," before receiving instructions to withdraw. Considering Longstreet's attitude since the moment he set foot on the mountain, it is doubtful these orders were authentic.[101]

Three general conclusions emerge from the murky evidence. First, most of the Confederate units seem not to have left the mountain until relatively late, say eleven o'clock or after.[102] Second, the brigades on the right, which had been defending Fox's Gap, withdrew by way of the the Rohrersville Road to Boonsboro, with Rosser's 5th Virginia Cavalry covering their rear. In the center—there no longer was a left—the Confederate units fell back directly on the National Road to Boonsboro; and Walker's South Carolina brigade assumed a defensive position at the foot of the mountain.[103] Third, all of the units paused after reaching Boonsboro for a period (for some it was up to several hours) to rest briefly and to sort out their tangled organizations.[104] Even though the withdrawal was carried out as expeditiously as conditions would allow, the delay may have been welcomed by Lee. In his dread, perhaps he hoped that something would turn up to allow him to change his mind.

As luck would have it, something did turn up. Although scarcely what Lee might have wanted, he received more bad news, and it caused him to modify his plans.

Within two hours of writing the eight o'clock dispatch to McLaws, Lee learned of the disaster at Crampton's Gap. He heard about it, moreover, from a source bound to have described it as an even greater catastrophe than it turned out to be in the end. When the Confederates had broken under the assault of the Sixth Corps, the infantry of Cobb and Mahone fled to the south toward the remainder of McLaws's command. At the same time, Thomas Munford and his dismounted cavalry turned north to retrieve the horses they had left on the road to Rohrersville. Munford was thus cut off from the battle before the arrival of McLaws and Stuart and the stabilizing of the Confederate line. He had made his way to Rohrersville, a hamlet seven miles south of Boonsboro, and there he sent a dispatch to Lee depicting the results as he knew them.[105]

At 10:15, realizing Munford's small force could accomplish little, Lee dictated a calm reply for Chilton's signature.[106] "Hold your position at Rohrersville, if possible, and if you can discover or hear of a practicable road below Crampton's Gap by which McLaws, at Weverton at present, can pass over the mountains to Sharpsburg, send him a messenger to guide him over immediately." Lee correctly saw that the one contribution Munford could make was to help McLaws escape his predicament. It is also apparent the news did not change Lee's mind that McLaws should break off operations against Harpers Ferry and flee for safety.

Awareness of this new crisis did, however, cause Lee to reexamine and modify his own plans. It no longer seemed acceptable for the troops at Boonsboro to retreat to Virginia and leave McLaws entirely to his own devices. Ten brigades, a quarter of the Army of Northern Virginia, must not be sacrificed without a fight. This reasoning also provided Lee the excuse—albeit a negative one—to postpone quitting his Maryland campaign. He may even have taken a perverse satisfaction from a development that stiffened his resolve to persevere in the teeth of a quirky fate.

Incredibly, Lee's first instinct was to continue the fight at Turner's Gap. He may have been prompted by rumors that noises indicated movement on the Federal line. Shortly before eleven o'clock, the Confederate commander issued orders that no doubt stunned Longstreet, if he saw them. Lee directed Evans's brigade, which was still in place near the Mountain House, to send out a reconnaissance to the day's battleground to "ascertain whether the enemy still occupied it or had retired." A small detachment of the Holcombe Legion lost its lieutenant in discovering the Federals had not budged an inch.[107] It was probably at about the same time that Lee learned a prisoner had been brought in from the Second Corps, indicating that the noises heard were a new Federal force relieving Hooker's tired men.[108]

The possibility of a fresh enemy corps poised to attack in the morning ended any thought of remaining at Turner's Gap. Lee probably had not placed much hope in continuing on the mountain in any case; and he decided on an alternative way of protecting McLaws even before he heard the results of the reconnaissance. He would stop at Keedysville, a village three miles southwest of Boonsboro on the road to Sharpsburg and Shepherdstown. There he would threaten the flank of Federal forces operating in Pleasant Valley against McLaws. If McClellan chose to move in force against Lee, the Potomac was a scant seven miles away. Apparently, Lee selected Keedysville from the map because of its central location. Whether or not the ground there was suitable for a defensive stand would have to be determined by the morning's light.

It was desirable that McLaws should know at once of the modified plans, and at 11:15 Lee dictated another dispatch to be sent over Chilton's signature. As in the case of all the previous evening's messages, this one eschewed the deferential language normally employed by Lee's staff when writing for their chief, and it reads instead as if it came directly from Lee's pen.[109]

"In addition to what has already been stated in reference to your abandonment of Weverton, and routes you can take," Lee dictated, "I will mention you might cross the Potomac, below Weverton, into Virginia." Hence, Lee had not changed his mind on one key point. He still expected McLaws to break off the operations against Harpers Ferry and abandon not only Weverton but also Pleasant Valley and Maryland Heights. He was simply providing McLaws with another route for escape.

"I believe there is a ford at the Point of Rocks, and at Berlin below," Lee wrote with an unusual tentativeness. That Lee was unable to write with positive certainty about the fords no doubt reflects the late hour, the confusion at headquarters, and the pressing sense of urgency. Apparently, he was not able to consult in a timely fashion with anyone who possessed knowledge of the region.[110] "But do not know whether either is accessible to you," Lee continued. "The enemy from Jefferson seem to have forced a passage at Crampton's Gap, which may leave all on the river clear." This puzzling statement seems to suggest not only that Lee did not fully rely on Munford's information, but also that he believed McLaws might not have heard about the battle at the gap. Lee was entirely correct, however, that the river was clear.

Then Lee got to his main reason for the dispatch. "This portion of the army will take position at Centreville, commonly called Keedysville, 2½ miles from Boonsborough, on the Sharpsburg road, with a view of preventing the enemy that may enter the gap at Boonsborough turnpike from cutting you off, and enabling you to make a junction with it." This is the key evidence in proving Lee had significantly modified his plan since writing to McLaws three hours earlier. No longer will Lee cross immediately into Virginia. Instead, he would stand at Keedysville, and his sole stated purpose is the protection of McLaws's command. "If you can pass to-night on the river road, by Harper's Ferry, or cross the mountain below Crampton's Gap toward Sharpsburg, let me know," Lee concluded, "I will be found at or near Centreville, or Keedysville, as it is called."

Thus, as Lee prepared to set out from Boonsboro, although he no longer intended to cross immediately into Virginia, he nevertheless still believed he was abandoning his campaign in Maryland. He had every reason to believe his instructions for McLaws and Jackson to abandon the siege of Harpers Ferry would be obeyed. McClellan would now have free access to the garrison, and the Federal army would be swelled by its numbers.[111] Clearly, the courier bearing Jackson's optimistic dispatch of 8:15 predicting the imminent capture of Harpers Ferry had not yet found his way through the darkness to Lee. It is also likely that none of the couriers from Stuart bearing a somewhat calmer view of McLaws's predicament had yet arrived, nor had the Confederate commander heard more from Thomas Munford at Rohrersville.

Around midnight, Lee set in motion the final details necessary for his retreat. He ordered Porter Alexander with the eighty wagons in the army's ordnance train to cross the river at Williamsport and then proceed south to Shepherdstown.[112] No doubt Lee prescribed the circuitous route in order to expedite the march by keeping the ford at Shepherdstown free for his main body. Lee called William Pendleton to headquarters and instructed him to disperse the Artillery Reserve. The battalion of Stephen Lee was to accompany the infantry to Keedysville, while Pendleton was to post the battalions of Thompson Brown and William Nelson on the Virginia side to guard the fords from Williamsport to Shepherdstown.[113]

No one with Lee on the night of the September 14 got more than random snatches of sleep. It must have been about midnight when the first Confederate regiments set out for Keedysville on the road leading southwest from the center of Boonsboro. Reasonable order had been restored to the units as they rested at the foot of the mountain, and the vanguard was assigned to Robert Rodes with his own and Colquitt's brigades, both of which had been withdrawn early from the Mountain House at Turner's Gap. After an interval, D. H. Hill followed with the remainder of his division—the brigades of Garland (now McRae), Ripley, and G. B. Anderson—which had made their way from the vicinity of Fox's Gap. Lee then inserted into the middle of his column all of the ordnance and supply wagons and ambulances still with the army. These vehicles so clogged the road that Stephen Lee could not get into Boonsboro to join the main army with his battalion of the Reserve Artillery. He had to take his guns across open fields and force his way into the line some distance from town.[114]

It was nearly three o'clock before the road was clear for Longstreet's men. Drayton's brigade from Fox's Gap led the way, followed by Kemper and Garnett from Turner's Gap. Lee had designated Hood's division (with G. T. Anderson attached) to be the rear guard, but Hood had to wait until Joseph Walker's brigade of South Carolinians was relieved. Walker had been ordered to remain halfway down the mountain on the National road to cover the withdrawal. Fortunately, there was now cavalry to take their place.

Several hours earlier Fitzhugh Lee had arrived in Boonsboro with the remainder of his brigade. Around four o'clock, he took up position at the foot of Turner's Gap and relieved Walker. Fitz Lee posted two guns of Pelham's Horse Artillery on a knoll by the National Road and supported them on each flank by dismounted troopers from the 3d Virginia Cavalry. He advanced skirmishers onto the mountain. The 4th Virginia, followed by the 9th Virginia, were held in column on the road in the rear.[115] Meanwhile, Rosser's 5th Virginia remained near the foot of Fox's Gap with the other section of Pelham's battery.[116] The 1,200 Virginia troopers now held the unenviable task of retarding the progress of the Federal host, which Fitz Lee himself estimated at 100,000.[117]

For the infantry and artillery it was an unwonted first for Lee's Army of Northern Virginia to stumble through the darkness seeking safety in retreat. In their midst, came an ambulance with outriders clearing a path for the army's commander. His Maryland campaign in shambles, Robert E. Lee grimly urged his men to keep in ranks and hurry onward.[118] Traveling on a different road, Porter Alexander remembered it as one of the most painful journeys of the war. Although Alexander alternately rode and walked, he found it impossible to stay awake. Without the luxury of a horse, countless foot soldiers dropped from exhaustion and crawled to the side to avoid being trampled. Some were able to catch up on the morrow, but many would be captured by the advancing Federals.[119] Even after the infantry began arriving at Keedysville, it appeared rest would not be possible. It was rumored that enemy cavalry held Sharpsburg just down the road.

In the final indignity of a long, harrowing day, the 1,300 Federal horsemen who had escaped from Harpers Ferry on the unguarded road at the foot of Maryland Heights, cut a swath through Lee's retreating columns. Although Grimes Davis had no purpose except to lead his men to the safety of Pennsylvania, with Lee's army moving on so many different roads, it would have defied odds if an encounter had not occurred. Lee learned only that a large Federal cavalry force was reported to be between him and the Potomac and within three miles of the position where he intended to make his temporary stand, and the Confederate commander ordered the units most conveniently at hand to clear away the threat.

Robert Rodes had arrived at Keedysville at about one o'clock with his own and Colquitt's brigades. After less than an hour's rest, the bone-tired Confederates who had held the left and center at Turner's Gap were pressed into service one more time. Rodes was halted on the road by Colonel Chilton, who said that Lee had changed his mind and only two regiments should be sent. No sooner had the 5th and 6th Alabama been selected, than a third set of orders arrived (this time from Longstreet) telling Rodes to proceed with both brigades. Army headquarters may also have been tired and confused, or Lee may have simply decided that after the warning he needed to secure his rear until Jackson could get up from Harpers Ferry. It was nearly daylight by the time Rodes reached Sharpsburg and found the cavalry long departed. He put his own brigade on the high ground overlooking the river southwest of town and allowed them to cook breakfast, while he sent Colquitt on to guard the ford below Shepherdstown.[120]

The Confederates were not to escape unscathed from the fugitive Federal cavalry column sweeping across their rear. Maj. Francis Little, commanding the 11th Georgia Infantry, had been left behind by Toombs to escort the trains from Hagerstown, but apparently Little was only aware of the conglomerate of wagons at Funkstown, which included the stores collected in Maryland and D. H. Hill's recently arrived vehicles from Boonsboro. Apprehending danger only from the north, the major formed his column with half of his regiment in the middle of these wagons and the other half in the rear and arranged for the 1st Virginia Cavalry to follow behind. Upon reaching the road to Williamsport, the head of Little's column intercepted Longstreet's reserve ordnance train and, unbeknownst to Little, followed in its wake. Thus, at daybreak Grimes Davis and 1,300 horsemen in blue discovered near Williamsport a two-mile-long line of wagons with all of its guards close to the rear. The Mississippi-born Davis used his Southern accent to order the unsuspecting civilian teamsters to turn aside onto the road to Greenscastle. The Federals purloined over half the wagons before scattered musket fire hurried them on their way to Pennsylvania.[121]

It might have been even worse for the Confederates on this hapless night. Pendleton, who was on his way to Williamsport with two battalions of the Artillery Reserve, would later estimate that he missed the enemy cavalry by less than an hour.[122] When word reached Lee from Pendleton and Little, it is not known whether the Confederate commander correctly understood there was only one enemy force causing the commotion in his rear. He ordered Robert Toombs, who had just arrived in Sharpsburg from Hagerstown, to send two regiments to protect the trains at Williamsport. In the end, these incidents may have played a role in persuading Lee that Keedysville was too far distant from the Potomac for comfort.[123]

It is doubtful whether Lee ever learned with any precision the human cost of his stand at the South Mountain gaps. In time, the best historical estimate would put the Confederates loss at nearly two thousand at Turner's Gap and almost one thousand at Crampton's Gap.[124] But these figures only begin the story. While they may closely approximate the casualties in the two battles, they do not reflect the full diminution of the Army of Northern Virginia on September 14, 1862. The heat, the forced marches, and the confusion of the retreats scattered thousands of Lee's soldiers across the countryside from Hagerstown to Pleasant Valley.

On this day a new factor emerged in the strategy calculations of the Maryland campaign. On September 2, Lee's army was an instrument of sufficient strength and mettle to justify his crossing the Potomac. From the 14th onward, however, his unrelenting demands blunted the weapon in his hands and reduced its power. It is questionable whether hereafter Lee could have successfully exploited the initiative, even if he had regained it. But it is also questionable whether Lee recognized his loss of potential. One thing, at least, is certain. He would be long in acknowledging it.

CHAPTER SEVEN

"We will make our stand on these hills"

Lee's Hope Renewed, September 15, 1862

FIRST LIGHT OF another fair but hot, dry day found Lee in Keedysville. In the normal way, September 15 never began for the Confederate commander, just as the 14th never ended. For the general, who had not gone to sleep, the two days blended seamlessly together, and Lee, who had rested at most a couple of hours the night before, must have been approaching physical and mental exhaustion.

Sleep need wait, however, until the crisis be resolved. In his three months' career as army commander, Lee had taken fate-defying risks a half-dozen times, and each time fate had winked at his contempt—until now. He had stripped the south Atlantic states of troops to concentrate strength at Richmond; he had divided his army to turn the enemy out of a strong position on the Chickahominy; he had detached Jackson to Gordonsville to confront Pope; he had sent Longstreet to join Jackson before there was certain knowledge that McClellan was withdrawing from the James; he had dispatched Jackson on the distant march through Thoroughfare Gap to gain the enemy's rear; and he had unleashed the entire army in furious assault on the plains of Manassas. All of these undertakings had entailed high risks. All had held moments of great tension and doubt. But, finally, all had ended gloriously for Confederate arms.

Seduced by the momentum of these hazardous successes, he had dared to defy the greatest odds of all. He had crossed the Potomac to pursue the chance of winning the war. Until the day before yesterday a smiling fortune had continued to grace his campaign. Then, within thirty-six hours, his plans had unraveled at a breathtaking pace. He had been too slow, and his foe too quick. And all at once—or so it must have seemed—he had been forced onto the defensive. Now, regrettably, he found himself being driven to Keedysville, a place he had never intended to visit.

Lee Stands at Sharpsburg

Indeed, as Lee was helped down from his ambulance among the pale shadows cast by first light at five o'clock in the morning and stepped into the single street of the Maryland hamlet, he faced imminent catastrophe.[1] He could see no opportunity—no matter how improbable—to seize and exploit. His army was too scattered, and the enemy too near at hand. Not only was the Army of Northern Virginia still dispersed widely on the missions assigned by Special Orders 191, but the one-third that Lee called his main body was neither in good shape nor well in hand. As the Confederate commander prepared to make his stand at Keedysville, the forces under his immediate control stretched from the foot of South Mountain on one line fourteen miles west to Williamsport and on another, slightly divergent line eleven miles southwest to Shepherdstown.

The reserve trains were crossing the Potomac at Light's Ford near Williamsport accompanied by the 11th Georgia Infantry and the 1st Virginia Cavalry; Pendleton was approaching Williamsport with two battalions of the Artillery Reserve; and the 15th and 17th Georgia were on their way from Sharpsburg for additional protection. Colquitt's brigade was near Boteler's Ford below Shepherdstown, and Rodes, with his own brigade and the 2d and 20th Georgia of Toombs, was just behind on the high ground southwest of Sharpsburg. In Keedysville, Lee had D. H. Hill with the brigades of McRae (Garland), Ripley, and G. B. Anderson, the artillery battalion of Stephen Lee, and most of the immediate trains of the army. Four brigades of D. R. Jones (Kemper, Garnett, Drayton, and Walker), along with Evans's brigade, were just straggling into the village, while Hood was forming the rear guard (Wofford, Law, and G. T. Anderson) to leave Boonsboro. Fitzhugh Lee at the foot of Turner's Gap was making first contact with the cautiously advancing skirmishers of Richardson's division of the Second Corps, and Rosser continued to watch Fox's Gap. Admittedly, all were working to a purpose and would soon be coming together, but all were also weary and much thinned in strength.

Of the world beyond Elk Ridge and the Potomac, Lee remained profoundly ignorant. He had still no reply from Jackson, nor any answer to the repeated dispatches to McLaws. Even Munford—only five miles away at Rohrersville and not blocked by natural barriers—had not responded. Lee could not be sure his messages of last night had gotten through; and he could not know, therefore, if Jackson were moving to his relief, or if McLaws were attempting to escape. Hoping a courier might have better luck in daylight, Lee told Colonel Long, his military secretary, to send another message to the endangered commander in Pleasant Valley.

"General Lee desires me to say," wrote Long to McLaws, indicating he composed the letter at Lee's behest, "that he sent several dispatches to you last night; he is in doubt that they have been received."[2]

"We have fallen back to this place [heading indicates Centreville, Md.] to enable you more readily to join us. You are desired to withdraw immediately from your position on Maryland Heights, and join us here." Thus, Lee had not changed his mind from last night's 11:15 dispatch. He expected the siege of Harpers Ferry to be abandoned, and he was making the defensive stand at Keedysville solely for the purpose of diverting the enemy's attention and protecting McLaws's flank.

"If you can't get off any other way," Long continued, using an informal contraction rare in headquarters messages, "you must cross the mountain. The utmost dispatch is required." Long was not clear whether the haste derived simply from McLaws's own precarious position, or because Lee feared a prolonged stand at Keedysville.

"Should you be able to cross over to Harper's Ferry," the message closed curiously, "do so and report immediately." This sentence, along with addressing the dispatch to Maryland Heights rather than Weverton, suggests, albeit very thinly, that Lee may have heard from one of the several messengers McLaws reported Jeb Stuart sent during the night. If this were the case, Lee probably had gotten a somewhat calmer view of the situation than the one he had received earlier from the limited knowledge of Munford. While Stuart should have depicted desperate conditions in Pleasant Valley, he could also have mentioned the triangular fire that had opened on Harpers Ferry. It is equally possible, however, that Lee (through Long) was merely being especially careful to be correctly understood. He would not want McLaws to think that he must come to Keedysville to the support of the main body, if other avenues of escape were open.

Lee's stay in Keedysville turned out to be a brief one, encompassed in the forty-five minutes between daybreak and sunrise. It was a busy one, however. In addition to authorizing the follow-up message to McLaws, he is known to have engaged in two other activities. He sought information on where to establish a defensive line with his infantry and artillery, and he received a dispatch from Munford. Indeed, it was news garnered

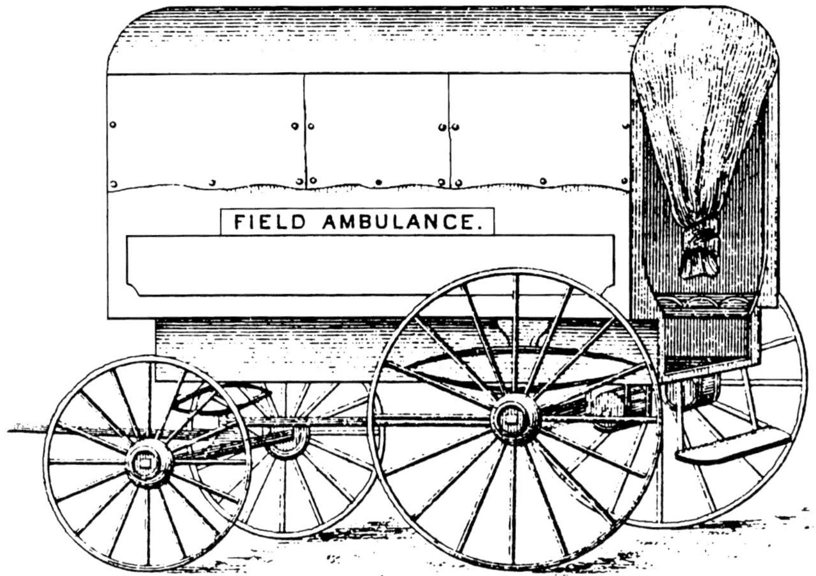

A Confederate ambulance. Because both of his badly injured hands were bandaged around splints, and one or both of his arms were in slings, Robert E. Lee traveled in a vehicle similar to this one from August 31 through September 15, 1862—for ten of the fourteen days he spent in Maryland. When he returned to Traveller's back on the 16th, he needed an orderly to hold the reins for him. With only a primitive spring suspension to absorb shocks, these wagons were infamous for their jolting ride. From *OR Atlas,* plate 174, p. 7.

Lee's view from the high meadow. Around 7:00 A.M. on September 15, 1862, Lee directed his ambulance to a plateau a mile west of Keedysville on the bluffs bordering the eastern banks of Antietam Creek. Looking south he could see no evidence of activity at Harpers Ferry. To the east he could see bluecoats pouring through Turner's Gap in South Mountain. With approximately this view to the west, he could see and appreciate the strength of a position at Sharpsburg as it would appear to the enemy. Here Lee received the Jackson dispatch of 8:00 the previous evening announcing the imminent surrender of Harpers Ferry. Later the same day, McClellan would in fact have very nearly this same view. Just right of center on the horizon is the tower built in the 1890s marking the right-angle turn in the Sunken Road. Photograph by David W. Lowe.

Lee's view from north Cemetery Hill. At the time of the battle, a small cemetery attached to the Lutheran church was located on the western slope of this hill, which is immediately east of Sharpsburg and the farthest north of the heights of Sharpsburg. After the war the National Cemetery was established on its crest and south of the Boonsboro Pike (which bisects the hill). According to tradition, Lee spent most of his four days in Sharpsburg in the area that is now the National Cemetery, from which point he could look toward both the Middle and Lower Bridges. It is likely, however, that Lee spent most of the morning of September 17 north of the pike, where he could catch glimpses of the fighting at the Dunkard Church and Sunken Road. The Hagerstown Pike enters from the left and runs north to the Dunkard Church (out of view to the right). Behind the pike is the Reel Ridge, where Lee intended to form his fall-back line for Jackson and the left flank before the arrival of McLaws and the repulse of Sedgwick. This is the route taken by Lee from Cemetery Hill to the Hagerstown Pike between 8:00 and 9:00 A.M. on September 17. Photograph by David W. Lowe.

Wartime Sharpsburg. This photograph from the western slope of Cemetery Hill, likely taken sometime after September 1862, shows Main Street heading west toward the Potomac and Shepherdstown. The cleft grove of woods in the center on horizon is where Lee pitched his headquarters tent, probably at about noon on September 16. On the morning of the battle, Lee rode down this street from his tent to take up observation on Cemetery Hill. Photograph from Reilly, *The Battlefield of Antietam.*

The Jacob H. Grove House in the late nineteenth century. Located at the square on Main Street, this house on September 15, 1862, may have provided Lee his first night's sleep in forty-eight hours. Heros von Borcke, Stuart's chief of staff, was writing dispatches in the living room midday on the 16th when Union artillery fire forced him to seek cover. It was probably about the same time that Lee changed his headquarters to a copse of trees a mile west toward Shepherdstown on the same road. He returned to the house, however, where, at around 3:00 P.M., while studying maps with Jackson and Longstreet, he received word of a dual threat: Federal troops were moving toward the Lower Bridge and had crossed the Antietam by the Upper Bridge. Legend had incorrectly located the war council of the evening of the 17th to this house. Courtesy of Miss Louise Grove, Sharpsburg, Maryland.

The Upper Bridge. From 1823 to 1863, fifteen limestone bridges of similar design were built over Antietam Creek by Irish immigrant laborers and funded by Washington County, Maryland. Three were in the immediate area of the battlefield. The farthest upstream (north), built in 1830 and known originally as the Hitt Bridge, carried the Keedysville Road to Williamsport. It was used by portions of the First, Second, and Twelfth Corps on September 16 and 17 to cross the Antietam. Veterans referred to it as the Sumner Bridge. It is the only one of the three still used by vehicular traffic today and is here seen as viewed from the north looking south. The Middle Bridge, built in 1824 (as the Orndorff Bridge) to convey the Boonsboro Turnpike, was over a mile and a half downstream. Known locally after the battle as the Lee Bridge—probably the only one used or even seen by Lee—it was destroyed by floods in 1891 and has been replaced by a modern structure. Photograph by David W. Lowe.

The Mumma vale, looking east from the eastern edge of the Dunkard Church plateau, where today the Antietam Battlefield Visitors Center is located. The Mumma house, fired on by Confederates of D. H. Hill's division on the 17th, has been rebuilt. It was this low ground that threatened Lee's strong position on Sharpsburg Heights. Immediately to the south (right), but not visible, is the Sunken Road; to the north (not visible) is the junction of the Smoketown Road and the Hagerstown Turnpike, where the Dunkard Church is located. Across this ground French's division of the Second Corps advanced to the attack. Photograph by David W. Lowe.

Lower Bridge, Confederate view. Built in 1836 to carry the road from Sharpsburg to Maple Swamp, this bridge was, by the eve of the fighting, known as the Rohrback Bridge. After September 17 it become the Burnside Bridge, and probably the single-most-famous feature of the battlefield. From the bluffs west of the bridge, including a small farm quarry that served as rifle pits, Georgians of Robert Toombs's brigade repulsed successive attacks by Burnside's Ninth Corps. This photograph, taken from the quarry and facing east, emphasizes the proximity of the Confederate defenders to the bridge and illustrates how easy it was for them to sweep the structure and the road approaching it with a destructive fire. Photograph by David W. Lowe.

from these two sources that persuaded Lee not to make a stand at Keedysville. Although the sequence cannot be confirmed, Lee likely first got word from Munford that no road existed over Elk Ridge to enable McLaws to march directly to join the main body. This information alone would have changed nothing. Lee had not selected Keedysville from the map because it would be near for McLaws—indeed, Sharpsburg would be slightly nearer—but because it would be closer to the flank of an enemy force operating against Pleasant Valley; and that strategic fact still mattered, even if McLaws had to escape by way of Weverton, Sandy Hook, or Harpers Ferry.[3]

Yet, almost simultaneously Lee learned (probably from engineers he had sent out to examine the terrain) that the position at Keedysville was not a good one from a tactical standpoint.[4] All of the high ground in the vicinity lay to the right, and there was no strong natural anchor for the left. In consequence, there would be three miles of relatively open ground to be guarded between Keedysville and the upper Potomac. Already uncomfortable about the security of his rear and flank because of the multiple rumors of marauding Federal cavalry, Lee decided to cross Antietam Creek and fall back about three miles to Sharpsburg. There he could form a line in a crook of the Potomac that would allow him to anchor each flank on the serpentine river. Moreover, Boteler's Ford would be but five miles distant and safely within the perimeter of his defense, safeguarding either retreat or the arrival of reenforcements from Jackson. Lee probably bypassed the bluffs lining the eastern bank of the Antietam, because the creek, although shallow enough to ford at most places, would have been within yards of any position formed on them and a considerable inconvenience to maneuvering. Lee was either unaware at this time that these eastern bluffs dominated the lower ridges west of the creek, or he believed the other factors more compelling.

It is also possible that Lee had now come very near returning to his intention of recrossing immediately into Virginia. When the orders were given to resume the march, all of the wagons at hand were instructed to continue across the Potomac. As the sun finally rose on the weary main body, it was still in Maryland, but its lengthening shadow was leaning toward home.

Lee himself could no longer abide the frustrating sense of lacking control over his own army. In advance of the troops, he boarded his ambulance and headed west to find a vantage point. About a mile from Keedysville, on the bluffs approaching the Antietam, he was driven to a high meadow that afforded an excellent view of the countryside in all directions. Immediately before him he saw Sharpsburg and its heights as they would soon appear to McClellan.[5] He grasped at once the immense defensive strength of the high ground east and south of the town, although he may have recognized that the rolling nature of the terrain obscured a full appreciation of any weaknesses. Then, looking almost due south through a telescope held by a staff member, Lee could also view the western slope of Maryland Heights at the end of Elk Ridge. At this hour—approaching eight o'clock—Confederate guns had been firing on Harpers Ferry for several hours, but Lee's angle of vision prevented him from seeing any sign of the bombardment, and the fourteen miles' distance precluded hearing its roar. Looking eastward through the glass, Lee could clearly see blue columns—it would have been Richardson's division of the Second Corps—descending South Mountain at Turner's Gap.

It is likely the old engineer started to feel somewhat better as soon as he was able to view the terrain surrounding him. Better was yet to come. A pot of hot coffee arrived as a gift from a sympathetic farmer's wife, and, as Lee enjoyed the refreshing brew, a courier who had been searching for army headquarters all through the confusing night galloped onto the meadow. He carried the 8:15 dispatch from Jackson that promised "complete success to-morrow." The coffee and the message banished Lee's tiredness. Hope sprang renewed in the imagination of the Confederate commander. Surely, under the circumstances, Jackson would have ignored the orders to abandon the siege. Now it appeared Harpers Ferry might be captured—a significant victory all by itself—and the glimmer of a chance that Jackson might still join the main body in Maryland in time to keep the campaign alive. Of course, there were gigantic *ifs*. Would McLaws be chased away from Maryland Heights and the garrison relieved? Could Lee hold on at Sharpsburg long enough for Jackson to finish the work at Harpers Ferry?

The first and foremost reason for Lee to attempt a defensive stand in Maryland continued to be the need to protect McLaws in Pleasant Valley. Indeed, that reason had now become even more important, since it might buy the time necessary to insure the capture of Harpers Ferry. Still, Jackson's message raised the possibility that the stand at Sharpsburg might become something more than a brief defensive parry before a final retreat. If Lee could reunite his army and escape the tactical box he was putting himself in at Sharpsburg, it might yet be possible to resurrect the campaign of maneuver in western Maryland. Lee would have to wait and judge events as they developed at Harpers Ferry and observe the enemy's advance in his own front. In the meantime, he had an increased motive to prepare the strongest possible defensive position behind the Antietam.

Visibly invigorated, and ready for the new day, Lee climbed back aboard his ambulance. The vehicle lurched and jolted across the high meadow and down its southern slope, returning the Confederate commander to the pike that led to Sharpsburg. Here, in response to the orders he had issued earlier, Confederate columns already clogged the road.

It was about 6:30, and the sun still sat on the rim of South Mountain, when D. H. Hill set out from Keedysville with the brigades of McRae (Garland), Ripley, and G. B. Anderson, heading westward to take up position at Sharpsburg. Two miles brought the troops to the handsome three-arched span built of grayish-white limestone that carried the Boonsboro Pike across the Antietam Creek and from its central location would be known as the Middle Bridge. Then, Hill's weary soldiers started to ascend a moderately steep three-quarter-mile grade, but officers stopped them halfway to the top and filed them to the right (north) onto a farm road that ran roughly parallel to the creek. Designated to hold the left flank of the new position, Hill formed his men in two lines facing east toward the Antietam, the direction from which it was natural to assume the enemy would approach.[6]

When Lee arrived, shortly after eight o'clock, he continued on past the farm road to the crest of the eminence, which afterward veterans would refer to as Cemetery Hill.[7] This was the most northerly of the series of ridges constituting the heights of Sharpsburg he had spotted from the high meadow, and here Lee established field headquarters. He at once confirmed the great natural strength of this high ground east and south of town would allow him to form a compact line that would defy the superior numbers of the enemy. But, he could now also recognize the most serious weakness of the position was its left flank. The northern slope of Cemetery Hill descended into half-mile-wide valley that ran behind his line on the heights and made it vulnerable to a tactical turning movement.

At some point after the dispatch from Jackson had revived his optimism, Lee must also have begun to appreciate another fact about Sharpsburg that heretofore had been of minor import. Not only did the Boonsboro Pike continue westward through the town to become the

Shepherdstown Road and lead toward safety in Virginia, but there was another highway that lead to hope rather than despair. Entering Sharpsburg from the north was the Hagerstown Pike, a road that would carry Lee to the town thirteen miles distant where he could regain the initiative and resume his campaign of maneuver. It was his avenue of escape without retreat.

As Lee constructed his defensive, he had two reasons, therefore, to look beyond the snug position on the heights and toward the north: he must protect his vulnerable left flank, and he must also keep open the road to Hagerstown. He ordered back D. H. Hill's two absent brigades from their positions near the Potomac. He chose Colquitt, the stronger of the two, to occupy a deeply eroded lane that traversed the entire width of the valley floor from the Hagerstown Turnpike to the northern foot of Cemetery Hill, where it connected at a right angle with the farm road from the Boonsboro Pike, already filled with Hill's troops. Thus, in effect, Lee refused his left flank. He placed Rodes's brigade in reserve along the Hagerstown Pike, where it supported both the left and the left-center.

Longstreet arrived ahead of his command at about 9:30 and found Lee on Cemetery Hill.[8] Lee presumably informed his senior subordinate about the dispatch from Jackson, the decision to stand at Sharpsburg, and the nature of the defensive line he was preparing. Whatever Longstreet thought of the news at the time, it fired him into energetic action. He took personal charge of posting the artillery that had started to arrive. He sent S. D. Lee's battalion to support Hill's line north of the Boonsboro Pike and placed the four companies of the Washington Artillery south of the road. Other batteries were squeezed into the line wherever possible. "Put them all in," Longstreet told the artillerists, "every gun you have, long range and short range." Old Peter wanted no masked batteries on this day, but hills frowning with cannon to intimidate the Federals.[9]

Later in the day, when Allen Cutts galloped up to report to Lee, there was no room for his battalion of thirty-two guns on Cemetery Hill. Cutts had been forgotten at Boonsboro, and he had left the town so late that he had been fired upon by Federal skirmishers. Detached from the army, he had traveled north toward Williamsport and after a morning of adventures had reached the field by way of the Hagerstown Pike. His men were now resting near a small German Baptist Brethren house of worship—known locally as the Dunkard Church—several hundred yards northwest of the sunken lane. Lee complimented Cutts on his escape and ordered him to remain near the church. The Confederate commander was no doubt glad of the extra strength to anchor the left flank.[10]

In the meanwhile, around ten o'clock, D. R. Jones arrived from Keedysville with three of his brigades.[11] As Kemper's brigade of Virginians reached the brow of Cemetery Hill, Lee turned them off to the south to form the right-center of the line. Perhaps to infuse his own newly found vigor into the troops, he called out to them as they passed, "We will make our stand on these hills."[12] Kemper and Drayton formed in immediate support of the Washington (La.) Artillery, and Garnett was put in their rear as reserve. Their line covered the Sharpsburg end of the road from Harpers Ferry that ran from the base of Maryland Heights, which Lee may have believed McLaws would use to rejoin the army.

At about the same time, Longstreet recalled Toombs's brigade from its position near the Potomac to cover the stone bridge (Rohrback) that spanned the Antietam a little over a mile downstream from the Boonsboro Pike. From the first, therefore, Lee determined that he would not defend the Middle Bridge, but he would prevent the Federals from crossing the Lower Bridge on the far right flank of his line. He would permit the enemy to cross the Antietam and attack his strong position on Sharpsburg Heights with the creek in their immediate rear. The Middle Bridge, moreover, would have been difficult to defend, since the bluffs along the eastern bank dominated the crossing and masked the approach of attackers. The Federals must not be allowed to carry the Lower Bridge, however; for, once across, they could not only turn the Confederate right flank but also sever communications with Harpers Ferry and cut off the only ford for returning to Virginia.

Fortunately for Lee, the Lower Bridge was better suited for defenders. Steep bluffs approached the banks on both sides of the creek and from the east forced attackers to approach along several hundred yards of road exposed to a raking fire. The position did not impress the officer charged with guarding the span, however. Col. Henry Benning was in immediate command of the 2d and 20th Georgia regiments (the 15th and 17th having been sent to Williamsport to guard trains), and he posted his men along the crest of the ridge at the western end of the bridge. Benning was painfully aware that the knee-deep creek was "fordable everywhere above and below the bridge." Supported by Eubank's Virginia battery of Lee's battalion, he built a rude breastworks from fence rails, took advantage of a small stone quarry, threw skirmishers across the Antietam, and awaited the worst.[13]

Around eleven, the last of the army, the four brigades of the rear guard, Wofford and Law (both under Hood), G. T. Anderson, and Evans began to arrive from Keedysville. Lee was apparently determined to keep the two feuding generals apart and found room for Evans (along with Anderson) in the center on the Boonsboro Pike, while Hood was placed on the far right of D. R. Jones and behind Toombs to guard the Lower Bridge.[14]

Lee now had every man and every gun in a compact two-mile line facing east, except for its left flank, which bent back at a right angle to connect with the Hagerstown Pike. By manning a series of short ridges that dominated the low ground rising from Antietam Creek, he was able to present an exceptionally strong front.[15] The hills bristled with over a hundred cannon in twenty-six batteries.[16] Although Lee may have had no more than 15,000 men with their colors at the moment, the fourteen brigades at Sharpsburg waved sixty-two regimental battleflags and deftly posted in open spaces gave the impression of twice their numbers.[17]

Still, as critics have been quick to point out, there were serious weaknesses in the position. First and most obvious, Lee violated the military axiom to fight only with open and easy avenues for retreat. With the Potomac enveloping 180 degrees in his rear, he could not retire without crossing the river, and the single ford within his perimeter at Boteler's was considered a rough passage and was situated behind his far right flank and not the center of his position. In addition, the C&O Canal was an obstacle that would have to be bridged.[18]

If Lee ignored these weaknesses, he did so because he had no choice. He could not have moved upriver in search of a better position—say, Williamsport—without abandoning McLaws as surely as if he had recrossed into Virginia; nor was there space on the Maryland side between the Potomac and Elk Ridge (nor any fords) if he had moved downriver in the other direction. No doubt, Lee's awareness of this potential problem had led him, first, to order Jackson to break off at Harpers Ferry and cover the crossing at Boteler's and, second, to send half of the Reserve Artillery to guard the fords at Williamsport, hoping to maintain an optional route for escape even though it lay outside of his perimeter. In any case, it must be remembered that Lee chose Sharpsburg as a stopgap position. If the news from Harpers Ferry were bad, it would probably be necessary to retreat to Virginia before a battle took place. If the news from Harpers Ferry were exceptionally good, he might be able to march northward to Hagerstown before battle occurred.

There was a tactical weakness of much greater immediate concern to the Confederate commander. While virtually impervious to a frontal assault, Lee's line was currently vulnerable on both flanks. Although he sat in a half-circle bend of the Potomac, his left fell a mile short of the river and was entirely in the air; his right was two miles from the river and rested on a tight loop of the more easily fordable Antietam; and, at least temporarily, he had no cavalry to picket the openings on his flanks. Lee had four brigades in second line and could have extended his front in one or the other direction, but he wisely elected to await developments before committing his reserves.

Thus, as the sun climbed to its meridian, Lee waited on Cemetery Hill for the arrival of the enemy and for word from Harpers Ferry. Here he received a disturbing report from Thomas Rosser of the 5th Virginia Cavalry. The Confederate commander learned that Fitz Lee had been routed in the streets of Boonsboro and was retreating northwest toward Hagerstown with three regiments of his brigade. This bad news was balanced somewhat by Rosser's word that with a single regiment he had been able to slow the Federal progress toward Keedysville to a crawl.[19]

Then, shortly after noon, a sweating courier on a heavily lathered horse arrived from Jackson. "Through God's blessing," Stonewall wrote in a dispatch of eight o'clock that morning, "Harper's Ferry and its garrison are to be surrendered."[20] With profound relief, Lee exclaimed, "This is indeed good news! Let it be announced to the troops." As even the privates in the ranks had grasped the desperation of their plight, the word was greeted with resounding cheers as galloping staff officers shouted it along the line.[21]

There was more to Jackson's dispatch, however, and the remainder confronted Lee with the critical decision that could no longer be postponed: "As [A. P.] Hill's troops have borne the heaviest part in the engagement, he will be left in command until the prisoners and public property shall be disposed of, unless you direct otherwise." In other words, did Lee judge the main body to be in such imminent danger that the fruits of the capture must be forfeited? "The other forces can move off this evening so soon as they get their rations. To what point shall they move? I write at this time in order that you may be apprised of the condition of things. You may expect to hear from me again to-day after I get more information respecting the numbers of prisoners, &c." Should Jackson move to prepare a new position in Virginia? Should he march to Shepherdstown to cover a recrossing? Or, should he join the main body at Sharpsburg?

Jackson had scarcely provided Lee with all the information necessary to make this critical decision. Did "other forces" include Walker and McLaws? Could either or both of these generals get their artillery off their mountains, cross their rivers, draw their rations, and leave by this evening? Considering the crawling pace of yesterday's march from Hagerstown, how long would it take for the reenforcements to cover the thirteen miles from Harpers Ferry? Given its most optimistic reading, Jackson's dispatch promised that five of the six divisions would be with the main body by noon tomorrow.

As was his wont, Lee read the message optimistically. And apparently he rendered his decision immediately and instinctively. He would retreat no farther. He would stand until his army was united, and then he would return to his campaign of maneuver. Although no trace of any reply to Jackson exists, it is inconceivable that Lee did not respond to Stonewall's specific request for direction. Nor, considering Jackson's subsequent actions, can there be any doubt about the substance of Lee's reply. He must have approved Jackson's leaving A. P. Hill at Harpers Ferry to dispose of the prisoners and public property, while ordering Stonewall to hasten to Sharpsburg with his other two divisions and the commands of McLaws and Walker.[22] Thus, between noon and one, Lee rendered final his decision to remain in Maryland.

Many years later, Porter Alexander, ensconced in hindsight's easy chair, pronounced the decision "the greatest military blunder that Gen. Lee ever made." According to the army's ordnance chief, Lee should have recognized that the "best *possible* outcome" of a stand at Sharpsburg was a "drawn battle." With most of the army already in Virginia, the Confederate commander should have terminated the campaign by recrossing the Potomac with Longstreet and D. H. Hill.[23]

At the time—and on the ground—matters appeared differently to Lee.

The Pursuit Ends

In addition to the welcome news of the surrender of Harpers Ferry, Lee was also persuaded to remain in Maryland by what he judged to be the cautious Federal advance from South Mountain. Later, in writing to President Davis, he would note pointedly, "The enemy did not pass through the gap until about 8 o'clock," adding, "their advance reached a position in front of us about 2 p.m."[24] Lee probably felt confident that his careful opponent would not launch a rash frontal assault against Sharpsburg Heights, a position comparable in strength to Malvern Hill in elevation, massed artillery, and infantry support in depth. McClellan would sniff the flanks and search for weaknesses—as Lee ought to have done at Malvern Hill—and consume the remainder of the 15th in reconnaissance.

Although Lee rightly divined his foe would not dash headlong across the Antietam, his guess was based on a faulty assessment of the enemy's advance from South Mountain. The Federals had, in fact, started their descent from Turner's Gap at dawn, and the appearance of blue infantry on the west bank of the Antietam two hours after Lee's last units had crossed the creek scarcely indicated a lackadaisical pursuit. Struggling through the same kind of heat and dust that had afflicted Longstreet's march the day before—while skirmishing with a dogged defense by Confederate cavalry and not knowing where they might encounter the enemy main body—the Federals had covered a respectable seven miles in eight hours.

When skirmishers of the First Corps discovered at daylight that the Confederates had retreated, Joe Hooker wisely brought forward Richardson's fresh division of the Second Corps to lead the advance.[25] The infantry had already deployed against Fitzhugh Lee's cavalry brigade at the foot of the mountain, when Pleasonton arrived with three regiments of Federal horse to hasten the pursuit. Fitz Lee sent the 4th and 9th Virginia on to Boonsboro to rest, probably intending to rotate rear guard responsibilities, while he attempted to inch backward with the 3d Virginia and the section of Pelham's artillery, taking advantage of every swell and knoll to retard the Northern advance. Pleasonton pushed aggressively forward, however, overlapping the Confederate flanks and hurling the 8th Illinois Cavalry against the center.

The 3d Virginia gave way and dashed unheralded into Boonsboro. The troopers of the 4th and 9th were caught unaware, sitting on the curbs holding the reins of their horses, and they could barely manage to mount, let alone form ranks in the narrow streets, before the mêleé engulfed them. Under repeated charges from the Yankees and the sniper fire of loyal citizens from windows and alleys, the three Rebel regiments emerged from Boonsboro in such a cloud of dust and confusion that riders banged into telegraph poles and impaled their horses on rock piles heaped by the roadside for repair of the National Turnpike. Rooney Lee, second oldest son of the army commander and colonel of the 9th, fell from his wounded horse and lay dazed as the enemy rushed past. He was not recognized and eventually crawled to safety in a small woods.[26]

Pleasonton reported the Confederates left behind thirty dead (some having been trampled to death), fifty wounded, a large number of prisoners, and two guns "when they broke and ran in every direction."[27] Fitz Lee finally stopped enough of his fugitives two miles west of town to mount a countercharge. He then continued on toward Hagerstown, hoping to pull the enemy after him in the wrong direction. The Federals were not fooled by the false spoor, however, and as soon as the Keedysville road had been cleared by Pleasonton's advance, Richardson's division set out in the direction recently taken by the Confederate main body. The Federals' progress was slowed by the necessity to break column and deploy in battleline to chase away Rosser's 5th Virginia Cavalry, which had fallen across their front in its retreat from the vicinity of Fox's Gap. By two o'clock Richardson's skirmishers had reached the west bank of the Antietam, and Hooker was scrutinizing Sharpsburg from— or very nearly from—the same high meadow where Lee had enjoyed breakfast coffee six hours earlier.

Excited Union loyalists in Boonsboro had led Hooker to believe—and he had so reported to McClellan—that the routed Confederate army was fleeing in confusion to cross the Potomac. High-ranking generals (D.H. Hill was mentioned) were said to be dead and Lee himself wounded. The rumors grew from partial truths. No doubt there had been extensive speculation to be heard among the soldiers about the retreat; the body of Samuel Garland had been escorted through the streets by his staff; and some may have seen Lee with bandages and sling, riding in an ambulance. Confirmation of the dissolute condition of the Rebel army seemed to come from the hundreds of stragglers captured during the morning and the scattering of the Confederate cavalry.

Great must have been Hooker's disappointment, therefore, as he applied his glass to the heights of Sharpsburg.[28] With upward of a hundred guns in view, supported by what he estimated to be 30,000 to 50,000 infantry, the fox chased to ground had turned out to be a tiger. With only 5,000 men at hand in Richardson's division, even the approaching 14,000 of the First Corps could not tempt "Fighting Joe" into assailing the cornered Lee before the arrival of strong reenforcements.

At daybreak on the 15th, George McClellan had the Army of the Potomac well in hand, and, although it stretched along eight miles of mountain front, it was ready—or so he thought—to press the victories of the previous day. Franklin, who held Crampton's Gap with the Sixth Corps (supported by Couch's division of the Fourth), was supposed to advance against McLaws in Pleasant Valley and attempt to relieve the garrison at Harpers Ferry. Hooker formed the right at Turner's Gap with the First Corps and Richardson's division of the Second Corps and was intended to advance on the National Road against the Confederate main body. Because McClellan expected Lee to stand at Boonsboro, he instructed Sumner with the remainder of the Second Corps (Sedgwick and French) and the Twelfth Corps (now under the newly arrived Joseph Mansfield) to follow Hooker as reserve.

As a result of the turning movement of the 14th, Burnside's Ninth Corps at Fox's Gap now constituted the Federal center, and McClellan understood that by a peculiar twist it was the center that now provided him with tactical flexibility. He intended Burnside to advance on the Old Sharpsburg Road to its junction with the Rohrersville Road, and then, pending developments, the Ninth Corps would either swing south (left) and support Franklin or march north (right) to the assistance of Hooker and Sumner at Boonsboro. Of Porter's Fifth Corps, only Sykes's division at Middletown was near at hand, and it was ordered to strengthen Burnside's column. Morell's division of the Fifth had just arrived at Frederick, and Humphreys's division of green regiments was learning the meaning of "forced" marches as it straggled to get from Washington into the campaign.

It is not the business of a commander to lead the vanguard of his army at any time, but this is especially true when he is advancing on several fronts and cannot know which one will become the critical point. During the morning, McClellan maintained headquarters at Bolivar near the eastern foot of Turner's Gap, where he monitored information and made necessary modifications in his plans. Some of the news was welcome, and other was not. Hooker reported the Confederates had abandoned Boonsboro and fled in a "perfect panic" for the Potomac. McClellan responded by ordering Hooker to press the pursuit and, if necessary, to let Sumner's fresh Second Corps take the lead. By midmorning, however, the signal station on Monument Hill wigwagged that the enemy could be seen forming line behind the Antietam. Shortly before noon, a dispatch arrived from Franklin announcing that McLaws seemed to be retiring from the Pleasant Valley front and that Harpers Ferry had probably surrendered.

These developments opened both opportunities and dangers for Federal prospects. If the early reports on the demoralization of the Confederate main body were true, then it was good news that Lee was attempting to stand at Sharpsburg. Nothing in the record of either Lee or his army had led McClellan to anticipate their precipitate retreat, however; nor had the condition of affairs at the close of the 14th—although clearly indicating a Union victory—suggested a Confederate rout to be imminent. Still, Burnside and Porter could now be diverted to Keedysville to join Hooker and Sumner. If all of the various units could be brought together in time and in decent shape, Lee might be forced into battle before he escaped or was reenforced. Even Franklin would now be free to rejoin the main army, assuming the rumors about Harpers Ferry were true. Unfortunately, Jackson's corps and the other Confederate divisions operating against Harpers Ferry would also be unleashed. Would Stonewall simply join Lee? Or would he cross the river to reenforce McLaws and operate against Franklin and the Federal left flank? Or would the general known to be Lee's favorite instrument for a turning movement show up someplace entirely unexpected, such as in McClellan's rear and between the Army of the Potomac and Washington?

Around noon, perhaps after hearing that Burnside's advance had been delayed, McClellan took a quick tour of the South Mountain battlefields, starting with Fox's Gap. Here he found Porter with Sykes's division waiting impatiently in the road, while the Ninth Corps finished cooking breakfast with rations that had just come up. It is probably true that Hooker outshone Burnside in the pursuit of the 15th, because Hooker had fresh troops to lead the advance, and Burnside did not. McClellan ordered the Ninth Corps to the side of the road, and he directed Porter to take the lead to Keedysville by way of the Old Sharpsburg Road. This would be but the first—and perhaps not the greatest—disappointment in the pursuit of Lee.

McClellan proceeded to Boonsboro, where he established headquarters by about 1:15. In retrospect, he would have been better off riding directly to Keedysville and taking personal command on the Antietam front. At this point, however, he was still thinking in terms of the unfolding strategic situation, and he awaited further news from Franklin to determine a course of action. By late afternoon, McClellan learned that Harpers Ferry had in fact surrendered and that the Confederates appeared to be withdrawing rapidly from Pleasant Valley. While this indicated that Jackson did not intend to cross the river and join with McLaws, it shed no light on what else he would do. Even now Stonewall with a portion of his force might be hurrying to Lee, or he might be consolidating his columns to operate at some other point on the Federal left flank. Franklin would have to remain to watch and report on developments at Harpers Ferry.

McClellan also heard from Hooker that Lee's position at Sharpsburg was a formidable one and that reenforcements were needed. Shortly after five, the Federal commander decided to move army headquarters to Keedysville and take immediate charge on the Antietam. No sooner did he emerge from Boonsboro, however, than he sensed that something was wrong. As he rode past regiment after regiment, first of the Second Corps and then of the First Corps, word spread of his approach, and the troops roared a mighty, continuous cheer. But why were the units still in a snarled column that stretched for miles along the Boonsboro Pike? At Keedysville, McClellan met Edwin Sumner, the army's senior corps commander and the general who should have exerted his authority to deploy the troops as they arrived. Sumner knew nothing of what was happening.

Together the two generals rode forward until they discovered a large group of officers congregated at the foot of a bluff bordering the Antietam, the vantage point that Hooker had discovered for viewing the Confederate position at Sharpsburg. Here, McClellan learned that except for Richardson's division, which had been the first to arrive and was deployed on either side of the Boonsboro Pike, only Sykes's division, which Porter had pushed to the front by a parallel road to the left, was in battleline. Hooker's First Corps had halted in its tracks on the Boonsboro Pike, blocking the advance of the remaining two divisions of Sumner's Second Corps. Even farther to the rear on the Old Sharpsburg Road and over two miles away, Mansfield's Twelfth Corps had stopped at the Nicodemus Mill near Springvale. None of the artillery had gone into battery except the guns of Tidball (A, 2d U.S.) and Pettit (B, 1st New York), which were exchanging shots with the Confederates.

Hooker reported that an hour earlier a large number of Confederate units had formed column and marched to the rear. Wondering if the enemy might be starting to retire, Hooker had sent an engineer upstream to search for a site to cross that would not be directly under the Confederate guns. He told McClellan that a number of fords and a stone bridge had been discovered. While the conference was in progress, Burnside and Cox rode up and reported the head of the Ninth Corps was finally at hand on the Old Sharpsburg Road.

The group—by now the size of a small regiment—climbed the hill to the high meadow, where first Lee and then Hooker had studied the heights across the Antietam. Almost at once Confederate long-range guns opened with enough accuracy to cause McClellan to order the ridge be cleared of all but himself and Fitz John Porter. With a coolness that even future critic Jacob Cox admitted to admiring at the time, McClellan continued to examine the enemy position with a "business-like air." Not surprisingly, the young engineer in blue saw much the same thing as the older engineer in gray had seen ten hours earlier. It would be bloody—perhaps even futile—to launch a direct frontal assault against Sharpsburg Heights, and unfortunately he saw no firm evidence of the retreat mentioned by Hooker. There seemed to be promise for a turning movement from the north, however, against the enemy's left.

Unfortunately, by the time McClellan descended from the plateau, less than an hour remained before sunset. Still, the Federal commander was able to take a number of important steps to prepare for the morrow. He ordered army headquarters to be established at a church at the western end of Keedysville, and then he personally supervised the posting of artillery along the Antietam bluffs. As the guns came into battery, they engaged in a long-range duel that once again demonstrated the superiority of the Federal long arm.

At the same time, McClellan took the first step in developing a tactical plan to move against Lee's left flank. Hooker's First Corps was sent a mile and a half upstream to bivouac in the fork between the Antietam and the Little Antietam. Hooker may have been thus chosen early to lead the force for a turning movement, simply because his men were first in line on the nearest road; but his selection also may have suited McClellan's growing appreciation of him as the army's most aggressive corps commander. At this time, McClellan seriously considered sending Pleasonton with the cavalry on a wide turning movement along the Williamsport Road from Boonsboro to Jones's Crossroads, where it intersected six miles to the north with the Hagerstown Pike. While Lee might have made this very move had the roles been reversed, it is revealing of the differences in the two commanders that McClellan decided against the plan because he did not want his cavalry operating at such a distance from the main body on the eve of battle.

In fact, McClellan kept all of the troops of the Army of the Potomac compactly together, pending further reconnaissance and planning. Sumner was advanced in the center and put in second line on either side of the Boonsboro Pike behind Richardson and Sykes. Burnside was ordered a short distance to the left and onto ground that was not yet well known. Mansfield was instructed to wait until daylight to advance. All things considered—the heat and the dust, the uncertainty over Harpers Ferry and Lee's movements, and the balkiness of individual subordinates—if the Army of the Potomac had not had a great day, neither had it been a bad one.[29]

The Surrender of Harpers Ferry

Harpers Ferry was the wild card in the day's strategy for both Lee and McClellan. Not merely its surrender—which Federal blunders had rendered a foregone conclusion—but its surrender at such an early hour would shape the remainder of the campaign for both sides. It decided Lee to remain at Sharpsburg and to attempt to resurrect his mission in Maryland; and it inhibited McClellan from focusing on the single task of defeating the Confederate main body behind the Antietam. It was an event that happened before its time, and it surprised all but the handful of Federal officers who decided to capitulate prematurely.

Although human endeavor is seldom exempt from error, an unusually large number of miscues plagued the Harpers Ferry story from the start. Robert E. Lee persistently underestimated the mischief that might arise from an expedition to clear his Valley communications. He anticipated the enemy forces would quickly flee for safety, and he failed to provide sufficient time, adequate artillery, or specific instructions looking to the coordination of a siege. Only on the last count can he be excused, since a capable and aggressive commander, Stonewall Jackson, was near at hand to take charge. Still, Lee was wrong to risk the fate of the campaign, which he believed critical to winning the war, on the speedy conclusion of Jackson's operations.

Only the greater blunders committed on the Federal side saved Lee from acute embarrassment. John Wool, the crusty old Mexican war veteran and professional soldier commanding the department, should have known better; even if better could not be expected from Secretary of War Edwin Stanton, a civilian wholly devoid of strategic sense and subject to fits of extreme anti-military bias. Both saw Harpers Ferry in a political rather than a military light. Fearing abandonment would be equated by the public with cowardice and dereliction of duty, they ordered the post to be held to the last man. Neither perceived that the town possessed virtually no strategic value in itself and was not worth the loss of a man, let alone 13,000. This at least McClellan understood. No Northern leader, however, including McClellan and Lincoln, saw the strategic value of a large Federal force on the flank and rear of the invading force. It did not matter where precisely the Federals were located—at Harpers Ferry, Martinsburg, Winchester, or wherever—as long as they threatened Lee's only feasible line of communications. Their duty should not have been to hold Harpers Ferry to the last man but to survive as long as possible to harass and annoy the enemy's rear.

The mistakes of Dixon Miles—even granting the considerable handicaps under which he labored—were arguably the worst of all. Although armed with a polyglot command of inexperienced, in some cases utterly green, regiments and saddled with unambiguously stupid orders, he managed to convert his difficult situation into a hopeless one. He made no attempt whatsoever to hold Loudoun Heights, and his palsied stand on Maryland Heights—reenforced only by troops not four weeks in uniform—lasted barely two hours. Moreover, although he reluctantly allowed his cavalry to escape during the night, he would listen to no proposal that his infantry try to find a weak point and fight its way out. In the end, however, the only bungle that really mattered was the one made by Miles between seven and eight o'clock on the morning of September 15. With the sound of artillery fire having been audible from Pleasant Valley on the 14th—and having almost certainly received a message from McClellan that help was near at hand—Miles endured no more than an hour's bombardment before deciding to surrender.[30]

Although Stonewall Jackson expected success on the 15th, he could not have anticipated victory to come so swiftly or bloodlessly. Unimpressed with the results of the bombardment on the previous day, he worked his men through the night to prepare for the assault he now believed would be necessary. Col. Stapleton Crutchfield, Jackson's chief of artillery, had finished posting a ten-gun battery across the Shenandoah on a ridge from which it could rake the enemy line on Bolivar Heights; and A. P. Hill had worked his division along the river to attack the flank from the same southeast direction. J. R. Jones had advanced a brigade on the other end of the line on the Potomac, and Lawton's division stood ready in the center.

As soon as light permitted sighting targets, near sunrise at 6:10, Confederate artillery opened with a roar from Jackson's positions and were followed by the battery on Maryland Heights. A patch of fog halfway down Loudoun Heights occluded the peninsula from the view of Walker's gunners, but they soon joined in with random fire based on their elevations of the day before.[31] To the eyes and ears of the anxious garrison, who had spent a long night dreading the fate dawn would bring, the three-way cross fire was terrifying. The savage commotion created by seventy cannon cowed the Federals beyond the damage caused. It is possible the only truly effective fire came from eight guns in Crutchfield's battery just east of the Shenandoah. While the remainder of Jackson's pieces had no advantage of elevation against Bolivar Heights, McLaws's battery (now reduced to two guns) was out of range on Maryland Heights, and Walker's four were firing blindly from Loudoun.[32] Still, the sight of orange-centered puffs of smoke on every side, the sound of explosions bouncing back and forth in the triple water gap, the feel of trembling earth, a handful of gruesome casualties, and a shortage of long-range artillery ammunition finished the garrison in an hour.[33]

Around 7:15, the weak Federal counterfire slackened and ceased altogether. When Jackson's guns fell silent, it was taken as the signal for the infantry assault to begin. A. P. Hill's men moved forward along the Shenandoah, and Lawton's division prepared to cross the open valley in front of Bolivar Heights. The troops of both commands anticipated heavy losses before carrying the enemy position. There was great cheering, therefore, when the sighting of white flags suspended the attack. In the interval of confirming the Federal intent to surrender, sporadic Confederate artillery fire mortally wounded Dixon Miles.[34] By eight o'clock Jackson felt certain enough of the outcome in his own mind to send his dispatch to Lee announcing Harpers Ferry is "to be surrendered."[35]

The same dispatch revealed that Jackson understood the urgency of the Confederate situation and had thought several steps ahead. He proposed to Lee that one division be left at Harpers Ferry to deal with the prisoners and public property, while the remaining five draw rations from the captured stores and be prepared to march the same evening to rejoin the main campaign at whatever point the Confederate commander designated. While awaiting Lee's decision, Jackson acted on the assumption that his suggestions would be approved. He named A. P. Hill as commissioner to accept the surrender and assigned Hill's division to guard the prisoners and secure the supplies. He instructed Hill to parole the garrison, allowing the officers to keep their sidearms, horses, and personal property. The enemy was to be issued two days' rations and sent marching as rapidly as possible in the direction of Washington.[36] By ten o'clock, Jackson had also signaled the good news to Maryland and Loudoun Heights and instructed McLaws and Walker to begin crossing their commands to Harpers Ferry.[37]

In midmorning, Jackson and his staff rode into the town. Around eleven o'clock an ebullient Jeb Stuart suddenly appeared. The cavalry chief had been with McLaws in Pleasant Valley and had galloped along the River Road and across the pontoon bridge to "congratulate old Stonewall on his splendid success." Although the first tentative report had long since been dispatched, Stonewall saw the opportunity to send a confirming message with details of the magnitude of the capture, and he requested Stuart to carry it to Lee. Jeb no doubt appreciated the chance to bear such glad tidings, and, without resting his horse, he hastened off with a single aide to find the Confederate commander. Either because he mistakenly believed the route would be shorter, or because he hoped to pick up Munford's brigade along the way, Stuart elected to travel on the Maryland side. Clattering back across the pontoon bridge, he followed the canal towpath until he struck the road to Antietam Furnace and Sharpsburg.[38]

Not much time passed—perhaps it was 11:30—before a courier arrived at Jackson's headquarters to deliver a long-delayed message. It was the dispatch Lee had written between eight and ten o'clock the night before from Boonsboro, during the short period in which he had intended to withdraw immediately from Maryland. The message ordered Stonewall to break off operations and march to Shepherdstown to cover the crossing of the main body. It is interesting to speculate how Jackson would have resolved his dilemma had he received these instructions before 7:30 that morning. Would he have disengaged at Harpers Ferry, when he felt victory was so near? Or, would he have disobeyed orders and risked the destruction of the main body in order to complete his work? Happily, the dilemma no longer existed. Now that the army could be speedily reunited, there was no need for Lee to return to Virginia. Jackson folded the dispatch, endorsed it—"I will join you at Sharpsburg"—and instructed a courier to deliver it as swiftly as possible to Lee.[39]

The ambiguity disappeared when Jackson received—at two o'clock or later—Lee's response to the eight o'clock victory announcement. The Confederate commander agreed that Jackson should retain a division at Harpers Ferry to parole prisoners and secure public property. After drawing rations, the remainder of the expeditionary forces should march that evening to join the main body at Sharpsburg.[40]

Nonetheless, it is apparent that Jackson did not wait for Lee's reply before taking further decisive action. The need for haste was too great. In name only was it the "main body" which Lee commanded. Two-thirds of the Army of Northern Virginia were still absent and remained divided by rivers and mountains. If the campaign were to be salvaged, Jackson must unite his forces quickly and reach Lee while strategic options remained open for the Confederates. Stonewall must take the initiative and trust his actions would meet with Lee's approval. Sometime around noon, therefore, he summoned McLaws and Walker to report in person to Harpers Ferry.

Not waiting for a joint conference—McLaws probably arrived around two—Jackson told each general the next order of business was to reunite with the main body in Maryland.[41] He had determined his own command and Walker's would follow several roads on the Virginia side that led to Boteler's Ford below Shepherdstown. Not only was the route better known, it was secure from enemy interference, and for Jackson and Walker it would be two miles shorter. When McLaws asked whether his command might stay north of the Potomac and go around Maryland Heights, Jackson made no reply, leaving the forces in Pleasant Valley free to pursue the route they preferred. If Stonewall instructed the generals to issue rations to their men, he did not offer to share the largess from Harpers Ferry with them. Moreover, considering later developments, he may not have emphasized the need for haste as clearly as he ought to have.[42]

After the war, McLaws recalled that during the interview he suggested to Jackson an alternative plan. He proposed that he be reenforced to attack Franklin and thus relieve Lee by threatening McClellan's flank. This strategy—which was such an obvious possibility that it hobbled the movements of both McClellan and Franklin—had already occurred to Jackson. Stonewall did not feel at liberty to pursue such a drastically divergent course, however. Aware that Lee might even then be preparing to cross into Virginia, he believed that direct and immediate support was necessary. The danger to the main body seemed too dire to trust to the uncertainties of an indirect threat. Besides, Jackson had already promised to join Lee in Maryland.[43]

McLaws could report to Jackson that his command was already in motion. The portly Georgian had spent his last morning in independent command in great anxiety and had leapt at the first chance to rejoin the army. The thunderous artillery fire from Harpers Ferry at sunrise had simply reminded him of his critical situation—at least as he perceived it. Believing retreat to be virtually impossible, he also thought he was confronted by a vastly superior force under Franklin in his front. In reality, both sides totaled about 12,000, although each believed itself outnumbered. Couch's division had arrived at Burkittsville, however, and Franklin had the potential to break through the Brownsville Gap on McLaws's flank.

During the morning of the 15th, Franklin did press forward with his skirmish line within two hundred yards of the Confederate position, and the illusion of a Federal assault seemed all too real. Both sides noticed when the firing ceased at Harpers Ferry, and some Southerners believed the Northern attack was suspended because of the silence. When the unnatural quietness was broken by a continuous wave of cheers that rolled down the Confederate lines, a Yankee climbed onto a stone wall and shouted, "What the hell are you fellows cheering for?" "Because Harper's Ferry is gone up, God Damn you," came the reply. "I thought that was it," said the bluecoat, as he jumped down from the wall.[44]

McLaws wasted no time in preparing to cross the Potomac. In spite of his query to Jackson about taking the Maryland route to Sharpsburg, he seems to have been intent from the first on joining the nearby Confederate forces. He immediately advanced a force to secure the pontoon bridge across the river; and he seemed determined to hold his Pleasant Valley line only long enough to cover the passage of his trains into Virginia. His wagons had already started to move when Jackson summoned him to Harpers Ferry. Upon his return, McLaws found Richard Anderson had withdrawn the infantry and formed a second line at the foot of the valley, still covering both Weverton and Sandy Hook. Franklin had not closely pursued the retreat, but neither was the command ready to cross the Potomac. Only a handful of the wagons had gotten across the pontoon bridge before it had become clogged with Federal prisoners being marched by A. P. Hill into Maryland for release. Not until two hours past midnight could McLaws start crossing his infantry. The head of his column marched on to Halltown and went into bivouac. The last of his command did not reach the new camp until eleven o'clock in the morning of the 16th.

Nine miles was the farthest any of McLaws regiments had to march to reach Halltown, and yet it took him twenty-one hours to complete the trip. Understandably, his men were exhausted from the strain of the almost-battle of the morning, the marching and countermarching during the day, and a night spent waiting in line to cross the bridge. On top of this, they could not draw rations from their wagons—which had little to offer, in any case—and soon discovered that all of the spoils of

Harpers Ferry had been disposed of by Jackson's men. Somewhere in the shuffle McLaws forgot—if he had ever been fully aware of—the urgent necessity of joining Lee. Uppermost in his mind in the hours to come would be rest and food for his men. However understandable, McLaws's modest journey did not bode well for Lee's expectation of a quick uniting of the Army of Northern Virginia.[45]

Nor, was McLaws's progress the only omen of ill. John Walker may have returned from Harpers Ferry reasonably early in the afternoon, and he may have gotten his division into column and on the road in good time, but he had not spent his two days at Loudoun Heights becoming familiar with the vicinity. He wasted time trying to cross the lower Shenandoah, where there were no fords, and finally had to countermarch and "go round the Mountain" and back to Key's Ford. Darkness was falling as he crossed the river, and, when he reached Halltown, he also put his men into camp for the night.[46]

Even Jackson's own command did not at first make such progress as would have lightened Lee's heart. A. P. Hill's division, of course, had become fully entangled in paroling 12,520 prisoners of war and "securing" public property. Apparently much of the food and clothing became secure when transferred to the stomachs, backs, and feet of individual soldiers without benefit of unnecessary middlemen such as quartermasters and commissaries. It is revealing that among the tons of captured equipage only 305 pairs of shoes, ninety pairs of socks and fourteen blankets were officially reported. Several North Carolina regiments took the opportunity to discard their smooth bore muskets and arm themselves with Springfield rifles on the spot. Although not the undisciplined orgy that had followed the capture of Manassas Junction, there was a danger that Hill's division—Jackson's largest—would bog down in the impedimenta and take longer than necessary to complete its task.[47]

Jackson himself must take part of the blame for the slow start of his other two divisions. Lawton and J. R. Jones did not receive orders to cook two days' rations until three o'clock, and apparently no time was set for their march to start. By quickly seizing rations in Harpers Ferry, Alexander Lawton was able to get off with the brigades of Walker (Trimble) and Douglass (Lawton) almost at once. Jubal Early, who was left behind with his own and Hays's brigade, was not able to procure and prepare food and leave until after dark. After a march of six miles, Early came upon the rear of Lawton, who had gone into camp near the

Shepherdstown Road and was still four miles shy of Boteler's Ford.[48] John R. Jones carried his men back to their old camp southwest of Halltown to prepare for the march and did not finish cooking rations until midnight.[49]

All in all, it was not an auspicious start to a swift reunion.

Lee's Resolve Strengthened

After reading Jackson's victory dispatch, Lee remained on Cemetery Hill. He had disposed of all the forces at hand, and once again he was compelled to await the development of events beyond his control. Symbolically, a staff member had to hold the telescope through which he watched for signs of the arrival of the enemy across the Antietam. His bandaged hands had become a metaphor for his military impotence. Perhaps it was the cumulation of two weeks of pain and the frustration of being cared for like an infant that began to tell on the Confederate commander. Possibly it was the continuous heat and dust or the lack of rest and the strain of two days of anxiety that began to wear on him. Or, perhaps he was particularly unhappy with the quality of intelligence he had gotten of late. Whatever the explanation, around one o'clock, when a brimming Jeb Stuart came galloping up on a foaming horse to proclaim the surrender of Harpers Ferry, Lee received him so brusquely that it amounted to a snub.

"We got 11,000 prisoners," exclaimed Stuart, leaping from his horse, "and all their commissary and quartermaster stores, including wagons and teams." Before replying a word to Stuart, Lee turned and instructed an orderly to walk the horse and not allow it to cool off too quickly. Then, turning back, he asked abruptly, "General, did they have any shoes?" Pointing to the 6th North Carolina of Law's brigade waiting on the nearby Boonsboro Pike to follow the rest of Hood's division to the right of the line, Lee went on, "These good men are barefoot."[50]

In spite of his curt response, Lee must have gotten valuable information from Stuart. While the details of the spoils could wait until a quieter hour, Lee needed to know if Jackson understood the demand for haste in marching to Sharpsburg and whether McLaws and Walker could also be counted on to arrive in a reasonable time. Stuart could not only answer these questions affirmatively, he could also reassure Lee that, in spite of suffering a rout at the close of the battle at Crampton's Gap, McLaws's command was intact and its wagons already approaching the Potomac. If Stuart's report on the state of affairs at Harpers Ferry when he left

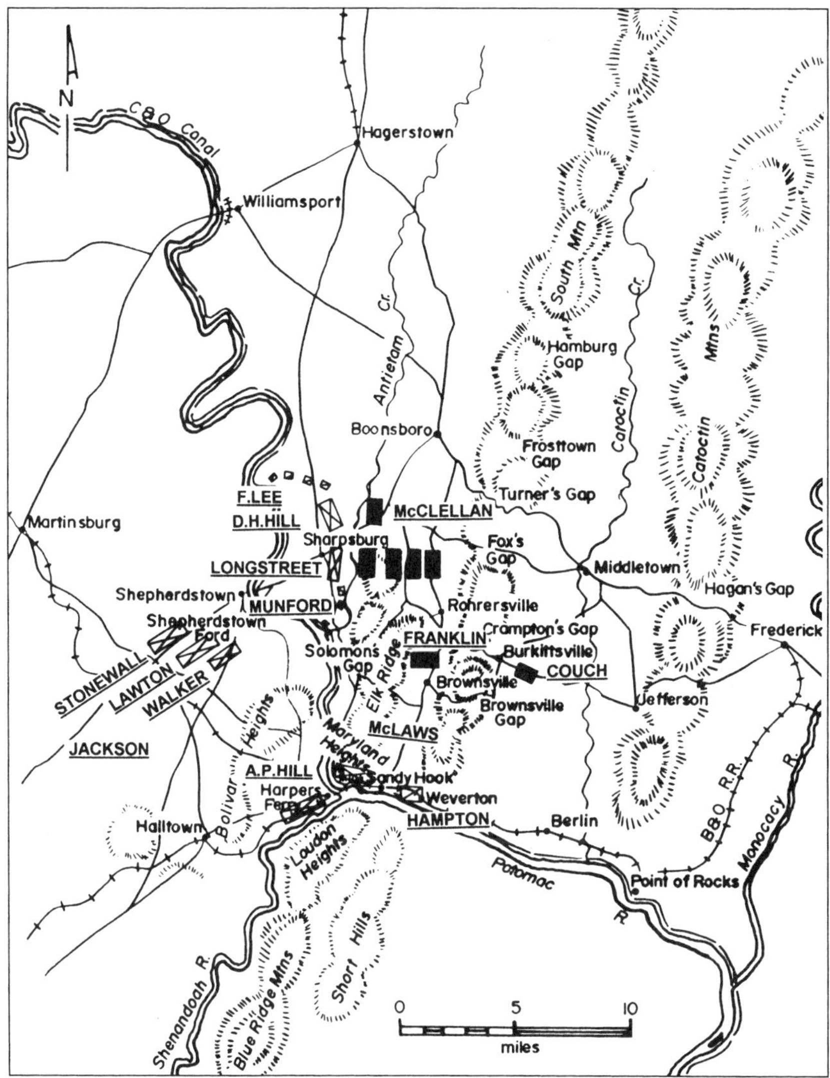

Concentration at Sharpsburg, September 15

turned out to be overly optimistic, it would not be his fault. In addition, due to his own ride by way of Antietam Furnace, Jeb could testify there was no Federal activity west of Elk Ridge to pose an immediate threat to Lee's far right flank.

Shortly thereafter Stuart departed for the left of the line on the Hagerstown Pike. Between 1:00 and 2:00 a third message arrived from Jackson. This time it was no more than a sentence. It was Lee's dispatch of the night before ordering Jackson to break off at Harpers Ferry and cover the retreat of the main body at Shepherdstown, which he had folded and endorsed, "I will join you at Sharpsburg." This brief note told Lee nothing he should not have already known, and it came after he had fully determined to maintain his position on the Antietam and make a bid to revive his campaign in Maryland. Still, it must have encouraged the Confederate commander and strengthened his resolve. The real meaning of the message was not only that Jackson understood the urgency of the moment, but also that Stonewall agreed with the decision and would bring his heart to the fight.[51]

By two o'clock the temperature had risen to seventy-nine degrees, and a deceptive calm had settled on Cemetery Hill as Lee and his soldiers waited for the appearance of the enemy. Occasionally, there had been the distant sound of small arms fire, but as yet no blue coats had been sighted on the Antietam. Then, a messenger from Tom Rosser came galloping up the hill and reported to Lee that Federal skirmishers were now approaching the creek.[52]

When the rest of Fitzhugh Lee's brigade had retreated northwest on the National Pike in an unsuccessful attempt to draw the main pursuit toward Hagerstown, Rosser's 5th Virginia—as it retired from Fox's Gap on the Old Sharpsburg Road—found itself the only Confederate force available to duel with the advance of the Federal infantry from Boonsboro to Keedysville. Although Rosser had only several hundred troopers, he held two important advantages that morning. Because Pleasonton had followed Fitz Lee, Richardson's 5,000-strong division had moved out of Boonsboro with neither horsemen, nor artillery. Rosser not only had greater mobility, he also had Capt. John Pelham with two guns of the Horse Artillery. While a portion of the 5th Virginia pushed tired Confederate stragglers on toward Sharpsburg, the remainder kept in close contact with Richardson's leading brigade under John Caldwell. By feinting attacks, the Confederates tormented their pursuers into consuming time in the deployment from column into line of battle. Finally, Richardson ended the game by throwing the 5th New Hampshire Infantry forward as a permanent skirmish line across his front.

Having won his point by reducing the enemy progress to an unremitting crawl, Rosser pulled back to Keedysville. He then reported to Lee on the Federal advance, as well as the rout of Fitz Lee at Boonsboro and the detour of the rest of the cavalry toward Hagerstown. With the 5th Virginia being the only cavalry available, the Confederate commander had ordered Rosser to keep a few skirmishers east of the creek and divide the remainder to cover each flank. It was one of these scouts that reported the arrival of the Federals on the Antietam.[53]

On the first sighting of the blue uniforms of the 5th New Hampshire, Stephen D. Lee opened from north of the Boonsboro Pike with five selected long-range pieces from his battalion. Some time passed before Richardson had the twelve guns of Capts. John Tidball and Rufus Pettit in position to reply. For most of the afternoon the fire on both sides was desultory, although it was sufficient to demonstrate once more the Federal advantage in artillery at long distance. When Hood ordered Lt. John Ramsay to advance a gun from Rowan's North Carolina battery to a knoll over three hundred yards to the front to shell a woods near the Lower Bridge, the young artillerist got off less than a dozen rounds before the enemy found his range. All of the rifled cannon in the Confederate line had to open to cover his hasty retreat. It was an ominous sight, therefore, late in the day for the Confederates to watch one after another "finely appointed batteries" wheel into position on the opposing bluffs.[54]

Offsetting good news came for the Confederates during the afternoon, however, with the arrival of more cavalry—an arm in which they in turn excelled—to cover the exposed flanks of the army. Fitz Lee emerged on the Hagerstown Pike with the three regiments that had been battered in the streets of Boonsboro and extended the left of the line from the Dunkard Church to the Potomac.[55] Meanwhile, Thomas Munford appeared at the Lower Bridge, having traveled since sunrise from Rohrersville to cross Elk Ridge and join the main body. He had with him only the remnants of the 2d and 12th Virginia, which had survived Crampton's Gap the day before; but, by stretching his line very thin, he was able to reach from the bridge south two and half miles to the confluence of the Antietam with the Potomac.[56]

Late in the afternoon, Lee may have been able to discern that such of the enemy as had deployed—only Richardson's division had done so at this point—had moved to the north of the Boonsboro Pike and slightly upstream. Whatever the cause, Lee decided the Confederate left was too weak; so he pulled Hood's division from the far right to strengthen the position on the flat ground near the Dunkard Church. As the brigades of Law and Wofford retired from the ridge opposite the Lower Bridge, their movement was plainly visible to the enemy, who opened on them with artillery. Suffering a number of casualties before he reached the shelter of trees that shielded him from view, Hood marched through Sharpsburg and north on the Hagerstown Pike. D. R. Jones stretched his division to the right to cover the vacated position.[57] It was Hood's movement Joe Hooker observed from the overlook east of the Antietam and—overestimating the force at 15,000—wondered if the Confederates were beginning a retreat.

Nothing could have been farther from Lee's mind, as the long day finally drew to a close. He was certainly tired from lack of rest—and probably irritable from the accumulation of pressures both great and minor—but the hope of regaining the strategic initiative must have revived his spirits. For the first time since Leesburg he established his headquarters indoors, sharing the Jacob Grove house in Sharpsburg with Longstreet, where he could sleep on a bed softer than his camp cot.[58] He even took the time to complete a letter he had started two days earlier in Hagerstown in reply to a report by Gustavus Smith "of the 4th instant."[59]

The dispatch is one of the blandest ever sent over Lee's name and does little more than acknowledge and approve actions taken by Smith. In fact, Lee may have done no more than to indicate in a general way what was wanted to a staff member for drafting.

"I am glad to learn that you have organized a force for the Rappahannock," the letter began, "which I hope will be sufficient for the present purposes. . . ." Indeed, for some time Lee had urged the Confederate presence be pushed as far north in central Virginia as possible.[60] Foremost, he wished to protect the frontiers he so recently liberated from marauding Federals. In addition, he may also have desired—as he would specifically state nine months later during the Gettysburg campaign—to exert pressure on Washington from the south and thereby prevent a total concentration against his own army above the Potomac.

"But I beg you will spare no effort to increase it," he continued, "and, if it acquires sufficient strength, that you will advance it beyond the Rappahannock, to cover that country from the raids of the enemy's cavalry as far as possible." Although Smith likely did not commit specific numbers to a letter that might be captured, he must have conveyed the notion that the force he had pushed forward was small. In actuality, totaling less than 1,600 in the 61st Virginia Infantry and three newly raised cavalry regiments, it was a token display of the flag. Nor was there reasonable expectation Smith could do better in the foreseeable future. He had but 25,000 men present for duty and the responsibility to cover both North Carolina and southeastern Virginia, including manning the defenses of Richmond and confronting the remainder of Burnside's force at New Berne.[61] The desiccation of Confederate strength in the mid-Atlantic derived directly from Lee's draining away units for the field army, and it was the ultimate testament of Jefferson Davis's faith in that army and its commander. Smith's weakness may have reminded Lee that the Confederacy could not afford to sacrifice the Army of Northern Virginia on foreign soil. Even more, however, it might have reminded Lee that he had virtually nothing to fall back on in Virginia and thus reenforced his belief that his only path to winning the war lay in pursuing the offensive strategy to its ultimate conclusion.

"The wounded at Warrenton must be brought back to a place of greater security whenever opportunity affords," the dispatch continued, "as soon as they can bear the transportation. They were only sent there temporarily." Lee here admitted he knew Smith would have no significant force to operate beyond the Rappahannock in the near future. He also divulged, however, a change that occurred in his own strategic thinking. Ten days earlier he had written to Davis that if the Maryland campaign failed he would fall back "to take a position about Warrenton."[62] Now, with the real possibility of failure confronting him, he gave no sign that Warrenton figured in his plans. This may be the first indication that Lee was already evolving an alternative strategy that would only emerge with clarity four days later. Even if forced from Maryland, he would remain on the upper Potomac to threaten Maryland and detain the enemy as far as possible from central Virginia.

Finally the dispatch closed with two topics close to Lee's heart. "I am glad you have given directions for the gathering up and forwarding to their regiments of the stragglers through the country, and hope you will speedily obtain enough labor to complete the works around Richmond."

The subjects covered in the letter to Smith must have seemed far removed from the worries pressing Lee on the heights of Sharpsburg. They might have provided him with a bit of perspective by reminding him of Richmond and the wider Confederacy. It may have occurred to him to be especially grateful—considering subsequent events—that Davis had not joined the army at Frederick. He might have gone so far as to speculate on the success of Confederate armies elsewhere. There is no evidence Lee had received any later news, after he had published the orders on September 6 announcing Kirby Smith's victory. It is impossible to tell whether he knew that Smith, Bragg, and Marshall were now all in Kentucky; that Loring had captured Charleston; or that Price was finally on the move in northern Mississippi. To the extent he had even the tiniest glimmer of such information, however, it is likely it stiffened his resolve against abandoning his own offensive.

Still, it is unlikely that the exhausted commander focused much attention on matters so far removed. If he did not take the first opportunity to rest, he probably spent the waning hours of the 15th reviewing the situation nearer to hand. He could not have helped but been pleased at the improvement of his situation since the previous night. Instead of stumbling through the darkness to Virginia in defeat, he held a strong defensive position and expected his army to be united on the morrow. In such a mind, having observed the strength of the position he held from the vantage point of the enemy and noting the late deployment of the Federals east of the Antietam, he expressed his belief that McClellan would not launch an major assault until the day after next.[63]

If Lee had known at ten o'clock that only two out of the twenty-seven brigades at Harpers Ferry were in motion to join him, he might have been less satisfied with his situation. Moreover, those two brigades (Lawton with Trimble and Douglass) would halt four miles short of Boteler's Ford; and, although Early and Hays had drawn their rations and were setting out to join Lawton, it seemed initially as though only a single division would get off on the 15th.[64] But, Stonewall Jackson was not yet through for the day. Setting out after dark himself, he must have issued a secondary round of orders to quicken his lethargic command. John R. Jones, who took ten hours to return his men to their old camp at Halltown and draw and cook rations, acted like a commander expecting to start the next morning. Instead, he broke bivouac after midnight, and the head of his division filed onto the Shepherdstown Road. Around one o'clock, John Walker roused his two brigades from a sound sleep and set out to follow Jones. The late starters joined Jackson and Lawton at the junction of the Shepherdstown and Boteler's Ford roads several hours later.[65] Thus, shortly before dawn, three of the six Confederate divisions at Harpers Ferry were within nine miles of Sharpsburg.

Although this late-hour effort showed plainly Jackson's intention to reach Lee in time to affect the outcome of the campaign, there were flaws in his execution that did not augur well for Lee's plans to regain the initiative. As soon became painfully clear, Stonewall had not conveyed a full sense of the emergency to LaFayette McLaws. With a quarter of the Army of Northern Virginia in his command, McLaws not only did not set out on the night of the 15th, but neither did he understand he was to start the following day.[66] On top of which, the men Jackson had poised to cross the Potomac were in miserable shape. Having prepared for and expected battle in the morning, all had their rest interrupted, and many got no sleep at all. When the driver of a gun in the Rockbridge Artillery was overcome with drowsiness and went sprawling from his horse, no one laughed. His example roused those around him and spared them a similar fate. Even Stonewall confessed it was a "severe night's march."[67] By the returns of September 1, Jackson should have had nearly 16,000 men with him that night, but his column shed stragglers as badly as had Longstreet and D. H. Hill on the retreat from Turner's Gap. He would carry scarcely 10,000 into Maryland in the morning.[68]

Soldiers are not brightly colored pins, and the hills they climb and the rivers they wade are not the flat, smooth paper of maps. Commanding a large nineteenth-century army and getting it to do what was wanted when it was wanted, and staying in good shape while doing it, was not an easy task—not for George McClellan and not for Robert E. Lee.

CHAPTER EIGHT

"All will be right"

Lee's Last Chance for Maneuver, September 16, 1862

TUESDAY, SEPTEMBER 16, was fated to be yet another hot day. But during the night, low pressure had crossed the Blue Ridge, raising the humidity considerably and bringing the promise of rain. The increasingly moist air had coalesced, and by dawn a heavy fog blanketed the valley of the Antietam. For more than two hours past daylight, the dense mist blinded both sides to any glimpse of their enemy, although they lay less than a mile from one another.

Ironically, the natural shroud only complemented the faulty perception the opponents already held of each other. Lee, who assumed much the greater part of the Army of the Potomac had arrived, must have thought 70,000 or 80,000 Federals lay enshrouded across the creek. Similarly, since McClellan believed he faced the Confederate main body, he projected at least 60,000 enemy on the hidden heights of Sharpsburg. The watery sun, which persisted until midday before disappearing behind overcast skies, would finally dissipate the fog. No sun would burn away the cloudy intelligence, however, and neither commander would pierce the misperceptions even after the fog lifted. McClellan actually had some 48,000 effectives on or within easy marching distance of the field. Lee had 25,000 effectives at or near at hand.[1]

Lee Sees a Window

Before daylight, Lee arose and breakfasted at the Jacob Grove house.[2] Refreshed by his first good night's sleep since the 12th, his natural bent to search for the best results asserted itself, and he resumed plotting to regain control of the campaign. If he were correct in his perception of last evening that McClellan would not hastily launch a frontal assault on a position so strong, he would have twenty-four hours to plan and initiate an alternative to his current dilemma. He need not either retreat to Virginia or stand dumbly on the defense at Sharpsburg. He would find a way not only to remain in Maryland but also to reclaim the initiative.

Happily, there were developments at hand that bolstered his optimism. In the first place, the fog guaranteed that even an aggressive foe would get a late start in reconnoitering and preparing an attack. Second, Confederate reenforcements were at hand. Jackson sent word that his men were already in motion and that the head of his column would be in the waters of the Potomac by dawn. Lee knew Boteler's Ford was but three miles away, and he could interpret the message to mean that the divisions of J. R. Jones, Lawton, and Walker were within an easy march and would join the main body early in the forenoon.[3]

With the prospect of an active day opening before him, Lee decided the time had come to return to the back of Traveller. He still could neither mount, nor dismount without help; and his horse had be led by an aide, since his bandaged hands could not hold the reins. Yet, merely being in the saddle again gave him a range and flexibility he had sorely missed for over two weeks.[4] At first light Lee rode back to Cemetery Hill, his vantage point of the previous day. The heavy fog prevented him seeing objects more than twenty feet away, so he left his horse and walked south of the Boonsboro Pike until he reached the advanced position of the Washington Artillery. For some time he paced among the guns from Louisiana, pausing occasionally and staring as if by force of will he might pierce the mysteries behind the drifting, milky curtain, or catch a sound that would tell him if the Federals were preparing for an assault.[5] Federal scouts—both infantry and cavalry—were across the Middle Bridge by this time; but the soft, blurred noises that may have come to Lee's ears did not suggest that a large body of men was on the move.[6] He could begin to hope he was right that McClellan would follow a shorter version of the slow but sure policy of the Federal campaign against Richmond and make the approach to the heights of Sharpsburg a battle of posts.

Although the thoughts of the Confederate commander, as he stood silent and alone in the morning mist, can never be recaptured with certainty, the information available to him at the time and the actions he subsequently took suggest he was pondering a return to the offensive. It is true the Army of Northern Virginia could not be fully reunited early on the 16th. Jackson in his dispatch had reported that McLaws and

Anderson remained in Pleasant Valley, and both divisions—which would be in some danger until they had crossed the Potomac—could not be expected before late afternoon or early evening. Moreover, A. P. Hill's division—assigned not only to parole the prisoners and secure the captured property but also to prevent the Federals from retaking Harpers Ferry—would likely not arrive before nightfall. Still, even though these three large divisions constituted a third of the army, they need not be with the main body at Sharpsburg to enable Lee to initiate an offensive maneuver. They could recross the river at Williamsport, or some point farther west, and unite with the army on the march.

In his thinking, Lee probably inclined, as he usually did, to a turning movement to the west that would carry him around the enemy's right flank. Certainly, in this case it was sound strategy. Due east, the Army of the Potomac occupied the bluffs of the Antietam and a defensive position as strong as the one Lee held at Sharpsburg. Directly southeast lay Pleasant Valley, which would be as much of a trap for the main body as it had been for McLaws. And there is no reason to believe Lee saw any attraction in a movement to the south, which would inevitably require crossing the Potomac, only three miles away. Certainly he would not want to return to Virginia in order to march east to Leesburg and recross the river lower down to threaten McClellan's rear. Such a move would place the Confederates between Washington's forts and McClellan's army. If he must go back to Virginia, a movement to the west to ford the upper Potomac might make some sense. Still, any return to Virginia would relieve the pressure on the Federals, and this Lee did not want to do. Even more, now that the Army of the Potomac was back in the field, it might be impossible to reenter Maryland a second time.

It must have made most sense to Lee to march north to Hagerstown. Here he could pick up exactly where he had left off three days before the Federals had foiled his plans. Here he could threaten both Pennsylvania and the right flank of the Federal army. He could rest his army a bit, await the arrival of McLaws and A. P. Hill, and finally bring McClellan to battle on ground advantageous to the Confederates. Equally important, this was the route that seemed to lay invitingly open to him. Nearly three miles of open, undefended ground lay between the Potomac and the Antietam to the north and northwest, and the Hagerstown Pike provided him a direct and reasonably good road to his objective.

There would be some danger in committing his entire army to a single column so near the presence of the enemy. It would be wise to investigate the existence of parallel roads, as well as to learn of possible fords in the rear of his route of march. It would also be prudent to shorten his column by sending off most of the wagons still with the army to join the reserve trains at Shepherdstown. These vehicles could recross the river farther to the west (the Williamsport fords were still guarded) and unite with the army at Hagerstown in a day or two.

How far Lee advanced his strategy as he paced among the guns at dawn cannot be known; but either then or before nine o'clock that morning, he issued two orders that revealed the direction his thinking had taken. First, he ordered a cavalry reconnaissance in force "up the Potomac" on the Maryland side. This was not a scout for additional fords for an escape from Sharpsburg, but a quest for information on routes to the north and northwest. Stuart considered the mission of sufficient importance that he led it himself, taking as many as three regiments from Fitzhugh Lee's brigade with him. Jeb left Heros von Borcke behind in Sharpsburg with ten couriers to coordinate the intelligence reports and feed the incoming information to army headquarters.[7]

Second, Lee ordered the wagons remaining with the army—which included the regimental, brigade, and divisional wagons that supplied food and ammunition directly to the men in the ranks and which had parked a mile west of Sharpsburg—to cross the Potomac and retire to Shepherdstown, where the reserve trains of the army and of D. H. Hill and Longstreet had already gathered. Had Lee been planning on the morning of the 16th merely to stand and offer battle at Sharpsburg, he would certainly have kept the nonreserve ordnance wagons to supply ammunition for the fighting, and he would have fed the men from the subsistence wagons before sending them off. Nor does it make sense to believe this was a step in retreating to Virginia, not when Lee believed Jackson, Walker, and McLaws were hurrying to Sharpsburg. Stripping away all cumbersome vehicles was, however, a logical preliminary for a swift movement through a narrow opening to the freedom for maneuver that lay beyond.[8]

How far Lee carried his ponderings during his predawn pacing is uncertain. Just before six o'clock, when the rim of the rising sun would have been visible had it not been for the fog, he returned to his horse along the Boonsboro Pike. By the smoldering embers of a dying campfire, he received a young lieutenant who rode up with a message from Longstreet. Lee listened intently to the information—perhaps a report on movements of the Federals in front—and then staring off into the gray mist and speaking as if to himself, he soliloquized: "All will be right, if McLaws gets out of Pleasant Valley."[9]

Lee and the Whims of War

As was their wont when serious work was at hand, the drums of Stonewall Jackson beat the long roll an hour before the rising of the sun. Jackson's old division under John R. Jones had only just reached the bivouac two miles from Shepherdstown after its night march from Harpers Ferry when ordered to fall in and form the head of the column. It was a groggy and subdued foot cavalry that continued to plod four miles through the darkness and crossed the Potomac at daybreak. Jones followed the canal towpath two miles west to strike the Shepherdstown Road and then headed three miles north to make camp in a "beautiful oak grove" on the left of the road a mile short of Sharpsburg. Only then did he allow his men to sink to the ground for their first rest in forty-eight hours.[10]

Lawton's division, which followed closely on the heels of Jones, fared somewhat better, as the brigades of Early and Hays had been able to snatch several hours of sleep, while the brigades under Marcellus Douglass and James Walker received what passed for a full night's rest for the troops of Stonewall.[11] John G.Walker's two-brigade division reached the rear of Jackson's column just as the head was setting out; but rather than pressing forward, Walker put his men into camp. They would not cross the Potomac until noon or shortly thereafter.[12]

After Jackson ensured the fording of the Potomac by his divisions was proceeding smoothly, he rode ahead to Sharpsburg. Around eight o'clock he found Lee with Longstreet on Cemetery Hill.[13] It is possible—although far from certain—that John Walker may have reported with him.[14] If so, Walker was soon dismissed, and Lee entered into serious conversation with his two chief lieutenants. It may be surmised that at this time Lee spoke briefly to Longstreet and Jackson of his intention to resume the offensive by working around the Federal right flank and marching in the direction of Hagerstown. In order to take advantage of Federal inactivity, he may have even proposed that the movement start as soon as Stuart could report the way was clear along the Potomac to the northwest. The suggestion—if made—may have taken aback the normally aggressive Jackson, who would have had to confess the previous night's severe march had rendered his men incapable of undertaking any new move without rest. Some such exchange would explain Lee's orders to Jackson to hold his divisions in bivouac west of Sharpsburg, rather than putting them immediately into the defensive line. Whatever specifically was said at this time, after the war Lee would recall of Jackson: "When he came upon the field, having preceded his troops, and learned my reasons for offering battle, he emphatically concurred with me." Along with Lee, Jackson understood what was at stake in Maryland; and neither wished to give up the campaign "without a struggle."[15]

Unfortunately, signs appeared almost immediately that suggested Lee's window of chance might be an illusion. Between eight and nine o'clock, after Jackson had departed to supervise the encampment of his men,[16] the fog began to lift from the Antietam valley.[17] The heavy guns of two Federal batteries opened on the troops of Longstreet and D. H. Hill along the brow of Sharpsburg Heights as soon as the gray infantry was exposed to view.[18] At nearly the same time, word also came in that enemy troops had crossed the bridge on the Boonsboro Pike.[19] Suddenly, Lee must have wondered if he had miscalculated. Did this activity portend that a Federal assault was imminent? True, such a threat ought not have worried Lee greatly. His position was nearly as strong as the enemy's had been at Malvern Hill, and Jackson's reserves were now at hand. If McClellan wished to dash Federal regiments headlong against the Confederate center, Lee could feel confident in the outcome. Still, an enemy attack would nail Lee to his position at Sharpsburg and prevent him from escaping to open ground more suitable for maneuver. More immediately pressing, however, he had sent away all of his ordnance wagons and might run out of ammunition in repelling an assault.

The development clearly bore close watching, although the imminence of an attack seemed to dissipate during the two hours from 9:00 to 11:00. The cannonading remained light, while the Confederates refused a response. The men of Longstreet and D. H. Hill, who were protected once they withdrew to the foot of the heights, suffered few casualties. Meanwhile, skirmishers who were pushed out from Evans's brigade could report that the Federals west of the Antietam seemed content to form a defensive bridgehead several hundred yards from the creek.[20] Ironically, there is no reason to believe anything more would have developed from this affair without Confederate provocation.

At eleven o'clock, Col. James B. Walton of the Washington Artillery, apparently on his own authority, ordered the heaviest Confederate pieces "all along" the line to respond to the "annoying" Federal fire. Of the forty or so Confederate guns ranged on the Sharpsburg heights, only a dozen had any hope of reaching their tormentors.[21] The lesson of the previous afternoon should have been fresh in Walton's mind, and it is not certain what he hoped to accomplish. Since he directed part of his fire against the Federal infantry with a toehold west of the Antietam, he may have wished to develop the enemy's intentions.[22]

Whatever his purpose, Walton at once got back more than he could handle. Four batteries of the Federal Artillery Reserve posted on the bluffs north of the Boonsboro Pike—each composed of six 20-pounders—immediately joined the two Federal batteries already firing.[23] Gen. D. H. Hill described the duel between the thirty-six Federal guns and the ten or twelve Confederate pieces that followed as "the most melancholy farce in the war."[24] It is highly doubtful Lee approved of the firing in the first place, and he soon ordered it to cease, so that the little ammunition on hand might be preserved for the "enemy infantry." After forty minutes, Walton—who by that time was probably grateful—received the order from Longstreet to cease firing and withdrew his guns behind the ridge.[25]

The Federals did not halt their bombardment, however, but continued firing for another thirty to sixty minutes, shifting their aim to the town. Heros von Borcke sat on the sofa of the Jacob Grove house placidly entering observations in his diary, when suddenly his peaceful world exploded around him. Shells pierced the roof and walls of the house, sending furniture flying in every direction and covering von Borcke with plaster. He quickly decided the time had come to transfer Stuart's headquarters to a more tranquil site. After some difficulty in finding his horse in the haze of dust and debris, and even greater trouble in picking his way through the street filled with overturned wagons and panic-stricken mules and teamsters, the Prussian stood on no ceremony in riding for the countryside.[26]

It was likely at this same time that Lee—who was seen walking through the village followed by his horse—decided to transfer his own quarters to his tent in a grove of woods three-quarters of mile outside the town on the north of the road to Shepherdstown.[27] Here, shortly after noon, Lee gathered with his senior generals to assess the situation. It was generally—albeit mistakenly—assumed that the bombardment was a prelude to a Federal assault.[28] As Lee awaited attack, the configuration of his army was not significantly different from the position he had assumed upon arrival on the morning of the 15th, except that it was longer and considerably stronger on the left flank, north along the Hagerstown Pike. The Confederate infantry and artillery presently occupied a line about two and a half miles in length, with two of the miles being securely posted on or immediately behind the high ridges west of the Antietam. The cavalry extended each flank more than a mile.

D. R. Jones's division held the right and right-center from the Lower Bridge to Cemetery Hill. The brigades of Evans and G. T. Anderson covered the Boonsboro Pike. North of the pike, D. H. Hill occupied the remainder of the ridge until it fell away in front of the Piper farm, at which point Hill's line bent westward in a ninety-degree angle toward the Hagerstown Pike. Hood's division was in the fields around the Dunkard Church on the left and carried the Confederate line to within a mile and a half of the Potomac.

The guns of the Washington Artillery and the batteries attached to D. R. Jones, Hood, and Evans, plus two of S. D. Lee's batteries (a total of forty-four guns in eleven batteries), supported the center and right. S. D. Lee had been ordered to shift four batteries of his battalion to the Dunkard Church during the night, so that the left was now supported by his guns and those of D. H. Hill's division and Cutts's and H. P. Jones's battalions of the Artillery Reserve (a total of seventy-six guns in seventeen batteries).[29]

Fitzhugh Lee's cavalry brigade—minimally the 9th Virginia and probably the 3d, 4th, and 5th, which had likely returned from Stuart's reconnaissance by this time as well—along with four guns of Pelham's Horse Artillery extended the left to the Potomac and observed the upper Antietam. On the right, Munford with the 2d and 12th Virginia and three guns of Chew's battery watched the creek from the Lower Bridge to Snavely's Ford more than a mile to the south.[30]

Since none of the cavalry reported any enemy movement on the flanks, Lee had to assume that the attack would come against the center. Apparently, he was sufficiently satisfied with the strength of his line to repulse an attack from that quarter that he did not disturb the slumber of Jackson's two divisions behind Sharpsburg. Nor did he feel compelled to rush Walker's division to the front line, as the head of that division—just then reaching the field—was allowed to go into camp to the west of Jackson, halfway between the Potomac and Sharpsburg.[31] Also, Lee could have—but did not—call upon the two battalions of the Artillery Reserve, which were just south of the Potomac. During the gloomiest part of the night of the 14th, when Lee had believed it would be necessary to retreat into Virginia, he had sent Pendleton with the battalions of Brown (twenty guns in five batteries) and Nelson (twenty-four guns in five batteries) to cross at Williamsport and guard the fords of the river. During the 15th Pendleton placed Brown at Williamsport, and by ten on the morning of the 16th he had positioned Nelson at Boteler's Ford south of Shepherdstown.[32] Although Lee was now determined not to recross into Virginia, he apparently believed Pendleton served a better purpose in guarding the communications of the still divided army than in joining the main body, which already had as many guns as it could usefully employ.

There were but two actions taken by Lee that indicate uneasiness on his part at the imminence of battle at midday on the 16th. First, at some point during the hour and a half cannonade, he sent a courier to Harpers Ferry with orders to McLaws to "hasten" his command to Sharpsburg.[33] Second, Lee may have been more concerned over the scarcity of ammunition than over the number of troops at hand for an impending battle. He must have regretted sending away the brigade and division ordnance wagons earlier in the morning, and—although there is no evidence extant—he probably sent orders for all of his ammunition wagons, except the reserve train, to return to Sharpsburg.[34]

Additionally, shortly after the cannonade halted, when the army chief of ordnance, Porter Alexander, rode into headquarters from Shepherdstown, Lee called him aside and ordered him to collect empty wagons and return at once to Harpers Ferry. Alexander was to expedite the removal of the captured guns and ammunition, sending all suitable calibers that could be used by the army to Sharpsburg and the remainder to Winchester. As there were no empty wagons at hand, Alexander returned to Shepherdstown, where he collected some empty vehicles and unloaded others from his own train and set out for Harpers Ferry.[35] It is revealing that Lee did not order the reserve train forward at this time and that he still viewed Winchester as his depot. Both facts argue that Lee believed the chance for maneuver had not entirely vanished from his Maryland campaign.

For the soldiers of the Army of Northern Virginia the 16th of September was a day of irritations and annoyances. All morning the sun had dodged a swelling legion of clouds, only to disappear entirely in an overcast sky around eleven at the start of the serious bombardment. By noon the day had become hot and muggy with few breezes to stir the leaden air. All of the men—whether they marched from South Mountain or Harpers Ferry—had arrived at Sharpsburg asleep on their feet and were now in line of battle for the second day. Rest had been fitful at best in the near presence of the enemy and from the veteran's unerring instinct of when a major battle was in the offing. Uneasiness came also from enduring an artillery fire they could not repay in kind and from the vague perception that their scattered army was not yet whole.[36]

On top of it all, the men were hungry. The commissary trains were parked across the Potomac inaccessible and useless. The breakfasts cooked by D. H. Hill's infantry on the morning of the 14th, and hastily stowed as the troops were rushed up South Mountain, remained uneaten in the wagons. After the last haversack was emptied, foraging parties picked fresh corn from the fields and fruit from the orchards.[37]

The commander of the Army of Northern Virginia was also compelled to endure several anxious but idle hours after the bombardment ceased around 12:30. There was nothing left for him to do that would directly affect his current situation, and he was forced to await the further actions of the enemy, the recuperation of Jackson's men, and the arrival of McLaws. To fill the time, Lee dictated a letter to Davis, his first after an untypical hiatus of three days.[38] Much had happened—most of it negative—since Lee had written to the president from Hagerstown on the 13th. The general, who was not above shaping the truth to put the best possible face on the calamities that had befallen the Army of Northern Virginia, could disguise the bad news; but he could not avoid conveying the impression that he and his army faced a grave crisis. The letter he wrote was highly unusual in the amount of strategic and tactical specifics included. It conveyed the impression of a commander reviewing recent history to justify in his own mind that he had rendered correct decisions.

"My letter to you of the 13th instant," he began in his customary fashion, "informed you of the positions of the different divisions of this army."[39] Lee then bluntly confessed that he had miscalculated on two important projections:

> Learning that night that Harper's Ferry had not surrendered, and that the enemy was advancing more rapidly than was convenient from Fredericktown, I determined to return with Longstreet's command to the Blue Ridge, to strengthen D. H. Hill's and Stuart's divisions, engaged in holding the passes of the mountains, lest the enemy should fall upon McLaws' rear, drive him from Maryland Heights, and thus relieve the garrison at Harper's Ferry.

Here Lee confirms what his words and actions at the time implied—that he was not seriously concerned about the delay at Harpers Ferry and the advance of the enemy until the night of September 13. He also makes clear that he had focused on Turner's Gap and that he believed the defense of that pass was the joint responsibility of D. H. Hill and

Stuart. It is not clear whether the use of "passes" was meant to refer to the multiple gaps at Boonsboro or that Stuart was additionally responsible for Crampton's and elsewhere. Lee also gives the erroneous impression that his main worry had been that the enemy would raise the siege of Harpers Ferry. Perhaps, now that he knew the magnitude of the capture in men and booty, he recognized it should have been a major concern. At the time, however, his own orders to McLaws had directed abandoning the operations.

Lee then went on to admit—again somewhat less than forthrightly—that he had reached South Mountain too late:

> On approaching Boonsborough, I received information from General D. H. Hill that the enemy in strong force was at the main pass on the Frederick and Hagerstown road, pressing him so heavily as to require immediate re-enforcements. Longstreet advanced rapidly to his support, and immediately placed his troops in position. By this time Hill's right had been forced back, the gallant Garland having fallen in rallying his brigade. Under General Longstreet's directions, our right was soon restored, and firmly resisted the attacks of the enemy to the last. His superior numbers enabled him to extend beyond both of our flanks, and his right was able to reach the summit of the mountain to our left, and press us heavily in that direction. The battle raged until after night; the enemy's efforts to force a passage were resisted, but we had been unable to repulse him.

Lee proceeded to interweave his second piece of bad news—the defeat of McLaws—with an explanation of his reaction to the crisis:

> Learning later in the evening that Crampton's Gap (on the direct road from Fredericktown to Sharpsburg) had been forced, and McLaws' rear thus threatened, and believing from a report from General Jackson that Harper's Ferry would fall next morning, I determined to withdraw Longstreet and D. H. Hill from their positions and retire to the vicinity of Sharpsburg, where the army could be more easily united.

In addition to Lee's somewhat vague rationalization for not retiring to Virginia in response to the unfavorable developments, this long and convoluted sentence contains two other interesting points. First, it reveals that Lee—in spite of his frequent study of maps—may have labored in some ignorance of Maryland geography. It is Fox's Gap that might loosely be described as on the "direct road" from Frederick to Sharpsburg. Crampton's Gap, on the contrary, lay in the direction of Harpers Ferry.

Second, and much more importantly, is Lee's explanation of his decision to march to Sharpsburg less than forty-eight hours after the decision was rendered. On the one hand, he implies that he knew of the imminent fall of Harpers Ferry at the very hour Jackson was writing the dispatch that would not arrive until twelve hours later. On the other, he makes no mention of the fact that for several hours on the night of the 14th he fully intended to abandon the campaign and return to Virginia. Nor does he reveal that his first revised plan had been to halt at Keedysville. In the same vein, he does not describe the final halt at Sharpsburg as a stand to confront the pursuing enemy but simply refers to its convenient location for reuniting his army. This open-ended statement—made shortly after midday on the 16th—may well reflect his continuing hope to break out of the defensive box at Sharpsburg and resume his campaign of maneuver in Maryland.

After thus abridging major developments to the point of distortion, Lee then related at some length a relatively minor tactical detail:

> Before abandoning the position, indications led me to believe that the enemy was withdrawing, but learning from a prisoner that Sumner's corps, which had not been engaged, was being put in position to relieve their wearied troops while the most of ours were exhausted by a fatiguing march and a hard conflict and I feared would be unable to renew the fight successfully in the morning, confirmed me in my determination.

It is interesting that Lee refers only to the freshness of the enemy and the exhaustion of the Confederate troops, while making no reference either to the superiority of Federal numbers or to the tactical weaknesses of the Confederate position at the end of the day. He leaves the impression that he would have renewed the fight at Turner's Gap on the 15th if the soldier from Sumner's corps had not been captured. To the extent the unnecessary inclusion of this incident in the letter to Davis reflects Lee's state of mind on the 16th—and is not merely a statement of bravado to disguise the disaster at South Mountain—it indicates he retained an attitude of combativeness and optimism about his chances in the Maryland campaign.

In contrast, when describing the withdrawal itself, Lee emphasized the apparent lack of aggressiveness of the Federals: "Accordingly the troops were withdrawn preceded by the trains without molestation by the enemy, and about daybreak took position in front of this place. The enemy did not pass through the gap until about 8 o'clock of the morning after the battle, and their advance reached a position in front of us about 2 p.m."

Lee was scarcely being realistic to find significance in the lack of "molestation" of a withdrawal made in the dead of night. Neither was he fair to criticize the enemy for taking six hours—while skirmishing—to make a march that took his own van five hours to complete without opposition. Nor was he honest in omitting mention of Pleasonton's sharp attacks at Boonsboro that scattered Fitz Lee's rear guard. Still, whether objectively accurate or not, Lee's description once again indicates his frame of mind on the 16th. He interpreted the enemy's movements as unnecessarily slow. It may well have been this observation that led Lee to predict the evening before that McClellan would not attack on the 16th. It is also possible that unconsciously Lee had read an awareness of his own extreme vulnerability on the night of the 14th and forenoon of the 15th into his unreasonable critique of the enemy's movements.

In any case, Lee then went on to present his sole piece of good news to counterbalance the several bad:

> Before their arrival, I received intelligence from General Jackson that Harper's Ferry had surrendered early in the morning. I enclose his report.[40] From a more detailed statement furnished by General Jackson's adjutant-general, it appears that 49 pieces of artillery, 24 mountain howitzers, and 17 revolving guns, 11,000 men fit for duty (consisting of twelve regiments of infantry, three companies of cavalry, and six companies of artillery), together with 11,000 small-arms, were the fruits of this victory.

Lee then made a curious statement regarding the current status of the expeditionary forces. "Part of General Jackson's corps has reached us," he wrote, "and the rest are approaching, except General A. P. Hill's division, left at Harper's Ferry to guard the place and take care of public property." In the first place, this gives an inaccurate view of army organization by implying the divisions of McLaws and Anderson (and perhaps even Walker) belonged permanently under Jackson. None of these divisions, however, ever were or ever would be under Jackson on the organizational chart. Lee can only have employed "corps" in the unusual way to mean the temporary grouping that resulted when Jackson's seniority gave him temporary command of the divisions which came together in the Valley expedition. Second, the statement indicated Lee was under the misunderstanding that McLaws was already on the march for Sharpsburg, whereas that commander would not start until after 3:00 in the afternoon. And, finally, Lee's reference to A. P. Hill being at Harpers Ferry not only to secure the captured goods but "to guard the place" indicates the Confederate commander believed Franklin might attempt to retake the town and that—at least as late the writing of this letter—Lee was willing to keep A. P. Hill at Harpers Ferry to prevent its recapture. This suggests that Lee viewed Franklin's presence in Pleasant Valley as a threat to the Confederate flank and communications with Winchester.

Lee then made a second comment that reflected directly on his current situation, and it was equally curious in its own way. "The enemy," he wrote, "have made no attack up to this afternoon, but are in force in our front." It is this sentence that confirms the letter was dictated in the early afternoon. This makes it all the more interesting that Lee makes no mention of the bridgehead established by the Federals west of the Antietam or of the heavy bombardment just ended. The statement is too bland to be interpreted with confidence, but it is possible he had again begun to lean toward the belief McClellan would not act on the 16th.

Lee ended his dispatch on a high note by repeating the good news he had to report. "This victory of the indomitable Jackson and his troops," he concluded with a flourish, "gives us renewed occasion for gratitude to Almighty God for His guidance and protection." Ironically, this—Lee's first effusive praise for Jackson—came on the fifth-week anniversary of the Confederate commander's decision of August 9 to send Longstreet to supersede the lagging Jackson in independent command at Gordonsville. Apparently, Thoroughfare Gap and Harpers Ferry had made Lee a believer in "Old Jack."[41]

In midafternoon, around three o'clock or so, Lee reconvened his council of war with Longstreet and Jackson, returning once more to the Jacob Grove house. It may well have been the information provided by Stuart's reconnaissance on the nature of the ground between the Potomac and the Hagerstown Pike that occupied the generals' attention as they studied maps of Maryland and Washington County.[42] It may also be that since the bombardment had ceased and McClellan had made no further aggressive move, they were again giving serious consideration to slipping away from Sharpsburg and marching north to Hagerstown. Such would be the most reasonable explanation for the meeting and for their examining such large-scale maps.

While Lee thus engaged in optimistic projections, his window for maneuver slammed shut once and for all. Around 3:30—and occurring almost simultaneously—Union artillery opposite the Middle Bridge recommenced the bombardment of Cemetery Hill; pickets from Toombs's brigade east of the creek reported that a Federal column was approaching the Lower Bridge, and a courier from Stuart dashed up to relate that the head of another enemy column was just then crossing the Antietam at the Upper Bridge and a nearby ford. It has been frequently asserted that McClellan telegraphed his punch to Lee on the afternoon of the 16th. In Lee's eyes there were three telegrams, and they contradicted one another in regard to where the enemy intended to attack. One message, however, was certain: the road to Hagerstown was closed.

The evening before Lee had predicted that "there would not be much fighting" on the 16th.[43] Implicitly, he believed McClellan would give him another twenty-four hours to escape from the box at Sharpsburg. Lee was wrong.

McClellan Shuts the Window

Although too swiftly for Lee's rising expectations, the First Corps's passage of the Antietam came a half-day later than George McClellan had wanted to open an offensive against the Confederate position at Sharpsburg. In two dispatches sent before eight A.M., McClellan expressed the hope he would be able to attack during the morning.[44] And he probably did. Ignorant of the true size of Lee's army, he nonetheless knew the odds would only worsen, as passing time allowed the Confederate troops from Harpers Ferry to alter the strategic balance. At daybreak on the 16th, there were two ineluctable uncertainties that hobbled the Army of the Potomac and prevented McClellan from launching an instantaneous, straight-ahead attack against the Confederates on the heights of Sharpsburg.[45]

First, at the strategic level, the surrender of Harpers Ferry had freed considerable Confederate forces for new operations. Stonewall Jackson had become a wild card in the hand being played by the two commanders. Although there was a report that the Confederates in Pleasant Valley (McLaws) were recrossing into Virginia, and rumors that part of Jackson's men had already joined Lee at Sharpsburg, McClellan could not ignore the potential of a turning movement against Federal communications. The number of Confederate divisions designated in Special Orders, No. 191, to operate against Harpers Ferry indicated that a powerful force sat on McClellan's flank. The fact that the force was commanded by Jackson, a proven master of rapid maneuver, elevated it to a threat McClellan must reckon seriously. McClellan could not know that Lee would simply instruct Jackson to march to Sharpsburg. Certainly, he could not commit the Army of the Potomac to battle on that optimistic assumption. However much the Federal commander might wish to order the Sixth Corps to join the main body on the Antietam, Franklin served a more valuable service in observing Jackson and complicating Confederate maneuvers.

Second, at the tactical level, and by far the most inhibiting uncertainty, it simply was not readily apparent how the Sharpsburg ridges frowning with guns might be successfully carried. McClellan confronted a quandary similar to the one Lee had twice faced during the summer. How was it possible to bring a campaign to a victorious closing against a foe that held a strong defensive position? At Malvern Hill, Lee had made the mistake of underestimating the enemy, and his frontal assault ended in heavy casualties and failure. On the morning of August 30, the Confederate commander had gone to the opposite extreme and decided not to attack John Pope but to undertake a new campaign of maneuver instead.

There is no evidence McClellan ever considered a frontal attack on Sharpsburg. Nor is there any indication that he intended to allow the Confederate army to withdraw to Virginia unpunished for its foray into Maryland. McClellan endeavored to find a third way. After studying the nasty piece of ground held by Lee's army, he devised a plan of battle that held out the promise of destroying the enemy but offered better odds of success and threatened fewer casualties than a head-on assault.

McClellan fully appreciated the strength of the position Lee had selected. He referred to it as "one of the strongest to be found in this region of the country, which is well adopted to defensive warfare."[46] There were three features of the topography that worked to Lee's advantage. In the first place, the peninsula formed by the confluence of the Antietam and the Potomac was dominated by the divide or high ground bordering the Antietam and running generally north and south. The presence of this ridge meant that a Federal attack made in a westerly direction—anywhere from the mouth of the Antietam to any point northward which the Confederates chose to defend—would likely be excessively bloody and bear an unacceptably high risk of failure. Lee's lines were on or just behind bluffs so near the creek at both the Lower and Middle Bridges as to argue against an attack at either point or anywhere in between. To cross the Antietam, it would be necessary to go upstream to the north and beyond the Confederate position. The solitary advantage the terrain offered McClellan were the bluffs east of the creek, which were slightly higher than those occupied by Lee on the west. The eastern bluffs afforded the longer reach of the Federal artillery an excellent opportunity to dominate the battleground, if the fighting did not move too far from the Antietam.

Second, although the squiggly course of the Potomac measured ten and a half miles from Mercerville on the extreme northern periphery of the battle area to the mouth of the Antietam on the south, those two points were only five and a half miles distant on a straight line. In other words, Lee sat in a crook of the Potomac that allowed him to anchor each end of his line on the river. This meant there was scant possibility of turning either of his flanks. Whether or not Lee had enough infantry and artillery to cover the entire five and a half miles at once was immaterial. The distances involved were so short that at the first sign of a flank movement the Confederates could easily rush troops to fill any interval to the river. Moreover, in the case of Lee's right, a turning movement would mean marching directly into the teeth of Confederate forces approaching from Harpers Ferry.

It is reasonable to assume that the negligible chance for success held out by a turning movement was one of the reasons McClellan did not probe either Confederate flank with his cavalry. Another reason, however, and the third feature of the topography that complicated planning an assault on Lee's position, was the rolling nature of the ground. The deeply cut ravines and widely scattered woods rendered reconnaissance by horsemen largely ineffective. The view McClellan possessed from the bluffs east of the Antietam and from his signal stations in the mountains provided the best intelligence he could hope to acquire of the Confederate position. Even then, although the Federals might catch glimpses of enemy troop movements, there were innumerable places affording screens behind which the size and intentions of the Confederates would remain hidden.[47]

McClellan's assessment of the difficult terrain confronting him undergird the plan of battle he devised. His offensive scheme was—as he believed it needed to be—an inventive one. As originally conceived, McClellan's plan called for an opening attack on one enemy flank. This initial assault was to accomplish two objectives: first, to discover if Lee intended to make a determined stand and to do so in a way less bloody than a frontal assault on the heights of Sharpsburg; and second—if Lee showed determination—to press the Confederates hard enough to make them strip their lines elsewhere in response to the threat. Then, McClellan planned for a follow-up attack several hours later on the opposite flank to take advantage of the thinned enemy ranks. He was willing to accept success where he found it, however, and "whenever either of these flank movements should be successful," he proposed to throw his best troops against what he assumed would be the much weakened enemy center. It was this final blow against the heart of Lee's line on Cemetery Hill—and not either of the flank attacks—which he expected to crush the Confederate army.[48]

McClellan's plan has been inaptly described as a double envelopment—in other words, as an attempt to roll up both wings of the enemy and then punch through the middle. The Federal commander never assumed, however, that he had the numbers necessary to make a double envelopment work successfully. On the contrary, all of the information he possessed indicated he faced a numerically equal foe. As a result, he intended to make probing attacks on each flank that would divert the Confederates' attention and cause them to rearrange and weaken their line. Initially, McClellan did not intend to commit more than a single corps to either flank attack; nor did he propose to launch the attacks simultaneously, or expect to be able to achieve surprise in either.

The position of Confederate troops and the lay of the ground made obvious which flank must be probed first and which second. Only by moving from the north against Lee's left could the Federals hope to cross the Antietam without suffering excessive losses from heavy artillery and musketry fire. Equally obvious, the natural strength of the Confederate right at the Lower Bridge made it unwise to attack there until after it had been weakened by the withdrawal of some of its defenders.

Since each of Lee's flanks rested on the Potomac, McClellan did not expect either attack could succeed as a turning movement to get into the Confederate rear. More modestly, he intended to enfilade the flanks of Lee's main line on Sharpsburg Heights. The opening attack would not continue westward after crossing the Antietam to discover the end of the Confederate line approaching the river. Instead, it would bear to its own left (east), keeping near the creek and aim for the end of the heights at the point where Lee's line turned west in front of the Piper farm. Thus, McClellan's object on the left was the hinge in the Confederate line, where D. H. Hill's division bent from facing the Antietam and ran westward to join the Hagerstown Pike. If the end of the high ground could be gained at this point, the remainder of Lee's line running southward would be rendered untenable.

Although the position might be difficult to carry, there were three decided advantages in trying. Since the attack would be made perpendicularly against Lee's main artillery line facing east, those Confederate guns would not be able to bear fully on the Federal troops. Conversely, by remaining relatively near the Antietam, the Federal columns could reap full advantage from their own heavy guns posted on the bluffs east of the creek, an advantage that would be forfeited if the assault were made too far to the west. Finally, as the attack progressed southward it would uncover the face of the remainder of the Army of the Potomac and free additional corps to join in the attack.

Likewise, McClellan planned that the second attack—the one on the Confederate right—should gain the crest of the bluffs behind the Lower Bridge and then bear to its right (north) to carry the heights from the opposite end. He intended to keep his attacks concentrated within covering range of his own artillery, connected with the remainder of his line, and protected from flank assaults. The plan was designed to attack an enemy believed to be of equal size who was entrenched in a strong defensive position.

Purpose also seems to have guided McClellan's choice of leaders and units to execute his plan. On the morning of the 16th the Federal line was sufficiently compact that he could have designated any corps, or combination of corps, to execute any part of his battleplan without causing undue confusion or delay. McClellan selected Joe Hooker, who had the reputation of being the most aggressive fighter in the army, to lead the risky opening attack from the north; and he chose Ambrose Burnside, probably his closest friend in the army, to command the assault from the south. Of middling and roughly equal strengths (12,000 and 14,000), Hooker's First Corps and Burnside's Ninth Corps were not the most settled units in the Army of the Potomac.[49] The First Corps (which had been McDowell's old Third Corps in Pope's army) had recently suffered heavy casualties at both Second Manassas and South Mountain, and according to Hooker its morale was shaky. Similarly, several divisions of the Ninth Corps had been engaged with significant losses at Second Manassas, Chantilly, and South Mountain; and the corps itself was a recent and as-yet-uncongealed amalgam of forces from scattered departments. Thus, McClellan's assignments for the flank attacks resembled each other in this regard: for both he selected strong commanders and more expendable corps.

He retained in the center to deliver the final, crushing blow Edwin Sumner's Second Corps and Fitz John Porter's Fifth Corps. These were the only corps present from the old Army of the Potomac of the Peninsula campaign and the units he knew best and trusted most. The Fifth Corps (9,000) was still suffering in numbers and morale from its disastrous repulse at Second Manassas just two weeks before, but it contained the division of regulars that McClellan considered the bedrock of the army. The Second Corps (18,000) was the largest and arguably the best corps with the army.

In rear of the center and east of Keedysville, McClellan held Joseph Mansfield's Twelfth Corps (8,000) in reserve. Mansfield, who previously served only in garrison duties, had commanded the army's smallest corps for only two days. Initially, McClellan probably intended to use the Twelfth Corps at whatever point on the line it was most needed.

McClellan had determined at least the broad outlines of his plan by eleven o'clock, when he set out with his staff to visit Burnside and put its first steps into effect. Riding south along the Federal line while the artillery of both armies shook the ground with their duel, he reconnoitered the area around the Lower Bridge with care, going beyond his picket line and drawing the fire of the enemy.

What McClellan found did not please him. Around noon he ordered the Ninth Corps into a new line in preparation for the attack on the morrow. Samuel Sturgis's division was to be brought forward to the rear slope of the high ground opposite the Lower Bridge. Isaac Rodman's division was to be sent a half-mile south to cover the road leading to Snavely's Ford and thus protect the left flank of the army. The divisions of Orlando Willcox and Eliakim Scammon were moved forward in close support. McClellan had the engineers mark the exact spot each unit was to occupy, and then before departing he spent some time discussing with Burnside the role the Ninth Corps was to play on the 17th.[50]

The fact that Burnside's staff did not conduct the various divisions of the Ninth Corps to their new positions until around 3:30 or so—

although it annoyed McClellan when he learned of the late hour and was perhaps an omen of delays to come—curiously worked to the Federal advantage. Lee was presented something of a dilemma when he learned of this move almost simultaneously with the news that a force was crossing the upper Antietam.

Satisfied at the time that his left was now secure and that the Ninth Corps would be well situated for its attack, McClellan rode back to his headquarters tent on the Boonsboro Pike west of Keedysville. Shortly after one o'clock, he sent orders to Hooker, whose First Corps was encamped a half-mile upstream in the forks of the Antietam and Little Antietam, to cross the creek and move into position to attack Lee's left in the morning.

Hooker's initial response was prompt, and his lead division under George Meade left camp by two o'clock.[51] After seeing his men well started, the First Corps commander rode to McClellan's headquarters to protest being sent all alone on a detached mission to attack the enemy. McClellan may have explained in greater detail the role of the First Corps in the larger plan for battle, but he did not commit additional forces to the probing assault on the Confederates' left.[52] Instead, he told Hooker that reenforcements could be requested after the attack had started and that Hooker would be in command of all support sent to him.

When Hooker returned to his corps, he found it moving slowly, and it was after three o'clock before Meade started cautiously crossing the Upper Bridge. According to instructions, Abner Doubleday's division was to ford a quarter-mile downstream, while James Ricketts and the artillery and trains were to follow Meade. The configuration of Hooker's advance suggests that McClellan wanted to put two divisions simultaneously west of the creek to forestall an ambush of the vanguard. After the crossing, Doubleday's division would be in place to dress on the Antietam and thus refuse the left flank of Meade and Ricketts as they advanced south along the western slope of the high ground. Inconveniently, the road from Keedysville to Williamsport, which carried Meade over the Upper Bridge, angled to the northwest and away from Sharpsburg. The column had climbed and descended the first ridge and was starting on the second, with Doubleday tearing down fences and valiantly trying to keep up as he dutifully marched through the rocky fields a hundred yards to the left of the road—but all in the wrong direction—when the Federal commander appeared with his staff to check on the progress of the movement. It is possible that Hooker, if left on his own, would have followed the Williamsport Road all the way to the Hagerstown Pike.

McClellan allowed the second crest to be cleared before he turned the column to the left and directed it south across the Hoffman farm. It was then shortly after four o'clock. Hooker took advantage of the visit to again plead his case for increasing the size of the attacking force, dramatically proclaiming, "the rebels would eat me up." Actually, Hooker would later remember that his dire prediction would come to pass if either he were not reenforced or "if another attack was not made on the enemy's right.[53] Apparently, McClellan did not go beyond the earlier offer that Hooker would be "at liberty" to ask for reenforcements the next day.

After McClellan departed, Meade turned left into the open country, but the contours of the ground carried him southwest, rather than south, and the lead brigade under Truman Seymour eventually struck the Smoketown Road. This small country lane finally channeled the First Corps in a southerly direction, although by this time the column was a mile and a half west of the Antietam. Instead of turning left and filling the interval to the creek, Doubleday's division continued westward. Marsena Patrick's brigade actually crossed Meade's rear, while the three remaining brigades were blocked by Ricketts's division, which followed Seymour down the Smoketown Road. Presumably, Hooker had decided his right flank was more vulnerable than his left and hence transferred Doubleday to the other side of his column. Eventually Patrick came under artillery fire before striking the Hagerstown Pike and halted on the northern edge of the Joseph Poffenberger farm. After dark Doubleday was reunited and his division faced westward along the pike.

With the Bucktails of the 1st Pennsylvania Reserve Rifles thrown forward as skirmishers, Meade advanced down the Smoketown road brushing aside pickets of the 9th Virginia Cavalry and two guns of Pelham's horse battery. Around 4:30, as Seymour crossed the Alfred Poffenberger farm and neared the East Woods, his brigade came under fire from a number of well-placed Confederate guns and from the infantry regiments of Hood's division, which had advanced from the Hagerstown Pike. Both the direction of the Confederate fire and the angle taken by the Smoketown Road—which bends forty-five degrees in the woods to join the Hagerstown Pike—pulled Seymour to the west.

After a spirited contest, Seymour stopped for the night at the western edge of the East Woods, about a half-mile from and facing the

Hagerstown Pike. Meade's other two brigades advanced on Seymour's right and halted on the Joseph Poffenberger farm along the northern edge of the North Woods, but they continued to front south. Immediately in their rear Doubleday faced west. Ricketts lagged somewhat behind and bivouacked on either side of the Smoketown Road in Seymour's rear. As night closed down, Hooker's front was compact, but he was vulnerable on both flanks. He had marched almost four miles, but he had not made much real progress. In its final position, the First Corps was only a mile on a straight line from where he had crossed the Antietam.

It was nearly five o'clock when McClellan recrossed the creek and transferred his headquarters to the Philip Pry farmhouse. The large brick home stood on a hill east of the Antietam, which afforded a panoramic view of the Confederate position at Sharpsburg. Indeed, it adjoined the ridge where Lee had stopped to study the terrain at dawn on the 15th and from which first Hooker and then McClellan himself had examined the enemy lines later the same afternoon. The Federal commander had a little over an hour—until about 6:15—to observe through the failing visibility of an overcast twilight what Lee's reaction would be to the threat posed by Hooker. And, although partially obscured by ravines and forests, a large force of Confederate infantry could be seen marching from south of Sharpsburg to the vicinity of the Dunkard Church. Pinprick flashes and the roll of musketry indicated serious fighting was taking place. The Federal heavy guns opened on the enemy, but the range was extreme and the effect of the shells could not be gauged. Darkness lessened but did not end the fighting, and the flare of bursting shells and burning fuses streaking the night sky set a grand but ominous prologue for the morrow's morning.

Although McClellan did not plan it that way, the lateness of Hooker's movement worked to the Federal advantage. Surprise had never been an objective and likely would not have been possible in any case. As it was, Hooker was now in place for an assault early in the morning, and Lee had all night to worry about the meaning of the various movements of the Army of the Potomac.

At the same time, McClellan himself had come to doubt one part of his plan. Although the repeated pleas of Hooker had not swayed him, the stubborn fighting in the East Woods, combined with the sighting of Confederate troops being transferred to the threatened flank strongly suggested that Lee intended to stand at Sharpsburg. While McClellan might welcome the shifting of enemy troops as a sign that his plan was already working, he had to be concerned that the odds would become too heavy against Hooker in the morning and the Confederates might indeed "eat . . . up" the First Corps. In consequence, not long after reaching the Pry house, McClellan decided to amend his plan and increase the numbers of the column opening the attack from the north.

As reenforcement, McClellan selected another unit he may have considered expendable. He chose the small Twelfth Corps under its newly arrived commander, Joseph Mansfield, which at the moment was the army's only reserve. At 5:50 McClellan sent orders through the wing commander, Edwin Sumner, for the Twelfth Corps to cross the Antietam and to report to Hooker. Sumner was directed to make certain the "artillery, ammunition, and everything else appertaining to the corps, be gotten over without fail to-night, ready for action early in the morning." In addition, Sumner was to have the Second Corps ready to move an hour before daylight, although where it was to march was not specified.[54]

Sumner, who did not wish to see the Twelfth Corps pass from his enlarged command, and who furthermore assumed the destination of the Second Corps would be the same as Mansfield's, requested permission for the two corps to cross the Antietam together that night. McClellan refused, however, to make further changes in his plan of operations before the battle started. The Federal commander was unwilling to commit two-thirds of his army to the opening attack and, at the same time, forfeit the prime striking force from the center. He not only rejected Sumner's request, but he specifically instructed that the Second Corps was not to march in the morning until receiving orders. Around midnight, Mansfield broke camp near Keedysville and set out to follow Hooker's route on the road to Williamsport, which crossed the Upper Bridge. It was around 2:30 in the morning when his two divisions went into camp on the Line and Hoffman farms about a mile and a half in Hooker's rear.

McClellan took one additional step on the evening of the 16th to prepare for the pending battle, and it was related to the shifting of the Twelfth Corps. Apparently, he was now satisfied that a majority of the Confederates at Harpers Ferry had either joined Lee or were on their way to Sharpsburg, and the Sixth Corps could now safely unite with the main body on the Antietam. McClellan ordered Franklin to leave a division to watch any enemy that might remain and march with the rest of his wing to Keedysville. Franklin would fill Mansfield's role as reserve, and the Sixth Corps could be employed to support either flank attack or the final, decisive assault on the center.

After making these adjustments, McClellan may have believed his plan was well launched. Nonetheless, there were serious, potential problems—which neither McClellan nor Hooker seemed to grasp—in the configuration of the forces poised for the opening attack. Not only was Seymour's brigade facing in the wrong direction, but a half-mile gap had opened with the remainder of Meade's division. Moreover, if the entire First Corps continued to dress right on the Hagerstown Pike, Hooker's advance in the morning would carry him about a mile too far west and behind the Antietam bluffs instead of against the hinge in Lee's line near the Piper farm. Hooker ran the risk of moving away from effective Federal artillery cover and the close support of the Second and Fifth Corps in the center.

After nine o'clock, in a light drizzle that had started to fall, Joe Hooker visited his picket line in the East Woods. He found the opposing lines so near the soldiers could hear the tread of the enemy, and a nervous gunfire erupted sporadically in the darkness. He returned to his headquarters in the Joseph Poffenberger barn determined to attack as early in the morning as possible, in order to catch the Confederates before they could be further reenforced. He dispatched a message to McClellan informing him of the decision and once again asked for more men. Curiously, when the Twelfth Corps arrived later in the night, Hooker would not advance it into line, neither would he bring it forward as close support. Since no campfires were allowed in the Army of the Potomac that night, an important opportunity was missed. Lee had no idea of Mansfield's presence.

Lee Accepts Battle at Sharpsburg

On the afternoon of the 16th, the five Virginia regiments of Fitz Lee's cavalry brigade had reunited for the first time in nearly a week and were covering the northern flank of the Confederate army. The 1st, 3d, 4th, and 5th regiments lay in the fields west of the Dunkard Church, resting from the rigors of reconnaissance and escorting trains.[55] The burden of picketing the ground between the Hagerstown Pike and the Antietam fell to the 9th Cavalry. Between 3:00 and 3:30, scouts of the 9th watched

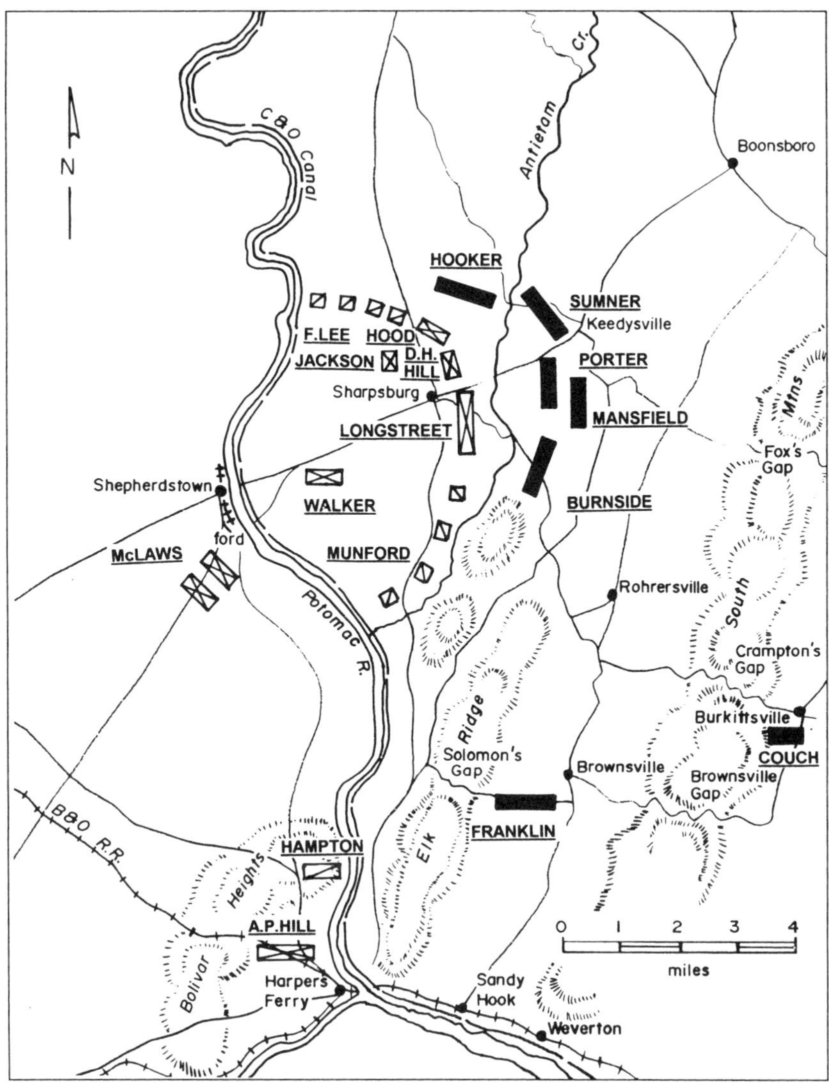

Pre-Antietam maneuvering, September 16

from a nearby cornfield as Doubleday's division splashed across the creek at Pry's Ford. Word was at once sent to Stuart at the Dunkard Church that the enemy was west of the Antietam, and the cavalry chief in turn dispatched a courier to inform Lee.[56]

Stuart's message concluded Lee's conference with Jackson and Longstreet at the Grove house in Sharpsburg. It made moot the study of the maps of Maryland and Washington County. The charts were rolled up and put away, and with them went Confederate hopes for escaping the box at Sharpsburg without a serious battle, or by withdrawing into Virginia. Federal troops west of the Antietam meant that a move to Hagerstown on the Maryland side of the Potomac was now out of the question. Also, the two armies had reached a level of tactical entanglement that virtually predestined heavy fighting.

If Lee had needed only to worry about the threat from the north, his situation would have been simple. His left wing was already relatively strong, with the division of Hood and the brigades of Colquitt and Ripley (D. H. Hill) for a front-line defense and the brigades of Rodes and Garland (D. H. Hill) in reserve along the Hagerstown Pike, totaling some 6,500. The infantry was supported by eighty-one guns, representing over half of the artillery present, and covered by Fitz Lee's brigade, which included nearly three-fourths of the cavalry then on hand.[57] In addition, Lee had the three divisions under Jackson and Walker bivouacked southwest of Sharpsburg available to send to the left if the demand arose.

Unfortunately, Lee had to deal with several other reports that considerably blurred the picture. In the center the artillery fire seemed to have gained in intensity,[58] and word came in at almost the same time that another heavy Federal column was moving on the southern flank toward the Lower Bridge.[59] Threatened at three points at once, Lee initially felt the need to respond to all three. Although it was highly unlikely that McClellan—or any commanding general for that matter—would open a battle with simultaneous assaults on both wings and the center, the threats seemed so imminent that Lee believed he must act, even while determining where the greatest danger lay.

Something of Lee's thinking can be induced from the response he ordered. First, he sent Jackson with the 2,000 men of J. R. Jones's division—the smallest of the three reserve divisions—north to support the left wing. Hence, in terms of size, Lee's initial response to Hooker was minimal, but in sending Jackson, who by seniority would take charge of all the forces on the left, he compensated for the lack of numbers. Second, he sent the division of Lawton (Ewell) of 5,000 men—the largest in reserve—to extend the right flank to the south and guard the Lower Bridge and the ford at Snavely's. Here Lawton would come under the supervision of Longstreet. Finally, Lee kept Walker's division of 4,500 at its bivouac southwest of Sharpsburg as the final reserve, available to be sent wherever needed.[60]

At the same time Lee started the divisions toward the endangered flanks, he also took steps to discover the nature and severity of the threats. Apparently, he could not tell from the first reports of the scouts—perhaps it was wishful doubt—whether the Federals had crossed the upper Antietam with a column of infantry for a serious flank attack or merely with a sizable body of cavalry. He ordered Stuart to uncover the enemy intent, even if it required attacking with Fitz Lee's brigade. Jeb was reluctant to engage a large cavalry force in the rolling and wooded terrain, and he asked his engineer, William Blackford, to take a handful of men to acquire the information for Lee.

Blackford worked his way under cover to the northeast until he reached an observation point from which he turned a "field glass of unusual size and power" on the skirmishers of Seymour's brigade (Meade) as they advanced down both sides of the Smoketown Road. As soon as he could distinguish the light-blue uniform trimming and bayonet scabbards of infantry, Blackford reported the bad news to Stuart. Although Stuart insisted upon being taken forward to confirm the conclusion with his own eyes, word soon was sent to Lee's headquarters that a large column of Federal infantry was advancing on the Smoketown Road.[61]

In some manner, Lee learned that the threat at the Lower Bridge, although real, was not imminent.[62] Something either in the hesitancy of Burnside's movements or the manner in which his troops seemed to go into bivouac for the night when they stopped allowed Lee to judge that the assault would not be made in the waning daylight hours of the 16th. By four o'clock or shortly thereafter he concluded the most pressing danger lay to the north, and he ordered Lawton's division to countermarch and join Jackson at the Dunkard Church.

Hood's small division—2,000 men in nine regiments of the brigades of William Wofford and Evander Law—had enjoyed twenty-four hours' rest from the rigors of the march from Hagerstown, the fighting at South Mountain, and the nocturnal retreat to Sharpsburg. Sent by Lee on the previous evening to strengthen the northern flank on the Hagerstown Pike, the division had bivouacked in the fields and woods around the Dunkard Church. Hood's placement reflected the fluidity Lee wished to maintain on this yet-unthreatened flank, which also represented the potential escape route to Hagerstown. Hood neither extended D. H. Hill's line along the Sunken Road westward toward the Potomac nor even put his men into line of battle. He camped parallel to the Hagerstown Pike, facing east, and was thus prepared to meet danger in any direction or to lead the march northward, if the opportunity arose.

Hood was with Stuart at the Dunkard Church when word came in from the 9th Virginia Cavalry around 3:30 that the Federals were crossing the Antietam. Apparently, he assumed that the enemy would most likely advance by way of the Hagerstown Pike, because he threw skirmishers from Wofford and Law forward to the southern edge of the plowed field beyond the D. R. Miller farm, facing north, dressing their left on the pike and their right in the edge of the East Woods. On the right of Hood's skirmishers, cavalry videttes of the 9th Virginia covered the Smoketown Road and the face of the East Woods, and even farther right a battalion of riflemen from Colquitt's brigade (D. H. Hill) extended the picket line toward the Antietam.

Thus, when Seymour's brigade (Meade) advanced south down the Smoketown Road, chance brought them against the center and the softest part of the Confederate skirmish line. The Pennsylvanians easily swept aside the horsemen and Pelham's two guns, crossed the Samuel Poffenberger farm, and entered the East Woods. As the detachments of the 9th Virginia galloped to the rear, Hood—who had retained his flexibility—swung into action. He moved Wofford's brigade by the left flank northward to the edge of the Miller Cornfield, dressing on the Hagerstown Pike and extending into the edge of the East Woods. Law marched due east through the grassy field in his front until he struck the Smoketown Road; and then, advancing northeast on both sides of the road, he entered the East Woods and formed at right angle to Wofford. Thus, it was the 5th Texas on Wofford's right and the left side of Law's brigade, which engaged Seymour in the spirited contest that lasted from five until darkness at 6:30. Three Confederate regiments stopped the advance of Hooker's First Corps.[63]

Sometime during the early afternoon—before there had been any hint of a developing battle—Jackson's men were roused from their rest in the grove of oaks southwest of Sharpsburg by the regimental bands striking up "Dixie." A thrill rippled through the camp, as Capt. William Poague of the Rockbridge Artillery later recalled, and soon thousands of voices lifted in "soul stirring music" until "harmony rolled and thundered through that little vale." Whether it was spontaneous or some wise head had sensed the need to invigorate the divisions, it worked as a tonic on the weary foot cavalry who had marched and fought more than any other units in the Eastern army since Jackson had launched his Valley campaign in May. By four o'clock, when Stonewall galloped back from Sharpsburg and the drums beat the long roll for assembly, they "felt ready for anything."[64]

As Lawton's division headed almost due east to protect the Lower Bridge, Jackson set out northeastward with J. R. Jones's division across the fields to the west of Sharpsburg. A march of two and a half miles carried Jackson to the Hagerstown Pike in the vicinity of the Dunkard Church by around five o'clock. Hood had vacated the area, and part of his division was already engaged in the East Woods. Jackson immediately formed for battle west of the pike in two lines, facing north. He posted the first line, composed of the brigades of Jones and Winder, as an extension of Wofford's brigade, which held the southern edge of the Miller Cornfield east of the pike, with Winder connecting with Wofford. The second line was drawn up parallel to the first and three hundred yards in its rear, with Taliaferro's brigade dressing on the pike and Starke's brigade immediately in its rear. Poague's Rockbridge Artillery wheeled into battery on a knoll several hundred yards in advance of the first line and engaged the guns of Hooker's corps.[65]

Jones's division did not become engaged after taking position, and it might be asked why the usually aggressive Jackson did not go on the offensive. After the war, Longstreet would point out that Hooker was isolated and vulnerable on the night of the 16th and that Jackson, Hood, and D. H. Hill could have combined to destroy him before help arrived.[66] After noting that Longstreet's hindsight in this instance was considerably more aggressive than the advice he customarily gave to Lee during the war, several pertinent observations can be made. First, Jackson brought only 2,000 men with him to the contest. He was fully cognizant that his four brigades had become two small ones and treated them as such. He adopted a narrow front and put Col. A. J. Grigsby in command of the consolidated first line and Brig. Gen. William Starke in charge of the second. In simplest terms, he did not have enough men to go on the offensive.

Second, he could scarcely have known the size of the Federal forces he faced. Posting his lines to the left of Wofford suggests that Jackson had heard from Stuart that—in addition to the enemy force already engaged in the East Woods—other Federal columns (Doubleday and two brigades of Meade) were advancing westward farther to the north, heading in the direction of the Hagerstown Pike. Hood was in contact with the enemy and not available, and D. H. Hill was too far away to effect coordination in the short time before darkness. Third, due to the threats perceived by Lee from the center and right at the time he issued orders to Jackson, it is entirely possible the Confederate commander himself put restrictions on the actions to be taken by his subordinate. In fine, Hooker had become vulnerable by veering too far from the Antietam, but Jackson had no way of knowing this, nor was he in any position to take advantage of it in any event.

It was nearly six o'clock and darkness was rapidly falling by the time the head of Lawton's division appeared near the Dunkard Church after its detour toward the Lower Bridge. Aware that his left flank was a mile and a half from the Potomac and hanging in the air, Jackson personally posted Early's brigade to face west and connect at right angle with his first line. It was totally dark by the time Hays's brigade was formed behind Early and the brigades of Lawton (Douglass) and Trimble (Walker) bivouacked in reserve in the fields south of the Dunkard Church.[67]

After Jones and Lawton were dispatched to strengthen the flanks and the war council was dismissed at the Grove house, Lee believed the die had been cast for battle. In later years Lee twice insisted that McClellan had "forced" battle on him at Sharpsburg.[68] The Confederate commander had fully intended to attack the Federal army after the Valley supply line had been cleared, his army reunited, and "McClellan was out where he could get at him." Now, the Army of Northern Virginia was still missing a third of its force, and it was McClellan who was doing the attacking. McClellan had shut down the possibility for maneuver in Maryland, and Lee refused to consider the alternative of recrossing into Virginia. All that remained was fighting. The best Lee could hope for was to win the coming battle and to win it in such a way that he could recapture the offensive when it was over.

In point of fact, whether or not Lee seriously considered them, he did possess two options beyond standing to deliver battle at Sharpsburg on the midafternoon of the 16th. It was indeed physically possible for him to withdraw to Virginia. This would be proven two days later, when, in the same hours available on the 16th, he recrossed the Potomac in miserable weather while encumbered with wounded and a larger number of troops and wagons. Second, such a withdrawal need not mean a final abandonment of the campaign, since he could immediately recross the Potomac and return to Maryland at some other point. That Lee recognized this second option existed would also be demonstrated two days later, when he adopted exactly this plan.

He must have believed that to leave Maryland now—for any reason—would be premature. Understanding that much of war is a trial of wills between opposing commanders, Lee refused to acknowledge tactical defeat even for strategic gain. From the start this campaign had aimed at delivering the final, crushing blow to Northern morale. He could not discourage his army and inspirit the enemy by allowing himself to be chased ignominiously from Maryland. He would not leave "without a struggle."[69] The stakes were too high.

Moreover, it is clear that Lee did not decide to stand at Sharpsburg believing he would be defeated or even that he would be forced to fight a drawn battle. He expected his army would be reunited in time for the start of the fighting in the morning, and he expected to win.

Lee spent the remainder of the 16th and many of the hours past midnight doing all that he could to prepare for every foreseeable contingency. He was concerned that the ammunition and subsistence at Shepherdstown be quickly and easily available to the army; and, no doubt, prudence also compelled him to prepare for a possible hasty retreat. There was little he could do to improve the rough passage of the Potomac at Boteler's, the only ford now open to the Confederates, but he could facilitate the crossing of the C&O Canal. He sent the following untimed orders through his adjutant to General Pendleton, who commanded the reserve artillery battalion and a small infantry force at the ford:

> The commanding general wishes you to have constructed immediately a wide bridge over the canal opposite the ford. You can either do it by making a bridge on a level with the tow-path or by digging the banks on either side so as to pass down and up easily, causewaying the bottom so as to make the crossing easy.
>
> [P.S.] Captain Johnson, Engineer, is sent forward, who will attend to the construction of the bridge.[70]

Two things Lee did not mention to Pendleton are of equal interest. First, he did not order Brown's Battalion of the Artillery Reserve (twenty guns) to be withdrawn from Light's Ford two miles below Williamsport, even though Hooker's advance had now blocked that crossing as an exit from Maryland for the Confederate army. This is a clue that as early as the 16th Lee valued Light's Ford for a possible quick reentry into Maryland should he be compelled to beat a tactical retreat. Second, he did not order Pendleton to send any of the guns from the two reserve battalions to the battlefield for the coming fight. Although it is true there were more than enough short-range guns at Sharpsburg, the dueling on both the 15th and 16th had demonstrated Lee's woeful lack of rifled pieces, and there were ten or more rifles with Pendleton.[71] It can only be speculated that at this time Lee felt the guns could be most usefully employed in guarding the fords against enemy cavalry raids. Moreover, it seems likely there was a lost message in which Lee directed Pendleton to have the captured guns and ammunition forwarded from Harpers Ferry.[72]

In a related matter of logistics, sometime during the late afternoon or evening, Lee ordered the return of at least some of the ordnance and subsistence trains from Shepherdstown. The wagons did not arrive before two or three o'clock in the morning, and they may have been held up by Pendleton's bridge building on the canal.[73]

In the two matters that ought to have been Lee's greatest concern—hastening the reunion of his army and strengthening his front lines at Sharpsburg—there is no evidence he took any additional steps for four or five hours after dispatching Lawton and Jones to meet the threats to the flanks. It may be he was awaiting further information to fully evaluate the tactical situation; and, in addition, he had no word on how near the divisions of McLaws and Anderson were to Sharpsburg.[74] Whatever the explanation, Lee seems to have been roused to action by an unusual request he received. Around eight o'clock John Hood rode up to headquarters and made an appeal that must have sounded strange coming from one of the hardest hitting division commanders in the army. He asked that his two brigades be relieved by fresh troops. Lee could not have failed but be impressed that Hood was so fully persuaded a fierce struggle was imminent and that his justly famous fighters would not give a good account of themselves in it.

Hood explained that his men had been "without food for three days, except a half ration of beef for one day, and green corn." Lee sympathized and may have promised the wagons would return during the night, but he had to tell Hood there were no troops that could be spared to relieve his brigades. Although McClellan had clearly committed to battle along the Smoketown Road—and the picket firing that continued into the night could probably be heard by the generals as they spoke—Lee refused to send Walker's division, his last reserve, to the left wing. Hood would have to find Jackson and see if he could provide relief.

Off into the darkness rode Hood on the task he must have found personally distasteful. After considerable difficulty, he found Jackson already asleep by the roots of a large tree. Hood awakened him and explained the situation. Yes, Stonewall responded, he had two brigades in reserve and would order Lawton (Douglass) and Trimble (Walker) to advance at once and relieve the hungry men. He extracted from Hood the promise of prompt support on the morrow, if it should be needed. There are two interesting points about this famous episode that have escaped comment. First, without seeming hesitation the two commanders agreed to one of the most difficult of military operations, to exchange, in the middle of the night, troops already in close contact with the enemy. Second, it reflected the ambiguity remaining in the command structure of the Army of Northern Virginia that Jackson doubted his own seniority would be sufficient to insure Hood's prompt support.

The interview between Jackson and Hood probably occurred around 9:00 and by 10:00 the vanguard of Lawton's Georgians under Marcellus Douglass were replacing the Texas brigade on the southern edge of the Miller Cornfield. During the next hour Trimble's brigade under James Walker relieved Law's men in the East Woods and plowed field on the right. Apparently, the delicate operation went off without a hitch, except the exchange no doubt heightened the nervousness of the pickets on both sides and contributed to the rumors that night attacks were made.

After putting his men into camp behind the Dunkard Church, Hood set out to find their rations and cooking utensils. Although the general blamed his troubles solely on the darkness, it is likely his wagons did not return from Shepherdstown until well after midnight. By the time he found them and got them forward, the battle, which broke with the dawn, prevented many of his men from cooking the dough they prepared.[75]

Although Lee had refused to commit John Walker's division to the left, Hood's visit may have awakened in the Confederate commander a keener awareness of his weakness for the coming battle. Not long after eight o'clock, he took a number of steps to improve his position. First, he ordered D. H. Hill to march Ripley's brigade from its position at the hinge in the Confederate line in front of the Piper farm to the northwest to protect the right flank of the new line that had been formed to oppose Hooker. Ripley advanced nearly a mile across open fields to the Mumma farm, faced his brigade due east toward the Antietam, and connected with the right of Law's brigade, before the latter was replaced by Trimble.[76]

Thus, in the final configuration adopted for the left flank on the night of the 16th—in a design too perfect to be coincidental—Lee formed a half-mile horseshoe protecting the Hagerstown Pike and its juncture with the Smoketown Road at the Dunkard Church. This highly unusual salient at the end of a battleline was probably intended to economize strength and to permit a flexible response to the enemy's main thrust wherever it might fall in the morning. Still, it left a gap of almost a mile unprotected between Jackson and the Potomac. After dark Stuart posted Pelham's horse battery in the middle of this ground on a dominating hill behind the Nicodemus farmhouse and advanced Fitz Lee's brigade to the rear slope of the hill as support. It is possible that the purpose of this formation—at least in part—was to create a trap. If the Federals smashed through Stuart's line to turn the Confederate left flank, they would find the Potomac on their right and the brigades of Early and Hays on their left.[77]

About the same time as the readjustment of Ripley's position, Lee also took steps to bring forward the various units absent from the field. Orders issued through Longstreet recalled the 11th Georgia (G. T. Anderson) and the 15th and 17th Georgia (Toombs) from their duty of guarding the wagontrains at Williamsport and Martinsburg.[78] More importantly, since nothing had yet been heard from McLaws, a second set of hurry-up orders was dispatched to the tardy forces from Pleasant Valley.

LaFayette McLaws seems not to have understood as fully as did Stonewall Jackson the depths of the crisis facing the Confederate army. Certainly, McLaws faced a plenitude of problems to distract him.[79] He had reached the Harpers Ferry pontoon bridge with his trains (including his wounded) in the lead and was ready to cross on the afternoon of the 15th. A long stream of paroled Federal prisoners were being pushed across the bridge into Maryland and prevented him from passing more than a portion of his wagons at random intervals. With Franklin threatening from the rear, and fearful that the enemy prisoners would reveal the Confederates were vulnerably bunched at the river, McLaws reformed a defensive line at the lower end of Pleasant Valley. Not until two o'clock in the morning was the way clear for the passage across the Potomac of the remainder of his wagons and the ten brigades in his and R. H. Anderson's divisions. The bridge had been damaged by the escaping Federal cavalry column the previous night and kept breaking into sections, causing delays until repaired. Once on the other side, he found the streets of Harpers Ferry clogged with men and vehicles that impeded his progress, and in the confusion he could locate no rations for his men.

It was at this point that McLaws, tired and likely much bothered, seems to have forgotten the injunction from Jackson almost precisely twenty-four hours before to rejoin the main body quickly. At eleven o'clock on the morning of the 16th, McLaws bivouacked his troops at Halltown, while he rode six miles west to Charlestown to see to the care of his wounded and to try to find food. He was thus engaged, when Lee's noontime order to hasten to Sharpsburg reached him. Returning to Halltown, McLaws broke camp by three o'clock in the afternoon. There was considerable grumbling among the men over the interruption of their rest and at missing their share of the booty from the capture of Harpers Ferry.[80]

As the column marched northwest on the Shepherdstown Road, the word somehow got abroad that Winchester was the destination. The idea of the friendly security and abundance of the Shenandoah Valley appealed to the discontented, and the rumor restored morale. As the gray twilight began to gather, thoughts turned homeward and thousands of voices lifted in the harmony of plantation songs, and "Rock the Cradle, Julie" and "We're Gwying Down the Newbury Road" echoed through the bordering forests. Six miles out from Halltown the vanguard came to a fork in the road, and the leading ranks were struck dumb with the realization they were heading toward the Potomac once more. Regiment by regiment, the column fell silent as it turned toward Maryland.[81]

With not even the last quarter-moon to light their way on this cloudy, misting night, McLaws called a halt to their creeping progress at about nine o'clock and put his men into camp. He believed he was about two miles from Boteler's Ford. It was some two hours later when Lee's second order reached him. This time the mandate was peremptory: McLaws and Anderson must immediately join the army. Around midnight—as a young ensign of the 32d Virginia would recall forty-four years later—the "very unwelcome, everlasting long roll" sounded, and the colonels rode about exhorting the groggy troops, "Hurry up, men! Hurry! Everything depends on being at the ford by daybreak." With but two miles to cover, McLaws did better than that. His van reached the river by 2:30 or so, and with soldiers holding torches to light the way, his men began the final, soggy chapter of this long and memorable night.[82]

It may be that the returning courier assured Lee that McLaws was at the Potomac three miles away and should easily arrive at Sharpsburg by dawn. This would explain why the Confederate commander was finally willing to commit his last reserves on the field to his front line. At three o'clock he ordered Walker's division from its camp southwest of the town to proceed due east across the Harpers Ferry Road to the ford of the Antietam on the Snavely farm, over a mile below the Lower Bridge.[83]

One uncertainty remained. Would A. P. Hill's division be up from Harpers Ferry in time? Lee would later recall that he "had hoped" Hill would arrive at Sharpsburg by the night of the 16th.[84] But, apparently, some confusion had developed along the chain of command. Since the bulk of the paroling was finished early on the 16th and the securing of captured property could have been completed by a small fraction of the division, there was no reason Hill could not have left during the afternoon. Moreover, since the firing along the Antietam was audible at Harpers Ferry, Hill had cause to hasten his departure. Yet, although Hill prepared his command for the march, there is no evidence he intended to leave before he had received orders to do so. Perhaps the continuing presence of a large Federal force (Franklin's Sixth Corps) in Pleasant Valley reminded him that his division was the sole protection against an enemy turning movement and the disruption of the Confederate supply lines.

After a night of worry over the multiple threats along the Antietam, Lee was prepared to abandon the communications he had just opened. Between three and four—well before any Confederate intelligence could have reported Franklin's 5:30 departure to join McClellan—the Confederate commander dispatched a courier to Harpers Ferry with instructions for A. P. Hill to bring the Light Division to Sharpsburg. The summons would arrive at 6:30 and within an hour Hill would be on the road. A long, hot march and an uncertain arrival time lay ahead.[85]

With the orders to A. P. Hill, Lee had done all that he could do to prepare. Around four o'clock, the head of McLaws's weary column approached Sharpsburg on the road from Shepherdstown, and McLaws rode forward to report in person.[86] Impressed by the urgency of his summons, McLaws later recalled his surprise that at this early hour there were neither signs nor sounds of a battle starting or that one had occurred the day before. When he entered the sleeping village, he could find no one who could tell him anything, even where to find Lee. Returning to rejoin his column, McLaws encountered Longstreet and staff, who were approaching Sharpsburg from the west. Longstreet promptly asserted his control over Anderson's division, ordering that it immediately be sent to a hill just beyond the town,[87] but he did not attempt to give instructions to McLaws, beyond pointing out that Lee's headquarters were in a grove along the Shepherdstown Road three-quarters of a mile west of Sharpsburg. On the way to Lee's tent, McLaws next encountered Jackson, who ordered him to post his division on the far right of the Confederate line. When McLaws finally reached army headquarters, Lee countermanded Jackson's order and directed the four brigades be held on the Shepherdstown Road.[88]

There are several interesting points to be drawn from this seemingly trivial episode. First, although McLaws is always listed in organizational charts as part of Longstreet's command during the Maryland campaign, he apparently was not under Longstreet's orders either prior to or on the 17th, and Jackson apparently assumed that he retained control of the forces engaged in the Valley expedition. Second, while Jackson may not have been aware that Walker's division had been sent to the far right about an hour earlier, even so, he was more concerned about the threat to the Lower Bridge than to his own front on the Hagerstown Pike. Third, with the separation of the two divisions for different destinations, R. H. Anderson's division became Longstreet's particular reserve, while McLaws's became Lee's, or a general reserve for the army. And, of greatest interest, Lee sent neither division to confront the attack by Hooker. This is yet another sign that Lee initially worried as much about his center and right as he did about his left. When daylight broke on the 17th, Lee was holding over a quarter of the forces he had at hand in general reserve; and, if the two brigades of Jackson (Early and Hays) and two of D. H. Hill (Rodes and Garland) that were not on the front line are included, then the total in reserve increases to over a third.

The posting of the Army of Northern Virginia at the start of the Battle of Antietam did not mirror the certainty of a general who had read and understood his opponent's mind. If Lee faced with calmness the reckoning that was to come at dawn, his peace of mind derived from his trust in the troops he commanded and his belief that the realities of this unequal war required him to chance his army in Maryland—and not from any insight into the intentions of McClellan.

CHAPTER NINE

"A hard day's work before us"

Lee's Bloodiest Day, September 17, 1862

When Lee awoke for the morning shortly after four o'clock, the weather was as uncertain as the fate of his army and the future of the Confederate cause. While the light drizzle had ceased, the air was warm and moist, and clouds shuttered tightly the black night sky. The scant rain had scarcely laid the deeply cumulated dust, and the coming day promised to be oppressively hot and humid if the sun broke through its shroud. Of course, Lee could not foresee what lay in store for the next fourteen hours. He could not know that his army stood on the verge of the bloodiest day in its four-year history or that it would stare into destruction's face four times before darkness again enfolded the Maryland countryside. But he did know that his offensive options had been taken away, and he recognized that he must perforce stand on the defensive and receive the blows of his foe. He could at this time see no way to regain control of his campaign. As a servant pulled on his boots for him and buttoned his tunic, it may have bemused Lee to compare his personal incapacity with his strategic helplessness.

Before Lee had finished his morning toilet, an aide announced the arrival of LaFayette McLaws from Harpers Ferry. Lee at once threw back the tent flap and hailed the dismounting Georgian, "Well, General, I am glad to see you." After briefly thanking McLaws for his part in the capture of Harpers Ferry, Lee went on—with perhaps the barest hint of reproach for the delayed arrival—"but we have I believe a hard day's work before us." It was then that Lee directed McLaws to bring his division down the Shepherdstown Road and halt it a quarter-mile short of the headquarters, "as the shells of the enemy fall about here." The men were to rest until needed. Diplomatically, McLaws pointed out that he had just been ordered by Jackson to take position on the right of the line. "Never mind that order," Lee replied, "but do as I told you and consider yourself especially under my orders."

McLaws rode off to relay Longstreet's orders to R. H. Anderson and then to rejoin his own division. He issued the barest minimum of instructions to his subordinates and thereafter lay down exhausted to fall asleep in the tall grass by the side of the road.[1]

After McLaws departed, Lee turned to another matter that was still playing on his mind. At 4:30 he sent a one-sentence dispatch to Pendleton: "I desire you to keep some artillery guarding each of the fords at Williamsport, Falling Waters, and Shepherdstown, and have some infantry with it if possible."[2] Since Pendleton had already been directed to guard these fords, it is uncertain why Lee felt compelled to repeat the orders. It is also curious that Lee continued to focus on the need to occupy Williamsport now that his road to that town was blocked by the Federal force on the Hagerstown Pike. It is possible the Confederate commander simply wanted to protect his rear against enemy cavalry raids by the forces from Hagerstown and Chambersburg. It seems likely, however, that he already had in mind the last-resort ploy to reenter Maryland at Williamsport should the luck of battle at Sharpsburg force him back into Virginia. It is also not clear where Lee believed Pendleton might come by infantry support, unless by commandeering stragglers as they chanced by.[3]

Such, apparently, were the thoughts that occupied the attention of Robert E. Lee as the Battle of Sharpsburg erupted.

Around 5:15 objects first became dimly distinguishable in the gray dawning. Musket fire—which had continued in a desultory patter throughout the night—suddenly flared north of Sharpsburg, signaling that the pickets in the East Woods and across the fields of the D. R. Miller farm were already probing each other. Within fifteen minutes the brightening light made distant targets visible, and the musketry then swelled into the rolling crash of regimental lines banging away at one another. Almost at once the small arms fire was reduced to background chatter by the ground trembling boom of a hundred cannon from Federal artillery on both sides of the creek. And so started Antietam with the overwhelming, deafening din that would characterize the next twelve hours and that would become the enduring memory for many of the soldiers who survived the most sanguinary day of the war.[4]

Lee probably heard the opening roar of the guns, while still at his tent on the Shepherdstown Road.[5] In his role as defender he was forced to guess the battleplan of the attackers. He could have had no authentic reports on enemy movements at the Middle or Lower Bridges at this time, since there were no such movements. It was possible, therefore, that McClellan intended simply a major assault from the north to turn or smash the Confederate left. But it was equally possible that McClellan wanted Lee to believe just that and weaken the Confederate line elsewhere to meet the threat from the north. With the Middle Bridge already in Federal hands and a large Federal force within dashing distance of the Lower Bridge, Lee dared not ignore the possibility that the attack along the Hagerstown Pike was a diversion to distract his attention.

In any case, Confederate fortunes on the left were in good hands. Jackson had held Pope's army at bay for two days at Manassas; and with Hood's division in reserve and several brigades of D. H. Hill nearby, affairs on the left could take care of themselves for the time being. Lee decided to return to his old observation post at Cemetery Hill. His decision to direct the battle from the right-center of his line is a curious affirmation of McClellan's plan of battle. Lee's presence opposite the Middle Bridge suggests that he was indeed still worried about the ultimate intentions of his opponent.

The Opening Attack by Hooker, 5:15 to 9:00 A.M.

Around five o'clock, when there was but the barest hint of a lighter sky above the rim of South Mountain, Joseph Hooker, accompanied by George Meade, left his quarters in the Joseph Poffenberger barn and rode to the far edge of the North Woods. The rain had ceased, but there would be no rosy dawn this day. Within fifteen minutes, while Hooker studied the ground in the brightening grayish light, the battle flared between Seymour and Walker (Trimble) in the East Woods and southern half of the D. R. Miller Cornfield. Within another fifteen minutes the First Corps artillery on Poffenberger Hill and the heavy reserve guns across the Antietam opened their duel with the Confederate artillery under Stuart on Nicodemus Hill and the guns of S. D. Lee on the high plateau opposite the Dunkard Church. At 5:30 Hooker cast the die for his attack.

The Federal corps commander decided his object would be the high flat ground from which S. D. Lee's artillery battalion was clearly visible almost a mile directly south in his front.[6] This plateau (on which the small white Dunkard Church was located) was truly a critical point. The ground to its front (east) fell away sharply to form the dale in which lay the Sunken Road and the hinge in D. H. Hill's line, meant to cover the flank of the bluffs crowning the Antietam. With this plateau in Confederate hands, a Federal assault could not have succeeded against the hinge

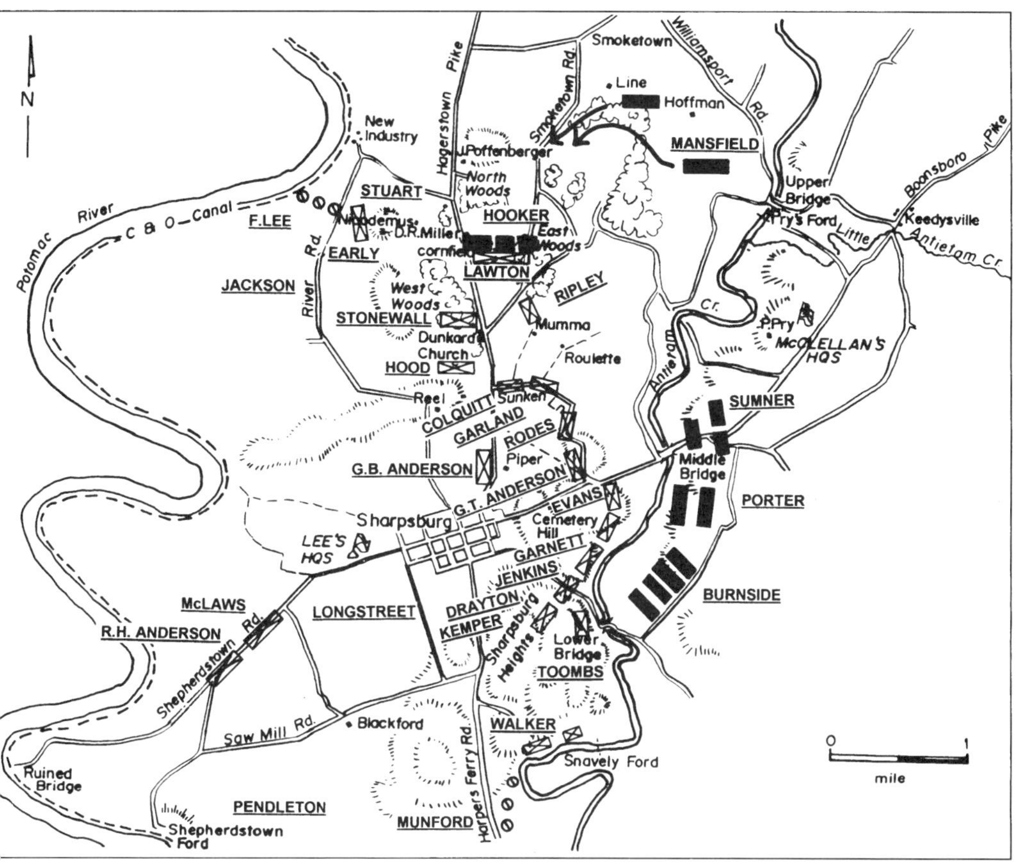

Battle of Sharpsburg, September 17, first phase

in Lee's line. Once it was occupied by the Federals, however, an attack on the Sunken Road almost could not fail. Unfortunately for Hooker, in order to get to the plateau, he had first to dispose of the salient Jackson had constructed a half-mile in its front for its protection.

Hooker could not have known the precise configuration of the Confederate squared mule shoe that awaited him, but he should have known he confronted a battleline and not the flank of the enemy.[7] He determined upon a two-pronged attack that—because the Smoketown Road angled southwestward to join the Hagerstown Pike at the Dunkard Church—would converge on the plateau. Seymour's brigade would advance southwest along the Smoketown Road, supported by Ricketts's division, while Doubleday's division, leaving one brigade facing west to refuse the right flank, would advance south with its right dressed on the Hagerstown Pike. The remaining two brigades of Meade's division would be held in reserve in the center. At the time these orders went out at about 5:30, Hooker also called for Mansfield to advance the Twelfth Corps to the front. The ferocity of the battle that followed may have taken even Hooker by surprise. In the two hours it took Mansfield to pull trigger, the First Corps was wrecked.

If Hooker failed to anticipate fully the fierce combat that would erupt when he tried to seize the Dunkard Church plateau, he was guilty of naively assuming the Confederates did not recognize the key to the defense of their entire line. Jackson must have been pleased when he saw the enemy intended to assail his salient directly on its face and upper right shank. Shortly after daybreak, he swung his left flank 180 degrees to the north by sending Early's brigade to support Stuart and the artillery on Nicodemus Hill. This position now became doubly important, as it allowed the Confederates to enfilade the western flank of the Federals advancing on both the Smoketown Road and the Hagerstown Pike; and it subjected them to a cross fire from the guns of S. D. Lee to the south.

From 5:30 until 6:00, the fighting was limited to the 900 Pennsylvanians in Seymour's Brigade and the 700 Alabamians, Georgians, and North Carolinians in Trimble's (Walker) Brigade in and near the East Woods.[8] Around six o'clock the 2,200 men in the brigades of Gibbon, Phelps, and Patrick of Doubleday's division, advancing along the eastern border of the Hagerstown Pike, reached the D. R. Miller farm buildings and engaged the 1,100 men in Lawton's (Douglass) brigade.[9] Seizing the opportunity thus presented, the 800 men in the first line of Jackson's division under J. R. Jones advanced obliquely to the Hagerstown Pike and poured a flank fire into Gibbon. Doubleday responded by throwing Patrick and half of Gibbon west of the pike and advancing Phelps to the left to connect with Seymour in the East Woods.[10]

It was at this point that the Battle of Antietam took on a life of its own, changing into the bestial savagery that characterized the entire morning and yielded the bloodiest day of the war. Jackson had never intended to mount a stationary defense of the plateau. His men had dug no trenches, nor had they thrown up even light breastworks for cover. Apparently, the whole point of the salient had been to afford Jackson the mobility to hurl his regiments against the attacking Federals. The nature of the battle that resulted was thus preordained. Offense and defense merged into one, as both Federals and Confederates became simultaneously the aggressors. Charge met charge and countercharge as each side poured their immediate reserves into the struggle.

By 6:30 Jackson had advanced his second line west of the pike and thrown Hays's brigade forward to fill a hole that opened between Lawton (Douglass) and Trimble (Walker). Hooker had brought Ricketts's division to the assistance of Seymour and committed Magilton and Anderson of Meade to the center. On a 500-yard front, 5,000 Confederates and 8,700 Federals delivered and stood to endure withering volleys of musketry, while each suffered heavily under the cross fire of the other's artillery. Of the 13,682 men engaged, 4,368 were casualties by seven o'clock, a staggering 32 percent.[11]

Yet the damage was far greater than the casualty lists suggest, for by no means did 68 percent of the men remain. With the command structures at all levels shattered, with a huge stream of stragglers flowing to the rear (including the uninjured helping wounded comrades), and with the smoke and confusion that engulfed the Cornfield and the East and West Woods, Jackson's two divisions had temporarily ceased to exist, and the skeleton that remained of the First Corps had not only lost all offensive punch, but it was incapable of withstanding another serious attack from its foe.

The slender evidence extant suggests that Jackson did not call upon Lee for reenforcements to meet the crisis that had developed on the left by seven o'clock. At the end of the morning's first phase, Stonewall still had cards of his own to play. He ordered Jubal Early to return with his brigade from the support of the artillery on Nicodemus Hill. Early was to replace Jackson's division (J. R. Jones), which had lost every general officer and had been reduced to 300 men under Col. Andrew Grigsby of the 27th Virginia. Early would also have to find and take command of the remnants of Ewell's division (Lawton), as a badly wounded Alexander Lawton had already been carried from the field. It would be Early's job to hold the left of the line west of the Hagerstown Pike.

To restore the empty right of the line along the Smoketown Road and in the East Woods, Jackson requested D. H. Hill to advance from the Sunken Road and vicinity. Hill, who understood the vital role his division played in covering the hinge in the Confederate line and securing the northern flank of the heights of Sharpsburg, had previously refused to commit more than Ripley's brigade to the support of Jackson's salient. Now, with catastrophe imminent, Hill ordered forward both Ripley and Colquitt and rode off in search of Lee for authorization to employ his other three brigades as well.

To fill the yawning hole in the center of the line where Lawton's brigade (Douglass) had held the Cornfield, Jackson summoned Hood, who was resting in the rear of the Dunkard Church, to redeem his pledge of the evening before.[12] When the call for help reached Hood's division, half of its men were still cooking the food and coffee that had taken all night to reach the front. Shortly after seven, with Law's brigade on the right and the Texas brigade on the left, the division marched east across the Hagerstown Pike and then wheeled to the northeast. Passing over the retreating fragments of Lawton (Douglass) and Trimble (Walker), Hood's 2,000 officers and men broke into the double-quick trot and slammed into the frazzled remnants of the First Corps in the now-bloody Cornfield and East Woods. At about the same time, Jubal Early formed his brigade at right angles to Doubleday's line in the West Woods. Hooker's First Corps, threatened from the west and smote in front, yielded the ground it had gained.

Although Law's brigade stalled after a modest advance in the East Woods, the Texas brigade (Wofford) swept through the Cornfield and sent units of Doubleday and Meade reeling back toward the North Woods. The uneven advance of the two brigades opened a gap; and, as Wofford emerged from the Cornfield into the grassy meadow in front of the Miller farmhouse, his right flank was in the air. Unluckily, at this moment, Early responded to orders to return to the Dunkard Church and marched his brigade to the south. Thus, the pressure was removed from Doubleday's right, so that the Federal forces west of the pike fell back only a short distance. Hence, Wofford found himself in a cul-de-sac and receiving fire from the front and both flanks simultaneously.

At this juncture critical for Federal fortunes, Hooker called for the support of the Twelfth Corps, which had been creeping forward along the Smoketown Road from its bivouac only a mile to the rear. Alpheus Williams's lead division of 4,700, fat with regiments in uniform less than a month, struck southwestward from the Smoketown Road and passed through the open fields between the North and East Woods and turned south to confront Hood. Gordon's brigade attacked Wofford in the Cornfield, while Crawford advanced into the Confederate gap in the center and struck Law in the East Woods. By now, Wofford's brigade, after engaging in a "contest rarely equaled in warfare" and suffering 64 percent casualties, including the 82 percent of the 1st Texas—the highest percentage casualties of any regiment in any battle of the Civil War—had melted into nothing.[13] Once again the center of Jackson's line could offer no resistance to its enemy.

Gordon's brigade and the right of Crawford's advanced cautiously over the blood-soaked ground strewn with human wreckage. With the confusion of the field, and the unsteadiness of the two-thirds of the men and officers who were utterly green, the division lost its cohesion. Finally, Williams was stalled in the Cornfield by half his numbers, when the 2,700 Confederates in the brigades of Ripley and Colquitt from D. H. Hill's division arrived to block his further progress.

The hapless Twelfth Corps lost overall coordination when its commander, Joseph Mansfield, fell mortally wounded shortly after 7:30 while posting the left of Crawford's brigade along the Smoketown Road in the East Woods. Consequently, George Greene's small division of 2,500 men was not deployed until forty-five minutes after Williams. Greene was weakened by a third when Goodrich's brigade was sent west across the Hagerstown Pike to confront the threat from Early, which no longer existed. About 8:15 the remaining two brigades, Tyndale and Stainrook, formed on Crawford's left and extended through and beyond the East Woods to the east.

At the same time, additional Confederate support appeared. Garland's brigade (McRae) of 750 men, the third of the reenforcements from D. H. Hill, arrived in the East Woods to relieve Law. The North Carolinians under McRae had not recovered from their mauling three days earlier at Fox's Gap; and, when one of their officers loudly observed that the Federal line extended well beyond their right flank, the demoralized brigade broke in confusion. The panic spread to the left, as each regiment saw the troops on its right retire, and by 8:30 the entire Confederate line east of the Hagerstown pike had peeled away.

At the height of Hood's fight, Jackson dispatched Sandie Pendleton, his only staff officer on the field, to "go forward and see how it goes." Pendleton set out on a mile ride to the front through "bullets whistling" so thick he "could almost see them," and from which he "never expected to come back alive." He found Hood, who said, "Tell General Jackson unless I get reinforcements I must be forced back." Stonewall now had no choice but to seek help, and he sent Pendleton to relay the message to Lee.[14]

About the same time, D. H. Hill drew a similar conclusion. Even the arrival of his last two brigades (Rodes and G. B. Anderson) would not be enough to secure victory on the left flank. Hill sent his adjutant, Maj. J. W. Ratchford, to army headquarters with a plea for additional troops.[15]

Thus, a little over two hours after the start of the battle, two staff officers were galloping toward Lee with the news that the left had collapsed for a second time. Once again the Cornfield, East Woods, and Hagerstown Pike had no Confederate defenders. Once again the way to the Dunkard Church plateau lay open to the enemy. But this time Jackson had no one left to plug the hole. If help were to come, it must come from Lee.

Fortunately for the Confederates, a lull settled temporarily over the left, the first break in three hours of desperate struggle. In this second phase of the fighting, the Federals had added 7,900 men of the Twelfth Corps to the conflagration; and the Confederates had poured in 5,400 in the five brigades of Hood and D. H. Hill. Of these 13,000 fresh troops, 4,300 were casualties—a percentage of 32.4, slightly higher than in the first phase. In all, during the three hours, 27,000 men had struggled over the same 160 acres and 8,700 (32.2 percent) had fallen.

Unfortunately for the Confederates, the Federals now held a much better position than before the intervention of Hood and the brigades from D. H. Hill. Most of Williams's shattered division was useless for the remainder of the day, but Greene's division of the Twelfth Corps remained disciplined and relatively fresh. While Goodrich's detached brigade secured the Federal right flank west of the Hagerstown Pike, Greene with his other two brigades moved across the fields to the east and parallel to the Smoketown Road, until he reached the Mumma farm buildings. Here he halted to replenish his ammunition.

With 1,700 men, Greene had thus advanced into the Mumma dale and was resting at the foot of the eastern slope of the Dunkard Church plateau. One of the new regiments of Crawford's brigade, the 125th Pennsylvania, with over 900 men and as strong as many brigades on either side, had lost its way and wandered down the Smoketown Road, crossed the Hagerstown Pike, and now held the Dunkard Church and the woods immediately thereabout. Even more threateningly, Federal artillery had moved onto the plateau itself. A superbattery of thirty-six guns, collected from the First, Second, and Twelfth Corps, formed a 300-yard line from the southern edge of the East Woods to the northern tip of the plateau opposite the Dunkard Church. Most ominously of all, the Second Corps, the biggest and generally most seasoned corps in the Army of the

Potomac, was on the march to the left. Its lead division under Sedgwick, 5,600 strong, was already approaching the East Woods.

The only good news for the Confederates was that all of these enemy units—Greene, the 125th Pennsylvania, the artillery, and Sedgwick—were facing in the wrong direction. During the first three hours of the battle and in spite of poor coordination and frequent setbacks, Joe Hooker had at least doggedly focused on the capture of the plateau that would secure the flank of a Federal assault on the hinge in Lee's line and from which artillery could fire on the rear of the Confederate guns on Cemetery Hill. Between 8:30 and 9:00 Hooker had been forced to leave the field because of a painful foot wound, and temporarily no one took his place in overall command on the Federal left.[16] The rudderless Federal attack was drawn off course by the angle in the Smoketown Road, the westward retreat of the Confederates in the direction of the West Woods, and the fire from the guns of Stuart and S. D. Lee, which were all now west of the pike.

All morning the axis of battle had run east-west, with the Federals facing south and the Confederates facing north. Shortly before nine o'clock, the axis rotated ninety degrees to stretch north-south, with the Federals facing west and the Confederates facing east. After securing the coveted plateau the Federals had turned their backs on it. Still, if Edwin Sumner employed his 15,000-strong Second Corps with a minimum of skill, it ought not matter whether he attacked to the west or to the south. With barely 1,200 Confederates under Early in line to the west, and but 2,000 in the last two brigades of D. H. Hill to the south along the Sunken Road, Sumner must surely punch through, whichever direction he chose. Whether Lee's line were broken at the hinge or enveloped on the flank, the Confederate position on the Antietam bluffs would be taken in the rear. By nine o'clock, McClellan's plan was on the verge of victory—although not as originally planned—and this was before Burnside had even stirred from his bivouac in front of the Lower Bridge.

Lee and the Morning Crises on the Left, 5:30 to 9:30 A.M.

Around 5:30, as the whispering skirmish flared into full-throated battle on the left, Lee rode slowly from his headquarters—the reins of his horse held by an orderly—and proceeded down the main street of Sharpsburg to his observation post on Cemetery Hill. By moving from point to point on this centrally located ridge, he could catch glimpses through the smoky shroud of so much of the fighting to the north as topped the rises of the undulating ground while keeping a careful watch on the Federal masses poised in his front and to the south.[17] For nearly two hours the advance and retreat of black-powder clouds and the rattle of musketry that accompanied them signaled the ebb and flow of a closely balanced contest.

Sometime during the early morning, the sun set its pattern for the day by appearing and disappearing in a generally cloudy sky, and the temperature began its rise to the midseventies, which perhaps because of the high humidity seemed even hotter. Perhaps also, the rising suspense, along with the prospect of imminent death or maiming, made the morning seem warmer in memory.

Lee spent most of these early hours just south of the Boonsboro Pike in the rear of Squires's battery of the Washington Artillery. Here he endured a triple cross fire from Hooker's guns behind the North Woods and from the long-range pieces of the Federal Artillery Reserve across the Antietam to the east and southeast. He also watched while a wave of human debris streamed south on the Hagerstown Pike and across the fields toward Sharpsburg from Jackson's battles in the Miller Cornfield and the East Woods. The Louisiana gunners were firing as fast as they could load, but only two of their four cannon were rifled, and they were making poor reply to their tormentors. Apparently, Lee became increasingly irritated by both the unequal artillery duel and the men he believed were shirking their duty. At one point he remarked acidly to battery commander Charles Squires, "Captain, our men are acting badly." Squires took the criticism personally and pointed out his men "were working their guns in excellent style." But Lee cut him off, "The infantry, sir, are straggling, they are straggling."[18]

The tension of these first hours spent watching victory totter wildly to and fro was broken by an incident so curious that many would remember it from a day full of overwhelming impressions. Not long after seven o'clock, D. H. Hill rode up to Lee, who had already been joined by Longstreet, to report that Jackson was seeking help and to request permission to send all five brigades of his own division to support the threatened left. The three generals crossed to the north side of the Boonsboro Pike and advanced to the crest of the ridge to observe the reported advance of Federal reenforcements—most likely the Twelfth Corps. They may also have witnessed something of Hood's attack, as it emerged from behind the Dunkard Church. Lee and Longstreet dismounted, and their staffs were ordered to remain behind so as not to attract the attention of Federal artillerists east of the Antietam with a

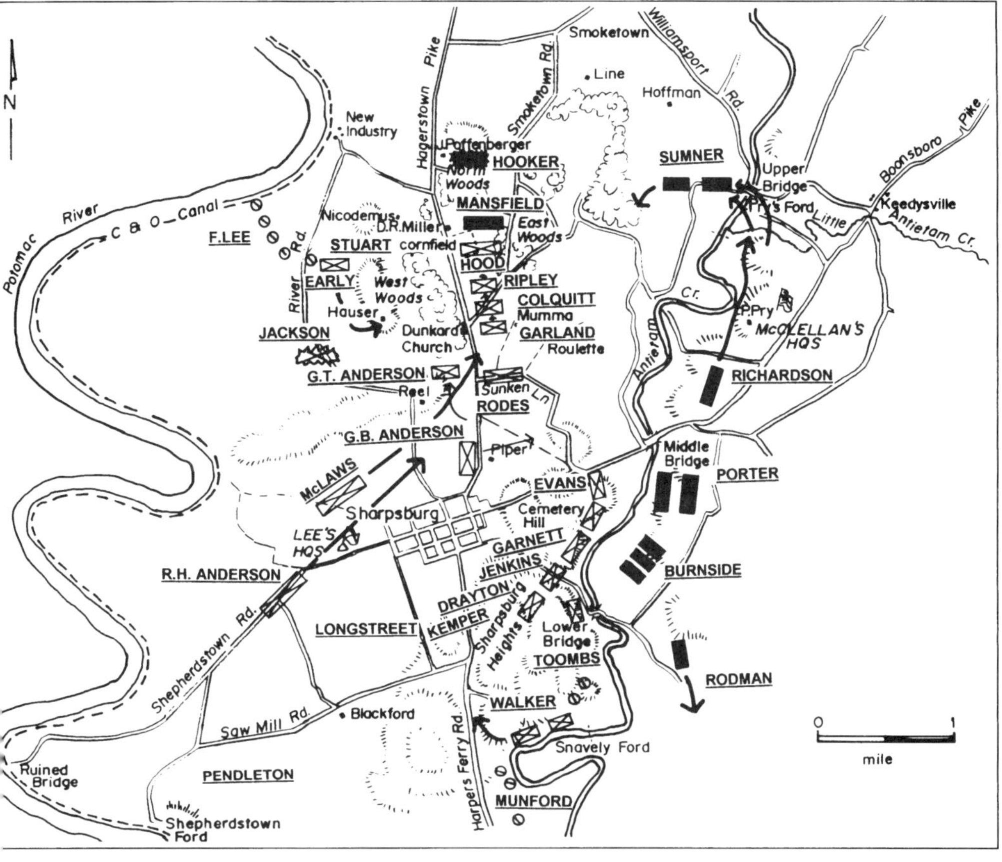

Battle of Sharpsburg, September 17, second phase

tempting target. Hill who was impatient to return to his command remained on horseback.

As the generals studied the ground beyond Jackson's line, Longstreet swung his glasses to the right and noticed a puff from the mouth of a solitary cannon. "There is a shot for you," he said to Hill, and in several seconds a shell allegedly aimed by Capt. Stephen Weed of Battery I, 5th U.S. Artillery, whizzed within feet of Lee, who was standing at the horse's head talking to Hill, cut off the horse's forelegs at the knees, and passed over the crest to explode in an infantry regiment, killing several soldiers. Hill's horse did not die immediately but dropped forward on its stumps, its muzzle in the grass and its rump high in the air. Hill made several desperate attempts to dismount in the usual way by throwing his leg backward, but he could not raise his leg high enough to clear a rubber coat and blanket strapped to the saddle. Although the moment was frightening, gruesome, and pathetic for horse lovers such as Lee, all three generals and their staffs broke the tension by laughing at the absurd spectacle, until Hill followed Longstreet's advice and threw his left leg forward and dismounted over the pommel.[19]

D.H. Hill's request presented Lee with a dilemma. Currently, only Ripley's brigade was near the scene of fighting and could be spared without serious derangement of the Confederate line. The remainder of Hill's division held the left-center and performed the important duty of covering the hinge that protected the northern flank of Sharpsburg Heights. Two hours into the battle, Lee was being asked to strip a vital section of his line to prevent another part from collapse.

Nonetheless, Lee agreed and approved the commitment of D. H. Hill's entire 5,500-man division to advance in Hood's wake. By this decision the Confederate commander abandoned his fall-back position in Sunken Road (Colquitt), his reserves on the Hagerstown Pike (Rodes and Garland), and the far left of his line on the heights opposite the Middle Bridge (George B. Anderson). In other words, all of those troops actually on the ground at the hinge in the Confederate line were being thrown into what had been Jackson's salient to the north.[20]

Beyond committing all of the forces already on the left, however, Lee's response to the first crisis was minimal. He was probably still too concerned with the threat to his center and right to risk any of the reserves that might soon be needed there. In any case, Lee did not touch any of the 3,000 men in McLaws's division a mile west of Sharpsburg, who constituted the general reserve for the army; or the 4,000 of R. H. Anderson, just outside of town, who formed Longstreet's reserve. Instead, he pulled George T. Anderson's 600-strong brigade from the center, where it rested in second-line support of Evans opposite the Middle Bridge, and sent it to reenforce Hood.[21]

The situation continued to change very rapidly, however, and the Confederate commander was granted but short grace from fate. Within thirty minutes—before eight o'clock—Lee received two messages from the left, and both came in the shape of pleas for additional support. It was probably Maj. J. W. Ratchford, D. H. Hill's adjutant, who first galloped up to army headquarters. His would have been slightly the milder of the two messages. According to Ratchford, he carried Hill's promise to "have the battle won before eleven o'clock," if Lee "would send him some help to meet the enemy's reinforcements." Mindful of the Federals poised opposite the Middle and Lower Bridges, Lee at first refused.

It was not until Capt. Sandie Pendleton, Jackson's adjutant, dashed up with Hood's dire prediction of the imminent collapse of the left that Lee relented. The fresh Federal force (Twelfth Corps) had punched gaping holes in the Confederate line and was threatening both of its flanks. This time Lee had no choice but to confront the crisis at hand and risk the disaster that might or might not materialize later on another part of the line. He sent Maj. Walter Taylor to summon McLaws's division from its brief two-hour rest west of town, and he sent Ratchford along to guide McLaws into position. Pendleton was dispatched back to Jackson with the word that help was on the way.[22] Then, within the next thirty minutes, as Jackson's patchwork line did in fact collapse, Lee sensed that McLaws's division might prove to be too little and too late.

Impelled by his growing concern and no doubt frustrated at his inability to gallop to the scene of danger, Lee set out on foot—trailing Traveller and his remaining staff behind—to cross the broken country on the northeastern outskirts of town. As he neared the Hagerstown Pike he encountered Capt. Thomas Carter and the King William Artillery, returning from the north. Carter, who was cousin to Lee, had been unable to find a suitable position to cover Rodes's brigade, now moving back into the Sunken Road; and, in order to reach high ground west of the Hagerstown Pike, he had been forced into the town's suburbs to find a break in the stone walls bordering the pike. According to the artillerist, Lee "seemed to fear that the whole left wing, then hard pressed and losing ground, would be turned, and that the enemy would gain possession of the range of hills some three-quarters of a mile to the left of Sharpsburg."[23]

Lee commandeered Carter and ordered him, with his battery and any other artillery that could be gathered, to occupy the range in question, the Reel Ridge. It seems that at this point—8:30 or so—Lee had conceded Jackson's line farther to the north was lost, and he set about to reconstruct a fall-back position. His choice was a wise one and revealed both his engineer's eye and his study of the county map. Lee must have known, perhaps through simple observation, that Rodes's brigade had barely passed the Sunken Road before encountering the retreating fragments of Colquitt and Garland. Robert Rodes had decided on his own authority to return his Alabama regiments to the shelter of the eroded roadbed. Lee may or may not have known that George B. Anderson's brigade was on the march from the Hagerstown Pike and would be available to take position on Rodes's right. Connecting at the Hagerstown Pike with the left of Rodes, the new line would run westerly past the

Reel farm to rest on another dramatic bend in the Potomac, which considerably shortened the front to be defended.

It was about this same time—and therefore probably while he was walking through the Sharpsburg outskirts—that Lee decided to take the ultimate risk. He dispatched his military secretary, Col. Armistead Long, to order Walker's division from guarding Snavely's Ford on the far right to the support of the nearly ruined left.[24]

Perhaps Lee was disheartened by the flood of wounded and the demoralized stragglers he found streaming past him to the safety of the town. Indeed, it was most likely on this dispiriting journey that he lost his temper when he spied a forager with a pig under his arm heading for the rear. Outraged at the spectacle of stealing and desertion at the very moment his army was crumbling, Lee arrested the man and sent him to Jackson for summary execution.[25] It may be that in this frame of mind, and with virtually no infantry left west of the Hagerstown Pike, that Lee decided nothing less than the most extreme response would save the army.

Perhaps, also, he reasoned it was now imperative that he shorten his line on both flanks and make his entire front more compact. Or, he may even have been counting on the imminent arrival of A. P. Hill from Harpers Ferry. What does not seem reasonable—in light of Lee's acute concern for the lower Antietam up to this point—is that he concluded McClellan would make no move in that direction simply because there had been no Federal action a scant three hours into the day.

A further complication in understanding Lee's decision to transfer Walker is the fact that R. H. Anderson's slightly larger division was not yet committed and nearer to hand. The most reasonable explanation is that Lee assumed R. H. Anderson would be needed to supplement Rodes's thin line along Sunken Road east of the Hagerstown Pike and that McLaws would be insufficient to hold the ground west of the pike. It is also possible—although there is no evidence to support the theory—that in bringing Walker to the left as well as McLaws and R. H. Anderson, Lee was toying with the eventual possibility of massing his forces to assume the offensive and smash through the Federal line, either to turn the enemy flank or to open an escape route to Hagerstown.[26]

However these various thoughts and others now unknowable played through Lee's mind, he took an inordinate chance in removing Walker. It was not simply that he exposed the right flank of D. R. Jones's division, it made the defense of the Lower Bridge difficult if not impossible. After all, Jones could refuse his flank by pulling his men back to other high ground, and the Lower Bridge would become relatively unimportant once the enemy was given Snavely's as an Antietam crossing. Of much greater importance was that Walker's removal uncovered Boteler's Ford and Lee's only practical escape route across the Potomac. And it did so at the very moment when it seemed likely that a retreat would be imminently necessary.

Yet, what other choices did Lee have? Either he had to rely on McLaws and R. H. Anderson alone to stabilize the left or else start his retreat immediately toward the Potomac. His judgment of the impending disaster apparently told him the that former would not solve his problem. Why he rejected retreat is only a bit less certain. He may have believed—with good cause—that to break off in the middle of a desperate battle and attempt to cross a canal and a major river would lead to an even greater catastrophe and the loss of most of his army. Or, Lee at this moment may have revealed—with the greatest clarity yet—the assumption undergirding his entire Maryland campaign: he believed the Confederacy now rode its highest tide and following it to its final eddy was imperative, even if it meant risking the destruction of the Army of Northern Virginia.

By the time Lee arrived on the Hagerstown Pike at nearly nine o'clock, all of his staff had been dispatched on errands, and he was accompanied by a single aide. Hoisted onto Traveller's back, the general—with the orderly holding the reins—set out at a slow pace northward on the pike toward the Dunkard Church. When he had gone about halfway to the church and reached the southern slope of the Reel Ridge, on which he intended to build his second line, he was accosted by a begrimed and agitated Col. Stephen D. Lee. The breathless colonel reported that his battalion of artillery had been wrecked by the morning's fighting, and he had left it only under the compulsory orders of General Hood to deliver a message. After repeated requests to Jackson had been to no avail, the crisis now impelled Hood to appeal directly to the commanding general. "Unless reinforcements were sent at once," said the artillerist, "the day was lost."

Sensing near panic in the usually cool gunner, Lee lowered his own voice and said, "Don't be excited about it Colonel, go tell General Hood to hold his ground, reinforcements are now rapidly approaching between Sharpsburg and the ford; tell him that I am now coming to his support." Perhaps due to partial misunderstanding, the colonel would not be mollified and replied, "General, your presence will do good, but nothing but infantry can save the day on the left." No doubt filled with forebodings, the artillerist set out to return to his men. Before he had gone a hundred yards, he heard General Lee shout, and looking back he saw him gesture to the head of a column approaching from the southwest at the double-quick. It was Cobb's brigade, the vanguard of McLaws's division.[27]

Lee apparently made no attempt to supervise the deployment of McLaws. Remanding tactical control to the hands of Jackson, Hood, and D. H. Hill, who had been on the field all morning, he turned back to the ridge near the Reel house. Here he saw that Carter had posted the King William Artillery and that Maj. Scipio Pierson, D. H. Hill's chief of artillery, had collected several other batteries. It was from this point Lee likely saw the initial success of McLaws against the Federal forces that had penetrated the West Woods and held the Dunkard Church.[28] He must have soon learned, however—and again it may have been by simple observation—that an enemy column just as large was taking position to move against the thin Confederate line east of the Hagerstown Pike. By this time, the head of Walker's division had arrived and had already been committed to supporting McLaws in the West Woods. Lee therefore played the last card remaining in his hand. He ordered R. H. Anderson's division, his last reserve of any sort on the field, to advance to the support of Rodes.[29]

Impelled by concern for the weakest part of the line, Lee rode across the Hagerstown Pike to the Sunken Road. Here he met D. H. Hill and the two generals rode along the waiting troops, warning of the impending attack and exhorting them to defend the country lane to the last extremity. Lee may have been heartened by the pledge of Col. John Gordon of the 6th Alabama that "these men are going to stay here, General, till the sun goes down or victory is won."[30] But, he was probably more encouraged to learn that Rodes's 800-man brigade was not alone in the road. George B. Anderson's much larger brigade (1,200) had arrived and taken position in the lane on the right, while Lt. Col. Christopher Sanders, who commanded the 350-man splinter that remained of Cobb's brigade after the debacle at Crampton's Gap, had failed to comprehend orders from McLaws and in consequence had wandered into the western end of the road at its juncture with the pike. Several hundred men from the brigades of Colquitt and Garland had rallied to fill the gap between Sanders and Rodes. In fine, a continuous line of about 2,600 men had settled into the natural rifle pit, which had been made stronger by the piling of fence rails above its northern shoulder.

By 9:30, Lee had committed 6,500 fresh troops in the divisions of McLaws and Walker and the brigade of G. T. Anderson to restore Confederate fortunes west of the Hagerstown Pike; while another 6,600—counting the approaching division of R. H. Anderson—had been designated to hold the line east of the pike. It would have to be enough. All that he had left were the 2,800 men in the six small brigades under D. R. Jones and Nathan Evans who stretched in a dangerously thin line from Cemetery Hill to the Lower Bridge—that and the hope that A. P. Hill with 6,000 or 7,000 men would soon arrive from Harpers Ferry. Leaving the tactical management of the fight on the left and left-center in the hands of his subordinates, Lee returned south on the Hagerstown Pike to the ridge on the Reel farm to watch and wait. He also helped to rally stragglers and send them back to their depleted commands. It was all that remained of any consequence that he could do.

McLaws and Walker Restore the Confederate Left, 9:00 A.M. to 1:00 P.M.

Some two hours earlier, Edwin Sumner, Second Corps commander, had paced the flagstone porch of the Pry farmhouse as the discharge of the nearby heavy guns rattled the window panes. Sumner was impatient to take his corps across the Antietam and join the fighting. Finally, reports of Hooker's unexpected early success seduced McClellan into making a major revision in the Federal plan of battle. Sensing that victory might be achieved solely with the attack on Lee's left flank—thus eliminating the need for the risky assaults at the Lower and Middle Bridges—McClellan decided to commit the Second Corps to press the gains made by Hooker. By 7:20, Sumner had his orders to cross the Antietam and throw his corps into the fray.[31]

The change in plans led to unforeseen complications. Time must be taken to relieve Richardson's division from its position immediately in front of the Middle Bridge by ordering up Morell's division of the Fifth Corps from Keedysville. Sumner had no intention of waiting, however, and he immediately set in motion the 11,000 men in his other two divisions. The corps commander rode with John Sedgwick in the van of the lead division, which was composed entirely of veterans and made good time in reaching the field. By 8:50, Sumner was forming the division in

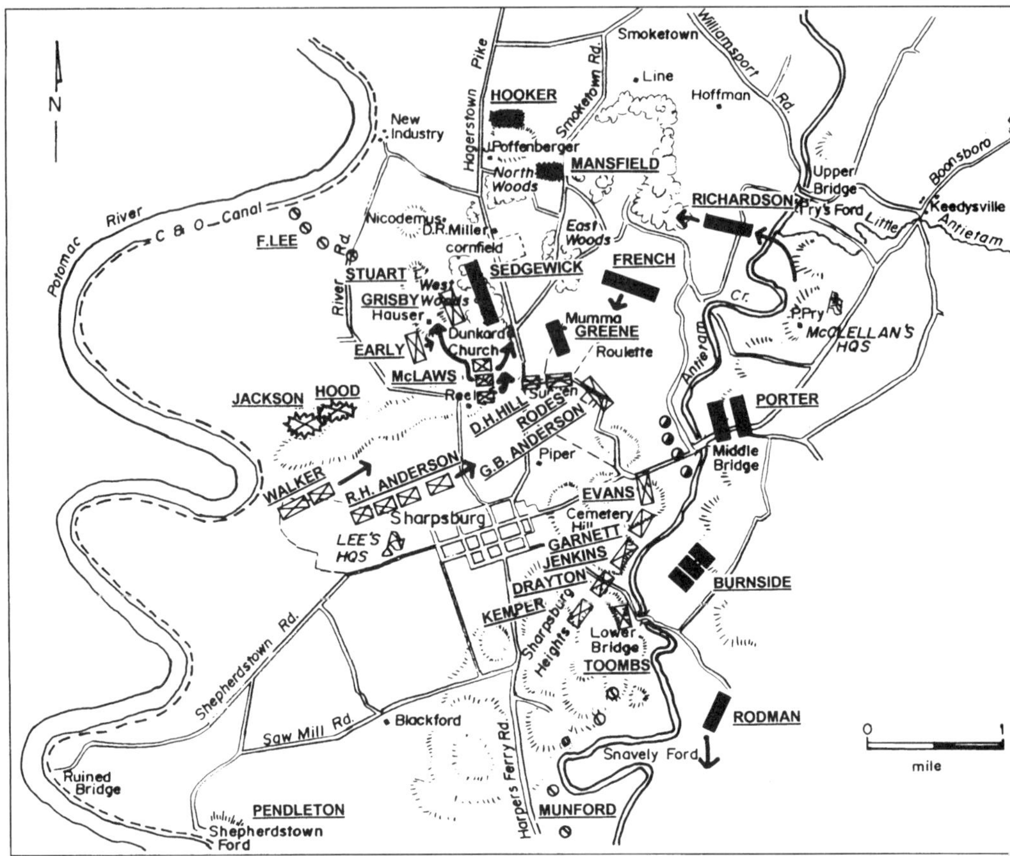

Battle of Sharpsburg, September 17, third phase

a brigade front of six long lines on the eastern edge of the East Woods. Unfortunately, the rear division under William French had been constituted only two days before. French could not move his men as efficiently as Sedgwick and a gap developed large enough to put the two units out of sight of one another.

Once again Sumner did not wait. Hearing that the enemy had retreated in disorder westwardly across the Hagerstown Pike, he grasped that a great opportunity existed if seized immediately. Having sent repeated orders to French to advance as quickly as possible and form on Sedgwick's left, Sumner marched Sedgwick through the East Woods and across the Miller Cornfield. In a very few minutes, the lead brigade under Willis Gorman had crossed the Hagerstown Pike and pierced the West Woods, where it encountered a light but deadly accurate fire from the front. In the next fifteen minutes, Napoleon Dana's brigade moved into the West Woods and closed on Gorman's rear, while Oliver Howard's brigade reformed its mingled lines along the pike. At approximately 9:20, disaster of the first magnitude struck Sedgwick. A withering fire erupted from the front and from the left flank, and the division was swept from the field, losing in twenty minutes nearly 40 percent of its men.

For the second time during morning, fortune taught a Federal general that she did not always favor the bold. Sumner did not, as has sometimes been alleged, march his lead division into a trap. He did, however, advance so far to the west that Sedgwick's entire left flank was in the air. Hence, as McLaws's Confederate division approached from the southwest to support a battle axis, which all morning had run perpendicular to the Hagerstown Pike, it was perfectly aligned to tear apart the flank of any Federal force parallel to that road. And Sedgwick formed in brigade front—his men packed tightly together in six long lines of nearly a thousand each—could not readily return fire.

It was the beginning of this attack against Sedgwick that Lee witnessed from the ridge where he was forming his fall-back line of artillery. The enemy force he saw east of the pike was French's division. Ironically, French arrived behind the Mumma farm minutes before the onslaught against Sedgwick. But, seeing Greene's division (Twelfth Corps) and believing it was Sedgwick's, French veered leftward and headed south toward the Sunken Road. By nine o'clock on September 17, there were not many happy coincidences that could have saved the Confederate left. Of the very few, one did occur.

The rout of Sedgwick's division was a great tactical victory for the Confederates. Indeed, in terms of losses inflicted upon the enemy and dramatic reversal of fortunes it was one of the greatest feats of Southern arms on any battlefield of the war. It is also remarkable that Stonewall Jackson and Jubal Early understood clearly and responded intelligently to the tangled tactical situation. Yet, withal, the execution of the Confederate assault on Sedgwick was so sloppy and inefficient as to attest that luck is as important in war as intelligence.

At 5:30—just as the battle proper opened between Trimble (Walker) and Seymour in the East Woods and through the eastern edge of the Miller Cornfield—Jackson decided to provide infantry support for the batteries Stuart had gathered on Nicodemus Hill and at the same time to fill part of the gap between the Confederate left and the Potomac. He accomplished both by swinging the left shank of his salient, the 1,100 men in Early's brigade, in a nearly 180-degree arc, first west to the Hauser Ridge and then north.[32] For about an hour, Early's men rested in relative security behind Nicodemus Hill, while the remainder of Jackson's two divisions gradually melted away under the fire of Hooker's attack. When Stuart noticed that Federal troops (Patrick and Gibbon of Doubleday) had crossed the Hagerstown Pike and were threatening to isolate his artillery from the main body, he pulled the guns back to Hauser Ridge closer to Dunkard Church and suggested that Early should assault the western flank of the intruding force.[33]

As Early was forming his line for attack, Stuart alerted him that Alexander Lawton had been severely wounded and that Jackson had called for him to return and assume command of Ewell's division. Early left the one-hundred-strong 13th Virginia to support the guns, and—taking a circuitous route to avoid enemy skirmishers—marched with the remainder of his brigade to the proximate point of his previous night's bivouac east of the Alfred Poffenberger house. It was around seven o'clock, when Early found Col. Andrew Grigsby with 300 men—all that remained of Jackson's (Jones's) division—preparing to charge Federal skirmishers that had penetrated the West Woods and were within three hundred yards of the Dunkard Church. Early formed in Grigsby's rear, and the combined forces swept the Federals back onto their main body (Patrick and Gibbon.) Seemingly without Early's knowledge, this attack closely coincided with the smashing assault of Hood's division east of the pike, and the two advances had no doubt mutually strengthened each other. Early advanced only half the distance northward that Hood covered, however, and thereby inadvertently exposed Hood's left flank along the pike.

From his new position, just west of the southern edge of the Cornfield, Early could see a discouraging number of Federals. In addition to the brigades (of Doubleday) immediately in his front, he watched the arrival and deployment of a fresh division (Williams's Twelfth Corps) east of the pike. Taking advantage of the temporary lull in the fighting, Early rode south and crossed the pike to find the rest of the division he now commanded. Here he discovered that the brigades of Lawton (Douglass), Trimble (Walker), and Hays existed only in the casualties on the field and the stragglers who had retired to the rear. He also observed that the Confederate forces east of the pike (Hood and the brigades of D. H. Hill) were beginning to fall back.

It must have been around eight o'clock when Early found Jackson and reported the dire situation from firsthand knowledge. Jackson promised to send for reenforcements and asked Early to hold on until they arrived. This was likely the origin of Jackson's urgent appeal to Lee that caused the Confederate commander to summon McLaws and start his own foot journey north to the scene of the crisis.

Within thirty minutes Early returned to his men and reformed his line, still perpendicular to the pike, with his own brigade resting on the road and Grigsby's command on the left. From this vantage, he observed a series of adverse events that boded disaster for Confederate fortunes. First, he saw a Federal force east of the pike moving past his right flank and toward his rear. This was the 125th Pennsylvania of Gordon's brigade, Williams's division, Twelfth Corps. The 125th was utterly green, having been mustered into service exactly one month and one day previously in Harrisburg.[34] It had gotten detached from its brigade, and all alone it was advancing in splendid ignorance down the Smoketown Road, a journey that, because of the sharp angle the road took in the East Woods, was carrying the regiment toward the Dunkard Church. With 700 men and officers, the 125th Pennsylvania no doubt appeared to Early to be a brigade.

Soon thereafter Early saw a Federal battery on the plateau just opposite the Dunkard Church open fire in the direction of Sharpsburg. He then realized that the entire area east of the pike had now fallen into enemy hands and that he was in danger of being cut off from the town. As the final and crowning complication, Early observed two long lines (Gorman's 1,700 men, the van of Sedgwick) emerge from the East Woods and then face west on a line that would carry them directly against his right flank. Simultaneously, the troops on the Smoketown Road (125th Pennsylvania) crossed the pike and occupied the woods around the Dunkard Church. It was now about nine o'clock.

While the East Woods force (Gorman) paused to dress its lines, Early sprang into action. He swung back his right so that his line was now in the edge of the West Woods and facing east. He correctly judged that the greatest immediate danger came from the enemy at the church. Not only would possession of the plateau threaten the flank and rear of Lee's line on the bluffs east of Sharpsburg, but the Federals there would prevent reenforcements from reaching the West Woods. Leaving Grigsby with the fragment of Jackson's (Jones's) division to confront and attempt to delay the column from the East Woods (Gorman), Early retired westward with his own brigade, traveling south behind the Hauser Ridge to mask his movements from observation. He then swung to the left, once again faced east, and opened fire on the Federal skirmishers around the church.

It was now about ten minutes past nine, and two brigades of Sedgwick (Gorman and Dana) had entered the woods on Early's left. They were being held by the desperate and deadly fire of Grigsby's valiant band and the need to wait for the third brigade (Howard), which had become disorganized just east of the pike. During the advance of Gorman's brigade its far left regiment, the 34th New York (311 officers and men) had become separated and taken up position along with the 125th Pennsylvania at the church. Thus, Early's 1,000 men now faced an approximately equal force in their immediate front. At this extraordinarily opportune moment, Early saw the van of his promised reenforcements approaching from the south along the Hagerstown Pike.

Early also saw the imminent mishap in the offing. If he continued his attack to the east, he would cross the face of the Confederates advancing from the south; and not only would the commands become entangled, but they might kill as many of each other as they did of the enemy. Early attempted to call off his assault, but the two Federal regiments—clearly grasping their own danger—were rapidly retreating from the woods. Early's men at first could not be restrained from pursuit. In order to avoid smashing into Early's flank, the brigade arriving from Sharpsburg veered east across the pike and followed the fleeing Federals. Observing another enemy brigade (Howard) enter the woods on his left, Early finally succeeded in pulling his own regiments back to the Hauser Ridge for reforming. It was now about 9:20, and Early suddenly observed a fresh Confederate force sweep across his front. It smashed into the flank of the three Federal brigades and sent them reeling to the north and west. It all happened so quickly that Early apparently did not participate in the rout.

It was Joseph Kershaw's brigade of South Carolinians that Early first saw approaching from the south. Around nine o'clock, after crossing the fields northwest of Sharpsburg, McLaws's men had reached the Hagerstown Pike just opposite its juncture with the Sunken Road.[35] They passed some distance in front of Robert E. Lee, who shouted to Col. Stephen D. Lee and pointed out their welcome arrival. McLaws, who apparently saw neither of the Lees, grasped the danger, if he did not understand the ground, and hastened to form a divisional front for an immediate advance. He sent Cobb's brigade (Sanders) to the far right to dress on the Hagerstown Pike and then attempted to form Kershaw, Barksdale, and Semmes, in that order, to the left (west). With the help of John Hood and Maj. J. W. Ratchford (D. H. Hill's adjutant), both of whom were on hand, McLaws at least got his men pointing in the right direction. In the din and confusion, however, Colonel Sanders, commanding Cobb's brigade, failed to hear all of the orders and continued across the pike to take up position in the Sunken Road. He thus became detached from the division for the remainder of the day.

Adding greater urgency to the moment and leading to further complications, McLaws could see a heavy Federal force entering the woods (probably Dana's brigade, Sedgwick's second line) and, not knowing he would first encounter the two isolated Union regiments around the church, reasoned that he must cross the open ground and enter the woods before the enemy had time to prepare. He therefore ordered his right to charge before his left had time to form completely.

Thus it was Kershaw's brigade, dressing its right on the Hagerstown Pike in lieu of the errant Cobb, that passed through the ranks of G. T. Anderson's brigade, which had arrived shortly before and had stalled short of the Dunkard Church. And it was Kershaw who came charging into the flank of the 125th Pennsylvania and 34th New York just as Early approached the two regiments from the front. Kershaw also saw the danger of friendly forces crossing paths, and he pulled his brigade to the right. This swerve carried the South Carolinians east of the pike and directly into the teeth of the southern end of the superbattery of guns from the First, Second, and Twelfth Corps, which had formed a line from the East Woods to the northern edge of the plateau. Not only was Kershaw's attack stopped, but his brigade was shattered by the artillery fire alone, losing 341 out of its 858 officers and men (40 percent).

Hence, McLaws's attack got off to a most inauspicious start, and more diversions were yet to come. As McLaws was forming for the assault, he received orders from Jackson to send support to the thin line still holding against the front of Sedgwick's division. McLaws detached Semmes's brigade on the far left and sent it behind the Hauser Ridge to reenforce the handful of men who still remained under Colonel Grigsby. When at last, around 9:20, McLaws was ready to advance, the only troops left in his divisional front were the four Mississippi regiments of Barksdale. Even then, this final brigade entered the West Woods diagonally from the southwest corner, and it initially followed Kershaw to the east in pursuit of the two retreating Federal regiments. Only when Barksdale began to receive fire from the north did he discover the large Federal force (Sedgwick) on his flank. While his right wing (17th and 21st Mississippi) continued eastward in Kershaw's wake, Barksdale changed front with his left two regiments (13th and 18th Mississippi) to confront the danger.

Still, this splinter of McLaws that finally found Sedgwick's flank would be enough. Charging squarely at right angles to Sedgwick, the 400 Mississippians, joined by the 600 Georgians of G. T. Anderson's brigade, which advanced to their support, poured a withering fire down the long, helpless Federal lines. Simultaneously, Semmes's 700 men trebled Grigsby's fire from the front. In the resulting firestorm, Sedgwick's 5,400 veterans melted into the terrain, suffering 2,200 casualties (40 percent) in about twenty minutes. As the Federal survivors raced for the safety of the North and East Woods, Stuart's cavalry and the 13th Virginia (left behind by Early) joined in the pursuit. So, too, did the other fresh Confederate forces that had just reached the field.

Walker's division had made good time in skirting south and west of Sharpsburg to reach the Hagerstown Pike near the Sunken Road by about 9:30.[36] Forming his line on the ground just vacated by McLaws, Walker put Manning's brigade on the right and Ransom's on the left. Preparing to advance, he received orders from Jackson to leave a force to fill the gap between the Sunken Road and the West Woods. Walker halted Manning and detached the 3d Arkansas and the 27th North Carolina to remain behind. Ransom charged ahead into the West Woods and joined the pursuit of Sedgwick.

By this time the chase after Sedgwick had become a jumble of units, and its progress became further disorganized by fences and the irregularities of the ground. Finally, the Confederates were stopped by the brigades of Crawford, Gordon, and Goodrich of the Twelfth Corps. Simultaneously raked by artillery fire from the Federal batteries on the Poffenberger Hill in front and on the flank by the superbattery and the long-range guns east of the Antietam, the patchwork wave of pursuers suffered heavily as they fell back west of the pike. In the meanwhile, Manning, with the remainder of his brigade, had the misfortune to encounter General Kershaw near the Dunkard Church. In ignorance of the developments of the rapidly unfolding situation, Kershaw ordered Manning's three regiments to charge directly across the pike in the path of his own ruined brigade, where they also were bloodily repulsed.[37]

This time, however, the repelling force east of the pike was not artillery alone. The brigades of Tyndale and Stainrook (Twelfth Corps) had advanced westward from the Mumma farm to support the guns. Moreover, their divisional commander, George Greene, had finally heard the now-obsolete news that Sedgwick was in the West Woods. Around 10:30, Greene followed the retreating regiments of Manning across the pike and occupied the woods around the church, assuming Sedgwick to be on his right. So incapacitated were the Confederates by this point that Greene was allowed to hold his advanced position for two hours.

Some of the Confederate units—such as those of Early, Grigsby, and Stuart—were exhausted from an interminable morning of severe fighting. Others—such as McLaws, Walker, and G. T. Anderson—had been scattered by detachments and disoriented by rapid deployment over unfamiliar ground in a meeting engagement. All had been disorganized by the nature of the complicated fighting, and all had suffered heavily. In time, a quilt-work line, which took little account of divisional structure, was patched together parallel to the pike and facing east. Such confusion still reigned, however, that many of the ranking Confederate officers, including the usually alert Jubal Early, were unaware of the presence of Greene's two brigades in their midst. Around 12:30, while Brig. Gen. Robert Ransom was absent searching for a stray regiment, his senior colonel (and older brother), Matthew Ransom, on his own initiative drove the Federals from the West Woods. Greene, who had at last learned of Sedgwick's repulse earlier, did not require much pushing.[38]

Thus for two hours the Federals occupied the entire Dunkard Church plateau, Hooker's original goal and the target of Federal attacks for much of the morning. The timing was ideal, as the occupation coincided with the assaults by Sumner's other two divisions on the the hinge in the Confederate line at the Sunken Road. Ironically, Federal attention was riveted almost exclusively to the west, and but a solitary battery contributed fire from this dominating position to the attempts by French and Richardson to carry the critical point of the Confederate left-center. So massive was the Federal artillery presence on this portion of the field, stretching from the plateau to the Poffenberger Hill, one captain was told that—"there were more batteries than could be used" and sent to the rear. If some of that power had been directed against the Confederate line in the Sunken Road already swept on the right from the guns east of the Antietam, it is possible that tactical change alone would have rendered a different outcome to the entire battle.[39]

The final spasm of fighting in the bloody half–square mile from the Dunkard Church to the North Woods occurred at around one o'clock. As William Franklin's Sixth Corps arrived on the field from Pleasant

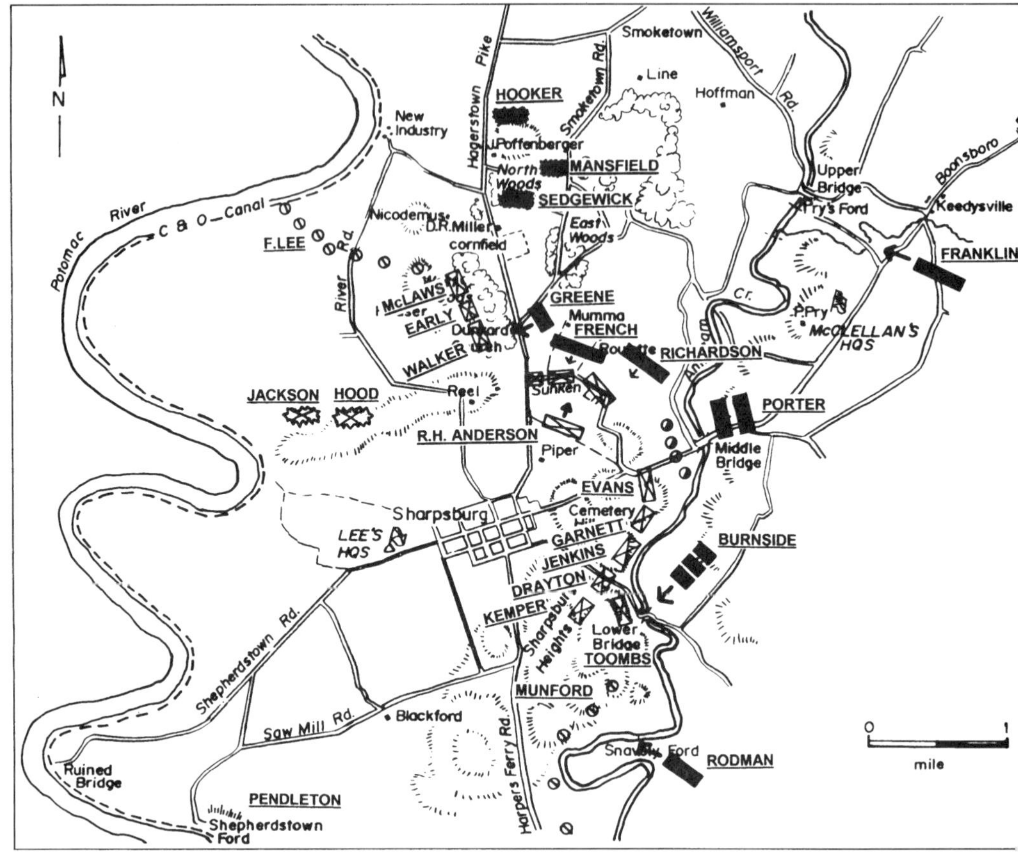

Battle of Sharpsburg, September 17, fourth phase

Valley and formed line to relieve the First, Second, and Twelfth Corps, one of its brigades accidentally brushed too close to the woods around the church. The five regiments under Col. William Irwin were repulsed with over a quarter of their men casualties.

Thus ended seven and a half hours of fighting over approximately 320 acres. In this, the battle's third phase (Sedgwick) and fourth phase (Greene and Irwin)—in sum, the fighting in the West Woods and around the Dunkard Church—the Federals had poured an additional 8,300 men into the fight and lost 2,500 (30 percent). In the only fighting during the day in which the Confederates enjoyed even a slight advantage, Lee had added 8,500 men and had suffered 2,000 casualties (23.7 percent). The total of new troops committed during the third and fourth phases was 16,727, and of these 4,481 (26.8 percent) were now casualties.[40]

The strengths for the combined four phases of the morning's fighting on the left show that 25,000 Federals fought 19,000 Confederates, or a ratio of about four Federals to every three Confederates. The combined casualties were 6,800 (27.3 percent) Federals and 6,400 (33.8 percent) Confederates. In all, 43,760 soldiers fought and 13,179 (30.1 percent) fell.

Federal Success on Four Fronts, 9:30 A.M. to 1:30 P.M.

At 9:15, after all three brigades of Sedgwick had crossed west of the Hagerstown Pike—and at almost the exact moment when Kershaw and Early attacked the 34th New York and 125th Pennsylvania at the Dunkard Church—William French's division of the Second Corps encountered Confederate skirmishers at the Roulette farm buildings in the dale of the Sunken Road. French was not irredeemably late, nor was he hopelessly out of place. He was on the eastern slope of the plateau and within 300 yards of the Dunkard Church. Had he attacked due west, he would have passed through Kershaw's shattered brigade and struck the flank of the Confederate forces, which were in the act of striking Sedgwick's flank.[41] The outcome from the tactical imbroglio that would have resulted is intriguing but moot, because French advanced south rather than west.

French was pulled southward because, unlike Sumner, he did take into account Greene's two brigades at the Mumma farm, and he may even have believed the units were part of Sedgwick's division and that he was supporting Sedgwick's left as instructed. Once French had advanced far enough to encounter enemy skirmishers at Roulette's, he no longer had the option of turning west, since that would have exposed his own left flank. Around 9:30, therefore, as Sedgwick's division began to break apart in the West Woods, French prepared to launch the first assault against the Confederate line in the Sunken Road.

On paper, French's 5,700 men held a better than two to one advantage over the 2,600 Confederate defenders. Severely mitigating factors rendered these odds meaningless: first, the division had been formed but three days before and lacked cohesion; second, almost 3,000 of its strength came from green regiments just mustered into the service; third, French attacked with a single brigade at a time; fourth, he made no attempt to maneuver but came frontally against the Sunken Road; and, fifth, the strong Confederate position amounted to natural rifle pits that had been strengthened by piled fence rails as breastworks.

The results were predictable. The old regiments fought valiantly in the highly unfavorable circumstances and on at least one occasion penetrated into the roadbed; but French's ninety minutes of disjointed attacks never seriously threatened to break the Confederate line. Indeed, after the arrival of the 3,300 men in R. H. Anderson's division around 10:15 to support D. H. Hill, the Confederates held a slight numerical advantage. By eleven o'clock French had suffered 30 percent casualties, exhausted most of his ammunition, and shattered the morale of his new division. As Richardson, the last division of the Second Corps, took up position on his left, French retired to the rear of the Roulette farm buildings.[42]

Unlike French, Israel Richardson had neither lost his way nor found it difficult to manage the march of the 4,000 men in his veteran regiments. The two hours that elapsed between his own deployment and that of Sedgwick resulted from McClellan's modification in the Federal plan of battle. As the infantry vanguard that followed the Confederates from South Mountain, Richardson had taken up position straddling the Boonsboro Pike immediately in front of the Middle Bridge on the afternoon of the 15th. He had remained in place until 7:30 on the morning of the 17th, an indication that McClellan originally expected the role of the Second Corps would be to strike the Confederate center, when success on either or both of the flanks justified the attack. After McClellan decided to commit the Second Corps to the escalating assault on the northern flank, he told Sumner that Richardson would not be available until replaced, but Sumner had chosen not to wait. Because it had taken nearly two hours for George Morell to break camp near Keedysville and advance his division of the Fifth Corps two miles, Richardson did not start his march to Pry's Ford until around 9:30. Consequently, whatever hypothesis might be constructed for the more efficient use of Sedgwick and French, Richardson could not have been on hand to support them, unless Sumner had been willing to await his relief.

It was ironic that the final large Federal force committed to the attack on the Confederate left and left-center would be the only one of the day to approximate the route originally envisioned by McClellan for his attack on this flank. Hugging the Antietam, Richardson's approach on French's left brought him opposite the eastern end of the Sunken Road and directly against the hinge in Lee's line. Indeed, Richardson's advance with a two-brigade front—Thomas Meagher on the right and John Caldwell on the left—initially caused him to overlap the eastern flank of the Confederates in the Sunken Road. The division was pulled slightly to the west, however, by the need to relieve French and by several small enemy counterattacks.

In the end, Richardson nearly repeated French's performance. Attacking over much the same ground and committing a single brigade at a time, he nearly exhausted Meagher and Caldwell without taking the road. Only with the advance of Col. John Brooke's five regiments, the last fresh brigade of the Second Corps, did the Confederates finally retreat from the Sunken Road. Shortly after one o'clock the Federals finally held the key to the field on the Confederate left.[43]

For the third time—and with the sun but midway in the heavens—the Army of Northern Virginia faced a crisis of survival on its left flank. Certainly, some criticism can be leveled against the higher command for the tactical management of the fight. Neither Longstreet, nor D. H. Hill, who were both present and directing throughout, seem to have coordinated their units effectively. In particular, the deployment of R. H. Anderson's division was confused and inefficient. Still, in the end, the Confederates mounted a defense of the Sunken Road of heroic dimensions. The 37.3 percent casualties suffered by the infantry ranked second only to the losses of Hood and D. H. Hill's other three brigades in the second phase of the fighting in the Cornfield and East Woods. Toward the close of the nearly unceasing three-hour struggle, Longstreet held the reins of the horses while his staff worked two guns of Miller's battery of the Washington Artillery; and Hill grabbed a musket and led a desperate countercharge by 200 hastily assembled stragglers.

In sum, in the fifth phase of the battle, the struggle for the Sunken Road, the Federals poured 10,565 fresh troops into the battle and suffered 3,020 casualties (28.6 percent). The Confederates added 6,723 new troops to the fray and lost 2,508 (37.3 percent) of them. Thus, at the end of the morning's fighting, 35,000 Federals had lost almost 10,000 (27.7 percent), while inflicting nearly 9,000 casualties (34.8 percent) on 26,000 Confederates. For seven and a half hours 61,000 men contended so fiercely for a mere three-quarters of a square mile that 19,000 (30.6 percent) of them were casualties.

Unfortunately for the Army of Northern Virginia, the hole in its left-center was only one dimension of the crisis it faced at midday on the 17th. At ten o'clock, just when affairs looked most promising on the Confederate left—after Sedgwick had been routed from the West Woods, and it appeared that sufficient forces were on hand to defend the Sunken Road—Federal forces mounted their first attack against the right,

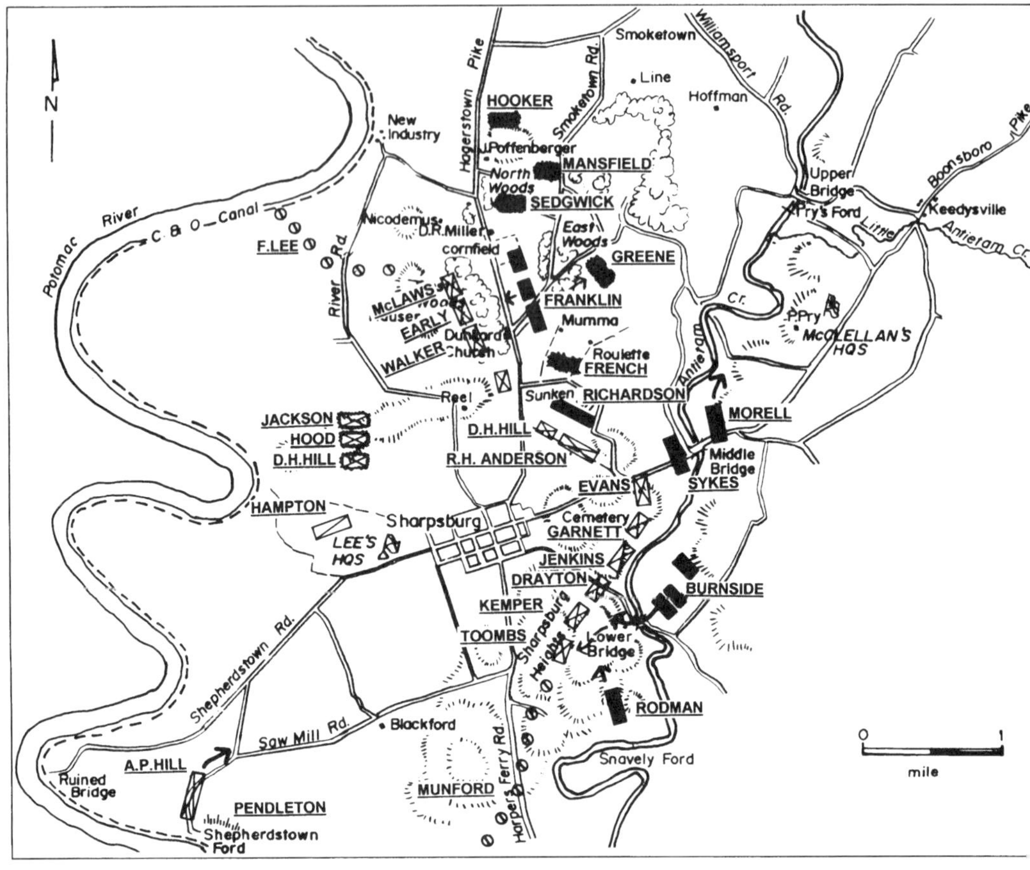

Battle of Sharpsburg, September 17, fifth phase

which Lee had stripped almost bare of troops. During the three hours that D. H. Hill and R. H. Anderson held back French and Richardson, 400 Georgians under Robert Toombs beat back repeated assaults by the Ninth Corps at the Lower Bridge. At one o'clock, however—and simultaneous with the loss of the Sunken Road—Burnside crossed the Antietam at both the bridge and Snavely's Ford. Lee had no reserves to meet the crisis at either end of his line. To win, the Federals had only to push.

McClellan's decision to commit Sumner to the attack on the Confederate left flank had fundamentally altered the Federal battleplan. Implicit in the decision to send the Second Corps to support Hooker was the further decision to suspend temporarily Burnside's attack on the Lower Bridge. Not only might the potentially bloody assault from the south be rendered unnecessary, but also Franklin's Sixth Corps was approaching the field from Pleasant Valley. Hence, although McClellan sent Burnside instructions at 6:30 to prepare to carry the bridge, he did not send the follow-up orders to launch the assault until almost three hours later.

By nine o'clock, or shortly before, news of an entirely different character was filtering in from the front. The cost of the Federal gains had been excessive. Both the First and Twelfth Corps were wrecked, and both of the corps commanders were wounded. Clearly, the hope for easy success had been a gossamer. The enemy remained in force at Sharpsburg and was fighting with fierce determination. Whereas the Second Corps had been sent to bolster promising successes by Hooker and Mansfield, it now appeared that Sumner was the only effective Federal force remaining on the northern portion of the field. Even without knowledge of the impending disaster to Sedgwick, McClellan concluded that the attack on the Confederate left by itself could not achieve final victory. After learning that Franklin's Sixth Corps was within a mile and a half of Keedysville, at 9:10 the Federal commander sent orders to Burnside "to open your attack."[44]

During the next hour, from 10:00 to 11:00, the news was of a decidedly mixed character. At ten o'clock the head of Baldy Smith's division (Sixth Corps) reached Keedysville. At the same time Burnside launched his first assault against the Lower Bridge. But, as the forenoon dragged on, the battle's center of gravity kept pulling McClellan's attention northward. Slowly the details of Sedgwick's catastrophe became known, and then followed the news that Richardson was replacing French's exhausted division. This meant the last fresh force on the field was being committed to the battle. Meanwhile, although Burnside had made a number of assaults, he had yet to cross a soldier west of the Antietam. It was during these anxious hours that McClellan sent a barrage of couriers to hasten Burnside's progress. Finally, at eleven-thirty, fearful that a Confederate counterattack might sweep away the Federal right, McClellan ordered Franklin to cross the Sixth Corps at Pry's Ford and to renew the assault on Sumner's front.

As noon approached, the Federal situation seemed to deteriorate to the point of three hours before. Once again there was but a single corps (Sixth) to sustain the attack from the north, although another (Second)—and this the biggest and best in the army—had been wrecked in the interval. Burnside had still not forced passage of the Antietam, and once again Porter remained the only reserve both to cover the center and to support Burnside's attack. There were no other infantry forces at hand. It was, perhaps, with such desperate thoughts running through his mind that McClellan queried Pleasonton, "Can you do any good by a cavalry charge?"[45]

The ninety minutes following 11:30 may have been the worst of the day for McClellan. Everywhere the battle was in doubt, and nowhere did he have troops that he believed he could safely spare to influence the outcome. Finally, at one o'clock, three events occurred almost simultaneously to break the stalemate. Richardson's division overran the Sunken Road, and Burnside crossed a division at Snavely's Ford and carried the Lower Bridge.

Ambrose Burnside had acted promptly upon the receipt shortly before seven of McClellan's orders to prepare for the attack on the southern flank. He had advanced Crook's brigade (Kanawha division), supported by Sturgis's division, as near the Lower Bridge as possible without exposing the men to enemy sharpshooters.[46] Rodman's division moved a short distance downstream toward Snavely's Ford and took lee in a ravine at the foot of Red Hill, a spur of Elk Ridge. Then the Ninth Corps waited while the commander of the Army of the Potomac twice revised his plan of battle.

McClellan's order to open the attack must have arrived at 9:45 or 9:50. By ten o'clock, Jacob Cox, the titular head of the Ninth Corps, launched the first attack against the Lower Bridge. It is not surprising that neither the first assault nor several subsequent ones were successful, nor even that a handful of Confederates could continually repulse 5,000 men in the brigade of Crook and the division of Sturgis. The narrow bridge admitted but five infantrymen in full gear across its width, and the road leading to it from the east ran parallel to the creek for almost a quarter of a mile. To the west the bluffs approached nearly to the banks of the Antietam. Not a man among Robert Toombs's 400 Georgians needed to be a sharpshooter. All that was required was the veteran's ability to load and fire efficiently to send 1,200 bullets a minute into a compact target a hundred yards or so distant.

What is surprising is that for nearly three hours the Ninth Corps attempted to cross the Antietam only at the Lower Bridge. In truth, looking at the sluggish, shallow stream today, it is easy to agree with Henry Kyd Douglas of Jackson's staff, who grew up at Ferry Hill plantation four miles to the west, and after the war wrote, "One thing is certain, they might have waded it that day without getting their waist belts wet at any place."[47] Clearly, the slight rain of the night before had been insufficient to turn the creek into a raging torrent. The fact remains that the professional engineers of the army had concluded the Antietam could be crossed only at the bridges and the fords, and Burnside cannot be seriously faulted for following their counsel.[48]

On the other hand, the discouraging prospects for taking the bridge, combined with the engineers' advice, ought to have made it a high priority to investigate the possibility of crossing at Snavely's Ford. Instead, while Federal regiments were being shattered in vain attempts to carry the bridge, Rodman's division did not advance until nearly one o'clock, "after resting some two hours and refreshing the men."[49] It is probable that both Burnside and Rodman, who believed, as did McClellan and the entire Army of the Potomac, that Lee's army was roughly equal in size to their own, assumed the important ford would be heavily guarded by enemy infantry and artillery. Indeed, had Rodman attempted to force passage with his 2,800 men before nine o'clock, he would have found his way blocked by John Walker's 3,800 Confederates. From the time of McClellan's order to open the attack onward, however, only the two undersized cavalry regiments of Munford's brigade, one company of South Carolina infantry, and a single battery of the Washington Artillery were available to protect the ford. When Rodman did start to cross the creek, news of his movement caused Toombs to begin to retire, and the 51st Pennsylvania and 51st New York (Ferrero's brigade, Sturgis's division) carried the Lower Bridge.

Still, the three hours it took the Ninth Corps to carry the Lower Bridge and ford the creek at Snavely's did not make their attack hopelessly late. Indeed, Burnside's success at one o'clock coincided neatly with the carrying of the Sunken Road.

By 1:20, therefore, allowing time for the news to filter back to headquarters, prospects had brightened considerably for McClellan. With Franklin in place on the right, Burnside on the move on the left, and Porter remaining fresh in the center, the Army of the Potomac was finally poised to execute his battleplan as originally devised.

Lee and the Midday Crisis, 9:30 A.M. to 2:00 P.M.

During the final hours of the forenoon, Robert E. Lee observed the oscillation of fortune's pendulum from the opposite end of its wide swing. When the Confederate commander completed his review of Rodes's brigade in the Sunken Road around 9:30, prospects on the left appeared brighter than at any time that morning. There is but sketchy evidence of

Lee's movements during the next two and a half hours, although he likely first returned to the ridge near the Reel house, where he had prepared his second line of defense with stray batteries of artillery.[50] From this position he would have learned of the brilliant success of McLaws's attack through the West Woods. He could have seen the beginning of the assault on the Sunken Road and observed R. H. Anderson's division marching to bolster its Confederate defenders.

Thus, between 10:00 and 10:30, when unwelcome word arrived of the Federal attack on the Lower Bridge, Lee felt sufficiently confident of affairs on the left to abandon them to Jackson, Longstreet, and D. H. Hill and to turn his own attention fully to the long-dreaded developments on the right. Lee spent the next ninety minutes circulating among Cemetery Hill, the town, and a knoll near his headquarters tent on the Shepherdstown Road. It is reasonable to assume he went first to his accustomed observation post on Cemetery Hill, where he might obtain a close view of the new threat and ponder the limited responses available to him.

Lee's success on the left had been dearly purchased at the expense of other parts of his line. Necessity had compelled him to do just what McClellan had wanted him to do. He had committed all of his reserves (McLaws and R. H. Anderson), weakened his center (G. T. Anderson), and stripped bare his far right (Walker). Now, to defend his entire front from the right flank of D. H. Hill at the Sunken Road southward, stretching along the Antietam bluffs past the Middle and Lower Bridges to Snavely's Ford (a distance of two miles on a straight line and much longer if conforming to the twisting terrain), Lee had scarcely 2,400 infantry and eleven batteries.[51]

It is possible that Lee may not have realized just how badly off he was. There is no evidence he had yet received the divisional returns he called for at Hagerstown on the 13th; and, even if he had, he may not have fully grasped the extraordinary diminution of his army during the last three days. He had at his disposal the division of D. R. Jones and the detached brigade of Nathan Evans. Two of the brigades (Drayton and Evans) had been in the field less than two months; and, as late as the trimonthly estimate of September 1, the full seven brigades had totaled 9,500 officers and men present for duty. Lee may have believed, therefore, that 5,000 to 6,000 infantry remained at hand. Still, even with this figure, which doubled reality, the Confederate commander must have known that he was in serious trouble. If he could not confine the Federals to the toehold at the Middle Bridge, the Confederate army would be split into halves; and, if he could not hold both the Lower Bridge and Snavely's Ford, he would lose his communications and his only line of retreat. Snavely's was but a mile and a half from Boteler's Ford on the Potomac.

Salvation lay in the arrival of A. P. Hill's division from Harpers Ferry. But where was Hill, and when would he arrive? It is possible Lee heard something of Hill's whereabouts from Wade Hampton, who reached Sharpsburg with his cavalry brigade shortly before noon.[52] Yet, it would have been better for Lee's peace of mind if he were kept unaware of Hill's progress. Even if couriers were pounding the roads with hourly reports of Hill's advance—and there is no evidence one way or the other—Lee could have learned only that his last reenforcements would reach the field around three o'clock. Since there was no reason to expect a break in the morning-long, unremitting assaults by the Federals, Hill might well come up too late to save the Army of Northern Virginia from destruction.

It was imperative that something be done in the meanwhile, but there seemed to be little of consequence Lee could do. Uncertain which looming disaster might first erupt—and aware that cavalry would be of limited value because of the terrain—he kept Hampton's 1,200 horsemen as a desperate last reserve near his headquarters on the Shepherdstown Road.[53] It was at this point that Lee and his staff started to devote most of their energy to rounding up stragglers and sending them back to the front.

In truth, "stragglers" is a poor term to describe the military debris then crowding Sharpsburg and its environs. Most of the shirkers and laggards had been shorn from the Army of Northern Virginia long before eleven o'clock on the morning September 17. Hour on hour of fighting of the most ferocious character had splintered organizations and blown away several levels of leadership. Disoriented knots of soldiers under junior officers wandered the roads and fields searching for ammunition, food, and orders. Lee personally posted Capt. James Nisbet and a fragment of the 21st Georgia (Trimble's brigade) as a barrier across the road near headquarters, ordering Nisbet to collect the able bodied and let only the wounded pass to Shepherdstown. Lee returned several times to remind Nisbet of the importance of his task. In the streets of Sharpsburg, the Confederate commander encountered Capt. Thomas Garrett of the 5th North Carolina (Garland's brigade) and commissioned him to collect all of the men who could be found regardless of command and report to General Evans on the Boonsboro Pike.[54]

In his search for defenders to cover the exposed right flank, Lee likely also discovered that batteries had retired from the contest and were roaming the rear unable to replenish their ammunition chests.[55] Not only was the loss of Longstreet's ordnance wagons coming back to haunt, but the road from Boteler's Ford was so blocked with traffic that supplies were reaching the front with great difficulty.[56] Lee took time, therefore, to send an urgent message to Pendleton in the rear:

> If you have fifteen or twenty guns, suitable for our purposes, which you can spare, the general desires you send them, with a sufficiency of ammunition. You must not take them from the fords if essential to their safety. Send up the stragglers. Take any cavalry about there and send up at the point of the sword. We want ammunition, guns and provisions.
>
> P.S. If you have not as many guns as wanted, to spare, send those of long range.[57]

It is most interesting to note that Lee gave not the slightest hint to Pendleton that the Artillery Reserve might soon need to cover the retreat of the army across Boteler's Ford. Nor did Lee relent in his insistence that the ford at Williamsport continue to be guarded. Indeed, there is nothing in the message that suggests Lee, even as his prospects for success approached their dimmest, considered abandoning his campaign in Maryland. On the contrary, the plea for provisions indicates just the opposite.

High noon found Lee back at Cemetery Hill to confront a new and ominous threat. During his absence the enemy had significantly expanded their toehold at the Middle Bridge. Federal artillery had crossed the Antietam. Despite the heavy fire of the Confederate batteries on Cemetery Hill, twenty-two guns had worked their way forward on both sides of the Boonsboro Pike, piece by piece, to the ridge several hundred yards west of the creek. Likely it was news of this unwanted development that had caused Lee to direct that Captain Garrett report with all the strays collected to Nathan Evans. To the extent Lee could observe or learn from the reports of Evans's skirmishers, the Federal artillery so far had been supported only by cavalry. Around noon, however, a body of infantry crossed the bridge, and the horsemen withdrew.[58]

Thus, as the sun reached and crossed its meridian, Lee stood on Cemetery Hill near Squires's Battery of the Washington Artillery, as it banged away at the enemy slowly encroaching against his center. Here he received report after report of increasingly bad news. Although it is uncertain Jackson sent word at this time, if he did, Stonewall could have only related that he was slowly pulling together into a defensive line the brigades disorganized by their pursuit of Sedgwick's division. But he would also have reported that long columns of fresh Federal troops (Franklin's Sixth Corps) were forming in front of the East Woods.

Word there was from Longstreet, but it was of the most startling sort. Chilton came galloping back from the left-center to announce that he had found Old Peter holding the reins of artillery horses, while his staff worked two guns. In answer to the query of what troops held his line, Longstreet had pointed to his half battery and a small nearby command and remarked, "There they are; but that regiment hasn't a cartridge."[59] Anything else witnessed by Chilton would have been equally discouraging, because it was about this time that D. H. Hill grabbed a musket and led 200 men in a desperate charge against the enemy.

Not long after Lee learned the news that his left-center was crumbling, he walked over to Colonel Walton of the Washington Artillery, who was standing nearby, and asked, "Well, Colonel, what do you make of the enemy? What is he going to do?" Although young Lt. William Owen, adjutant of the battalion, who overheard the exchange, remembered that he spoke "in his quiet way," Lee's calm masked desperation. Walton, of course, had little knowledge of the overall tactical situation, and he merely remarked that the Federals seemed to be shifting a battery farther to the right. At that moment a courier dashed up and thrust forward a message toward the Confederate commander. Lee could not hold the paper because of his bandages and not a single member of his staff remained at hand, so adjutant Owen took the note and read it aloud: "The enemy is moving a six-gun battery to our right, evidently with the intention of covering with it their crossing. [Signed] Johnson, Engineer Officer."[60]

This message meant much more to Lee than it did to Owen. Although the language is somewhat veiled, Lee must have earlier sent one of his engineering officers to observe enemy activity at Snavely's Ford, and the Confederate commander understood the somber portent of the note.[61] McClellan's intentions were now becoming all too clear. The movements against the Middle and Lower Bridges apparently were feints to hold his attention while the Federals turned his right flank. Lee took the only countermeasure open to him. He sent Owen on a mission to move Eshleman's company of the Washington Artillery, one of the two batteries covering the Lower Bridge, to return the fire of the Federal battery and protest the crossing of the ford.

Now all of the pieces for the pending doom were present. And by one o'clock—or as shortly thereafter as it took for the bad news to reach Lee—the pieces began to snap together. On the left-center the Federals overran the Sunken Road; and on the right, not only did the Federals ford the creek at Snavely's, but by flanking Toombs they also uncovered the Lower Bridge. Lee's most desperate moments were at hand. All of the worst possible eventualities had become events, and A. P. Hill was still at least two hours away. Overarching all, the enemy at Snavely's Ford were virtually astride Confederate communications and might even prevent Hill from reaching the field of battle. The time for last desperate measures had arrived. With a boost to Traveller's back, Lee set out for the left to find Stonewall Jackson.

In spite of his desperate circumstances—indeed, because his straits were so dire Lee intended nothing less than to assume the offensive. Several times since arriving at Sharpsburg, he had flirted with the notion of escaping from his box by slipping between McClellan and the upper Potomac. Now his attention was drawn back to the area between the river and the Hagerstown Pike, because that was where the largest, most cohesive part of his army had survived. As chance would have it—or was it more than simply luck?—that was also where his hardest marcher and best offensive lieutenant commanded.

As Lee rode among the troops who had collected in the fields behind the Dunkard Church, he carefully assessed the fighting capability of the units he passed.[62] Spying a three-gun battery that appeared much the worse for the morning's wear, he called out for its commander. Up stepped Capt. William T. Poague of the Rockbridge Artillery to report. Lee asked about the battery's ammunition supply and its condition for a new fight, particularly inquiring about its mobility. The captain replied optimistically for any engagement in the immediate area, but "for any rapid movement," he had to confess, he had only horses enough to move a single gun. As the Confederate commander pondered this reply, his attention was summoned by a begrimed, powder-streaked youth among the gunners.[63]

Either Lee had not recognized the Rockbridge Artillery or, in his intense distraction, he had forgotten his special relationship to the unit. It is even possible that at this moment of supreme crisis in his country's destiny Lee had consciously excluded all personal concerns from his mind. Whatever the explanation, it seems he would have ridden away from the battery without asking after the fate of his youngest son, if Robert E. Lee, Jr., had not spoken up from the ranks. "General," asked Rob, "are you going to send us in again?" (Poague would remember the question as being posed with greater pathos, "You are not going to put us in again in our crippled condition, are you?") What internal grief the reply cost the father can only be guessed. "Yes, my son," said Lee, pointing across the Hagerstown Pike, "you all must do what you can to help drive those people back."

Around one o'clock Dr. Hunter McGuire, medical director for Jackson's command, left his hospital at the Smith farm near Lee's headquarters and rode to the left in search of Stonewall. McGuire found Jackson near the Dunkard Church and offered his chief peaches from his saddlebags. While Jackson, who said he had eaten nothing all day, devoured the peaches "ravenously," the doctor mentioned the thinness of the Confederate lines and tactfully suggested it might be prudent to start transferring the wounded south of the Potomac. There must have been moments during the morning when Jackson himself believed the Confederates were on the verge of being chased out of Maryland, and he had pointedly commented to McLaws several hours before that "God has been very kind to us this day."[64] But the crisis seemed to be past. This was just after Irwin's errant brigade had been repulsed, and Jackson correctly assessed the lull that had settled over that portion of the field. "I think they have done their worst," he told McGuire, "and there is now no danger of the line being broken."[65]

Jackson had less than an hour to enjoy his illusory satisfaction. Sometime between 1:30 and 2:00, Lee found him and apprised him of the impending disaster on the right. The Confederate commander wanted to know if Jackson could undertake an offensive against the Federal forces east of the Hagerstown Pike. Lee could give him Hampton's fresh brigade of cavalry and perhaps some of the stragglers that had been collected in the rear, but for the most part Jackson would have to rely on the infantry and artillery already on hand. It cannot be known whether Lee broached the notion of a turning movement at the start, or whether the idea became a necessity because Jackson contended a frontal attack could not succeed. In any case, if the plan emerged from joint discussion, or was simply dictated by Lee, in the end Jackson was commissioned to get past the enemy's flank with a column composed primarily of cavalry and artillery to attack the enemy's rear. At the sound of small arms fire, the brigades belonging to McLaws and Walker in the West Woods were to attack to the east.[66]

In retrospect Lee's plan seems quixotic. Why not strip Jackson's line of infantry and artillery and rush them to the right? Indeed, why not dismount Hampton's troopers and send them to the right? After all, it was the right that was threatened. At the same time, Lee could have pulled back the remainder of the troops on the left to the Reel Ridge and shortened his lines. This no doubt would have been the best defensive tactics available to him. If it be objected that such measures would take too long, it is difficult to believe that Lee thought the turning movement could be accomplished in less time.

On top of all, it is hard to see why Lee thought the plan would significantly relieve the pressure on his right. The turning movement would imperil only the Federal forces west of the Antietam and, if wildly successful, might drive them back across the creek. Without crossing the Antietam, the Confederates could not threaten McClellan's communications or the main Federal army. The attack was not likely, therefore, to send a shock wave that would cause the instantaneous collapse of the Federal assault on the right. Nor would it regain Lee access to his only escape route, Boteler's Ford, which he was about to lose.

Indeed, Lee's plan makes sense only if viewed as an attempt to open a new path for escape. If the Federal forces parallel to the Hagerstown Pike could be pushed back to or across the Antietam, Lee could try to pull his shattered army northward toward Hagerstown. This, too, would have its risks. Considerable material of the army would almost certainly be lost, and A. P. Hill's division might have to beat a hasty and costly retreat. Yet, if Lee could reach Hagerstown, he would have the protected fords at Williamsport behind him, and his campaign in Maryland would still be alive. Tomorrow would then be more than another day. It would be another opportunity.

It must have been close to two o'clock by the time Lee left Jackson and set out across the fields northwest of Sharpsburg to return to his headquarters tent on the Shepherdstown Road. He no doubt shifted his observation post in order to have a better view of the far right. On his arrival, he found there was still no sign of A. P. Hill's division, but there was moderately good news of another sort. After retiring from the Cornfield and the East Woods, John Hood had rallied a fragment of his division and established a skirmish line in the shape of a V. Stragglers had been passed down to the point, where they were formed into makeshift units under unfamiliar officers. Hood was now returning to the Dunkard Church area with several thousand men in what became known as the "stragglers' brigade." Inspired by the sight of the column as it passed him on the road, Lee shouted loudly enough to be heard by several companies at a time, "Men, I want you to go back on the line, and show that the *stragglers* of the Army of Northern Virginia, are *better than the best troops of the enemy*."[67]

Then, Lee settled down to wait for word from Jackson and A. P. Hill and to keep an eye on the Federal forces at the Lower Bridge and Snavely's Ford.

If Stonewall Jackson thought Lee's plan was quixotic, no evidence of the fact has survived. He set about in earnestness to make it work. He decided he would remain in the West Woods to coordinate the frontal assault and assigned Jeb Stuart to command the turning column. Considering the circumstances, Jackson collected a respectable force for Stuart.[68] In addition to the cavalry of Hampton and Fitz Lee, he borrowed the 48th North Carolina Infantry from Manning's brigade, and he assembled a patchwork battalion of artillery from various batteries. After dispatching the motley division to the northwest, Jackson rode along the line in the woods alerting his subordinates to prepare their men for an attack across the Hagerstown Pike. Anticipating there would be preliminary cannonading, Jackson was careful to specify that musketry would be the signal for the attack. "When you hear the rattle of my small arms," he directed, "this whole line must advance."[69]

While visiting the 35th North Carolina, Jackson noticed an enemy battery on a nearby hill, and he ordered Col. Matthew Ransom to capture it to clear the way for the attack to come. Ransom replied that he would follow any orders Jackson gave him, but he did not believe his regiment could carry the battery. He had already tried it once and failed, and when he had neared the crest he had seen what appeared to be the greater part of the Federal army behind the hill. Jackson could not let this ominous news pass unverified. He asked Ransom, "Have you a good climber in your command?" The famous incident that followed has been related in inimitable fashion by the regimental historian of the 35th North Carolina:

> Colonel Ransom called for volunteers, and Private Wm. S. Hood, Company H, jumped up and said he could climb. Jackson picked out a tall hickory tree and told him to go up it. Hood pulled off his

shoes in a jiffy and went up like a squirrel. When he got near the top Jackson, sitting on his horse under the tree, asked him: "How many troops are over there?"

Hood uttering an exclamation of amazement, replied: "Oceans of them."

Jackson sternly said: "Count the flags, Sir!"

Hood began: "One, two, three, four, etc., etc.,"

General Jackson repeating after him the numbers until he had counted thirty-nine, when Jackson said: "That will do, come down, sir."

All this time the enemy's sharpshooters were firing at Hood.[70]

Jackson had heard enough to excuse the 35th North Carolina from charging the Federal battery. Even more, what he had learned did not bode well for Lee's plan. It would not have been unreasonable for Jackson to assume the "ocean" of flags represented 20,000 or more enemy awaiting him across the pike. Nor, would he have been far off the mark in such an estimate, although only the 7,300 men in five of Franklin's six brigades of the Sixth Corps had not already been mauled by the day's fighting. Against this enemy horde, Jackson would be fortunate to muster 5,000 in his line in the West Woods.[71] Having stripped his batteries of their best guns for Stuart, he would also be weak in artillery and would have few if any pieces capable of following the infantry in their advance. Jackson may have been heartened to learn that Lee had forwarded a stragglers' brigade several thousand strong under Hood to his support. Yet, when taken all together, Stonewall must have known that the success of Lee's plan would depend entirely on Stuart's ability to panic the enemy and throw them into disarray.

By three o'clock Stuart had assembled a long column at the Cox farm on the River Road about three-quarters of a mile west of the Nicodemus Hill. In the full force under his command he had nine regiments of cavalry (2,600) and three of infantry (1,300). He also had the nine pieces of artillery Jackson had collected from various batteries, as well as the full batteries of French and Branch of Walker's division, or a total of twenty-one guns.[72] At the start he divided his forces to protect his own flank during the turning movement. He sent the twelve guns under French and Branch to Nicodemus Hill and moved the infantry slightly to the east to support them. Then, with the nine stray guns, which he had put under Capt. John Pelham's command, and the cavalry, he headed north on the River Road.

The three regiments of Fitz Lee's brigade, with the 4th Virginia in the lead, advanced nearly a mile until they reached the tiny hamlet called New Industry situated on the banks of the Potomac; it is at this point the river makes a radical swing eastward and approaches to within seven hundred yards of the Hagerstown Pike. Stuart thus discovered that the route to the north was open. Masked by the high ground on his right, his entire force might escape without notice. No explanation has ever been offered why Stuart did not continue northward to Bakersville and then east to gain the rear of the Federal right flank. Instead, he halted Fitz Lee at New Industry and sent Pelham with the artillery east on the road that connected with the Hagerstown Pike. After going a few hundred feet, Pelham went into battery on an eminence to the left of the road and parallel to the pike and but a short nine hundred yards from the artillery of the First Corps posted on the dominating Poffenberger Hill. Even as Pelham took up his position, the Federals erupted with a "most terrific fire," and within fifteen minutes the Confederates guns were driven to seek shelter.[73] In a vain attempt to support their beleaguered colleagues, the batteries of French and Branch started firing from Nicodemus Hill. They got off only a few rounds before they too were forced to retire.

The almost instantaneous silencing of the Confederate artillery stopped Stuart in his tracks. Hampton halted well short of New Industry, and the 48th North Carolina—after double-quicking to its new position on the left—never fired a shot. After thirty to forty-five minutes spent pondering the situation, Stuart ended the turning movement and retired with his force to his former position. By four o'clock Lee's plan was dead.

William Poague, who accompanied his gun from the Rockbridge Artillery on the mission, noted in his memoirs that some of the officers had protested to Pelham at the idea of opening fire on the strong Federal position. "Oh, we must stir them up a little," Pelham had replied with a laugh, "and then slip away." With some pointedness, Poague commented, "And so we did stir them up, and with a vengeance they soon stirred us out." When the reports of Jackson and Stuart became available after the war, Poague would excuse Pelham and assume the escapade had been Stuart's "method of determining whether McClellan's flank could be turned."[74] If so, it was a most peculiar method indeed. On the contrary, it would seem to be another instance, similar to both

Evelington Heights and Chantilly, when Stuart had failed in a serious responsibility because of his penchant for "stirring up" the enemy at an inappropriate moment.

Both Lee and Jackson make plain in their reports that they intended a turning movement, and Stuart in his report admits he understood his objective.[75] Longstreet and Walker even remembered Jackson talking of the purpose to get past the enemy and attack in the rear, which by definition is part of a turning movement.[76] In performance, however, Stuart executed a flank attack rather than a turning movement. After demonstrating that three cavalry regiments and nine guns could get past the Federal flank, Stuart turned east and frontally assaulted the end of the enemy line. Whether or not his entire force could have slipped behind the protection of the high ground will never be known. Nor is it possible to guess what success would have met a Confederate attack from the north or northwest. In truth, it is highly doubtful that a cavalry force and nine guns might have accomplished much against the massed Federal artillery that could have been easily swung around to confront them. And it is unlikely that the 1,300 infantry and additional twelve guns Stuart might have taken with him would have made a difference.

Still, it was not Stuart's place to decide in advance that Lee's plan would not work. Especially was it incumbent upon him to put forth a full effort to make the plan work in light of the fact that the survival of the Army of Northern Virginia seemed to hinge on his success.

The word that reached Jackson sometime between 4:00 and 4:30 was that the Federal line stretched almost to a "remarkable bend" in the Potomac and that enemy artillery so covered the short distance remaining as to render a turning movement impossible.[77] This news caused Jackson, who had become convinced during the delay of the difficulties facing a frontal attack, to suspend all plans for an offensive on the left. As he rode along the line to alert his subordinates that the attack had been canceled, he encountered Longstreet and Walker in conference on the ridge south of the Dunkard Church and opposite the Sunken Road.

It seems that earlier in the afternoon, Longstreet had decided—without consultation with Lee or Jackson—that the Federals were so demoralized as to justify a Confederate counterattack from the West Woods.[78] Learning that Ransom's brigade had been directed to launch an assault, Walker found Longstreet and explained the planned turning movement in progress. Longstreet had withdrawn his order, and the two generals were awaiting the sound of Stuart's attack when Jackson rode up with the bad news.[79]

At that point all plans for any offensive were dropped. If the survival of the Army of Northern Virginia had in fact depended solely upon aggressive action being undertaken on its left—as Lee believed to be the case when he ordered the turning movement—the army would have ceased to exist by four o'clock on the afternoon of September 17. Luckily for Lee, three developments offset Stuart's failure. McClellan's deliberateness, Burnside's delay, and A. P. Hill's arrival twisted fortune one more time before darkness fell.

Burnside's Attack and Lee's Final Crisis, 2:00 to 5:00 P.M.

At Federal headquarters the cautious optimism triggered by the simultaneous successes at the Sunken Road, Lower Bridge, and Snavely's Ford began to evaporate within an hour. Instead of the sound of roaring rifles from troops pressing the advantages gained at any of these three points, an ominous lull settled over the field by two o'clock. Only the occasional crackle of skirmishers' muskets accompanied the artillery continuo played along the line. To the south, for reasons unknown to McClellan, Burnside's men were not moving forward from the bridge, and to the north Franklin had formed a division for attack but was not advancing it.

Half of the mystery was soon explained when an aide galloped into the Pry yard. He was fresh from Sumner's field headquarters behind the East Woods and had just witnessed a heated argument between the two corps commanders on the right. Franklin wanted to attack, but Sumner absolutely forbade it, and both were appealing to the army commander to settle the dispute. McClellan recognized that the decisive moment of the battle had arrived. He dispatched Col. Thomas M. Key, judge advocate general of the Army of the Potomac, with peremptory orders to Burnside to carry the bluffs and advance on Sharpsburg. Then, McClellan called for his horse and set out for the Upper Bridge. He was prepared, if necessary, to personally direct the attack on the Confederate left.[80]

Sometime between 2:30 and 3:00 McClellan arrived on the scene behind the East Woods.[81] What he observed as he approached the battlefield must have prepared him to believe the excessively gloomy report he heard from Sumner. Not only did he observe ample evidence along the route of the 10,000 casualties already suffered by his army, but also, in witnessing Sedgwick's veterans break and run when a single shell exploded nearby, he had convincing proof of the unsteadiness of the troops which had survived the firestorm. Apparently, Sumner swore that the First, Second, and Twelfth Corps were finished, at least temporarily, as fighting units. If Franklin's attack failed, he warned, there would be nothing to stop the Confederates from destroying all four corps. Even more, there was no visible sign of weakness in the Confederate line in the West Woods and no reason to expect that Franklin's 9,000 men could accomplish what 30,000 had wrecked themselves in attempting all morning.

Based on his own observations and Sumner's tale of woe, McClellan decided to cancel the assault. In fact, so strongly did Sumner present the case for the thinness of the Federal line from the North Woods to the Sunken Road and the potential for the success of a Confederate counter-attack, that McClellan stripped his center of half its defenders by ordering the brigades of Charles Griffin and Thomas Stockton (Morell's division, Fifth Corps) to march to Franklin's support.[82] Ironically, Sumner was at least partly right. At almost the very same moment, Lee was indeed planning a counterattack. The turning movement under Stuart stemmed from desperation, however, not from strength, and it would die aborning.

When McClellan suspended Franklin's attack, he also abandoned his overall tactical plan for the battle. No longer would there be simultaneous attacks on the enemy flanks; nor would there be any significant support to send to Burnside on the left. Only 5,000 men remained in the center to cover the Artillery Reserve, the trains, and the communications of the army.[83] On the basis of the changed circumstances, it would have been reasonable for McClellan to cancel Burnside's attack. There would not be sufficient time, however. As McClellan finished his visit with Sumner, the Ninth Corps simultaneously launched its assault on Sharpsburg.

The 51st Pennsylvania and 51st New York regiments carried the Lower Bridge at a little past one o'clock. Immediately thereafter, Jacob Cox, field commander for the Ninth Corps, crossed over Sturgis's division (Nagle and Ferrero) and Crook's brigade (Kanawha division), about 5,000 men, to the eastern bank of the Antietam. These three brigades had been engaged since 10:00 in futile assaults on the bridge. Once across the Antietam, they discovered their ammunition was depleted, and Sturgis reported "his men so exhausted by their efforts as to be unfit for an immediate advance." Certainly, this was true in the case of Edward Ferrero's brigade, which had suffered casualties (29.3 percent) approaching the level of the forces engaged to the north. James Nagle and George Crook (losing 14.4 and 4.0 percent, respectively) should have been relatively fresh; and, clearly, someone was derelict in coordinating the logistics of the Ninth Corps.[84] Nevertheless, Cox was compelled to request, and Burnside to approve, a delay until ammunition wagons and Willcox's fresh division could be brought up from the rear.

It required two hours for the 3,000 men of Willcox to get into position and for Sturgis's men—who were, after all, only to be held in reserve at the bridge—to replenish their ammunition.[85] Apparently, the delay also retarded the progress of the Ninth Corps's left wing. The 3,700 men of Rodman's division (Harland and Fairchild) and Hugh Ewing's brigade (Kanawha division) had suffered virtually no casualties in crossing Snavely's Ford under the fire of a single battery, the videttes of Munford's cavalry, and a handful of infantry skirmishers. Yet, Rodman also took two hours to work his way upstream to the bridge.

Finally, at three o'clock (at almost exactly the time that Stuart set out on his expedition, that McClellan decided to suspend the offensive on the right, and a half-hour after A. P. Hill arrived in advance of his division to report at Lee's headquarters) the Ninth Corps launched its assault. In a front line 5,800 strong, with Rodman on the left and Willcox on the right, supported by the 2,800 men of the Kanawha division, Jacob Cox angled his attack to the northwest toward Sharpsburg. Unaware that McClellan had abandoned the overall battle plan, Cox set out to execute his part of the program by clearing the heights in front of Sharpsburg and uncovering the Middle Bridge.[86]

In about an hour, the Ninth Corps advanced three-quarters of a mile and had come near to achieving its objective. By four o'clock Benjamin Christ and Thomas Welsh of Willcox had secured the eastern and southern slopes of Cemetery Hill, and their skirmishers had driven the Confederate artillery off that dominating crest. Harrison Fairchild's brigade (Rodman) had driven the Confederate infantry (D. R. Jones) from the ridges and through the ravines south of town and into the streets of Sharpsburg. At the same time—although with absolutely no coordination with Cox—Capt. Hiram Dryer advanced the 4th U.S. Infantry along the Boonsboro Pike to the northeastern slope of Cemetery Hill.[87]

Unfortunately for the Federals, as Cox's line advanced farther from the Antietam, its left flank floated higher and higher into the air. No

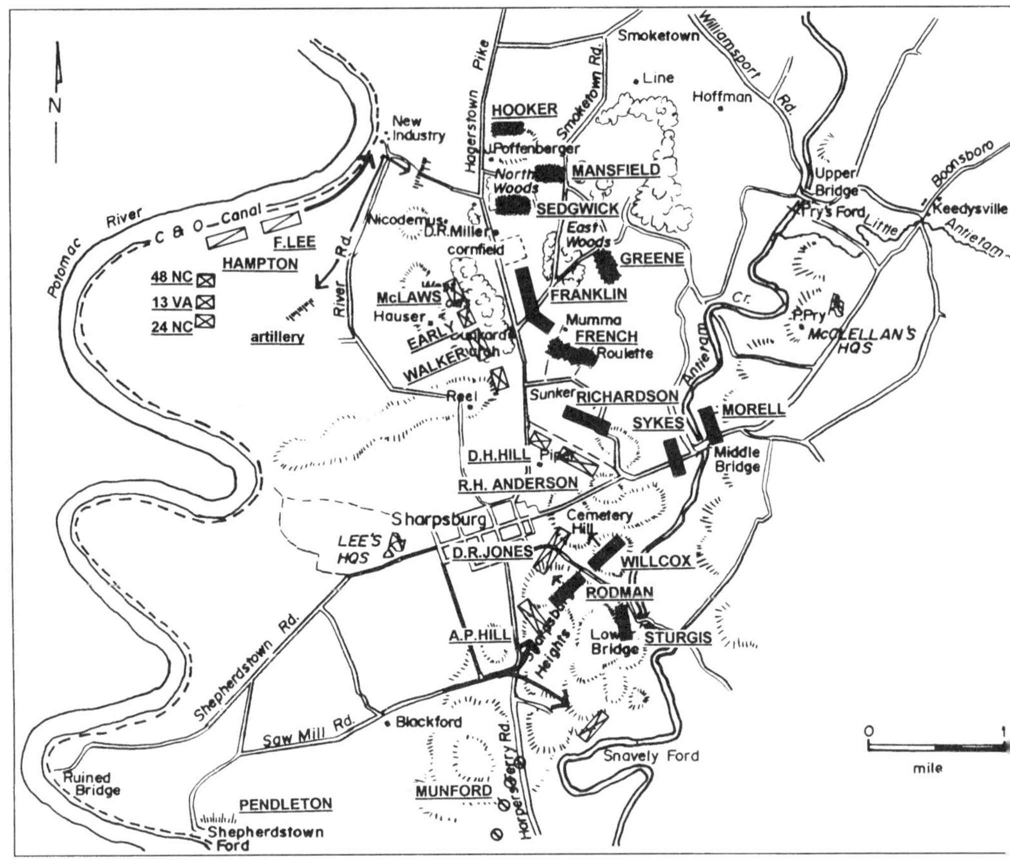

Battle of Sharpsburg, September 17, sixth phase

explanation has ever been offered as to why Cox should have kept two divisions of fourteen regiments in reserve and not used any of them to protect his flank. In one final twist, fate turned against the Union. A. P. Hill's division arrived from Harpers Ferry at just the right time and in exactly the right place to take advantage of the Federal carelessness.

Lee, after returning from the meeting with Jackson, did not return to his observation post on Cemetery Hill. Not only was the position now swept by Federal batteries west of the Antietam, but it no longer afforded Lee a view of his greatest threat. He found a knoll south of the Shepherdstown Road near his headquarters tent that allowed him to observe both D. R. Jones directly to the east as well as the approaches to Sharpsburg from the Lower Bridge and Snavely's Ford. He must have been relieved to learn that in his hour's absence the enemy column at the ford had not advanced west to cut Confederate communications but had merely moved slowly north to join the troops at the Middle Bridge. For some unknown reason, the combined enemy forces did not then immediately launch their attack, and Lee was spared a few more precious minutes.

He needed every moment. He had less than 3,000 infantry to defend his center and right, from the Middle Bridge all the way south to the Potomac. On paper he had nearly seventy guns in the battalions of Walton, Frobel, and Jones and the batteries of Boyce and Wise; but some of these guns had been disabled, and others had been forced to leave the line in search of ammunition. He could not expect success from what he had at hand. He had to rely on there being time for the arrival of A. P. Hill, or relief to come from Jackson's turning movement.

At 2:30, up the knoll galloped A. P. Hill, accompanied by his staff. He reported that his division had just started to cross the Potomac and was about an hour behind. "General Hill I was never so glad to see you," exclaimed Lee, who made no attempt to disguise the relief in his voice, "you are badly needed. Put your force in on the right as soon as they come up."[88]

Powell Hill may well have told Lee he brought only five of his six brigades, leaving four Georgia regiments under Col. Edward Thomas to continue wagoning captured stores from Harpers Ferry. But, he must have either failed to mention at all or else seriously understated the bedraggled condition of his men after their forced march. Had Lee known that but 3,200 infantry would reach the field as reenforcements, it is improbable he would have split the column. Perhaps believing 5,000 were approaching, Lee instructed Hill to send the first three brigades to the support of D. R. Jones but to detach the last two to guard the Antietam Furnace Road against the approach of additional Federal forces from Snavely's Ford, or from the bridge near the mouth of the Antietam. He assigned Capt. Osmun Latrobe, inspector general on D. R. Jones staff, to guide the latter into position.[89]

There is no indication that Lee then or at any time thereafter expressed dissatisfaction to Hill about his tardiness in reaching Sharpsburg. Still, Lee did write to Davis that he had "hoped" Hill would have arrived on the night of the 16th, and one of the most enduring impression Lee carried from Sharpsburg was that his army was "not all on the ground until late in the day."[90] Apparently, Lee believed that Hill would leave Harpers Ferry at the earliest opportunity, while Hill understood that he was to await instructions. In the absence of evidence, Hill cannot be solely blamed for the misunderstanding. He can be faulted, however, for failing to anticipate Lee's order to march. Although he completed the paroling of the prisoners on the 16th, Hill exhibited a reluctance easily understood in any Confederate to forfeit a single piece of the captured stores.[91] Still, when the sounds of battle became clearly audible in Harpers Ferry at dawn,[92] the very best of commanders on a detached mission would have made full preparations to march to the roaring cannon at moment's notice. Jackson might even have left without instructions.

Lee's orders arrived at 6:30, and the head of Hill's column set out at 7:30. Certainly an hour is not an inordinate amount of time to go from camp to march, but just as certainly it indicates the division was not standing at arms and awaiting only the command to move. On top of which, Hill inexplicably chose to ignore the relatively straight and easy road that ran from Halltown west toward Shepherdstown, which all of the other divisions had employed, and instead he set out on the torturously winding river road.

Finally, even if the distance covered did amount to seventeen miles as Hill claimed in his report—and the Confederate's own map makes the route appear five or so miles shorter[93]—the eight hours consumed meant that Hill made little better time than Franklin had from Pleasant Valley. While it is true Hill had the Potomac to ford and midday hours to endure, these factors are insufficient to justify the myth that has grown up about the miraculous double-quick march for the salvation of Lee. Nor would they explain why Franklin's men arrived in excellent shape to fight, while Hill shed 40 percent of his troops along the route. It seems that the timeliness of Hill's appearance at Sharpsburg has stifled a number of pointed questions that might otherwise have been asked.[94]

Yet, ironically, had Hill arrived earlier, there is no guarantee his impact would have been nearly so beneficial. On the one hand, had Hill been present at one o'clock, he might have stopped Rodman from crossing Snavely's Ford and Sturgis from carrying the Lower Bridge. In that case, there would have been no late-afternoon crisis. On the other hand, if Hill had arrived at any time before one o'clock, Lee might have been compelled to commit his division to the defense of the Sunken Road. In that event, there would have been no way to stop Burnside and the Army of Northern Virginia might have been destroyed by four.

It is also true—and this Lee must have grasped on the spot—the mere appearance of Hill with his staff would not save the Confederate right. In the hour or more required for Hill's troops to come up, the day and the army could still be lost. As the minutes dragged on—and while Lee waited in vain for word of Jackson's turning movement—it began to seem that Federal inertia alone might save the Confederates on the southern front. Then, at three o'clock, long lines of blue began to advance northward from the Lower Bridge. D. R. Jones's four small brigades, outnumbered four to one, could cover only half of the enemy's front and were pushed inexorably back on Sharpsburg. Simultaneously, Federal infantry began to creep forward from the Middle Bridge along the northern edge of the Boonsboro Pike. Richardson's battery, the last of the Washington Artillery that remained in the center, under heavy fire and out of ammunition, was compelled to abandon Cemetery Hill.

Galvanized by the emergency, Lee and his staff and all the higher officers at hand grabbed every soldier who could stand and fire and every gun with wheels and horses and shoved them to the front. Fragments of the divisions of D. H. Hill and R. H. Anderson, men who had already been through several battles during the day, were pressed into impromptu companies and forwarded to Evans in the center. Masking his own unease, the Confederate commander called out to sixty-six survivors of the 1st North Carolina (Ripley), as they were about to enter battle for the third time, "Go in cheerfully boys." At this time, Stephen Lee opportunely returned with twelve guns and fresh ammunition and was rushed to Cemetery Hill. For the support of Jones on the right there was no infantry, but Richardson and Miller of the Washington Artillery and Read's battery (McLaws) were hurried to the south. Yet, as four o'clock neared, it seemed that nothing would stop the enemy's advance from the Lower Bridge.[95]

Into this broiling sea of confusion rode Lt. John Ramsay with the right section of Reilly's battery (Hood). He had spent hours in the rear searching for ammunition for his two 10-pounder Parrotts. With his limbers full, he was approaching Sharpsburg from the west on the Shepherdstown Road, when Lee spied him and his telescope. "What troops are those?" asked Lee, pointing to a line almost in the southeastern outskirts of Sharpsburg. Ramsay uncased his glass and handed it to the general. "Can't use it," said Lee, holding up his bandaged hands. Ramsay quickly dismounted and adjusted his lens. "They are flying the United States flag." Lee then pointed to a line farther to the west and almost at right angles to the first and asked, "What troops are those?" Scanning to the right, Ramsay replied, "They are flying the Virginia and Confederate flags." Said Lee, "It is A. P. Hill, from Harpers Ferry."[96]

Even then it appeared Hill may have arrived too late. Shortly after four, D. R. Jones reported in person that his line had broken. His men were retreating through the streets of Sharpsburg, and the town was lost. This was bad news for Lee to digest. It meant that Evans's brigade and S. D. Lee's guns on Cemetery Hill were lost, and communication with Jackson's wing had been all but severed. Happily, Jones's news was about twenty minutes old and midst the fast-breaking events was obsolete. Even as Lee pondered his next move, Capt. Robert Troup of Toombs's staff dashed up and breathlessly reported that the enemy was in full retreat. He said that General Toombs believed the Federals could be driven back across the Antietam if there were some artillery support available. "What!" exclaimed Jones. "Haven't the enemy got Sharpsburg?" Upon Troup's assurance that the situation had been completely reversed, Lee said, "Tell General Toombs to take any guns he can find, and use them as he thinks best."[97]

Lee could not let slip this opportunity to inflict even greater harm on the enemy. From nearby he summoned Charles Squires of the Washington Artillery, who had been driven from Cemetery Hill and was now engaged in rallying yet another stragglers' brigade. "Capt. Squires," ordered the Confederate commander, "gather up every rifled gun you can find, take them wherever you find them and proceed with them to General Toombs of Georgia."[98]

In spite of Robert Toombs's exuberant pronouncement of victory, however, he and his men had made merely a contribution to the repulse of the Ninth Corps. Greater roles had belonged to the men of A. P. Hill and to luck.

After leaving Lee, A. P. Hill rode into Sharpsburg and at the small village square turned right onto the Harpers Ferry Road, which ran behind and parallel to D. R. Jones's defensive line. He conferred with Jones, learning the precise position of the troops he was to support, and discovered that there was a shorter route for his men to take than the one he had followed. All of the forces arriving from Harpers Ferry previously had traveled almost due north to the Shepherdstown Road. About midway on this road, however, Hill could turn to the right and follow the Saw Mill Road east to the Harpers Ferry Road. Not only would this halve the distance, but it would bring his division up on the right of Kemper's Brigade, the far right of Jones's line.

It cannot be known for certain whether Hill set out to return to his men before or after the Federals started their advance from the Lower Bridge at three o'clock. In either case, Hill behaved as if he fully recognized the value of every moment. He rode down the Saw Mill Road to the Blackford farm, where Thomas Munford had established headquarters.[99] He then hurried his division across the Potomac without giving the men time to wring the water from their socks and trousers.[100] It is revealing that Hill worked from the rear to hasten the arrival of his division and that he committed each brigade piecemeal as soon as it cleared the river, rather than waiting to accumulate his strength for greater impact. While this can be explained in part by the urgency of the situation, it also indicates that Hill understood his men were expected to perform the relatively simple task of extending the Confederate defensive line and could be put into position by Jones or Kemper. Had Hill anticipated that his division would be called upon to execute an independent, full-scale attack on the flank of the enemy, he might have waited to have several brigades in hand, and it is almost certain the impetuous officer would have been on hand to direct the assault.

Of course, had Hill waited even a quarter-hour for any reason, he might have been too late. Happily, his largest brigade, the 1,000-strong five South Carolina regiments of Maxcy Gregg, was in the van. At 3:40, when Gregg entered the Harpers Ferry Road, he found that no Confederate line existed for him to support. He saw only the shards of Toombs's brigade, which appeared demoralized and heading for the rear. Even then, D. R. Jones's division was falling back into the streets of Sharpsburg. As Gregg headed north, he saw to the east that the enemy had overrun the Pee Dee Artillery, which was attached to his brigade and had preceded him onto the field. He also saw the enemy line was at right angles to his own and presenting its vulnerable flank. Needing no further inducements, Gregg swung to his right and cautiously advanced through a forty-acre cornfield toward the Federals he could no longer see.[101]

A. P. Hill's arrival had not gone undetected. At three o'clock, the Federal signal station on Red Hill alerted Burnside's headquarters: "Look out well on your left; the enemy are moving a strong force in that direction."[102] Because of the mortal wounding later of Isaac Rodman, who commanded the Federal left wing, it is uncertain whether this message was relayed to the front in time. From whatever alarm, Rodman did attempt to refuse his flank and sent a force into the forty-acre cornfield from the east. Unfortunately this critical duty—of being the left regiment of the left brigade of the left division of the left corps of the Army of the Potomac—this day fell on the one-month-old 16th Connecticut. The green regiment would have barely known what to do had it been standing on a level field and closely supported by friends on either side.

Instead, it found itself alone in a hilly field of tall, standing corn catching glimpses of blue uniforms through the stalks in its front. It approached much too close to Gregg's brigade, and then it broke under a withering fire.

As the panic-stricken Connecticut soldiers fled from the field, they disrupted the lines of the 4th Rhode Island Infantry, which was marching to their support. When the Rhode Islanders halted to reform, they spotted what appeared to be United States flags in the corn in front of them. Three volunteers carried the regimental colors to within twenty feet of the indeterminate force before a blaze of musketry settled the question. The 4th Rhode Island briefly returned the fire, while officers searched the acres of corn for support. When none could be found, orders were given to retire, but the withdrawal soon became a confused race for safety.[103]

As viewed from the Confederate perspective, the climax to Antietam's fury was even more routine. According to Alexander Haskell, Gregg's adjutant, "We had three pitched battles with Burnside. In the two first, he charged us and was driven back. In the third, we charged him and drove him from the field."[104] While Gregg only drove two regiments from the field, the collapse of Harland's brigade exposed the left flank of Fairchild, whose men had carried the ravine south of Cemetery Hill and whose skirmishers were entering the side streets of Sharpsburg. When Branch's North Carolinians came down the Harpers Ferry Road and veered east they struck the 8th Connecticut and the left end of Fairchild's line. Against the veteran Federals, Branch did not meet with the same easy success. Indeed, Fairchild retired only when he realized that an enemy force (Gregg) was threatening his rear.[105]

In the confused fighting that followed, Cox seems never to have considered joining with Sykes's regular infantry on the Boonsboro Pike—which was within hailing distance of his right—and thereby uncovering the Middle Bridge for reenforcements from Porter. This movement would have fulfilled McClellan's requirements, and it almost certainly would have brought assistance to the Ninth Corps from the center. Instead, Cox ordered Willcox, the division on the right, to retrace the route southeast to the high ground around the Lower Bridge, while he brought Sturgis forward to cover the retreat.

Additional assaults by Archer's brigade, Toombs, and the reformed units of D. R. Jones (the latter having hurried through the side streets of the village and down the Harpers Ferry Road) contributed little to the closing scenes of the battle. A. P. Hill's last two brigades (Pender and Field) were sent to watch Snavely's Ford, as ordered by Lee, and did not participate in the repulse. Nevertheless, by six o'clock or shortly thereafter, Cox had pulled his entire force back to a semicircle around the western edge of the Lower Bridge. By the time Captain Squires had collected nine long-range guns and reported to Toombs, the light was failing and there was no opportunity to drive the Federals across the Antietam.[106] In fine, it was the thousand men in Gregg's brigade that stopped the Ninth Corps and saved the Army of Northern Virginia.

In the sixth and final phase of the battle of Antietam each side committed comparatively large numbers of fresh troops, but each also suffered lighter casualties than in any other phase of the fighting. The 6,600 Confederates in the commands of D. R. Jones, Evans, A. P. Hill, and the various artillery units on the right and center suffered 1,226 casualties for a rate of 18.6 percent. On the Federal side, the Ninth Corps and elements of the Fifth Corps and the Horse Artillery totaled nearly 15,000 and lost 2,462 for an even lighter 16.6 percent. Several Federal exceptions must be noted: Ferrero suffered 29.3 percent in carrying the bridge; and, in rates exceeding even most of the carnage on the northern front, Harland and Fairchild lost 33.4 percent and 48.3 percent respectively, as the target of Hill's flank attack.

Lee had been right. September 17 was indeed a hard day's work. The Army of Northern Virginia fought like a wounded beast driven to its lair. It waged an aggressive, open field defense, and it paid an excessively high price. The Confederates suffered 31.4 percent casualties compared to the 24.4 percent of the Federals, who nominally were on the offense.

But—and who is to say for certain—it may well have been Confederate aggressiveness that saved the Southern army. Surely, the assaults by Hood, McLaws, and A. P. Hill were not merely justified but unavoidable. Even the smaller offensives, however—the attacks by Jackson, Hays, Ripley, Colquitt, Early, Ransom, Cooke, D. H. Hill, and others—exuded a confidence and determination that dissuaded the Federals from committing their last reserves in a desperate final bid for victory.

For both sides, Sharpsburg was a compact field of concentrated fury. In twelve hours, 82,000 men fought over less than a 1,000 acres. Nearly 23,000 (27.1 percent) fell casualty by the time the sun sank behind the western bluffs bordering the Potomac.

For the Confederates, Sharpsburg was a cruel field for reasons beyond bullet and shot and shell. By a quirk of nature, the ground most heavily contested was virtually devoid of running water. And, to complete the misery, many of the subsistence wagons that Lee had ordered away the previous morning never found their regiments and brigades. In consequence, most of the Confederates fought—and many died—this "longest, saddest" day with empty stomachs and throats parched from thirst.[107]

Night of Reckoning

Night became shroud, mercifully cloaking the swath of destruction and misery that stretched two miles southward from the North Woods to the Lower Bridge. Its darkness enfolded the dead, whose corpses lay in rows in the Miller Cornfield as they had stood in regimental ranks, strewed the fields and woods around the Dunkard Church, and thickly carpeted the bed of the Sunken Road. It also hid from view the piteous sight of the writhing wounded who lay suspended between life and death. And it veiled the exhausted living, few of whom slept, while some quested through the carnage for friends or pilfered for small treasures. Yet, this darkness never reached the pitch blackness usual in farm lands, as the horizon, blushing murky red from the burning buildings in Sharpsburg, cast a fittingly hellish tinge to the landscape. But, in the end, Antietam closed as it had begun—with the overwhelming impression of sounds. Silent now were the guns. Swelling the chorus of the night were the voices of human agony.[108]

Less is known about Lee at sunset and the hours immediately following than at any other time of the day. He neither sent or received any written messages that have survived; nor, so far as can be determined, did he venture forth from the field across the road from his tent on the Shepherdstown Road. Instead, in the hours of twilight, after dispositions had been made to secure the thin lines, the leadership of the army drifted instinctively toward the commanding general. Some, no doubt, came expecting to receive orders to withdraw during the night into Virginia. Many must have doubted the campaign in Maryland could be continued. All brought tales of the day's staggering losses and of the handful of survivors.

Lighted by the lurid glow from a burning farmhouse on the edge of the field, the group increased in size as each general arrived with several staff officers. Jackson came, along with both Hills, Early, Hood, D. R. Jones, and the artillerists Walton and S. D. Lee. In the center, surrounded by his own staff, Robert E. Lee spoke individually with each arriving general, asking in a quiet voice, "How is it on your part of the line?" The answers, according to Col. Stephen Lee, who much later would claim to have been close enough to hear the conversations, were unvaryingly grim. When John Hood, visibly shaken, reported that he had no command, Lee responded with equal emotion, "Great God! General Hood, where is your splendid division?" With a suggestion of bitterness, Hood answered, "They are lying on the field where you sent them." None of the generals were optimistic about continuing the fight on the morrow, and some suggested retreat.[109]

Looking around the group, Lee noticed a face was missing, and asked anxiously, "But where is Longstreet?" Maj. Charles Venable, aide-de-camp, replied, "I saw him at sun down, all right." As if on summons, Old Peter rode up just then, trailing a cloud of smoke from the cigar he habitually carried clenched between his teeth during a battle and lighted only after the fighting stopped. He had been delayed in tending wounded and helping a family whose home was burning in Sharpsburg. "Ah! here is Longstreet," said Lee coming forward and throwing his arm around the shoulder of his senior lieutenant, "here's my old war-horse! Let us hear what he has to say."[110] If Lee expected a more optimistic report, he was disappointed. Longstreet said his front was manned by "little better than a good skirmish line," and he advised returning to Virginia before daylight.[111]

It seems unlikely that Lee could have anticipated good news from his generals. He had seen too much of the day's battle. He knew full well that his army had been on the verge of destruction four times. He could not have forgotten that he had been compelled to commit his last reserves by ten in the morning or that only the providential hesitation of the Federals and the timely arrival of A. P. Hill had reprieved the Army of Northern Virginia from certain annihilation. Of course, he could not know precisely what casualties he had suffered or how many men remained. He may have even discounted somewhat the reports of his generals as the exaggerations of men fresh from a day's work that had indeed been hard. It is possible, therefore, that Lee did not realize that at that moment his army had melted to less than 25,000 men of all arms.

Still, Lee had seen too many broken, shattered regiments not to understand the weakness of his manpower in general terms. He knew that among the forces with him only the brigades of Pender and Field (A. P. Hill) had not been heavily engaged. He also knew that the only additional force within supporting distance was Thomas's brigade at Harpers Ferry and that recent experience suggested that Thomas could not be brought up by daylight. Moreover, by this time the Confederate commander had certainly received Jackson's report on the failed turning movement—even the junior officers in the outer circle were saying "what a pity" Stonewall "had not been able to get around the flank of the enemy this afternoon"[112]—and thus he knew that the route northward to Hagerstown was closed. This meant he had but two options. Either he must retreat, or else he must stand another day to receive the attacks of the Federals. The choice could not be delayed. If the decision were to be retreat, the movement would have to commence at once.

After several long minutes of silence engulfed the inner group, Lee announced his decision in words to the following effect: "Gentlemen, we will not cross the Potomac to-night. You will go to your respective commands, strengthen your forces; send two officers from each brigade towards the ford to collect your stragglers and get them up. I have had the proper steps taken to collect all the men who are in the rear. If McClellan wants to fight in the morning I will give him battle again. Go!"[113]

Lee never felt the need to justify or even to explain his decision to stand at Sharpsburg an additional day. In his report he would write only, "We awaited without apprehension the renewal of the attack."[114] In his several postwar conversations on the Maryland campaign he did not refer to the subject. The best explanation must come, therefore, from an understanding of Lee's intentions in the Maryland campaign and how that campaign exemplified his strategy for winning the war.

Both the tenor of Lee's instructions and the speed of his choice indicate he had made up his mind before hearing the reports from his officers. This conclusion is not surprising, since he could have heard nothing from his subordinates that would have justified his decision. Indeed, Lee could not have elected to remain at Sharpsburg on the basis of anything he knew about his tactical situation or based on the advice of any military axiom he had ever learned. With his skeletal army, he chose to stand an additional day on the peninsula of a major river with a single ford for escape—and that a rough and rocky passage preceded by a precipitous canal to cross. Nor is it possible that Lee any longer believed the Army of the Potomac was too demoralized to give a good account of itself, or, as some have hypothesized, that he confidently divined McClellan's timidity. No rational general would have staked the existence of his army merely on the assumption that his opponent—a general who had just savagely attacked both flanks and reduced the Confederate army to a husk—would not attack at all on the following day.

And Lee was not irrational. He was not even bold or audacious, at least not in the sense that boldness and audacity are commonly understood to encompass taking risks that might be avoided. Lee was a desperate leader of a desperate cause who made a desperate decision to stand at Sharpsburg on September 18. It was not the first desperate decision he had made, and it would not be the last, although it may have been his most outrageous. It differed in degree but not in essence from his decisions to divide his army and attack north of the Chickahominy on June 26; to send Longstreet to Gordonsville on August 9, days before there was good cause to believe McClellan was leaving the James; to detach Jackson on a twenty-five-mile sweep from the main body to gain Pope's rear on August 24; to cross the Potomac and carry the war into enemy territory on September 4 and, indeed, from virtually every major strategic decision he had been compelled to render since September 13, when the unexpected advance of the Federal army had forced him to stand at South Mountain with a badly divided army.

The fact that fate had favored each one of these desperate ventures does not make it necessary to believe that Lee had beguiled himself into believing he could do no wrong, and the enemy could do no right. Lee understood that no single victory could win the war for the South, except the last one in a long series of successes that had incrementally demoralized the North to the point of abandoning the war. After the herculean Confederate effort of the springtime to conscript, mobilize, and concentrate its maximum force, Lee had gambled on using that strength in a maximum effort to create a tide of victories. And he had succeeded. He also knew—at least vaguely—that the tide had expanded beyond the Virginia front. Other armies of the Confederacy were on the march northward. He must have believed the best chance for winning the war was at hand. He may have reasonably doubted that such a combination of strength and good fortune could ever again be assembled.

In the brutal light of reality, Lee must have believed that even the total loss of the small army that remained with him at Sharpsburg would be no greater blow to the Confederate cause than for that army to be chased ignominiously out of Maryland after a one-day battle. If he decided to retreat and to abandon the field on the night of the 17th, he would hand the Federals an unqualified victory of immense proportions. The North's jubilation would not only fuel Northern determination to carry on the war, but the revelation of the vincibility of Lee and his army might bolster Northern morale through uncountable defeats in the future.

Yet, if he decided to stand another day, good things as well as bad might result. The Federals might not attack, or a way might be found to beat off their assaults if they did. An opportunity might even yet be seized to turn the enemy's right flank. At the very least, if the army survived, an orderly and disciplined retreat could be planned and executed. And the extra day would give the Confederates the chance ever after to argue that they had not been chased ingloriously out of Maryland.

There was, of course, another and persuasive counterargument to Lee's decision that can be paraphrased in the ancient epigram, "the general who runs away lives to fight another day." There were important reasons to preserve the core of the Army of Northern Virginia and to avoid risking its total destruction. Without the core, it would be difficult and time consuming to rally the stragglers collecting at Winchester and wandering throughout northern and central Virginia. And without these veterans, the handful of troops remaining at Richmond could not mount a serious defense of the capital. Federal forces would even be freed for transfer to the West to be used against the other Confederate offensives.[115]

All such arguments, if they occurred to Lee, may have carried little weight with the Confederate commander for one simple reason. He may have correctly doubted it would be possible for his exhausted army to cross safely into Virginia in the nine hours before daylight. There had been absolutely no preparation, and to locate the troops after the day's confused fighting and to organize their withdrawal in darkness may have been impossible. It had been difficult enough at South Mountain, where there had been a smaller force, no rough ford to cross, and the wagons and artillery had already been dispersed. Now, the men were tired, there was considerable artillery, and a large portion of the trains had passed back into Maryland during the day. There was good cause to believe that waiting a day could not lead to a disaster worse than attempting a hasty retreat.

Thus, although Lee never justified or explained his decision to stand at Sharpsburg an additional day, reasonable explanations do emerge from an understanding of both the particular and the overall situations he confronted on the night of the 17th. Moreover, in a general way he would offer insight after the war, when, in response to critics who charged him with incurring too great risks, he said, "such criticisms were obvious, but that the disparity of force between the contending armies rendered the risks unavoidable."[116]

• • •

Interestingly, no officer raised objection to Lee's decision, and no question was asked about its implementation. The commanders quietly returned to their troops and undertook whatever they could to prepare for resisting a Federal attack on the morrow. When the word reached Stuart that the army was to stand and offer battle another day, it seems to have caught him by surprise. Belatedly, he became uneasy over the security of the Confederate left flank. He commissioned Heros von Borcke, his chief of staff, to establish a double line of pickets, infantry behind cavalry, to close the gap to the Potomac River.[117]

Even later, Stuart began to worry about Nicodemus Hill, which the batteries of French and Branch had abandoned during the unsuccessful turning movement late in the afternoon. The hill lay a half-mile beyond the newly retracted Confederate line that bent at a forty-five-degree angle behind the Dunkard Church in the direction of Sharpsburg. If the enemy crowned its prominence with artillery during the night, they would be able to enfilade the Confederates as far as Sharpsburg itself.

Around midnight Stuart found Jackson asleep on the ground across the Shepherdstown road from Hunter McGuire's hospital at the farm of Capt. David Smith. Jackson, who well knew the importance of the hill from the morning's fighting, dispatched Henry Kyd Douglas to find an infantry force to secure it from the Federals. Douglas set out in the darkness across the fields, making steady progress until he neared the Dunkard Church, where his horse spooked at the smell of blood and the bodies littering the ground. Douglas dismounted, fighting back his own nausea, until he found Jubal Early and was given a picked detail of fifty men to accomplish his mission.

At first impression through the murky gloom, it appeared that the Federals had already occupied the hill, and the soldiers crept forward ready to wrest possession at the point of the bayonet. But the enemy turned out to be tree stumps, and no one was hurt in this, the final action of the Battle of Antietam.[118]

CHAPTER TEN

"Until none but heroes are left"

Antietam Endgame, September 18–21, 1862, and After

THE BATTLE AT Sharpsburg on September 17, 1862, did not end the Maryland campaign. Robert E. Lee would not let it end. Four days earlier—when McClellan was battering at the passes of South Mountain and the Army of Northern Virginia was still widely divided—Lee had declined to accept defeat as final. Every day since then, he had continued to exert his every effort to keep his offensive alive. So, even now—with his back to the Potomac and great gaping holes rent in his reunited army—he again refused to be vanquished. On the night of Antietam, Lee may have intended no more than to stand on the defensive one more day. But by the next morning his deep sense of an irretrievable opportunity slipping from his grasp bent his thoughts once more toward seizing the initiative. Then, although balked at every turn, for over a month following would he attempt to breathe life into his failed campaign. Not gracefully did Lee yield the tide of Confederate fortune.

Lee Defies Fate, September 18

A dull, gray dawn spread sullenly over the blasted, blood-drenched fields of Antietam. Smoke drifted from campfires and the cooling ashes of houses and barns to thicken the leaden air of the somber morning. The Confederate soldiers awoke fully expecting another battle.[1] Their brief war experience taught them that when unentrenched armies remained within several hundred yards of one another, the fighting was irresistibly renewed. Along the Chickahominy and at Second Manassas the two forces had clawed at each other day after day until one had yielded and reached safe haven. But Antietam had been a different kind of battle. Its concentrated fury knocked the wind from both armies. Although sharpshooters soon peppered the scant two hundred yards separating the lines and hindered the parties trying to carry off the wounded and bury the dead, the cannon remained silent on the 18th. Neither side wished to provoke the other.[2]

There is no record of what the Confederate soldiers—stunned and dazed by the shock of the furious battle—said to one another, as they lay waiting for the Federal attack. A young Virginian of Walker's division may have captured the prevailing mood, when he wrote in his diary the simple requiem, "Yesterday was an awful day for the 30th Regt." He may also have expressed a disturbing doubt that was common, when reflection on the battle caused him to conclude, "I don't think we gained anything yesterday."[3]

Lee would claim in his official report that "we awaited without apprehension the renewal of attack."[4] And, indeed, he had strengthened his position from the night before. Nearly 6,000 estrays had been collected and returned to the ranks, and several of the batteries left at Harpers Ferry were ordered to Sharpsburg.[5] Ammunition had been brought forward from Shepherdstown to replenish the caissons and cartridge boxes, and rations were issued to the troops, many of whom had not seen their commissary wagons for four days.[6] And Lee had constricted the Confederate front, making it shorter and more compact. It now stretched in the north from the Cox farm on the Potomac to run behind the Dunkard Church and past the Reel Ridge and barely cover Sharpsburg at Cemetery Hill and then wend southward to Snavely's Ford.

Still, although strengthened, it was not strong. There was nothing fancy about the new position. Gone were the salients and hinges. This was merely a thin curved line that barely covered the entrails of the Army of Northern Virginia, and there were no reserves. Although Lee's numbers can never be certainly known, at most 30,000 manned the front, and the count was likely nearer to 25,000. If only arithmetic mattered, the question would be resolved by a simple formula: the 35,000 of yesterday minus the 10,000 casualties plus the 6,000 returned stragglers would put 31,000 in the ranks on the 18th. There were, however, thousands of men who would never be listed among the official casualties but who were not with their units this morning. Some had suffered minor wounds and would return so soon they would not be counted among the wounded. Others were helping friends who had been wounded. Some were lost, and some were hiding. Slivers of evidence suggest that a quarter or more of Lee's soldiers who should have been present for duty the morning after Antietam were not.[7]

Only the brigades of Pender and Field (A. P. Hill) had not been heavily engaged the day before; and most of the men collected in the

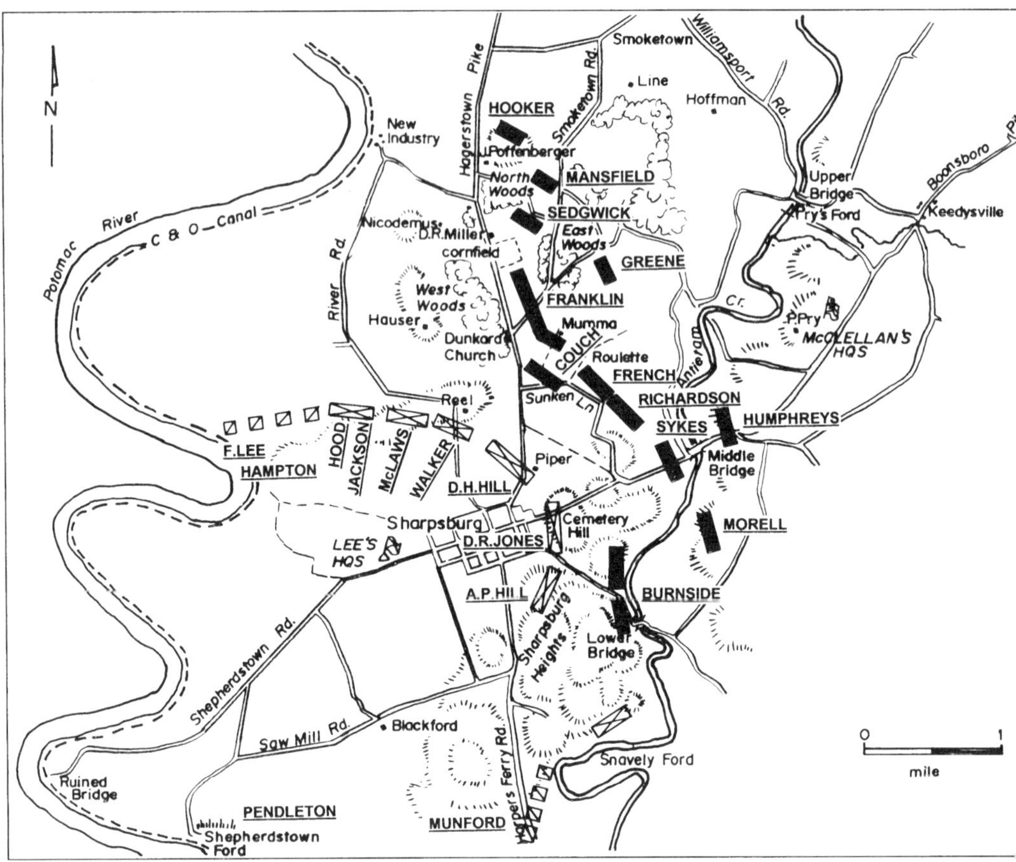

Sharpsburg, the morning after, September 18

rear had been stragglers from the forced marches from Harpers Ferry of McLaws's, R. H. Anderson's, and A. P. Hill's divisions. Certainly, the brigades of Longstreet and Jackson remained woefully weak. Even allowing that only the worst examples were cited in the reports and memoirs, the numbers known are pitiful indeed: less than a hundred each in the brigades of Hays and Garnett, 120 in Evans's, 200 each in Armistead's and Trimble's, and 250 in Lawton's. In all, of Lee's thirty-nine infantry brigades, on the morning of the 18th, twenty had less than 400 men each.[8]

In addition, the battle had wrecked the command structure of the army. Considering how close Jackson, Longstreet, and even Lee himself had come to the fighting at times, the Confederacy was extraordinarily fortunate not to have lost any of the three. The subordinate structure did not escape the cataclysm. Through death, wounds, or devolution the

Army of Northern Virginia lost three of its nine division commanders, nineteen of its thirty-nine brigade commanders, and eighty-six of its 173 regimental commanders. In sum, almost one-half (48.9 percent) of the line commanders in the army bore a new level of responsibility on the morning after Antietam.

As an inevitable result, officers with rank appropriate to their authority—already scarce when the army entered Maryland—had all but disappeared in the battle. One division was now led by a colonel; twenty brigades by colonels; four brigades by lieutenant colonels or majors; and three brigades by captains. Of the 173 regiments, only twenty-two (12.7 percent) were headed by full colonels. Twenty-two brigades did not have a single regiment led by a full colonel, and five of these had captains commanding all of their regiments. On September 18, Lee had only twenty-seven general officers to command the infantry, artillery, and cavalry of his army.[9]

Although the precise details of the ruin were no doubt obscured for days, the general impression must have been inescapable at once. It certainly was plain to Stuart and his staff as they rode along the attenuated line at dawn, where on the left it seemed as if there was "hardly one man to a rod of ground."[10] It was obvious to D. H. Hill, who ordered Maj. J. W. Ratchford, his adjutant, to consolidate the two anemic North Carolina brigades of his division and to take command of both.[11] And it seems to have been clear to Lee's most aggressive fighter as well. Just after the break of day, Jackson mounted and rode from the Shepherdstown Road north across the fields to the vicinity of the Dunkard Church. He approached Sam Hood and asked, "Hood, have they gone?" Upon learning the enemy had not, Stonewall said simply, "I hoped they had" and rode off to inspect his thin lines.[12]

Early on this grim, gray morning the Confederates had perhaps only two advantages in their favor. First was their task. They had only to defend; and if attacked they had no choice but to fight for their survival. Second was the soldiers themselves. Walter Taylor described the men who stood with Lee on the 17th as "the very flower of the Army of Northern Virginia."[13]

And, indeed, they were. Before there had been time for them to season as veterans, or even to shrink their stomachs or callous their feet, they had been called upon to wage three major campaigns in two and three-quarters months. In a bare eighty-three days, they had freed their capital, driven the Federals from Virginia, and crossed the Potomac into the enemy's land. The chaff had long since been winnowed from the grain. Now, with the eighty-fourth day, the bloodiest day of the war, the army had been sifted one final time. Surely, the men who stood in line at Sharpsburg on the 18th must have been among the toughest soldiers who ever fought for any country.

Writing with acid, Harvey Hill declared, "The skulkers and cowards had straggled off, and only the bravest and truest men of my division had been left."[14] A twenty-three-year-old lieutenant from South Carolina would express the same thought more poetically in a letter to his parents five days later: "Our army is small, but fights gloriously. . . . none but heroes are left."[15] Such quality was worth many times the numbers.

Far less is known about Lee's activities at any time on the 18th than on the day of the battle, and almost nothing certain has survived of his movements during the early morning. Presumably he arose before first light, as was his custom on days of critical operations, and spent several hours preparing for an enemy assault. When it became evident the Federals would not repeat their dawn attack of the previous day, he apparently needed to occupy the slowly passing minutes. At 6:30 he dictated a dispatch to President Davis. This letter—in effect a preliminary report on the Battle of Sharpsburg—affords a rare opportunity to glimpse Lee's initial understanding of what had happened the day before. Written while the bloom was fresh on the chaos, his account is vague and at places confused.

"On the afternoon of the 16th instant the enemy, who, you were informed on that day, was in our front, opened a light fire of artillery upon our line."[16] In his usual fashion, Lee connected with his last report so that Davis might know if any intervening message failed to get through. It is not surprising that in retrospect he remembered the cannonade of the 16th as "light."

"Early next morning," he continued, "it was renewed in earnest, and large masses of the Federal troops that had crossed the Antietam above our position assembled on our left and threatened to overwhelm us. They advanced in three compact lines." This certainly is not an apt description of Hooker's attack on the Miller Cornfield and the East Woods; nor is it an accurate version of the assaults by the First, Twelfth, and Second Corps. Possibly this is a telescoped recollection of Hooker's advance on the afternoon of the 16th, or it may even have been Lee's memory of Sedgwick's three brigades attacking the West Woods.

"The divisions of Generals McLaws, R. H. Anderson, A. P. Hill, and Walker had not arrived the previous night, as I had hoped, and were still beyond the Potomac." This clearly implies that all four of the divisions named were south of the river when Hooker opened his attack at 5:30. But Walker, of course, had arrived at noon or shortly thereafter on the 16th, and Lee would correct this mistake in his final report.[17] McLaws had reported to Lee in person at about 4:30 on the morning of the 17th, while the head of his column was immediately behind him and the rest of his division and R. H. Anderson's were in the act of crossing the Potomac. In this case too, Lee—although not as far off the mark as with Walker—nevertheless leaves the wrong impression. It may be that Lee was still so upset on the 18th over what he considered to be the slow reuniting of his army—which he believed to be a major contributing factor to the demise of his campaign—that it colored his recollection of events. In his final report, Lee avoided mentioning the precise time of McLaws's arrival, but three years after the war he made a remark that indicated the matter still rankled. He would recollect "battle was given at Sharpsburg with a tired and weakened force (about 35,000 men) and not all on the ground till late in the day."[18]

Continuing his dispatch to Davis, Lee went on, "General Jackson's and General Ewell's divisions were thrown to the left of Generals D. H. Hill and Longstreet." This mistakenly implies Jackson deployed his two divisions after Hooker's attack commenced, when he had taken position on the left the night before and was in the fight from the start.

"The enemy advanced between the Antietam and the Sharpsburg and Hagerstown turnpike and was met by General Hill's and the left of General Longstreet's divisions, where the contest raged fiercely, extending to our entire left." Here Lee erroneously gives the impression that Hooker's attack fell on the Sunken Road and then spread west to the Miller Cornfield and the Dunkard Church. Also note that neither here nor elsewhere in this report does Lee even hint that any subordinate commanded more than a division on the field; nor does he anywhere indicate that he knew which Federal Corps or division was attacking at what point.

Lee concludes his summary of the morning fighting as follows:

> The enemy was driven back and held in check, but before the divisions of McLaws, Anderson, and Walker, who, upon their arrival on the morning of the 17th, were advanced to support the left wing and center, could be brought into action, that portion of our lines was forced back by superior numbers. The line after a severe conflict was restored and the enemy driven back, and our position maintained during the rest of the day.

In this ambiguous and confused narration, Lee lumps together the attacks of Mansfield and Sumner—imparting to them a simultaneity that escaped the Federal generals—and inaccurately implies a coordinated counterattack by the Confederate reenforcements. He also suggests ("the line . . . was restored") that he regained everything he had lost. On the contrary, the Federals wrested control from the Confederates of the Miller Cornfield, the East Woods, the Dunkard Church plateau east of the Hagerstown Pike, and the Sunken Road. Lee's reference to maintaining the position for the remainder of the day masks the fact that no serious fighting occurred after one o'clock. He also fails to mention the repulse of Stuart's attempt to turn the enemy flank. Finally, he repeats his mistake in regard to Walker, although this time he is technically correct in regard to the arrival of McLaws and R. H. Anderson.

Lee then described Burnside's attack as follows:

> In the afternoon the enemy advanced on our right, where General Jones' division was posted, who handsomely maintained his position. General Toombs' brigade, guarding the bridge over Antietam Creek, gallantly resisted the approach of the enemy, but his superior numbers enabling him to extend his left, he crossed below the bridge, and assumed a threatening attitude on our right, which fell back in confusion. By this time, between three and four o'clock p.m., General A. P. Hill with five of his brigades had reached the scene of action, drove the enemy immediately from the position they had taken, and continued the contest until dark, restoring our right, and maintaining our ground.

Lee's summary, although general in the extreme, is basically accurate. He has now admitted that both wings of his army were at one time broken. He also correctly asserts that the Federal crossing at Snavely's Ford made it impossible to hold the Lower Bridge. He even comes close to pinpointing the arrival time of A. P. Hill. Apparently, his displeasure with D. R. Jones was momentary, as he is willing to share equally the credit between Jones and Toombs for holding the right until help arrived.

The dichotomy in Lee's accounts of the morning fighting on the left and the afternoon fighting on the right no doubt derived largely from the fact that he had devoted most of his attention to the right and that much of the battle there had come under his personal observation.

Yet, it is also true that the morning action was in fact much more confused than that of the afternoon.

It is not surprising Lee should have a murky comprehension of the battle less than twelve hours after its conclusion. It would be many months before he received any formal written reports. He had nothing more to go on than several sketchy oral reports and his own observations and impressions. It is perhaps a bit surprising he understood the fighting on the right as well as he did. The importance in critiquing Lee's early report, however, is not to catch him in mistakes. Rather, it is to serve as an important reminder of a simple fact that no Civil War commander could escape, but which many historians ignore. Perfect clarity of understanding was impossible, and even reasonable clarity usually came long after decisions had to be rendered.

In addition to Lee's not having a clear picture of the battle, three other conclusions can be drawn from the dispatch to Davis. First, the Confederate commander was unhappy that the divisions of McLaws, R. H. Anderson, and A. P. Hill had not been on hand by the night of the 16th. Second, he fully comprehended how close his army had come to extinction at Sharpsburg. And, third, he maintained that the Army of Northern Virginia had everywhere restored its line by the end of the day. Whether he believed this last point or simply attempted to put a favorable twist on events for Davis cannot be known.

What Lee did not mention is of even greater interest than what he did. He wrote nothing of his horrendous losses or of the thinness of his remaining line. He did not admit that his expedition into Maryland was all but dead. Nor did he touch upon the question of what he might do next. Still, no absolute importance can be attached to anything missing in Lee's dispatch, because the letter exists only as an extract copied from the original. It is at least possible that something genuinely startling was censored from the dispatch. A less sensational explanation would be that Davis wished to share important news from the army in Maryland with selected others and had his private secretary copy the pertinent sections for restricted circulation. Then, the extract survived and the original did not.[19] More than most, the loss of this document is to be regretted.

Lee and his thin line of infantry and artillery awaited a battle that never came. Yet, the Federal failure to renew the fighting on the 18th was a much nearer thing than has been generally recognized. McClellan had indeed ordered an attack for the early morning. Sometime around twilight of the 17th, the Federal commander paid a second visit to his right in the vicinity of the North Woods. He listened and then assented to corps commander William Franklin's proposal for a dawn assault to seize Nicodemus Hill for Federal artillery, to be followed by an attack of the entire Sixth Corps on the West Woods and Dunkard Church.[20] At this time, McClellan had reason to expect that more than 28,000 reenforcements would be available, and the prospects of success for continuing the offensive a second consecutive day must have seemed reasonable.

McClellan worked throughout the first part of the night to ensure that these fresh troops would reach the field at an early hour. The first step he took was to hasten the advance of Andrew Humphreys's newly organized third division of the Fifth Corps, which had reached Frederick on the morning of the 17th. During the course of the battle, Humphreys had already been sent a series of orders urging him to join the army as soon as possible; but now he was instructed to shorten his rest halts, force his march through the night, and arrive by daylight.[21] Second, McClellan reached out to tap the state troops—believed to number 15,000—that Pennsylvania governor Andrew Curtin had assembled to defend the Cumberland Valley from invasion. He ordered Brig. Gen. John F. Reynolds, who had been detached from the Army of the Potomac to command these forces and had reached Hagerstown, to march at once for Keedysville.[22] And, finally, at midnight he ordered Couch's division (Fourth Corps)—left behind to occupy Maryland Heights and watch Harpers Ferry—to march at once through Pleasant Valley and join Franklin on the right of the line as near to daylight as possible.[23]

At some point during the late night, McClellan changed his mind and decided to suspend, but not cancel, the attack by Franklin. His reasons can be surmised. Cooler reflection away from the heat of the battlefield must have convinced him that Couch could not march twelve miles in twelve hours through the darkness from Maryland Heights, much less Humphreys cover twice the distance from Frederick. The value of the latter division was in any case open to serious doubt, as seven of Humphreys's eight regiments were green units, less than a month old. On top of this, McClellan learned that ammunition for both small arms and artillery was dangerously low and that shells for the long-range 20-pound Parrotts had been exhausted in the heavy cannonading of the 17th.[24] In other words, any attack at daylight would have to be made with the troops at hand—some 18,000 men in the Fifth and Sixth Corps—

without adequate cover of artillery support. It seemed plain that the First, Second, Ninth, and Twelfth Corps were unfit for immediate offensive operations. In the circumstances, postponement made sense.

As late as eight o'clock in the morning, McClellan still seriously believed he would "probably" attack on the 18th.[25] Instead, a series of unfortunate developments caused him to stretch the postponement to a full twenty-four hours. In the first place, although both Couch and Humphreys arrived in good time during the morning, only Couch was in sound condition to take part in an offensive. Humphreys had shed a third of his men along the route from Frederick, and he reached Keedysville with but 5,000 of his 7,200 troops.[26] Although Humphreys later asserted confidence that his men would have given a good account of themselves, the previous day's dismal performance of similarly green regiments—not subjected to a brutal all-night march—contradicted his claim.

Next, John Reynolds arrived from Hagerstown. He had been unable to persuade any of the Pennsylvania militia regiments to march for the battlefield. Curtin's men refused to advance beyond Hagerstown in defense of their home state. It did not much matter, however, since Reynolds's entire force consisted of one-week-old state militiamen, many of whom were as unfamiliar with guns as all were with army discipline.

Third, McClellan learned nothing about the enemy that encouraged him to believe an attack would succeed. Lee's army stood defiantly in place to receive assault. There were no indications of a Confederate retreat, and the signal stations reported that troops were still being crossed from the Virginia side.[27]

Fourth, telegrams from Washington demonstrated that the War Department had taken seriously his need for ammunition. But, due to the enemy destruction of the B&O bridge over the Monocacy, the special train that had been dispatched immediately upon receipt of his request had been forced to detour to Harrisburg, and it would not reach Hagerstown until noon. After transfer to wagons, the ammunition would not be able to reach the army before nightfall.[28]

Fifth, after repeated demands from Burnside for support in order to hold the left flank at the Lower Bridge, McClellan felt compelled to send him Morell's division of the Fifth Corps. And, in truth, the southern flank was now more vulnerable after the withdrawal of Couch from Pleasant Valley.[29] Nevertheless, this meant that Sykes's 3,600 men and Humphreys's exhausted regiments were the only infantry available to protect the center, the army's trains, and communications.

And, on top of all of this, McClellan fell ill on the 18th with a severe case of dysentery, a recurring disease that had plagued him since his days in the Mexican War. For two days it would be difficult for him to leave his tent, let alone to ride about the field.[30] Such malady could only affect his ability to make decisions.

In consequence of these developments, McClellan waited until 5:45 in the afternoon to reissue the orders for Franklin to capture Nicodemus Hill. The attack was to be made early the next morning by one brigade, but it was to be supported by the entire Sixth Corps, including Couch's division. Two hours later, McClellan ordered the First and Ninth Corps to support the movement by advancing their pickets "at an early hour."[31]

What was lost by the twenty-four hour postponement can never be known. Still, several observations can be made. There are good grounds for believing that the First, Second, Ninth, and Twelfth Corps and Humphreys's exhausted, green division would not have been useful for an offensive.[32] There are no good grounds—even in hindsight—for believing the 24,000 men in the Fifth and Sixth Corps (including Couch) could have defeated, let alone destroyed, Lee's 25,000. Moreover, McClellan had no way of knowing Lee had so few men. Every assault of the previous day had been repulsed with losses of one-quarter to one-third. An unsuccessful attack on the 18th with similar losses might well have rendered the Army of the Potomac incapable of stopping Lee from resuming the Confederate invasion of the North. McClellan had everything to lose and only a blind shot chance of victory for return. He made the opposite decision of Lee's, but from the same motive. Because he believed duty to his cause demanded it, he would stand on the defensive until he had a reasonable certainty for success.

In a career filled with controversy, McClellan's decision not to attack on September 18 would became one of his most fiercely criticized actions. It provides a curious counterpoint to the fact that Lee's decision to remain on the 18th is one of but a handful of actions taken by the Confederate commander that even his veterans would second guess. In truth, both may have erred in the light of hindsight. But it is difficult to conclude that either can be seriously faulted for their decisions in light of what they knew at the time and of how each interpreted his responsibility as commander of the major army of his nation. Lee believed he was compelled to take unreasonable risks. McClellan believed he was prohibited from doing so. Each may have been correct.

• • •

As the hours dragged on and the expectation of renewed fighting faded, life gradually returned to normal in the ranks. Around nine o'clock the sun broke through the clouds. Soldiers of both armies boiled coffee, cooked rations, and smoked pipes.[33] Most of the wounded within the lines had already been carried to the rear, but the burial parties continued their grim work. At many places, small groups from each side hoisted white flags and attempted to reach the dead and wounded in the no-man's-land between the lines. When not discouraged by picket fire, these parties of mercy were sent back by officers of rank who insisted that flags of truce must be authorized at army headquarters.[34] Since neither commander would admit to the other that he had forsworn attacking, no official truce was ever established.

For Robert E. Lee, returning to normality meant asking once again if there were not some way to salvage his campaign in Maryland. He could not assume that because the Federals did not attack early they would not attack at all. More battles than not so far in the war had started past midday, including his own attacks along the Chickahominy, Pope's on August 30, and McClellan's on September 16.[35] He did know, however, that he had been provided a breathing spell and the time to grasp the initiative, if he could find the place.

It must have been obvious to Lee that a direct assault on any part of the Federal front was out of the question; and to his rear and right lay only Virginia. All that remained was to make another attempt to punch through to the north between the Potomac and the Hagerstown Pike. Lee may have speculated that the abortive turning movement by Stuart and Jackson of the previous afternoon had failed only because the Confederates had been outgunned by Federal artillery. Furthermore, Stuart did discover that a narrow opening existed between the river and the enemy's flank. There was some reason to believe, therefore—especially for one desperate to keep his Maryland campaign alive—that if the Confederates massed their own artillery to cover the movement, a second attempt might succeed.

In midmorning Lee rode to the left to confer with Jackson. He found Stonewall near a twenty-five-gun battery in the rear of the Dunkard Church, relaxing over a cup of captured Yankee coffee and talking with Jeb Stuart.[36] The substance of the meeting that followed can only be known from the actions that were subsequently taken because of it. In essence, Lee wanted Jackson to amass fifty cannon and crush the Federal flank. Whether the Confederate commander ordered Jackson to make the attack and Jackson found a subtle way to demure, or Lee merely proposed the plan and Jackson openly expressed opposition, cannot be known. What is certain is that Jackson did not believe the attack could succeed. His belief was probably based on yesterday's experience and may have been seconded by Stuart. It is also certain that Lee refused to take as final the word of two of his most trusted subordinates. Apparently, the disagreement came to focus on the question of whether or not the power of Confederate artillery could change the unhappy results of the previous day. Lee was at last persuaded to seek the expert opinion of a respected artillery officer.

The Confederate commander returned to his own headquarters and dispatched a courier to summon Col. Stephen D. Lee. Upon the gunner's arrival, the general addressed him simply, "Colonel Lee, I wish you to go with this courier to General Jackson, and say that I sent you to report to him." Puzzled, the artillerist asked, "Shall I take my batteries with me?" "No," responded the general, "just say that I told you to report to him, and he will tell you what he wants."

Jackson turned out to be equally mysterious. "Colonel Lee," he said, "I wish you to take a ride with me," and taking along but a single aide, the three men rode to the foot of Nicodemus Hill. They dismounted and climbed slowly to the crest, trying to avoid the fire of nearby enemy sharpshooters. The hill was littered with "wrecked caissons, broken wheels, dead bodies, and dead horses," gruesome vestiges of the fierce fighting it had witnessed the day before. Continuing in his cloaked manner, Jackson said, "Colonel, I wish you to take your glasses and carefully examine the Federal line of battle." Following instructions, Lee slowly swept the horizon with his field glasses. He saw a discouraging number of batteries "unlimbered and ready for action" behind a "strong skirmish line" and supported by a "dense mass of infantry." He was viewing the infantry of the 15,000-strong Sixth Corps (including Couch's Division) and the combined artillery of the First, Second, Sixth, and Twelfth Corps. "General," he said finally, showing he also knew how to veil his language, "that is a very strong position, and there is a large force there."

"Yes," said Jackson. Suddenly the conversation took an ugly turn. "I wish you to take fifty pieces of artillery and crush that force, which is the Federal right. Can you do it?" Startled beyond response, Lee returned to his binoculars for an even more careful scrutiny of the enemy position. He counted more than fifty guns, saw that difficulties of terrain would work against the Confederates, and with a sinking spirit knew the task was impossible. After a long pause, an extraordinary exchange—at least as Colonel Lee remembered it thirty-four years later—then occurred.

"Yes, General" [said the artillerist, evading the main question]. "Where shall I get the fifty guns?"

"How many have you?"

"About twelve out of the thirty I carried into action the day before."

"I can furnish you some, and General Lee says he can furnish some."

"Shall I go for the guns?'

"No, not yet. Colonel Lee can you crush the Federal right with fifty guns?"

"General, I can try. I can do it if anyone can."

"That is not what I asked you, sir. If I give you fifty guns, can you crush the Federal right?"

"General, you seem to be more intent upon my giving you my technical opinion as an artillery officer, than upon my going after the guns and making the attempt."

"Yes, sir, and I want your positive opinion, yes or no."

Colonel Lee returned once more to his field glasses, although he long since knew the answer he must give. After a considerable while, with Jackson scrutinizing him closely, he finally replied, "General, it cannot be done with fifty guns and the troops you have near here."

Instantly, Jackson was satisfied. The small party descended the hill and started back toward the rear of the Dunkard Church. The colonel felt that he had failed a test of some kind, and mortification overcame him at the thought some other officer might be given the assignment. He begged to be allowed to make the attempt, but Jackson brushed off his chivalric concern by remarking that his bravery was not in question. Jackson then ordered the colonel to report to the commanding general and describe in detail everything that had occurred.

With rising misgivings, Colonel Lee returned to General Lee's headquarters. As instructed, he described all that he had seen and all that had been said. He concluded by stating that Jackson had positively compelled him to give a technical opinion in regard to the chances of the assault. When he stated that he believed the attack must fail, the colonel thought he saw "a shade come over General Lee's face."[37]

The interview ended, and so did any further hope of Robert E. Lee for avoiding a return to Virginia.

(One thing should be noted in passing, although it is a small matter when compared to the brilliant achievements that history has expected of its Civil War commanders. Simply by not pulling back an inch on the 18th and by having Franklin ready to attack, McClellan exerted enough pressure to thwart Lee's last attempt to stay in Maryland.)

Williamsport, the Last Gambit, September 18–19

Even then, Lee did not abandon all hope for his campaign. It is a measure of his determination that he turned almost at once from the failed movement to crush the Federal right to implement a different stratagem to keep alive his offensive. If he must return to Virginia, he did not have to remain there. He would withdraw from Maryland but only to return by way of Williamsport to execute an even wider turning movement.[38] It is not unlikely that for some days he had held this option in reserve as a last resort. This would explain his concern in guarding Light's Ford with a battalion of the Artillery Reserve even after that crossing was inaccessible to him from the Maryland side. No doubt concerned over the double passage of the Potomac, as well as over the unfortunate boost any return to Virginia might give to enemy morale, he had refused to exercise this option so long as any alternative remained. Now, however, he had accumulating evidence that the enemy was receiving heavy reenforcements and so, even continuing to stand on the defensive, had disappeared as an alternative.[39] It was the Williamsport maneuver or abject retreat.

By late morning or early afternoon of the 18th, Lee settled on the broad outlines of his plan. He would recross the Potomac at Boteler's Ford and march west to Martinsburg and then north to Williamsport. It was a distance of some twenty-five miles, and the army ought to be back in Maryland by the 20th or the 21st at the latest. This would put him but six miles from Hagerstown and the rear of McClellan's right flank. Because the Federals had a good view of movements behind Confederate lines from their signal station on Red Hill due east of the Lower Bridge,[40] it would be necessary to wait for darkness to start withdrawing the troops. True, it had taken three days to cross into Maryland, and there was but the single rocky ford for the recrossing. Still, the army was much smaller now, and its reserve ordnance wagons and much of the Reserve Artillery were already on the other side. By carefully preparing in advance and by starting the trains during daylight, he ought to be able to accomplish it in one night and the following morning.

A greater concern was that McClellan might take actions that would disrupt or even foil the plan. First, the enemy might pursue so closely that the tail of the Confederate army would be destroyed at Shepherdstown. Second, Lee might arrive at Williamsport only to find Light's Ford held by a strong Federal force. The Confederate commander evolved a scheme to solve both problems at once. He would rush a force to Williamsport in advance to secure a foothold for reentry and at the same time divide the enemy's attention to relieve pressure on the withdrawal of the main body. The advance force would have to be cavalry, and it would lessen the bottleneck at Boteler's if a different ford could be found for its crossing the Potomac. If there was a danger in calling attention to Williamsport a day or so ahead of his intended recrossing there, Lee seems not to have worried about it.

Sometime around noon, Lee discussed his strategy with Jackson. Whether Stonewall agreed with the entire plan or not, he at least offered no objections to it. On the contrary, he sent orders to his topographical engineer, Jed. Hotchkiss, to reconnoiter the river in their rear for other fords that might be used.[41] At two o'clock Lee rode to Longstreet's bivouac. He discovered that his old "war horse" had just taken the "liberty" of sending a note "suggesting a withdrawal to the south side of the Potomac." How much of the pending plan Lee revealed to Longstreet is not clear, but the two did discuss the details of preparation for the retreat.[42] In addition, Lee held several meetings with Stuart during the afternoon. As a result, Jeb ordered his engineer, William Blackford, to examine the Potomac in their rear above Boteler's to find a ford for cavalry. Blackford was not told the purpose of his mission, nor was he permitted to inquire among civilians for information.[43]

An unforeseen and unwanted complication arose during the afternoon. Amidst the thunder of nature's own cannonade, the skies opened to a torrential downpour and provided yet another example for those who believed the heavens wept over every major battlefield. The rain then settled into a light drizzle, which continued into the night, and turned the roads into slippery and treacherous quagmires. There was some little comfort in the thought these same roads would render pursuit more difficult, and the lowering clouds would bring on darkness sooner.

In spite of the weather, the preparations went forward and instructions were issued for a disciplined retreat. Orders were sent back to Pendleton at the ford to halt all traffic coming from Virginia and to prepare to assist the crossing.[44] All usable property of the army was to be secured, even to the extent of recovering guns abandoned between the lines. In some cases tubes were removed from damaged carriages and slung under wagons for removal.[45] Cannoneers were again admonished not to ride their guns, and all officers were adjured to be "occupied constantly in getting everything along."[46] As many as possible of the wagons bearing supplies, ammunition, and wounded were to start for the river at once.[47] It was hoped that the roads would be clear by nine o'clock for the infantry and artillery.

Longstreet's divisions in the center were to be the first to pull back, and, after crossing the river, they were to form line of battle on the south bank, joining Nelson's battalion of the Artillery Reserve already in position there. Next to follow were Jackson's divisions from the left, which were not to stop but continue on beyond Shepherdstown on the road to Martinsburg and eventually to Williamsport. Finally, A. P. Hill, with the freshest division in the army, was to cover the retreat, retiring slowly and presenting a fighting front toward the enemy until the river was reached. Last of all, Fitzhugh Lee with his own and Munford's cavalry brigades and a single battery of long-range guns was to bring up the rear.[48]

It soon became apparent there were too many vehicles with the army to withdraw in the time allotted; yet there were not enough wagons to carry all of the wounded who were unable to walk. As a result, there was a traffic jam that severely tested the thin Confederate logistical skills, and the army was compelled to abandon an unfortunately large number of its casualties. When word spread that many of the unfit were to be left behind, friends stopped at the hospitals to say goodbye, and all except those with the most desperate injuries tried to make private arrangements to get away and avoid becoming prisoners.[49] Almost at once, the roads, lanes, and cow paths leading to the ford were choked with wagons, ambulances, litters, and soldiers held on horseback and leaning on the shoulders of comrades. Horses with their riders slipped and fell and vehicles mired fast in the mud.[50]

The creeping lines merged at the single passage of the Potomac only to enter the neck of a very narrow bottle. The refugees had first to cross a makeshift bridge over the canal and then slide down a steep bank to the river. The water was cold, waist deep, and a half-mile wide. The riverbed was stony and strewn with boulders. On the Virginia side loomed another high bank and a narrow road that wound along the base of a cliff. With the early twilight, fog descended on the Potomac valley. Bonfires were lighted on each bank to keep the crawling column from drifting into deeper water, while mounted horsemen bearing torches formed a chain of human buoys midst the huge rocks.[51]

When nine o'clock arrived, Longstreet saw that the roads immediately in his rear were clear, and he pulled first Evans's brigade and then D. R. Jones's division from the line. At a prearranged signal the men rose silently from their bivouac and slipped to the rear, leaving their campfires blazing to deceive the enemy. Longstreet thus initiated the time-ordered, sequential withdrawal of the main body and added the press of infantry and artillery against the mouth of the bottle. Jackson's men took their place in line, and by midnight A. P. Hill retired to form a defensive line on the high ground southwest of Sharpsburg.[52]

The addition of the disciplined soldiers and officers of the line actually helped lessen the confusion and hasten the passage into Virginia. Lee took station on the Maryland bank, while Jackson spent most of the night on horseback in the middle of the river. The acclaimed master of the hour was Maj. John Harman, Jackson's quartermaster and legendary mover of mules, who was credited with "cussin'" the army across that night.[53] The unsung heroes were the soldiers themselves. Constantly shouting out the numbers of their regiments or the names of their batteries, they kept their organizations intact.[54] Although several wagons were lost in the canal and a gun slipped into a ravine on the Virginia side, providentially there were no drownings reported.[55]

Longstreet's infantry started crossing at two o'clock and Jackson's at daylight.[56] By then the skies had cleared, and the rising sun promised a bright, warm day. At 8:00 the ford was almost clear of wagons, and the turn came for A. P. Hill and the rear guard. The brigades of Field and Pender crossed first, followed by Archer and Branch. Maxcy Gregg's men maintained a battleline facing the enemy until the very last; and when his men entered the water, he left two companies of the 14th South Carolina behind as skirmishers. In the middle of the fog-enshrouded river, Gregg found a horseless wagon of wounded that had been abandoned by its teamsters. "My men," he shouted, lifting his hat, "it is a shame to leave these poor fellows in the water! Can't you take them over the river?" At once a dozen volunteers grabbed the ambulance and pulled it to the southern bank, while the rest of the brigade cheered and sang "Carry Me Back to Old Virginia."[57]

Far to the rear, on the hill a mile west of Sharpsburg where the commanding general had pitched his headquarters tent during the battle, Fitzhugh Lee waited with a squadron of cavalry and a 10-pounder Parrott under Lt. John Ramsay. Longstreet's order requiring a battery to support the cavalry had passed down through Colonel Walton to Adjutant Owen of the Washington Artillery, who had selected

Capt. James Reilly's North Carolina battery; and thus the unwelcome task had finally descended upon the hapless lieutenant with his single piece. So far there had been no sign of enemy pursuit. When word arrived about 6:30 that the Confederate rear guard had reached the river, Fitz Lee called in his pickets and ordered Ramsay to elevate his gun and lay his longest fuses. One, two, three farewell shells went hurtling toward the enemy. Before the third had exploded, the head of a column of Federal cavalry emerged from Sharpsburg. Lee's troopers mounted, and Ramsay limbered his gun and ordered, "Trot, march!" But there was no trot left in the tired men and horses. The last Confederates walked away from Sharpsburg.[58]

One unit that almost did not escape was the 2d Virginia Cavalry. When the orders for the withdrawal were issued, Munford's brigade was scattered across the countryside. The 7th Virginia was on the left with Lee's brigade, and the 12th Virginia, near Sharpsburg, had been selected by Stuart for the Williamsport expedition. The 2d Virginia, under Munford's personal supervision, was skirmishing with the Federal cavalry on the extreme right, all the way down the Antietam to its mouth at the canal. Hence, the courier with notice of the withdrawal never found Munford, and it was nearly daylight when the colonel rode into Sharpsburg and discovered from Fitz Lee that the army had gone. Munford quickly returned, gathered up his scattered regiment, and hastened for Boteler's.[59]

Around ten o'clock, the last units of the Army of Northern Virginia—Fitz Lee and Ramsay, Munford and the 2d Virginia, and the two companies of the 14th South Carolina—converged on Boteler's Ford. In midpassage they came under the fire of Federal skirmishers. Pendleton's guns opened from the cliffs on the Virginia side and easily dissuaded the enemy from following.[60] According to army tradition, Robert E. Lee watched from the southern bank until the last soldier had crossed.[61] He and his army had pulled off a minor miracle of logistics. But his mind was not focused entirely on the safety of his army. As far as he was concerned, he was still in the midst of his Maryland campaign. He had merely completed a successful change of base.

While the Army of Northern Virginia successfully withdrew from the pen at Sharpsburg and entered into an open space for maneuver; Stuart's expedition to Williamsport got off to an equally promising start, although not without confronting serious difficulties of its own. As

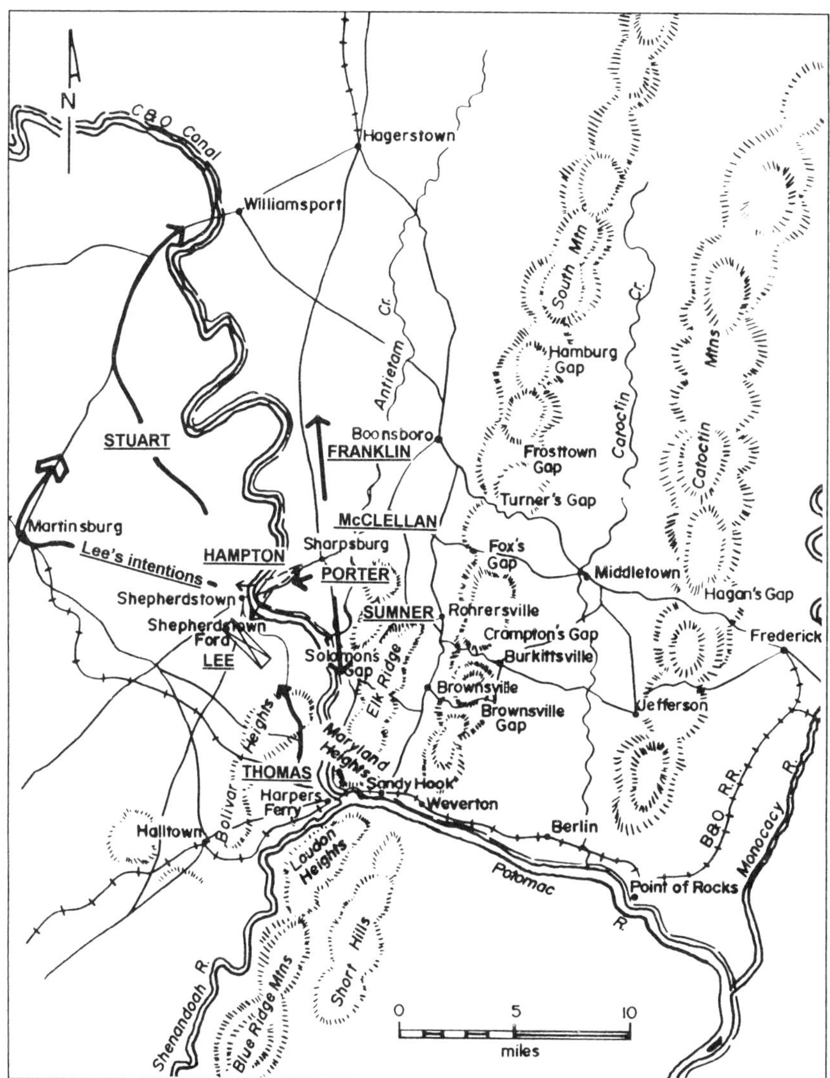

Retreat from Sharpsburg, September 18–20

bidden by his chief, Lt. William Blackford set out in the late afternoon with a party of twenty horsemen to find a crossing suitable for cavalry. The closest known opportunity was Shepherd's Ford, which lay only four miles by road upriver from Shepherdstown on the Virginia side. Unfortunately, because the meandering Potomac ran almost due north to south at this point, Shepherd's lay behind the Federal lines in Maryland.

Forbidden to seek help from local residents, Blackford had no recourse except to ride along the bank looking for places that appeared to be shallower than others. He then plunged into the river until the water became too deep. He was wet to the neck by the time he found a low dam of loose rocks that had been built as a fish trap. For ten or fifteen yards below the dam the water reached only to the horse's girth, although beyond this narrow channel it dropped quickly to a depth that covered the saddle. Blackford crossed and recrossed several times to check for hidden pitfalls. Rocks and brush obstructed his way and the current was rapid; but it was getting dark, and it was the best he could do. Posting a trooper on the bank and dropping others off at intervals, he returned to report to Stuart.[62]

Apparently, Stuart was not pleased by Blackford's description of the crossing at the fish trap dam. Perhaps awaiting better news from Jed. Hotchkiss, the cavalry commander delayed his departure. Finally, at ten o'clock he detailed Blackford to lead Hampton's brigade to the obscure ford, while he set out with the rest of his staff, the 12th Virginia of Munford's brigade, and Pelham's Horse Artillery for Boteler's. If Jeb was attempting to spare himself a difficult journey, he was only partially successful. He soon became engulfed in the roiling wave of humanity converging on the ford. Stuart's booming commands to clear the way were met with jeers and rude rejoinders from teamsters who had no idea who it was harassing them. Five times von Borcke went down in the mud with his horse, and once Stuart fell under a wagon and narrowly escaped serious injury. Along the way, the cavalry chief encountered Hotchkiss, who had just returned from Virginia and was looking for Jackson. Unwillingly, the engineer was turned back into the churning column as a guide. He was of no value until the river had finally been cleared, when he was able to take Stuart to the headquarters of General Pendleton.[63]

Having been at Shepherdstown since the 15th and responsible for the defense of the Potomac fords, Pendleton should have given Stuart several pieces of information useful for the cavalry expedition. First, although Lee had repeatedly directed that Light's Ford at Williamsport be guarded, Pendleton had found trouble keeping Col. J. Thompson Brown's battalion of the Artillery Reserve at the crossing. Brown had withdrawn to Martinsburg on the 17th; and, although he had promised to return the same day, it seems clear that by the night of the 18th no Confederate force held the ford. Not only did Federal cavalry now occupy Williamsport, but Federal pickets had appeared opposite Shepherd's Ford four miles above Shepherdstown. Pendleton had been compelled to remove Ancell's Fluvanna Artillery of Nelson's battalion from Boteler's Ford to counter the latter threat. This meant that Stuart might have to fight his way back across the Potomac. On the positive side, Pendleton could report that Brown's five batteries of twenty guns, as well as some 400 infantry, were in the Martinsburg area, and all could be employed to support the operation. Impressed with the growing dangers he faced, Stuart decided to press on through the night with the several hundred troopers of the 12th Virginia and Pelham's guns. Following the River Road through the village of Hard Scrabble toward the mouth of the Opequon, he covered nearly half the distance to Williamsport before halting for an hour's rest.[64]

In the meanwhile, Lieutenant Blackford had easily followed his human chain of scouts and guided Hampton's brigade to the fish trap on the Potomac. Thereafter, the crossing turned into a nightmare. Here there were no bonfires or torches, and in the heavy fog each horseman could only see and follow the man immediately in his front. The head of the column kept close to the dam and made it successfully through the narrow channel safely. The swift current irresistibly inched each rider downstream, however, and the trailing regiments found themselves in swimming water. Men and horses were lost. The experience was "even worse than fighting," according to Capt. Rufus Barringer of the 1st North Carolina. Not privy to the grand strategy being pursued, Barringer assumed the enemy had cut the brigade off from the army, and they had been compelled to plunge blindly into the river to escape capture. Hampton, who presumably knew something of the objective of his mission, kept his men in the saddle all night.[65]

In spite of taking an hour's rest, it was Stuart who reached Williamsport first. Arriving around noon, he dashed across Light's Ford with the 12th Virginia and chased a squadron of Federal cavalry from the town. Shortly thereafter reenforcements increased his strength to a respectable size. Not only did Hampton arrive with five regiments of cavalry by way of Mason's Ford, but from Martinsburg came the 2d and 10th Virginia Infantries, a battalion of the 11th Georgia Infantry, a section of Hupp's Salem Artillery, and a section of Watson's Richmond Howitzers. In total, the expeditionary column included about 1,500 cavalry, 400 infantry, and up to fourteen guns.[66]

Stuart spread his forces in a semicircle on the ridges outside Williamsport, and he pushed a reconnaissance under von Borcke to within two miles of Hagerstown before it encountered serious resistance.

During the whole of the 19th, the Confederates had only to contend with a portion of the Federal cavalry that had escaped from Harpers Ferry and was operating out of Hagerstown. As night fell, it appeared that Lee had acquired his foothold for reentry into Maryland.

There was one rub. In zealous pursuit of creating a diversion, Stuart flaunted his numbers, fired artillery needlessly to disperse mere handfuls of enemy skirmishers, and spread widely the word that Lee was close behind with the entire Army of Northern Virginia. Lee had better not take too long in coming, or the diversion half of his plan might foil the turning movement half. Stuart nevertheless was pleased at a job well done, and he rewarded himself by throwing a party with music and dancing for the belles of Williamsport.[67]

Checkmate at Shepherdstown, September 19–21

Although conducted with considerable stealth, the withdrawal of the Army of Northern Virginia did not go unnoticed. Shortly before midnight, pickets of the Second Corps heard the rumble of Confederate artillery moving westward and the sound of trees being felled, and Edwin Sumner correctly concluded that the enemy was retiring and obstructing roads to delay pursuit. As a consequence of this report, McClellan canceled the planned attack by Franklin and the Sixth Corps at daylight. He ordered instead that Pleasonton send cavalry scouts on the roads leading west and south and that the First, Second, Fifth, and Sixth Corps push forward skirmish lines to determine if the enemy had retired.[68]

As the Federal infantry pickets probed cautiously through the fog at sunrise on the 19th, they found only dead and wounded Confederates. The cavalry, however, encountered Fitzhugh Lee and Ramsay's gun just west of Sharpsburg, and it was not immediately clear what the foe was doing. By 8:30, McClellan had enough information to conclude the enemy had entirely abandoned their line of the day before, but he did not yet know if they had recrossed the Potomac or merely fallen back to an interior line to cover a recrossing. In either case, McClellan was now certain the Confederate offensive in Maryland was over, and he wired to Halleck, "We may safely claim a complete victory." In order to be prepared to attack any new position Lee might have assumed, the Federal commander kept his front intact and moved his whole line forward as a unit.[69]

By 10:30, Pleasonton's cavalry had scoured the countryside and opened fire on the only enemy to be found, the tail of the Confederate column as it crossed the river at Boteler's. Lee's precipitous retreat indicated to McClellan that the Federal attacks on the 17th—the effects of which had been in doubt—had indeed crippled the Confederate army. "Our victory was complete," he telegraphed to Halleck. "The enemy is driven back into Virginia."[70] Too ill to mount a horse, the Federal commander climbed into an ambulance and rode through Sharpsburg and toward the Potomac to reconnoiter. During his hour's ride he confronted the critical question of how he would respond to Lee's withdrawal.

There is no indication McClellan seriously considered pursuing the Confederates across the Potomac. Sixteen days before, he had taken command of two badly demoralized armies, one fresh from a devastating defeat and both in need of rest and refitting. In two weeks' time he had marched a hundred miles and won two major battles, the last of which, the bloodiest day of the war, had consumed a quarter of the men engaged. He had accomplished his mission. He had removed the emergency that had compelled the army to take the field before it was ready. With a patchwork force—including a fifth of its men so green they made McDowell's soldiers at Bull Run look like seasoned veterans—he had repulsed the enemy at the peak of their summer's victories. He had been responsible for seeing that the most important prong of the Confederate multifront offensive had been the first to shatter. The North could now concentrate on the West.

So long as Lee remained in Maryland, the Army of the Potomac had no alternative but to continue to fight. Now that Lee had gained maneuverability in the open spaces south of the river, it would require a new campaign to bring him to bay. Immediate pursuit into Virginia made no more sense than one wounded beast crawling after another into its lair. And any new campaign required time for rest, reorganization, and refitting. Just one day before, four of the six corps had been unfit for mounting an attack. The command structure of the army was in ruin, and all manner of supplies and munitions were nearly exhausted. Sections of the B&O Railroad and the C&O Canal had been destroyed, and both bridges at Harpers Ferry had been blown up. Finally, there remained the crucial question of whether a new campaign should be undertaken in willy-nilly pursuit of the enemy or be planned to advance on lines most advantageous for an offensive.

By 11:30 McClellan had decided upon his response. He would put the Army of the Potomac into camp to recuperate before launching a new offensive. But he did take two steps to gain immediate advantage from the Confederate withdrawal. First, he sent the Twelfth Corps to seize

Maryland Heights in anticipation of reoccupying Harpers Ferry and to make sure the enemy did not return. Second, after learning that a sizable Confederate force remained at Boteler's on the Virginia side, he ordered his strongest corps (the Sixth) to take position opposite the ford. Franklin was to open fire and "do the enemy all the damage possible," but he was not to "attempt to cross the river without further orders." In even more explicit language, chief of staff Randolph Marcy informed Pleasonton, "General McClellan directs me to say that he does not propose to cross the river, and that he does not desire you to do so, unless you see a splendid opportunity to inflict great damage upon the enemy without loss to yourself."[71] The Federal commander was concerned—and not without justification, as events would prove—that enthusiasm might carry an inadequate force into a trap.

Before even the first of these orders were dispatched at 11:45, information arrived that caused McClellan to modify his arrangements. It was word of Stuart's expedition, and it came in the exaggerated news that 4,000 infantry and six guns were moving on Williamsport, while a column of 10,000 infantry was marching on the same point from Winchester. While McClellan repeated the details as he received them, it is clear that he did not credit the numbers. He dispatched Couch's division of less than 6,000 effectives, along with 2,000 cavalry and six batteries, with every confidence that their force would be sufficient to drive "the rebels back into Virginia." He probably viewed Stuart's move as the diversion that, in half measure, it was.[72]

Nevertheless, exercising his normal caution, McClellan ordered Franklin to be prepared to march to Williamsport with his two remaining divisions. This meant the Sixth Corps would be unavailable to harass the Confederate force at Boteler's Ford. Consequently, McClellan turned to his next-freshest force, the two veteran divisions of the Fifth Corps. Fitz John Porter was apparently given the same cautionary advice as Pleasonton, and with the same proviso that he might seize a sound opportunity to harm the enemy. Late in the afternoon, Porter arrived opposite the ford to find three batteries of the Horse Artillery engaged in a duel with the enemy guns across the river. For reasons never satisfactorily explained, Porter ordered Pleasonton to retire to Sharpsburg with the cavalry. He then lined the canal and river banks with sharpshooters and nineteen guns under Col. Henry Hunt of the Artillery Reserve.

With riflemen picking off Confederate gunners, the Federals opened a devastating artillery fire across the river. Because the enemy seemed to wither under the fire, and because there seemed to be few infantry supports, Porter decided just such an opportunity existed as was permitted by his discretionary orders. He quickly issued instructions for the selection of a battalion of volunteers from each of the divisions of Sykes and Morell to dash across the ford and "secure some of the enemy artillery." In the haste, word never reached Sykes, and only the 4th Michigan Infantry and sixty men of the 1st U.S. Sharpshooters, about 400 men in all, crossed into Virginia at twilight.

Nonetheless, the impact of this small body on the detachment of the vaunted Army of Northern Virginia guarding the ford went beyond anything Porter could have anticipated. The Confederate infantry threw down their arms and ran in panic, and many gunners abandoned their pieces. Only the fall of night saved the Confederates from a disaster of the first magnitude. Darkness prevented the Federals from seeing the trophies that were theirs for the taking, and they returned to the safety of the Maryland side, hauling only two cannon with them.[73]

This small action impressed both Porter and Hunt that the retreating Confederates were in disarray, and their reports convinced McClellan that a much larger opportunity existed to damage the demoralized foe. The Federal commander authorized Porter to cross both Sykes's and Morell's divisions in the morning. It is evident from the fact no orders were issued to the other corps to prepare to follow Porter that McClellan had not changed his mind about following with the army after Lee into Virginia. He intended only for Porter to secure the ford and to capture as much of the enemy artillery as possible. Still, it is also clear that McClellan understood the potential the enemy's panic had revealed. Correcting the error made by Porter in casually returning the cavalry to the rear, McClellan ordered Pleasonton to be at the ford by daylight with his entire force, including the Horse Artillery. He directed Pleasonton to push "as rapidly as possible" after the enemy. And, while cautioning against "incurring too great risk," he encouraged the cavalry commander, "If great results can be obtained, do not spare your men or horses."[74]

Events were occurring elsewhere, however, which—much as Lee had intended they would—hobbled Federal plans for pursuit. News from up the river turned ugly during the early evening. McClellan learned not only that Williamsport had fallen but that a Confederate force had approached within several miles of Hagerstown. He could not ignore this threat to his flank and rear. His first reaction was to order Couch at 8:15 to force march a brigade through the night to reach Williamsport by daylight. Next, at 9:30 he sent a dispatch to John Reynolds, who had returned to Hagerstown, calling upon him to support Couch with the Pennsylvania militia. No doubt Reynolds's recent observations on the unreliability of the raw state levies left the Federal commander dissatisfied with these arrangements. At 11:00—just one hour after he had directed Pleasonton to personally supervise the pursuit of the Confederates from Shepherdstown with all of his cavalry and artillery—McClellan substantially modified the orders. Now, Pleasonton was to send half of his force and two batteries to report to Porter at daylight. With the other half of his command and two batteries, the cavalry chief was to proceed immediately to the crossing of the Williamsport Road and the Hagerstown Pike and join with Couch's advance on Williamsport.[75]

As dawn broke on September 20, Fitz John Porter discovered no horsemen had reported to the ford. While sending back to headquarters to find out what happened to the cavalry, Porter dispatched the 4th Michigan and 62d Pennsylvania from Griffin's Brigade with Lt. Charles Hazlett and the unhitched horses from his battery to haul three more enemy guns from across the river. At seven o'clock Porter decided he could wait no longer and ordered his two divisions to start fording the Potomac. In two hours, 3,000 men in three small brigades, under the personal supervision of Brig. Gen. George Sykes, had reached the Virginia side. Without cavalry or artillery, Sykes pushed cautiously ahead until, at 9:15, his skirmishers encountered Confederate infantry about three-quarters of a mile from the river.

The small affair that followed, known as the Battle of Shepherdstown, was over in an hour. A. P. Hill, who had returned with his division, charged with nearly double the numbers into the advancing Federals. Sykes quickly sought and immediately received permission to retire to the Maryland side. The units from the Fifth Corps conducted the withdrawal skillfully and with little loss—with one exception. The 118th Pennsylvania was a new regiment armed with condemned Enfield rifles. Half of its 737 men heard only the snap of their percussion cap when they pulled trigger, and the regiment broke in panic and lost 269 casualties (36 percent) before reaching safety.[76]

McClellan concluded that the reports of the death of the Army of Northern Virginia had been considerably exaggerated. After learning Couch had chased the interlopers at Williamsport back across the river by nightfall, the Federal commander was satisfied that the Maryland campaign was over.

During the withdrawal, Lee for the first time operated as if his entire army were organized into two corps, one under Longstreet and the other under Jackson. Throughout the summer he had experimented with the structure of his army in order to perfect it. There are indications that at one time he was inclined to divide his force into thirds and was testing subordinates to find another officer qualified to command above the divisional level. It is also possible, however, that Lee hesitated to bifurcate the army, because he harbored doubts about Jackson's abilities based on Stonewall's sluggish performance during the Seven Days and his refusal to seize the initiative against Pope on the Rapidan for almost a month. Second Manassas, Harpers Ferry, and Sharpsburg had removed all questions about Jackson, while no commander of a division had exhibited talents worthy of promotion. Lee had decided, therefore, to divide the army into halves and was awaiting only a suitably quiet time to undertake the reorganization. Informally he started to operate with the two-wing structure on the night of September 18.[77]

Lee had, in fact, played leapfrog with Longstreet and Jackson to execute the skillful withdrawal from Maryland. Longstreet had retired first with half of the army, while Jackson covered Sharpsburg. After crossing the Potomac, Longstreet sent a portion of his command on toward Martinsburg and with the remainder formed a defensive line along the Virginia bank, while Jackson forded the river. Just after sunrise, Longstreet had replaced his own men with Jubal Early's division (Ewell). Apparently, at around ten o'clock—when the last of A. P. Hill's infantry and Fitz Lee's cavalry crossed and Pleasonton opened with sharpshooters and artillery—Lee, Jackson, and Longstreet were all still in the area of the ford. None of the three interpreted the firing as anything more than a feeble farewell from an exasperated foe. Indeed, after the war, Lee recalled that he "believed Gen. McClellan had been so crippled at Sharpsburg, that he could not follow the Confederate army into Virginia immediately." Lee and Jackson rode on with the army, and Longstreet remained only long enough to instruct Early to retire but leave the brigades of Lawton and Armistead to support Pendleton and the artillery.[78]

Even in retrospect, the dispositions made for guarding the ford should have been adequate. Pendleton, who had been responsible for the crossing for four days, should have known the ground well; and his artillery force, Nelson's battalion of the Artillery Reserve, had been increased by the most servicable pieces from throughout the army. He had been left with forty-four guns—only thirty-three of which could he even suitably place on the bluffs along the river—and for their support he had not only the two infantry brigades but Munford's cavalry brigade as well.[79] Moreover, Pendleton was not charged with preventing the entire Federal army from crossing the Potomac. His mission was to protect the rear of the Confederate army for the remainder of the 19th, while it rested preparatory to marching on Williamsport the following day. If Lee had not made this clear in person during the morning, he sent instructions that spelled it out in the afternoon: "The commanding general says that if the enemy is in force in your front you must retire tonight. If not in force, being merely an artillery force, withdraw the infantry forces, directing them to rejoin their respective divisions on the march tomorrow, a few guns and a small cavalry force being sufficient to guard the fords."[80]

In other words, Pendleton was to withdraw during the night of the 19th either his entire force, if seriously pressed by the enemy, or all but a token force, if not.

Brig. Gen. William Nelson Pendleton, Episcopal minister and Lee's chief of artillery, was weakened by illness and exhausted from his labors in the Maryland campaign. He may have been infected by the demoralization of the retreat, and he had no experience in the coordination of combined arms or in confronting the enemy in semi-independent command. His inadequate performance of his responsibilities on the 19th would tarnish his reputation for the remainder of the war.

Pendleton committed three cardinal mistakes. First, he failed to count his men.[81] To an artillerist, the number of soldiers in a battery was usually of relative importance. If a gun were servicable, it mattered little how many extra gunners were available. It may have been the assumption that a battery was a battery that led Pendleton to believe that, in infantry, a regiment was a regiment and a brigade a brigade. In this case, however, he had been assigned two brigades worn down to the size of infantry battalions. There were only 400 men in Lawton's brigade under Col. John H. Lamar and another 200 in Armistead's brigade under Col. James G. Hodges.[82] In addition, Thomas Munford almost certainly had not more than 200 cavalrymen in his brigade.[83] When Porter's sharpshooters opened a galling fire on the Confederate gunners, battery commanders called for riflemen to return the fire, and later Munford called for support for the right flank downstream. Pendleton responded to the requests by ordering a regiment here and there until he unknowingly stripped the ford itself to 200 defenders.[84]

Second—and this was inexcusable for an artillerist—he failed to provide a sufficiency of ammunition for his guns. In the late afternoon, battery after battery reported they had consumed all on hand. It was at this point that Pendleton made his third and worst mistake. He should have started to retire his guns, since he knew his orders called for him to withdraw the bulk of his force during the night under any circumstances. Instead, he assumed the sight of his men pulling back would induce the Federals to cross the Potomac. Incredibly, he then concluded that if his mute batteries would simply stand and suffer fire another hour or so until darkness fell, his problem would be solved. It did not occur to Pendleton that guns which suddenly fell silent would also invite the enemy across the river. And he does not seem to have taken into account the added difficulty he would face in extracting his guns from the bluffs at night. Had Pendleton simply pulled back at sunset, he would have fulfilled his orders and averted disaster.

Around 5:30 the Federals opened a tremendous fire of artillery and small arms from the Maryland shore, and the company of the 1st U.S. Sharpshooters dashed into the Potomac and were soon followed by the 4th Michigan. To the tired, demoralized Confederates it seemed as if the entire Army of the Potomac was about to engulf them. The Georgians of Lawton's brigade who remained at the ford fled for safety; so too did a majority of the gunners. Even some who managed to limber their pieces abandoned them when they discovered they must run a gauntlet of Federal fire several hundred yards back from the river.[85]

In the gathering "deep dusk," Pendleton, who had taken post on the main road from the ford but out of sight of the river, noticed Confederate infantry rushing past him.[86] He learned from the fugitives that the enemy had crossed to the Virginia side, and he assumed all of the artillery not already on the road and moving to the rear was lost. He was, of course, helpless. It would probably have been better for his reputation had he ridden into the melee at the ford, risking capture, and attempted at least to save a gun or two. Instead, he did the most sensible thing under the circumstances. He sent an aide to the ford while he set out to find reenforcements from the main body.

Thus began a nightmarish seven-hour odyssey of confusion and frustration. In the end, Pendleton would travel not more than four or five miles in a straight line. But how much distance he covered with wrong turns and blind alleys is unknowable. In his search through the dark for someone in authority who would take responsibility, Pendleton was shunted up and down the command hierarchy of the army. In moving inland, Lee had avoided the clogged streets of Shepherdstown by advancing over country roads from the ford to strike the pike to Martinsburg, and he had put Jackson's corps in the lead in preparation for the march back into Maryland by way of Williamsport. Hence, the closest units to the river belonged to Longstreet's command.[87]

First, Pendleton stumbled into the bivouac of Roger Pryor, who had succeeded to the command of R. H. Anderson's division. Pryor, an antebellum fire-eating politician, who at the moment was in over his head nearly as far as Pendleton, "thought the responsibility too serious for him to assume" and referred the artillery chief to General Hood, who was next down the road. Pendleton found Hood's staff, but he was told Hood was too "unwell" to be disturbed. No one knew where Longstreet might be found. At this point, Pendleton had no recourse but to forget about the troops nearest at hand and proceed on toward Jackson's corps. Around midnight he found D. H. Hill and reported that the enemy had forced passage of the river and captured thirty guns of the Artillery Reserve. Whether he asked Hill for troops and Hill declined, or Pendleton had by this time forsaken hope from any but the commanding general and simply asked directions to Lee, is not clear. In either case, he found no help. Hill neither offered to return on his own authority nor knew the whereabouts of Lee.[88]

Pendleton pressed on through the night until at last he encountered Jackson's camp. In Stonewall he finally found someone ready to take action. Jackson roused his staff and prepared to return to the river in person, but he did not immediately issue orders for any of his troops to march for the ford. Instead, he referred Pendleton to Lee, who had bivouacked nearby. Although Jackson would likely not have been deterred by the darkness, he may have hesitated for fear of disrupting Lee's plans for the movement on Williamsport the next day. Moreover, since Longstreet was nearer the river, Lee might prefer to send Longstreet's troops.[89]

It must have been at least one o'clock, and perhaps later, when Pendleton reached Lee's tent. Awakened from what may have been his best sleep in a week, the Confederate commander heard that all of his Reserve Artillery had been captured by the enemy. "All?" Lee asked. "Yes, General," Pendleton responded, "I fear all."[90] For the sake of covering his reputation, if not merely to submit a complete report, Pendleton must have related to Lee the full details of the skeletal size of the infantry brigades, the demoralization of the men, and his inability to find anyone who would assume authority. Here, scattered throughout Pendleton's sad story, was clear and unmistakable evidence—too plain for Lee to miss—that he had fought his army beyond human endurance.

What now was Lee to do? Of course, nothing could be accomplished before daylight, but the decision that would set the army in motion must be made immediately. Could he accept the loss of so much artillery without attempting to recover it? Still, although the loss of thirty guns certainly hurt, Jackson had captured more than that at Harpers Ferry. Moreover, the strong possibility existed—contrary to what Lee had assumed—that McClellan's army had not been crippled and that it would be necessary to fight a major portion, if not all, of it to get the guns back. The latter thought raised an even darker specter. The Confederate army lay but five miles from the river; and, if the Federals undertook an energetic pursuit at daylight, it might not be a matter of attacking to regain lost property but of fighting for the survival of the army.

Was this to be the end of his campaign? Must he abandon his plans to move on Williamsport and recross the Potomac? In the predawn hours of September 20, Lee may have finally asked himself the question most generals would have asked days before. Of what use was it to continue an offensive with an army unable to fight?

In the end, Lee decided he must turn back. There was a chance the Federals had mounted a mere raid and the guns might be recovered. Even if the enemy had crossed in force, the Confederates must at least act to protect the rear of their own army. Before the break of day, Lee issued orders to Jackson to return to the ford and take with him all four of his divisions if necessary. Jackson was to attack the enemy—and authorized to call upon Longstreet for help—unless Stonewall judged the greater part of the Army of the Potomac to be across the river. Lee also alerted Longstreet to have his corps ready to march at dawn.[91]

To fill the remaining hours before daylight, Lee dictated a dispatch to Davis. Although briefer than usual, he attempted to put the best face on recent developments. After indicating he had not written to the president on the 19th, Lee explained why he had withdrawn from Maryland: "Since my last letter to you of the 18th, finding the enemy indisposed to make an attack on that day, and our position being a bad one to hold with a river in rear, I determined to cross the army to the Virginia side."[92]

Lee fails to mention his intelligence that the Federals were receiving heavy reenforcements—a cause to which he would give prominence in his final report. On the surface the two reasons he does mention seem to carry little weight. Why should the enemy *not* attacking on the 18th contribute to the decision to withdraw? Also, since Lee had refused to notice the Potomac was in his rear for three days, why did it matter on the 18th? Probably, this is Lee's convoluted way of acknowledging that his position had been a bad one all along and that he had reached the limit of how long he could maintain it.

Lee then described the recrossing and his next intended move: "This was done at night successfully, nothing being left behind, unless it may have been some disabled guns or broken-down wagons, and the morning of the 19th found us satisfactorily over on the south bank of the Potomac, near Shepherdstown, when the army was immediately put in motion toward Williamsport."

Lee is less than candid in omitting reference to the numerous wounded that were abandoned. Also, he plainly states the entire army is on its way to Williamsport. He continued: "Before crossing the river, in order to threaten the enemy on his right and rear and make him apprehensive for his communications, I sent the cavalry forward to Williamsport, which they successfully occupied."

Here Lee acknowledges the dual purpose of the Stuart expedition. Jeb was to obtain a foothold and to create a diversion. Apparently he saw no contradiction in calling McClellan's attention to the point of intended reentry. Also, this is evidence that Stuart had by this time reported the noon occupation of Williamsport.

Lee then turned to the bad news he found difficult to disguise: "At night the infantry sharpshooters, left, in conjunction with General Pendleton's artillery, to hold the ford below Shepherdstown, gave back, and the enemy's cavalry took possession of that town, and, from General Pendleton's report after midnight, I fear much of his reserve artillery has been captured."

There is much of interest in Lee's contemporaneous account of the fiasco on the night of the 19th. First, he remembers only having left sharpshooters to support the artillery. Second, he is under the mistaken impression that Federal cavalry had crossed the river and captured Shepherdstown. Third, his use of "after midnight" probably means

Pendleton reached him closer to midnight than dawn. Finally, he confirms that Pendleton did initially give an exaggerated estimate of the loss of guns.

Lee closed with an admission that his next move was in some doubt: "I am now obliged to return to Shepherdstown, with the intention of driving the enemy back if not in position with his whole army; but, if in full force, I think an attack would be inadvisable, and I shall make other dispositions."

Lee has already indicated he believed the Federal raid of the previous night had been carried out by cavalry. Nevertheless, having just crossed his own army over the river in a single night, he had to credit the possibility that McClellan could do the same. Moreover, Lee's use of "whole army" and in "full force" probably should not be taken literally. He likely meant only to admit that the Confederate army in its weakened condition could not attack a major portion of the enemy forces.[93] There is no evidence of what, if anything specific, he had in mind with his intriguing reference to "other dispositions."

As soon as the overcast skies of the 20th lightened, Lee went in search of Jackson. No one seemed to know where Stonewall could be found, and as Lee rode from camp to camp he discovered that D. H. Hill had just received orders from Jackson to march to Boteler's Ford. Hill did not recognize the name and asked Lee for clarification. Nor did Lee understand this was one of the local names for the Shepherdstown Ford.[94] Hill was at a loss on how to proceed and asked the commanding general for different orders. Lee was unwilling, however, to interfere with Jackson's plans. No matter how often Hill asked, Lee would only respond that he was to follow Jackson. Maj. J. W. Ratchford, Hill's adjutant, would later claim, "I never saw a man more confused." And Hill himself would comment on Lee, "I have never seen him exhibit such indecision and embarrassment."[95]

It would be surprising if the burdens of the long summer's campaign had not finally worn Lee down. The last week of unending crises and lack of sleep must have taken an especially heavy physical toll on the Confederate commander. It is possible that the disappearance of Jackson and the unintelligible orders left Lee temporarily disoriented. If so, the confusion did not last long. After leaving Hill, Lee dispatched a courier to Shepherdstown Ford to get a report from Jackson while he set out himself to find Longstreet and prepare the rest of the army to come to Stonewall's aid if needed. One last time during this campaign, Lee's lack of personal mobility frustrated his ability to make personal observations and to exert direct control.

It must have been nearly nine o'clock by the time Longstreet collected his scattered brigades several miles back from the ford. In ignorance of how the force might be needed, Lee ordered Longstreet to form a defensive line along the Charlestown Pike. In the meantime, the Confederate commander had dispatched a second aide to acquire news from Jackson. By 9:30, the unmistakable roll of musketry indicated a battle in progress, and Lee gave way to impatience and rode toward the river. He had proceeded but a short distance when he encountered a courier from Jackson bearing the brief message, "With the blessing of Providence, they will soon be driven back." Lee read into the message all he needed to know: McClellan had not crossed the entire Federal army into Virginia. Jackson had the situation well in hand, and the commanding general turned back to his headquarters to contemplate what, if anything, remained of his campaign.[96]

Jackson had set out without an escort in the predawn blackness to reconnoiter the situation at the ford. He discovered that conditions were not nearly as bad as painted by Pendleton. Maj. William Nelson, who had remained at his post, had gotten off most of the guns. The enemy had hauled but few across the river, before retiring to the Maryland side. Stonewall may have watched Griffin's daybreak raid, which netted several more cannon. Still, it was not until seven o'clock that the enemy started to cross the Potomac in earnest. Whether Jackson had left behind orders to be delivered or sent them after receiving Lee's instructions is not known. In either case, Jackson's division commanders did not receive directions to march to Boteler's Ford until 6:30. A. P. Hill apparently understood where he was expected to go and set out promptly. Both D. H. Hill and Early (Ewell's division) were confused by the use of the local name for the ford and lost time before deciphering their destination. Maj. J. W. Ratchford, D. H. Hill's adjutant, rode to the ford, found Jackson, and confirmed the intent of the orders.[97]

In the meanwhile, Jackson must have watched as the Federals crossed one and then a second brigade of infantry, while a third seemed poised to ford the river. He gauged that A. P. Hill's division would be adequate to the task at hand, and he knew exactly where to deploy the regiments for maximum effect. Around nine o'clock, A. P. Hill arrived at the junction of the Charlestown Pike with the Trough Road about a mile from the ford. He immediately formed his division into two lines, with the brigades of Pender, Gregg, and Thomas in the first and Archer, Lane (Branch), and Brockenbrough (Field) in the second. Advancing along either side of the Trough Road, his skirmishers encountered the enemy about three-quarters of a mile from the river.

Sykes successfully withdrew Lovell's brigade of regulars with light loss, and Warren's brigade arrived in Virginia only to return at once to Maryland. The battle, such as it was, occurred west of the Trough Road between A. P. Hill's center and left and Barnes's Federal brigade of Morell's division and lasted about an hour. Although there were 4,000 Confederates and 3,000 Federals on the field, the fighting occurred between 3,000 and 1,700, respectively. Early's division arrived in time to form in support, but it did not engage in the fighting. A. P. Hill suffered all but six of his 261 casualties in the brigades of Pender, Gregg, Archer, and Branch. On the Union side, 321 of the total of 363 casualties were borne by Barnes's brigade, and 269 of those were from the 118th Pennsylvania.[98]

The Battle of Shepherdstown was a minor affair in terms of numbers engaged and lost, but for Stonewall Jackson it was a small gem of tactical execution. He reacted quickly and intelligently, and, without overstepping the bounds of his authority, he was prepared to act when the orders came. Then, with a minimum of force, Jackson achieved a complete victory. All but five of the captured cannon were recovered, and Stonewall ended any thought the Federals had of exploiting a confused Confederate army in retreat.[99]

In spite of the morning's easy victory, Lee could not discount the possibility that McClellan might make another attempt to force passage of the Potomac. The Federal artillery continued a furious barrage throughout the day, and Lee held his army in readiness to repel an assault. Jackson's men took refuge in the ravines and gullies on the bluffs, while Longstreet's troops remained in line two miles inland. Around five o'clock the troops away from the river formed column for the rear, but the regiments in sight of the enemy awaited the cover of darkness to slip away. Fitzhugh Lee's cavalry took their place at the ford.

The direction the army marched indicated that Lee had not yet abandoned his hope of reentering Maryland at Williamsport. Instead of moving due south toward Winchester, the "tired, sleepy and nearly worn-out" Confederates stumbled through the night to bivouac in the early morning hours on the Opequon Creek in the vicinity of Martinsburg.

As late as midnight, Jackson's headquarters wagons shifted to Tabler's Mill, two miles west of the town on the road to Williamsport.[100]

It is clear that much had happened on the 19th and 20th to give Lee pause and to cause him to reevaluate his plans. In the emergency, only A.P. Hill's men had performed well. Elsewhere there had been confusion and hesitation. The horrendous straggling had continued unabated since the return to Virginia. Longstreet had been compelled to threaten a column with artillery to force men back into line.[101] It is also evident that the dire condition of the army was on Lee's mind on the 20th. Both articles of General Orders, No. 107, issued that afternoon, reflected his concern. First, in order to get an accurate count of the number of men he commanded, something he lacked throughout the Maryland campaign, he directed that field returns be made at once. Second, aware of the fearful attrition in the officer corps, he ordered that promotions be made immediately to fill the gaping holes rent by illness and battle.[102]

Of equal, if not greater, importance was the bad news that arrived from Stuart. All day on the 20th, Pleasonton's two brigades of cavalry and Couch's three brigades of infantry had slowly closed around Stuart's semicircle covering Williamsport. By late afternoon, it had become obvious to the troopers in the ranks that the time had arrived for retreat. Stuart had a different notion, however. If he could not hold Williamsport for Lee, he might throw the enemy into a turmoil and create opportunities for the future. Judging the Federals to be weakest in the center on the Hagerstown Pike, at twilight he ordered Hampton's brigade to break through and gain the enemy's rear. Hampton, who was convinced he confronted the greater part of the Army of the Potomac, unsuccessfully tried to talk Stuart out of the plan. In the darkness, Hampton's horsemen could find no point at which they did not encounter overwhelming opposition, and Jeb finally relented. By the light of burning buildings on the riverfront, the last Confederates left Maryland soil by eleven o'clock. Stuart continued six miles to the southeast toward Martinsburg before making camp for the night, and early the next morning he and his command rejoined the main army.[103] Even if Stuart did not send advance word to Lee, the commanding general learned upon the arrival of his cavalry chief that reentry into Maryland at Williamsport was no longer an option.

Sometime during the night of the 20th or early on the morning of the 21st, Lee finally admitted his Maryland campaign was over. Although the news from Stuart may have been the final straw, his realization that he no longer had an army that could execute his commands was probably the decisive consideration. Otherwise, given his past record, Lee likely would have immediately looked elsewhere to recross the Potomac. But, he did no such thing. Instead, he finally yielded. As he put it with some understatement in his final report, "The condition of our troops now demanded repose."[104] Later in the day he dictated a dispatch to Davis that was, in effect, an epitaph for the campaign and the hopes he had carried across the Potomac.

"As stated to you yesterday," he opened, with the second direct confirmation that he had intended reentering Maryland, "the march of the army toward Williamsport was arrested."[105] He was then able to write a happy conclusion to the crisis he had reported the previous day:

> General Jackson's corps was turned back toward Shepherdstown, to rectify occurrences in that quarter. Only one or two brigades of the enemy's infantry with cavalry had crossed the river, none of whom had entered Shepherdstown. They displayed a large force of artillery on the opposite bank. General A. P. Hill's division pushed forward, and soon drove them across the river, when this army resumed its march. Only four pieces of artillery fell into the hands of the enemy, which they had carried across the river before they were attacked by A. P. Hill.

Lee's summary of the action is generally accurate, except he implies his army left Shepherdstown immediately after the battle. Also, the Federals would claim they captured five cannon. He next gave a long and needlessly detailed account of the loss of Longstreet's ordnance wagons to Federal cavalry on the night of the 14th. The paragraph seemed designed to forestall critical fire from the rear. Why he waited six days to report the incident is unknown.

Then, Lee cut to the heart of why he believed his campaign had stalled short of victory. "The army is resting today on the Opequon, below Martinsburg," he wrote. "Its present efficiency is greatly paralyzed by the loss to its ranks of the numerous stragglers." For Lee to complain about straggling was not new. He had been preoccupied with the problem since taking field command, and he had employed equally blunt language on the subject in his letter to Davis on September 7. This is the first occasion, however, on which he claimed that straggling "paralyzed" his army.

He went on to make an enigmatic observation. "A great many men belonging to the army never entered Maryland at all; many returned after getting there, while others who crossed the river kept aloof." It is certainly true that many of his soldiers did not cross the Potomac. But, the explanation for thousands of these men was Lee's own orders that those trying to catch up with the army be diverted to the stragglers camp in Winchester. It is also certain that from September 14 onward the unauthorized absences increased dramatically due to exhaustion from forced marches and the scavenging for food caused by hunger. There is no particular reason to believe that a significant number of soldiers returned on their own to Virginia, however, or that there were more than the usual number of shirkers—common to both armies—who disappeared when the fighting started. In this regard, the Maryland campaign was unusual only in that once the ranks were departed, it was sometimes more difficult to rejoin them.

"I have taken every means in my power from the beginning to correct this evil," he continued, "which has increased instead of diminished."[106] And his record since taking command supports his statement. "The stream has not lessened since crossing the Potomac, though the cavalry has been constantly employed in endeavoring to arrest it." It is certainly noteworthy that in Lee's opinion the hemorrhaging had not slowed since the return to Virginia.

"As illustrative of the fact," he went on, "I inclose a report just received from General J. R. Jones, who was sent to Winchester to arrest stragglers at that point while the army was at Sharpsburg." Although no report from J. R. Jones has been found, its bleak message can be inferred from a dispatch sent nearly a week later. Jones had discovered the country to be overrun with strays, including among them an "astonishing" number of officers. Through the "constant" labor of cavalry sweeps, he claimed to have returned 5,000 or 6,000 men to the army. No doubt the majority of this number, for which Jones took credit, were simply convalescents from earlier battles waiting at Winchester for the first opportunity to rejoin their commands. It seems that neither Jones nor Lee drew fine distinctions when it came to stragglers.[107]

Lee then underscored for Davis the adverse effect of straggling on his ability to plan and execute strategy. "It occasions me the greatest concern in the future operations of the army," he lamented, "for it is still my desire to threaten a passage into Maryland, to occupy the enemy on this frontier, and, if my purpose cannot be accomplished, to draw them into the Valley, where I can attack them to advantage."

In this key sentence, Lee reveals how far he has lowered his sights in a single day. He no longer pretends he is capable of entering Maryland but only that he hopes to remain close enough to the Potomac to "threaten" recrossing and thereby keep the Federals out of Virginia. Even this is not stated confidently, and he is compelled to present a fall-back plan to lure the enemy into the Shenandoah Valley.

Flushed with disappointment from the campaign he had just abandoned, Lee urged draconian measures upon the president. "Some immediate legislation, in my opinion, is required, and the most summary punishment should be authorized. It ought to be construed into desertion in the face of the enemy, and thus brought under the Rules and Articles of War." Lee's suggestion raises the grim specter of half of the army attempting to execute the other half.

At the moment he wrote, Lee may have believed that the situation was so serious as to require such an extreme response. Certainly, he could cite dire illustrations to support his case:

> To give you an idea of its extent in some brigades, I will mention that, on the morning after the battle of the 17th, General Evans reported to me on the field, where he was holding the front position, that he had but 120 of his brigade present, and that the next brigade to his, that of General Garnett, consisted of but 100 men. General Pendleton reported that the brigades of Generals Lawton and Armistead, left to guard the ford at Shepherdstown, together contained but 600 men. This is a woeful condition of affairs, and I am pained to state it, but you ought not be ignorant of the fact, in order, if possible, that you may apply the proper remedy.

It is revealing that Lee's first example derived from personal observation and occurred on the morning of the 18th. Thus, he must then have had a good idea of the weakness of his army before he ordered its withdrawal from Maryland.

Lee continued with an incisive glimpse into the aggressive attitude that drove both him and his strategy. In effect, Lee demanded that every soldier in his army be a hero:

> It is true that the army has had hard work to perform, long and laborious marches, and large odds to encounter in every conflict, but not greater than were endured by our revolutionary fathers, or than what any army must encounter to be victorious. There are

> brilliant examples of endurance and valor on the part of those who have had to bear the brunt in the battle and the labor in the field in consequence of this desertion of their comrades.

Finally returning to a more practical level, Lee outlined his plans for the immediate future. He wrote almost wistfully, "I hope by a few days' rest, if it is possible to give it, and the regular issue of rations, to restore the efficiency of the army for the work before it." Lee here admits for the second time that his army is at present incapable of undertaking serious operations. This time, however, the admission is buried within a general statement that radiates, albeit dimly, the return of his natural optimism.

"The enemy I know has suffered on his side," he asserted, "especially his infantry, as they have been driven in all encounters." Typically, in search of the best case, Lee appreciates the damage suffered by the enemy army as well as his own. Still, it would be interesting to know if he engaged in conscious exaggeration in claiming Federal infantry had "been driven in all encounters." His case might barely be stretched to cover Sharpsburg by focusing exclusively on the repulse of Sedgwick and of Burnside, but it is difficult to see how he could have been thinking at all of the fights at either Turner's or Crampton's Gaps.

Tempering even this mild optimism with reality, Lee noted, "His artillery is numerous and powerful, and his re-enforcements arrive daily." Nonetheless, he promised, "I shall endeavor at least to detain him on this frontier and to give him sufficient employment."

The Confederate commander then added what must have seemed—even to him—to be an understatement. "If re-enforcements, clothing, and shoes could be forwarded to the army, it would be of the greatest benefit."

Lee concluded his melancholic dispatch by lifting his eyes from his own immediate theater for the first time in two weeks. "I have not heard of General Loring for some time, nor do I know whether he is employed in the Valley of the Kanawha or where. From such information as I get, I believe the enemy has pretty much withdrawn from Western Virginia.

Did Lee consciously refrain from mentioning Bragg and Kirby Smith?

The plain theme of Lee's letter was his recognition that he has driven the wheels off of his army. He had no recourse but to pause for repair. In this regard, it is interesting to speculate how many men he could have carried with him back across the Potomac at Williamsport. The question is moot, since movements by the Federal commander at both Shepherdstown and Williamsport blocked the move. For one final time in the Maryland campaign, McClellan and the Army of the Potomac—if they failed the expectations of the armchair generals in Washington—again thwarted Lee.

Echoes of Maryland

Lee returned to Virginia, but he could not dismiss western Maryland from his mind. During the previous three weeks he had gained a new insight into the grand strategy of the struggle. He had long recognized that the Confederacy would lose the war on the James River. He now believed the South must win the war—if indeed it could win it—in the Hagerstown or Cumberland Valleys. The only way to guarantee access to all of Virginia's vital resources was to conduct his campaigns beyond its borders. If Richmond were never so safe as when its defenders were absent, the Confederate capital would be safest when Federal forces were wholly occupied with the defense of their own capital. The upper Potomac was the only platform from which he could free all of Virginia and exert irresistible pressure on Washington. Even more, victories gained on Northern soil would demoralize Northerners more quickly and shake their confidence in their government.

As Lee made plain just four days after he had abandoned his first campaign in Maryland, he would have initiated his second immediately if he could. To Jefferson Davis he wrote on the 25th:

> When I withdrew from Sharpsburg into Virginia, it was my intention to recross the Potomac at Williamsport, and move on Hagerstown, but the condition of the army prevented [it]; nor is it yet strong enough to advance advantageously.
>
> In a military point of view, the best move, in my opinion, the army could make would be to advance upon Hagerstown and endeavor to defeat the enemy at that point. I would not hesitate to make it even with our diminished numbers, did the army exhibit its former temper and condition; but, as far as I am able to judge, the hazard would be great and a reverse disastrous. I am, therefore, led to pause.[108]

On the same day, in a letter of congratulations to William Loring in western Virginia on the capture of Charleston, Lee revealed how anxious he was to continue the war north of the Potomac. Having heard that Loring's next object was to be Ravenswood on the Ohio River,

Lee argued that a move on that frontier would be barren of results. Instead, he urged Loring to advance on Morgantown and enter western Pennsylvania. Or, optionally, he offered a plan for joint cooperation: "It will depend upon circumstances whether we will be able to recross into Maryland, but, should you operate down the Potomac, endeavor to keep yourself advised of the movements of this army and notify me of your position. Probably a combined movement into Pennsylvania may be concerted."[109]

Without doubt Lee dabbled in fantasy to expect Loring's ragtag 5,000-man army to surmount more than 200 miles of rugged mountains and valleys and threaten the flank of the Army of the Potomac. It was a fantasy born of desperation. Two considerations exerted tremendous pressure on Lee to act immediately. First, however little he might have known while in Maryland about Confederate operations in other theaters, he was bound to have gained information since his return to Virginia.[110] Everywhere else the Confederate tide continued to rise. Three armies—Bragg, Kirby Smith, and Marshall—marched across Kentucky. Breckinridge was on the move from Mississippi to join them, and Price and Van Dorn were preparing to enter west Tennessee. Only the Army of Northern Virginia was failing in its role.

Moreover, looking simply to his own theater, if Lee did not press the initiative, he would lose it. And, if he lost the initiative, he would be forced to fall back on the defensive and imperil the brilliant gains of the summer. The enemy was badly hurt. Now was the time to press on to final victory. "The enemy has suffered from straggling as well as ourselves (I believe to a greater extent)," he observed on the 24th, "but his numbers are so great he can afford it; we cannot."[111] It was the same thinking that had launched the Maryland campaign, and it would press Lee on to drink the last, bitter dregs of hope.

Events had pushed Lee backward from one less attractive alternative to another. He had stood at Sharpsburg only to find a way to break out of the box and regain the initiative. He had withdrawn from Sharpsburg only to recross immediately at Williamsport. And now he abandoned the Williamsport movement only after promising himself he would require but a few days to refit before launching a new campaign to recross the Potomac.

Plainly, it was with the intention of a rapid reentry into Maryland that Lee threw himself into revitalizing the Army of Northern Virginia.

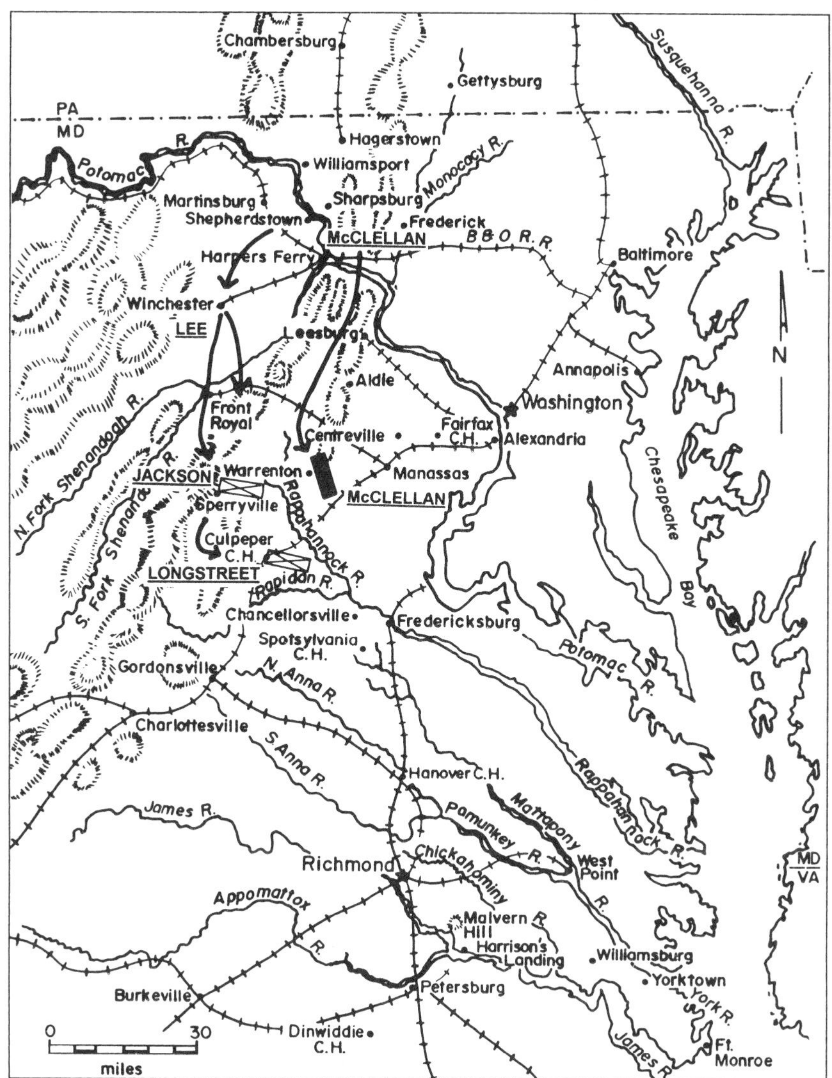

Echoes of Maryland

From the 21st to the 25th, he looked into nearly every branch of his army and took measures to restore potency and increase efficiency. He endeavored not only to repair the losses of the recent campaign but also to apply the lessons he had learned in it. First and foremost, he worked to fill the depleted ranks of the infantry regiments. He cast a tight net to gather in stragglers, convalescents, and conscripts.[112] He also issued orders—not altogether new—to correct the scourge of straggling by enforcing morning roll calls and establishing provost guards for both camp and the march.[113]

Having at last gained full confidence in Jackson and Longstreet, Lee made permanent, albeit informally, the organization of the entire army into two wings. Although it would take over a month to confirm the promotions and sort out the internal details of the bifurcation, the army would hereafter operate as two corps.[114] One branch of the service Lee deemed to require immediate and thorough attention. With several brilliant exceptions, the performance of the Confederate artillery had been abysmal in Maryland. Lee set on foot the consolidation of batteries and the weeding out of incompetent officers. He also tried to get more long-range cannon and ammunition so that the artillery would not be so woefully outgunned in future duels.[115]

Lee recognized that the deterioration of his army had derived in no small degree from the inadequate supplies of food and clothing, especially shoes. He increased his efforts to fill the deficiencies both from local sources and from Richmond. He even took the time to suggest to Davis that the Commissary Department forsake bulky barrels to transport hard bread and in the future emulate the Federals by using small, light boxes.[116]

Inevitably, Lee would be disappointed. The kind of healing "repose" demanded by the frazzled Army of Northern Virginia could not be obtained in a handful of days. The men who remained in the ranks described themselves as "worn out" and "broken down." Theirs was a fatigue that reached beyond the body and seeped into the soul. A few nights' sound sleep might restore aching legs and feet, but only the passing of weeks could soften memories of the horrors they had witnessed and smooth nerves made raw from repeatedly facing death or maiming. "I hope that this campaign is ended," confessed T. J. Goree, Longstreet's aide, "for although I am as anxious as any one for the war to be brought to a close, yet I do not want to see any more fighting this fall." Lee must have begun to sense this truth in his dispatch to Davis on the 25th, when he wrote that the army did not "exhibit its former temper."[117]

Neither could the thousands of stragglers scattered across northern Virginia be gathered in and distributed to their units in a matter of days. Custis Lee, the Confederate commander's eldest son, who was traveling from Richmond on a special mission from Jefferson Davis, first encountered the stream of estrays as far south as Harrisonburg, and he observed the numbers only increased as he made his way northward to Winchester and Martinsburg.[118] Robert Chilton, the army's adjutant, estimated that 40,000 errant Confederates were absent from the army and wandering the roads and fields in all directions.[119]

Moreover, although Lee dismissed "diminished numbers" as not deterring him from a new campaign, the field returns submitted to him on September 22d must have weighed heavily in his decision. Even after the return of over 10,000 men, he still commanded an army but half the size he had first carried into Maryland, and insignificantly larger than the one with which he had made his stand five days earlier at Sharpsburg. He could not cross the Potomac again with only 36,000 effectives—especially when it was doubtful the term "effectives" aptly described his men.[120]

Thus it came to pass on September 26—a "day cool and sad"—that Lee acknowledged the ultimate failure of his campaign. When he realized it would not be possible to renew offensive operations in the foreseeable future, he let slip through his fingers the last slender option to final defeat. "Not deeming it prudent . . . to re-enter Maryland," he withdrew his army from the near vicinity of the Potomac and went into more permanent camps ten miles farther south at Bunker Hill and Winchester.[121] All that was left to him now was posturing and bluffing a menace to the upper Potomac that he was powerless to fulfill.

Slowly, as the autumn passed and the days grew cooler, the army mended. More than 16,000 men swelled the ranks before the next returns on September 30, and another 12,000 joined before October 10th. By the middle of November, the army had grown to 85,000 present for duty, its greatest strength since the eve of the Seven Days.[122]

Improvement came not only in the swelling numbers. In three months of aggressive operations Lee had already imprinted his will on the Army of Northern Virginia by forging it into an offensive weapon. Now, he seized the opportunity provided by the surcease in campaigning to shape its efficiency. Company roll calls each morning and incessant daily drills brought a semblance of military professionalism to the fractious volunteer force. By the end of November, the ranks had discovered a new source for satisfaction. Along with their pride as fighters, they belatedly felt a confidence in themselves as soldiers.[123]

The spirit also mended, although the Maryland campaign left a bitter taste in the mouths of the Confederates. After singing a heartfelt "Carry

Me Back to Old Virginia" as they recrossed the Potomac, for a long while after they shouted down any band attempting to play "Maryland, My Maryland."[124] By focusing narrowly on (first) the capture of Harpers Ferry, (second) the miracle of withstanding three times their numbers at Sharpsburg, and (third) McClellan's refusal to renew the attack on September 18, the Confederates gleaned all the silver they could from the Maryland campaign. But they could not escape entirely the admission of failure. "I suppose it will be generally concluded," confessed Walter Taylor, "that our march through . . . Maryland was decidedly meteoric." Sandy Pendleton, Jackson's chief of staff, admitted to his mother, "I think the Maryland campaign has not been very successful." More bluntly, Brig. Gen. William Dorsey Pender told his wife in referring to the Potomac, "My only regret is that we crossed it in the first place." Succinctly, Lee's oldest son, Custis, reported to President Davis, "They got the worst of it."[125]

Physically, Lee healed about as slowly as his army. It was nearly a month after the battle at Sharpsburg before he regained a measure of control over his everyday life. On October 12, he would write to his wife: "My hands are improving slowly, and, with my left hand, I am able to dress and undress myself, which is a great comfort. My right is becoming of some assistance, too, though it is still swollen and sometimes painful. The bandages have been removed. I am now able to sign my name. It has been six weeks to-day since I was injured, and I have at last discarded the sling."[126]

How long it took for the soul to heal cannot be known. The least of Lee's worries was the carping criticism of the politicians and editors from their armchairs at home. As Davis wrote to him on September 28, "The feverish anxiety to invade the North has been relieved by the counterirritant of apprehension for the safety of the capital in the absence of the army, so long criticized for a 'want of dash.'" Certainly the Confederate commander did not need to worry about losing the trust of Davis. "I am alike happy," the president assured him, "in the confidence felt in your ability, and your superiority to outside clamor, when the uninformed assume to direct the movements of armies in the field." And as balm for the general who had accepted fortune's dare and lost, he concluded, "In the name of the Confederacy, I thank you and the brave men of your army for the deeds which have covered our flag with imperishable fame."[127]

On October 29 the president wrote candidly to Kirby Smith, "The results in Kentucky have been to me a bitter disappointment."[128] So far as is known, Jefferson Davis never wrote or spoke such words to Robert E. Lee. It is difficult to believe his regret over Maryland was less, however.

In general orders that were read aloud at the head of each regiment, Lee passed on to the troops the gratitude of their president. Using the dramatic prose requisite on such occasions, the general proclaimed: "History records few examples of greater fortitude and endurance than this army has exhibited." In this document there was no mention of shirkers, laggards, or cowards. And since there was no admission of failing in Maryland, there was no need to ascribe reasons for failure. Buried within the text, however, Lee did mention that the army had resisted three times its own number at Sharpsburg. Readers and listeners could infer that only the vast preponderance of the enemy had cut short the expedition.[129]

One by one the days of good weather for campaigning slipped by, as Lee spent his quietest October of the war. He watched helplessly as McClellan refitted the Federal army, trained the new regiments, and refused to move hastily into a new campaign. Lee had been reduced to his inferior aim of continuing a threatening pressure on the upper Potomac. He hoped Federal fear of another Confederate incursion into western Maryland would compel the enemy to base any new campaign on Harpers Ferry. As early as September 24, Lee wrote, "If we cannot advance into Maryland, I hope to draw [McClellan] into the valley, where I think we can operate to advantage." If the Federals could be lured into the Shenandoah, they would be drawn away from Richmond, and, as their communications lengthened, they would be made vulnerable to maneuver.[130]

In truth, however, Lee anticipated the enemy would not be so foolish. Lee did not fear McClellan, but he did respect both his opponent's deliberateness and grasp of strategy. He fully expected the Federal army would utilize its advantage in numbers to leave a strong detachment in western Maryland and embark a large force for the James. On the 28th he told Davis: "My great anxiety is, lest, with other troops, General McClellan may move upon Richmond. At present there is no way I can endanger his safety. I have been in hopes that he would cross the river and move up the valley, where I wish to get him, but he does not seem so disposed."[131]

Unable to learn anything from reconnaissances and spies about McClellan's intentions, on October 8 Lee sent Stuart on a raid across the Potomac. Crossing above Williamsport, the Confederate cavalry drove on to Chambersburg before completing a circuit of the Federal army and returning by way of White's Ford at Leesburg. In spite of Stuart's intelligence that "McClellan has detached no part of his army eastward, but, on the contrary, has been receiving re-enforcements," Lee continued to believe that the Federals would make the obvious best move.[132] As late as October 22d, he would write Davis that he supposed McClellan "will do little more this fall than to organize and instruct his new troops, and, as the winter advances, prepare to advance south of the James, which now seems to me his most probable plan."[133]

What Lee did not know was that McClellan wanted to make the obviously best move, but he was prevented by the unallayable fear of the Lincoln government of uncovering the front of Washington. Nor would the Federal commander have the luxury of awaiting the late winter or early spring to start a new campaign. On October 26 the Army of the Potomac commenced crossing the river at Berlin. It soon became apparent to Lee, however, that McClellan could not be enticed into the Shenandoah Valley. Instead, the Federal commander advanced southward with his usual deliberation. Advancing on the east side of the mountains, he blocked the gaps behind him and thus isolated the Valley and neutralized a large chunk of central Virginia. McClellan's course carried him toward Gordonsville and the vital Virginia Central Railroad, and ultimately it would have brought him to Richmond from the northwest.

It would have been an interesting campaign. Eventually, the Federal army would have been in the open, trailing long supply lines in its rear. Lee would have had abundant opportunities for maneuvering. Whether McClellan's deliberate dispositions could have forestalled Lee's turning movements must remain moot. By November 7, the Army of the Potomac had reached Warrenton, and Lee had responded by dividing the wings of the Army of Northern Virginia. Jackson was at Sperryville, and Longstreet was twenty-five miles to the southeast at Culpeper Court House.

If Lee had a plan on that day beyond observing and waiting for an opportunity, it has been lost to history. About this time, he wrote to Custis, "I am operating to baffle the advance of the enemy and retain him among the mountains until I can get him separated that I can strike him to advantage."[134] Idleness was being enforced upon the general who believed that idleness was fatal to the Confederate cause. In terms of strategic freedom—although certainly not of geography—Lee had been returned to where he started six months before. The initiative was firmly back in the hands of the enemy.

On November 7, Lincoln removed McClellan from command and replaced him with Ambrose Burnside, a general who was willing to pursue the direct overland route to Richmond by way of Fredericksburg. First, of course, Burnside would have to get past Fredericksburg.

October saw the Confederate tide ebb. William Rosecrans's Federal army stopped Price and Van Dorn at Iuka and Corinth in Mississippi before they ever got to Tennessee. Bragg fought a tactically indecisive battle with Don Carlos Buell at Perryville on October 8 and then fled from Kentucky, taking Kirby Smith with him and leaving Humphrey Marshall to find his own way back to Virginia. On October 15, Loring was removed from command, and the offensive in western Virginia stalled at Charleston. By the 24th no Confederate force anywhere was on the offensive.

Thus closed the third phase of the Civil War, and with it ended the last period in which the Confederacy came reasonably close to approaching the field strength of the Federals. The aggressive multifront campaign was expensive for the Confederacy. The total casualties of 25,000 represented 2.1 percent of the Southern military pool.[135] Still, the shift in advantage was greater than these figures show. In spite of an amendment to the Conscription Act on September 27, which extended the draft age from thirty-five to forty-five, the odds against the South shifted sharply.[136] By the end of 1862, the Confederacy would have only 447,000 men in the field, compared to the Federals 918,000. From the much more favorable ratio of three to four in June, the South would slip to one to two in December.[137]

In the expenditure of human resources, Lee was clearly the chief culprit. His casualties of 10,316 men at Sharpsburg on the 17th was only eighty-one shy of the combined losses of Van Dorn, Price, Smith, and Bragg in all of their battles in the west during the summer and fall.[138] More impressive than the cold statistics, however, was the degree to which the Maryland campaign crippled the Army of Northern Virginia. The general—who from the moment he assumed field command had thought and planned entirely in terms of the offensive—for the next seven months would remain on the defensive.

FINALE

"We have tried the utmost"

Lee's Venture Risked and Lost

"According to General Hill's account," huffed Robert E. Lee, "if another dispatch had been lost, the South would have been victorious!" Lee spoke with such heated animation as to suggest his innocent questioner had touched upon a festering sore that refused to heal.

It was, otherwise, a typical wintry morning in 1868, and a freshly lighted fire blazed in the hearth of the office of the president of Washington College. Edward Gordon, clerk of the small liberal arts school in Lexington, had reported to the large windowless room in the basement of the chapel at eight o'clock, as he did each morning for instructions and a review of the day's plans. After the conclusion of the brief business, Gordon asked Lee if he had read D. H. Hill's recent article entitled "The Lost Dispatch."

Much to the astonishment of Gordon—since the general had never before discussed the war—Lee then held forth at length on the reasons for the expedition into Maryland and on the causes for the failure of the campaign. On the surface, Lee was indignant over Hill's attempt to recast history for self-serving purposes by arguing that the loss of Special Orders, No. 191, had harmed the Federals and aided the Confederates.[1] But there also glimmered through Lee's excitement on this February morning his dismay that someone else should attempt to explain what he himself had intended or presume to depict what had been in his own mind.

Lee was experiencing his second loss of control over the Maryland campaign. He had lost the direction of operations when the Army of the Potomac entered Frederick on September 12, 1862. With the passing of the entire campaign—whether he fully understood it before or not—he had also lost control over the telling of the story.[2]

He, who alone had decided to cross the Potomac, to stand at South Mountain and Sharpsburg, and to retire into Virginia, now became merely one primary source among others. He, who alone knew why he had rendered the critical decisions, was reduced to the role of witness and his memory to the status of testimony. There was nothing ironic in the transformation, however.

There can be no irony in the inevitable. Lee and the Maryland campaign had become history. And their meaning had passed into the hands of historians.

Verdicts of History

As Lee explained them during the campaign, the reasons for the failure of his operations in Maryland were plain and uncomplicated. As the enemy's legions had swollen, Confederate numbers had dwindled. And between the two, Lee had been most distressed over the straggling that had reduced his army to offensive impotence. "This was the main cause of its retiring from Maryland," he explained to Davis, "as it was unable to cope with advantage with the numerous host of the enemy." In regard to the poor response of Marylanders, he maintained that his stay was too short to encourage a people "so completely trodden under foot."[3]

Although Lee claimed to know of the finding of S.O. 191 within sixteen hours of McClellan's reading them, in his wartime writings he did not attribute the failure of the campaign to the lost orders. Perhaps, he deemed it unseemly to emphasize the importance of an event that cast some of his subordinates in a bad light but about which there was much mystery. In any case, even in his final report, which did not appear until eleven months after the battle and after McClellan's testimony had made the matter public knowledge, Lee still understated the significance of the lost orders. Holding to the arrival of Federal reenforcements and the exhaustion of the Confederate army as the causes of his failure, he dismissed the incident in two and a half sentences as an unwelcome but surmountable annoyance: "In the mean time events transpired in another quarter which threatened to interfere with the reduction of the place [Harper's Ferry]. A copy of the order directing the movement of the army from Fredericktown had fallen into the hands of General McClellan, and disclosed to him the disposition of our forces. He immediately began to push forward rapidly."[4]

It was the publication of D. H. Hill's article three years after the close of the war that prodded Lee into declaring that the enemy's good fortune had been the pivotal event in the campaign. The conversation with Gordon on the morning of February 15, 1868, was only his opening salvo. Later the same morning Lee reiterated his opinions in similar words to William Allan, a professor of applied mathematics and former ordnance officer of the Army of Northern Virginia. Six days later, Lee put his views into somewhat more restrained language in a letter to D. H. Hill; and, finally, two months later he reverted to the subject again in a second, briefer conversation with Allan.

The message in the three conversations and the letter are clear. Lee called the enemy's discovery of his plans "a great misfortune"[5] and "a great calamity."[6] He asserted, "It is probable that the loss of the dispatch changed the character of the campaign."[7] And he confessed, "Sharpsburg was forced on him by McClellan finding out his plans and moving quickly in consequence."[8]

It is also clear that Lee did not believe that his postwar views represented a change of opinion. He wrote to Hill, "at the time the order fell into Genl McClellan's hands, I considered it a great calamity & subsequent reflection has not caused me to change my position."[9]

Lee admitted that his inferior numbers and the exhaustion and separation of his army were the immediate causes for his return to Virginia, but these conditions resulted from McClellan's too-rapid advance, which in return resulted from the knowledge the Federal commander gained from S.O. 191:

> Had the Lost Dispatch not been lost, and had McClellan continued his cautious policy for two or three days longer, I would have had all my troops concentrated on the Maryland side, stragglers up, men rested and intended then to attack McClellan, hoping the best results from [the] state of my troops and those of the enemy. Tho' it is impossible to say that victory would have certainly resulted, it is probable that the loss of the dispatch changed the character of the campaign.[10]

Hence, to Lee the Federal discovery of Special Orders, No. 191, became the defining cause of Confederate failure in the Maryland campaign. Nowhere did Lee at any time indicate any misgivings about undertaking the expedition, nor did he second-guess any of his decisions during its course. The implication in all of his statements is clear: he believed his actions were correct, and he would have done it all over again in much the same way. Indeed, it is likely that his belief that only a trick of fate had foiled his plans encouraged him to cross the Potomac nine months later and, in fact, to try it again.

Lee's execution of the Gettysburg campaign might seem to raise doubts about his truthfulness on this point. It might be asked whether the modifications he incorporated into his operations during his second incursion into the North were not derived from lessons he had learned from his first expedition and were not, therefore, strong presumptive evidence that he did realize (whether he admitted it or not) that he had made mistakes in the fall of 1862. In June 1863, Lee would cross the Potomac at Williamsport much farther to the west. He would ignore the Federal garrison at Harpers Ferry. He would make no effort to rouse Marylanders to rebellion. And he would intend from the start to penetrate deeply into Pennsylvania.

Certainly, it is possible that some of these changes resulted, at least in part, from his earlier experiences. It is just as possible, however, that Lee was simply responding to vastly different circumstances in 1863. Lee perceived—and correctly so—that the Army of the Potomac after Chancellorsville was not the disorganized and demoralized force that had cowered in Washington's forts in September 1862. Also, the second time Lee crossed the Potomac, he did so because Confederate fortunes elsewhere, particularly at Vicksburg, were so dire that he needed to gain a victory to relieve the pressure in the West. For both reasons, when Lee headed north a second time he did not intend to stay for a protracted period but to bring his campaign to a rapid resolution. He was, therefore, far less concerned about wagoning supplies from Virginia and was even willing to contemplate abandoning his communications altogether.

Thus, it is conceivable that Lee never believed he made any serious mistake in the Maryland campaign. And it is possible that he went to his grave in 1870 convinced that only a quirk of fate in September of 1862 had denied him victory and the Confederacy its best chance at independence.

It might have provided Lee some comfort to know that by and large the history written during the next thirteen decades would be kind to him and his conduct of the Maryland campaign. Certainly, when measured against the scorn heaped upon George B. McClellan, historians have been gentle with Robert E. Lee. For that reason, it is surprising to note the observation of Douglas Southall Freeman, Lee's preeminent biographer, that the first three weeks of September 1862 "have been the most criticized of Lee's military career."[11] If Freeman is correct, Lee has escaped from the scythe of history with superficial scratches.

No doubt, Lee's high approval derives in part from the simple fact that much of the writing about the Maryland campaign has been authored by Confederates and their spiritual descendants. Three members of Lee's staff (Walter Taylor, Charles Marshall, and Armistead Long) established the framework of the Confederate interpretation.[12] Other veterans (such as Jubal Early, Jed. Hotchkiss, and William Allan) elaborated the thesis.[13] Not all veterans went so far as Early and claimed the entire campaign to be a "substantial victory" for the South.[14] But, in near unison, the former soldiers proclaimed that Lee had been correct in crossing the Potomac and that his masterful tactical conduct had won the Battle of Sharpsburg—or at least fought it to a draw.

The ex-Confederates had to admit that Lee had fallen short of his strategic goals in entering Maryland. The citizens of the state had not flocked to his colors; the Army of Northern Virginia had not remained north of the Potomac until the close of the season of active operations; and the Army of the Potomac had not been routed in a Manassas-like defeat. To excuse these failures the Southerners merely adopted Lee's explanations, although they pushed them well beyond the claims of their old commander. The veterans whittled down the Confederate army until, in the most extreme estimate, only 29,000 men of all arms stood with Lee at Sharpsburg on the 17th.[15] At the same time, they expanded the importance of the lost orders until their loss took on the role of divine intervention. Looking back in 1906 and contemplating the Federal discovery of S.O. 191, Walter Taylor would lament, "It looks as if the good Lord had ordained that we should not succeed."[16]

The only significant contrary opinion came, not surprisingly, from James Longstreet. Having advised against several of Lee's decisions at the time they were made, Longstreet remained consistent by criticizing many of them after the war. According to the senior subordinate in the Army of Northern Virginia, the major mistake committed by his commander was to violate the basic military principal to keep an invading force united while in enemy territory. Longstreet had vocally opposed an expedition to clear the lower Shenandoah Valley on September 6 and again, although less directly, in the Frederick war council on September 9. And, in looking back, he would insist, "The great mistake of the campaign was the division of Lee's army."[17] Curiously, Longstreet's criticism is an inside-out version of the standard Confederate explanation of the campaign's ill success; the difference is that Longstreet was willing to assert that Lee committed an error rather than blame the failure on the bad luck of the loss of S.O. 191.

Longstreet found other faults in Lee's conduct of the campaign as well. He recognized the need to protect McLaws in Pleasant Valley; but he believed—again, as he advised at the time—that once McClellan reached the foot of South Mountain, Lee should have retired immediately to Sharpsburg rather than standing at Turner's Gap.[18] In his memoirs, Longstreet would claim (although there is no evidence in this instance that he said so at the time) that once Harpers Ferry had surrendered and McLaws was safe, there was no longer any reason for the Confederates to remain north of the Potomac. Lee should have withdrawn on the night of the 15th to join Jackson in Virginia.[19]

Still, withal, it is important to note that Longstreet warmly approved of the grand strategy of the expedition into Maryland. He recognized that September 1862 offered a moment of opportunity that had to be seized and pressed to the fullest, and he shared in the high aspirations for the campaign.[20] Indeed, he would declare, "If General Lee had kept his army together, he could not have been defeated."[21] Longstreet disagreed only with Lee's lower level of campaign strategy. In conformity with his views at other times and places, Longstreet believed the Confederates should have found a way to make the Federals do the attacking. As he said to Lee in Hagerstown on the night of the 13th, "General, I wish we could stand still and let the damn Yankees come to us!"[22]

The Confederate interpretation did not die with the last veteran. It has survived in various guises to the present day. Three widely read and admired biographies have both preserved and disseminated the view that the expedition into Maryland was thwarted by unkind fate. Clifford Dowdey, in his popular *Lee*, concluded, "In this occasion . . . the element of luck entered" to balk "Lee's audacity."[23] And Col. G. F. R. Henderson, in his *Stonewall Jackson and the American Civil War*, a British work published at the turn of the century and still frequently cited by scholars, wrote, "If the lost order had not fallen into McClellan's hands, Lee in all probability would have had ample time to select his battlefield and concentrate his army; there would have been no need of forced marches, and consequently much less straggling."[24]

By a considerable margin, the most respected study of Lee and one of the most influential works in all of Civil War literature has been Douglas Southall Freeman's four-volume *R. E. Lee: A Biography*. Freeman devoted sixty-five pages of his second volume to a detailed analysis of the major strategic and tactical decisions made by Lee in the Maryland campaign. Although Freeman defended Lee's most significant decisions (to cross the Potomac and to stand at South Mountain and Sharpsburg), the historian admitted that the Confederate commander might have done some things differently (such as reduce Harpers Ferry before entering

Maryland). Freeman also recognized that Lee courted high risk when "he carried worn out men across the Potomac."[25]

Nonetheless, the conclusion of Freeman's careful examination is familiar: ". . . the unsuccessful outcome of the operations in Maryland will be found to hinge upon the unexpected rapidity and assurance of the Federal movements on and after September 13th."[26] In other words, all of the things Lee might have done differently would not have mattered, according to Freeman, if Special Orders, No. 191, had not fallen into McClellan's hands.

The most recent biographer of the Confederate commander, Emory M. Thomas, has produced the ablest portrait yet of Lee the man and his human side. While Thomas's approach eschews a close analysis of strategic and tactical decisions rendered by the general, he does pose the question of why Lee decided to stand at Sharpsburg. Among several speculations, he seems to favor the answer that Lee may have tried "to pursue an offensive goal—the destruction of the enemy—by means of defensive tactics." In overall terms, believing that fundamental differences in strategy separated Lee and Davis, Thomas views the Maryland campaign as Lee's attempt to win the war through offensive operations in spite of the president's defensive policies.[27]

Lee's reputation and the judgment on his conduct have fared curiously in the hands of the four historians who have written monographs devoted exclusively to the Maryland campaign. All four historians—Francis Palfrey, Ezra Carman, James Murfin, and Stephen Sears—for somewhat different reasons, focus considerably more attention on George McClellan than they do on Robert E. Lee. Indeed, an anti-McClellan animus is the common hallmark of these studies. The most that can be said of their treatment of Lee is that none of the four are seriously critical of him.

Francis Palfrey, who participated in the battle as lieutenant colonel of the 20th Massachusetts in Sedgwick's division, published *The Antietam and Fredericksburg* in 1882. He wrote before the volume in the *Official Records* pertaining to Antietam had been printed, and his coverage of the entire Confederate role in the campaign is scant and confused. Although Palfrey penned paragraphs of scathing comments on McClellan, he rendered no judgments on any of Lee's actions. The single clue that suggests the lapse of twenty years had started to cool the New Englander's partisanship is his passing reference to the "indomitable Lee."[28]

Ezra Carman is a peculiar case. He, too, was a veteran of the battle, having commanded as colonel the 13th New Jersey in Williams's division. He possessed considerable advantages over not only Palfrey but also every other student who has attempted to write on the Maryland campaign. For many years Carman served as historian on the Antietam National Battlefield Board. As such, he toured the field with returning veterans and corresponded extensively with others. The mountain of primary source material he gathered permitted him to write the texts of the battlefield cast-iron plaques and, as well, to determine the position of troops on the Cope's maps published in 1904. Carman also wrote a lengthy history of the entire campaign that has never been published but may be found among his papers in the Library of Congress.

Like Palfrey, Carman is highly critical of McClellan. Unlike Palfrey, Carman gives a roughly balanced attention to both the Federal and Confederate sides of the story. His manuscript is, in fact, a treasure of anecdotal and tactical information on Lee and the Army of Northern Virginia. But Carman neither analyzes Lee's decisions nor offers judgment on them. It is not until the very end of the narrative—and then only in context of what Southern newspapers wrote after the battle—that Carman's opinion may be surmised. "It was fully admitted," he concluded, "that the campaign was both a political and military blunder."[29]

No less curious is what has happened to Lee in the hands of the two recent historians, James Murfin and Stephen Sears, who published studies a hundred years and more after the campaign. Although Murfin's *Gleam of Bayonets* and Sear's *Landscape Turned Red* differ in many regards, their treatment of Lee is sufficiently similar to allow them to be considered in tandem. Both authors are aggressively anti-McClellan to the point that it colors their interpretation of Lee. Picking up on a minor theme in the Confederate interpretation, which suggested that Lee understood McClellan, Murfin and Sears turn the claim into a leitmotif of the campaign.[30]

All of Lee's decisions that might have been foolhardy in another time and place become justified because McClellan was his opponent. According to Murfin, the Confederate commander had "McClellan marked," so that "it was almost as if Lee was pulling the strings of a Federal puppet."[31] Sears asserts, upon "learning of McClellan's reappointment to command," that Lee "was confident that time was on his side."[32] In this version, Lee's boldness—which Sears describes as the "calculating instincts of a riverboat gambler"—is a perfect foil for McClellan's timidity.[33] Whether or not it was true in the field at the time, it is certainly true that Lee has been extremely fortunate to have McClellan as his opponent in historical literature.

The only serious criticism of Lee's conduct of the Maryland campaign has come from a small group of historians who argue with the premise upon which the campaign itself was based. A handful of commentators have maintained that the grand strategy of the Confederacy should have been defensive. The South should have husbanded its resources and adopted a Fabian policy. Lee, with his constant pressing of the offensive, bled his country to death. The Confederacy could not afford such an aggressive strategy and would "have fared better had it not possessed" a Robert E. Lee.[34]

A first glimmer of this view—although certainly minus any bias against Lee himself—can be traced to the opinions of a few disappointed veterans in the immediate wake of the battle. Sharpsburg had snapped the skein of decisive Confederate victories in the East, and it set some to wondering if the South had attempted too much. "Our Army has shown itself incapable of invasion," mused Dorsey Pender, brigadier in A. P. Hill's division, "and we had better stick to the defensive." Thinking in a wider context, Jed. Hotchkiss of Jackson's staff, asserted, "Defense is our true policy," and, he concluded, "we gain by delay and the enemy loses." Looking back from the additional experience gained at Gettysburg, a captain of the 27th North Carolina had no trouble in drawing the moral: "I think the battle of Sharpsburg ought to have taught us a lesson. We have no business invading the enemy's territory."[35]

Such voices, a minority at the time, were lost after the war in the mythology of the Lost Cause. Not until 1907 would a veteran sound a variation on this theme. E. Porter Alexander, Lee's chief ordnance officer during the campaign, opined that it was not possible for a Confederate army to operate in western Maryland or Pennsylvania "for any length of time." He asserted that supplies adequate to a force large enough to contend on the battlefield could not be provided by wagon through the Shenandoah Valley. "Whenever we crossed the Potomac going northward," he concluded, "we were as certain to have to recross it coming southward, in a few weeks, as a stone thrown upward is certain to come down." Alexander was not opposed to an aggressive strategy, but he believed any offensive must be sufficiently strong and focused to bring about a quick victory.[36]

• • •

In 1913 George Bruce, a veteran of the 20th Massachusetts, delivered a paper on "The Strategy of the Civil War," which opened a frontal assault on Lee and Lee's military conduct. Bruce assumed that the determination of the North to pursue the struggle to the end was evident from the first. "If the resolution of the one [side] was equal to that of the other," he argued, "it would be easy to calculate the end of a war where the losses on each side in every contest were equal."[37] It was clear to Bruce that the Confederacy necessarily had to pursue a strategy that aimed to suffer fewer casualties than the North.

Lee could never be ranked with the great captains of history, according to Bruce, because the Confederate commander pursued a strategy that ran contrary to the interests of his country. As Bruce would have it, "Lee never looked at the war in a broad, general way, his mind being absorbed upon a single campaign with slight references to its bearings upon or relation to other operations."[38] Indeed, the Confederate commander was guilty of more than mere shortsightedness. "He supplemented . . . the principle of aggressive warfare" because it "was congenial to his impulsive nature." The disastrous result, as seen by Bruce, was that one year and seven days after taking field command, Lee had waged six of the war's greatest battles and suffered 82,200 in killed and wounded, while during the same period his enemy had lost but 74,720.[39]

Periodically, over the last eighty years, Bruce's ideas have been dusted off, adapted, and used to advance interpretations critical of Lee in particular or the Confederacy in general. In the 1930s, the British military historian, Maj. Gen. J. F. C. Fuller employed the Brucian argument to show that Grant was a much better general than Lee. In the 1960s, Thomas Connelly used it to demonstrate that the Confederacy wasted its resources in the Eastern theater and lost the war by ignoring the West. In the 1980s, Grady McWhiney utilized it as part of his larger theory that the Confederacy was obsessed with making open field assaults, an obsolete mode of warfare that led to huge losses the South could not afford. Finally, in 1992, in a straightforward attempt to debunk the Lee myth, Alan Nolan would repeat and elaborate Bruce's basic arguments.[40]

Although these five writers pursued distinctly different agenda, they all agreed on certain fundamental points about Lee: first, he had no grand strategy; second, he focused narrowly on the defeat of his opponent of the moment and was willing to pay whatever price it cost to do so; and third, his aggressive conduct not only hastened the demise of the Confederacy but may also have been a major contributing cause of it.

In a curious way the verdicts of history have thus come full circle. In the end, both critics and admirers make personality paramount in their interpretation of Lee: neither credits him with a realistic understanding of the war or with the rational pursuit of a plan to win it.[41]

Lee's Overland Campaign of 1862—A Shore Too Far

From June 26 through September 20, 1862, the first three months of his command in the field, Robert E. Lee conducted three separate offensive campaigns. Each had a distinct aim. Lee did not plan them all in advance at one sitting. He did not plot his move against McClellan on the Chickahominy as the first step toward the Potomac. Nonetheless, Lee's three operations do connect to make one larger campaign. As events evolved, Lee lifted his eyes from one freed frontier to the next. One campaign grew naturally from the other, and when completed they formed an organic whole. What started as a campaign to relieve Richmond became a campaign to win the war.

Lee took command in the field as a pragmatist. During the first year of the war he had the time and the opportunity to form a comprehensive view of the struggle. He came to recognize that the Confederacy had at best a long-shot chance to gain independence. He knew that the imbalance of resources that existed between the North and the South, coupled with the laws of mathematics, worked inexorably against his country. He recognized that as long as the North remained determined to subdue the South, the Confederacy could not win the war. Confederate victory could come only from a Union abandonment of the conflict.

Lee knew also that by June 1 the North had demonstrated more than a sufficient will to win, if the war were waged on Northern terms. McClellan's reliance upon engineering, artillery, and the navy played to Northern strengths, minimized Northern losses, and permitted the North to succeed with far less than full mobilization.

Lee aimed to change the terms on which the war was waged. In all three campaigns, he employed open field maneuvers to neutralize engineering and to allow infantry and cavalry to decide the outcome, rather than artillery and ships. For Lee, maneuvering was never an end in itself but the means to gain advantage for attacking the enemy. It did not appear to Lee that a defensive strategy could lead to the demoralization of the North. Especially if it meant the loss of the resources of Virginia and Tennessee, the South could not continue the conflict long enough for the North to become demoralized. Only the infliction of heavy losses and the belief that an interminable struggle lay ahead might discourage the supporters of the Union.

As the campaign of 1862 evolved, Lee perceived the growing likelihood that he was forging the very chain of humiliating defeats that might cause the North to abandon the effort to subdue the South. This awareness caused him to push his army relentlessly forward and to cross the Potomac in search of final victory. Further, he knew that with the April Conscription Act the Confederacy had exerted its maximum effort to bring troops into the field, while the new Federal call in August barely tapped the froth from the North's reservoir of strength. The infantry divisions that arrived at Leesburg from Richmond on September 2 represented the last reenforcements Lee could expect for a long, long time. Then, on top of all of this, after entering Maryland he learned that in the West Confederate armies were on the march toward the Ohio. He concluded that the Confederate tide was swelling to its flood, and he was led to take risks that would otherwise have been unacceptable.

In his overland campaign of 1862, Lee marched 150 miles and waged three of the war's bloodiest battles.[42] In three months he spent most of the human capital his country had gathered at great exertion and placed at his disposal. He lost 45,000 killed, wounded, and captured in the fighting and abandoned at least another 30,000 crippled and starving along the dusty roads of Virginia and Maryland.[43] Three times he divided his army in the face of the enemy, and on three occasions he fought major battles with the odds in numbers heavily against him.[44]

Does this record open Lee to the charge of butchery? Does it confirm the prophecy of the staff officer who claimed Lee's very "name might be audacity"? Or does it validate Harry Heth's conclusion that Lee was "the most aggressive man in his army," or make apt Longstreet's description of Lee as the "up-and-at-'em" style of fighter, who "found it hard, the enemy in sight, to withhold his blows"?[45] Indeed, when the huge casualties alone are considered, these characterizations of Lee—no doubt largely intended as compliments—seem to be justified.

When Lee's overland campaign is dismantled into its constituent parts, however, when his decisions are examined one by one and viewed in the light of what he knew and what he intended to achieve, the image of a berserk warrior swirling a broadsword above his head dissolves into mist. Lee never lost sight of how limited were his means nor of how barren were "successes that inflict no loss upon the enemy beyond the actual loss in battle."[46] Throughout the entire three months—whenever circumstances would permit—he sought to use maneuver to gain heavy victories through easy fighting.

It was not audacity Lee displayed in the Maryland campaign but a fierce determination born of a realistic appraisal of his country's chances. One time only did he falter. On the night of the 14th, in the gloom of the defeat at Turner's Gap, he decided he must retreat from Maryland. Within four hours he found in the need to protect McLaws in Pleasant Valley the excuse to keep his campaign alive. Thereafter, he persevered until his army no longer responded to his orders.

Lee's stand at Sharpsburg derived not from a single decision but from a series of decisions. He took up position on the heights of Sharpsburg on the early morning of the 15th to protect the rear of McLaws and to await the outcome of the operations at Harpers Ferry. At noon he learned of the fall of Harpers Ferry. Thereafter, for the next twenty-seven hours he was not "standing" at Sharpsburg at all; he was simply pausing while his army reunited. He intended to seize the initiative and renew his offensive. During this period he still held the ford at Williamsport, and the road to Hagerstown was open. It was not until three o'clock on the afternoon of the 16th, when Stuart's scouts reported blue columns crossing the upper Antietam, that Lee became boxed in at Sharpsburg. Only then did he grudgingly relent to stand on the defensive and receive battle.

Lee's election to remain an additional day after the furious battle had ripped his army apart; and, finally, his determination to withdraw to Virginia only to recross the Potomac at once at Williamsport were indeed choices fraught with great risk. They were not, however, bold decisions. They were desperate decisions.

Lee's campaign—the larger one that stretched from Beaver Dam Creek on June 26 to Shepherdstown on September 20—represented a calculated attempt to restore Confederate resources, to demoralize the North, and to win the war in the summer of 1862. Interestingly, this larger campaign invites comparison with Federal operations from the Wilderness to Cold Harbor, commonly called Grant's Overland campaign of 1864. Both were elements of a multiprong offensive on several fronts. Both were attempts to reach an ultimate victory by ignoring the usual rest periods between battles for reorganization and refitting. Both were excessively costly, Lee suffering 45,000 casualties to Grant's 60,000. Both relied upon a succession of turning movements that culminated in heavy battles. Each ended in failure when the army on the offensive became unable to continue at the same ruinous pace. In 1864 Grant settled into the siege of Petersburg, and in 1862 Lee spent the fall and winter on the passive defense.

There are differences between the two overland campaigns, however, and the differences militated against the Confederates. Unlike Grant, Lee was under a pressing need to minimize casualties. Unlike Lee, Grant did not have to worry about a single enemy victory undermining his entire campaign. Grant failed in his May 1864 operations either to capture Richmond or destroy the Army of Northern Virginia; but, when he concluded he retained the initiative. Moreover, his new position on the James was far superior to his opening one on the Rappahannock. Hence, Grant only partially failed because he partly succeeded.

Lee, on the other hand, failed fully. It is true that he restored for a time all of the resources of Virginia to the use of the Confederacy. It is also true that the capture of Harpers Ferry reduced enemy strength by 11,000 soldiers and provided a treasure of badly needed ordnance and supplies for the South. Neither, however, was of more than passing importance. Antietam loosened the coil of tension from the summer's successes, which Lee had counted upon to catapult him to final victory. Even more, the Confederate retreat from Maryland restored Northern morale, a result exactly the opposite sought by Lee. James Longstreet was correct: "At Sharpsburg was sprung the keystone of the arch upon which the Confederate cause rested."[47]

Lee took his tide at its flood, as the Bard adjured, and still he lost his ventures. He spent Confederate resources that could never be replaced, and his actions inevitably raise the question of whether they were worth the cost. Even if the initial decision to cross the Potomac can be defended, how can the risks at South Mountain and Sharpsburg be justified? For some—then and later—they cannot.

But for Lee all of the decisions formed a single strand, and all were woven into single tapestry. He judged that the Confederacy had reached the fulcrum of its fate. He believed it was necessary to risk all because a similar opportunity most likely would never come again.

Was he right? It is a judgment impossible to make with a finality that beggars debate. History cannot objectively assess alternative hypotheses or judge the paths not taken. At most, history can isolate Lee's assumptions and, where information permits, second-guess them.

Lee's first and most basic assumption is also the easiest to dispatch. His belief that without foreign intervention the South could not defeat the North unless the North lost the will to fight seems axiomatic. The only possible way for the Confederacy standing alone to have neutralized the overwhelming odds it faced would have been to resort entirely to guerrilla warfare. Since this would have meant the abandonment of slavery and the plantation system, it was an unacceptable option and was never seriously considered. Within the constraints of the diplomatic situation and its own culturally framed war aims, the South could win only if the North gave up the struggle.

Lee's second assumption is more open to debate. Was offense (or offensive-defensive) the strategy best suited to demoralize the enemy? Granted, if the defense could be conducted in such a way as to guarantee all the battles fought would be like a Fredericksburg or a Cold Harbor, it would be possible for the side on the defensive to even the odds, to demoralize the enemy, and to win the war. But, when the enemy elected to pursue a defensive-offensive strategy—such as did McClellan and Grant in their sieges of Richmond and Petersburg—the passive defensive lost most of its advantages and all of its charms. It was one thing to seize and entrench a position of such importance to the enemy that the enemy was compelled to assault the entrenchments; it was quite another to be nailed to the defense of a position of such great importance to oneself that initiative and maneuver were forfeit.

The point in question was not one of abstract military theory. It was a concrete historical situation. By June of 1862, Lee (as well as Davis and many others) believed that the Confederacy had nearly been driven beyond its means for sustaining the war. Considering the South's loss of territory, resources, and morale by that date, the belief was not unreasonable.

Lee's third assumption is the most problematic of all. Was there any strategy—offensive or defensive—the South could have pursued that would have persuaded the North to abandon the contest? Looking back in hindsight, it does not seem as if Northern support for restoring the Union ever became so wobbly or wore so thin that any action taken by the Confederacy would have caused the North to accept secession. It seems that each defeat merely stiffened Northern determination to dig deeper, and every delay merely quickened impatience for victory. Hence, Lee was probably wrong.

Still, whether the offensive or defensive strategy would have produced the better results, or whether anything the South could have done would have been effective, are not questions that even now can be definitively answered. Even less could they be answered by Lee in 1862—

except by trial. He read a pattern into the news reaching him from the North, and he based his actions on the conclusions he drew that there was at least a slender chance the North might tire of the struggle. The most that can be asked today is whether his assumption was a reasonable one. The best answer would seem to be—considering especially his minimal options—that it was.

Finally, was Lee correct in believing that the Confederate tide was cresting in September 1862? Certainly, in view of the South's strength mobilized and concentrated in the field, the morale of its soldiers and citizens, and its collateral offensives on other fronts, it is reasonable to believe that the Confederacy was approaching its apogee on that date. But, was it also reasonable to incur extraordinary risks on the assumption that there would not be other, equally attractive opportunities in the future? Once again, no definitive answer is possible. History can only look to subsequent events and judge if Lee likely was correct.

Would it be possible to put together another string of Confederate victories in Virginia? Yes, Fredericksburg and Chancellorsville served nicely to dampen Federal morale. Neither, however, was a rout such as Second Manassas, which led to Federal troops huddling in the environs of Washington. And neither disrupted Federal offensives elsewhere.

Would it be possible to put together another army of offensive strength? Yes, the bottom of the barrel could be scraped several times more. But never again would the number of Confederates mobilized be so high or would the odds bear so lightly against the South.

Would it be possible to find another opening for the Army of Northern Virginia to cross the Potomac? Yes, in eight months' time the opportunity would again arise.

Would it be possible to launch the second attempt coincident with Confederate offensives in the West? No. Indeed, when Lee next crossed the Potomac, Confederate fortunes in the Western theater—at Vicksburg and Chattanooga—would be on the verge of collapse.

Would the Confederates ever again come so close to the one final push that might have knocked the North out of the war? Probably not.

Thus, although he failed, Lee was right more often than he was wrong. In light of what he could know and based upon reasonable assumptions, he usually made the correct decision. He was right to undertake a turning movement across the Potomac to press his summer's victories to a successful conclusion. He was right to divide his army in order to press on with his campaign and at the same time clear the enemy garrisons from his communications. In this case, it was his timing that was wrong. He needed first to defeat the Federal army under McClellan that was moving out from Washington before separating his own forces.

Lee was right also to stand at South Mountain and at Sharpsburg in an attempt to resurrect his failing campaign. His decision to remain at Sharpsburg on September 18 was at least half-right. To the extent that it was based on the likely inability to withdraw the Army of Northern Virginia safely on the night of the 17th, the decision was inevitable. To the degree that it was an attempt to salvage morale, it may be argued. But to the extent the last stand was based on the hope to renew the campaign, it was quixotically unreal.

Only in his belief that he could immediately reenter Maryland at Williamsport on the 20th or 21st was Lee wholly wrong. By that point he no longer commanded an army capable of offensive operations. The battle at Shepherdstown spared him the humiliation of discovering that only a corporal's guard would have followed him back across the Potomac. After the close of the war, in one of the few boasts about himself ever attributed to Lee, the Confederate commander said of his soldiers, "I believe I got out of them all they could do or all any men could do."[48] Certainly, this was true in the Maryland campaign.

Hence, in all of his major strategic decisions save one, Lee was right. He recognized the high tide of the Confederacy even as it crested, and he rode that tide to its farthest swell. For two and a half years more he would search futilely for another way to crush Northern morale. He and other Confederate leaders would rationalize their chances to win independence through the election of 1864 and beyond. Shortly after Appomattox, Lee likened his efforts to those of "a man breasting a wave of the sea, who, as rapidly as he clears a way before him, is enveloped by the very water he has displaced."[49]

In the end, Northern determination proved greater than Southern resources. The tide ran too shallow, and the shore stretched too far.

Notes

Introduction. "On such a full sea . . ."

1. *New York Times*, Oct. 20; quoted in William Allen Frassanito, *Antietam: The Photographic Legacy of America's Bloodiest Day* (New York: Charles Scribner's Sons, 1978), 16.

2. The battlefield parks in order of founding were: Chickamauga (1890), Antietam (1890), Shiloh (1894), Gettysburg (1895), and Vicksburg (1899). See Charles W. Snell and Sharon A. Brown, *Antietam National Battlefield and National Cemetery, Sharpsburg, Maryland: An Administrative History* (Washington, D.C.: National Park Service, U.S. Department of the Interior, 1986), 92. The Gettysburg battlefield commission appointed by the secretary of war actually started its work in May 1893. See U.S. War Department, Gettysburg National Military Park Commission, *Annual Reports to the Secretary of War, 1893–1901* (Washington, D.C.: GPO, 1902), 5.

3. From the 1896 Annual Report of Secretary of War Daniel S. Lamont, cited in Snell, *Antietam Administrative History*, 90. The great disparity in expenditures and acreage derived from the philosophy of Maj. George B. Davis, the second president of the Antietam Battlefield Board, who believed it ncessary to acquire only enough land to build roads marking the lines of the Union and Confederate armies. See also Harry A. Butowsky, "Nomenclature Used in the National Parks," *Cultural Resources Management Bulletin* 2 (1979): 3, 7–8.

4. It is impossible to arrive at a precise comparison of the attendance for the two parks. Figures available since 1934, as published in annual and decennial National Park Service reports, show wide swings in the total for each park on a year to year basis and a variety of counting methods employed over time. The peak difference occurred in 1936, when Gettysburg outdrew Antietam 50 to 1. In recent years, the disparity has more or less settled into a 3 to 1 pattern. See U.S. Department of the Interior, National Park Service, *Statistical Reports* [title varies] (Washington, D.C.: GPO, 1940–); available in the library of the Harpers Ferry National Historical Park, Harpers Ferry, West Virginia.

5. Even today Gettysburg has more than 380 cannon, although some are in storage. The number of cannon at Antietam began gradually increasing in the late 1950s; currently there are forty.

6. Snell, *Antietam Administrative History*, 146–48.

7. By the mid-1960s, there were more than forty books on Gettysburg, including memoirs and secondary studies but not counting (where identifiable) guide books, government reports, monument dedications, and excursion souvenirs. Works in the omitted categories would treble the number, but such items (although fewer in number) exist also for Antietam. See Richard Allen Sauers, *The Gettysburg Campaign, June 3–August 1, 1863: A Comprehensive, Selectively Annotated Bibliography* (Westport, Conn.: Greenwood Press, 1982).

8. Francis Winthrop Palfrey, *The Antietam and Fredericksburg* (New York: Charles Scribner's Sons, 1882). Palfrey later published additions, corrections, and second thoughts in "The Battle of Antietam," in *Papers of the Military Historical Society of Massachusetts* (hereafter *PMHSM*) 3 (1903): 1–26. Isaac Winter Heysinger, *Antietam and the Maryland and Virginia Campaigns of 1862, From the Government Records, Union and Confederate, Mostly Unknown and Which Now First Disclosed the Truth* (1912; reprint, Gaithersburg, Md.: Olde Soldier Books, 1987). Edward James Stackpole, *From Cedar Mountain to Antietam, August–September, 1862* (Harrisburg: Stackpole, 1959).

9. Ezra Ayers Carman, "The Maryland Campaign of 1862," Carman Papers, Library of Congress, Washington, D.C. For details of Carman's life, see John Connor Scully, "Ezra Carman: Soldier and Historian" (master's thesis, George Mason University, 1997).

10. Bruce Catton, *This Hallowed Ground: The Story of the Union Side of the Civil War* (Garden City, N.Y.: Doubleday & Company, 1956). Catton entitled his chapter on the summer of 1862 "The Turning Point" and his subchapter on Antietam "High-Water Mark" (see p. 161).

11. James V. Murfin, *Gleam of Bayonets: The Battle of Antietam and the Maryland Campaign of 1862* (New York: Thomas Yoseloff, 1965). Stephen W. Sears, *Landscape Turned Red: The Battle of Antietam* (New Haven: Ticknor & Fields, 1983). Perry D. Jamieson, *Death in September: The Antietam Campaign* (Fort Worth: Ryan Place Publishers, 1995).

12. The local studies, all by John William Schildt: *Antietam Hospitals* (Chewsville, Md.: Antietam Publications, 1987); *Drums along the Antietam* (Parsons, W.Va.: McCain Printing, 1972); *Four Days in October* (Privately published, 1978); *Monuments at Antietam* (Frederick, Md.: Great Southern Press, 1991); *Mount Airy—The Grove Family Homestead* (Chewsville, Md.: Antietam Publications, 1992); *Roads to Antietam*, 2d rev. ed. (Shippensburg, Pa.: Burd Street Press, 1997); *September Echoes, the Maryland Campaign of 1862: The Places, The Battles, The Results* (Middletown, Md.: Valley Register, 1960). The photo study is Frassanito's *Antietam: The Photographic Legacy*. The seminar papers are included in: Gary W. Gallagher, ed., *Antietam: Essays on the 1862 Maryland Campaign* (Kent, Ohio: Kent State Univ. Press, 1989). The original articles: Mark A. Snell, ed., *"Antietam: The Maryland Campaign of 1862: Essays on Union and Confederate Leadership," Civil War Regiments* 5, no. 3 (1997). The eyewitness accounts are in John Michael Priest, *Antietam: A Soldiers' Battle* (Shippensburg, Pa.: White Mane Press, 1989). The guide books include Jay Luvaas and Harold W. Nelson, eds., *The U.S. Army War College Guide to the Battle of Antietam: The Maryland Campaign of 1862* (Carlisle, Pa.: South Mountain Press, 1987); and John Michael Priest, *Antietam: The Soldiers' Battlefield, A Self-Guided Mini-Tour* (Shippensburg, Pa.: White Mane Press, 1994). The artillery study is Curt Johnson and Richard C. Anderson, Jr., *Artillery Hell: The Employment of Artillery at Antietam* (College Station: Texas A&M Univ. Press, 1995). The South Mountain monograph is John Michael Priest, *Before Antietam: The Battle for South Mountain* (Shippensburg, Pa.: White Mane Press, 1992). The Harpers Ferry monographs include Paul R. Teetor, *A Matter of Hours: Treason at Harper's Ferry* (Rutherford, N.J.: Fairleigh Dickinson Univ. Press, 1982); and Allan L. Tischler, *The History of the Harpers Ferry Cavalry Expedition, September 14 & 15, 1862* (Winchester, Va.: Five Cedars Press, 1993). The bibliography is D. Scott Hartwig's *The Battle of Antietam and the Maryland Campaign of 1862: A Bibliography* (Westport, Conn.: Meckler, 1990).

13. Sauers, *Gettysburg Bibliography*. The comparison of numbered items is mentioned by Hartwig in his *Antietam Bibliography* (xi).

14. Stephen W. Sears, "The Last Word on the Lost Order," in *Experiences of War: An Anthology of Articles from MHQ, The Quarterly Journal of Military History* (New York: Dell, 1992), 7.

15. Murfin, *Gleam of Bayonets*, 206.

16. Henry Heth, "Causes of Lee's Defeat at Gettysburg," *Southern Historical Society Papers* (hereafter *SHSP*) 4 (1877): 159–60.

17. John William Jones, *Personal Reminiscences, Anecdotes, and Letters of Gen. Robert E. Lee* (New York: D. Appleton, 1876), 242.

18. Edward Meade Earle, ed., *Makers of Modern Strategy: Military Thought from Machiavelli to Hitler* (Princeton: Princeton Univ. Press, 1943), 17.

Reprise. "From the interior to the frontier": Lee Reaches the Potomac, September 1, 1862

1. U.S. War Department, *The War of the Rebellion: A Compilation of the Official Records of the Union and Confederate Armies*, 128 vols. (Washington, D.C.: GPO, 1880–1901), ser. 1, vol. 12, 2:647, 744 (hereafter cited as *OR;* citations are to series 1 unless otherwise stated). Neither the reports of Jackson or Stuart mention hours. Stuart tacitly admitted not having reported previously by stating, "Next morning I returned by way of Frying Pan, to connect with General Jackson and inform him of the enemy as far as ascertained." According to two recent historians, the Stuart-Jackson meeting occurred at either 8:00 or 9:00 in the morning, but neither cites any evidence to support his claim. See Joseph W. Whitehorne, "A Beastly, Comfortless Conflict: The Battle of Chantilly, September 1, 1862," *Blue & Gray Magazine* 4 (1987): 17; and Robert Ross Smith, "Ox Hill: The Most Neglected Battle of the Civil War," in *Fairfax County and the War Between the States* (Fairfax County, Va.: Civil War Centennial Commission, 1961): 29. On the other hand, Heros von Borcke, who had been with Stuart at Frying Pan, observed that "the morning of the 1st of September passed off quietly enough"—before mentioning that he and his chief rode to join Stonewall. Moreover, the Prussian staff officer states that the orders for the reconnaissance came from Jackson "about noon." See Heros von Borcke, *Memoirs of the Confederate War for Independence*, 2 vols. (New York: Peter Smith, 1938), 1:170–71.

2. Stuart's report, *OR*, vol. 12, 2:744.

3. Ibid. Jermantown is the correct historical spelling for the small community, although Civil War maps frequently refer to it as Germantown.

4. R. R. Smith, "Ox Hill," 43–44. There is no existing evidence on how Jackson discovered the approach of Reno, but since Robertson's brigade was patrolling the area, it's reasonable to assume cavalry scouts of his brigade provided the warning.

5. For firsthand testimony on the ferocity of the storm on September 1, see Joseph L. Harsh, *Sounding the Shallows: A Confederate Companion for the Maryland Campaign of 1862* (Kent, Ohio: Kent State Univ. Press, 1999), chap. 1.

6. This brief summary is based on the admirable tactical studies by R. R. Smith, "Ox Hill," and Whitehorne, "Chantilly," the latter unfortunately undocumented.

7. James Longstreet, *From Manassas to Appomattox: Memoirs of the Civil War in America*, ed. James I. Robertson, Jr. (Bloomington: Indiana Univ. Press, 1960), 194. D. R. Jones led Longstreet's column, as he reported he advanced the brigades of Toombs and G. T. Anderson into the woods in support of Jackson. *OR*, vol. 12, 2:580. This is confirmed by Osmun Latrobe, in his September 1 diary entry, Virginia Historical Society, Richmond.

8. Pender to wife, Sept. 2, William Dorsey Pender, *The General to His Wife: The Civil War Letters of William Dorsey Pender to Fanny Pender*, ed. William Woods Hassler (Chapel Hill: Univ. of North Carolina Press, 1965), 170.

9. Lee broke up his headquarters at Manassas on the afternoon of the 31st, but it is not clear where he spent the night. See Douglas Southall Freeman, *R. E. Lee: A Biography*, 4 vols. (New York: Charles Scribner's Sons, 1934–35), 2:342; D. M. Perry, "The Time of Longstreet's Arrival at Groveton," in Robert Underwood Johnson and Clarence Clough Buel, eds., *Battles and Leaders of the Civil War*, 4 vols. (New York: Thomas Yoselof, 1956), 2:527 (hereafter *B&L*); William Willis Blackford, *War Years with Jeb Stuart* (New York: Charles Scribner's Sons,

1945), 135; and Luther Wesley Hopkins, *From Bull Run to Appomattox: A Boy's View* (Baltimore: Fleet-McGinley, 1908), 50.

10. The sole source for this interview is a memoir by Thomas Munford, who fixes its time by recalling that it started to rain just as he left Lee. The account is plausible except for one detail. According to Munford, when Lee uttered the word "crush," he crumpled the Janney letter in his hand for emphasis. This, of course, Lee was incapable of doing on September 1 because of his injured hands. See Thomas Taylor Munford, "Lee's Invasion of Maryland," in *Addresses Delivered before the Confederate Veterans Association of Savannah, Ga.*, 5 vols. (Savannah: Braid & Hutton, 1893–1902), 3:36–37 (hereafter cited as *ACVAS*).

11. The dispositions made after the battle may be worked out from the reports of A. P. Hill (p. 672), Early (p. 715), and H. J. Williams (p. 1011) in *OR*, vol. 12, 2.

12. Robert Edward Lee, *The Wartime Papers of R. E. Lee*, ed. Clifford Dowdey and Louis H. Manarin (Boston: Little, Brown, 1961), 312.

1. "We cannot afford to be idle": Lee's Strategic Dilemma, September 2–3

1. Although called the "Seven Days," the battle that raged from Beaver Dam Creek (June 26) to Malvern Hill (July 1) actually lasted six days, including June 28, when there was no significant fighting. The Federals usually added the fight at King's School House on the 25th to get seven days, while the Confederates added their pursuit to Harrison's Landing on July 2. In either case, what is called the Seven Days Battle was really five days of fighting over six days. Also, from this point forward, all references to weather in the Maryland campaign are derived from Harsh, *Sounding the Shallows*, chap. 1.

2. Longstreet, *From Manassas to Appomattox*, 195; Latrobe, Diary, Sept. 2.

3. Stuart's report, *OR*, vol. 12, 2:744–45; Hampton's report, *OR*, vol. 19, 1:822; von Borcke, *Memoirs* 1:173–74; George Michael Neese, *Three Years in the Confederate Horse Artillery* (New York: Neale, 1911), 114; and Henry Brainard McClellan, *I Rode with Jeb Stuart* (Bloomington: Indiana Univ. Press., 1958), 108–9.

4. Longstreet, *From Manassas to Appomattox*, 195, is the source for cavalry reports coming in "from time to time." It is presumed that Longstreet would not have been privy to these reports had he not spent some time waiting at Lee's headquarters. Similarly, Jackson wrote in his report: "By the following morning the Federal Army had entirely disappeared from our view, and it soon appeared, by a report from General Stuart, that it had passed Fairfax Court-House and had moved in the direction of Washington City." See *OR*, vol. 12, 2:647. It is possible, of course, that Lee forwarded the reports of Stuart to Longstreet and Jackson. It would have been more efficient—and more usual—for the three to have conferred and awaited the reports together. One of the surprising observations of this current study is the considerable time and effort spent by Lee in consulting his superiors and subordinates.

5. Pope to Halleck, Sept. 2, *OR*, vol. 12, 2:87. Pope claimed that his "whole force" was "less than 60,000 men." Undoubtedly, he was not counting the Second and Sixth Corps in these figures. According to the morning reports for September 2, Pope's army, including Sumner and Franklin (with Couch's division of the Fourth Corps attached), totaled 93,095. See John Owen Allen, "The Strength of the Union and Confederate Forces at Second Manassas" (master's thesis, George Mason University, Fairfax, Virginia, 1993), 114.

6. Pope to Halleck and Halleck to Pope, both Sept. 2, *OR*, vol. 12, 3:796–97.

7. Circular, Headquarters Army of Virginia, Fairfax Court House, Sept. 2, ibid., 2:86–87; also in ibid., 2, see the reports of Pope (p. 46); Heintzelman (p. 414); Gates of the 80th New York, Hooker's force (p. 377); Torbert of Hooker's force (p. 538); Bayard (p. 91); Beardsley (p. 272); Lloyd of the 6th Ohio Cavalry (p. 278); and the Itinerary of the Fifth Corps (p. 465).

Note that neither Couch's division nor Beardsley's cavalry brigade were provided for in Pope's Circular.

8. On September 3, Lee wrote to Davis, "Yesterday about noon [the enemy] evacuated Fairfax Court House, taking the roads as reported to me, to Alexandria & Washington." In the absence of this comment, it would have been natural to assume that several hours would have elapsed before Lee learned of the retreat, making it mid- or late afternoon. It is unlikely, however, that Lee would have misremembered within twenty-four hours the time he received such important information. Note that the sentence quoted is not in the mangled version of this dispatch printed in *OR*, vol. 12, 2:559–60, which is also missing other text. See the full document in Lee, *Wartime Papers*, 269–70.

9. Although Oliver Howard would claim he commanded the rear guard, his statement that "after passing Fairfax Court House we were not molested by the Confederates" indicates he was out of touch with what was happening. The disagreeable task of fending off the enemy while pushing wagons and stragglers forward in the dark actually fell to the 1st Minnesota of Alfred Sully and the 71st Pennsylvania of Isaac Wistar. See Oliver Otis Howard, *Autobiography of Oliver Otis Howard, Major-General*, 2 vols. (New York: Baker and Taylor, 1907), 1:269; Rufus Barringer, "Ninth Regiment (First Cavalry)," in *Histories of the Several Regiments and Battalions from North Carolina in the Great War 1861–1865*, ed. Walter Clark, 5 vols. (Wendell, N.C.: Broadfoot's Bookmark, 1982), 1:421 (hereafter *North Carolina Regiments*); Ulysses Robert Brooks, *Stories of the Confederacy* (Columbia, S.C.: State Company, 1912), 74–77; and, for a very full account, Isaac Jones Wistar, *Autobiography of Isaac Jones Wistar, 1827–1905, Half a Century in War and Peace* (Philadelphia: Wistar Institute of Anatomy and Biology, 1937), 388–93.

10. In *OR*, vol. 12, 2 see the reports of Stuart (pp. 744–45) and Lloyd of the 6th Ohio Cavalry (p. 278); also see Hampton's report, ibid., vol. 19, 1:822; Jedediah Hotchkiss, *Make Me a Map of the Valley: The Civil War Journal of Stonewall Jackson's Topographer*, ed. Archie McDonald (Dallas: Southern Methodist Univ. Press, 1973), 78; and von Borcke, *Memoirs* 1:173–74, where the account is somewhat confused. Such lavish attention from Stuart, including an honorary commission in the Confederate army, would eventually lead to Antonia Ford being arrested for spying and sent to the Old Capital Prison in Washington. See Nan Netherton, et al., *Fairfax County, Virginia: A History* (Fairfax: County Board of Supervisors, 1978), 356.

11. Lee's report, *OR*, vol. 19, 1:144.

12. For further discussion of Lee's view that action was imperative at this time, see Harsh, *Sounding the Shallows*, chap. 5, sect. A.

13. Longstreet, *From Manassas to Appomattox*, 195.

14. These figures were reported by a U.S. Army board of engineers in November/December 1862, *OR*, vol. 21:904. Lee could not have known the precise numbers, of course, but the Confederates possessed a surprisingly full appreciation of the works, as is evidenced by the fact Johnston's army—when evacuating Manassas in March—left behind a "very accurate outline of the fortifications in and about Washington." See U.S. Congress, *Report of the Joint Committee on the Conduct of the War*, 3 vols. (Washington, D.C.: GPO, 1863), 1:244.

15. For Lee's written comments on the inadvisability of attacking Washington, see Harsh, *Sounding the Shallows*, chap. 5, sect. B.

16. Robert Edward Lee [Jr.], *Recollections and Letters of General Robert E. Lee by His Son* (Garden City, N.Y.: Garden City Publishing, 1924), 416. Lee is quoted as saying Fort Wade, but there was no such fort, and Fort Ward was just behind his cousin Cassius Lee's home on "the Hill" near the Alexandria Seminary, where he was visiting.

17. Robert Edward Lee, "Letter from General R. E. Lee [to William M. McDonald]," *SHSP* 7 (1879): 445 (hereafter cited as Lee, "McDonald Letter"). For further comments on the supply problem in Fairfax, see Harsh, *Sounding the Shallows*, chap. 5, sect. C.

18. For further comments on the strategic unsoundness of remaining in Fairfax County, see Harsh, *Sounding the Shallows*, chap. 5, sect. D.

19. There is no direct proof that Lee consulted with Longstreet and Jackson on September 2. There is strong circumstantial evidence that he spoke with both about strategy matters on either the 2d or the 3d; and it makes sense to believe that Lee would have held some of the consultations on the afternoon of the 2d, before he issued orders for the move to Leesburg.

20. That Lee did not mention the option to retire southward in either his wartime or postwar writings and conversations that have survived is probably an indication of how obvious it was to him that the move would have been wrong. After the war, Charles Marshall of Lee's staff did discuss the possibility but rejected it. See Charles Marshall, *An Aide-de-Camp of Lee*, ed. Maj. Gen. Sir Frederick Maurice (Boston: Little, Brown, 1927), 145, 147–48. The option is more briefly dismissed by William Allan, "Strategy of the Campaign of Sharpsburg or Antietam, September, 1862," *PMHSM* 3 (1888): 76; and by Bradley Tyler Johnson, "First Maryland Campaign," *SHSP* 12 (1884): 502.

21. Gary W. Gallagher, ed., *Lee the Soldier* (Lincoln: Univ. of Nebraska Press, 1996), 13. For further discussion of Lee's views on invading the North in September 1862, see Harsh, *Sounding the Shallows*, chap. 5, sect. E.

22. Lee to Davis, Feb. 3, 1864, Lee, *Wartime Papers*, 667.

23. Actually, Lee's strict enforcement of discipline on his army in both the Maryland campaign of 1862 and the Pennsylvania campaign of 1863 is strong presumptive evidence that he did understand that a policy of destruction was counterproductive to what he sought to obtain.

24. On September 3, Lee would write to Davis, "The army is not properly equipped for an invasion of an enemy's territory." See *OR*, vol. 19, 2:590.

25. The Confederates may have had a somewhat exaggerated expectation of the lushness of Loudoun. In the spring, the head of the commissary bureau estimated that northern Virginia and the Potomac about Loudoun could supply an army of 100,000 men. Cole to Johnston, May 13, 1862, ibid., vol. 11, 2:513. That wagons loaded with food donated by civilians in Loudoun appeared from nowhere at Chantilly may have strengthened the impression. See George Wise, *History of the Seventeenth Virginia Infantry, C.S.A.* (Baltimore: Kelly, Piet & Company, 1870), 106–7. Nevertheless, the 8th Census makes clear that Loudoun was in the top 5 percent of Virginia counties in agricultural production. See U.S. Census Bureau, *Agriculture of the United States in 1860: Compiled from the Original Returns of the Eighth Census* (Washington, D.C.: GPO, 1864), 154–63.

26. For further discussion on Lee's views on a westward movement, see Harsh, *Sounding the Shallows*, chap. 5, sect. F.

27. T. A. B. Corley, *Democratic Despot: A Life of Napoleon III* (New York: Clarkson N. Potter, 1961), 239–49.

28. Whether or not a Confederate victory in Kentucky or Ohio, achieved while Lee remained inactive in northern Virginia, would have provided impetus for British action is not at all clear. An excellent recent study of foreign affairs during the Civil War is Paul David Crook, *The North, the South, and the Powers, 1861–1865* (New York: Wiley, 1974).

29. For a discussion of Lee's views on the likelihood of foreign help for the Confederacy, see Joseph L. Harsh, *Confederate Tide Rising: Robert E. Lee and the Making of Southern Strategy, 1861–1862* (Kent, Ohio: Kent State Univ. Press, 1998), 57, 186–87. For a further discussion of the absence of foreign affairs considerations in Lee's decision to enter Maryland, see Harsh, *Sounding the Shallows*, chap. 5, sect. G.

30. In addition to these seven, Lee would cross the Potomac, and John C. Breckinridge would be belatedly ordered northward for Kentucky from operations against Baton Rouge. Hence, a total of nine columns would be part of the offensive.

31. Bragg was in titular command of five of the columns: his own, Van Dorn's, Price's, Smith's, and Marshall's. Once he left Mississippi, however, Bragg lost all control of Van Dorn

and Price. Even in Kentucky, the three armies (Bragg, Smith, and Marshall) never physically united, and Bragg was never able to exert more than marginal coordination over their operations.

32. Davis to Bragg, Sept. 4, *OR*, vol. 16, 1:711.

33. "Bragg ought immediately to advance," Lee to Randolph, June 19, *OR*, vol. 11, 3:609. Ten days later Secretary Randolph ordered Bragg, "Strike the moment an opportunity offers." See Randolph to Bragg, June 29, ibid. Neither Lee nor Randolph specified where the blow should fall.

34. Bragg to Cooper, July 23, ibid., vol. 17, 2:655–56; and Aug. 1, ibid., vol. 16, 2:741.

35. Lee wrote: "If the impression made by Morgan in Kentucky could be confirmed by a strong infantry force, it would have the happiest effect. If he is obliged to fall back, the reaction may produce the same result as in Missouri. Where is Genl Marshall? Now is the time for him to go in. But if Bragg could make a move, or with E. K. Smith & Loring, it would produce a great effect. Do you think anything can be done?" Lee to Davis, July 26, Lee, *Wartime Papers*, 238.

36. Davis to Bragg, Aug. 5, Jefferson Davis, *The Papers of Jefferson Davis*, 8 vols. to date (Baton Rouge: Louisiana State Univ. Press, 1971–), 8:322. In fact, the following day, Davis temporarily prohibited Marshall from advancing on Kentucky on the grounds Morgan had already fallen back. Davis to Marshall, Aug. 6, *OR*, vol. 16, 2:745. Actually, Davis had already written to Smith, "The junction with Genl. Bragg if effected in time will I trust enable the two armies to crush Buell's column and advance to the recovery of Tennessee and the occupation of Kentucky." See *Papers of Jefferson Davis* 8:305. As the campaign evolved without first crushing Buell, Davis nonetheless fully approved its course. See Davis to Bragg, Sept. 4, *OR*, vol. 16, 2:711; and Oct. 17, *Papers of Jefferson Davis* 8:448.

37. Smith to Bragg, Aug. 9 and 11th, *OR*, vol. 16, 2:748, 751; also, for a version of the plan after it had been more fully developed, Marshall to Randolph, Sept. 7, ibid., vol. 52, 2:347–48.

38. Bragg to Smith, Aug. 10, ibid., vol. 16, 2:748–49. On August 27, Bragg would write to Van Dorn and Price, "we shall confidently expect to meet you on the Ohio and there open the way to Missouri." See ibid., 782–83. Bragg's ready agreement with Smith must probably be viewed in the light that Kentucky was not a new idea but already existed as a goal after the defeat of Buell. The likelihood of prior discussions—in person or in lost letters—can be read between the lines of the Bragg-Smith correspondence.

39. Randolph's undated endorsement on Loring to Randolph, Aug. 11, received Aug. 14, ibid., vol. 12, 3:927. Smith sent a version of the plan to Davis that may have reached Richmond by this time. See Kirby Smith to Davis, Aug. 11, *Papers of Jefferson Davis* 8:332.

40. News of Smith's invasion of Kentucky was not known in New York until the morning of the 3d. See George Templeton Strong, *The Diary of George Templeton Strong*, ed. Allan Nevins, 4 vols. (New York: Macmillan, 1952), 3:252. Jefferson Davis did not learn of the victory at Richmond, Kentucky, until the evening of the same day. See Davis to Bragg, Sept. 4, *OR*, vol. 16, 2:711. Curiously, the chief clerk of the Confederate War Department, who closely followed the course of the war through official dispatches, newspapers, and rumor, would not record in his diary news of Smith's victory until September 10. See John Beauchamp Jones, *A Rebel War Clerk's Diary at the Confederate States Capital*, 2 vols. (Philadelphia: J. B. Lippincott, 1866), 1:152.

41. Lee to Davis, Sept. 3, *OR*, vol. 19, 2:591. This dispatch is discussed in detail in the final section of this chapter.

42. Figures are aggregate present and absent for June 30, 1862. See Harsh, *Confederate Tide Rising*, 13, 178–79, 212n22.

43. Proclamation of July 1, Abraham Lincoln, *Collected Works*, ed. Roy P. Basler, 9 vols. (New Brunswick, N.J.: Rutgers Univ. Press, 1953–55), 5:296–97. On Lee's knowledge of the new call see his letter to Davis, Sept. 3, *OR*, vol. 19, 2:590. News of Lincoln's call had been in the newspapers since early July, but exactly how Lee learned of it is not known.

44. If the new call were fully met, the Federal armies would total 924,000 from a pool of 4,453,114 or 20.75 percent. The South's 477,000 from its pool of 1,197,489 represented 39.83 percent. Military pools are discussed in Harsh, *Confederate Tide Rising*, 178, 212n20.

45. General Orders, No. 94, War Department, Adjutant General's Office, Aug. 4, 1862, *OR*, ser. 3, vol. 2:291–92. The militia draft fell considerably short, raising only 87,588 men, but it served its purpose by spurring volunteering. The call for volunteers, would oversubscribe at 421,465. Ibid., vol. 4:1264–65. Hence, by the end of 1862, the North would have 918,121 men in the field, while the South's total had fallen to 446,622, yielding a ratio of 2.06 to 1. See Thomas Leonard Livermore, *Numbers and Losses in the Civil War in America* (Dayton, Ohio: Morningside, 1986), 47. All figures are aggregate present and absent.

46. On September 2, the Army of Virginia (including artillery and cavalry) and the Army of the Potomac (not including headquarters staff, reserve artillery, or cavalry) totaled 93,095 officers and men present for duty. See Allen, *Second Manassas Strengths*, 114. Additional forces (including McClellan's staff, Couch's division, Cox's division, Hunt's Artillery Reserve, the handful of Pleasonton's cavalry that had arrived from the Peninsula, and the few old units still attached to the defenses of Washington) would have added no more than 17,000.

47. Lee knew of the fragmented nature of the Federal forces and believed them weakened and demoralized. See Lee to Davis Sept. 3, *OR*, vol. 19, 2:590–91; and Maryland campaign report, ibid., 1:144. After the war, Lee would acknowledge his assessment of the Federal army as "disorganized and demoralized" and that he counted on this to give him an edge in battle. See Gallagher, ed., *Lee the Soldier*, 26; also see p. 8.

48. On August 30, there were twenty-four new regiments at Washington; a few more may have arrived by September 2. They averaged about 750 each, present for duty.

49. The forces under Jackson were the divisions of Ewell, Jackson, and A. P. Hill and Robertson's cavalry brigade. Longstreet took with him his own division (which he had organized into two demidivisions under Kemper and Wilcox) and the divisions of D. R. Jones and Hood and Fitz Lee's cavalry brigade. Lee ordered forward on the 15th the division of R. H. Anderson, which acted as general reserve without being attached to either wing in the field.

50. For the sake of clarity in this paragraph and those following, the names used for the commanders of the infantry divisions retained in Richmond are those of the men who commanded them when they joined Lee on September 2. For the record, however, they had gone through several permutations. *D. H. Hill's division* was Hill's during the Seven Days. When he left to command the district of North Carolina, the division for a while was under its senior brigadier Roswell Ripley and then briefly under G. W. Smith when he returned from sick leave. And finally, just as it headed north, Hill was returned to its command. *Walker's division* was Holmes's forces from North Carolina during the Seven Days. It was called D. H. Hill's while he commanded the District of North Carolina but fell to its senior brigadier, John Walker, after Hill returned to his old command. *McLaws's division* was two-thirds of the force under Magruder during the Seven Days.

51. Cooper to G. W. Smith, Aug. 17, *OR*, vol. 12, 3:932.

52. Randolph to Lee, Randolph to Davis, and Cooper to G. W. Smith, all Aug. 17, ibid., 932–33. Before hearing from Lee, Randolph anticipated the order by offering to assemble McLaws's division at the railroad.

53. Lee to Cooper, Aug. 18, ibid., 935.

54. Davis to Lee, Aug. 18, ibid. It should be remembered that G. W. Smith was briefly in command of D. H. Hill's old division. For the movements of the Ripley/Colquitt brigades, see G. W. Smith to Pendleton, ibid., 965; Susan Pendleton Lee, *Memoirs of William Nelson Pendleton* (Harrisonburg, Va.: Sprinkle Publications, 1991), 204–5; Henry Walter Thomas, *History of the Doles-Cook Brigade, Army of Northern Virginia, C.S.A.* (Atlanta: Franklin Printing and Publishing, 1903), 68, 469; and Calvin Leach, Aug. 19–Sept. 2, Diary, Southern Historical Collection, University of North Carolina, Chapel Hill.

55. Randolph to Lee, Aug. 19, *OR*, vol. 12, 3:936–37.

56. Lee to Randolph, Aug. 19, ibid., 937.

57. Both units had been under orders for Gordonsville. On Hill's three brigades, see Laura Elizabeth Battle, *Forget-me-nots of the Civil War: A Romance Containing Reminiscences and Original Letters of Two Confederate Soldiers* (St. Louis: Fleming Printing, 1909), 71–73; and John S. Tucker, "The Diary of John S. Tucker: Confederate Soldier from Alabama," ed. Gary Wilson, *Alabama Historical Quarterly* 43 (1981): 18. On the Artillery Reserve, see Pendleton to wife, Aug. 19, 22, S. P. Lee, *Memoirs*, 204; G. W. Smith to Pendleton, Aug. 18, and Melton to Pendleton, Aug. 19, *OR*, vol. 12, 3:965.

58. Hill was transferred from commanding the District of North Carolina to his old division. Hill's report, *OR*, vol. 19, 1:1019. On McLaws's division, see James Dinkins, *1861 to 1865, by an Old Johnie: Personal Recollections and Experiences in the Confederate Army* (Cincinnati: Robert Clarke, 1897), 52; and Mike M. Hubbert, "The Travels of the 13th Mississippi Regiment: Excerpts from the Diary of Mike M. Hubbert of Attala County (1861–1862)," ed. John E. Fisher, *Journal of Mississippi History* 45 (1983): 305. The arrival of Hampton is projected.

59. G. W. Smith to Randolph, Aug. 31, *OR*, vol. 12, 3:948.

60. Pendleton to wife, Aug. 27, S. P. Lee, *Memoirs*, 205–6.

61. Davis to Lee, Aug. 26, *OR*, vol. 12, 3:945. For further discussion of this Lee-Davis exchange, see Harsh, *Confederate Tide Rising*, 143–44.

62. At least the 44th Georgia (Ripley) and 3d North Carolina (Ripley) reached Manassas by the afternoon of the 30th; see H. W. Thomas, *Doles-Cook Brigade*, 469; and William Lord DeRosset, "Additional Sketch Third Regiment," in *North Carolina Regiments* 1:223. The brigades may not have been kept intact on the march, however, as the 1st North Carolina (Ripley) seems not to have arrived in Gainesville until the 31st. See Leach, Diary, Aug. 31. Draughton Haynes of the 49th Georgia was marching north to rejoin Thomas's brigade of A. P. Hill's division and traveled with the 6th Georgia of Colquitt's brigade. He recorded in his diary that on one of the days (either August 28 or 29), "The day has been warm and we have come no less than 25 miles." See Draughton Stith Haynes, *The Field Diary of a Confederate Soldier, Draughton Stith Haynes, While Serving with the Army of Northern Virginia, C.S.A.* (Darien, Ga.: Ashantilly Press, 1963), 13–14.

63. Pendleton to wife, Aug. 27, S. P. Lee, *Memoirs*, 206.

64. The Virginia Central was in operation from Hanover Junction to Gordonsville and the Orange and Alexandria from Gordonsville to Rapidan Station, where the bridge over the river had been destroyed. It is also possible that Richmond authorities ordered these roads kept relatively clear to facilitate transport of Walker's division from Petersburg, since it had the farthest to travel.

65. Hubbert, "Diary," 306. For additional details, see D. H. Hill's report, *OR*, vol. 19, 1:1019; D. H. Hill to G. W. Smith, ibid., vol. 12, 3:948; Tucker, "Diary," 18–19; Battle, *Forget-me nots*, 74–75; Dinkins, *Recollections*, 52–53; DeRosset, *North Carolina Regiments* 1:216; Henry Robinson Berkeley, *Four Years in the Confederate Artillery: The Diary of Private Henry Robinson Berkeley*, ed. William H. Runge (Chapel Hill: Univ. of North Carolina Press, 1961), 25–26; and D. Augustus Dickert, *History of Kershaw's Brigade, With Complete Roll of Companies, Biographical Sketches, Incidents, Anecdotes, etc.* (Wilmington, N.C.: Broadfoot Publishing, 1990), 142, although the dates are not reliable in the latter.

66. Two telegrams of Walker to G. W. Smith, *OR*, vol. 12, 3:948–49; John George Walker, "Jackson's Capture of Harper's Ferry," in *B&L* 2:604; James Augustus Graham, "27th Regiment," in *North Carolina Regiments* 2:430–31; William H. S. Burgwyn, "35th Regiment," in ibid., 601; J. M. Waddill, "46th Regiment," in ibid. 3:66; and Isaac Hirsch, Aug. 25–Sept. 2, Diary, Fredericksburg Area Museum and Cultural Center, Fredericksburg, Virginia

67. The numbers break down as follows: forces north of the James, 12,933 officers and men present for duty; south of the James (excluding North Carolina), 4,740. There were some

7,500 men in the Cape Fear and Kinston districts of North Carolina, but these were mostly in green regiments and were beyond effective supporting distance of Richmond. See *OR*, vol. 18:750, 751, 759, 764; William H. S. Burgwyn, "Clingman's Brigade," in *North Carolina Regiments* 4:482; C. G. Elliott, "Martin-Kirkland Brigade," in ibid., 527; and Louis G. Young, "Pettigrew-Kirkland-MacRae Brigade," in ibid., 556.

68. Once again, battalions, independent companies, and batteries have been consolidated into abstract regiments of ten companies for the purpose of this summary. The figures for the Army of Northern Virginia are taken from the table of organization in *OR*, vol. 19, 1:803–10, as modified by Allen, "Second Manassas Strengths," and from a large number of other scattered, miscellaneous sources. See Harsh, *Sounding the Shallows*, chap. 2. The total number of Confederate regiments in the field must be approximate because of the ambiguity as to when some units were mustered in and others disbanded. The figure used comes from an ongoing study based on the *OR*. Joseph H. Crute, *Units of the Confederate States Army* (Midlothian, Va.: Derwent Books, 1987); Stewart Sifakis, *Compendium of the Confederate Armies*, 10 vols. (New York: Facts on File, 1991–92); and various state studies, memoirs, and regimental histories.

69. Lee had more regiments on September 2 than he had during the Seven Days, as he had added the brigades of Evans and Drayton and various individual regiments (5th and 8th Florida, etc.), and had lost only the brigade of Junius Daniel. See Leon Walter Tenney, "Seven Days in 1862: Numbers in Union and Confederate Armies before Richmond" (master's thesis, George Mason University, 1992). It was also larger by about five consolidated regiments than his army at Gettysburg, which was composed of 2,005 companies. See John W. Busey and David G. Martin, *Regimental Strengths and Losses at Gettysburg*, 2d rev. ed. (Hightstown, N.J.: Longstreet House, 1986), 129.

70. This is not to deny the primacy of excitability, amateurishness, and inexperience in dealing with large numbers that characterized the reports of both civilians and civilian soldiers in the Civil War. It is meant only to suggest there was some basis in fact for the exaggerated accounts in the Maryland campaign. It should also be noted that regiments on both sides were raised to number about 1,000. Because of disease, desertion, and detachments, however, even regiments that had seen no combat seldom numbered more than 750 after several weeks in camp.

71. Allen, "Second Manassas Strengths," 187, 205.

72. These regimental averages have been worked up from the raw figures in Allen, "Second Manassas Strengths," 186–202. For the purpose of meaningful comparison only full infantry regiments have been included, i.e., artillery and cavalry and infantry companies and battalions have been excluded. All figures are for officers and men, present for duty. More often than not, Confederate figures are found stripped down by excluding officers and extra-duty men. Because of poor Confederate record keeping, only about 25 percent of the regimental strengths in Allen are on or about September 1. The remainder are estimates. The figures that do exist tend to confirm the estimates, however.

73. Hampton's brigade is included here in Stuart's division. The grand total proves by the addition of eight for general headquarters. Allen, "Second Manassas Strengths," 186. For a breakdown of the estimate by divisions, see Harsh, *Sounding the Shallows*, chap. 5, sect. H.

74. For a discussion of other strengths historians have assigned to the Army of Northern Virginia on September 2, see ibid.

75. On September 2, 1862, Lee had 184.7 infantry regiments, including battalions consolidated into ten company regiments. See note 68 above. Cavalry was excluded in this analysis because of its relative insignificance in battle. Artillery was omitted because of ambiguities arising from the difficulty of tracing batteries. For the purposes of this comparison the following were considered major battles: First Bull Run, Williamsburg, the Valley campaign, Seven Pines, Seven Days, Cedar Mountain, and Second Manassas. See Harsh, *Sounding the Shallows*, chap. 3.

76. According to muster rolls in the War Department Collection of Confederate Records (RG-109, DNA), on or about September 1 conscripts had been assigned in the following numbers to these North Carolina regiments: 1st North Carolina (354); 2d North Carolina (147); 3d North Carolina (511); 5th North Carolina (541); 18th North Carolina (90); 23d North Carolina (262); and 48th North Carolina (31). For the 48th North Carolina, see also, W. H. H. Lawhon, "48th Regiment," in *North Carolina Regiments* 3:116. In addition, the historian of the 15th North Carolina (Cobb's brigade) reported his regiment had received 250 conscripts before leaving Richmond, which would have been pre–August 19. H. C. Kearny, "15th Regiment," in ibid. 1:739. Hence, the approximate figure 2,200 is used in the text. Some conscripts joined later at Frederick: 7th North Carolina (130) (James Sidney Harris, "7th Regiment," in ibid., 372); 18th North Carolina, "large number" (William H. McLaurin, "18th Regiment," in ibid. 2:32); and perhaps others. In the case of the 18th, however, it is not clear if this is simply a misdated reference to the ninety conscripts of September 1 or an additional batch. It should also be noted that the conscripts joining the 18th North Carolina were without arms until supplied after the capture of Harpers Ferry.

77. In summary: three brigades had fought in five major battles; three had fought in four; nine had fought in three; twelve had fought in two; and thirteen had fought in one. There are several reasons this sort of comparison cannot be pressed too far without much greater (and probably excessive) refinement: (1) even after considered essentially settled, many of the brigades lost or gained a regiment; (2) in some cases individual regiments were lightly engaged, while the brigade was more heavily engaged (e.g., several of Walker's regiments at Malvern Hill); and (3) minor battles not included provided major engagements for several brigades (e.g., the Texas Brigade at Eltham's Landing). See Harsh, *Sounding the Shallows*, chap. 3.

78. Both Lee and Johnston—although the latter more so—dragged their feet in responding to Jefferson Davis's insistence that battle-tested brigades be rearranged to put units from the same state together as required by Confederate law. Yet both were willing to move brigades and restructure divisions. Lee would make three important divisional changes during the Maryland campaign by consolidating Kemper with D. R. Jones and Wilcox with R. H. Anderson and by restoring Hood to command and returning Evans's brigade to independent status.

79. In summary: four divisions had fought in four major battles; three had fought in three; one had fought in two; and three had fought in one. In this comparison Kemper and Wilcox are counted as two divisions, even though they fought as one at Seven Pines and in the Seven Days. The same cautions outlined for brigades (see note 77 above) apply to the comparison of divisions as well. See ibid. Note that preliminary research on the Army of the Potomac in the Maryland campaign indicates that Federal organizations at all levels were inferior in experience and continuity to the Army of Northern Virginia.

80. It is true that Longstreet had separated his own bulky division into three demi-divisions under Kemper, Wilcox, and D. R. Jones. He could not have done this without Lee's knowledge and approval, but it is not clear that Lee either initiated the move or saw it as increasing Longstreet's command level—at least not before August 9.

81. For a further discussion of the corps structure of the Army of Northern Virginia in Sept. 1862, see ibid., chap. 5, sect. I.

82. Nevertheless, both A. P. Hill and Longstreet had units weak in officers. Pender's brigade (Hill) had only three field officers present, where there should have been twelve, and many of the companies were commanded by corporals. See Graham Daves, "22nd Regiment," in *North Carolina Regiments* 2:169. William Wood of the 19th Virginia of Pickett's brigade (Longstreet) would remember that "officers were scarce. Many of them were at home or in hospitals, sick or wounded . . . and in some instances two companies were thrown into one temporarily, in order to have a commissioned officer to command." Wood himself in this

manner came to command Companies A and I of his regiment, William Nathaniel Wood, *Reminiscences of Big I* (Jackson, Tenn.: McCowat-Mercer Press, 1956), 33–34.

83. Commanders and attrition based on the organizational tables compiled by Ezra Carman, "Maryland Campaign," chap. 11, Carman Papers. The number of infantry regiments is a bit smaller in this instance because of the inappropriateness of consolidating and including battalions for this purpose.

84. For further discussion of the officer corps of the Army of Northern Virginia, see Harsh, *Sounding the Shallows*, chap. 5, sect. J.

85. Edward Alexander Moore, *The Story of a Cannoneer under Stonewall Jackson, in Which Is Told the Part Taken by the Rockbridge Artillery in the Army of Northern Virginia* (New York: Neale Publishing, 1907), 125; see also John H. Worsham, *One of Jackson's Foot Cavalry, His Experiences and What He Saw during the War, 1861–1865* (Jackson, Tenn.: McCowat-Mercer Press, 1964), 81–82.

86. For further discussion of the condition of the reenforcing columns from Richmond, see Harsh, *Sounding the Shallows*, chap. 5, sect. K.

87. McLaws to wife, Sept. 4, McLaws Papers, Southern Historical Collection, University of North Carolina, Chapel Hill. For more on wagons and rations, see Derosset, *North Carolina Regiments* 1:224; and T. D. Lattimore, "34th Regiment," in ibid. 2:585.

88. For further discussion of the condition of the Army of Northern Virginia in September 1862, see Harsh, *Sounding the Shallows*, chap. 5, sect. L.

89. It is likely the baggage trains with the clothing of Jackson and Longstreet never crossed the Potomac with the army and did not rejoin it until it returned to Virginia in late September. Lattimore, *North Carolina Regiments* 2:585. The reenforcements from Richmond were probably in somewhat better shape, as Ransom's brigade left their camp equipage in Richmond but held on to extra clothes and blankets until they were lost at Sharpsburg. Garland S. Ferguson, "25th Regiment," in ibid., 296–97. For illustrative memoirs on the lack of shoes and sore feet, see Leach, Diary, Aug. 28; Marion Hill Fitzpatrick, *Letters to Amanda, from Sergeant Major Marion Hill Fitzpatrick, Company K, 45th Georgia Regiment* (Culloden, Ga.: Privately published, 1976); McLaws to wife, Sept. 4, McLaws Papers, University of North Carolina; multiple examples cited in Murfin, *Gleam of Bayonets*, 94–95; and the informative analysis by Robert K. Krick, "The Army of Northern Virginia in September 1862: Its Circumstances, Its Opportunities, and Why It Should Not Have Been at Sharpsburg," in Gallagher, ed., *Antietam Essays*, 40–41.

90. Lee's order appears in William Miller Owen, *In Camp and Battle with the Washington Artillery of New Orleans: A Narrative of Events during the Late Civil War, from Bull Run to Appomattox and Spanish Fort* (Boston: Ticknor and Company, 1885), 126; see also McLaurin, *North Carolina Regiments* 2:31–32. Another ordnance weakness of which Lee must have been aware was the large number of smooth bore muskets still in use in his army. According to McLaurin, the 18th North Carolina did not exchange their smooth bores for rifles until the capture of Harpers Ferry. Edward Porter Alexander estimated that half the army went into the Maryland campaign with the older, less accurate, and shorter range smooth bores. *Military Memoirs of a Confederate: A Critical Narrative*, ed. T. Harry Williams (Bloomington: Indiana Univ. Press, 1962), 223.

91. Johnson, "Maryland," 507.

92. McKim to mother, June 24, Randolph Harrison McKim, *A Soldier's Recollections: Leaves from the Diary of a Young Confederate* (New York: Longman's, Green, 1910), 119; Pender to Wife, Sept. 2, Pender, *The General to His Wife*, 171; Pendleton to wife, Aug. 31, S. P. Lee, *Memoirs*, 209; Armistead Lindsay Long, *Memoirs of Robert E. Lee, His Military and Personal History* (Philadelphia: J. M. Stoddart, 1886), 205; and Chamberlayne to mother, Sept. 6, and to sister, Sept. 8, John Hampden Chamberlayne, *Ham Chamberlayne, Virginian, Letters and Papers of an Artillery Officer in the War for Southern Independence, 1861–1865* (Richmond: Press of the

Dietz Printing Company, 1932), 102, 104. Also see, Dickert, *History of Kershaw's Brigade*, 142–43, for the high morale in his brigade as it marched from Richmond.

93. Lewis Henry Steiner, *Report of Lewis H. Steiner, M.D., Inspector of the Sanitary Commission, Containing a Diary Kept during the Rebel Occupation of Frederick, Md.* (New York: Anson D. F. Randolph, 1862), 17.

94. For a brief discussion of various types of turning movements, see Harsh, *Confederate Tide Rising*, 67–71.

95. In his report, Lee would write: "The condition of Maryland encouraged the belief that the presence of our army, however inferior to that of the enemy, would induce the Washington Government to retain all its available force to provide against contingencies, which its course toward the people of that State gave it reason to apprehend." And he went on to state directly: ". . . we expected to derive . . . assistance in the attainment of our object from the just fears of the Washington Government." See *OR*, vol. 19, 1:144.

96. For further discussion of Lee's entry into Maryland as a turning movement, see Harsh, *Sounding the Shallows*, chap. 5, sect. M.

97. After the war, Lee explained to William Allan that he acted to clear his communications through the Shenandoah Valley "to be in proper position for battle, when he chose or should be forced to deliver one." Gallagher, ed., *Lee the Soldier*, 13. Edward C. Gordon would recall that Lee's eyes flashed when he said: "I went into Maryland to give battle." Douglas Southall Freeman, *Lee's Lieutenants: A Study in Command*, 3 vols. (New York: Charles Scribner's Sons, 1942–44), 2:717. In an earlier memorandum of this conversation, Gordon wrote that Lee said that after the reduction of Harpers Ferry, he "intended then to attack McClellan." Gallagher, ed., *Lee the Soldier*, 26.

98. For a further discussion regarding Lee's expectations of the resources of western Maryland, see Harsh, *Sounding the Shallows*, chap. 5, sect. N.

99. According to Bradley Johnson, in his meeting at Leesburg on the evening of the 4th, Lee remarked that he had promised Davis to "relieve Virginia of the presence of these two armies." Johnson, "Maryland," 504. Three times after the war Lee used the word "relieve." Gallagher, ed., *Lee the Soldier*, 7, 13; and Lee, "McDonald Letter," 445. In his report, he employed "freed." *OR*, vol. 19, 1:144.

100. Beginning in December 1860, a series of commissioners from various Southern states had visited Maryland, but they had been unable to persuade Governor Thomas Hicks to call a special session of the legislature to consider secession. After the Baltimore riots in April, the state was heavily garrisoned by Federal troops. Hence, Confederates were able to believe that Marylanders had never had the opportunity to express their desire to secede. These events, as well as later incidents (including the arrest of the legislators), are covered in great detail in chapter one of Ezra Carman's unpublished study, "The Maryland Campaign," Carman Papers, Library of Congress; *The American Annual Cyclopaedia and Register of Important Events*, 14 vols. (New York: D. Appleton, 1862–75), 1:360, 442–48. Estimates are that approximately 20,000 Marylanders served in the Confederate army and navy during the war. See Daniel D. Hartzler, *Marylanders in the Confederacy* (Westminster, Md.: Family Line Publications, 1986), 1–3; and William Worthington Goldsborough, *The Maryland Line in the Confederate States Army* (Gaithersburg, Md.: Olde Soldiers Books, 1987), 329.

101. Congressional Joint Resolution on Maryland, Dec. 21, 1861, *OR*, ser. 4, vol. 1:805–6. Davis's statement of war aims for the benefit of Great Britain and France in Hunter to Mason and Slidell, Feb. 8, 1862, in U.S. Navy Department, *Official Records of the Union and Confederate Navies in the War of the Rebellion*, 31 vols. (Washington, D.C.: GPO, 1894–1927), ser. 2., vol. 3:333–36.

102. Allan, who had served as ordnance officer in the Army of Northern Virginia, taught at Washington College and for a while came into nearly daily contact with Lee. He made at least two memoranda of conversations with Lee, but neither includes this quotation, found in

his *The Army of Northern Virginia in 1862* (Dayton, Ohio: Morningside House, 1984), 200n.1. Allan recalled the quotation when discussing Lee's decision of August 24, 1862, to send Jackson on the raid behind Pope, but he makes it relatively clear that Lee himself made the statement to apply generally. It should be noted Allan does not put any part in quotation marks. Douglas Freeman (without other attribution than Allan) gives the above as a direct quote of Lee's words and claims it was made in direct response to the move of August 24, *R. E. Lee* 2:302. The sentiment should be given credence but the words not taken as Lee's precisely. The thought closely reflects Lee's view that the war was not winnable by remaining on the defensive or by failing to seize and press the initiative.

103. That Lee's move to Leesburg was preliminary to and distinct from his final decision to enter Maryland is shown in his letter to Davis on the following day: "I therefore determined, while threatening the approaches to Washington, to draw the troops into Loudoun, where forage and some provisions can be obtained, menace their possession of the Shenandoah Valley, and, if found practicable, to cross into Maryland." Lee to Davis, Sept. 3, *OR*, vol. 19, 2:590.

104. "The purpose, if discovered," Lee wrote, "will have the effect of carrying the enemy north of the Potomac, and, if prevented, will not result in much evil." Lee to Davis, Sept. 3, *OR*, vol. 19, 2:590. This sentence has sometimes been misunderstood by historians as referring to the move into Maryland, and they have marveled at Lee's cool remark that it was riskless. He was, however, referring only to the movement to Leesburg.

105. Further reasons for assuming the strategy council occurred on September 2, include: (1) Longstreet recorded discussing the possibility of entering Maryland with Lee before the decision was made. He remembered that Lee's hesitation was over the question of supplies, but he gives no date or place for the meeting. See James Longstreet, "The Invasion of Maryland," in *B&L* 2:663. (2) Jackson was clearly involved at some point in the considerations as is evidenced by his discussion with Bradley Johnson on the subject of entering Maryland during the ride to Leesburg on the 4th. See Johnson, "Maryland," 502–3. Also, Jackson's report makes it clear he knew of Stuart's intelligence on the 2d, which information likely came from Lee and implies consultation. See *OR*, vol. 12, 2:647. (3) It makes sense to assume that any consulting would have occurred while the decision was most open for discussion, and that would have been before orders were issued for the march to Leesburg. Whether Lee talked with the officers together or separately cannot be known; and, of course, it is entirely possible that more than one such meeting took place.

106. Longstreet, *From Manassas to Appomattox*, 200–201.

107. William W. Hassler, *Colonel John Pelham, Lee's Boy Artillerist* (Richmond: Garrett & Massie, 1960), 77. For further discussion of Jackson's views on invasion, see Harsh, *Sounding the Shallows*, chap. 5, sect. O.

108. Longstreet would claim both in his report and in his postwar memoirs that his command started its march on the 2d, but he is clearly in error, as contemporaneous reports confirm all units of the army took up the march on the morning of the 3d. Jackson used the road that ran directly north from Ox Hill. Longstreet probably took the road from Chantilly, although the one from Saunders' Toll Gate is a possibility. If the latter is the case, Longstreet's men had a longer march of three or four miles. See Longstreet, *From Manassas to Appomattox*, 195; Alexander Hunter, "A High Private's Account of the Battle of Sharpsburg," *SHSP* 10 (1882): 507; G. Wise, *History of the Seventeenth Va.*, 107, who mistakenly refers to Guilford Station on the Gum Spring Road; H. W. Thomas, *History of the Doles-Cook Brigade*, 221, 469; Jubal Anderson Early, *War Memoirs, Autobiographical Sketch and Narrative of the War Between the States*, ed. Frank E. Vandiver (Bloomington: Indiana Univ. Press, 1960), 134; and John A. Ramsay, "Additional Sketch Tenth Regiment, Light Batteries A, D, F [E] and I," in *North Carolina Regiments* 1:572–73. Also see in *OR*, vol. 19, 1, Jackson (pp. 647–48), Longstreet (p. 839), Jones (p. 885), Johnston (p. 1002), and Williams (p. 1011). Allan agreed that all of the marching orders for the 3d were issued on the 2d (*Army of Northern Virginia*, 323–24).

109. Owen, *In Camp and Battle*, 129.

110. Only the orders to Hill have survived, but they reflect the ones to McLaws. See *OR*, vol. 19, 2:588. McLaws was to take the Gum Springs Road. Hill was to find one north from Pleasant Valley or go back to the Gum Springs Road. Since contemporary maps show no road from Pleasant Valley, it is possible Hill retraced his steps and followed McLaws. See also, Edward Porter Alexander, *Fighting for the Confederacy: The Personal Recollections of General Edward Porter Alexander*, ed. Gary W. Gallagher (Chapel Hill: Univ. of North Carolina Press, 1989), 136; and Pendleton's report, *OR*, vol. 19, 1:829.

111. Stuart's report implies reasonably specific instructions from Lee, which were probably verbal. See *OR*, vol. 19, 1:814; see also, Hampton's report, ibid., 822; and von Borcke, *Memoirs* 1:177–78.

112. Each side numbered about 160, although Munford claimed that forty of his men did not participate in the charge. Capt. Sam Means's Loudoun Rangers—natives of the area—were in Leesburg to attend the funeral of one of their members, not to arrest John Janney, as had been reported to Lee. Munford pursued them to Waterford, eight miles to the north. Then, as ordered by Lee, Munford proceeded in company of a commissary officer to scavenge for cattle up the river to Lovettsville. See the reports of Stuart and Munford in *OR*, vol. 12, 2:745, 749; and Stuart's report, *OR*, vol. 19, 1:814; see also, H. B. McClellan, *I Rode with Jeb Stuart*, 109; and Briscoe Goodhart, *History of the Independent Loudoun Virginia Rangers, U.S. Vol. Cavalry (Scouts), 1862–65* (Washington, D.C.: Press of McGill & Wallace, 1896), 40–44.

113. Special Orders, No. 187, Hdqtrs. Dept. of Northern Virginia, Sept. 2, 1862, *OR*, vol. 19, 2:589. The exactness with which Stuart carried out Lee's instructions is uncertain. The entire 6th Virginia Cavalry of Robertson's brigade was left behind at Centreville "to collect arms, &c." and missed the Maryland campaign. Munford's report, ibid., 1:825. But whether this was in lieu of or in addition to the unfit from all commands is not clear.

114. The Special Orders (cited in note 113) named Capt. William Allen, 1st Virginia, but the "Additions and Corrections" in the *OR Index* volume (p. 1150) changes the spelling to Allan. This would have been William Allan who was Jackson's ordnance officer and postwar author of *Army of Northern Virginia*.

115. Chilton to Randolph, Sept. 2, *OR*, vol. 19, 2:588. Chilton explained that Lee could not communicate directly, as would have been appropriate, because of "an injury, by accident, which temporarily disables both hands."

116. For the sources for all conclusions relating to weather see Harsh, *Sounding the Shallows*, chap. 1.

117. Of the contemporaneous accounts dealing with the main body, only a member of the Washington Artillery recorded an early start on the 3d. Owen, *In Camp and Battle*, 129. Osmun Latrobe, staff officer to D. R. Jones, noted a 9:00 A.M. start. Latrobe, Diary, Sept. 3d, typescript, Virginia Historical Society, Richmond. Maj. Hazael Williams, acting commander of Winder's Brigade, reported setting out at 10 A.M. *OR*, vol. 19, 1:1011. Note, however, Williams is one day off for nearly a week in his report. These sources combined suggest Longstreet's men may have commenced their march slightly earlier than Jackson's. If so, this may have set the stage for Stonewall's irascible impatience the next morning, which in turn led to the arrest of A. P. Hill. See discussion in chapter 2. On the flank, McLaws's division did start quite early. See note 121.

118. It should be noted that only one of Lee's communications of the 2d bore a heading that revealed his headquarters as "Ox Hill, Little River Turnpike." See *OR*, vol. 19, 2:588. The dispatches on the morning of the 3d were headed "Near Chantilly" and "Chantilly." See *OR*, vol. 19, 2:589–90; and Lee, *Wartime Papers*, 269–70. Since Chantilly and Ox Hill are within two miles of each other, it is most likely the various headings refer to a single headquarters as located by different staff members who prepared the dispatches. It is next most likely that Lee maintained his headquarters at Ox Hill, near the front, for most of the 2d, while considering

the pursuit of Pope and his other options and then, in late afternoon or early evening, retired a short distance west on the turnpike to establish camp for the night. It is least likely Lee spent the night at Ox Hill and broke camp on the morning of the 3d only to stop a short distance down the road to dictate letters.

119. Lee to Randolph, Sept. 3, *OR*, vol. 19, 2:589–90. Lee believed that over 400 conscripts were available in Fauquier alone.

120. Lee to Davis, Sept. 3, Lee, *Wartime Papers*, 269–70. The version in *OR*, vol. 12, 2:559–60, omits four sentences. Note Lee's opening sentence—in his usual style—confirms it was his first report since the morning of August 30. This informed the president that no intervening reports had been lost in transit.

121. On McLaws's division see McLaws to wife, Sept. 4th, McLaws Papers, University of North Carolina; Hubbert, "Diary," 307; Dinkins, *Recollections*, 53; James Dinkins, "Griffith-Barksdale-Humphrey Brigade and Its Campaigns," *SHSP* 32 (1904): 255. On D. H. Hill, see: H.W. Thomas, *History of the Doles-Cook Brigade*, 221, 469; Tucker, "Diary," 19; and Leach, Diary, Sept. 3. Federal knowledge of the nighttime occupation of Leesburg is reported in Banning to Wool, Sept. 4, *OR*, vol. 19, 2:179.

122. Hunter, "Sharpsburg," 506–7; Worsham, *Foot Cavalry*, 81–82; and von Borcke, *Memoirs* 1:178.

123. Von Borcke, *Memoirs* 1:177–78. No report from Fitzhugh Lee has been found for this period. Federal correspondence reflects no activity at all in front of Alexandria on the 3d. See *OR*, vol. 19, 2:169–74. George McClellan had been named commander of the defenses of Washington on September 2d; but for whatever reason (whether lack of trust or lack of authority), he made no attempt to use the cavalry of Pope's Army of Northern Virginia to probe the Confederates. Late in the day, the Union commander did have the small cavalry force that had arrived from the Peninsula under Alfred Pleasonton in place south of the Potomac. In any case, the Federal high command was receiving fairly accurate information from a stream of stragglers and released prisoners that indicated Lee was moving west toward Dranesville.

124. On the 3d's march in general, see Carman, "Maryland Campaign," Carman Papers, chap. 2, p. 119. On the cavalry, see von Borcke, *Memoirs* 1:179; James Ewell Brown Stuart, *The Letters of Major General James E. B. Stuart*, ed. Adele H. Mitchell (N.p.: Stuart-Mosby Historical Society, 1990), 262–63; Neese, *Three Years in the Confederate Horse Artillery*, 110; and Brooks, *Stories of the Confederacy*, 77. On Longstreet, see G. Wise, *History of the 17th Va.*, 107; Hunter, "Sharpsburg," 507; Owen, *In Camp and Battle*, 129; Ramsay, *North Carolina Regiments* 1:573; Latrobe, Diary, Sept. 3; and Mildred Aurelia Austin, *Georgia Boys with "Stonewall" Jackson—James Thomas Thompson and the Walton Infantry* (Athens: Univ. of Georgia Press, 1967), 45–46. On Jackson, see in *OR*, vol. 19, 1 the reports of Williams (p. 1011) and Early (p. 965). Also see Hotchkiss to wife, Sept. 8th, Hotchkiss Papers, Library of Congress; Hotchkiss, *Make Me a Map*, 78; Henry Kyd Douglas, "Stonewall Jackson in Maryland," in *B&L* 2:620; Cooke, *Jackson*, 308; Willam Thomas Poague, *Gunner with Stonewall, Reminiscences of William Thomas Poague*, ed. Monroe F. Cockrell (Jackson, Tenn.: McCowat-Mercer Press, 1957), 41 (including the dry-shod gunners); James Madison Scates, "The Civil War Diary of James Madison Scates," *Virginia Social Science Journal* 2 (1967): 13–14; Chamberlayne, *Letters*, 102; and McRae's report, *Supplement to the Official Records of the Union and Confederate Armies*, ed. Janet B. Hewett, et al., est. 100 vols. (Wilmington, N.C.: Broadfoot Pub. Co., 1994–), 3:573. On the Artillery Reserve, see Berkeley, *Diary*, 26; and on Walker, see Hirsch, Diary, Sept. 2–3.

125. Lee to Davis, Sept. 3, *OR*, vol. 19, 2:590–91, headed "Headquarters Alexandria & Leesburg Road, Near Dranesville." In his memoirs, Armistead Long gives the date as the 2d, and it is possible that Lee dictated the dispatch at Ox Hill and then retained it for twenty-four hours. Much, if not all, of the thinking recorded in the letter probably did occur to Lee as early as the 2d. Still, it is most likely that Long, who had become nearly blind and was writing

largely from memory, simply got the date wrong by one day. See Long, *Memoirs of Robert E. Lee*, 204.

126. For a further discussion of the Confederate view of the superiority of the Army of Northern Virginia, see Harsh, *Sounding the Shallows*, chap. 5, sect. P.

127. Less than 30,000 of the new Federal troops had reached Washington by Sept. 3. The story of the green regiments will be examined in a future study of the Federal side of the Maryland campaign.

128. For a more extended explanation by Lee of his belief that idleness hurt the Confederates, see the excerpt from his letter to Davis, June 25, 1863, in ibid., sect. A.

129. For a discussion of Lee's appreciation of the fears of Lincoln and Stanton, see Harsh, *Confederate Tide Rising*, 188.

130. Lee would write in his report of wishing "to prolong a state of affairs in every way so desirable." *OR*, vol. 19, 1:144. Also, after the war, in February 1868, he remarked to William Allan that a reason for crossing the Potomac had been "to live for a time" on Maryland supplies; and in April of the same year he told Allan he had to clear his communications through the Shenandoah Valley "in order to remain for any time" in Maryland. See Gallagher, *Lee the Soldier*, 7, 13.

131. Northern newspapers were not only assuming that Jackson would invade Maryland, they were also reporting that Kirby Smith's army was within forty miles of Cincinnati. See Strong, *Diary* 3:251–52; also the *New York Tribune*, *Washington Star*, and *Baltimore Sun* for Sept. 2 and 3. Lee was either without Northern newspapers for some days, or, if he did read them, he did not rate highly a raid by Kirby Smith or associate Smith's advance with Bragg. It might be noted in passing that Porter Alexander's notion that Lee should have shifted troops west to reenforce Bragg instead of entering Maryland—which was inherently impractical in any case—was rendered impossible by Lee's ignorance. See Alexander, *Military Memoirs of a Confederate*, 220–21.

132. It is ironic that some historians have been quick to castigate McClellan for believing Bragg or Beauregard was joining Lee during the Maryland campaign, overlooking the fact that Lee suggested just such a juncture and that the Confederate commander believed the reverse rumor to be true. In Federal eyes, such a shift helped explain the large numbers being reported for Lee. It is likely neither side yet quite knew how to evaluate the potentials and limitations the railroad had introduced in warfare in regard to mobility.

133. Marshall, *Aide-de-Camp of Lee*, 66–67. For extended statements by Lee indicating that he realized his success had disrupted Federal plans and caused them to withdraw forces to protect Washington, see Harsh, *Sounding the Shallows*, chap. 5, sect. Q.

134. Even had Lee magically acquired a copy of the *Washington Daily National Intelligencer* of the 3d, he would have learned only that McClellan had been named to command the capital's defenses.

135. A rumor would gain currency in the ranks that shoeless men had been ordered to remain in Virginia. See G. Wise, *History of the 17th Va.*, 108. No such order has been found. It is possible some soldiers did not enter Maryland for this reason, and a few may have even discarded their shoes to become eligible to stay behind. See Priest, *South Mountain*, 4–5. Nonetheless, thousands of barefoot soldiers did cross the Potomac. As will be discussed below, Lee made every effort to acquire shoes in Frederick, Hagerstown, and Williamsport for the thousands of barefoot men who were with him.

2. "More fully pursuaded": Lee Crosses the Potomac, September 4–6, 1862

1. Jed. Hotchkiss called the 4th "a very fine day" and noted a detour was necessary to cross Goose Creek. Hotchkiss, *Make Me a Map*, 78. The same source contains most of the

essentials for the September 4 movements of Jackson's command, but it should be supplemented by Hotchkiss to wife, Sept. 8, Hotchkiss Papers; Henry Kyd Douglas, *I Rode with Stonewall, Being Chiefly the War Experiences of the Youngest Member of Jackson's Staff from the John Brown Raid to the Hanging of Mrs. Surratt* (Chapel Hill: Univ. of North Carolina Press, 1940), 146; Early, *War Memoirs*, 134; Poague, *Gunner with Stonewall*, 41; George H. Mills, "16th N.C. Regiment, Additional Sketch," in *North Carolina Regiments* 4:164; E. A. Moore, *The Story of a Cannoneer*, 129; H. W. Thomas, *History of the Doles-Cook Brigade*, 221; and in *OR*, vol. 19, 1 the reports of Jackson (p. 648), Early (p. 966), Neal (p. 1003), and Williams (p. 1001). For Longstreet's command see D. R. Jones's report in *OR*, vol. 19, 1:885; Owen, *In Camp and Battle*, 129; Austin, *Georgia Boys*, 46; Latrobe, Diary, Sept. 4; and G. Wise, *History of the Seventeenth Va.*, 107. The latter two sources specify the Robert Newton Harper farm (then Newton Hall, now Cardock Hall) as the point of bivouac.

2. Von Borcke, *Memoirs* 1:180; Stuart's report, *OR*, vol. 19, 1:814; and Stuart to wife, and Stuart to Randolph, Sept. 4, Stuart, *Letters*, 263–65. As a minor exception to the inactivity, a small body of Hampton's troopers scouted down the Potomac to a point almost opposite Georgetown, skirmishing with an equally small group of Federal cavalry. Brooks, *Stories of the Confederacy*, 77.

3. It is uncertain whether Lee or Stuart chose Robertson and why he was elected for the mission. Neither Stuart nor Jackson believed Robertson competent, and the 4th would be his last day in command before being transferred to North Carolina. His brigade had been reduced to two regiments by the detachment of the 2d Virginia to Leesburg, the 6th Virginia to collect arms at Manassas, and the 17th Virginia Battalion on an unspecified expedition. In *OR*, vol. 19, 1, see the reports of Stuart (p. 814), Munford (p. 825), and Robertson (p. 828); see also, Neese, *Three Years in the Confederate Horse Artillery*, 110–11. This cavalry demonstration is discussed below as a diversion for D. H. Hill's raid across the Potomac.

4. The abbreviated version followed here is the one accepted by James I. Robertson, Jr., *General A. P. Hill: The Story of a Confederate Warrior* (New York: Random House, 1987), 130–32, which is based on the firsthand account found in the Jed. Hotchkiss Papers in the Library of Congress. For a substantially different firsthand account see Douglas, *I Rode with Stonewall*, 146–47. See also, Alexander, *Fighting for the Confederacy*, 141–42; Mills, *North Carolina Regiments* 4:164–65; and Berry Benson, *Berry Benson's Civil War Book, Memoirs of a Confederate Scout and Sharpshooter*, ed. Susan Williams Benson (Athens: Univ. of Georgia Press, 1962), 25.

5. Hood's arrest probably occurred on either the 3d or 4th, since he remembered it as having been after the march to Maryland had commenced. See John Bell Hood, *Advance and Retreat, Personal Experiences in the United States and Confederate States Armies*, ed. Richard N. Current (Bloomington: Indiana Univ. Press, 1959), 38–39; and Joseph Benjamin Polley, *A Soldier's Letters to Charming Nellie* (New York: Neale Publishing, 1908), 83; and Stuart's report, *OR*, vol. 12, 2:738. The Texas brigade was at the Stone House on the Warrenton Turnpike on the 31st, which would have been approximately the correct position for its scouts to have taken the wagons from Stuart's men near the Stone Bridge over Bull Run. See Ramsay, *North Carolina Regiments* 1:572; and Harsh, *Confederate Tide Rising*, 165. Longstreet apparently had a preference for divisions of three brigades, having divided his own division in half two months earlier. It must be assumed that Lee was at least aware of the Evans/Hood arrangement, and perhaps Longstreet had asked his approval, but it did not last long, as Evans had reverted to command of an unattached brigade by September 17. Lee was less enamored of symmetry and more concerned with ability of individual officers.

6. Hotchkiss, *Make Me a Map*, 78; James B. Sheeran, *Confederate Chaplain: A War Journal of Rev. James B. Sheeran, C.SS.T., 14th Louisiana, C.S.A.*, ed. Rev. Joseph T. Durkin (Milwaukee: Bruce Publishing, 1960), 23–24; on the General Orders, see note 13.

7. For a discussion of the conclusion that few of Lee's men refused to participate in the Maryland campaign, see Harsh, *Sounding the Shallows*, chap. 6, sect. A.

8. Allan, *Army of Northern Virginia*, 326; Sheeran, *Confederate Chaplain*, 23–24; James Fitz James Caldwell, *The History of a Brigade of South Carolinians, Known First as "Gregg's," and Subsequently as "McGowan's Brigade"* (Philadelphia: King & Baird, 1866), 69; Gilbert Moxley Sorrel, *Recollections of a Confederate Staff Officer*, ed. Bell Irvin Wiley (Jackson, Tenn.: McCowat-Mercer Press, 1958), 98; and Worsham, *Jackson's Foot Cavalry*, 81–82.

9. Robert Healy, "Letter," in *B&L* 2:621 (note); Long, *Memoirs of Robert E. Lee*, 205; Worsham, *Jackson's Foot Cavalry*, 82; Haynes, *Diary*, 15; Simpson to sister, Sept. 24, in Richard Wright and Taliaferro N. Simpson, *"Far, Far from Home": The Wartime Letters*, ed. Guy R. Everson and Edward H. Simpson, Jr. (New York: Oxford Univ. Press, 1994), 147; Mac Wyckoff, *History of the 2nd South Carolina Infantry: 1861–1865* (Fredericksburg, Va.: Sergeant Kirkland Museum and Historical Society, 1994), 40; and a collection of anecdotes in Sears, *Landscape Turned Red*, 70.

10. For a discussion of Lee's decision to send D. H. Hill into Maryland on September 4, see Harsh, *Sounding the Shallows*, chap. 6, sect. B.

11. For a discussion of the details of D. H. Hill's crossing of the Potomac, see ibid.

12. Harrison's three daughters were leaning out an upstairs window and observed Lee's arrival. Many years later one—unfortunately which one is not clear—would commit her recollections to paper. Harrison Family Memoirs, typescript Loudoun County Museum, Leesburg, Virginia. Dr. Jackson left a record of his memories: Samuel K. Jackson, Essays, Virginia Historical Society, Richmond. The Harrison home is also mentioned by Walter Herron Taylor, *General Lee, His Campaigns in Virginia, 1861–1865, with Personal Reminiscences* (Norfolk: Nusbaum Book and News, 1906), 118.

13. Headquarters Army of Northern Virginia, Leesburg, Sept. 4, 1862, *OR*, vol. 19, 1:592–93. The quote is from Long, *Memoirs of Robert E. Lee*, 205–6.

14. For a discussion of Confederate artillery present in the Maryland campaign, see Harsh, *Sounding the Shallows*, chap. 6, sect. C.

15. For a discussion of the batteries left at Leesburg, see ibid.

16. Wood, *Reminiscences of Big I*, 34. Colonel Strange suspended the arrest the following morning, but Wood refused to resume command until after a court of inquiry. The disagreement ended tragically with the colonel's death at South Mountain.

17. Lee to Davis, Sept. 4, *OR*, vol. 19, 2:591–92.

18. Davis to Lee, Aug. 30, *Papers of Jefferson Davis* 8:367–69. This previously unpublished letter reveals the growing strain felt by Davis from the exposed condition of Richmond. In the closing sentence, the president makes an intriguing but mysterious reference to Lee's "hope of having the service of Genl Johnston in the field with you." The letter that was enclosed by Davis has been lost—possibly on purpose, since it identified a traitor—and its contents must be reconstructed from Davis's comments.

19. Long, *Memoirs of Robert E. Lee*, 205.

20. Lee's report, *OR*, vol. 19, 1:144. On the ordnance train, see Porter Alexander's *Military Memoirs of a Confederate*, 219, 223. As part of the preparation for Maryland, Alexander replenished all of the army's ammunition, and then he ran his empty wagons back to Gordonsville, where they were refilled. He continued to convoy ammunition throughout the campaign and would claim "we were able to meet all demands." Ibid, 219; see also, Alexander, *Fighting for the Confederacy*, 128, 136. There is evidence that some batteries were unable to engage at Sharpsburg because the caissons were empty, but the failure may have come at a lower level of distribution.

21. It is known that D. H. Hill and McLaws were ordered to unload their subsistence trains so the wagons could be used to collect additional supplies. S.O., No. 187, Sept. 2, Hdqtrs,

Dept. of Northern Virginia, *OR*, vol. 19, 2:589. And Thomas Munford, after the capture of Leesburg, was ordered up the Potomac in the company of a commissary officer to purchase cattle. Munford's report, ibid., vol. 12, 2:749. It is likely these were but a small part of the actions taken by Lee to secure food.

22. It is unfortunate that the telegram is lost, as not only might it shed additional light on Lee's thinking, but its date and hour (the latter being usual on telegrams) would be important in establishing the chronology of Lee's decision. If Lee sent the wire on the 3d from Dranesville, it might be necessary to revise substantially the analysis of his progress toward deciding to enter Maryland. In the absence of the telegram, however, contextual evidence—including the very tentative proposal of the 3d—would suggest the wire was sent at about the same time Lee wrote the dispatch of the 4th.

23. *The National Cyclopedia of American Biography*, 9 vols. (New York: James T. White, 1892–99), 9:305–6; see also, Lee to Davis, Sept. 12, *OR*, vol. 19, 2:605. Murfin, apparently following Nevins, misidentifies the ex-governor as E. Loring Lowe and mistakenly states that he did travel with the army. See Murfin, *Gleam of Bayonets*, 105; and Allan Nevins, *The War for the Union*, 4 vols. (New York: Charles Scribner's Sons, 1959–71), 2:217.

24. Lee to Davis, Sept. 9, 12, *OR*, vol. 19, 2:603, 605.

25. The *Baltimore Sun* for September 4 may have been the first Northern newspaper Lee had seen since leaving Richmond. It is the first he mentions. For other news he might have derived from a close reading of this paper, see later in this chapter, including note 84.

26. Bradley Tyler Johnson (1829–1903) graduated from the College of New Jersey (Princeton) in 1849, was elected district attorney of Frederick County in 1851, was defeated in bid as state comptroller in 1857, and served as state Democratic party chairman from 1859–60. See unsigned biography of Johnson in Johnson Papers, Duke University, Durham, North Carolina; also, *National Cyclopedia of American Biography* 4:182; William C. Davis, ed., *The Confederate General*, 6 vols. (N.p.: National Historical Society, 1991), 3:172–79; and Johnson's report of Second Manassas in *OR*, vol. 12, 2:664–68.

27. Gallagher, ed., *Lee the Soldier*, 7. This is additional evidence that Lee consulted with his chief subordinates on either the 2d or 3d or perhaps both.

28. Johnson, "Maryland," 502–5. A daughter of the Harrison household remembered Stonewall's visit but implied it was earlier in the day. See Harrison, Memoir, 1. It is certainly possible Jackson met with Lee more than once on the 4th. For a brief but perceptive evaluation of the meeting, see D. Scott Hartwig, "Robert E. Lee and the Maryland Campaign," in Gallagher, ed., *Lee the Soldier*, 333–34.

29. For a statistical breakdown of slavery in Maryland's population, see Harsh, *Sounding the Shallows*, chap. 6, sect. D.

30. In the governor's race, Augustus Williamson Bradford received 57,498 votes, while Congressman Benjamin Chew Howard polled only 26,086 and carried only four counties (Talbot, Calvert, Charles, and St. Mary's). The state Senate had thirteen Unionists and eight whose opponents identified them as Secessionists, but seven of the latter had not been up for election and had carried over. The House, where all members were newly elected, was Unionist 68 to 8. See *The Tribune Almanac for 1862* (New York: New York Tribune Association, 1861), 59; also *The American Annual Cyclopaedia, 1861*, 442–49; and *National Cyclopedia of American Biography* 4:136, 9:307–8.

31. It should be pointed out that Johnson had an ax to grind in his postwar account. There was some anti-Maryland sentiment in the Army of Northern Virginia after Sharpsburg because of the failure of her citizens to respond to the opportunity given them. It is not unlikely Johnson had rehearsed this argument a number of times with accusatory colleagues before the struggle ended. It should also be noted that Lee had demonstrated his awareness of the political sensitivity on the issue of Maryland and Marylanders at the very beginning of

the war. See his four letters to Stonewall Jackson and one to James Mason in May of 1861 in Lee, *Wartime Papers*, 20–33.

32. Johnson, "Maryland," 504–5. Lee presumably meant the armies of Pope and McClellan, although Johnson—willing to grant Lee's unbounded genius—seems to have believed he meant the Federal and Confederate armies.

33. For further discussion of Lee's strategy to cross the Potomac east of the mountains, see Harsh, *Sounding the Shallows*, chap. 6, sect. E.

34. *OR*, vol. 19, 1:38–39, 117–18, 124; ibid., 2:172–81; and ibid., vol. 51, 1:785–88. This account—and others that follow at intervals—of daily Federal activities is no more than a brief summary of the subject, which is intended to form a separate series of studies. A general understanding of enemy operations is necessary, however, to give context to Confederate intelligence and strategy.

35. Harrison, Memoir, 1–2; and S. K. Jackson, Essays, 2–3. For additional sources on Stonewall Jackson, see note 37; and on Jeb Stuart, note 45.

36. Conflicting evidence leaves the timing of the events of the morning of the 5th open to some question. The usually reliable Hotchkiss recorded (*Make Me a Map*, 78), "We started about sunrise" and places Jackson at the head of the column as it reached the Potomac. Both Harrison, Memoirs, and von Borcke, *Memoirs* 1:183, insist Jackson met with Lee during the morning. Worsham (*Jackson's Foot Cavalry*, 82) remembered the Stonewall brigade as crossing between nine and ten o'clock. The historian of the 16th North Carolina recalled Pender's brigade "fell in" at about 10:00 and reached the ford at 2:00, but since A. P. Hill's division was the second to cross, the fact is only indirectly related to the timing of Jackson's division. Mills, *North Carolina Regiments* 4:164. The version in the text assumes Lee arose about 5:30 and finished breakfast by 7:00, which would allow time for the conference and the prayer meeting and for Jackson to be back with his command by 9:00. It is also assumed that Jackson anticipated the march and ordered his camp struck before he left to meet with Lee to receive his final orders, including his destination.

37. Hotchkiss, *Make Me a Map*, 78; von Borcke, *Memoirs* 1:184–85; Carman, "The Maryland Campaign," chap. 3, pp. 126–28; Douglas, *I Rode with Stonewall*, 147, and "Maryland," 620; Allan, *Army of Northern Virginia*, 326; plus an on-site study of Leesburg by John Divine.

38. To the sources in note 37 add: (see for naked legs) Haynes, *Diary*, 15, and William Augustus McClendon, *Recollections of War Times, by an Old Veteran while under Stonewall Jackson and Lieutenant General James Longstreet* (Montgomery, Ala.: Paragon Press, 1909), 128–29; (see for Harmon's swearing) John Daniel Imboden, "Incidents of the First Bull Run," in *B&L* 1:238 (note); (in general see) Early, *War Memoirs*, 135; E. A. Moore, *The Story of a Cannoneer*, 128–29; and Poague, *Gunner with Stonewall*, 41.

39. Early, *War Memoirs*, 134–35; Hotchkiss, *Make Me a Map*, 78; Hotchkiss to wife, Sept. 8, Hotchkiss Papers; Worsham, *Jackson's Foot Cavalry*, 82; Carman, "Maryland Campaign," chap. 3, p. 131, Carman Papers; and Early's report, *OR*, vol. 19, 1:966. Lt. Robert Healy (55th Virginia) remembered Field's brigade of A. P. Hill did not bivouac until two in the morning (Healy, "Letter," 62n.); and according to a member of Hill's artillery, the march ended at 12:30 (Chamberlayne, *Letters*, 102); but a member of the 49th Georgia (Thomas's brigade, Branch) recorded 11:00 P.M. for the bivouac (Haynes, *Diary*, 15).

40. Jackson's report, *OR*, vol. 19, 1:952; and Jackson to Branch, Sept. 5, ibid., 2:594. It is possible that Jackson sent similar orders—which have not survived—to Starke, commanding the Stonewall division, and to Lawton, commanding Ewell's. In light of Jackson's flat statement about his lack of cavalry, it seems likely the company of horsemen from Cobb's Legion that had been serving with A. P. Hill's division and were detached by orders dated the 5th had been left behind at Leesburg. See S.O. No. 188, Hdqrts Dept. of Northern Virginia, Sept. 5, 1862, ibid., 595.

41. After the war Lee made clear the temporary nature of the arrangement, commenting "that when Genl. Jackson afterward crossed he had taken command of all the troops then north of the Potomac and thus for a time Genl. Hill was immediately under his command." Gallagher, ed., *Lee the Soldier*, 26.

42. Jackson to Hill, Sept. 5, *OR*, vol. 19, 2:593; Daniel Harvey Hill, "The Lost Dispatch," *Land We Love* 4 (1867–68): 274; Hill's report, *OR*, vol. 19, 1:1019; and Carman, "Maryland Campaign," chap. 3, p. 131, Carman Papers. Hill's fifth brigade, G. B. Anderson, had not returned from its mission of firing on trains opposite Berlin and was still in Virginia. See Walter Lee to mother, Battle, *Forget-me-nots*, 74–75; Tucker, "Diary," 19; and James T. Shinn, Diary, Sept. 6, vol. 76 in Edwin Augustus Osborne Papers, Southern Historical Collection, University of North Carolina, Chapel Hill. There is also firsthand testimony that the 1st North Carolina of Ripley's brigade did not cross until September 6. See Leach, Diary, Sept. 5, 6. According to rumors in Frederick, the Confederates were going into camp on the Moffat farm. See Steiner, *Diary*, 7.

43. Hotchkiss to wife, Sept. 8, Hotchkiss Papers.

44. Carman, "Maryland Campaign," chap. 3, p. 131, Carman Papers.

45. Von Borcke, *Memoirs* 1:182–85; Stuart's report, *OR*, vol. 19, 1:814; and Brooks, *Stories of the Confederacy*, 77–78.

46. In this first battle of Poolesville—and the first action of the Maryland campaign—the Confederates lost three killed and four wounded; the Federals had eight or nine wounded among their captured. See von Borcke, *Memoirs* 1:185–86; Stuart's report, *OR*, vol. 19, 1:814–85; Carman, "Maryland Campaign," chap. 3, pp. 129–30; and Pleasonton to Marcy, Sept. 5, 11:30 P.M., *OR*, vol. 19, 2:186.

47. Lack of evidence does not prove that an event did not happen. Stuart may, in fact, have been in touch with Jackson; but certainly Stonewall acted as if he had either not heard from Stuart at all or had not received information from the cavalry leader that he found comforting. See von Borcke, *Memoirs* 1:185–86; and Carman, "Maryland Campaign," chap. 3, pp. 129–30. Hampton's brigade did not set out until near sunset. It passed through Leesburg and crossed the Potomac by moonlight. See Brooks, *Stories of the Confederacy*, 77–78; and Hampton's report, *OR*, vol. 19, 1:822.

48. In 1860 Montgomery County had a population of 18,322 with 5,421 slaves (29.6 percent); Frederick County had 3,243 slaves (7.0 percent) out of a total of 46,591. U.S. Census Bureau, *8th Census*, 1:210–14.

49. Mills, *North Carolina Regiments* 4:164.

50. The quotes in the two preceding paragraphs are from Caldwell, *Gregg's Brigade*, 69; Douglas, *I Rode with Stonewall*, 146–48; and Hotchkiss, *Make Me a Map*, 79. Anecdotes on the subject of the army's discipline and its reception in Maryland (September 5–9)—and the two are normally intertwined—have been conveniently and extensively collected in Murfin, *Gleam of Bayonets*, 100–12; Sears, *Landscape Turned Red*, 83–85, et seq.; and Priest, *South Mountain*, 11–12, et seq. Also useful are Polley, *Letters*, 80–81, 82; Sheeran, *Confederate Chaplain*, 24; Wood, *Reminiscences of Big I*, 34–35; Sorrel, *Recollections of a Staff Officer*, 98–99, 103; Healy, "Letter," 621; Early, *War Memoirs*, 134–35; E. A. Moore, *Cannoneer under Stonewall*, 130; J. B. Moore, "Battle of Sharpsburg," *SHSP* 27 (1899): 211; Brooks, *Stories of the Confederacy*, 79–80; G. Wise, *History of the 17th Va.*, 108; J. T. Thompson to parents, Oct. 1, in Austin, *Georgia Boys*, 52; Chamberlayne to mother, Sept. 6, and to sister, Sept. 8, Chamberlayne, *Letters*, 103, 104; Hubbert, "Diary," 307; Fleming to aunt, Oct. 24, Francis Philip Fleming, "Francis P. Fleming in the War for Southern Independence: Soldiering with the 2nd Florida Regiment," ed. Edward C. Williamson, *Florida Historical Quarterly* 27 (1949–50): 45; James Henry Lane, "28th Regiment," in *North Carolina Regiments* 2:473; and James A. Weston, "33rd Regiment," in ibid., 553. The best analysis from the citizens' point of view may be found in Richard Duncan, "Marylanders and the Invasion of 1862," in John T. Hubbell, ed.,

Battles Lost and Won: Essays from Civil War History (Westport, Conn.: Greenwood Press, 1975), 183–96. From among the conflicting reports, Duncan concludes: "Unionists received them coolly, and many who sympathized with the southern cause held aloof from identifying themselves" (p. 184).

51. In *OR*, vol. 19, 1 see the reports of Pendleton (p. 829) and R. L. Walker (p. 984); in *OR*, vol. 19, 2 Order No. —, Headquarters Artillery Corps, Leesburg, Sept. 5 (p. 595), and Pendleton to Lee, Oct. 2, (pp. 650–51); and also Pendleton to wife, Aug. 31, S. P. Lee, *Memoirs*, 208, 210.

52. Quote is from Neese, *Three Years in the Horse Artillery*, 111–12; the description of Big Spring is from Randolph Abbott Shotwell, *The Papers of Randolph Abbott Shotwell*, ed. J. G. Roulhac Hamilton, 3 vols. (Raleigh: North Carolina Historical Commission, 1929–36), 1:310. See also G. Wise, *History of the 17th Va.*, 107–8; Ramsay, *North Carolina Regiments* 1:572–73; Owen, *In Camp and Battle*, 129; Latrobe, Diary, Sept. 5; and Hubbert, "Diary," 307.

53. Harrison, Memoirs, 2, where the timing of these visits is ambiguous. The half-day of the 4th was too busy to allow much socializing, however, and it is likely Fitz Lee arrived in Leesburg with Stuart on the 5th. It is possible that Rob did visit on the 4th. The young Harrison daughters accompanied Lee on his visit to Janney. On Janney's presentation see Freeman, *R. E. Lee* 1:465–68.

54. Special Orders, No. 188, Headquarters Dept. of Northern Virginia, Sept. 5, 1862, *OR*, vol. 19, 2:595.

55. It is doubtful Lee knew—or would have been pleased had he known—that on the previous day Stuart had written directly to the secretary of war with "some recommendations" for changes in the cavalry command. Jeb lamely excused outflanking his chief by claiming "General Lee is too busy and they apply to routine of my own command." Stuart to Randolph, Sept. 4, Stuart, *Letters*, 264–65.

56. Lee to Davis, Leesburg, Sept. 5, *OR*, vol. 19, 2:593–94. Lee sent an extraordinary twenty-one dispatches and telegrams to Davis in the twenty-six days from September 3 through 28. Thereafter, he more frequently wrote to the War Department (either the secretary or the adjutant general) than the president, relapsing into corresponding with Davis approximately once a week.

57. Echoing the cautious prediction of Johnson, Lee would state in his report: "The difficulties that surrounded them were fully appreciated, and we expected to derive more assistance in the attainment of our object from the just fears of the Washington Government than from any active demonstration on the part of the people, unless success should enable us to give them assurance of continued protection." *OR*, vol. 19, 1:144.

58. On Loring and Jenkins, see in ibid., vol. 12, 3, Lee to Randolph, Aug. 25 (p. 943); Randolph to Loring, Aug. 29 (p. 946); Loring to Randolph, Aug. 29 (p. 946); Loring to Randolph, Sept. 1 (p. 949); and Loring's report in ibid., vol. 19, 1:1073–74.

59. Lee to Davis, Sept. 7, ibid., vol. 19, 2:596; and Hirsch, Diary, Sept. 5–6.

60. McClellan's reports, *OR*, vol. 19, 1:25–26, 38; and Federal correspondence, ibid., vol. 12, 3:811–13, vol. 19, 2:182–89; and ibid., vol. 51, 1:788–90. Specifically, see Wool to Miles, Sept. 5, and Binney's report (on White) in ibid., vol. 19, 1:523, 533.

61. Worsham, *Jackson's Foot Cavalry*, 82; Hotchkiss, *Make Me a Map*, 79; and Carman, "Maryland Campaign," chap. 3, pp. 131–32.

62. Jackson's usual mount, the famous Little Sorrel, had been "temporarily stolen." Henry Kyd Douglas is the primary source for this incident, *I Rode with Stonewall*, 147–48; and idem, "Maryland," 620–21. It is also recorded by Jed. Hotchkiss, *Make Me a Map*, 79, and in a letter to his wife on September 8, Hotchkiss Papers. He relates that Stonewall returned to horseback later in the day.

63. Wm. Jackson to Branch, Sept. 6, *OR*, vol. 19, 2:595. Presumably similar orders to establish pickets and sentinels were sent to Lawton. Hotchkiss records that Jackson was then

sufficiently recovered to ride "to a point above the Monocacy Bridge" (*Make Me a Map*, 79). According to George Mills, *North Carolina Regiments* 4:164, Pender's brigade (Branch) went into line around noon; John Chamberlayne recorded the time as 1 P.M. for Branch's artillery. Letter to mother, Sept. 6, Chamberlayne, *Letters*, 102. See also Jubal Early in "Barbara Frietchie—Refutation of Whittier's Myth," *SHSP* 7 (1879): 436; and Early, *War Memoirs*, 135; H. W. Thomas, *History of the Doles-Cook Brigade*, 221; Tucker, "Diary," 19; Carman, "Maryland Campaign," chap. 3, pp. 131–32. And see also in *OR*, vol. 19, 1, Jackson's (pp. 952–53), Early's (p. 966), and McGowan's (p. 987) reports.

64. Carman, "Maryland Campaign," chap. 3, p. 132; Faithful's report, *OR*, vol. 51, 1:136–37. See especially the diary of Dr. Lewis H. Steiner, an inspector for the U.S. Sanitary Commission, who arrived in Frederick on the night of the 5th and remained until after the arrival of the Federal army. Steiner's journal entries were first published in 1863 as part of his report to the commission in pamphlet form. It is has been reprinted in abridgment in Richard Harwell, ed., *The Union Reader* (New York: Longmans, Green, 1958), 158–74. Citations herein are to the original publication. See Steiner, *Diary*, 7–8.

65. Quotes are from Steiner, *Diary*, 7–8; see also Carman, "Maryland Campaign," chap. 3, p. 131; D. H. Hill's report, *OR*, vol. 19, 1:1019; and Hill in "Lost Dispatch," 274. There was a rumor in the ranks—apparently incorrect—that Jackson sent a message to "Abe." Chamberlayne to mother, Sept. 6, Chamberlayne, *Letters*, 102.

66. Quotes are from Steiner, *Diary*, 8–9; see also Worsham, *Jackson's Foot Cavalry*, 82; Jackson's report, *OR*, vol. 19, 1.952–53; and Carman, "Maryland Campaign," chap. 3, p. 131. The usually reliable Worsham misplaces the march in the late evening.

67. Steiner, *Diary*, 9–10; Early, "Barbara Frietchie," 436; H. J. Williams (who gets the date wrong) in *OR*, vol. 19, 1:1011; and Douglas, *I Rode with Stonewall*, 149–50. The quote is from Mills, *North Carolina Regiments* 4:164.

68. Steiner, *Diary*, 9–11; and hospital information from Worsham, *Jackson's Foot Cavalry*, 82. See also, Duncan, "Marylanders," 184–86; Hotchkiss, *Make Me a Map*, 79; Sheeran, *Confederate Chaplain*, 24–28; Tucker, "Diary," 19; and Poague, *Gunner with Stonewall*, 41–42; and the collections of anecdotes in Sears, *Landscape Turned Red*, 85–87; and Murfin, *Gleam of Bayonets*, 106–10.

69. D. R. Jones's report, *OR*, vol. 19, 1:885. Apparently, Jones at first believed his own three brigades and those of Kemper were to continue to be treated as independent divisions, and he elevated Robert Toombs to the command of the former (Toombs, Drayton, and G. T. Anderson). See Toombs's report, *OR*, vol. 19, 1:888. It is doubtful this was the intention of either Lee or Longstreet, however, and Toombs seems not to have exercised authority outside of his own brigade in the campaign that followed. Capt. Osmun Latrobe of Jones's staff, noted "10.15 A.M., the moment we touched the Old State." Latrobe, Diary, Sept. 6.

70. On the September 6 crossing in general, see Longstreet, *From Manassas to Appomattox*, 201; and "Maryland," 663; D. R. Jones's report, *OR*, vol. 19, 1:885; Long, *Memoirs of Robert E. Lee*, 206–7; G. Wise, *History of the Seventeenth Va.*, 106, who misplaces the crossing at Noland's Ferry; Owen, *In Camp and Battle*, 130–31; Price to mother, Sept. 10, Robert J. Trout, *With Pen and Saber: The Letters and Diaries of J. E. B. Stuart's Staff Officers* (Mechanicsburg, Pa.: Stackpole Books, 1995), 96; Carman, "Maryland Campaign," chap. 3, p. 132; and two sources who misdate the crossing, (on the 5th) Polley, *Letters*, 80, and (on the 7th) Ramsay, *North Carolina Regiments* 1:573.

71. Letter of Capt. Matthew Nunnally of the 11th Georgia (G. T. Anderson's brigade) in Austin, *Georgia Boys*, 50; see also, Wyckoff, *2nd S.C.*, 40–41.

72. Latrobe, Diary, Sept. 6.

73. On Barksdale's brigade, see Hubbert, "Diary," 307. The crossing of the trains and the miscellaneous artillery is speculative. Ordnance Chief Porter Alexander remembered crossing with Brig. Gen. Paul Semmes, which would place the ordnance train on September 6

(*Fighting for the Confederacy*, 137). On the other hand, the usually reliable diary of Adj. William Owen records the Washington Artillery as crossing on the 7th (*In Camp and Battle*, 131). Hence, Longstreet's artillery reserve, including S. D. Lee's battalion, may have crossed with Pendleton on the following day.

74. Louise Porter Daly, *Alexander Cheves Haskell: The Portrait of a Man* (Norwood, Mass.: Plimpton Press, 1934), 76; also on dustiness, see Neese, *Three Years in the Horse Artillery*, 112.

75. On the Reserve Artillery, see Pendleton to wife, Sept. 6, S. P. Lee, *Memoirs*, 210–11; and report, *OR*, vol. 19, 1:829. Walker's report is silent on the doings of the 6th, but after the war he would state that he "reached the vicinity of Leesburg" on the night of the 6th ("Harper's Ferry," 604). This contradicts Lee's nearly contemporaneous claim that Walker arrived at Leesburg on the evening of the 5th. Lee to Davis, Sept. 7, *OR*, vol. 19, 2:591. The diary of a private in the 30th Virginia provides a compromise answer. Isaac Hirsch records arriving within seven miles of Leesburg on the evening of the 5th—at which point Walker probably reported to Lee. On the 6th, the division marched through Leesburg and camped at the Big Spring. Hirsch, Diary, Sept. 5–6. George Washington Ball's farm thus acquired the unusual—and perhaps unique—role of hosting the entire infantry of the Army of Northern Virginia within four successive nights.

76. Munford's movements are inferred from his artillery, see Neese, *Three Years in the Horse Artillery*, 112–13.

77. On G. B. Anderson's brigade see Shinn, Diary, Sept. 4–6. The historian of the 12th North Carolina (Garland's brigade of D. H. Hill) mentioned that a "large detachment" from the regiment was left behind at the crossing as rear guard and did not rejoin until after the battle of South Mountain. See Walter Alexander Montgomery, "12th Regiment," *North Carolina Regiments* 1:627. This raises the possibility that other detachments may have been strewn in the wake of Lee's army, a weakening factor not related to straggling.

78. After the war, in referring to himself, Lee would simply recall: "He came on with the remainder of the army as soon as he could." Gallagher, ed., *Lee the Soldier*, 7. It is not unlikely that Lee was traveling in an unmarked ambulance, and few were aware of his crossing. The usually careful Douglas Freeman reported that Lee was riding with A. P. Hill when approaching the river. Hill ordered troops out of the road to make way for the commanding general, but Lee refused to trouble the men and "turned his horse out of the road." See *R. E. Lee* 2:355, citing Theo Hartman, "Some Incidents of Army Life," *Confederate Veteran* 30 (1922): 45. Not only was the arrested Hill at Monocacy Junction by this time, but Lee, of course, could not ride a horse. Robertson's biography of Hill accepts the story but places it on September 3 on the march from Dranesville, when it was still impossible for Lee to have been on horseback. Robertson, *A. P. Hill*, 129–30. Either the tale is apocryphal, or it occurred at a much different time.

79. Lee to Davis, Sept. 6, *Wartime Papers*, 296. It is not certain whether the telegraph had been connected to Leesburg or the message had to be carried to the wires at Warrenton, Culpeper, or even Rapidan Station.

80. Duncan, "Marylanders," 193. It might be noted that the Confederates would continue to damage the canal at every opportunity. On September 14, as he prepared to take Maryland Heights, LaFayette McLaws ordered Roger Pryor to destroy the section of the waterway at Weverton. McLaws's report, *OR*, vol. 19, 1:856.

81. Longstreet, *From Manassas to Appomattox*, 201–2; and in "Maryland," 663. Longstreet is actually much more positive in his memoirs, stating that Lee asked him to organize a force for the capture of Harpers Ferry. Since Lee had written to Davis just the day before that he had no doubt the Federals would flee when they perceived their plight, it is highly unlikely he would not give them a bit of time to develop their perceptions. Moreover, both of Longstreet's accounts of this conversation are so prescient as to raise doubts about their entire reliability. According to Longstreet, he predicted that (1) the expedition would be time consuming;

(2) the enemy would learn of the division of forces; and (3) they would move against the Confederates in time to catch them fragmented. There is no reason to doubt the basic outline of the conversation, but there is cause to believe that hindsight colored the details of his recollections. Longstreet first mentioned this incident—in a briefer and less omniscient form—in a letter to D. H. Hill a year before the appearance of the *Century* article. See Longstreet to D. H. Hill, Feb. 22, 1885, D. H. Hill Papers, Library of Virginia, Richmond.

82. Henry Alexander White, *Robert E. Lee and the Southern Confederacy, 1807–1870* (New York: Haskell House, 1968), 200; Hotchkiss, *Make Me a Map*, 79; Douglas, *I Rode with Stonewall*, 148–49. There is evidence that Lee did not remain entirely confined to his tent. Douglas reported taking his mother to meet the general. Lt. William Owen got up a party of locals and was received by Lee. Owen, *In Camp and Battle*, 130–31. Pvt. James Power Smith recalled dining with the Confederate commander in a private home in Frederick in *With Stonewall Jackson in the Army of Northern Virginia* (Gaithersburg, Md.: Zullo and Van Sickle Books, 1982), 16.

83. General Orders, No. 103, Hdqrtrs. Army of Northern Virginia, Sept. 6, 1862, *OR*, vol. 19, 2:596. These orders do not include the hour or location in their heading, but it is assumed Lee issued them in the afternoon after his arrival near Frederick, for the following reasons: (1) the observant Dr. Steiner mentions the announcing of a provost marshal in the afternoon (*Diary*, 162); and (2) the orders included information that may have been received by Lee after his arrival (see note 86).

84. *Baltimore Sun*, Sept. 4. On Lee's reading this paper, see note 25; on Stuart and the captured documents, see note 86. On the following day, September 7, Walter Taylor of Lee's staff would write to his sister: "The Yankee papers of the 6th exhibit a gloomy picture for our enemy. Just now it does appear as if God was truly with us. All along our lines the movement is onward. Ohio, Maryland, they expect to see invaded. We are here & I trust Kirby Smith will ere long shell Cincinnati." *Lee's Adjutant: The Wartime Letters of Colonel Walter Herron Taylor, 1862–1865*, ed. R. Lockwood Tower, with John S. Belmont (Columbia: Univ. of South Carolina Press, 1995), 43. This passage suggests something of what Lee might have known. Unfortunately, it is not possible to tell whether Taylor (or Lee) read the papers of September 6 on the 6th or the 7th. It does seem, however, as though Lee and those around him knew only of Kirby Smith's advance and not much about even that.

85. The conference occurred between Lee and Jackson alone, and nothing is known of their conversation. Douglas, *I Rode with Stonewall*, 148–49; and in "Maryland," 620.

86. Von Borcke, *Memoirs* 1:187–88; and see in *OR*, vol. 19, 1 Myer's (p. 118), Stuart's (p. 815), and Hampton's (p. 822) reports. What was in the courier's pouch is not known. Stuart described the contents as dispatches from Davis, but no letters from Davis to Lee after the one dated August 30 (which Lee received on September 4) have survived until the one dated the 7th. Moreover, Lee usually acknowledged receipt of letters from the president. The next day, however, Lee would mention only having received one dated the 1st from G. W. Smith. It is possible that in addition to this dispatch from Smith, the courier also delivered messages from the secretary of war and/or the adjutant general, including news of Kirby Smith's victory at Richmond, Kentucky, and possibly even some word on Bragg and Marshall. There is a highly romantic variation of this story provided by an anonymous member of the 2d South Carolina Cavalry of Hampton's brigade. According to this version, the courier from Richmond had somehow joined Stuart's column and been provided a one-man escort, perhaps as a guide. The two men had "incautiously" ridden ahead of the main body and been captured by the Federal signal party. The escort escaped and alerted Hampton's vanguard. A rescue squad was immediately dispatched and discovered the Federals had stopped to make a social call on a local farmer's daughter. Hence, the dispatches were retrieved. Brooks, *Stories of the Confederacy*, 78–79.

87. Gallagher, ed., *Lee the Soldier*, 7–8. Also after the war, Lee would recall the cavalry screen set up in this meeting as follows: "Stuart with his cavalry was close up to the enemy and doing everything possible to keep him in ignorance and to deceive him by false reports, which he industriously circulated." Ibid., 25–26. See also Fitzhugh Lee, *General Lee* (New York: D. Appleton, 1894), 201; and Alexander, *Fighting for the Confederacy*, 140. Von Borcke seems to suggest that Stuart established his screen on the 6th (*Memoirs* 1:191), but this is apparently contradicted by the reports in *OR*, vol. 19, 1 of Stuart (p. 815), Hampton (p. 822), and Munford (p. 825).

88. This summary of Federal activities is from McClellan's report, *OR*, vol. 19, 1:38–39; and the correspondence in ibid., 2:189–99; and ibid., vol. 51, 1:790–96.

3. "In this I was disappointed": Lee Revises His Strategy, September 7–9, 1862

1. Latrobe, Diary, Sept. 7. Barksdale's brigade, apparently the tail of the column, had stopped short of Buckeystown, and a member recorded marching nine miles to reach Monocacy Junction. Hubbert, "Diary," 307.

2. McRae's report in *Supplement to the Official Records of the Union and Confederate Armies*, ed. Janet B. Hewitt, et al., est. 100 vols. (Wilmington, N.C.: Broadfoot Publishing, 1994–), 3:573 (hereafter cited as *SOR*); also Nunnally in Austin, *Georgia Boys*, 50; and Neese, *Three Years in the Horse Artillery*, 113.

3. Caldwell, *History of a Brigade of South Carolinians*, 69; G. Wise, *History of the Seventeenth Va.*, 110; D. R. Jones's report, *OR*, vol. 19, 1:885; Leach, Diary, Sept. 7; Haynes, *Diary*, 16.

4. Pender to wife, Sept. 7, Pender, *The General to His Wife*, 172; Lang to cousin, Sept. 7, David Lang, "Civil War Letters of Colonel David Lang," ed. Bertram H. Groene, *Florida Historical Quarterly* 54 (1976): 343; Hotchkiss to wife, Sept. 8, Hotchkiss Papers; Chamberlayne to mother, Sept. 6, Chamberlayne, *Letters*, 103; Nunnally in Austin, *Georgia Boys*, 50.

5. Owen, *In Camp and Battle*, 131–32; Charles Winder Squires, "'Boy Officer' of the Washington Artillery—Part I," *Civil War Times Illustrated* 14 (May 1975): 17. This latter should be checked against the original memoirs in the W. H. T. Squires Papers, Southern Historical Collection, University of North Carolina, Chapel Hill.

6. Lee to Davis, Sept. 7, *OR*, vol. 19, 2:596–97.

7. Walker, "Harper's Ferry," 604; and Waddill, *North Carolina Regiments* 3:67. Much light is shed on the obscure movements of Walker's division by Hirsch, Diary, Sept. 6, 7, 8. On G. B. Anderson's brigade, see Shinn, Diary, Sept. 7.

8. Pendleton to wife, Sept. 10, S. P. Lee, *Memoirs*, 211; and report in *OR*, vol. 19, 1:829. The usually reliable adjutant of the Washington Artillery, William Owen, recorded in his diary that Walton's battalion crossed the Potomac on the 7th (*In Camp and Battle*, 131). It is assumed Lee's battalion may have been with them.

9. For testimony on the rich provisions in Maryland and the resourceful methods of the soldiers, see Owen, *In Camp and Battle*, 131; Early, *War Memoirs*, 135; Dickert, *History of Kershaw's Brigade*, 151–52; J. P. Smith, *With Stonewall Jackson*, 16; E. A. Moore, *The Story of a Cannoneer*, 132–33, who met many of his friends in Frederick; Alexander, *Fighting for the Confederacy*, 139; S. P. Lee, *Memoirs*, 211; Lang to cousin, Sept. 7, Lang, "Letters," 343; Poague, *Gunner with Stonewall*, 41–42; Thompson to parents, Oct. 1, Austin, *Georgia Boys*, 52. On the "nice lot of champagne in Maryland and cheap," see Longstreet to J. E. Johnston, Longstreet Papers, Duke University, Durham; also see Owen, ibid. Alexander Hunter, who has often been quoted on the scarcity of food in the army, referred primarily to the closing days of the Second Manassas campaign and confessed, "we fared better in the rich fields of Maryland" ("Sharpsburg," 507–8).

10. Alexander, *Fighting for the Confederacy*, 139–40; Hunter, "Sharpsburg," 509; Sheeran, *Confederate Chaplain*, 28–30; Steiner, *Diary*, 11–13; E. A. Moore, *Story of a Cannoneer*, 130–37; Pender, *The General to His Wife*, 172–74; Duncan, "Marylanders," 185–86; Hotchkiss to wife, Sept. 8, and to brother, Sept. 28, Hotchkiss Papers.

11. On the following day Jed. Hotchkiss would observe, "our line of couriers is not fully established." Letter to wife, Sept. 8, Hotchkiss Papers.

12. Not too much weight can be put on this last point, however, since it is not known at what hour Lee dictated the dispatch. He may have learned of the skirmish later in the day.

13. Von Borcke, *Memoirs* 1:191–92; and Blackford, *War Years with Jeb Stuart*, 140.

14. In *OR*, vol. 19, 1 see the reports of Stuart (p. 815), Hampton (p. 822), and Munford (p. 825); also, Pleasonton to Marcy, Sept. 7, ibid., 2:201; Neese, *Three Years in the Horse Artillery*, 113; Brooks, *Stories of the Confederacy*, 81; and H. B. McClellan, *I Rode with Jeb Stuart*, 110, who mistakenly puts Munford at Poolesville on the 7th.

15. Lee to Randolph, Sept. 7, *OR*, vol. 19, 2:139–40.

16. Part of Funk's report may be found in Harmon to Cooper, Sept. 5, ibid., 594. What Funk was doing in the vicinity of Winchester is unclear. So far as is known, his regiment had not been detached from the Stonewall brigade in which it served. Lee's enclosure, which was noted as not found by the compilers of the *OR*, may have been White to Halleck, Sept. 3, ibid., vol. 12, 2:768.

17. Lee to G. W. Smith, Sept. 7, ibid., vol. 19, 2:599.

18. Lee to Davis, Sept. 7, ibid., 597–98. It should be noted in passing that the Federals faced equally severe problems with straggling. On September 9 McClellan would issue lengthy orders using language very similar to Lee's—including the accusation of cowardice—to attempt to correct the evil. See General Orders, No. 155, Hdqtrs. Army of the Potomac, Camp near Rockville, Md., Sept. 9, 1862, ibid., 226–27.

19. Pender to wife, Sept. 28, 19 (in sequence quoted), Pender, *The General to His Wife*, 179, 175–76.

20. G. Wise, *History of the Seventeenth Va.*, 115–16. A classic story that provides insight into the straggling problem is related by John Casler of the 33d Virginia of the Stonewall brigade. In December 1862, while returning from an AWOL visit to Winchester, Casler encountered a two-man detail from his company on a mission to recover eight deserters from their ranks. The "absentees were all good soldiers, but they were tired of the infantry." When tracked down at their homes, the men said they would return only if guaranteed a transfer to the cavalry. Casler, incidentally, was himself absent for two weeks on this jaunt without the knowledge of the officers of his regiment. See John Overton Casler, *Four Years in the Stonewall Brigade* (Dayton, Ohio: Morningside Bookshop, 1971), 119–20.

21. The seemingly wild Bragg story probably derived from the fact that the Army of Mississippi was now on the move in eastern Tennessee and its destination was unknown. It should also be remembered that just four days earlier Lee had reported to Davis that a portion of Buell's troops were in Washington. Once again, the presence of railroads made possibilities uncertain.

22. Federal movements for September 7 have been summarized from reports of Halleck (p. 4) and McClellan (pp. 38–39) in *OR*, vol. 19, 1, and the correspondence in ibid., 2:199–209; ibid., vol. 51, 1:796–99; and ibid., vol. 16, 2:495–97, 500.

23. Lee to Davis, Sept. 8, ibid., vol. 19, 2:600–601.

24. Hirsch, Diary, Sept. 7, 8. There is a possibility that some of Walker's regiments did not cross the Potomac until the 8th. Graham, *North Carolina Regiments* 2:431. On Walker's version of his reporting to Lee, see this chapter, below.

25. Pendleton's report, *OR*, vol. 19, 1:829; and Cutts to Pendleton, with enclosure from Chilton, Sept. 8, ibid., 2:599–600. Cutts would remain with Hill throughout the campaign, including the battle at Sharpsburg.

26. Hotchkiss, *Make Me a Map*, 79–80; G. Wise, *History of the Seventeenth Va.*, 110; and Owen, *In Camp and Battle*, 131–32. Wise places the destruction on the 9th, but Owen and Hotchkiss (who is the most careful of the three) give the 8th. Details of the repair are from the B&O Railroad's Annual Report, cited in Duncan, "Marylanders," 193.

27. Federal activities are summarized from McClellan's report, *OR*, vol. 19, 1:39–40; and correspondence in ibid., 2:207–18, vol. 51, 1:799–800; and unpublished documents in the McClellan Papers, Library of Congress, Washington, D.C. The figures for the Army of the Potomac are a rough estimate of the number of present for duty.

28. In addition to the sources in note 27 above, see Pleasonton's report, *OR*, vol. 19, 1:208.

29. In ibid. see the reports of Stuart (p. 815) and Hampton (p. 822); see also, Barringer, *North Carolina Regiments* 1:421; von Borcke, *Memoirs* 1:193–97; and Blackford, *War Years with Jeb Stuart*, 140–42. Blackford gives September 11 as the day of the ball; but as this is patently too late, von Borcke's date has been followed. This particular attack, of course, came too late for Lee to have learned about it before he wrote to Davis.

30. Munford's report, *OR*, vol. 19, 1:825; H. B. McClellan, *I Rode with Jeb Stuart*, 110–11; and Neese, *Three Years in the Horse Artillery*, 113–16. The 6th Virginia was still at Gainesville and the 17th Virginia Battalion on detached service. The 7th Virginia was at Urbana, however, and it is not clear why it did not accompany Munford on his mission.

31. Chilton to Cooper, Sept. 8, *OR*, vol. 19, 2:601.

32. It might be argued that Lee composed a bland report to avoid causing Davis undue concern. Yet, although the Confederate commander sometimes omitted details for the sake of security, he was not wont to sugarcoat his news. He had certainly pulled no punches in his blunt dispatch of the previous day on the serious results of straggling.

33. Lee to Davis, Sept. 12, 13, ibid., 604–5, 605–6.

34. Proclamation to Marylanders, ibid., 1:601–2; see also Douglas, *I Rode with Stonewall*, 150–51; Long, *Memoirs of Robert E. Lee*, 207–9. No reference to the proclamation by Marshall has been found. That Jefferson Davis was in error in believing Lee issued the document in response to the president's own suggestion is discussed below. Porter Alexander's (*Military Memoirs of a Confederate*, 225) assertion that Lee came to see himself as deliverer of Maryland—and determined to stand at Sharpsburg in part for this reason—is discounted in light of (1) the conference with Bradley Johnson on the 4th, (2) Lee's restrained language in regard to Maryland in subsequent dispatches to Davis, and (3) the realistic tone of the proclamation itself.

35. Johnson's proclamation may be found in Clement A. Evans, ed., *Confederate Military History: A Library of Confederate States History*, 12 vols. (Atlanta: Confederate Publishing, 1899), 2:90–91; Steiner, *Diary*, 14–15; or a slightly variant version in the *Washington Daily National Intelligencer*, Sept. 13. For the proclamation issued by Maryland governor Augustus Bradford also on the 8th, see ibid., Sept. 10. The pronouncements of White and Heard are in Steiner, *Diary*, 16–17. It should be noted that the closing paragraph of Lee's proclamation echoed the resolution of the Confederate Congress of December 1861, which declared that no peace should be reached until Marylanders had the chance to decide freely their own fate. Johnson's proclamation specifically refers to that congressional resolution and settles the question as to whether Confederate military leaders were aware of it.

36. Evans, ed., *Confederate Military History* 2:87–91; Special Orders, No. 186, Adj. and Insp. General's Office, Richmond, Aug. 11, *OR*, ser. 4, vol. 2:42; Steiner, *Diary*, 12–13; Hotchkiss, *Make Me a Map*, 79; and for the numbers of volunteers, Duncan, "Marylanders," 188–89. For further discussion of Confederate recruitment of Marylanders see Harsh, *Sounding the Shallows*, chap. 6, sect. F.

37. Lee to Davis, Sept. 8, *OR*, vol. 19, 2:600. No response by the president is known. The rapid and unsuccessful conclusion of the campaign rendered Lee's proposal moot.

38. For Lee's views on foreign intervention see Harsh, *Confederate Tide Rising*, 57, 186–87; and idem, *Sounding the Shallows*, chap. 5, sect. G. It was Bradley Johnson, while in the process of trying to deflect criticism from Marylanders for their cool response, who attempted to show there were other grand results that might have flowed from the Maryland campaign. He made an effort, moreover, to demonstrate that foreign question shaped Lee's strategy. Johnson, "Maryland," 505. Careful historians, such as D. S. Freeman, have avoided implying Lee had foreign affairs in mind when he crossed the Potomac.

39. Latrobe, Diary, Sept. 7; Leach, Diary, Sept. 7; Hubbert, "Diary," 307; and Harvey Judson Hightower, "Letters from . . . A Confederate Soldier, 1862–1864," ed. Dewey W. Grantham, Jr., *Georgia Historical Quarterly* 40 (1956): 177.

40. Lee to Davis, Sept. 9, 1862, *OR*, vol. 19, 2:602. The reasoning adopted for the presumed sequence of Lee's writings and meetings for the day will be discussed as each occurs. This dispatch is placed first, simply because there are reasons to believe the other events happened afterward; and it is given a relatively early hour to allow time for the many other events to transpire.

41. I transposed the fourth and fifth sentences of Lee's dispatch to allow for a better continuity of discussion.

42. Steiner, *Diary*, 12–19; Hubbert, "Diary," 307; Cooke, *Jackson*, 310–12; and Duncan, "Marylanders," 185–87, where it is noted that the merchants with patience got partial reimbursement the following spring, when speculators bought up the Confederate scrip at forty cents on the dollar.

43. This estimate is present for duty, the appropriate category in this case, since all present ate whether or not they were combat effectives. About 5,500 has been deducted from the September 1 estimate based on trimonthly returns. This is a generous deduction, considering the easy marches since that date and the three to four days rest (depending on the unit) at Frederick. It also should be noted that several thousand recruits from North Carolina joined the army at that latter city. Figures are based on Allen, "Second Manassas Strengths," 186.

44. *Washington Daily National Intelligencer*, *Washington Star*, *Baltimore Sun*, and *Baltimore American*, all for Sept. 8 and 9.

45. Lee to Davis, Sept. 9, *OR*, 19, 2:602–3. It is assumed this dispatch was the second of the two to Davis: because, (1) had Lee known of the letter from Davis when he first wrote, there would have been no need for a second dispatch; and (2) Lee's brief discussion of strategy herein seems to be an elaboration of his remarks in the other dispatch (e.g., he does not feel it necessary to explain that scanty supplies in the Frederick area are behind his move toward Hagerstown).

46. *Papers of Jefferson Davis* 8:389n.1.

47. Davis to John Forsyth, July 18, 1862, ibid. 8:295. Secretary of War George Randolph would, of course, have had access to the same current information available to Davis. But having joined the cabinet in March 1862, Randolph could not have possessed the same historical perspective as the president, who had been pressing aggressive strategies since the decision to open fire on Sumter.

48. Davis to Lee, Sept. 7[?], *OR*, vol. 19, 2:598–99. For further discussion of the dating of this letter see Harsh, *Sounding the Shallows*, chap. 6, sect. G. The belief that Lee, in spite of his politeness, did not want Davis to visit the army is shared by the president's latest biographer in a recent essay. See William C. Davis, "Lee and Jefferson Davis," in Gallagher, ed., *Lee the Soldier*, 296–97; although the story is told without such an interpretation in Davis's *Jefferson Davis: The Man and His Hour* (New York: Harper Collins Publishers, 1991), 468–69.

49. Walker's memoir first appeared as an article in *Century Magazine* 32 (1886): 296–308, and was later reprinted in *B&L* 2:604–11. Walker's report, written on October 7, 1862, was published in *OR*, vol. 19, 1:912–14, but not until 1887, and it is possible he did not have a copy for reference. On the other hand, the report was also printed in *Our Living, Our Dead* 1 (1874–75): 225–28, and presumably submitted by Walker himself.

50. Hirsch, Diary, Sept. 7, 8, 9, 10; and Walker's report, *OR*, vol. 19, 1:912.

51. Hill, "Lost Dispatch," 274.

52. The mission is confirmed in S.O. 191, *OR*, vol. 19, 2:604; Hirsch, Diary, Sept. 9, 10; Graham, *North Carolina Regiments* 2:431; Burgwyn, ibid., 601; Waddill, ibid. 3:67; and Walker's report, *OR*, vol. 19, 1:912–13. Remember that D. H. Hill had tried unsuccessfully to destroy the aqueduct on September 4–5.

53. Walker's report, *OR*, vol. 19, 1:913. Hirsch, Diary, Sept. 10, suggests that a portion of Walker's division actually started north on the march back to Frederick before being halted and turned south toward the Potomac. For an excerpt from Walker's report that contradicts his later article, see Harsh, *Sounding the Shallows*, chap. 6, sect. H.

54. LaFayette McLaws, "The Maryland Campaign," in *ACVAS* 3:5.

55. Lee to Davis, Sept. 7, *OR*, vol. 19, 2:596–97. The reference to orders is to S.O. 191, analyzed in detail below.

56. Lee to Davis, Sept. 12, and two dispatches of the 9th, in *OR*, vol. 19, 2:604–5, 602–3.

57. Lee to Davis, Sept. 7, ibid., 597–98.

58. Chilton to Cooper, Sept. 8, ibid., 601.

59. Gallagher, ed., *Lee the Soldier*, 8, 26.

60. It is tempting to speculate that Walker at this point superimposed knowledge he gained after the war about the Pennsylvania campaign of 1863.

61. Lee's report, *OR*, vol. 19, 1:145; and Lee, "McDonald Letter," 445.

62. Eighteen years after a conversation with Lee, Rev. Edward C. Gordon recalled, "the estimate he gave me of Gen. McClellan—the substance of which was that he was an able but timid commander." Freeman, *Lee's Lieutenants* 2:716–17. It should be noted that in a memorandum taken down the day of the conversation, however, "caution" is the word Gordon has Lee use to describe movements of the Federal army. Gallagher, ed., *Lee the Soldier*, 25. On Lee's reliance on the demoralization and disorganization of the Federal army, see Lee to Davis, Sept. 3, *OR*, vol. 19, 2:590; and Gallagher, ed. *Lee the Soldier*, 8, 26. Also, it should be noted that in his conversations and letters of 1868, Lee frequently refers to McClellan and McClellan's army and makes no reference to when or how he learned who the Federal commander in the campaign would be. In his correspondence at the time, however, he makes no mention of McClellan; and even in his report written ten months later, he does not name McClellan, until discussing events of September 13. *OR*, vol. 19, 1:146.

63. Longstreet's book appeared in 1896, Taylor's in 1906, Alexander's in 1907, and Allan's posthumously in 1892. Long's memoir appeared in 1886, the same year as Walker's article; and Marshall's only comments specifically on the Maryland campaign were written in 1877.

64. Letters from Johnson and Douglas, "Stonewall Jackson's Intentions at Harper's Ferry," *B&L* 2:615–18. The substance of the controversy will be discussed below.

65. Freeman, *R. E. Lee* 2:359–61, n. 46. It is possible that Freeman himself came to have some doubts, as in 1943 he would write: "If Lee's hopes were correctly set forth in J. G. Walker's account of an interview." *Lee's Lieutenants* 2:160n.30.

66. W. C. Davis, ed., *Confederate General* 6:89; and Special Orders, No. 264, Adj. and Inspector General's Office, Richmond, Va., Nov. 11, 1862, *OR*, vol. 14:679.

67. Both quotes from Lee to Davis, Sept. 12, *OR*, vol. 19, 2:604–5. Lee would write much the same thing in his report ten months later: "It had been supposed that the advance upon Fredericktown would lead to the evacuation of Martinsburg and Harpers Ferry, thus opening the line of communication through the Valley." Ibid., 1:145.

68. For a discussion of Lee's knowledge on the situation at Harpers Ferry, see Harsh, *Sounding the Shallows*, chap. 6, sect. I.

69. See Franklin McIntosh Myers, *The Comanches, A History of White's Battalion, Virginia Cavalry* (Baltimore: Kelly, Piet, 1871), 107–9, where it is stated White remained near Harpers Ferry until the 12th, when he retired east to Waterford in Loudoun County. John Walker

would report, however, the presence of White's company at the foot of Loudoun Heights on the morning of September 13 with the signal party from Jackson, raising the possibility that White remained to cooperate with Jackson for several days. See Walker, "Harper's Ferry," 608.

70. Gallagher, ed., *Lee the Soldier*, 13; and Lee to Davis, Sept. 12, *OR*, vol. 19, 2:605.

71. As related above, John Walker alleged that Jackson arrived near the end of his own interview with Lee and that his two seniors soon "turned to the subject of the capture of Harpers Ferry." Also, still according to Walker, Jackson accepted the assignment enthusiastically, swapping pleasantries with Lee about revisiting his "friends" in the Valley. If indeed Walker were present at the start of the war council, and if there were any discussion of Harper's Ferry in his presence, it must have been of a very general nature and probably limited to a recognition that the Federal garrisons posed a threat that must be resolved. After all, it will be recalled, in about twelve hours Walker would demonstrate his ignorance of the Harpers Ferry expedition by deciding to abandon his attempt to destroy the aqueduct and join the army on its supposed march to Hagerstown. See Walker, "Harper's Ferry," 606.

72. Hotchkiss, *Make Me a Map*, 80; D. H. Hill to Dabney, July 21, 1864, Robert L. Dabney Papers, cited in Hal Bridges, *Lee's Maverick General, Daniel Harvey Hill* (New York: McGraw Hill, 1961), 161n.40; also Robert Lewis Dabney, *Life and Campaigns of Lieut.-Gen. Thomas J. Jackson (Stonewall Jackson)* (New York: Blelock, 1866), 549.

73. Longstreet remembered he found the two generals discussing the expedition, and "both heartily approving it." Since he entered the meeting at nearly its closing, however, this is not proof Jackson had not initially entered objections. Longstreet, "Maryland," 663.

74. Lee's report, *OR*, vol. 19, 1:145; Gallagher, ed., *Lee the Soldier*, 8, 25; and Robert Edward Lee, "A Lee Letter on the 'Lost Dispatch,' and the Maryland Campaign of 1862," ed. Hal Bridges, *Virginia Magazine of History and Biography* 66 (1958): 165. (In these postwar recollections Lee's memory telescopes events, and he specifies McClellan as his opponent.) A member of Stuart's staff would write on the following day: "The main body of the enemy is about 10 miles from Washington at a place called Rockville, which they are fortifying rapidly." Price to mother, Sept. 10, Trout, *With Pen and Saber*, 97. If this is a reflection of Stuart's views, it explains why Lee believed there would be ample time to clear the Valley.

75. McLaws, "The Maryland Campaign," 5.

76. Lee's report, *OR*, vol. 19, 1:145; Lee, "D. H. Hill Letter," 164; Lee, "McDonald Letter," 445.

77. Gallagher, ed., *Lee the Soldier*, 8. In a later conversation Lee also said: "to capture the detached force at Harpers Ferry was the object of his movement then." Still, the reference is to the Federal force and not the place. Ibid., 13.

78. As the first Confederate commander at Harpers Ferry, Jackson had even prematurely violated Maryland soil to occupy the heights. See the correspondence between Lee and Jackson in Lee, *Wartime Papers*, 17–29, passim.

79. These underlying assumptions have been intuited from S.O. 191 themselves and from Longstreet's elucidation of them. The quotation is from Longstreet, "Maryland," 663. After the war, LaFayette McLaws would assert: "It is evident from the whole tenor of the order that little, if any delay, was contemplated at Harper's Ferry; certainly a siege was not in the programme." McLaws, "The Maryland Campaign," 7.

80. Longstreet gave two slightly varying accounts of his participation in the conference in "Maryland," 663, and later in *From Manassas to Appomattox*, 202–3. In his earlier version, Longstreet stated vaguely that the conference occurred "a day or two" after reaching Frederick, and only in the account farther removed from the event did he seem to imply the improbable date of the 7th. In all other respects, the version in *Battles and Leaders*, although brief, has the sharper details of the two.

81. Longstreet would write: "My suggestion upon finding that he and Jackson were bent on the surrender of Harper's Ferry, was that he should use his entire army in the affair."

Longstreet to D. H. Hill, June 6, 1885, D. H. Hill Papers, Library of Virginia. On Lee's thinking see Gallagher, ed., *Lee the Soldier*, 8; and Lee, "D. H. Hill Letter," 165.

82. McLaws, "The Maryland Campaign," 5–6.

83. These figures are all present for duty and have been rounded down slightly from those of September 1 to allow for straggling in the interim and the arrival of conscripts at Frederick. Allen, "Second Manassas Strengths," 186.

84. For a discussion of the number and fate of copies of S.O. 191, see Harsh, *Sounding the Shallows*, chap. 6, sect. J.

85. This copy is in "Orders and Circulars Issued by the Army of the Potomac and the Army and Department of Northern Virginia, C.S.A., 1861–1865," RG-109. It is inked with the round stamp "Printed War Records, 1861–1865." It is merely a reasonable assumption that this copy was originally the one mentioned by Lee as being included in the dispatch to Davis of September 12 (*OR*, vol. 19, 2:605), which Davis then sent to Adj. Gen. Samuel Cooper. If not, if separate copies were sent to both Davis and Cooper, then Harsh, *Sounding the Shallows*, chap. 6, sect. J, needs to be amended to read ten copies.

86. In ser. 1, vol. 79, McClellan Papers, Library of Congress, with envelope bearing the inscription: "This is the original order found and on which McC. was able to plan his movements to South Mt. & Antietam." The signature, "W. C. P.," indicates William C. Prime, editor of *McClellan's Own Story* (New York: Charles L. Webster, 1887).

87. D. H. Hill Personal Papers, North Carolina State Archives, Raleigh, where the copy—with Morrison's certification written along the margin—is kept in the vault. There is a photocopy in the D.H. Hill Papers, Southern Historical Collection. Hill's most extensive comments on this topic are in his "Lost Dispatch"; but see also "Address of General D.H. Hill," in *SHSP* 13 (1885): 269; "The Battle of South Mountain, or Boonsboro': Fighting for Time at Turner's and Fox's Gaps," *B&L* 2:567; and D. H. Hill to Longstreet, Feb. 11, 1885, Longstreet Papers, Duke University, Durham, North Carolina.

88. Gallagher, ed., *Lee the Soldier*, 8; Chilton to Davis, Dec. 7, 8, 1874, *Jefferson Davis, Constitutionalist: His Letters, Papers, and Speeches*, ed. Dunbar Rowland, 10 vols. (Jackson: Mississippi Department of Archives and History, 1923), 7:409–12; Chilton to D. H. Hill, June 22, 1867, D. H. Hill Personal Papers, North Carolina State Archives; Venable and Taylor in Walter Herron Taylor, *Four Years with General Lee* (Bloomington: Indiana Univ. Press, 1962), 66–67. And also Marshall to D. H. Hill, Nov. 11, 1867, and Chilton to D. H. Hill, Jan. 1, 1868, both in D. H. Hill Papers, Library of Virginia.

89. Longstreet, *From Manassas to Appomattox*, 213; and Walker, "Harper's Ferry," 607.

90. Chilton to Davis, Dec. 7, 8, 1874, Rowland, ed., *Jefferson Davis* 7:409–12; and Gallagher, ed., *Lee the Soldier*, 26. The spy theory was advanced by D. H. Hill and his adjutant J. M. Ratchford, see Bridges, *Lee's Maverick General*, 97–98. The plausibility of the theory was buttressed by Ratchford's recollection that "a spy acting as a Confederate courier was discovered near Harper's Ferry and was at once hung to a limb of a tree on the road side." See J. M. Ratchford, Memoir, 36, in D.H. Hill, Jr., Personal Papers, North Carolina State Archives. Since Ratchford could not have witnessed firsthand an event at Harpers Ferry and offers no corroboration, this story may be no more than thirty-year-old army scuttlebutt. Interestingly, Osmun Latrobe of D.R. Jones's staff recorded in his diary for August 20: "Marched through Stevensburg, Hung a spy on the Road" (Latrobe, Diary). On the one hand, this proves such things did happen; on the other, it might be the very incident the army was still talking about and Ratchford remembered being discussed. At the time Ratchford would have been at Hanover Junction.

91. Location of Hill's headquarters is from A. C. Avery, "Memorial Address on the Life and Character of Lieut.-Gen. D.H. Hill," *SHSP* 21 (1893): 136. The location of the finding of the orders is from Richard C. Datzman, "Who Found Lee's Lost Dispatch," Lost Orders

File, Antietam National Battlefield Library, Sharpsburg, Maryland. On Hill's activities on September 10, see chapter 4.

92. *OR*, vol. 19, 2:603–4.

93. Douglas, *I Rode with Stonewall*, 150.

94. R. Channing Price of Stuart's staff, in a letter to his mother dated September 10, gave an explanation from the ranks of the Frederick merchants' change of heart: "There is an abundance of everything in Frederick & some who went up Saturday evening [6th] got anything they wanted, boots, clothing, hats etc. Monday & yesterday [8th and 9th] on account of difficulty of money or as some say because our Quarter Master had pressed everything, it was difficult to find a store open." Trout, *With Pen and Saber*, 96–97.

95. Taylor, *General Lee*, 125n; see also Harrison Family Memoirs, 2, Loudoun Museum.

96. Taylor to Davis, Sept. 10, *OR*, vol. 51, 2:617.

97. Murfin, *Gleam of Bayonets*, 331, claims that Lee sent just the first two articles to Cooper on September 16; however, then he cites the Lee-DNA copy, which is a complete version of all ten articles.

98. Taylor, *General Lee*, 120–21; quote is from Taylor, *Letters*, 43–44.

99. Paxton to Branch, Sept. 10, *OR*, vol. 19, 2:604; and Sorrel, Circular, Headquarters Right Wing, Sept. 9, ibid., vol. 51, 2:616. Sunrise for September 10 was 5:44 A.M., according to John Gruber, *J. Gruber's Hagers-town Town and Country Almanack for the Year of Our Lord 1862* (Hagerstown: John Gruber, 1861).

100. *OR*, vol. 19, 1:145.

101. D. H. Hill, "Lost Dispatch," 277, 278.

102. Gallagher, ed., *Lee the Soldier*, 26–27.

103. Ibid., 8. When Lee wrote to D. H. Hill a week later, he tempered his anger and stated simply: "when it became necessary to dislodge the Federal troops occupying Martinsburg and Harper's Ferry, he was by verbal instructions placed in command of the expedition." Lee, "Hill Letter," 164.

104. Lee to Davis, Sept. 12, *OR*, vol. 19, 2:605.

105. McLaws's report, ibid., 1:852.

106. Hirsch, Diary, Sept. 9; and Walker, "Harper's Ferry," 606.

107. Allen, "Second Manassas Strengths," 201–2. Munford was absent the 6th Virginia Cavalry, the 17th Virginia Cavalry battalion and probably a portion of the 12th Virginia Cavalry. See Munford's report, *OR*, vol. 19, 1:825.

108. Taylor, *General Lee*, 125n.

109. The details of the McLaws-Lee conference are from McLaws, "The Maryland Campaign," 5–6. There is also an outline memorandum—briefer and with no additional information—that may have been used in the preparation of the address in the McLaws Papers, Southern Historical Collection.

110. Unfortunately, this account is virtually verbatim from S.O. 191. Nonetheless, it suggests McLaws remembered Lee saying nothing that differed from the wording in the document.

111. The fact that Lee seriously underestimated the size of the Harpers Ferry garrison has not previously been suspected. McLaws's recollection of Lee's statement is supported by Jeb Stuart, who in his report, wrote: "Friday [Sept. 12], the day on which, by the calculation of the commanding general, Harper's Ferry would fall, had passed, and, as the garrison was not believed to be very strong at that point, I supposed the object already accomplished." *OR*, vol. 19, 1:816.

112. The details of the Anderson-Lee conference are from R. H. Anderson to D. H. Hill, Nov. 14, 1867, D. H. Hill Personal Papers, North Carolina State Archives.

113. The meetings with McLaws and Anderson might seem to lend credence to John Walker's claim that Lee explained the Harpers Ferry expedition to him earlier in the day. It

will be remembered, however, that Walker's report makes it clear he did not know of his part in the expedition until he received S.O. 191 late on the night of the 9th. It should also be pointed out that in the McLaws-Anderson meetings Lee spoke strictly on a need-to-know basis and did not engage in a discussion of the grand strategy of the campaign.

114. The only order to survive is a circular from Longstreet's headquarters setting the hour of departure for five the next morning. Its warning that "troops will be in readiness to move promptly at that hour" probably meant that rations were cooked on the night of the 9th. *OR*, vol. 51, 2:616. That Jackson issued orders the night before can be inferred from a correction sent out the following morning. Paxton to Branch, Sept. 10, ibid., vol. 19, 2:604.

115. Von Borcke, *Memoirs* 1:199. The official reports of Stuart, Hampton and Munford (no report from Fitz Lee for the campaign has been found) shed little light on September 9–11. Stuart's engineer, William Blackford, recalled in his memoirs, "It was the 11th of September before we were disturbed in our enjoyment of these scenes and pleasant associations at Urbana." Blackford, *War Years with Jeb Stuart*, 140.

116. Federal movements on the 9th have been summarized from *OR*, vol. 19, 1:39, 2:218–32, and vol. 51, 1:801–4.

4. "Intercept such as may attempt escape": Lee's Best-Laid Plans, September 10–12, 1862

1. Johnson, "Maryland," 513; Hotchkiss, *Make Me a Map*, 80; Evans, ed., *Confederate Military History* 3:339; Haynes, *Diary*, 16. The formation of marching by the side of the trains is confirmed by a survivor of the 6th North Carolina of Law's brigade in Neill Ray, "6th Regiment," *North Carolina Regiments* 1:306.

2. Lewis Henry Steiner (1827–1892) attended the University of Pennsylvania Medical School. He retired from the practice of medicine to teach chemistry at the Maryland College of Pharmacy and assist in editing the *American Medical Monthly*. He joined the U.S. Sanitary Commission in August 1861 and rose to become chief inspector for the Army of the Potomac and acting associate secretary of the Commission. He was in charge of the relief efforts after the Battle of Antietam. At the close of the war he headed the schoolboard for Frederick County and then served as the first librarian of the Enoch Pratt Free Library in Baltimore. See *The Papers of Frederick Law Olmstead*, ed. Jane Turner Censer, vol. 4 (Baltimore: Johns Hopkins Univ. Press, 1986), 144n.1.

3. Steiner, *Diary*, 19–20. For further scattered references to black servants traveling with the Army of Northern Virginia in the Maryland campaign, see Dinkins, *Recollections*, 53–54; idem, "Barksdale's Brigade," 264; Alexander, *Fighting for the Confederacy*, 127; N.S. Smith, "Additional Sketch Thirteenth Regiment," *North Carolina Regiments* 1:695; H.B. McClellan, *I Rode with Jeb Stuart*, 109; Dickert, *History of Kershaw*, 151–52; Scates, "Civil War Diary," 14; Sheeran, *Confederate Chaplain*, 20; Hotchkiss, *Make Me a Map*, 82; Hotchkiss to wife, Sept. 17, and to brother, Sept. 28, Hotchkiss Papers; and Pender to wife, Sept. 25, Pender, *The General to His Wife*, 177–78.

4. Steiner, *Diary*, 20–21. For a discussion of Steiner's comments on the physical condition of the Confederates, see Harsh, *Sounding the Shallows*, chap. 7, sect. A.

5. Steiner, *Diary*, 19–20; Allen, "Second Manassas Strengths," 186. See chapter 1 (note 72) for a discussion of Confederate regimental strengths. Steiner's estimate was roughly supported by civilian Jacob Englebrecht, who noted in his diary, "the whole number [for the two days] at about seventy thousand." Schildt, *Roads to Antietam*, 41. Priest, *South Mountain*, 65, suggests that Lee deliberately marched his army through Frederick in columns of four in order to dupe "spies" into believing it was larger than it was. A more likely explanation, however, would be the narrowness of the streets. In any case, a careful observer such as Steiner—who counted regiment by regiment—was not likely to be fooled by such a ploy. Sixty-three

batteries should have passed before Steiner's scrutiny with approximately 280 cannon, which would make his 150 guns stamped "U.S." represent about half the total.

6. Steiner, *Diary*, 20; Early, "Barbara Frietchie," 437. It is evident that Barbara Frietchie, heroine of the John Greenleaf Whittier poem, did not confront Stonewall Jackson, but little else is certain about her story—whether she waved a flag on the 10th or not, whether she was bedridden or not, etc. On Frietchie see Douglas, *I Rode with Stonewall*, 151–52; idem, "Maryland," 622; George O. Seilheimer, "The Historical Basis of Whittier's 'Barbara Frietchie,'" *B&L* 2:618–19; John Greenleaf Whittier, "A Correction from Mr. Whittier," *Century Magazine* 32 (1886): 783; Johnson, "Maryland," 514–15; Valerius Ebert, "Letter from Mrs. Frietchie's Nephew," *SHSP* 7 (1879): 438–39; W. Gordon McCabe, "The Real Barbara Frietchie: Ninety-Six Years Old, Bedridden and Never Defied Stonewall Jackson," *SHSP* 27 (1899): 287–89; J. P. Smith, *With Stonewall*, 15; Alexander, *Fighting for the Confederacy*, 140; Sorrel, *Recollections of a Confederate Staff Officer*, 102–3; Murfin, *Gleam of Bayonets*, 118–19; Sears, *Landscape Turned Red*, 93; Schildt, *Roads to Antietam*, 41–42; and Priest, *South Mountain*, 61–62. Robert Michael Pennefather, "The Historical Investigation of Barbara Frietchie" (master's thesis, George Mason University, 1995), makes clear that, while the confrontation with Jackson almost certainly did not occur, there are strong arguments on both sides of the story of whether Frietchie waved the flag at the Confederates or not.

7. After recovering from a wound suffered in the Seven Days, Jones had rejoined the army several days earlier in Frederick and superseded William Starke, who returned to command of the Louisiana brigade.

8. Paxton to Branch, Sept. 10, *OR*, vol. 19, 2:604.

9. [Daniel T. Carraway,] "Lieutenant-General A. P. Hill: Some Reminiscences of the Famous Virginia Commander," *SHSP* 19 (1891): 180; Robertson, *A. P. Hill*, 134–35.

10. Poague, *Gunner with Stonewall*, 43.

11. Douglas first covered this incident in an article ("Maryland") for *Century Magazine* in June 1886 (later reprinted in *B&L* 2:622). He stated it somewhat differently in the memoirs he revised in the late 1890s but which were not published until 1940 as Douglas, *I Rode with Stonewall*, 151.

12. Douglas, *I Rode with Stonewall*, 151–52; and idem, "Maryland," 622.

13. Munford's report, *OR*, vol. 19, 1:825; William Naylor McDonald, *A History of the Laurel Brigade, Originally the Ashby Cavalry of the Army of Northern Virginia and Chew's Battery* (Baltimore: Sun Job Printing Office, 1907), 94; and Curtin to Halleck, 3:30 P.M., Sept. 10, *OR*, vol. 19, 2:247. It is not likely that Stuart would have increased the cavalry assigned to Jackson without Lee's approval. Since Longstreet would also receive a regiment (the 1st Virginia) instead of a squadron, it is probable that Lee decided overnight that he had provided insufficient cavalry for the expedition.

14. Caldwell, *The History of a Brigade of South Carolinians*, 69–70, who remembered the orders were read to the troops at their first rest.

15. Douglas, *I Rode with Stonewall*, 152; idem, "Maryland," 622; and Duncan, "Marylanders," 189.

16. Douglas, *I Rode with Stonewall*, 152; idem, "Maryland," 622; Early, *War Memoirs*, 135; idem, report in *OR*, vol. 19, 1:966; H. W. Thomas, *History of the Doles-Cook Brigade*, 221; Worsham, *One of Jackson's Foot Cavalry*, 83; Hotchkiss, *Make Me a Map*, 80; and Williams's report, *OR*, vol. 19, 1:1011, with its misdate of the 11th. A member of Gregg's South Carolina brigade remembered stopping "about three or four p. m." Being at the rear of the column, however, they would have started later and been subject to delays. Caldwell, *History of a Brigade of South Carolinians*, 70. It is possible that Thomas's brigade (A. P. Hill) continued forward and camped on South Mountain. See Haynes, *Diary*, 16–17.

17. In his report, Jackson covers his idleness during the remaining eight hours of daylight with the written equivalent of mumbling. He lumps together the marches of the 10th

and the 11th to take advantage of the greater progress on the latter day: "my command left the vicinity of Frederick City on the 10th, and, passing rapidly through Middletown, Boonsborough, and Williamsport, recrossed the Potomac into Virginia, at Light's Ford, on the 11th." *OR*, vol. 19, 1:953. Of course, in denying there was a delay, he offers no explanation of why there was one. That the road from Boonsboro to Williamsport was macadam is in Evans, ed., *Confederate Military History* 3:338.

18. Douglas, *I Rode with Stonewall*, 152.

19. For a discussion of the sources for Jackson's near capture, see Harsh, *Sounding the Shallows*, chap. 7, sect. B.

20. Quotes are from Steiner, *Diary*, 20; and Hotchkiss, *Make Me a Map*, 80. See also Hunter, "Sharpsburg," 508, and Longstreet, *From Manassas to Appomattox*, 205, who remember the rendition of the tune as "rollicking." According to a staff officer, D. R. Jones's division did not commence the march until 10:00 A.M. Latrobe, Diary, Sept. 10.

21. The bivouac of Longstreet's troops is confirmed in G. Wise, *History of the 17th Va.*, 110; Carman, "The Maryland Campaign," chap. 6, p. 314, and chap. 7, p. 373; Ramsay, *North Carolina Regiments* 1:573; Owen, *In Camp and Battle*, 135; and Latrobe, Diary, Sept. 10. In his 1890s memoirs, Longstreet would claim he passed through Turner's Gap and camped at the western base of South Mountain. Either he misremembered, or he continued on after his troops stopped and made headquarters near Jackson. See *From Manassas to Appomattox*, 206. The reports of both Longstreet and Lee treat Longstreet's march to Hagerstown as a continuum, making it impossible to distinguish the progress of a specific day; see *OR*, vol. 19, 1:839 (Longstreet) and 145 (Lee).

22. Freeman states flatly that Lee accompanied Longstreet, but he cites no supporting evidence, *R. E. Lee* 2:364.

23. Longstreet, *From Manassas to Appomattox*, 205.

24. Undated memorandum, McLaws Papers, Southern Historical Collection; McLaws, "Maryland," 7, where McLaws incorrectly states that he followed the army reserve trains, probably confusing them with Longstreet's reserve trains. See also, Hubbert, "Diary," 307; Wyckoff, *History of the 2nd S.C.*, 41; and Simpson, *Far, Far from Home*, 147. After the war, McLaws would imply this half-day delay was of great significance to the outcome of the expedition. This is open to serious doubt, however, in light of the way events transpired.

25. The official reports of McLaws and his subordinates are vague on the movements of this column prior to the morning of the 12th; *OR*, vol. 19, 1:852–85. Even McLaws's postwar memoir ("Maryland," 7) lacks detail: "On reaching Middletown we turned to the left, and, marching until after dark, camped for the night." Also ambiguous is Simpson, *Far, Far from Home*, 149. Evidence that McLaws passed through Burkittsville on the 10th and camped at the foot of the Brownsville Pass comes from Longstreet, although it is not clear how he would have known (*From Manassas to Appomattox*, 206), and the history of Kershaw's brigade, where the date is incorrectly given as the 11th (Dickert, *History of Kershaw's Brigade*, 147), and is confirmed in Carman, "Maryland Campaign," chap. 6, p. 345. Somewhat confusing the picture is the diary entry of Mike Hubbert, a soldier in the 13th Mississippi of Barksdale's brigade, which records that he reached Middletown at midnight and went into camp near there. Perhaps at this point Barksdale was bringing up the rear of the column. See Hubbert, "Diary," 307.

26. "Our cavalry captured five of the yankee Cavalry as they passed through Burketsville." See Hubbert, "Diary," 307. Which cavalry had been assigned to McLaws, or even whether he had received a regiment, as had Jackson and Longstreet, or merely the squadron specified in S.O. 191, is unknown.

27. Alexander, *Military Memoirs of a Confederate*, 228; idem, *Fighting for the Confederacy*, 142; and Pendleton's report, *OR*, vol. 19, 1:829; and Pendleton to his wife, Sept. 10, 13, S. P. Lee, *Memoirs*, 211–12. For a discussion of the size of the trains with the Army of Northern Virginia, see Harsh, *Sounding the Shallows*, chap. 7, sect. C.

28. The erroneous implication in the official reports—although nowhere clearly stated—is that the entire army, including D. H. Hill, marched through and left Frederick on the 10th. The quote is from Shinn, Diary, Sept. 10; see also Leach, Diary, Sept. 10; and the description of Hill's march through town on the 11th in Steiner, *Diary*, 21–22. The discovery that D. H. Hill did not pass through Frederick on the 10th but stopped in the southeastern outskirts is important for another reason. If he bivouacked for the night in the fork between the road from Monocacy Junction (Georgetown Turnpike) and the road from Ijamsville, which he probably did, then his headquarters would have been in the vicinity of the location where S.O. 191 would be found on the morning of the 13th.

29. In his postwar memoir, Walker does not mention his decision to return to Lee, possibly because it casts doubt on his alleged foreknowledge of the Harpers Ferry expedition. Walker, "Harper's Ferry," 606–7. In his more candid official report, he acknowledges being on the verge of marching when S.O. 191 arrive. *OR*, vol. 19, 1:912–13. It would appear, however, that a portion of his division had actually commenced the return march and was halted after several miles. See Graham, *North Carolina Regiments* 2:431–32; and Hirsch, Diary, Sept. 10, 11.

30. In addition to the sources in note 29 above, see Waddill, *North Carolina Regiments* 3:67.

31. Von Borcke, *Memoirs* 1:199; and Neese, *Three Years in the Confederate Horse Artillery*, 116. At least one member of Stuart's staff—who was at Urbana on the 10th—would not even be aware that the army was marching away from Frederick on that very day. Price to mother, Sept. 10, Trout, *With Pen and Saber*, 97.

32. Federal movements have been summarized from McClellan's report, *OR*, vol. 19, 1:42–43; and Federal correspondence in ibid., vol. 19, 2:232–52, and vol. 51, 1:805–13.

33. Caldwell, *History of a Brigade of South Carolinians*, 70; and Douglas, "Maryland," 623. Douglas is silent on how and when Jackson learned of the Martinsburg garrison.

34. Caldwell, *History of a Brigade of South Carolinians*, 70; and Worsham, *One of Jackson's Foot Cavalry*, 84.

35. The ford is described in Caldwell, *History of a Brigade of South Carolinians*, 70; and Neese, *Three Years in the Confederate Horse Artillery*, 124 (at a later crossing on September 15). See also Poague, *Gunner with Stonewall*, 43; Douglas *I Rode with Stonewall*, 155–56; idem, "Maryland," 623. Rain is mentioned in Hotchkiss, *Make Me a Map*, 80; and Hirsch, Diary, Sept. 11.

36. In *OR*, vol. 19, 1, see the reports of Jackson (p. 953), Early (p. 966), A. P. Hill (p. 980), and Williams (p. 1011). Also see, Hotchkiss, *Make Me a Map*, 80; Poague, *Gunner with Stonewall*, 43; Caldwell, *History of a Brigade of South Carolinians*, 70; Worsham, *One of Jackson's Foot Cavalry*, 84; Dabney, *Life and Campaigns of Jackson*, 551; Early, *War Memoirs*, 135–36; Douglas, *I Rode with Stonewall*, 156; H. W. Thomas, *History of the Doles-Cook Brigade*, 221–22; and Paxton to Branch, Sept. 11, *OR*, vol. 19, 2:604; and James Cooper Nisbet, *Four Years on the Firing Line* (Jackson, Tenn.: McCowat-Mercer Press, 1963), 101. Many years after the war, Henry Kyd Douglas would maintain that it was Jackson's object to drive the Martinsburg garrison back to Harpers Ferry and thus "corral" them along with the other Federal troops in "that military pen." See Douglas, "Maryland," 623. There is no contemporary evidence to support this notion, however, and the fact Jackson formed his line so far from Martinsburg suggests he hoped to catch the garrison, rather than drive them.

37. Haynes, *Diary*, 17.

38. Hotchkiss, *Make Me a Map*, 80.

39. G. Wise, *History of the 17th Va.*, 110; Owen, *In Camp and Battle*, 135–36.

40. The timing of Lee's decision to march on to Hagerstown is a conjecture based on: (1) Longstreet's known early arrival in Boonsboro; and (2) the fact that Longstreet's column marched only a short distance toward Hagerstown on the 11th. It is reasonable to assume that Lee spent some time in Boonsboro evaluating reports and reaching his decision. It is entirely

possible, however, that Lee changed his mind on the 10th and some other problem caused the lack of progress on the 11th.

41. Quote from Gallagher, ed., *Lee the Soldier*, 8. In his official report ten months later, Lee wrote: "A report having been received that a Federal force was approaching Hagerstown from the direction of Chambersburg, Longstreet continued his march to the former place, in order to secure the road leading thence to Williamsport, and also to prevent the removal of stores which were said to be in Hagerstown." *OR*, vol. 19, 1:145. No earlier contemporaneous reference to the Federal threat by Confederates has been discovered. After the war, Lee would twice refer to his decision to move on to Hagerstown and each time would mention only the allure of the supply of flour. See ibid., 8, 26. The Federals in the Chambersburg area were the vanguard of the Pennsylvania militia, which Governor Curtin had called out to repel the threatened invasion.

42. In his report Lee would write: "it had not been intended to oppose its [the Federal army's] passage through the South Mountains, as it was desired to engage it as far as possible from its base." *OR*, vol. 19, 1:145.

43. Latrobe, Diary, Sept. 11; Carman, "History of the Maryland Campaign," chap. 7, p. 373; Toombs's report, *OR*, vol. 19, 1:888; and G. Wise, *History of the 17th Va.*, 110, who suggests that the tail of the column may have stopped well short of Funkstown. For a charming, if somewhat romanticized, account of the Confederate occupation of Hagerstown, Leighton Parks, "What a Boy Saw of the Civil War—With Glimpses of General Lee," *Century Magazine* 70 (1905): 259–60.

44. For a discussion of D. H. Hill, that the trains of the "whole army remained with him at Boonsboro, see Harsh, *Sounding the Shallows*, chap. 7, sect. D.

45. Steiner, *Diary*, 21–22. While Hill would claim to have but 5,000 men at South Mountain three days later, the September 1 trimonthly estimate gives him 10,137 (including Cutts's artillery battalion) present for duty; Allen, "Second Manassas Strengths," 206, 209. Steiner estimated the division to number 8,000.

46. Nothing is to be learned of September 11 in Hill's postwar article, "South Mountain," 560, or in the reports of Hill and his subordinates, *OR*, vol. 19, 1:1019–52. However, see Shinn, Diary, Sept. 11, and Leach, Diary, Sept. 11, both in the Southern Historical Collection; and George Gorman, ed., "Memoirs of a Rebel, Part I," *Military Images* 3 (1981): 4, where the date is one day early.

47. McLaws, "Maryland," 7, 19.

48. This statement is based on the fact that Kershaw reported his brigade, as McLaws's lead unit, set out from Brownsville at the western foot of South Mountain on the morning of September 12. *OR*, vol. 19, 1:862. And a diarist in Barksdale's brigade, the rear unit, recorded marching ten miles to reach Brownsville. Hubbert, "Diary," 307–8. In his own report, McLaws makes the simple but enigmatic statement: "I reached the valley on the 11th." *OR*, vol. 19, 1:852.

49. Walker's report, *OR*, vol. 19, 1:913; and in "Harper's Ferry," 607; Waddill, *North Carolina Regiments* 3:67; and Hirsch, Diary, Sept. 11, 12.

50. Stuart's report, *OR*, vol. 19, 1:815.

51. Stuart's report, ibid. Unfortunately, no report for the Maryland campaign has been found from Fitzhugh Lee. Although he sometimes sheds light on his own cavalry operations in his biography of his uncle, he does not do so in this instance. See F. Lee, *General Lee*.

52. In *OR*, vol. 19, 1, see the reports of Stuart (p. 815) and Hampton (p. 822): see also von Borcke, *Memoirs* 1:199–200, who mistakenly reports Fitz Lee as passing through Urbana; and Brooks, *Stories of the Confederacy*, 81, where the anonymous author incorrectly states that Hampton did not leave Urbana until late afternoon.

53. In *OR*, vol. 19, 1, see the reports of Stuart (p. 815) and Munford (p. 825). The action is covered in detail in Neese, *Three Years in the Confederate Horse Artillery*, 116–17, and to a lesser

extent in von Borcke, *Memoirs* 1:200–201. In his report, Stuart ignores the skirmish and implies that Munford had left for Jefferson to cover the rear of McLaws, a movement that would not occur until the following day.

54. Lee to Stuart, 2:30 P.M., Sept. 12, James Ewell Brown Stuart Papers, Henry E. Huntington Library, San Marino, California.

55. Von Borcke, *Memoirs* 1:201–2.

56. Federal movements are summarized from McClellan's report, *OR*, vol. 19, 1:42; and the correspondence in ibid., 2:252–70 and vol. 51, 1:813–21.

57. This distribution is partly conjecture, although the positions of Jones, Ramsay's battery (Evans), the pickets, and the reserve trains are relatively certain. Lee's headquarters were outside of town, but they may have been with Jones on the Williamsport Road. See, in ibid., vol. 19, 1, the reports of Longstreet (p. 839) and Jones (p. 885); see also, Parks, "What a Boy Saw," 259; G. Wise, *History of the 17th Va.*, 110–11; Ramsay, *North Carolina Regiments* 1:573; Alexander, *Fighting for the Confederacy*, 142; Pendleton to wife, Sept. 13, S. P. Lee, *Memoirs*, 211; and Latrobe, Diary, Sept. 12. Interesting anecdotal accounts are in Tischler, *Harpers Ferry*, 92; and Priest, *South Mountain*, 86–88.

58. On Jackson, see Douglas, "Letter," 617; on McLaws, see Long to McLaws, Sept. 13, *OR*, vol. 19, 2:606. The lack of communication from Walker is conjectured on the basis of: (1) the absence of evidence of any such; (2) Walker's lack of cavalry; and (3) the fact that news from Walker would have had to travel the greatest and most convoluted distance to reach Lee.

59. Lee to Davis, *OR*, vol. 19, 2:604–5.

60. It might be noted that Lee enclosed a copy of S.O. 191 in this dispatch to Davis. For speculation on this copy as the lost orders, see Harsh, *Sounding the Shallows*, chap. 7, sect. E.

61. Washington County's 4.8 percent slave population was one-third less even than Frederick's (7 percent). See U.S. Census Bureau, Eighth Census, *Population of the United States in 1860*, 210–14.

62. Pendleton to wife, Sept. 13, S. P. Lee, *Memoirs*, 211–12. For a similar assessment of the citizens of Frederick, see Chamberlayne to sister, Sept. 8, Chamberlayne, *Letters*, 104–5.

63. Examples of both the generosity and the coolness may be found in Sears, *Landscape Turned Red*, 96–97; Ramsay, *North Carolina Regiments* 1:573; Austin, *Georgia Boys*, 50; and Owen, *In Camp and Battle*, 135. Only Alexander Hunter would remember the reception as warmer in Hagerstown than in Frederick; see Hunter, "Sharpsburg," 511.

64. Hagerstown, unlike Frederick, had time to prepare for its occupation and send away its bank specie, railroad cars, and the like. See Duncan, "Marylanders," 189–90.

65. See the tables in U.S. Census Bureau, *Agriculture of the United States in 1860*, 72–73.

66. G. Wise, *History of the 17th Va.*, 111; Owen, *In Camp and Battle*, 136; and Pendleton to wife, Sept. 13, S. P. Lee, *Memoirs*, 212.

67. Although it is reasonable to assume that by this time Lee had learned from Stuart or through Northern newspapers that McClellan was in command of the Army of the Potomac, there is no contemporary evidence to prove it. From this point forward in the text McClellan's name will be used synonymously with Army of the Potomac in Lee's thinking.

68. Orders and Circulars of the Army of Northern Virginia, RG-109, National Archives. For some reason the editors of the *OR* chose not to publish this circular.

69. In either case, the rush of events would deny Lee the information he sought until four days after he had returned to Virginia. See returns dated Sept. 22, *OR*, vol. 19, 2:621.

70. Gallagher, ed., *Lee the Soldier*, 26.

71. Ibid., 8.

72. Lee's report, *OR*, vol. 19, 1:145.

73. Carman, "Maryland Campaign," chap. 3, p. 315; *Richmond Dispatch*, Sept. 20, 1862; *Papers of Jefferson Davis* 8:381n.8, 389n.1; and Joab Goodson, "Letters of Captain Joab Goodson, 1862–64," ed. Stanley H. Hoole, *Alabama Review* 10 (1957): 130.

74. Lee to Stuart, Sept. 12, 2:30 P.M., Hagerstown, Stuart Papers. It is assumed that the untimed dispatch to Davis was written earlier, because it still locates the Federal garrison at Martinsburg.

75. See note 14 for evidence of orders on the rate of march. These may have been embodied in an unnumbered circular or in General Orders, No. 105 or 106, which have not been found. There are no gaps in the special orders in the collection in RG-109.

76. Hotchkiss, who would have been riding with the headquarters staff, implied in his diary that Jackson learned of White's evacuation after the Confederates were on the march the next morning. Hotchkiss, *Make Me a Map*, 80.

77. In *OR*, vol. 19, 1, see the reports of Jackson (p. 953) and A. P. Hill (p. 980); see also, Longstreet, *From Manassas to Appomattox*, 205–6; Caldwell, *History of a Brigade of South Carolinians*, 70; Hotchkiss, *Make Me a Map*, 80; Haynes, *Diary*, 18; and Worsham, *One of Jackson's Foot Cavalry*, 84. No separate report of the captures was rendered, although A. P. Hill reported "a large quantity," and Caldwell remembered "sutler's goods and government provisions . . . in abundance." It may be assumed that most of the goods reported as captured at Winchester and Martinsburg by Maj. W. J. Hawks, Jackson's chief commissary, were taken at the latter place. *OR*, vol. 19, 1:961.

78. Caldwell, *History of a Brigade of South Carolinians*, 70; also, Hotchkiss, *Make Me a Map*, 80; and Dabney, *Life and Campaigns of Jackson*, 551. The fullest account, perhaps somewhat gilded, is in Douglas, *I Rode with Stonewall*, 156–58; and idem, "Maryland," 623. The suggestion that the version by Douglas is somewhat exaggerated may be found in Dennis E. Frye, "Henry Kyd Douglas Challenged by His Peers," *Civil War* (Sept. 1991): 42, 44.

79. Douglas, *I Rode with Stonewall*, 156–57.

80. Lee to Stuart, Sept. 12, 2:30 P.M., Hagerstown, Stuart Papers.

81. Early's report, *OR*, vol. 19, 1:966; Hotchkiss, *Make Me a Map*, 80; H.W. Thomas, *History of the Doles-Cook Brigade*, 221; Early, *War Memoirs*, 136; Douglas, *I Rode with Stonewall*, 158; and Worsham, *One of Jackson's Foot Cavalry*, 84. It will be recalled that Lige White's scouts had been operating in the vicinity of Martinsburg for some days, but there is no indication that Jackson made any attempt to use them for intelligence. White's command, now increased to two companies, crossed the Shenandoah on the night of the 12th, moving toward Waterford and effectively out of the remainder of the campaign. Myers, *Commanches*, 109–10.

82. McLaws's report, *OR*, vol. 19, 1:852; McLaws, "Maryland," 8–9; Aiken's report, *SOR* 3:564; Carman, "Maryland Campaign," chap. 6, p. 318.

83. McLaws, "Maryland," 8–9; and Aiken's report, *SOR* 3:564.

84. Dickert, *History of Kershaw's Brigade*, 147–48.

85. Dinkins, "Barksdale's Brigade," 257.

86. In addition to the sources cited in notes 82–85, see in *OR*, vol. 19, 1, the reports of Kershaw, quoted in the text (pp. 862–63), and Nance (p. 867); and Hubbert, "Diary," 308.

87. McLaws makes it clear in his report that his first contact with anyone came from Jackson on the afternoon of the 13th. *OR*, vol. 19, 1:854.

88. See Walker's report, ibid., 913; and Walker, "Harper's Ferry," 607–8. See also Graham, *North Carolina Regiments* 2:432–33; and Hirsch, Diary, Sept. 12, 13.

89. Stuart's report, *OR*, vol. 19, 1:816; Duncan, "Marylanders," 189, citing the *Baltimore American* of September 13; and Stager to McClellan, Sept. 12, *OR*, vol. 19, 2:275. The brief comments in the diary of Lt. Col. William Carter (3d Virginia Cavalry), quoted in Tischler, *Harpers Ferry Cavalry Expedition*, 246, are of some help.

90. Stuart's report, *OR*, vol. 19, 1:816. Stuart's comment underscores McLaws's recollection that Lee estimated the Harpers Ferry garrison to number 3,000 to 4,000 ("Maryland," 5).

91. In *OR*, vol. 19, 1, see the reports of Stuart (p. 816) and Munford (p. 825). See also Neese, *Three Years in the Confederate Horse Artillery*, 117–8. Neese's reference to a

twelve-mile journey indicates Munford went from Monocacy Junction to Frederick on his way to Jefferson.

92. In *OR*, vol. 19, 1, see the reports of Pleasonton (p. 209), Burnside (p. 416), Stuart (pp. 815–16), and Hampton (pp. 822–23). See also, Steiner, *Diary*, 172–73; Brooks, *Stories of the Confederacy*, 82–83; Jacob Dolson Cox, *Military Reminiscences of the Civil War*, 2 vols. (New York: Charles Scribner's Sons, 1900), 1:271–72; David Waldhauer, "The Affair at Frederick City: A Correction of General Johnson's Account," *SHSP* 13 (1885): 417–18; and George Nolan Saussy, "Lee's Army, an Address," *CVAS* (1893): 73–74. It is likely that a squadron of the 2d South Carolina Cavalry supported the provost guard (bringing the total force to 150), but how close it was is uncertain. In his report Hampton credits Capt. J. F. Waring of the Jeff. Davis Legion with leading the charge; but in the postwar article cited above, Capt. David Waldhauer of the same unit claims to have been in command. The latter presents evidence that makes his statement credible.

93. In *OR*, vol. 19, 1, the reports of Stuart (p. 816) and Hampton (p. 823). See also Stuart to wife, Sept. 12, Stuart, *Letters*, 265–66; Johnson, "Maryland," 517; Blackford, *War Years with Jeb Stuart*, 142–43; Brooks, *Stories of the Confederacy*, 83; and von Borcke, *Memoirs* 1:202–5. Johnson supplies the local name of "Hagan's" for the gap in the Catoctins. It should be noted that both von Borcke and Bradley Johnson are unusually misleading in their accounts of the day.

94. Quote from Leach, Diary, Sept. 12; also see, Shinn, Diary, Sept. 12; Tucker, "Diary," 19; and Gorman, "Memoirs," 4. Tucker observed "many warm sympathizers" in Boonsboro, but Gorman reported that "but few families" did not have "brothers or sons in the Yankee army."

95. D. H. Hill, "South Mountain," 560; and see in *OR*, vol. 19, 1, the reports of Hill (p. 1019), Ripley (p. 1031), Rodes (pp. 1033–34), McRae (p. 1039), Grimes (pp. 1048–49), Griffith (p. 1049), and Colquitt (p. 1052). A perusal of these reports and the sources cited in note 94 makes only two things clear: (1) the National Pike beyond Boonsboro and toward Hagerstown and Williamsport (an unlikely route for escaping Federals) was guarded; and (2) there was no infantry at South Mountain until the evening of the 13th.

96. Lane's North Carolina battery accompanied Colquitt to Boonsboro. See Colquitt's report, *OR*, vol. 19, 1:1052; Colquitt to D. H. Hill, July 4, 1885, D. H. Hill Personal Papers, North Carolina State Archives. See also the brief memoir by Colquitt's acting aide, Lt. George D. Grattan, which makes it clear the brigade did not move to the mountain until the 13th: "The Battle of Boonsboro Gap or South Mountain," *SHSP* 39 (1914): 34.

97. Stuart's report, *OR*, vol. 19, 1:816.

98. This summary of Federal activities is from ibid., 26, 2:270–80, vol. 51, 1:821–26. The quotations are from Burnside to Halleck and McClellan, 5:30 A.M., and McClellan to Halleck, 10 A.M., ibid., vol. 19, 2:272–73, 270–71.

99. Lincoln to McClellan, 5:45 P.M., Sept. 12, ibid., 270.

100. Marcy to Burnside, 11 P.M., Sept. 12, ibid., vol. 51, 1:823–24.

5. "More rapidly than convenient": Lee's Plans Unravel, September 13, 1862

1. Lee to Davis, Sept. 16, *OR*, vol. 19, 1:140.

2. Gallagher, ed., *Lee the Soldier*, 25.

3. Long to McLaws, Sept. 13, *OR*, vol. 19, 2:606. The dispatch is not timed, but the phrase "will be . . . by noon today" places it in the morning. It is noteworthy that Lee did not attach his own name to the letter. This procedure followed the military protocol of communicating with subordinates through staff, but Lee did not always follow the standard form and frequently wrote directly to Jackson, Longstreet, Stuart, G. W. Smith, etc.

4. Taylor, *General Lee*, 120; and *Papers of Jefferson Davis* 8:389n.1.

5. The resolution, debate, and vote are printed in "Proceedings of the First Confederate Congress," *SHSP* 46 (1928): 106–7, 120–25. See also, *Richmond Dispatch*, Sept. 13; and Carman, "Maryland Campaign," chap. 3, p. 137. The resolution passed the House as originally worded by a vote of 56 to 13 on September 12, although twenty-nine representatives voted for an amendment to strike the final phrase. Apparently, Lee returned to Virginia before the Senate could consider the issue. Davis could not have known of the final outcome by the time he wrote the letter that Lee received on the morning of the 13th. Even if Davis had sent his message by telegraph—and its apparent length and probable inclusion of the proclamation argues against this—it could have gone no farther than Warrenton by wire.

6. Lee to Davis, Sept. 13, *OR*, vol. 19, 2:605–6.

7. Davis to Lee, Sept. 7[?], ibid., 598–99. Given in abridged form in *Papers of Jefferson Davis* 8:386, where it is dated September 12—too late for Lee to have received it on the 13th.

8. Louis Manarin, "A Proclamation 'To the People of ——,'" *North Carolina Historical Review* 41 (1964): 246–47. Subsequently, an unexplained copy of the proclamation with Pennsylvania filled in in the blank would surface in the papers of a collector.

9. Resolution of Sept. 12, *OR*, ser. 4, vol. 2:82.

10. Curiously, Davis, in his memoirs, with access to both his own draft and Lee's proclamation, would assert that the former was the basis for the latter. Not only are the contents of the two dissimilar, but the chronology makes the claim impossible. See Jefferson Davis, *The Rise and Fall of the Confederate Government*, 2 vols. (New York: D. Appleton, 1881), 2:333. On September 14 Braxton Bragg issued a proclamation to Kentuckians. It also seems not to have been based on the Davis draft, and it makes no mention of the Mississippi River, *OR*, vol. 16, 2:822–23.

11. Reference is to the paragraphing in the version in Lee, *Wartime Papers*, 306–7.

12. Lee's report, *OR*, vol. 19, 1:151. On the 75,000 estimate, see chapter 1.

13. Tenney, "Seven Days in 1862," 133.

14. Lee's casualties at Second Manassas totaled 9,474, almost twice the 5,000 he estimated in this dispatch. See "The Opposing Forces at Second Bull Run, August 16th–September 2nd, 1862," *B&L* 2:500.

15. In place of the standard phrase "Your obedient servant," Lee closed this dispatch to Davis in an unusually personal manner: "With sincere wishes for your health and prosperity, I am most respectfully and truly yours."

16. Pendleton to Davis, Sept. 13, Hagerstown, abridged in *Papers of Jefferson Davis* 8:390–91.

17. Stuart's report, *OR*, vol. 19, 1:817.

18. Lee to Stuart, Sept. 13, Stuart Papers.

19. Certificate of Maj. John F. Edwards, Chief Commissary, Oct. 10, 1885, McLaws Papers, Southern Historical Collection. On the cutting of the C&O Canal, see McLaws's report, *OR*, vol. 19, 1:856.

20. McLaws, "Maryland," 11.

21. Ibid., 10–11.

22. Aiken's report, *SOR* 3:565–67.

23. See Carman, "Maryland Campaign," chap. 6, pp. 318–19; and in *OR*, vol. 19, 1, see the reports of McLaws (pp. 853–54), Kershaw (pp. 863–64), Nance (pp. 867–68), and Ford (p. 548). On Barksdale, see Dickert, *A History of Kershaw's Brigade*, 148–49; Dinkins, *Personal Recollections and Experiences*, 54; "Barksdale's Brigade," 257–59; and Hubbert, "Diary," 308.

24. McLaws report, *OR*, vol. 19, 1:853–54.

25. McLaws to Chilton, [illegible] P.M. [no date], McLaws Papers, Virginia Historical Society. The illegible hour might be "$1\frac{1}{2}$." There is no evidence this dispatch ever reached Lee.

26. McLaws, "Maryland," 10–11; and McLaws's report, *OR*, vol. 19, 1:854.

27. McLaws, "Maryland," 11; McLaws's report, *OR*, vol. 19, 1:854.

28. Hubbert, "Diary," 308.

29. McLaws, "Maryland," 11; McLaws's report, *OR*, vol. 19, 1:854.

30. For a discussion of Walker's activities on September 13 and the evidence bearing thereon, see Harsh, *Sounding the Shallows*, chap. 7, sect. F.

31. McLaws's report, *OR*, vol. 19, 1:854. It is assumed that Jackson sent a similar message to Walker, although Walker made no mention of a courier. See Harsh, *Sounding the Shallows*, chap. 7, sect. F.

32. This account of Jackson's forces on the 13th is from the following reports in *OR*, vol. 19, 1: Jackson (p. 953), Crutchfield (p. 962), Early (p. 966), A. P. Hill (p. 980), Williams (p. 1011), and E. Pendleton (p. 1016). See also Poague, *Gunner with Stonewall*, 43; Worsham, *One of Jackson's Foot Cavalry*, 84; Early, *War Memoirs*, 136; H. W. Thomas, *History of the Doles-Cook Brigade*, 221–22; Caldwell, *History of a Brigade of South Carolinians*, 70–71; Chamberlayne, *Letters*, 109; and Robertson, *A. P. Hill*, 135–36. For the shoeless anecdote, see Sheeran, *Confederate Chaplain*, 30.

33. Hotchkiss, *Make Me a Map*, 80–81; Douglas, "Maryland," 625; Douglas, *I Rode with Stonewall*, 158; Dabney, *Life and Campaigns of Jackson*, 551–52; and Cooke, *Jackson*, 321–22.

34. Steiner, *Diary*, 24–25. Curiously, although Steiner had been in effect a spy within enemy lines for a week, there is no indication he sought out McClellan or anyone in the Army of the Potomac to report on the strength, condition, or intentions of the Confederates.

35. Frederick to Harpers Ferry by way of Jefferson and Knoxville was nineteen miles and to Hagerstown by the National Turnpike was twenty-seven miles. The closest route from Hagerstown to Harpers Ferry would have been twenty-nine miles by way of Sharpsburg and Shepherdstown. Although it would appear closer to go from Sharpsburg to Antietam Furnace and Sandy Hook, the meandering roads actually add eight miles to the distance.

36. Summary of Federal movements based on the reports in *OR*, vol. 19, 1: by McClellan (pp. 26, 40, 44–45), Pleasant (p. 209), Franklin (pp. 378–79), Slocum (p. 380), Burnside (pp. 416–17), Fairchild (pp. 449–50), and Munford (p. 825); and the following orders, all from Marcy on the evening of the 12th, in ibid., vol. 51, 1:821–25, to Sumner, Porter, Franklin, Couch, Burnside, and Pleasonton.

37. Stuart's report, ibid., vol. 19, 1:816.

38. Almost nothing is known of Pelham's brush with danger. Reports have not been found for either Fitz Lee or McReynolds. See von Borcke, *Memoirs* 1:212–13. The historian of the 1st New York Cavalry recalled no significant fighting. See William Harrison Beach, *The First New York (Lincoln) Cavalry, From April 19, 1861, to July 7, 1865* (Milwaukee: Burdick & Allen, 1902), 170.

39. Munford's report, *OR*, vol. 19, 1:825–26; and Neese, *Three Years in the Confederate Horse Artillery*, 118–19.

40. In *OR*, vol. 19, 1, the reports of Stuart (pp. 816–17) and Hampton (p. 823); and see also von Borcke, *Memoirs* 1:206–8. Stuart believed there were two brigades of enemy infantry, but there was only Harland's. Because Hart's South Carolina Horse Artillery fought in sections, von Borcke reported two Confederate batteries.

41. In *OR*, vol. 19, 1, reports of Stuart (pp. 816–17) and D. H. Hill (p. 1019); also see Lee to Stuart, Sept. 13, 12:45 P.M., Stuart Papers; and D. H. Hill to Longstreet, Feb. 11, 1885, Longstreet Papers, Duke University.

42. Essentially harmonious accounts of the affairs at Hagan's Pass and Middletown may be found in *OR*, vol. 19, 1, in the reports of Pleasonton (p. 209), Stuart (pp. 816–17), and Hampton (pp. 823–24); and in von Borcke, *Memoirs* 1:205–12; and Brooks, *Stories of the Confederacy*, 83–85. Although Hampton maintained there was not the "slightest confusion in the

ranks" of the 1st North Carolina, the rout is described in detail by von Borcke. Bradley Johnson, the Frederick native, supplies the local name "Koogle's" for the covered bridge. Johnson, "Maryland," 522.

43. The first quote is from Stuart's report, *OR*, vol. 19, 1:817; the second is from Lee's postwar recollections as recorded in Gallagher, ed., *Lee the Soldier*, 26. Additional details of what Stuart learned and where he learned it are from Carman, "Maryland Campaign," chap. 7, pp. 393–94, which is discussed further in this chapter.

44. When Stuart submitted his report, almost a year and a half later, after events had proven his error in judgment, he would simply refer to Crampton's Gap, "which I had reason to believe was as much threatened as any other." *OR*, vol. 19, 1:817.

45. In ibid. see the reports of Stuart (p. 817), Hampton (p. 824), and Munford (p. 826); see also, Neese, *Three Years in the Confederate Horse Artillery*, 119; and Brooks, *Stories of the Confederacy*, 85–86. Stuart implies he sent Hampton off just before South Mountain, but Hampton makes it clear he left directly from Catoctin Creek. Neese's word is accepted that the nearly fatal clash between friendly forces occurred not at Burkittsville but in the gap itself.

46. D. H. Hill to Longstreet, Feb. 11, 1885, Longstreet Papers, Duke University.

47. Colquitt to D. H. Hill, July 4, 1885, D. H. Hill Personal Papers, North Carolina State Archives.

48. D. H. Hill to Longstreet, Feb. 11, 1885, Longstreet Papers, Duke University; and Grattan, "Boonsboro," 34. Grattan was acting aide to Colquitt at the time, and his account—although dismissed by Bridges (*Lee's Maverick General*, 291n.6) as "not very reliable"—accords with other versions except in one major respect. Grattan's insistence that Garland's brigade did not appear until the morning is discussed below.

49. Rosser to Hill, July 10, 1883, D. H. Hill Papers, Library of Virginia. See also Stuart's report, *OR*, vol. 19, 1:817; von Borcke, *Memoirs* 1:212–13. Fox's Gap is sometimes referred to in primary sources as Braddock's Gap.

50. None of these messages has been found. Their general content has been surmised from the reactions of Hill and Lee (as discussed below) and from D. H. Hill to Longstreet, June 8, 1885, Longstreet Papers, Duke University.

51. D. H. Hill to Longstreet, Feb. 11, 1885, Longstreet Papers, Duke University.

52. After the war Hill would believe that the pro-Lee clique among Confederate veterans intentionally used him as a scapegoat for the failure of the Maryland campaign, in a manner similar to their use of Longstreet to explain defeat at Gettysburg. See D. H. Hill to Longstreet, May 21, 1885, and subsequent letters, Longstreet Papers, Duke University.

53. D. H. Hill to Longstreet, letters of Feb. 11, June 8, July 30, 1885, Longstreet Papers, Duke University. In *OR*, vol. 19, 1, see the reports of Stuart (p. 817) and D. H. Hill (p. 1052); also see D. H. Hill, "South Mountain," 560. In fairness to Hill, it might be noted that Lee interpreted a similar dispatch from Stuart to mean the infantry would merely assist the cavalry in holding Turner's Gap. See Lee to Stuart, 12:45 P.M., Sept. 13, Stuart Papers.

54. In addition to the sources cited in note 53, see Colquitt to D. H. Hill, July 4, 1885, D. H. Hill Personal Papers, North Carolina State Archives; and Colquitt's report, *OR*, vol. 19, 1:1052. In both his report and his postwar article, D. H. Hill clearly implies that he sent Garland back to the mountain at the same time he sent Colquitt and withdrew his other three brigades to Boonsboro; but these other actions Hill did not take until eight o'clock or later.

55. The quotes are from Grattan, "Boonsboro," 36; and Colquitt to Hill, July 4, 1885, D. H. Hill Personal Papers, North Carolina State Archives. See also Colquitt's report, *OR*, vol. 19, 1:1052; and the 1885 statement by Lt. Col. Emory F. Best in the Longstreet Papers, Duke University, which refers to September 13 as the 14th. Hal Bridges (*Lee's Maverick General*, 102) doubts Grattan's story about the campfires, entirely on the basis of Stuart's assertion that the enemy had taken pains all day to conceal themselves. There is no evidence the

Federals took any special measures aimed at secrecy, however, and Stuart's claim may have derived from the rolling and wooded nature of the terrain; or, the cavalry chief may simply have been attempting to cover his erroneous intelligence.

56. Colquitt to Hill, July 4, 1885, Hill Personal Papers, North Carolina State Archives; Hill to Longstreet, Feb. 11, 1885, Longstreet Papers, Duke University; Gallagher, ed., *Lee the Soldier*, 8, 26. On G. B. Anderson, see Shinn, Diary, Sept. 13; and Gorman, "Memoirs," 4. On Ripley see Leach, Diary, Sept. 13, which must have been written on the 14th; and Thruston's report, *SOR* 3:584.

57. Colquitt to Hill, July 4, 1885, and Alfred Iverson to Hill, D. H. Hill Personal Papers, North Carolina State Archives. George Grattan maintained correctly that Garland's brigade did not appear on the mountaintop until sunrise. Grattan must have either been away delivering messages or asleep when Garland conferred with Colquitt. Grattan, "Boonsboro," 35–36.

58. Steiner, *Diary*, 25. There is no indication Steiner attempted to meet personally with McClellan.

59. McClellan to Lincoln, Sept. 13, 12 P.M., *OR*, vol. 19, 1:281. The story of the finding of S.O. 191, as well as McClellan's analysis and use of them, are both historiographical controversies of considerable proportion in their own right. Because these are essentially Federal topics, they will be treated in detail in a later volume. Only so much of the story as is necessary to an understanding of its impact on Lee and Confederate strategy is given here.

60. Marcy to Pleasonton, Sept. 13, 3 P.M., ibid., vol. 51, 1:829.

61. McClellan to Lincoln, Sept. 13, 12 P.M., ibid., vol. 19, 1:281.

62. The figures for Federal strength are present for duty and are derived from Allen, "Second Manassas Strengths," 114; and from the returns of Sept. 20, 1862, *OR*, vol. 19, 2:336.

63. This is not a typographical error.

64. This summary of McClellan's information and his strategy is based on McClellan to Franklin, Sept. 13, 6:20 P.M., *OR*, vol. 19, 1:45–46; and fragment in ibid., vol. 51, 1:826–27; and McClellan to Halleck, Sept. 13, 11 P.M., ibid., vol. 19, 2:281–82.

65. In spite of S.O. 191's reference to D. H. Hill as a division commander, the Federals had gotten the notion that Hill commanded a corps. The error may have derived from half-understood reports that reflected the fact Hill had commanded the reenforcing column from Richmond in late August. See McClellan to Halleck, Sept. 15, 8 A.M., ibid., 294; also Banks's October 20 estimate of the organization and strength of Lee's army, in ibid., 453; and McClellan's summary of it, in ibid., 1:67.

66. This is the dispatch known only by Lee's reply. Lee to Stuart, 12:45 P.M., Sept. 13, Stuart Papers.

67. Stuart's report, *OR*, vol. 19, 1:817.

68. The quotation was remembered by Lee and is from Gallagher, ed., *Lee the Soldier*, 26. The remainder of the account is from Carman, "Maryland Campaign," chap. 7, pp. 393–94, which appears to be based on uncited firsthand testimony (perhaps from a member of Stuart's staff).

69. It is assumed that Stuart wrote to Lee at the same time he wrote to D. H. Hill and that it would have taken a courier no more than two hours to reach Lee in Hagerstown. It is possible, however, that Stuart wrote a message to Lee while still at Bolivar, and the courier took longer to deliver it. See Carman, "Maryland Campaign," chap. 7, p. 394.

70. Gallagher, ed., *Lee the Soldier*, 26.

71. For further discussion of the conclusions in the text concerning Lee's information on the night of the 13th and the sources upon which they are based, see Harsh, *Sounding the Shallows*, chap. 7, sect. G.

72. There is no hard evidence of any specific information from Jackson to Lee on the 13th; there is only Henry Kyd Douglas's general claim that Stonewall kept a constant relay of couriers to apprise Lee of his situation. Douglas, "Letter," 617. In spite of the difficulty Jack-

son experienced in establishing communications with McLaws and Walker on the 13th, he knew generally that both were in place and that by the afternoon McLaws occupied Maryland Heights. It is possible the optimism Jed. Hotchkiss expressed in his diary—"We have the enemy surrounded and hope to take them tomorrow"—may have been shared by Stonewall. Hotchkiss, *Make Me a Map*, 81. How much of this, if any, Jackson passed on to Lee cannot be known.

73. For a further discussion of Lee's plans on the night of September 13, see Harsh, *Sounding the Shallows*, chap. 7, sect. H.

74. This entire interview is documented solely by three slightly variant versions as recorded by Longstreet, *From Manassas to Appomattox*, 219–20; in "Maryland," 665–66; and finally in a letter to D. H. Hill; June 6, 1885, D. H. Hill Papers, Library of Virginia, cited by D. H. Hill in "South Mountain," 560. This is one of those occasions when Longstreet's recollections seem to suggest self-serving hindsight and perhaps ought to be accepted with some caution. His claimed prescience would be more impressive if it accorded more closely with the geography of western Maryland.

75. Allan, *Army of Northern Virginia*, 345. In his 1868 conversation, Lee seems to give evidence only of a message to Jackson on the night of the 14th. See Gallager, ed., *Lee the Soldier*, 8. It makes sense to believe there would have been one on the night of the 13th, however; and Allan's opinion, since he also recorded the conversation, deserves weight.

76. T. M. R. Talcott to McLaws, Sept. 13, 10 P.M., *OR*, vol. 19, 2:607.

77. This dispatch has not been found, and D. H. Hill makes no mention of it in his official report. He paraphrases it in "South Mountain," 560 (which is quoted), and also in a letter to Longstreet, Feb. 11, 1885. In another letter to Longstreet, July 30, 1885, Hill stated that the dispatch was at that time in "my papers." Both letters are in the Longstreet Papers, Duke University.

78. In *OR*, vol. 19, 1, see the reports of Stuart (p. 817) and Ripley (p. 1031). Also see, Thruston's report, *SOR* 3:584; and Leach, Diary, Sept. 13.

79. Lee, "Hill Letter," 165; and Gallagher, ed., *Lee the Soldier*, 26. Lee first mentioned that he knew at the time the document was a copy of S.O. 191 in a letter eight months earlier. See Lee to D. H. Hill, June 12, 1867, Lee Family Papers, Virginia Historical Society. See also Harsh, *Sounding the Shallows*, chap. 7, sect. I.

80. For a discussion of Lee's knowledge of the loss of S.O. 191 and his reaction thereto, see ibid.

81. Lee to Stuart, Sept. 14, Stuart Papers.

82. Lee "Hill Letter," 165.

83. Lee to McLaws, Sept. 14, 1862, Hagerstown, *OR*, vol. 19, 2:608. The dispatch is untimed, and it must be speculation that it was sent in tandem with the message to Stuart.

84. See D. H. Hill's articles: "Lost Dispatch," 275–78; "Address," 269; and "South Mountain," 569–70; and "The Lost Dispatch—Letter from General D. H. Hill," *SHSP* 13 (1885): 421–22.

6. "The day has gone against us": Lee Stands at the Mountain Gaps, September 14, 1862

1. Common sense argues that Longstreet must have issued orders, and they are in one instance confirmed. See the report of Toombs, *OR*, vol. 19, 1:888.

2. On reveille, see G. Wise, *History of the 17th Va.*, 111; recording daylight were Owen, *In Camp and Battle*, 136; and Longstreet, *From Manassas to Appomattox*, 220.

3. In *OR*, vol. 19, 1, see the reports of Little (p. 911), D. R. Jones (p. 885), and Toombs (p. 888). Longstreet makes clear that the 11th Georgia of G. T. Anderson's brigade was left behind through haste. See Longstreet, *From Manassas to Appomattox*, 220.

4. Latrobe, Diary, Sept. 14. Reilly's battery, attached to Hood, marched into Hagerstown at 10:00 to procure and cook rations; at 1:00 a courier brought orders to "proceed in a gallop" to South Mountain. See Ramsay, *North Carolina Regiments* 1:573.

5. Pendleton's report, *OR*, vol. 19, 1:829–30; Pendleton to wife, Sept. 22, S. P. Lee, *Memoirs*, 212; and Alexander, *Fighting for the Confederacy*, 142.

6. Lee's place near the head of the column is inferred from Porter Alexander's claim that they left "early" (*Fighting for the Confederacy*, 142); and Lee's actions upon arrival at Boonsboro indicate he was among the first on the scene. For a discussion of Lee's mode of travel on the 14th, see Harsh, *Sounding the Shallows*, chap. 8, sect. A.

7. Curiously, the weather records kept in Frederick do not support the veterans' memories. The temperature reached only seventy-three by 2:00 P.M. on the 14th. The 13th and 14th were, in fact, among the cooler days of the month. On the 14th, in Frederick, the skies were 30 percent overcast at 7:00A.M.; but 100 percent by 2:00 P.M. On weather in the campaign, see Harsh, *Sounding the Shallows*, chap. 1.

8. Quotes from Longstreet's report, *OR*, vol. 19, 1:839; and Longstreet, "Maryland," 666; see also Longstreet, *From Manassas to Appomattox*, 220; and Longstreet to D. H. Hill, June 15, 1885, D. H. Hill Papers, Library of Virginia. For other comments on the hot and fatiguing march, see in *OR*, vol. 19, 1, the reports of Lee (p. 147), Garnett (p. 894), and McMaster (p. 945); also the postwar comment of Lee in Gallagher, ed., *Lee the Soldier*, 8.

9. Sgt. W. H. Andrews noted in his journal that the 1st Georgia Regulars of G.T. Anderson's brigade "doublequicked back to South Mountain." See Andrews, *Diary of W. H. Andrews, 1st Sergt. Co. M, 1st Georgia Regulars, from February, 1861, to May 2, 1865* (East Atlanta, 1891), 7. If Longstreet, in order to make up for lost time, did indeed subject his men to double-time for even part of the way, it would explain why they arrived in such a frazzled condition. Double-quicking the entire distance would have gotten the vanguard to Boonsboro by ten o'clock, or at least the handful still on their feet.

10. D. H. Hill probably sent more than one message, but he reported the one to Longstreet. Hill's report, *OR*, vol. 19, 1:1021. It is also possible the message mentioned by Lee was, in fact, the one addressed to Longstreet. Lee to Davis, Sept. 16, *OR*, vol. 19, 1:140. See note 22 below. On the sights and sounds of the Battle of South Mountain, see Harsh, *Sounding the Shallows*, chap. 8, sect. B.

11. Long, *Memoirs of Robert E. Lee*, 215.

12. Hood, *Advance and Retreat*, 39; and Joseph Benjamin Polley, *Hood's Texas Brigade, Its Marches, Its Battles, Its Achievements* (New York: Neale Publishing, 1910), 114. Later in the day, S.O. 193 officially but "temporarily suspended" Hood's arrest and freed his division from Evans's control. *OR*, vol. 19, 2:609. No mention was ever made of the matter again, and the temporary became permanent.

13. D. H. Hill to Longstreet, July 30, 1885, Longstreet Papers, Duke University.

14. On Colquitt's report see Hill, "South Mountain," 561. On the posting of Colquitt's brigade, see Harsh, *Sounding the Shallows*, chap. 8, sect. C; on Hill's knowledge of Longstreet's march to his relief, see ibid., chap. 8, sect. D.

15. For a discussion of the strength of D. H. Hill's division, see Harsh, *Sounding the Shallows*, chap. 8, sect. E.

16. This account of D. H. Hill's early-morning activities is from his report, *OR*, vol. 19, 1:1019–22; postwar memoir, "South Mountain," 560–61; and also the following letters: Hill to Longstreet, Feb. 11, 14 (reprinted in *SOR* 3:583–84, where it is misdated 1888), June 5, 8, July 30, 1885, Longstreet Papers, Duke University. See also, Hill to C. C. Buel, *Century* Collection, New York Public Library; Colquitt to Hill, D. H. Hill Personal Papers, North Carolina State Archives; and the 1885 statement by Lt. Col. Emory Fiske Best, Longstreet Papers, Duke University, reprinted in *SOR* 3:580–82.

17. Rosser to D. H. Hill, July 10, 1885, D. H. Hill Papers, Library of Virginia.

18. Pleasonton may have been the only Federal who understood the terrain sufficiently to grasp the opportunity missed. In *OR*, vol. 19, 1, see the reports of Pleasonton (p. 210), Cox (p. 458), and Scammon (p. 461).

19. Rosser to D. H. Hill, July 10, 1885, D. H. Hill Papers, Library of Virginia.

20. Garland's fight is covered in *OR*, vol. 19, 1, in the reports of McRae (pp. 1039–43) and Ruffin (pp. 1045–47); in Montgomery, *North Carolina Regiments* 1:626–28; N. S. Smith, ibid. 1:695–96; Thomas F. Toon, "20th Infantry," ibid. 2:115–16; V. E. Turner, "23rd Infantry," ibid. 2:219–22; and also in R. V. Minor, "Letter," *B&L* 2:566n; and in H. C. Wall, "The 23rd North Carolina Infantry: Historical Sketch," *SHSP* 25 (1897): 163–64. See also the following letters: Ruffin to Hill, Aug. 4, 1885, and McRae to Hill, Aug. 21, 1885, D. H. Hill Papers, Library of Virginia; Hill to Longstreet, Feb. 14, 1885, Longstreet Papers, Duke University; Hill to C. C. Buel, Dec. 10, 1885, *Century* Collection; and Iverson to Hill, Aug. 23, 1885, D. H. Hill Personal Papers, North Carolina State Archives.

21. This interesting glimpse into Hill's understanding of the situation at the time may be found in his "South Mountain," 564–65, and is confirmed in comments he made on the 14th to Lt. Col. Thomas Ruffin. See Ruffin to Hill, Aug. 4, 1885, D. H. Hill Papers, Library of Virginia.

22. Hill, "South Mountain," 564, 566; see also, Hill to Longstreet, Feb. 14, and June 5, 1885, Longstreet Papers, Duke University.

23. D. H. Hill to Longstreet, Feb. 14, 1885, Longstreet Papers, Duke University. The message alluded to is probably the one received by Lee as he was approaching Boonsboro. See note 10.

24. On G. B. Anderson's fight, in *OR*, vol. 19, 1, see the reports of Grimes (pp. 1048–49), Griffith (pp. 1049–50), and Sillers (pp. 1050–51); and Matthew Manly, "2nd Regiment," *North Carolina Regiments* 1:166; and Edwin Augustus Osborne, "4th Regiment," ibid. 1:244–45. See also, Gorman, "Memoirs," 4–5; Walter Lee to Mother, Sept. 29, 1862; Battle, *Forget-me-nots*, 76; and Shinn, Diary, Sept. 14.

25. In *OR*, vol. 19, 1, see the reports of Ripley (pp. 1031–32) and Rodes (pp. 1033–34). Hal Bridges (*Lee's Maverick General*, 110n.30) argues the two brigades arrived at 11:00 A.M., but the time seems a bit early in light of Rodes's report of receiving orders "toward noon."

26. This summary of Federal operations on the morning of the 14th is from the reports in *OR*, vol. 19, 1, of Pleasonton (pp. 209–10), Burnside (p. 417), Willcox (p. 428), Cox (pp. 458–59), Scammon (pp. 461–62); and heavily from Cox, *Military Reminiscences* 1:277–85.

27. The quote is from Burnside's report, *OR*, vol. 19, 1:417.

28. The exchange of notes and Lee's reaction is recorded in Hill's report, ibid., 1020; and Longstreet, *From Manassas to Appomattox*, 224.

29. On the futile and exhausting march of the three brigades, see Longstreet, *From Manassas to Appomattox*, 224, 225; G. Wise, *History of the 17th Va.*, 111; Latrobe, Diary, Sept. 14; and in *OR*, vol. 19, 1, the reports of Jones (pp. 885–86), Garnett (p. 894), Hunton (p. 898), and Jos. Walker (pp. 905–6). Walker indicates the column reached the church on the Old Sharpsburg Road and turned around because the firing from the direction of Fox's Gap had ceased. Longstreet incorrectly implies that D. R. Jones accompanied Drayton and G. T. Anderson, rather than Kemper, Garnett, and Walker. Also, it is likely Lee gave the order for Jones to return, as Longstreet by then would have been on the mountain with Hill.

30. Hill's quote is from Longstreet, *From Manassas to Appomattox*, 222. See also Hill, "South Mountain," 569; and in *OR*, vol. 19, 1, the reports of G. T. Anderson (pp. 908–9) and Ripley (pp. 1031–32). In addition, on Ripley's aberration, see H.W. Thomas, *History of the Doles-Cook Brigade*, 68–69, 469; Andrews, *Diary*, 7; Thruston's report, *SOR* 3:584–86; Leach, Diary, Sept. 14; DeRosset, *North Carolina Regiments* 1:224–25; and idem, "Letter," *B&L* 2:569n., excerpted from "Ripley's Brigade at South Mountain," *Century Magazine* 33 (1886): 308–9.

31. Rodes himself uses the term "muskets" in reporting his strength. *OR*, vol. 19, 1:1034. It is a term used by Confederates to denote fighting men only and therefore excludes officers, staff, extra-duty men, and attached artillery. Sometimes it derived from a count of the muskets in line of battle and, therefore, even excluded those detached as skirmishers, although it is not clear whether Rodes made this latter deduction. If the 15,000 men of the Federal First Corps are reduced in similar fashion to make the comparison fair, they had about nine thousand "muskets."

32. On Rodes's fight see Rodes's report, *OR*, vol. 19, 1:1034–36; Robert E. Park, "Letter," *B&L* 2:572–73n.; Edwin L. Hobson, "Letter," *SHSP* 25 (1897): 105n.; Tucker, "Diary," 20; and the unusual side view in Alexander, *Fighting for the Confederacy*, 142–43.

33. Longstreet's report, *OR*, vol. 19, 1:839; and in *From Manassas to Appomattox*, 227; and "Maryland," 666.

34. On Evans's fight see Longstreet, *From Manassas to Appomattox*, 224; and in *OR*, vol. 19, 1, the reports of Evans (p. 939), Stevens (pp. 941–42), McMaster (p. 945), Wallace (p. 946), Hilton (pp. 948–49), Durham (pp. 949–50); also, McMaster to D. H. Hill, July 11, 1885, D.H. Hill Papers, Library of Virginia.

35. On Hood's fight see Hood's report, *OR*, vol. 19, 1:922; in Ramsay, *North Carolina Regiments* 1:573; Ray, ibid. 1:306–7; and Hood, *Advance and Retreat*, 40–41.

36. On D. R. Jones's arrival and fight, see the sources cited in note 29; and, in addition, in *OR*, vol. 19, 1, the reports of Cabell (pp. 899–900), Brown (p. 901), W. D. Stuart (pp. 902–3), Corse (p. 904), and Jos. Walker (pp. 905–6); see also, Wood, *Reminiscences of Big I*, 35–36; and Hunter, "Sharpsburg," 511. On Colquitt's fight, see Colquitt's report, *OR*, vol. 19, 1:1052–53; Grattan, "Boonsboro," 41–43; D. H. Hill to Longstreet, Feb. 11, 1885, and statement by Lt. Col. Emory F. Best [1885] both in Longstreet Papers, Duke University; and Colquitt to Hill, July 4, 1885, D. H. Hill Personal Papers, North Carolina State Archives. It was allegedly this fight that earned John Gibbon's western regiments the sobriquet "Iron Brigade." New research not only casts doubt on this incident, but also shows that Walter Phelps's brigade (Hatch) was already known by that nickname. See Thomas G. Clemens, "Black Hats off to the Original Iron Brigade," *Columbiad: A Quarterly Review of the War between the States* 1 (1997): 46–58.

37. Hotchkiss, *Make Me a Map*, 81.

38. For the strength of Federal and Confederate forces at Harpers Ferry, see Harsh, *Sounding the Shallows*, chap. 8, sect. F.

39. Jackson's report, *OR*, vol. 19, 1:953; and Hotchkiss, *Make Me a Map*, 81. Walker had been in signal contact with McLaws. Jackson to McLaws, Sept. 14, 7:20 A.M., mentions a dispatch from McLaws but is unclear whether it was received that morning or the night before. *OR*, vol. 19, 1:607.

40. Jackson to McLaws, Sept. 14, 7:20 A.M., *OR*, vol. 19, 2:607.

41. Some of the details in the dispatch are of greater interest to Walker than to McLaws. See also the convincing case made by Douglas, "Letter," 617–18.

42. For the controversy see Walker, "Harper's Ferry," 609–10; Johnson, "Letter," 615–16; and Douglas, "Letter," 617–18. As will be discussed below, however, Walker went on to make immodest claims of precipitating the surrender of Harpers Ferry and saving Lee's army that do not stand up to scrutiny and provide another example of the unreliability of the general's recollections.

43. Bartlett's report, *OR*, vol. 19, 1:958–59; all of the signal messages discussed below are from this source.

44. There is an unaccountable minor mystery about the number of Walker's guns. Contradicting the message received by Bartlett, Walker reported carrying five pieces (three Parrotts and two rifles) up the mountain. Ibid., 913. Curiously, Pvt. Isaac Hirsch in his diary noted only three guns, entry for September 14. Since the 30th Virginia left the mountain during the

night, however, Hirsch is not a close witness. On the other hand, Jed. Hotchkiss, who was with the guns, noted in his diary: "We opened on them in the P.M. from Loudoun Heights, with 3 pieces of artillery." See Hotchkiss, *Make Me a Map*, 81. It may be that five or six guns were carried up the mountain, but only three were employed—or employed at any one time.

45. In light of the dispatches Lee sent to McLaws in the morning and on the evening of the 13th, it is reasonable to assume he sent a similar warning to Jackson, even though it has not been found. Jackson refers to receipt of such a message in a dispatch to Lee of 8:15 P.M. on the 14th, but—since he implies it was just received—it may have been a follow-up, as will be argued below. *OR*, vol. 19, 1:951.

46. It cannot be known if Bartlett relayed the message to McLaws via Loudoun Heights, or if he were able to send it directly to Maryland Heights. If the latter were the case, it is all the more interesting that no messages were recorded as received from McLaws during the 14th.

47. For a discussion of Walker's claim to have forced the issue at Harpers Ferry, see Harsh, *Sounding the Shallows*, chap. 8, sect. G.

48. In *OR*, vol. 19, 1, see the reports of Bartlett (p. 859) and McLaws (p. 854).

49. Jackson's report, ibid., 953. For a note on the effect of the bombardment, see Harsh, *Sounding the Shallows*, chap. 8, sect. H.

50. Jackson summarized his tactics in his report, *OR*, vol. 19, 1:954. For further discussion of the evolution of Jackson's plan, see Harsh, *Sounding the Shallows*, chap. 8, sect. I.

51. On Lawton's movements see the reports in *OR*, vol. 19, 1, of Jackson (p. 954) and Early (p. 966); see also, Nisbet, *Four Years on the Firing Line*, 101; H. W. Thomas, *History of the Doles-Cook Brigade*, 222; and Early, *War Memoirs*, 136–37.

52. On J. R. Jones's movements, see the reports in *OR*, vol. 19, 1, of Jackson (p. 954), Jones (p. 1007), Williams (p. 1111), and Pendleton (p. 1016); see also, Poague, *Gunner with Stonewall*, 43; Worsham, *One of Jackson's Foot Cavalry*, 84–85; and E. A. Moore, *The Story of a Cannoneer*, 138. Although Jackson reported only the movement of Winder's brigade under Grigsby, it is clear from the other reports that Jones also advanced Starke's Louisiana brigade along the Potomac flank at about eight o'clock.

53. On A. P. Hill's movements, see the reports in *OR*, vol. 19, 1, of Jackson (p. 954), Hill (p. 980), Walker (p. 984), Lane (p. 985), McGowan (p. 987), Hamilton (p. 991), Perrin (p. 993), Edwards (pp. 997–98), Brown (pp. 998–99), Archer (p. 1000), Neal (p. 1003), Pender (p. 1004), and Thomas (p. 1006). In *SOR* 3, see the reports of McRae (pp. 574–75) and McIntyre (pp. 576–77). See also Chamberlayne, *Letters*, 109; Caldwell, *History of a Brigade of South Carolinians*, 71; Harris, *North Carolina Regiments* 1:372; Benjamin H. Cathey, "16th Regiment," ibid., 759; Thomas H. Sutton, "18th Regiment," ibid. 2:70; Robert Healy, "2nd Letter," *B&L* 2:626–27; Haynes, *Diary*, 19; and Robertson, *A. P. Hill*, 126.

54. On the placement of the Crutchfield superbattery see the reports in *OR*, vol, 19, 1, of Jackson (p. 954) and Crutchfield (p. 962).

55. The dispatch has been lost, but after the war Lee recalled sending a message "to hurry up Jackson" in the late afternoon or early evening of the 14th. Gallagher, ed., *Lee the Soldier*, 8. That Lee's memory did not telescope this dispatch with one sent on the 13th is suggested by Jackson's reply to Chilton, who sent all three messages, which have survived, from Lee at Boonsboro on the 14th. On the contrary, the dispatches from Hagerstown on the 13th were sent out over the names of Lee and Long.

56. Henry Kyd Douglas anticipated that he could leave Jackson's headquarters immediately after dark (about 6:30), ride the eleven miles to his home at Ferry Hill just beyond Shepherdstown, visit with his family, and return to camp by midnight. Of course, he knew the route well; and because he stayed longer than expected, he did not actually return until three in the morning. Douglas, *I Rode with Stonewall*, 159–60. Lee's courier probably left Boonsboro at about 5:00 and had an hour and a half of daylight.

57. Jackson to Chilton, 8:15 P.M., Sept. 14, *OR*, vol. 19, 1:951.

58. Edward Moore of the Rockbridge Artillery recalled hearing "heavy cannonading across the Maryland border, apparently eight or ten miles from us." E. A. Moore, *Story of a Cannoneer*, 142–43.

59. Although Jackson continued to send signals to McLaws throughout the day, there is not a single message from McLaws recorded by Signal Officer Bartlett. *OR*, vol. 19, 1:958–59.

60. While there is no evidence to support the speculation, it may be that Jackson's learning somewhat later that night of McLaws's plight motivated him to take the somewhat risky step of posting Crutchfield across the Shenandoah. Crutchfield admitted that "this position, although commanded perfectly by Bolivar Heights, yet secured a fire into the rear of the enemy's works." *OR*, vol. 19, 1:962. It would also seem that the decision to post the ten guns was made only after night had fallen. There is one indication Jackson may have expected the capitulation of Harpers Ferry early on the 15th. According to John Esten Cooke, Jackson signaled to McLaws and Walker: "I have occupied and now hold the enemy's first line of intrenchments, and, with the blessing of God, will capture the whole force early in the morning." Cooke, *Jackson*, 324. Cooke's statement is rendered suspect for two reasons: first, Cooke implies the signal was sent after dark; second, the message is not among those in the report Bartlett claims includes all signals sent from Jackson's headquarters.

61. Rosser to D. H. Hill, July 10, 1885, D. H. Hill Papers, Library of Virginia.

62. Heros von Borcke wrote that he and Stuart did not arrive until the afternoon. The reports of Stuart, Munford, and Hampton all agree, however, that Stuart arrived in the morning. The timing allowed in the text gives Jeb the benefit of the doubt; for, if he arrived much after ten, then his subsequent actions would have been even less fathomable. See von Borcke, *Memoirs* 1:215; and in *OR*, vol. 19, 1, the reports of Stuart (p. 817), Hampton (p. 824), Munford (p. 826), and Price to Mother, Sept. 18, Trout, *With Pen and Saber*, 99–100.

63. Munford's report, *OR*, vol. 19, 1:826–27; Allen, "Second Manassas Strengths," 193, 202; and John H. Thompson, "Historical Address of the Former Commander of Grimes's Battery," *SHSP* 34 (1906): 152.

64. In *OR*, vol. 19, 1, see the reports of Stuart (p. 818) and Hampton (p. 824).

65. According to Heros von Borcke, he accompanied Pryor and Stuart on a reconnaissance to the top of the ridge, where they could see perfectly into Harpers Ferry. While it is possible that Pryor and Stuart ascended Weverton Cliffs at the end of South Mountain, as this would have afforded them a view downriver to see if McClellan were approaching, they would not have been able to look up the river into Harpers Ferry. It is likely von Borcke confused the later climb up Maryland Heights with McLaws, which is discussed in note 66.

66. The visit to Pryor is recorded only in von Borcke, *Memoirs* 1:215–16, where a somewhat confused account (see note 65) has Stuart leaving for McLaws's headquarters at nearly dark. In his report, Stuart implies he proceeded directly from Crampton's Gap to Maryland Heights. *OR*, vol. 19, 1:818.

67. In *OR*, vol. 19, 1, see the reports of Stuart (p. 818) and McLaws (p. 854); also see, A. H. McLaws to McLaws, 2 P.M. Sept. 14, *OR*, vol. 19, 2:608; and McLaws, "Maryland," 12–13.

68. In addition to the sources cited in note 67, see von Borcke, *Memoirs* 1:216–17.

69. McClellan to Franklin, 6:20 P.M., Sept. 13, *OR*, vol. 19, 1:45–46.

70. This summary of the movements of the Federal left wing is derived from the following reports in *OR*, vol. 19, 1, Franklin (pp. 376–78), Slocum (pp. 380–81), Smith (p. 401), and Hancock (pp. 405–6), and also, the Itineraries (pp. 378–79), which contain information clarifying the reports.

71. See the report of Montague, 32d Va., ibid., 881.

72. Neese, *Three Years in the Confederate Horse Artillery*, 120. Stuart could not have arrived from Boonsboro, conferred, withdrawn Hampton, and left Crampton's Gap much before 10:00. According to Neese, the first sighting occurred "at about ten."

73. Neese, *Three Years in the Horse Artillery*, 120.

74. Munford, *OR*, vol. 19, 1:826.

75. In ibid. see the reports of Semmes (p. 873), Manly (p. 876), and Montague (pp. 881–82). Even Munford admitted it looked for awhile as if the enemy intended to attack Semmes at Brownsville Gap. (p. 826).

76. In ibid. see the reports of Munford (pp. 826–27) and Holt (pp. 876–77). Parham's regiments, which are estimated to have numbered 850 present for duty on September 1, may have been weakened by detachments as well as straggling. Allen, "Second Manassas Strengths," 193. Holt's fighting strength is given in ibid., 861, and likely is minus the two companies he sent back to the valley. Federal casualties are from ibid., 183. It might be noted in passing that the boat howitzers of Grimes's battery were ineffective due to their short range (Munford's report), and one of Chew's four rifled guns became disabled after two rounds. Neese, *Three Years in the Confederate Horse Artillery*, 121.

77. On the actions of Cobb and his brigade, see in *OR*, vol. 19, 1, the reports of Munford (pp. 826–27) and Cobb (pp. 870–71). Timothy J. Reese has a study of Cobb and his brigade underway that reveals both in a more favorable light. See his "Howell Cobb's Brigade at Crampton's Gap," *Blue & Gray Magazine* 15 (1998): 6–21, 47–56. If Reese's book fulfills the promise of his unannotated article, a major reevaluation of this battle will be required.

78. Cobb simply reported that he first selected his two strongest regiments, which would have been the 16th Georgia and the 15th North Carolina. In *OR*, vol. 19, 1, see Cobb's report (p. 870) and the returns for the brigade (p. 861).

79. The losses in Parham's regiments cannot be isolated, although Munford reported they suffered heavily. The 10th Georgia of Semmes lost one-third; and Cobb's brigade lost 690 out of 1,341, or 51.5 percent. Ibid., 861. Supposedly, the presence of a large number of conscripts in the 15th North Carolina added to the confusion in that regiment. Kearney, *North Carolina Regiments* 1:740.

80. Von Borcke, *Memoirs* 1:217; and in *OR*, vol. 19, 1, see the reports of Cobb (pp. 870–71), Stuart (pp. 818–19), McLaws (pp. 854–55), and Semmes (p. 873). See also McLaws, "Maryland," 13–14.

81. McLaws's report, ibid., 856.

82. In ibid. see the reports of McLaws (p. 855), Kershaw (p. 864), Semmes (p. 873), and Barksdale (p. 883); also see Hubbert, "Diary," 308. McLaws implies that Barksdale and Kershaw withdrew during the night, but their reports make clear they did not move until daylight. Barksdale erroneously states the 13th.

83. This somewhat romanticized episode is discussed further below.

84. Carman, "Maryland Campaign," chap. 9, pp. 569–70; and McLaws, "Maryland," 17–18. See also endorsement on original of Chilton to Munford, Sept. 14, 10:30 P.M., McLaws Papers, University of North Carolina. After the war, Richard H. Anderson would recall spending "the most difficult time of it under Maryland Heights at the foot of Pleasant Valley until Jackson cleared away the road for us." R. H. Anderson to D. H. Hill, Nov. 14, 1867, D. H. Hill Personal Papers, North Carolina State Archives.

85. Longstreet's report, *OR*, vol. 19, 1:839; and Longstreet in "Maryland," 666 (first quote); and idem, *Memoirs*, 227 (second quote). It was perhaps the negative impression made by Longstreet in this message that caused Lee after the war to imply the defeat was Hill's fault: "Genl. Hill *ought to have* had all of his troops up at the mountain, while in fact part were back in Boonsboro." Gallagher, ed., *Lee the Soldier*, 26. Considering that it was Lee who had scattered the army all over western Maryland and had himself been slow to waken to the danger of McClellan's advance, he was not being very charitable to Hill.

86. In *OR*, vol. 19, 1, see the reports of Pendleton (pp. 829–30), Barnwell (p. 837), and the tables (pp. 836–37); see also Pendleton to wife, Sept. 22, S. P. Lee, *Memoirs*, 212. Apparently, there were enough six-gun batteries to carry the Artillery Reserve average above four.

87. This is the message Jackson must have received by 8:00 in order to pen his reply by 8:15. See the discussion in notes 55–57.

88. Hood, *Advance and Retreat,* 41.

89. For further discussion of the war council at the Mountain House, see Harsh, *Sounding the Shallows,* chap. 8, sect. J.

90. For further discussion of Lee's decision to retreat to Virginia, see ibid., sect. K.

91. The existence of the lost eight o'clock dispatch to Jackson, which had not previously been suspected, is asserted with positive assurance by Ezra Carman, "Maryland Campaign," chap. 9, pp. 506–7. His description of Jackson receiving the message the following morning is discussed below.

92. Chilton to McLaws, 8:00 P.M., Sept. 14, *OR,* vol. 51, 2:618–19. It is not clear why Lee thought McLaws would be at Weverton.

93. In ibid., vol. 19, 1, see the reports of Toombs (p. 888), Little (p. 911), and D. H. Hill (p. 1025). See also Carman, "Maryland Campaign," chap. 9, pp. 507–12. Toombs received orders from his division commander, D. R. Jones, at about 10:00. It is interesting that D. H. Hill sent his trains to Hagerstown, and Lee—who must have passed them on the road—did not countermand the order. It is a strong indication that through midday Lee still intended Hagerstown to be his base.

94. Longstreet, *From Manassas to Appomattox,* 227.

95. Corse's report, *OR,* vol. 19, 1:904.

96. Hood, *Advance and Retreat,* 41; Hood's report, dated Sept. 27, *OR,* vol. 19, 1:922.

97. Carman, "Maryland Campaign," chap. 8, p. 497.

98. Sorrel, *Recollections of a Confederate Staff Officer,* 101–2; Ratchford, Memoir, 37–38, North Carolina State Archives; and D. H. Hill, "South Mountain," 579–80.

99. H. W. Thomas, *History of the Doles-Cook Brigade,* 68–69.

100. A. S. Cutts, "Cutts' Battalion at Sharpsburg," *SHSP* 10 (1882): 430.

101. Ripley's report, *OR,* vol. 19, 1:1032.

102. On the late withdrawal, see in *OR,* vol. 19, 1: 4:00 A.M., Walker for Jenkins's brigade (p. 906); sometime after midnight, Stevens of Evans's brigade (p. 942); and 11:00, Rodes (p. 1036). For between 9:00 and midnight, see DeRosset (of Ripley), *North Carolina Regiments* 1:225; 11:00 P.M., Owen (of Washington Artillery), *In Camp and Battle,* 137; "about 9 o'clock," Gorman (of G. B. Anderson), "Memoirs," 5. Also see three sources on Ripley's brigade: "ten to twelve," DeRosset, "South Mountain," 309; "about 11 P.M.," Thruston's report, *SOR* 3:585; and "about 10 o'clock," Leach, Diary, Sept. 14.

103. Carman, "Maryland Campaign," chap. 8, p. 497.

104. On the rest pause at Boonsboro, see Ramsay, *North Carolina Regiments* 1:573; Corse of Kemper's brigade, *OR,* vol. 19, 1:904, and vol. 51, 1:169; 44th Georgia of Ripley's brigade, H. W. Thomas, *History of the Doles-Cook Brigade,* 469; Cutts, "Cutts' Battalion," 430; 17th Virginia of Kemper's brigade, G. Wise, *History of the 17th Va.,* 114. Capt. John C. Gorman (2d North Carolina, G. B. Anderson's brigade), remembered resting near Boonsboro until four o'clock. Gorman, "Memoirs," 6.

105. Munford's report, *OR,* vol. 19, 1:827; idem, "Maryland," 52.

106. Chilton to Munford, 10:15 P.M., Sept. 14, *OR,* vol. 19, 2:609, addressed to Rohrersville. Original, with endorsement "None found," in McLaws Papers, University of North Carolina.

107. Stevens's report, *OR,* vol. 19, 1:942.

108. Lee to Davis, Sept. 16, ibid., 140. Apparently, only a brigade of Sedgwick's division was involved. McClellan's report, ibid., 52.

109. Chilton to McLaws, 11:15 P.M., Sept. 14, ibid., 2:608. No specific place addressed. Since Lee dictated this dispatch less than an hour after ordering the reconnaissance by Evans, it is possible he had not awaited the results.

110. Henry Kyd Douglas was absent with Jackson, and Bradley Johnson probably was as well. Charles Marshall hailed from too-distant Baltimore. Capt. Alexander Heard's company of Frederick recruits may have been left behind in Hagerstown. Still, it is remarkable that Lee could not find expert advice on so important a point.

111. For further discussion of Lee's decision to retreat to Virginia, see Harsh, *Sounding the Shallows*, chap. 8, sect. K.

112. Alexander, *Military Memoirs*, 234; also *Fighting for the Confederacy*, 144.

113. In *OR*, vol. 19, 1, see the reports of Pendleton (p. 830) and Barnwell (p. 838); see also Pendleton to wife, Sept. 22, S. P. Lee, *Memoirs*, 212–13. It was at this point that Lee and Pendleton probably assumed Cutts's battalion was still subject to the orders of D. H. Hill, while the latter assumed Cutts had reverted to the artillery reserve. See Cutts, "Cutts' Battalion," 430–31. Once again, there is no mention of H. P. Jones or his battalion, but presumably he remained with D. H. Hill. See Harsh, *Sounding the Shallows*, chap. 7, sect. D.

114. Carman, "Maryland Campaign," chap. 9, pp. 514–15, where it is evident that Carman worked from uncited testimony from survivors of the march, including Stephen D. Lee.

115. Ibid., 525. The 1st Virginia was absent in Hagerstown with the trains.

116. Ibid., 523.

117. No report for the campaign by Fitz Lee has been found; but see the accounts in H. B. McClellan, *I Rode with Jeb Stuart*, 124; and George William Beale, "Maryland Campaign, The Cavalry Fight at Boonsboro Graphically Described, The Ninth Virginia and Eighth Illinois Regiments Cross Sabers," *SHSP* 25 (1897): 276–77; and the excellent details in Carman, "Maryland Campaign," chap. 9, pp. 523, 525. Less useful are F. Lee, *Lee*, 205; and Johnson, "Maryland," 523–24. The estimate of Lee's brigade is from Allen, "Second Manassas Strengths," 201; and Fitz Lee's estimate of the Federals is recorded in Owen, *In Camp and Battle*, 136.

118. Owen, *In Camp and Battle*, 137; Carman, "Maryland Campaign," chap. 9, pp. 517–18.

119. Alexander, *Fighting for the Confederacy*, 144. Commissary Sergeant John Tucker of the 5th Alabama recorded in his journal: "Never saw so much straggling in all my life." Tucker, "Diary," 20.

120. Rodes report, *OR*, vol. 19, 1:1036. Additional details from Carman, "Maryland Campaign," chap. 9, pp. 513–14.

121. The Federals claimed "over sixty wagons." See Wool to Halleck, Sept. 15, *OR*, vol. 19, 1:758–59; and William M. Luff, "March of the Cavalry from Harper's Ferry, September 14, 1862," in *Military Essays and Recollections, Papers Read before the Commandery of the State of Illinois, Military Order of the Loyal Legion of the United States*, 4 vols. (Chicago: A. C. McClurg, 1891–1907), 2:47. The Confederates admitted to losing forty-five. See Lee to Davis, Sept. 21, *OR*, vol. 19, 1:142; Alexander, *Military Memoirs*, 234, 236; and idem, *Fighting for the Confederacy*, 144. A convenient summary of the anecdotes of this romantic night escape may be found in John W. Mies, "Breakout at Harper's Ferry," *Civil War History* 2 (1956): 13–28; and Tischler, *Harper's Ferry*, which is well researched. Additional details from the Confederate side are from Carman, "Maryland Campaign," chap. 9, pp. 509–11, which cites the "historian of the 11th Georgia."

122. Pendleton's report, *OR*, vol. 19, 1:830. Coincidentally, Maj. Walter Taylor had returned to Hagerstown from his S.O. 191 mission to Leesburg and Winchester on the night of September 14. He had scarcely gone to sleep in a room at the Hamilton Hotel when a ruckus outside his window alerted him to the news that a battle had occurred at South Mountain and the Confederates were retreating toward the Potomac. Taylor set out for Sharpsburg; but overcome with weariness, he spent the rest of the night asleep behind a hayrick along the road. Apparently his sleep was extraordinarily deep, because he discovered the next morning that Davis and the 1,300 Federal horseman had passed within feet of him during the night. Taylor, *General Lee*, 121–22.

123. Toombs's report, *OR*, vol. 19, 1:888; Carman, "Maryland Campaign," chap. 9, p. 509. Toombs sent the 15th and 17th Georgia under Col. W. T. Williams to Williamsport, and the regiments did not rejoin him until the afternoon of the 17th during the attack by Burnside.

124. The report of Confederate casualties in the Maryland campaign by Surgeon LaFayette Guild, medical director of the Army of Northern Virginia, printed in *OR*, vol. 19, 1:810–13, is defective in three ways: (1) it omits some regiments and brigades of infantry, and includes no cavalry or Reserve Artillery; (2) it includes killed and wounded but omits captured and missing; and (3) it is not broken down by battle or engagement. After years of study, Ezra Carman put Confederate losses at 1,932 at Turner's Gap and 962 at Crampton's Gap. Carman, "Maryland Campaign," chap. 26, p. 2. Carman accepts the Federal losses as 1,813 at Turner's and 533 at Crampton's, as compiled by the editors of the *Official Records* from nominal lists and returns. *OR*, vol. 19, 1:183–88.

7. "We will make our stand on these hills": Lee's Hope Renewed, September 15, 1862

1. Lee's daylight arrival in Keedysville is from Carman, "Maryland Campaign," chap. 9, pp. 517–18.

2. Long to McLaws, Sept. 15, Headquarters, Centreville, Maryland (addressed to Maryland Heights), *OR*, vol. 19, 1:609–10.

3. Carman, "Maryland Campaign," chap. 9, pp. 507, 518–19. This information is not found in Munford's report, and, along with additional details relating to Munford's brigade, it suggests that Carman had available postwar testimony from Munford or a staff member close to the cavalry commander. The analysis of Lee's thinking given above differs slightly from that reached by Carman, who believed Munford's message freed Lee to retire to Sharpsburg. Carman understood Lee to stand at Keedysville only to threaten the flank of an enemy moving on McLaws, if the latter's command crossed Elk Ridge; he ignored the fact that McLaws's escape—in whatever direction—had to be protected.

4. Carman, "Maryland Campaign," chap. 9, p. 518. Carman indicates only that Lee was dissatisfied with the Keedysville position. Since Lee had neither the time nor the mobility to examine the ground himself, it makes sense to assume he had the engineers on his staff reconnoiter the terrain, one of the traditional tasks of the engineers. Oliver T. Reilly, age five at the time, remembers watching the Confederates retreat through Keedysville for hours. He also recalled that staff officers rode through the town warning the citizens to flee, as there was likely to be "a battle . . . fought over the town." See Reilly's *The Battlefield of Antietam* (Hagerstown: Hagerstown Bookbinding and Printing, 1906), unpaginated [p. 25].

5. This detailed account of Lee's reconnaissance is based on information in Carman, "Maryland Campaign," chap. 9, pp. 518–20. Carman cites no source. For such intimate details (the coffee and the contents of the dispatch), however, he must have had testimony from someone on Lee's staff. As to location, Carman says only that the high meadow was near McClellan's future headquarters. It may have been the flat ridge immediately southwest of the Pry farmhouse, today sometimes known as the Kefauver overlook.

6. On the bridge—soon known as the Middle or Lee bridge—as well as the other bridges on the battlefield, see Helen Ashe Hays, *The Antietam and Its Bridges: The Annals of an Historic Stream* (New York: G. P. Putnam's Sons, 1910). On D. H. Hill's taking up position at Sharpsburg, the best source is Carman, "Maryland Campaign," chap. 9, pp. 514–15. For corroborating (if sometimes confused) details, see in *OR*, vol. 19, 1, the reports of D. H. Hill (p. 1022), Ripley (p. 1032), and Rodes (p. 1036). See also, in *North Carolina Regiments* 1, Cowan (p. 184), DeRosset (p. 225), Osborne (p. 246), and Montgomery (p. 627); and Tucker, "Diary," 20; Thruston's report, *SOR* 3:586; H. W. Thomas, *History of the Doles-Cook Brigade*, 469; Shinn, Diary, Sept. 15; and Ratchford, Memoir, 39. Ripley's comment that he posted his own,

G. B. Anderson's, and Garland's (McRae) brigades under orders of Longstreet and in the "temporary absence" of D. H. Hill apparently refers to a rearrangement of the line later in the day.

7. This is the hill just east of Sharpsburg, which roughly parallels Antietam Creek. Today it is the site of the Antietam National Cemetery, south of the Boonsoboro Pike, and the civilian Mountain View Cemetery, north of the same road. There is no evidence that the name Cemetery Hill was used at the time of the battle, but veterans did employ it in their recollections. See Carman, "Maryland Campaign," chap. 9, p. 520. It is a convenient sobriquet that deserves resurrection. Moreover, it is not anachronistic, since the cemetery for the nearby Lutheran Church was located there in September 1862.

8. On Longstreet's arrival see ibid. Less helpful is Longstreet himself in his report, *OR*, vol. 19, 1:839–40; *From Manassas to Appomattox*, 233–36; and "Maryland," 666–67. He mistakenly implies in the memoirs that both he and Hill arrived during the afternoon. There is evidence that Longstreet visited the battlefield after the war, and he may have given additional verbal details to Carman at that time. Reilly, *Battlefield* [p. 20].

9. On the posting of the Confederate artillery, see Carman, "Maryland Campaign," chap. 9, pp. 515–16, 521–22. Quote is from William Owen (adjutant of the Washington Artillery), *In Camp and Battle*, 138. See also Ramsay, *North Carolina Regiments* 1:573–74; and in *OR*, vol. 19, 1, the reports of S. D. Lee (p. 844), Walton (p. 848), and Frobel (p. 925). For discussion of a possible variation by Squires's battery of the Washington (La.) Artillery, see note 53 below.

10. Cutts, "Cutts' Battalion," 430–31; and some additional details in Carman, "Maryland Campaign," chap. 9, p. 524. Around sunrise, Cutts rode from his camp west of Boonsboro back to town and found the army gone and the enemy near. He also discovered Lloyd's North Carolina battery in a field, its horses unharnessed and its men asleep. Cutts ordered the battery to join him and set off on an adventure that eventually brought him down the Hagerstown Pike to the Dunkard Church. Lloyd's battery was in such poor condition it had been left behind at Frederick by Walker's division, and after the campaign it would be disbanded for having lost a gun and two caissons without firing a shot. See Ransom to Chilton, Sept. 25, *OR*, vol. 19, 1:921.

11. On the arrival of D. R. Jones's division the greatest detail may be found in Carman, "Maryland Campaign," chap. 9, p. 520. Scanty coverage is provided in Latrobe, Diary, Sept. 15; Hunton's report, *OR*, vol. 19, 1:898; Wood, *Reminiscences of Big I*, 37, which says the 19th Virginia had no food with them; G. Wise, *History of the 17th Va.*, 114, which says his regiment was allowed to cook and eat breakfast at "Kistersville"; and Hunter, "Sharpsburg," 511–12, and "Sharpsburg, II," 10–11, which provides a dubiously detailed account of foraging on the march and has his regiment arriving "late in the evening." Joseph Walker's brigade (Jenkins) is not accounted for by Carman or the reports. It may have arrived later with Hood and the rear guard. In any case, by the afternoon it was in line with the other brigades of D. R. Jones south of the Boonsboro Pike.

12. William Henry Morgan, *Personal Reminiscences of the War of 1861–5, In Camp, en Bivouac, on the March, on Picket, on the Skirmish Line, on the Battlefield, and in Prison* (Lynchburg: J. P. Bell, 1911), 141. This dramatic incident—which has been a favorite with historians (see Freeman, *R. E. Lee* 2:378)—may be the product of army folklore. It was recorded five decades after the fact by Pvt. William Henry Morgan, who was absent from his regiment during the Maryland campaign and only heard the story from comrades sometime after he returned to the army on September 25. Morgan belonged to Company C, 11th Virginia, Kemper's brigade, D. R. Jones's division.

13. On the posting of Toombs, see in *OR*, vol. 19, 1, the reports of Toombs (p. 888); and in ibid., vol. 51, 1, Benning (pp. 161–62), Lewis (p. 165), and Cumming (p. 168). Also see, Carman, "Maryland Campaign," chap. 9, 521.

14. On the arrival of the rear guard, the most comprehensive coverage is found in Carman, "Maryland Campaign," chap. 9, p. 522. Also see in *OR*, vol. 19, 1, the reports of G. T. Anderson (p. 909), Hood (p. 922), Wofford (p. 927), Law (p. 937), Evans (p. 939), Hilton (p. 949), and Durham (p. 950). Also see Hood, *Advance and Retreat*, 41; and Ray, *North Carolina Regiments* 1:307.

15. D. H. Hill's postwar complaint that Longstreet hogged the high ground while he got "the flats" is misleading in two respects. First, whether Lee assigned Hill the position north of the Boonsboro Pike or Hill selected it for himself, the decision was made hours before the arrival of Longstreet. Second, two-thirds of Hill's line was on a ridge (even if lower than Cemetery Hill), and only the far left, which ran along the Sunken Road to connect with the Hagerstown Pike, was on relatively flat ground. See Hill to his son, Joseph, 1886, cited in Bridges, *Lee's Maverick General*, 116.

16. The tables in *OR*, vol. 19, 1:836–37, verify eighty-nine guns in twenty-one of the batteries, and twenty guns are estimated for the remaining five batteries. See also, C. Johnson, *Artillery Hell*, 125–28.

17. The 11th, 15th, and 17th Georgia, absent guarding the trains, have been deducted. Hooker estimated he saw 30,000 Confederates on the afternoon of the 15th. Hooker's report, *OR*, vol. 19, 1:217.

18. For sample criticisms of Lee's stand at Sharpsburg on September 15, see Murfin, *Gleam of Bayonets*, 205–6; Stephen W. Sears, "Getting Right with Robert E. Lee: How To Know the Unknowable Man," in *The Civil War: The Best of American Heritage*, ed. Stephen W. Sears (Boston: Houghton Mifflin, 1991), 49; and Jeffry D. Wert, *General James Longstreet: The Confederacy's Most Controversial Soldier—A Biography* (New York: Simon & Schuster, 1993), 191.

19. Carman, "Maryland Campaign," chap. 9, p. 523.

20. Jackson to Lee, 8:00 A.M., Sept. 15, *OR*, vol. 19, 1:951. For further discussion of Jackson's announcement to Lee of the fall of Harpers Ferry, see Harsh, *Sounding the Shallows*, chap. 8, sect. L.

21. On Lee's comment and the cheering, see Owen, *In Camp and Battle*, 138; while Longstreet, *From Manassas to Appomattox*, 228, confirms the time in general terms, as does Latrobe, Diary, Sept. 15.

22. No one, except Carman, has inferred the necessary existence of the missing message from Lee to Jackson in response to the news of the surrender of Harpers Ferry, nor that it must have answered Jackson's questions—and in so doing rendered final the decision to stand at Sharpsburg. Without citation, Carman makes the simple assertion: "Having concluded to receive battle on the Antietam, Lee replied to Jackson's dispatches by ordering him to join him as quickly as possible." Carman, "Maryland Campaign," chap. 9, p. 564.

23. Alexander, *Fighting for the Confederacy*, 145–46. Porter's memoirs are valuable for testimony on events he personally witnessed, but he was not a careful student of the Maryland campaign. His entire sweeping judgment is based on the erroneous notions that neither did Lee order Jackson from Harpers Ferry nor did McClellan appear on the Antietam until September 16.

24. Lee to Davis, Sept. 16, *OR*, vol. 19, 1:140.

25. This summary of the Federal advance from Turner's Gap is from Carman, "Maryland Campaign," chap. 9, pp. 526–46; McClellan, *Own Story*, 584–87; Cox, *Military Reminiscences* 1:297–300; from *OR*, vol. 19, 1, the reports of Pleasonton (p. 210) and Hooker (pp. 216–17); and from the correspondence in ibid., 47, 2:294–307, and vol. 51, 1:834–38.

26. Confederate details of the cavalry fight in Boonsboro are from Carman, "Maryland Campaign," chap. 9, pp. 529–31; George William Beale, *A Lieutenant of Cavalry in Lee's Army* (Boston: Gorham Press, 1918), 45–46; the same author's "Maryland," 277–78; and H. B. McClellan, *I Rode with Jeb Stuart*, 124–26. F. Lee, *Lee*, 205, is not helpful.

27. Considering the large number of stragglers left behind by the main body the night before, it is not certain all of the casualties came from Fitz Lee's brigade; nor is it clear the two guns were those of Pelham. At least one might have been abandoned by Lloyd's North Carolina battery. See note 10.

28. Hooker ought not have been completely surprised, however, for he had received a report at ten o'clock that the Confederates had formed a line at Sharpsburg. He may have been alerted by McClellan who had information from the signal station just established at the Washington monument on South Mountain. Hooker's report, *OR*, vol. 19, 1:217. In his report, Hooker estimated the strength of the Confederates at 30,000; while in his testimony before the Committee on the Conduct of the War he put the figure at 50,000. *Joint Committee on the Conduct of the War Report* 1:580–81.

29. It should be noted in passing that in 1876 the Military Historical Society of Massachusetts commissioned a committee report on the "Alleged Delay in Concentration of the Army of the Potomac under McClellan at Antietam . . . ," John Chipman Gray, "Report of . . . ," in *PMHSM* 14:1–3. While a full discussion of the report must await the next study (Federal strategy), suffice it here to mention the committee worked before publication of the *Official Records*, and the value of its report is limited to several firsthand observations, which are included.

30. For a discussion of what Miles could have known on the morning of the 15th, see Harsh, *Sounding the Shallows*, chap. 8, sect. M.

31. On whether Harpers Ferry was fog enshrouded on the morning of Sept. 15, see ibid., sect. N.

32. Sixty-eight guns would seem to represent the maximum number brought to bear by the Confederates on the morning of the 15th. The inefficiency of the eight guns of McLaws and Walker has been discussed; moreover, McLaws had removed two of his guns from Maryland Heights during the night. Jackson had a total of sixty-two guns distributed in seventeen batteries. It is not certain all were used. Crutchfield apparently employed only eight of the ten he carried across the Shenandoah; and of those remaining with Jackson at least twelve were of such short range (6–pounders) as to be ineffective. In *OR*, vol. 19, 1, see the tables (pp. 806–8, 836–39) and Crutchfield's report (p. 962). According to Jennings Wise, the Letcher Artillery of A. P. Hill had been left in Richmond, which would be four fewer guns available to Jackson. Jennings Cropper Wise, *The Long Arm of Lee; or, The History of the Artillery of the Army of Northern Virginia*, 2 vols. (Lynchburg: J. P. Bell, 1915), 281.

33. Killed and wounded for the Federals during the entire siege totaled only 217, and 173 of these occurred among the units that fought on Maryland Heights on the 12th and 13th. The difference of forty-four must be increased to the fifty to sixty range for the morning of the 15th to allow for several casualties suffered during the bombardment, for example seven killed in the 126th New York. Sixty casualties out of 12,737 represents 0.00471 percent, or less than one-half of 1 percent. It might be noted that on the day after the surrender, Porter Alexander concluded, "from all my experience of artillery fire scattered over a considerable territory, as it was here, I should not have anticipated so speedy a surrender. I should have thought it would take a day, or possibly more, to force surrender." Alexander, *Fighting for the Confederacy*, 145.

34. For Confederate tactical operations in general on the morning of the 15th, see Jackson's report, *OR*, vol. 19, 1:955; Douglas, *I Rode with Stonewall*, 161–62; and idem, "Maryland," 625–26. On A. P. Hill's division, see in *OR*, vol. 19, 1, the reports of A. P. Hill (pp. 980–81), Walker (p. 984), Lane (p. 985), McGowan (p. 987), Perrin (p. 993), Edwards (pp. 997–98), Brown (pp. 998–99), Archer (p. 1000), Neale (p. 1003), Pender (p. 1004), and Thomas (p. 1006). See also Harris, *North Carolina Regiments* 1:372; Cathey, ibid., 760; Sutton, ibid., 2:70; Healy, "Second Letter," 626–27; Chamberlayne, *Letters*, 109; Daly, *Portrait of a*

Man, 78–79; Haynes, *Diary*, 19–20; and Caldwell, *History of a Brigade of South Carolinians*, 71–72. On Lawton's division, see Early's report, *OR*, vol. 19, 1:966; Powers, *North Carolina Regiments* 2:155–56; H. W. Thomas, *History of the Doles-Cook Brigade*, 222; Nisbet, *Four Years on the Firing Line*, 102; Sheeran, *Confederate Chaplain*, 31; and Early, *War Memoirs*, 137. On J. R. Jones's division, see in *OR*, vol. 19, 1, the reports of J. R. Jones (p. 1007), Williams (pp. 1011–12), and Pendleton (p. 1016). See also, Poague, *Gunner with Stonewall*, 43–44; Worsham, *One of Jackson's Foot Cavalry*, 85; and E. A. Moore, *Story of a Cannoneer*, 138–39.

35. For a discussion of the timing of the surrender of Harpers Ferry, see Harsh, *Sounding the Shallows*, chap. 8, sect. O.

36. In *OR*, vol. 19, 1, the reports of Jackson (p. 955), Hawks (p. 961), and A. P. Hill (pp. 980–81). For discussion of Jackson's paroling of the Harpers Ferry garrison, see Harsh, *Sounding the Shallows*, chap. 8, sect. P.

37. The telegraph, which the Federals had not destroyed, was used to notify McLaws. McLaws report, *OR*, vol. 19, 1:855. The signal to Walker is assumed. A member of the 30th Virginia noted hearing the news by 10:00 A.M. Hirsch, Diary, Sept. 15.

38. The quote is from von Borcke, *Memoirs* 1:221–22; see also Stuart's report, *OR*, vol. 19, 1:819; H. B. McClellan, *I Rode with Jeb Stuart*, 123–24; and Carman, "Maryland Campaign," chap. 9, pp. 564–65. William Blackford indicated the staff believed Stuart had taken Hampton and Munford with him to Sharpsburg. Stuart had already decided to leave Hampton behind to cover McLaws's crossing and to protect the forces remaining at Harpers Ferry, however, but he may have mentioned picking up Munford along the way. Blackford, *War Years with Jeb Stuart*, 147; and von Borcke, *Memoirs* 1:224.

39. For a discussion of Jackson's message to Lee at noon of the 15th, see Harsh, *Sounding the Shallows*, chap. 8, sect. Q.

40. The message from Lee has never been found, nor is there any direct evidence that it ever existed. Yet, the probability Lee sent it is very high. Jackson's eight o'clock dispatch contained questions that demanded answers. It might be argued Jackson's endorsement that he was coming to Sharpsburg could have arrived very quickly and obviated the need for Lee to direct Stonewall's march. Even so—and it is not likely it arrived that quickly—Lee needed to tell Jackson whether there was time to secure the men and materials captured and to draw rations, or whether the emergency was so great that the expeditionary forces must ignore all else and rush to Sharpsburg.

41. McLaws's report, *OR*, vol. 19, 1:855; Walker, "Harper's Ferry," 610–11. McLaws mentions being summoned, while Walker only remarked on visiting Harpers Ferry. McLaws's meeting can be pegged at about two o'clock, since it is known that Lt. Thomas S. B. Tucker, a member of McLaws's staff, returned with Jackson's summons about one o'clock. Carman, "Maryland Campaign," chap. 10, p. 571. The time of Walker's meeting cannot be determined.

42. McLaws, "Maryland," 18. When measured on the Confederate map in War Department, *The Official Atlas of the Civil War*, intro. Richard J. Sommers (New York: Arno Press, 1978), Plate 29, p. 1, the distance from Halltown to Sharpsburg by way of Sandy Hook and the Maryland side is at least thirteen miles, as compared to eleven on the Virginia side by way of Boteler's Ford. Actually both routes were indeterminately longer than they appear on the map, since the roads on both sides were so hilly and winding as to add many miles.

43. Carman, "Maryland Campaign," chap. 10, pp. 571, 581–82. McLaws concluded that Jackson was under orders to march to join Lee, implying Lee's response to the victory dispatch had already arrived. This seems less likely than the interpretation given in the text above. Carman also writes that he had been assured by members of Jackson's staff that Stonewall discussed the possibility of crossing into Pleasant Valley to defeat Franklin.

44. The anecdote is from William Blackford of Stuart's staff, who, with Stuart, was present with McLaws at the time. Blackford, *War Years with Jeb Stuart*, 145. For further information on the cavalry, see in *OR*, vol. 19, 1, the reports of Stuart (p. 819) and Hampton (p. 824);

see also von Borcke, *Memoirs* 1:219–21; and Blackford, *War Years with Jeb Stuart*, 144–47. On the divisions of McLaws and Anderson, see in *OR*, vol. 19, 1, the reports of McLaws (pp. 855–56), Kershaw (p. 864), and Barksdale, who gets the day wrong (p. 883); see also Kearney, *North Carolina Regiments* 1:739–41; Dinkins, "Barksdale's Brigade," 259; and Dickert, *History of Kershaw's Brigade*, 150.

45. Carman, "Maryland Campaign," chap. 10, pp. 571–72; McLaws's reports, *OR*, vol. 19, 1:855–56, 857; McLaws, "Maryland," 18; Hubbert, "Diary," 309; Dinkins, "Barksdale's Brigade," 259, and Dinkins, *Personal Recollections and Experiences*, 55. After the war, McLaws's chief commissary testified that upon application to the "proper office of Genl. Jackson's command," he was told "the captured stores had been distributed to others." Statement by J. F. Edwards, McLaws Papers, University of North Carolina. The possibility that McLaws may have exaggerated his problems and the time consumed in crossing the bridge in order to cover his later tardiness is raised by an entry in Jed. Hotchkiss's diary: "McLaws' Division came over, from Md. Heights, at midnight and he remained near Hall Town the rest of the night" (*Make Me a Map*, 82).

46. The quote is from Hirsch, Diary, Sept. 16; see also in *North Carolina Regiments*, 2, Graham (p. 433) and Burgwyn (p. 601). For Walker's version—which as usual puts the best possible face on the events—see *OR*, vol. 19, 1:914; and "Harper's Ferry," 610–11.

47. In *OR*, vol. 19, 1, see the Harpers Ferry returns (p. 549), Jackson's report (p. 955), Harman's report (pp. 960–61), Hawks's report (p. 961), and Crutchfield's report (p. 962). Jackson claimed to capture seventy-three cannon, although the Federals admitted to the loss of only forty-seven, of which seven had been spiked. (McIlvaine's report, p. 548.) Ham Chamberlayne, who was in charge of the captured guns—at least until Porter Alexander arrived—seems to verify the Federal position in a letter to his sister of September 22, when he states the number of cannon to be forty-six. Chamberlayne, *Letters*, 110. Moreover, on September 16, Lee reported to Davis the capture of only forty-nine guns. *OR*, vol. 19, 1:141. The difference seems to be explained by whether or not the mountain howitzers were counted as cannon. The historian of the 34th North Carolina remembered that the prisoners were marched to the Maryland side before being counted, paroled, and released. Lattimore, *North Carolina Regiments* 2:585. Thirteen thousand small arms were captured, including those turned in by the prisoners. On the regiments who traded up from smooth bores to rifles, see Harris (7th North Carolina), *North Carolina Regiments* 1:372; and McLaurin (18th North Carolina), ibid., 2:32.

48. Early's report, *OR*, vol. 19, 1:967; Powers, "21st Regiment, Additional Sketch," *North Carolina Regiments* 2:156; Nisbet, *Four Years on the Firing Line*, 102; and Early, *War Memoirs*, 139; H. W. Thomas, *History of the Doles-Cook Brigade*, 222. Time was also taken on the evening of the 15th to destroy the B&O railroad bridge and to prepare to destroy the pontoon bridge. Hotchkiss, *Make Me a Map*, 82, implies both bridges were destroyed that night. The pontoon bridge remained, however, as McLaws did not finish crossing until 11:00 the next morning and was followed by Hampton. Since the demolition was carried out by the engineers, however, it should not have affected the start of any of the troops to Sharpsburg. It is an interesting question as to why Miles had not destroyed the pontoon bridge himself on the 14th.

49. In *OR*, vol. 19, 1, see the reports of J. R. Jones (p. 1007) and Williams (p. 1011); see also, E. A. Moore, *Story of a Cannoneer*, 143; and Worsham, *One of Jackson's Foot Cavalry*, 86, the latter being the only source to imply an early evening start.

50. This story is pieced together from Stuart's report, *OR*, vol. 19, 1:819; H. B. McClellan, *I Rode with Jeb Stuart*, 123–24; and Carman, "Maryland Campaign," chap. 9, pp. 564–65. The conversation is from Carman, who cites Lt. Col. Samuel McDowell Tate of the 6th North Carolina as source.

51. For Jackson's writing of this message, see Harsh, *Sounding the Shallows*, chap. 8, sect. Q. There is nothing to pinpoint the time of its arrival, but it makes sense to believe it came between Stuart's arrival and the time when the enemy appeared on the Antietam. It

should be noted that Henry Kyd Douglas theorized that Jackson's endorsed message was the deciding factor in Lee's determination to stand at Sharpsburg. Although Carman accepts this interpretation, it has not been followed in the text above, where it is seen as simply reaffirming Lee in his decision. As previously stated, Lee must have decided somewhat earlier when he answered Jackson's victory dispatch of eight o'clock. See note 22.

52. D. S. Freeman mistakenly has Lee studying maps when Fitz Lee informs him of the arrival of the Federals. Freeman, *R. E. Lee* 2:379. Freeman transposed the events of the following day, when Lee learned of Hooker's crossing the Antietam, as is clear in the source Freeman cited. White, *Robert E. Lee*, 211.

53. Carman "Maryland Campaign," chap. 9, p. 523 (which is plainly based on testimony from Rosser), 532–33 (probably derived from a veteran of the 5th New Hampshire). For a note on Charles Squires, Washington Artillery, and his claim to form the rear guard, see Harsh, *Sounding the Shallows*, chap. 8, sect. R.

54. In *OR*, vol. 19, 1, see the reports of S. D. Lee (p. 844), Walton (p. 848), and Frobel (p. 925). The quote is from Longstreet, *From Manassas to Appomattox*, 234. The anecdote is from Ramsay, *North Carolina Regiments* 1:573–74, who puts the incident at 10:00 in the morning—which was not only before the battery had arrived, but some four or five hours before there were any Federal guns to fire on it.

55. Carman, "Maryland Campaign," chap. 9, pp. 530–31. Carman has F. Lee arriving in the evening, but that seems in error, as part of his brigade traveled and arrived with Cutts's battalion of artillery.

56. Carman, "Maryland Campaign, chap. 9, pp. 523–24. It is noteworthy that previous accounts of the Battle of Antietam have confined Munford to the Lower Bridge and Snavely's Ford, missing the point that he extended Lee's line all the way to the Potomac. Munford's official report ends with Crampton's Gap, and Carman's account is based on postwar testimony from the colonel.

57. Carman, "Maryland Campaign," chap. 9, p. 565; in *OR*, vol. 19, 1, the reports of Hood (pp. 922–23), Wofford (p. 927), and Law (p. 937). See also, Ray, *North Carolina Regiments* 1:307. Francis Palfrey ("Battle of Antietam," 2) incorrectly implies Hood proceeded directly from Keedysville to the Dunkard Church.

58. Owen, *In Camp and Battle*, 139. It is possible Lee intended to sleep in the Widow Herr's house at Boonsboro on the night of 14th.

59. Lee to G. W. Smith, Sept. 15, Hagerstown, Md., *OR*, vol. 19, 1:609. Smith's report has not been found, but its contents are easily inferred from Lee's reply. On the inconsistency of the date and location of this letter, see Harsh, *Sounding the Shallows*, chap. 8, sect. S.

60. Lee to G. W. Smith, Sept. 7, and Lee to Davis, Sept. 13, *OR*, vol. 19, 2:599, 606.

61. From a reference table compiled from *OR*, vol. 18:750, 751, 759, 764; and for the breakdown of the brigades of Clingman, Martin, and Pettigrew, see *North Carolina Regiments* 4:482, 552, 556. The command on the Rappahannock included the 61st Virginia, the 13th Virginia Cavalry, the 14th Virginia Cavalry Battalion, and the 2d North Carolina Cavalry. The organizational chart in *OR*, vol. 19, 1:804, assigns the 61st Virginia to Mahone's brigade of R. H. Anderson's division, but the regiment did not join the Army of Northern Virginia until after the end of the Maryland campaign.

62. Lee to Davis, Sept. 5, *OR*, vol. 19, 2:593.

63. Owen, *In Camp and Battle*, 139. The adjutant of the Washington Artillery quartered in a house across the street from Lee and either heard the remark or heard it repeated.

64. Early's report, *OR*, vol. 19, 1:967; Early, *War Memoirs*, 139; Nisbet, *Four Years on the Firing Line*, 102; and Powers, *North Carolina Regiments* 2:156.

65. On Jackson see Hotchkiss, *Make Me a Map*, 82; Douglas, *I Rode with Stonewall*, 165; and Douglas, "Maryland," 627. On J. R. Jones see in *OR*, vol. 19, 1, the reports of Jones (p. 1007) and Williams (p. 1011); and also, E. A. Moore, *Story of a Cannoneer*, 143. On Walker

see Walker's report, *OR*, vol. 19, 1:914; Walker, "Harper's Ferry," 610–11; Burgwyn, *North Carolina Regiments* 2:601; Graham, ibid., 433; and Hirsch, Diary, Sept. 15. Although J. R. Jones may have set out without additional orders, Walker had put his division to bed and would not likely have marched without subsequent orders.

66. It might also be argued that Jackson should have foreseen and prevented the bottleneck caused by the Federal prisoners on the pontoon bridge that delayed McLaws's crossing, and, as well, that he should have seen to providing rations for both McLaws and Walker. A. P. Hill's division, of course, was expected to remain behind at Harpers Ferry. On the other hand, it is possible that Hampton's brigade—the only relatively fresh cavalry—should have been hastened to Sharpsburg on the night of the 15th. The fault here would belong more to Stuart than Jackson, however.

67. E. A. Moore, *Story of a Cannoneer*, 143; and Jackson's report, *OR*, vol. 19, 1:955.

68. September 1 estimate from Allen, "Second Manassas Strengths," 186; September 16 estimate, assumed to be nearly the same as for the 17th, from Carman, "Maryland Campaign," chap. 23, pp. 27, 34.

8. "All will be right": Lee's Last Chance for Maneuver, September 16, 1862

1. Figures are from Carman, "Maryland Campaign," chap. 13, p. 20, and chap. 26, passim. Carman gives Lee 15,600 in Longstreet and Hill and 10,300 in the reinforcements under Jackson and Walker, for a total of 25,900 infantry, cavalry, and artillery. It is important to emphasize that these figures are for "fighting effectives," a category in which the extra-duty men have been subtracted. Previously in the text the figures most often have represented "present for duty," because this is the category most easily obtained and most comparable for the two sides. The latest "present for duty" numbers for Lee's army are for September 1, however; and these figures have become so obsolete by the 16th—due to straggling, casualties, and nonexistent field records—that they can no longer provide a fair basis for comparison. For a discussion of the various categories used to express strengths in Civil War armies, see Harsh, *Sounding the Shallows*, chap. 9, sect. A.

2. For a discussion of where Lee slept on the night of September 15–16, see Harsh, *Sounding the Shallows*, chap. 9, sect. B.

3. Carman, "Maryland Campaign," chap. 13, p. 18, where it is not clear whether Jackson's message arrived before or after Lee left his headquarters.

4. For a discussion of Lee's return to riding Traveller, see Harsh, *Sounding the Shallows*, chap. 9, sect. C.

5. The fog and its density are in several anecdotes related by Carman, which apparently derive from both Confederate and Federal (including Nelson A. Miles) sources. Carman, "Maryland Campaign," chap. 8, pp. 1, 4–5; also see note 19 below. It is confirmed in two contemporary telegrams of McClellan: McClellan to Halleck, 7:00 A.M., *OR*, vol. 19, 2:307–8; and McClellan to Franklin, 7:45 A.M., ibid., vol. 51, 1:839. On the contrary, Adj. William Owen of the Washington Artillery, in an account based on a wartime diary, wrote that at daylight the Federals were "in plain view" on the eastern bluffs of the Antietam. Owen, *In Camp and Battle*, 140.

6. The unopposed crossing of the Middle Bridge by Federal cavalry around daylight is from Carman, "Maryland Campaign," chap. 8, p. 21. See also note 19 below. It is curious that Lee had pickets out from Toombs's brigade east of the Antietam at the Lower Bridge (*OR*, vol. 19, 1:162) but did not establish any pickets—even on the west bank—at the Middle Bridge. Perhaps, the open nature of the ground at the latter had seemed to obviate the necessity of videttes.

7. Stuart makes no mention of the morning of the 16th whatsoever in his official report, but the reconnaissance is recorded in both von Borcke, *Memoirs* 1:226 (quoted in the text

above) and Blackford, *War Years with Jeb Stuart,* 148. Stuart may have taken the 3d, 4th, and 5th Virginia Cavalry—or some portion or combination thereof—with him. The 9th Virginia remained on the Hagerstown Pike near the Dunkard Church to guard the left flank of the line, while the 1st Virginia had not yet returned from escorting Longstreet's reserve wagons to Williamsport. See Beale, "Maryland," 278–79; and Carman, "Maryland Campaign," chap. 10, p. 512, and chap. 13, pp. 34–35.

8. For a discussion of Lee's sending trains to Virginia, see Harsh, *Sounding the Shallows,* chap. 9, sect. D.

9. Carman, "Maryland Campaign," chap. 13, p. 18.

10. For Jones leading the column, see Early, *War Memoirs,* 139. For the brutal fifteen-mile night march, which included the six miles from Halltown to the juncture of the Shepherd's Ford and Shepherdstown Roads, see Poague, *Gunner with Stonewall,* 44 (quoted in text); the reports in *OR,* vol. 19, 1, of Jackson (p. 955), J. R. Jones (p. 1007), Pendleton (p. 1016), Williams (pp. 1011–12). See also, Worsham, *One of Jackson's Foot Cavalry,* 86; E. A. Moore, *Story of a Cannoneer,* 143. The route via the canal towpath mentioned by Williams of the 5th Virginia is confirmed on the map by Lt. S. Howell Brown published in *OR Atlas,* plate 29, p. 1.

11. On Lawton's division see the reports in *OR,* vol. 19, 1, of Early (p. 967) and Hays (p. 978). See also, Early, *War Memoirs,* 139; Nisbet, *Four Years on the Firing Line,* 102; and H.W. Thomas, *History of the Doles-Cook Brigade,* 222.

12. For a discussion of Walker's march from Harpers Ferry, see Harsh, *Sounding the Shallows,* chap. 9, sect. E.

13. For a discussion of Jackson's arrival in Sharpsburg, see ibid., sect. F.

14. For a discussion of Walker's arrival in Sharpsburg, see ibid., sect. E.

15. Although there should be no doubt that Jackson reported personally to Lee, this meeting is recorded only by Henry Kyd Douglas in his memoirs. Having remained behind, Douglas left Harpers Ferry "very early on the morning of the 16th" and rode to Sharpsburg by way of Shepherdstown. Since Douglas was traveling through the neighborhood where he grew up, he certainly could have covered the twenty miles by 7:30 or 8:00 if he had left by 4:00. When Douglas arrived, Jackson was already on Cemetery Hill and in conversation with Lee and Longstreet. Douglas makes no mention of Walker being present. Douglas, *I Rode with Stonewall,* 166. The quotation ending the paragraph is from Lee to Mrs. Jackson, Jan. 25, 1866, Lee Family Papers, Virginia Historical Society. Without mentioning the letter, the quotation is paraphrased in Dabney, *Life and Campaigns of Jackson,* 570. There is a transcribed copy in the Hotchkiss Papers, Library of Congress.

16. For the "Miss Fairfield" breakfast incident, see Harsh, *Sounding the Shallows,* chap. 9, sect. F.

17. The latest report of fog in a contemporary document is McClellan to Franklin at 7:45 A.M., *OR,* vol. 51, 1:839. McClellan describes it as "so dense I have not yet been able to determine" whether the Confederates had abandoned Sharpsburg.

18. According to George Sykes, it was Weed's Battery I of the 5th U.S. Artillery (Sykes's division, Fifth Corps) and Benjamin's Battery E of the 2d U.S. Artillery (Willcox's division, Ninth Corps) which "opened a lively cannonade upon such of the enemy as could be seen." These guns were posted on the ridge south of the Boonsboro Pike, and Weed recorded his battery opened around nine o'clock. In *OR,* vol. 19, 1, see the reports of Sykes (pp. 350–51), Weed (p. 353), and Benjamin (p. 436)

19. Carman, "Maryland Campaign," chap. 13, pp. 21–22. The first crossing of the Middle Bridge occurred at about daybreak, when Lt. Col. Nelson A. Miles led two companies each from the 61st and 64th New York on a reconnaissance to determine if the Confederates had retreated. Miles advanced six hundred yards west of the Antietam and almost into the lines of George T. Anderson's brigade. A captured picket alerted the Federals to the danger, and they quickly recrossed the creek. Because of the fog, the thick dust in the road that deadened foot-

falls, and the measures taken by Miles to enjoin silence, it is doubtful that the Confederates ever knew of this penetration. The second crossing occurred after seven o'clock in response to a fear that the Confederates might attempt to destroy the bridge and thus impede an attack on the center. Capt. Hiram Dryer advanced four companies of the 4th U.S. regulars several hundred yards west of the creek and took position behind a barn on the left of the road. In *OR*, vol. 19, 1, see the reports of Buchanan (p. 356) and Dryer (p. 356); see also Carman, "Maryland Campaign," chap. 13, pp. 27–28.

20. Nathan Evans is the only Confederate commander who reported skirmishing in the vicinity of the bridge. The Federal side is reported by Dryer of the 4th U.S. In *OR*, vol. 19, 1, see the reports of Dryer (p. 356) and Evans (p. 939).

21. For a discussion of the artillery bombardment of September 16, see Harsh, *Sounding the Shallows*, chap. 9, sect. G.

22. Walton mentions only firing at the enemy batteries, but Dryer reports suffering casualties from fire directed at his men. *OR*, vol. 19, 1:357. It is possible he was an accidental target, however, and his casualties resulted from Confederate shells falling short.

23. Hunt's report, ibid., 206. The batteries were Langner's, von Kleiser's and Wever's of the German (1st) New York Artillery and Taft's 5th New York Battalion.

24. D. H. Hill's report, ibid., 1026. Walton insisted he silenced some of the Federal batteries—there is no evidence to support his claim—but he admitted his guns could not even reach all of them. Ibid., 849. Frobel noted that Reilly's battery soon ran out of rifled ammunition, and he confessed the cannonade was "without any perceptible result" on the enemy. Ibid., 925. The Federals did suffer casualties, however, including Maj. Albert Arndt, commanding the New York battalion, who was mortally wounded. Ibid., 206. There is no indication that Federal firing focused on any particular target. It played on the entire Confederate line from the Sunken Road in the north and along the heights of Sharpsburg, and it was remembered by most as "heavy" or "considerable." See note 36 below; and Harsh, *Sounding the Shallows*, chap. 9, sect. G.

25. Owen, *In Camp and Battle*, 140–41; and Walton's report, *OR*, vol. 19, 1:848–49.

26. Von Borcke noted the family had finally been persuaded to take refuge in the cellar (*Memoirs* 1:226–27).

27. Lee was spotted on foot amid the shells by Adj. William Owen of the Washington Artillery. Owen, *In Camp and Battle*, 141. Owen no doubt misremembered that Lee was "leading his horse by the bridle," however. It seems unlikely that a man with injured and bandaged hands would be holding the reins of a frightened horse. Although there is no direct evidence that Lee shifted his headquarters at this time, the speculation is a reasonable one. He would be at his new site shortly after noon.

28. Von Borcke, *Memoirs* 1:229; and Shinn, Diary, Sept. 16. That Lee shared in this view is suggested by Owen's quoting him as telling the artillerists "to keep the artillery ammunition for the enemy's infantry only" (*In Camp and Battle*, 141).

29. Eubank (three guns) has been added to the count in note 21 to reach the total for the center and the right. For the left, it is assumed: S. D. Lee had fifteen guns in four batteries; Cutts had twenty-six guns in five batteries; D. H. Hill had sixteen guns in four batteries; and H. P. Jones had fifteen guns in four batteries. See *OR*, vol. 19, 1:836–37; Cutts, "Letter," 430–31; and note 44 in chapter 4 above.

30. Stuart's report, *OR*, vol. 19, 1:819–20; Beale, *Lieutenant of Cavalry*, 46–47; McDonald, *History of the Laurel Brigade*, 95; and Battlefield Plaque No. 320. The latter is one of almost four hundred tablets placed on the battlefield in the 1890s by the Antietam National Battlefield Board. The text was composed by Ezra Carman and based on recollections of survivors.

31. Hirsch, Diary, Sept. 16. Walker himself may have reported to Lee at this time, as he gives noon as the time in his alternate version in his second *Century Magazine* article. It is even

possible that Jackson—after seeing to the encampment of his own men and made anxious by the cannonade—rode back to hurry up Walker. This scenario would harmonize Jackson's initial early arrival with Walker's claim that he rode from the river with Stonewall to report to Lee.

32. In *OR*, vol. 19, 1, see the reports of Pendleton (p. 830) and Barnwell (pp. 837–38); see also, Pendleton to wife, Sept. 22, S. P. Lee, *Memoirs*, 212–13.

33. The order has not survived but is reported by McLaws, *OR*, vol. 19, 1:857. The timing is calculated by working backward, allowing three and a half to four hours for the courier to travel the fifteen miles to Harpers Ferry; for the order to be forwarded seven miles to Charlestown, where McLaws had gone for provisions; and for McLaws to return to Harpers Ferry by three o'clock. This schedule is sufficiently tight that the possibility must be allowed that Lee sent the order before the serious cannonade started at 11:00.

34. This is speculation, but it is reasonable because: (1) the wagons were ordered back at some time before the morning of the 17th; and (2) Lee had the scarcity of ammunition on his mind at this time as is evidenced by both his comments in the streets of Sharpsburg to preserve the artillery ammunition for the enemy infantry (Owen, *In Camp and Battle*, 141); and (3) the assignment to Porter Alexander (see note 35). For the commissary wagons not being available during the 16th, see D. H. Hill's report, *OR*, vol. 19, 1:1025; and Wood, *Reminiscences of Big I*, 37. That they were parked two miles in the rear by midnight, see G. Wise, *History of the 17th Va.*, 115. Also, Hood would—although with difficulty—locate his wagons and bring them up to the Dunkard Church during the night. Hood, *Advance and Retreat*, 42.

35. Alexander, *Fighting for the Confederacy*, 147–48; and *Military Memoirs*, 242. It should also be noted that Lee was in effect responding to Jackson's request—made in a report probably given Lee early in the morning—that Lee send the army's chief ordnance and commissary officers to Harpers Ferry. See Jackson to Lee, Sept. 16th, *OR*, vol. 19, 1:951–52; also note 40 below. The need for artillery ammunition was probably made more acute by the capture of Longstreet's forty-five wagons, although these same would have been in Shepherdstown at this time and unavailable even if not captured.

36. For a discussion of the artillery bombardment, see Harsh, *Sounding the Shallows*, chap. 9, sect. G. On the sense of a major battle pending, see E. A. Moore, *Story of a Cannoneer*, 145; and Shinn, Diary, Sept. 16. For speculation in the ranks about the reuniting of the army, see Douglas, *I Rode with Stonewall*, 166.

37. For the lack of commissary trains on the 16th, see note 34. A veteran of the 1st North Carolina (Ripley's brigade) recalled that he and his fellows "fared abundantly on green corn and pumpkins." Hamilton A. Brown, "1st Infantry (State Troops)," *North Carolina Regiments* 1:141. Rodes's brigade had gone through the town on the 15th and, because camped near the temporary park of the trains, got a "scanty meal." After marching back to the Antietam's bluffs, Rodes's men subsisted on "green corn." Rodes's report, *OR*, vol. 19, 1:1036. See also Tucker, "Diary," 20; and Shinn, Diary, Sept. 16.

38. It is not clear whether Lee dictated the letter from his field headquarters or whether it was at this time that he returned to the Grove house in Sharpsburg, where he would hold a war council later in the afternoon.

39. Lee to Davis, Sept. 16, Sharpsburg, Md., *OR*, vol. 19, 1:140.

40. According to *OR*, vol. 19, 1:140n., "not found." The reference is probably to Jackson to Lee, Sept. 16, in ibid., 951–52. It is likely that Jackson wrote this report before joining Lee. Whether he sent it on ahead or delivered it in person is unknown.

41. On March 6, 1863, Jed. Hotchkiss recorded in his diary the following remark of Jeb Stuart: "He says Gen. Lee came to us at Gordonsville with rather a low estimate of Jackson's ability;—but now he often wishes he had many Jacksons" (*Make Me a Map*, 118).

42. Carman, "Maryland Campaign," chap. 13, p. 34; and White, *Robert E. Lee*, 211. If Lee was fortunate and had the most up-to-date local map, it would have been *A Map of Washington*

Co., Maryland. Exhibiting the Farms, Election Districts, Towns, Villages, Etc. From Actual Survey by Thomas Taggart (Hagerstown: McKee and Robertson, 1859).

43. Owen, *In Camp and Battle*, 139. These are the words of Owen, who does not claim to quote Lee directly.

44. McClellan to Halleck, 7:00 A.M., *OR*, vol. 19, 2:307–8; and McClellan to Franklin 7:45 A.M., ibid., vol. 51, 1:839.

45. Around midday of September 16 is the point at which it becomes necessary to pay somewhat closer attention to the details of Federal operations. Otherwise, Lee's strategic and tactical situations, both as he perceived them and as they actually existed, cannot be fully understood, nor can his responses to them be fairly judged. Nevertheless, a full consideration of the Federal point of view must await the next study. The summary in this section, unless otherwise noted, is based on the correspondence in *OR*, vol. 19, 2:307–11 and vol. 51, 1:838–40 and the reports in vol. 19, 1, of McClellan (pp. 29–31, 54–56), Myer (p. 122), Fisher (p. 128), Hooker (pp. 217–18), Sumner (p. 275), Franklin (p. 376), Burnside (pp. 418–19), and Cox (pp. 423–24). See also the testimony before the Joint Committee on the Conduct of the War in *Report*, 1, of McClellan (pp. 431–32), Hooker (p. 581), Sumner (p. 368), Franklin (p. 626), and Burnside (p. 640); the postwar recollections in *McClellan's Own Story*, 587–91; Cox, *Military Reminiscences*, 1:304–5; and some information in Carman, "Maryland Campaign," chap. 13, which is not to be found elsewhere.

46. McClellan's final report, *OR*, vol. 19, 1:54.

47. McClellan mentions—albeit not elaborately—all of these tactical problems in his final report and his memoirs. Ibid., and repeated in *McClellan's Own Story*, 587–88. He simply does not state in blunt words: "This was a tough tactical nut to crack, and it took some time to figure out a plan."

48. Unfortunately, the original offensive scheme has been obscured by subsequent changes. McClellan himself contributed to the confusion because he never clearly and fully explained his plan all in one place and because in his several partial explanations he allowed modifications made later to appear to be part of the plan as originally devised on the morning of the 16th. McClellan explained his plan on five different occasions: (1) in a telegram to Halleck on the 17th, while the battle was raging (*OR*, vol. 19, 2:312); (2) in his preliminary report, dated October 15, 1862 (ibid., 1:30); (3) in testimony before the Joint Congressional Committee on the Conduct of the War on March 2, 1863 (*Report* 1:431–32); (4) in his final report, dated August 4, 1863 (*OR*, vol. 19, 1:55); and (5) in his memoirs, which were unfinished at the time of his death (*McClellan's Own Story*, 587–90).

49. The strengths given here and immediately below for corps on September 16 are slightly larger than the figures calculated by Ezra Carman for effective strengths in the fighting on the 17th to allow for the inevitable prebattle straggling that always occurred.

50. Nothing is known of this conversation, except Cox's much later recollections that Burnside: (1) seemed to think Hooker had finagled the independent command to further his career; and (2) received from McClellan the impression that the attack of the Ninth Corps was to be something of a diversion. Cox, *Military Reminiscences*, 1:303, 307.

51. This summary of Hooker's movements is from the reports in *OR*, vol. 19, 1, of McClellan (p. 55), Hooker (p. 217), Hofmann (p. 235), Williams (p. 239), Richardson (p. 263), and Meade (p. 268); the reports in ibid., vol. 51, 1, of Dick (p. 150) and McGee (p. 156); also, the testimony before the Joint Committee on the Conduct of the War, *Report*, 1, of McClellan (p. 440) and Hooker (p. 581). Also see *McClellan's Own Story*, 590–91; and Carman, "Maryland Campaign," chap. 13, pp. 31–49. It is likely that McClellan had discussed these orders earlier in the morning while visiting with Hooker.

52. Hooker later misremembered that McClellan promised that the attacks were to be made simultaneously with his own on the center and right. Joint Committee on the Conduct of the War, *Report* 1:581. See note 53 below.

53. This statement is inconsistent with Hooker's claim that McClellan had promised the simultaneous attack earlier; see note 52. All of the quotes in this paragraph are from Hooker's report, *OR*, vol. 19, 1:217.

54. Ruggles to Sumner, Sept. 16, 5:50 P.M., ibid., vol. 51, 1:839.

55. The 3d, 4th, and 5th regiments—or a portion of them—had reconnoitered the ground along the upper Potomac with Stuart during the morning. See note 7. The 1st Virginia had been detailed on the 10th to accompany Longstreet to Hagerstown and on the 14th had escorted the trains to Virginia. After spending the night of the 15th at Harrisville, it had come by way of Martinsburg and Shepherdstown to rejoin its brigade. Carman, "Maryland Campaign," chap. 9, p. 512.

56. Ibid., chap. 13, pp. 33–35; and Beale, "Maryland," 278–79.

57. These figures, as are all strengths in the remainder of this section, are from Carman, "Maryland Campaign," chap. 26. As in the case of the Federal numbers in the preceding section, the strengths have been slightly increased to allow for prebattle straggling. The artillery mentioned in this paragraph refers to the battalions of Cutts, Pierson, Stephen Lee, and Pelham's horse battery.

58. Although it would have been a clever move on McClellan's part to renew the heavy artillery fire in the center to coincide with Hooker's crossing the Antietam, there is no indication in the Federal reports that any but a sporadic fire continued during the afternoon. Carman, however, insists that artillery fire on Cemetery Hill was a factor in Lee's thinking at this time. Carman, "Maryland Campaign," chap. 13, p. 34. It is possible that Lee magnified the continued, routine firing in the general excitement over threats to both his flanks.

59. Jacob Cox's recollection that he heard the firing from Hooker's fight as he moved into position (*Military Reminiscences* 1:305), as well as McClellan's complaint that Burnside did not carry out the movement until near sunset (*OR*, vol. 19, 2:308), indicate the largest part of the Ninth Corps movements came several hours later. Carman's assertion that Lee heard of the threat on the right simultaneously with the news of Hooker on the left might seem inaccurate, therefore, except for the fact that Lee reacted as if he heard both reports at nearly the same time. Carman, "Maryland Campaign," chap. 13, p. 34. It must be assumed that a portion of Burnside's move, particularly that of Sturgis and Crook near the bridge itself, was carried out between three and four o'clock.

60. This assumes that even if Lee did not have precise figures for his divisions, he at least had an approximate understanding of their comparative strengths. It is also interesting to note that at this late date Lee remained flexible in the corps or wing structure of his organization. At the time he made the decision, he must have believed he was separating for the coming battle the two divisions that had formed the core of Jackson's command since the Valley campaign of the spring. Lee could have postponed the split—and perhaps avoided it altogether—by sending Walker to the right and holding Lawton in reserve. Possibly, he recognized that Walker's men had been the last to arrive and decided to give them more rest. Citations for these movements are given below, where they are discussed in greater detail.

61. Blackford, *War Years with Jeb Stuart*, 147–49. Blackford's observation point can be generally located by his reference to Pelham's guns, which are known to have been at the northwest corner of the Samuel Poffenberger woods, where they were firing down the Smoketown Road. Carman, "Maryland Campaign," chap. 13, p. 34.

62. It would be reasonable to assume that Lee ordered Thomas Munford to carry out a similar reconnaissance on the right flank, but no documentation has been found. The only evidence of Confederate perception of the threat posed by Burnside are brief mentions in the reports in *OR*, vol. 19, 1, of Walton (p. 849), Toombs (p. 890), and Cumming (vol. 51, 1:168).

63. This summary of the action on the Smoketown Road on the late afternoon of the 16th is from the following sources: in ibid., vol. 19, 1, the reports of S. D. Lee (pp. 844–45), Hood (p. 1023), Wofford (pp. 927–28), Ruff (pp. 929–30), Turner (p. 936), and Law (p. 937). Also see

Ray, *North Carolina Regiments* 1:307; Beale, "Maryland," 278–79; Hood, *Advance and Retreat,* 41–42; and Carman, "Maryland Campaign," chap. 13, pp. 34–41.

64. Poague, *Gunner with Stonewall,* 44–45.

65. Summary of Jackson and Jones from the following sources: in *OR*, vol. 19, 1, the reports of Jackson (p. 955), Jones (p. 1007), Poague (p. 1009), Pendleton (p. 1016), Williams (p. 1012), and Wilson (p. 1014); also in Worsham, *One of Jackson's Foot Cavalry,* 86; E. A. Moore, *Story of a Cannoneer,* 146–47; Poague, *Gunner with Stonewall,* 45; and Carman, "Maryland Campaign," chap. 13, pp. 41–42.

66. Longstreet, *From Manassas to Appomattox,* 237.

67. This summary of the actions of Lawton are from the following sources: in *OR*, vol. 19, 1, the reports of Jackson (p. 955), Early (p. 967), Lowe (p. 975), Walker (p. 976), and Hays (p. 978). See also Early, *War Memoirs,* 140; Nisbet, *Four Years on the Firing Line,* 102; H.W. Thomas, *History of the Doles-Cook Brigade,* 222; and Carman, "Maryland Campaign," chap. 13, p. 42.

68. Gallagher, ed., *Lee the Soldier,* 13; and Freeman, *Lee's Lieutenants* 2:717. In the latter Lee is said to have commented that the discovery of S.O. 191 by McClellan "caused him to act as to force a battle on me before I was ready."

69. Lee to Mrs. Jackson, Jan. 25, 1866, Lee Family Papers, Virginia Historical Society.

70. Chilton to Pendleton, Sept. 16, S. P. Lee, *Memoirs,* 224. The order was probably sent between four and six o'clock in the afternoon. Apparently the canal had been cut and drained of water, and Lee knew it.

71. In *OR*, vol. 19, 1, see the reports of Pendleton (p. 830) and Barnwell (p. 838). Also see Pendleton to wife, Sept. 22, S. P. Lee, *Memoirs,* 213; and J. Wise, *Long Arm of Lee,* 1:292–93.

72. Pendleton sent Stapleton Crutchfield to Harpers Ferry to forward guns and ammunition to Sharpsburg. Apparently, on the 17th Crutchfield and Porter Alexander, whom Lee had earlier ordered to supervise sending ordnance to Shepherdstown or Winchester, would work at something of cross-purposes. Crutchfield's report, *OR*, vol. 19, 1:962–63; and Alexander, *Military Memoirs,* 271.

73. At least this is the hour that Hood would find his subsistence wagons, as is explained below.

74. It is possible that Lee issued orders to Walker to strengthen the right but not to march until early the following morning. See note 83 below for a discussion.

75. The sources for Hood and his men are: in *OR*, vol. 19, 1, the reports of Hood (p. 923), Wofford (pp. 927–28), Ruff (pp. 929–30), Turner (p. 936), and Law (p. 937); also Ray, *North Carolina Regiments* 1:307; and Hood, *Advance and Retreat,* 41–42. The sources for Jackson and Lawton's men are in *OR*, vol. 19, 1, the reports of Jackson (p. 955), Early (p. 967), Lowe (p. 975), and Walker (p. 976); also in Early, *War Memoirs,* 141; Nisbet, *Four Years on the Firing Line,* 102; and H. W. Thomas, *History of the Doles-Cook Brigade,* 222. Containing additional details on the exchange is Carman, "Maryland Campaign," chap. 13, pp. 47–48. According to an anecdote in Carman (p. 46), after dark Fitz Lee brought his men to the rear of the Nicodemus Hill and then climbed the hill and lay down to sleep by a tree, where he was soon joined by Jackson. If true, this is where Hood would have found Jackson. The story must be doubted, however, as it would have had Stonewall bedding down almost a quarter-mile in advance of his infantry line. Still, this would explain Hood's difficulty in finding Jackson. Another witness has Stonewall spending at least part of the night in the Jacob Grove house in Sharpsburg. Price to mother, Sept. 18, Trout, *With Pen and Saber,* 100.

76. The fact that Col. James Walker reported forming on Ripley's left helps place the timing of this event. Although there is no evidence to indicate it, it is unlikely that Lee left unguarded Ripley's original position. The brigade of Garland (McRae), or more likely that of G. B. Anderson, was probably moved to protect the hinge at the end of the high ground. See Ripley's report, *OR*, vol. 19, 1:1032; Thruston's report, *SOR* 3:586; DeRosset, *North Carolina*

Regiments 1:225; H. W. Thomas, *History of the Doles-Cook Brigade*, 469; and Carman, "Maryland Campaign," chap. 13, p. 47.

77. Stuart's report, *OR*, vol. 19, 1:819; von Borcke, *Memoirs* 1:229; Beale, "Maryland," 279–80; Blackford, *War Years with Jeb Stuart*, 149; and Carman, "Maryland Campaign," chap. 13, pp. 42, 46. For a further discussion of Confederate cavalry on the evening of September 16, see Harsh, *Sounding the Shallows*, chap. 9, sect. H.

78. In *OR*, vol. 19, 1, see the reports of Toombs (p. 891) and Little (p. 911).

79. The two most important sources for this account of McLaws's problems and his responses are McLaws, "Maryland," 19, 24; and McLaws's report in *OR*, vol. 19, 1:857. Supplemental information is derived from the reports in ibid. of Kershaw (pp. 864–65) and Nance (p. 869); and Gibson's report in *SOR* 3:568. See also Emmet M. Morrison, "Fifteenth Virginia at Sharpsburg," *SHSP* 33 (1905): 101; James B. Lacy, "The Fifteenth Virginia, Composed of Richmond, Henrico and Hanover Boys," *SHSP* 27 (1899): 49; Dickert, *History of Kershaw's Brigade*, 150; Taylor, *General Lee*, 130; Hubbert, "Diary," 309; and Certificate by J. F. Edwards, Oct. 10, 1885, McLaws Papers, Duke University.

80. Caldwell, *History of a Brigade of South Carolinians*, 73. As was usually the case, some individuals found a way to fare quite well. John T. Parham, "Thirty-second at Sharpsburg, Graphic Story of Work Done on One of the Bloodiest Fields," *SHSP* 34 (1906): 251. Others, however, complained of a small slice of unsalted beef and three hardtack crackers. Dinkins, "Barksdale's Brigade," 259.

81. Dinkins, "Barksdale's Brigade," 259–60; also, idem, *Personal Recollections*, 55–57.

82. Parham, "Thirty-second at Sharpsburg," 250–51; Carman, "Maryland Campaign," chap. 17, p. 194.

83. In his 1886 article for *Century Magazine* ("Sharpsburg," *B&L* 2:675), John Walker claimed he received Lee's order at 4:00 in the afternoon for execution at 3:00 the following morning. Because of the general unreliability of this account, as previously noted, and because the claim is not corroborated by Walker's wartime report (*OR*, vol. 19, 1:914) or any other source that has been found, it has not been incorporated into the text above. Nevertheless, there is nothing inherently suspect about this statement. If Lee did issue the orders at 4:00 the previous afternoon, the following slight modification in interpretation would be necessary: it would mean that when Lee countermarched Lawton from Snavely's Ford to join Jackson on the left, the Confederate commander remained extremely concerned about the threat to the Lower Bridge. Unwilling to commit Walker, his last reserves, until the situation on the Hagerstown Pike became clearer, Lee was willing, however, to issue advance orders, which could always be revoked. When it became certain that both McLaws and Walker would be on hand as reserves for the opening of the battle, Lee allowed the orders to stand. See also, W. N. Rose, "24th Regiment," *North Carolina Regiments* 2:275; Lawhon, ibid., 3:116; Carman, "Maryland Campaign," chap. 13, p. 19; and Hirsch, Diary, Sept. 17.

84. Lee to Davis, Sept. 18, *OR*, vol. 19, 1:141.

85. In ibid., the reports of A. P. Hill (p. 981) and Franklin (p. 376); and a vague reference in Taylor, *General Lee*, 130. Such specifics as are known of Lee's order must be derived from the statement by A. P. Hill in his report: ". . . at 6.30 a.m., I received an order from General Lee to move to Sharpsburg." Since "heavy cannonading was heard this day [16th], up the river, on the Maryland side," Hill must have anticipated he would soon receive such an order, and he was able to get a quick start. Caldwell, *History of a Brigade of South Carolinians*, 73.

86. McLaws indicated he reached the vicinity of Lee's headquarters "about sunrise" (report) and "before sunrise" (article). His positive assertion that the battle had not commenced places his arrival at between 4:00 and 5:00. The above account of McLaws and Anderson is based entirely on McLaws's report (*OR*, vol. 19, 1:857–58), his postwar article ("Maryland," 24), and information McLaws provided to Ezra Carman (Carman, "Maryland Campaign," chap.17, pp. 194–95), except where supplemented as noted. A diary entry by a

member of the 13th Mississippi (Barksdale) confirms: "Our Division crossed the Potomac . . . at daybreak." Hubbert, "Diary," 309.

87. For a discussion of R. H. Anderson's division and its arrival at Sharpsburg, see Harsh, *Sounding the Shallows*, chap. 9, sect. I.

88. Antietam Battlefield Plaque No. 363 confirms that Cobb's brigade (Sanders) of McLaws bivouacked "near General Lee's headquarters west of Sharpsburg."

9. "A hard day's work before us": Lee's Bloodiest Day, September 17, 1862

1. This detailed account of McLaws's arrival is entirely from Carman, "Maryland Campaign," chap. 17, p. 105. Less detailed versions may be found in McLaws's report, *OR*, vol. 19, 1:857–58; and McLaws, "Maryland," 24. Lee twice stated that McLaws's division arrived after the battle had started. Lee to Davis, Sept. 18; and Lee's report, *OR*, vol. 19, 1:141, 148. Since McLaws reported ahead of his division, this is not strictly a contradiction.

2. Lee to Pendleton, Sept. 17, *OR*, vol. 19, 1:610.

3. Whatever caused Lee to repeat his orders, his uneasiness was not without foundation. At some unknown point during the day, J. Thompson Brown and the artillery battalion guarding Williamsport retired to Martinsburg. Brown to Pendleton, Sept. 17, ibid., 2:610–11. This dispatch implies, however, that Pendleton ordered Brown to return to Williamsport.

4. Two extended comments on the sounds of Antietam may be found in Longstreet, *From Manassas to Appomattox*, 241; and Neese, *Three Years in the Confederate Horse Artillery*, 125.

5. For a discussion of Lee's movements on Sept. 17, see Harsh, *Sounding the Shallows*, chap. 9, sect. J.

6. Carman, "Maryland Campaign," chap. 15, pp. 54–55. Today, the battlefield Visitors Center is located on the eastern edge of the plateau, overlooking the dale in which the Mumma farm is located.

7. Ezra Carman in his manuscript history (ibid., 55) claims Hooker believed he could turn the Confederate left flank simply by advancing parallel to the Hagerstown Pike. While it is true that Seymour's approach from the northeast and encounter in the East Woods might have suggested the Confederates were presenting a flank to Hooker, there was other evidence that strongly indicated the contrary. In the first place, both Walker (Trimble) and Lawton (Douglass) had triggered picket fire during the night, when they replaced Hood's brigades. Secondly, the heavy artillery fire from Nicodemus Hill west of the Hagerstown Pike proved the Confederate presence on Hooker's right.

8. The account of the tactical maneuvering in the Battle of Antietam included in the remainder of this chapter is an extremely abbreviated summary of a vast and complicated story. It is hoped that a future study in this series will tell that story as fully as evidence will allow its reconstruction. In the present work only enough has been included to make intelligible Lee's role in the battle and the context in which he made decisions of importance to his strategy. Full documentation of such a condensed version would be unattractive, even if possible. Not only every sentence, but many phrases and some words would require their own footnotes—and these citations would be long and discursive. Hence, only generalized notes are given here, with the expectation that the fault will be rectified in a fuller tactical study. The reader is also alerted that condensation has required a certain amount of "rounding off" not merely in strengths and losses but also in oversimplifying unit actions. For example, the sentence cited above should have been expanded or a footnote added to show that the right of Lawton's brigade also engaged Seymour. Such detail would be exceedingly tedious and detract from the focus on the strategy of the Maryland campaign.

9. The strengths of both Confederate and Federal units are from Carman, who devotes his entire chapter 23 of his "Maryland Campaign" to the topic.

10. The most basic sources used for this summary of the first phase (Jackson-Hooker) were Carman, "Maryland Campaign," chaps. 15 and 16; Federal First Corps reports in *OR*, vol. 19, 1:213–75 and in vol. 51, 1:139–56; Confederate reports for Jackson's and Ewell's divisions in ibid., vol. 19, 1:956–79, 1006–18; and the newly published reports in *SOR* 3:514–15, 533–46. Additional information not to be found elsewhere has been derived from the Antietam Battlefield Plaques located along the Hagerstown Pike, Mansfield Avenue, Smoketown Road, and Cornfield Avenue. See also, Thomas Clemens, ed., "A Brigade Commander's First Fight: The Letters of Colonel Walter Phelps, Jr., During the Maryland Campaign," in Snell, ed., *Antietam*, 59–72.

11. The casualties of both Confederate and Federal units are from Carman, who devotes his entire chapter 24 of his "Maryland Campaign" to the topic. See Harsh, *Sounding the Shallows*, chap. 9, sect. K, for further details.

12. The most basic sources used for this summary of the second phase (Hood-Mansfield) were Carman, "Maryland Campaign," chap. 16; and in *OR*, vol. 19, 1, the Twelfth Corps reports (pp. 474–518), Hood's division (pp. 922–38), and the three brigades of D. H. Hill (pp. 1022–23, 1031–33, 1039–54); the report in *SOR* 3:562–64; W. R. Hamby, "Texas Brigade at Sharpsburg," in Polley, *Texas Brigade*, 129–34; Hood, *Advance and Retreat*, 42–44; and George E. Otott, "Clash in the Cornfield: The 1st Texas Volunteer Infantry in the Maryland Campaign," in Snell, ed., *Antietam*, 73–123. Also see the Battlefield Plaques along Mansfield Avenue, Smoketown Road, Hagerstown Pike, Starke Avenue, and Sunken Road. Jackson's coordination is conjectured, but it must be noted that Hood in his memoirs reports receiving orders from Lawton; also, there is evidence D. H. Hill was involved in directing the fight on the left.

13. Battlefield Plaque No. 324; and William Freeman Fox, *Regimental Losses in the Civil War, 1861–1865: A Treatise on the Extent and Nature of the Mortuary Losses in the Union Regiments*, (Albany: Albany Publishing, 1889), 36, 556.

14. Alexander S. Pendleton to mother, Sept. 21, S. P. Lee, *Memoirs*, 216. Sandie was the son of Rev. William Nelson Pendleton, who commanded Lee's Reserve Artillery.

15. Ratchford, Memoir, 40, D. H. Hill, Jr., Personal Papers.

16. On Hooker's retirement see Carman, "Maryland Campaign," chap. 16, p. 175.

17. For a discussion of Lee's movements on September 17, see Harsh, *Sounding the Shallows*, chap. 9, sect. J.

18. Squires, "Boy Officer," 19.

19. For a discussion of the wounding of D. H. Hill's horse and its implications, see Harsh, *Sounding the Shallows*, chap. 9, sect. L.

20. It is the assumption of the paragraph in the text that Jackson and D. H. Hill understood the importance of the Sunken Road as both a fall-back defensive position and the hinge in the Confederate line, and they sought Lee's permission before removing all of the troops in the area. It is certainly possible, however, that in the emergency Jackson assumed he had the authority—especially since Hill had been under his command at the beginning of the campaign—and simply notified Lee of the significant change in troops dispositions. In the latter event, Lee approved after the fact, when he made no effort to hold back any of Hill's troops. The theory of Hill visiting Lee before the commitment of any but Ripley's already advanced brigade would make the case for prior approval somewhat stronger. In any case, it is important to note that all five of D. H. Hill's brigades were ordered to support Hood. Rodes's report, *OR*, vol. 19, 1:1036–37; and Battlefield Plaque No. 385. Because only three (Ripley, Colquitt, and Garland) got into the action, it has mistakenly been assumed that they were the only intended support.

21. See G. T. Anderson's report, *OR*, vol. 19, 1:909; Battlefield Plaque No. 323; and Carman, "Maryland Campaign," chap. 17, p. 192, where no precise time is given, but it is clearly implied that Lee ordered Anderson earlier than McLaws. Lee's selection of G. T. Anderson

may have been influenced by the fact the brigade had been temporarily attached to Hood during the retreat from South Mountain.

22. Ratchford, Memoir, 39–40, D. H. Hill, Jr., Personal Papers; A. S. Pendleton to mother, Sept. 21, S. P. Lee, *Memoirs*, 216. Neither dispatch has been found, and both may have been oral. For further discussion of Jackson's call for reinforcements and the summoning of McLaws, see Harsh, *Sounding the Shallows*, chap. 9, sect. M.

23. Carter's report, *OR*, vol. 19, 1:1030; Carman, "Maryland Campaign," chap. 17, pp. 192–93, which seems to be based on additional information—perhaps from a Lee staff member or from Carter himself.

24. Another order that does not exist and may have been oral. In his report Walker records receiving the order "soon after 9 a.m." *OR*, vol. 19, 1:914. Both Brig. Gen. Robert Ransom (ibid., 919) and Pvt. Isaac Hirsch (Diary, Sept. 17) note the time of the start of the march as about 9:00; and in his postwar article, Walker claims to have received the order "about 9" ("Sharpsburg," 676). Carman writes that Lee's order reached Walker at "nearly or quite 9 a.m." ("Maryland Campaign," chap. 17, p. 243). Inexplicably, the Battlefield Plaques state the division left Snavely's Ford "between 8 and 9 a.m." (Nos. 360, 362, 367, and 374). The weight of evidence indicates, therefore, that Lee sent the order around 8:30; it reached Walker around 9:00, and the division moved shortly thereafter.

25. Long, *Memoirs of Robert E. Lee*, 222. Allegedly, Jackson simply put the man back in the forefront of battle, and, when the soldier acquitted himself bravely, did not pursue the matter.

26. That Lee would consider exactly such a turning movement later in the day and again on the 18th makes such a possibility worth considering.

27. Stephen Dill Lee, "New Lights on Sharpsburg," *Richmond Dispatch*, Dec. 20, 1896. Prior to publishing the newspaper article, Lee provided versions of the story to Ezra Carman for "Maryland Campaign," chap. 17, p. 193; and Henry A. White for *Robert E. Lee*, 218. Lee's official report confirms the generalities without mentioning the details of the meeting with the Confederate chief. *OR*, vol. 19, 1:845. R. E. Lee's reference to "between Sharpsburg and the ford" is intriguing. It could possibly mean he was expecting A. P. Hill at a much earlier hour than his actual arrival. It is far more likely, however, that the Confederate commander was only referring to either McLaws or Walker, or both, who were coming from west of Sharpsburg, than that he was thinking of a force newly arrived from Shepherd's Ford. Certainly, he could have had no authentic information that A. P. Hill was at or approaching Shepard's at nine in the morning.

28. Carter's report, *OR*, vol. 19, 1:1030–31.

29. On R. H. Anderson's division, see Harsh, *Sounding the Shallows*, chap. 9, sect. I.

30. John Brown Gordon, *Reminiscences of the Civil War* (New York: Charles Scribner's Sons, 1903), 84; Bridges, *Lee's Maverick General*, 118; and Freeman, *R. E. Lee* 2:391. Rodes's brigade had been on its way to the East Woods when it fell back to the Sunken Road upon encountering the retreating remnants of Ripley, Colquitt, and Garland.

31. Sources for Sumner and the early actions of the Second Corps are Carman, "Maryland Campaign," chap. 17, pp. 181–85; Samuel Storrow Sumner, " The Antietam Campaign," in *PMHSM* 14 (1918): 10–11; Gray, "Report," ibid., 2–3; E. V. Sumner's report, *OR*, vol. 19, 1:275–76; and his testimony before the Joint Committee on the Conduct of the War, *Report* 1:368; and Francis Amasa Walker, *History of the Second Army Corps in the Army of the Potomac* (New York: Charles Scribner's Sons, 1886), 99–119. Unfortunately, this order has not been found, and—as in the case of so many of Lee's orders—may have been oral rather than written. The timing but not the text of the order is given in Sumner's report. It would be most revealing to know the precise language of the instructions. The interpretation in the text accepts for the most part the conclusions about Sumner reached by Marion Vincent Armstrong

in his perceptive "A Failure of Command? A Reassessment of Edwin V. Sumner and the Federal II Corps at Antietam," in *Leadership and Command in the American Civil War*, ed. Steven E. Woodworth (Campbell, Calif.: Savas Woodbury, 1996), 67–145.

32. The account in the text, until noted otherwise, is from the superbly detailed report of Jubal Early, *OR*, vol. 19, 1:967–71. Although not without minor faults, there is no finer, more accurate contemporary description of the morning's battle. The events obviously made a clear, indelible impression on Early's mind.

33. On Stuart and the cavalry on the Confederate left, see Stuart's report, ibid., 819–20; von Borcke, *Memoirs* 1:229–31; H. B. McClellan, *I Rode with Jeb Stuart*, 129–31; Blackford, *War Years with Jeb Stuart*, 149–51; and Beale, "Maryland," 279–80. Although much has been made of the importance of Stuart's twenty-five or so guns on Nicodemus Hill, it would seem that he held the position for little more than an hour. It must have been between 6:30 and 7:00 that he abandoned the prominence and withdrew to Hauser Ridge, which is nearer the Dunkard Church.

34. Information on the 125th Pennsylvania is from Higgins's report, *OR*, vol. 19, 1:491–93; and *History of the One Hundred and Twenty-fifth Regiment Pennsylvania Volunteers, 1862–1863* (Philadelphia: J. B. Lippincott, 1906), 51–85.

35. The basic sources used for this summary of the third phase (McLaws-Sedgwick) were Carman, "Maryland Campaign," chap. 17, pp. 180–98; in *OR*, vol. 19, 1, the reports from McLaws's division (pp. 857–84) and Sedgwick's (pp. 305–23); McLaws, "Maryland," 25–27; and the Battlefield Plaques along the Hagerstown Pike and Confederate Avenue. For a good, brief description of the tactical fighting, see Ted Alexander, "Forgotten Valor: Off the Beaten Path at Antietam," *Blue & Gray Magazine* 12 (1995): 8–19, 48–64.

36. The sources for the march, deployment, and fighting of Walker's division are in *OR*, vol. 19, 1, the reports of Walker (pp. 914–16), Hall (pp. 918–19), and Ransom (pp. 919–20). Also in Walker, "Sharpsburg," *B&L* 2:676–77; Carman, "Maryland Campaign," chap. 17, pp. 243–45; Hirsch, Diary, Sept. 18; in *North Carolina Regiments*, 2, Rose (p. 275), Ferguson (pp. 296–97), and Burgwyn (p. 601); Lawhon, *North Carolina Regiments* 3:116–17; and Battlefield Plaques Nos. 360, 362, 367, 374, 388. For a discussion of claims put forward by Walker, see Harsh, *Sounding the Shallows*, chap. 9, sect. N.

37. Kershaw's report, *OR*, vol. 19, 1:865.

38. The basic sources used for this summary of the fourth phase (Walker-Greene-Irwin) were Carman, "Maryland Campaign," chap. 17, pp. 243–45 and chap. 19, pp. 5–9. In *OR*, vol. 19, 1, the reports from Walker's division (pp. 914–21), G. T. Anderson's brigade (pp. 909–12), Greene's division (pp. 504–16), and selected reports of the Sixth Corps (pp. 376–79, 402–5, 409–16). The reports in *SOR* 3:519–22, 550–54. Also, the Battlefield Plaques along the Smoketown Road, Hagerstown Pike, Cornfield Avenue, Confederate Avenue, and Branch Avenue.

39. When Greene's division advanced around 10:30 to occupy the Dunkard Church woods, Capt. John Tompkins felt sufficiently relieved of danger from the west that he turned his Battery A, 1st Rhode Island Artillery to the southeast and opened on the Sunken Road, which French's division had been attacking for an hour. Tompkins retired at 12:00, having exhausted his ammunition. He was replaced by Charles Owen's Battery G, 1st Rhode Island Artillery. Owen expended a mere seventy-five rounds and directed them at an enemy battery near Sharpsburg. It was Owen who earlier was sent to the rear of the Mumma farm buildings as excess guns by Maj. F. N. Clarke, Sumner's chief of artillery. See the reports of Tompkins and Owen in *OR*, vol. 19, 1:308–9, 325–26.

40. The figures for phase four include Armistead—who participated in the repulse of Greene—within the Confederate figures, but does not include any of the five unemployed brigades of Franklin among the Federal totals, or the 7th Maine Infantry of Irwin, which suffered its casualties primarily later in the afternoon.

41. Depending upon French's deployment in such a move and his exact timing, he would have either also struck Walker's flank or been struck in his own flank by Walker. The possible results from a tactical situation in which three flanking movements (four counting Kershaw-Early and the Dunkard Church regiments) cross paths must approach infinity, and it would be nonsense to predict an outcome.

42. The basic sources used for this summary of French's assault on the Sunken Road were Carman, "Maryland Campaign," chap. 18. In *OR*, vol. 19, 1, the reports for D. H. Hill's division (pp. 1023–53), R. H. Anderson (pp. 884–85), and French (pp. 323–37). See the Confederate reports in *SOR* 3:568–70 and 584–89. See also the Battlefield Plaques along the Sunken Road and the Hagerstown Pike.

43. For Richardson's assault see, in addition to the Confederate sources cited in note 42, the Federal reports in *OR*, vol. 19, 1:277–305; and several plaques on the Boonsboro Pike.

44. Ruggles to Burnside, Sept. 17, 9:10 A.M., ibid., 844.

45. McClellan to Pleasonton, Sept. 17, 11:45 A.M., George Brinton McClellan, *The Civil War Papers of George B. McClellan: Selected Correspondence, 1860–1865*, ed. Stephen W. Sears (New York: Ticknor & Fields, 1989), 467.

46. The basic sources used for the summary of the sixth and final phase (Burnside–A. P. Hill) were Carman, "Maryland Campaign," chap. 21. In *OR*, vol. 19, 1, the Ninth Corps reports (pp. 419–74), D. R. Jones's division (pp. 886–908), and A. P. Hill's division (pp. 981–1005). In ibid., vol. 51, 1, the supplemental reports (pp. 161–69). In *SOR* 3, the Federal reports (pp. 531–33, 555–62) and the Confederate reports (pp. 571–80). Also see Cox, *Military Reminiscences* 1:308–53; Burnside's testimony before the Joint Committee on the Conduct of the War, *Report* 1:640–42; and the Battlefield Plaques on Rodman Avenue, Branch Avenue, the Harpers Ferry Road, and at Burnside Bridge. Additional sources are cited, below, where appropriate.

47. Douglas, *I Rode with Stonewall*, 172.

48. This issue—regrettably, like most enigmatic points in Civil War history—has fallen into the hands of loyalists to one or another general and led to much finger pointing and vituperation. In truth, neither Burnside nor McClellan can be fairly blamed—if indeed there is blame to allot—for misconstruing the fordability of the Antietam. It was the job of neither to tramp the banks of the creek in search of a crossing. The entirely nonpartisan mystery that remains to be solved is why the engineers of the Army of the Potomac decided the stream could be crossed only at the bridges and the fords. While the simple possibilities of slothfulness or excessive duties cannot be dismissed out of hand, engineering was a Federal forté, and it is difficult to imagine what tasks would have been given a higher priority. Certainly, a reconnaissance had been carried out and had discovered a small aqueduct and at least one dam. It is possible that certain permanent features—such as the proximity of the bluffs to the banks—have not been given sufficient weight by later critics, or that some condition obtained on the 17th—such as damming for mills—disappeared after the war. One consideration worthy of giving pause is that Lee's defensive posture (especially the posting of Toombs and Walker) suggests the Confederates also believed the Antietam would be crossed easily only at the bridges and the fords.

49. Fairchild's report, *OR*, vol. 19, 1:451.

50. Ezra Carman, "Maryland Campaign," chap. 21, p. 53, has Lee remaining at the Reel house until early afternoon, which is highly unlikely in light of the sightings cited below.

51. Later in the afternoon this force would be somewhat larger with the return of G. T. Anderson, the 15th and 17th Georgia of Toombs, the missing half of the 11th Georgia, and the collection of stragglers and pieces of batteries from the left. All told these additions may have amounted to 1,000 men.

52. Carman, "Maryland Campaign," chap. 19, p. 39. It is known that Hampton crossed into Harpers Ferry just before the pontoon bridge was destroyed on the 16th. He recrossed at

the mouth of the Antietam, rather than at Shepherd's Ford, but he still ought to have brought some news of Hill.

53. It will be recalled that the Jeff. Davis Legion was already serving on the left with Fitzhugh Lee's Brigade.

54. Nisbet, *Four Years on the Firing Line*, 106–7; and Garrett's report, *OR*, vol. 19, 1:1044–45. If Nisbet's memoir is adjusted for his error in believing Trimble's brigade (Walker) did not retire from the East Woods until 1:00, it would put his first encounter with Lee between 11:00 and 12:00. Jackson had struggled all morning with the problem of shattered units, and he had employed his own staff, as well as members of the Rockbridge Artillery and the 9th Virginia Cavalry to collect stray soldiers. E. A. Moore, *Story of a Cannoneer*, 149; Beale, "Maryland," 280.

55. Frobel's report, *OR*, vol. 19, 1:925; also Ramsay, *North Carolina Regiments* 1:574–76. The artillery ammunition shortage apparently existed in spite of Porter Alexander's boast that he kept the army fully supplied at all times. Alexander, *Fighting for the Confederacy*, 126.

56. Cooke, *Jackson*, 333.

57. R. H. Chilton to Pendleton, Sept. 17, *OR*, vol. 19, 1:610; also S. P. Lee, *Memoirs*, 225. Carman placed this untimed dispatch at "midday." Carman, "Maryland Campaign," chap. 21, p. 35. It is additionally persuasive that it was sent before one o'clock—and the loss of the Lower Bridge and Snavely's Ford—because: (1) of the request for long-range guns; and (2) after that time the route from Shepherd's Ford would have been vulnerable.

58. The infantry was the 400 men in Poland's battalion of regulars. See Carman, "Maryland Campaign," chap. 20; and Battlefield Plaque No. 77.

59. Longstreet, "Maryland," 669–70. The infantry was the 27th North Carolina and 3d Arkansas (Manning's brigade), but Longstreet was apparently aware only of John Cooke's 27th North Carolina. Confirmation of Longstreet and staff working as artillerists—without mention of Chilton—may be found in Longstreet, *From Manassas to Appomattox*, 250; Long, *Memoirs of Robert E. Lee*, 219; Cooke, *Jackson*, 335; Sorrel, *Recollections of a Confederate Staff Officer*, 106–7; and contemporaneous mention is made in Walton's report, *OR*, vol. 19, 1:850. After the war, legend expanded the account to have Longstreet pulling the lanyards. See two unidentified newspaper clippings in Latrobe Papers, Virginia Historical Society.

60. Owen, *In Camp and Battle*, 150–51. According to Owen, "One hand was in a sling, it not having recovered from the accident at second Manassas; the other held his field-glass." This implies that one hand was healthy, which was not the case. It is likely Owen misremembered about the left hand. It is also possible (if a convoluted possibility) that Lee's less damaged left hand was more loosely bandaged and did permit holding and using binoculars—that is field glasses. A telescope (field glass) required two hands and should have been out of the question.

61. Owen regularly saved official documents coming into his hands as the basis for Walton's official reports. It is possible, therefore, that he retained this order either as a memento or because there was no one else present to whom to give it. It is perhaps more likely, however, that he gave it to a member of Lee's staff for headquarters' records and reproduced its contents from memory. The fact that the Johnson in question was probably Capt. Samuel Johnston gives credence to this view. See Longstreet's report, *OR*, vol. 19, 1:842. If the latter is the case, important parts may be missing. However that may be, this document is a perfect example of the myriad of hastily scribbled notes, reports, and orders written during battle by both Confederates and Federals that were discarded, lost, or destroyed and have not survived. No doubt some of them, if they existed, would radically change the historical appreciation of persons and events of the Civil War.

62. Lee's visit to the left at 1:30 to confer with Jackson has not been previously guessed and cannot be firmly documented. Yet it makes sense. It is clear that Lee ordered the attempted turning movement. In *OR*, vol. 19, 1, see the reports of both Lee (p. 151) and Jackson

(pp. 956–57); see also, Longstreet, *From Manassas to Appomattox*, 257. Of course, it is possible that Lee could have summoned Jackson to headquarters or sent a written or oral order without a meeting. The meeting is likely, however, since Lee would have wanted Jackson's view on the prospects for success, as well as the opportunity to discuss an order with such a large measure of inherent discretion. That Lee went to Jackson is suggested by the circumstantial evidence provided in the meeting with his son and, to a somewhat lesser extent, by the story of Hood's straggler brigade. See below for both.

63. For a discussion of Lee's meeting with his youngest son, see Harsh, *Sounding the Shallows*, chap. 9, sect. O.

64. Quoted in George Francis Robert Henderson, *Stonewall Jackson and the American Civil War* (New York: Longmans, Green, 1949), 533.

65. Hunter McGuire, "General T. J. ('Stonewall') Jackson, Confederate States Army: His Career and Character," *SHSP* 25 (1897): 95, 101; and Schildt, *Antietam Hospitals*, 38.

66. The conclusion is hypothesized on the basis of the situation as known at the time and the actions Jackson would then take.

67. James Steptoe Johnston, "A Reminiscence of Sharpsburg," *SHSP* 8 (1880): 528–29. Rev. J. S. Johnston, who during the battle was a courier on the staff of Evander Law, is the only source for this incident. Johnston places its time at four o'clock, but Hood makes it plain that Lee ordered the reformed division back to the Dunkard Church area much earlier in the afternoon. Hood's report, *OR*, vol. 19, 1:923, where Hood makes no reference to the episode. Johnston's claim that the stragglers' brigade numbered 5,000 has been scaled down to credible proportions. Johnston recalled the morale of the stragglers was high, and he believed they would have fought well if called upon. After darkness the organization melted away, as the men drifted back to their own organizations.

68. The details of this little known attempt at a turning movement were first put together by Ezra Carman, "Maryland Campaign," chap. 19, pp. 34–41, including, apparently, information from participants not to be found elsewhere. Scattered references to the movement are given in *OR*, vol. 19, 1, in the reports of Lee (p. 151), Stuart (p. 820, where the dates 17th and 18th are confused), Walker (pp. 915, 916), Ransom (p. 920), Jackson (p. 956), and Poague (p. 1010). See also Poague, *Gunner with Stonewall*, 47; F. Lee, *General Lee*, 214; von Borcke, *Memoirs* 1:232; Lawhon, *North Carolina Regiments* 3:117; and Walker, "Sharpsburg," 679–80. Very brief secondary accounts may be found in White, *Robert E. Lee*, 221–22; and Evans, ed., *Confederate Military History* 3:354.

69. Walter Clark in *Wilmington (N.C.) Messenger*, Oct. 7, 1894, quoted in Carman, "Maryland Campaign," chap. 19, p. 36. Reprinted in 1901, Clark, "Sharpsburg," *North Carolina Regiments* 5:78.

70. Quoted from Burgwyn, *North Carolina Regiments* 2:603–5. A shorter version is given in Clark, ibid., 5:71. The number of flags observed by Private Hood—thirty-nine and still counting—would not have been impossibly high. There were twenty-seven regiments in Franklin's Sixth Corps alone. Moreover, scattered units of the First, Second, and Twelfth Corps would have been within sight, and Hood probably counted all the flags he saw, including those of batteries and the double and triple sets of colors carried by some units.

71. This allows 1,000 for Ransom's Brigade (minus the 24th North Carolina); 500 in the two remaining regiments of Manning (46th North Carolina and 30th Virginia); 1,500 for McLaws's three brigades after their heavy losses; 700 for Armistead; 900 for Early; and several hundred for the divisions of Jackson and Ewell. G. T. Anderson had returned to the Boonsboro Pike by this time.

72. Carman, "Maryland Campaign," chap. 19, p. 39. Carman gives Stuart only seven cavalry regiments, but his arithmetic does not prove this. According to Carman, Stuart had Hampton's brigade, three regiments from Fitz Lee's (including the 4th Virginia), and the errant 7th Virginia Cavalry of Munford's brigade. If Hampton were missing the Cobb Legion

and the Jeff. Davis Legion; or if Carman did not count them because they were battalions, then the figure seven would be correct. Carman also identifies six of the nine guns from Jackson as follows: one from Poague, two from Raines, and three from Brockenbrough. French and Branch were six-gun batteries. The 48th North Carolina (Manning) may have been the strongest regiment in Lee's army with 900 men. It was the only infantry sent by Jackson, but Stuart still had on hand the 13th Virginia (100) left by Early and the 24th North Carolina (300), which had strayed from Ransom's brigade during the pursuit of Sedgwick.

73. Poague's report, *OR*, vol. 19, 1:1010.

74. Poague, *Gunner with Stonewall*, 47–48.

75. All from *OR*, vol. 19, 1: Lee wrote, "to turn the enemy's right" (p. 151); Jackson, "with a view of turning the Federal right" (p. 956); and Stuart, "to turn the enemy's right" (p. 820).

76. Longstreet, *From Manassas to Appomattox*, 257; and Walker, "Sharpsburg," 679.

77. Jackson's report, *OR*, vol. 19, 1:956–57.

78. This remarkable claim—that Longstreet would order an attack without asking Lee and that he would do it on Jackson's sector of the field without consulting Jackson—would be open to serious doubt if vouched for only in Longstreet's *From Manassas to Appomattox*, 256–57. It is confirmed, however, in the reports of Walker and Ransom, *OR*, vol. 19, 1:916, 920.

79. Walker gives a embellished account of this meeting in his memoirs, "Sharpsburg," 679–80. He claims that Jackson reported Stuart had found the Federal right "securely posted on the Potomac." Walker also indicates Jackson was much disappointed and quotes Stonewall as lamenting, "It is a great pity,—we should have driven McClellan into the Potomac." Whether or not Jackson had entertained such high hopes for the attack may be doubted, and it is certainly unlikely that Stonewall expected a contortionist feat such as would have been represented by an attack from the west and north driving the enemy westward into the Potomac. The bare bones of the meeting are confirmed in Walker's wartime report (*OR*, vol. 19, 1:916) and in Longstreet, *From Manassas to Appomattox*, 256–57.

80. William Foster Biddle, "Recollections of McClellan," *United Service* n.s. 11 (1894): 468; and Stephen W. Sears, *George B. McClellan: The Young Napoleon* (New York: Ticknor & Fields, 1988), 314–15.

81. This dramatic incident and its problematic timing will be discussed in detail in a future study.

82. *McClellan's Own Story*, 601; McClellan's report and Griffin's report, *OR*, vol. 19, 1:62, 349.

83. Sykes's division and Barnes's brigade of Morell's Fifth Corps remained in the center. Warren's small brigade, probably less than 500 men, had already been moved south to cover the Lower Bridge from west of the Antietam.

84. Cox, *Military Reminiscences* 1:345. It is interesting that in the much more severe fighting on the right flank—which occurred across the creek and at a greater distance from the reserve trains—there is only one known instance (Greene's hour wait at the Mumma farm) of the exhaustion of ammunition delaying the fighting.

85. Cox's argument that Willcox's movement compared favorably with the advance of Mansfield and Franklin does not bear close scrutiny. Cox, *Military Reminiscences* 1:345–46.

86. See note 46.

87. The basic sources used for this summary of Federal activities at the Middle Bridge were Carman, "Maryland Campaign," chap. 20, pp. 2–37. In *OR*, vol. 19, 1, the reports of the Fifth Corps (pp. 538–68) and Pleasonton (pp. 211–12); and the supplemental reports in ibid., vol. 51, 1:137–39; and *SOR* 3:515–19, 524–30. Also, the Battlefield Plaques along the Boonsboro Pike.

88. Carman, "Maryland Campaign," chap. 21, p. 59, quoted without attribution. The run-on sentence has been broken in two. Alexander Haskell gives a variant account that cannot,

however, be trusted, as it has Lee greeting Hill on the banks of the Potomac. Haskell, *Portrait of a Man*, 79–80.

89. Longstreet, *From Manassas to Appomattox*, 261; D. R. Jones's report, *OR*, vol. 19, 1:887.

90. Lee to Davis, Sept. 18, *OR*, vol. 19, 1:141; and Gallagher, ed., *Lee the Soldier*, 8.

91. It is sometimes stated that on the 17th Hill left Edward Thomas's brigade behind at Harpers Ferry to complete the paroling of prisoners and to guard captured supplies; but the paroling was completed the day before. Also, there is the curious possibility that Hill actually started for Sharpsburg on the 16th. A member of the 49th Georgia recorded in his diary on the 16th: "We left Bolivar this morning, immediately after the paroled prisoners went off and marched due west for $2\frac{1}{2}$ miles and were then ordered back and now we are stationed on the suburbs of Harpers Ferry awaiting orders. We are to remain for the purpose of guarding commissary stores." Haynes, *Diary*, 20.

92. Indeed, the fighting on the afternoon and evening of the 16th had been heard in Harpers Ferry. Caldwell, *History of a Brigade of South Carolinians*, 73; and Hotchkiss, *Make Me a Map*, 82.

93. Map of Harper's Ferry and Sharpsburg, by Lt. S. Howell Brown, *OR Atlas*, plate 29-1.

94. Hal Bridges in his biography of D. H. Hill raises the question that A. P. Hill perhaps ought to have set out earlier. *Lee's Maverick General*, 125.

95. Quote is from Leach, Diary, Sept. 17. On the desperate, patchwork defense of the center and right before the arrival of A. P. Hill, see in *OR*, vol. 19, 1, the reports of S. D. Lee (pp. 845–46), Walton (p. 850), Read (pp. 866–67), D. R. Jones and his subordinates (pp. 885–912), Evans and his subordinates (pp. 939–50), D. H. Hill (pp. 1024–25), and Colquitt (p. 1054). See also Longstreet, *From Manassas to Appomattox*, 252–54; and Carman, "Maryland Campaign," chap. 20, pp. 18–19 and chap. 21, p. 53.

96. Ramsay, *North Carolina Regiments* 1:575.

97. Henry Lewis Benning, "Notes on the Battle of Sharpsburg," *SHSP* 16 (1888): 394.

98. Squires, "Boy Officer," 20.

99. Carman, "Maryland Campaign," chap. 21, p. 59.

100. One semi-comic but nearly tragic consequence of this haste was related many years later by Berry Benson. After Gregg's brigade's successful attack had been halted and the South Carolinians found it necessary to retreat, Benson discovered he could not run. One trouser leg had split and, weighted with water, wrapped itself around his other leg with each step he took. Only by stopping under heavy fire and tearing off the trouser leg did he escape. Benson, *Civil War Book*, 28–29.

101. McGowan's report, *OR*, vol. 19, 1:988; Haskell, *Portrait of a Man*, 80. See also note 46.

102. Y. Y. Y. to Burnside, *OR*, vol. 19, 1:138.

103. In ibid. see the reports of Harland (pp. 453–54) and Curtis (pp. 456–57).

104. Haskell, *Portrait of a Man*, 81.

105. Carman, "Maryland Campaign," chap. 21, pp. 68–70. Frank A. Bond, apparently a captain on Pender's staff, many years later claimed that he carried word to Lee that a Federal brigade had crossed a ford of the Antietam. Lee answered that no troops were available and that it would be necessary to trust to Providence. When Bond returned to his post, the Federals were retreating back across the ford. Because no reference has been found to a Federal brigade crossing after the arrival of A. P. Hill, let alone one recrossing by ford, the incident has not been used. Bond, "General Lee Trusting in Providence at Antietam," *Century Magazine* 33 (1886): 309.

106. Squires, "Boy Officer," 20. According to Squires there was a curious anticlimax to his mission. Toombs, who may only have been awaiting a moment of glory to cap his military career and allow him to retire from the army, anxiously asked the young gunner, "Squires, what was said of me at headquarters?" Assured that it was "the talk of the army that he had

held the whole of Burnside's corps in check all day," the Georgia politician composed a bombastic boast about the prowess of his accomplishments to be delivered to Lee. Squires carried the message back to the Confederate commander. Lee, without replying to Squires, turned to David R. Jones nearby and said, "Do you hear that Gen. Jones?" Since Jones had not only reported his division (including Toombs) "broken to pieces" but that Sharpsburg had fallen to the enemy, Squires assumed Lee's comment a severe criticism. He added, "This rebuke to Gen. Jones was, in my opinion, one of the causes of his death soon after." Jones would indeed suffer a heart attack a month after Antietam, retire from the army, and die on January 15, 1863. Whether "Mars' Robert's" displeasure contributed to Jones's physical decline may be doubted.

107. Quote is from Henry Lord Page King, Diary, Sept. 17, Southern Historical Collection. On the lack of food, see D. H. Hill's report, *OR*, vol. 19, 1:1025; and statement by J. F. Edwards, McLaws's commissary chief, McLaws Papers, University of North Carolina. On the lack of water, see DeRosset, "South Mountain," 309; and Thruston's report, *SOR* 3:588. The only significant running water on the battlefield proper is the small stream at the southern foot of Cemetery Hill, which joins the Antietam just above the Lower Bridge.

108. On the dead from Lawton's Georgia brigade seeming to be in formation see McGuire, "Jackson," 101; and Hotchkiss, *Make Me a Map*, 130–31. On the dead and wounded around the Dunkard Church, see Walker, "Sharpsburg," 681; and Douglas, *I Rode with Stonewall*, 174–75. On the search for wounded and pilfering, see Walker, "Sharpsburg," 681; and Douglas, *I Rode with Stonewall*, 174. On the extensive conflagrations in Sharpsburg and the reddening of the horizon, see Longstreet, *From Manassas to Appomattox*, 262; and "Maryland," 671; Owen, *In Camp and Battle*, 157; von Borcke, *Memoirs* 1:233, 235; Blackford, *War Years with Jeb Stuart*, 151; E. A. Moore, *Story of a Cannoneer*, 154–55; Neese, *Three Years in the Confederate Horse Artillery*, 126; Squires, "Boy Officer," 20.

109. For a discussion of Lee's war council on the evening of September 17, see Harsh, *Sounding the Shallows*, chap. 9, sect. P.

110. Owen, *In Camp and Battle*, 157; Longstreet, *From Manassas to Appomattox*, 262; and Longstreet, "Maryland," 671–72.

111. S. D. Lee, *New Lights on Sharpsburg*, 12.

112. Owen, *In Camp and Battle*, 157.

113. S. D. Lee, *New Lights on Sharpsburg*, 12.

114. *OR*, vol. 19, 1:151.

115. For a discussion of Lee's news of distant events, see Harsh, *Sounding the Shallows*, chap. 9, sect. Q.

116. Allan, *Army of Northern Virginia*, 200n.1.

117. Von Borcke, *Memoirs* 1:234–35.

118. Douglas, *I Rode with Stonewall*, 174–76. That Jackson spent the second night in a row without a tent and slept on the ground was not unusual. It is curious, however, that three members of his staff (Jed. Hotchkiss, Sandy Pendleton, and Dr. Hunter McGuire) slept at Shepherdstown. Was Jackson already moving his wounded into Virginia? Hotchkiss, *Make Me a Map*, 82–83.

10. "Until none but heroes are left": Antietam Endgame, September 18–21, 1862, and After

1. Blackford, *War Years with Jeb Stuart*, 151; Owen, *In Camp and Battle*, 158; Hubbert, "Diary," 309; Mills, *North Carolina Regiments* 4:166; and von Borcke, *Memoirs* 1:238. Heros von Borcke even entered in his diary the presentiment of his own death in the battle he fully expected.

2. For a discussion of firing on September 18, see Harsh, *Sounding the Shallows*, chap. 10, sect. A.

3. Hirsch, Diary, Sept. 18.

4. Lee's report, *OR*, vol. 19, 1:151. After the war, Lee supposedly said he was "expecting and indeed hoping for another attack." John William Jones, *Life and Letters of Robert Edward Lee, Soldier and Man* (New York: Neale Publishing, 1906), 195; see also, J. W. Jones, *Personal Reminiscences*, 239.

5. For a discussion of the Confederate stragglers brought up by the morning of September 18, see Harsh, *Sounding the Shallows*, chap. 10, sect. B.

6. On ammunition see Carman, "Maryland Campaign," chap. 22, p. 5; and Owen, *In Camp and Battle*, 158–59. On food see von Borcke, *Memoirs* 1:236–37, 238 (where Jackson is glimpsed drinking Yankee coffee); Brig. Gen. Maxcy Gregg breakfasted on roasted corn from the forty-acre cornfield. Haskell, *Portrait of a Man*, 82. Hotchkiss claimed that all of the wagons crossed from Shepherdstown in the morning, but this is probably an exaggeration (*Make Me a Map*, 83).

7. Carman, "Maryland Campaign," chap. 22, p. 7, concludes that Lee did not "exceed 35,000." In the most precise figure ever likely to be reckoned, Carman puts Lee's losses for September 16–18 at 10,316 (chap. 26, p. 2).

8. The cavalry division of three brigades, including eleven regiments and two legions, has not been counted for this purpose. For a discussion of the strength of the Army of Northern Virginia on September 18, see Harsh, *Sounding the Shallows*, chap. 10, sect. C.

9. The casualties among commanding officers has been extracted from a detailed Table of Organization compiled by Ezra Carman, "Maryland Campaign," chap. 11.

10. H. B. McClellan, *I Rode with Jeb Stuart*, 132. Stuart's early-morning ride is also mentioned in Blackford, *War Years with Jeb Stuart*, 151; and von Borcke, *Memoirs* 1:237.

11. Ratchford, Memoir, 45–46, D. H. Hill, Jr., Personal Papers.

12. Hood, *Advance and Retreat*, 45. Henry Kyd Douglas's claim that Jackson "seemed ready for fight at the drop of a hat" is apparently based on an assessment of the general's nature, rather than on any specific evidence from the 18th. Douglas, *I Rode with Stonewall*, 179.

13. Taylor, *Four Years with General Lee*, 73. William Allan wrote, ". . . if Confederate numbers were much reduced, it was the very flower of that army that remained." Allan, "Strategy of the Campaign of Sharpsburg," 94.

14. D. H. Hill's report, *OR*, vol. 19, 1:1025. That Hill held much the same sentiments on the 18th is attested by two incidents. He made a rallying speech to the survivors of G. B. Anderson's brigade and referred to them as the "faithful few." Shinn, Diary, Sept. 18. Then, when riding with Capt. Stephen Thruston of the 3d North Carolina, he proclaimed, "My dear sir, we have too many cowards in our army." DeRosset, "South Mountain," 309.

15. Haskell, *Portrait of a Man*, 84. This oft-quoted phrase was used by Clifford Dowdey as a chapter title for Sharpsburg in his biography *Lee* (Boston: Little, Brown, 1965).

16. Lee to Davis, Sept. 18, 6:30 A.M., Sharpsburg, Maryland, *OR*, vol. 19, 1:141; and Lee, *Wartime Papers*, 311.

17. Lee's report, *OR*, vol. 19, 1:148.

18. Gallagher, ed., *Lee the Soldier*, 8.

19. The file copy at the National Archives (RG-109) is marked: "An extract truly copied from the original. Sept. 24, 1862. Burton N. Harrison Private Secretary." It might be noted that week-old news would not have been very fresh, and the date of the extract might be seen as adding slight weight to the theory that something was intentionally excised from the message.

20. William Buel Franklin, "Notes on Crampton's Gap and Antietam," in *B&L* 2:597; and Douglas, *I Rode with Stonewall*, 176.

21. This and other information in this section on Humphreys is from *OR*, vol. 19, 1:368–74, vol. 51, 1:843–44, 847.

22. Reynolds's information is from ibid., vol. 19, 2:329, 330; and Edward J. Nichols, *Toward Gettysburg: A Biography of General John F. Reynolds* (1958; reprint, Gaithersburg, Md.: Olde Soldiers Books, 1987), 134. Reynolds to Halleck, Sept. 19, *OR*, vol. 19, 2:332, makes clear that none of the militia went to Sharpsburg with Reynolds.

23. Marcy to Couch, Sept. 17, 12:00 A.M., *OR*, vol. 51, 1:844.

24. On ammunition see ibid., vol. 19, 1, Hunt's report (p. 207), 2:312–14, 321–23; and vol. 51, 1:840–42, 845–47.

25. McClellan to Halleck, ibid., vol. 19, 2:322; and telegram and letter to wife, McClellan, *Civil War Papers*, 469, all dated 8:00 A.M., Sept. 18. Also at about 7:30, McClellan told Humphreys that the question of attacking that day had not yet been decided. *OR*, vol. 19, 1:373.

26. The figure of less than 5,000 is derived from Humphreys's admission that during an hour and a half rest a "considerable" portion of his stragglers came up and brought his division to 6,000. Humphreys's report, *OR*, vol. 19, 1:373.

27. McClellan's preliminary report and repeated in his final report, ibid., 32, 67. McClellan had Pleasonton probing the center and both flanks at dawn, but there is no indication he received any useful information from the cavalry. Marcy to Pleasonton, ibid., vol. 51, 1:848–49. The Confederate reenforcements were probably the continuing collection of estrays, but would also have included the artillery brought up from Harpers Ferry. See note 5.

28. Watson to McClellan, 10.00 A.M.; and Ripley to McClellan, 12:30 P.M., ibid., 2:322, 323.

29. The condition of the Ninth Corps is a matter of some dispute. Burnside would testify before the Joint Congressional Committee on the Conduct of the War five months after the battle (March 1863) that his command could have resumed the offensive and that he recommended to McClellan that an attack be made at five in the morning. *Report* 1:641–42. In August of the same year, McClellan wrote in his final report that Burnside gave the impression he could not hold the west bank of the Antietam and needed a fresh division to cover his possible retreat. *OR*, vol. 19, 1:66. Burnside's case has been recently reargued by William Marvel in *Burnside* (Chapel Hill: Univ. of North Carolina Press: 1991), 145–48. What is most needed but still is lacking is a study focusing on the condition of the Ninth Corps. In its absence, it might simply be noted that: (1) whatever Burnside may have said on the evening of the 17th, Morell was sent on Burnside's request on the 18th for purely defensive purposes; and (2) McClellan would not have spared Morell from the center if the Federal commander had not been convinced either by Burnside's testimony or his own personal observations that the Ninth Corps might not hold without it.

30. McClellan to Hooker, Sept. 20, *OR*, vol. 19, 1:219; and McClellan to wife, Sept. 20, 9:00 A.M., McClellan, *Civil War Papers*, 473. Sears, *George B. McClellan*, 321, says McClellan was suffering from neuralgia; Paul E. Steiner, *Medical-Military Portraits of Union and Confederate Generals* (Philadelphia: Whitmore, 1968), 16–17, concluded, however, that the illness was dysentery.

31. Marcy to Franklin, 5:45 P.M.; and Marcy to Meade, 7:40 P.M., with note on verbal orders to Burnside; *OR*, vol. 51, 1:847, 848.

32. A future study will attempt an evaluation of the condition of the Army of the Potomac similar to the one made of the Army of Northern Virginia herein, including damage to the command structure. It might be pointed out, however, that Meade went on record on the 18th on the condition of the First Corps: "To resist an attack in our present strong position I think they may be depended upon, and I hope they will perform duty in case we make an attack, though I do not think their *morale* is as good for an offensive as a defensive movement." Ibid., vol. 19, 1:66.

33. Longstreet's comment in Reilly, *Battlefield of Antietam*, 20; Shinn Diary, Sept. 18; also David Hunter Strother, *A Virginia Yankee in the Civil War, The Diaries of David Hunter Strother,*

ed. Cecil D. Eby, Jr. (Chapel Hill: Univ. of North Carolina Press, 1961), 113. At least some brigades did not see their subsistence wagons on the 18th, however. Andrews, *Diary*, 7; and Thruston's report, *SOR* 3:588.

34. For a discussion of flags of truce both in general and specifically on September 18, see Harsh, *Sounding the Shallows*, chap. 10, sect. D.

35. Late-starting battles that might be noted: Mechanicsville (3:00 P.M.), Gaines's Mill (1:00 P.M.), Savage's Station (4:00 P.M.), Frayser's Farm (2:30 P.M.), Malvern Hill (1:30 P.M.), Porter at Second Manassas (2:30 P.M.), and Hooker on Sept. 16 (2:00 P.M.).

36. Von Borcke, *Memoirs* 1:237–38. For a further discussion of the Lee-Jackson meeting, see Harsh, *Sounding the Shallows*, chap. 10, sect. E.

37. For a discussion of the proposed turning movement on September 18, see ibid.

38. For a discussion of Lee's intended reentry into Maryland via Williamsport, see ibid., sect. F.

39. In *OR*, vol. 19, 1, see the reports of Lee (p. 151) and Longstreet (p. 841); also see Longstreet, *From Manassas to Appomattox*, 263.

40. Owen, *In Camp and Battle*, 159.

41. Hotchkiss, *Make Me a Map*, 83. After the war, Lee assured Mrs. Jackson that her husband had concurred both in offering battle at Sharpsburg and in withdrawing from Maryland: "When I determined to withdraw across the Potomac, he also concurred." Lee to Mrs. Jackson, Jan. 25, 1866, Lee Family Papers, Virginia Historical Society. This technically leaves open, however, the question of Jackson's approval of the recrossing at Williamsport. It is even possible that Lee did not share with Jackson the intent to recross, in which case Hotchkiss's search for optional fords was simply for the purpose of relieving the pressure at Boteler's Ford.

42. Longstreet's report, *OR*, vol. 19, 1:841, where there is no indication that Lee mentioned the aim of reentering Maryland; although the reference to Federal reenforcements and the failure to turn the Federal right (albeit on the 17th) suggests the strategic situation was discussed by the two generals. This is a rare instance in which Longstreet fails to develop in his *Century* article or memoirs an incident mentioned in his official report.

43. Blackford, *War Years with Jeb Stuart*, 142. The multiple meetings between Stuart and Lee are inferred from the fact that Stuart was on his way to see Lee when he gave Blackford the instructions to find the ford.

44. Pendleton's report, *OR*, vol. 19, 1:830; Alexander, *Military Memoirs*, 272; and idem, *Fighting for the Confederacy*, 149.

45. Poague, *Gunner with Stonewall*, 48–49; and Squires, "Boy Officer," 20.

46. Information is from the only written order for the withdrawal to have survived, Longstreet to Walton, *OR*, vol. 51, 2:620; and in slightly altered version, Owen, *In Camp and Battle*, 159.

47. E. A. Moore, *Story of a Cannoneer*, 156–57. Apparently, perhaps because of the weather, Lee does not seem to have been concerned that Federal observers would spot the retreating wagons.

48. Longstreet, *From Manassas to Appomattox*, 263–64; Owen, *In Camp and Battle*, 159–60; and Stuart's report, *OR*, vol. 19, 1:820.

49. For a discussion of the wounded Lee left behind, see Harsh, *Sounding the Shallows*, chap. 10, sect. G.

50. Dickert, *History of Kershaw's Brigade*, 160; Hotchkiss, *Make Me a Map*, 83; and von Borcke, *Memoirs* 1:240–41.

51. G. Wise, *History of the 17th Va.*, 119; Owen, *In Camp and Battle*, 160–61; Hotchkiss, *Make Me a Map*, 83; Clark, *North Carolina Regiments* 5:79; J. B. Moore, "Sharpsburg," 212; and Pendleton's report, *OR*, vol. 19, 1:830.

52. For a discussion of the timing of the Confederate withdrawal, see Harsh, *Sounding the Shallows*, chap. 10, sect. H.

53. Freeman, *R. E. Lee* 2:406; McLaws, "Maryland," 27; Jackson's report, *OR*, vol. 19, 1:957; Hotchkiss, *Make Me a Map*, 83; and Douglas, *I Rode with Stonewall*, 180.

54. J. B. Moore, "Sharpsburg," 213.

55. Owen, *In Camp and Battle*, 161; Hotchkiss, *Make Me a Map*, 83.

56. In *OR*, vol. 19, 1, see the reports of Longstreet (p. 841) and Early (p. 972).

57. For the operations of the infantry rear guard see the reports in ibid. of A. P. Hill (p. 981), Lane (p. 986), McGowan (p. 988), and Perrin (p. 994). For the Gregg incident see H. B. McClellan, *I Rode with Jeb Stuart*, 133–34.

58. Ramsay, *North Carolina Regiments* 1:576–77; and Ramsay to Julius Ramsay, Sept. 23, John Andrew Ramsay Papers, Southern Historical Collection.

59. H. B. McClellan, *I Rode with Jeb Stuart*, 132–33, 134, where the story is related as affecting Munford's entire brigade. It is certain, however, that the 12th Virginia left with Stuart for Williamsport on the night of the 18th; and it seems unlikely the 7th, on the far left throughout the battle, had rejoined its brigade.

60. H. B. McClellan, *I Rode with Jeb Stuart*, 132–33, 134; Ramsay, *North Carolina Regiments* 1:576–77; and in *OR*, vol. 19, 1, the reports of Pendleton (p. 831) and McGowan (p. 989).

61. McLaws, "Maryland," 27; and Walker, "Sharpsburg," 682. For a discussion of Walker's claim to have conversed with Lee in the middle of the Potomac, see Harsh, *Sounding the Shallows*, chap. 10, sect. I.

62. Blackford, *War Years with Jeb Stuart*, 152; Barringer, *North Carolina* 1:421.

63. Von Borcke, *Memoirs* 1:241, and Hotchkiss, *Make Me a Map*, 83.

64. Brown to Pendleton, Sept. 17, *OR*, vol. 19, 2:610–11; in ibid., 1, the reports of Pendleton (p. 830) and Barnwell (p. 838). See also, Hotchkiss, *Make Me a Map*, 83; and von Borcke, *Memoirs* 1:241.

65. In *OR*, vol. 19, 1, see the reports of Stuart (p. 820) and Hampton (p. 824). See also Blackford, *War Years with Jeb Stuart*, 153; and Barringer, *North Carolina Regiments* 1:421.

66. On the Confederate force assembled at Williamsport, see Harsh, *Sounding the Shallows*, chap. 10, sect. J.

67. On Stuart's operations at Williamsport see in *OR*, vol. 19, 1, the reports of Stuart (pp. 820–21) and Hampton (p. 824). See also Carman, "Maryland Campaign," chap. 25, p. 13; Blackford, *War Years with Jeb Stuart*, 153–54; H. B. McClellan, *I Rode with Jeb Stuart*, 134–35. The greatest detail, including the musical ball, is to be found in von Borcke, *Memoirs* 1:242–47.

68. Marcy to Sumner, 4:00 A.M., Marcy to Franklin and Meade, 4:30 A.M., and Marcy to Pleasonton, 4:00 A.M., in *OR*, vol. 51, 1:849–50, 852; and Marcy to Porter, untimed, in ibid., vol. 19, 1:331.

69. McClellan to Halleck, 8:30 A.M., *OR*, vol. 19, 1:330; and Marcy to Sumner, Franklin, Burnside, Porter, Meade, and Davis, 8:45 P.M., ibid., vol. 51, 1:849. The circular is incorrectly marked "p.m." The movement only makes sense while McClellan still expected he might have to confront a Confederate line in Maryland. Moreover, the Twelfth Corps is assigned a position, but it was ordered to Harpers Ferry at noon.

70. McClellan to Halleck, Sept. 19, 10:30 A.M., ibid., vol. 19, 2:330.

71. In ibid., vol. 51, 1, all Sept. 19, Marcy to Meade, 12:30 P.M. (p. 849); Marcy to Sumner, 12:15 P.M. (p. 850); Marcy to Sumner, 5:00 P.M. (p. 850); Marcy to Franklin, 11:45 A.M. (p. 851); and Marcy to Pleasonton, 1:15 P.M. (p. 853). Also McClellan to Halleck, Sept. 19, 1:30 P.M., ibid., vol. 19, 1:68 (time from McClellan, *Civil War Papers*, 470).

72. Marcy to Franklin, Sept. 19, 11:45 A.M., and Marcy to Couch, untimed but presumably the same hour, ibid., vol. 51, 1:851, 852.

73. This summary of Fifth Corps operations on the evening of the 19th and the morning of the 20th, except where otherwise noted, is from the official reports in *OR*, vol. 19, 1:339–55, 361–68; Carman, "Maryland Campaign," chap. 22, pp. 9–19, and chap. 25, passim; and William Henry Powell, *The Fifth Army Corps (Army of the Potomac), a Record of Operations during the*

Civil War in the United States of America, 1861–1865 (New York: G. P. Putnam's Sons, 1896), 293–302.

74. Marcy to Porter, Sept. 19, 10:45 P.M., *OR*, vol. 19, 2:331; and Marcy to Pleasonton, Sept. 19, 10:00 A.M., ibid., vol. 51, 1:853.

75. See the following dispatches of Sept. 19, in ibid., vol. 51, 1, Marcy to Couch, 8:15 P.M. (p. 851); Marcy to Reynolds, 9:30 P.M. (p. 852); and Marcy to Pleasonton, 11:00 P.M. (p. 853).

76. In addition to the sources cited in note 73, see the dispatches of Sept. 19 in ibid., vol. 19, 2, Pleasonton to Marcy, 6:30 A.M. (p. 334); Sykes to Porter, 9:15 A.M. (pp. 334–35); and Marcy to Porter, 10:30 A.M. (p. 334); also see Marcy to Porter, 9:00 A.M., ibid., vol. 51, 1:854.

77. As has been seen, Lee almost reached the two-corps structure at Second Manassas, except for keeping R. H. Anderson as an independent reserve. He had not integrated the reenforcements from Richmond (Walker, McLaws, and D. H. Hill) into the commands of Longstreet and Jackson even through the battle on the 17th. See note 81 of chapter 1. On Lee's misgivings about Jackson see Lee to Davis, Oct. 2, *OR*, vol. 19, 2:643–44; and Hotchkiss, *Make Me a Map*, 18. The two-corps structure would not be formally recognized in orders until November, after promotions were made to lieutenant general. On September 28, Davis wrote to Lee that the law was to be passed, but Lee may have been aware of it earlier. Ibid., 633.

78. Lee to Mrs. Jackson, Jan. 25, 1866, Lee Family Papers, Virginia Historical Society. In *OR*, vol. 19, 1, see the reports of Pendleton (p. 831), Longstreet (p. 841), Jackson (p. 957), and Early (p. 972). Also see Early, *War Memoirs*, 153; Longstreet, *From Manassas to Appomattox*, 263; and G. Wise, *History of the 17th Va.*, 120.

79. For a detailed account of the guns and their positions, see Barnwell's report, *OR*, vol. 19, 1:838.

80. Chilton to Pendleton, Sept. 19, ibid., 2:612; and S. P. Lee, *Memoirs*, 225.

81. Douglas Freeman entitled a chapter in *Lee's Lieutenants* "Pendleton Fails to Count His Men" (2:226–35). It is a solid, detailed analysis of Pendleton's actions that does not, however, discuss the larger issues involved for either the Confederates or Federals.

82. This unusual pairing of a brigade from Ewell's division (Lawton) with one from R. H. Anderson (Armistead) came about accidentally. On the 17th, as Anderson moved to support the Sunken Road, Armistead was detached and ordered to reenforce McLaws's division at the Dunkard Church. With the wounding of both Armistead and Anderson, the brigade of five Virginia regiments had fallen under the control of Jubal Early, who had succeeded to the command of Ewell's division, and it remained with him through the withdrawal into Virginia. It is known from Early's report that Lawton's brigade numbered about 400 on the 19th, and, since Pendleton claimed his infantry totaled 600, this would leave 200 for Armistead's brigade. Reports of Pendleton and Early in *OR*, vol. 19, 1:832, 972. For further discussion of the two brigades, see note 85 below.

83. At most, Munford had the 2d and 7th Virginia Cavalry, if, that is, the 7th had returned from its duty with Fitz Lee on September 17. The 12th Virginia was absent on Stuart's Williamsport expedition.

84. In addition to Pendleton's report, ibid., 832; see also the two dispatches from Hodges to Pendleton, both September 19, ibid., 2:612, 613.

85. It is interesting that several contemporary sources single out Lawton's Georgians in a way that suggests Armistead's Virginians were more heroic. In fact, all of Armistead's regiments had been detached to distant points and only the Georgians remained at the ford. An excellent view of the panic among the gunners may be found in J. B. Moore, "Sharpsburg," 214–15.

86. Except where otherwise noted, Pendleton's actions on the 19th and 20th are from his report, *OR*, vol. 19, 1:830–34; and Pendleton to his wife, Sept. 22, S. P. Lee, *Memoirs*, 213–15.

87. This is apparent from the sequence in which Pendleton encountered units; but also see in *OR*, vol. 19, 1, the reports of Early (p. 972) and A. P. Hill (p. 981); also see Early, *War Memoirs*, 162; and G. Wise, *History of the 17th Va.*, 120.

88. In his report and letter, Pendleton names only Pryor and Hood, but in the latter document he adds that afterward "I was referred to another and another." *OR*, vol. 19, 1:833–34; and S. P. Lee, *Memoirs*, 214. Pendleton's brief interview with D. H. Hill is revealed in an 1864 letter by Hill to Robert L. Dabney, in Bridges, *Lee's Maverick General*, 128; and in Ratchford, Memoir, 46–47, D. H. Hill, Jr., Personal Papers. It would seem that Pendleton at some point encountered Osmun Latrobe of D. R. Jones's staff. After hearing the alarming news, Latrobe set out on his own and found Longstreet, who sent him to report to Lee. Here Latrobe had no success, however, recording that he "hunted till 12 oclk ineffectually." Latrobe, Diary, Sept. 19.

89. Mary Anna Jackson, *Memoirs of Stonewall Jackson by His Widow*, 2d ed. (Louisville: Prentice Press, 1895), 345; Douglas, *I Rode with Stonewall*, 184; Lee to Mrs. Jackson, Jan. 25, 1866, Lee Family Papers, Virginia Historical Society.

90. Lee to Mrs. Jackson, Jan. 25, 1866, Lee Family Papers, Virginia Historical Society; Freeman, *R. E. Lee* 2:407; and idem, *Lee's Lieutenants* 2:232–33.

91. Lee to Davis, Sept. 20, 1862, *OR*, vol. 19, 1:142; and Lee to Mrs. Jackson, Jan. 25, 1866, Lee Family Papers, Virginia Historical Society. Four years after the event, Lee wrote as if he intended an unrestricted attack. The document written at the time makes clear, however, that he would not have attacked a major portion of the Army of the Potomac.

92. Lee to Davis, Sept. 20th, *OR*, vol. 19, 1.142. The dispatch is not timed. Internal evidence indicates it was written before Lee left his headquarters around dawn to ride back toward Shepherdstown.

93. After the war, Lee would seem to remember much more bellicose intentions that contradict his contemporary statement: "From his [Pendleton's] statement, I thought it possible, that the Federal army might be attempting to follow us, and I sent at once to Gen. Jackson to say, that in that event, I would attack it." Lee to Mrs. Jackson, Jan. 25, 1866, Lee Family Papers, Virginia Historical Society. His postwar dropping of the proviso "if not in full force" may have come from telescoping or from faulty memory. It would not seem to have any bearing on the controversy mentioned in note 99 below.

94. Reference is to the ford several miles downstream from Shepherdstown that throughout the present study has been called Boteler's Ford. Local Virginians referred to it as Boteler's Ford, since one of the area's most prominent residents, Congressman Alexander Boteler, had a farm nearby. Many Marylanders, on the other hand, knew the crossing as Blackford's Ford. Apparently, D. H. Hill and Lee knew only the name that appeared on most maps, Shepherdstown Ford.

95. D. H. Hill to Robert L. Dabney, July 19, 1864, in Bridges, *Lee's Maverick General*, 128; and Ratchford, Memoir, 46–47, D. H. Hill, Jr., Personal Papers.

96. In addition to the sources cited in note 95, see Lee to Mrs. Jackson, Jan. 25, 1866, Lee Family Papers, Virginia Historical Society; and M. A. Jackson, *Memoirs of Stonewall Jackson*, 344–45. Kemper's brigade returned two miles toward the river (G. Wise, *History of the 17th Va.*, 120); but the rest of D. R. Jones's division remained on the Charlestown Pike (Latrobe Diary, Sept. 20). It is also possible that McLaws's division moved back to the pike. See Hubbert, "Diary," 310.

97. M. A. Jackson, *Memoirs of Stonewall Jackson*, 344–45; A. P. Hill's report, *OR*, vol. 19, 1:982; Bridges, *Lee's Maverick General*, 129. Jackson's old division (now under Colonel Grigsby) was so small, probably 500 or fewer men, that it attracted little attention during this affair. Jubal Early suggests in passing, however, that the division did return and was in the rear of his own. Early's report, *OR*, vol. 19, 1:972. The movement of Ripley's brigade of D. H. Hill as far as the Charlestown Pike is confirmed in Leach Diary, Sept. 20.

98. Federal sources on the Battle of Shepherdstown are cited in note 73, to which should be added Alfred A. Woodhull, "Letter of July 21, 1886," in *B&L* 2:672–73. For Confederate sources, see in *OR*, vol. 19, 1, the reports of Jackson (p. 957), Early (p. 972), A. P. Hill (p. 982), Lane (p. 986), McGowan (pp. 989–90), Hamilton (p. 992), Perrin (p. 995), McCorkle (p. 997), Brown (p. 999), Archer (p. 1001), Pender (pp. 1004–5), and Thomas (p. 1006). In *SOR* 3, see the reports of McRae (pp. 575–76) and McIntosh (p. 577). See also Carman, "Maryland Campaign," chap. 25; Early, *War Memoirs*, 162; Chamberlayne, *Letters*, 115–18; Cathey, *North Carolina Regiments* 1:761; Lane, ibid., 2:474; J. B. Moore, "Sharpsburg," 215–16; Scates, "Diary," 14; Haynes, *Diary*, 20–21; and Fitzpatrick, *Letters*, 21. Also useful was the hand-drawn map courtesy of Mr. John Divine of Leesburg.

99. For a further discussion of the Battle of Shepherdstown, see Harsh, *Sounding the Shallows*, chap. 10, sect. K.

100. Quote is from G. Wise, *History of the 17th Va.*, 121. For a discussion of Confederate movements after the Battle of Shepherdstown on September 20, see Harsh, *Sounding the Shallows*, chap. 10, sect. L.

101. Owen, *In Camp and Battle*, 162. On Dorsey Pender's use of the sword on stragglers, see McIntosh's report, *SOR* 3:579.

102. Not published in the *OR*, see Orders and Circulars Issued by the Army of the Potomac and the Army and Department of Northern Virginia, C.S.A., 1861–1865, RG-109, National Archives.

103. In *OR*, vol. 19, 1, see the reports of Stuart (p. 821) and Hampton (p. 824); and for a much more detailed account see von Borcke, *Memoirs* 1:247–57.

104. Lee's report, *OR*, vol. 19, 1:152.

105. Lee to Davis, Sept. 21, Camp on the Opequon, near Smoketown, ibid., 142.

106. This sentence has been transposed for the sake of topical continuity.

107. Jones to Lee, Sept. 27, ibid., 2:629–30. It would be interesting to know if Lee sent Jones back to Virginia on the night of the 17th as part of his preparations for renewed fighting the next day. For a further discussion of the depot at Winchester, see Harsh, *Sounding the Shallows*, chap. 10, sect. M.

108. Lee to Davis, Sept. 25, Camp on the Opequon, near Smoketown, *OR*, vol. 19, 2:626–27. The first paragraph quoted is the clearest of all Lee's statements in regard to what he intended to do before the Battle of Shepherdstown intervened.

109. In ibid., 1, see Lee to Loring, Sept. 25 (pp. 625–26); and for the secretary of war's support for Lee's plan, see Randolph to Loring, Sept. 30 (pp. 637–38).

110. For a discussion of Lee's information on September 21–25, see Harsh, *Sounding the Shallows*, chap. 10, sect. N.

111. In *OR*, vol. 19, 2, see Lee to G. W. Smith, Sept. 24 (pp. 624–25). On October 1 Lee wrote of the Federal army: "It will require some time for it to recover from the battles of Boonsborough and Sharpsburg, in which they must have lost heavily." Lee to G. W. Smith, ibid., 640.

112. In ibid., 2, see Chilton to Cooper, Sept. 23 (pp. 621–22); Lee to Davis, Sept. 23 (pp. 622–23); Lee to G. W. Smith, Sept. 24 (pp. 624–25); Taylor to G. W. Smith, Sept. 25 (p. 627); and J. R. Jones to Paxton, Sept. 27 (pp. 629–30).

113. In ibid. see Lee to Myers, Sept. 21 (p. 614); Special Orders, No. 196, Headquarters Army of Northern Virginia, Sept. 21 (pp. 614–15); Lee to Davis, Sept. 22 (pp. 617–18); Lee to Longstreet and Jackson, Sept. 22 (pp. 618–19); and Lee to Randolph, Sept. 23 (p. 622).

114. On Lee's informal but permanent division of the army into two wings, see in ibid.: Field Returns of Sept. 22 (p. 621); Lee to Longstreet and Jackson, Sept. 22 (pp. 618–19); and Special Orders, No. 201, Sept. 26, Headquarters Army of Northern Virginia (pp. 628–29), in which there is allusion to the right and left wings of the army. Also see Circular, Headquarters,

Right Wing, Army of Northern Virginia, Sept. 26, ibid., vol. 51, 2:627. Lee would formally recommend the promotion of Longstreet and Jackson to the rank of lieutenant general on October 2, although the internal reorganization of the two corps would take longer. In ibid., vol. 19, 2, see Lee to Davis, Oct. 2 (pp. 643–44); Lee to Randolph, Oct. 27 (pp. 683–84); and Special Orders, No. 234, Army of Northern Virginia, Nov. 6 (pp. 698–99).

115. In ibid., vol. 19, 2, see Chilton to Baldwin, Sept. 21 (p. 613); Taylor to Pendleton, Sept. 23 (p. 623); and Lee to Pendleton, Sept. 23 (pp. 623–24). For results that point to earlier action by Lee, see Lee to Randolph, Sept. 28 (p. 632); Lee to Randolph, Oct. 4 (pp. 646–47); Pendleton to Lee, Oct. 2 (pp. 647–52); and Special Orders, No. 209, Headquarters Army of Northern Virginia, Oct. 4 (pp. 652–54).

116. In ibid. see Lee to Myers, Sept. 21 (p. 614); Lee to Davis, Sept. 23 (p. 623); and Lee to Pendleton, Sept. 23 (pp. 623–24).

117. The first quotation is from Goree to mother, Oct. 10, Thomas Jewett Goree, *Longstreet's Aide: The Civil War Letters of Major Thomas J. Goree*, ed. Thomas W. Cutrer (Charlottesville: Univ. Press of Virginia, 1995), 99. The final quote is from Lee to Davis, Sept. 25, *OR*, vol. 19, 2:626–27. On the "worn out" condition of the Army of Northern Virginia, see Walter Taylor to sister, Sept. 21, Taylor, *Letters*, 44–45; Haynes, *Diary*, 21; Hubbert, "Diary," 310; Andrews, *Diary*, 7; McIntire's report, *SOR* 3:577–78; Pender to wife, Sept. 22, 25, Pender, *The General to His Wife*, 176, 177; and Hotchkiss to brother, Sept. 28, Hotchkiss Papers. On the condition of the artillery, in *OR*, vol. 19, 2, see Jones to Pendleton, Sept. 29 (p. 613), and Pendleton to Lee, Oct. 2 (pp. 647–52); and on lack of medical supplies, see Guild to Moore, Oct. 9 (pp. 659–60).

118. Custis Lee to Davis, Sept. 25, Martinsburg, *Papers of Jefferson Davis* 8:405–6.

119. Chilton to Davis, Sept. 25, ibid., 404. Chilton's figure is by no means impossibly high. Ezra Carman estimated that Confederate straggling in Maryland alone exceeded 20,000 ("Maryland Campaign," chap. 26, p. 3). To this figure must be added not only those who straggled after the army returned to Virginia but also the convalescent thousands who had been unable to cross the Potomac to join their commands. Moreover, 34,000 men would return to the ranks by November 10. Field Returns, *OR*, vol. 19, 2:713.

120. Field Returns, Sept. 22, *OR*, vol. 19, 2:621.

121. The first quote is from Hotchkiss, *Make Me a Map*, 85. In *OR*, vol. 19, 2, for the Lee quote, see Lee to Davis, Sept. 25 (pp. 633–34); and for the movement see Special Orders, No. 201, Sept. 26, Headquarters Army of Northern Virginia (pp. 628–29). At the time, Walter Taylor wrote: "I believe my Chief was most anxious to recross into Maryland but was persuaded by his principal advisors that the condition of the army did not warrant such a move. This is conjecture on my part. I only know of his opinion & *guess* why he did not follow it." Taylor to sister, Sept. 28, Taylor, *Letters*, 45–46.

122. In *OR*, vol. 19, 2, see Field Returns for Sept. 22 (p. 621), Sept. 30 (p. 639), Oct. 10 (p. 660), Oct. 20 (p. 674), and Nov. 11 (p. 713).

123. On improvement of the army, see Chamberlayne, *Letters*, 117; Hotchkiss, *Make Me a Map*, 85; Alexander, *Fighting for the Confederacy*, 155; Thompson to parents, Oct. 1, Austin, *Georgia Boys*, 52; Lee to Randolph, Oct. 9, *OR*, vol. 19, 2:658; Taylor to brother, Oct. 15, Taylor, *Letters*, 48; Cage to wife, Oct. 18, William L. Cage, "The Civil War Letters of William L. Cage," ed. T. Harry Williams, *Louisiana Historical Quarterly* 39 (1956): 124.

124. Taylor to sister, Sept. 21, 28, Taylor, *Letters*, 44–46.

125. Taylor to sister, Sept. 21, ibid., 44; A. S. Pendleton to mother, Sept. 21, S. P. Lee, *Memoirs*, 217; Pender to wife, Sept. 28, Pender, *The General to His Wife*, 180; and Custis Lee to Davis, Sept. 25, *Papers of Jefferson Davis* 8:406. In the same letter quoted, Taylor was somewhat disingenuous, when he wrote: "We do not boast a victory—it was not sufficiently decisive for that."

126. Lee [Jr.], *Recollections*, 79; the letter is not headed, but date is confirmed internally.

127. In *OR*, vol. 19, 2, see Davis to Lee, Sept. 28 (pp. 633–34); and Lee acknowledged receiving on the night of Oct. 1, Lee to Davis, Oct. 2 (p. 643).

128. Davis to K. Smith, Oct. 29, *Papers of Jefferson Davis* 8:468.

129. General Orders, No. 116, Headquarters Army of Northern Virginia, Oct. 2, *OR*, vol. 19, 2:644–45.

130. In ibid. see Lee to G. W. Smith, Sept. 24 (pp. 624–25), and Lee to Davis, Sept. 28 (pp. 626–27).

131. In ibid. see Lee to Davis, Oct. 2 (pp. 643–44), in which Lee does not specify an enemy move up the James. However, he is responding to a rumor mentioned by Davis in a letter of September 28 (pp. 633–34). Lee's focus on a possible enemy move on the James is made clear in the October 9 dispatch to G. W. Smith (p. 658) and another to Davis on October 22 (p. 675).

132. In ibid. see Lee to Stuart, Oct. 8 (p. 55); quote is from Lee to Randolph, Oct. 14 (p. 51). Charles Marshall testified that Lee sent Stuart on the Maryland raid "expressly to ascertain if any preparations were being made to move General McClellan's army again by sea to Richmond." Marshall added, "Later in the year when we were on the Rappahannock General Lee was constantly watching for any indication of such a movement" (*Aide-de-camp to Lee*, 147–48).

133. In *OR*, vol. 19, 2, quote is from Lee to Davis, Oct. 22 (p. 675); see also, Lee to G.W. Smith, Oct. 24 (pp. 679–80).

134. Lee to Custis Lee, Nov. 10, Lee, *Wartime Papers*, 333.

135. Confederate casualties of 13,912 in the Maryland campaign are from Carman, "Maryland Campaign," chap. 26, p. 2. Confederate casualties in the West of 10,397 are from *B&L* 2:29–30, 736, 759–60; and Patricia L. Faust, ed., *Historical Times Illustrated Encyclopedia of the Civil War* (New York: Harper & Row, 1986), 630. For details of the Confederate losses in Maryland, see Harsh, *Sounding the Shallows*, chap. 10, sect. P.

136. *OR*, ser. 4, vol. 2:160.

137. January 1, 1863, mobilized strength figures from Livermore, *Numbers and Losses*, 47.

138. Lee's loss on September 17 was 10,316, compared to the West's total 10,397. See sources in note 135.

Finale. "We have tried the utmost": Lee's Ventures Risked and Lost

1. An hour after Gordon left, Lee raised the subject with William Allan, a mathematics professor and former ordnance officer in the Army of Northern Virginia. Both Gordon and Allan made memoranda of Lee's remarks, and the manuscripts of both are currently in the William Allan Books in the Southern Historical Collection, University of North Carolina, Chapel Hill. In 1943, when the memoranda were still in the possession of Allan's son, Douglas Freeman published transcriptions as an appendix in volume two of *Lee's Lieutenants*, 715–23. Recently they have been reprinted in Gallagher, ed., *Lee the Soldier*, 7–9, 25–27. Lee's testimony on various aspects of the campaign, as embodied in these memoranda and others, have already been incorporated at appropriate points in the present work, and the more recent printed version has been cited.

2. Lee's letter to Mrs. Jackson in January 1866 and his gentle attempts to correct Dabney's manuscript biography of Stonewall Jackson indicate that he had already learned of the corrosive effect of history. Lee to Mrs. Jackson, Jan. 25, 1866, Lee Family Papers, Virginia Historical Society. It seems likely, moreover, that his decision in the summer of 1865 to write his own history of the Army of Northern Virginia was his attempt to control the story. See Allen W. Moger, "General Lee's Unwritten 'History of the Army of Northern Virginia,'" *Virginia Magazine of History and Biography* 71 (1963): 341–63.

3. In *OR*, vol. 19, 2, see Lee to Davis, Sept. 23 (pp. 622–23), and Lee to Davis, Oct. 2 (pp. 643–44); see also Lee to Randolph, Sept. 30 (pp. 636–37), and General Orders, No. 116, Headquarters Army of Northern Virginia, Oct. 2 (pp. 644–45.)

4. Quote is from Lee's report, ibid., 1:146; reasons for leaving Maryland are given on pp. 151–52. Because Lee does not mention in his report his intention of recrossing the Potomac at Williamsport, the reasons for leaving Maryland become, by default, the reasons for ending the campaign.

5. Gallagher, ed., *Lee the Soldier*, 26.

6. Lee, "Hill Letter," 164.

7. Gallagher, ed., *Lee the Soldier*, 8.

8. Ibid., 13.

9. Lee, "Hill Letter," 164. James Longstreet seems to corroborate Lee's statement by writing, "General Lee was not satisfied with the result of the Maryland campaign, and seemed inclined to attribute the failure to the Lost Dispatch" ("Maryland," 674).

10. Gallagher, ed., *Lee the Soldier*, 8.

11. Freeman, *R. E. Lee* 2:409–10. William Allan was the first to make this point, and he identified the same areas of controversy as Freeman. Allan, *Army of Northern Virginia*, 440.

12. Taylor, *Four Years with General Lee* and *General Lee;* Marshall, *Aide-de-Camp to Lee;* and Long, *Memoirs of Robert E. Lee.* Marshall would attempt much fuller coverage in his planned life of Lee, but he never finished it, portions were published posthumously in 1927.

13. Early, *War Memoirs;* Allan, *Army of Northern Virginia;* for Hotchkiss, see *Confederate Military History*, vol. 3.

14. Early, *War Memoirs*, 159. Indeed, many years before, in addressing an audience at Washington College, Early had proclaimed the campaign "a grand success." Gallagher, ed., *Lee the Soldier*, 52. Yet, the Confederate commander's own nephew, Fitzhugh Lee, would state flatly that "General Lee's Maryland campaign was a failure." He would add that the expedition "demonstrated" that the Confederate "army, without reenforcements, was too small for offensive operations." F. Lee, *General Lee*, 215–16. The latter remark suggests that—at least in retrospect—Fitz Lee believed his uncle should have rested and refitted the army after Second Manassas.

15. Early, *War Memoirs*, 156. Although he tried, Walter Taylor was never able to reduce the figure below 35,000. See Taylor, *Four Years with General Lee*, 73; and *General Lee*, 135; see also, "Sharpsburg or Antietam," in John William Jones, comp., *Army of Northern Virginia Memorial Volume* (Richmond: J. W. Randolph & English, 1880), 344–45.

16. Taylor, *General Lee*, 125.

17. Longstreet, "Maryland," 673. Longstreet would make the same statement more obliquely in his book *From Manassas to Appomattox*, 289. Privately, D. H. Hill agreed, writing to Longstreet after the war, "Do you know I always dreaded that scattering method of Lee? I said to my brother at the beginning of the Penn. campaign, we are going to be ruined by dispersals, as we were before." D. H. Hill to Longstreet, June 5, 1885, Longstreet Papers, Duke University. Porter Alexander was even more critical of Lee, but his views were so far outside the Confederate tradition that they are treated separately below.

18. Longstreet, "Maryland," 665–66; and *From Manassas to Appomattox*, 219–20. Other Confederates more delicately suggested Lee might have been brash to stand at Sharpsburg. Walter Clark wrote: "It showed a boldness the success of which future ages may admire, but which will not justify an attempt to imitate" (*North Carolina Regiments* 5:591). Even William Allan—who in 1886 totally rejected the notion—by 1892 admitted that "in the light of subsequent events . . . there is much to be said" for Longstreet's view that Lee should have retired

to Virginia, rather than standing at South Mountain. Five years later, Allan would confess to a Northern audience that "this course would have been the best one." See Allan, "First Maryland Campaign, Review of General Longstreet," *SHSP* 14 (1886): 102–3; *Army of Northern Virginia*, 441; and "Sharpsburg," 102.

19. Longstreet, "Maryland," 666–67; idem, *From Manassas to Appomattox*, 228–29.

20. Longstreet, *From Manassas to Appomattox*, 279, 285.

21. Longstreet, "Maryland," 673.

22. Gallagher, ed., *Lee the Soldier*, 8.

23. Dowdey, *Lee*, 304. Dowdey admitted that "strategically . . . the drawn battle was a loss" (p. 316).

24. Henderson, *Stonewall Jackson*, 552.

25. Freeman, *R. E. Lee* 2:411–12. For a discussion of Freeman's criticism of Lee, see Harsh, *Sounding the Shallows*, chap. 10, sect. O.

26. Freeman, *R. E. Lee* 2:410. In a recent essay on the Army of Northern Virginia in the Maryland campaign, historian Robert K. Krick accepted only part of Freeman's view. Krick wrote: "Lee's decision to move into Maryland cannot be rationally gainsaid. . . . The difficulties that his shrunken army faced could not deter him from grasping the moment. Ten days later, when fate had denied Lee and his army the circumstances he had sought, he fought the battle of Sharpsburg, or Antietam. That fight he should not have made. The effort to find the right set of circumstances, however, he had to make." Later, Krick reemphasized his unhappiness over Lee's decision to give battle at Sharpsburg: "His decision to make that stand was a bad one, probably his worst of the war" ("Army of Northern Virginia in September 1862," 36–37, 55).

27. Emory M. Thomas, *Robert E. Lee: A Biography* (New York: W. W. Norton, 1995), 261. Charles P. Roland also offers a judicious, if brief, evaluation in "The Generalship of Robert E. Lee," in Grady McWhiney, ed., *Grant, Lee, Lincoln and the Radicals: Essays on Civil War Leadership* (Evanston, Ill.: Northwestern Univ. Press, 1964), 38–42; and his more recent *Reflections on Lee: A Historian's Assessment* (Mechanicsburg, Pa.: Stackpole Books, 1995), 44–48. The most extended treatment of the subject since Freeman may be found in Scott Hartwig, "Robert E. Lee and the Maryland Campaign," in Gallagher, ed., *Lee the Soldier*, 331–55. Hartwig's well-written and insightful examination appeared after the present work was completed, and, although there are points of disagreement, there are also many areas of substantial agreement.

28. Palfrey, *The Antietam*, 123.

29. Quote from Carman, "Maryland Campaign," chap. 26, p. 6. The Cope's Maps, as they are popularly known, are U.S. Engineer Corps, *Atlas of the Battlefield of Antietam, Prepared under the Direction of the Antietam Battlefield Board* (Washington, D.C.: GPO, 1904), with a 2d rev. ed. in 1908. They are reproduced in part in Murfin, *Gleam of Bayonets*.

30. Early suggestions of Lee's clairvoyance may be found in Allan, *Army of Northern Virginia*, 441–42; and Freeman, *R. E. Lee* 2:106.

31. Murfin, *Gleam of Bayonets*, 205–6.

32. Sears, *Landscape Turned Red*, 66. Neither Murfin nor Sears seeks to discover when Lee learned it was McClellan who led the opposing army.

33. Sears, *Landscape Turned Red*, 66–67. A weakness of such psychohistory is that it shuts out the need for further inquiry into the reasons Lee rendered his decisions. Sears would make clearer his admiration for Lee in a later essay. Sears, "Getting Right with Robert E. Lee," 44–53.

34. Thomas L. Connelly, "Robert E. Lee and the Western Confederacy: A Criticism of Lee's Strategic Ability," *Civil War History* 15 (1969): 132.

35. Pender to wife, Sept. 22, Pender, *The General to His Wife*, 176; Hotchkiss to brother, Sept. 28, Hotchkiss Papers; Strayhorn to sister, July 11, 1863, "Letters of Thomas Jackson

Strayhorn," ed. Henry McGilbert Wagstaff, *North Carolina Historical Review* 13 (1936): 313.

36. Alexander, *Military Memoirs*, 221–22. Alexander supported his common-sense observation with a quixotic solution. He suggested that Lee should have entrenched Jackson behind the Rappahannock and then gone with Longstreet via Richmond-Bristol-Chattanooga to reenforce Bragg (p. 220). Alexander also called Lee's decision to stand at Sharpsburg "the greatest military blunder that Gen. Lee ever made." Alexander, *Fighting for the Confederacy*, 145.

37. George Anson Bruce, "The Strategy of the Civil War," in *PMHSM* 13 (1913): 468. Fifteen years earlier, in his survey history of the war, John Codman Ropes, also a member of the Military Historical Society of Massachusetts, had sharply criticized Lee's decision to give battle at Antietam: "This decision to stand and fight at Sharpsburg, which General Lee took on the evening of the 14th of September,—just after his troops had been driven from the South Mountain Passes—is beyond controversy one of the boldest and most hazardous decisions in his whole military career. It is in truth so bold and so hazardous that one is bewildered that he should even have thought seriously of making it." Ropes, *The Story of the Civil War: A Concise Account of the War in the United States of America between 1861 and 1865*, 2 vols. (New York: G. P. Putnam's Sons, 1894–98), 2:349. Note that Ropes's confused understanding of the chronology of Lee's decision may have contributed to his bewilderment.

38. Bruce, "Strategy," 471.

39. Ibid., 467. Elsewhere Bruce referred to "the impulsive nature of Lee, his audacity. . . ." (p. 453). He was clearly elaborating on the assessment of Lee made by Longstreet: "As commander he was much of the Wellington 'Up-and-at-'em' style. He found it hard, the enemy in sight, to withhold his blows." Longstreet, *From Manassas to Appomattox*, 287–88.

40. John Frederick Charles Fuller, *Grant & Lee, A Study in Personality and Generalship* (New York: Charles Scribner's Sons, 1933); Grady McWhiney and Perry D. Jamieson, *Attack and Die: Civil War Military Tactics and the Southern Heritage* (Tuscaloosa: Univ. of Alabama Press, 1982); and Alan T. Nolan, *Lee Considered: General Robert E. Lee and Civil War History* (Chapel Hill: Univ. of North Carolina Press, 1991); and Connelly, "Lee and the Western Confederacy," *Civil War History* 15 (1969): 197–213. McWhiney expressed the interpretation in less elaborate form in an earlier article, "Who Whipt Whom?" Confederate Defeat Reexamined," *Civil War History* 11 (1965): 5–26. As well known as Connelly's critique is the sharp rejoinder by Albert Castel, "The Historian and the General: Thomas L. Connelly vs Robert E. Lee," *Civil War History* 16 (1970): 215–28.

41. Charles Marshall must stand as a preeminent exception to this generalization. Marshall's exposition of Lee's strategy and his insistence that the Confederate commander consistently pursued that strategy throughout the war is discussed in Harsh, *Confederate Tide Rising*, chap.2.

42. The battles were the Seven Days, Second Manassas, and Antietam.

43. The casualty totals come from the Seven Days (20,135), Cedar Mountain (1,365), Second Manassas (9,474), in *B&L* 2:317, 496, 500; and for the Maryland campaign (13,912), Carman, "Maryland Campaign," chap. 26, pp. 1–2; for a grand total of 44,886. The straggling is an estimate for the entire three months. On Maryland see Longstreet, "Maryland," 674; and Carman, "Maryland Campaign," chap. 26, p. 3. For further details on the Maryland casualties, see Harsh, *Sounding the Shallows*, chap. 10, sect. P.

44. Lee divided his army when he sent A. P. Hill, D. H. Hill, and Longstreet north of the Chickahominy, Jackson through Thoroughfare Gap, and the expeditions to clear the Federal garrisons from the lower Shenandoah Valley. He was outnumbered at Second Manassas, South Mountain, and Antietam.

45. Alexander, *Military Memoirs*, 110–11; Heth, "Letter," 156–57; Longstreet, *From Manassas to Appomattox*, 287–88. For a perceptive explanation of Lee's aggressiveness, set within the context of Southern culture and expectations, see Gary W. Gallagher, "Another Look

at the Generalship of Robert E. Lee," in Gallagher, ed., *Lee the Soldier*, 275–89. Although a generally favorable view of Lee, Gallagher nonetheless finds Lee's determination to remain in Maryland after September 15 one of a handful of the general's "unfortunate decisions" (p. 282).

46. Lee to Davis, Jan. 10, 1863, Lee, *Wartime Papers*, 389.

47. Longstreet, "Maryland," 674.

48. William Preston Johnston, "Memorandum of Conversations between Robert E. Lee and William Preston Johnston, May 7, 1868 and March 18, 1870," ed. W. G. Bean, *Virginia Magazine of History and Biography* 73 (1965): 478.

49. Saunders, Memorandum of Conversation, Lee [Jr.], *Recollections and Letters*, 233.

Bibliography

Unpublished Sources

Manuscript Collections

Antietam National Battlefield Board. Antietam Studies. Record Group 94, Records of the Adjutant General's Office, 1780s–1917. National Archives, Washington, D.C.

———. Papers. Record Group 92, Records of the Office of the Quartermaster General. National Archives, Washington, D.C.

Allan, William. Books. Southern Historical Collection. University of North Carolina, Chapel Hill.

Carman, Ezra Ayers. Papers. Library of Congress, Washington, D.C.

———. Papers. New-York Historical Society, New York.

Century Collection. New York Public Library, New York.

Confederate Archives. Record Group 109, War Department Collection of Confederate Records. National Archives, Washington, D.C.

Harrison Family. Memoirs. Typescript. Loudoun Museum, Leesburg, Virginia.

Hill, Daniel Harvey. Papers. Southern Historical Collection. University of North Carolina, Chapel Hill.

———. Papers. Virginia Historical Society, Richmond.

———. Papers. Library of Virginia, Richmond.

———. Personal Papers. North Carolina State Archives, Raleigh.

Hill, Daniel Harvey, Jr. Personal Papers. North Carolina State Archives, Raleigh.

Hirsch, Isaac. Diary. Fredericksburg Area Museum and Cultural Center. Fredericksburg, Virginia.

Hotchkiss, Jedediah. Papers. Library of Congress, Washington, D.C.

Jackson, Samuel K. Essays. Virginia Historical Society, Richmond.

Johnson, Bradley Tyler. Papers. Duke University, Durham, North Carolina.

King, Henry Lord Page. Diary. Southern Historical Collection. University of North Carolina, Chapel Hill.

Latrobe, Osmun. Diary (typescript and photocopy). Virginia Historical Society, Richmond.

Leach, Calvin. Diary. Southern Historical Collection. University of North Carolina, Chapel Hill.

Lee, Robert Edward. Lee-Davis Correspondence. Library of Virginia, Richmond.
———. Lee Family Papers. Virginia Historical Society, Richmond.
———. Lee Headquarters Collection. Virginia Historical Society, Richmond.
———. Official Telegrams. Duke University, Durham, North Carolina.
———. Papers. Library of Congress, Washington, D.C.
Longstreet, James. Papers. Duke University, Durham, North Carolina.
———. Papers. Southern Historical Collection. University of North Carolina, Chapel Hill.
McClellan, George Brinton. Papers. Library of Congress, Washington, D.C.
McLaws, LaFayette. Papers. Duke University, Durham, North Carolina.
———. Papers. Southern Historical Collection. University of North Carolina, Chapel Hill.
———. Papers. Virginia Historical Society, Richmond.
Osborne, Edwin Augustus. Papers. Southern Historical Collection. University of North Carolina, Chapel Hill.
Ramsay, John Andrew. Papers. Southern Historical Collection. University of North Carolina, Chapel Hill.
Ratchford, J. W. Memoirs. Daniel Harvey Hill, Jr., Personal Papers. North Carolina State Archives, Raleigh.
Ropes, John Codman. Papers. Boston University, Boston.
Shinn, James T. Diary. Edwin Augustus Osborne Papers. Southern Historical Collection. University of North Carolina, Chapel Hill.
Squires, Charles Winder. Memoirs. W. H. T. Squires Papers. Southern Historical Collection. University of North Carolina, Chapel Hill.
Stiles, Joseph Clay. Papers. Henry E. Huntington Library. San Marino, California.
Stuart, James Ewell Brown. Papers. Henry E. Huntington Library. San Marino, California.
U.S. Weather Bureau. Records of Surface Land Observations, 1819–1941. Record Group 27, Records of the Weather Bureau. National Archives, Washington, D.C.

Unpublished Studies

Allen, John Owen. "The Strength of the Union and Confederate Forces at Second Manassas." Master's thesis. George Mason University, 1993.
Antietam National Battlefield Plaques. Typescript at Visitors Center, Sharpsburg, Maryland.
Carman, Ezra Ayers. "The Maryland Campaign of 1862." Carman Papers. Library of Congress, Washington, D.C.
Datzman, Richard C. "Who Found Lee's Lost Dispatch." Lost Orders File, Library, Visitors Center. Antietam National Battlefield Site, Sharpsburg, Maryland.
Pennefather, Robert Michael. "The Historical Investigation of Barbara Frietchie." Master's thesis. George Mason University, 1995.
Scully, John Connor. "Ezra Carman: Soldier and Historian." Master's thesis. George Mason University, 1997.
Tenney, Leon Walter. "Seven Days in 1862:Numbers in Union and Confederate Armies before Richmond." Master's thesis. George Mason University, 1992.

Newspapers

Baltimore American
Baltimore Sun
New York Times
New York Tribune
Richmond Dispatch
Richmond Examiner
Richmond Times
Richmond Whig
Washington Daily National Intelligencer
Washington Star

Published Sources: Books, Articles, Pamphlets, Broadsides

Addresses Delivered before the Confederate Veterans Association of Savannah, Ga. 5 vols. Savannah: Braid & Hutton, 1893–1902.

Alexander, Bevin. *Lost Victories: The Military Genius of Stonewall Jackson.* New York: Henry Holt, 1992.

Alexander, Edward Porter. *Fighting for the Confederacy: The Personal Recollections of General Edward Porter Alexander.* Ed. Gary W. Gallagher. Chapel Hill: Univ. of North Carolina Press, 1989.

———. *Military Memoirs of a Confederate: A Critical Narrative.* Ed. T. Harry Williams. Bloomington: Indiana Univ. Press, 1962.

Alexander, Ted. "Forgotten Valor: Off the Beaten Path at Antietam." *Blue & Gray Magazine* 13 (1995): 8–19, 48–64.

Allan, William. *The Army of Northern Virginia in 1862.* Dayton: Morningside House, 1984.

———. "Confederate Artillery at Second Manassas and Sharpsburg." *Southern Historical Society Papers* 11 (1883): 289–91.

———. "First Maryland Campaign, Review of General Longstreet." *Southern Historical Society Papers* 14 (1886): 102–18.

———. "Memoranda of Conversations with General Robert E. Lee." In Gallagher, ed., *Lee the Soldier,* 7–24.

———. "Memorandum of Conversation with Robert E. Lee, April 15, 1868." In Marshall, *Aide-de-Camp of Lee,* 248–52.

———. "Memorandum of Conversation with Robert E. Lee, February 15, 1868." In Freeman, *Lee's Lieutenants* 2:720–21.

———. "Roster of the A.N.V. [at Second Manassas and Sharpsburg]." *Southern Historical Society Papers* 11 (1883): 474–75.

———. "Strategy of the Campaign of Sharpsburg or Antietam, September, 1862." *Papers of the Military Historical Society of Massachusetts* 3 (1888): 73–103.

———. "Strategy of the Sharpsburg Campaign." *Maryland Historical Magazine* 1 (1906): 247–71.

Amann, William Frayne, ed. *Personnel of the Civil War.* 2 vols. New York: Thomas Yoseloff, 1961.

America: History and Life—A Guide to Periodical Literature. Santa Barbara, Calif.: Clio Press, 1964–.

The American Annual Cyclopaedia and Register of Important Events. 14 vols. New York: D. Appleton, 1862–75.

The Annals of the War, Written by Leading Participants, North and South, Originally Published in the Philadelphia Weekly Times. Philadelphia: Times Publishing, 1879.

Andrews, W. H. *Diary of W. H. Andrews, 1st Sergt. Co. M, 1st Georgia Regulars, From February, 1861, to May 2, 1865.* East Atlanta: Privately printed, 1891.

Armstrong, Marion Vincent. "A Failure of Command? A Reassessment of Edwin V. Sumner and the Federal II Corps at Antietam." In Woodworth, ed., *Leadership and Command in the Civil War,* 67–145.

Arnold, Thomas Jackson. "The Lost Dispatch—A War Mystery." *Confederate Veteran* 30 (1922): 317.

Austin, Mildred Aurelia. *Georgia Boys with "Stonewall" Jackson—James Thomas Thompson and the Walton Infantry.* Athens: Univ. of Georgia Press, 1967.

Avery, A. C. "Memorial Address on the Life and Character of Lieut.-General D. H. Hill." *Southern Historical Society Papers* 21 (1893): 110–50.

Barringer, Rufus. "Ninth Regiment (First Cavalry)." In Clark, ed., *North Carolina Regiments* 1:417–43.

Battle, Laura Elizabeth. *Forget-me-nots of the Civil War: A Romance Containing Reminiscences and Original Letters of Two Confederate Soldiers.* St. Louis: Fleming Printing, 1909.

Beach, William Harrison. *The First New York (Lincoln) Cavalry, From April 19, 1861, to July 7, 1865.* Milwaukee: Burdick & Allen, 1902.

Beale, George William. *A Lieutenant of Cavalry in Lee's Army.* Boston: Gorham, 1918.

———. "Maryland Campaign, 'the Cavalry Fight at Boonsboro' Graphically Described, the Ninth Virginia and Eighth Illinois Regiments Cross Sabers." *Southern Historical Society Papers* 25 (1897): 276–80.

Beall, James F. "Twenty-first Regiment." In Clark, ed., *North Carolina Regiments* 2:129–46.

Beers, Henry Putnam. *Guide to the Archives of the Government of the Confederate States of America.* Washington, D.C.: GPO, 1968.

Bennett, R. T. "Fourteenth Regiment." In Clark, ed., *North Carolina Regiments* 1:705–32.

Benning, Henry Lewis. "Notes on the Battle of Sharpsburg." *Southern Historical Society Papers* 16 (1888): 393–95.

Benson, Berry. *Berry Benson's Civil War Book: Memoirs of a Confederate Scout and Sharpshooter.* Ed. Susan Williams Benson. Athens: Univ. of Georgia Press, 1962.

Beringer, Richard E., Herman Hattaway, Archer Jones, and William N. Still, Jr. *Why the South Lost the Civil War.* Athens: Univ. of Georgia Press, 1986.

Berkeley, Henry Robinson. *Four Years in the Confederate Artillery: The Diary of Private Henry Robinson Berkeley.* Ed. William H. Runge. Published for the Virginia Historical Society. Chapel Hill: Univ. of North Carolina Press, 1961.

Berrier, H. R. "Company B, Tenth Virginia Cavalry." In Clark, ed., *North Carolina Regiments* 5:627–28.

Biddle, William Foster. "Recollections of McClellan." *United Service* n.s. 11 (1894): 460–69.

Blackford, William Willis. *War Years with Jeb Stuart.* New York.: Charles Scribner's Sons, 1945.

Blake, Joel C. "Letters of Joel C. Blake." Ed. J. Russell Reaver. *Apalachee* 5 (1957–62): 5–25.

Blosser, Susan Sokol, and Clyde Norman Wilson, Jr. *The Southern Historical Collection: A Guide to Manuscripts.* Chapel Hill: Univ. of North Carolina Library, 1970. With Supplement to 1975 (1976).

Boatner, Mark Mayo. *The Civil War Dictionary.* New York: David McKay, 1959.

Bond, Frank A. "General Lee Trusting in Providence at Antietam." *Century Magazine* 33 (1886): 309.

Boritt, Gabor S., ed. *Why the Confederacy Lost.* New York: Oxford Univ. Press, 1992.

Bridges, Hal. *Lee's Maverick General, Daniel Harvey Hill.* New York: McGraw Hill, 1961.

Brooks, Ulysses Robert, ed. *Stories of the Confederacy.* Columbia, S.C.: State Company, 1912.

Brown, Hamilton A. "First Regiment (State Troops)." In Clark, ed., *North Carolina Regiments* 1:135–56.

Bruce, George Anson. "Lee and the Strategy of the Civil War." In Gallagher, ed., *Lee the Soldier,* 111–38.

———. "The Strategy of the Civil War." In *Papers of the Military Historical Society of Massachusetts* 13 (1913): 391–483.

Burgwyn, William H. S. "Clingman's Brigade." In Clark, ed., *North Carolina Regiments* 4:481–500.

———. "Ransom's Brigade." In Clark, ed., *North Carolina Regiments* 4:569–79.

———. "Thirty-fifth Regiment." In Clark, ed., *North Carolina Regiments* 2:591–628.

Busey, John W., and David G. Martin. *Regimental Strengths and Losses at Gettysburg.* 2d rev. ed. Hightstown, N. J.: Longstreet House, 1986.

Butowsky, Harry A. "Nomenclature Used in the National Parks." *Cultural Resources Management Bulletin* 2 (1979): 3, 7–8.

Caffey, Thomas E. *Battle-fields of the South, from Bull Run to Fredericksburg, with Sketches of the Confederate Commanders, and Gossip of the Camps, by an English Combatant.* New York: John Bradburn, 1864.

Cage, William L. "The Civil War Letters of William L. Cage." Ed. T. Harry Williams. *Louisiana Historical Quarterly* 39 (1956): 113–30.

Caldwell, James Fitz James. *The History of a Brigade of South Carolinians, Known First as "Gregg's," and Subsequently as "McGowan's Brigade."* Philadelphia: King & Baird, 1866.

[Carraway, Daniel T.] "Lieutenant-General A. P. Hill: Some Reminiscences of the Famous Virginia Commander." *Southern Historical Society Papers* 19 (1891): 178–83.

Casler, John Overton. *Four Years in the Stonewall Brigade . . . Containing the Daily Experiences of Four Years' Service in the Ranks from a Diary Kept at the Time.* 4th rev. ed., Jed. Hotchkiss and James I. Robertson, Jr. Dayton, Ohio: Morningside Bookshop, 1971.

Castel, Albert. "The Historian and the General: Thomas L. Connelly vs Robert E. Lee." *Civil War History* 16 (1970): 215–28. Also in Gallagher, ed., *Lee the Soldier,* 209–23.

Cathey, Benjamin H. "Sixteenth Regiment." In Clark, ed., *North Carolina Regiments* 1:751–69.

Catton, Bruce. *This Hallowed Ground: The Story of the Union Side of the Civil War.* Garden City, N.Y.: Doubleday, 1956.

Chamberlayne, John Hampden. *Ham Chamberlayne, Virginian: Letters and Papers of an Artillery Officer in the War for Southern Independence, 1861–1865.* Ed. C. G. Chamberlayne. Richmond: Press of the Dietz Printing Co., 1932.

Clark, Walter, ed. *Histories of the Several Regiments and Battalions from North Carolina in the Great War 1861–1865, Written by Members of the Respective Commands.* 5 vols. Wendell, N.C.: Broadfoot's Bookmark, 1982. Cited herein as *North Carolina Regiments.*

———. "Sharpsburg." In Clark, ed., *North Carolina Regiments* 5:71–82.

———, et al. "Report of the Sharpsburg Battlefield Commission." In Clark, ed., *North Carolina Regiments* 5:587–92.

Clemens, Thomas G. "Black Hats off to the Original Iron Brigade." *Columbiad: A Quarterly Review of the War Between the States* 1 (1997): 46–58.

———, ed. "A Brigade Commander's First Fight: The Letters of Colonel Walter Phelps, Jr., During the Maryland Campaign." In Snell, ed., *Antietam,* 59–72.

Cole, Garrold L. *Civil War Eyewitnesses: An Annotated Bibliography of Books and Articles, 1955–1986.* Columbia: Univ. of South Carolina Press, 1988.

C.S. Congress. *Proceedings of the First Confederate Congress, Second Session in Part.* Published as *Southern Historical Society Papers,* 46 (1928).

Confederate Veteran. 40 vols. Nashville: United Confederate Veterans, 1893–1932.

Connelly, Thomas Lawrence. "Robert E. Lee and the Western Confederacy: A Criticism of Lee's Strategic Ability." *Civil War History* 15 (1969): 116–32. Also in Gallagher, ed., *Lee the Soldier,* 189–207.

Cooke, John Esten. *Robert E. Lee.* New York: G. W. Dillingham, 1899.

———. *Stonewall Jackson.* New York: G. W. Dillingham, [ca. 1899].

Corley, T. A. B. *Democratic Despot: A Life of Napoleon III.* New York: Clarkson N. Potter, 1961.

Cowan, John, and James I. Metts. "Third Regiment." In Clark, ed., *North Carolina Regiments* 1:177–214.

Cox, Jacob Dolson. *Military Reminiscences of the Civil War.* 2 vols. New York: Charles Scribner's Sons, 1900.

Crawford, Samuel Wylie. *The Genesis of the Civil War: The Story of Sumter, 1860–1861.* New York: Charles L. Webster, 1886.

Crook, Paul David. *The North, the South, and the Powers, 1861–1865.* New York: Wiley, 1974.

Crute, Joseph H., Jr. *Confederate Staff Officers, 1861–1865.* Powhatan, Va.: Derwent Books, 1982.

———. *Units of the Confederate States Army.* Midlothian, Va.: Derwent Books, 1987.

Cuffel, Charles A. *History of Durell's Battery in the Civil War (Independent Battery D, Pennsylvania Volunteer Artillery.): A Narrative of the Campaigns and Battles of Berks and Bucks Counties' Artillerists in the War of the Rebellion, from the Battery's Organization, September 24, 1861, to Its Muster Out of Service, June 13, 1865.* Philadelphia: Craig, Finley, 1903.

Cutts, Allen Sherrod. "Cutts' Battalion at Sharpsburg." *Southern Historical Society Papers* 10 (1882): 430–31.

Dabney, Robert Lewis. *Life and Campaigns of Lieut.-Gen. Thomas J. Jackson (Stonewall Jackson).* New York: Blelock, 1866.

Daly, Louise Porter. *Alexander Cheves Haskell: The Portrait of a Man.* Norwood, Mass.: Plimpton, 1934.

Daniel, John Warwick, ed. *Life and Personal Reminiscences of Jefferson Davis by Distinguished Men of His Time.* Baltimore: Eastern Publishing, 1890.

Darter, Lewis J., Jr. *List of Climatological Records in the National Archives.* Special List No. 1. Washington, D.C.: GPO, 1942.

Daves, Graham. "Twenty-second Regiment." In Clark, ed., *North Carolina Regiments* 2:161–80.

Davis, George Breckenridge. "The Antietam Campaign." In *Papers of the Military Historical Society of Massachusetts* 3:27–72.

Davis, Jefferson. *Jefferson Davis, Constitutionalist: His Letters, Papers, and Speeches.* Ed. Dunbar Rowland. 10 vols. Jackson: Mississippi Department of Archives and History, 1923.

———. *The Papers of Jefferson Davis.* Ed. Lynda Lasswell Crist and Mary Seaton Dix. 8 vols. to date. Baton Rouge: Louisiana State Univ. Press, 1971–95.

———. *The Rise and Fall of the Confederate Government.* 2 vols. New York: D. Appleton, 1881.

———. "Robert E. Lee." *Southern Historical Society Papers* 17 (1889): 362–72.

Davis, William C. *Jefferson Davis: The Man and His Hour.* New York: Harper Collins, 1991.

———. "Lee and Jefferson Davis." In Gallagher, ed., *Lee the Soldier,* 291–305.

———, ed. *The Confederate General.* 6 vols. N.p.: National Historical Society, 1991.

DeRosset, William Lord. "Additional Sketch Third Regiment." In Clark, ed., *North Carolina Regiments* 1:215–28.

———. [Letter on South Mountain.] In Johnson and Buel, eds., *Battles and Leaders* 2:569n.

———. "Ripley's Brigade at South Mountain." *Century Magazine* 33 (1886): 308–9.

Dickert, D. Augustus. *History of Kershaw's Brigade, with Complete Roll of Companies, Biographical Sketches, Incidents, Anecdotes, etc.* Rev. ed. Intro. Mac Wyckoff. Wilmington, N.C.: Broadfoot Publishing, 1990.

Dinkins, James. *1861 to 1865, by an Old Johnie, Personal Recollections and Experiences in the Confederate Army.* Cincinnati: Robert Clarke, 1897.

———. "Griffiths-Barksdale-Humphrey Brigade and Its Campaigns." *Southern Historical Society Papers* 32 (1904): 250–74.

Dornbusch, Charles Emil. *Military Bibliography of the Civil War.* 3 vols. New York: New York Public Library, 1961–72. Vol. 4 (supplement). Ed. Robert K. Krick. Dayton, Ohio: Morningside Press, 1987.

Douglas, Henry Kyd. *I Rode with Stonewall, Being Chiefly the War Experiences of the Youngest Member of Jackson's Staff from the John Brown Raid to the Hanging of Mrs. Surratt.* Chapel Hill: Univ. of North Carolina Press, 1940.

———. "Stonewall Jackson in Maryland." In Johnson and Buel, eds., *Battles and Leaders* 2:620–29.

———. "Stonewall Jackson's Intentions at Harper's Ferry." In Johnson and Buel, eds., *Battles and Leaders* 2:617–18.

Dowdey, Clifford. *Lee.* Boston: Little, Brown, 1965.

Duncan, Richard. "Marylanders and the Invasion of 1862." *Civil War History* 9 (1965): 370–83. Also in Hubbell, ed., *Battles Lost and Won,* 183–96.

Earle, Edward Meade, ed. *Makers of Modern Strategy: Military Thought from Machiavelli to Hitler.* Princeton: Princeton Univ. Press, 1943.

Early, Jubal Anderson. "Barbara Frietchie—Refutation of Whittier's Myth." *Southern Historical Society Papers* 7 (1879): 435–39.

———. "The Campaigns of Gen. Robert E. Lee." In Gallagher, ed., *Lee the Soldier,* 37–73.

———. *War Memoirs, Autobiographical Sketch and Narrative of the War Between the States.* Ed. Frank E. Vandiver. Bloomington: Indiana Univ. Press, 1960.

Ebert, Valerius. "Letter from Mrs. Frietchie's Nephew." *Southern Historical Society Papers* 7 (1879): 438–39.

Elliott, C. G. "Martin-Kirkland Brigade." In Clark, ed., *North Carolina Regiments* 4:527–49.

Evans, Clement Anselm, ed. *Confederate Military History: A Library of Confederate States History.* 12 vols. Atlanta: Confederate Publishing, 1899. Vol 2: *Maryland.* By Bradley Tyler Johnson. Vol. 3: *Virginia.* By Jedediah Hotchkiss.

Experiences of War: An Anthology of Articles from MHQ, the Quarterly Journal of Military History. New York: Dell, 1992.

Farwell, Byron. *Stonewall: A Biography of General Thomas J. Jackson.* New York: W. W. Norton, 1992.

Fairfax County and the War Between the States. Fairfax County, Va.: Civil War Centennial Commission, 1961.

Faust, Patricia L., ed. *Historical Times Illustrated Encyclopedia of the Civil War.* New York: Harper & Row, 1986.

Ferguson, Garland S. "Twenty-fifth Regiment." In Clark, ed., *North Carolina Regiments* 2:291–301.

Fitzpatrick, Marion Hill. *Letters to Amanda from Sergeant Major Marion Hill Fitzpatrick, Co. K, 45th Georgia Regiment . . . To His Wife Amanda Olive Elizabeth White Fitzpatrick, 1862–1865.* Culloden, Ga.: Privately published, 1976.

Fleming, Francis Philip. "Francis P. Fleming in the War for Southern Independence. Soldiering with the 2nd Florida Regiment." Ed. Edward C. Williamson. *Florida Historical Quarterly* 27 (1949–50): 38–52, 143–55, 205–10.

Flowers, George Washington. "Thirty-eighth Regiment." In Clark, ed., *North Carolina Regiments* 2:675–97.

Fox, William F. *Regimental Losses in the Civil War, 1861–1865: A Treatise on the Extent and Nature of the Mortuary Losses in the Union Regiments, with Full and Extensive Statistics Compiled from the Official Records on File in the State Military Bureaus and at Washington.* Albany: Albany Publishing, 1889.

Franklin, William Buel. "Notes on Crampton's Gap and Antietam." In Johnson and Buel, eds., *Battles and Leaders* 2:591–97.

Frassanito, William Allen. . . . *Antietam: The Photographic Legacy of America's Bloodiest Day.* New York: Charles Scribner's Sons, 1978.

Freeman, Douglas Southall. *Lee's Lieutenants, a Study in Command.* 3 vols. New York: Charles Scribner's Sons, 1942–44.

———. *R. E. Lee: A Biography.* 4 vols. New York: Charles Scribner's Sons. 1934–35.

Frothingham, Thomas Goddard. "The Crisis of the Civil War, Antietam." *Massachusetts Historical Society Proceedings* 56 (1922–23): 173–208.

Frye, Dennis E. "Drama between the Rivers: Harpers Ferry in the 1862 Maryland Campaign." In Gallagher, ed., *Antietam,* 14–34.

———. "Henry Kyd Douglas Challenged by His Peers." *Civil War* (Sept. 1991): 40–46.

———. "The Siege of Harper's Ferry." *Blue & Gray Magazine* 5 (1987).

Fuller, John Frederick Charles. *Grant and Lee: A Study in Personality and Generalship.* New York: Charles Scribner's Sons, 1933.

Gallagher, Gary W. "Another Look at the Generalship of Robert E. Lee." In Gallagher, ed., *Lee the Soldier,* 275–89.

———. "The Autumn of 1862: A Season of Opportunity." In Gallagher, ed., *Antietam,* 1–13.

———. "The Maryland Campaign in Perspective." In Gallagher, ed., *Antietam,* 84–94.

———, ed. *Antietam: Essays on the 1862 Maryland Campaign.* Kent, Ohio: Kent State Univ. Press, 1989.

———, ed. *Lee the Soldier.* Lincoln: Univ. of Nebraska Press, 1996.

Gibson, Drury P. "Letters from a North Louisiana Tiger." Ed. Debra Nance Laurence. *North Louisiana Historical Association Journal* 10 (1979): 130–47.

Goldsborough, William Worthington. *The Maryland Line in the Confederate States Army.* Reprint ed. with index. Gaithersburg, Md.: Olde Soldiers Books, 1987.

Goodhart, Briscoe. *History of the Independent Loudoun Virginia Rangers, U.S. Vol. Cav. (Scouts), 1862–65.* Washington, D.C.: McGill & Wallace, 1896.

Goodson, Joab. "The Letters of Captain Joab Goodson, 1862–64." Ed. Stanley H. Hoole. *Alabama Review* 10 (1957): 126–53.

Gordon, Edward C. [Letter to William Allan, November 18, 1886.] In Freeman, *Lee's Lieutenants* 2:716–17.

———. "Memorandum of a Conversation with General R. E. Lee." In Freeman, *Lee's Lieutenant* 2:717–19. Also in Gallagher, ed., *Lee the Soldier,* 25–27.

Gordon, John Brown. *Reminiscences of the Civil War.* New York: Charles Scribner's Sons, 1903.

Goree, Thomas Jewett. *Longstreet's Aide: The Civil War Letters of Major Thomas J. Goree.* Ed. Thomas J. Cutrer. Charlottesville: Univ. Press of Virginia, 1995.

Graham, James Augustus. "Cooke's Brigade." In Clark, ed., *North Carolina Regiments* 4:501–12.

———. "Twenty-seventh Regiment." In Clark, ed., *North Carolina Regiments* 2:425–63.

Grattan, George D. "The Battle of Boonsboro Gap or South Mountain." *Southern Historical Society Papers* 39 (1914): 31–44.

Gray, John Chipman. "Report of Major John C. Gray, Jr., for the Committee on Investigation of the Alleged Delay in Concentration of the Army of the Potomac under McClellan at Antietam, and the Causes of the Delay of the Second Army Corps in Entering the Battle of Antietam." In *Papers of the Military Historical Society of Massachusetts* 14 (1918): 1–3.

Gruber, John. *J. Gruber's Hagers-town Town and Country Almanack for the Year of Our Lord 1862*. Hagerstown: John Gruber, 1861.

Hamby, W. R. [Texas Brigade at Sharpsburg.] In Polley, *Texas Brigade*, 129–34.

Harris, James Sidney. "Seventh Regiment." In Clark, ed., *North Carolina Regiments* 1:361–86.

Harsh, Joseph L. *Confederate Tide Rising: Robert E. Lee and the Making of Southern Strategy, 1861–1862*. Kent, Ohio: Kent State Univ. Press, 1998.

———. *Sounding the Shallows: A Confederate Companion for the Maryland Campaign of 1862*. Kent, Ohio: Kent State Univ. Press, 1999.

Hartman, Theo. "Some Incidents of Army Life." *Confederate Veteran* 30 (1922) 45–46.

Hartwig, D. Scott. *The Battle of Antietam and the Maryland Campaign of 1862: A Bibliography*. Westport, Conn.: Meckler, 1990.

———. "Robert E. Lee and the Maryland Campaign." In Gallagher, ed., *Lee the Soldier*, 331–55.

Hartzler, Daniel D. *Marylanders in the Confederacy*. Westminster, Md · Family Line Publications, 1986.

Harwell, Richard Barksdale, ed. *The Union Reader*. New York: Longmans, Green, 1958.

Hassler, William Woods. *Colonel John Pelham, Lee's Boy Artillerist*. Richmond: Garrett & Massie, 1960.

Hattaway, Herman, and Archer Jones. *How the North Won the Civil War: A Military History of the Civil War*. Urbana: Univ. of Illinois Press, 1983.

Haynes, Draughton Stith. *The Field Diary of a Confederate Soldier, Draughton Stith Haynes, While Serving with the Army of Northern Virginia, C.S.A.* Darien, Ga.: Ashantilly, 1963.

Hays, Helen Ashe. *The Antietam and Its Bridges: The Annals of an Historic Stream*. New York: G. P. Putnam's Sons, 1910.

Healy, Robert. [Letter on March into Maryland.] In Johnson and Buel, eds., *Battles and Leaders* 2:621n.

———. [Letter on Harpers Ferry] In Johnson and Buel, eds., *Battles and Leaders* 2:62–27n.

Heitman, Francis Bernard. *Historical Register and Dictionary of the United States Army, from Its Organization, September 29, 1789, to March 2, 1903*. 2 vols. Washington, D.C.: GPO, 1903.

Henderson, George Francis Robert. *Stonewall Jackson and the American Civil War*. New York: Longmans, Green, 1949.

Hennessy, John J. *Return to Bull Run: The Campaign and Battle of Second Manassas*. New York: Simon & Schuster, 1993.

Heth, Henry. "Letter from Major-General Henry Heth, of A. P. Hill's Corps, A.N.V." *Southern Historical Society Papers* 4 (1877): 151–60.

Hewett, Janet B., et al., ed. *Supplement to the Official Records of the Union and Confederate Armies*. Est. 100 vols. Wilmington, N.C.: Broadfoot Publishing, 1994–.

Heysinger, Isaac Winter. *Antietam and the Maryland and Virginia Campaigns of 1862, from the Government Records, Union and Confederate, Mostly Unknown and Which Now First Disclosed the Truth.* New York: Neale Publishing, 1912.

Hightower, Harvey Judson. "Letters from Harvey Judson Hightower, A Confederate Soldier, 1862–1864." Ed. Dewey W. Grantham, Jr. *Georgia Historical Quarterly* 40 (1956): 174–89.

Hill, Daniel Harvey. "Address of General D. H. Hill." *Southern Historical Society Papers* 13 (1885): 259–76.

———. "The Battle of South Mountain, or 'Boonsboro': Fighting for Time at Turner's and Fox's Gaps." In Johnson and Buel, eds., *Battles and Leaders* 2:559–81.

———. "The Lost Dispatch." *Land We Love* 4 (1867–68): 270–84.

———. "The Lost Dispatch—Letter from General D. H. Hill." *Southern Historical Society Papers* 13 (1885): 420–23.

History of the One Hundred and Twenty-fifth Regiment Pennsylvania Volunteers, 1862–1863, by the Regimental Committee. Philadelphia: J. B. Lippincott, 1906.

Hobson, Edwin L. [Letter on South Mountain.] *Southern Historical Society Papers* 25 (1897): 105n.

Hood, John Bell. *Advance and Retreat: Personal Experiences in the United States and Confederate States Armies.* Ed. Richard N. Current. Bloomington: Indiana Univ. Press, 1959.

Hopkins, Luther Wesley. *From Bull Run to Appomattox: A Boy's View.* Baltimore: Fleet-McGinley, 1908.

Hotchkiss, Jedediah. *Make Me a Map of the Valley: The Civil War Journal of Stonewall Jackson's Topographer.* Ed. Archie McDonald. Dallas: Southern Methodist Univ. Press, 1973.

Howard, Oliver Otis. *Autobiography of Oliver Otis Howard, Major-General.* 2 vols. New York: Baker & Taylor, 1907.

Hubbell, John T., ed. *Battles Lost and Won: Essays from Civil War History.* Westport, Conn.: Greenwood, 1975.

Hubbert, Mike M. "The Travels of the 13th Mississippi Regiment: Excerpts from the Diary of Mike M. Hubbert of Attala County (1861–1862)." Ed. John E. Fisher. *Journal of Mississippi History* 45 (1983): 288–313.

Hunt, Roger D., and Jack R. Brown. *Brevet Brigadier Generals in Blue.* Gaithersburg, Md.: Olde Soldiers Books, 1990.

Hunter, Alexander. "A High Private's Account of the Battle of Sharpsburg." *Southern Historical Society Papers* 10 (1882): 503–12; 11 (1883): 10–21.

Imboden, John Daniel. "Incidents of the First Bull Run." In Johnson and Buel, eds., *Battles and Leaders* 1:229–39.

Jamieson, Perry D. *Death in September: The Antietam Campaign.* Civil War Campaigns and Commanders Series. Fort Worth: Ryan Place Publishers, 1995.

Jackson, Mary Anna. *Memoirs of Stonewall Jackson by His Widow.* 2d ed. Louisville: Prentice, 1895.

Johnson, Bradley Tyler. "First Maryland Campaign." *Southern Historical Society Papers* 12 (1884): 500–537.

———. "Stonewall Jackson's Intentions at Harper's Ferry." In Johnson and Buel, eds., *Battles and Leaders* 2:615–16.

Johnson, Curt, and Richard C. Anderson, Jr. *Artillery Hell: The Employment of Artillery at Antietam.* College Station: Texas A&M Univ. Press, 1995.

Johnson, Robert Underwood, and Clarence Clough Buel, eds. *Battles and Leaders of the Civil War . . . Being for the Most Part Contributions Based upon "The Century Magazine War Series."* 4 vols. New York: Thomas Yoseloff, 1956.

Johnston, James Steptoe. "A Reminiscence of Sharpsburg." *Southern Historical Society Papers* 8 (1880): 526–29.

Johnston, William Preston. "Memorandum of Conversations between Robert E. Lee and William Preston Johnston, May 7, 1868 and March 18, 1870." Ed. W. G. Bean. *Virginia Magazine of History and Biography* 73 (1965): 474–84. Also in Gallagher, ed., *Lee the Soldier*, 29–34.

Jones, Archer. *Civil War Command and Strategy: The Process of Victory and Defeat.* New York: Free Press, 1992.

———. "Military Means, Political Ends: Strategy." In Boritt, ed., *Why the Confederacy Lost*, 43–77.

Jones, John Beauchamp. *A Rebel War Clerk's Diary at the Confederate States Capital.* 2 vols. Philadelphia: J. B. Lippincott, 1866.

Jones, John William. "Did Cutts' Battalion Have Sixty Guns at Sharpsburg?" *Southern Historical Society Papers* 10 (1882): 190.

———. *Life and Letters of Robert E. Lee, Soldier and Man.* New York: Neale Publishing, 1906.

———. *Personal Reminiscences, Anecdotes, and Letters of Gen. Robert E. Lee.* New York: D. Appleton, 1876.

———, comp. *Army of Northern Virginia Memorial Volume.* Richmond: J. W. Randolph & English, 1880.

Jones, Wilbur D., Jr. "Who Lost the Lost Orders? Stonewall Jackson, His Courier, and Special Orders No. 191." In Snell, ed., *Antietam*, 1–26.

Kearney, H.C. "Fifteenth Regiment." In Clark, ed., *North Carolina Regiments* 1:733–49.

Kegel, James A. *North with Lee and Jackson: The Lost Story of Gettysburg.* Mechanicsburg, Pa.: Stackpole Books, 1996.

Krick, Robert K. "The Army of Northern Virginia in September 1862: Its Circumstances, Its Opportunities, and Why It Should Not Have Been at Sharpsburg." In Gallagher, ed., *Antietam*, 35–55.

———. *Lee's Colonels: A Biographical Register of the Field Officers of the Army of Northern Virginia.* 3d rev. ed. Dayton, Ohio: Morningside Bookshop, 1991.

Lacy, James B. "The Fifteenth Virginia, Composed of Richmond, Henrico and Hanover Boys." *Southern Historical Society Papers* 27 (1899) 48–51.

The Land We Love. A Monthly Magazine Devoted to Literature, Military History and Agriculture. 6 vols. 1866–69.

Lane, James Henry. "Twenty-eighth Regiment." In Clark, ed., *North Carolina Regiments* 2:465–84.

Lang, David. "Civil War Letters of Colonel David Lang." Ed. Bertram H. Groene. *Florida Historical Quarterly* 54 (1976): 340–66.

Lattimore, T. D. "Thirty-fourth Regiment." In Clark, ed., *North Carolina Regiments* 2:581–90.

Lawhon, W. H. H. "Forty Eighth Regiment." In Clark, ed., *North Carolina Regiments* 3:113–24.

Lee, Fitzhugh. *General Lee.* New York: D. Appleton, 1894.

Lee, Robert Edward. "A Lee Letter on the 'Lost Dispatch,' and the Maryland Campaign of 1862." Ed. Hal Bridges. *Virginia Magazine of History and Biography* 66 (1958): 161–66.

———. "Letter from General R. E. Lee [to William M. McDonald]." *Southern Historical Society Papers* 7 (1879): 445–46.

——— *The Wartime Papers of R. E. Lee.* Eds. Clifford Dowdey and Louis H. Manarin. Boston: Little, Brown, 1961.

Lee, Robert Edward [Jr.]. *Recollections and Letters of General Robert E. Lee, by His Son.* Enlarged ed. Garden City, N.Y.: Garden City Publishing, 1924.

Lee, Stephen Dill. "New Lights on Sharpsburg." *Richmond Dispatch,* December 20, 1896.

Lee, Susan Pendleton. *Memoirs of William Nelson Pendleton, by His Daughter.* Enlarged ed. Harrisonburg, Va.: Sprinkle Publications, 1991.

Levin, Alexandria Lee. "A Wounded Confederate Soldier's Letter from Fort McHenry." *Maryland Historical Magazine* 73 (1978): 394–96.

Lincoln, Abraham. *Collected Works.* Ed. Roy P. Basler. 9 vols. New Brunswick: Rutgers Univ. Press, 1953–55.

Livermore, Thomas Leonard. *Numbers and Losses in the Civil War in America.* Corrected ed. Dayton, Ohio: Morningside, 1986.

Long, Armistead Lindsay. *Memoirs of Robert E. Lee: His Military and Personal History, Embracing a Large Amount of Information Hitherto Unpublished.* Philadelphia: J. M. Stoddart, 1886.

Longstreet, James. *From Manassas to Appomattox, Memoirs of the Civil War in America.* Ed. James I. Robertson, Jr. Bloomington: Indiana Univ. Press, 1960.

———. "The Invasion of Maryland." In Johnson and Buel, eds., *Battles and Leaders* 2:663–74.

Luff, William M. "March of the Cavalry from Harper's Ferry, September 14, 1862." In *Military Essays and Recollections* 2:33–48.

Luvaas, Jay, and Harold W. Nelson, eds. *The U.S. Army War College Guide to the Battle of Antietam: The Maryland Campaign of 1862.* Carlisle, Pa.: South Mountain Press, 1987.

McAlpine, Newton. "Sketch of Company I, 61st Virginia Infantry, Mahone's Brigade, C.S.A." *Southern Historical Society Papers* 24 (1896): 98–108.

McCabe, James Dabney. *Life and Campaigns of General Robert E. Lee.* Atlanta: National Publishing, 1870.

McCabe, W. Gordon. "The Real Barbara Frietchie: Ninety-six Years Old, Bedridden and Never Defied Stonewall Jackson." *Southern Historical Society Papers* 27 (1899): 287–89.

McClellan, George Brinton. *The Civil War Papers of George B. McClellan: Selected Correspondence, 1860–1865.* Ed. Stephen W. Sears. New York: Ticknor & Fields, 1989.

———. *McClellan's Own Story: The War for the Union, the Soldiers Who Fought It, the Civilians Who Directed It, and His Relations to It and to Them.* New York: Charles L. Webster, 1887.

McClellan, Henry Brainard. *I Rode with Jeb Stuart: The Life and Campaigns of Major General J. E. B. Stuart.* Ed. Burke Davis. Bloomington: Indiana Univ. Press, 1958.

McClendon, William Augustus. *Recollections of War Times, by an Old Veteran while under Stonewall Jackson and Lieutenant General James Longstreet: How I Got in and How I Got out.* Montgomery, Ala.: Paragon Press, 1909.

McDonald, William Naylor. *A History of the Laurel Brigade, Originally the Ashby Cavalry of the Army of Northern Virginia and Chew's Battery.* Baltimore: Sun Job Printing Office, 1907.

McGuire, Hunter. "General T. J. (Stonewall) Jackson, Confederate States Army: His Career and Character." *Southern Historical Society Papers* 25 (1897): ivn., 90–112.

McKim, Randolph Harrison. *A Soldier's Recollections: Leaves from the Diary of a Young Confederate, with an Oration on the Motives and Aims of the Soldiers of the South.* New York: Longman, Green, 1910.

McLaurin, William H. "Eighteenth Regiment." In Clark, ed., *North Carolina Regiments* 2:15–64.

McLaws, LaFayette. "The Maryland Campaign." In *Address Delivered before the Confederate Veterans Association of Savannah, Ga.* 3:5–30.

McMurray, Richard M. *Two Great Rebel Armies: An Essay in Confederate Military History.* Chapel Hill: Univ. of North Carolina Press, 1989.

McPherson, James M. *Drawn with the Sword: Reflections on the American Civil War.* New York: Oxford Univ. Press, 1996.

MacRae, James C., and Charles Maney Busbee. "Fifth Regiment." In Clark, ed., *North Carolina Regiments* 1:281–92.

McWhiney, Grady. "Who Whipt Whom? Confederate Defeat Reexamined." *Civil War History* 11 (1965): 5–26.

———, ed. *Grant, Lee, Lincoln and the Radicals: Essays on Civil War Leadership.* Evanston, Ill.: Northwestern Univ. Press, 1964.

McWhiney, Grady, and Perry D. Jamieson. *Attack and Die: Civil War Military Tactics and the Southern Heritage.* Tuscaloosa: Univ. of Alabama Press, 1982.

Manarin, Louis. "A Proclamation To the People of ——." *North Carolina Historical Review* 41 (1964): 246–51

Manly, Matthew. "Second Regiment." In Clark, ed., *North Carolina Regiments* 1:157–76.

A Map of Washington Co., Maryland: Exhibiting the Farms, Election Districts, Towns, Villages, etc.: From Actual Survey by Thomas Taggart. Hagerstown: McKee and Robertson, 1859.

Marshall, Charles. *An Aide-de-Camp of Lee, Being the Papers of Colonel Charles Marshall, Sometimes Aide-de-Camp, Military Secretary, and Assistant Adjutant General on the Staff of Robert E. Lee, 1862–1865.* Ed. Sir Frederick Maurice. Boston: Little, Brown, 1927.

Marvel, William. *Burnside.* Chapel Hill: Univ. of North Carolina Press, 1991.

Maurice, Frederick Barton. *Robert E. Lee, the Soldier.* New York: Houghton, Mifflin, 1925.

Mies, John W. "Breakout at Harper's Ferry." *Civil War History* 2 (1956), 13–28.

Military Essays and Recollections, Papers Read before the Commandery of the State of Illinois, Military Order of the Loyal Legion of the United States. 4 vols. Chicago: A. C. McClurg, 1891–1907.

Mills, George H. "Sixteenth Regiment, Additional Sketch." In Clark, ed., *North Carolina Regiments* 4:137–219.

Minor, R. V. [Letter on South Mountain.] In Johnson and Buel, eds., *Battles and Leaders* 2:566n.

Mitchell, Mary Bedinger. "A Woman's Recollections of Antietam." In Johnson and Buel, eds., *Battles and Leaders* 2:686–94.

Moger, Allen W. "General Lee's 'Unwritten History of the Army of Northern Virginia.'" *Virginia Magazine of History and Biography* 71 (1963): 341–63.

Montgomery, Walter Alexander. "Twelfth Regiment." In Clark, ed., *North Carolina Regiments* 1:605–52.

Moore, Edward Alexander. *The Story of a Cannoneer under Stonewall Jackson, in Which Is Told the Part Taken by the Rockbridge Artillery in the Army of Northern Virginia.* New York: Neale Publishing, 1907.

Moore, J. B. "Battle of Sharpsburg." *Southern Historical Society Papers* 27 (1899): 210–19.

Morgan, William Henry. *Personal Reminiscences of the War of 1861–5: In Camp, en Bivouac, on the March, on Picket, on the Skirmish Line, on the Battlefield, and in Prison.* Lynchburg: J. P. Bell, 1911.

Morrison, Emmett M. "Fifteenth Virginia at Sharpsburg." *Southern Historical Society Papers* 33 (1905): 99–110.

Munden, Kenneth White. *Guide to Federal Archives Relating to the Civil War.* Washington, D.C.: GPO, 1962.

Munford, Thomas Taylor. "Lee's Invasion of Maryland." *Addresses Delivered before the Confederate Veterans Association of Savannah, Ga.* 3:35–55.

Murdock, Eugene C., ed. *The Civil War in the North: A Selective Annotated Bibliography.* New York: Garland Publishing, 1987.

Murfin, James V. *The Gleam of Bayonets: The Battle of Antietam and the Maryland Campaign of 1862.* New York: Thomas Yoseloff, 1965.

Myers, Franklin McIntosh. *The Comanches: A History of White's Battalion, Virginia Cavalry, Laurel Brig., Hampton Div., A.N.V., C.S.A.* Baltimore: Kelly, Piet, 1871.

National Cyclopedia of American Biography. 9 vols. New York: James T. White, 1892–99.

Neese, George Michael. *Three Years in the Confederate Horse Artillery, by . . . a Gunner in Chew's Battery.* New York: Neale Publishing, 1911.

Netherton, Nan, et al. *Fairfax County, Virginia: A History.* Fairfax: County Board of Supervisors, 1978.

Nevins, Allan. *The War for the Union.* 4 vols. New York: Charles Scribner's Sons, 1959–71.

Nevins, Allan, James I. Robertson, Jr., and Bell I. Wiley, eds. *Civil War Books: A Critical Bibliography.* Baton Rouge: Louisiana State Univ. Press, 1967–69.

Nichols, Edward J. *Toward Gettysburg: A Biography of General John F. Reynolds.* Reprint. Gaithersburg, Md.: Olde Soldiers Books, 1987.

Nisbet, James Cooper. *Four Years on the Firing Line.* Ed. Bell Irvin Wiley. Jackson, Tenn.: McCowat-Mercer, 1963.

Nolan, Alan T. *Lee Considered: General Robert E. Lee and Civil War History.* Chapel Hill: Univ. of North Carolina Press, 1991.

Olmsted, Frederick Law. *Defending the Union: The Civil War and the U.S. Sanitary Commission, 1861–1863.* Ed. Jane Turner Censer. Vol. 4 in *The Papers of Frederick Law Olmsted.* Baltimore: Johns Hopkins Univ. Press, 1986.

"The Opposing Forces at Cedar Mountain, Va., August 9th, 1862." In Johnson and Buel, eds., *Battles and Leaders* 2:495–96.

"The Opposing Forces at Corinth, Miss., October 3rd and 4th, 1862." In Johnson and Buel, eds., *Battles and Leaders* 1:337.

"The Opposing Forces at Iuka, Miss., September 19th, 1862." In Johnson and Buel, eds., *Battles and Leaders* 2:736.

"The Opposing Forces at Perryville, Ky., October 8th, 1862." In Johnson and Buel, eds., *Battles and Leaders* 2:29–30.

"The Opposing Forces at Second Bull Run, August 16th–September 2nd, 1862." In Johnson and Buel, eds., *Battles and Leaders* 2:497–500.

"The Opposing Forces in the Seven Days' Battles, June 25th–July 1st, 1862." In Johnson and Buel, eds., *Battles and Leaders* 2:313–17.

Osborne, Edwin Augustus. "Fourth Regiment." In Clark, ed., *North Carolina Regiments* 1:229–80.

Otott, George E. "Clash in the Cornfield: The 1st Texas Volunteer Infantry in the Maryland Campaign." In Snell, ed., *Antietam*, 73–123.

Ould, Robert. "The Exchange of Prisoners." In *Annals of the War*, 32–59.

Our Living and Our Dead, Devoted to North Carolina—Her Past, Her Present and Her Future. 4 vols. Raleigh, 1874–76.

Owen, William Miller. *In Camp and Battle with the Washington Artillery of New Orleans: A Narrative of Events during the Late Civil War, from Bull Run to Appomattox and Spanish Fort.* Boston: Ticknor, 1885.

Palfrey, Francis Winthrop. *The Antietam and Fredericksburg.* Campaigns of the Civil War Series. Vol. 5. New York: Charles Scribner's Sons, 1882.

———. "The Battle of Antietam." In *Papers of the Military Historical Society of Massachusetts* 3:1–26.

Papers of the Military Historical Society of Massachusetts. 16 vols. Boston, 1881–1918.

Parham, John T. "Thirty-second [Virginia] at Sharpsburg, Graphic Story of Work Done on One of the Bloodiest of Fields, Forty-five Per Cent Loss." *Southern Historical Society Papers* 34 (1906): 250–53.

Paris, Louis Phillipe Albert d'Orleans, comte de. *History of the Civil War in America.* 4 vols. Philadelphia: Porter & Coates, 1876–88.

Park, Robert E. [Letter on South Mountain.] In Johnson and Buel, eds., *Battles and Leaders* 2:572–73n.

Parker, Francis M. "Thirtieth Regiment." In Clark, ed., *North Carolina Regiments* 2:495–505.

Parks, Leighton. "What a Boy Saw of the Civil War—With Glimpses of General Lee." *Century Magazine* 70 (1905): 258–64.

Parrish, T. Michael, and Robert M. Willingham, Jr., eds. *Confederate Imprints: A Bibliography of Southern Publications from Secession to Surrender.* Austin: Jenkins Publishing, n. d.

———. "The R. E. Lee 200: An Annotated Bibliography of Essential Books on Lee's Military Career." In Gallagher, ed., *Lee the Soldier*, 561–93.

Pender, William Dorsey. *The General to His Wife: The Civil War Letters of William Dorsey Pender to Fanny Pender.* Ed. William Woods Hassler. Chapel Hill: Univ. of North Carolina Press, 1965.

Perry, D. M. "The Time of Longstreet's Arrival at Groveton." In Johnson and Buel, eds., *Battles and Leaders* 2:527.

Poague, William Thomas. *Gunner with Stonewall, Reminiscences of William Thomas Poague . . . A Memoir Written for His Children in 1913.* Ed. Monroe F. Cockrell. Jackson, Tenn.: McCowat-Mercer, 1957.

Polley, Joseph Benjamin. *Hood's Texas Brigade, Its Marches, Its Battles, Its Achievements.* New York: Neale Publishing, 1910.

———. *A Soldier's Letters to Charming Nellie.* New York: Neale Publishing, 1908.

Powell, William Henry. *The Fifth Army Corps (Army of the Potomac): A Record of Operations during the Civil War in the United States of America, 1861–1865.* New York: G. P. Putnam's Sons, 1896.

Powers, L. E. "Twenty-first Regiment, Additional Sketch." In Clark, ed., *North Carolina Regiments* 2:147–59.

Priest, John Michael. *Antietam: A Soldiers' Battle.* Shippensburg, Pa.: White Mane, 1989.

———. *Antietam: The Soldiers' Battlefield, a Self-Guided Mini-Tour.* Shippensburg, Pa.: White Mane, 1994.

———. *Before Antietam: The Battle for South Mountain.* Shippensburg, Pa.: White Mane, 1992.

Ramsay, John Andrew. "Additional Sketch Tenth Regiment, Light Batteries A, D, F [E] and I." In Clark, ed., *North Carolina Regiments* 1:551–82.

Ray, Neill W. "Sixth Regiment." In Clark, ed., *North Carolina Regiments* 1:293–335.

Reese, Timothy J. "Howell Cobb's Brigade at Crampton's Gap." *Blue & Gray Magazine* 15 (1998): 6–21, 47–56.

Reilly, Oliver T. *The Battlefield of Antietam.* Hagerstown: Hagerstown Bookbinding and Printing, 1906.

"Relative Numbers . . . Sharpsburg or Antietam." In J. W. Jones, *Army of Northern Virginia Memorial Volume,* 344–45.

Robertson, James I., Jr., *General A. P. Hill: The Story of a Confederate Warrior.* New York: Random House, 1987.

———. *Stonewall Jackson: The Man, the Soldier, the Legend.* New York: Macmillan Publishing, 1997.

Roland, Charles P. "The Generalship of Robert E. Lee." In McWhiney, ed., *Grant, Lee, Lincoln and the Radicals,* 31–71. Also in Gallagher, ed., *Lee the Soldier,* 159–87.

———. *Reflections on Lee: A Historian's Assessment.* Mechanicsburg, Pa.: Stackpole Books, 1995.

Ropes, John Codman. *The Story of the Civil War: A Concise Account of the War in the United States of America between 1861 and 1865.* 2 vols. New York: G. P. Putnam's Sons, 1894–98.

Rose, W. N. "Twenty-fourth Regiment." In Clark, ed., *North Carolina Regiments* 2:269–90.

Roulhac, Thomas R. "Forty-ninth Infantry." In Clark, ed., *North Carolina Regiments* 3:125–49.

Sauers, Richard Allen. *The Gettysburg Campaign, June 3–August 1, 1863: A Comprehensive, Selectively Annotated Bibliography.* Westport, Conn.: Greenwood, 1982.

Saussy, George Nolan. "Lee's Army, An Address." In *Addresses Delivered before the Confederate Veterans Association of Savannah, Ga.* 1:67–88.

Scates, James Madison. "The Civil War Diary of James Madison Scates." *Virginia Social Science Journal* 2 (1967): 3–20.

Schildt, John W. *Antietam Hospitals.* Chewsville, Md.: Antietam Publications, 1987.

———. *Drums along the Antietam.* Parsons, W.Va.: McClain Print., 1972.

———. *Four Days in October.* Privately published, 1978.

———. *Monuments at Antietam.* Frederick, Md.: Great Southern, 1991.

———. *Mount Airy—The Grove Family Homestead.* Chewsville, Md.: Antietam Publications, 1992.

———. *Roads to Antietam.* 2d rev. ed. Shippensburg, Pa.: Burd Street Press, 1997.

———. *September Echoes: The Maryland Campaign of 1862, the Places, the Battles, the Results.* Middletown, Md.: Valley Register, 1960.

Sears, Stephen W. *George B. McClellan: The Young Napoleon.* New York: Ticknor & Fields, 1988.

———. "Getting Right with Robert E. Lee: How To Know the Unknowable Man." In Sears, ed., *The Civil War,* 44–53.

———. *Landscape Turned Red: The Battle of Antietam.* New Haven: Ticknor & Fields, 1983.

———. "The Last Word on the Lost Order." In *Experiences of War,* 197–210.

———, ed. *The Civil War: The Best of American Heritage.* Boston: Houghton Mifflin, 1991.

Seilheimer, George O. "The Historical Basis of Whittier's Barbara Frietchie." In Johnson and Buel, eds., *Battles and Leaders* 2:618–19.

Sheeran, James B. *Confederate Chaplain: A War Journal of Rev. James B. Sheeran, C.SS.T., 14th Louisiana, C.S.A.* Ed. Rev. Joseph T. Durkin. Milwaukee: Bruce Publishing, 1960.

Shotwell, Randolph Abbott. *The Papers of Randolph Abbott Shotwell.* Ed. J. G. Roulhac Hamilton. 3 vols. Raleigh: North Carolina Historical Commission, 1929–36.

Sifikas, Stewart. *Compendium of the Confederate Armies.* 10 vols. New York: Facts on File, 1991–92.

Simpson, Richard Wright, and Taliaferro N. Simpson. *"Far, Far from Home": The Wartime Letters of Dick and Tally Simpson, Third South Carolina Volunteers.* Ed. Guy R. Everson and Edward H. Simpson, Jr. New York: Oxford Univ. Press, 1994.

Smith, James Power. *With Stonewall Jackson in the Army of Northern Virginia.* Gaithersburg, Md.: Zullo and Van Sickle Books, 1982.

Smith, N.S. "Thirteenth Regiment, Additional Sketch." In Clark, ed., *North Carolina Regiments* 1:689–99.

Smith, Robert Ross. "Ox Hill: The Most Neglected Battle of the Civil War." In *Fairfax County and the War Between the States,* 18–64.

Snell, Charles W., and Sharon A. Brown. *Antietam National Battlefield and National Cemetery, Sharpsburg, Maryland: An Administrative History.* Washington, D.C.: National Park Service, 1986.

Snell, Mark A., ed. "Antietam, the Maryland Campaign of 1862: Essays on Union and Confederate Leadership." *Civil War Regiments: A Journal of the American Civil War* 5, no. 3 (1997).

Sorrel, Gilbert Moxley. *Recollections of a Confederate Staff Officer.* Ed. Bell Irvin Wiley. Jackson, Tenn.: McCowat-Mercer, 1958.

Southern Historical Society Papers. 52 vols. Richmond, 1876–1959.

Squires, Charles Winder. "'Boy Officer' of the Washington Artillery—Part I." *Civil War Times Illustrated* 14 (1975): 10–24.

Stackpole, Edward James. *From Cedar Mountain to Antietam, August–September, 1862: Cedar Mountain, Second Manassas, Chantilly, Harpers Ferry, South Mountain, Antietam.* Harrisburg: Stackpole, 1959.

Steiner, Lewis Henry. *Report of Lewis H. Steiner, M.D., Inspector of the Sanitary Commission, Containing a Diary Kept during the Rebel Occupation of Frederick, Md., and an Account of the Operations of the U.S. Sanitary Commission during the Campaign in Maryland, September 1862.* New York: Anson D. F. Randolph, 1862.

Steiner, Paul E. *Medical-Military Portraits of Union and Confederate Generals.* Philadelphia: Whitmore, 1968.

Strayhorn, Thomas Jackson. "Letters of Thomas Jackson Strayhorn." Ed. Henry McGilbert Wagstaff. *North Carolina Historical Review* 13 (1936): 311–34.

Strong, George Templeton. *The Diary of George Templeton Strong.* Ed. Allan Nevins. 4 vols. New York: Macmillan, 1952.

Strother, David Hunter. *A Virginia Yankee in the Civil War: The Diaries of David Hunter Strother.* Ed. Cecil D. Eby, Jr. Chapel Hill: Univ. of North Carolina Press, 1961.

Stuart, James Ewell Brown. *The Letters of Major General James E. B. Stuart.* Ed. Adele H. Mitchell. N.p.: Stuart-Mosby Historical Society, 1990.

Summers, Festus Paul. *The Baltimore and Ohio in the Civil War.* New York: G. P. Putnam's Sons, 1939.

Sumner, Samuel Storrow. "The Antietam Campaign." In *Papers of the Military Historical Society of Massachusetts* 14 (1918): 5–18.

Sutton, Thomas H. "Eighteenth Regiment, Additional Sketch." In Clark, ed., *North Carolina Regiments* 2:65–78.

Sypher, Joseph Rinehart. *History of the Pennsylvania Reserve Corps: A Complete Record of the Organization, and of the Different Companies, Regiments and Brigades, Containing Descriptions of Expeditions, Marches, Skirmishes and Battles, Together with Biographical Sketches of Officers and Personal Records of Each Man during His Term of Service.* Lancaster: Elias Barr, 1865.

Taylor, Walter Herron. "The Battle of Sharpsburg." *Southern Historical Society Papers* 24 (1896): 267–74.

———. *Four Years with General Lee.* Ed. James I. Robertson, Jr. Bloomington: Indiana Univ. Press, 1962.

———. *General Lee, His Campaigns in Virginia, 1861–1865, with Personal Reminiscences.* Norfolk: Nusbaum Book and News, 1906.

———. *Lee's Adjutant: The Wartime Letters of Colonel Walter Herron Taylor, 1862–1865.* Ed. R. Lockwood Tower. Columbia: Univ. of South Carolina Press, 1995.

Teetor, Paul R. *A Matter of Hours, Treason at Harper's Ferry.* Rutherford, N.J.: Fairleigh Dickinson Univ. Press, 1982.

Thomas, Emory M. *Bold Dragoon: The Life of J. E. B. Stuart.* New York: Harper & Row, 1986.

———. *Robert E. Lee: A Biography.* New York: W. W. Norton, 1995.

Thomas, Henry Walter. *History of the Doles-Cook Brigade, Army of Northern Virginia, C.S.A., Containing Muster Rolls of Each Company of the Fourth, Twelfth, Twenty-first and Forty-fourth Georgia Regiments, with a Short Sketch of the Services of Each Member, and a Complete History of Each Regiment, by One of Its Own Members, and Other Matters of Interest.* Atlanta: Franklin Printing and Publishing, 1903.

Thompson, John H. "Historical Address of the Former Commander of Grimes' Battery." *Southern Historical Society Papers* 34 (1906): 149–55.

Tischler, Allan L. *The History of the Harpers Ferry Cavalry Expedition, September 14 & 15, 1862.* Winchester, Va.: Five Cedars, 1993.

Toon, Thomas F. "Twentieth Regiment." In Clark, ed., *North Carolina Regiments* 2:111–27.

Torrence, Leonidas. "The Road to Gettysburg, The Diary and Letters of Leonidas Torrence of the Gaston Guards." Ed. Haskell Monroe. *North Carolina Historical Review* 36 (1959): 476–517.

The Tribune Almanac for the Years 1838 to 1866. 2 vols. New York: New York Tribune Association, 1868.

Trout, Robert J. *With Pen and Saber: The Letters and Diaries of J. E. B. Stuart's Staff Officers.* Mechanicsburg, Pa.: Stackpole Books, 1995.

Tucker, John S. "The Diary of John S. Tucker: Confederate Soldier from Alabama." Ed. Gary Wilson. *Alabama Historical Quarterly* 43 (1981): 5–33.

Turner, V. E., and Henry Clay Wall. "Twenty-third Regiment." In Clark, ed., *North Carolina Regiments* 2:181–268.

U.S. Census Bureau. *Agriculture of the United States in 1860: Compiled from the Original Returns of the Eighth Census.* Washington, D.C.: GPO, 1864.

———. *Manufactures of the United States in 1860: Compiled from the Original Returns of the Eighth Census.* Washington, D.C.: GPO, 1865.

———. *Population of the United States in 1860: Compiled from the Original Returns of the Eighth Census.* Washington, D.C.: GPO, 1864.

———. *Statistics of the United States (Including Mortality, Property, etc.) in 1860: Compiled from the Original Returns of the Eighth Census.* Washington, D.C.: GPO, 1866.

U.S. Congress. *Report of the Joint Committee on the Conduct of the War.* 3 vols. Washington, D.C.: GPO, 1863.

U.S. Department of the Interior. National Park Service. *Statistical Reports* [title varies]. Washington, D.C.: GPO, 1940–.

U.S. Engineer Corps. *Atlas of the Battlefield of Antietam, Prepared under the Direction of the Antietam Battlefield Board.* Washington, D.C.: GPO, 1904. 2d rev. ed., 1908.

U.S. Navy Department. *Official Records of the Union and Confederate Navies in the War of the Rebellion.* 31 vols. (including sep. bound index). Washington, D.C.: GPO, 1894–1927.

U.S. War Department. *The Official Military Atlas of the Civil War: Atlas to Accompany the Official Records of the Union and Confederate Armies.* Intro. Richard J. Sommers. New York: Arno, 1978.

———. *The War of the Rebellion: A Compilation of the Official Records of the Union and Confederate Armies.* 128 vols. Washington, D.C.: GPO, 1880–1901.

———. Gettysburg National Military Park Commission. *Annual Reports to the Secretary of War, 1893–1901*. Washington, D.C.: GPO, 1902.

Vandiver, Frank Everson. *Mighty Stonewall*. New York: McGraw-Hill, 1957.

von Borcke, Heros. *Memoirs of the Confederate War for Independence*. 2 vols. New York: Peter Smith, 1938.

Waddell, A. M. "General George Burgwyn Anderson—The Memorial Address of Hon. A. M. Wadell, May 11, 1885." *Southern Historical Society Papers* 14 (1886): 387–97.

Waddill, J. M. "Forty-Sixth Regiment." In Clark, ed. *North Carolina Regiments* 3:63–82.

Walcott, Charles Folsom. *History of the Twenty-first Regiment Massachusetts Volunteers in the War for the Preservation of the Union, 1861–1865, with Statistics of the War and of Rebel Prisons*. Boston: Houghton, Mifflin, 1882.

Waldhauer, David. "The Affair at Frederick City: A Correction of General Johnson's Account." *Southern Historical Society Papers* 13 (1885): 417–19.

Walker, Francis Amasa. *History of the Second Army Corps in the Army of the Potomac*. New York: Charles Scribner's Sons, 1886.

Walker, John George. "Harper's Ferry and Sharpsburg." *Century Magazine* 32 (1886): 296–308.

———. "Jackson's Capture of Harper's Ferry." In Johnson and Buel, eds., *Battles and Leaders* 2:604–11.

———. "Report of Brig. General Walker of the Battle of Sharpsburg." *Our Living, Our Dead* 1 (1874–75): 225–28.

———. "Sharpsburg." In Johnson and Buel, eds., *Battles and Leaders* 2:675–82.

Wall, H. C. "The 23rd North Carolina Infantry: Historical Sketch." *Southern Historical Society Papers* 25 (1897): 151–76.

Wallace, Lee A., Jr. *A Guide to Virginia Military Organizations, 1861–1865*. 2d rev. ed. Lynchburg: H. E. Howard, 1988.

Wert, Jeffry D. *General James Longstreet: The Confederacy's Most Controversial Soldier—A Biography*. New York: Simon & Schuster, 1993.

Weston, James A. "Thirty-third Regiment." In Clark, ed., *North Carolina Regiments* 2:537–80.

Wharton, Rufus W. "First Battalion (Sharpshooters)." In Clark, ed., *North Carolina Regiments* 4:225–42.

White, Henry Alexander. *Robert E. Lee and the Southern Confederacy, 1807–1870*. New York: Haskell House, 1968.

Whitehorne, Joseph W. "A Beastly, Comfortless Conflict: The Battle of Chantilly, September 1, 1862." *Blue & Gray Magazine* 4 (1987): 7–23, 46–56.

Whittier, John Greenleaf. "A Correction from Mr. Whittier." *Century Magazine* 32 (1886): 783.

Wiggins, Octavious A. "Thirty-seventh Regiment." In Clark, ed., *North Carolina Regiments* 2:653–74.

Williams, R.S. "Thirteenth Regiment." In Clark, ed., *North Carolina Regiments* 1:653–87.

Winfree, Waverly K., ed. *Guide to the Manuscript Collections of the Virginia Historical Society*. Richmond: Virginia Historical Society, 1985.

Wise, George. *History of the Seventeenth Virginia Infantry, C.S.A.* Baltimore: Kelly, Piet, 1870.

Wise, Jennings Cropper. *The Long Arm of Lee: or, The History of the Artillery of the Army of Northern Virginia, with a Brief Account of the Confederate Bureau of Ordnance.* 2 vols. Lynchburg: J. P. Bell, 1915.

Wistar, Isaac Jones. *Autobiography of Isaac Jones Wistar, 1827–1905: Half a Century in War and Peace.* Philadelphia: Wistar Institute of Anatomy and Biology, 1937.

Wood, William Nathaniel. *Reminiscences of Big I.* Ed. Bell Irvin Wiley. Jackson, Tenn.: McCowat-Mercer, 1956.

Woodhull, Alfred A. [Letter on Antietam, July 16, 1886.] In Johnson and Buel, eds., *Battles and Leaders* 2:671n.

———. [Letter on Shepherdstown, July 21, 1886.] In Johnson and Buel, eds., *Battles and Leaders* 2:672–73n.

Woodworth, Steven E. *Lee and Davis at War.* Lawrence: Univ. of Kansas Press, 1995.

———. *Leadership and Command in the American Civil War.* Campbell, Calif.: Savas Woodbury Publishers, 1996.

Worsham, John H. *One of Jackson's Foot Cavalry, His Experiences and What He Saw during the War, 1861–1865, Including a History of "F Company," Richmond, Va., 21st Regiment Virginia Infantry, Second Brigade, Jackson's Division, Second Corps, A.N. Va.* Ed. Bell Irvin Wiley. Jackson, Tenn.: McCowat-Mercer, 1964.

Wyckoff, Mac. *History of the 2nd South Carolina Infantry: 1861–1865.* Fredericksburg, Va.: Sergeant Kirkland Museum and Historical Society, 1994.

———. *History of the 3rd South Carolina Infantry: 1861–1865.* Fredericksburg, Va.: Sergeant Kirkland Museum and Historical Society, 1995.

Young, Louis G. "Pettigrew-Kirkland-MacRae Brigade." In Clark, ed., *North Carolina Regiments* 4:555–68.

Index

Abingdon, Va., 106
Aiken, David Wyatt (CSA, col.), 224
Alabama, 28
Alabama troops, 265
—artillery: Bondurant, 236
—infantry: 5th, 296, 384; 6th, 296
Alexandria, Va., 21, 52, 67, 90; Federal raids from, 221; Federal toehold, 19, 79
Alexandria, Loudoun, and Hampshire Railroad (Va.), 51
Alexander, Edward Porter (CSA, lt. col.), 45, 63; critic of offensives, 488; critic of Sharpsburg stand, 308; ignores Walker's memoirs, 193; with Lee, 254; meets with Lee, 338; ordnance train, 76; returns to Harpers Ferry for ordnance, 338; ride to Keedysville, 295; secret service money, 108; to recross Potomac, 294
Allan, William (CSA, capt.), 50, 53, 140, 143, 195, 481–82, 484; biography, 509–10n.102
Anderson, George Thomas (CSA, gen.), 289
Anderson, Richard Heron (CSA, gen.): defends Pleasant Valley, 320; friend of McLaws, 165; Lee explains S.O. 191 to, 165; in Pleasant Valley, 202; underemployed by McLaws, 278
Anderson, Robert (USA, lt. col.), 373
Anderson's (G. B.) brigade: arrives at Sharpsburg, 303; Battle of Boonsboro, 257, 259, 264; crosses Potomac, 71, 112; forms line in Sunken Road, 381, 384; at Keedysville, 299; march to Buckeystown, 112; march to Keedysville, 294; ordered to be ready, 236; ordered to left, 380; second phase (Sharpsburg), 375
Anderson's (G. T.) brigade, 337; arrives at Sharpsburg, 306; Battle of Boonsboro, 264–65; at Boonsboro, 299; departs Hagerstown, 254; fourth phase (Sharpsburg), 393; march to Boonsboro, 254; march to Keedysville, 295; midday crisis, 401; ordered to left, 380; on Sept. 16th, 364; third phase (Sharpsburg), 391–92
Anderson's (R. H.) division: added to McLaws, 150; advance to Sunken Road, 402; Battle of Shepherdstown, 460; crosses Potomac, 103; crosses to Harpers Ferry, 365; enlarged by Wilcox's division, 178; fatigue, 43; fifth phase (Sharpsburg), 396; Hagerstown original object, 149; held in reserve, 382; holds Sunken Road, 398; Lee protects, 249; Lee's preliminary report, 434–37; Longstreet orders into reserve, 367; march through Frederick, 169–72; march to Big Spring, 92; march to Monocacy Junction, 111; midday crisis, 401; officer cadre, 42; ordered to Sunken Road, 384; orders for Valley expedition, 159–60; outside corps structure, 41; in Pleasant Valley, 278; regimental numbers and strengths, 37–39; Second Manassas, 41; sent to Gordonsville, 34; separated from McLaws, 369; sixth phase (Sharpsburg), 419; strength on Sept. 18th, 432; to abandon Pleasant Valley, 289
The Antietam and Fredericksburg, 486
Antietam Battlefield, 2, 3; attendance, 497n.4; founding, 497n.2
Antietam BattleWeld Board, 4, 487
Antietam, Battle of. *See* Sharpsburg, Battle of
Antietam Creek (Md.): bluffs along, 345–46, 371, 377, 401; deceptive terrain of, 346; First Corps crosses, 350–51; fog on Sept. 16th, 330–31, 333, 335; Lee decides to stand behind, 301; military geography of, 301, 345–46; Stuart's turning movement, 408
Antietam Furnace, Md., 202; escape route for McLaws, 247; Stuart's route, 318

Appomattox Court House, Va., 2, 496
Archer's brigade, 447; Battle of Shepherdstown, 465; sixth phase (Sharpsburg), 422
Arkansas troops, infantry: 3d, 392
Arlington Heights, Va., 130
Armistead, Lewis Addison (CSA, gen.), 74, 106
Armistead's brigade: Battle of Shepherdstown, 458; at foot of South Mountain, 284; in Pleasant Valley, 202; recrosses Potomac, 457; strength on Sept. 18th, 432; weakness, 469
Army of Mississippi (CSA), 27, 30, 61
Army of Northern Virginia (CSA): abandons Boteler's Ford, 455; abandons wounded, 446; aggressive fighting of, 423; almost destroyed, 437; artillery on Cemetery Hill, 555n.32; artillery reorganized, 72–73; baggage trains, 44; battle axis changes, 397; bivouacs at Martinsburg, 467; blacks in, 169–71; brigades' experience, 40; casualties at Second Manassas, 38, 218, 220–21; casualties compared to West, 479; Circular (Sept. 12th), 194; clothing shortage, 44–45, 138; combat experience, 39–40; condition on Sept. 18th, 430–34; confidence, 45–46; conscripts, 171, 507n.76; corps structure, 40–41, 220, 457, 474, 581n.77, 583–84n.114; crosses the Potomac, 71, 76, 80, 83, 86–90, 103; discipline, 117, 474; divisions' experience, 40; enemy cavalry in rear, 295–96; enters Frederick, 101–2; failure in Maryland, 1; fatigue, 43; fighting quality, 45–46; flanks secure on Sept. 16th, 346; Frederick war council, 145–52; General Orders No. 102, 72–75; General Orders No. 103, 106–7; green diet, 44, 118; growing weakness, 287; Hagerstown as destination, 78; heroic qualities, 433; hinge in line, 348, 370–71; holds nearly all Confederate forces in East, 327; hunger, 44, 338; lacks supplies, 60; large reserve on Sept. 16th, 367; learns of Harpers Ferry's surrender, 307; Lee describes weakness of, 469; Lee orders trains to Virginia, 333, 362; Lee risks before S.O. 191 lost, 167; Lee strips right flank, 382; Lee uncertain of strength, 218–20; Lee visits left flank, 381; left flank collapses, 381; logistics, 53; loses artillery duel on Sept. 16th, 335–36; loses guns, 459; main body, 149–51, 159, 163–64, 178, 183–85, 190, 254, 260, 283; marching conditions, 85; marching guidelines, 175; march through Frederick, 168–72, 185–86; march to Keedysville, 294; march to Leesburg, 51–54; Maryland reception, 518–19n.50; midday crisis, 397–98, 403; morale, 32, 39, 45–46, 48; move to Gordonsville, 33; move to Winchester, 474; number of regiments, 37–38; Oct. artillery reorganization, 474; officer cadre, 41–43, 433; ordnance shortage, 45, 60, 63, 76, 403; ordnance train, 52, 55, 76; pillage proscribed, 73; preparations for Maryland, 72–75; preparations for Sept. 18th, 428; progress on Sept. 10th, 177; protects Frederick, 102–3; provost guard, 74; quartermaster, 114; reception in Maryland, 90–92, 112–14; recruits, 138–39; regiments' experience, 39–40; regimental strengths, 37–38, 170, 185–86; remains at Boteler's Ford, 465; to rest at Hagerstown, 138; rests on Monocacy, 111, 113; retires from Potomac, 475; retreat from Turner's Gap, 290–91; to return to Virginia after Boonsboro, 288; Richmond retains convalescents, 123; right flank weak, 416; risk of retreat on Sept. 17th, 428; routed at Crampton's Gap, 282; rumors in ranks, 69; safety of trains, 333; saved by Gregg's brigade, 423; secure on Sept. 13th, 241; shoe shortage, 45, 60, 64, 138, 322, 513n.135; sick left in Frederick, 196; soldiers visit Frederick, 102; Special Orders No. 188, 93–94 (*see also* Special Orders No. 191); Steiner's comments on, 170–71, 185–86; straggling, 116–19, 138, 218–19; straggling after Turner's Gap, 295; straggling proscribed, 73–75; strength, 170–71, 185–86, 194,484
—strength on: June 1st, 220; Sept. 2d, 33–37, 39, 65; Sept. 10th, 531–32n.5; Sept. 13th, 219–20; Sept. 15th, 306; Sept. 16th, 559–60n.1; Sept. 17th, 171, 220; Sept. 18th, 431–33; Sept. 22d, 475; Sept. 30th, 475; Oct. 10th, 475; strong position on Sept. 15th, 328; subsistence, 114, 123, 124; subsistence shortage, 76; subsistence train, 70; supplies from Hagerstown, 193; supply line, 33–34, 136; tensions in on Sept. 16th, 338; third wing, 32–37, 42–43; trains, 169–72, 179, 221, 508n.89, 562nn.34, 37; trains at Keedysville, 299; trains captured, 296; trains reduced, 72; trains to recross Potomac, 289, 294, 333, 362; tri-monthly report, 39, 329; turning movement on Sept. 18th, 441–43; views on invasion,

69–70; wagon shortage, 44; weakness on Sept. 20th, 466; weak record keeping, 218–19; widely dispersed, 299; Williamsport expedition, 448–52; Williamsport turning movement, 444–45; withdrawal from Sharpsburg, 445–48; worn out, 474
Army of Northern Virginia in 1862, 140
Army of the Potomac (USA): advance from Frederick, 212, 229–30; advance from Turner's Gap, 308–15; advance from Washington, 119, 121, 129–30, 148, 163, 167, 181, 189, 209–11; Burnside replaces McClellan, 479; after Chancellorsville, 483; on Chickahominy, 118; crosses Potomac on Oct. 26th, 478; delay in naming commander, 130–31; demoralized, 111; enters Frederick, 480; Fifth Corps joins, 210; Fifth Corps ordered to join, 189; Lee plans to turn, 332; in McLaws's rear, 244; midday success, 401; no campfires on Sept. 16th, 354; ordered to occupy Frederick, 189; ordnance shortage, 438–39; presses Confederate rear, 213; progress on Sept. 15th, 310–15; proves not demoralized, 426; pursuit on Sept. 19th, 452–56; reaches Warrenton, 478; reaches Washington, 75; right flank weak, 414; stalls on Boonsboro Pike, 313; strength on Sept. 13th, 239; strength on Sept. 16th, 559n.1; Stuart's turning movement, 408; Sumner as possible commander, 98; thwarts Williamsport move, 470–71; too-rapid advance, 224, 269, 271, 274; triple threat on Sept. 16th, 344; in Washington, 62
Army of Virginia (USA): at Second Manassas, 370; in Washington, 62
Artillery (CSA): Lee reorganizes, 72–73
Artillery Reserve. *See* Reserve Artillery
Atlantic Ocean, 126
Augusta County, Va., 48

Baggage trains (CSA), 49, 72, 508n.89
Ball, George Washington (CSA, farmer), 66
Baltimore, Md., 100, 110; as Confederate destination, 111–12, 119, 140, 192; convention (1860), 81; newspapers, 79; rail link to Washington, 46; riots (1861), 49; rumored uprising (1862), 112, 124; safe by Sept. 12th, 210, 229; tourists from, 92
B&O Railroad (Md.–Va.), 104; damage to, 111, 139, 453; D. H. Hill to destroy, 71; Harpers Ferry bridge, 202; Jackson disrupts, 182–83; Jackson to seize, 158; last train to Frederick, 169; Monocacy bridge, 88–89, 100, 121, 439; not at Hagerstown, 139; vulnerable, 47
Baltimore Sun, 79, 106, 116
Banks, Nathaniel Prentiss (USA, gen.): defenses of Washington commander, 120; rumored at Darnestown, 114
Banks Corps. *See* Twelfth Corps (USA)
Barksdale, William (CSA, gen.), 203
Barksdale's brigade: at Leesburg, 55; captures Maryland Heights, 224; march from Richmond, 36; march to Maryland Heights, 201–3; on Maryland Heights, 276; ordered to Pleasant Valley defensive line, 284; third phase (Sharpsburg), 391
Barnes's brigade: Battle of Shepherdstown, 465
Barnesville, Md., 104, 114, 122, 210; Federals capture, 167
Barringer Rufus (CSA, capt.), 451
Bartlett, Joseph (CSA, capt.), 270–71
Battles and Leaders of the Civil War, 143
Bayard's brigade, 19
Beauregard, Pierre Gustave Toutant (CSA, gen.), 28, 49
Beaver Creek, Md., 285; Longstreet to march to, 247, 250
Beaver Creek Heights, Md., 254
Benning, Henry Lewis (CSA, col.), 305
Berkeley and Hampshire Turnpike (Va., W. Va.), 183
Berlin, Md., 71, 104; McClellan crosses Potomac from, 478; possible escape route for McLaws, 293
Berlin Turnpike (Md.), 204
Best's Grove, Md.: Lee's headquarters, 105, 112; Stuart at, 108
Between the Hills, Va., 226
Big Spring (Va. farm), 92; D. H. Hill at, 55; Jackson at, 66–67, 86; Longstreet at, 86; McLaws at, 55; Walker at, 104, 112
Blackford, William Willis (CSA, capt.), 244, 249; observes Hooker's crossing, 357; Williamsport expedition, 449–50; Williamsport turning movement, 445
Blackford farm: sixth phase (Sharpsburg), 420
Blackford's Ford (Potomac). *See* Boteler's Ford
Black Horse Troop (Va. cav.), 88, 175–76
Blacksburg, Va., 93
Bloody Lane. *See* Sunken Road
Blue Ridge Mountains (Va.), 11, 76, 82, 192, 201, 330
Bolivar, Md., 233, 260; McClellan's headquarters at, 311

Bolivar Heights (Va., W. Va.), Confederates move against, 273–74, 317; Federal defenses on, 228; Jackson examines, 272; on Sept. 14th, 268–71

Bonaparte, Charles Louis Napoleon (Napoleon III), 25

Bonaparte, Napoleon (Napoleon I), 45

Boonsboro, Md., 258, 260, 285–86, 292–94; Confederate forces at, 224; destination of Confederate main body, 150; D. H. Hill at, 214; D. H. Hill's object, 162; escape route for McLaws, 244, 251; Jackson's camp, 175; Jackson's near capture, 176–77; Longstreet's original object, 159; Longstreet's route, 183; McClellan's headquarters at, 312; McClellan thinks Confederate main body at, 240; possible site for reunion, 163–64; Stuart reaches, 234; trains at, 190; Unionist citizens, 310

Boonsboro, Battle of: Burnside takes command, 262; casualties, 297; Confederate defeat at, 267; Confederate retreat from, 290–91, 294–97; D. H. Hill learns of Longstreet's arrival, 264; D. H. Hill plans counterattack, 265; D. H Hill urges Longstreet to hurry, 264; fighting ends, 287; Lee not on field, 256, 284–85; Longstreet's return to, 254; Longstreet takes command, 266; McClellan takes command, 283; main account of, 256–67; sounds of, 254–55; started by Pleasonton, 260–61. *See also* Fox's Gap; Frosttown Gap

Boonsboro Pike (Md.), 285, 293; Federals advance on, 404; Lee near, 322; Lee visits, 331; Richardson leaves, 396; sixth phase (Sharpsburg), 415, 418, 422; terrain at Sharpsburg, 303–4

Boonsboro–Rohrersville Road (Md.), 281

Boonsboro, skirmish of, 309–10; casualties, 310

Boonsboro Valley, Md., 250

Boswell, James Keith (CSA, capt.), 173

Boteler, Alexander (CSA, cong.), son of, 202

Boteler's Ford (Potomac), 289, 337; Confederates abandon, 455; confusion of names, 463; congested on Sept. 17th, 404; Jackson nears, 322, 328, 331; Lee needs to defend, 301; rough passage, 426, 446; Williamsport expedition, 448–49; Williamsport turning movement, 444–45

Braddock Road (Va.), 19

Bradford, Augustus Williamson (Md. gov.), 82

Brady, Mathew, 1

Bragg, Braxton (CSA, gen.), 61–62; Davis sends proclamation to, 217; multiprong invasion, 27–31, 106, 131, 327, 472, 479; rumored in Valley, 119; unmentioned by Lee, 470

Branch, Lawrence O'Bryan (CSA, gen.): as division commander (Jackson), 68, 88, 173

Branch's brigade: Battle of Shepherdstown, 465; Chantilly, 12; sixth phase (Sharpsburg), 422; withdrawal from Sharpsburg, 447

Branch's division. *See* Hill's (A. P.) division

Brawner Farm (Groveton, Va.), Battle of, 42

Breckinridge, John Cabell (CSA, gen.): multiprong invasion, 131, 472

Bristoe Station, Va., 220

Brockenbrough's brigade. *See* Field's brigade

Brookeville, Md., 121, 130, 210

Brooklyn, N.Y., 77

Brooke, John Rutter (USA, col.), 397

Brooke's brigade: fifth phase (Sharpsburg), 397

Brooks's brigade: at Crampton's Gap, 279, 282

Brown, John (USA, abol.), 276

Brown, John Thompson (CSA, col.): Williamsport expedition, 450

Brown's artillery battalion: to guard Williamsport, 294, 357, 361; Williamsport expedition, 450; Williamsport turning movement, 444

Brownsville Gap (South Mountain), 179; Federals threaten, 279; McLaws's route, 187; Semmes defends, 231, 280–81

Brownsville, Md.: Wilcox ordered to, 279

Bruce, George Anson (historian): critic of Lee, 489

Buckeystown, Md., 134; Jackson at, 88–89; Longstreet at, 103; Sixth Corps marches to, 230; Walker at, 120

Buell, Don Carlos (USA, gen.), 28–29, 62, 479

Bull Run, Battle of. *See* First Bull Run; Second Manassas

Burkittsville, Md., 206, 280; Confederates abandon, 231; confused with Purcellville, 272; Federals attack from, 279; McLaws's route, 179, 201; Munford retreats to, 231

Burnside, Ambrose Everett (USA, gen.), 118, 167; arrives on the Antietam, 313; attack suspended, 399; carries Lower Bridge, 400; to lead attack, 348; Lee's preliminary report, 436; McClellan orders to attack, 399, 413; on morning of Sept. 15th, 311; replaces McClellan, 479; reports to McClellan, 209; second phase (Sharpsburg), 377; situation on Sept. 18th, 439; sixth

phase (Sharpsburg), 400–401; slow to carry Lower Bridge, 399, 571n.48; S.O. 191 makes cautious, 252; takes command at Turner's Gap, 262–63; in Washington, 62
Burnside Bridge. *See* Lower Bridge
Burnside's command (right wing): Battle of Boonsboro, 258–59, 261–67, 292; to carry Turner's Gap, 240; at Cracklinton, 167; ordered to Frederick, 189; possible relief for Harpers Ferry, 210; progress on Sept. 12th, 209
Burnside's Corps. *See* Ninth Corps (USA)

Cabinet (British), 26
Caldwell, John Curtis (USA, gen.): fifth phase (Sharpsburg), 397; pursuit from Boonsboro, 324
Caldwell's brigade: fifth phase (Sharpsburg), 397
Camp Hill, Va. (W. Va.), 270
Carman, Ezra Ayers (USA, col.), 4; as historian, 487
"Carry Me Back to Old Virginia," 182, 447, 475–76
"Carry the war into Africa," 23–24, 51
Carter, Thomas Henry (CSA, capt.), 381
Catoctin Creek (Md.), 232
Catoctin Furnace, Md., 206
Catoctin Mountains (Md.), 189, 207, 22; Jackson's route, 175
Catton, Bruce (historian), 3–4
Cemetery Hill, 431; Confederate artillery on Sept. 16th, 337, 344; Lee abandons, 416; Lee arrives, 303; Lee on Sept. 15th, 307, 324; Lee on Sept. 16th, 331–33; Lee on Sept. 17th, 370, 377–78, 402; naming, 553n.7; sixth phase (Sharpsburg), 415, 419, 422
Centerville, Md. *See* Keedysville, Md.
Centreville, Va., 17; fortifications, 11–12
Century Magazine, 143
Chain Bridge (Potomac), 19
Chain Bridge Road (Va.), 18–19
Chamberlain, Samuel (USA, capt.), 90
Chambersburg, Pa., 173–74, 369; Federal threat from, 183; as Lee's destination, 78, 133, 140, 188, 190–91, 194; Stuart's raid, 478
Chancellorsville, Battle of, 483, 495
Chantilly, Va., 17, 21
Chantilly, Battle of. *See* Ox Hill, Battle of
Chantilly Plantation (Va.), 11
Charleston, S.C., 81
Charleston, Va. (W. Va.), 97, 479
Charlestown, Va. (W. Va.): McLaws visits, 365
Charlestown Turnpike (Va., W. Va.), 228, 464
Charlottesville, Va., 24, 95, 123
Chattanooga, Tenn., 28, 495
Cheek's Ford (Potomac), 71, 112; Walker's division to cross at, 161
Chesapeake Bay, 24, 82
Chesapeake and Ohio Canal (Md.), 136; cost to repair, 105; damage to, 104–5, 223, 453; D. H. Hill to disrupt, 71; obstacle in Lee's rear, 306, 426; Pendleton to bridge, 361; tow path, 88; vulnerable, 47. *See also* Monocacy Aqueduct
Chickahominy River (Va.), 16, 28, 298, 427, 430, 441
Chilton, Robert Hall (CSA, col.), 238, 256, 274, 291, 293, 405, 475; signs S.O. 191, 164
Christ's brigade: sixth phase (Sharpsburg), 415
Circular of Sept. 12th (CSA), 194
Clarksburg, Md., 122
Clausewitz, Karl von, 9
Cobb, Howell (CSA, gen.): courier from McLaws, 282; courier from Munford, 282; hesitation on Sept. 14th, 281; ordered to hold mountain gaps, 278; takes command at Crampton's Gap, 282
Cobb's brigade: arrives at Hagerstown Pike, 384; defeated at Crampton's Gap, 282; forms line at Sunken Road, 384; march to Maryland Heights, 202–3; march to Crampton's Gap, 282; occupies Sandy Hook, 225; ordered to Brownsville, 277–78; reaches Brownsville, 281; retreat from Crampton's Gap, 291; third phase (Sharpsburg), 391
Cockey family: in Urbana, 166, 188
Coggins Point, Va., expedition, 41
Colquitt, Alfred Holt (CSA, col.): confers with Garland, 236; focuses on Turner's Gap, 275; misled by Stuart, 234; occupies Turner's Gap, 234, 256; perceives danger, 235–36; warns D. H. Hill, 235–36
Colquitt's brigade. *See* Rains's brigade
Comus, Md., 122
Confederate president. *See* Davis, Jefferson
Confederate States: aim to liberate Maryland, 57–58, 216; assesses Maryland campaign, 476; chances for victory, 490–91; concentration of forces, 32–33, 298, 491; conscription, 32, 54, 479, 491; forces defending Richmond, 326; independence, 15, 253; Lee's peace proposal, 126–27; Maryland expectations, 509n.100; multiprong invasions, 62, 131; odds faced, 31–32, 65, 479, 504nn.44, 45; Potomac as

Confederate States (*cont.*)
boundary, 48; recruits, 138–39; regiments in field, 39; resources, 491; scrip, 113; use of blacks in army, 169–71; view Maryland as suppressed, 47–48; views of Maryland campaign, 1–2, 70, 82, 493–94

Confederate strategy: "carry the war into Africa," 23–24; critics of, 488–89; defensive, 494; dilemma of Sept. 2–3, 19–25; and foreign affairs, 26; Frederick war council, 145–52; invasion of North, 23–24, 216; Lee goes on defensive, 253; Lee intends to attack McClellan, 195; Lee loses initiative, 168, 198–99; Lee's overland campaign, 490–96; Leesburg option, 50–51; Maryland campaign assessed, 493–94; Maryland option, 46–50; move against Washington, 22–23; move to west, 24; multiprong invasions, 14–20, 62, 427, 470, 472, 479, 522n.84; Richmond conference (Aug.), 36; turning movements, 20, 46–47, 76, 210, 260, 314, 406–13, 436, 441–45; withdraw to south, 23. *See also* Maryland campaign

Congress (CSA): on Maryland campaign, 539n.5; Maryland resolutions (1861), 49, 216; minority opposes Pennsylvania invasion, 216; rejects peace commission, 216; resolution on Mississippi River, 218

Connelly, Thomas L. (historian), 489

Connecticut troops, infantry: 8th, 230, 422; 11th, 230; 16th, 421

Conrad's Ferry (Potomac), 67

Conscription (CSA), 32, 54, 491, 507n.76

Conscripts (CSA), 40

Cooke, John Rogers (CSA, col.), 226

Cooper, Samuel (CSA, gen.), 34. *See also* Lee-Cooper correspondence

Cope's maps, 487

Corinth, Miss., 28, 479

Cornfield. *See* Miller (D. R.) Cornfield

Corse, Montgomery Dent (CSA, col.), 290

Couch's division, 19, 84; advance against Lee, 130; arrives at Burkittsville, 320; to carry Crampton's Gap, 240; at Licksville Crossroads, 279; march to Barnesville, 210; march to Jefferson, 279; march to Licksville Crossroads, 230; march to Offutt's Crossroads, 99, 109; morning of Sept. 15th, 311; ordered to Keedysville, 438–39; ordered to Williamsport, 454; planned attack on Sept. 19th, 439; situation on Sept. 18th, 439; turning movement on Sept. 18th, 442; at Williamsport, 466

Cox, Jacob Dolson (USA, gen.): arrives at Sharpsburg, 313; at Fox's Gap, 258–59, 261–62, 295; commander of Kanawha Division, 206; occupies Frederick, 206–7; plans for Fox's Gap, 262–63; sixth phase (Sharpsburg), 400–401, 414, 422; warned by Moor, 261–62; in Washington, 62

Cox's Corps. *See* Ninth Corps (USA)

Cox's division. *See* Kanawha division

Cox farm (Sharpsburg), 410, 431

Cracklintown, Md.: Burnside captures, 167

Crampton's Gap (South Mountain), 213–15, 260–61; McLaws's route, 179; Munford's brigade retreats to, 231

Crampton's Gap, Battle of, 274; casualties, 297; Cobb takes command, 282; Confederate forces at, 280–81; Confederate retreat from, 291; Confederates routed at, 278–79, 282; early threat ignored, 275–76; Federal delay at, 280–81; Franklin's wing at, 279–80; geography, 257; Lee's ignorance of, 287; McLaws hesitates, 278; McLaws orders Cobb to hold mountain gaps, 278; McLaws's defensive plans, 276–78; main account of, 275–84; Munford's defense of, 275, 280–82; R. H. Anderson's division in Pleasant Valley, 278; Stuart misperceives McClellan's plan, 278

Crawford's brigade: fourth phase (Sharpsburg), 392; second phase (Sharpsburg), 374–75

Crook, George (USA, col.): at Fox's Gap, 262; sixth phase (Sharpsburg), 400

Crook's brigade: at Fox's Gap, 262; sixth phase (Sharpsburg), 414

Crutchfield, Stapleton (CSA, col.), 274, 316

CSS *Richmond*, 61

Culpeper Court House, Va., 23, 69, 478; supply line, 95; Taylor's visit, 155–56

Cumberland, Md., 97, 137; route for Federal fugitives, 174

Cumberland Gap (Ky.–Tenn.), 29

Cumberland Valley (Pa.), 471

Cumberland Valley Railroad (Pa.–Md.), 185

Curtin, Andrew Gregg (Pa. gov.), 209, 438–39; news of Confederates, 181

Cutts, Allen Sherrod (CSA, lt. col.): arrives at Sharpsburg, 304–5; near capture, 290

Cutts's artillery battalion, 553n.10; arrives at Sharpsburg, 304–5; attached to D. H. Hill, 161; at Battle of Boonsboro, 260; on left on Sept. 16th, 337; at Monocacy Junction, 120; near capture, 290

Damascus, Md., 122, 130
Dana, Napoleon Jackson Tecumseh (USA, gen.), 386
Dana's brigade: third phase (Sharpsburg), 386, 390
Darnestown, Md., 91, 114, 129; Franklin at, 160
Davis, Benjamin Franklin ("Grimes") (USA, col.), 284
Davis, Jefferson (CSA, pres.): approval of Maryland campaign, 64, 70, 75; approves entry into Pennsylvania, 219; consoles Lee, 476; diplomatic instructions on Maryland, 49; discretion to generals, 27; excited by Lee's proposal, 131–32; Lee sends proclamation to, 217; military policy, 27, 36–37; multiprong invasions, 27–30; on entering Pennsylvania, 77–78; Proclamation to Pennsylvania and Ohio, 217; proposes proclamation, 216–18; proposes visit, 131–32; report from Pendleton, 222; return to Richmond, 156; sends proclamations to Bragg and K. Smith, 217; statement of expanded war aims, 49; sends third wing to Lee, 36; tells K. Smith of disappointment, 477; trip to Warrenton, 215–16; visited by Pendleton, 36–37. *See also* Lee-Davis correspondence; Lee-Davis relationship
Democratic party, 77, 81
Department of Southwestern Virginia (CSA), 97
Department of the South (USA), 117
DeRosset, William Lord (CSA, col.), 290
Difficult Run (Va.), 12, 17, 19
District of North Carolina (CSA), 35, 37
"Dixie," 102, 358
Doles, George Pierce (CSA, col.), 290
Doles's brigade. *See* Ripley's brigade
Doubleday's division: attack on Sept. 16th, 351–52; crosses Antietam, 350, 355; first phase (Sharpsburg), 371–72; second phase (Sharpsburg), 374; third phase (Sharpsburg), 388
Double envelopment, 347
Douglas, Henry Kyd (CSA, lt.), biography, 173; challenges Walker's memoirs, 143; Jackson's near capture, 176–77; Jackson's ruse, 173; refutes Walkers claims, 269; retakes Nicodemus Hill, 429; signal courier, 272; views on Lower Bridge, 400
Douglass, Marcellus (CSA, col.): arrives Sharpsburg, 334; on Sept. 16th, 363
Douglass's brigade. *See* Lawton's brigade
Dowdey, Clifford (historian), 485
Downey, Stephen W. (USA, lt. col.), 176–77
Dranesville, Va., 51–52, 66, 70; Battle of, 56–57
Dranesville dispatch, 57–65
Drayton's brigade: arrives at Sharpsburg, 305; at Keedysville, 299; Battle of Boonsboro, 264–65; departs Hagerstown, 254; march to Boonsboro, 254; march to Keedysville, 294; midday crisis, 401
Drovers' Inn (Dranesville), 57
Dryer, Hiram (USA, capt.): sixth phase (Sharpsburg), 415
Dunkard Church (Sharpsburg), 431; Cutts ordered to, 304–5; Federal Sept. 18th attack, 438; first phase (Sharpsburg), 370, 388; fourth phase (Sharpsburg), 392; Hood at, 357; Hood transferred to, 325; Jackson reaches on Sept. 16th, 359; Lee's preliminary report, 435–36; second phase (Sharpsburg), 374, 376, 388; stragglers' brigade, 408; Stuart at, 355; third phase (Sharpsburg), 389; turning movement of Sept. 18th, 441, 443
Dunkard Church plateau: first phase (Sharpsburg), 370, 372; fourth phase (Sharpsburg), 393; Lee's preliminary report, 436; second phase (Sharpsburg), 376–77

Early, Jubal Anderson (CSA, gen.), 42: fourth phase (Sharpsburg), 393; historiography, 484; in Frederick, 171–72; reports to Jackson, 388–89; second phase (Sharpsburg), 377, 388; third phase (Sharpsburg), 387–88; war council on Sept. 17th, 424
Early's brigade: arrives Sharpsburg, 334; fifth phase (Sharpsburg), 395; first phase (Sharpsburg), 372, 388; fourth phase (Sharpsburg), 393; march to Sharpsburg, 321, 328; reaches Dunkard Church on Sept. 16th, 360; retakes Nicodemus Hill, 429; second phase (Sharpsburg), 373–74
Early's division. *See* Ewell's division
East Woods, 408; first phase (Sharpsburg), 370, 372–73, 387; Lee's preliminary report, 434, 436; McClellan visits, 413–14; second phase (Sharpsburg), 373–77; Sixth Corps arrives, 405; skirmish on Sept. 16th, 351–52; third phase (Sharpsburg), 385, 389, 392
Election of 1864, 496
Eleventh Corps (USA), 18; rumored in Maryland, 129–30
Elk Ridge (Md.), 201–4; held by McLaws, 224; no Federals west of, 323; sixth phase (Sharpsburg), 400

Emancipation Proclamation, 1, 4
Emmittsburg Road (Md.), 102, 172
Estrays. *See* Straggling
Europe, 25
Evans, Nathan George (CSA, gen.): arrests Hood, 68–69; division commander (Longstreet), 68–69; Lee keeps apart from Hood, 306
Evans's brigade, 337; arrives at Sharpsburg, 306; at Frosttown Gap, 266-267; guards Middle Bridge, 380; at Keedysville, 299; midday crisis, 401, 405; no support remains for, 385; reconnaissance at Turner's Gap, 292; sixth phase (Sharpsburg), 420; skirmish on Sept. 16th, 335; strength on Sept. 18th, 432; weakness, 469; withdrawal from Sharpsburg, 447
Evans's division: crosses Potomac, 103; depart from Hagerstown, 254; march through Frederick, 177; march to Boonsboro, 254; march to Hagerstown, 183–85; occupies Hagerstown, 190
Evelington Heights, Va., 412
Ewell, Richard Stoddert (CSA, gen.), 42
Ewell's division (CSA), 175; arrives in Sharpsburg, 334; Battle of Shepherdstown, 464–65; Lee's preliminary report, 435; march through Frederick, 173; march to Martinsburg, 199–200; march to North Mountain Depot, 182; march to Sharpsburg, 321, 328; at Monocacy Junction, 99–100; move on Bolivar Heights, 273; nears Potomac, 331; officer cadre, 42; ordered to Dunkard Church on Sept. 16th, 357; ordered to Lower Bridge on Sept. 16th, 356; Ox Hill, 11, 14; progress on Sept. 13th, 228; progress on Sept. 15th, 316–17; reaches Dunkard Church on Sept. 16th, 360; recrossing Potomac, 457; replaces Hood on Sept. 16th, 363; second phase (Sharpsburg), 373
Ewing's brigade: sixth phase (Sharpsburg), 415

Fairchild, Harrison Stiles (USA, col.), 230
Fairchild's brigade: sixth phase (Sharpsburg), 415, 422
Fairfax, Va.: war council, 49
Fairfax County, Va., 11, 16, 24; bareness, 21–22, 59
Fairfax Court House, Va., 11, 12, 14, 19, 58
Fairfax Station, Va., 22
Faithful William (USA, capt.), 100
Falling Waters, Va., 369
Falls Church, Va., 84
Farnsworth, John Franklin (USA, col.), 122
Farnsworth's brigade, 233, 242
Fauquier County, Va., 11; resources, 48
Featherston's brigade: at foot of South Mountain, 284
Ferrero's brigade: sixth phase (Sharpsburg), 415
Field's brigade: Battle of Shepherdstown, 465; Ox Hill, 12; sixth phase (Sharpsburg), 422; strength on Sept. 18th, 431; withdrawal from Sharpsburg, 447
Fifth Corps (USA): Battle of Shepherdstown, 456; fifth phase (Sharpsburg), 396; fresh for Sept. 18th, 438; joins McClellan, 210; morning of Sept. 15th, 311; only reserve in center, 399; ordered ahead of Ninth Corps, 312; ordered to Boteler's Ford, 454; ordered to join McClellan, 189; pursuit on Sept. 19th, 452; retreat to Washington, 18–19; veteran unit, 349
Fifth phase, Battle of Sharpsburg (Sunken Road), 395–97; casualties, 397
First Bull Run, Battle of, 20, 40, 453
First Corps (USA-Potomac), 348; advance against Lee, 121; advance from Turner's Gap, 309–10; bivouac on Sept. 16th, 354; condition on Sept. 16th, 348; condition on Sept. 18th, 439; crosses Antietam, 344, 350–51; demoralized, 414; first phase (Sharpsburg), 370, 373; fourth phase (Sharpsburg), 394; at Frosttown Gap, 263, 266; in Frederick, 239; joins Burnside, 109; Lee's preliminary report, 434; McClellan orders up the Antietam, 314; march to Brookeville, 121; march to Frederick, 230; march to New Market, 210; march to the Antietam, 313; Ox Hill, 12; pursuit on Sept. 19th, 452; retreat to Washington, 19; rumored advance, 129–30; second phase (Sharpsburg), 374–75; third phase (Sharpsburg), 391; to attack on Sept. 19th, 440; turning movement on Sept. 18th, 442; wrecked, 399
First Corps (USA-Virginia). *See* Eleventh Corps (USA)
First phase, Battle of Sharpsburg (Hooker-Jackson), 370–73, 387–88; casualties, 373
First Manassas. *See* First Bull Run
Flint Hill, Va., 12, 14, 17–19
Ford, Antonia, 19, 501n.10
Foreign mediation, 26
Forrest, Nathan Bedford (CSA, gen.), 28
Fort Buffalo, Va., 14

Fort Monroe, Va.: Federal toehold, 19
Fort Ward, Va., 21
Fourth Corps (USA). *See* Couch's division
Fourth phase, Battle of Sharpsburg (Dunkard Church), 392–94; casualties, 394–95
Fox's Gap (South Mountain): Confederates retreat from, 291, 310; Federals carry, 287; Federals use for turning movement, 260; fighting at, 257–65; Garland defends, 258–59; Garland routed, 259; G. B. Anderson arrives at, 259; geography of, 236, 257; Jackson's route, 173; Rosser leaves, 324; Rosser occupies, 234, 257–58
France, 49; possible intervention, 4, 25–26
Franklin, William Buel (USA, gen.): alerts McClellan of Harpers Ferry's surrender, 311–12; commands at Crampton's Gap, 279–80; does not press McLaws, 320; fears Jackson move up Pleasant Valley, 319; fourth phase (Sharpsburg), 393; McClellan's orders to, 279; morning of Sept. 15th, 311; ordered to Sharpsburg, 353; relieved, 98; to attack on Sept. 18th, 438; to attack on Sept. 19th, 440; to carry Crampton's Gap, 240; to watch Harpers Ferry, 313
Franklin's command (left wing): at Crampton's Gap, 279–80; march compared to Longstreet's, 279; march to Darnestown, 166; progress on Sept. 12th, 209; to carry Crampton's Gap, 240
Franklin's Corps. *See* Sixth Corps
Frederick, Md., 260; anxious over Confederates, 100; Confederate cavalry line, 187; Confederates abandon, 214; Confederate soldiers visit, 102–3; Confederates march through, 168–72; Confederates protect, 106; council of war, 145–52; Davis's proposed visit, 132; fall of, 235, 480; Federals concentrate on, 230; home of B. Johnson, 81; home of E. Lowe, 77; McClellan's entry, 229, 237; merchants, 128; message time to Hagerstown, 196; occupied by Federals, 213; passes to visit, 154–55; provisions dwindle, 128, 146; reception of Confederates, 113–14; shoes for Confederates, 194; skirmish at, 206–7; Stuart predicts fall of, 188–89; supply line, 136; Union sympathizers, 171–72; welcomes Union troops, 207
Frederick County, Md.: resources, 48, 193; slave population, 91; subsistence from, 124; unionist sympathies, 81–82
Frederick Herald, 125
Frederick–Harpers Ferry Road (Md.), 214–15
Frederick–Urbana Road (Md.), 100
Fredericksburg, Va., 22, 35, 494–95; fall back to, 23
Fredericksburg, Battle of, 3, 147
Freeman, Douglas Southall (historian), 483; on Lee in Maryland, 485; uses Walker's memoirs, 143–44
French, William Henry (USA, gen.), 385–86, 396
French's division: fifth phase (Sharpsburg), 396–98; morning of Sept. 15th, 311; third phase, 385–89
Frietchie, Barbara, 171–72, 532n.6
Frobel's artillery battalion: sixth phase (Sharpsburg), 417
Front Royal, Va.: supply line, 95, 123
Frosttown Gap (South Mountain), 260, 263–66; fighting at, 263, 265–66; Meade carries, 287; military geography of, 236, 257, 265–66
Frying Pan Farm, Va., 11, 51
Fuller, Joseph Frederick Charles (historian), 489
Funk, John (CSA, col.), 116
Funkstown, Md., 289; Lee's headquarters, 222; Longstreet's route, 190
Furnace Hill, Va. (W. Va.), 268

Gainesville, Va., 57, 96, 123
Garland, Samuel, Jr. (CSA, gen.): confers with Colquitt, 236; confers with Rosser, 258; killed, 258, 310
Garland's brigade: arrives at Sharpsburg, 303; at Keedysville, 299; Battle of Boonsboro, 257–59, 261–62, 264; crosses Potomac, 71; Federals could turn at Fox's Gap, 261; forms line in Sunken Road, 381, 384; in reserve on Sept. 16th, 356; march to Keedysville, 294; ordered to left, 380; ordered to South Mountain, 236–37; routed at Fox's Gap, 259; second phase (Sharpsburg), 375; seen by Moor, 261; stragglers, 403
Garnett, Richard Brooke (CSA, gen.), 93
Garnett's brigade. *See* Pickett's brigade
Garrett, Thomas (CSA, capt.), 403–4
General Orders, No. 102, 72–75
General Orders, No. 103, 106–7
General Orders, No. 107, 466
General Orders, No. 116, 477
Geneva, N.Y., 225
Georgia, 61
Georgia troops:
—artillery: Read, 419
—cavalry: Cobb Legion, 233

Georgia troops (*cont.*)
—infantry: 2d, 299, 305; 4th, 243, 257, 290; 10th, 281; 11th, 254, 289, 296, 299, 364; 15th, 299, 305, 364; 16th, 281–82; 17th, 299, 305, 364; 20th, 299, 305; 21st, 403; 24th, 281–82; 49th, 87; 53d, 280; Cobb Legion, 281–82
German Americans, 82, 193
Gettysburg (film), 5
Gettysburg, Pa., 100; rumored Confederate object, 209
Gettysburg, Battle of: battlefield, 2–3; compared to Sharpsburg, 2–5
Gettysburg, campaign of, 326; and Maryland rebellion, 483; compared to Maryland campaign, 482–83; Harpers Ferry in, 483; Lee's intentions in, 483; Williamsport in, 483
Gibbon's brigade: first phase (Sharpsburg), 372, 388; second phase (Sharpsburg), 388; at Turner's Gap, 263, 267
"The Girl I Left Behind Me," 177
Gladstone, William Ewart, 26
Gleam of Bayonets, 487
Goggin, James (CSA, maj.), 278
Goodrich's brigade: fourth phase (Sharpsburg), 392; second phase (Sharpsburg), 375–76
Goose Creek, Va., 66
Gordon, Edward C., Rev., 195, 480–81
Gordon, John Brown (CSA, col.): speech to Lee, 384
Gordon's brigade: fourth phase (Sharpsburg), 392; second phase (Sharpsburg), 374; third phase (Sharpsburg), 389
Gordonsville, Va., 33, 221, 298, 427, 478
Goree, Thomas Jewett (CSA, capt.), 474
Gorgas, Josiah (CSA, col.), 96
Gorman Willis Arnold (USA, gen.), 386
Gorman's brigade: third phase (Sharpsburg), 386, 389–90
Grant, Ulysses Simpson (USA, gen.), 7
Great Britain, 49; possible intervention, 4, 25–26
Great Lakes, 139
Green diet, 44, 118
Green regiments, 389, 395, 421, 439, 453, 456, 504n.48, 513n.127
Greene, George Sears (USA, gen.), 375, 393
Greene's division: fifth phase (Sharpsburg), 395; fourth phase (Sharpsburg), 393; second phase (Sharpsburg), 375–76; third phase (Sharpsburg), 387
Gregg, Maxcy (CSA, gen.), 421; withdrawal from Sharpsburg, 447
Gregg's brigade, 67; Battle of Shepherdstown, 464–65; occupies Martinsburg, 199; sixth phase (Sharpsburg), 421; withdrawal from Sharpsburg, 447
Grigsby, Andrew Jackson (CSA, gen.): commands Jackson's first line on Sept. 16th, 359; second phase (Sharpsburg), 373, 388; third phase (Sharpsburg), 389, 391
Grigsby's brigade. *See* Stonewall brigade
Griffin, Charles (USA, gen.), 414; relieved, 98
Griffin's brigade: Battle of Shepherdstown, 456, 464; ordered to support Franklin, 414
Grove (Jacob Hess) house, 355–56, 360; as Lee's headquarters, 326; Sharpsburg war council on Sept. 16th, 343–44; as Stuart's headquarters, 336; under artillery fire, 336
Groveton, Battle of. *See* Brawner Farm
Guild, Lafayette (CSA, med. dir.), 196, 221; defective casualty report, 552n.124
Gum Springs Road (Va.), 55

Hagan's Gap (Catoctin Mountains), 1755, 207, 222; skirmish at, 232
Hagerstown, Md., 369; army to reunite at, 136–37, 163; as Confederate base, 188, 190–91, 194, 222; Confederates depart, 254; Confederates occupy, 190; Federal ammunition via, 439; as Lee's aim, 78, 192; Lee's planned move to, 133; Longstreet at, 214; Longstreet departs, 254; message time to Frederick, 196; not Jackson's object, 176; object of Lee's revised strategy, 332; Pleasonton pursues F. Lee to, 324; reception of Confederates, 193; route closed to Lee, 356; shoes for Confederates, 194; Stuart's turning movement, 408; supplies in, 146; supply of flour, 183; Taylor's visit, 156; Williamsport expedition, 451; Williamsport turning movement, 444
Hagerstown Pike (Md.): first phase (Sharpsburg), 371–72; fourth phase (Sharpsburg), 392; Hood defends on Sept. 16th, 358; Hooker aims toward, 350; Lee's preliminary report, 436; Lee visits, 381–84; second phase (Sharpsburg), 373–74, 388; Stuart's turning movement, 408–9; terrain at Sharpsburg, 303–4; third phase (Sharpsburg), 386–87, 391; turning movement on Sept. 18th, 441
Hagerstown Valley (Md.), 471

Halleck, Henry Wager (USA, gen.): at Corinth, 28, 49; fears for Washington's safety, 119; and Harpers Ferry, 98; military theorist, 111; news of Confederates, 181; Pope's retreat, 18; as success, 7; telegram from Miles, 190
Halltown, Va. (W. Va.), 227, 238, 320–21; A. P. Hill's route, 418; McLaws bivouacs, 365
Hamburg Gap (South Mountain), 241, 290; 4th Georgia defends, 248; military geography of, 257
Hammond's Mills, Va. (W. Va.), 182
Hampton, Wade (CSA, gen.): brigade commander (Stuart), 206–7; Stuart sends to Crampton's Gap, 233, 242–43
Hampton's brigade, 283; arrives in Sharpsburg, 403; covers Leesburg march, 52; at Crampton's Gap, 275; crosses Potomac, 89–90; at Dranesville, 67; at Hyattstown, 115; Hyattstown skirmish, 122; kept in reserve, 403; leaves Crampton's Gap, 280; march from Richmond, 34–37; march to Frederick, 107; march to Leesburg, 56; Munford almost fires on, 233–34; operations on Sept. 13th, 231–35; Poolesville skirmish, 90; regimental numbers and strengths, 37–39; ride to Frederick, 188; sent to Weverton, 276; skirmish at Frederick, 206–7; skirmish at Hagan's Gap, 232; Stuart's turning movement, 408; welcomed in Poolesville, 90–91; at Williamsport, 466; Williamsport expedition, 450–51
Hancock's brigade: at Crampton's Gap, 279
Hanover Junction, Va., 35
Hard Scrabble, Va. (W. Va.), 451
Harland, Edward (USA, col.), 230
Harland's brigade, 242; sixth phase (Sharpsburg), 415, 422
Harman, John Alexander (CSA, maj.), 87; withdrawal from Sharpsburg, 447
Harpers Ferry, Va. (W. Va.), 259; bridges, 202; as Confederate crossing point, 80, 83; Confederate forces to cooperate at, 213–14; Confederates to capture, 136; escape route, 225; Federal cavalry at, 162; Federals shift responsibility, 98; firing heard at, 240; garrison expected to flee, 146, 148; geography of, 227, 268; Jackson decides to move on, 199–200; Jackson devises siege, 227–28; Jackson takes command, 227–28; Jackson to intercept fugitives, 158; Lee and Longstreet consult on, 105; Lee awaits capture, 195; Lee counts on surrender of, 245; Loring to protect, 97; McClellan learns of role in S.O. 191, 238; McClellan's dilemma in relieving, 239; McLaws ignorance of, 165; McLaws's original object, 159–60; McLaws remains at on Sept. 13, 225; McLaws to capture, 159–60; Maryland Heights is key to, 148–49, 160; ordered not to surrender, 201; receives Winchester garrison, 79; relief by McClellan, 215; size of garrison, 137; as threat, 24, 50, 105
Harpers Ferry, siege of, 293–94; attack delayed, 268–69; bombardment on Sept. 15th, 316–17; bridges at, 557n.48; cavalry escape from, 284, 295–96; civilians to evacuate, 268; Confederate fire deficient, 273; Confederates isolate, 270; Confederates move against Bolivar Heights, 273–74; fate sealed on Sept. 14th, 275; Federal blunders, 315–16; Federal casualties, 555n.33, 557n.47; Federal property captured, 321; garrison paroled, 317; Jackson confuses details, 272; Jackson examines Bolivar Heights, 272; Jackson opens firing, 273; Jackson revises plan, 270–71; Jackson sends battery to Shenandoah, 274; Jackson's original plan, 267–69; McLaws learns enemy in rear, 271; McLaws's defensive line, 282; as McLaws's escape route, 301; main account of, 267–75, 315–22; Miles surrenders, 316; odds at, 268; pontoon bridge, 318, 320, 364; proposed flag of truce, 268; rapid Federal advance in relief of, 269, 271, 274; Walker's claims, 143, 269–71; wild card in strategy, 315, 344
Harpers Ferry–Sharpsburg Road (Md.), 420, 422
Harpers Ferry–Shepherdstown Road (Va., W. Va.), 365
Harrisburg, Pa., 47, 78, 139–41, 181; Federal ammunition via, 439
Harrison, Henry T., 71–72
Harrisonburg, Va., 474; supply line, 136
Harrison Hall (Leesburg), 71–72; prayer meeting, 86; war council, 81
Harrison's Landing, Va., 15
Hartwig, D. Scott (historian), 4, 587n.27
Harvard Law School (Mass.), 81
Haskell, Alexander Cheves (CSA, capt.), 422
Hatch's division: at Turner's Gap, 263, 267, 287
Hauser Ridge: first phase (Sharpsburg), 387–88; third phase (Sharpsburg), 391
Haymarket, Va.,

Hays's brigade: arrives in Sharpsburg, 334; first phase (Sharpsburg), 373; march to Sharpsburg, 321, 328; reaches Dunkard Church on Sept. 16th, 360; strength on Sept. 18th, 432; third phase (Sharpsburg), 388

Hazlett, Charles Edward (USA, lt.): Battle of Shepherdstown, 456

Healy, Robert (CSA, lt.), 70

Heard, John (Md. pol.), 125

Hedgesville, Va. (W. Va.), 199

Henderson, George Francis Robert (historian), 485

Henrico County, Va. *See* Richmond, Va.

Hermitage, Md., 77

Herr, Widow, 287

Heysinger, Isaac Winter (USA, capt.), 4

Hill, Ambrose Powell (CSA, gen.), 275; confers with D. R. Jones, 420; headquarters at Blackford farm, 420; Jackson arrests, 67–68, 74; Lee expects on Sept. 16th, 366; Lee expects earlier, 417; Ox Hill, 11–14; relieved from arrest, 173; reports to Lee, 417; sends parolees across pontoon bridge, 320; surrender commissioner, 317; under arrest, 88; war council of Sept. 17th, 424

Hill, Daniel Harvey (CSA, gen.), 261; advises retreat from Turner's Gap, 267, 287–88; alerted by Stuart, 235; appreciates crisis, 256; article on lost orders, 158, 480–81; Battle of Shepherdstown, 460, 463; at Best's Grove, 105; blamed for lost campaign, 235, 451n.42; Boonsboro war council, 287; buys cornfield, 71, 73, 91; calls for Lee's help, 255; commands rearguard of Valley expedition, 161; commands Richmond reenforcements wing, 35–37; on Confederate heroic qualities, 434; confers with Longstreet, 256; consolidates brigades, 433; copies of S.O. 191, 152–53; discovers urgency, 259; enters Frederick, 101–2; Federals could turn at Fox's Gap, 261; fifth phase (Sharpsburg), 398; focuses on Turner's Gap, 275; forms line of extra-duty men, 259; guards Harpers Ferry routes, 208; his copy of S.O. 191 lost, 153; horse killed, 379–80; ignores Walker's memoirs, 140; Jackson opens communications with, 88–89; Jackson's brother-in-law, 89; Jackson's confidant, 147; joins Lee, 54; learns of Frederick's fall, 208; learns of Longstreet's arrival, 264; leaves no force at Turner's Gap, 208; Lee orders to take personnel command at Turner's Gap, 248; midday crisis, 401, 405; march to Leesburg, 55; not in Lee's confidence, 135; ordered to Leesburg, 52; orders Colquitt to Turner's Gap, 235; orders Garland to Turner's Gap, 236; orders Ripley to Turner's Gap, 248; plans counterattack, 265; possible wing commander, 41; rides to Mountain House, 256; rides with Lee down Sunken Road, 384; rumored killed, 30; second phase (Sharpsburg), 373; sends Garland to Fox's Gap, 258; sends to Lee for help, 376; sent copy of S.O. 191 by Jackson, 152–53; strength for Valley expedition, 150–51, 161; temporarily commands Jackson's wing, 85–86, 100; temporarily under Jackson's command, 153; to send Stuart help, 222–23; underestimates urgency, 256; urges Longstreet to hurry, 264; war council on Sept. 17th, 424; warned by Colquitt, 235-36. *See also* Lee–D. H. Hill correspondence

Hillsborough, Va., 205, 226

Hill's (A. P.) division, 175; bedraggled, 417; discipline, 91; guarding Harpers Ferry, 332, 342; Jackson leaves at Harpers Ferry, 307; leaves for Sharpsburg, 366; Lee divides, 417; Lee's preliminary report, 434, 436; march compared to Franklin's, 418; march from Harpers Ferry, 418; march through Frederick, 173; march to Martinsburg, 182–83, 199–200; at Monocacy Junction, 99–100; move on Bolivar Heights, 273–74; needed at Sharpsburg, 385, 403, 416–17; officer cadre, 40–42; ordered to Sharpsburg, 366; Ox Hill, 11–12, 14; progress on Sept. 13th, 228; progress on Sept. 15th, 316–17; recrosses Potomac, 457; secures Federal property, 321–22; straggling, 118; strength on Sept. 18th, 431; Stuart's turning movement, 408; timeliness of arrival, 418; under Branch, 173; withdrawal from Sharpsburg, 447 *See also* Hill's (D. H.) division

Hill's (D. H.) division, 40; arrives at Sharpsburg, 303; artillery, 72; Battle of Boonsboro, 256–67; Battle of Shepherdstown, 460, 464; at Boonsboro, 197; crosses Potomac, 71, 76, 80, 83; Cutts attached to, 120; fatigue, 43; few casualties on Sept. 16th, 335; fifth phase (Sharpsburg), 396; holds Sunken Road, 377; at Keedysville, 299; lacks cavalry, 163; Lee's preliminary report, 435; line at Sunken Road on Sept. 16th, 357; march from Richmond, 34–37; march through Frederick, 185–86; march to Boonsboro, 207; march to

Keedysville, 294; midday crisis, 401; at Monocacy Junction, 99–100; no progress on Sept. 10th, 179–80; object to guard Harpers Ferry routes, 185–86; operations on Sept. 13, 235–36; ordered to left flank, 380; orders for Valley expedition, 161–62; outside command structure, 41; progress on Sept. 10th, 534n.28; progress on Sept. 11, 186; progress on Sept. 12th, 207; as rearguard in Valley expedition, 149; regimental numbers and strengths, 37–39; remains at Boonsboro, 185–86; retreat from Boonsboro, 290–91; second phase (Sharpsburg), 373–77; secure on Sept. 13th, 240–41, 244–45; sixth phase (Sharpsburg), 419; strength, 170–71, 185–86; strength on Sept. 18th, 433; watching Harpers Ferry roads, 235; west of Boonsboro, 214

Hilton Head, S.C., 117

Hindsight in history, 6–10

Hirsch, Isaac (CSA, pvt.), 134

Historiography, 483–84

Hodges, James Gregory (CSA, col.): Battle of Shepherdstown, 458

Hoffman, John, farm: bivouac of Twelfth Corps, 353; route of First Corps, 351

Holmes, Theophilus Hunter (CSA, gen.), 41

Holt, Willis Cox (CSA, maj.), 281

Hood, John Bell (CSA, gen.): Battle of Shepherdstown, 460; Boonsboro war council, 287; division commander (Longstreet), 43; Evans arrests, 68–69; finds relief from Jackson, 363; Jackson hopes Federals are gone, 433; Lee keeps apart from Evans, 306; returned to command, 256, 544n.12; searches for food, 363; seeks relief from Lee, 362–63; sends to Lee for help, 383; skirmish on Sept. 16th, 357–58; stragglers' brigade, 408; Stuart's turning movement, 410; third phase (Sharpsburg), 391; war council on Sept. 17th, 425

Hood, William S. (CSA, pvt.), 409

Hood's (Texas) brigade (CSA): arrives at Sharpsburg, 306; at Boonsboro, 299; captures wagons, 69; demands Hood's return, 256; retires from line on Sept. 16th, 363; second phase (Sharpsburg), 374–75; skirmish on Sept. 16th, 357–58; transferred to Dunkard Church on Sept. 15th, 325

Hood's division, 295; arrives at Sharpsburg, 306; at Boonsboro, 299; bivouacs at Dunkard Church, 363; Evans commands, 103; at Fox's Gap, 266, 284, 287; holds Confederate left on Sept. 16th, 356; retires from line on Sept. 16th, 363; retreat from Turner's Gap, 290; second phase (Sharpsburg), 374, 388; skirmish on Sept. 16th, 357–58; transferred to Dunkard Church on Sept. 15th, 325

Hooker, Joseph (USA, gen.): at Chantilly, 12; crosses Antietam, 350–51; first phase (Sharpsburg), 370, 372, 388; at Frosttown Gap, 263, 292; headquarters in J. Poffenberger's barn, 354; Lee's preliminary report, 434, 436; McClellan offers support to, 350; McClellan orders to press pursuit, 311; McClellan visits on Sept. 16th, 350–51; in McClellan's battle plans, 567n.7; message to McClellan, 354; observes Hood's transfer, 326; pleads for support, 351; pursues Lee to Sharpsburg, 310; reports to McClellan, 310–11, 313; second phase (Sharpsburg), 374, 377; to lead attack, 348; visits McClellan's headquarters, 350; visits pickets on Sept. 16th, 354; vulnerable on Sept. 16th, 359

Hotchkiss, Jedediah (CSA, capt.): critic of offensives, 488; historiography, 484; on Loudoun Heights, 267; makes map of Washington County, 147; march to Frederick, 89; Williamsport expedition, 450; Williamsport turning movement, 445

House of Commons (British), 26

Howard Benjamin (Md. pol.), 82

Howard, Oliver Otis (USA, gen.), 386, 501n.9

Howard's brigade: third phase (Sharpsburg), 386, 390

Hubbert, Mike (CSA, sgt.), 36

Huger, Benjamin (CSA, gen.), 41

Humphreys's division: arrives on Sept. 18th, 438–39; created, 210; morning of Sept. 15th, 311; planned Sept. 19th attack, 439 Hunt, Henry Jackson (USA, col.), 454–55

Hunter's Mill, Va., 52

Hyattstown, Md., 115; Confederate cavalry line, 187–89; Confederates abandon, 188; skirmish at, 122

Ijamsville Crossroads, Md., 210

Illinois troops, cavalry: 8th, 118, 122, 230, 309; Chicago Dragoons, 206

Indiana troops: cavalry (3d), 122, 230; infantry (27th), 237

Irwin's brigade: at Crampton's Gap, 279; fourth phase (Sharpsburg), 394

Iuka, Miss., 479

Jackson, Samuel K. (CSA, phys.), 72, 85
Jackson, Thomas Jonathan (CSA, gen.): advice on Maryland, 51; agrees to relieve Hood, 363; announces surrender of Harpers Ferry, 317; arrests A. P. Hill, 67–68, 74; aware of South Mountain fighting, 274; Battle of Shepherdstown, 460–61, 463–64; believes left is safe, 407; at Best's Grove, 105; brother-in-law of D. H. Hill, 89; brush with Federal cavalry, 176–77; buys cornfield, 91; cancels turning movement, 413, 426, 574n.79; commands half of army, 474; commands left on Sept. 17th, 370; communicates with D. H. Hill, 88–89; copies of S.O. 191, 152–53; correct not to attack on Sept. 16th, 359–60; crosses Potomac, 85; debates point to recross Potomac, 173–75; decides to move on Harpers Ferry, 199–200; defense of Monocacy Junction, 100; devises Harpers Ferry plan, 267; disciplinarian, 67–68, 74; Early reports to, 388–89; examines Bolivar Heights, 272; excellent performance at Shepherdstown, 465; first phase (Sharpsburg), 373, 387; forms mule-shoe defense, 364; has flags counted, 409–10; hopes Federals are gone, 433; idle at Martinsburg, 240; initially opposes Valley expedition, 147; injured, 100; isolates Miles, 270; knowledge of Harpers Ferry, 227; learns of McLaws and Walker, 228; Lee alerts of danger, 287; Lee approves Harpers Ferry plan, 318; Lee calls indomitable, 343; Lee orders to lift Harpers Ferry siege, 318; Lee orders turning movement, 407–8; Lee's appreciation of grows, 457; McLaws suggests move in Pleasant Valley to, 319; march to Chantilly, 11; march to Frederick, 88–89; march to Sharpsburg, 328–29; Martinsburg original object, 158–59, 214; meets with McLaws and Walker, 319; midday crisis, 401, 405; mobbed at Martinsburg, 199; modifies S.O. 191, 182; mule-shoe salient of, 371, 373; opens contact with McLaws, 225; ordered to cross Potomac, 85; orders firing at Harpers Ferry, 273; orders for capture of Harpers Ferry, 268–74; orders McLaws to Lower Bridge, 367; orders march to Leesburg, 66; out of touch with McLaws and Walker, 223; Ox Hill battle, 11–13; Ox Hill meeting, 18; pass for church, 102; prepares to join Lee at Sharpsburg, 318–19; progress on Sept. 10th, 175–76; progress on Sept. 11th, 182–83; progress on Sept. 12th, 199–200; receives gifts, 91; recrossing Potomac, 457; repairs Confederate left, 373; reports to Lee, 107; reports to Lee on Cemetery Hill, 334, 560n.60; restores A. P. Hill, 173; restores battery commanders, 173; revises plan for Sept. 14th, 270–71, 273–74; rides with Lige White, 89; ruse in Frederick, 173; seals fate of Harpers Ferry, 275; Second Manassas, 41, 370; second phase (Sharpsburg), 373; sends battery across Shenandoah, 274; sends Lee advice, 307; sends signal party to Walker, 226, 267; sends S.O. 191 to D. H. Hill, 152–53; sends to Lee for help, 375; sent to command left, 356; Seven Days, 40; at Sperryville, 478; strength for Valley expedition, 150–51, 159; Stuart covers crossing, 86, 88, 518n.47; Stuart's turning movement, 406–13; supports Lee's strategy, 334–35; takes command at Harpers Ferry, 227–28; takes entire command on Valley expedition, 157; tells Lee of Harpers Ferry's surrender, 307; in temporary command of D. H. Hill, 85–86, 153; third phase (Sharpsburg), 387, 391; to disrupt B&O, 158; to intercept Harpers Ferry fugitives, 158; to join Lee at Sharpsburg, 318; to move against Harpers Ferry, 198; turning movement on Sept. 18th, 441–43; turning movement to Chantilly, 1; uses Virginia roads to Sharpsburg, 319; Valley campaign, 22, 28; verbal instructions from Lee, 158; views of B. Johnson, 80–81; views on where to cross Potomac, 81–85; war council of Sept. 17th, 424; warns of Federal advance, 270–71; Williamsport turning movement, 445; withdrawal from Sharpsburg, 447. *See also* Lee–Jackson correspondence
Jackson's command (wing): arrives in Sharpsburg, 334; assigned 7th Virginia Cavalry, 163; combat experience, 358; crosses Potomac, 86–88; fatigue, 43; fatigue on Sept. 15th, 328–29; Frederick war council, 147–52; Harpers Ferry signal station, 270–71; at Manassas, 220; march through Frederick, 168–72; march to Frederick, 88–89; march to Leesburg, 55–56; march to Sharpsburg, 321–22, 328–29; nears Potomac, 331; officer cadre, 42; ordered to Leesburg, 51; orders for Valley expedition, 157–59; Ox Hill, 11–14, 16; progress on Sept. 10th, 175–76; progress on Sept. 11th, 182–83; progress on Sept. 12th, 199–200; progress on Sept. 13th,

227–28; progress on Sept. 15th, 316; recrossing Potomac, 457; regimental numbers and strengths, 37–39; remains at Boteler's Ford, 465; in reserve on Sept. 16th, 356, 358; rests on Sept. 16th, 337; secure on Sept. 13th, 240–41, 244–45; strength, 170–71; strength on Sept. 15th, 328–29; strength on Sept. 18th, 432; supports Lee's stand at Sharpsburg, 324; temporarily under D. H. Hill, 100; threat to Federal flank, 344–45; to rejoin army, 163; Walker interview, 144; withdrawal from Sharpsburg, 446

Jackson's division: arrives in Sharpsburg, 334; first phase (Sharpsburg), 370, 373; fourth phase (Sharpsburg), 393; Lee's preliminary report, 435; march through Frederick, 168–73; march to Dunkard Church, 359; march to Frederick, 99–100; march to Leesburg, 80; march to Martinsburg, 182, 199–200; march to North Mountain Depot, 182; march to Sharpsburg, 321–22, 328; move on Bolivar Heights, 273–74; nears Potomac, 331; officer cadre, 42; ordered to Dunkard Church, 356; Ox Hill, 11-12, 14; progress on Sept. 13th, 227–28; progress on Sept. 15th, 316; second phase (Sharpsburg), 373, 388; third phase (Sharpsburg), 389; in van of crossing Potomac, 86–88; weakness, 359

James River (Va.), 37; Lee fears new move on, 477–78; stalemate on, 15

James Walker's brigade. *See* Trimble's brigade

Jamieson, Perry D. (historian), 4

Janney, John (Va. pol.), 14; Lee visits, 93

Jefferson, Md., 137, 215, 280; occupied by Munford, 206; Sixth Corps at, 279; skirmish at, 234; Walker's proposed route, 180

Jenkins, Albert Gallatin (CSA, gen.), 27, 30, 97, 131

Jenkins's brigade (CSA): Battle of Boonsboro, 264; at Keedysville, 299; retreat from Turner's Gap, 291, 295

Jermantown, Va., 12

Johnson, Bradley Tyler (CSA, col.), 42; army's quality, 45; biography, 80–81, 516n.26; challenges Walker on Harpers Ferry, 143; enters Frederick, 101–2; ignores Walker's memoirs, 140; influence on Lee, 94, 114; on Lee's aims in Maryland, 83; proclamation by, 125; refutes Walker's claims, 269

Johnson, Edward (CSA, gen.), 116

Johnston, Joseph Eggleston (CSA, gen.), 22, 40; on entering Maryland (1861), 49

Johnston, Samuel R. (CSA, capt.), 361, 405, 572n.61

Joint Congressional Committee on the Conduct of the War (USA), 95

Jones, David Rumph (CSA, gen.): Lee rebukes, 575–76n.106; reports line broken, 419; war council on Sept. 17th, 424

Jones, John Robert (CSA, gen.), 80–81; arrests stragglers, 468; division commander (Jackson), 173; march to Sharpsburg, 328

Jones's artillery battalion: on left on Sept. 16th, 337; sixth phase (Sharpsburg), 417

Jones's (D. R.) division, 337; alone defends right flank, 382; arrives at Sharpsburg, 305; Battle of Boonsboro, 264; covers Lower Bridge on Sept. 15th, 326; departs Hagerstown, 254; expanded, 103; at Frosttown Gap, 267; at Keedysville, 299; Lee's preliminary report, 435–36; march through Frederick, 177; march to Boonsboro, 254; march to Hagerstown, 183–85; midday crisis, 401; no support remains, 385; occupies Hagerstown, 190; officer cadre, 42; sixth phase (Sharpsburg), 415–16, 418, 421–22; withdrawal from Sharpsburg, 447

Jones's (J. R.) brigade: enters Frederick, 102; forms line on Sept. 16th, 359; march to Frederick, 99

Jones's (J. R.) division. *See* Jackson's division

Kanawha Division (USA): commander Jacob Cox, 206; at Fox's Gap, 259, 261–62; McClellan repositions on Sept. 16th, 349; occupies Frederick, 206–7; sixth phase (Sharpsburg), 414

Kanawha Valley, Va. (W. Va.) 20, 30, 97

Kearneysville, Va. (W. Va.), 176

Kearny, Philip (USA, gen.), 13

Kearny's division, 13

Keedysville, Md., 293, 294; Confederate stand at, 299; Lee at, 298–301; Lee decides to stand at, 293–94; Lee decides not to stand at, 301; McClellan concentrates at, 312; McClellan's headquarters at, 313, 350; Morell leaves, 396

Keedysville–Williamsport Road (Md.), 350–51

Kemper's brigade: arrives at Sharpsburg, 305; Battle of Boonsboro, 264; at Keedysville, 299; march through Frederick, 177; march to Keedysville, 294–85; occupies Hagerstown, 190; on Monocacy, 121; retreat from Turner's Gap, 290; sixth phase (Sharpsburg), 420

Kemper's division, 74; merged, 103; officer cadre, 42
Kentucky, 48, 249; border, 30; Davis's proclamation ignores, 217; invasion of, 26, 28–30; rumors of sympathy, 29
Kernstown (Va.), Battle of, 93
Kershaw, Joseph Brevard (CSA, gen.), 390
Kershaw's brigade: captures Maryland Heights, 224; fifth phase (Sharpsburg), 395; fourth phase (Sharpsburg), 392; march to Burkittsville, 179; march to Maryland Heights, 201–3; on Maryland Heights, 203, 278; ordered to Pleasant Valley defensive line, 284; third phase (Sharpsburg), 391
Key, Thomas Marshall (USA, col.), 413
Key's Ford (Shenandoah), 161, 198, 204–5
Koogle's Bridge (Middletown), 232, 261
Knoxville, Md., 215, 283
Knoxville, Tenn., 28–29

Lamar, John Hill (CSA, col.), 458
Landscape Turned Red, 488
Lane's brigade. *See* Branch's brigade
Latrobe, Osmun (CSA, capt.), 417
Laurel Brigade. *See* Munford's brigade
Law, Evander McIvor (CSA, col.): skirmish in East Woods on Sept. 16th, 357–58
Law's brigade: arrives at Sharpsburg, 306; at Boonsboro, 299; retires from line on Sept. 16th, 363; second phase (Sharpsburg), 374–75; skirmish in East Woods on Sept. 16th, 357–58; transferred to Dunkard Church, 325
Lawton, Alexander Robert (CSA, gen.): division commander (Jackson), 42; march to Sharpsburg, 321, 328; second phase (Sharpsburg), 388; wounded, 373
Lawton's brigade (CSA): Battle of Shepherdstown, 458; first phase (Sharpsburg), 372–73; march to Sharpsburg, 328; reaches Dunkard Church on Sept. 16th, 360; recrossing Potomac, 457; replaces Hood on Sept. 16th, 363; second phase (Sharpsburg), 372–73; strength on Sept. 18th, 432; third phase (Sharpsburg), 388; weakness, 469
Lawton's division. *See* Ewell's division
Lee Bridge (Antietam). *See* Middle Bridge
Lee, Fitzhugh (nephew of Robert E.) (CSA, gen.), 411; on National Pike, 119; raid to Westminster, 205; reaches Sharpsburg, 325; Stuart's turning movement, 411; at Turner's Gap, 295; visits uncle, 93; withdrawal from Sharpsburg, 447–48
Lee, George Washington Custis (son of Robert E.) (CSA, gen.): visits Winchester, 474
Lee, Mary Custis (Mrs. Robert E.), 29
Lee, Robert Edward (CSA, gen.): abandons Cemetery Hill, 416; abandons wounded, 446; active operations, 61, 66, 70–71; admits Harpers Ferry might not be captured, 251; admits Maryland campaign is over, 466; against invasion, 60; aggressive nature, 491–92; alerts Jackson to danger, 287; and A. P. Hill's arrival, 382; approves Jackson's Harpers Ferry plan, 308, 318; approves Rappahannock force, 326; arrives at Leesburg, 71–72; as general in chief, 28; asks about Loring, 470; asks for former governor Lowe, 77; asks for strength returns, 194; assesses defensive line at Keedysville, 300–301; assesses midday crisis, 404–5; assesses opening attack, 369–70; assumes Davis's approval, 64; assumes Valley garrisons will flee, 148; authorizes attack east of mountains, 222–23; Battle of Shepherdstown, 460, 463; believes Federals move on Harpers Ferry, 215; believes greatest threat at Turner's Gap, 248, 250; believes Pope in command, 79; believes Valley evacuated, 115–17; best cases view, 470, 472; at Best's Grove, 105; bolsters left flank, 380; blames lost orders, 212; blames straggling, 467–68; blames worsening odds, 481; boldness, 5–6; Boonsboro war council, 287; butchery charge, 491–92; calls Longstreet Old War Horse, 425; cancels Williamsport move, 471; causes straggling, 118–19; cautions Stuart on retreat, 197; cautious on entering Pennsylvania, 219; on Cemetery Hill on Sept. 15th, 307, 324; on Cemetery Hill on Sept. 16th, 331–33; on Cemetery Hill on Sept. 17th, 370, 377–78, 402; changes base, 448; coffee from farmer's wife, 302; collects stragglers, 403; commits all of reserves, 402; concerned for McLaws and Walker, 322; concerned not to leave prisoners, 196; concerned over Federal advance, 213; confers on Harpers Ferry, 521–22n.81; confers with Jackson on Sept. 18th, 441–42; confers with Longstreet, 246; confusing description of army organization, 343; consoled by Davis, 476; consults Longstreet on Harpers Ferry, 105; corps structure, 40–41, 222; credits Longstreet with saving Turner's Gap, 340; criticized for stand at

Sharpsburg, 306–7; critics of strategy of, 489; crosses Potomac, 104, 298; countermands Jackson's order, 368; counts on Harpers Ferry to surrender, 245; Davis approves entry into Pennsylvania, 249; death, 483; decides against return to Virginia, 293; decides against withdrawal on Sept. 17th, 426; decides Jackson to join at Sharpsburg, 308; decides to end Maryland campaign, 287–88; decides to enter Maryland, 66, 70–71, 75–76, 80; decides to move to Hagerstown, 534–35n.40, 535n.41; decides to retreat from Turner's Gap, 287–88; decides to stand at Keedysville, 293–94; decides to stand behind Antietam, 301; decides to stand on Sept. 18th, 426; decides where to cross Potomac, 84; defends Richmond at a distance, 471; defensive line on Sept. 15th, 306; and demoralization of North, 490; depends on McClellan's weaknesses, 112; on decision to retire to Sharpsburg, 340–41; describes Battle of Boonsboro, 339–40; describes capture of Harpers Ferry, 342; describes Battle of Crampton's Gap, 340; describes Federal pursuit to the Antietam, 342; describes Sept. 13th situation, 339; desperation, 492; determination, 223, 241, 245, 252–53, 298, 361, 383, 427–30, 441, 443, 492; difficulties in obtaining supplies, 128; directs Stuart to hold Turner's Gap, 250; discounts Maryland uprising, 114; discourages Davis's visit, 131–33; distorts recent events, 339–43; divides Longstreet's command at Turner's Gap, 264; does not mention multiprong invasions, 470; does not mention Walker, 214; does not plan to offer battle at Sharpsburg, 333; does not underestimate McClellan, 426; doubts final success of S.O. 191, 251; Dranesville dispatch, 57–65; ends campaign against Pope, 16–19; on enemy demoralization, 57; enters Leesburg, 71–72; errs in dividing army, 166–67; establishes headquarters at Grove house, 326; estimate of Federal force, 330; expects A. P. Hill on Sept. 16th, 366; expects A. P. Hill sooner, 417; explains Maryland campaign, 480–83; explains S.O. 191 to McLaws, 164–65; explains S.O. 191 to R. H. Anderson, 165; explains Williamsport intentions, 462; fears new move on James, 477–78; Federal triple threat on Sept. 16th, 344; flanks secure on Sept. 16th, 346; focuses on Turner's Gap, 275; focus of responsibility, 9; on foreign intervention, 26; forms line on Reel Ridge, 381; forms stragglers' brigade, 408–9; Frederick war council, 145–52; at Funkstown, 190; General Orders No. 102, 72–75; General Orders No. 103, 106–7; goes into battle with large reserves, 367; goes to Gordonsville, 29, 33; grand strategy, 19–21, 31, 47, 60, 110–11, 116, 127, 135–43, 440, 471, 490–91; greets A. P. Hill, 417; growing appreciation of Jackson, 457; growing weakness of army, 297; Hagerstown as destination, 78, 133, 192; headquarters at Harrison Hall, 71–72; hears opening of battle, 369; hindsight, 7; historiography, 483–89; holds R. H. Anderson in reserve, 382; hopes to lure Federals into Valley, 477; ignorance of Crampton's Gap, 287; ignores straggling, 65; influence of B. Johnson on, 94; influence of foreign affairs on, 126; in Hagerstown, 229; in high meadow, 301–2; injured hands, 66, 72, 85, 136, 368, 476, 500n.10, 561n.27, 572n.60; instructs Stuart, 107–8; intends long stay in Maryland, 78; intends to attack McClellan, 195; intentions at Shepherdstown, 582n.93; invasion of North, 23–24; issues orders to cross Potomac, 85; Jackson reports to on Sept. 16th, 560n.16; Jackson supports strategy, 334–35; on Jackson's Maryland plan, 49; at Keedysville, 298–301; keeps Hood with army, 69; and killing of D. H. Hill's horse, 379–80; knowledge of Confederate views on invasion, 48–49; knowledge of Federal commander, 130–31, 141–42; knowledge of multiprong invasions, 27–28, 30–31, 62; learns Federals cross Upper Bridge, 344, 356; learns Federals hold Middle Bridge, 335; learns Frederick to fall, 197, 208; learns Harpers Ferry will surrender, 302; learns McLaws cannot use Solomon's Gap, 301; learns Martinsburg abandoned, 196–97; learns of Crampton's Gap, 291; learns of Federal arrival on Antietam, 324; learns of Frederick's fall, 222; learns of Harpers Ferry's surrender, 307; learns of loss of S.O. 191, 242–44, 248–49; learns of McClellan's return, 536n.67; learns of Sharpsburg's losses, 425–26; learns of Western success, 106–7; leaves Keedysville, 301; Leesburg option, 50–51; Leesburg visitors, 92; Leesburg war council, 80–85; liberation of Maryland as aim, 94; lopsided news, 191–92; loses initiative in Maryland, 168, 198–99, 252–53;

Lee, Robert Edward (*cont.*)
loses temper, 382; on lost orders, 481–82; McClellan forces battle at Sharpsburg, 360; McClellan forces battle at Sharpsburg, 360; on McClellan's return, 85; marching guidelines, 175; march to Leesburg, 70–71; meeting with Jackson-Longstreet on Sept. 2d, 500n.4, 502n.19, 510n.105, 516n.27; meets Carter, 381; meets Ramsay, 419; meets Rob (son), 407; meets S. D. Lee, 383–84; meets Stuart on Sept. 15th, 322–23; meets with E. P. Alexander, 338; meets with Jackson-Longstreet on Sept. 16th, 334, 343–45; men believe in, 45; mild rebuke of Walker, 112; minimal response on Sept. 16th, 337; miscalculates Harpers Ferry, 315; misperceives Maryland geography, 340–41; modifies campaign strategy, 195; modifies S.O. 191, 178, 183–85; move against Washington, 20–22, 58–59; movements in late morning of Sept. 17th, 402; moves to corps structure, 474; move to west, 24; move to Winchester, 474; names provost marshal, 74; on new enemy troops, 58; on news of multiprong invasions, 327; news from Richmond, 106–7; newspaper editors, 7; no word from McLaws, 223; odds faced, 31–32; operates army in halves, 457; opposes idleness, 61; opposes return to Virginia, 149; optimism, 43, 57, 330, 470; options on night of Sept. 16th, 360; orders A. P. Hill to Sharpsburg, 366; orders army's rear protected, 296–97; orders batteries from Harpers Ferry, 431; orders cavalry reunited, 93–94; orders D. H. Hill's to left, 380; orders D. H. Hill to take personal command at Turner's Gap, 248; orders G. T. Anderson's to left, 380; orders Jackson to lift Harpers Ferry siege, 318; orders for Leesburg, 51–53; orders McLaws into reserve, 368; orders McLaws to abandon siege, 284, 289, 293–94, 300; orders McLaws to go into reserve, 367; orders McLaws to hurry, 213, 247, 365; orders McLaws's to left, 381; orders Munford to hold Rohrersville, 291–92; orders Pendleton to bridge canal, 361; orders Pendleton to guard Potomac fords, 369; orders promotions, 466; orders reconnaissance at Turner's Gap, 292; orders reconnaissance on Sept. 16th, 357; orders R. H. Anderson's to Sunken Road, 384; orders Ripley to East Woods, 363; orders scout up Potomac, 333; orders straggler shot, 382; orders Stuart to warn McLaws, 198, 247; orders trains back to Sharpsburg, 338, 362; orders trains to Virginia, 333; orders turning movement on Sept. 17th, 407–8; orders wagon guards to Sharpsburg, 364; orders Walker to left, 382; orders Walker to Snavely's Ford, 366; overland campaign of 1862, 15, 490–96; ordnance shortage, 76; Ox Hill, 12–14; Ox Hill meeting, 18; passes through Frederick, 178; peace proposal, 126–27; plans move to Hagerstown, 128–29, 133; plans return to Hagerstown, 332; plans to engage Federals west of mountains, 195; plans to resume offensive, 331–33, 344; plans to threaten Maryland, 468; plans unravel, 242, 298; plans Valley expedition, 147–48; possible move through Hamburg Gap, 241; postwar comments, 585n.1; on Potomac crossing point, 192; as pragmatist, 490; prefers Turner's Gap to Sharpsburg, 246; preliminary battle report, 434–37; prepares for battle, 361–64; prepares for Maryland campaign, 52–53, 72–75, 77; prepares for Maryland reentry, 472–74; prepares for retreat from Turner's Gap, 285; president of Washington College, 480; proclamation on Maryland campaign, 477; proclamation to Marylanders, 124–25, 195; proposes clearing Valley, 146; proposes entering Maryland, 57–65; proscribes pillage, 73; proscribes straggling 73–75; protects McLaws, 249–51, 292; purchases supplies, 113; quiet October, 477; rallies stragglers on Reel Ridge, 385; reacts to D. H. Hill's article, 158, 480–81; reasons for S.O. 191, 192; receives Davis's proclamation, 216–18; on reception in Hagerstown, 193; reduces trains, 72; reevaluates Williamsport move, 461; refers to Jackson as indomitable, 343; refuses to commit Walker to left, 362–63; rejects Longstreet's advice, 246; remains at Boteler's Ford, 465; reorganizes artillery, 72–73; report from Jackson, 107; report on Longstreet's captured wagons, 467; report on Maryland campaign, 481; report on Second Manassas, 54; report on Sharpsburg withdrawal, 462; report on Shepherdstown, 467; reprimands McLaws, 213; requests returns, 466; requests supplies, 474; resists returning to Virginia, 332; response to Sept. 16th threats, 356; restores Hood, 256; retains hope on Sept. 16th, 338; reticence, 135; retires from Potomac, 474; retreat from Boonsboro, 290–91, 294–97; returns to

Boonsboro, 254; returns to Shepherdstown Road, 408; returns to Traveller, 331; reviews line at Sunken Road, 401; revises fall-back plan, 327; revises strategy, 244–45, 249, 466–67; in Richmond, 29; ride to Keedysville, 295; rides Traveller toward Dunkard Church, 383; on risk taking, 50; risks army before S.O. 191 lost, 167; route to Hagerstown closed, 356; rumored wounded, 310; satisfied with S.O. 191, 185; seeks Davis approval, 75; seeks every advantage, 219; sees arrival of A. P. Hill, 419; sees danger to McLaws, 215; sees early reunification of army, 308; sees McLaws's timely arrival, 390; sends artillery to Toombs, 420; sends for ordnance, 404; sends Jackson to command on left, 356; sends proclamation to Davis, 217; sends White to scout Valley, 146; on Sept. 16th, 331–33; in Sharpsburg on Sept. 17th, 402–3; Sharpsburg stand supported by Jackson, 324; Sharpsburg war council on Sept. 16th, 355–56; Special Orders No. 188, 93–94 (*see also* Special Orders No. 191); splits A. P. Hill's division, 417; splits main body, 183–85; stands against odds, 253; stands at Sharpsburg, 492, 496; stands to protect McLaws, 285, 300; stays at foot of Turner's Gap, 256, 284–85; straggling, 65, 94, 116–19, 218–19; straggling angers, 378; strategic dilemma, 14–15, 19–25; strategy assessed, 493–96; strategy of exhaustion, 20–21; strategy of Valley expedition, 147–49; strength of position on Sept. 15th, 328; strips right flank, 382; Stuart warns of Frederick's fall, 188–89; and Stuart's turning movement, 406–13; subsistence shortage, 76; success in failure, 8; suggests laws on straggling, 469; supplies from Hagerstown, 193; supply problems, 22; takes risks, 427; tests McLaws, 160; threatens Baltimore and Washington, 192; told of defeat at Boonsboro, 267; transfers headquarters to Shepherdstown Road, 336; tries to salvage campaign, 330–33, 430; troops from West, 61; trusts Stuart and D. H. Hill to hold Turner's Gap, 242; turning movement on Sept. 18th, 441–43; turning movements, 20, 46–47, 66, 76; unaware of Federal advance, 121–22; uncertain of Federal plans, 367; uncertain of strength, 218–20; uncertain of Walker's location, 112; unconcerned on Sept. 12th, 198; underestimates Federal advance, 129–30, 148, 165–67, 191, 195, 212, 252; underestimates Harpers Ferry garrison, 530n.111; urges Loring to Shenandoah, 30, 96–97; use of cavalry, 52–53, 162–63; use of newspapers, 79, 106–7; verbal instructions to Jackson, 158; view of Federal inactivity, 343; view of McClellan, 140–42; views Franklin as threat to communications, 343; views Sharpsburg as enemy will see, 302; visits Alexandria, 21; visits Dunkard Church, 406–7; visits Jackson, 572–73n.62; visits J. Janney, 93; visits Reel Ridge, 402; visits Squire's battery, 404; visits Sunken Road, 384; Walker interview, 133–45; walks to Hagerstown Pike, 381; war council on Sept. 17th, 424–29; on weakness of army, 469; Williamsport option, 360; Williamsport turning movement, 444–45; withdrawal from Sharpsburg, 445–48; withdraw to south, 23. *See also* Lee–Cooper correspondence; Lee–Davis correspondence; Lee–Davis relationship; Lee–A. P. Hill correspondence; Lee–D. H. Hill correspondence; Lee–G. W. C. Lee correspondence; Lee–G. W. Smith correspondence; Lee–Jackson correspondence; Lee–Longstreet correspondence; Lee–Loring correspondence; Lee–McLaws correspondence; Lee–Mrs. Lee correspondence; Lee–Munford correspondence; Lee–Pendleton correspondence; Lee–Randolph correspondence; Lee–Stuart correspondence

Lee, Robert Edward "Rob," Jr. (son of Robert E.) (CSA, pvt.): crosses Potomac, 88; visits father, 93, 407

Leesborough, Md., 109

Lee, Stephen Dill (CSA, col.): artillery fire on Sept. 15th, 325; meets Lee, 383–84; sixth phase (Sharpsburg), 419–20; third phase (Sharpsburg), 390; turning movement on Sept. 18th, 442–43; war council on Sept. 17th, 424

Lee, William Henry Fitzhugh "Rooney" (son of Robert E.) (CSA, gen.): visits father, 93; wounded, 309–10

Lee–A. P. Hill correspondence: Sept. 17th, 366

Lee–Cooper correspondence: Sept. 8th, 123

Lee–Davis correspondence, 308; Aug. 26th, 36; Aug. 30th, 75; Sept. 3d, 30, 54–55, 57–65; Sept. 4th, 75–80, 83, 516n.22; Sept. 5th, 94–97; Sept. 6th, 104; Sept. 7th, 112–19; Sept. 8th, 120–27; Sept. 9th, 127–33; Sept. 11th, 192–96; Sept. 12th,

Lee–Davis correspondence (*cont.*)
158–59; Sept. 13th, 215–22; Sept. 16th, 212, 339–43; Sept. 18th, 434–37; Sept. 20th, 461–63; Sept. 21st, 467–70; Sept. 25, 471; Sept. 28th, 476–77; Oct. 22, 478
Lee–Davis relationship, 57, 486; on Maryland proclamation, 124; on reinforcements, 33
Lee–D. H. Hill correspondence: Sept. 13th, 236–37, 244, 248; Sept. 14th, 255, 259, 271; Feb. 21, 1868, 482
Lee–G. W. C. Lee correspondence: Nov. 7, 478
Lee–G. W. Smith correspondence: Sept. 7th, 116–17; Sept. 15th, 326–27; Sept. 24th, 472
Lee–Jackson correspondence: Sept. 11th, 192; Sept. 12th, 196–97, 199–200; Sept. 13th, 245, 247, 542–43n.72, 547n.45; Sept. 14th, 271, 274–75, 286–88, 294, 547n.55; Sept. 15th, 302, 307–8, 317–18, 322–24, 554n.22, 556n.40, 557–58n.51; Sept. 20, 464
Lee–Longstreet correspondence: Sept. 13th, 246; Sept. 14th, 285; Sept. 16th, 333
Lee–Loring correspondence: Sept. 25th, 471
Lee–McLaws correspondence: Sept. 13th, 213–15, 223, 225, 247, 250–51; Sept. 14th, 271, 282–84, 289, 293, 299; Sept. 15th, 300; Sept. 16th, 338, 365
Lee–Mrs. Lee correspondence: Oct. 12th, 476
Lee–Munford correspondence: Sept. 14th, 291–92; Sept. 15th, 300–301, 552n.3
Lee–Pendleton correspondence: Sept. 16th, 361–62; Sept. 17th, 369, 404; Sept. 19th, 450
Lee–Randolph correspondence: Sept. 7th, 116
Lee–Stuart correspondence: Sept. 11th, 188–89, 214; Sept. 12th, 196–98, 208; Sept. 13th, 222–23, 232, 234–35, 242–44; Sept. 14th, 249–50, 283, 294; Sept. 15th, 300; Sept. 16th, 355
Lee–Walker interview, 133–145
Lee's artillery battalion: arrives at Sharpsburg, 304–5; on Confederate left on Sept. 16th, 337; crosses Potomac, 112; first phase (Sharpsburg), 370; at Keedysville, 299; march to Keedysville, 294; sixth phase (Sharpsburg), 420
Lee's brigade, 234, 337; at Alexandria, 57; Chantilly, 11; covers Confederate left on Sept. 16th, 356; covers march to Leesburg, 52; crosses Potomac, 89–90; detachments for Valley expedition, 163; at Dranesville, 67; at New Market, 115; operations on Sept. 13th, 231; Poolesville skirmish, 90; pursues Pope, 16–19; reaches Sharpsburg, 325; rearguard at Turner's Gap, 295, 299; rearguard on Sept. 20th, 465; recrossing Potomac, 457; returns to Boonsboro, 257, 275; reunited, 354; rides to Frederick, 107; skirmish at Boonsboro, 310–24; Stuart's turning movement, 411; welcomed in Poolesville, 90–91; Westminster mission, 188, 205; withdrawal from Sharpsburg, 446–48
Lee's Bridge (Antietam). *See* Middle Bridge (Antietam)
Leesburg, Va., 52; abandoned, 133; Confederate march to, 51–54; Confederates enter, 66; Davis to visit, 131; D. H. Hill passes through, 71; Lee considers move to, 24, 50–51, 59; Munford's mission, 14; skirmish, 52–53; supply line, 147, 156; Taylor visits, 155–56; war council, 80–85; welcomes Confederates, 55, 70, 92
Leesburg Turnpike (Va.), 51, 55
Lexington, Ky., 29
Liberal party (British), 26
Liberty, Md., 188
Library of Congress (Washington, D.C.), 152
Licksville Crossroads, Md., 210, 230, 279
Light division. *See* Hill's (A. P.) division
Light's Ford (Potomac), 182, 299; Williamsport expedition, 450; Williamsport turning movement, 444–45
Lincoln, Abraham (USA, pres.): Bragg rumor, 119; call for militia (1861), 49; call for troops (July 1862), 32; Emancipation Proclamation, 1, 4; Harpers Ferry mistakes, 315; relieves McClellan, 479; relieves Porter, Franklin, and Griffin, 98; for speedy war, 20; as success, 7–8; telegram to McClellan, 209, 237; weak in strategy, 22
Lincoln administration: anxiety over Maryland, 47, 94; Confederate peace proposal, 126; fear for Washington, 61, 70–71, 136, 142
Lincoln, Mary Todd (Mrs. Abraham), 237
Line (George) farm: Twelfth Corps bivouac, 353
Little River Turnpike (Va.), 11–12, 17, 51–52
Long, Armistead Lindsay (CSA, col.), 57, 76, 213–15, 223, 300; courier to Walker, 382; historiography, 484
Longstreet, James (CSA, gen.), 259, 261; advice on Maryland, 51; advises retreat from Turner's Gap, 267; advises stand at Sharpsburg, 246; approves entering Maryland, 484; arrives at Sharpsburg, 304; Battle of Shepherdstown, 463–64; at Best's Grove, 105; Boonsboro war council, 287; Chantilly, 13; commands half of army, 474;

confers with D. H. Hill, 256; confers with Lee, 246, 521–22n.81; copy of S.O. 191, 152–53; critical of Jackson on Sept. 16th, 359; critical of Lee, 484; at Culpeper, 478; decides retreat is necessary, 285, 287; D. H. Hill urges to hurry, 264; Frederick war council, 149–52; at Funkstown, 190; headquarters at Grove house, 326; heroic leadership, 397, 405; historiography, 484; ignores Walker's memoirs, 140, 143; and killing of D. H. Hill's horse, 379–80; Lee calls Old War Horse, 425; with Lee on Cemetery Hill on Sept. 16th, 334; Lee consults on Harpers Ferry, 105; midday crisis, 401, 405; modifies S.O. 191, 149–52; objects to going to Hagerstown, 183–84; objects to stand at Turner's Gap, 246; offers Wilcox for Valley expedition, 178; on Maryland campaign as watershed, 493; opposes division of army, 149–50; opposes stand at South Mountain, 484; ordered to cross Potomac, 85–86; ordered to Leesburg, 51; orders artillery duel to end, 336; orders R. H. Anderson into reserve, 367; Ox Hill meeting, 18; recrossing Potomac, 457; retreat from Turner's Gap, 291; Second Manassas, 30, 41; sent to Gordonsville, 33; serves artillery, 572n.59; Seven Days, 40; Seven Pines, 40; Stuart's turning movement, 412; takes command at Turner's Gap, 266, 285; urges main body stay at Boonsboro, 150; Williamsport turning movement, 445; withdrawal from Sharpsburg, 447; war council on Sept. 17th, 425. *See also* Lee–Longstreet correspondence

Longstreet's command (wing): arrives at Sharpsburg, 304; assigned 1st Va. Cavalry, 163; Battle of Shepherdstown, 460, 463; crosses Potomac, 103; departs Hagerstown, 254; fatigue, 43; few casualties on Sept. 16th, 335; at Hagerstown, 197, 214; Hagerstown original object, 149; at Manassas, 220; march through Frederick, 177; march to Big Spring, 92; march to Boonsboro, 254, 545n.29; march to Hagerstown, 183–85, 190; march to Keedysville, 294; march to Leesburg, 55–56, 67; march to Monocacy Junction, 111; officer cadre, 42; orders for Valley expedition, 159; ordnance wagons captured, 296, 467; Ox Hill, 12; progress on Sept. 10th, 177–78; progress on Sept. 11th, 183–85, 190; recrossing Potomac, 457; regimental numbers and strengths, 37–39; remains at Boteler's Ford, 465; retreat from Turner's Gap, 290–91; safe on Sept. 13th, 240–41, 244–45; strength, 170–71; strength on Sept. 18th, 432; wagon's captured, 404; withdrawal from Sharpsburg, 446

Loring William Wing (CSA, gen.): captures Charleston, 327; Lee congratulates, 471; Lee directs to Martinsburg, 96–97; Lee requests news of, 470; multiprong invasions, 27, 29–30, 131; relieved from command, 479

Lost orders. *See* Special Orders No. 191

Loudoun County, Va., 11, 48; Lee's option, 59; nearby fords, 83; supply rich, 24, 51, 59, 502n.44

Loudoun Heights (Blue Ridge Mountains), 201; artillery fire from, 316–17, 546–47n44; on Sept. 14th, 268–71; rugged terrain, 226; signals established, 225, 227; undefended, 316; view from, 222; Walker occupies, 226; Walker's object, 161, 204; Walker's role on, 149

Loudoun Rangers, 14, 52

Loudoun Valley (Va.),

Louisiana troops, artillery: Eshleman, 405; Miller, 397, 419; Richardson, 419; Squires, 378, 404; Washington, 51, 112–13, 304, 331, 417

Lovell's brigade: Battle of Shepherdstown, 465

Lovettsville, Va., 161; Walker's route, 204

Lowe, Enoch Louis (Md. former gov.), 77, 113, 124, 131, 195–96; to Winchester, 156

Lower (Burnside) Bridge (Antietam), 118; Confederates occupy on Sept. 15th, 325–26; delay in carrying, 571n.48; Federal intentions at, 370; Federals carry, 398, 400, 406; Lee's preliminary report, 436; McClellan visits on Sept. 16th, 349–50; midday crisis, 401, 405; military geography of, 305, 345–46, 400; second phase (Sharpsburg), 377; situation on Sept. 18th, 439; sixth phase (Sharpsburg), 414, 416, 418, 420, 422; strength of position, 347; threat abates, 357; threatened on Sept. 16th, 344, 356; Toombs ordered to, 305; vulnerable, 382–83; Williamsport, turning movement, 444

Lurray, Va.: supply line, 95, 123, 136

Lynchburg, Va., 24, 34, 95

McClellan, George Brinton (USA, gen.), 292; abandons battle plans, 414; advance against Lee, 109, 119, 121, 167, 229–30; advance from Turner's Gap, 308–15; aims to relieve Harpers Ferry, 241; Antietam battle plans,

McClellan, George Brinton (*cont.*) 347–49; Antietam grand tactics, 344–54; approves Burnside's Sept. 14th plans, 263; battle plans, 563n.48; believes Confederate main body at Boonsboro, 240; cancels Sept. 18th attack, 438–40; cautious approach to the Antietam, 309; cautious approach on Sept. 16th, 331; claims victory, 452–53; complications of Harpers Ferry for, 315; concentration at Keedysville, 312; confusing reports, 108–9; considers sending Pleasonton on turning movement, 314; considers Sixth Corps attack, 413–14; crosses Antietam on Sept. 16th, 350–51; crosses Potomac at Berlin, 478; decides against new campaign, 453; decides main effort to be at Turner's Gap, 240; decides secondary effort to be at Crampton's Gap, 240; delay in naming to field command, 130–31; dilemma of relieving Harpers Ferry, 239; entry into Frederick, 229; establishes signal stations, 84; estimate of Confederate force, 330; expects Lee to stand at Boonsboro, 311; as failure, 8; fears Jackson turning movement, 210; final Burnside orders, 413; focus of responsibility, 9; forces Lee to battle at Sharpsburg, 360; forces South Mountain, 430; forms Antietam line on Sept. 15th, 314; grand strategy, 440; Harpers Ferry mistakes, 315; at Harrison's Landing, 15; headquarters at Bolivar, 311; headquarters at Boonsboro, 312; headquarters at Keedysville, 350; headquarters at Pry house, 352–53; headquarters in Frederick, 237; hinge in Lee's line his object, 348; historiography, 483, 486–87; Hooker visits headquarters, 350; ill on Sept. 18th, 440; impatience with Burnside, 399; initiative passes to, 210–11, 252; Jackson threatens flank on Sept. 16th, 344–45; learns Confederates divide army, 229; learns Harpers Ferry unsurrendered, 240; learns of Confederate crossing, 84; learns of French and Richardson, 399; learns of Harpers Ferry's surrender, 311–12; learns of Ninth Corps delay at Fox's Gap, 312; learns of Sedgwick's route, 399; learns of threat to Hagerstown, 455; learns of threat to Williamsport, 454; learns reasons Lee divides army, 238; Lee's views on, 85, 140–42; Lincoln relieves, 479; meets Sumner at East Woods, 413–14; meets Sumner at Keedysville, 313; misled by terms of S.O. 191, 238–39, 260; moves headquarters to Keedysville, 313; moves headquarters to Rockville, 119; moves to Urbana, 210; on nature of Jackson's recrossing, 229; new James move blocked, 478; news of Confederates on Sept. 10th, 181; news of Confederates on Sept. 11th, 189–90; news of Confederates on Sept. 12th, 209–11; offers support to Hooker, 350–51; orders Couch to Williamsport, 454; orders Fifth Corps to Shepherdstown, 454; orders Second Corps to support Hooker, 385; orders First Corps to cross Antietam, 350; orders First Corps up the Antietam, 314; orders for Franklin at Crampton's Gap, 279; orders Hooker to press pursuit, 311; orders Pennsylvania militia to Keedysville, 438; orders Pleasonton to verify S.O. 191, 239; orders Porter to precede Burnside, 312; orders Sixth Corps to Sharpsburg, 353; orders Sixth Corps to Shepherdstown, 454; orders Twelfth Corps to support Hooker, 353; perception of Confederate strength, 239; plans for Sept. 14th, 240–41; plans for Sept. 15th, 310–15; plans to attack on Sept. 18th, 438; plans to attack on Sept. 19th, 440; plans to carry Turner's Gap, 260; possession of S.O. 191 reported by Stuart, 233, 242–43, 248–49; progress before finding S.O. 191, 230; pursuit on Sept. 19th, 452–56; puzzled by Confederates, 209; receives S.O. 191, 237; reception in Frederick, 237; reduces Lee's options, 210–11; refuses to send Second Corps on Sept. 16th, 353; relief of Harpers Ferry, 215; relieved, 2; restores morale, 84, 99; revises battle plans, 352–53, 385, 399, 414, 414; rides to East Woods, 413–14; scouts Confederate artillery, 313–14; second visit to East Woods, 438; seizes initiative, 229–30; selection of attacking units, 348; sends Twelfth Corps to Maryland Heights, 453; Seven Days, 111; siege of Richmond, 59; sixth phase (Sharpsburg), 401; S.O. 191's information, 237; S.O. 191's omissions, 238; strategic defense of Washington, 22; suggests Pleasonton attack, 399; suspects Confederate move on Harpers Ferry, 209; suspends Burnside's attack, 398; takes command at Turner's Gap, 263; telegram from Lincoln, 209; telegram to Lincoln, 237; thwarts Lee, 444; thwarts Williamsport move, 470–71; timidity, 5–6; too rapid an advance to South Mountain, 269, 271, 274; tours South Mountain battlefields, 312;

unable to destroy Confederates, 241; understands military geography, 95; views Sharpsburg from Lee's earlier vantage, 314; visits First Corps, 350–51; visits Ninth Corps, 349–50; visits Sharpsburg, 453; withdrawal from James, 33–34, 41

McGuire, Hunter (CSA, surg.), 407, 429

Machiavelli, Niccolo, 7

McLaws, LaFayette (CSA, gen.), 257, 259, 261, 287; adds R. H. Anderson's division, 150; arrival at Sharpsburg, 566–67n.86, 567n.1; assesses position after Crampton's Gap, 283–84; attacks at West Woods, 401; believes outnumbered, 319; brings guns to Maryland Heights, 271; captures Maryland Heights, 224; copy of S.O. 191, 152–53; crosses to Harpers Ferry, 557n.56; decides on desperate defense, 283–84; defensive line in Pleasant Valley, 282; defensive plan for South Mountain, 276–78; delays leaving Harpers Ferry, 328; disobeys Lee, 284; encounters Longstreet-Jackson, 366–67; falls behind schedule, 204; Federals in rear of, 226; at first unconcerned for rear, 278; friend of R.H. Anderson, 165; heavy responsibilities, 179; ignorance of affairs, 200; ignorance of Harpers Ferry, 165; Jackson signals on Sept. 14th, 270–71; Jackson to cooperate, 200; joins Lee, 55; lacks information, 223–24; learns enemy in rear, 271; learns of Harpers Ferry's surrender, 317; learns of Jackson's approach, 225; leaves escape route, 225; Lee explains S.O. 191 to, 164–65; Lee orders to abandon Maryland Heights, 284, 289, 293–94, 300; Lee orders to hurry, 213, 247; Lee protects, 292; Lee reprimands, 213; Lee sees as endangered, 215; Lee's preliminary report, 435; Lee tests, 160; makes contact with Walker, 225; march to Sharpsburg, 365; meets with Jackson, 319; not in Lee's confidence, 135; ordered to Leesburg, 52; orders Cobb to hold mountain gaps, 278; orders from Jackson, 269–71; orders Wilcox to Brownsville, 279; out of touch with Lee, 191–92, 223; out of touch with McLaws and Walker, 223; pulls back in Pleasant Valley, 311–12; reports to Lee, 367–68; rides up Maryland Heights, 276; signals to Jackson through Walker, 271; slow to rejoin Lee, 320–21, 365; S.O. 191 deadlines, 198; S.O. 191 complications, 186–87; Stuart to warn, 198, 247; on straggling, 44; suggests Jackson move in Pleasant Valley, 319; tactical plans, 201–2; third phase (Sharpsburg), 391–92; to capture Maryland Heights, 159–60; to capture Harpers Ferry garrison, 160; trapped in Pleasant Valley, 282–84; underemploys R.H. Anderson, 278; visits Charlestown, 365; withdrawal from Pleasant Valley, 319

McLaws's command: approaches Sharpsburg, 366; bivouacs near Potomac, 365; crosses into Harpers Ferry, 320; enlarged by Wilcox's division, 178; fatigue on Sept. 15–16th, 320, 365; fords Potomac, 365; lacks cavalry, 163; Lee protects, 250–51; march through Frederick, 169–72, 178; march to Halltown, 365; orders for Valley expedition, 159–60; progress on Sept. 10th, 179, 533n.25; progress on Sept. 11, 187; progress on Sept. 12th, 201–4; progress on Sept. 13th, 223–26; progress on Sept. 15th, 320; rear exposed, 188; rear threatened, 274–75; strength for Valley expedition, 150–51, 160, 170–71, 178; subsistence shortage, 223; to rejoin army, 163; vulnerable on Sept. 13th, 241, 244–45

McLaws's division: arrives at Hagerstown Pike, 384; artillery, 72; at Big Spring, 92; crosses Potomac, 103; fourth phase (Sharpsburg), 393; free to rejoin Lee, 308; Lee protects, 249; Lee's preliminary report, 435–37; march from Richmond, 34–37; march to Leesburg, 55; march to Monocacy Junction, 111; midday crisis, 401; ordered to left, 381; outside corps structure, 41; progress on Sept. 13th, 223–26; regimental numbers and strengths, 37–39; strength on Sept. 18th, 432; third phase (Sharpsburg), 387, 390–91

McRae, Duncan Kirkland (CSA, col.): commander Garland's brigade (D.H. Hill), 258, 375

McRae's brigade. *See* Garland's brigade

McReynolds, Andrew Thomas (USA, col.), 230–31

McWhiney, Grady (historian), 489

Magilton, Albert Lewis (USA, col.), 373

Magruder, John Bankhead (CSA, gen.), 41

Mahone's brigade (CSA), 202; at Crampton's Gap, 202, 275, 281, 291

Malvern Hill, Va., 309, 345

Manassas battlefield: abandoned arms, 96, 123, 220

Manassas, Battle of. *See* First Bull Run; Second Manassas

Manassas Junction, Va., 15, 24; supply line, 136
Manassas-Centreville-Fairfax line, 22
Manning, Vannoy Hartrog (CSA, col.): fourth phase (Sharpsburg), 392
Manning's brigade. *See* Walker's (J. G.) brigade
Mansfield, Joseph King Fenno (USA, gen.): first phase (Sharpsburg), 372; morning of Sept. 15th, 311; mortally wounded, 375; new to command, 349
Mansfield's Corps. *See* Twelfth Corps (USA)
Marcy, Randolph Barnes (USA, gen.), 459
Market Street (Frederick), 101, 172
Marshall, Charles (CSA, col.): historiography, 484; ignores Walker's memoirs, 140; on Lee, 61–62; proclamation to Marylanders, 124
Marshall, Humphrey (CSA, gen.): multiprong invasions, 27, 29–30, 106, 131, 327
Martinsburg, Va. (W. Va.), 225; abandoned by Federals, 199; Confederates to capture, 136; Federal garrison, 24; garrison expected to flee, 146, 148; Jackson approaches, 182–83; Jackson's original object, 148, 158–59; Lee bivouacs at, 467; Lee directs Loring to, 96–97; McClellan learns role in S.O. 191 of, 238; occupied by Confederates, 199; size of garrison, 137, 213–14; threat to supply line, 145–47, 316; White sent to, 116; Williamsport expedition, 450; Williamsport turning movement, 444, 465
Martinsburg–Shepherdstown Road (Va., W. Va.), 460
Martinsburg–Williamsport Road (Va., W. Va.), 446
Maryland, 26; Confederate aim to liberate, 48–49, 57–58, 94; Confederate debts, 113; Confederate view as suppresses, 48–49, 82; Confederate volunteers, 125, 288; Davis's proclamation ignores, 217; German Americans, 82; hospitality, 91–92; Lee ponders entering, 57–65; Lee's reasons for entering, 57–65; legislature, 82; maps of, 344, 356; political conditions, 81–82; political vulnerability, 47; proclamation by Lee, 124–25; proclamations issued, 525n.35; provisions dwindle, 128; reception of Confederates, 90–92, 112–14, 518–19n.50; Southern sympathizers, 81–82; subsistence from, 77; unionism, 516n.30; uprising unlikely, 82, 114; western Maryland, 48, 77, 81–82, 110, 193, 196
Maryland campaign of 1862: analysis of S.O. 191, 152–64; cavalry preparations, 52–53; Chambersburg as Lee's aim, 78; comparative army strengths, 330, 344; compared to Gettysburg, 482–83; Confederate congressional resolution on, 216, 539n.5; Confederate critics, 586–87n.18, 587n.26; Confederate interpretations, 485; Confederate reception in Maryland, 90–92; Confederates cross Potomac, 86–88, 103–4; Confederates trapped at Sharpsburg, 356; Confederate strength, 170–71, 185–86; Confederate strategic aims, 48–50; Confederate volunteers, 125; Davis approves Pennsylvania entry, 219; Davis's approval, 64; D. H. Hill crosses Potomac, 86–88; drama of, 8; Federals find S.O. 191, 237–38; Frederick war council, 145–52; Hagerstown as Lee's aim, 78; Harpers Ferry becomes siege, 227–28; historiography, 1–10, 483–89; initiative shifts to Federals, 252; Jackson's march to Frederick, 88–89; Jackson takes command at Harpers Ferry, 227–28; Lee admits over, 466; Lee decides against return to Virginia, 293; Lee decides on, 66, 70–71, 75–76, 80; Lee decides to end, 287–88; Lee decides where to cross Potomac, 84; Lee explains, 480–83; Lee intends to attack McClellan, 195; Lee loses initiative in, 168, 198–99, 253; Lee modifies strategy, 195, 244–45, 249; Lee orders Potomac crossed, 85; Lee proposes, 57–65; Lee reports, 481; Lee's determination in, 241, 245, 252; Lee's peace proposal, 126–27; Lee's proclamation, 124–25; Lee's strategy, 123, 127, 183–85, 195; Lee seeks approval, 75; Lee tries to salvage, 245–46, 253, 302–3; Longstreet crosses Potomac, 103; loss blamed on D. H. Hill, 235; loss of S.O. 191, 152–53; McClellan's battle plans, 347–49; McClellan seizes initiative, 229–30; McClellan's grand tactics, 344–54; march to Leesburg, 66–70; Maryland provisions dwindle, 128; not for liberation, 83, 94; not invasion, 60, 76–78, 83, 139–40; preliminary raid for, 52, 66, 70–71, 76; preparation for, 72–75; proclamations issued, 525n.35; railroads in, 9; risks of, 60–61; in shambles, 295; Sharpsburg war council on Sept. 16th, 355–56; solution to Lee's dilemma, 47; strategy assessed, 493–94; Stuart's performance in, 114–15, 121–22, 129–30, 166–67, 180, 185, 188–89, 205; supplies in Hagerstown, 193; telegraph in, 9; as turning movement, 46–47; Walker interview, 133–45; war's watershed, 493; watershed of,

168, 252. *See also* Boonsboro, Battle of; Crampton's Gap, Battle of; Harpers Ferry, siege of; Sharpsburg, Battle of; Shepherdstown, Battle of; Valley expedition
Maryland Heights (South Mountain), 201–4, 213, 227, 300; artillery fire from, 316–17; key to Harpers Ferry, 148–49, 160, 200; McClellan learns role in S.O. 191, 238; McLaws abandons, 284; McLaws brings guns to, 271; McLaws captures, 224; McLaws to capture, 159–60; rugged terrain of, 203, 224; on Sept. 14th, 268–71; signal station, 84; skirmish, 203; Twelfth Corps occupies, 453; weakly defended, 316
"Maryland! My Maryland," 86, 102, 476
Maryland troops (CSA), 49; infantry (1st), 80, 125
Maryland troops (USA): cavalry (1st), 176; Coles battalion, 53; Potomac Home Brigade battalion, 100
Mason-Dixon Line, 78
Mason's Ford (Potomac): Williamsport expedition, 451
Mason's Island, Md., 86
Massachusetts troops, 49; cavalry (1st), 98, 117, 230
Meade, George Gordon (USA, gen.): first phase (Sharpsburg), 370; on Sept. 16th, 351
Meade's division: bivouacs on Sept. 16th, 354; crosses Antietam, 350; first phase (Sharpsburg), 372; at Frosttown Gap, 266–67, 282; skirmish on Sept. 16th, 351–52, 358
Means, Samuel (USA, capt.), 14
Meagher, Thomas Francis (USA, gen.), 397
Meagher's brigade: fifth phase (Sharpsburg), 397
Mercersville, Md., 346
Mexican War, 141, 440
Michigan troops: infantry (4th), 455–56, 459
Midday crisis, Battle of Sharpsburg, 401–6
Middle (Lee) Bridge (Antietam), 303; bombardment on Sept. 16th, 344; Federal intentions, 370; Federals seize, 331, 560–61n.19; Federals threaten from on Sept. 16th, 356; guarded by Evans's brigade, 380; midday crisis, 401, 405; military geography of, 345–46; Morell replaces Richardson at, 385; sixth phase (Sharpsburg), 415–16, 418, 422
Middlebrook, Md.: Sumner to, 166
Middleburg, Md., 79; Confederate advance, 130, 194
Middletown, Md., 137, 231, 262–63; Jackson confuses, 272; Jackson's route, 157, 173–76; McLaws's route, 159, 178; skirmish at, 232; Stuart abandons, 242; Stuart at, 207, 232; Sykes at, 311; Walker's proposed route, 180
Middletown Valley (Md.), 213–14, 222, 250; Federals appear in, 236
Miles, Dixon (USA, col.): discovers danger, 189–90; firing heard from, 240; holds through Sept. 14th, 268–75; mistakes, 316; mortally wounded, 317; news of Confederates, 181; ordered to hold Harpers Ferry, 99; relief for, 230; telegram to Halleck, 190; surrender demanded, 268
Military geography, 78–79, 95
Military intelligence, 9–10, 38, 79, 141–42
Miller (David R.) farm: first phase (Sharpsburg), 372; second phase (Sharpsburg), 374; skirmish on Sept. 16th, 358
Miller (D. R.) Cornfield: first phase (Sharpsburg), 370, 373, 387; Lee's preliminary report, 434–36; second phase (Sharpsburg), 374–77; on Sept. 16th, 358; stragglers' brigade, 408; third phase (Sharpsburg), 386, 388
Mississippi, 131
Mississippi troops: cavalry (Jeff. Davis Legion), 207, 232
—infantry: 13th, 284, 393; 17th, 392; 18th, 122, 393; 21st, 393
Mississippi River, 28; Confederate resolution on, 218
Missouri, 48
Mobile, Ala., 28
Monocacy Aqueduct (C&O), Md., 71, 181; undamaged, 105; Walker mission, 135–37, 180
Monocacy Junction, Md., 100, 105; bridge, 111; Jackson at, 100; Longstreet at, 111; McLaws at, 111; R. H. Anderson at, 111
Monocacy River (Md.), 77; line of, 112; valley, 99
Montague, Edgar Burwell (CSA, col.), 280
Montgomery County, Md.: slave population, 91
Monument Hill (South Mountain), 311
Moor, August (USA, col.): captured, 206–7; warns Cox, 261
Moor's brigade: occupies Frederick, 206–7
Moore, Edward Alexander (CSA, pvt.), 43
Morell's division: march to Brookeville, 210; morning of Sept. 15th, 311; ordered to

Morell's division (*cont.*)
support Franklin, 414; replaces Richardson's division, 385, 396; at Shepherdstown, 455; situation on Sept. 18th, 439
Morgan, John Hunt (CSA, col.), 28–29, 503n.35
Morgantown, Va (W. Va.), 472
Morrison, Joseph G. (CSA, capt.), 152
Mountain House (Turner's Gap), 234, 292, 294; D. H. Hill's headquarters, 256, 258-59, 264, 266, 287; lookout station, 259
Multiprong invasions. *See* Confederate strategy
Mumma (Samuel) farm: fifth phase (Sharpsburg), 395; second phase (Sharpsburg), 376; third phase (Sharpsburg), 387
Mumma dale: first phase (Sharpsburg), 370; second phase (Sharpsburg), 376–77
Munford, Thomas Taylor (CSA, col.), 11, 287, 293–94, 552n.3; Battle of Shepherdstown, 458; brigade commander (Stuart), 93, 104; calls on McLaws for help, 280; commands at Crampton's Gap, 275–76; defense of Crampton's Gap, 280–82; guards Snavely's Ford, 337; Lee orders to cover McLaws's retreat, 291–92; Lee orders to hold Rohrersville, 291–92; reaches Sharpsburg, 325; retreat from Crampton's Gap, 291; tells Lee McLaws cannot use Solomon's Gap, 301. *See also* Lee–Munford correspondence
Munford's brigade, 175, 251; almost fires on Hampton, 233–34; Battle of Shepherdstown, 458; at Big Spring, 92; Chantilly, 11; covers Leesburg march, 52–53; at Crampton's Gap, 275; defense of Crampton's Gap, 280–82; detachments for Valley expedition, 163; falls back to Burkittsville, 231; falls back to Crampton's Gap, 231; guards right flank, 558n.56; operations on Sept. 13th, 231-32, 234; Pimmitt Run action, 67, 71; Poolesville abandoned, 122; pursues Pope, 17; reaches Sharpsburg, 325; rearguard for crossing, 89, 104; retires to Rohrersville, 291; ride to Jefferson, 206; ride to Urbana, 115; at Rohrersville, 299; on Sept. 16th, 337; sixth phase (Sharpsburg), 401, 420; skirmish at Sugar Loaf, 180–88; Stuart seeks, 318; Williamsport expedition, 450; withdrawal from Sharpsburg, 446, 448
Murfin James V. (historian), 4, 487
Myer farm (Md.), 153, 180
Nagle's brigade: sixth phase (Sharpsburg), 414
Narrows, Va., 97
National Archives (Washington, D.C.), 152
National Pike (Md.), 115, 119, 130, 157, 167, 182–83, 260, 264, 295; D. H. Hill's route, 208; Federals advance on, 236; Jackson's route, 173–76; Longstreet's return to Boonsboro on, 254; Longstreet's route, 190; Stuart's defense of, 188, 233; under repair, 309
Neersville, Va., 226
Neese, George Michael (CSA, corp.), 92
Nelson, William (USA, gen.), 106
Nelson, William (CSA, maj.), 464
Nelson's artillery battalion: to guard Boteler's Ford, 294, 337; Williamsport expedition, 451; withdrawal from Sharpsburg, 446, 458
New Hampshire troops: infantry (5th), 324
New Industry Md., 411
New Jersey troops: infantry (14th), 100
New Market, Md., 115, 210; Confederate cavalry line, 187–89; Federals occupy, 189
Newton Hall, Va., 67
New York, N.Y., 78
New York Times, 1
New York troops: artillery (B, 1st), 313; cavalry (1st), 230
—infantry: 9th, 230; 34th, 390–91, 395; 51st, 401, 414; 89th, 230; 103d, 230; 126th, 225
Nicodemus Hill (Heights): Confederates retake, 429; first phase (Sharpsburg), 370, 372, 387; object of Federals on Sept. 18th, 438; object of Federals on Sept. 19th, 440; second phase (Sharpsburg), 373; on Sept. 16th, 364; Stuart's turning movement, 410; turning movement on Sept. 18th, 442
Nicodemus Mill, Md., 313
Ninth Corps (USA): advance against Lee, 129–30; approaches Turner's Gap, 236; arrives at the Antietam, 313; condition on Sept. 16th, 348; condition on Sept. 18th, 439, 578n.29; crosses Potomac, 84; delays in pursuit, 312; forms Antietam line on Sept. 15th, 311; at Fox's Gap, 259, 262–66; in Frederick, 230, 239; to Leesborough, 109; McClellan repositions on Sept. 16th, 349–50; march to Brookeville, 121; moves on Turner's Gap, 242; occupies Frederick, 206–7, 210; Ox Hill, 12; repulse, 470; retreat to Washington, 19; to Seventh Street, 99; situation on Sept. 18th, 439; sixth phase (Sharpsburg), 400–401, 414, 420, 422; to attack on Sept. 19th, 440; in Washington, 62

Nisbet, James Cooper (CSA, capt.), 403
Nolan, Alan T. (historian), 489
Noland's Ferry (Potomac), 71
North Anna River (Va.): troop buildup, 35–37
North Carolina, 61; Confederate weakness in, 326; conscripts, 40; District of, 35, 37
North Carolina State Archives (Raleigh), 153
North Carolina troops, 321
—artillery: Lane, 234–45; Rowan, 325, 419, 448
—cavalry: 1st, 19, 232, 451
—infantry: 1st, 419; 3d, 38; 4th, 179; 5th, 258, 403; 6th, 322; 15th, 281; 27th, 226, 392, 488; 35th, 409; 48th, 226, 409
North Mountain Depot (Va., W. Va.), 182
North Woods, 414; first phase (Sharpsburg), 370; second phase (Sharpsburg), 374; third phase (Sharpsburg), 391

Official Records, 143, 154, 217, 486
Offutt's Crossroads, Md., 99, 109
Ohio, 29–30
Ohio River, 39, 40, 97, 106, 131, 249, 471
Ohio troops, infantry: 11th, 206; 28th, 261
Old Sharpsburg Road (Md.), 173–76, 258, 262, 264; Ninth Corps advances on, 311
Opequon Creek (Va.), 228, 465, 467
Orange and Alexandria Railroad (Va.), 22, 505n.64
Orange Court House, Va., 34, 44
Overland campaign: 1862, 490–96; 1864, 492–93
Owen, William Miller (CSA, lt.), 405, 447
Ox Hill, Va., 11–12, 17–18, 30, 120
Ox Hill, Battle of, 11–15, 59, 62, 223, 412; casualties, 13, 220, 348–49
Ox Road (Va.), 51

Palfrey, Francis Winthrop (USA, lt. col.), 3; as historian, 486
Palmerston, John Henry Temple (Viscount), 26
Pamunkey River (Va.), 35
Parham, William Allen (CSA, lt. col.), 231
Parham's brigade. *See* Mahone's brigade
Parr's Ridge (Md.), 121
Patrick, Marsena Rudolph (USA, gen.), 351
Patrick's brigade: first phase (Sharpsburg), 372, 388; second phase (Sharpsburg), 388; on Sept. 16th, 351
Patrick Street (Frederick), 172
Paxton, Elisha Franklin (CSA, maj.), 88
Pelham, John (CSA, maj.): nearly captured, 231; Stuart's turning movement, 411
Pelham's horse artillery. *See* Virginia troops, artillery
Pender, William Dorsey (CSA, gen.), 476; critic of offensive, 488; orders discipline, 91; Ox Hill, 13; on straggling, 118
Pender's brigade, 102; Battle of Shepherdstown, 464–65; sixth phase (Sharpsburg), 422; strength on Sept. 18th, 431; withdrawal from Sharpsburg, 447
Pendleton, Alexander Swift (CSA, capt.), 476; courier to Lee, 375, 381
Pendleton, William Nelson (CSA, gen.), 294; Battle of Shepherdstown, 457–61; biography, 458; copy of S.O. 191, 152–53; crosses Potomac, 112; favorable view of Lee, 222; on German Americans, 193; guards Potomac fords on Sept. 16th–17th, 337, 369; Lee reports his loss of guns, 462–63; near capture, 296; ordered to Beaver Creek, 285; ordered to reorganize artillery, 73; reorganizes artillery, 92; reports at Frederick, 120; reports to Davis, 222; visits Davis, 36–37; Williamsport expedition, 450–51; withdrawal from Sharpsburg, 445. *See also* Lee–Pendleton correspondence
Peninsula, the (Va.), 22
Peninsula campaign, 3
Pennsylvania: border, 187, 290; Davis's apparent object, 217; deep penetration of, 123, 139–40; Jackson's aim, 81; Jackson's ruse, 173; Lee to enter, 77–79; Lee threatens, 84; Loring to enter; as rumored destination, 69, 112–13; rumors of Federal flight to, 116–17, 119; Susquehanna railroad bridge, 139
Pennsylvania troops
—cavalry: 4th, 230; 6th, 230; 8th, 230; 12th, 230
—infantry: 51st, 401, 414; 62d, 456; 71st, 19; 118th, 456, 465; 125th, 377, 389, 391, 395; militia, 438–39; Reserve Corps, 266; 1st Rifles, 351
Petersburg, Va., 35, 37
Pettit, Rufus D. (USA, capt.), 313, 325
Phelps's brigade: first phase (Sharpsburg), 372
Philadelphia, Pa., 47, 78, 140
Pickett, George Edward (CSA, gen.), 93
Pickett's brigade: Battle of Boonsboro, 264; commander Richard Garnett, 74, 93; at Keedysville, 299; march to Keedysville, 295; strength on Sept. 18th, 432
Pierson's artillery battalion: forms line on Reel Ridge, 384
Pillage proscribed, 73

Pimmitt Run, Va., action at, 67, 71
Piper (Henry) farm, 354
Pittman, Samuel Emlen (USA, col.), 238
Pleasant Valley, Md., 201–4, 226, 393; escape route for McLaws, 244, 247, 251; Federals enter, 278; held by McLaws, 224; McClellan learns role in S.O. 191, 238; McLaws approaches, 187; McLaws suggests Jackson move on, 319; Stuart in, 317
Pleasant Valley, Va., 52
Pleasanton, Alfred (USA, gen.): advance from Turner's Gap, 309; and Confederate feint, 84; confusing reports, 109; ignorant of Confederate march from Frederick, 181; pursues F. Lee to Hagerstown, 324; pursuit on Sept. 19th, 452; retires from Boteler's Ford, 454; sends for Ninth Corps, 261; skirmish at Boonsboro, 309–10; S.O. 191 makes cautious, 252; starts fighting at Fox's Gap, 260; to verify S.O. 191, 239; at Williamsport, 466
Pleasonton's division: advance to South Mountain, 230; attack in center suggested, 399; capture of Sugar Loaf, 189; and Confederates recrossing Potomac, 457; crosses Potomac, 84; occupies Frederick, 207, 239; occupies New Market, 189; occupies Urbana, 189; reconnoiters Confederates, 119, 121–22; scouts Confederate crossing, 98; split to pursue Confederates, 456
Poague, William Thomas (CSA, capt.), 358, 406–7, 411; arrested, 88
Poffenberger (Alfred) farm: second phase (Sharpsburg), 388; on Sept. 16th, 351
Poffenberger (Joseph) farm: on Sept. 16th, 351
Poffenberger (Samuel) farm: on Sept. 16th, 358
Poffenberger Hill: first phase (Sharpsburg), 370; fourth phase (Sharpsburg), 392–93; Stuart's turning movement, 411
Point of Rocks, Md., 71; possible escape route for McLaws, 293; reports Confederate crossing, 84; Walker recrosses at, 180, 187, 204
Poolesville, Md.: Federals advance to, 129; Federals capture, 118, 122, 142–43; reports Confederates crossing, 84; skirmish, 90, 114–15; welcomes Stuart, 90
Pope, John (USA, gen.), 142, 298; defense of Fairfax Court House, 12, 14; on the Rapidan, 30, 33–35; relieved, 84, 98; report on Second Manassas, 98; retreat to Washington, 11, 16–19, 23, 58; in Washington, 79
Porter, Fitz John (USA, gen.): Battle of Shepherdstown, 455–56, 458; joins McClellan in scouting Confederate artillery, 314; march to Boteler's Ford, 454; morning of Sept. 15th, 311; relieved, 98; Second Manassas, 30
Port Hudson, La., 131
Potomac River (Md.), 270, 292; condition at crossing, 86–87; Confederate boundary, 48; Confederates debate crossing point, 80–85; crossings of Sept. 6th, 103; D. H. Hill crosses, 71; fish trap dam, 450–51; at Harpers Ferry, 201; Jackson crosses, 86; Lee crosses, 104, 298, 480; Lee decides where to cross, 84; Lee ponders crossing point, 50; obstacle in Lee's rear, 306–7; Pendleton guards fords of, 337; Sharpsburg in crook of, 346; stalemate, 15; turning movement on Sept. 18th, 441; valley, 85; Williamsport turning movement, 445
Price, Sterling (CSA, gen.): multiprong invasions, 27–28, 30, 106, 131, 327–28, 472
Princeton College (N.J.), 81
Proclamation to Marylanders, 124–25, 195, 217
Pry (Philip) house: McClellan's headquarters, 352–53, 385, 413
Pry's Ford (Antietam): Doubleday crosses at, 355; Richardson crosses at, 396
Pryor, Roger Atkinson (CSA, gen.): Battle of Shepherdstown, 460; Stuart visits, 276
Pryor's brigade: march to Weverton, 202–3; at Weverton, 202, 278, 284
Pryor's division. *See* R. H. Anderson's division
Purcellville, Va., 272

Rains's (Colquitt's) brigade, 380; Battle of Boonsboro, 256, 259, 261, 263, 265, 267; crosses Potomac, 71; fatigue, 43; forms line in Sunken Road, 381, 384; holds Confederate left on Sept. 16th, 356; march from Richmond, 34; march to Keedysville, 294; march to Sharpsburg, 294; near Boteler's Ford, 299; occupies Turner's Gap, 234; ordered to Sunken Road, 304; second phase (Sharpsburg), 374; seen by Moor, 261; skirmish on Sept. 16th, 358; to watch Turner's Gap, 208; vulnerable to be turned at Fox's Gap, 261
Ramsay, John Andrew (CSA, lt.), 325; meets Lee, 419; withdrawal from Sharpsburg, 447–48

Randolph, George Wythe (CSA, sec. of war), 36, 96. *See also* Lee–Randolph correspondence
Randolph, Robert (CSA, capt.), 88
Ransom, Matt Whitaker (CSA, col.), 393; Stuart's turning movement, 409
Ransom, Robert, Jr. (CSA, gen.): fourth phase (Sharpsburg), 392–93
Ransom's brigade: fourth phase (Sharpsburg), 392–93; Stuart's turning movement, 412
Rapidan River (Va.), 30, 35, 53, 96; railroad bridge, 53, 95, 123, 220; stalemate, 18
Rapidan Station, Va., 37, 65, 123, 136, 187
Rappahannock River (Va.), 35, 37; as fallback, 23; railroad bridge, 95; stalemate, 18
Ravenswood, Va. (W. Va.), 97, 471
Ratchford, James Wylie (CSA, maj.), 152, 433; Battle of Shepherdstown, 463; courier to Lee, 376, 380
Red Hill (Elk Ridge), 400; signal station, 421, 444
Reel Ridge: Confederate line on Sept. 18th, 431; Lee's fall back line, 381; Stuart's turning movement, 408
Reinforcing column from Richmond, 33–37
R. E. Lee: A Biography, 485–86
Reno, Jesse Lee (USA, gen.): D. H. Hill to attack, 223; at Fox's Gap, 262; mortally wounded, 265
Reno's Corps. *See* Ninth Corps
Reserve Artillery, Army of Northern Virginia (CSA), 444, 458; arrives at Frederick, 120; Battle of Shepherdstown, 460; at Boteler's Ford, 454; crosses Potomac, 112; departs Hagerstown, 254; at Frederick, 190; at Gainesville, 57; guards Potomac fords, 306, 404; Hagerstown original object, 149; held at Boonsboro, 254; in main body, 150; march from Richmond, 34–37; march through Frederick, 169–72; march to Boonsboro, 254; march to Hagerstown, 185; march to Williamsport, 299; near capture, 296; ordered to Beaver Creek, 285; ordered to Leesburg, 52; regimental numbers and strengths, 37–39; remains in Leesburg, 104; reorganized, 73; strength, 170–71; trains to recross into Virginia, 294; Williamsport expedition, 450; withdrawal from Sharpsburg, 448 Reynolds, John Fulton (USA, gen.), 438–39
Rhode Island troops: infantry (4th), 230, 422
Richardson, Charles (CSA, maj.), 92
Richardson's division: advance from Turner's Gap, 299, 302, 309–10; attacks Sunken Road, 398; carries Sunken Road, 400; fifth phase (Sharpsburg), 396–97; forms Antietam line on Sept. 15th, 314; march to the Antietam, 313, 324–25; replaced by Morell, 385
Richmond (Ky.) Battle of, 30, 106
Richmond, Va., 298; defenses of, 37, 61, 65, 505–6n.67; Lee defends at a distance, 471; lines of advance on, 95; Lowe's residence, 77; McClellan's advance on, 25; safety of, 61; supplies from, 22, 24, 53, 95; threatened from James, 61; to retain convalescents, 123; under siege, 59, 110; vulnerable, 75, 221–22, 326; war council, April 1862, 49; war council, August 1862, 36–37
Ricketts, James Brewerton (USA, gen.): on Sept. 16th, 351
Ricketts's division: crosses Antietam, 350; first phase (Sharpsburg), 371; at Frosttown Gap, 266; skirmish on Sept. 16, 351–52
Ridgeville, Md.: Federals capture, 167
Ripley, Roswell Sabine (CSA, gen.): awakens Stuart, 248; to command at Fox's Gap, 260; retreat from Turner's Gap, 290–91
Ripley's brigade: arrives at Sharpsburg, 303; Battle of Boonsboro, 257, 259, 263–65; crosses Potomac, 71; fatigue, 43; holds Confederate left on Sept. 16th, 356; at Keedysville, 299; march from Richmond, 34; march to Keedysville, 294; ordered to East Woods, 363; ordered to Turner's Gap, 248; readiness for Turner's Gap, 236; retreat from Turner's Gap, 290–91; retreats to Sunken Road, 381; second phase (Sharpsburg), 373, 375; sent to Fox's Gap, 259–60
River Road, Md., 91, 202, 215, 318; held by McLaws, 224; as McLaws's escape route, 283; Stuart's turning movement, 410; Williamsport expedition, 451
Robertson, Beverly Holcombe (CSA, gen.), 84; Pimmitt Run action, 67, 71; relieved, 93
Robertson's brigade. *See* Munford's brigade
Rockingham County, Va.: resources, 48
"Rock the Cradle, Julie," 365
Rockville, Md., 99, 109, 121, 141, 148; Federal advance to, 129; McClellan establishes headquarters at, 119
Rodes, Robert Emmett (CSA, gen.): at Frosttown Gap, 260, 264–65
Rodes's brigade, 380; Battle of Boonsboro, 257, 259, 263, 267; crosses Potomac, 71; march to Keedysville, 294; march to Sharpsburg, 296; ordered to Hagerstown

Rodes's brigade (*cont.*)
Pike, 304; readiness for Turner's Gap, 236; in reserve on Sept. 16th, 356; second phase (Sharpsburg), 375; sent to Frosttown Gap, 260, 264–65; at Sharpsburg, 299
Rodman, Isaac Peace (USA, gen.), 401; mortally wounded, 421
Rodman's division: McClellan repositions on Sept. 16th, 349; sixth phase (Sharpsburg), 400, 415, 418
Rogers, John D. (CSA, capt.), 152
Rohrersville, Md., 291, 294; escape route for McLaws, 244, 251; Munford leaves, 325
Rohrersville–Boonsboro Road (Md.), 291, 311
Romney, Va. (W. Va.), 93
Ropes, John Codman (historian), 588n.37
Rosser, Thomas Lafayette (CSA, col.): alerts Lee, 307, 324; alerts Stuart, 275; confers with Garland, 258; covers Lee's flanks on Sept. 15th, 324; delays Federal advance from Boonsboro, 324; ordered to Fox's Gap, 275; rearguard from Fox's Gap, 299, 310; on Stuart's indifference, 234
Roulette (William) farm: fifth phase (Sharpsburg), 395
Rush, Richard H. (USA, col.), 231
Russell, John (Lord), 26

Sanders, Christopher Columbus (CSA, lt. col.), 384, 391
Sander's brigade. *See* Cobb's brigade
Sandy Hook, Md., 203, 225, 277–78, 281, 283; Confederates fall back to, 320; escape route for McLaws, 247, 251
Saw Mill Road (Md.): sixth phase (Sharpsburg), 420
Scammon, Eliakim Parker (USA, gen.): at Fox's Gap, 261
Scammon's brigade: at Fox's Gap, 259, 261–62
Scott, Winfield (USA, gen.), 141
Sears, Stephen W. (historian), 487–88
Second Bull Run. *See* Second Manassas, Battle of
Second Corps (USA-Potomac): advance from Turner's Gap, 299, 302, 309; conditions on Sept. 18th, 439; crosses Potomac, 84; demoralized, 414; fifth phase (Sharpsburg), 396; forms Antietam line on Sept. 15th, 314; fourth phase (Sharpsburg), 394; in Frederick, 239; Lee's preliminary report, 434, 436; march to Darnestown, 181; march to Frederick, 230; march to Rockville, 99, 109; march to the Antietam, 313; march to Urbana, 210; morning of Sept. 15th, 311; ordered to support Hooker, 385; preparatory orders, 353; pursuit on Sept. 19th, 452; retreat to Washington, 18–19; rumored advance, 129–30; second phase (Sharpsburg), 376–77; third phase (Sharpsburg), 385, 391; at Turner's Gap, 292, 341; turning movement on Sept. 18th, 442, veteran unit, 349, wrecked, 399
Second Corps (USA-Virginia). *See* Twelfth Corps (USA)
Second Manassas, Battle of, 3, 13, 68–69, 81, 223, 298; casualties, 38, 218, 220–21; compared to Sharpsburg, 430, 441; Jackson at, 370; Lee's victory, 11, 26, 75
Second phase, Battle of Sharpsburg (Hood-Mansfield), 373–77, 388; casualties, 376–77
Sedgwick, John (USA, gen.), 385–86
Sedgwick's division: Confederate pursuit, 405; demoralized, 414; fifth phase (Sharpsburg), 395–97; fourth phase (Sharpsburg), 92–93; Lee's preliminary report, 434; morning of Sept. 15th, 311; retreat to Washington, 19; routed, 387, 397, 470; second phase (Sharpsburg), 377; third phase (Sharpsburg), 385, 390, 392
Semmes, Paul Jones (CSA, gen.): arrives late at Crampton's Gap, 282; brigade commander (McLaws)
Semmes's brigade: guards Brownsville Gap, 202, 231, 276, 280; third phase (Sharpsburg), 391
Seneca, Md., 129
Seneca Creek (Md.), 109
Seven Days, Battle of, 1, 25, 80, 125, 500n.1
Seven Pines (Va.), Battle of, 28
Seymour, Truman (USA, gen.): on Sept. 16th, 351
Seymour's brigade: advance on Smoketown Road, 351–52; bivouac on Sept. 16th, 354; first phase (Sharpsburg), 370, 372, 387; skirmish on Sept. 16th, 358
Shaara, Michael (novelist), 5
Sharpsburg, Md., 118, 157, 292–93; Federals in side streets of, 419; Longstreet prefers to Turner's Gap, 246; route for Federal fugitives, 174
Sharpsburg (Antietam), Battle of: artillery duel on Sept. 15th, 325; artillery duel on Sept. 16th, 335–36, 344; battle axis changes, 377; casualties, 373, 376–77, 394–95, 397, 423, 433; cavalry of little use, 346; compared to Gettysburg, 2–5; Confederate line on Sept. 18th, 431; Confederate officer casualties, 433; Confederate ordnance

shortage, 403; Confederate strength, 171, 220; Confederate withdrawal, 445–48; in crook of Potomac, 346; deceptive terrain, 346; exhausted both sides, 430; fifth phase (Sunken Road), 395–97; first phase (Hooker-Jackson), 370–73, 387–88; flags of truce on Sept. 18th, 441; fourth phase (Dunkard Church), 392–94; historiography, 1–10; Jackson commands on left, 370; Lee assesses opening attack, 370; Lee on Cemetery Hill, 303, 307, 324, 331–33, 370, 377–78, 402; Lee's postwar comments on, 480; Lee's preliminary report, 434–35; midday crisis, 401–6; military geography of, 303, 306–7, 345–46; opening fire, 369; second phase (Hood-Mansfield), 373–77, 388; sixth phase (Lower Bridge), 400–401, 414–23; Stuart's turning movement, 406–13; third phase (West Woods), 385–92; tourists, 2–3; war council on Sept. 16th, 343–44; war council on Sept. 17th, 424–29. *See also* Maryland campaign of 1862

Sharpsburg–Harpers Ferry Road (Md.), 202–3

Sharpsburg Heights (Md.): compared to Malvern Hill, 309, 345; strength of, 303, 331, 347; third phase (Sharpsburg), 389; viewed by Hooker, 310

Shenandoah River (Va.), 198, 228, 273–74

Shenandoah Valley (Va.): Confederate scouting, 146; Federal evacuation, 79–80, 96, 115–17; Federal toehold, 20; goal for Loring, 30; supply line, 48, 79–80, 84, 95, 105, 111, 122–23, 133–34, 136, 146

Shenandoah Valley campaign (1862), 80

Shepherdstown, Va. (W. Va.), 202, 288, 292, 369, 459; A. P. Hill's route, 418; Jackson ordered to, 318; Reserve Artillery to guard, 294; route for Federal fugitives, 174; supply line, 136; Williamsport expedition, 450; Williamsport turning movement, 445

Shepherdstown, Battle of, 455–61, 463–65; casualties, 465; Lee reports, 467

Shepherdstown Ford. *See* Boteler's Ford

Shepherdstown Road (Md.): Lee establishes headquarters on, 338, 369; McLaws's route, 368; terrain of Sharpsburg, 303–4

Sherman, William Tecumseh (USA, gen.): as success, 7

Sheridan, Philip Henry (USA, gen.): as success, 7

Shiloh (Tenn.), Battle of, 1, 28

Short Hills, Va., 201, 226

Sixth Corps (USA), 274; advance against Lee, 130; approaches Keedysville, 399; arrives East Woods, 405; attack suspended, 414; carries Crampton's Gap, 291; at Crampton's Gap, 279–80; crosses Pry's Ford, 399; fourth phase (Sharpsburg), 393; fresh on Sept. 18th, 438; march to Barnesville, 181; march to Buckeystown, 230; march to Licksville Crossroads, 210; march to Offutt's Crossroads, 119; march to Tennallytown, 109; morning of Sept. 15th, 311; needed in Pleasant Valley, 345; ordered to East Woods, 399; ordered to Sharpsburg, 353; outflanks Confederates on Sept. 14th, 282; Ox Hill, 12; presence threatens Harpers Ferry, 366; pursuit on Sept. 19th, 452; retreat to Washington, 18; Stuart's turning movement, 410; to attack on Sept. 18th, 438; to attack on Sept. 19th, 440; to carry Crampton's Gap, 240; to watch Harpers Ferry, 313; turning movement on Sept. 18th, 442

Sixth phase, Battle of Sharpsburg (Lower Bridge), 400–401, 414–23; casualties, 423

Slavery, 1, 4, 170

Slocum, Henry Warner (USA, gen.): at Crampton's Gap, 279

Slocum's division: at Crampton's Gap, 279

Smith, David, farm, 407, 409

Smith, Edmund Kirby (CSA, gen.): Davis sends proclamation to, 217; multiprong invasions, 27–30, 131, 327, 472, 479; unmentioned by Lee, 470; victory announced, 106

Smith, Gustavus Woodson (CSA, gen.), 36; command at Seven Pines, 40; to cover Warrenton, 221; on Maryland offensive, 49

Smith, William Farrar (USA, gen.): at Crampton's Gap, 279

Smith's division: at Crampton's Gap, 279, 282; reaches Keedysville, 399

Smoketown Road (Md.): First Corps advances on, 351–52, 357; first phase (Sharpsburg), 371–72; second phase (Sharpsburg), 373–77; third phase (Sharpsburg), 389

Snavely's Ford (Antietam), 337; Confederate line on Sept. 18th, 431; Federals carry, 398, 400; Federal threat to on Sept. 16th, 356; Lee's preliminary report, 436; midday crisis, 401, 405; sixth phase (Sharpsburg), 400–401, 416, 418, 422; unguarded, 405; vulnerable, 382; Walker ordered to, 366

Solomon's Gap (Elk Ridge), 202–3, 281; only a notch, 283

Sorrel, Gilbert Moxley (CSA, maj.), 290
South Carolina, 61, 90
South Carolina troops, 266, 295
—artillery: Boyce, 417; Hart, 233, 275; Pee Dee, 421
—cavalry: 2d, 206
—infantry: 2d, 224; 3d, 203, 224; 7th, 203, 224; 8th, 203, 224; 14th, 447; Holcombe Legion, 292
South Mountain (Md.), 213, 427; casualties, 297, 348; Confederate defeat, 430; held by McLaws, 224; Jackson's route, 175; Lee's postwar comments on, 480; Longstreet's route, 183; McLaws's route, 201
South Mountain, Battle of. *See* Boonsboro, Battle of; Crampton's Gap, Battle of
Special Orders No. 188, 93
Special Orders No. 191, 133; addressed to D. H. Hill, 237; ambiguous picture of Confederate organization, 238; authenticity of, 238; based on wrong assumptions, 267–68; blamed by Confederate historians, 485–86; causes Pleasonton caution, 252; citizen overhears McClellan, 233, 242–43, 248–49; compared to Pope's lost dispatch, 238; complicates Federal strategy, 345; copy given to McClellan, 237; deadlines, 190, 198; delays, 200, 204–5, 208, 299; delivered to Walker, 137, 180; enables McClellan's victory, 482; evolution of contents, 145–52; Federal garrisons do not flee, 186–87; gaps in information, 238; how lost, 152–53; importance overrated, 252; information revealed to McClellan, 237; issued hastily, 151–52, 166; Jackson confuses details, 272; Jackson's discretion, 173; Jackson modifies, 182; Jackson to Martinsburg, 214; Lee blames, 212, 212–82; Lee doubts final success of, 251; Lee learns of loss of, 242–44, 248–49; Lee modifies, 183–85, 196; Lee risks army before loss of, 167; Lee satisfied with, 185; Longstreet's modifications, 149–52; Longstreet opposes, 484; McLaws leaves Federal escape route, 225; misleading terms, 238–39, 260; no strengths given, 238; original form, 147–49; poorly written, 154–55, 159–60, 163, 166; reasons for, 192; sequence of columns, 161; seven copies, 152; in shambles, 298; spy theory, 529n.90; surviving copies, 152–53; textual analysis, 152–64; weaknesses appear, 186–87
Sperryville, Va., 478
Springvale, Md., 313
Squires, Charles Winder (CSA, capt.): Lee orders to collect guns, 420; sixth phase (Sharpsburg), 423
Stackpole, Edward J. (historian), 3
Stafford, Leroy Augustus (CSA, col.), 42
Stainrook's brigade: fourth phase (Sharpsburg), 392; second phase (Sharpsburg), 375
Stanton, Edwin McMasters (USA, sec. of war): Harpers Ferry mistakes, 315; weak in strategy, 22
Starke, William Edwin (CSA, gen.): commands Jackson's second line, 359
Starke's brigade: forms line on Sept. 16th, 359; move on Bolivar Heights, 273
Starke's division. *See* Jackson's division
Staunton, Va., 48, 96
Stevens, Isaac Ingalls (USA, gen.), 13
Steiner Lewis Henry (USA, phys.): biography, 169, 520n.64, 531n.2; comments on quality of Confederates, 170–71, 185–86; on Confederate strength, 220; family farm, 237; McClellan's entry into Frederick, 229; observes Confederates march through Frederick, 169–72; observes D. H. Hill's division, 185–86; observes reactions of Frederick citizens, 171–72
Stevens's brigade. *See* Evans's brigade
Stevens's division, 12, 62; Ox Hill, 117
Stockton, Thomas Baylies Whitmarsh (USA, col.), 414
Stockton's brigade: temporarily ordered to support Franklin, 414
Stonewall brigade: forms line on Sept. 16th, 359; march through Frederick, 173; move on Bolivar Heights, 273
Stonewall division. *See* Jackson's division
Stonewall Jackson in the American Civil War, 485
Straggling, 44–45; angers Lee, 378; caused by Lee, 118–19; as cowardice, 117–18; Lee arrests straggler, 382; Lee blames officers, 219; Lee collects stragglers, 403; Lee ignores, 65; Lee's dispatch on, 116–19; Lee's orders on, 94; proscribed, 73–75; after Sharpsburg, 431; Stuart to prevent, 162–63; after Turner's Gap, 295; Walker interview, 138
Strange, John Bowie (CSA, col.), 74–75
Stuart, Flora (Mrs. J. E. B.), 67
Stuart, James Ewell Brown (CSA, gen.), 287; abandons Urbana, 188–89; abandons Williamsport, 466; alerts D. H. Hill, 232; alerts Lee of Federals west of Antietam, 356; alerts Lee of Frederick's fall, 207;

alerts McLaws to River Road, 276; ambiguous notice of loss of S.O. 191, 235, 242; authorized to call on D. H. Hill, 222–23; awakened by Ripley, 248; believes Valley Expedition on time, 230; at Best's Grove, 105; bivouacs at Middletown, 207; buys time for D. H. Hill, 232; captures Federal dispatches, 107, 522n.86; Chantilly, 11, 13, 16; clash with White, 146; copy of S.O. 191, 152–53; at Crampton's Gap, 275–76; crosses Potomac, 89–90; dance at Frederick, 188–89; decides Federals will move on Harpers Ferry, 233, 242; departs for Crampton's Gap, 257; detaches Rosser at Fox's Gap, 257, 275; at Dunkard Church, 355; fails to turn flank, 411–12, 426; first phase (Sharpsburg), 370, 388; focuses on Crampton's Gap, 275; growing concern, 205; ignorant of S.O. 191 delays, 205; ignores Rosser's alert, 275; instructed by Lee, 108; learns of danger at Crampton's Gap, 233; learns of loss of S.O. 191, 233; learns of Ninth Corps pursuit, 231; leaves Crampton's Gap, 280; Lee cautions, 197; Lee orders to hold Turner's Gap, 250; Lee reports at Williamsport, 462; Lee's preliminary report, 436; letter to War Department, 67; line on Catoctin Mountains, 231; march to Leesburg, 52–53, 56–57; meets Lee at Frederick, 107–8; meets Lee in Leesburg, 85; meets Lee on Sept. 15th, 322–23; in Middletown Valley, 214; misleads Colquitt, 234; misperceptions, 230–31, 275–76, 278; news for Lee, 322; ordered to scout Hooker on Sept. 16th, 357; party at Williamsport, 452; Pennsylvania raid, 478; performance in Maryland, 114–15, 121–22, 129–30, 166–67, 180, 185, 188–89, 205, 275–76; Poolesville skirmish, 114; posts Pelham on Nicodemus Hill, 364; prepares for Sept. 18th, 429; provides cavalry detachments, 162–63; pursues Pope, 16–19, 23; reconnaissance on Sept. 16th, 559–60n.7; returns to Crampton's Gap, 282; rides to Boonsboro, 234; rides to Crampton's Gap, 250; rides to Frederick, 107; rides to Weverton, 276; rides up Maryland Heights, 276; second phase (Sharpsburg), 388; sends Hampton to Crampton's Gap, 233, 242–43; shifts line to northwest, 187–89; to guard roads from Harpers Ferry, 198; to warn McLaws, 198; at Turner's Gap, 234; turning movement, 406–13, 426, 441–42, 573nn.68, 71, 573–74n.72; underestimates Federal force pursuing, 242; visits Jackson at Harpers Ferry, 317; visits McLaws, 276; visits Pryor, 276; warns Lee of Frederick's fall, 188–89; Williamsport expedition, 448–52; Williamsport turning movement, 445. *See also* Lee–Stuart correspondence

Stuart's division: captures wagons, 69; covers Jackson's crossing, 71; covers Leesburg march, 52–53; covers rear of Valley expedition, 162–63; fails to keep in touch with Jackson, 88; fourth phase (Sharpsburg), 393; operations on Sept. 10th, 180–81; operations on Sept. 11, 187–89; operations on Sept. 12th, 205–7; operations on Sept. 13th, 230–35; ordered to cover crossing, 86; orders for Valley expedition, 162–63; regimental numbers and strengths, 37–39; strength for Valley expedition, 150–51, 162, 170–71; strength on Sept. 18th, 433; third phase (Sharpsburg), 392; to bring up stragglers, 162–63; to remain east of mountains, 149

Stuart's turning movement, 406–13

Sturgis, Samuel Davis (USA, gen.), 414

Sturgis's division: McClellan repositions on Sept. 16th, 349; sixth phase (Sharpsburg), 400, 414

Sugar Land Run, Va., 57, 80

Sugar Loaf Mountain (Md.), 107, 122; Confederate cavalry line, 187–89; Federals capture, 189; signal station, 84; skirmish at, 180, 188

Sumner Bridge. *See* Upper Bridge (Antietam)

Sumner, Edwin Vose (USA, gen.): commander Second Corps, 166; fifth phase (Sharpsburg), 395; Lee's preliminary report, 435–36; meets McClellan at Keedysville, 313; meets McClellan at the East Woods, 413–14; morning of Sept. 15th, 311; pleads for orders, 385; possible commander of Army of the Potomac, 98; pursuit on Sept. 19th, 452; requests orders to cross Antietam, 353; second phase (Sharpsburg), 377; third phase (Sharpsburg), 386

Sumner's command (center): to Middlebrook, 166; progress on Sept. 12th, 209

Sumner's Corps. *See* Second Corps (USA)

Sunken Road, 414; Colquitt occupies on Sept. 15th, 304; Confederate line formed in, 381–82; fifth phase (Sharpsburg), 395–96; first phase (Sharpsburg), 370; fourth phase (Sharpsburg), 392–93; Lee visits, 384; midday crisis, 401; R. H. Anderson ordered

Sunken Road (*cont.*)
to, 384; second phase (Sharpsburg), 373, 377; third phase (Sharpsburg), 387, 391
Susquehanna River (Pa.), 139,142
Sykes's division: advance against Lee, 130; Battle of Shepherdstown, 455–56, 465; forms Antietam line on Sept. 15th, 314; in Frederick, 239; march to Frederick, 230; march to Rockville, 121; march to the Antietam, 313; march to Urbana, 210; morning of Sept. 15th, 311; situation on Sept. 18th, 439; sixth phase (Sharpsburg), 422

Tabler's Mill, Va. (W. Va.), 406
Talcott, Thomas M. R. (CSA, maj.), 247
Taliaferro's brigade: forms line on Sept. 16th, 359; in van of crossing, 86
Taylor, Walter Herron (CSA, maj.), 433, 476; courier to McLaws, 381; Davis mission, 133, 155–57, 215, 551n.122); historiography, 484; ignores Walker's memoirs, 140, 143; super visor of orders, 155, 164; Winchester as object, 155
Tennallytown, D.C., 109, 119
Tennessee, 29
Texas brigade. *See* Hood's brigade
Texas troops, 285
—infantry: 1st, 374–75; 5th, 358
Third Corps (USA-Potomac): retreat to Washington, 19
Third Corps (USA-Virginia). *See* First Corps (USA)
Third phase, Battle of Sharpsburg (West Woods), 385–92; casualties, 394–95
Third phase of the war, 27, 31–32; closing of, 479
Thomas, Emory M. (historian), 486
Thomas's brigade: Battle of Shepherdstown, 465; left at Harpers Ferry, 417, 425, 575n.1
Thoroughfare Gap (Bull Run Mountains), 30, 35, 96, 162, 427
Three Springs, Md., 88–89, 105; Jackson at, 91; Longstreet at, 103
Tidball, John Caldwell (USA, capt.), 313, 325
Toombs, Robert Augustus (CSA, gen.): asks Lee for support, 420; counterattacks, 575–76n.106
Toombs's brigade: Lee's preliminary report, 436; march to Hagerstown, 185; occupies Hagerstown, 190; ordered to Lower Bridge, 305; ordered to Sharpsburg, 289; outflanked, 406; remains at Hagerstown, 254; on Sept. 16th, 364; sixth phase (Sharpsburg), 400, 422; threatened on Sept. 16th, 344; two regiments sent to Williamsport, 297
Traveller: Lee returns to, 331; Lee rides to Dunkard Church, 383
Trenton, N.J., 2
Trimble's brigade: first phase (Sharpsburg), 370, 372–73, 387; march to Sharpsburg, 321, 328; officer cadre, 42; reaches Dunkard Church on Sept. 16th, 360; replaces Hood on Sept. 16th, 363; stragglers, 403; strength on Sept. 18th, 432; third phase (Sharpsburg), 388
Trough Road (Va., W. Va.), 464–65
Troup, Robert (CSA, capt.), 420
Tupelo, Miss., 28–29
Turner's Gap (South Mountain), 213–15, 260, 274, 286, 292; D. H. Hill's route, 207; dilemma for McClellan, 239; geography of, 236, 257, 259–60; Jackson's route, 175; Longstreet against standing at, 246; Longstreet's route, 183. *See also* Boonsboro, Battle of
Turning movements, 20, 46–47, 76, 210, 260, 314, 406–13, 436, 441–45
Twelfth Corps (USA): advance against Lee, 130; bivouacs behind Hooker, 353; condition on Sept. 18th, 434, 436; crosses Antietam, 353; crosses Potomac, 84; demoralized, 414; first phase (Sharpsburg), 372; forms Antietam line on Sept. 15th, 314; fourth phase (Sharpsburg), 392, 394; in Frederick, 237, 239; march to Frederick, 230; march to Ijamsville Crossroads, 210; march to Rockville, 99, 109; march to the Antietam, 313; morning of Sept. 15th, 311; ordered to support Hooker, 353; in reserve, 349; retreat to Washington, 19; rumored at Darnestown, 114; second phase (Sharpsburg), 374; sent to Maryland Heights, 453; third phase (Sharpsburg), 387–88, 391; turning movement on Sept. 18th, 442; wrecked, 399
Tyndale's brigade: fourth phase (Sharpsburg), 392; second phase (Sharpsburg), 375

United States: call for troops (1862), 32; conscription, 32; forces in the field, 31; green troops, 58; new troops, 32, 100; odds faced, 31–32, 65; use of black troops, 32; views of Md. campaign, 2
United States Military Academy, 222
United States Sanitary Commission, 169

United States troops:
—artillery: A, 2d, 313; M, 2d, 122; I, 5th, 379
—cavalry: 5th, 230; 6th, 230; green regiments, 225
—infantry: 4th, 415
—sharpshooters: 1st, 455, 459
Unity, Md.: Federals occupy, 122
Upper (Sumner) Bridge (Antietam): First Corps crosses, 344, 350
Upper Potomac: Jackson threatens, 22; as Lee's object, 471; threat to Washington, 24
Upton's Hill, Va., 18
Urbana, Md., 115; abandoned, 188; cavalry dance, 122; skirmish at, 188; Stuart rests at, 166; Stuart's headquarters, 108, 188

Valley campaign (Shenandoah), 358–59
Valley expedition: behind schedule, 191, 223; deadlines, 158, 160–61; delays on Sept. 13th, 228; D. H. orders, 161–62; hurried preparations, 166; Jackson devises siege, 227–28; Jackson's freedom of route, 157; Jackson's orders, 157–59; Jackson's start untimed, 157; Jackson takes command, 227–28; Lee decides to end, 287–88, 293–94; Lee errs in dividing army, 166–67; Lee misjudges Federal advance, 166–67; Lee plans, 147–49; Lee's concern, 215; Lee's lopsided news of, 191–92; Lee's verbal instructions, 158;
Lee tries to salvage, 245–46; Longstreet's orders, 159; McLaws's orders, 159–60; Martinsburg as Jackson's original object, 158–59; regiments to carry axes, 164; sequence of columns, 161; strategy of, 147–49; strengths of columns, 150–51, 159–62; Stuart's orders, 162–63; use of cavalry, 162–63; Walker's orders, 161. *See also* Harpers Ferry, siege of; Special Orders No. 191
Valley garrisons: cause Lee to divide army, 192; Lee expects to flee, 192; merged, 201, 224; threat to Confederate supply line, 189. *See also* Harpers Ferry; Martinsburg
Valley of Virginia, 212–13
Valley Pike (Va.): route for Federal fugitives, 174
Van Dorn, Earl (CSA, gen.): multiprong invasions, 27–28, 30, 106, 131, 472
Venable, Charles (CSA, maj.), 425
Vestal Gap, Va., 226
Vicksburg, Miss., 483, 495
Vienna, Va., 18
Virginia, 261, 293; western, 29
Virginia Central Railroad, 22, 34, 48, 478, 505n.64
Virginia Military Institute, 258
Virginia troops (CSA)
—artillery: Branch, 270, 410; Chew, 67, 92, 122, 188, 231, 337; Eubank, 305; Fluvanna, 451; French, 270, 410; Grimes, 275, 280; King William, 381; Pelham, 18, 231, 295, 324, 337, 351, 358, 364; Richmond Howitzers, 451; Rockbridge, 43, 182, 329, 358, 406; Salem, 451; Wise, 417
—cavalry: 1st, 163, 181, 185, 289, 296, 299, 354; 2d, 52, 93, 188, 231, 280, 325, 337, 448; 3d, 295, 309–10, 337, 354; 4th, 88, 295, 309–10, 337, 354, 411; 5th, 115, 234, 257–58, 261, 275, 291, 295, 307, 310, 324, 337, 354; 6th, 221; 7th, 67, 122, 163, 175–76, 180, 183, 448; 9th, 93, 295, 309–10, 337, 351, 354–55, 358; 12th, 67, 122, 188, 231, 280, 325, 337, 448, 450–51; White's battalion, 537n.81
—infantry: 2d, 228, 451; 6th, 281; 10th, 86, 228, 451; 12th, 281; 13th, 388, 392; 15th, 280; 17th, 118, 290; 19th, 74–75; 21st, 102; 27th, 373; 30th, 134, 226, 431; 32d, 280, 365; 42d, 102; 48th, 102; 55th, 70; 61st, 326; 1st battalion, 102
Virginia troops (USA): cavalry (Loudoun Rangers), 14, 52
von Borcke, Heros (CSA, maj.), 451; at Crampton's Gap, 282; at Dranesville, 67; Fairfax Court House, 19; flees Grove house, 336; Urbana dance, 115, 122

Walker, James Alexander (CSA, col.): arrives in Sharpsburg, 334; commander Trimble's brigade (Ewell), 42; on Sept. 16th, 363
Walker, John George (CSA, gen.), 287, 435; aqueduct mission, 135–37; biography, 144; date of reporting to Lee, 134–35; fails to destroy aqueduct, 180; falls behind schedule, 204–5; guns on Loudoun Heights, 270; Harpers Ferry controversy, 269–71; increased responsibilities, 204; isolation, 226; Jackson sends signal party to, 267; Jackson signals on Sept. 14th, 270–71; Jackson to cooperate, 200; learns of Harpers Ferry's surrender, 317; Lee's mild rebuke, 112; march to join Lee, 34–37; march to Sharpsburg, 328; meets with Jackson, 319; memoirs, 134, 143–45; memoirs not used by veterans, 140, 143; not mentioned by Lee,

Walker, John George (*cont.*) 214; opens fire at Harpers Ferry, 273; ordered to Leesburg, 52; out of touch with Jackson and McLaws, 223; out of touch with Lee, 223; receives copy of S.O. 191, 137; recrosses Potomac, 180; report of, 134; signal party from Jackson, 226; S.O. 191 complications, 186–87; S.O. 191 deadline, 198; slow to rejoin Lee, 321; Stuart's turning movement, 412

Walker's (Joseph) brigade: fourth phase (Sharpsburg), 392–93; Stuart's turning movement, 409

Walker's division, 214; arrives Sharpsburg, 334; arrives West Woods, 384; artillery, 72; camp at Big Spring, 104; crosses Potomac, 112, 134; fourth phase (Sharpsburg), 392–93; on Franklin's flank, 240; free to rejoin to Lee, 308; given no cavalry, 163; Lee orders to left, 382; Lee's preliminary report, 435–36; march from Richmond, 34–37; march to Buckeystown, 112, 120; march to Frederick, 134; march to Leesburg, 104, 521n.75; march to Sharpsburg, 328; midday crisis, 401; mistaken for A. P. Hill, 225; nears Leesburg, 98; nears Potomac, 331; ordered to Snavely's Ford, 366, 566n.83; orders for Valley expedition, 161; out of touch with Lee, 191–92; outside of corps structure, 41; progress on Sept. 10th, 180; progress on Sept. 11th, 187; progress on Sept. 12th, 204; progress on Sept. 13th, 226; rear exposed, 188; regimental numbers and strengths, 37–39; in reserve on Sept. 16th, 356; rests on Sept. 16th, 337; secure on Sept. 13th, 240–41, 244–45; on Sept. 18th, 431; signals on Loudoun Heights, 225; sixth phase (Sharpsburg), 401; strength, 170–71; Stuart's turning movement, 410; timing in Valley expedition uncertain, 161, 193; to rejoin army, 163; at Warrenton, 57; whereabouts uncertain, 112

Walton, James Burdge (CSA, col.), 405; starts artillery duel on Sept. 16th, 335–36; war council on Sept. 17th, 424; withdrawal from Sharpsburg, 447

Walton's artillery battalion. *See* Louisiana troops: Washington Artillery

War council on Sept. 17th, 424–29

War Department (CSA): and multiprong invasions, 29; Stuart's letter to, 67. *See also* Lee–Randolph correspondence

War Department (USA): creates battlefield parks, 2; records, 217

Warren, Edward Tiffin Harrison (CSA, col.), 42

Warren's brigade: Battle of Shepherdstown, 465

Warrenton Junction, Va., 53, 57; Davis visits, 215–16; as fallback position, 95; hospitals, 123, 221, 327; supply line, 95; Taylor's visit, 155–56

Warrenton Turnpike (Va.), 53; Ox Hill, 11, 14

Washington Artillery Battalion. *See* Louisiana Troops: Washington Artillery

Washington College (Va.), 480

Washington, D.C.: armies concentrate at, 83; communications to west, 70, 80; Federal raids from, 221; fortifications, 11, 14, 18, 21, 58–59, 120, 332; ground in front of, 22–23; Halleck fears for safety of, 119; McClellan in command of, 84; rumored Confederate destination, 111–12, 119, 140; safe by Sept. 12th, 210, 229; troop concentration, 32; vulnerable, 46

Washington County, Md.: maps of, 344, 356; resources, 48

Washington–Frederick Road (Md.), 188

Washington Star, 79

Weed, Stephen Hinsdale (USA, capt.), 379

Welsh's brigade: sixth phase (Sharpsburg), 415

"We're Gwying Down the Newbury Road," 365

Westminster, Md., 229, 234; F. Lee's raid, 205

West Point. *See* United States Military Academy

West Woods, 438; fifth phase (Sharpsburg), 395; first phase (Sharpsburg), 373; fourth phase (Sharpsburg), 392–93; Lee's preliminary report, 434; second phase (Sharpsburg), 374; Stuart's turning movement, 408–9, 412; third phase (Sharpsburg), 386–87, 389

Weverton, Md., 201, 203, 300; Confederates fall back to, 320; as McLaws's escape route, 301; occupied by Pryor, 278

Weverton Cliffs, Md.: held by McLaws, 224; occupied by Wright, 284

Weverton Gap (South Mountain), 283: possible escape route for McLaws, 293

White, Elijah Viers (CSA, capt.): calls for volunteers, 125; clash with Stuart, 146; enters Frederick, 101; rides with Jackson, 88–89; sent to scout Valley, 146

White, Julius (USA, gen.), 119, 166; discovers danger, 189–90; evacuates Winchester, 79; flees to Harpers Ferry, 201; moves to Martinsburg, 99; reports, 116

White House Plantation, Va., 35
White's Ford (Potomac), 93, 112; Lee selects, 85
White's cavalry battalion. *See* Virginia troops: White's cavalry
Whiting, Charles Jarvis (USA, maj.), 230–31
Whiting, William Henry Chase (CSA, gen.), 36
Whiting's division, 40
Wilcox's brigade: ordered to Brownsville, 279; ordered to Pleasant Valley, 284
Wilcox's division: crosses Potomac, 103; merged with R. H. Anderson, 178; officer cadre, 42
Willcox, Orlano Bolivar (USA, gen.): at Fox's Gap, 262
Willcox's division: at Fox's Gap, 262; McClellan repositions on Sept. 16th, 349; sixth phase (Sharpsburg), 415, 422
Williams, Alpheus Starkey (USA, gen.): sends S.O. 191 to McClellan, 237
Williams's Corps. *See* Twelfth Corps (USA)
Williams's division: second phase (Sharpsburg), 374–75; third phase (Sharpsburg), 388
Williamsport, Md., 183–85, 285, 297, 305, 337, 408; Confederate trains to, 289; Jackson's route, 174, 182; Lee explains intent, 462; nearby fords, 83; as reentry option, 361, 369, 444–45; Reserve Artillery to guard, 294; shoes for Confederates, 194; Stuart abandons, 466; Stuart's expedition, 448–52; Stuart's Pennsylvania raid, 478
Williamsport–Hagerstown Road (Md.), 455–56
Winchester, Va.: depot, 92, 96, 105, 111, 116, 146; Federals evacuate, 78, 83, 116, 138, 199; garrison, 24, 50; Loring to protect, 97; stragglers collected, 428, 468; supply line, 95, 123, 133, 136; Taylor's visit, 155–56; threat to supply line, 316
Wingfield, T. H. (CSA, surg.), 196
Winder's brigade. *See* Stonewall brigade
Wofford, William Tatum (CSA, col.): skirmish on Sept. 16th, 357–58
Wofford's brigade. *See* Hood's brigade
Wood, William Nathaniel (CSA, lt.), 74
Wool, John Ellis (USA, gen.): Bragg rumor, 119; and Harpers Ferry, 98; Harpers Ferry mistakes, 315
Woolten, Dr. (USA, phys.), 196
Wright, Ambrose Ransom (CSA, gen.), 202
Wright's brigade: at Weverton Cliffs, 202–3, 284;

York River (Va.), 35
Yorktown, Va., 49